Scottish Record Society

Melrose Parish Registers of Aptisms, Marriages, Proclamations of Marriages, Session Minutes (1723-1741) and Mortuary Rolls. 1642-1820

Editor: Charles S. Romanes

Alpha Editions

This edition published in 2020

ISBN : 9789354037030

Design and Setting By
Alpha Editions
www.alphaedis.com
email - alphaedis@gmail.com

PREFACE.

THE RECORDS relating to the parish of Melrose in the General
Register House, Edinburgh, now printed, consist of certain
volumes containing Baptisms, Proclamations of Marriages, Session
Minutes, and a Mortuary Roll.

The entries relating to Baptisms begin on the 28th August
1642 and have been fairly well recorded. There are blanks in
these Registers between 18th April 1686 and 2nd November 1690,
18th October 1713 and 3rd January 1714, 21st April 1720 and
28th May 1720, 15th August 1722 and 7th October 1722, and
between 8th September 1723 and 24th November 1723. From
that date until 1st March 1741 the Baptisms are intermixed with
Proclamations of Marriages and Session Minutes.

The Baptisms seem to be carefully recorded until 30th July
1769, when for a considerable period they are entered out of order.
No explanation can be offered for this peculiar condition of the
Record, which continues until 1820, when the present volume closes.

The Register of Proclamations of Marriages and Marriages
begins on 30th June 1642. There are blanks in the Register
between 22nd December 1650 and 14th September 1651, 27th
November 1656 and 2nd January 1657, 26th April 1657 and 27th
October 1657, 12th November 1657 and 8th May 1659, 28th April
1666 and 7th November 1690. This Register is fairly well kept
until the close of the present volume. Testimonials or church
certificates are recorded for the period from 4th October 1652 to
13th May 1666.

From the Session Records in the hands of the Session Clerk,

Melrose, through the kindness of the Rev. R. J. Thompson, M.A., Minister of the Parish, the Editor has been able to supply a number of Baptisms, Marriages, and records of Mortcloths extracted from such Minutes and a Mortuary Roll from 25th December 1760 to 21st August 1781.

The second Mortuary Roll from 8th September 1781 to 30th December 1804 is in the Register House.

The chief portions of the Session Minutes from 1st November 1642 are in the hands of the Session Clerk, Melrose.

Melrose Parish Registers.

—◆—

I.—Record of Baptisms.

BAPETESMS.

George Blaickie.
Jon Wilsone.
James Bowie.
Walter Dalgleish.
Jon Baine.

Twa Blainslies.

———

Thomas Meill.
—— Pyper.
George Pringall.
James Lettham.
William Wallace.
Thomas Smith.
George Shell.
Wm. Anderson.
James Wallace.
James Meil.
Nicoll Bowar.
Thomas Bowstan.
James Hwnttar.
Jon Dawedson.
Alexander Feshar.
Wm. Clarke.
Andrew Penman.
Robert Laidla.
Andrew Reynoldson.
Jon Dawedson.
George Turner.
Thomas Hunter.
James Marre.

Note.—The above names appear on the first page of the Record without explanation. They are probably the elders of the Church.

———

1642.

Aug. 28. Adam Linlighgow in Melros, a dachter named Margreat ; witnesses, Andro Paterson, Jon Wallace.

„ 31. John Thomson in Galtonsyd, a.d.n. Margreat ; w. James and Thomas Marre.

Sept. 1. George Blakie in Melros, twa twines, Jenett and Margreat, b. ; w. Jon Wallace, Adam Linlighgow.

„ 4. William Barrie in Galtonsyd, a.d.n. Agnes ; w. James Mylles, Jon. Barrie.

„ 10. Jn. Lawrie in Melros, a.s.n. Wm.; w. James and Robert Mylles.

„ 13. Andro Meane in Newsteid, a.s.n. Andro : w. Andro Sklaiter, Thomas Maine.

„ 18. Thomas Walch in Newsteid, a.d.n. Helen : w. Wm. Fisher, Wm. Meaine.

„ 27. John Notman in Comislie, a.d.n. Allison ; w. Thomas Turner, Wm Tait.

Oct. 4. Robert Sklaiter in Eildon, a.s.n. Robert : w. Richard Sklaiter, James Meaine.

1642.

Oct. 4. Andro Lookup in Damzelton, a.s.n. Wm.: w. Wm. Hud, Thomas
Lookup.

„ 16. James Mouddie in Darnick, a.s.n. John; w. John Drumond, Andro
Smith.

„ 23. Andro Bowiston in Bridgend, a.d.n. Jenett; w. John Uscher, John
Hownam.

„ 23. Andro Smith in Darnick, a.s.n. Wm.: w. George Hownam, John
Drumond.

„ 25. Mathew Walker in Darnick, a.d.n. Issobell; w. James Heiton,
Thomas Drumond.

„ 25. Thomas Lookup in Melros, a.s.n. Thomas; w. Thomas Linlighgow,
Wm. Wallace.

„ 27. Thomas Marre in Darnick, a.s.n. Nicoll; w. Thomas Linlighgow,
James Marre.

„ „ Thomas Morton in Galtonsyd, a.d.n. Jenet; w. James Bowiston,
Thomas Clerk.

Nov. 8. James Riddall in Newtoun, a.s.n. James; w. John Riddall, Thomas
Mill.

„ „ James Vair in Newtoun, a.s.n. Thomas; w. Nicoll Mill, Nicoll
Ker.

„ 15. Nicoll Schisholme, a.d.n. Marian; w. Andrew Cook, Wm.
Schisholme.

„ 21. Thomas Ormiston, a.d.n. Jenett; w. Wm. Ormiston, Andrew
Ormiston.

Dec. 2. George Barrie, a.s.n. David; w. Mr. David Fletcher, Wm. Ormiston,
Wm. Edgar.

„ 4. George Shibball in Eilden, a.d.n. Margreat: w. James Meanie,
Wm. Schisholme.

„ 17. Andrew Hownam in Bridgend, a.s.n. Andrew: w. John Uscher, John
Moffat.

„ „ Jon Drumond, a.d.n. Margreat; w. James Mouddie, Andro Smith.

„ 19. John Wright, a.d.n. Margreat; w. Thomas Law, Robert Law.

1643.

Jan. 8. Thomas Paterson in Galtonsyd, a.d.n. Isobel; w. James Marre, Gawin
Martin, John Birckart.

„ 9. Jon Vair in Melros, a.d.n. Jeane; w. James Vair, Wm. Watson.

„ „ John Bicket in Damzelton, a.d.n. Margreat; w. James Ealies, William
Ridfourd.

„ 22. John Uscher in Darnick, ——; w. Andrew Kennydie, John
Messt.

Feb. 6. Richard Meane in Newsted, a.d.n. Elizabeth; w. Andrew and John
Meanes.

„ 8. William Fisher in Darnick, a.s.n. William; w. Michall Fischer,
Thomas Linlithgow.

„ 8. William Wryght in Galtonsyd, a.d.n. Jenett; w. James Mean,
Thomas Maban.

„ „ James Freir in Galtonsyd, a.s.n. Archibald; w. Robert Freir, Robert
Mylles.

„ 11. William Wallace in Melros, a.s.n. George: w. Mitchell Fischer,
Thomas Lithgow.

„ 13. James Lithgow in Ridpeth, a.s.n. William: w. Mitchell Fischer,
William Fischer.

„ 16. Thomas Bowsting in Galtonsyd, a.s.n. James; w. Thomas and James
Bowstings.

„ 21. Robert Freir in Newsted, a.d.n. Isobel; w. Andrew Sclaiter, Andrew
Meane.

Mar. 1. Robert Meane in Newsted, a.s.n. Alexander; w. James and John
Meanes.

„ 12. Robert Whyte in Newtoune, a.d.n. Bessie: w. Henrie Cochrane,
Nicoll Mill.

1643.
Mar. 14. James Ballantyn in Langhaugh, a.s.n. James ; w. Andro Darling, Peter
    Darling.
  „ „ Andrew Ormiston in Langlee, a.d.n. Janie ; w. Hew Bell, Thomas
    Lithgow.
  „ „ Thomas Law in Melros, a.d.n. Margreat ; w. Jon Wright, Robert Law.
  „ 22. Robert Freir in Galtonsyd, a.d.n. Margreat ; w. James Marr, James
    Freir.
April 3. Alexander Ridpeth in Melros, a.d.n. Agnes ; w. Wm. Ormistoune, Wm.
    Edgar.
  „ 8. William Edgar in Melros, a.s.n. William ; w. Thomas Lithgow, Alexr.
    Fischer.
  „ 9. Robert Brown in Newsteid, a.d.n. Margreat ; w. George Meane,
    Thomas Welch.
  „ 21. James Merton in Westhouses, a.d.n. Agnes ; w. Walter Maban, Wm.
    Couper.
  „ 23. Nicoll Mersser in Bridgend, a.d.n. Bessie ; w. Jon Urscher, Jon Wright.
  „ 24. Thomas Hiton in Westhouses, ane nephoy, bap. his name Georg ;
    w. Robert and Andrew Hitons.
  „ 28. Andrew Cook in Melrose, a.s.n. Andrew ; w. Wm. Edgar, Andrew
    Sklaiter.
Maii 7. Robert Lithgow in Eildown, a.d.n. Agnes ; w. Richard Sklaiter, John
    Bower.
  „ „ James Gray in Blanislie, a.s.n. John ; w. John Sunnes, Jon. Blakie.
  „ „ Andrew Hoome in Newsted, a.d.n. Jon ; w. Andro Sklaiter, Andro
    Meine.
  „ 8. Robert Trotter in Housbayer, a.s.n. James ; w. Thomas Lithgow,
    William Wallace.
  „ „ James Wallace in Melros, a.s.n. James ; w. William Edgar, Nicoll
    Mosse.
  „ 24. Gawin Richardsonne in Housbyre, a.d.n. Bessie ; w. James Darling,
    James Henrysone.
  „ 30. James Ealies in Damzelton, a.s.n. William ; w. Andrew Paterson,
    Wm. Lithgow.
June 3. Alexander Ealies, fornicator with Issobell Hobkirk, a.s.n. Georg ;
    w. George Holiewall, James Lithgow.
  „ 3. William Wright in Housbyres, a.d.n. Elizabeth ; w. David and
    Thomas Robertsons.
  „ 5. Thomas Gill in Commyslie, a d.n Bessie ; w. Adam Newtoun,
    Thomas Gill.
  „ 9. Robert Bunzie in Newtown, a.d.n. Bessie ; w. Thomas Bunzie,
    Andrew Wilson.
  „ 22. James Marre in Gatonsyd, a.d.n. Isobell : w. Robert Freir, Jon
    Holievall.
Julii 9. Richard Moss in Darnick, a.s.n. Wm.; w. Jon Moss, Nicoll Moss.
  „ 20. Andro Darling in Westhouses, a.d.n. Mary ; w. Wm. Bell, Jon Scott.
  „ 27. Adam Newtoun in Comyslie, a.d.n. Marion ; w .Thomas and James
    Fairgreives.
  „ 30. Thomas Maben in Darnick, a.d.n. Margreat ; w. Thomas Law, Jon
    Maben.
Aug. 7. James Bowsting in Galtonsyd, a.d.n. Bessie : w. Wm. Ormystoun,
    James Marre.
  „ 13. George Hownam in Dernick, a.d.n. Margreat ; w. James Fischer,
    John Hownam.
Sept. 4. Johne Maban in Melros, a.s.n. Walter : w. Jon Waugh, Walter
    Maben.
  „ 14. William Fischer in Draygrang, a.d.n. Helen : w. Thomas Lithgow,
    William Wallace.
  „ „ Jon Mersser in Eildoun, a.d.n. Janet ; w. Jon Waugh, Jon Bell.
  „ „ Bernard Mersser in Bridgend, a.d.n. Agnes ; w. Wm. Mersser, Jon
    Hownam.

1643.

Sept. 14. Andrew Mersser in Darnick, a.s.n. Nicoll; w. Robt. Mersser, Jon Mersser.

  „ 23. Nicoll Mill in Newtoune, a.d.n. Isobell; w. Wm. Ker, Wm. Holwall.

  „ 23. Wm. Browne in Newstead, a.d.n. Janet; w. Thomas Mersser, Robert Browne.

Oct. 2. Curbert Robertsone in Newstead, a.s.n. Andrew; w. Andrew Sklaiter, David Meine.

  „ 2. Andrew Hiton, fornicator with Bessie Meine, a.d.n. Mary; w. Nicoll Mill, Alexander Hastie.

  „ 8. Wm. Henderson in Langshaw Mill, a.s.n. Thomas; w. Thomas Gill, Jon Notman.

  „ 15. Thomas Martin in Galtonsyd, fornicator with Janet Barrie, a.d.n. Agnes; w. James Marre, Jon Holiewell.

  „ 24. Wm. Wright in Galtonsyd, a.s.n. Jon; w. Jon Pringell of Williamlaw, Wm. Ormiston.

  „ 25. Robert Pringell of Blindlie, a.s.n. Henrie; w. Jon Pringle, Thomas Lithgow.

  „ 29. Thomas Marre in Darnick, a.s.n. Thomas; w. Jon Uscher, James Fisher.

  „ 30. Jon Hownam in Bridgend, a.d.n. Chrystian; w. George Bowsting, Jasper Battie.

Nov. 6. Alexr. Hiton in Newsteid, a.s.n. Alexander; w. Henrie Cochrane, Williame Ker.

  „ 27. William Mein in Newsteid, a.s.n. Thomas; w. Thomas Lithgow, Robert Mein.

Dec. 9. Johne Edgar in Melros, twa daughters n. Jeane and Isobell; w. Thomas Lithgow, Wm. Wallace, Wm. Edgar, Alex. Ealies.

  „ 24. James Mein in Eildoune, a.s.n. James; w. Richard Sklaiter, Jon Bower.

  „ „ Robert Mersser in Darnick, a.d.n. Issobell; w. Nicoll Moss, Jon Uscher.

1644.

Jan. 8. Thomas Marre in Galtonsyd, a.d.n. Agnes; w. James Marre, Rot. Freir.

  „ 13. Andrew Paterson in Melros, a.s.n. James; w. Wm. Bower, Jon Bower.

  „ „ William Lambe in Eildoune, a.s.n. Jon; w. James Meine, George Sybball.

Feb. 11. Andrew Cink in Dernick, a.d.n. Janet; w. Wm. Fischer, Nicoll Scholme.

  „ 15. Andrew Mersser in Dernick, a.s.n. Andrew; w. Nicoll Moss, Jon Moss.

  „ 22. Thomas Mill, fornicator with Agnes Ker, a.s.n. Jon; w. Henrie Cochrane, James Stennous.

  „ „ Nicoll Moss in Dernick, a.s.n. Wm.; w. Wm. Edgar, Wm. Fischer.

  „ 26. Nicoll Mersser in Dernick twa dochters n. Malie and Jonet; w. Nicoll Moss, Andro Mersser.

Mar. 10. Jon Mein in Newsteid, a.s.n. Jon; w. Thomas Benzie, David Mein.

  „ 16. George Merten in Galtonsyd, a.d.n. Margreat; w. Gawin Merten, James Merten.

  „ 25. Hew Bell in Langlie, a.d.n. Anna; w. Thomas Lithgow, Wm. Wallace.

Apryll 14. Archibald Moffat, fornicator with Issobell Moffat, their s.n. Archibald; w. Rot. Moffat, James Stoddart.

  „ 27. Bernard Welsone in Newsteid, a.d.n. Jonet; w. Wm. Mein, James Mein.

  „ 28. Nicoll Ker in Newsteid, a.s.n. Jon; w. Jon Oynes, Mark Troumble.

Mai 9. Jon Scott in Westhouses, a.s.n. Jon; w. Jon Holiewell, Wm. Couper.

  „ 14. George Hoy in Galtonsyd, a.d.n. Issobell; w. James Marre, Robert Freir.

1644.

Maii 19. James Stennous in Newtoun, a.d.n. Bessie ; w. Nicoll Mill, Richard
    Sklaiter.

,, 31. James Cairncros in Hillslope, a.s.n. Jon ; w. Wm. Cairncros, Alexr.
    Anderson.

June 9. Richard Sklaiter in Eildoune, a.s.n. Rot. ; w. Thomas Sklaiter, James
    Mein.

,, ,, Robert Braidie in Eildoune, a.d.n. Agnes ; w. Rob. Sklaiter, James
    Mein.

,, 13. Andrew Mein in Newsteid, a.d.n. Issobell ; w. Andrew Sklaiter,
    George Mein.

,, ,, Robert Forfer in Newsteid, a.s.n. Williame ; w. Curbert Bowie,
    Thomas Bowie.

,, 15. Robert Clerk in Galtonsyd, a.s.n. Jon ; w. George Holiewall, James
    Freir.

,, 27. Thomas Laidla in Allanschaws, a.d.n. Bessie ; w. Jon Moffet,
    Archibald Moffet.

,, last. Gawane Martine in Melros, a.d.n. Elizabeth ; w. Wm. Edgar,
    Walter Donaldson.

Julii 2. Robert Ormistoune in Galtonsyd, a.d.n. Margreat ; w. Rot. Philp,
    Wm. Couper.

,, 29. William Martoune in Westhouses, a.d.n. Janet ; w. Robert Wood,
    Thomas Robertson.

,, ,, James Vair in Newtoune, a.d.n. Isobell ; w. Thomas Ker, Alexander
    Hitone.

,, 15. James Ker in Damzeltoune, a.d.n. Jonet ; w. James Ealies, Andro
    Paterson.

,, ,, Thomas Bower in Eildonne, a.d.n. Agnes ; w. Richard Sklaiter, Jon
    Bower.

Aug. 4. William Laidla in Newtoune, a.s.n. Johne and s.n. Jon ; w. Thomas
    Stennous, Wm. Young.

,, 20. Andrew Mein in Melros, a.d.n. Jeane ; w. David Mein, James
    Wallace.

,, 25. Robert Trotter in Housbyres, a.s.n. Alexr. ; w. Thomas Lithgow,
    Wm. Wallace.

,, ,, Nicoll Cochrane in Newtoune, a.s.n. Nicoll ; w. Nicoll Mill, Thomas
    Stennous.

Sept. 1. Andrew Mein in Newsted, a.s.n. Andro ; w. Henrie Cochrane, Andro
    Sklaiter.

,, 8. John Holliewall in Galtonsyd, a.d.n. Jonet ; w. James Marre, James
    Freir.

,, 22. Adame Lithgow in Melros, a.s.n. Jon ; w. James Lithgow, Hew Bell.

,, 29. James Symsone in Newsteid, a.d.n. Margreat ; w. Wm. Symsone,
    Jon Symsone.

Oct. 12. Jon Drumond in Galtonsyd, a.d.n. Issobell ; w. James Freir,
    Robert Mylles.

,, 21. Jon Blakie in Comysliehill, a.s.n. Jon ; w. Jon Sunnous, George
    Turner.

Nov. 2. Walter Urscher in Bridgend, a.s.n. Jon ; w. Jon Urscher, Jasper
    Baittie.

,, ,, Nicoll Mersser in Bridgend, a.s.n. Wm ; w. Andrew Bowsting, Jon
    Hownam.

,, 10. Andrew Patersone in Damzeltoun, a.s.n. Andro ; w. James Bounzie,
    Adam Lithgow.

,, ,, William Bower in Melros, a.d.n. Jonet ; w. Jon Bower, James Ealies.

Dec. 1. James Mein in Newsteid, a.s.n. Robert ; w. Alexr. Mein, David Mein.

,, last. Georg Holiewall in Galtonsyd, a.d.n. Jonet ; w. Thomas Maban,
    Thomas Bowsting.

1645.

Jan. 14. Georg Blakie in Melross, a..n. Georg ; w. Johne Wallace, Edame
    Lithgow.

1645.

Jan. 23. Wm. Wryght in Housbyres, a.d.n. Jonet ; w. Robert Trotter, Thomas Robersone.

" 30. James Mosse in Galtonsyd, a.d.n. Euphame ; w. Wm. Hoy, James Bowsting.

" " Robert Philip in Galtonsyd, a.d.n. Agnes ; w. James Freir, Thomas Mabau.

Feb. 11. Richard Mein in Newsted, a.s.n. Andro ; w. Alexr. Main, Andrew Mein.

" " Jon Bowsting in Galtonsyd, a.d.n. Marg. ; w. James Freir, Thomas Law.

" " Jon Martin in Melros, a.s.n. Thomas ; w. Thomas Lithgow, Thomas Martin.

Mar. 1. Andrew Cuik in Melros, a.d.n. Issobell ; w. Wm. Edgar, Andrew Sklaiter.

" " Williame Kennydie in Darnick, a.d.n. Jeane ; w. Andrew Kennydie, James Hitone.

" 23. James Riddall in Newtoune, a.d.n. Jonet ; w. Nicoll Milne, Thomas Stenous.

April 4. Jon Uscher in Dernick. a.d.n. Jonet ; w. James Hiton, Andrew Kennedie.

" 13. William Swanstoun in Thripwod, furnicator with Issobell Patersone, a.d.n. Janet ; w. Jon Moffet, James Moffet.

" 23. William Fischer in Dernick, a.d.n. Jeane ; w. Andrew Kennedie, Jon Hownam.

" last. Alexander Dobsone in Bolsid, a.s.n. Jon ; w. Jon Dobsone, Andrew Tunno.

Maii 1. Robert Scot in Melros, twa twines, baptised a sonne name Frances, and a dochter, name, Jeane ; w. Thomas Law, Andro Sklaiter.

" 4. Thomas Welch in Newstead, a.d.n. Margreat ; w. Andro Sklaiter, Robert Forsin.

" 7. Thomas Pringell in Comislichill, a.s.n. Jon ; w. Patrick Blakie, James Murray.

" 9. Jon Scott in Westhouses, a.s.n. Jon ; w. Nicoll Mill, John Holiwall.

" 27. Alex. Mein in Newsted, a.d.n. Agnes ; w. David Mein, James Mein.

June 8. Jn. Noltmaine in Hagbourne, furnicator with Margt. Blakie, a.s.n. James ; w. James Duke, James Turner.

" 24. James Meine in Faldonnesyde, a.d.n. Margarett ; w. Thomas Lithgow, James Murray.

" 20. Adame Young in Newtoune, a.s.n. Adame ; w. Nicoll Mill, Henrie Cochrane.

" 29. Nicoll Kar in Newtoune, a.d.n. Agnes ; w. William Forsane, Adame Young.

" 30. James Luckupe in Melross, a.s.n. Jon ; w. George Elliott, Andrew Mene.

July 22. Patrick Luckupe in Melross, a.d.n. Marrjorie ; w. Jon Barrey, Gawine Meilne.

" 22. Andrew Sklaitour in Newsteid, a.s.n. Thomas ; w. James Meine, Jon Meine.

" 22. Jon Thomsone in Galtonsyde, a.s.n. Johne ; w. Robert Holywell, Robert Phillipe.

" 30. Thomas Ormistoune in Galtonsyde, a.s.n. William ; w. Williame Ormistoune, Hew Bell.

Aug. 3. Williame Lambe in Yldoune, a.s.n. Richard ; w. James Meine, Richard Sclatour.

" 3. James Freir in Galtonsyde, a.s.n. Alexander ; w. Robert Freir, George Helliwelle.

" 3. John Meine in Newstead, a.d.n. Issobell ; w. Andro Meine, Nicoll Cochrane.

" 8. Richard Moss in Darnock, a.d.n. Jannet ; w. Johne Moss, Nicoll Moss.

1645.

Aug. 10. William Darling in Buckholme, a.d.n. Bessie : w. George Pringill,
Edward Darling.

" 15. Robert Sclatour in Yldoune, a.d.n. Agnes : w. Richard Sclater,
Williame Meine.

" 22. Johne Messer in Darnock, a.d.n. Jennett : w. Williame Fischar,
Thomas Mar.

" 24. George Dagleish in Hagbourne, a.d.n. Catherine ; w. Jon Pringill, Mr.
James Hunter.

" 24. William Moffett in Thripwoode, a.s.n. Johne ; w. James Moffett,
George Romanes.

" 29. Andrew Meine in Newsteid, a.s.n. Johne ; w. Jon Maine, Jon Maine (*sic*).

" 29. Williame Helliweell in Darnock, a.s.n. Johne ; w. William Spotiswood,
Andro Messer.

" 31. Williame Scheill in Blainslie, a.s.n. Williame ; w. George Scheill,
William Hall.

Sept. 22. Androw Willsone in Newsteid, a.s.n. Johne ; w. Johne Meine, Androw
Meine.

" 22. Thomas Lookupe in Mclreiss, a.s.n. Johne (?) ; w. Johne Crament,
Mark Halyburton.

" 27. Robert Turner, servant to my Lord Haddingtoune, a.s.n. James ; w.
Johne Turner, Richard Alexander.

" 27. William Fischar in Drygrange, a.d.n. Eupham ; w. Johne Fischar,
Thomas Lithgow.

" 28. George Suinneyis in Mosshouses, a.d.n. Helene : w. James Dawsone,
Williame Smith.

" 28. James Stenhouse in Newtoune, a.s.n. Androw ; w. Thomas Stenhouse,
Thomas Karr.

Nov. 5. Mark Martine in Westhouses, a.s.n. Robert ; w. Robert Martine,
Gawine Martine.

" 5. Androue Smith in Darnock, a.d.n. Agnes ; w. Williame Fischar,
Williame Mersser.

" 5. Thomas Drummond, sodger in Buccleugh's regiment, a.s.n. Thomas ;
w. Johne Moss, Johne Drummond.

" 5. Thomas Bousteane in Melroise, a.s.n. Michaell, forn ; w. William
Wallace, Andrew Bousteane.

" 22. Williame Chisholme in Yldone, a.d.n. Elizabeth ; w. Richard Sclatour,
James Meine.

" 27. Johne Marr in Melroise, a.d.n. Issobell ; w. Richard Sclatour, Johne
Wryght.

Dec. 9. Nicoll Chisholme in Darnock, a.d.n. Marrione ; w. Andrew Cuik,
William Chisholme.

" 9. James Gleiss residenter in Melroise, a.d.n. Issobell ; w. Thomas
Lithgow, Johne Edgar.

" 26. James Thomline in Gattensyde, a.s.n. James ; w. James Hietonne,
Johne Hietonne.

" 26. James Dousone in Mosshouses, a.s.n. Williame ; w. John Fischarr,
Robt. Trotter.

" 27. Johne Meine in Newsteid, a.d.n. Issobell ; w. Robert Meine, Williame
Andersone.

" 27. Thomas Patersone, sodger in the Londiang regiment, a.d.n. Agnes,
died ; w. Williame Marr, Johne Bickett.

1646.

Jan. 7. James Wauch in Melroiss, a.d.n. Margarett ; w. Williame Bower, John
Bower, forn.

" 14. Matthew Walker in Buccleuchis' regiment, a.d.n. Margarett : w.
James Hietoune, Johne Hietoune.

" 18. Robt. Browne in Newsteid, a.d.n. Issobell ; w. Johne Meine, Androu
Meine.

" 18. Williame Anderson in Shelbrig (?) in Gallowsheilds parosch, a.d.n.
Issobell ; w. John Andersone, Thomas Dobson.

1646.

Jan.   18.   Androu Heitoune in Neutoune, a.d.n. Alysone ; w. Walter Donaldsone, Jon Wallace.

 ,,   18.   James Edgar in Newsteid, a.s.n. James ; w. Thomas Laidlay, Thomas Milne.

 ,,   22.   Andrew Merser in Darnock, a.d.n. Margarett ; w. Androu Sclatour, Johne Wallace.

 ,,   22.   Johne Davidsone in Ershngtoune, a.s.n. Thomas ; w. Williame Edgar, Andrew Paterson.

 ,,   23.   James Meine in Newsteid, a.s.n. Johne ; w. Jon Meine, Androu Sclatoun.

Feb.   6.   Andreu Meine in Gattensyde, a.d.n. Alison ; w. James Freir, Thomas Boustoune.

 ,,   ,,   Andruo Hietoune in Westhouses, a.s.n. Thomas ; w. Thomas Hietoune, Jon Scott.

 ,,   8.   William Karr in Neutoune, a.s.n. Johne ; w. Nicoll Cochrane, Thomas Stenhouse.

 ,,   22.   Mr. Johne Lithgow, a.s.n. Thomas ; w. Johne Scott, Johne Pringill.

 ,,   22.   Williame Fischar in Darnick, a.d.n. Marrion ; w. Alexander Fischar, William Fischar.

 ,,   22.   Robert Leithane in Yldcine, a.s.n. Robert ; w. Andreu Patersone, Richard Sclatour.

Mar.   7.   Cuthbert Bower in Newsteid, a.d.n. Jannet ; w. Johne Meine, Thomas Marr.

 ,,   15.   James Hietoune in Darnock, a.s.n. James ; w. George Griersone, John Uscher.

 ,,   15.   James Romanus in Blainslie, a.d.n. Heillene ; w. James Davidsone, Edward Romanus.

 ,,   15.   Thomas Browne in Faundonesyde, in Gallowsheilds parosch, a.d.n. Issobell ; w. James Meine, Jon Mebane.

 ,,   22.   Rot. Clark in Gattonsyde, a.d.n. Margarett ; w. Robert Freir, Jon Helliwall.

 ,,   22.   Jon Bickett in Danzeltoun, a.s.n. Rodger ; w. James Eillis, Jon Watsone.

 ,,   22.   Thomas Wryt in Caldsheils, in Gallowsheilds parosch, a.d.n. Elizabeth ; w. Jon Idingtoune, George Wallace.

 ,,   22.   Wm. Hoy in Gattensyde, a.d.n. Issobell ; w. George Hoy, George Helliwall.

 ,,   29.   James Bousteane, in Westhouses, a.s.n. Thomas ; w. Thomas Purvess, George Helliwall.

Apryll 5.   George Mersser in Darnock, a.s.n. Johne ; w. Nicoll Moss, Johne Moss.

 ,,   5.   Johne Wilsone in Gallosheills, &c., a.s.n. Johne ; w. Jon Creibs, Phillip Darling.

 ,,   5.   George Scheill in Gallowsheills, &c., a.s.n. Marrione ; w. Androu Wilsone, William Darling.

 ,,   12.   Thomas Hoy in Colmeslichill, a.d.n. Agnes ; w. Jon Blaikie, Patrick Aitkine.

 ,,   26.   James Blaikie in Colmyslichill, a.s.n. Thomas ; w. Jon Souneyis, Jon Turner.

 ,,   26.   Robt. Law in Melrois, a.s.n. James ; w. Andreu Davidsone, Johne Wrycht.

 ,,   26.   Andreu Mersser in Darnock, a.s.n. George ; w. George Messr, Nicoll Moss.

Maii   3.   Thomas Eillis in Danzeltoune, a.d.n. Katherine ; w. Jon Bickett, James Eillis.

 ,,   10.   Wm. Wryt in Gattonsyde, a.d.n. Elizabeth ; w. Jon Wryt, Jon Meine.

 ,,   10.   Wm. Edgar in Melrois, a.s.n. Johne ; w. Johne Edgar, Wm. Wallace.

 ,,   10.   Wm. Scheill in Blanslie, a.s.n. Wm. ; w. George Scheill, Wm Hall.

1646.

Maii 27. Jon Hair in Melrois, a.d.n. Issobell ; w. Androu Patersone, Rt. Law.

June 21. Nicoll Mersser in Darnock, a.s.n. Nicoll ; w. Nicoll Moss, Jon Mersser.

July 12. Rot. Pringill of Blindlie, a.d n. Elizabeth ; w. James Cockburne, Peter Darling.

,, 12. Johne Helliwall in Gattonsyd, a.s.n. Johne ; w. Jon Helliwal, Rot. Mylnes.

,, 12. Nicol Mersser in Darnock, a.s.n. Johne ; w. Jon Mersser, Nicol Moss.

,, 19. Wm. Ormistoun in Gattonsyde, a.s n. Thomas ; w. James Marr, Johne Wryt.

,, 26. James Stoddart in Thripwood, a.d.n. Issobell ; w. Jon Moffett, Thomas Laidlaw.

,, 31. Richard Sclatour in Newsteid, a.s.n. Robert ; w. Jon Meine, Rot. Mersser.

Aug. 16. Androu Kennedie in Darnock, a.s.n. Wm ; w. Nicoll Moss, Wm. Fischar.

,, 23. Charles Clark in Gattonsyde, a.s.n. Wm. ; w. James Marr, James Bousteane.

,, 28. James Lukupe in Gattensyde, a.s.n. Patrick ; w. James Marr, James Bousteane.

Sept. 8. Wm. Karr in Newtoune, a.d.n. Elizabeth ; w. Nicoll Mylne, Henrie Cochrane

,, 27. Richard Sclatour in Williamlaw, a.s.n. Williame ; w. Richard Sclatour, Robert Meine.

,, 27. James Deipo in Williamlaw, a.d.n. Margarett ; w. Jon Deipo, Jon Blaikie.

Oct. 2. Androu Patersone in Melrois, a.d.n. Christiene ; w. Andrew Patersone, Robert Law.

,, 9. James Meine in Newsteid, a.s.n. David ; w. David Meine, Rot Meine.

,, 16. Thomas Lyell in Blainslie, a.d n. Agnes ; w. George Sheill, Edward Darling.

,, 18. George Hoy in Gattonsyde, a.d.n. Agnes ; w. James Marr, Wm. Hoy.

,, ,, Jon Wattsone in Danzeltoun, a.s.n. Wm ; w. James Eillis, Androu Peaterson.

,, 25. Johne Drumment in Bankmill, a.d.n. Marrione ; w. Androu Cairn-cross, Richd. Allexr.

,, 25. Wm. Davidsone in Laudopmuir, a.d. Eupha ; w. Thomas Freirgreiff, Hew Bell.

Nov. 3. Robert Bunzie in Newsteid, a.s.n. Andrew : w. Rot. Meine, Alexr. Meine.

,, 13. James Symsone in Newsteid, a.d.n. Marrione ; w. Wm. Symsone, Jon Symsone.

,, 15. Wm. Taitt in Buckholme, a.s.n. Johne, w. Alexr. Eilliss, Rot. Trotter.

,, 15. James Meine in Yldoun, a.d.n. Jennett ; w. Wm. Chisholme, Richard Sclatour.

,, 20. Rot. Meine in Newsteid, a.d.n. Bessie : w. Androw Meine, Alexr. Meine.

,, 29. George Bowstoun in Bridgend, a.s.n. Johne ; w. Johne Hownam, Nicol Meine.

,, ,, Nicol Cochrane in the Newtoun, a.d.n. Isobel : w. Nicol Milne, Thomas Chisholm.

Dec. 4. Alexr. Heittoun in Newtoun, a.s.n. Andro ; w. Nicol Miln, Andro Cochrane.

,, 6. Hew Bell of Langlie, a.s.n. Thomas ; w. Thomas Lithgow, William Fischer.

,, ,, Robert Trotter in Howsebyres, a.s.n. Thomas ; w. Alexr. Ellis, John Edgar.

,, 27. John Dimmack in Gatonside, a.d.n. Janet ; w. James Mar, James Bowsting.

,, ,, John Scot in Melros, a.s.n. Johne ; w. Johne Wright, George Blaickie.

1647.

Jan.   1. Andro Lukup, a.d.n. Isobel ; w. Andrew Patersone, James Lukup.

  ,,   ,, Richard Schlaiter, a.d.n. Janet ; w. Robert Meine, John Bowar.

  ,,   8. Jas. Ellis in Danzeltoun, a.d.n. Isobel ; w. Androu Patersone, Thomas Ellis.

  ,,   10. Thomas Patersone in Gallowshields, a.d.n. Agnes ; w. Johne Lorimer, Johne Mason.

  ,,   ,, James Wallace in Melros, a.d.n. Helene ; w. William Wallace, Alexr. Ellis.

Feb.   5. James Cairncross of Hilslope, a.d.n. Isobel ; w. Nicol Milne, Nicol Cairncross.

  ,,   21. George Wallace, a.s.n. Thomas ; w. Thomas Lithgow, Adam Lithgow.

  ,,   25. Andro Cuik, a.s.n. David ; w. Mr. David Fletcher, James Lithgow.

  ,,   28. William Bowar, a.s.n. William ; w. Johne Wallace, John Bowar.

  ,,   ,, David Thomson, a.d.n. Margret ; w. George Pringle, Johne Frater.

Mar. 18. Johne Notman, a.s.n. Thomas ; w. Thomas Laidlay, Thomas Wark.

  ,,   28. Johne Lawrie, a.s.n. Johne ; w. Nicoll Miles, Andro Miles.

  ,,   ,, Robert Schlaiter, of Galashills, a.d.n. Marie : w. George Friar, William Malor.

April 11. James Mar, a.s n. James ; w. James Bouston, Johne Halliwell.

  ,,   18. James Meine in Newsteid, a.s.n. Andro ; w. Andro Meine, Robert Meine.

  ,,   ,, James Meine in Fadonside, a.s.n. James ; w. Thomas Lithgow, Johne Meine.

  ,,   ,, Johne Hettoun in the Bridgend, a.s.n. Leonard ; w. Johne Uscher, George Hettoun.

  ,,   ,, Johne Hittoun in Darnick, a.d.n. Janet ; w. Andro Boustoun, Andro Smith.

  ,, last. Thomas Feirgrieve in Choislie, a.s.n. William ; w. William Cairncross, Thomas Jacks.

May   2. Adam Trumbal in Newsteid, a.s.n. George ; w. Andro Schlaiter, Andro Boustoun.

  ,,   ,, Andro Bowstoun in Bridgend, a.s.n. Johne : w. Johne Hownam, Andro Chisholm.

  ,,   9. Bartholomew Walker, a.s.n. Janet ; w. William Edgar, Alexr. Redpath.

  ,,   24. Robert Blaickie in Hackburn, a.s n. Patrick ; w. Patrick Blaikie, Patrick Aitken.

June 27. Thomas Heitton, a.d.n. Isabel ; w. Andro Hutton, George Pringle.

  ,,   ,, Thomas Miles, a.d.n. Jean ; w. Bartholomew Walker, John Hae.

July   2. Robert Bradie, a.s.n. James ; w. Richard Sclater, Johne Bowar.

  ,,   ,, John Wright, a.d.n. Agnes ; w. Thomas Carr, William Wright.

  ,,   4. Richard Lyes, a.d.n. Isobel ; w. Robert Lyes, William Sandelands. A testimonial from Mr. John Newlands.

  ,,   10. Bernard Wilson, a d.n. Christane ; w. Andro Schlater, Andro Meine.

  ,,   12. Andrew Cuik, a.d.n. Isobel ; w. Nicoll Chisholme, William Chisholme.

  ,,   ,, John Boustoun, a.d.n. Alison ; w. Robert Trotter, James Boustoun.

  ,,   17. Richard Boustoun, a.d.n. Margaret ; w. James Fischer, James Symson.

  ,,   ,, John Sore ?, a.s.n. James ; w. James Mar, John Holywell.

  ,, last. Andro Stewart, a.d.n. Isobel ; w. Richard Schlaiter, George Merser.

  ,,   ,, George Davidson, a.d.n. Isobel ; w. Johne Lyel, William Stirling.

Aug. 10. Johne Moffet, a.s.n. Archibald ; w. Archibald Moffet, James Moffet.

Sept. 12. William Laidlay, a.s.n. James ; w. Thomas Stenhouse, William Ker.

  ,,   19. William Messer, a.s.n. Peter ; w. Archibald Moffet, James Moffet.

  ,,   ,, Andro Morar, a.s.n. John ; w. Johne Morar, Robert Morar.

  ,,   27. Thomas Schlaiter, a.d.n. Isobel ; w. Robert Trotter, James Dawson.

Oct. 10. William Laidly, a.d.n. Isobel ; w. William Ladly, James Riddell.

  ,,   18. Thomas Welch, a.s.n. William ; w. Robert Meine, Andro Schlaiter.

  ,,   ,, William Cairncross, a.s.n. James ; w. Nicol and George Cairncrosses.

  ,,   18. Nicoll Chishom, a.s.n. James ; w. Andro Cuik, William Chishom.

  ,,   ,, William Hunter, a.d.n. Heilene ; w. James Kerr, Nicol Hunter.

1647.
Oct. 18. William Cairncrose, a.s.n. James ; w. Adam Lithgow, George Blackie.
Nov. 7. William Wilson, a.d.n. Aignes ; w. Bernard Wilson, James Messer.
„ 16. Andro Cairncrosse, a.s.n. William ; w. James Huetson, Patrick Etkine.
„ 20. James Mophet, a.s.n. Robert ; w. William Mophet, Johne Mophet.
„ „ Nicoll Kerr, a.s.n. Nicoll ; w. William Kerr, Nicoll Cochrane.
„ „ Johne Thomson, a.s.n. James ; w. James Cairncrosse, Andro Mylles.
Dec. 5. Johne Cochrane, a.s.n. Johne ; w. Johne Mosse, Johne Usher.
„ 10. Robert Forson, a.s.n. James ; w. Andro Slaitter, Andro Meine.
„ 12. William Fisher, a.s.n. Johne ; w. John Fisher, Olr. Fisher.
„ „ Johne Purviouse, a.s.n. Johne ; w. Adam Walker, Adam Paterson, a testimoniell from the elder of Gallowshelles.
„ 17. Andro Kerre, a.d.n. Janet ; w. Walter Donelson, Thomas Buie.
„ 24. James Eilisie, a.d.n. Margret ; w. Thomas Lithgow, Olr. Eilise.
„ last. George Pattersone, a.d.n. Isobell ; w. Johne Purviuse, John Pattersone, a testimonial from ye elders of Gallowshilles.

1648.
Jan. 2. Andro Meine, a.d.n. Isobell ; w. Johne Meine, Andro Sclaitter.
„ „ George Dalgleishe, a.s.n. Johne ; w. Johne Pringell, Andro Pringell, baptised in the Stoll.
„ 7. Thomas Loukup a.d.n. Margrat ; w. Thomas Lithgow, William Wallace.
„ 9. Alr. Clapperton, a.s.n. Alr.; w. Adam Clapperton, Andro Darline.
„ 23. Robert Philipe, a.d.n. Isobell ; w. Thomas Ormiston, William Hay.
„ „ Charles Clark, a.d.n. Agnes ; w. Johne Holliwell, John Drummant.
Feb. 1. George Merten, a.s.n. Johne ; w. Mathew Walker, James Fisher.
„ 4. William Wright, a.s.n. Johne ; w. Johne Wright, James Boustoun.
„ 27. Andro Ruttlage, a.s.n. Johne ; w. Thomas Freirgrive, Richard Oliver.
„ „ Johne Shill, a.s.n. William ; w. Johne Pringell, Andro Pringell.
Mar. 3. Thomas Eilse, a.s.n. Robert ; w. James Lithgow, William Fisher.
„ 5. Johne Blaikie, a.s.n. James ; w. James Cairncross, Thomas Freirgrive.
„ 10. William Mabane, a.d.n. Janet ; w. John Freir, Thomas Gill.
„ 19. James Freir, a.d.n. Isobell ; w. Robert Freir, James Boustoun.
„ „ Andrew Riddell, a.s.n. James ; w. James Riddell, Thomas Riddell.
„ last Andro Smith, a.s.n. Andro ; w. James Muddie, Nicoll Mosse.
„ „ William Chisme, a.s.n. Thomas ; w. Thomas Chisme, Nicoll Chisme.
„ „ George Howie in Gallowsheils, s.n. Robert ; w. William Wilson, Thomas Watson, ane testimoniall from Johne Anderson, elder.
April 16. Andro Thomsone, Gollowsheils, s.n. James ; w. Johne Blaikie, Wm. Maine, ane testimoniall from Johne Frein.
„ „ Robert Hislope, s.n. Robert ; w. Andro Hislope (?, Johne Helliwell.
„ „ Andro Waker, a.s.n. Walter ; w. Gaven Waker [*torn*].
„ last. James Bouston, d.n. Isobell ; w. Thomas Purvous, James Bouston.
„ „ Andro Hiton, a.s.n. Andro ; w. Johne Wallace, Nicoll Mill.
„ „ Andro Davison, a.d.n. Margrat ; w. Andro Davison, Andro Patersoune.
„ „ George Sunase, a.s.n. George ; w. Thomas Freirgreive, Richard Oliver.
„ „ George Kirkwood in Gallowshiels, a.s.n. Wm. ; w. James Ballantyne, Wm. Meban, ane testimoniall from Johne Freir.
May 13. James Cairncross [entry unfinished].
May 22. Alr. Freiden in Gallowsheils, a.d.n. Bessie ; w. Thomas Dobson, Robert Patterson, ane testimoniall from George Freir.
„ „ George Pringall in Gallowsheilds a.s.n. Charles ; w. George Freir, Gaven Pattersone, ane testimoniall from George Freir.
„ 29. Bernard Wilson, a.d.n. Margrat ; w. William Wilson, Johne Meine. Andro Hislop, a.s.n. Wm. ; w. Wm. Smith, Richard Oliver.
June 29. John Peirson in Gallowsheilds, a.d.n. Issobel ; w. David Thomson, George Dowson, ane testimoniall from John Freir.
July 2. William Merser, a.d.n. Janet ; w. John Merser, Nicoll Merser.

1648.

July 9. Richard Freter in Gallowsheilds, a.d.n. Janet ; w. Johne Crux, John
          Freter ; ane testimoniall from Johne Freir.

,,   ,, William Wallace, a.s.n. Johne ; w. John Wallace, Adam Lithgow.

,,   ,, Robert Mein, a.d.n. Janet ; w. Andro Tono, Alr. Mein.

,, 14. Thomas Ridfurd, a.d.n. Isobell ; w. Robert Ridfurd, Wm. Ridfurd.

,, 30. Thomas Watson in Gallowsheilds, a.d.n. Janet ; w. Thomas Turner,
          Johne Cratch, ane testimoniali from John Frier.

Aug. 6. William Broune, a.d.n. Anna ; w. John Mein, Robert Broun.

,, 18. Gaven Merten, a.s.n. John ; w. Johne Mertin, Alr. Ridpethe.

,, 20. Thomas Ormiston, a.s.n. Thomas, a.d.n. Isobell ; w. James Ormiston,
          Wm. Ormiston.

,, ,, Thomas Vair, a.d.n. Margrat ; w. Nicoll Mill, Wm. Lindsay.

,, 25. Robert Clerk, a.d.n. Marie ; w. Robert Freir, James Bowson.

,, ,, William Fisher, a.s.n. John ; w. William Fisher, Alr. Fisher.

,, 27. Thomas Vair, a.s.n. Thomas ; w. Aler. Hiton, Andro Hiton.

,, ,, Thomas Mar, a.s.n. Robert ; w. John Usher, Wm. Messer.

Sept. 1. James Davison, a.s.n. Thomas ; w. Thomas Turner, Richard
          Alexander.

,, 3. Andro Mein, a.s.n. Andro ; w. Thomas Bowstoune, Thomas Merten.

,, 17. William Anderson in Gallowsheilds, a.s.n. Georg ; w. Andro Peco,
          Wm. Mein, ane testamoniall from John Freir.

,, ,, William Thine, a.s.n. Thomas ; w. John Pringle, Edward Darling.

,, ,, John Waddell, d.n. —— ; w. James Cairncros, James Mein.

,, ,, Richard Sclaitter, a.d.n. Margrat ; w. John Pringle, Thomas Purvious.

,, 24. Robert Meban, a.s.n. James ; w. Thomas Drammnt, Andro Loukup in
          Bowdon.

Oct. 22. Thomas Pringl, a.d.n. Marion ; w. Johne Blaikie, John Pringell.

,, 29. James Simpson, a.s.n. James ; w. John Simpson, Wm. Cairncros.

Nov. 3. Andro Sclaitter, a.d.n. Isobell ; w. John Meine, Robert Meine.

,, 5. John Hunom, a.s.n. Johne ; w. John Hunom, John Mosse.

,, 10. James Lithan, a.s.n. Johne ; w. John Lithan, Thomas Bowston.

,, 14. George Gill, a.d.n. Bessie ; w. John Sheill, James Tait, bap. in stoll.

,, 29. James Lithgow, a.s.n. John ; w. Thomas Lithgow, Mr. Alex. Hume.

,, ,, William Tait, a.d.n. Margrat ; w. James Mein, Alr. Giles.

,, ,, Adam Newton, a.d.n. Janet ; w. Patrick Etkin, Thomas Freirgreive.

,, ,, Thomas Darling, a.d.n. Barbara ; w. Edward Darling, George
          Romanous.

,, ,, William Cairncros, a.d.n. —— ; w. James Cairncross, William
          Davisone.

Dec. 3. Mr. David Fletcher, a.d.n. Christian ; w. Thomas Lithgow, Mr. John
          Lithgow.

,, 17. James Loupwp, a.d.n. Jenot ; w. Thomas Loukwp, Patrick Loukwp.

,, 22. Thomas Boustain, a.s.n. James ; w. Wm. Reidfurd, James Boustain.

,, 29. Rot. Broune, a.s.n. John ; w. Jon Mein, Wm. Browne.

,, ,, Andro Boustain, a.d.n. Margrat ; w. William Fischer, George
          Boustain.

1649.

Jan. 5. George Cairncrose, a.s.n. George ; w. Wm. Cairncrose, Nicol
          Cairncrose.

,, ,, Thomas Wauch, a.d.n. Margrat ; w. James Davidson, Richard
          Alexander.

,, 12. James Merten, a.d.n. Margret ; w. Thomas Heiton, James Paterson.

,, ,, Richard Mein, a.d.n. Elspith ; w. Jon Mein, Andro Mein.

,, 19. Jon Turnbul, a.d.n. Bessie ; w. Jon Moffet, James Moffet.

,, ,, Thomas Hay, a.d.n. Isobel ; w. James Howatson, Jon Howatsone.

Feb. 4. Jon Dobson in Gallowsheilds, haveing a testimoniall from the elders
          a.s.n. Jon ; w. George Dobson, Alex. Dobsone.

,, ,, James Thomson, a.s.n. Andro ; w. Andro Darling, Wm. Hilsone.

,, ,, Robert Leithone, a.d.n. Jean ; w. Richart Sclatter, James Mein.

,, 11. Wm. Lamb, a.d.n. Janet ; w. Richart Sclatter, James Mein.

1649.

Feb. 17. Rot. Wilson in Gallowsheilds, a.s.n. Hew ; w. Hew Scot, Thomas
Watson, who produced a testimoniall from the elders.

,, 22. James Mein, a.s.n. Rot. ; w. Rot. and Andro Meines.

Mar. 4. George Hoy, a.d.n. Margret : w. Wm. Hoy, James Boustoun.

,, 11. Patrick Aytken, a.s.n. James ; w. Richart Alexr., Thomas Purves.

,, ,, James Hunter, a.s.n. Jon ; w. James Mein, James Davidson.

,, 16. Georg Pringal, a.s.n. Rot. : w. Rot. Pringall, Thomas Haton.

,, ,, Georg Couper, a.d.n. Margret ; w. Wm. Couper, Jon Halliwell.

,, 23. Georg Hoy, a.d.n. Isobel ; w. George Hoy, Thomas Boustain.

Apr. 1. Thomas Hutone, a.s.n. Andro ; w. Thomas Heiton, Andro Heiton.

,, 6. James Wallace, a.d.n. Isobel ; w. Wm. Wallace, Thomas Loukwp.

,, ,, Edward Romanos, a.s.n. Jon : w. Georg Romanos, Jon Moffet.

,, 15. James Wauch, a.s.n. Jon ; w. Wm. Bowar, Jon Bowar.

,, 22. Andro Richart, a.d.n. Ann ; w. Andro Heiton, Thomas Heiton, testimoniall from the elders of Gallowsheilds.

,, ,, Richard Boustain, a.s.n. Hew ; w. Jon Boustan, Wm. Fischer.

,, 29. James Bouar, a.d.n. Margret ; w. Jon Boue, elder, Jon Boue, younger.

May 5. Andro Mersar, a.d.n. Jenot ; w. Jon Wallace, James Wallace.

,, ,, Mathew Walker, a.s.n. Jon ; w. Jon Heiton, Andro Heiton.

,, ,, George Paterson, a.d.n. Margret : w. Edward Darling, Edward
Romanos.

,, 13. Jon Bichat, a.d.n. Issobel : w. James Eileis, Andro Eileis.

,, 24. Andro Kennadie. a.d.n. Margret ; w. Nicoll Moss, George Mudie.

,, ,, Thomas Myles, a.d.n. Isobell ; w. Jon Hounam, Nicol Merser.

June 8. James Mein, a.d.n. Isobel : w. Andro Mein, Jon Moffet.

,, 24. Wm. Bel, a.d.n. Agnes ; w. Hew Bel, Rot. Freir.

,, ,, Edward Darling, a.s.n. George ; w. Edward Romanos, Thomas Bel.

,, 29. Thomas Droumond, a.d.n. Jenot : w. Jon and Andro Droumonds.

,, ,, James Pringall, a.s.n. James ; w. Wm. Tait, Rt. Turnor.

July 13. Robt. Ormeston, a.d.n. Jean ; w. Robt. Freir, James Boustain.

,, ,, Wm. Hoy, a.d.n. Margret ; w. George Berton, Thomas Holliwall.

,, 29. Andro Trumbel, a.d.n. Agnes ; w. Rot. Whyt, Wm. Laidlow.

Aug. 10. Rot. Trotter, a.s.n. Janet ; w. Alexr. Eileis, James Mein.

,, 26. Wm. Laidlow, a.d.n. Janot ; w. Jon Laidlow, Wm. Ker.

Sept. 2. Andro Wilson, a.s.n. Andro : w. Rot. Forsan, Jon Mein.

,, ,, Bartholomew Walker, a.d.n. Isobel ; w. Thomas Reidfurd, Robert Bow.

,, 9. Thomas Couchram, a.d.n. Jenot : w. Nicol Mylne, Harie Couchrain.

,, ,, George Boustain, a.s.n. Rot. ; w. Rot. Mein, Andro Mein.

,, ,, Andro Paterson, a.d.n. Cristian ; Wm. Bowar, Jon Wallace.

,, ,, Agnes Ker's child baptised att the apoyntment off the presbitree : w.
Adam Younge. Thomas Ker.

,, last. Thomas Jack, a.d.n. Isobel ; w. Wm. Eileis, Wm. Fischer.

Oct. 7. Wm. Ormiston, a.s.n. Andro ; w. James Bowstain. Thomas Ormiston.

,, 28. Jon Drowmand, a.d.n. Isobell ; w. Andro Smith, Richard Bowar.

Nov. 2. Rot. Myls, a.d.n. Bessie ; w. Rot. Freir, Hendrie Myls.

,, 4. Thomas Loukwp, a.s.n. Andro : w. Jon Loukwp, Rot. Loukwp.

,, 11. George Blaikie, a.s.n. Jon ; w. Adam Lythgow, Mark Blaikie.

,, 18. Ritchardt Sclatter, a.s.n. Thomas : w. Rot. Mein, Jon Bowar.

,, ,, James Bunze, a.d.n. Agnes ; w. Andro Mein, Adam Trumble.

,, ,, Rot. Freir, a.d.n. Agnes ; w. Wm. Bell, James Freir.

,, 23. Andro Hislop, a.d.n. Margret ; w. Richart Alexr., Wm. Sim.

Dec. 4. William Fischer, a.d.n. Isobel ; w. Alexr. Fischer, Andro Mein.

,, 16. Nicol Cairncrose, a.d.n. William ; w. James Mein, James

,, ,, James Mein, a.s.n. Rot. : w. Andro Sclaiter, Jon Mein.

,, 20. Jon Wright, a.s.n. John ; w. James Lythgow, Wm. Fischer.

1650.

Jan. 7. Andro Heiton, a.s.n. Andro ; w. Thomas Heiton, elder, Thomas
Heiton, younger.

,, ,, Andro Cuik in Darnick, a.d.n. Helen ; w. Nicol and Andro Chisholmes.

,, 25. Mungo Donalson, a.s.n. Walter : w. Jon. Mein, Wm. Fischer.

1650.
Feb.   1. James Eileis, a.d.n. Helen ; w. William Wallace, Alexr. Fischer.
Mar.   3. Hendrie Myls, a.d.n. Isobel ; w. James Freir, Jon Holliwall.
  ,,   .. Hew Bell, a.d.n. Isobel ; w. Wm. Fischer, Rot. Pringall.
  ,,   .. Thomas Bowie, a.d.n. Isobel ; w. Rot. Mein, Wm. Fischer.
  ,,   22. Wm. Boustain, a.s.n. Robert ; w. Wm. Bell, James Boustain.
  ,,   .. Rot. Blaikie, a.s.n. Michel ; w. Robert Blaikie, George Messer.
  ,,   24. James Eileis, a.d.n. Margret ; w. James and Thomas [*torn*].
  ,,   31. William Davidson, a.s.n. Jon ; w. James Paterson, William **Cairn-**
            crose.
  ,,   .. Andro Mein, a.d.n. Jenot ; w. Thomas Boustain, James Leithan.
April   5. Gilbert Ker, a.d.n. Bessie ; w. Andro Davidson, Cudbert Bowie.
  ,,   7. Jon Watson, a.s.n. Wm. ; w. Wm. Cairncrose, Jon Pringall.
  ,,   14. Rt. Merton, a.s.n. Robert ; w. **Jon** Holiwall, Georg Frier.
  ,,   .. James Lithgow, twa twines, n. Andro and Agnes ; w. Wm. Bel, **Hew**
            Bell.
  ,,   26. Jon Mercer, a.s.n. ; w. Jon Hownam, Nicol Mercer.
  ,,   .. Patrick Blaikie, a.d.n. Margret ; w. James Howetson, Jon Pringall.
  ,,   28. Thomas Welch, a.s.n. Robert ; w. Jon Main, Robert Forsan.
  ,,   .. Rot. Braidie, a.s.n. Walter ; w. Richart Sclatter, Georg Sibbald.
May   3. Georg Moodie, a.d.n. Isobell ; w. Andro Kennadie, Patrick Blaikie.
  ,,   .. Wm. Swanston, a.s.n. Wm. ; w. James Davidson, Patrick Aitkin.
  ,,   19. James Tauding, a.s.n. Andro ; w. Wm. Hoy, Jon Mabon.
  ,,   .. Wm. Moffet, a.d.n. Bessie ; w. Jon Hall, James Moffet.
  ,, last. Adam Trumble, a.s.n. Jon ; w. Jon Mein, Andrew Sclatter.
June   9. Rot. Rod, a.d.n. Margret ; w. Jon Pringall, James Rolmanhous.
  ,,   18. Thomas Pringall, a.s.n. Thomas ; w. Thomas Freirgreive, Jon Blaikie.
  ,,   25. Alexr. Bowstain, a.d.n. Janet ; w. Nicol Mosse, Andro Kennedie.
  ,,   28. James Mein, a.d.n. Barbara ; w. Wm. Wallace, James Cairncrose.
July   5. James Riddell, a.s.n. Jon ; w. Nicol Mill, Wm. Laidlow.
  ,,   28. James Bowstain, a.s.n. James ; w. James Freir, James Wilson.
Aug.   1. Andro Phamp, a.s.n. Andro ; w. Rot. Mein, Alexr. Eileis.
  ,,   9. Wm. Bell, a.s.n. Thomas ; w. Rot. Freir, James Boustain.
  ,,   11. Walter ——, a.d.n. Jean ; w. Wm. Ormiston, James Boustain.
  ,,   17. Andro Mein, a.d.n. Bessie ; w. Bernard Mein, Rt. Mein.
  ,,   .. Wm. Bowar, a.d.n. Margret ; w. Jon Bowois, elder and younger.
Nov.   28. Andro Heiton, a.s.n. Jon ; w. Jon Mein, Alexr. Heiton.
  ,,   .. Georg Mercer, a.d.n. Alison ; w. Andro Kennadie, Andro Mercer.
Dec.   15. Janet Freir, a.d.n. Isobel ; w. Rt. Freir, Rot. Clark.
  ,,   27. Wm. Rutherfuird, a.d.n. Isobel ; w. Jon Rutherfuird, Gawen Merton.
1651
Jan.   19. Thomas Mylne, a.d.n. Alison ; w. Nicol Mylne, James Riddell.
Feb.   2. Walter Schaw, a.s.n. James ; w. Andro Wilson, Rot. Forsan.
  ,,   .. Thomas Heiton, a.d.n. Helen ; w. Andro Heiton, Georg Moodie.
Mar.   22. James Wallace in Melros, a.d.n. Margaret ; w. Wm. **Wallace**,
            Alexander Ellis.
  ,,   .. Bernard Wilson, a.s.n. Thomas ; w. John Mein, Andre Mein.
  ,,   .. William Wallace in Blainslie, a.d.n. Catherine ; w. Thomas **Lyell**,
            Wm. Dick.
  ,,   30. James Mein, a.s.n. Wm. ; w. Robert and Andro Mein.
  ,,   .. Thomas Ellis, a.s.n. James ; w. James Ellis, Andro Paterson.
Apr.   4. Andro Hardie, a.s.n. Adam ; w. Adam Hardie, Nicol Moffet.

[*At this point the record stops, a new volume begins, and some of the above*
entries are repeated.]

BOOKE OF BAPTISMES
1651. No. 4.

Followies the names and witnesses to the childreine baptised within the Kirk of Melrose the yeirs of God underwritten—

Thay are to say,

1651.

Mar. 22. James Wallace, a.d.n. Margaret ; w. Wm. Wallace, Alexr. Eleis.
   ,, ,, Bernard Wilsone, a.s.n. Thomas ; w. Jon Mein, Andro Mein.
   ,, penult. Wm Wallace, a.d.n. Catherine ; w. Thomas Lyell, Wm. Dick.
Apr. 4. James Mein, a.s.n. Wm. ; w. Andro Mein, Rot. Mein.
   ,, ,, Thomas Elleis, a.s.n. James ; w. Alexr. and Da. Elleis.
   ,, ,, Andro Kennedie, a.s.n. Andro ; w. Andro Kennedie, Nicol Moss.
   ,, ,, Andro Messr, a.s.n. Thomas ; w. Andro Sclaitter, Andro Messr.
   ,, 6. Wm. Hoy, a.s.n. George ; w. Wm. Hoy, George Hoy.
   ,, 13. James Pringall, a.s.n. Johne ; w. George Pringall, Johne Pringall.
June 4. William Cairncross, a.d.n. Jonatt ; w. William Wallace, George Kar.
   ,, 4. Johne Benatte, a.d.n. Margaret ; w. William and George Holliewall.
   ,, ,, George Baittie, a.d.n. Mart. ; w. Gesper Battie, Johne Romain.
   ,, 29. Thomas Raidfurd, a.s.n. Johne ; w. William Wallace, Wm. Edgar.
July 9. James Cairncross, a.d.n. Jeane ; w. Jon Pringall, Thomas Fergreive.
   ,, 20. Nicol Couhran, a.s.n. Johne ; w. Nicol Milne, Redchart Sclatter.
   ,, 27. George Freir, a.s.n. Robert ; w. Rot. Freir, Wm. Bell.
   ,, ,, Robert Heslope, a.s.n. James ; w. James Bowstone, Johne Haliewooll.
   ,, ,, James Semson, a.d.n. Agnezes ; w. James Semson, Johne Semson.
   ,, ,, Thomas Myldes, a.s.n. Thomas ; w. Johne Howname, William Fischer.
Aug. 6. James Lythgow, a.d.n. Margaret ; w. Thomas Lythgow, David Rodger.
   ,, last. Andro Cuik, a.s.n. Robert ; w. Andro Sclatter, Johne Mein.
Sept. 21. Thomas Darling, a.d.n. Margaret ; w. Edward Darling, Edward Rolmainhous.
   ,, 28. George Pringall, a.s.n. George ; w. Thomas and Andro Heiton.
   ,, ,, James Mein, a.s.n. Alexr. ; w. Redchard and Andro Meines.
Oct. 3. Adam Turnbull, a.s.n. Andro ; w. Johne Mein, Andro Turnbull.
Nov. 16. Andro Penman, tuo s.n. Johne and Thomas ; w. Johne Bowar, Wm. Bowar.
   ,, ,, Robert Ormeston, a.d.n. Issobell ; w. Wm. and Thomas Ormeston.
   ,, ,, Johne Haliewooll, a.s.n. Rot. ; w. Johne and Robert Haliewooll.
Dec. 7. Rot. Trotter, a.d.n. Issobell ; w. Alexr. Eilies, Johne Bunzie.
   ,, 21. James Howatson, a.s.n. Johne ; w. Patrick Blaikie, Johne Turneor.
   ,, 26. Alexr. Fischer, a.s.n. William ; w. James Lythgow, Wm. Fischer.
   ,, ,, George Uschar, a.s.n. Johne ; w. Johne and Nicol Moss.
   ,, ,, Robert Lowkwp, a.d.n. Jenatt ; w. Johne Bowar, Thomas Lowkwp.
1652.
Jan. —- Thomas Bowie, a.s.n. James ; w. Robert Forsan, Culbert Bowie.
Feb. 8. Andro Mein, a.s.n. Andro ; w. Andro Sclaitter, Andro Mein.
   ,, ,, Hendrie Myldes, a.d.n. Bessie ; w. Robert Myldes, Johne Haliewoll.
   ,, 13. Alexr. Mein, a.s.n. Andro ; w. Robert and Andro Meines.
   ,, ,, Markie Blaikie, a.d.n. Isobell ; w. Wm. and George Blaikie.
   ,, 28. Andro Tuno, a.d.n. Jean ; w. Andro Duncanson, Mr. Wm. Wilkie.
Mar. 12. Wm. Wauch, a.s.n. Wm. ; w. Thomas Lowkup, Wm. Edgar.
   ,, ,, Margaret Eillies, a.d.n. Isobell ; w. Alexr. Eillies, James Eillies.
   ,, 19. James Riddall, a.s.n. Mungow ; w. Thomas Milne, Nicoll Couchran.
   ,, 21. Thomas Vair, a.d.n. Issobell ; w. Thomas and Nicoll Milnes.
   ,, 21. Wm. Turnbull, a.s.n. James ; w. James and Johne Mertones.

1652.

April 2. Mungow Donaldson, a.s.n. Johne ; w. Jon Mein, Rot. Mein.
  „ „ Wm. Scott, a.s.n. Adam : w. Johne and Johne Bowars.
  „ 4. Andro Heitton, a.s.n. Johne ; w. Stene Bulmain, Wm. Fischer.
  „ „ James Corsbie, a.d n. Helene ; w. George and John Halliewoolls.
  „ 11. George Hoy : a d.n. Helen ; w. Wm. Hoey, Thomas Wilson.
  „ 18. Andro Mein, a.s.n. Redchart ; w. Johne Mein, James Mein.
  „ „ Wm. Bell, a.s. and a.d.n. Thomas and Agnezes ; w. ——.
  „ 25. Thomas Watson, a.d.n. Marian ; w. Wm. Ingleis, George Scot.
  „ 30. Alexr. Heiton, a.s. and a.d.n. Thomas and Mart. ; w. Nicoll Milne
          Nicoll Couchran.
  „ „ Georg Pringall, a.s.n. James ; w. Walter and Alexr. Pringall.
  „ „ Thomas Ormeston, a.d.n. Margaret ; w. Wm. and Andro Ormeston.
June 13. Thomas Mein, a.d.n. Jonett ; w. Rot. and Andro Meines.
  „ „ Hewie Wilson, a.d.n. Helene ; w. Thomas Lowkwp, Thomas Law.
  „ 13. Thomas Mar, a.d.n. Aleson ; w. Johne Bouston, Retchart Bowston.
  „ 20. Robert Freir, a.s.n. Georg ; w. Wm. Bell, James Freir.
  „ „ Johne Denantt. a.s.n. Johne : w. Ridchart Alexander, Thomas
          Turneor.
  „ 25. John Wilson in Gallosheills, a.s.n. Adam ; w. George Kirkup,
          Mungow Donaldson.
  „ 27. John Jonston, a.s.n. John ; w. Johne Turneor, Johne Dennantt.
July 4. Robert Bunzie, a.s.n. Robert ; w. Robert Mein, Johne Bunzie.
  „ 18. Wm. Fischer, a.d.n. Jonatt ; w. Johne Fischer, Wm. Fischer.
  „ „ Johne Pringill, a.s.n. Johne ; w. James Davidson, Edward Darling.
  „ „ Thomas Dobson, a.d.n. Grisall ; w. James Messr ; George Dobson.
  „ 23. Ridchart Sclaitter, a.d.n. Mart. ; w. Robert and Andro Meines.
Aug. 8. Hewie Brodarstaines, a.d.n. Helene ; w. Thomas Lyell, Johne
          Pringall.
  „ 13. John Wright, a.s.n. George ; w. Thomas Law, Mongow Donaldson.
  „ 22. Thomas Jack, a.s.n. James ; w. Johne and Nicol Moss.
  „ „ Thomas Cowchran, a.d.n. Issobell ; w. Nicoll Cowchran, Nicoll Mien.
  „ „ Wm. Laidlaw, a.d.n. Jonnett ; w. Nicoll Miln, Johne Laidlaw.
  „ 29. Edward Darling, a.s.n. Andro ; w. Thomas Darling, Edward Rolmain-
          hous.
  „ „ Thomas Lyell, a.s.n. Wm. ; w. Edward Darling, Edward Rolmain-
          hous.
Sept. 3. George Blaikie, a.d.n. Janett ; w. James Lythgow, Adam Lythgow.
  „ 5. John Pringall, a.s.n. John ; w. James Mein, Thomas Pringall.
  „ „ Andro Merser, a.s.n. James ; w. Andro Merser, John Heittone.
  „ 10. Thomas Miln, a.s.n. Mongow ; w. Nicoll and John Miln.
  „ 10. Wm. Wallace, a.s.n. James ; w. John and James Wallace.
  „ 12. Robert Ingales, a.d.n. Helene ; w. James Moffit, James Stoddert.
  „ „ James Wattson, a.s.n. Alexr. ; w. Andrew Paterson, Mungo Donaldson.
  „ 19. James Davidson, a.s.n. Wm. ; w. James Greive, Wm. Hall.
Oct. 3. James Lythgow, a.s.n. James ; w. Mr. John Lythgow, James Eillies.
  „ „ Andro Cairncroce, a.d.n. Elesbath : w. James Mein, Ridchart
          Alexander.
Oct. 8. Mr. David Flescheor, a.d.n. Jonatt ; w. Mr. Thomas Wilkie, James
          Lythgow.
  „ „ John Rathie, a.d.n. Jonett ; w. John and Wm. Meins.
  „ „ Andro Pringill, a.s.n George ; w. Jon and Robert Pringall.
  „ 15. Georg Wilson, a.s.n. Wm. ; w. John Hownam, John Rathie.
  „ 15. Johne Nottman, a.s.n. George ; w. Johne Jonston, Wm. Smeth.
  „ 29. John Messr., a.s.n. Andro ; w. John Hownam, John Messr.
  „ „ Wm. Camb, a.s.n. George ; w. Ridchart Sclaitter, Alexr. Uschar.
  „ „ Adam Heislop, a.s n. John ; w. John Pringill, George Messr.
Nov. 5. Andro Mein, a.d.n. Marie ; w. John Mein, Alexr. Mein.
  „ 7. Thomas Stenhous, a.s.n. Thomas ; w. Ridchart Sclaitter, Nicol
          Miln.
  „ 12. Andro Reidpeth, a.s.n. Alexr. ; w. Alexr. Reidpeth, Wm. Edgar.

1652.
Nov. 19. Rot. Kar in Faldonsyd, a.d.n. Jonett ; w. James Lithgow, Wm.
      Fischer.
  ,, 21. Wm. Ormeston, a.s.n. Wm.; w. James Bowston, Robert Clark.
Dec. 5. Thomas Wilson, a.s.n. Adam ; w. [*torn*], Wm. Bell.
  ,, ,, Thomas Loukup, a.s.n. Wm.; w. Rot. Mein, Wm. Edgar.
  ,, 17. James Mein, a.d.n. Agnus ; w. Rot. Mein, Jon Mein.
  ,, ,, Patrick Atcken, a.d.n. Jeane ; w. James Feirgreive, Thomas Feirgreive.
1653.
Jan. 2. James Howatson, a.d.n. Jonett; w. James Howatson, Johne Howatsone.
  ,, 21. John Bychet, a.d.n. Jonett ; w. Andro Patson, James Eilies.
  ,, ,, George Modie, a.s.n. Johne ; w. Patrick Blaikie, James Fischer.
  ,, ,, Thomas Jonston, a.s.n. Thomas ; w. James Bowstone, Johne
      Holiwooll.
  ,, 23. James Mein, a.d.n. Jonatt ; w. Ridchart Mein, Ridchart Sclaitter.
  ,, ,, Rot. ——, a.d.n. Marion ; w. Andro Bowston, Johne Hownam.
  ,, 30. James Gillies, a.d.n. Agnus ; w. James Lythgow, Alexr. Eillies.
  ,, ,, Alexr. Uscher, a.s.n. Johne ; Jon Moss, Johne Uscher.
Feb. 18. James Wallace, a.d.n. Jonatt ; w. Alexr. Eillies, Wm. Edgar.
  ,, ,, Johne Bowston, a.s.n. Johne ; w. Rt. Freir, Wm. Bell.
Mar. 4. James Lethem, a.d.n. Issobell ; w. Thomas and James Bouston.
  ,, 6. Thomas Feirgreive, a.d.n. Jean ; w. James Feirgreive, James Mein.
  ,, 11. Alexr. Fischer, a.d.n. Grissell ; w. James Lythgow, Johne Fischer.
  ,, 13. Wm. Swanston, a.d.n. Margaret ; w. Ridchart Alexander, Johne
      Merton.
  ,, ,, James Rolmainhous, a.d.n. Helene ; w. Johne Pringill, Edward
      Rolmainhous.
  ,, 18. Johne Mar, a.s.n. Thomas ; w. Andro Mein, Johne Mein.
      Edward Kar, a.s.n. Thomas ; w. Thomas Turneor, Johne Jonstone.
  ,, 26. James Browne, a.d.n. Jenet ; w. Thomas Forgreiw, Andro Achesone.
  ,, ,, Thomas Turner, a.s.n. Johne ; w. Thomas Forgrew, John Turneor.
  ,, ,, Thomas Pringall, a.d.n. Agnes ; w. Thomas Forgreive, John Pringall.
  ,, ,, William Trumbull, a.d.n. Christian ; w. James Mertone, Johne
      Huname.
April 17. Berball Waker, a.s.n. Johne ; w. Thomas Loukup, Wm. Edgar.
  ,, ,, Johne Drumand, a.d.n. Hellen ; w. Thomas Drumond, Edward
      Drowmand.
  ,, 24. Andro Achesone, a.s.n. George ; w. Thomas Forgrew, Alexr. Turner.
May 1. Wm. Chesolem, a.d.n. Jenet ; w. Wm. Fischer, Ed. Cheselme.
  ,, ,, Johne Holiwall, a.s.n. Robert ; w. Robert Holiwall, Johne Holiwall.
  ,, 15. Rot. Lethem, a.s.n. Rot. ; w. Recheard Sclatter, Georg Seball.
  ,, 22. Wm. Fischar, a.d.n. Margaret ; w. John Ficher, James Lithgow.
  ,, 22. John Frater, a.s.n. George ; w. John Wilsone, Mungo Donaldsone.
  ,, 22. John Messer, a.d.n. Issobel ; w. Nicoll Messer, Wm. Merssr.
  ,, 22. James Fischer, a.s. to wit William ; w. Wm. Fischer, Wm. Mein.
June 26. Robert Mabon, a.s.n. Walter ; w. Andrew Paterson, Andrew Lookup.
  ,, 26. James Bunzie, a.s.n. Thomas ; w. John Mein, John Bunzie.
July 16. Andrew Boustoune, a.d.n. Issobell ; w. Andrew Cuik, John Huname.
  ,, 16. Alexr. Bowden, a.d.n. Issobell ; w. Wm. Fischer, Malze Walker.
  ,, 16. James Riddell, a.d.n. Alesone ; w. Nicoll and Thomas Milns.
  ,, 16. Andrew Sclaitter, a.s.n. Thomas ; w. John Mein, Andrew Holme.
  ,, 16. William Johnstoun, a.s.n. Wm. ; w. Richart Sclaitter, Edward Darling.
  ,, 16. Bertie Mein, a.d.n. Isobel ; w. Richard Sclaitter, George Siball.
  ,, 16. Thomas Law, a.d.n. Christiane ; w. Alexr. Eles, James Wallace.
  ,, 16. Rot. Holiwall, a.d.n. Isobel ; w. John Holiwall, Wm. Bell.
  ,, 16. George Beattie, a.s.n. Andro ; w. John Howname, Nicol Merssr.
Aug. 12. Rot. Browne, a.d.n. Christiane ; w. John Mein, Wm. Browne.
  ,, ,, Rot. Lader, a.s.n. Williame ; w. Edward Romainhous, John Pringall.
  ,, ,, Wm. Reidfurd, a.d.n. Margaret ; w. Archald Moffet, Tho. Reidfurd.
  ,, ,, Andrew Heitoune, a.s.n. Thom ; w. Stein Bullman, Alexr. Elles.
  ,, 28. Johne Bunzie, a.d.n. Issobell ; w. James Lidderdaill, Alexr. Elleis.

1653.
Sept. 11. Rot. Lees, a.d.n. Elizabeth ; w. Johne and Andro Pringall.
  ,,   ,, James Elles, a.s.n. Walter ; w. Alexr. and James Elles.
  ,,   ,, Mongo Donaldsone, a.s.n. Walter ; w. Wm. Sweit, Wm. Kar.
  ,,   ,, Patrick Lowkup, a.d.n. Margaret ; w. Johne Burne, Thomas Lukup.
Oct. 8. Thomas Gray, a.d.n. Agnes ; w. Rot. and Williame Forgrieve.
  ,,   ,, George Freir, a.s.n. George ; w. James Bowstone, Ro. Miles.
  ,,   ,, Wm. Greitsone, a.s.n. Agnes ; w. Williame Leittone, George Hey.
  ,,   ,, Johne Romainhous, a.d.n. Heillein ; w. Edward and James Romainos
  ,,   16. Wm. Clerk, a.d.n. Hellen ; w. Wm. Fischer, Wm. Hoy.
  ,,   ,, Robert Mertoune, a.d.n. Issobell ; w. James and Johne Mertounes.
  ,,   ,, Wm. Renek, a.d.n. Margaret ; w. Johne and Wm. Fischer.
  ,,   23. William Scot, a.s.n. Thomas ; w. Thomas Forgrew, James Mein.
  ,,   ,, Johne Bunzie, a.s.n. James ; w. Johne and James Bunzie.
Nov. 18. William Cairncrosse ; a.s.n. James ; w. ——.
Dec. 4. William Martoune, a.s.n. William ; w. James Boustine, Thomas
            Boustine.
  ,,   11. James Boustine, a.s.n. James ; w. James and Thomas Boustines.
  ,,   18. James Sympsone, a.d.n. Margaret ; w. Richard Sclaitter, John
            Symsone.
1654.
Jan. 1. Nicol Darling, a.d.n. Jeane ; w. James Darling, Richard Alexander.
  ,,   8. Andrew Meine, a.d.n. Helein ; w. Thomas Boustain, Wm. Martine.
  ,,   13. Andrew Cuik, a.s.n. Androw ; w. Wm. and Andrew Chismes.
  ,,   ,, Thomas Drumand, a.d.n. Issobell ; w. Androw Patersone, James
            Eilise.
  ,,   20. John Blaikie, a.d.n. Margaret ; w. James Meine, Thomas Turner.
  ,,   22. Robert Browne in the parish of Gallowsheels, a.d.n. Marioune ; w.
            Wm. Freir, John Wilsone.
  ,,   22. Johne Johnston, a.d.n. Jenet ; w. Richard Alexander, Thos. Turner.
  ,,   27. Robert Trotter, a.s.n. Robert ; w. James and Alexr. Eilice.
  ,,   29. James Turner, a.d.n. Margaret ; w. Richard Alexander, Thomas
            Turner.
Feb. 17. James Eilice, a.s.n. Alexr.; w. Alexr. Elice and James Lithgow.
  ,,   ,, Andrew Cuick, a.s.n. Williame ; w. Wm. Edgar
  ,,   26. James Lithgow, a.s.n. William ; w. Alexr. Elice, Wm. Fischer.
  ,,   ,, John Scott, a.s.n. Robert ; w. John and Robert Hollywall.
Mar. 3. a.d.n. Issobell ; w. Alexr. Elice, James Elice [*no parents given*].
  ,,   12. Andrew Wilsone, a.d.n. Bessie ; w. Robert Forson, James Mersare.
  ,,   ,, Robert Clark, a.d.n. Jeane ; w. James Boustain, Robert Ormistoune.
  ,,   17. John Lythgow, a.d.n. Margaret ; w. Edward Darling, John Pringle.
  ,,   17. James Feirgreive, a.s.n. Williame ; w. Thomas Feirgreive, James
            Meine.
  ,,   31. Nicol Marsar, a.d.n. Isobell ; w. John Hounop, Walter Ushar.
Apr. 2. James Frier, a.d.n. Agnes ; w. Robert Freir, James Boustine.
  ,,   7. Andrew Kennedie, a.s.n. William ; w. James and William Fischer.
  ,,   14. Andrew Tunno, a.d.n. Margaret ; w. Alexr. Usher, Mungo
            Donaldson.
  ,,   21. Thomas Darling, a.d.n. Christiane ; w. Edward Darling, John Pringle.
  ,,   28. Thomas Milne, a.d.n. Isobell ; w. Nicol Milne, James Milne.
  ,,   ,, John Hallywoll, a.d.n. Margaret ; w. James Boustine, Wm. Bell.
  ,,   30. Alexr. Meen, a.d.n. Agnes ; w. James Boustine, Wm. Bell.
May   5. Thomas Lookup, a.d.n. Isobell ; w. Wm. Edgar, John Wallace.
  ,,   9. Robert Ormestoune, a.d.n. Bessie ; w. Adam Darling, John Wright.
June 4. Robert Freir, a.s.n. John ; w. James Freir, John Halliwoll.
  ,,   18. John Moffet, a.d.n. Marie ; w. Archibald and William Moffets.
July 28. Margaret Blaikie, a.s.n. James ; w. Alexr. Eilies, George Blaikie.
Aug. 7. James Bouer, a.s.n. John ; w. John Bouer, James Meen.
  ,,   13. Andrew Penman, a.s.n. James ; w. John Bouer, John Bouer.
  ,,   13. William Browne, a.s.n. James ; w. James Meen, Robert Meen.
  ,,   27. George Mersar, a.s.n. Andrew ; w. Andrew Kennedie, Nicol Mersar.

1654.
Aug. 27. William Moffet, a.s.n. William ; w. James Moffet, James Stodderet.
Sept. 15. William Macdougall, a.s.n. William ; w. Wm. Fisher, Patrick Riddell.
  ,, 30. Thomas Boustine, a.s.n. Thomas ; w. James Boustine, Thomas Boustine.
  ,, ,, Andrew Turnbull, a.d.n. Christian ; w. James Riddell, John Milne.
Oct. 7. Patrick Redfoord, a.s.n. James ; w. Alexr. and James Eilies.
  ,, ,, William Bell, a.d.n. Agnes ; w. James Lythgow, James Boustine.
Dec. 31. John Mertine, a.d.n. Margaret ; w. Andrew and John Mertine.
1655.
Jan. 12. Robert Halliwoll, a.d.n. Isobell ; w. John and John Hallwolls.
  ,, 18. John Haitlie, a.d.n. Helen ; w. Alexr. Haitlie, John Mabane.
  ,, 20. John Cochran, a.d.n. Anne ; w. John Mosse, John Herwune.
  ,, 28. John Greirsoune, a.d.n. Bessie ; w. William Heitoune, George Boge.
Feb. 2. Mungo Donaldsonne, a.s.n. Peter ; w. Williame Sweet, John Fraiter.
  ,, 2. James Riddell, a.s.n. Andrew ; w. Nicoll and Thomas Milns.
  ,, 11. Thomas Milds, a.d.n. Isabell ; w. John Halliwoll, James Boustine.
  ,, 11. George Boe, a.d.n. Jenet ; w. Nicol Miln, Thomas Cochrane.
  ,, 18. James Corsbie, a.s.n. James ; w. George Bartoune, William Hoie.
  ,, 18. George Mudie, a.s.n. George ; w. James and William Gilberts.
  ,, 23. Andrew Mersar, a.s.n. Andrew ; w. Andrew Heitoun, Andrew Mersar.
Mar. 2. Walter Riddell, a.d.n. Jean ; w. John Fisher, James Lithgow.
Apr. 2. William Turnbull, a.s.n. Andrew ; w. James and John Mertines.
  ,, 2. Alexr. Coshar, a.d.n. Janet ; w. Alexr. Eilies, William Edgar.
  ,, 8. Walter Vetch, a.d.n. Elizabeth ; w. William How, James Boustine.
  ,, 22. Thomas Wilsone, a.d.n. Elizabeth ; w. Mark Blaikie, Andrew Tunno.
  ,, 22. William Scot, a.s.n. William ; w. Thomas Freirgreive, James Meen.
  ,, 27. James Lithgow, a.d.n. Catharine ; w. Alexr. Eilies, John Meen.
  ,, 29. George Deuare, a.s. presented be John Blaikie, n. Andrew ; w. James Boustine, William Howe.
May 11. James Mein, a.s.n. James ; w. Richard Sclaiter, John Bower.
  ,, 13. Andrew Pringle, a.s.n. Andrew ; w. John Pringle, Andrew Pringle.
  ,, 18. James Broune, a.d.n. Agnes ; w. William Darling, Andrew Stewart.
  ,, 20. Thomas Eilice, a.d.n. Margaret ; w. Andrew Paterson, Andrew Loukup.
  ,, 20. George How, a.d.n. Jenet ; w. William How, Thomas Wilsone.
  ,, 25. Hew Wilsone, a.d.n. Bessie ; w. Thomas Loukup, James Waugh.
  ,, 27. John Bell, a.s.n. John ; w. James Mersar, Culbert Bowie.
June 7. William Tait, a.d.n. Bessie ; w. Alexr. Eilies, James Eilies.
  ,, 17. Christian Wilsone, a.d. presented by James Burne, n. Agnes ; w. Alexr. Eilies, Robert Trotter.
  ,, 24. Andrew Kennedie, a.d.n. Jean ; w. George Mudie, James Fischare.
  ,, 27. Alexr. Heitoun, a.s.n. William ; w. Thomas Stennais, Andrew Heitoun.
July 1. James Leithane, a.s.n. Thomas ; w. James Boustane, Thomas Boustane.
  ,, 6. Thomas Redford, a.d.n. Helen ; w. Alexr. Eilies, Alexr. Ushare.
  ,, 8. Nicoll Cochran, a.d.n. Agnes ; w. Nicoll Miln, Andrew Meine.
  ,, 20. William Fishar, a.d.n. Christian ; w. John and Robert Mains.
Aug. 24. Andrew Mein, a.d.n. Agnes ; w. John Benzie, James Mein.
Sept. 2. Daniell Herrisone, a.d. presented by Mungo Donaldson, n. Jean ; w. James Karre, James Eilice.
  ,, ,, John Miln, a.s.n. Mungo ; w. Nicoll and Thomas Miln.
  ,, ,, George Sheill, a d.n. Janet ; w. Andrew Patersone, Mark Blaikie.
  ,, 23. John Maban, a.s.n. Williame ; w. William Fishure, James Mein.
  ,, 30. William Messar, a.s.n. Nicoll ; w. Nicoll Messar, James Fishare.
Oct. 2. Robert Meen, a.s.n. John ; w. Andrew Wilson, Andrew Mein.
  ,, 7. Andrew Hertoun, a.d.n. Agnes ; w. Andrew Lithgow, George Hounam.
  ,, 12. Thomas Gray, a.s.n. Robert ; w. Robert Forsan, Alexr. Mein.
  ,, 26. ——— Johnstoune, a.s.n. George ; w. Thomas Turner, John Blackie.

1655.
Nov. 1. Thomas Stennis, a.d.n. Marione ; w. Richart Sclaitter, Nicoll Milne.
  ,, 4. Thomas Lookup, a.d.n. Helen, w. Robert and John Meen.
  ,, ,, John Maxwell, a.s.n. James, w. Mungo Donaldson, Thomas Redford.
  ,, ,, Andrew Chisholme, a.s.n. Robert. w. John Fenwick, James Hunter.
  ,, ,, Robert Clark, a.s.n. Andrew, w. James Boustine, Williame Howe.
  ,, 12. Andrew Paterson, a.d.n. Christian ; w. Andrew Paterson, John Bowar.
  ,, 18. James Mein, a.d.n. Janet ; w. John and Robert Meins.
  ,, 25. Robert Bounzie, a.d.n. Janet ; w. Robert Mein, James Bounzie.
  ,, ,, Alexr. Wod, a.d.n. Margt. ; Andrew Darling, James Parre.
Dec. 2. Thomas Cochrane, a.d.n. Annaple ; w. Nicol Miln, Nicol Cochrane.
  ,, ,, Robert Halliwall, a.d. presented by James Cairncross, n. Jenie ; w. Robert Mein and John Halliwall.
1656.
Jan. 1. John Boware, a.s.n. James ; Richard Sclaiter, John Bouar.
  ,, 4. Patrick Redford, a.s.n. Patrick and a.d.n. Isobell ; w. Wm. Edgare, Thomas Lookup.
  ,, 11. John Miln. a.s.n. Robert ; w. Nicol Miln, Thomas Miln.
  ,, ,, John Hounam, a.d.n. Isabell ; w. John Houname, Nicol Mercere.
Feb. 8. John Bunzie, a.s.n. James ; w. John Meen, James Lidderdaine.
  ,, ,, James Feirgreive, a.d.n. Bessie ; w. Thomas Feirgreive, Richard Alexander.
  ,, ,, Robert Lies, a son presented by Robert Lies, n. John ; w. John Lies, Robert Lund.
  ,, 24. James Eilice, a.s.n. James ; w. James Lithgow, Alexr. Eilice.
  ,, 29 John Lithgow, a.d.n. Catherine ; w. John Shillinglaw, Wm. Hall.
Mar. 9. Robert Sheel, a.d.n. Elizabeth ; w. James Boustain, Adam Darling.
  ,, 16. George Cairncross, a.d.n. Janet ; w. Robert Breadie, John Bouar.
  ,, ,, Thomas Bald, a.s.n. Walter ; w. William Fischar, Robert Wright.
  ,, 23. William Ranwick, a.s.n. William ; w. John and William Fischars.
  ,, 30. Hendrie Mylds, a.d.n. Helene ; w. John Haliewell, Robert Meen.
  ,, ,, Wm. Laidlaw, a.d.n. Margaret ; w. John Laidlaw, Thomas Miln.
Apr. 4. Robert Blaikie, a.s.n. George ; w. John Merser, Andro Pringle.
  ,, 4. Andrew Smith, a.s.n. James ; w. George Houname, John Thomsone.
  ,, ,, Robert Browne, a.d.n. Agnes ; w. John and Robert Meines.
  ,, 20. Wm. Cairncross, a.s.n. John ; w. John Meen, Nicol Miln.
  ,, ,, James Fishar, a.s.n. Nicholl ; w. Georg Griersone, Wm. Fishar.
  ,, 27. James Steinesone, a.s.n. John ; w. Richard Sclaiter, Thomas Pringle.
May 11. Robert Law, a.s.n. Robert ; w. Andrew and Peter Darlings.
  ,, 11. Thomas How, a.d.n. Margaret ; w. James Moffat, Robert Laidlay.
  ,, 18. John Blakie, a.d.n. Isabell ; w. James Meine, Thomas Turner.
  ,, ,, George Boustine, a.s.n. Andrew ; w. Andrew Chisholm, John Johnstoune.
  ,, ,, Robert Martoune, a.s.n. David ; w. John Martoune, James Martoune.
  ,, 23. John Marre, a.s.n. John ; w. Robert Mein, Andrew Marre.
  ,, ,, James Eilies, a.s.n. James ; w. Alexr. Eilies, Robert Trotter.
June 1. Nicol Ushar, a.d.n. Isabel ; w. Nicol Merser, Walter Ushar.
  ,, 6. William Lamb, a.s.n. John ; w. John Bouar, Richard Sclaitter.
  ,, ,, Robert Maban, a.s.n. Robert ; w. Thomas Drummond, Mungo Donaldson.
  ,, 8. Andrew Mein, a.d.n. —— ; w. Adam Hislope, James Deipo.
  ,, 8. George Martoune, a.s.n. William ; w. Wm. Martoune, Wm. Wright.
  ,, 29. Nicol Mersar, a.s.n. Thomas ; w. Robert Meen, James Mersar.
  ,, 29. Wm. Martoune, a.s.n. John ; w. James Boustine, Wm. Bell.
July 11. John Leies, a.s.n. William ; w. Rot. Lies, George Messer.
  ,, 13. Thomas Harwell, a.s.n. Thomas ; w. John Harwel, James Bowstoune.
  ,, 22. Andrew Sclater, a.d.n. Jonet ; w. John and Rot. Meines.
  ,, 24. William Clerk, a.d.n. Margret ; w. Wm. Fishar, Wm. Hoy.
Aug. 8. Bartholome Waker, a.s.n. James ; w. Alexr. and James Eleisis.
  ,, 17. James Malkomtosh, a.s.n. Andrew ; w. George Grierson, Wm. Spotswood.

1656.

Aug. 24. Johne Bunzie, a.d.n. Agnes ; w. Rot. Alexander, Rot. Mein.
  ,,   29. Andrew Pringle, a.d.n. Eliz. ; w. John Pringle, George Messer.
  ,, last. Adam Trumble, a.s.n. Thomas ; w. John Bounzie, John Mein.
Sept. 7. Robert Stirling, a.d.n. Issobell ; w. Edward Darling, Thomas Lyon.
  ,,   ,, George Freir, a.d.n. Issobell ; w. Rot. Freir, Wm. Hoy.
  ,, 28. James Lithgow, a.d.n. Helene ; w. Mr. John Lithgow, Alexr. Helliburton.
Oct. 20. James Mein, a.d.n. Agnes ; w. Alexr. Clerk, James Eleis.
  ,, 25. Walter Riddell, a.d.n. Eupham ; w. Wm. Fishar, James Walace.
Nov. 2. Thomas Bowstoun, a.s.n. Jon ; w. James and Thomas Boustons.
  ,,   8. Andrew Richard, a.s.n. Richard ; w. Walter Welch, Thomas Heitton.
  ,, 21. Andrew Mein, a.s.n. Alexr. ; w. John and Andrew Meins.
  ,,   ,, John Halliwall, a.d.n. Janet ; w. John and Thomas Halliwall.
  ,, 23. Thom. Bouston, a.d.n. Janet ; w. Thomas and James Bouston.
  ,, 30. Thomas Myles, a.s.n. James ; w. Ro. Myles, Adam Lithgow.
Dec. 5. Andrew Tunno, a.d.n. Dina ; w. Mr. Jon Currie, Wm. Edger.
  ,, 15. Wm. Messer, a.s.n. George ; w. George and John Messers.
  ,, 28. Wm. Anderson, a.d.n. Janet ; w. John Maxwell, Wm. Wallace.

1657.

Jan. 2. James Mein, a.s.n. Johne ; w. John and Robert Meins.
  ,,   2. John Halliwell, a.d.n. Hellein ; w. John and Robert Halliwells.
  ,,   .. James Turner, a.s.n. George ; w. Thomas and George Turners.
  ,,   9. Robert Bunzie, a.d.n. Agnes ; w. Alexr. and Rot. Meins.
  ,, 11. William Fishar, a.s.n. Robert ; w. John and William Fishars.
  ,, 11. Thomas Welch. a.s.n. Andrew ; w. John and James Meins.
  ,, 16. Andrew Cuike, a.s.n. John ; w. John Mein, Mungow Donaldson.
  ,, 25. Mungow Donaldson, a.d.n. Catherin ; w. John Crooker, Wm. Sueet.
  ,, 25. John Ushar, a.s.n. John ; w. John Moss, Alexr. Ushar.
Feb. 6. Wm. Bell, a.d.n. Janet ; w. James Boustain, Wm. Hoy.
  ,,   ,, James Mein, a.d.n. Margt. ; w. Wm. Cairncross, Richard Sclater.
  ,, 22. Michael Fishar, a.s.n. Andrew ; w. Andrew Kennedie, Wm. Fishar.
  ,,   .. Merkie Mein, a.d.n. Aleson ; w. Richard Sclater, John Bowar.
Mar. 15. Robert Rae, a.d.n. Margt. ; w. John Moffat, Andrew Sclater.
  ,,   ,, Alexr. Heiton, a.d.n. Aleson ; w. Andrew Heiton, George Sibbald.
  ,, 22. George Sheill, a.d.n. Bessie ; w. Andrew Sclaiter, Andrew Paterson
  ,, 29. Andrew Drumond, a.d.n. Isobell ; w. John and Thomas Drumonds.
  ,,   ,, William Turnbill, a.s.n. Stein ; w. James and John Mertens.
Apr. 5. Robert Wright, a.s.n. Robert ; w. Thomas and John Wrights.
  ,, 12. Andrew Stewart, a.s.n. And. ; w. John Pringle, George Mersar.
  ,, 12. James Depo, a.s.n. James ; w. James Moffat, Adam Haislop.
  ,, 19. John Frater, a.s.n. John ; w. John Cruix (?), Mungo Donaldson.
  ,, 26. Richard Sclaiter, a.d.n. Aleson ; w. John and Robert Meins.
  ,, 26. Wm. Swanston, a.d.n. Bessie ; w. John Marten, John Blaikie.
May 13. Jon Pringle, a.s.n. Thomas ; w. James Moffat, Wm. Moffat.
  ,, 14. Michaell Gibson, a.s.n. David ; w. Wm. Edgar, Mungow Donaldson.
  ,,   .. Umqll. Pat Ridford, a.d.n. Margt. presented by Thomas Lookup ; w. Wm. Edgar, James Lookup.
  ,, 17. James Merser, a.d.n. Issobell ; w. Andro Tunno, John Mean.
  ,, 24. Rot. Halliwell, a.s.n. Thomas ; w. James Boustan, Thomas Halliwell.
  ,, last. Thos. Mill, a.s.n. James ; w. John Mill, Mungo Mill.
  ,,   ,, John Mill, a.d.n. Aieson ; w. James and Archibald Moffats.
June 5. John Braidie, a.d.n. Margt. ; w. John Bowe, Robert Braidie.
  ,,   7. James Lookup. a.d.n. Issobell ; w. Thomas and Andrew Lookup.
  ,, 21. George Lowrie, a.d.n. Helien ; w. Robert and James Meine.
  ,,   ,, George Baittie, a.d.n. Marion ; w. Walter Uschar, Nicoll Merser.
  ,, 22. John Scot, a.d.n. Margt. ; w. Rot. and James Meins.
July 5. James Turner, a.s.n. George ; w. Tho. and George Turners.
  ,, 10. Andrew Smith, a.d.n. Margt. ; w. Andrew and William Kennedie.
  ,, 12. James Corsbie, a.d.n. Isobell ; w. Wm. and George Hoyes.
  ,,   ,, James Bowston, a.d.n. Isobell ; w. James and Thom. Bowstons.

1657.
July 12. William Ballenden, a.s.n. Thomas; w. Thomas Fiergreive, John Blaikie.
  „   17. Mr. David Fletcher, a.d.n. Elizt.; w. Mr. Thomas Wilkie, Mr. James Fletcher.
  „   „   Mark Blaikie, a.s.n. George; w. George and Wm. Blaikies.
  „   „   Rot. Soudon, a.d.n. Alison; w. John Lithgow, Andro Mar.
  „   19. Thomas Mein, a.d.n. Alison; w. John Mein, John Bower.
  „   „   George Usher, a.d.n. Marion; w. Walter and Alexr. Fishers.
  „   25. John Fiergreive, two d.n. Margt. and Janet; w. Thomas Fiergreive, James Darling.
Aug.   9. Alexr. Fishar, a.s.n. Wm.; w. Wm. and Michaell Fisher.
  „   „   George Paterson, a.s.n. Andrew; w. James Paterson, James Murray.
  „   22. James Ridpath, a.d.n. Isobell; w. Wm. Edgar, Alexr. Ridpath.
  „   „   John Brown, a.s.n. Robert; w. Wm. Wallace, John Wallace.
  „   30. George Moody, a.s.n. James; w. Wm. Uschar, George Hownam.
Sept. 25. James Lithgow, a.s.n. David; w. Mr. David Fletcher, Alexr. Halliburton.
  „   25. Jon Romainhous, a.d.n. Katherin; w. Edward Romainhous, Jo. Murray.
  „   29. Wm. Wallace, a.d.n. Janet; w. John Wallace, Edward Lithgow.
Oct. 25. Alexr. Usher, a.s.n. James; w. John Moss, George Usher.
  „   30. John Bell, a.s.n. ——; w. Cuthbert Bowie, James Bowie.
Nov.   1. Tho. Stenhous, a.s.n. Wm.; w. Wm. Haistie, Richart Slaiter.
  „   6. John Pringle, a.d.n. Agnes; w. James Corsbie, Wm. Hoy.
  „   13. Robt. Halliwell, a.d.n. Jn.; w. Rot. Mein, John Halliwell.
  „   15. John Merser, a.d.n. Margt.; w. John Hounam, Nicol Merser.
  „   15. George Martin, a.d.n. Geo.; w. John Bell, Alexr. Ursher.
  „   22. Isabell Anderson, a.d.n. Issobell, presented by Mungo Donaldson; w. Wm. Anderson.
Dec.   7. Robert Freir, a.d.n. Maricowne; w. Wm. Hoy, James Boustan.
  „   14. Alexr. Vetch, a.s.n. Harie; w. George Harvie, John Bridge.
  „   25. James Martin, a.d.n. Margt.; w. John Martin, John Maxwell.
1658.
Jan. 10. Rot. Clark, a.s.n. Robert; w. Richard and Andrew Ormistons.
  „   25. Andrew Marr, a.s.n. James; w. James Bouston, Wm. Bell.
  „ last. James Waugh, a.s.n. Wm.; w. George Blaikie, John Bower.
  „   31. Andrew Messer, a.d.n. Margt.; w. Andrew and John Heittons.
Feb.   5. George Hoy, a.s.n. Wm.; w. Wm. Hoy, Thomas Willson.
  „   5. John Heiton, a bastard son, n. Andrew; w. Andrew Heiton, John Fishar.
  „   7. James Simson, a.s.n. Jon; w. James Simson, Robert Maben.
  „   12. Thomas Lookup, a.s.n. Jon; w. Andrew and James Lookup.
  „   22. Jn. Mein, a.s.n. Ja.; w. Rot. and Jon Mein.
  „   28. Jon Dinnont, a.s.n. Jon; w. Rot. and Wm. Hall.
Mar.   7. Thom. Kerr, a.d.n. Jannet; w. Wm. Kerr, Jon Mill.
  „   12. Jon Mill, a.s.n. Wm.; w. Jon Mein, Mungo Mill.
  „   14. Jon Bowar, a.s.n. Jon; w. Ja. Bowar, Jon Bowar.
  „   21. Andr. Heitton, a.d.n. Margt.; w. Andr. Merser, Jon Heitton.
  „   „   Nicoll Ushar, a.s.n. Jon; w. Jon Hownam, Nicoll Merser.
  „   26. Rot. Kairner (?) in Bowdon, a.s.n. Rot.; w. Patrick Bullman, George Bourstonne.
  „   28. Ja. Caldwells, a.d.n. Agnes; w. Jon Bowie, Richart Sklaitter.
  „   „   Wm. Greinson, a.d.n. Margt.; w. Wm. Fisher, George Buy.
Aprill 9. Wm. Merser, a.s.n. George; w. Andrew and Nicoll Mersers.
  „   16. Rot. Fletcher, a.d.n. Issobel; w. Jon Fletcher, Chares Rutherfurd.
  „ last. Jon Hownam, a.s.n. Alexr.; w. Jon Hownam, Walter Ushar.
May   11. George Cairncross, a.d.n. Alison; w. Richd. Sclaiter, Rot. Braidie.
  „   23. Wm. Fishar, a.d.n. Hellen; w. Jon and Wm. Fishars.
  „   „   Hendrie Myles, a.d.n. Janet; w. Jon and Thomas Halliwells.
  „   28. Jon Lithgow, a.s.n. Edward; w. Andrew Mair, Rot. Laidlaw.

1658.
May 28. Tho. Welch, a.s.n. Rot. ; w. Nicoll Merser, Jas. Mein.
June 10. Thom. Freirgreive, a.d.n. Alison ; w. Ja. Freirgreive, Jon Blaikie.
  ,, 19. Robert Forsan, a.s.n. Robert ; w. Robert Mein, Jon Mein.
  ,, 20. Jon Johnstoune, a.d.n. Janet ; w. Tho. and George Turners.
  ,, ,, Walter Riddell, a.s.n. Wm. : w. Wm. Edgar, Thomas Watson.
July 2. Tho. Ridfurd, a.d.n. Issobell ; w. Adam Lithgow, Mungo Donaldson.
  ,, 8. Tho. Wilson, a.s.n. Thomas ; w. George and Wm. Hoys.
  ,, ,, Jas. Eileis, a.s.n. George ; w. James and Thomas Eileis.
  ,, ,, Andrew Penman, a.s.n. James ; w. John and James Bowers.
  ,, 28. James Adamson, a.d.n. Marie ; w. James Murray, Edward Darling.
  ,, 31. George Dewar, a.d.n. Margt. ; w. Thomas Turnor, George Turnor.
Aug. 15. Andrew Olipher, a.d.n. Agnes ; w. Jon Bouston, James Olipher.
  ,, ,, James Eileis, a.d.n. Barbara ; w. Robert Trotter, James Mein.
Sept. 19. Walter Taitt, a.s.n. Jon ; w. George Ushar, Wm. Taitt.
  ,, ,, George Turnor, a.s.n. Jon ; w. Robert Turnor, Jon Sunnais.
Oct. 3. John Riddell, two d.n. Janet and Heilein ; w. Nicoll Cochran, Jon Mill.
  ,, ,, Mr. Wm. Dowguid, a.d.n. Katherin ; w. Andrew and Archd. Darlings.
  ,, ,, Thomas Halliwell, a.s.n. Andro ; w. John and Alexr. Halliwells.
  ,, 17. Rot. Bunzie, a.d.n. Alison ; w. R. Mein, John Bunzie.
  ,, last. Andro Eileis, a.d.n. Issobell ; w. Thos. and Jas. Eileis.
  ,, ,, George Mitchell, a.s.n. Wm. ; w. Wm. Fishar, Wm. Fishar.
  ,, ,, Jon Mose, a.d.n. Jaine ; w. Rot. and Jon Meins.
Nov. 5. Tho. Cochran, a.s.n. Tho. ; w. Jon Riddell, Jon Mill.
  ,, 12. Rot. Ridfurd, a.d.n. Barbara ; w. Wm. Wight, Tho. Ker.
  ,, 19. Wm. Taitt, a.d.n. Margt. ; w. Wm. Tait, Wm. Scot.
  ,, 21. Ja. M'Kala, a.d.n. Jessie ; w. Jon Windrim, Wm. Mackala.
  ,, ,, Ja. Wallace, a.s.n. Jon ; w. Jon and Jas. Wallaces.
Dec. 3 Mark Purvis, a.d.n. Issobell ; w. Andro and Jon Meins.
  ,, 10. Jon Bunzie, a.s.n. Jon ; w. James Bunzie, John Meins.
  ,, 26. Jas. Simpson, a.d.n. Bessie ; w. Jas. and Jon Simpsons.
1659.
Jan. 9. Nicoll Bower, a.d.n. Mariown ; w. Andrew Murray, Jon Bower.
  ,, 14. Mich. Gibson, a.d.n. Eliz. ; w. Wm. Edgar, Jas. Ker.
  ,, ,, Jon Mill, a.d.n. Issobell ; w. Thos. and Jon Mills.
  ,, 21. Wm. Trumbill, a.d.n. Issobell ; w. Ja. and Jon Martens.
  ,, ,, Rot. Sheill, a.d.n. Margt. ; w. Tho. and Wm. Boustons.
  ,, 28. Andro Bowston, a.s.n. Androw ; w. And. and Nicoll Mersers.
  ,, 30. Wm. Mercer, a.s.n. Thomas ; w. Jas. and Jon Mersers.
Feb. 13. Thos. Myles, two d.n. Issobell and Hellen ; w. Hendrie and Rot. Myles.
  ,, 19. Nicoll Cairncroce, a.s.n. Walter ; w. Wm. Cairncroce and Jas. Moffat.
  ,, 25. Ja. Bower, a.d.n. Hellen ; w. Jon and Nicoll Bowers.
Mar. 6. And. Young, a.s.n. Androw ; w. Androw Darling, Rot. Law.
  ,, 13. Rot. Law, a.d.n. Marion ; w. Andrew Darling, Andro Young.
  ,, 18. Rot. Halliwell, a.d.n. Margt. ; w. John and Rot. Halliwells.
  ,, 27. Jon Lyes, a.d.n. Marion ; w. Rot. and Wm. Leis.
  ,, ,, Wm. Darling, a.d.n. Margt. ; w. Adam Darling, Rot. Ormiston.
April 1. Androw Martin, a.s.n. Androw ; w. Androw Lookup, Geo. Martin.
  ,, 10. Thomas Merser, a.s.n. Wm. : w. Ja. and Wm. Mersers.
  ,, 12. Ja. Mein, a.s.n. Jon ; w. Jon Mein, Jon Bunzie.
  ,, 24. Ja. Mein, a.s.n. Andro ; w. Rot. and Jon Meins.
  ,, ,, Rot. Halliwell, a.s.n. Jon ; w. Jon and Thos. Halliwells.
  ,, 24. Rot. Sheill, a.d.n. Hellen : w. Jon Belle and Wm. Bouston [*entry struck out*].
  ,, 29. Wm. Fishar, a.s.n. James ; w. Jon and Wm. Fishars.
  ,, 29. Jon Forgreive, a.s.n. Johne ; w. Hendrie and Thos. Myldes.
May 8. Jas. Mein, a.d.n. Issobell ; w. Jon and Rot. Meins.
  ,, ,, Jon Bunzie, a.d.n. Janet ; w. Johne Bunzie, Jas. Merser.
  ,, 20. Robert Rae, a.s.n. Robert ; w. Jas. Moffat, Robert Rae.

1659.

May 22. Jon Moss, a.s.n. Jon ; w. Jon Moss, Wm. Fishar.
,,   ,, Wm. Bell, a.s.n. Wm. ; w. James Bouston, Rot. Freir.
June 5. James Fishar, a.d.n. Margt. ; w. Jon Moss, Androw Kennedie.
,, 10. Jas. Browne, a.s.n. Thos. ; w. Thos. Law, George Blakie.
,, 12. Mark Blaikie, a.s.n. David ; w. Wm. Edgar, Adam Lithgow.
July 1. James Lithgow, a.s.n. James : w. Mr. David Fletcher, Alexr. Hally-
        burton.
,, ,, James Leithane, a.s.n. Thomas ; w. James Bouston, Wm. Hoy.
,, 3. Wm. Rennick, a.s.n. Thomas ; w. Jon and Wm. Fishars.
,, 10. Rot. Lawder, a.s.n. Robert ; w. Jon and Jas. Rolmanhous.
,, 15. Jas. Mein, a.d.n. Elspeth ; w. Jas. Lithgow, Jas. Eiles.
,, 23. Andrew Stewart, a.d.n. Bessie ; w. Thos. Foirgreive, Wm. Laidlaw.
,, ,, James Lookup, a.d.n. Margt. : w. Thos. and Andro Lookups.
,, 25. Thomas Laidlaw, a.s.n. Thomas ; w. Jon and Thos. Milnes.
,, 29. David Unes (?) in Lussuden, a.s.n. David ; w. Jon and Jas. Bunzies.
Aug. 21. Thomas Darling, a.d.n. Heillen ; w. Edward and Jon Darlings.
,, ,, Wm. Clerk, a.d.n. Margt. ; w. Wm. Fishar, Robert Freir.
,, ,, James Mein, a.d.n. Alison : w. Richard Frater, Thos. Mein.
,, 28. Mongo Milne, a.d.n. Christian ; w. Jon and Thos. Milnes.
Sept. 5. Wm. Fletcher in Bowden, a.d.n. Margaret ; w. George Paterson, Jon
        Fletcher.
,, 5. Jon Laidlaw, a.d.n. Agnes ; w. Wm. Fishar, Robert Laidlaw.
,, 5. Nicoll Eiles, a.s.n. James ; w. Jon Laidlaw, James Eillies.
,, 25. Jon Bower, a.d.n. Margaret : w. Jon and Jas. Bowers.
Oct. 2. Wm. Wallace, a.d.n. Margaret ; w. James Eilies, John Wallace.
,, 7. Robert Holywell, a.s.n. Jon : w. Rot. and Jon Meines.
,, 11. Gedeon Jackson, a.d.n. Heillin ; w. Mr. David Fletcher, Wm. Edgar.
,, 23. Wm. Hoge in Bowden, a.d.n. Christian : w. George Benatyne, Jas.
        Wallace.
,, 28. Thos. Milne, a.d.n. Alison ; w. Jon and Wm. Milnes.
Nov. 1. Jon Wilkie, a.s.n. John ; w. Jas. MacKalla, John Winterhope.
,, 18. Thos. Bowie, a.d.n. Agnes ; w. Alexr. Usher, Alexr. Ridpeth.
,, ,, John Gibson, a.s.n. David ; w. Michael Gibson, David Gibson.
Dec. 9. Adam Turnbull, a.d.n. John ; w. John Bunzie, Andrew Turnbull.
,, ,, Thos. Vair, a.d.n. Issobell ; w. John and Thos. Vair.
,, 16. Andro Mein, a.d.n. Marie ; w. Rot. Mein, James Mein.

1660.

Jan. 6. Thos. Law, a.d.n. Christian ; w. Jon Bouston, Michael Gibson.
,, ,, George Merten, a.d.n. Isobel : w. David Fletcher, Andro Merten.
Feb. 15. Mr. Wm. Deweatt, a.s.n. Wm. ; w. Mr. Wm. —— (?), Andrew Darling.
,, ,, Wm. Merser, a.d.n. Margt. ; w. Nicol and Jon Mersers.
,, 24. Rot. Forsan, a.d n. James ; w. Jon Duncan, Thos. Bowie.
,, ,, Walter Hall, a.s.n. Wm. : w. Rot. Forsan, Andrew Cuik.
Mar. 9. Jon Milne, a.d.n. Christian : w. Thos. and Jon Milnes.
,, 16. Thos. Myldes, a.s.n. Jon ; w. Rot. Mildes, Jon Holiwall.
,, 18. George Sheill, a.s.n. Jon : w. Tho. Dobson, George Sheill.
,, 23. Jon Riddell, a.d.n. Janett ; Jon and Thos. Milnes.
,, ,, Wm. Bouston, a.d.n. Margt. ; w. Jas. Bouston, John Holiwall.
,, 30. Jas. Hunter, a.s.n. Thos. ; w. Thos. Hunter, Richard Sclaitter.
April 15. Jon Penman, a.d.n. Christian ; w. Jon Bower, Androw Penman.
,, ,, Wm. Wallace, a.s.n. George ; w. Jas. and George Wallace.
,, ,, Jas. Bunzie, a.d.n. Janet ; w. Jon and Rot. Bunzie.
,, ,, Rot. Merton, a.d.n. Janet ; w. Wm. Hoy, Jon Freir.
,, 29. Bertie Mein, a.s.n. Rot. ; w. Richart Sclaitter, James Huntar.
,, ,, Wm. Hog in Bowdon, a.d.n. Margt. ; w. Andro Penman, Wm.
        Turnbull.
May 4. Thomas Lookup, a.d.n. Isobell ; w. James and Andro Lookups.
,, 6. Rot. Holiwall, a.s.n. Jon : w. Jon and Rot. Holiwalls.
,, 6. George Ushar, a.d.n. Margt. ; w. Jon and Alexr. Ushers.
,, 13. Wm. Bulman, a s.n. Andro : w. Andro Riddell, Andro Bulman.

1660.

May 20. Andro Drumond, a.s.n. Jon ; w. Jon Drumond, Jon Houñam.
,, 27. Wm. Anderson, a.s.n. Jon ; w. Mungo Donaldson, Thos. Williamson.
June 3. Jon Ushar, a.d.n. Margt. ; w. Walter and Jon Ushars.
,, 10. James Turner, a.d.n. Thomas ; w. Thos. and George Turners.
,, ,, John Bickett, a.s n. Jon ; w. Thos. Wilson, Rot. Freir.
July 15. George Mein, a.d.n. Margt. ; w. Rot. Philp, Wm. Hoy.
Aug. 11. Gideon Jackson, a.d.n. Christian ; w. Alexr. Hebron, Wm. Edgar.
,, 28. Jas. Haitlie, a.s.n. Rot. ; w. Adam Heslop, Rot. Wright.
Sept. 9. James Edmeston, a.s.n. Andro ; w. James Donaldson, George Taylor.
,, 16. John Mercer, a.s.n. Jon ; w. James Mercer, David Mein.
,, ,, John Cochran, a.d.n. Mary ; w. Wm. Fisher, George Alexander.
,, 22. Alexander Ushar, a.d.n. Marion ; w. Jon Messer, Walter Ushar.
,, 27. Androw Mare, a.s.n. Andrew ; w. James Bouston, Wm. Hoy.
Oct. 14. Rob. Clerk, a.s.n. William ; w. Andrew Darlin, Rob. Ormiston.
,, ,, Rob. Benzie, a.d.n. Issobell ; w. Rob. Mein, John Benzie.
,, 21. John Halliwall, a.d.n. Jenett ; w. Rob. Mein, Rob. Holliwall.
Nov. 9. John Fisher, a.s.n. James ; w. James Lythgow, Rob. Trotter.
,, ,, William Moffat, a.d.n. Helen ; w. James Moffat, Archibald Moffat.
,, 16. James Bowie, a.d.n. Margaret ; w. Cudbard Bowie, Thomas Bowie.
,, 18. William Marrer, a.s.n. James ; w. James and John Marrer.
,, 23. George Ormiston, a.s.n. John ; w. John Bell, Thomas Eiles.
,, ,, James Martin, a.s.n. John ; w. John Martin, Robert Watson.
,, 25. Walter Riddell, a.s.n. Robt. ; w. Wm. Edgar, John Notman.
,, 30. George Cairncrose, a.s.n. Wm. ; w. Rot. Braidie, Richart Sclaiter.
,, ,, John Marrer, a.s.n. George ; w. John Hounen, Nicoll Marrer.
,, ,, Andro Hyton, a.d.n. Marion ; w. Thomas Hyton, Wm. Bulman.
Dec 13. John Bell, a.d.n. Margret ; w. Cudbard and James Bowie.
,, ,, Mathew Fishar, a.d.n. James ; w. Wm. Fishar, Andro Kenedie.
,, 23. Andro Oliver. a.s.n. James ; w. James Oliver, Gasper Marrer.
,, 28. James Lounie in Galashiels, a.s.n. John ; w. Markie Blaikie, John Fiergreive.
,, ,, Andrew Martin, a.d.n. Issobell ; w. Andrew Lookup, George Martin.

1661.

Jan. 4. Alexr. Waithman, a.d.n. Helen ; w. Alexr. Wallace, Wm. Spotswood.
,, 11. George Alexander, a.s.n. Jon ; w. Wm. Fishar, Andro Derlin.
,, 18. Rob. Mein, a.d.n. Issobell ; w. Rot. Mein, John Halliwall.
,, ,, Stevin Martin, a.s.n. James ; w. Andro and John Hytons.
,, 27. George Monday, a.s.n. John ; w. Wm. Fishar, Culbard Bouie.
Feb. 1. Rot. Maban, a.d.n. Isobell ; w. Andro Lookup, Thomas Droumond.
,, 3. Thomas Stenous, a.d.n. Margret ; w. Richard Sclaitter, John Mill.
,, ,, James Mein, a.d.n. Janet ; w. Rot. and John Bounzies.
,, ,, James Bouar, a.d.n. Margret ; w. John Pringle, Andro Droumond.
,, 10. John Hounim, a.d.n. Margret ; w. John Hounim, John Marrer.
,, 24. John Lermont, a.d.n. Issobell ; w. John Maban, Adam Darling.
Mar. 8. Wm. Cusan, a.s.n. Wm. ; w. John Moffet, Wm. Spotswood.
,, ,, James Corsbie, a.s.n. John ; w. Wm. Hoy, Wm. Bouston.
,, ,, Andro Bouston, a.d.n. Jannet ; w. John Hounim, Andro Mercer.
,, 29. Rob. Mein, a.d.n. Agnas : w. Rob. and Andro Mein.
,, ,, Nicol Bowar, two sons n. John and James ; w. John Bowar, Thomas Mein.
,, ,, Andro Kennedie, a.s.n. Wm. ; w. George Monday, Wm. Fishar.
,, ,, Wm. Mertin, a.s.n. James ; w. James Paterson, James Martin.
April 12. Wm. Darling, a.d.n. Jean ; w. Adam Darling, James Donaldson.
,, 21. Rob. Holliwall, a.d.n. Helen ; w. John and Thomas Halliwalls.
,, 26. Andro Mein, a.d.n. Helen ; w. Rob. and James Meins.
,, 28. George Turnere, a.d.n. Margret ; w. Thomas and James Turneres.
,, ,, Jean Blaikie, a.s.n. Alexr. ; w. John Rathie, Thomas Law.
,, ,, Mark Purves, a.d.n. Issobell ; w. Rot. Mein, John Bounzie.
May 3. John Denant, a.d.n. Christian ; w. George and Wm. Hoys.
June 2. George Mein, a.s.n. Andro ; w. Adam Mein, James Mein.

1661.
June 7. George Pringle, a.s.n. George ; w. Thomas Bouston, James Ker.
  „   9. Thomas Watson, a.d.n. Marie ; w. Edwart Romanos, John Greive.
  „   „ John Laidlaw, a.s.n. James ; w. James Eiles, Andro Lookup.
  „ 14. Andro Marrer, a.s.n. James ; w. Andro Hyton, Jon Hyton.
  „ 16. Wm. Tate, a.s.n. James ; w. Andro Thomson, John Trotter.
  „ 30. Henrie Myles, a.d.n. Jannet ; w. John and Robert Haliwalls.
July 14. Thomas Holiwall, a.d.n. Issobell ; w. John and Rob. Holiwalls.
  „ 16. Wm. Borthik, a.s.n John ; w. John Hall, James Moffet.
Sept. 8. Michael Gibson, a.s.n. John ; w. John Bowar, Thomas Bowie.
  „ 15. Robert Sheil, a.s.n. Robert ; w. John Bell, Adam Darling.
Oct. 20. John Benzie, a.d.n. Jennet ; w. Rob. Mein, James Ledderdam.
  „   „ Thomas Cochrane, a.s.n. Henrie ; w. John Mill, Nicol Cochran.
  „ 25. Nicol Usher, a.d.n. Marion ; w. John Hounim, Walter Usher.
  „ 27. John Mein, a.s.n. Robert ; w. Rob. Freir, James Freir.
Nov. 3. Wm. Bell, a.d.n. Jennet ; w. Rob. Freir, Andro Mar.
  „   „ John Mertin, a.s.n. John ; w. George Berton, John Dinnant.
  „   8. John Fiergreive, a.d.n. Helen ; w. Wm. Edgar, George Ormiston.
  „   „ John Lees, a.d.n. Bessie ; w. Robt. and Michel Lees.
  „   „ James Moffat, a.d.n. Jean ; w. George Dewar, Geo. Alexander.
  „   „ James Eiles, a.d.n. Agnes ; w. Richard and John Sclaitters.
1662.
Jan. 3. James Merser, a.s.n. Andro ; w. James and Thomas Merser.
  „   5. Wm. Merser, a.d.n. Hellen ; w. Nicol and George Mersers.
  „ 12. Wm. Merser, a.s.n. James ; w. James and Thomas Mersers.
  „ 19. Wm. Wallace, a.s.n. Wm. ; w. James and George Wallaces.
Feb. 16. Wm. Paterson, a.d.n. Marion ; w. Wm. Fishar, Andro Thomson.
  „   „ Andro Richart, a.d.n. Helen ; w. George Pringle, Wm. Darling.
  „ 23. James Mein, a.d.n. Issobell ; w. Nicoll and John Sclaitters.
  „   „ John Milne, a.d.n. Christian ; w. John and Thomas Milnes.
Mar. 9. Ja. Smith, a.d.n. Margret ; w. Jas. and George Turners.
  „ 21. Ja. Mertoune, a.d.n. Margrat ; w. Ja. Mertane, Ja. Mabone.
  „   „ Tho. Wilsone, a.s.n. James ; w. Wm. and Jas. Hoye.
  „   „ Rot. Helliwill, a.s.n. Rot. ; w. Jo. and Tho. Helliwill.
April 4. Rot. Forsane, a.s.n. Patrick ; w. Patrick Duncan, Wi. Forsane.
  „   6. Jo. Messer, a.s.n. Jo. ; w. Jo. Helliwil, Rot. Milles.
  „   „ Rot. Milles, a.s.n. Ja. ; w. Ja. Messer, Geo. Mein.
  „ 11. Jo. Mille, a.s.n. Mungo ; w. Ja. and Mungo Milles.
  „ 20. Ja. Bunzie. a.s.n. Rot. ; w. Jo. Bunzie, Rot. Meine.
  „   „ Jo. Penman, a.d.n. Jennet ; w. Andro Penman, Ja. Buie.
May 4. George Blakie, a.d.n. Margrat ; w. Adam Lithgow, Mark Blakie.
  „   „ W. Wright, a.s.n. William ; w. Ja. Boustoune, Ja. Messer.
  „ 22. Rot. Wright, a.d.n. Margrat ; w. Adam Hislope, George Turner.
  „   „ Jo. Bunzie, a.d.n. Margrat ; w. Jo. and Ja. Messers.
  „ 18. Mitchill Fisher, a.d.n. Heiline ; w. Edgar and Wm. Fisher.
June 1. Jo. Mein, a.d.n. Agnus ; w. Rot. and Andro Meins.
  „ 15. Thos. Ladly, a.s.n. James ; w. Thomas Mille, Ja. Lidlie.
  „ 29. Jo. Mosse, a.s.n. Nicol ; w. Jo. Mosse, William Edgar.
  „   „ Gideon Jackson, a.d.n. Christiane ; w. Jo. and George Pringell.
  „   „ Tho. Gray, a.s.n. James ; w. Tho. Buie, Rot. Forsane.
July 8. George Wallace, a.d.n. Marion ; w. Ja. and Wm. Wallaces.
  „   „ Ja. Buie, a.s.n. Jon ; w. Culbert and Tho. Buie.
Aug 10. ——, a.s.n. Jo. ; w. Tho. Boustone, Rot. Freir.
  „ 17. George Pringle, a.s.n. Francis ; w. Ja. Ker, Rot. Mertone.
  „ 29. James Meine, a.d.n. Jeanet ; w. Rot. Mein, John Bunzie.
Sept. 21. George Mertoune, a.s.n. Wm. ; w. James and Androw Mertouns.
  „ 30. Robert Leyes, a.d.n. Cathren ; w. John and Androw Leyes.
  „   „ Wm. Wallace, a.s.n. Geo. ; w. Rot. and George Wallace.
Oct. 8. Thomas Milne, a.s.n. Wm. ; w. John and Wm. Milnes.
  „ 16. John Uschar, a.s.n. Walter ; w. Walter and Geo. Ushars.
  „ 21. Thomas Crukis, a.d.n. Bessie ; w. John and Rot. Leyess.

1662.

Oct. 21. John Mein, a.s.n. Wm. ; w. Rot. and Andrew Meines.
" " Wm. Milne, a.s.n. Nicoll ; w. John and Thos. Milnes.

1663.

Jan. 2. Stephan Mertoune, a.d.n. Christian ; w. Jas. and John Mertounes.
" 11. Rot. Law, a.d.n. Jeanet ; w. Thos. Law, Androw Darling.
" " George Sheill, a.d.n. Hellen ; w. Andro Penman, Mark Blaikie.
" 16. Wm. Anderson, a.s.n. Alexr. ; w. James Ker, Thomas Law.
" 18. James Meine, a.s.n. Thomas ; w. Rot. Meine, John Bunzie.
" " Rot. Bunzie, a.s.n. John ; w. Rot. and Andro Meines.
" 23. James Wallace, a.s.n. Thomas ; w. James Ker, Thomas Mar.
" 25. Andro Darling, a.s.n. John ; w. John Fletcher, George Alexander.
Feb 13. John Trotter, a.d.n. Barbara ; w. James Lithgow, James Ealleis.
April 3. Alexr. Fischar, a.s.n. John ; w. Wm. Fishar, Michall Fisher.
" " Wm. Ciark, a.d.n. Jeanet ; w. Walter Veitch, Robert Ormestoune.
" 10. James Corsbie, a.s.n. Wm. ; w. George Bertoune, Wm. Hoy.
" " James Mertoune, a.s.n. James ; w. James Mertoun, John Mertoun.
" " Andro Penman, a.d.n. Margret ; w. John and James Bowars.
" 12. Rot. Laidlaw, a.d.n. Marion ; w. John Laidlaw, Wm. Laidlaw.
" " George Uschar, a.d.n. Issobell ; w. John Mosse, Walter Uschar.
" " Walter Riddell, a.s.n. Thomas ; w. Rot. Wright, Adam Hislope.
" 26. James Gourlaw, a.d.n. Issobell ; w. Nicole Cochrane, John Milne.
" " John Mersser, a.d.n. Barnie ; w. John Hounam, Nicole Mersser.
" " Andro Merser, a.d.n. Issobell ; w. Andro Heitoune, John Heitoune.
May 10. John Bell, a.d.n. Alison ; w. James Myldes [*name illegible*].
" " Thomas Mein, a.d.n. Marton ; w. John Ker [*name illegible*].
" 17. Rot. Mein, a.d.n. Janet ; w. Rot. Mein, John Mein.
" " Androw Boustoun, a.d.n. Helen ; w. John Messer, Nicol Messer.
" 22. John Marshall, a.s.n. Johne ; w. James Mertine, Wm. Wallace.
June 1. Johne Fishar, a.d.n. Agnes ; w. Wm. Fishar, Michael Fishar.
" " George Mein, a.d.n. Alison ; w. Wm. Hoy, Rot. Mein.
" " William Rannick, a.d.n. Sarah ; w. Andrew Smith, John Moss.
" 18. Andrew Hittone, a.d.n. Helen ; w. John Hittone, Nicol Messer.
" 20. Michael Fisher, a.s.n. William, born 19th ; w. Wm. Fishar, Andrew Kennedie.
July 26. James Lindsay, a.d.n. Elspeth ; w. Walter Haitley, Wm. Bell.
" 31. Robert Turup, a.s.n. James ; w. Edward Darling, James Donaldsone
Aug. 9. Robert Halliwall, a.s.n. John ; w. John Halliwall, Andrew Mar.
" " John Lidlay, a.s.n. Alexander ; w. James Eiles, Thomas Dobson.
" 16. Gideon Jackson, a.d.n. Jein ; w. James Douglasse, Mr. George Hepburne, Alexr. Hepburne.
" " Robert Clerk, a.d.n. Helen ; w. Wm. Hoy, Robert Ormistoun.
" " John Lerment, a.d.n. Elspeth ; w. James Peterson, Wm. Martein.
" " Johne Wilsone, a.d.n. Jennet ; w. John Mosse, Walter Wishart.
" " George Turner, a.s.n. [*entry unfinished*].
" 30. Thomas Bowie, a.d.n. Jennet ; w. James Bowie, John Bell.
" " William Wryght, a.s.n. Wm. ; w. James Bousten, Wm. Howie.
Oct. 25. George Alexander, a.s.n. Alexr. ; w. Wm. Fisher, James Moffet.
" " William Martine, a.d.n. Jennet ; w. Robert Freir, James Boustin.
" 30. Robert Mein, a.s.n. Androw ; w. Androw Mein, Bernard Mein.
Nov. 6. George Meirtaine, a.s.n. John ; w. John Bell, Andro Mertine.
" " Bartholomew Mein, a.s.n. Richard ; w. Robert Lithgow, James Hunter.
" 20. Johne Brown, a.s.n. Johne ; w. Andrew Penman, James Gourlay.
" " Andrew Mein, a.s.n. Andrew ; w. Robert Mein, John Mein.
" 25. James Mein, a.s.n. Andrew ; w. Rot. Mein, Andrew Mein.
" " Thomas Mill, a.d.n. Annabell ; w. Johne Mill, Thomas Mill.
Dec. 4. Johne Pringall, a.s.n. William ; w. Tho. Watson, Wm. Pringall.
" " John Vair, a.s.n. Thomas ; w. John Bowar, Thomas Mein.
" " George Dewar, a.d.n. Jennet ; w. George Turner, James Moffet.
" " Adam Trumbull, a.d.n. Jennet ; w. Robert Mein, Androw Mein.

1663.
Dec. 18. John Halliwall, a.d.n. Jennet ; w. John Mosse, Robert Halliwell.
  ,,   25. James Edgar, a.s.n. Robert ; w. Wm. Edgar, Henrie Myls.
    1664.
Jan. 15. Thomas Notman, a.d.n. Jennet ; w. Thomas Turner, George Turner.
  ,,   ,, John Ruthet, a.d.n. Issobell ; w. John Mill, Thomas Mill.
  ,,   29. Thomas Myls, a.s.n. Henrie ; w. John Halliwall, Thomas Halliwall.
  ,,   ,, Andrew Marr, a.s.n. Andrew ; w. Thomas Bouston and Andrew ——.
Feb. 5. Andrew Martine, a.s.n. Andrew ; w. Andrew Lookup, George Martine.
  ,,   12. James Eilies, a.d.n. Margaret : w. Andrew Lookup, George Eilies.
  ,,   19. John Mill, a.d.n. Agnes ; w. Thomas Mill, John Mill.
  ,,   ,, William Mill, a.d.n. Jennet ; w. John Mill, Thomas Mill.
  ,,   21. Alexander Newtoun, a.s.n. John ; w. Rot. Young, Thomas Law.
  ,,   ,, Johne Pringall, a.s.n. George : w. James Moffet, Archibald Moffet.
Mar. 4. James Macintosh, a.s.n. William ; w. Wm. Spottswood, Walter Aire.
  ,,   ,, Henrie Myls, a.d.n. Annabell ; w. Johne Lawrie, Thomas Halliwell.
  ,,   ,, Alexander Waithman, a.d.n. Margaret ; w. William Spotswood, Walter Ushart.
  ,,   ,, Thomas Litle, a.d.n. Margaret ; w. Edward Darling, George Eyles.
  ,,   13. George Wallace, a.s.n. William ; w. George Wallace, Wm. Wallace.
  ,,   20. Johne Gill, a.s.n. Thomas : w. Thomas Gill and —— Mill (*sic*).
  ,,   ,, James Lawrie, a.d.n. Katherine ; w. James Mill, John Penman.
  ,,   ,, Andrew Rannaldsone, a.s.n. Johne ; w. Johne Mosse, Johne Mosse (*sic*).
  ,,   27. Patrick Lookup, a.d.n. Issobell ; w. Thomas Lookup, Wm. Fisher.
  ,,   ,, Johne Meine, a.d.n. Jennet ; w. Robert Meine, Alexr. Meine.
Apr. 3. George Cairnecrose, a.d.n. Margaret ; w. Robert Braiddie, Johne Bower.
  ,,   10. George Muddie, a.d.n. Margaret : w. John Fisher, Androw Chishome.
  ,,   ,, James Turner, a.d.n. Jennet ; w. George Turner, Thomas Turner.
May 8. Johne Martine [*entry unfinished*].
  ,,   ,, Ja. Edgar, a.s.n. Johne ; w. Ja. Eleis, Wm. Edgar.
  ,,   ,, John Mein, a.s.n. Thomas ; w. Robert Freir, William Hoy.
  ,,   ,, George Boustoun, a.d.n. Issobell ; w. Andrew Boustoun, Andrew Boustoun.
  ,,   29. George Blaikie, a.d.n. Elizabeth ; w. Thomas Law, George Muddie.
June 8. Wm. Bell, twines, a.s.n. Hugh, a.d.n. Issobell ; w. James Lithgow, Wm. Bell.
  ,,   17. Thomas Halliwall, a.d.n. Helen ; w. John Halliwall, John Scot.
July 3. John Dalgleish, a.s.n. John ; w. Johne Hall, James Moffet.
  ,,   ,, John Penman, a.d.n. Jennet ; w. Andrew Penman, James Fisher.
  ,,   ,, James Bunie, a.s.n. Johne ; w. Johne Bunie, Robert Mein.
  ,,   ,, Robert Dickson, a.s.n. John ; w. William Tait, John Watson.
  ,,   10. Robert Forsone, a.d.n. Margaret ; w. William Forsane, John Duncan.
  ,,   ,, James Carswalls, a.d.n. Alison ; w. Richard Sclatter, Robert Mein.
  ,,   15. William Wallace, a.s.n. James ; w. James Wallace, George Wallace.
  ,,   23. Thomas Darling, a.s.n. George ; w. George Tailer, Edward Darling.
  ,,   25. James Moffet, a.d.n. Jennet ; w. James Moffet, John Bell.
  ,,   ,, Thomas Redfoord, a.s.n. George ; w. Adam Lithgow, James Mill.
Aug. 7. George Blaickie, a.s.n. George ; w. James Eilies, Mark Blaickie.
  ,,   14. William Mertonne, a.s.n. William ; w. William Bell, William Hoy.
  ,,   ,, John Wilsone, a. [*entry unfinished*].
  ,,   ,, James Bowie, a. ——: w. Johne Bowie, William Edgar.
Sept. 4. William Grierson, a.d.n. Agnes ; w. Wm. Spotswood, John Moss.
  ,,   ,, Thomas Gray, a.s.n. Robert ; w. Thomas Bowie, Robert Forson.
  ,,   ,, Thomas Wilkison, a.s.n. Alexander ; w. Alexander Wilkison, James Elies.
  ,,   18. Johne Freirgreive, a.s.n. Gideon ; w. Culbert Bowie, Michael Gibson.
  ,,   ,, George Pringall, a.d.n. Jennet ; w. James Bowie, James Elies.
Oct. 2. John Bowar, a.d.n. Helen ; w. Michael Gibson, Nicol Bowar.

1664.
Oct.   2. William Borthwick, a.s.n. William ; w. Johne Hall, Robert Knight.
,,   9. George Eleis, a.s.n. James ; w. Adam Lithgow, James Eleis.
,,   ,, James Mein, a.s.n. Johne ; w. Richard Sclatter, John Sclatter.
,,   31. John Mein, a.s.n. John ; w. Robert Mein, Andrew Mein.
Dec.   11. John Uscher, a.s.n. Walter ; w. Walter Uscher, George Uscher.
,,   23. Robert Halliwall, a.s.n. George ; w. John Halliwall, John Mosse.
,,   30. George Turner, a.d.n. Janet ; w. John Laidlay, William Laidlay.
,,   ,, Stephen Martine, a.s.n. Johne ; w. James Martine, Andro Heitton.
1665.
Jan.   14. Androw Drummond, a.d.n. Agnes : w. Johne Drummond, John
          Drummond.
Mar.   6. Gideon Jackson, a.d.n. Margaret ; w. George Pringall of Torwoodlee,
          George Pringall of Buckholme, Francis Hepburne.
May   24. John Mosse, a.d.n. Helen ; w. John Mosse, Wm. Edgar.
June   9. William Anderson a.d.n. [*entry unfinished*].
,,   ,, John Whrekie (?), a.s.n. John ; w. John Bouston, Thomas Law.
,,   18. Waltter Redall, a.d.n. Jenatt : w. Georg Turner, Adam Heslope.
July   2. Andro Hownam, a.s.n. Andro ; w. John Hownam, Georg Hownam.
,,   14. George Ushar, a.d.n. Helen ; w. John Moss, Walttar Ushar.
,,   29. James Meil, a.d.n. Isobell ; w. John Meile, John Tamson.
Aug.   13. John Dawedson, a.d.n. Kattren ; w. Robartt Mein, Alexander
          Anderson.
,,   ,, Nicol Bowar, a.s.n. Retchertt ; w. Retchertt Sclattar, John Bowar.
,,   20. James Gowrla, a.s.n James ; w. Necoll Cowhran, William Messar.
Sept.   3. George Turnar, a.d.n. Bessie ; w. Thomas Turnar, Adam Heslop.
Oct.   8. John Mein, a.s.n. Robartt ; w. Alexander Mein, Andro Mein.
,,   15. Robartt Benyze, a.d.n. Helin ; w. John Bonyze, Georg Mein.
,,   22. Robartt Mein, a.d.n. Margratt ; w. Andro and John Meins.
,,   ,, Weliam Bowstan, a.d.n. Aleson ; w. Thomas Boustan, John Holie-
          wall.
,,   30. John Mein, a.s.n. John ; w. Robartt Trottar, Andro Mein.
Nov   5. John Hoge, a.d.n. Isobell ; w. Robartt Young, Andro Phape.
,,   19. James Mertton, a.d.n. Jenett ; w. John Mertton, Thomas Hownam.
,,   ,, John Drowmand, a.s.n. John ; w. John Drowmand, Andro Drowmand.
,,   26. Robartt Mein, a.s.n. Weliam ; w. John Mein, Andro Mein.
Dec.   1. James Wallace, a.d.n. Jenett ; w. James Wallace, Weliam Wallace.
,,   ,, John Baynze, a.d.n. Bessie ; w. John Baynze, Adam Trownball.
,,   ,, John Mein, a.d.n. Margratt ; w. Robartt Mein, Robartt Frer.
,,   ,, Robartt Phaw, a.s.n. Adam : w. James Patterson, Georg Cowpar.
,,   24. James Edgar, a.d.n. Margratt ; w. James Elles, Weliam Edgar.
,, last. John Maxwell, a.d.n. Agnose ; w. Georg Wallace, Weliam Anderson.
1666.
Jan.   1. James Marr, a.d.n. Jennet ; w. Androw Marr, James Bowstoune.
,,   ,, Harrie Pringell, a.s.n. Andrew ; w. Andrew Pringell, Andrew Urshart.
,,   14. Robt. Hallywill, a.d.n. Margaret ; w. Johne Hallywill, Whalter Uscher.
,,   21. Robt. Spotswood, a.d.n. Mart. ; w. Andrew and Wm. Spotswoods.
,,   22. James Edgar, a.d.n. Anna ; w. Wm. Edgar, James Elies.
,,   26. Andrew Ronaldsone, a.d.n. Mart. : w. Wm. Ronaldson, John Mosse.
Feb.   4. George Sheill, a.s.n. Thomas ; w. Thomas Wilkison, James Elies.
,,   11. Andrew Olifer, a.d.n. Issobell : w. James Olifer, John Boustoune.
,,   15. Mr. John Scot of Langshaw, a.s.n. Francis : w. George Pringell,
          James Pringell of Cumselie.
,,   23. Mr. Alexr. Bisset, mr., a.d.n. Chrystiane ; w. Johne Ker, James Eles.
,,   25. Johne Hallowwill, a.d.n. Margaret ; w. Markie Blackie, John Fier-
          grieve.
Mar.   11. Nicle Mescer, a.s.n. James ; w. George Turner, Robt. Wright.
,,   ,, Whalter Rutherfoord, a.s.n. Johne ; w. Adame Knox, James Turner.
,,   24. Robt. Engles, a.s.n. Robt. ; w. Her. Ingles, Robt. Main.
,,   28. Wm. Bowstoune, a.s.n. Thomas : w. Thomas and James Bowstounes.
,,   ,, John Dalgleish, a.s.n. Wm. ; w. Johne Har, James Moffet.

1666.

April 1. George Martin, a.s.n. Robt. ; w. Wm. Bell, George Wallace.

,,   8. George Wallace, a.s.n. James ; w. James Ker, William Wallace.

,, 28. Andrew Marr in Gattonsyd, a.s.n. Andrew ; w. James Boustone, James Mar.

,,   ,, Thomas Hallowwill, a.s.n. Andrew ; w. Andrew Schisme, Johne Hallowwill.

,, 30. Johne Ker, a.d.n. Margaret ; w. George Pringell of Buckholme, Mr. Andrew Ker of Kippilaw.

,,   ,, James Engles, a.d.n. Mart. ; w. Hendrie and Robt. Engles.

,,   ,, Thomas Wilkison, a.s.n. James ; w. Alexr. Lithgow of Drygrange, James Elies.

,,   ,, George Mein, a.s.n. Wm. ; w. Andrew Mein, John Mein.

May 3. Whalter Dalgleish, a.s.n. Robert ; w. Nicle Mescer, John Mosse.

,,   4. James Mein, a.d.n. Issobell ; w. Andrew Mein, James Elies.

,, 20. Andrew Mein, a.s.n. Robt. ; w. John and James Meins.

,,   ,, Georg Elies, a.d.n. Thomas ; w. James Elies, John Sklater.

,, 27. John Dunce, a.d.n. Helene ; w. Thomas Watson, John Thin.

,, 29. Patrick Lookeup, a.s.n. John ; w. Johne Ker, Thomas Lookeup.

June 10. George Howname, a.d.n. Issobell ; w. Nicle and John Mescers.

,,   ,, Michaell Gibsone, a.s.n. Hendrie ; w. Markie Blackie, Thomas Lookeup.

,, 29. Andrew Huttone, a.s.n. Andrew ; w. Adam Lithgow, George Bullman.

July 1. Robt. Marr, a.s.n. James ; w. James and Jon Kers, portioners of Melrosse.

,, 20. John Freirgreive, a.s.n. Johne ; w. Markie Blackie, George Wallace.

,,   ,, Robt. Clark, a.s.n Wm. ; w. James Boustoune, Thomas Boustoune.

,, 29. George Mein, a.s.n. James ; w. Robt. Mein, Johne Hollowill.

Aug. 5. Alexr. Thomson, a.s.n. James ; w. James Pringell, Alexr. Riddell.

,, 17. Wm. Mairtone, a.s.n. James ; w. Adam and Wm. Darlings.

,, 19. Wm. Mairtone, a.s.n. Patrick ; w. James and Thomas Boustones.

,,   ,, George Mescer, a.s.n. George ; w. Nicle and Wm. Mersers.

,,   ,, Thomas Bowie, a.d.n. Agnes ; w. Wm. and Robt. Forsans.

,, 26. Robt. Lumbsdaill, a.s.n. Robt. ; w. Adam Hislop, James Turner.

,, 30. And. Fischer, a.d.n. Elizabeth ; w. Wm. and Michael Fischares.

,,   ,, Wm. Wallace, a.s.n. Wm. ; w. George and James Wallaces.

Sept. 4. Robt. Philp, a.d.n. Mart. ; w. Rot. Trotter, Whalter Vaitch.

,, 23. James Mein, a.d.n. Mart. ; w. Andrew and Johne Meins.

,,   ,, John Vair, a.d.n. Jeane ; w. John and Robt. Sklatters.

,, 30. James Mein, a.d.n. Jeane ; w. Nicle Bowar, Thomas Mein.

,,   ,, Wm. Tait, a.d.n. Jennet ; w. Johne Turner, Alexr. Trotter.

,,   ,, John Bell, a.d.n. Issobell ; w. James Messer, Wm. Bell.

,,   ,, George Elies, a.d.n. William ; w. Adam Lithgow, James Elies.

,,   ,, James Blackie, a.d.n. Thomas ; w. Thomas Blackie, John Mairtine.

Oct. 7. Johne Sheill, a.d.n. Agnes ; w. George Sheill, Edward Darling.

,, 14. Andrew Mairtone, a.d.n. Elizabeth ; w. George Mairtone, John Bell.

Nov. 11. Alexr. Lithgow of Drygrange, a.s.n. James ; w. Mr. John Lithgow, James Elies.

,, 19. Wm. Bell, a.s.n. Thomas, a.d.n. Anna ; w. Robt. Frier, Andrew Marr.

,, 25. Wm. Luckup, a.s.n. Andrew ; w. Thomas and Patrick Luckups.

,,   ,, Thomas Forrest, a.s.n. Johne ; w. Thomas and Johne Purvesses.

,, 29. John Marrtaine, a.s.n. George ; w. James and John Mairtaines.

Dec. 1. Alexr. Young, a s.n. Johne ; w. Johne Johnstone, John Thin.

,,   6. George Ormeston, a.s.n. Robt. ; w. Johne and Thomas Bells.

,,   ,, William Wallace, a.s.n. Michaell ; w. George Wallace, Markie Blackie.

,,   ,, Stephane Mairtaine, a.d.n. Margaret ; w. Andro and Johne Hyttones.

,, 20. Thomas Mylne, a.d.n Agnes ; w. John and Wm. Mylnes.

,, 28. John Penman, a.s.n. Johne ; w. Mr. Wm. Fletcher, James Martine.

1667.

Jan. 4. George Hownam, a.d.n. Helen ; w. Johne and Wm. Fishers.

1667.

Jan.   4. John Hoy, a.s.n. William ; w. George Hoy, Andrew Marr.
,,   ,, James Moffat, a.d.n. Jennit ; w. Wm. Fischer, Thomas Mescer.
,,   6. John Fischer, a.d.n. Issobell ; w. Wm. Fischer, James Mein.
,, 27. George Lawrie, a.s.n. Robt. ; w. Johne Lawrie, Johne Friergrieve.
,,   ,, Thomas Mairtaine, a.s.n John ; w. John and James Mairtaines.
,, 31. Thomas Stennows, a.d.n. Marion ; w. Johne Mylne, Nicle Cochrane.
Feb.   3. Andrew Penman, a.s.n. George ; w. George Wallace, George Mairtain.
,, 10. James Hunter, a.s.n. James ; w. Thomas Hunter, James Mein.
,,   ,, Robt. Forsan, a.s.n. John ; w. Johne Mein, Johne Duncane.
,, 15. William Wryght, a.d.n. Issobell ; w. Robt. Mein, Andrew Marr.
,, 17. Alexr. Wadman, a.s.n. Nicle ; w. William Spotswood, George Elies.
,, 22. George Hoy, a.s.n. William ; w. James Bowstoune, Andrew Marr.
,,   ,, James Bowie, a.d.n. Issobell ; w. Johne and Thomas Bells.
Mar.   3. Alexr. Newtone, a.d.n. Helene ; w. William Wallace, James Milne.
April 30. John Turner, a.d.n. Helene ; w. Wm. Tait, George Turner.
May   3. Thomas Gray, a.s.n. Wm. ; w. Markie Blackie, George Wallace.
,, 26. Thomas Lookup, a.s.n. Thomas ; w. Thomas Lookup, Thomas Law.
,,   ,, William Borthwick, a.s.n. Thomas ; w. Johne Wallace, James Moffat.
June   7. William Sklaitter, a.d.n. Elizabeth ; w. John Lithgow, John Laidlie.
,, 23. Johne Fleck, a.s.n. Robt. ; w. Robt. Fleck, Johne Bowstone.
,, 28. Johne Wilsone, a.s.n. Johne ; w. Johne Frater, John Pringell.
,,   ,, Robt. Law, a.s.n. Thomas ; w. Thomas Law, Andrew Darling.
,, 30. James Bunzie, a.s.n. James ; w. John Bunzie, John Mein.
July   7. Thomas Reidford, a.d.n. Jennet ; w. Adam Lithgow, Whalter Bell.
,, 10. Wm. Bowhill, a.s.n. James ; w. Thomas Law, Thomas Bowhill.
,, 14. Johne Darling, a.s.n. Andrew ; w. John Pringell, Thomas Darling.
,, 21. John Thomson, a.s.n. Patrick ; w. Robt. Hollowill, Andrew Drummond.
,,   ,, Thomas Turner, a.d.n. Mart. ; w. George Turner, Adam Hislope.
,,   ,, John Gibsone, a.d.n Helene ; w. James Bowar, Michael Gibsone.
,, 28. John Sklaitter, a.s.n. Richart ; w. John and Alexr. Meins.
Aug. 11. George Blackie, a.d.n. Jennit ; w. James Elies, Markie Blackie.
,, 18. George Muddie, a.d.n. Isobell ; w. Willian Fishar, William Spotswood.
,, 25. John Barton, a.s.n. Johne ; w. Andrew Marr, Whalter Vaitch.
,,   ,, —— Thomson, a.d.n. Jennit ; w. Wm. and George Moffats.
Sept. 1. William Mylne, a.s.n. Johne ; w. Johne and Thomas Mylnes.
,,   8. Robt. Marr, a.s.n. Johne ; w. John Karr, Johne Marr.
,,   ,, James Robertson, a.d.n. Agnes ; w. John and Thomas Mylnes.
,,   ,, Thomas Mylne, a.d.n. Agnes ; w. Johne Sklaitter, John Vair.
,, 15. George Uscher, a.d.n. Mart. ; w. Johne Mosse, Whalter Uscher.
,, 29. Robt. Bunzie, a.s.n. Robt. ; w. John Bunzie, James Mein.
,,   ,, And. Oliver, a.s.n. Andrew ; w. Andrew Chisholme, Thomas Law.
Oct. 13. Wm. Anderson, a.s.n. Thomas ; w. Mungow Donaldson, James Patterson.
Nov. 8. James Edgar, a.s.n. James ; w. Janes Elles, William Edgar.
,, 10. Thomas Bell, a.s.n. John ; w. John Bell, Thomas Law.
Dec. 1. James Mein, a.s.n. Weliam ; w. James Mein, John Boynze.
,,   6. Thomas Mabon, a.s.n. Thomas ; w. Robert Mein, John Mabon.
,,   ,, Andro Hownam, a.d.n. Jennett ; w. Nicol Mesar, George Hownam.
,,   8. John Drowmond, a.s.n. George ; w. John Drowmond, Andro Drowmond.
,, 20. John Bownyze, a.d.n. Bessie ; w. John Bownyze, James Bownyze.
       Robartt Reddall, a.s.n. Jenatt ; w. Weliam Feschar, John Mein.
,, 27. James Mein, a.s.n. James ; w. Andro Mein, George Mein.
,, 29. Andro Hownam, a.s.n. John ; w. John Hetton, John Feshar.

1668.

Jan.   3. Rot. Mein, a.s.n. James ; w. Rot. Middlemist, John Mein.
,, 21. John Mercer, a.s.n. Bernard ; w. John Mercer, Lochbruar ?) —— Turnbull.

1668.

Jan. 26. John Scheill, a.s.n. William ; w. William Gibson, George Sheill.
  „ 26. Patrick Luckhope, a.s.n. Thomas ; w. William Luckhop, Thomas Law.
Feb. 16. Wm. Luckhop, a.d.n. Marion ; w. Thomas and Andrew Luckhop.
  „ „ James Milne, a.d.n. Christine ; w. John and Thomas Milnes.
  „ 18. John Hogge, a.d.n. Jean and Issobell ; w. Adam Lithgow, Rot. Young.
Mar. 1. James Milne, a.s.n. Nicoll ; w. Johne and Thomas Milnes.
  „ „ William Mercer, a.s.n. John ; w. Thomas Law, Thomas Mercer.
      [*The above two entries are deleted in the Record.*]
  „ „ Mr. Alex. Cro, a.s.n. Rot. ; w. John Pringle of Williamlaw and Mr. Robt. Heittoun (?).
  „ „ George Wallace, a.s.n. Michael ; w. Andro and James Edgar.
  „ 8. Andrew Drummond, a.d.n. Marion ; w. Johne Drummond, John Thomson.
  „ 27. Alexr. Lithgow of Drygrange, a.s.n. Gavin ; w. Gavin Elleis, Thomas Williamson, Ja. Elleis.
  „ 29. Wm. Pringle, a.s.n. Wm. ; w. John Thin, Thos. Watsone.
Apr. 5. Thomas Myles, a.s.n. Thomas ; w. Henrie and Robt. Myles.
  „ „ George Martine, a.s.n. George ; w. Andro and James Martine.
  „ 5. Nicoll Mercer, a.d.n. Margt. ; w. Thomas Turner, James Smyth.
  „ „ Robt. Spotswood, a.s.n. Wm. ; w. John Mosse, Andrew Heitton.
  „ 12. James Boustoun, a.d.n. Margt. ; w. Andrew Marr, James Boustoun.
  „ 19. Thomas Laidlaw, a.s.n. Thomas ; w. John Milne, Thomas Stenhouse.
  „ „ John Mylne, a.d.n. Agnes ; w. Mungo and James Mylne.
  „ 26. George Martine, a.s.n. Andrew ; w. John Bell, Andrew Martine.
  „ „ John Lythgow, a.d.n. Agnes ; w. Andrew Marr, Rot. Laidlaw.
May 14. Wm. Sclettar, a.s.n. Andrew ; w. Andrew Cook, Andrew Sclettar.
  „ „ Robt. Laidlaw, a.s.n. Rot. ; w. John and Andrew Marr.
  „ 26. Rot. Mein, Bostland (?), a.d.n. —— ; w. Andrew and James Meins.
  „ 28. Mr. Alexr. Bisset, a.s.n. Rot. ; w. Mr. John Somerville, Mr. James Knox.
June 3. James Darling, a.s.n. Andro ; w. Andrew Darling, John Frater.
  „ 7. Rot. Mein, a.s.n. George ; w. John Mein, John Sclettar.
  „ 12. James Corson, a.s.n. George ; w. Andro Marr, Wm. Bowstoune.
  „ „ Andrew Merser, a.d.n. Isabel ; w. Andro Heiton, John Merser.
  „ „ John Moss, —— ; w. John Hislope, Andw. Moss.
July 16. John Symentone, a.s.n. James ; w. George Pringle, Thomas Law.
  „ 23. James Mylne, a.d.n. Jennet ; w. Thos. and John Mylne.
Aug. 6. James Halyburton, a.s.n. James ; w. John and James Hardie.
  „ 18. Wm. Mein, a.s.n. John ; w. John and Andro Meins.
  „ 26. James Mein, a.d.n. Agnes ; w. Wm. and John Meins.
Sept. 27. John Riddell, a.d.n. Janet ; w. John Vair, elder and younger.
  „ „ John Laidley, a.d.n. Agnes ; w. James Elies, James Edgar.
Oct. 4. George Hownam, a.s.n. John ; w. John Mercer, John Hownam.
  „ 11. John Mein, a.d.n. Isabel ; w. John and Andro Mein.
  „ 23. Robert Wallace, a.s.n. George ; w. Wm. and George Wallaces.
  „ „ James Guill, a.d.n. Jennet ; w. John Mylne, Thomas Stenhouse.
Nov. 8. John Guill, a.d.n. Margt. ; w. Nicoll Cochran, Thomas Mylne.
  „ „ Robert Holiwall, a.s.n. John ; w. John and Andro Mosses.
  „ 20. Mungo Mylne, a.d.n. Agnes ; w. John and Thomas Mylnes.
  „ 22. James Hall, a.s.n. David ; w. David Hall, Andrew Phaup.
Dec. 6. John Halliwall, a.s.n. Rob. ; w. John and Robt. Halliwalls.
  „ 15. John Freirgrieve, a.s.n. Wm. ; w. James Edgar, George Wallace.
  „ 20. Stephen Heitone, a.d.n. Agnes ; w. Andro and James Heittons.
1669.

Jan. „ Andro Fishar of Housebyre, two sons named John and James ; w. Wm. Fishar, Alexr. Lithgow of Drygrange.
  „ 9. Stephen Martine, —— ; w. Andrew and James Heittouns.
  „ 20. —— [*entry blank in Record*].

1669.

Jan. 30. James Mein, smyth, a.s.n. Andro ; w. John and Andro Meins.
,, last. Rot. Clark, a.d.n. Margt. ; w. Wm. Bell, Andro Marr.
Feb. 14. James Mein in Eildoune, a.d.n. Agnes ; w. John Wair, Nicoll Bowar.
,, ,, John Turner in Calfhill, a.d.n. —— ; w. Charles and James Watsons.
,, 19. Wm. Bell, a.s.n. Thomas ; w. Andro Marr, Robert Mercer.
,. 26. Georg Mercer, a.d.n. Issobell ; w. Wm. Mercer, Andro Heitton.
,, ,, Androw Mein, a.d.n. Agnes ; w. James and Rot. Meins.
Mar. 2. Wm. Bowstone, a.s.n. George ; w. Thos. and Georg Bowstones.
,, 19. Wm. Darling, a.s.n. Wm. ; w. Adam Darling, John Donaldsone.
,, 23. Thomas Mein, a.s.n. James ; w. Rot. Mein, Nicoll Bowar.
April 2. Wm. Waker, a.d.n. Jean ; w. Georg Hownam, Wm. Fischar.
,, 4. John Mein, maltman, a.s.n. William ; w. Androw Mein, Wm. Fischar.
,, 16. John Sclatter in Eildoun, a.d.n. —— ;
May 2. Walter Dalgleish, a.d.n. Elspeth ; w. Alexr. Dalgleish, Andro Heitton.
,, 6. John Dawsone, a.s.n. James.
,, 21. Archibald Freir, a.s.n. Rot. ; w. Rot. and James Freirs.
June 6. James Martine, a s.n. Thomas ; w. Patrick Lukup, John Laitheed.
July 2. James Darling, a.d.n. Issobell ; w Andrew Darling, Wm. Darline.
,, 7. John Merser in Bridgend : w. Nicoll Mercer, George Hownam.
,, 18. Thomas Vair, a.d.n. Isobell ; w. John Mylne, James Vair.
,, ,, Walter Riddell, a.s.n. Andro ; w. Wm. Tait, Walter Scot.
Aug. 16. Wm. Martine, a.s.n. Thomas ; w. James and Thomas Boustounes.
,, 29. John Mylne, a.d.n. Alison ; w. Thomas Stenhouse, Thos. Mylne.
,, ,, Wm. Anderson, a.d.n. Jennet ; w. James and Andro Patisones.
Sept. 12. Thomas Bell, a.s.n. Thomas ; w. John Bell, Thomas Law.
,, ,, James Tailfoore, a.s.n. James ; w. John Sclettar, Nicoll Bowar.
,, ,, Alexr. Mein, a.d.n. Maria ; w. Andro Mein, John Mein.
,, 19. John Merser, a.s.n. Androw ; w. Alexr. Redpath, Andro Heitton.
,, ,, Wm. Martine, a.s.n. John ; w. James Paterson, James Darling.
Oct. 3. George Mein, a.d.n. Agnes : w. Rot. Phillip, Thomas Halliwall.
,, 8. James Mein, a.d.n. Magt. ; w. Robt. and Thomas Meins.
,, 24. James Edgar, a.s.n. Robert ; w. James Eilleis, Wm. Edgar.
,, 27. John Karr, a.s.n. Thomas ; w. Mr. Wm. Mein, Thomas Wilkiesone.
Nov. 5. Wm. Guill, a.s.n. Thomas ; w. Wm. Anderson, James Paterson.
,, 16. John Mein, masone, a.d.n. Jennet ; w. Robt. Bunzie, John Mein.
,, 30. Alexander Lithgow of Drygrange, a.d.n. Magdalene ; w. Mr. James Elleis, Thomas Wilkieson.
Dec. 21. John Vair, a.d.n. Agnes ; w. James Mercer, Nicoll Bowar.
1670.
Jan. 11. John Heitton, a.s.n. John ; w. Andrew and —— Heittons.
,, ,, Thomas Guill, a.s.n. Wm. ; w. George Mertin, John Guill.
,, 18. Robert Hastie, a.s.n. Thomas ; w. George and Thomas Hasties.
,, 28. Mr. Thomas Byres, a.s.n. Alexr. ; w. Wm. and James Edgars.
Feb. 1. George Blackie, a.s.n. Thomas ; w. Thomas Lythgow, Adam Lythgow.
,, 16. James Turner in Newsteid, a.s.n. —— ; w. John and Thomas Bells.
Mar. 6. John Fisher in Darnick, a.s.n. John ; w. Andrew Heitton, Patrick Loukup.
,, 29. Wm. Anderson, a.d.n. Isobell ; w. Wm. Loukup, James Paterson.
,, ,, Thomas Bouston in Gattonsyde, a.d.n. Jannet ; w. Andro Marr, Rot. Mein.
April 3. James Lithgow, a.d.n. —— ; w. Walter Riddell, Adam Hyslop.
,, 4. William Bowstoun, a.d.n. Janet : w. Thomas Boustoun, Waltar Vaitch.
,, 10. Thomas Lythgow, a.s.n. Anna ; w. James Eillies, John Karr.
,, 13. George Hownam, a.s.n. Andro : w. Andro Drummond, John Hownam.
,, 23. Thomas Stenhouse, a.s.n. John ; w. Nicoll Cochrane, John Milne.
May 10. Nicoll Cochrane, a.s.n. Nicoll ; w. Thomas Stenhouse, James Milne.
,, 17. Andrew Howname, a.s.n. George ; w. George Hownam, John Heittone.
June 5. Michael Gibsone, a.d.n. Margaret ; w. Thomas Bell, Thomas Law.

1670.

June   5. George Turner, a.d.n. Jean ; w. Wm. Bell, Wm. Taitt.

July   10. John Guill, a.s.n. John ; w. Thomas and John Milnes.

„   17. Alexander Waithman, a.s.n. Thomas ; w. Andrew Heitton, John Moss.

Aug.   7. Andrew Martine, a.s.n. Wm. ; w. George and James Martines.

„   13. Thomas Wilkieson, a.d.n. Katherine ; w. James Eilleis, Alexander Lithgow.

Sept.   4. Wm. Loukup, a.s.n. John ; w. Patrick and Thomas Loukups.

„   20. John Heittone, a.s.n. John ; w. Andrew and John Heitons.

„   25. James Edgar, a.s.n. James ; w. James Eileis, Thomas Wilkiesone.

Oct.   9. Patrick Loukup, a.s.n. Wm. ; w. Andro Tunno, James Edgar.

„   18. Alexr. Newtone, a.s.n. Alexr. ; w. Patrick Loukup, John Lithead.

Nov.   6. John Frater, a.s.n. —— ; w. Andrew and James Darlings.

„   12. John Moss, a.d.n. Isobell ; w. Andro Kennedie, Andro Chisholme.

„   „ George Martine, a.d.n. Margaret ; w. Andro and James Martines.

„   „ Andrew Mein called "Kill," a.s.n. Andro ; w. John and Andro Mein.

„   „ James Milne, a.d.n. Alisone ; w. John Milne, John Stenhouse.

„   20. Charles Watson, a.s.n. Walter ; w. Wm. Bell, Andro Tunno.

1671.

Jan.   17. Thomas Mathesone, a —— ; w. Adam and James Edgar.

„   28. Wm. Milne, a.s.n. Wm. ; w. John and Thomas Milnes.

„   „ John Hogg, a.s.n. John ; w. John Leithead and Mark Blaikie.

Feb.   5. Andro Olivar, a.d.n. Jannet ; w. Thomas Law, Andro Wallace.

„   7. Archibald Freir, a.d.n. Isobel ; w. Rot. and James Friers.

„   15. John Mein, a.s.n. John ; w. Robert Mein, Walter Vaitch.

„   20. John Haliwall, a.s.n. John ; w. George Chisholm, Andro Haliwall.

Mar.   12. John Barton, a.s.n. Robt. ; w. Robt. Mein, Wm. Cook.

„   13. John Lindsay, a.s.n. John ; w. Andrew Marr, Walter Vaitch.

„   21. John Stenhouse, a.s.n. James ; w. James Milne, John Penman.

„   29. Andrew Howname, a.d.n. Isabel ; w. George Howname, elder and younger.

April   5. Thomas Marr, a.d.n. Alison ; w. Andro Marr, Robt. Mein.

„   13. Thomas Bighet, a.d.n. Margaret ; w. James Milne, Thomas Drummond.

„   „ Andro Paterson, a.s.n. Andro ; w. Thomas Drummond, Wm. Guill.

„   17. James Smith, a.d.n. Jean ; w. Nicoll Mercer, James Moffat.

May   10. James Milne, a.d.n. Margaret ; w. John and Thomas Milnes.

„   21. John Mein, multerer, a.s.n. John ; w. John and Andro Meins.

June   5. James Robertson, a.d.n. Janet ; Rot. Mein, Nicoll Bowar.

„   11. Mr. Alexr. Bissett, a.d.n. Agnes ; w. George Pringle of Buckholme Mr. Rot. Main.

„   23. Thomas Lithgow, a.s.n. John ; w. James Eilles, Mr. John Lythgow.

July   17. Nicoll Bowar, a d.n. Margaret ; w. James and Thomas Meins.

Aug.   7. Rot. Myles, a.s.n. Thomas ; w. Thomas and Henrie Myles.

„   18. George Blaikie, a.d.n. Isobel ; Adam Lythgow, Mark Blaikie.

„   30. John Mein, ostler, a.s.n. Robert ; w. John and James Meins.

„   „ John Milne, elder, a.s.n. John.

Sept.   7. Thomas Drummond, a.d.n. Isobell ; w. Rot. Maben, James Patsone.

„   13. Thomas Mein, a.d.n. Alison ; w. Rot. and James Meins.

Oct.   9. Andro Kennedie, a.s.n. Rot. ; w. Mr. Robert Main, Thomas Wilkiesone.

Nov.   8. Peter Darling, a.d.n. Jennet ; w. Adam and James Darling.

Dec.   9. Wm. Martine, a.s.n. John ; w. James and Andro Martines.

1672.

Jan.   16. James Darling, a.d.n. Jean ; w. Peter Darling, George Pringle.

„   26. Wm. Turner, a.s.n. John ; w. George and Thomas Turners.

„   31. Alexr. Mein, a.d.n. Agnes ; w. John and Andro Meins.

Feb.   10. George Mein, a.d.n. Agnes ; w. Mark Blaikie, John Haliwell.

Mar.   3. John Sclaitter, a—— ; w. John and Rot. Mein.

„   17. Andrew Mercer, a.s.n. John ; w. Andro and George Mercers.

1672.

Mar. 17. Nicoll Bowar, a.s.n. John ; w. Rot. and James Meins.

„ 24. Andro Mercer, wright, a.d.n. Agnes ; w. John Moss, Andro Chisholm.

April 7. Nicoll Cochrane, a.d.n. Jannet ; w. John Milne, Thomas Stenhouse.

„ 9. Andro Marr. a.d.n. Jennet ; w. Thomas Wilkiesone, Thomas Bouston.

„ 14. John Hoy, a d.n. Isabell ; w. Wm. Bouston, Andro Marr.

„ „ James Lindsay, a.d.n. Margaret ; w. Walter Vaitch, Thomas Boustone.

„ 21. John Ushar, a.s.n. James ; w. James Ushar, Andro Mercer.

May 12. Thomas Laidlay, a.d.n. Jannet ; w. Thomas and John Milnes.

„ 14. Thomas Vaitch, a.s.n. John : w. Adam Lythgow, James Mylne.

„ 29. Thomas Livingstone, a.d.n. Isobell ; w. John Stirling, John Thin.

June 9. John Mein, maissone, a.d.n. Margt. ; w. John and James Meines.

„ „ Thomas Martine, a. d.n. Margt. ; w. James Martine, Thomas Drummond.

„ 16. George Martine, a.d.n. Marion ; w. James and Andro Martines.

„ 20. John Milne, a.d.n. Jennet ; w. Nicoll Cochrane, Wm. Mylne.

„ 23. Thomas Lythgow, a.d.n. Marion ; w. Francis Scott, Mr. John Lythgow.

„ 25. Wm. Mylne, messenger (?), a.s.n. Nicoll ; w. James Mylne, Adam Lythgow.

„ 30. Thomas Loukup, younger, a.s.n. John ; w. Patrick and Andrew Loukups.

July 7. Andro Howname, weaver in Darnick, a.s.n. James ; w. Andro and John Heittons.

„ 7. Bernard Mein in Newsteid, a.d.n. Isobell ; w. Andro and John Meins.

„ 16. John Hogg, weaver in Melrose, a.d.n. Jean ; w. James Karr and George Wallace.

„ 21. Thomas Darling in Blanislie, a.s.n. John ; w. Edward Darling, Wm. Greive.

„ 28. George Turna, a.s.n. John ; w. Adam Hislop, Wm. Taitt.

Aug. 4. Rot. Spotswood, a.d.n. Agnes ; w. Andrew Chisholme, John Fishar.

„ 7. Thomas Drummond, a.s.n. Andro ; w. James and Thomas Martines.

„ 25. Wm. Martine in Westhouses, a.d.n. Bessie ; w. Wm. Ormiston, Adam Darling.

Sept. 1. Mr. Thomas Byres, a.d.n. Margaret ; w. Mr. Rot. Main, Thomas Lythgow.

„ „ John Bowar, a.d.n. Magt.; w. John and Thomas Bells.

„ „ George Frier in Gallowshiels, a.d.n. Isobell ; w. Wm. Karr, Wm. Williamsone.

„ „ Wm. Moffat in Threepwood, a.s.n. John ; w. Archibald and James Moffat.

„ 3. John Trotter, a.d.n. Margaret ; w. Walter Vaitch, Wm. Bell.

„ 8. Robert Frier, a.s.n. John ; w. Rot. and Archibald Friers.

„ 29. Charles Watsone, a.d.n. Jean ; w. Wm. Fisher, Tho. Watsone.

„ „ Thomas Bell, a.d.n. Elizabeth ; w. John Bell, Thomas Law.

Oct. 17. Wm. Mylne, a.s.n. John ; w. John and Thos. Mylnes.

„ 22. James Mein in Eildon, a.s.n. ——— ; w. Rot. and Thos. Meins.

Nov. 3. John Symentone, a.s.n. John ; w. Thos. Law, Rot. Gardner.

„ „ Wm. Browne, a.d.n. Margt.; w. George Turner, James Pringle.

„ 12. Thomas Mein, a.d.n. Margt.; w. Rot. and James Meins.

„ „ Wm. Loukup, a.d.n. Isabel ; w. James Paterson, Thomas Drummond.

„ 17. Henrie Wallace, a s.n. Andro, a.d.n. Marie ; w. Andro Tunno, Andro Wallace.

„ „ John Fischer, a.s.n. John ; w. Andro Heittone, Andro Chisholme.

„ 18. James Lambe, a.d.n. Issobell ; w. John Fischer, John Mein.

„ 24. John Mein Webster in Darnick, a.s.n. John ; w. Andro and George Hounam.

„ 25. James Edgar, a.d.n. Isobell ; w. James Eillies, Thomas Wilkiesone.

Dec. 1. John Davidsone, a——— ; w. James Moffat, John Purves.

1672.
Dec. 10. James Bowie, a——; w. John and Thomas Bells.
  „   13. Rot. Halliwall, a.s.n. Andro; w. John Moss, John Halliwall.
  „   19. Patrick Loukup, a.d.n. Margt.; w. Thomas Loukup, Thomas Law.
  „   24. Andro Mein, a.s.n. Andro; w. John Mein, James Mercer.
1673.
Jan.   6. Thomas Bicket, a.d.n. Marion; w. Thomas Drummond, Wm.
            Loukup.
  „   18. John Mercer Lochbreast, a.s.n. Bernard; w. George and Andrew
            Boustones.
Feb.   2. Andro Mein, a.d.n. Jennet; w. Rot. and John Meins.
  „   13. Thomas Myles, a.s.n. James; w. Andrew Marr, Henrie Myles.
  „   24. George Pringle, coblyman, a.s.n. George; w. Sir .Thomas   Karr,
            George Pringle, Buckholm.
  „   „ John Stenhouse, a.s.n. ——; w. John Mylne, Thomas Stenhouse.
Mar.   2. Andro Penman, a.s.n. Rot.; w. John Penman, James Bowar.
  „   11. Andrew Pringle, cobleman, a.s.n. George: w. Alexr. Mein, George
            Pringle.
  „   22. Alexr. Waithman, a.s.n. Thomas; w. George Eillies, Andro Heittone.
  „   24. John Martine, a.s.n. ——; w. Stephen and Andro Martines.
April 1. Thomas Mabon, a.d.n. Jennet; w. Thomas Boustone, Rot. Mein.
  „   6. John Sklettar, a.s.n. Wm.; w. Andro and Wm. Sklettars.
  „   15. Mongo Mylne, a.d.n. Issobell; w. John and Wm. Mylnes.
May   18. John Mylne, Laird, a.d.n. ——; w. Mungo and Wm. Mylnes.
  „   „ George Mein, a.d.n. ——; w. John Mein, Rot. Bunzie.
  „   25. John Heitton, a.d.n. Jennet; w. Andro Heitton, John Moss.
  „   26. John Mein, maltman, a.d.n. Isobel; w. Wm. Fishar, Andro Mein.
  „   „ John Heittone, a.d.n. Jennet; w. Andro Heittone, John Moss.
June   8. George Ormistone, a.d.n. Helen; w. John and Thomas Bells.
  „   20. Alexander Lythgow of Drygrange, a.s.n. Charles; w. Mr. John
            Lythgow, Francis Scott of Langshaw.
  „   29. John Moss, a.s.n. Andro; w. Andro Chisholme, John Fishar.
July 12. James Mylne, two d.n. Issobel and Margaret; w. Nicol Cochrane,
            Thomas Mylne.
  „   „ ——Wintrope in Newtoune, a.s.n. Alexr.; w. James and John Mylne.
  „   27. Thomas Bouston, a.d.n. Jennet; w. Andrew Marr, James Boustone.
  „   „ Wm. Laing, a.d.n. Kathrine; w. George and James Eillies.
Aug. 10. Wm. Simson, a.d.n. Margaret: w. Rot. Foregrieve, Wm. Mercer.
  „   17. James Mein, called "Brown James," a.s.n. James; w. Thomas Mein,
            Nicol Bowar.
  „   23. John Mylne, ostler, a.s.n. John; w. John and Wm. Mylnes.
  „   26. Thomas Wilkieson, a.d.n. Margt.; w. James Eillies, James Edgar.
  „   31. Walter Vair, a.d.n. Margt.; w. John Moss, Andrew Chisholme.
  „   „ James Bowar, called fermer, a.s.n. Thomas: w. Thomas and James
            Meins.
Sept. 21. Andro Olivar, a.s.n. Rot.; w. John Mein, James Bowar.
Oct. 20. John Hoy, a ——; w. George Hay, Andro Marr.
Nov.   9. Andro Fishar, a.s.n. Andrew; w. Andrew Lythgow, Wm. Fisbar.
  „   16. Wm. Mercer in Bridgend, a.s.n Nicoll: w. Nicol Mercer, George
            Hownam.
  „   „ Alexander Clapperton, a.d.n. Issobel; w. James Lambe, John Moss.
Dec.   7. Andrew Chisholme, a.d.n. Margt.; w. John Moss, Andrew Rennald-
            sone.
  „   14. John Thomson, called "Stumper," a.s.n. Thomas: w. Thos. and Wm.
            Boustouns.
1674.
Jan. 15. John Guill, a.s.n. John; w. John Mylne, and Wm. Guill.
  „   16. Thomas Lythgow, a.s.n. Walter; w. Mr. John Lythgow Francis
            Scott of Langshaw.
  „   27. Andrew Frier, a.s.n. Andrew; w. Rot. Frier, Andrew Halliwall.
Feb. 15. Wm. Grierson, a.d.n. Jennet; w. John Moss, Andrew Heittone.

1674.
Feb. 15. James Murray, a.d.n. Helen ; w. Andro and George Boustones.
  ,, 17. John Hoy in Gattinsyde, a.d. —— ; w. Andrew Halliwall, John Lourie.
  ,, 19. Rot. Forsan, a.s.n. Charles ; w. John Mein, James Bunzee.
  ,, 27. Mr. Alexr. Bisset, a.s.n. Alexr. ; w. Alexr. Lythgow, Thos. Wilkieson.
Mar. 4. George Wallace, a.s.n. William ; w. Wm. Wallace, James Lamb.
  ,,   8. Charles Watson, a.d.n. Elizabeth ; w. Wm. Fishar, Thomas Watson.
  ,, 22. Walter Dalgleish, a.d.n. Magt. ; w. John Mose, Alexr. Dalgleish.
April 5. Bernard Mein, a.s.n. Andrew ; w. Andrew and John Mein.
  ,,   7. Nicoll Bowar, a.s.n. Nicol ; w. John Vair, James Mein.
  ,, 14. John Mein, weaver, a.s.n. John ; w. James Mein, John Heittone.
  ,, 21. George Hoy, *cister*, a.d.n. Margt. ; w. Archibald Frier, Andrew
           Marr.
May 10. Alexr. Mein, a.s.n. Andro ; w. John and Andrew Meins.
  ,, 29. Rot. Middlemist, a.s.n. Robert ; w. Thomas Mein, Nicoll Bowar.
June 6. George Blaikie, a.d.n. Christine ; w. Mark Blaikie, Adam Lythgow.
  ,, ,, Thomas Martine, a.d.n. Jannet ; w. John and James Martines.
  ,, 13. Wm. Notman, a.d.n. Margaret, begotten in adulterie ; presented by
           Wm. Ormiston, Archd. Moffat, George Moffat.
  ,, 21. John Thin, a.d.n. Agnes ; w. John Stirling, James Grieve.
  ,, 29. James Edgar, a.d.n. Helen ; w. James Eilies, Thos. Wilkieson.
July 5. Rot. Spottiswood, a.s.n. —— ; w. John Moss, Andrew Kennedie.
  ,, 19. Wm. Muddie, a.s.n. John ; w. John Moss, John Mudie.
  ,, ,, Thomas Myles, a.d.n. Jannet ; w. Henrie Myles, John Mabon.
  ,, ,, Wm. Martine, a.d.n. —— ; w. Thomas Martine, younger, Rot.
           Martine.
  ,, 21. Thomas Laidley, a.d.n. Alison ; w. Wm. Laidley, James Mylne.
  ,, 26. Thomas Bouston, wynd, a.d.n. Jennet ; w. Andro Marr, Rot. Mein.
Aug. 2. Thomas Loukup, a.d.n. Agnes ; w. Patrick and Andro Loukup.
Sept. 6. John Riddell, a.d.n. Alison ; w. John and Thomas Mylnes.
  ,, 20. David Cook, a.d.n. —— ; w. Rot. Ormiston, James Lamb.
Oct. 6. John Karr, a.s.n. Robert ; w. Mr. Andrew Karr of Kippielaw, Thomas
           Wilkieson.
Nov. 15. John Sheill, a.d.n. Jean ; w. Thomas Law, James Lambe.
  ,, 22. Andrew Renaldsone, a.s.n. Wm. ; w. John Moss, Andrew Chisholme.
  ,, ,, John Mein, a.d.n. Margt. ; w. James and Rot. Meins.
  ,, 29. George Lowrie, a.s.n. Thomas ; w. Mr. John Scletter, Robt. Leithane.
Dec. 10. James Lambe, a.s.n. James ; w. Michael Gibson, James Wallace.
  ,, ,, Thomas Drummond, a.d.n. Jennet ; w. Andro Mercer, Rot. Maben.
  ,, 22. Rot. Halliwall, a.s.n. Thomas ; w. Andrew and George Mercers.
1675.
Jan. 9. Mr. Thomas Byers, a.d.n. Jean ; w. Mr. Alexr. Bisset, George
           Wallace.
  ,, 17. Andrew Pringle, a.s.n. Rot. ; w. George Pringle, elder and younger.
Feb. 2. George Pringle, cobleman, a.d.n. Margt. ; w. Wm. Sclatter, John
           Mein.
  ,, 28. Thomas Mein, a.d.n. Isobel ; w. Andrew and Rt. Meins.
Mar. 3. Rot. Freir, a.d.n. Issobel ; w. Archibald and James Friers.
  ,, ,, John Sclettar, a.d.n. Marion ; w. John Mein, George Lowrie.
  ,,   9. Rot. Leithane, a.s.n. John ; w. John Mein, Rot. Middlemist.
  ,, 14. James Scott, a.s.n. Rot. ; w. Andro Heitton, John Leitheed.
  ,, 16. Wm. Loukup, a.d.n. Margt. ; w. Patrick Loukup, James Paterson.
  ,, 20. James Lindsay, a.d.n. Elspeth ; w. Walter Vaitch, Andrew
           Cairncrose.
  ,, 23. John Ushar, a.d.n. Isobel ; w. George Mercer, Michael Usher.
May   9. John Lythgow, a.d.n. Margt. ; w. James Eillies, Alexr. Lythgow,
           Drygrange.
  ,, 14. John Main, maltman, a.d.n. Elizabeth ; w. Wm. Fishar, Andrew
           Mein.
June 20. Andro Houname, a.s.n. John ; w. John and Andrew Houname.
  ,, ,, John Mein, masone, a.d.n. Isobell ; w. John and Rot. Meins.

1675.
July   1. —— Philip in Gattonsyde, a.s.n. Rot.; w. Waltar Vaitch, Thos. Boustone.
,,   3. —— Dickson, a.s.n. John, begotten in fornication with —— Wallace; w. James Wauch, John Bonzie.
,,   8. John Milne, elder, a.s.n. Nicoll; w. George and Wm. Milne.
,,   20. Robert Bunzie, two sons named Thomas and Wm.; w. John and James Bunzie.
,,   28. Andrew Wright, a.s.n. Andrew; w. Wm. Mertoune, Rt. Myles.
Aug.   3. Thomas Pringle, a.s.n. John; w. John Bell, John Bowar.
,,   ,, Patrick Loukup, a.s.n. Patrick; w. Thos. and Andro Loukup.
,,   8. George Turner, a.s.n. —— ; w. Nicoll Cairncrose, James Edgar.
,,   ,, John Davidson, a.d.n. Marion; w. John Waugh, John Haitlie.
,,   15. Nicoll Merser, a.d.n. Isobell; w. Wm. Merser, George Hounem.
,,   24. James Marr, —— ; w. Andro Marr, Thos. Bustoun.
Sept. 18. Andrew Mein, a.s.n. Rot.; w. James Wauch, George Merser.
Oct. 12. Thomas Boustone, a.d.n. Jannet; w. Andro Marr, Rt. Mein.
,,   17. Alexr. Lythgow of Drygrange, a.s.n. Andrew; w. Andrew Plumar, Wm. Lythgow.
,,   28. John Stenhouse, a.d.n. Margaret; w. James Milne, James Wauch.
,,   ,, Thomas Lythgow, a.s.n. Thomas; w. Francis Scott and Alexr. Lythgow, Drygrange.
Nov.   2. Andrew Frier, a.d.n. Alison; w. Rot. and James Friers.
,,   14. John Ushar in Darnick, a.s.n. Wm.; w. James Ushar, Michael Fishar.
,,   ,, John Cockburn, a.s.n. Wm.; w. Andro Rennaldson, Waltar Vair.
,,   ,, Walter Vair, a.d.n. Margt.; w. Andro Merser, Andro Renaldson.
,,   16. Wm. Wright, —— ; w. Andro Marr, Archibald Freir.
,,   21. Thomas Mylne, a.s.n. John; w. John and Wm. Mylne.
Dec. 12. Wm. Merser, —— ; w. Nicol Merser, George Hounam.
,,   19. John Bowar, a.d.n. Agnes; w. John and Thomas Bell.
,,   26. Andro Chisholme, a.s.n. Wm.; w. John Moss, Andrew Renaldson.
1676.
Jan.   4. James Wallace, a.d.n. Margt.; w. Wm. and George Wallace.
,,   9. John Martine, a.s.n. Andro; w. Wm. Merser, George Boustone.
,,   16. John Guill, a.d.n. Jannet; w. John Milne, Mungo Milne.
,,   ,, Umqle Wm. Lowrie, a.d.n. Helen; w. George and John Lowrie.
Feb.   6. George Houname, a.s.n. Leonard; w. Wm. and John Mersers.
Mar. 14. Thomas Bicket, —— ; w. Wm. and David Cook.
,,   19. Andrew Stevensone, a.s.n. Andrew; w. Walter Vaitch, Rt. Ormiston.
,,   26. Edward Darling, a.s.n. John; w. James Greive, Adam Darling.
,,   ,, James Forsythe, —— ; w. Mr. John Taitt, John Symentone.
April 9. Thomas Matheson, a.d.n. Isobel; w. Andro Marr, Thomas Boustone.
,,   23. John Heittone, a.d.n. Margt.; w. John Mein, Andro Ushar.
,,   30. Umqle George Mercer, a.s.n. Charles; w. Andro and Wm. Mercers.
May   20. George Mein, a.s.n. David; w. John and James Mein.
,,   23. Andro Mein, a.s.n. Nicoll; w. John and James Mein.
,,   28. Rot. Halliwalls, a.d.n. Jannet; w. John Fishar, Andro Mercer.
June   9. Thomas Mein, a.s.n. Andro; w. Nicoll Bowar, John Sclatter.
,,   15. John Karr, a.d.n. Martha; w. Thomas Wilkieson, James Eillies.
,,   25. Thomas Darling, younger, in Blainslie, a.s.n. Edward; w. John Darling, James Smith.
July   9. George Wallace, a.d.n. Isobell; w. Wm. Wallace, Andro Wallace.
,,   16. John Sclaitter, a.d.n. Agnes; w. John Marr, Thomas Mein.
,,   23. John Wright, a.s.n. John; w. John Barton, Thos. Bouston.
Aug.   8. John Johnstone, a.s.n. John; w. Thomas and John Darlings.
,,   13. James Bunzie, a.d.n Agnes; w. John Mein, John Bunzie,
,,   14. Andrew Kennedie, a.s.n. James; w. Andro Chisholme and George Blaikie.
,,   24. Alexr. M'Faiden, a.d.n. Anne; w. Thomas Williamson, Thoma Matheson.

1676.

Aug. 27. John Heittone, a.d.n. Isobell ; w. Andro Heittone, Stephen Martine.
Sept. 10. Mr. Alexr. Bisset, minister, a.s.n. George.
" " John Moss, a.s.n. James ; w. Andro Heitton, Andro Chisholm.
Oct. 1. James Grieve, a.s.n. James ; w. John Stirling, John Darling.
" " Archibald Moffat, a.s.n. Robt. ; w. Archibald Moffat, elder, Peter Moffat.
" " George Lowrie, a.s.n. George ; w. John Sclaitter, James Mein.
" 10. Robt. Ormstone, a.d.n. Jennet ; w. David and Wm. Cooks.
" 22. Walter Dalgleish, a.d.n. Marion ; w. John Moss, John Dalgleish.
" " George Merser, a.s.n. Andro ; w. Andrew Merser, Thomas Drummond.
" " Rot. Leithan, a.d.n. Alisone ; w. John Sclaitter, James Mein.
" " Thomas Lukup, a.d.n. Christin ; w. Patrick Lukup, Andro Lukup.
" 29. Wm. Laing, a.d.n. Magt. ; w. Adam Lythgow, John Rathie.
Nov. 5. John Mein, a.d.n. Elizabeth ; w. Alexr. Mein, Wm. Fishar.
" 7. Adam Turnbull, a.s.n. Thomas ; w. John and James Bunzie.
" 10. James Frier, a.s.n. Robert ; w. Rot. and Archibald Frier.
" " John Mein, a.s.n. Andro ; w. James and John Mein.
" 21. James Lambe, a.d.n. Anna ; w. Thomas Law, Andrew Olivar.
" 26. John Mein, Cuddibutts, a.d.n. Marion ; w. James and John Mein.
Dec. 17. Thomas Laidlay, a.s.n. John ; w. John Mylne, Andro Heittone.

1677.

Jan. — George Martine, a.d.n. Elizabeth ; w. John Bell, Andro Martine.
" 14 Bernard Mein, a.d.n. Andro ; w. Andro and John Mein.
" " Alexr. Lythgow of Drygrange, a.s.n. Andro ; w. John and Thos. Lythgow.
Feb. 11. Rot. Mein, tennant in Gattonsyde, a.s.n. Robert ; w. John and Andro Meins.
" 18. Walter Vaitch, a.d.n. Margaret ; w. Rot. Ormstone and James Edgar.
" 20. Andro Smyth, a.s.n. John ; w. John Fisher and Andro Hounem.
" 25. Georg Blaikie, a.d.n. Jean ; w. Adam Lythgow and Mark Blaikie.
Mar. 1. Georg Pringle, natural son to Buckholm, two daughters n. Agnes and Alison ; w. Andro and George Pringle.
" 2. Wm. Scott, a.s.n. Wm. ; w. David Cook and Adam Lythgow.
" 20. Wm. Bowstone, "Whister," a.d.n. Margaret ; w. Thos. Bowstone, John Mabon.
" 25. John Slettar, a.s.n. Andro ; w. John and Thos. Mein.
" 27. Thomas Blaikie, a.d.n. Eupham ; w. John and James Meins.
May 19. Robert Spotswood, a.d.n. Issobell ; w. John Fisher and Andro Mercer.
" 29. Andro Wright, a.s.n. John ; w. Thos. and Robert Myles.
" " Robert Bowston, "Bucat," a.s.n. John ; w. Thos. Bowston and Alex. Trotter.
June 10. Wm. Mudie, a.d.n. Jennet ; w. John Mudie and Andro Heittone.
" 15. Andro Fisher, a.d.n. Anna ; w. Mr. John Lauder and Michaell Fisher.
" " Jean Cairncrosse, a.s.n. James, presented by Thomas Mylne ; w. Wm. Cook and David Cook.
" 17. Wm. Bowar, a.s.n. Wm. ; w. John Bell, John Bowar.
July 1. John Ushar, a.s.n. Walter ; w. John Moss, Andro Heittone.
" 8. Andro Lythgow, a.s.n. John ; w. John Lythgow, Andrew Moffat.
" 10. Thomas Mathiesone, a.d.n. Mary ; w. Andro Marr, Robert Mein.
" 15. John Mylne, elder, a.s.n. Robert ; w. Thomas Mylne, Adam Lythgow.
" 20. James Waugh in Melrose, a.s.n. James ; w. James Mylne, John Bowar.
" 29. James Bowar, fermer, a.s.n. John ; w. John Sclettar, James Mein.
Aug. 5. Andro Mercer, Wynd, ——— ; w. John and Andro Heittone.
" 12. Andro Drumnond, a.s.n. John ; w. Andro and Wm. Mercer.

1677.

Aug. 19. Andro Pringle, a.s.n. James ; w. Patrick Lukup, George Pringle.
Sept. 7. Thomas Bell, a.d.n. Jennet ; w. John Bell, John Bowar.
,, 9. John Wright, a.d.n. Isobell ; w. Georg Barton, Andrew Marr.
,, ,, James Murray, a.s.n. Robert ; w. James Mylne, Michaell Gibsone.
,, 10. James Lindsay, a.d.n. ——— ; w. Walter Vaitch, Rot. Ormstone.
Oct. 19. Wm. Mercer in Bridgend, a.s.n. Wm. ; w. George Hownam, Nicoll Mercer.
,, 21. John Mein, ostler, a.s.n. James ; w. James and John Meins.
Nov. 11. Wm. Mertine, a.s.n. Wm. ; w. Adam Darling, Wm. Fisher.
,, 14. Archibald Frier in Gattonsyd, a.s.n. James ; w. Henrie and Thos. Myles.
,, 17. James Edgar, a.s.n. Adam ; w. James Ellies, John Lythgow.
,, 29. Georg Mein, Wynd, a.d.n. Christin ; w. James Mercer, Alexr. Mein.
Dec. 17. John Broune and Annie Pringle, a.s.n. Robert ; w. Georg Pringle of Blindlee, Ned Wallace.
,, 20. Archibald Frier, a.s.n. Georg ; w. Robert and James Frier.
,, 23. John Symontone, a.s.n. Patrick ; w. John Pringle, Wm. Pringle.
,, 27. Robert Pringle, tailzer, a.s.n. Georg ; w. George and Andro Pringle.
1678.
Jan. 8. Agnes, d. to Issobell Ormstone, begotten in fornication with Nathaniell Cranstoun in Smailholm, presented by Walter Vaitch ; w. Rot. Ormston, Wm. Cuik.
,, 15. James Frier, a.s.n. Charles ; w. Robert and Archibald Friers.
,, last. John Mein, Wynd, a.d.n. Christin ; w. James and John Meins.
Feb. 3. Rot. Halliwall, a.d.n. Isobel ; w. John Halliwall, John Ushar.
Mar. 5. Andro Unes, a.d.n. Isobel ; w. John Martine, Adam Hyslop.
,, 10. James ——— in Bentmylne, a.s.n. James ; w. Wm. Fisher, Walter Scott.
,, 15. Stephen Heitton, a ——— ; w. James Martine, Andro Heitton.
,, 30. James Bunzie, a.s.n. Rot. ; w. John and Rot. Bunzies.
April 6. Andro Bunzie, notar (?), a.s.n. Rot. ; w. James Merser, John Bunzie.
,, 7. Patrick Lukup, a.s.n. Wm., baptised by Mr. Lennock ; w. Wm. Wallace, John Huntar.
,, 19. Andrew Martine, a.d.n. Christine ; w. George and James Martines.
May 10. Mr. Thomas Byres, a.d.n. Christin ; w. John Purves and George Wallace.
,, 12. Nicoll Bowar in Eildoune, a ——— ; w. John Vair, Thomas Mein.
,, 23. Andro Mercer, Baitsheill (?), a.s.n. Andro ; w. Andro Mercer, George Mercer.
,, 29. Nicoll Mercer in Mosshouses, a.s.n. George ; w. George Mercer, Michaell Pearsone.
June 2. John Mein, Townhead, a.s.n. James ; w. John Mein, Andro Sclettar.
,, 16. Alexr. M'Fadzean, a.d.n. Isobell ; w. Adam Darling, Andro Pringle.
,, ,, Michaell Pearson, a.s.n. John ; w. Nicoll and George Mercers.
,, 20. Thomas Wilkieson, a.d.n. Anna ; w. James Eillies, John Lythgow.
,, ,, John Bell, a.d.n. Jennet ; w. Thomas Bell, John Bowar.
,, ,, Robert Cook, a.d.n. Jennet ; w. Wm. and David Cook.
,, 23. Andro Rennaldson, a.d.n. Marie ; w. John Moss, Andro Heitton.
,, 30. Rot. Martine in Gattonsyde, a.d.n. Isobell ; w. Rot. Mein, James Leithane.
July 7. James Paterson in Gallowshiells ; w. James Ballandane, Wm. Wilsone.
,, 25. James Lambe, a.s.n. George ; w. ———.
Aug. 11. John Mercer, " Pett," a.d.n. Margt. ; w. John Bell, James Bowie.
,, 17. James Freirgreive, a.d.n. Jean ; w. Alexr. Trotter, Rot. Mercer.
,, ,, Rot. Fa, baillie in Melrose ; w. Mr. Rot. Maine, Thomas Wilkiesone.
Sept. 8. John Moss in Darnick, a.d.n. Helen ; w. Andro Rennaldson, Andro Chisholme.
,, 26. Rt. Ormiston, ——— ; w. David and Wm. Cooks.
Oct. 7. George Mercer, Baitshiells (?), a.s.n. James ; w. James Wauch, Andro Mercer.

1678.
Oct. 13. Andro Wright, merchant in Gattonsyde ; w. Thomas Maben, John
      Halliwall.
  „   „   Wm. Davidson, a.d.n. Issobel ; w. Rot. and Archibald Freirs.
Nov. 1. John Mein, Cuddiebutts, a.d.n. Margt. ; w. Thomas Bunzie, Andro
      Mein.
  „ 26. Wm. Mercer in Bridgend, a.d.n. Margt. ; w. Nicoll Mercer, George
      Hownem.
  „ 28. Thomas Mein in Eildoune, —— ; w. James and Rot. Meins.
Dec. 12. Thomas Bouston, a.d.n. Isobell ; w. Andro Marr, Rot. Mein.
  „ 22. Rot. Bouston, a.d.n. Jennet ; w. Alexr. Trotter, Rot. Mercer.
  1679.
Jan. 12. John Heittone, called " Corkens," a.d.n. —— ; w. Andro Heitton,
      John Moss.
  „ 19. George Lowrie, a.d.n. Helen ; w. John Sclaitter, James Mein.
Feb. 2. George Mercer, a.s.n. John ; w. John Moss, Andro Rennaldsone.
  „   9. Mark Shillinglaw, a.s.n. Andro ; w. Wm. Shillinglaw, Michael
      Gibsone.
  „ 23. John —— in Gattonsyde, —— ; w. John and Rot. Scotts.
  „   „ John Karr, a.s.n. John ; w. John Karr of Shaw, Patrick Lukup.
Mar. 2. Rot. Leithane, a.s.n. Thomas ; w. John Sclaitter, Rot. Mein.
  „   „ James Moffatt, a.d.n. Issobell ; w. Thomas Bowie, Wm. Cook.
April 1. John Fisher, a.s.n. Michael ; w. Andro and Andro Hownams.
  „   „ Wm. Mudie, a.s.n. James ; w. Andro Mercer, Nicol Waithman.
  „   „ James Martin, a.s.n. Wm. ; w. Alexr. Maxwell, Patrick Lukup.
  „   „ Rot. Smith, a.s.n. John ; w. Andro Chisholme, Andro Heittone.
  „ 15. Andro Mercer, a.s.n. John ; w. John Fischar, George Mercer.
  „ 19. Thomas Lythgow, a.s.n. James ; w. Rot. Faa, James Eilles.
  „ 25. Thomas Blaikie, a.d.n. Jennet ; w. John Mein, James Mein.
May 2. Mr. Alexr. Bissett, a.d.n. Marione ; w. George Pringle, Rot. Faa.
  „   3. George Blaikie, a.d.n. Marion ; w. Thomas Wilkiesone, John
      Mein.
  „ 11. Andro Smith, a.s.n. Andro ; w. Georg Mercer, Andro Rennaldsone.
  „   „ Alexr. Waithman, a.s.n. Alexr. ; w. Wm. Mudie, Andro Heittone.
June 8. John Maben in Gallosheills, a.d.n. Agnes ; w. Wm. Williamsone,
      James Ballandean.
  „ 29. Archibald Frier, a.d.n. Agnes ; w. James Frier, Thomas Bowstone.
July 6. James Scott in Langhaugh, a.d.n. Helen ; w. Andro Darling, Wm.
      Wilsone.
  „ 25. James Waugh, a.s.n. Georg ; w. John Bell, Wm. Cook.
Aug. 2. James Friergrieve, a.d.n. —— ; w. Alexr. Trotter, Wm. Mercer.
  „ last. Andro Kennedie, a.d.n. Jennet ; w. Andro Renaldsonne, Andro
      Chisholm.
  „ last. John Paterson, a.d.n. Issobell ; w. Rot. Frier, Archibald Frier.
Sept. 7. Andro Drummond, a.s.n. Andro ; w. John Thomsone, John Ushar.
  „ 20. James Purvis, a.s.n. Thomas ; w. Georg Mercer, John Patersone.
  „   „ Wm. Bowar, a.s.n. Wm. ; w. James Edgar, Andro Olivar.
Oct. 5. Andro Olivar, a.s.n. Andrew ; w. Wm. Bowar, Michael Gibsons.
  „   „ James Lindsay, a.d.n. Jean ; w. Walter Vaitch, Thomas Bowstone.
  „ 12. James Frier, a.d.n. Jennet ; w. Archibald and Rot. Friers.
  „ 19. Thomas Lukup, a.s.n. Andrew ; w. Patrick Lukup, Andro Lukup.
  „ 26. John Heittone, a.d.n. Agnes ; w. John Bowar, John Sclaitter.
  „   „ Robert Mein, a.d.n. Issobell ; w. John and Andro Meins.
  „   „ Wm. Mercer, " Hall," a.s.n. Andro ; w. Andro Mercer, Andro
      Kennedie.
  „ last. Wm. Fishar, a.d.n. Jean ; w. Wm. Cook, James Edgar.
  „   „ John Bell, a.d.n. Marione ; w. Thomas Bell, John Bowar.
Nov. 21. James Edgar, a.s.n. Alexr. ; w. Thomas Wilkiesone, James Elles.
  „   „ David Cook, a.s.n. Andrew ; w. Wm. and Rot. Cooks.
  „ 23. Wm. Sclaitter, a.d.n. Issobell ; w. John Mein, Adam Turnbull.
Dec. 14. John Mein, a.d.n. Jennet ; w. Wm. Fischar, Andro Mein.

1679.

Dec. 14. Wm. Moss, a.s.n. John ; w. John Moss, Walter Dalgleish.
„ 17. Rot. Sclatter, a.d.n. —— ; w. John Sclaitter, Rot. Mein.

1680.

Jan. 7. James Murray, a.d.n. Jennet ; w. Georg and Andro Martins.
„ „ Thomas Bighet, a.d.n. Issobell ; w. Thomas Drummond, Rot. Mabone.
„ 15. Wm. Broun, a.d.n. Jennet ; w. Alexr. Maxwell, Georg Sheill.
„ „ John Stenhouse, a.d.n. Issobell ; w. James Milne, James Waugh.
„ 25. James Broun, a.s.n. Wm. ; w. James Mercer, John Mein.
Feb. 8. Andro Hownam, a.s.n. Andro ; w. John Mercer, Andro Rennaldsone.
Mar. 4. James Martine, a.s.n. Georg ; w. John Tait, Michael Pearsone.
„ 21. Rot. Mertone, a.d.n. —— ; w. James Leithan, Rot. Mertone.
„ „ James Mercer, "Peoll," a.d.n. Elizabeth ; w. Andro Heittone, Georg Mercer.
„ 23. Thomas Mercer, a.d.n. Issobell ; w. Wm. Cook, James Edgar.
„ 26. Francis Dickson, a.s.n. Alexr. ; w. John Andersone, Thomas Mylne.
April 9. James Alexander, a.d.n. Issobell ; w. Georg Sheill, John Stenhouse.
„ 15. James Bunzie, a.d.n. Barbara ; w. Rot. and Thomas Trotters.
„ 20. Thomas Bowar, a.d.n. Agnes ; w. James Broun, Alexr. Rutherfoord.
„ 27. Rot. Mein, a.s.n. Thomas ; w. John Leithane, James Bunzie.
May 2. John Halliwall, a.s.n. Georg ; w. Andro and Georg Mercers.
„ 9. Alexr. MacFadzean, a.s.n. —— ; w. Adam Darling, James Maxwell.
„ 16. James Turner, a.s.n. Thomas ; w. John Pringle, James Fisher.
June 6. John Mudie, a.s.n. James ; w. Wm. Mudie, Andro Mercer.
„ „ Andro Fisshar of Housbyres, a.d.n. Margaret ; w. Wm. Fisshar, Andro Mercer.
„ „ Andro Pringle, a.d.n. Violet ; w. George Pringle, Adam Darling.
„ 13. John Taitt, a.s.n. James ; w. Georg Turner, Michael Fischar.
„ 20. Alex. Rutherfoord, a.s.n. John ; w. Wm. Broun, Wm. Cook.
„ 27. John Ushar, a.s.n. Thomas ; w. John Moss, Andro Chisholme.
July 2. John Wright, a.s.n. Georg ; w. Andro Marr, John Moss.
„ 11. Rot. Leithane, a.s.n. Georg ; w. John Sclaitter, Wm. Sclaitter.
„ 18. Nicoll Bowar, a.s.n. Nicoll ; w. Thomas Mein, James Bowar.
Aug. 10. James Lamb, a.s.n. Rot. ; w. Georg Wallace, James Milne.
„ „ Thomas Bunzie, a.d.n. Margaret ; w. John Mein, John Bunzie.
„ 29. Alexr. Heittone, a.d.n. Issobell ; w. James Bowar, John Haliwall.
„ last. Rot. Cook, a.s.n. Wm. ; w. David and Wm. Cooks.
Sept. 3. Georg Pringle, "Bull," a.s.n. James ; w. Andro Pringle, Thomas Leithane.
„ 11. Rot. Mein in Eildone, a.d.n. Issobell ; w. John Sclaitter, Thomas Mein.
„ 17. John Lyes in Gallosheills parish ; w. Rot. and Thomas Lyes.
„ 28. Thomas Mein in Eildone, a.d.n. Alisone ; w. John Sclaitter, Rot. Mein.
Oct. 19. Margaret Pearson, a.s.n. John, presented by Alexr. Clapperton ; w. Georg Wallace, Wm. Cook.
„ 24. John Heittone, a.d.n. Issobell ; w. Andro Chisholme, John Mein.
Nov. 4. Patrick Lukup, a.d.n. Helen ; w. Thomas Lukup, James Murray.
„ 14. John Sclaitter, a.d.n. Issobell ; w. John Riddell, Wm. Sclaitter.
„ 23. John Lythgow, a.d.n. Helen ; w. Alexr. Lythgow, James Eilles.
Dec. 12. James Olivar in Bouden, a.d.n. —— ; w. Andro and James Olivar.
„ 28. Andro Bunzie, a.s.n. Johne ; w. John Bunzie, Wm. Fischar.

1681.

Jan. 7. Thomas Lythgow, a.s.n. Rot. ; w. John Lythgow, Thomas Wilkiesone.
„ 12. Andro Wright, a.d.n. ; w. Thomas and John Mebens.
„ 23. Georg Mercer, a.d.n. Issobell ; w. John Moss, Andro Renaldsone.
„ 30. Andro Smith, a.d.n. Jennet ; w. Andro Smith, Georg Mercer.
Feb. 20. Rot. Bowstone, "Vicar," a.d.n. Issobell ; w. Andro Broun, Rot. Mercer.
Mar. 13. Andro Mercer, a.d.n. Issobell ; w. Thomas Drummond, Georg Mercer.
„ 20. Wm. Mercer, a.d.n. Issobell ; w. Georg Hownam, Nicol Mercer.

1681.

Mar. 27. James Maxwell, a.s.n. Georg ; w. Alexr. Mack, Faldean, Andro Pringle.

,, 29. John Mein, called "Cuddiebuts," a.d.n. Agnes ; w. Rot. and John Meins.

April 9. Georg Frier, a.s.n. Thomas ; w. Archibald and Ja. Friers.

,, 24. John Heittone, a.d.n. Jennet ; w. Andro and John Heittons.

May 1. John Mein, a.d.n. Issobell ; w. John and Andro Meins.

,, 8. Georg Howname, a.d.n. Jennet ; w. Nicoll Ushar, John Mudie.

,, 20. Alexr. Patersone of Old Melrose, a.s.n. Thomas ; w. Rot. Faa, Alexr. Lythgow.

,, 29. Georg Lowrie, a.s.n. John ; w. John Sclaitter, Rot. Leithane.

June 5. —— Cuik in Housebyre, a.s.n. Andro ; w. Alexr. Trotter, Rot. Frier.

,, ,, John Frier, a.d.n. Issobell ; w. Rot. Mein, Thomas Ma— .

,, ,, Wm. Smith, a.s.n. Andro ; w. Andro Smith, younger and elder.

,, ,, Georg Mercer, a.d.n. Jennet ; w. James and Andro Mercers.

,, 12. John Currie, a.s.n. Rot. ; w. Rot. Fa, Thomas Wilkiesone.

,, · ,, Ja. Bowie, a.d.n. Jennet ; w. Ja. and Thomas Bowies.

,, 29. James Turner in Blainslie, a.s.n. Edward ; w. John Darling, John Stirling.

July 3. James Mein, a.d.n. Issobell ; w. Thos. and Rot. Meins.

,, 16. Thomas Rennick, a.s.n. Thomas ; w. Georg Wallace, Wm. Cook.

,, 29. Mr. Alexr. Bisset, a.s.n. James ; w. Rot. Fa, Thomas Lythgow.

,, ,, Walter Veitch, —— ; w. Rot. Ormstone, Thomas Bowstone.

Aug. 7. Rot. Mercer, a.s.n. Georg ; w. Andro Fishar, Andro Marr.

,, 19. Thomas Blaikie, a.s.n. Thomas ; w. John and James Meins.

Sept. 9. Wm. Riddell, a.s.n. John ; w. John Mein, John Bunzie.

,, 11. John Marr, a.s.n. Andro ; w. Thomas Drummond, Andro Mercer.

,, ,, James Bowar, a.d.n. Issobell ; w. Nicoll and James Bowars.

,, 18. Rot. Mein, a.d.n. Agnes : w. John and Georg Meins.

,, ,, John Mein, called " Sober," a.s.n. —— ; w. James and John Meins.

,, 25. Rot. Frier, a.d.n. Margaret ; w. Alexr. Trotter, Rot. Mercer.

Oct. 2. Walter Karr, a.s.n. Andro ; w. James Milne, John Lowrie.

,, 11. James Martine, a.s.n. Wm. ; w. Georg Wallace, Alexr. Maxwell.

,, 28. Andro Kennedie, a.d.n. Jean ; w. John Moss, Andro Renaldsone.

Nov. 5. Thomas Bunzie, —— ; w. John Bunzie, Adam Turnbull.

,, ,, Georg Mein, a.s.n. James ; w. John Mein, James Broune.

,, 6. Andro Olivar, a.s.n. John ; w. Wm. Bowar, Michael Gibsone.

,, ,, James Lindsay, a.d.n. Christin ; w. Andro Marr, Walter Vaitch.

,, 19. James Frergrieve, a.s.n. John ; w. Thomas Hardy, Rot. Hilsone.

,, 20. John Moffat, a.d.n. Helen ; w. Thomas Moffat, Rot. Scott.

,, 26. Thomas Bowstone, Wynd, a.d.n. Issobell ; w. Andro Marr, Rot. Mein.

,, ,, John Bowar, a.s.n. John ; w. John and Thomas Bells.

Dec. 8. Alexr. Mein, a.s.n. Andro ; w. Andrew and Ja. Meins.

,, ,, Thomas Bell, a.s.n. Thomas : w. John Bell, John Bowar.

,, 21. John Mein, maltman, a.s.n. John ; w. Alexr. and Andro Meins.

1682.

Jan. 1. Rot. Faa, baillie of Melrose, a.s.n. Charles ; w. Thomas Wilkiesone, James Edgar.

,, 3. John Heitton, a.s.n. Andro ; w. James Bowar, Andro Heittone.

,, 13. James Bunzie, a.s.n. Alexr. ; w. John Bunzie, Alexr. Trotter.

,, 19. James Edgar, two daughters named Agnes and Barbara ; w. Thomas and John Lythgows.

,, 29. Thomas Wilkiesone, a.s.n. Thomas ; w. Rot. Faa, baillie, Alexr. Lythgow.

,, last. Georg Blaikie, a.s.n. Charles ; w. John Mein, John Mylne.

Feb. 12. Wm. Mercer, Hall, a.d.n. Jennet ; w. Andro and John Mercers.

Mar. 12. Rot. Walker in Gallasheills, two sons named Alexr. and Thomas ; w. Hew Darling, James Ballandane.

,, 19. James Murray, a.s.n. Wm. ; w. Georg and Andro Martines.

,, 26. Archibald Frier, a.d.n. Helen ; w. Henrie and Thomas Myles.

April 2. Wm. Bowstone, a.d.n. Jennet ; w. Thomas Bowstone, Walter Vaitch.

1682.

April 4. Alexr. McFadzean, a.d.n. Jennet ; w. Andro Pringle, Rot. Martine.
  ,, 6. James Lyes, a.d.n. Jennet ; w. Georg Blaikie, Michael Gibsone.
  ,, 9. Rot. Haddon, a.d.n. Jennet ; w. James Murray, Wm. Cook.
  ,, 11. Rot. Martine, a.s.n. Rot. ; w. Rot. Ormston, Andro Pringle.
  ,, 16. Rot. Martine in Gattonsyd, a.d.n. Margaret ; w. James Leithan, John Taitt.
  ,, last. John Wright, a.s.n. John ; w. Georg Barton, John Hoy.
May 12. David Cook, a.s.n. Alexr. ; w. Wm. and Rot. Cooks.
  ,, 21. Thomas Darling, a.s.n. John ; w. James Watsone, John Darling.
  ,, ,, John Taitt, a.d.n. Issobell ; w. Georg and Thomas Turners.
  ,, 23. Thomas Mathiesone, a.s.n. John ; w. Andro Marr, Andro Halliwall.
  ,, 27. John Symentone, a.s.n. Andro ; w. Thomas Law, Wm. Ballandane.
  ,, 28. Andro Drummond, a.d.n. Issobell ; w. John Thomson, John Welch.
June 2. Andro Lukup, a.s.n. Thomas ; w. Thomas Law, Thomas Lukup.
July 9. Thomas Scott, a.s.n. Andro ; w. Wm. Wilson, James Ballandane.
  ,, ,, James Cossar, a.s.n. James ; w. Georg Turner, Rot. Cossar.
  ,, 16. Andro Mein, " Kill," a.s.n. James ; w. John Mein, Andro Wilson.
  ,, ,, Thomas Mein, a.d.n. Marion ; w. James and Rot. Meins.
  ,, 18 Alexr. Patersone, a.s.n. Robert ; w. James Eillies, Alex. Lythgow of Drygrange.
  ,, 21. John Mein, Massone, a.d.n. Jennet ; w. Andro and John Meins.
  ,, 28. Thomas Bunzie, younger, a.d.n. Margaret ; w. John and Andro Bunzies.
Aug. 4. Andro Mein, elder, a.s.n. Henrie ; w. James and Alexr. Meins.
  ,, 6. Wm. Drummond, a.d.n. Jennet ; w. Wm. Mercer, John Thomson.
  ,, ,, John Maben, a.d.n. Jennet ; w. John and Wm. Mabens.
  ,, 12. John Frier, a.d.n Jennet ; w. Archibald and James Friers.
  ,, 17. James Marr, a.s.n. Andro ; w. Andro Marr, Thomas Bowstone.
  ,, 21. John Mein, called "Cuddiebutts," a.s.n. Robert ; w. Wm. and Rot. Meins.
  ,, ,, David Mein, a.d.n. Agnes ; w. Rot. Mein, Wm. Riddell.
  , 24. Rot. Sclettar, a.d.n. Jennet ; w. John Sclettar, James Meins.
  ,, ,, William Mylne, a.d.n. Christin ; w. John Myles, younger and elder.
Sept. 10. James Frier, a.d.n. Issobell ; w. Rot. and John Friers.
  ,, 24. James Broune, a.d.n. Agnes ; w. James Mercer, Georg Mein.
  ,, 29. Andro Wilsone, a.d.n. Jennet ; w. Thomas Lythgow, Rot. Mein.
Oct. 8. John Bourhill, a.s.n. Mark ; w. Rot. Ridfoord, Adam Lythgow.
  ,, ,, Andro Pringle, a.d.n. Violet ; w. George Pringle, Rot. Mertone.
  ,, ,, Thomas Mercer, a.s.n. Nicoll ; w. James Mercer, James Bunzie.
  ,, 9. John Mein, glover, a.d.n. Margaret ; w. Georg and Wm. Meins.
  ,, 22. Alexr. Heittone, a.d.n. Agnes ; w. James Bowar, Rot. Halliwall.
  ,, 23. Andro Turnbull, a.s.n. John ; w. Nicoll Bowar, James Mercer.
  ,, ,, James Lamb, a.s.n. John ; w. James Mylne, James Edgar.
  ,, 26. John Carter, a.s.n. Nicoll ; w. Peter and Georg Moffatts.
  ,, ,, Georg Bartone, a.d.n. Issobell ; w. John Hoy, Thomas Halliwell.
  ,, 31. Thomas Stenhouse, a.d.n. Agnes ; w. John and Wm. Mylnes.
Nov. 10. John Bell, a.d.n. Agnes : w. James Bowar, Thomas Bell.
  ,, 13. Wm. Mein, smyth, a.d.n. —— ; w. Georg and John Meins.
  ,, 29. John Lowrie, a.s.n. John : w. Henrie and Thomas Myles.
Dec. 7. Thomas Drummond, —— ; w. Andrew Mercer, Andro Smyth.
  ,, 8. Wm. Hobkirk, a.s.n. Nicoll ; w. Thomas Stewart, Thomas Bowie.
  ,, 16. Thomas Martine, a.s.n. Nicoll ; w. James and Georg Martines.
1683.
Jan. 7. John Hoy, a.s.n. John ; w. Thomas Mathiesone, John Wright.
  ,, 14. Georg Frier, a.s.n. Rot. ; w. Archibald and Rot. Friers.
  ,, 18. Thomas Bicket, a.d.n. Jennet ; w. John Lowrie, Thomas Drummond.
  ,, 21. James Laidlaw, a.s.n. Mongo ; w. Wm. Mylne, Wm. Karr.
  ,, 28. James Forsyth, a.s.n. Rot. ; w. John Forsyth, Rot. Hilsone.
  ,, ,, Georg Pringle in Langhaugh, a.s.n. Rot. ; w. Wm. Wilsone, John Frater.
Feb. 25. James Bowar, a.d.n. Jennet ; w. Nicoll and James Bowars.

1683.

Mar. 12. James Bowie, wright, a.d.n. Margaret ; w. James and Thomas Bowies.

  ,,   27. Rot. Ormstone, a.s.n. Rot. ; w. David and Wm. Cooks.

  ,,   29. John Hunter, a.d.n. Issabell ; w. Thomas Hunter, James Broune.

April 1. Georg Turner, a.d.n. Marione ; w. Georg Mudie, Alexr. Trotter.

  ,,   ,, Wm. Smyth, a.d.n. Jennet ; w. Andro Smyth, Andro Hownem.

May 10. Walter Keirr, a.d.n. Margt. ; w. Thomas and James Bowies.

  ,,   15. James Ballandane, younger, in Langhaugh, two twins, —— ; w. James Ballandane, elder, Wm. Wilsone.

  ,,   ,, Rot. Cook, a.d.n. Helen ; w. David and Wm. Cooks.

  ,,   23. John Dalgleish, a.s.n. Alexander ; w. Alexr. and Walter Dalgleish.

June 10. John Wright, a.d.n. Issobell ; w. Andro Marr, John Hoy.

  ,,   17. John Fuird, a.s.n. James ; w. Wm. and John Notmans.

  ,,   19. John Ushar, a.s.n. John ; w. Andro Heitton, John Moss.

July 8. Thomas Sudden, a.s.n. Rot ; w. Georg and Rot. Mercers.

  ,,   10. Wm. Sybbald, a.d.n. —— ; w. James and Rot. Meins.

  ,,   22. Thomas Lythgow, a.d.n. Elizabeth ; w. Rot. Faa, baillie, Thomas Wilkiesone.

Aug. 4. Patrick Lukup, a.d.n. Maria ; w. Thomas Law, Thomas Lukup.

  ,,   21. Alexr. Patersone of Old Melrose, a.s.n. William ; w. Rot. Faa, baillie, Thomas Wilkiesone.

Sept. 9. James Cochrane, a.d.n. Issobell ; w. Andro Kennedie, Androw Hownem.

  ,,   20. John Mein, a.d. ——, (*sic.*) Andrews John ; w. Andrew and Alexr. Meins.

  ,,   23 John Mercer, a.s.n. Andrew ; w. Wm. and John Mercers.

Oct. 7. George Mercer, merchant, a.d.n. Jennett ; w. John Moss, Andrew Renaldsone.

  ,,   13. Rot. Sclatter, a.d.n. Marion ; w. John Sclatter, Rd. Mein.

  ,,   21. Rot. Leithane. a.s.n. James ; w. Georg Lowrie, Thomas Mein.

  ,,   28. John Guill, a.s.n. John ; w. John Mylne, Thomas Stenhouse.

Nov. 2. Androu Bunzie, a.s.n. James ; w. John Bunzie, James Mercer.

  ,,   4. John Cairncrosse, a.d.n. Jennett ; w. Andro and James Marrs.

  ,,   ,, Andro Hownem, —— ; w. Georg Mercer, Georg Hownom.

  ,,   5. Rot. Mein, Townhead, a.d.n. Margaret ; w. Alexr. and John Meines.

  ,,   20. Thomas Heittone, a.d.n. Margaret ; w. James Caldwalls, Andro Heittone.

  ,,   24. Andro Mercer, a.d.n. Jennet ; w. Thomas Drummond, Rot. Maben.

  ,,   25. John Broune, a.s.n. James ; w. Georg and Rot. Mercers.

Dec. 1. James Lambe, ——, begotten in adulterie, presented be James Bowar; w. Wm. and David Cooks.

  ,,   18. Wm. Laing, a.s.n. David ; w. James Bowie, Michael Gibsone.

  ,,   ,, Thomas Drummond, a.s.n. Andro ; w. Andro and Wm. Smyths.

  ,,   ,, James Mercer, "Pooll," a.d.n. Issobell ; w. Androw and Georg Mercers.

1684.

Jan. 10. Andro Fischer of Housbyres, a.d.n. Anna ; w. Andro Mercer, John Moss.

  ,,   12. Georg Mein, a.s.n. James ; w. James Mercer, John Mein.

  ,,   26. Rot. Riddell, a.d.n. Agnes ; w. Andro Bunzie, John Mein.

Feb. 15. Rot. Mein, a.s.n. James ; w. Georg and John Meines.

  ,,   ,, John Mein, glover, —— ; w. Georg and John Meines.

  ,,   16. John Lythgow, a.d.n. Agnes ; w. Georg Pringle of Blindlie, James Edgar.

  ,,   24. Wm. Mercer, a.s.n. Georg ; w. Georg and Rot. Mercers.

Mar. 2. James Fiergreive, a.d.n. Jennet ; w. Thomas Hardie, Georg Turner.

  ,,   9. Rot. Mercer, a.s.n. Androw ; w. Andro Marr, Georg Mercer.

  ,,   19. James Corser, a.s.n. John ; w. Thomas Stewart, Thomas Hardy.

  ,,   23. Wm. Ecles, a.d.n. Issobell ; w. Andro Heitton, John Myln.

  ,,   30. John Marr, a.s.n. James ; w. Thomas Drummond, Thomas Turnbull

1684.

Mar. 31. Rot. Faa, baillie, a.d.n. Margaret ; w. Alexr. Lythgow of Drygraing,
        Alexr. Patersone.

April 1. Andro Kennedie, a.s.n. Charles ; w. Androw Reinaldsone, Georg
        Mercer.

,, ,, Rot. Merten, a.d.n. Issobell ; w. James Maxwell, Adam Darling.

,, 9. Wm. Moss, a.d.n. Alison ; w. John Moss, Andro Reinaldsone.

,, ,, Georg Lowrie, a.s.n. Thomas ; w. John Sclettar, Rot. Leithane.

May 14. Georg Rolmainhouse, Dukdub, a.s.n. Edward ; w. John Pringle,
        Alexr. Dicksone.

June 10. Wm. Martine, younger, a.s.n. John ; w. Andro Marr, Wm. Martine.

,, 17. Georg Pringle, a.s.n. Wm. ; w. Francis Pringle, Wm. Bowstone.

,, ,, Walter Vaitch, a.d.n. Margaret ; w. Francis Pringle, Wm. Bowstone.

July 6. Wm. Drummond, a.s.n. Andro ; w. Wm. and John Mercers.

,, 13. Thomas Mercer, a.s.n. Georg ; w. James Mercer, James Bunzie.

,, 18. Androw Lukup, a.d.n. Margaret ; w. Thomas Bell, Thomas Law.

,, 21. Francis Pringle, a.d.n. Violet ; w. James Wauch, Rot. Martine.

,, 26. Thomas Mylne, a.d.n. Agnes ; w. Thomas Stennes, James Turnbull.

,, 27. James Maxwell, a.s.n. James ; w. Andro Ritchie, Rot. Mertine.

Aug. 2. Georg. Blaikie, a.d.n. Katherine ; w. Adam Lythgow, Thomas
        Lythgow.

,, 10. Andro Olivar, a.d.n. Jennet ; w. Thomas Bell, Wm. Bowar.

,, ,, Thomas Bunzie, Claymyre, a.s.n. John ; w. Andro and John Bunzies.

,, 12. James Leithane, a.s.n. John ; w. James Edgar, Thomas Leithane.

,, 17. James Martine, a.s.n. Rot. ; w. Thomas and Georg. Martins.

,, 31. Andro Bowstone, a.s.n. Andro ; w. Andro Chisholme, Andro Mercer.

,, ,, Wm. Riddell, a.s.n. Andro ; w John Mein, Wm. Fischer.

Sept. 7. James Marr, a.s.n. Rot. ; w. Andro Marr, Rot. Mein.

,, ,, Rot. Marr, a.s.n. Thomas ; w. Thomas Wilkieson, Ja. Waugh.

,, 14. Thomas Kennedie, a.s.n. Thomas ; w. John Moss, Andro Ronaldsone.

,, 30. —— Mein, a.d.n. ; Marion ; w. Mr. Thomas Byres, Wm. Cook.

Oct. 5. Thomas Leithane, a.s.n. James ; w. James Leithane, James Edgar.

,, 11. John Bell, a.s.n. Alexr. ; w. James Bowie, Thomas Bell.

,, 12. James Frier, a.d.n. Agnes ; w. Rot. and Archibald Friers.

,, 13. Georg Mein, Calender, a.s.n. Cornelius ; w. John and Wm. Meins.

,, 18. Thomas Bunzie, a.d.n. Agnes ; w. John and Rot. Bunzie.

,, 26. Wm. Welsch, a.d.n. Issobell ; w. Andro Renaldsone, John Moss.

,, 28. John Moffatt, a.s.n. Rot. ; w. Rot. Scott, Thomas Maben.

Nov. 28. John Taitt, two twins ——; w. John Hoy, Rot. Martin.

,, 30. James Martine, a.s.n. Stephen ; w. Georg and James Martins.

,, ,, Thomas Sudden, a.s.n. James ; w. Rot. and Nicol Mercers.

Dec. 1. James Edgar, a.d.n. Elizabeth ; w. Rot. Faa, Thomas Wilkiesone.

,, 4. Thomas Mathiesone, a.s.n. Thomas ; w. Andro Marr, John Hoy.

,, 7. Baptised Jennet, dtr. to ——; w. Andro Ritchie, James
        Maxwell.

,, 26. John Frier, a.s.n. Rot. ; w. Rot. and John Friers.

1685.

Jan. 8. James Bowar, a.d.n. Margt. ; w. Nicoll and James Bowars.

,, 15. John Milne, a.s.n. James ; w. John and James Milnes.

Feb. 25. James Kyll, a.d.n. Margaret ; w. Walter Kyll, Wm. Sandilands.

Mar. 4. Ye deceist Alexr. Patersone, a.s.n. Alexr. ; w. Rot. Faa, M.
        Duncansone.

,, 12. Wm. Milne, a.d.n. Agnes ; w John and James Milnes.

,, 13. Nicoll Bowar, a.s.n. James ; w. Patrick Lukup, Richard Mein.

,, 15. James Laidlay, a.s.n. John ; w. Thomas Stenhouse, John Milne.

,, 24. Wm. Mein, smith ; a.s.n. Androw ; w. Mr. Andro and John Meins.

,, 29. Georg Mercer, a.s.n. John ; w. Andro Mercer, John Stenhouse.

,, ,, Andro Ritchie, a.d.n. Issobell ; w. James Dewar, —— M'Fadzean.

April 5. Thomas Patersone, a.s.n. Thomas ; w. John Sclatter, James
        Caldwalls.

1685.
April 5. David Cook, a.s.n. Wm. ; w. Wm. Cook, Walter Fleeming.
   ,,   11. Walter Karr, a.d.n. Jean ; w. James Bowie, John Dalgleish.
   ,,   20. Wm. Scott, a.s n. Wm. ; w. Andro Pringle, Andro Mein.
May   3. Wm. Rolmainhouse, a.d.n. Katharine ; w. John Stirling, Wm. Cook.
   ,,   8. Mr. Alexr. Bisset, a.d.n. Geiles ; w. Mr. James Faa, Rot. Faa.
   ,,   10. Georg Frier, —— : w. Thomas Boustone, James Frier.
   ,,   19. Rot. Faa, a.d.n. Jennet ; w. Thomas Wilkiesone, James Edgar.
   ,,   26. Thomas Stewart, a.d.n. Margaret ; w. Wm. Hobkirk, Charles Stewart.
June   7. James Patersone, a.s.n. David ; w. James Friergreive, Georg Turner.
   ,,   21. John Pringle, a.d.n. Anna ; w. Wm. Wilsone, James Ballandean
   ,,   28. John Burhill, a.s.n. Thomas ; w. Georg Blaikie, James Lamb.
   ,,   ,, Archibald Frier, weaver, a.s.n. Rot. ; w. Rot. and James Friars.
July   2. Thomas Mein, a.d.n. Margaret ; w. James Mein, Wm. Sybbald.
   ,,   5. Georg Bartone, a.s.n. Georg ; w. John Hoy, Archibald Frier.
   ,,   ,, John Ushar, a.d.n. Helen ; w. John Heittone, Andro Kennedie.
   ,,   12. Wm. Smith, a.d.n. Helen ; w. Andro Smith, Wm. Mercer.
   ,,   ,, Wm. Mercer, a.d.n. Issobell ; w. Wm. and Andro Smiths.
   ,,   16. Francis Pringle, a.d.n. Helen ; w. Andro and Georg Pringles.
   ,,   20. Andro Lukup, a.d.n. Margaret ; w. Patrick and Thomas Lukup.
   ,,   23. Wm. Laing, a.s.n. Joseph ; w. James Eiles, Georg Blaikie.
   ,,   28. Andro Turnbull, a.s.n. Nicoll ; w. Nicoll Bowar, John Bunzie.
   ,, last. Wm Sybbald, a.s.n. Andro ; w. Wm. Cook, John Sybbald.
Aug.   2. Wm. Davidsone, a.s.n. John ; w. John Pringle, John Rolmainhouse.
   ,,   11. Andro Mein, a.s.n. Richard ; w. James and John Meins.
   ,   13. James Pringle, a.s.n. John ; w. John Pringle, Georg Rolmainhouse
   ,,   19. James Blaikie, a.d.n. Margaret ; w. Andro Tunno, Georg Wallace
   ,,   23. John Mein, a.s.n. John ; w. John and Andro Meins.
   ,,   27. John Lownie, a.d.n. Issobell ; w. James Eilles, John Stenhouse.
   ,,   28. Wm. Boustone, a.s.n. Wm. ; w. Thomas and Wm. Boustones.
Sept.   6. Thomas Moffatt, —— ; w. John Ridfoord and Edward Lythgow.
   ,,   25. Wm. Hopkirk, —— ; w. Georg and Andro Martines.
   ,,   ,, Andro Kennedie, a.d.n. Margaret ; w. Rot. Faa, Thomas Wilkiesone.
Oct.   4. John Heittone, a.d.n. Bessie ; w. James Bowar, Andro Heittone.
   ,,   8. Charles Blaikie, a.d.n. Jennet ; w. Wm. Hopkirk, Michael Gibsone.
   ,,   11. James Bowar, fermer, a.d.n. Issobell ; w. James Bowars, elder and
          younger.
   ,,   18. John Waker, a.s.n. Wm. ; w. Wm. Lythgow, James Eilles.
   ,,   24. Issobell Boustone, her husband being dead, —— ; w. Thomas
          Boustone, Rot. Philip.
Nov.   3. Andro Smith, a.d.n. Issobell ; w. Wm. and Andro Smiths.
   ,,   8. Thomas Heittone, a.d.n. Alisone ; w. James Caldwalls, John Sclatter.
   ,,   ,, James Young, a.d.n. Jennet ; w. John Young, John Moss.
   ,,   27. Rot. Sclatter, a.s.n. Wm. ; w. John Sclatter, Wm. Sybbald.
Dec.   1. Rot. Mein, *alias* James his Robert, a.s.n. John ; w. Georg and John
          Meins.
   1686
Jan.   3. Georg Cockburn, a.s.n. Georg ; w. Adam Darling. Rot. Martine.
   ,,   20. Thomas Stenhouse, a.s.n. John ; w. John and Thomas Milnes.
   ,,   24. John Mercer, Lochbreast, a.s.n. John ; w. Andro and Wm. Mercers.
Feb.   5. Rot. Riddell, a.d.n. Jennet ; w. John Mein, Andro Sclatter.
   ,,   9. Thomas Drummond, a.d.n. Agnes ; w. John Marr, Andro Smith.
   ,,   21. John Foord, a.d.n. Jennet ; w. James Smith, Peter Moffat.
   ,,   ,, John Marr, a.s.n. Andrew ; w. Thomas Drummond. James Turnbull.
   ,,   ,, John Mein, glover, a.s.n. Rot. ; w. Georg and Andro Meins.
Mar.   7. Andro Notman, a.s.n. John ; w. John Fuird, John Notman.
   ,,   14. James Cochrane, a.s.n. Rot. ; w. Walter Vair, Wm. Mercer.
April 9. Andro Pringle, a.d.n. Issobell ; w. Francis Pringle, John Howname.
   ,,   18. Georg Mercer, a.d.n. Marion ; w. John Moss, Andro Rennaldsone.

The following two entries are made in pencil, and are in a handwriting of a very much later period :—

1646, Elisabeth or Bessie ;
1653, and Agnes, daughters to Thos. Grey, Appletreeleaves.

The Register is blank till 1690.

1690.

Nov. 2. Wm. Boustone, weaver in Gattonsyde, a.s.n. William; w. John and Georg Bartones.

,, 9. Andro Turnbull in Newsteid, a.d.n. Jennet ; w. John Mein, James Mein.

,, 18. Mr. Andro Mein, a.d.n. Agnes ; w. Rot. Faa, Mr. Mark Duncansone.

,, 23. Rot. Martine, weaver in Gattonsyde, a.d.n. Margaret ; w. Wm. Martine, James Leithane.

Dec. 7. Nicol Mercer in Darnick, a.s.n. Wm. ; w. James Fischer, Wm. Mercer.

,, 28. Rot. Sclatter, in the parishe of Lessudden, a.s.n. Robert ; w. Robt. Fairbairn, Richard Sclaitter.

1691.

Jan. 4. Rot. Leithane in Eildone, a.d.n. Issobell ; w. Wm. Milne, Alexr. Mein.

,, 18. Alexr. Mein in Eildone, a.s.n. Thomas ; w. Nicoll Bowar, John Drummond.

,, ,, John Wilkiesone in the parishe of Gallosheills, a.s.n. Wm. ; w. John Shortreid and Wm. Hadden, who are also cautioners that he shall satisfie the church when required.

,, ,, John Sheill in Melrose, a.d.n. Helen ; w. James Hunter, Wm. Hopkirk.

,, ,, Wm. Hopkirk in Melrose, a.d. —— ; w. John Penman, Georg Blaikie.

Feb. 8. Wm. Drummond in Bridgend, a.s.n. Wm. ; w. Andro Turnbull, Wm. Mercer.

,, — Thomas Robiesone in Gallosheills, a.d.n. Issobell ; w. Andro Robiesone, Georg Blaikie.

,, 22. Wm. Kennedie in Darnick, a.s.n. Wm. ; w. Androw Rennaldsone, John Moss.

Mar. 8. John Bowar in Eildone, a.s.n. Nicoll ; w. Nicoll Bowar, James Bowar.

,, 9. Thomas Turner, a s.n. Georg ; w. Georg Turner, Georg Chisholme.

,, ,, James Lees in Danzeltoune, a.s.n. James ; w. James Bowie, John Dasone.

,, 15. John Moodie in Threepwood, a.d.n. Jean ; w. Edward Lythgow, Georg Moodie.

,, 17. James Marr in Gattonsyde, a.s.n. Wm. ; w. Rot. Mein, Thomas Bowstone.

,, 29. Thomas Laidlay, a.s.n. Wm. ; w. James Marr, John Turner.

,, ,, James Leithane in Gattonsyde, a.d.n. Margaret ; w. James Marr, Thomas Leithane.

,, 31. Rot. Wilson in Langhaugh, a.s.n. John ; w. Wm. Wilsone, Georg Fraitter.

April 26. Thomas Leithane in Gattonsyde, a.s.n. Thomas ; w. James Marr, James Leithane, there.

May 10. Andro Knox in Drygrange, a.d.n. Margaret ; w. John Sheill. Adam Knox.

,, ,, John Mein, a.s.n. William ; w. John Boswald, John Mercer.

,, 17. John Braiden in Easterlanglie, a.s.n. Alexr. ; w. James Dewar, Alexr. Braiden, there.

May the last. Georg Proffite in Melrose, a.s.n. Rot. and a.d.n. Elizabeth ; w. James Phaup, James Mein, there.

June 7. John Marr in Melrose, a.s.n. Rot. ; w. James Patersone, Thomas Drummond, there.

,, ,, Thomas Bowstone in Gattonsyde, a.s.n. John ; w. Thomas Bowstone, James Marr, there.

,, 21. John Mein, younger, masone in Newsteid, a.s.n. John ; w. Alexr. Mein Rot. Mein, there.

1691.

July 5. James Sounhouse in Blainslie, a.s.n. Wm. ; w. John Wallace, John Stirling, there.

" " John Bowstone in Appletreeleaves, a.d.n. Marie ; w. Georg Fraiter, Wm. Wilson in Langhaugh.

" 9. John Penman in Melrose, a.s.n. John ; w. James Sympsone, James Patersone, there.

Aug. 8. Thomas Heittone in Eildone, a.d.n. Agnes ; w. John Sclaitter, Nicoll Bowar, there.

" 16. Georg Lies in Kilnow, in the parish of Gallosheills, a.s.n. Rot. ; w. Rot. and Wm. Lies.

" 23. Georg Mein in Newsteid, a.s.n. Georg ; w. John and James Meins there.

" " Alexr. Dicksone in Blainslie, a.s.n. Rot. ; w. John Wallace, and Rot. Mercer, elders.

" 26. Adam Harvie in Bowdone, a.s.n. Adam ; w. Georg Walker, Wm. Murray.

" " Thomas Sheill in Gattonsyde, a.d.n. Agnes ; w. Thomas Mathesone, Rot. Philip, there.

Sept. 6. Wm. Elliot in Gallosheills, a.d.n. Katharine ; w. Mr. Georg Hall, John Donaldsone, there.

" " James Eilles, weaver in Melrose, a.d.n. Elizabeth ; w. Georg and John Ushars in Darnick.

" " John Bald in Bowdone, a.s.n. Andro ; w. Andro Bald, Henrie Wallace, there.

" " Georg Muidie in Threepwood, a.d.n. Margaret ; w. Archibald Moffat, John Muidie, there.

" " Wm. Darling in Blainslie, a.d.n. Margaret ; w. Thomas Darling, John Wallace, there.

" " James Bowstone in Gattonsyde, a.d.n. Agnes ; w. James Marr, Thomas Mathesone.

" 20 Georg Frier in Gattonsyde, a.d.n. Helen ; w. Thomas Mathesone, Robt. Frier, there.

" " Andro Baittie in Bridgend, a.s.n. Georg ; w. Andro Turnbull, Wm. Mercer, there.

Oct. 5. Thomas Mertone in Danzeltoune, a.s.n. Thomas ; w. James Patersone, James Mein.

" " Rot. Halliwall in Gattonsyde, a.d.n. Jennet ; w. Andro and Rot. Halliwalls there.

" 11. John Gibsone in Melrose, a.s.n. Rot. ; w. Wm. Mein, Michael Gibsone, there.

" " Wm. Scott in Newsteid, a.s.n. James ; w. Wm. and Georg Meins there

" 25. Georg Grhame in Newsteid, a.d.n. Jean ; w. John Mein, glover, John Mercer.

" " Wm. Fuirgreive in Eildone, a.s.n. John ; w. James Caldwalls, Gideon Fuirgreive.

" " James Blaikie in Melrose, a.s.n.——— ; w. Andro Tunno, Georg Blaikie, there.

Nov. 1. Thomas Ormistone, weaver in Melrose, a.s.n. Georg ; w. John Bell, Georg Pringle, there.

" " Andro Ormistone in Gallosheills, a.s.n. Thomas ; w. John Mabon, Walter Thomson.

" 8. Georg Hoge in Hagburn, a.s.n. Rot. ; w. Alexr. Thomson in Whitlaw, James Hoge in Craigend.

" " John Ushar in Darnick, a.s.n. Alexr. ; w. Andro Rennaldsone, John Ushar, there.

" " Thomas Mercer in Danzeltoune, a.s.n. Thomas ; w. James Patersone, Wm. Guill, there.

" 26. George Fraim in Drygrange, a.s.n. William ; w. Andro Knox there, John Mein in Old Melrose.

" 29. James Bowie, wright in Melrose, a.s.n. Thomas ; w. James Bowie, millar, James, his son, there.

D

1691.

Dec. 6. John Ushar in Bridgend, a.s.n. Thomas ; w. Andro Turnbull there James Bowie in Melrose.

„ 20. James Mercer, tailzeor in Newsteid, a.s.n. Wm. ; w. Nicol Cochrane, John Mein, hostler, there.

„ 29 John Stirling, younger, in Blainslee, a.s.n. John : w. John Stirling, Thomas Darling, there.

„ „ Wm. Rohnainhouse in Blainslee, a.s.n. James ; w. John Wallace, James Darling, there.

1692.

Jan. 24. James Penman, glover in Melrose, a.s.n. Rot. ; w. Andro Penman, John Penman, there.

Feb. 12. John Holyburton, younger, of Muirhouselaw, a.s.n. Thomas ; w. John Holyburton, elder of Muirhouselaw, Mr. Mark Duncansone of Greatlaws.

„ 14. Francis Pringle in Drygrange boathouse, a.s.n. James ; w. Andro Knox in Drygrange, Georg Pringle in Earlstoune.

„ „ John Moffatt in Mosshouses, a.d.n. Euffan ; w. Andro Ritchie there, Alexr. Mein.

„ 21. Robt. Fairbairn in Eildone, a.d.n. Margaret ; w. John Sclaitter, Nicol Bowar, there.

„ „ James Hunter in Melrose, a d.n. Jennet ; w. John Bell, James Bowie, there.

„ „ Wm. Clapperton in Gallosheills, a.s.n. Rot. ; w. John Hilsone there, Georg Hoge in Hagburne.

Mar. 1. Robt. Mercer in Williamlaw, a.d.n. Alisone ; w. John Mercer, James Marr.

„ 13. John Ormistone, weaver in Melrose, a.d.n. Elizabeth : w. John Bell, Thomas Ormistone, there.

„ 20. Andro Wilsone, masone in Newsteid, a.d.n. Marie ; w. John and Georg Meins there.

April 3. John Freir in Gattonsyde, a.s.n. John ; w. Rot. Mein, Thomas Bowstone, there.

„ „ Andro Knox in Drygrainge, a.s.n. Robt. ; w. James Blaikie, James Huntar in Melrose.

„ „ John Sympsone in Darnick, a.d.n. Issobell ; w. John Ushar, James Mein.

„ „ Wm. Laidlay in Newtoune, a.d.n. Helen ; w. Nicol Cochrane, Thomas Stenhouse, there.

„ 17. James Fishar in Darnick, a.d.n. Euffan : w. Wm. Fischar, Androu Mercer, there.

„ 24. Robt. Freir in Gattonsyde, a.s.n. Archibald : w. James and John Freirs there.

May 1. Robt. Marr in Darnick, a.d.n. Christian ; w. John Ushar, Nicol Mercer, there.

„ „ Robt. Mertone in Westhouses, a.d.n. Elizabeth ; w. Andro Pringle, Alexr. M'Faidzeon, there.

„ „ John Dunnand in Gattonsyde, a.d.n. Margaret ; w. Rot. Dunnand there, Georg Pringle in Langhaugh.

„ 8. Nicol Milne in Darnick, a.s n. Wm. ; w. Nicol Cochrane, James Huntar.

„ „ James Mathesone in Gattonsyde, a.d.n. Margaret ; w. Thomas Matheson, John Halliwell, there.

„ 11. John Wallace in Blainslee, a.s.n. James : w. Thomas Darling there, Georg Chisholme in Colmslee.

„ 18. Wm. Cairncrosse of Langlee, a.s.n. Andro : w. Walter Cairncrosse of Hilslope, John Cairncrosse, his brother, there.

June 5. James Wallace, merchant in Melrose, a.d.n. Anna : w. James Blaikie, James Huntar, there.

„ „ James Taitt in Westerlanglee, a.s.n. Archibald : w. Rot. and John Brouns in Trinleeknow.

1692.

June 5. John Bowstone in Apletreeleaves, a.d.n. Jennet ; w. John Young
there, Wm. Darling in Easterlanglee.

,,   7. James Fishchar in Sorrowlesfield, a.s.n. Rot. ; w. Rot. Fischar in
Cleckmae, Androw Knox in Drygrange.

,, 14. Issobell Mercer in Darnick, a.s.n. Andro ; w. Androw and Wm.
Mercers there.

,, 19. Wm. Moss in Darnick, a.s.n. Androw ; w. Andro Rennaldsone, John
Ushar, there.

,, 26. Androw Notman in Mosshouses, a.s.n. James ; w. Andrew Ritchie
there, James Mein in Melrose.

July 3. Wm. Martine in Gattonsyde, a.s.n. Wm. ; w. Wm Martine, James
Myles, there.

,,   4. Georg Chisholme in Colmesleehill, a.d.n. Agnes ; w. Wm. Wilsone in
Langhaugh, Georg Hoge in Hagburn.

,, 10. John Mercer in Newsteed, a.s.n. John ; w. James Mein in Melrose,
Georg Mein in Newsteid.

,, ,, John Stoddert in Apletreeleaves, a.s.n. James ; w. Georg Fraiter in
Langhaugh, Thomas Darling in Blainslee.

,, 17. Thomas Cochrane in Newtoune, a.s.n. John ; w. Thomas Stenhouse,
Nicol Cochrane, there.

,, 27. Andrew Mein, Tounhead in Newsteed, a.s.n. Georg ; w. Georg Mein,
John Mercer, there.

,, ,, Wm. Bell in Gattonsyde, a.d.n. Jennet ; w. James Marr, Thomas
Mathesone, there.

,, ,, Rot. Wedderstoune in Colmeslee, a.s.n. John ; w. James Marr in
Gattonsyde, David Thomsone in Colmeslee.

,, last. James Gray in Melrose, a.s.n. Wm. ; w. Georg and John Sheills there.

Aug. 14. Thomas Bunzie, mason in Newsteed, a.s.n. John ; w. James Bunzie,
weaver, John Bunzie, father to the said Thomas, there.

,, ,, John Sheill, weaver in Melrose, a d.n. Jennet ; w. Georg Sheill, James
Mein, there.

,, 21. John Braiden in Easterlanglee, a.s.n. James ; w. Wm. Darling, Alexr.
Braiden, there.

,, ,, Adam Davidsone, smith in Melrose, a.d.n. Jennet ; w. David Hendersone, Andrew Dasone, there.

,, last. Walter Scott in Gattonsyde, a.d.n. Margaret ; w. Thomas Moffat,
Rot. Mein, there.

,, ,, John Drummond in Eildone, a.d.n. Margaret ; w. Alexr. Mein, Nicol
Bowar, there.

,, ,, James Sympsone, glover in Melrose, a.d.n. Issobell ; w. John and
Androw Penmans.

Sept. 18. John Mein in Old Melrose, a.d.n. Marie ; w. John Ecles in Smal-
holme Hospital, John Mein in Newsteid.

,, ,, Robert Lamb in Newsteid, a.s.n. James ; w. John ——, John Mein.

,, ,, James Myles in Gattonsyde, a.d.n. Issobell ; w. Thomas Myles, John
Symervail, there.

,, 25. Andrew Bunzie, weaver in Newsteid, a.s.n. Thomas ; w. John and
Thomas Bunzie there.

,, 28. Andrew Dasone, a.s.n. Andrew ; w. John Dasone, Andrew Penman,
there.

,, ,, Thomas McDugal in Nether Langshaw, a.s.n. James ; w. Thomas
Laidlay, Andrew Dicksone.

Oct. 2. James Mein, mason in Newsteid, a.s.n. Alexander ; w. John ——,
John Mein, there.

,, 9. John Bunzie in Newtoun, a.s.n. Robert ; w. Robert Bunzie, his father,
John Milne in Newtoune.

,, 12. Thomas Laydlie in Blainslee, a.d.n. Margrat ; w. Wm. and Andrew
Darlings there.

,, 16. John Spotwood in Newmilne, in the paroche of Stow, a.d.n. Isobel ;
w. Alexander Spotwood there, Thomas Darling in Blainslee.

1692.

Nov. 6. Andro Mein, alias Bridgend, mason in Newsteid, a.d.n. Margat ; w. Nicol Cochrane, Robert Mein.

,, ,, William Greistone, weaver in Darnick, a.s.n. Robert ; w. John Ushar, Andrew Rennaldsone, there.

,, ,, William Eiles, weaver in Melrose, a.s.n. Georg ; w. James——, James Eiles, weavers there.

,, ,, John Forrest in Westhouses, a.s.n. Thomas ; w. Thomas Mathesone in Gattonsyde, Andrew Turnbul in Bridgend.

,, ,, John Mein, glover in Newsteid, a.d.n. Jennet ; w. John Mercer, William Mein, there.

,, 9. Andrew Notman in Kaidslee, a.s.n. Alexander ; w. John Rollmain-house, James Burlee, there.

,, 18. William Hopkirk in Melrose, a.d.n. Elizabeth ; w. ——.

,, 20. William Mein, weaver in Newsteid, a.s.n. James ; w. Georg Mein, weaver there, James Mein in Melrose.

Dec. 4. James Olivar in Melrose, a.s.n. John ; w. Andrew Olivar, John Mein.

,, 18. John Wright in Gattonsyde, a.d.n. Marion ; w. John Hoy, Georg Bartone, there.

,, ,, John Ushar, weaver in Darnick, a.s.n. Andrew ; w. John Moss, Andrew Rennaldsone.

,, ,, Thomas Thomsone, a.d.n. Jennet ; w. John Thomsone, Georg Pringle in Gattonsyde.

,, 25. Robert Martine, weaver in Gattonsyde, a.d.n. Alisone ; w. James Leithane, William Martine, there.

,, ,, John Turnbull, mason in Eildone, a.d.n. Margat ; w. Robert Mein in Gattonsyde, James Mein in Melrose.

,, ,, William Riddel in Newsteid, a.d.n. Alisone ; w. John Sclaitter in Eildone, John Mein in Newsteid.

,, ,, Andrew Dickson in Langshaw, a.d.n. Jennet ; w. Robert Martine, James Marr in Gattonsyde.

1693.

Jan. 1. William Fischar in Gattonsyde, a.s.n. Alexander ; w. James Fischar in Darnick, John Forrest in Westhouses.

,, 15. Georg Mercer in Darnick, a.s.n. Robert ; w. Andrew Rennaldsone, John Ushar, there.

,, ,, Thomas Moffat in Threepwood, a.d.n. Euffan ; w. Peter Moffatt there, John Moffat in Mosshouses.

,, 24. Michael Persone, herd in Langshaw, a.d.n. Helen ; w. Rott. Mercer in Calfhill, James Pearsone in Upslaw, his brother.

,, ,, Andrew Tutop in Langshaw Milne, a.d.n. Elizabeth ; ——.

Feb. 5. William Smith in Darnick, a.s.n. Andrew ; w. Andrew ——, Andrew Smith, there.

,, ,, Mungo Dalgleish in Gattonsyde, a.s.n. John ; w. Thomas Myles, Thomas Matheson, there.

,, 12. William Hoyie, gardiner in Gattonsyde, a.d.n. Issobell ; w. John Hoyie, John Thomsone.

,, ,, Robert Bunzie, weaver in Newsteid, a.d.n. Christian ; w. James and John Bunzie there.

,, 19. Robert Mercer in Westerlanglee, a.s.n. Nicol ; w. James Tait, Andrew Mercer, there.

,, 26. William Cook in Melrose, a.d.n. Alisone ; w. James Huntar, David Cook, there.

,, ,, William Mercer in Darnick, a.s.n. John ; w. John Moss, John Ushar, there.

,, ,, Michael Wallace in Melrose, a.s.n. William ; w. James Wallace there, Thomas Bowstone in Gattonsyde.

Mar. 5. Andrew Bowstone in Bridgend, a.s.n. Robert ; w. George and Andrew Mercers in Darnick.

,, 12. Andrew Ritchie in Mosshouses, a.s.n. Andrew ; w. John Naiper, younger, Andrew Notman, there.

1693.

Mar. 23. Robert Mein in Newsteid, a.s.n. John ; w. John ——, John Meins, there.

,,   ,,   William Bowar in Melrose, a.s.n. William ; w. Andrew Olivar, James Olivar, there.

,,   ,,   Robert Sclaitter in Eildone, a.d.n. Margat ; w. John Sclaitter, Nicol Bowar.

,,   26. James Sunhouse in Blainslee, a.s.n. John ; w. John Stirling, James Dickson in Langshaw.

,,   ,,   Robert Pringle in Blainslee, a.s.n. George ; w. John Wallace, Thomas Darling.

April 2. John Bowar in Eildone, a.d.n. Christian ; w. Nicol Bowar, James Bowar, there.

,,   ,,   George Pringle, tailzeor in Gattonsyde, a.s.n. Francis ; w. Francis and Hendrie Pringles.

,,   4. John Laudor in Blainslee, a.s.n. William ; w. Thomas Darling, John Wallace, there.

,,   ,,   James Turner there, a.s.n. Thomas ; same witnesses.

,,   ,,   Thomas Laidley in Langshaw Milne, a.s.n. Robert ; same witnesses.

,,   ,,   John Petrah in Threepwood, a.d.n. Margat ; same witnesses.

,,   9. James Lindsey in Gattonsyde, a.d.n. Jean ; w. Rot. Ormistone, Andrew Linsay, there.

,,   16. Rot. Leithane in Eildone, a.s.n. Robert ; w. Nicol Bowar, William Sybbald, there.

May   7. John Turner in Ladupmuir, a.s.n. John ; w. George Turner in Buckholme, Andrew Mercer in Westerlanglees.

,,   14. Thomas Bunzie in Newsteid, a.d.n. Jennet ; w. John ——, John Meins, elders there.

,,   ,,   Bap. Elizabeth, d. to the deceased William Waugh in Melrose, holden up by James Sympsone in Melrose ; w. James Blaikie, James Huntar, there.

,,   28. Huge Bowstone, shoemaker in Darnick, a.s.n. William ; w. Robert Marr, John Ushar, there.

June   4. William Fairly in Overlangshaw, a.s.n. James ; w. Thomas Mathesone, Thomas Darling, elders.

,,   15. Alexr. Mein in Eildone, a.s.n. Richard ; w. Nicol Bowar, William Sybbald.

,,   ,,   Nicol Waithman in Darnick, a.s.n. Thomas ; w. Andrew Rennaldsone, James Mein.

,,   17. John Mercer in Bridgend, a.d.n. Margat ; w. John Ushar, George Howname, there.

July   2. Thomas Boustoune in Gottonsyde, a.d.n. Margat ; w. Thomas Bowstone, John Cairncros, there.

,,   ,,   William Kennedy, smith in Darnick, a.s.n. David ; w. John Ushar, Andrew Rennaldsone, there.

,,   16. Robert Scott in Gattonsyde, a.d.n. Margat ; w. Andrew Halliwell, William Martine, there

,,   21. William Rollmainhouse in Blainslee, a.d.n. Agnes ; w. William and James Stirling there.

,,   24. Thomas Boustoune, younger, in Gattonsyde, a.s.n. Robert ; w. Rot. Mein, Thomas Bowstoune, Wind, his father, there.

,,   29. William Drummond in Bridgend, a.s.n. John.

Aug.   6. Thomas Leithan in Gattonsyde, a.d.n. Elizabeth ; w. James Leithan, James Edgar.

,,   ,,   James Laidley in Newtoune, a.s.n. Thomas ; w. James Edgar, John Milne.

,,   13. James Dewar in Blainslee, a.d.n. Margat ; w. Thomas ——, Thomas Darlings, there.

,,   17. John Sandilands in Langshaw Milne, a.d.n. Jennet ; w. Thomas Laidlay, Thomas Watsone, there.

Sept.   3. Hendrie Gibsone in Melrose, a.d.n. Agnes ; w. Michael Gibsone, William Cook, there.

1693.

Sept. 3. Andrew Mein, Townhead, a.s.n. Robert ; w. George Mein, his father, William Mein, his brother.

" 10. Edward Lythgow of Newhouses, a.d.n. Isobel ; w Wm. and John Lythgow, his brethren.

" 24. James Leithane in Gattonsyde, a.s.n. James ; w. Thomas Leithan, Rot. Martine, there.

" " James Penman in Melrose, a.s.n. William ; w. Andro and John Penmans there.

Oct. 1. Alexr. M'Fadzen in Westhouses, a.s.n. James ; w. Andro Turnbul, William Martine, there.

" 14. John Gibsone in Melrose, a.s.n. John ; w. Michael Gibsone there, Richard Mein in Eildone.

Nov. 5. James Mercer, tailzeor in Newsteid, a.d.n. Christian ; w. Richard Mein in Eildone, John Mein, elder in Newsteid.

" " John Marr in Danzeltoune, a.d.n. Jennet ; w. James Patersone, Thomas Drummond, there.

" 12. John Sympsone in Darnick, a.d.n. Jennet ; w. John Moss, Andrew Rennaldsone.

" 19. James Gray, a.d.n. Margat ; w. James Huntar, James Blaikie.

" 23. James Fischar in Gattonsyde, a.d.n. Margat.

" " Wm. Elliot in Eildone, a.s.n. Gavin ; w. William Sybbald Nicol Bowar, there.

" " Thomas Davidsone in Drygrange, a.d.n. Magdalen ; w. Rot. Mein, masone in Newsteid, James Mein in Melrose.

Dec. 17. John Mein in Old Melrose, a.d.n. Isobell ; w. John and James Mein.

" " George Gramslay, a.d.n. Euffan ; w. as before.

" 24. James Huntar in Melrose, a.d.n. Agnes ; w.——.

" 31. John Penman in Melrose, a.d.n. Isobel.

1694

Jan. 7. William Cairncross of Langlee, a.d.n. Elizabeth ; w. Buckholme and Greatlaws.

" " Andrew Wilsone in Newsteid, a.s.n. Andrew.

" 21. James Marr in Gattonsyde, a.d.n. Katherine ; w. Andrew Marr, his father, Andrew Marr, his brother.

Feb. 18. Rot. Halliwall in Gattonsyde, a.d.n. Mary ; w. Andro Halliwal, Rot. Halliwall, there.

Mar. 4. Andrew Baitie in Bridgend, a.d.n. Helen ; w. Andro Turnbull, John Mercer, there.

" " Andrew Fischar in Newsteid, a.s.n. John ; w. John——, John Mein, there.

" 11. William Bell in Gattonsyde, a.d.n. Margat ; w. John Mein, elder in Newsteid, John Mein there.

" " James Bowstoune in Gattonsyde, a.d.n. Christian ; same witnesses.

" 18. Thomas Ormistoune in Melrose, a.s.n. Robert ; w. John and Rot. Ormistoune, his brethren.

April 8. Wm. Moss, weaver in Darnick, a.d.n. Agnes ; w. John Moss, Andrew Rennaldsone.

" " John Mercer, masone in Newsteid, a.s.n. James ; w. John Bunzie, Newtoun, James Mein in Melrose.

" " Thomas Gardiner in Melrose, a.d.n. Elizabeth ; w. Alexander Andersone, James Mein in Melrose.

" " Rot. Harvie, glover in Melrose, a.s.n. Adam ; w. John Mabone, James Paterson, there.

" " John Mein, glover in Newsteid, a.d.n. Agnes ; w. John Mein in Old Melrose, John Mein, masone in Newsteid.

" " Mungo Dalgleish in Gattonsyde, a.d.n. Elizabeth ; w. James Marr Thomas Matheson, there.

" 10. James Drover in Hagburn, a.d.n. Elizabeth ; w. George Hoge there, John Stodhart in Appletreeleaves.

" " James Pringle in Blainslee, ——; w. Thomas Darling, John Wallace, there.

1694.

April 15. Henrie Myles in Gattonsyde, a.d.n. Marion ; w. Wm. Fischar, James Myles, there.

,, ,, John Bunzie, gardiner in Newsteid, a.d.n. Isobell ; w. James Bunzie, his father, James Mercer, there.

,, ,, Andrew Riddel in Newtoune, a.d.n. Jennet ; w. John Riddel, Nicol Cochrane, there.

,, 22. Wm. Hopkirk in Melrose, a.d.n Helen ; w. James Huntar, James Blaikie, there.

,, 29. John Frier in Gattonsyde, a.d.n. Jennet ; w. Thomas Bowstone, Archibald Freir, there.

May — Wm. Stirling in Blainslee, a.s.n. John ; w. John Stirling, George Moffat, there.

,, 18. Andrew Lukup in Melrose, a.d.n. Mary ; w. Thomas and Patrick Lukup.

,, 20. James Bowie, wright in Melrose, a.s.n. James.

,, 27. James Mathesone, couper in Gattonsyde, a.s.n. John ; w. John Halliwall, John Drummond, there.

,, ,, Adam Davidsone, smith in Melrose, a.d.n. Helen, w. James Wallace, James Bowie, there.

June 10. James Vair in Newtoune, a.s.n. Thomas ; w. Nicol Cochrane, Thomas Vair, there.

,, ,, John Rollmainhouse in Blainslee, a.d.n. Elizabeth ; w. John Wallace, James Pringle.

,, ,, John Milne, younger in Newtoun, a.s.n. John ; w. John Milne, his father, Nicol Cochrane.

,, 17. Nicol Mercer in Darnick, a.d.n. Jennet ; w. James Fisher there, Henrie Gibsone in Melrose.

July 1. Thomas Halliwall in Gattonsyde, a.s.n. Andrew ; w. James Marr, Thomas Mathesone.

,, 8. John Purvis in Hagburn, a.d.n. Jennet ; w. George Hoge, Wm. Lees.

,, ,, James Wallace in Melrose, a.d.n. Jennet ; w. James Blaikie, John Mabone, there.

,, 22. Hendrie Pringle in Gattonsyde, a.d.n. Jennet ; w. George and Francis Pringle there.

,, ,, David Hendersone in Melrose, a.d.n. Marion ; w. John Mabone, Rot. Harvie, there.

,, ,, Andrew Mein, " Kill," in Newsteid, a.s.n. John ; w. Bernard Mein, Alexr. Mein, there.

,, ,, John Ushar in Bridgend, a.d.n. Jennet ; w. Thomas Ushar, Andrew Martine.

,, ,, Thomas Heittone in Newsteid, a.d.n. Isobell ; w. Alexr. and Bernard Meins.

,, 31. The deceased James Mein, Wind, in Newsteid, a.s.n. James ; w. James Mein, Wm. Karr.

,, ,, Wm. Karr in Newtoune, a.s.n. Thomas ; w. John Mein, James Stewart.

,, ,, Thomas Darling, younger, in Blainslee, a.s.n. James ; w. Thomas Darling, elder, Thomas Laidlay, there.

,, ,, John Steel (?) in Blainslee, a.d.n. Mary ; same witnesses.

,, ,, Wm. Martine in Gattonsyde, a.s.n. William ; same witnesses.

Aug. 7. Thomas Turner in Williamlaw, a.d.n. Elizabeth ; w. George Turner, his father, Thomas Laidlay.

,, 19. Andrew Mein, Bridgend, in Newsteid, a.s.n. Andrew : w. John and Rot. Meins, his brethren-in-law.

,, ,, James Eiles, weaver in Melrose, a.d.n. Isobell ; w. James Eiles, Walker-raw, George Ushar.

,, ,, Nicol Milne in Darnick, a.s.n. James ; w. James Huntar, John Mercer.

,, ,, James Blaikie in Melrose, a.d.n. Marion : w. Mr. George Byres, James Mein.

1694.

Sept. 2. James Sympsone in Melrose, a.s.n. William ; w. John and [*torn*] Penmans there.

" " John Drummond in Gattonsyde, a.d.n. Margaret ; w. Rot. Mein, Rot. Dinnand, there.

" 9. John Bunzie in Newtoun, a.s.n. John ; w. James Wallace, James Mein.

" " Thomas Bunzie, masone in Newsteid, a.s.n. Thomas ; w. John and Rot. Bunzies there.

" 16. [*torn*] Wallace in Melrose, a.s.n. Thomas, baptized by Mr. Georg Milligen, minister of Bowden ; w. Rot. Harvie, John Mabon, there.

" 29. John Ovens, herd in Newsteid, a.s.n. James ; w. James and John [*torn*].

" " Wm. Eiles, weaver in Melrose, a.s.n. Wm. ; w. James ——, James Eiles, weavers there.

Oct. 7. Michael Wallace in Melrose, a.s.n. Thomas ; w. James ——, James Wallace, there.

" " John Stodhart in Gledswood, a.s.n. John ; w. James [*torn*], Georg Fraiter.

" 14. Thomas Cochrane in Newtoune, a.d.n. Isobell ; w. Nicol Cochrane, Thomas Stenhouse, there.

" 17. Walter Scot in Gattonsyde, a.d.n. Agnes ; w. James [*torn*], Thomas Mathesone.

" 28. James Myles in Gattonsyde, a.s.n. Wm. ; w. James Marr, Thomas Mathesone, there.

Nov. 4. David Mein in Newsteid, a.s.n. James ; w. John Mein, John Sclaitter.

" " Wm. Drummond, a.s.n. Wm. ; w. Andrew Turnbull, John Drummond.

" 13. Thomas Martine in Danzeltoun, a.s.n. George ; w. James Martine, James Patersone.

" " Wm. Martine, weaver in Gattonsyde, a.s.n. Rot. ; w. Jon Martine, Thomas Stenhouse in Newtoune.

" 25. Wm. Eccles in Newtoune, a.s.n. John ; w. Nicol [*torn*], Thomas Stenhouse, there.

" " Wm. Laidlay there, a.d.n. Isobell ; same witnesses.

Dec. 6. Thomas Laidlay in Whitlaw, a.d.n. Marion, baptized in Stow ; w. [*torn*], John Turners.

" 9. Rot. Fairbairne in Eildone, a.d.n. Marion ; w. John Scot, James Mein.

" " John Forrest in Mosshouses, a.d.n. Isobell ; w. George Pringle, James Mein.

" " John Sheil, weaver in Melrose, a.s.n. George ; w. [*torn*] Lyes, Andro Dasone, there.

" " Andrew Dasone in Melrose, a.s.n. John ; w. John Sheil, Andro Dason.

" " John Greistone in Darnick, a.s.n. Andrew ; same witnesses.

" 16. James Dasone in Danzieltoune, a.s.n. John ; w. Andro Dasone, Alexr. Mein.

1695.

Jan. 13. Mr. Mark Duncansone of Greatlaws, a.s.n. Andrew ; w. John Halliburtoune of Muirhouselaw, Mr. Andrew Duncansone.

" " Rot. Mein, maltman in Newsteid, a.d.n. Jennet ; w. John Mein, John Bunzie, there.

" " John Bunzie, masone in Eildoune, a.s.n. Thomas ; w. [*torn*], John Mein.

" " Walter Dalgleish in Darnick, a.d.n. Isobell ; w. John Dalgleish, Michael Gibsone. These were baptized by Mr. Mulligen, minister of Bowdoune.

" 15. Rot. Mercer in Calfhill, a.s.n. Rot.

" 19. George Pringle, tayler in Gattonsyde, a.s.n. James ; w. Francis Pringle, his brother, Hendrie Pringle, there.

1695.

Jan. 26. Rot. Lamb in Westboathouse, a.s.n. Wm. ; w.——

,, ,, John Ormistone, weaver in Melrose, a.s.n. Robert ; w. Thomas and Rot. Ormistone there.

,, ,, Wm. Mercer, a.d.n. Helen ; w. John and William Meins.

,, ,, Nicol Waithman in Darnick, a.s.n. Nicol ; w. Thomas and John Ormistones.

Feb. 24. Thomas Mercer in Danzieltoune, a.s.n. Nicol ; w. James Patersone, Wm. Gill, there.

Mar. 10. Helen Bowar in Melrose, a.s.n. John ; holden up by her father.

,, 17. John Ushar, weaver in Darnick, a.s.n. James ; w. Andro Mercer, Andrew Rennaldsone, there.

,, ,, Wm. Mein in Newsteid, a.s.n. Andrew ; w. Georg Mein, his father, James Mein, there.

,, ,, John Halliwall, Nuk, in Gattonsyde, a.s.n. Rot. ; w. Thomas and Thomas Halliwalls there.

,, 24. Thomas Thomsone in Darnick, a.s.n. John ; w. John Thomsone, Henrie Pringle, there.

,, ,, John Martine in Melrose, a.d.n. Elizabeth Martine ; w. Andro Martine, James Mein.

,, ,, Wm. Livingstone, a.d.n. Jennet, holden up by Andro Martine ; same witnesses.

,, 31. John Vogan in Newtoune, a.d.n. Margat ; w. Nicol Cochrane, John Gill, there.

,, ,, Wm. Darling in Easterlanglee, a.d.n. Jean ; w. John Darling, his brother, Francis Braiden, there.

,, ,, Wm. Darling in Blainslee, a.d.n. Marion ; w. Thomas Darling, Thomas Laidlay, there.

April 14. James Laidley in Newtoune, a.d.n. Margaret ; w. Thomas Stenhouse, John Milne, there.

,, ,, Wm. Bowar in Melrose, a.d.n. Jennet : w. James Huntar, Wm. Brown, there.

May 5. Mungo Purvis in Melrose, a.s.n. James ; w. James ——, James Eiles.

,, 12. Thomas McDougall in Old Melrose, a.s.n. William ; w. James Mein, Thomas Garner in Melrose.

,, ,, Andrew Mein in Newsteid, a.s.n. Cornelius Mein ; w. George Mein, his father, Wm. Mein, his brother.

,, 26. James Oliver, cordiner in Melrose, a.d.—— ; w. Andro Oliver, Mr. George Byres, there.

,, ,, Thomas Davidsone in Gattonsyde, a.s.n. James ; w. George Pringle, Thomas Boustone, there.

Note.— The said James Boustone also became cautioner (*sic*) for the foresaid Thomas Davidson, that he should bring a testimonial from Mertone.

June 23. Rot. Pringle in Blainslee, a.d.n. Jennet ; w. James Mein, Mr. George Byres in Melrose.

,, 25. James Fischar in Darnick, a.d.n. Agnes ; w. John Moss, Andro Rennaldsone, there.

July 14. George Grhamsley in Darnick, a.s.n. George ; w. Andro and John Mercers there.

,, ,, George Freir in Gattonsyde, a.s.n. Rot. ; w. James Marr, Thomas Mathesone, there.

[*torn*] Thomas Sheil in Gattonsyde, a.d.n. Isobell ; w. George [*torn*] Darnick.

[*same day*] James Penman in Melrose, a.d.n. Margaret ; w. Andrew and Rot. Penmans, there.

Aug 18. James Linsday in Gattonsyde, a.s.n. John ; w. Rot. Mein, Thomas Boustone, there.

,, ,, Wm. Stirling in Blainslee, a.s.n. George ; w. John——, John Stirlings, there.

,, ,, George Rodger in Drygrange, a.d.n. Margaret ; w. Andrew Lithgow Rot. Fischar in Old Melrose.

1695.

Aug. 25. Wm. Cook in Melrose, a.d.n. Isobell ; w. James Eiles, Mr. Thomas Byres, there.

" " Henry Gibsone in Melrose, a.d.n. Jean ; w. Michael and John Gibsone there.

" " Thomas Leithane in Gattonsyde, a.s.n. Thomas ; w. James Leithan, Wm. Hoyie.

" 27. Wm. Cairncroce of Langlee, a.s.n. Hugh ; w. Walter Cairncross in Hilslope, Mr. Hugh Gray, his brother-in-law.

Sept. 1. John Symervall in Gattonsyde, a.d.n. Margaret ; w. Rot. and Thomas Halliwall there.

" 8. John Mein, glover in Newsteid, a.d.n. Elizabeth ; w. James Trotter there, Nicol Bowar in Eildone.

" 22. John Gibsone in Melrose, a.s.n. Rot. ; w. Michael and Henry Gibsones there.

" " Thomas Halliburtone in Gattonsyde, a.s.n. Andrew ; w. Walter Halliburtone, Andro Marr, there.

" 29. Rot. Bunzie, weaver in Newsteid, a.s.n. Robert ; w. James Bunzie there, Wm. Bowstone in Melrose.

Oct. 6. James Gray in Melrose, a.s.n. James ; w. James Bowie, James Wallace, there.

" 20. Mark Hoyie in Kelso, a.s.n. Thomas ; w. Georg and James Blaikies in Melrose.

" 22. James Huntar in Melrose, two daughters named Jennet and Agnes ; w. Mr. Mark Duncansone, Mr. Andrew Duncansone, there.

" 27. Wm. Hoyie in Gattonsyde, a.d.n. Margaret ; w. Andrew Marr, Thomas Mathesone, there.

" 29. Thomas Laidlay in Blainslee, a.d.n. Elizabeth ; w. Thomas Darling, John Wallace, there.

Nov. 23. Walter Cairncroce of Hilslope, a.s.n. ——.

" " James Wadderstone in Colmslee, ——.

[Dec. ?] 3. Wm. Milne in Eildone, a.s.n. John ; w. Alexr. Mein, Wm. Sibbald.

Dec. 3. Rot. Halliwall in Gattonsyde, a.d.n. Margaret ; w. Andrew Halliwall, Patrick Thomsone, there.

" " Wm. Lees in Colmsleehill, a.d.n. Katharine ; w. Alexr. Horsbrugh, John Hall, there.

" 15. James Bowstone, Dukedub, a.s.n. Thomas ; w. James Marr, Thomas Mathesone, there.

" " Wm. Kennedie in Darnick, a.d.n. Elizabeth ; w. Nicol Cochrane, Rot. Mein.

1696.

Jan. 10. Wm. Hopkirk in Melrose, a.s.n. Alexander ; w. James Blaikie, James Huntar, there.

" 12. Rot. Leithane in Eildone, a.s.n. John ; w. John Sclaitter, Rot. Sclaitter, there.

" " Rot. Sclaitter in Eildone, a.d.n. Alisone ; w. John Sclaitter, Nicol Bowar, there.

" " Wm. Wallace in Melrose, a.d.n. Elizabeth ; w. James and James Wallaces there.

" 19. Thomas Garner in Melrose, a.d.n. Agnes ; w. James Huntar, James Mein, there.

" 26. James Mercer, tailzer in Newsteid, a.s.n John ; w. Rot. and John Bunzie there.

" " James Lethan in Gattonsyde, a.d.n. Isobell ; w. James Marr, Thomas Leithane, there.

" " Wm. Fischar in Gattonsyde, a.d.n. Helen ; w. James Fischar in Darnick, James Dicksone in Langshaw.

Feb. 2. Hugh Bowstone in Darnick, a.d.n. Isobel ; w. John Usher, Andrew Rennaldsone, there.

" 9. Wm. Riddel, millar in Newsteid, a.s.n. William ; w. John ——, John Meins.

1696.

Feb. 23. James Trotter in Newsteid, a.s.n. Wm. ; w. Rot. and John Meins there.

"   " Rot. Harvie, glover in Melrose, a.d.n. Margaret ; w. John Mabone, James Wallace, there.

Mar. 8. John Ushar in Bridgend, a.s.n. James ; w. James Bowie, Thomas Ushar.

"   " Thomas Bowstone, weaver in Gattonsyde, a.d.n. Helen ; w. James Marr, Thomas Matheson, there.

" 15. Wm. Bell in Gattonsyde, a.d.n. Elizabeth ; w. Wm. Darling, James Wright, there.

" 24. John Milne, younger, in Newtoune, a.s.n. Mungo ; w. John and Mungo Milne, there.

" 29. Henry Myles in Gattonsyde, a.d.n. Margaret ; w. Thomas Myles, Alexr. Thomsone, there.

"   " Wm. Elliot in Eilldone, a.s.n. George ; w. Rot. Patersone, Alexr. Mein.

April 5. James Dasone in Danzieltone, a.s.n. Alexr. ; w. Alexr. Mein, Andrew Dasone.

"   " Rot. Bunzie, Melrose, a.d.n. Jennet ; w. James Bowie, John Bunzie, there.

"   8. Andrew Steel in St. Leonards, in the paroche of Lauder, a.s.n. John ; w. Thomas Laidlay, Thomas Darling.

"   " John Steel in Blainslee, a.d.n. Elizabeth ; same witnesses.

"   " Wm. Woodhall in Blainslee, a.d.n. Margaret ; same witnesses.

" 12. James Blaikie in Melrose, a.d.n. Jennet ; w. Andro Turnbull in Bridgend, George Blaikie in Melrose.

" 19. James Mathesone in Gattonsyde, a.s.n. Robert ; w. Archibald Frier, Thomas Mathesone, there.

"   " John Mercer in Bridgend, a.s.n. Nicol ; w. James Huntar, Andro Mercer.

" 26. Rot.—— in Melrose, a.d.n. Agnes ; w. James Mein, James Lythgow, there.

May 3. Mark Dow in Redpath, a.d.n. Jean ; w. John Rodger there, Thomas Garner in Melrose.

" 10. Wm. Martine, younger, in Gattonsyde, a.s.n. Rot. ; w. Thomas Martine, John Somervail, there.

"   " John Martine in Melrose, a.s.n. George ; w. Andro Martine, James Murray, there.

" 26. Rot. Fraitter in the paroche of Henderleithane, a.d.n. Jennet ; w. Thomas Darling, Thomas Laidlay.

"   " John Moodie in Threepwood, a.d.n. Isobell ; same witnesses.

" 31. Wm. Greistone in Darnick, a.d.n. Elizabeth ; w. Andrew Rennaldsone, John Ushar.

June 16. Edward Lythgow in Newhouses, a.s.n. John ; w. John Lythgow, his brother, George Hall.

"   " Thomas Bunzie in Newsteid, a.d.n. Elizabeth ; w. James Trotter, John Mein, there.

" 28. James Pringle in Blainslee, a.d.n. Elizabeth ; w. Thomas Darling, John Thin, there.

July 12. Thomas Ormistone, weaver in Melrose, a.s.n. John ; w. John Ormistone, his brother, James Mein, there.

Aug. 13. Alexr. Laidlay in the paroche of Drummelzear, a.s.n. William——.

" 22. John Bunzie, masone in Newtoune, a.d.n. Helen ; w. Rot. Bunzie, Mungo Milne.

" 27. Wm. Darling in Westhouses, a.d.n. Margaret ; w. Alexr. Mathesone, Thomas Darling.

Sept. 6. Mr. Mark Duncansone of Greatlaws, a.s.n. John ; w. the Laird of Muirhouselaw, elder and younger.

" 20. John Mercer, masone in Newsteid, a.s.n. David ; w. James Mein in Melrose, Mr. George Byres there.

" 27. John Frier in Gattonsyde, a.s.n. Alexr. ; w. Rot. Mein, Thomas Bowstone, there.

1696.

Sept. 27. Andrew Mein, Townhead in Newsteid, a.d.n. Mary ; w. Georg Mein, his
        father, Wm. Mein, his brother, there.

Oct.   4. Andrew Mein, Bridgend in Newsteid, a.s.n. Robert ; w. Nicol Mein,
        James Mein, there.

  „ 11. Thomas Bowstone, Burnbraehead in Gattonsyde, a.s.n. John ; w.
        Andrew Bowstone, his brother, John Frier, there.

  „ „ Rot. Marr in Darnick, a.s.n. Andro ; w. Andrew Mercer, Andrew
        Rennaldsone, there.

  „ „ Michael Wallace in Melrose, a.s.n. James, presented by Thomas
        Bowston ; w. James Bowstone, William Wallace.

  „ 18. Rot. Walker in Melrose, a.s.n. Rot. ; w. James Mein, Mr. George
        Byres, there.

  „ 25. Thomas Lukup in Melrose, a.s.n. John : w. Andro Lukup, Wm.
        Lukup.

Nov. 1. David Hendersone in Melrose, a.d.n. Margaret.

  „ „ John Ovens in Newsteid, a.d.n. Jennet ; w. Rot. Bunzie, James Mein.

  „ 15. John Stodhart in the paroch of Mertone. a.s.n. George ; w. James
        Mein, &c.

  „ „ Wm Martine, weaver in Gattonsyde, a.s.n. James ; w. Rot. Martine,
        James Marr, there.

  „ 22. Wm. Hoyie in Gattonsyde, a.s.n. George ; w. Andrew Marr, Thomas
        Bowstone, there.

  „ 29. Patrick Thomsone in Gattonsyde, a.s.n. John ; w. Rot. Halliwell, Rot.
        Mein, there.

Dec. 13. John Greistone in Darnick, a.d.n. Margaret ; w. Wm. Greistone,
        John Ushar.

  „ 20. James Wallace in Melrose. a.s.n. Patrick ; w. Wm. Gill, Wm. Wallace.

  „ „ James Wallace, merchant, a.d.n. Hannah ; Wm. Wallace, James Blaikie.

1697.

Jan. 3. Adam Davidsone in Eildone, a.s.n. John ; w. Wm. Sibbald, James Mein.

  „ „ James Myles in Gattonsyde, a.d.n. Isobell ; w. James Marr, Thomas
        Myles.

  „ 17. Rot. Mein, maltman in Newsteid, a.d.n. Margaret ; w. John Mein,
        Wm. Fischar, there.

  „ 24. Alexr. Dalgleish in Darnick, a.s.n. Walter ; w. John Dalgleish, Wm.
        Chisholme, there.

Feb. 15. Rot. Stirling in Blainslee, a.s.n. Rot. ; w. John and John Stirlings
        there.

  „ 26. John Dinnant in Gattonsyde, a.s.n. John ; w. James Marr, Wm.
        Hoyie, there.

  „ „ Nicol Waithman in Darnick, a.s.n. Walter ; w. John Ushar, Andrew
        Renaldsone, there.

  „ „ Thomas Bunzie in Newsteid, a.s.n. James ; w. John Bunzie, his father,
        John Mein, there.

Mar. 7. Andrew Beattie in Bridgend, a.d.n. Margaret ; w. ——, Andrew
        Turnbull.

  „ 28. Francis Braiden in Easterlanglee, a.d.n. Jennet : w. Nicol Cochrane,
        Nicol Bowar.

  „ „ George Rodger in Drygrainge, a.s.n. Rot. ; w. Rot. Fischar, &c.

  „ „ Andrew Wilsone in Newsteid, a.d.n. Agnes. These baptised by
        Mr. Wm Veek (?) (Vietch.)

April 11. James Young, weaver in Gattonsyde, a.d.n. Helen, baptised by Mr.
        George Johnstone ; w. John Bartine, Thomas Bartine.

  „ „ John Bunzie, garner in Newsteid, a.s.n. John : w. James and Rot.
        Bunzie.

  „ „ John Forson there, a.s.n. John : w. Rot. Forson, John Bunzie, there.

May 9. Walter Scott in Gattonsyde, a.s.n. Thomas ; w. Rot. Scott, John
        Moffat, there.

  „ 23. Wm Cairncross of Langlee, a.d.n. Euffan ; w. Walter Cairncross of
        Hilslope, Andrew Fischar of Housebyre.

1697.

May 27. Rot. Scott in Gattonsyde, a.d.n. Helen ; w. James Marr, Wm. Hoyie.

„ 30. Rot. Wedderstone in Colmslee, a.s.n. James ; w. Alexr. and Rot. Trotters.

June 20. John Moffatt in Langshaw, a.s.n. James ; w. James Thin, John Moodie.

July 18. John Bunzie, masone in Eildon, a.s.n. James ; w. Rot. and James Bunzies, his brothers.

„ 25. George Pringle in Westerboathouse, a.d.n. Mary ; w. James Mein, James Huntar.

„ „ Alexr. Lyal, weaver in Melrose, a.d.n. Elspeth ; w. James Blaikie, James Huntar.

Aug. 1. Michael Parsone in Sorrowlesfield, a.s.n. James ; w. James Marr, James Parsone in Westerhousebyre.

„ 22. James Moss in Ridpeth, in the paroche of Earlstone, a.s.n. Thomas ; w. John Broun of Park, Rot Patersone.

Note.— Thomas Litle had a childe baptised at Ligertwood, being brought forth on the seventh month, and James Darling, wright, became cautioner for that he should make satisfaction.

Sept. 12. Nicoll Milne in Darnick, a.d.n. Margaret ; w. Andrew Mercer there, James Mein in Melrose.

„ „ George Darline in Blainslie, a.s.n. Thomas ; w. Thomas and Thomas Darlines there.

„ 20. Wm. Bell in Galtonsyde, a.s.n. William ; w. Wm. Hopkirk and Rot. Hill in Melrose.

„ 27. Wm. Laidlaw in Newtoun, a.s.n. William ; w. Mungo Milne and —— there.

Oct. 10. Andrew Mein in Newsteid, a.d.n. Jennet ; w. James Blaikie, James Mein in Melrose.

„ 17. James Mattheson in Galtonsyde, a.d.n. Mary ; w. Archibald Friar, John Dinnand, there.

„ „ Wm. Scot in Darnick, a.s.n. Andrew ; w. George Mein, John Mein.

„ 22. Wm. Mein in Newsteid, a.s.n. George ; w. George and John Meins there.

„ 24. Wm. Fiergrieve in Eildon, a.s.n. James ; w. Rot. Laury, Thomas Hiton, there.

„ „ Thomas Davidson in Galtonside, a.d.n. Margaret ; w. James and Andrew Marres there.

Nov. 7. Wm. Darline in Easterlanglie, a.d.n. Margaret ; w. John Darline, Francis Bredan.

„ 14. John Turnbull in Galtonside, a.s.n. Andrew ; w. John and Wm. Meins.

„ 28. Wm. Hopkirk in Melrose, a.d.n. Helen ; w. James Blaikie, Rot. Hislop, there.

„ „ James Penman in Melrose, a.d.n. Christin ; w. Andrew and Rot. Penmans there.

Dec. 5. James Dauson, a.s.n. James ; w. Alexr. Mein in Eildon, Andrew Dauson.

„ „ Henry Pringle in Galtonside, a.s.n. James ; George Pringle, Thomas Bowston.

„ 19. Henry Gibson in Melrose, a.s.n. Michael ; w. Michael and John Gibsones there.

„ „ Andrew Dauson in Melrose, a.d.n. Margaret ; w. James Penman, James Dauson.

1698.

Jan. 2. Rot. Bunzie, miller in Melrose, a.s.n. James ; w. James Bowie, John Bunzie

„ 4. Wm. Kirkwood in Blainslie, a.s.n. John ; w. Thomas Laidlaw, Thomas Darline, there.

„ „ John Notman in Mosshouses, a.s.n. Thomas ; w. James Thynne, Rot. Mercer.

1698.

Jan. 4. John Peaco, a.s.n. Andrew ; w. John Mabon, Rot. Hislop.

,, ,, Thomas Laidlaw in Blainslie, a.d.n. Alison ; w. James Marr, Wm. Hoy.

,, ,, Thomas Martine in Galtonside, a.d.n. Margaret ; w. Wm. Martine, John Sommervaill.

,, 16. James Laidlaw in Newtown, a.d.n. Christin ; w. John Milne, Nicoll Cochran, there.

,, ,, John Milne, younger, in Newtoun, a.d.n. Christin ; w. John Milne, Nicoll Cochran, there.

,, 30. Mungo Blaikie, gardiner in Galtonside, a.d.n. Marion ; w. James Marr, Wm. Laidlaw.

Feb. 1. James Trotter in Newsteid, a.s.n. Robert; w. Rot. Fisher, James Phaup.

,, — Alexr. Dalgleish and Margaret Vair in Darnick, a.s.n. John Dalgleish ; w. Wm. Chisholme, John Dalgleish.

,, — Rot. Lamb and Elizabeth Wilson in Westhouses, a.d.n. Agnes Lamb : w. Thomas Matthesone, Wm. Williamsone, there.

,, 8. Andrew Toudhope and Jennet Dicksone in Blainslie, a.d.n. Marion Toudhope ; w. John Wallace, Alexr. Dicksone, there.

,, ,, Wm. Stirling and Elizabeth Moffet in Blainslie, a.s.n. James Stirling ; w. John Moffet, John Stirling.

,, 13. Wm. Martine and Isabell Mildes in Galtonside, a.d.n. Jennet Martine ; w. John Sommervaill, Thomas Martine.

,, 17. James Turner and Jean Huntar in Hagburn, a.s.n. George Turner ; w. John Moodie, James Thynne.

,, 20. James Mein and Jennet Pursell in Newsteid, a.d.n. Margaret Mein ; w. David Pursell, John Mein.

,, 27. Gilbert Wailsh and Elizabeth Falla in Darnick, Lairdsland, a.s.n. Thomas Wailsh ; w. Wm. and John Mercers in Darnick.

,, ,, George Mercer and Jean Marre in Darnick, a.d.n. Helen Mercer ; w. Wm. Mercer, John Marre.

Mar. 1. Wm. Darline and Margaret Matthesone in Westhouses, a.d.n. Jean Darline ; w. Wm. Cairncroce, Thomas Matthesone.

,, 20. Andrew and Agnes Bunzies in Newsteid, a.s.n. Alexr. Bunzie ; w. John Bunzie there, Rot. Scot in Galtonside.

,, ,, Thomas Hahburton and Margaret Black in Galtonside, a.s.n. Wm. Haliburton ; w. James and Andrew Marres there.

,, 27. John Sommervaill and Isabell Martine in Galtonside, a.s.n. George Sommervaill ; w. Thomas Martine there, and Wm. Livingstone in Lauder parish.

April 10. Andrew Turnbull and Marion Laidlaw in Bridgend, a.d.n. Jennet Turnbull ; w. James Blaikie in Melrose, Thomas Laidlaw in Blainslie.

,, 17. Rot. Fairbairn and Alison Sclater in Eildon, a.d.n. Alison Fairbairn ; w. John Sclater there, James Mein in Melrose.

,, ,, Rot. Hervy and Janet Mabon in Melrose, a.d.n. Jean Hervy ; w. John Mabon, James Mein, there.

,, ,, James Fisher and Isabell Moss in Darnick, a.d.n. Isabell Fisher ; w. Nicoll Milne there, John Mabon in Melrose.

,, ,, James Bowie and Isabell Jaque in Melrose, a.s.n. Thomas Bowie ; w. James Bowie, John Mabon, there.

,, ,, James Grieve and Jean Allane in Blainslie, a.s.n. James Grieve ; w. John Stirling, Hugh Allane, there.

,, 24. John Forrest and Annable Mildes in Longshaw, a.s.n. Henry Forrest ; w. George and James Dicksones, there.

,, ,, John Ushar and Elizabeth Thomson in Bridgend, a.s.n. George Usher ; w. John Usher, his brother, James Mein in Melrose.

May 1. James Marre and Alison Hog in Galtonside, a.s.n. Alexr. Marre ; w. Andrew and Andrew Marres, there.

,, 15. Wm. Romainhouse and Agnes Pringle in Blainslie, a.d.n. Margaret Romainhouse ; w. Thomas Darline, John Wallace, there.

,, 25. George Grahamsley and Jennet Allie in Darnick, a.s.n. Andrew Grahamsley ; w. Wm. Chisholme, Rot. Marre, there.

1698.

June 5. Wm. Eliot and Margaret Patersone in Eildon, a.s.n. Robert Eliot ; w. Alexr. Mein there, George Patersone in Gallasheills.

„ 12. John Mein and Isabell Sibbald in Newsteid, a.d.n. Grizell Mein ; w. Wm. and John Sibbaldes in Eildon.

„ 19. Wm. Drummond and Isabell Usher in Bridgend, a.d.n. Isabell Drummond ; w. Andrew Turnbull, Nicoll Mercer, there.

„ „ James Blaikie and Margaret Turnbull in Melrose, a.d.n. Isabell Blaikie ; w Andrew Turnbull in Bridgend, Stephen Martine in Darnick.

„ „ James Gray and Margaret Simson in Melrose, a.d.n. Jennet Gray ; w. James Bowie, John Sheill, there.

July 3. Wm. Mercer and Mary Dalgleish in Westerlonglee, a.s.n. John Mercer ; w. Andrew Mercer there, Alexr. Dalgleish in Darnick.

„ „ Patrick Hastie in Longhaugh, a.d.n. Catharin Hastie, begotten in fornication with Agnes Paterson there ; w. James Blaikie, James Mein in Melrose.

„ 24. John Haliwall and Christin Dinnand in Galtonside, a.d.n. Jean Haliwall ; w. Thomas Bowstone, Thomas Sheill, there.

„ „ Thomas Bowstone and Helen Cairncroce in Galtonside, a.d.n. Margaret Bowstone ; w. John Cairncroce in Redpath, Andrew Cairncroce in Galtonside.

„ „ Thomas Sheill and Margaret Mein in Galtonside, a.s.n. Thomas Sheill ; w. John Haliwall, Thomas Bowstone, there.

„ „ Alexr. Mein and Jennet Milne in Eildon, a.d.n. Alison Mein ; w. Wm. Eliot, Wm. Milne, there.

„ „ Mr. Mark Duncansone of Greatlawes, and Elizabeth Haliburtone, a.s.n. Thomas Duncansone ; w. John Haliburton, younger of Muirhouslaw, Mr. Andrew Duncansone in Melrose.

„ 31. Thomas Cochran and Isabell Milne in Newtown, a.d.n. Agnes Cochran ; w. John Milne, John Riddel, there.

Aug. 3. John Simson and Elizabeth Swanstone in Darnick, a.s.n. William Simson ; w. Andrew Rennaldson, John Usher, there.

„ „ John Gibsone and Elizabeth Philip in Melrose, a.d.n. Margaret Gibson ; w. Rot. and Rot. Philips in Galtonside.

„ 21. Thomas Ormistone and Jennet Pringle in Melrose, a.s.n. Thomas Ormistone ; w. John Ormistone, Thomas Lucup, there.

„ „ Andrew Mein and Mary Bunzie in Newsteid, a.s.n. William Mein ; w. George and William Meins there.

Sept. 4. John Martine and Elizabeth Wood in Melrose, a.d.n. Margaret Martine ; w. Andrew Martine, John Mabon, there.

„ „ Thomas Bowstone and Isabell Mabon in Galtonside, a.d.n. Isabell Bowstone ; w James Marre, Andrew Bowstone, there.

„ 7. John Moodie and Margaret Moffat in Threepwood, a.d.n. Margaret Moodie ; w. Archibald and Peter Moffets there.

Oct. 2. Richard Bower in Eildon, a.s.n. John Bower, baptized at Bowden, begoten in fornication with Jean Patersone ; w. George White, John Hope, in the parish of Bowden.

„ 9. Henry Cochran and Jennet Riddell in Newtown, a.s.n. Thomas Cochran ; w. Nicoll Cochran, Andrew Hiton, there.

„ „ James Richardson and Isabell Gray in Darnick, a.s.n. James Richardson ; w. John Haliwall, Andrew Rennaldsone, there.

„ „ Rot. Haliwall and Jennet Haliwall in Galtonside, a.d.n. Isabel Haliwall ; w. Andrew Haliwall, Patrick Thomsone, there.

„ 16. John Friar and Isabell Mein in Galtonside, a.d.n. Isabell Friar ; w. Rot. and Thomas Bowstones there.

„ 23. James Simson and Christin Penman in Melrose, a.s.n. John Simson ; w. John Penman, Wm. Cook, there.

„ 30. John Glendinning and Jennet Bower in Eildon, a.d.n. Margaret Glendinning ; w. Nicoll Bower, elder and younger, there.

Nov. 13. Thomas Gill and Isabell Ellies in Newtoun, a.d.n. Jennet Gill ; w. John Riddell, Nicoll Cochran, there.

1698.

Nov. 20. Rot. Walker and Elizabeth Bennet in Melrose, a.d.n. Elizabeth Walker ; w. James Huntar, James Blaikie, there.

,, ,, Thomas Lucup, younger, and Agnes Miller in Melrose, a.d.n. Jean Lucup ; w. Patrick and Andrew Lucups, there.

,, 22. John Purvis and Isabell Taitt in Williamlaw, a.s.n. James Purvis ; w. Thomas Hardie, Alexr. Horsburgh, there.

,, ,, Alexr. Horsburgh and Jennet Lauder, a.s.n. John Horsburgh ; w. Thomas Hardie and John Purvis, all in Williamlaw.

,, ,, Richard Robson and Jennet Pringle in Blainslie, a.s.n. James Robsone ; w. James Robsone there, Thomas Mathesone in Westhouses.

Dec. 6. Wm. Hoy and Isabell Hoy in Galtonside, a.s.n. Thomas Hoy ; w. James Marre, Rot. Bowstone, there.

,, 7. James Mercer and Jennet Bunzie in Newsteid, a.s.n. Robert Mercer ; w. Rot. Bunzie, Wm. Mein, there.

,, 25. Wm. Cook and Elizabeth Brotherstons in Melrose, a.s.n. Andrew Cook ; w. David Cook, James Simson, there.

,, ,, George Friar and Isabell Dewer in Galtonside, a.s.n. James Friar ; w. John Friar, Wm. Martine, there.

,, ,, Wm. Martine and Isabel Marre in Galtonside, a.s.n. Robert ; w. Rot. Martine, James Marre, there.

,, 27. Thomas Darline and Mary Stenhouse in Blainslie, a d.n. Marion Darline ; w. Thomas Darline, elder, Thomas Laidlaw, there.

1699.

Jan. 1. John Sibbald and Beatrice Rutherfoord in Eildon, a.d.n. Jean Sibbald ; w. Wm. Sibbald there, John Mein in Newsteid.

,, ,, Wm. and Margaret Meins in Newsteid, a.s.n. David Mein ; w. George Mein there, James Mein in Melrose.

,, ,, Francis Bryden and Margaret Bower in Easterlonglie, a.d.n. Helen Bryden ; w. Nicoll and Richard Bowers in Eildon.

,, 8. Rot. Bunzie and Alison Bowston in Newsteid, a.d.n. Margaret Bunzie ; w. Wm. Bowstone, George Pringle.

,, 29. Mungo Purvis and Margaret Ellies in Melrose, a.d.n. Helen Purvis ; w. James Ellies, elder and younger, there.

,, ,, Wm. Ellies and Agnes Murray in Melrose, a.d.n. Isabell Ellies ; w. James Ellies, elder and younger, there.

,, ,, Wm. Cairncroce of Westerlonglie, and Mary Gray, a.d.n. Mary Cairncroce ; w. Walter Cairncroce of Hilslop, James Blaikie.

Feb. 12. Wm. Hoy and Margaret Wilson in Galtonside, a.d.n. Agnes Hoy ; w. John and George Hoys there.

,, 18. James Hunter and Jennet Usher in Melrose, a.s.n. James Hunter ; w. Mr. Andrew Duncansone, James Bowie, there.

,, 28. Rot. Mercer and Alison Mar in Calfhill, a.s.n. John Mercer ; w. Walter Cairncroce of Hilslop, Simon Watherston.

,, ,, —— Brown —— in Blainslie ; w. ——.

Mar. 5. Wm. Darling and Alison Lees in Easterlonglie, a.s.n. James Darling ; w. John Darling, Francis Bryden.

,, 19. James Bowstone and Margaret Chisholme in Galtonside, a.s.n. John Bowstone ; w. James and Andrew Mars there.

,, ,, Thomas Gardiner and Mary Scott in Melrose, a.d.n. Agnes Gardner ; w. James Phaup, James Mein, there.

,, 21. James Thynne and Marion Hunter in Mosshouses, a.s.n. John Thynne ; w. John and William Thynnes in Blainslie.

,, 23. Andrew Lythgow and Margaret Tod in Drygrainge, a.d.n. Elizabeth Lythgow ; w. James Edgar, James Ellies.

April 9. Rot. Mar and Margaret Waugh in Darnick, a.s.n. Rot. Mar ; w. Patrick Lookup, Rot. Hyslop.

,, ,, Thomas Thomsone and Margaret Thomsone in Galtonside, two sons n. Robert and William Thomsones ; w. George Pringle, Wm. Thomsone.

1699.

April 10. Thomas Scot and Jean Friar in Melrose, a.s.n. Robert Scott; w. John and James Lythgow there.

,, ,, James Wallace and Anna Waugh in Melrose, a.d.n. Elspeth Wallace; w. Wm. Gill, Andrew Patersone.

,, ,, Henry Myles and Isabell Tait, a.d.n. Marion Myles; w. Wm. Fisher, James Myles, there.

May 7. Rot. Mein and Margaret Karr in Newsteid, a.d.n. Elizabeth Mein; w. Wm. Fisher, Rot. Eliot, there.

,, ,, Walter Scott and Agnes Moffet in Galtonside, a.s.n. Thomas Scott; w. Wm. Hoy, John Moffet, there.

,, 18. Wm. Darling and Isabell Moffet in Blainslie, a.s.n. Wm. Darling; w. Thomas Darling, Thomas Laidlaw, there.

,, ,, George Darling and Agnes Smith in Blainslie, a.d.n. Marion Darling; same witnesses.

,, ,, Alexr. Fisher of Claikmae and Mary Simson, a.d.n. Helen Fisher; same witnesses.

June 11. Wm. Chisholme and Isabell Usher in Darnick, a.d.n. Margaret Chisholme; w. John Usher, James Blaikie.

,, 25. Rot. Scott and Margaret Bunzie in Galtonside, a.s.n. John Scott; w. John Moffet, Andrew Bunzie.

July 23. James Young and Isabell Berton in Galtonside, a.d.n. Margaret Young; w. John and Thomas Bertons

,, ,, Wm. Bower and Margaret Mercer in Melrose, a.s.n. John Bower; w. Wm. Brown and John Bower.

,, 30. John Wright and Isabell Bichot in Darnick, a.s.n. John Wright; w. George Hownam, John Drummond, younger, there.

Aug. 20. Adam Lothian and Alison —— in Blainslie; w. Thomas Darling, Thomas Laidlaw, there.

,, 27. Wm. Greistone and Elspeth Ramsey in Darnick, a.d.n. —— Greistone; w. Andrew Rennaldsone, John Usher, there.

,, ,, Andrew and Agnes Meins in Newsteid, a.d.n. Jennet Mein; w. James Hunter, James Blaikie.

Sept. 10. John Ormiston and Rachell Cowan in Melrose, a.d.n. Helen Ormistone; w. John Bell, Thomas Ormistone, there.

,, 27. Andrew Wilson and Jennet Laury in Newsteid, a.s.n. Robert Wilson; w. George Moodie, James Mein.

,, 30. Mungo Blaikie and Christian Laidlaw in Galtonside, a.d.n. Helen Blaikie; w. Andrew Mar, Walter Halyburtone, there.

,, ,, James Lindsey and Helen Clerk in Galtonside, a.d.n. Helen Lindsey; w. Rot. Ormistone, Andrew Lindsey, there.

Oct. 8. Wm. Milne and Agnes Sclater in Eildon, a.d.n. Agnes Milne; w. Wm. Cook, Nicoll Cochran.

,, ,, Henry Gibson and Isabell Fisher in Melrose, a.s.n. John Gibson; w James Fisher, Nicoll Mercer in Darnick.

,, ,, John Sheill and Isabell Purvis in Melrose, a.s.n. John Sheill; w. George Shiell, Mungo Purvis, there.

,, 22. Thomas Bunzie and —— Bunzie in Newsteid, twins n. John and Jennet Bunzies; w. Rot. Elliot, Wm. Mein, there.

,, 29. Rot. Pringle and Jennet Mein in Newsteid, a.s.n. Andrew Pringle; w. Wm. Mein, James Mein.

,, ,, George Pringle and Margaret Newtoun, a.s.n. John Pringle; same witnesses.

Nov. 1. John Remainhouse and Margaret Litle in Blainslie, a.d.n. Margaret Remainshouse; w. Wm. Brown, Wm. Kirkhope.

,, ,, William Brown and Jennet Hardie in Blainslie, a.d.n. Eupham Brown; w. John Remainhouse, Wm. Kirkhope.

,, ,, Wm. Swanston and Christian Brotherstones, a.d.n. Margaret Swanston; w. John Remainshouse, Wm. Brown, all in Blainslee.

,, ,, Wm. Kirkhop and Margaret Martine in Blainslie, a.s.n. George Kirkhop; w. Wm. Swanston, Wm. Brown, there.

F

1699.

Nov. 1. John Blaikie and Marion Lythgow, a.s.n. Robert Blaikie ; same witnesses.

,, 5. John and Jennet Mabons in Melrose, a.s.n. William Mabone ; w. Charles Blaikie, James Ellies, there.

Dec. 19. Thomas Laidlaw and Helen Darling in Blainslie, a.d.n. Margaret Laidlaw ; w. Edward Darling, John Thynne, there.

,, 24. John Forsan and Agnes Culbertson in Newsteid, a.s.n. James Forsan ; w. Rot. Eliot, James Rennaldson.

,, 31. Wm. Mercer and Mary Dalgleish in Westerlonglie, a.d.n. Isabell Mercer ; w. Andrew Mercer there, Robert Hislop, beddell.

1700.

Jan. – . Walter Tait and Alison Niell in Darnick, a.s.n. Adam Tait ; w. John Usher, James Ellies.

,, 21. John Mercer and Mary Mein in Newsteid, a.d.n. Jennet Mercer ; w. Wm. Mein, James Mein.

,, ,, Alexr. Maxwell and Isabell Gray in Melrose, a.d.n. Mary Maxwell ; w. John Mabon, John Gibson, there.

,, 28. John Sclater and Agnes Mein in Eildon, a.s.n. John Sclater ; w. Robert Fairbairn, James Hunter.

Feb. 4. James Mein and Elizabeth Hiton in Newtoun, a.d.n. Jennet ; w. Andrew Hiton, Nicoll Cochran, there.

,, ,, Ye deceased Alexr. Dalgleish and Margaret Vair in Darnick, a.s.n. Alexr. Dalgleish, presented by John Dalgleish in Melrose ; w. William Chisholme, Wm. Mercer.

,, ,, Alexr. Lyall and Margaret Bower in Melrose, a.s.n. Thomas Lyall ; w. John Dalgleish, Wm. Gill.

,, 11. Richard Bower and Jean Patersone in Eildon, a.s.n. Nicoll Bower ; w. Nicoll Bower, Alexr. Mein, there.

,, 18. Ye deceased Henry Pringle and Jennet Cranstone in Galtonside, a.s.n. Henry Pringle ; w. Robert Bowstone, Wm. Hoy, there.

,, 25. John Dinnand and Mary Haliwall in Galtonside, a.d.n. Isabell Dinnand ; w. Robert Philip, James Mattheson, there.

,, 26. Wm. Karr and —— Brown in Newtoun, a.d.n. Janet Karr; w. Nicoll Cochran, John Riddell, there.

Mar. 24. James Rennaldson and Isabell Leadhouse in Darnick, a.s.n. Andrew Rennaldson ; w. Andrew Rennaldsone, Wm. Chisholme, there.

May 5. Andrew Drummond and Mary Brown in Darnick, a.s.n. John Drummond ; w. John Drummond, Gilbert Welch.

,, 14. Wm. Darling and Isabell Moffet in Blanislie, a.s.n. Thomas Darling ; w. Thomas Darling, Thomas Laidlaw, there.

,, ,, John Simmontoun and Marion Notman in Colmeslie, a.d.n. Margaret Simontoun ; w. James Thynne, Robert Mercer.

,, 19. David Henderson and Christian Milne in Melrose, a.d.n. Christian Henderson ; w. John Mabon, James Simson, there.

,, ,, Agnes Brown, a.d.n. Marion, begoten in fornication. and presented by Thomas Brown ; w. George Chisholme, Robert Mercer.

June 16. John Mein and Isabell Sibbald in Eildon, a.d.n. Agnes Mein ; w. John Sibbald, Robert Hislope.

,, 30. John Thurbrand and Elizabeth Forsyth in Longshaw ; w. Thomas Laidlaw, John Ritchie, there.

,, ,, James Blaikie and Margaret Turnbull in Melrose, a.s.n. Mark Blaikie ; w. James Hunter, Mr. Andrew Patersone, there.

July 14. Thomas Gardner and Mary Scott in Melrose, a.s.n. William Gardner ; w. David Cook, Robert Hislop, there.

,, 28. James Fisher and Isabell Moss in Darnick, a.d.n. Isabell Fisher ; w. Andrew Moss, Andrew Rennaldson, there.

Aug. 4. Wm. Chisholme and Isabell Usher in Darnick, a.d.n. Christian Chisholme ; w. John Usher, Andrew Rennaldson, there.

,, 11. John and Isabell Milnes in Newtoun, a.d.n. Isabell Milne : w. John Milne, Nicoll Cochran, there.

1700.

Aug. 11. Thomas Laidlaw and Eupham Matthie in Longshaw, a.d.n. Jennet Laidlaw ; w. John Thurbrand, George Mathie, there.

,, 25. Wm. Darling and Alison Lees in Easterlonglie, a.s.n. Andrew Darling ; w. John Darling, Francis Bryden.

,, 29. John Notman and Margaret Irvine in Kedzliedoors, a.s.n. John Notman ; w. James Mar, John Wallace.

Sept. 15. George Mercer and Jean Mar in Darnick, a.s.n. James Mercer ; w. Wm. Mercer, James Rennaldson, there.

,, 22. Alexr. Mein and Jennet Milne in Eildone, a.s.n. James Mein ; w. Wm. and John Milnes there.

,, ,, James Dauson and Agnes Mein in Eildon, a.d.n. Margaret Dauson ; w. Alexr. and Richard Meins there.

,, ,, Mr. Mark Duncanson of Greatlaws and Elizabeth Haliburtoun, a.s.n. Mark Duncanson ; w. John Haliburtoun, elder and younger of Muirhouslaw, Mr. Andrew Duncanson, minister at Lauder, John Duncanson in Melrose.

Oct. 13. John Usher and Elspeth Thomson in Bridgend, a.s.n. John Usher ; w. Andrew Turnbull, James Bowie.

,, 20. Robert Philip and Margaret Sclater in Galtonside, a.d.n. Margaret Philip ; w. John Gibson, Richard Sclater.

,, ,, Thomas Lookup and Agnes Miller in Melrose, two daughters, n. Elisabeth and Mary Lookups ; w. Patrick and Andrew Lookups there.

,, 22. ——,   w. ——.

,, ,, ——,   w. ——.

,, 27. John Karr and Isabell Wait in Housbyre, a.s.n. James Karr ; w. ——.

Nov. 3. Thomas and Margaret Thomsons in Galtonside, a.s.n. Robert Thomson ; w. George Pringle, Nicoll Milne.

,, 17. William Darling and Margaret Matthieson in Westhouses, a.s.n. William Darling ; w. Thomas Matthison, Wm. Hunter.

,, ,, Henry Cochran and Jennet Riddell in Newtoun, a.s.n. John Cochran ; w. James Laidlaw, James Mein, there.

,, 19. Thomas Turner and Alison Murray in Mosshouses, a.s.n. John Turner ; w. Andrew Chisholme, John Hatlie, there.

,, ,, Wm. Sterling and Elizabeth Moffet Blainslie, a.d.n. Agnes Sterling, w. James and John Sterlings there.

,, ,, Robert Watherstone and Jennet Duncan in Housbyre, a.s.n. Robert Watherstone ; w. Robert Trotter, Robert Davidsone, there.

,, 24. Thomas Martine and Jennet Runshiman in Galtonside, a.d.n. Margaret Martine ; w. Wm. Martine, elder and younger, there.

Dec. 8. Andrew and Agnes Meins in Newsteid, a.d.n. Elisabeth Mein ; w. James Mein, Thomas Bunzie, there.

,, ,, James Matthison and Jennet Halliwall in Galtonside, a.d.n. Jennet Matthison ; w. John Dinnand, Archibald Friar, there.

,, ,, John Bunzie and Marion Mein in Eildon, a.d.n. Margaret Bunzie ; w. Wm. Sibbald, Richard Mein, there.

,, 26. John Moodie and Elisabeth Moffet in Threepwood, a.d.n. Elisabeth Moodie ; w. Peter and Robert Moffets there.

,, ,, Robert Brown and Margaret Sommervaill in Colmesliehill, a.s.n. William Brown ; w. John Moodie, Robert Sterling.

,, ,, Robert Sterling and Marion Lythgow in Threepwood, a.s.n. John Sterling ; w. John Moodie, Andrew Lythgow, there.

1701.

Jan. 5. Andrew Lythgow and Margaret Tod in Drygrainge, a.s.n. Alexander Lythgow ; w. Alexr. Trotter of Housbyre. James Ellies of Huntliewood, James Wilkieson, James Edgar.

,, 19. Francis Bryden and Margaret Bower in Easterlanglie, a.d.n. Margaret Bryden ; w. Robert Bunzie, Robert Hislope in Melrose.

,, ,, James Mercer and Jennet Bunzie in Newsteid, a.s.n. Robert Mercer ; w. Robert Bunzie, Robert Hislope.

1701.

Jan. 21. George Darling and —— in Blainslie, ——; w. ——.

,,   26. John Sibbald and Beatrix Rutherfoord in Eildon, a.s.n. William Sibbald ; w. Andrew Rennaldson, Robert Hislope.

,,   28. Lieutennant Thomas Fairbairn and Grizell Karr, a.d.n. Christian Fairbairn ; w. Robert Fisher, Mr. Thomas Rutherfoord.

Feb. 9. Richard Bower and Jean Paterson in Eildon, a.s.n. Nicoll Bower ; w. Nicoll Bower, John Glendinning, there.

,,   ,, Alexr. Fisher and Mary Simson, baptised at Earlstoun, a.d.n. —— Fisher ; w. Mr. Thomas Rutherfurd, George Pringle.

,,   27. Walter Haliburton and Margaret Davidson in Galtonside, twins n. John and Walter Haliburtons ; w. Wm. Hoy, Thomas Haliburton, there.

Mar. 16. Wm. Ellies and Agnes Murray in Melrose, a.d.n. Isabell Ellies ; w. James Ellies, elder and younger, there.

,,   29. John Mercer and Mary Mein in Newsteid, a.d.n. Jennet Mercer ; w. John Marchell, Andrew Aiton in Melrose.

April 6. James Simson and Christian Penman in Melrose, a.s.n. Alexander Simson ; w. Thomas Walker, Alexr. Bell, there.

,,   ,, John Haliwall and Christian Dinnand in Galtonside, a.d.n. Jennet Haliwall ; w. Thomas Haliwall, John Dinnand, there.

,,   ,, Richard Robson and Jennet Pringle in Blainslie, a.d.n. Elisabeth Robson ; w. John Wallace, Thomas Laidlaw, there.

,,   13. Robert Paterson and Helen Muirhead in Sorrowlesfield, a.d.n. Helen Paterson ; w. Robert Hislop and Mr. Andrew Paterson.

,,   ,, John and Jennet Mabons in Melrose, a.d.n. Margaret Mabon ; w. Robert Hervie, Charles Blaikie, there.

,,   ,, John Martine and Elisabeth Wood in Melrose, a.s.n. Andrew Martin ; w. Andrew Martine, John Mabon, there.

,,   ,, Robert Pride and Jean Horn in Whitlaw, a.s.n. Thomas Pride ; w. Thomas Hardie, George Darling.

,,   24. Mungo Purvis and Margaret Ellies in Melrose, —— Purvis ; w. James Ellies, elder and younger, there.

,,   30. John Thynne and Agnes Milne in Blainslie, a.s.n. John Thynne ; w. Thomas Laidlaw, John Wallace, there.

,,   ,, Thomas Litle and Margaret Darling in Blainslie, a.d.n. Jennet Litle ; same witnesses.

May 11. James Mar and Alison Hog in Galtonside, a.s.n. Thomas Mar ; w. Andrew Mar, Thomas Bowstone and Wm. Hoy, there.

,,   ,, Robert Bunzie and Isabel Bowie in Melrose, a.d.n. Isabell Bunzie ; w. James Bowie, John Bunzie.

June 1. Nicoll Mercer and Agnes Fisher in Darnick, a.s.n. Andrew Mercer ; w. Andrew Mercer, James Fisher, there.

,,   ,, Thomas Walker and Jean Blaikie in Melrose, a.d.n. Christian Walker ; w. James Simpson, Charles Blaikie, there.

,,   ,, Mr. Alexr. Grey of Delduff, and Elizabeth Porteous, for present living in Westhouses, a.s.n. Alexander Grey ; w. Hugh Cairncroce, younger of Hilslope, Mr. Hugh Grey.

,,   29. Wm. Martine and Isabell Myles in Galtonside, a.s.n. Thomas Martine ; w. Thomas Martine, James Myles, there.

,,   ,, John Gibson and Elizabeth Philip in Melrose, a.s.n. John Gibson ; w. Wm. Mein, Robert Philip.

July 2. John Wallace and Elspeth Marjoriebanks in Blainslie, a.d.n. —— Wallace ; w. Thomas Laidlaw, Thomas Darling, there.

,,   6. Thomas Bowstone and Helen Cairncroce in Galtonside, a.d.n. Helen Bowstone ; w. John Cairncroce, John Barton.

,,   14. Wm. Vair and —— in Newtoun, a.s.n. Thomas Vair ; w. Mungo and Nicoll Milnes there.

,,   ,, Thomas and —— Ingles in Melrose, a.d.n. Mary Inglis ; w. Patrick Lukup, Robert Hislop, there.

,,   20. George Brown and Isabell Laing in Blainslie, a.s.n. William Brown ; w. James Stirling, Wm. Thynne, there.

1701.

Aug. 24. Thomas Haliburton and Margaret Black in Galtonside, a.d.n. Isabell Haliburton ; w. James Mar, Walter Haliburton, there.

Nov. 23. David Brown and Isabell Williamson in Buckholme, a.s.n. David Brown ; w. George Chisholme, Thomas Brown.

  „   „ Robert Walker and Elizabeth Bennet in Danieltoun, a.d.n. Jean Walker ; w. James Bowie, James Oliver.

  „   30. Robert Hervie and Helen Manderson in Melrose, a.d.n. Helen Hervie ; w. John Mabon, Robert Hislop, there.

Dec. 11. Andrew Mercer and Margaret Hervie in Westerlanglie, a.s.n. Andrew Mercer ; w. John and Wm. Mercers.

  „   31. George Hoy and Jennet Redpath in Galtonside, twins n. Alison and Agnes Hoys ; w. John and Wm. Hoys there.

  „   „ Robert Philip and Margaret Sclater in Galtonside, a.s.n. Robert Philip ; w. Robert and John Bowstones there.

1702.

Jan. 13. James Sterling and Margaret Sommervail in Blainslie, a.s.n. John Sterling ; w. John Sterling, John Sommervail.

  „   „ James Mein and Elisabeth Hiton in Newtoun, a.s.n. James Mein ; w. John Riddell, Nicoll Cochrane, there.

  „   31. James Rennaldson and Isabell Leadhouse in Darnick, a.d.n. Jennet Rennaldson ; w. John Mercer, Wm. Rennaldson, there.

Feb. 7. Andrew Dauson and Margaret Penman in Melrose, a.s.n. James Dauson ; w. James Blaikie, Robert Penman, there.

  „   8. John Drummond and Alison Mein in Darnick, a.d.n. Elisabeth Drummond ; w. Alexr. and Richard Meins.

  „   „ James Bowstone and Margaret Chisholme in Galtonside, a.d.n. Alisone Bowstone ; w. James and Andro Mars there.

  „   „ John Sclater and Agnes Mein in Eildon, a.d.n. Isabell Sclater ; w. Wm. and John Sibbalds there.

  „   15. Walter Tait and Alison Niell in Darnick, a.s.n. William Tait ; w. John Ushar, Wm. Tait.

  „   „ Wm. and Margaret Meins in Newsteid, a.d.n. Margaret Mein ; w. John Mercer, James Mein.

  „   22. Thomas Scott and Jean Friar in Melrose, a.d.n. Barbara Scott ; w. James Blaikie, James Hunter, there.

  „   24. Thomas Laidlaw and Helen Darling in Blainslie, a.d.n. Katharin Laidlaw ; w. Edward Darling, John Moffet, there.

  „   „ James Steell and Elisabeth Wilson in Calfhill, a.s.n. James Steell ; w. James Laidlaw, John Pearson.

Mar. 1. Andrew Drummond and Mary Brown in Darnick, a.s.n. William Drummond ; w. John Drummond, John Hiton, there.

  „   12. Wm. Milne and Agnes Sclater in Eildon, a.s.n. Thomas Milne ; w. Alexr. Mein, John Milne, there.

  „   „ Andrew Haliday and Jennet Bain in Eildon, a.d.n. Mary Haliday ; w. Wm. Sibbald, James Hunter.

  „   „ Wm. Chisholme and Isabell Usher in Darnick, a.s.n. Andrew Chisholme ; w. John Usher, Robert Bunzie.

April 7. John Sclater and Isabell Litle in Blainslie, a.s.n. William Sclater ; w. James Stirling, George Darling, there.

  „   „ John Steell and Isabell Thomson in Blainslie, a.s.n. John Steell ; same witnesses.

  „   „ John Thurbrand and Elizabeth Forsyth in Longshaw, a.s.n. Robert Thurbrand ; same witnesses.

  „   12. Alexr. Layall and Mary Bower in Melrose, a.s.n. Thomas Layall ; w. James Blaikie, James Hunter.

  „   19. Wm. and Isabell Hoys in Galtonside, a.s.n. George Hoy ; w. James Hoy, Alexr. Knox, there.

  „   „ James Blaikie and Margaret Turnbull in Melrose, a.s.n. Robert Blaikie ; w. James Hunter, Mr. Andrew Patersone.

  „   26. John Bartleman and Mary Bunzie in Newsteid, a.d.n. Isabell Bartleman ; w. Robert Bunzie, Robert Hislope.

1702.

May 13. Thomas Martine and Mary Young in Danieltoun, a.s.n. —— Martine ; w. James and Andrew Patersons there.

,, 5. William Nicolson, baillie, and Lilias Pringle in Melrose, a.s.n. Thomas Nicolson ; w. James Ellies of Huntliewood, James Wilkieson.

,, 10. Thomas Gardner and Mary Scott in Melrose, a.d.n. Jean Gardner ; w. David and Alexr. Cooks there.

,, 17. John Moffet and Helen Liderdale in Ouplaw, a.s.n. James Moffet, bap. at Stow ; w. Archibald and James Moffets.

,, 24. James Grey and Margaret Simson in Melrose, a.d.n. Margaret Grey ; w. James and James Bowies there.

June 7. James Bowie and Marion Bell in Melrose, a.d.n. Anna Bowie ; w. James Hunter, Robert Bunzie and Alexr. Bell, there.

,, 21. James Penman and Agnes Thomson in Melrose, a.s.n. William Penman ; w. James Blaikie, Robert Hervie, there.

July 5. Wm. Bower and Margaret Mercer in Melrose, a.d.n. Elisabeth Bower ; w. James Wallace, Wm. Brown, there.

,, 9. James Richardson and Isabell Grey in Darnick, a.d.n. Elisabeth Richardson ; w. John Haliwall, George Wight, there.

,, 28. Mr. Alexr. Grey of Delduff and Elisabeth Porteous, a.s.n. James Grey and a.d.n. Jean Grey ; w. Hugh Cairncroce of Hilslope, Mr. Hugh Grey.

Aug. 9. David Henderson and Christian Milne in Melrose, a.s.n. William Henderson ; w. John Mabon, James Simson, there.

,, 12. Thomas Thynne and Jean Montgomery in Whitlaw, a.s.n. George Thynne ; w. Thomas Hardie, James Thynne.

,, ,, Andrew Ritchie and Margaret —— in Bentmill, a.d.n. Christian Ritchie ; w. Thomas Hardie, younger, Alexr. Horsburgh.

,, 23. Wm. Clerk and Margaret Kedzie in Galtonside, a.d.n. Alison Clerk ; w. James Mar, Andrew Mar, there.

,, ,, George Pringle, boatman, and Margaret Newton, a.d.n. Jennet Pringle ; w. Mr Hugh Grey, Thomas Williamson.

Sept. 6. Mr. Mark Duncanson of Greatlaws and Elisabeth Haliburton, a.d.n. Margaret Duncanson ; w. John Haliburton, younger, of Muirhouslaw, John Duncanson, James Bowie and Mr. Andrew Paterson.

,, ,, Nicoll Milne and Christian Blaikie in Melrose, a.d.n. Christian Milne ; w. Charles Blaikie, John Coat.

,, 27. Robert Scott and Elisabeth Paterson in Danieltoun, a.s.n. James Scott ; w. James Patersone, Robert Hervie.

Oct. 6. John Thynne and Agnes Milne in Blainslie, a.d.n. Christian Thynne ; w. Thomas Laidlaw, Wm. Thynne.

,, ,, Alexr. Dickson and Helen Mercer, a.s.n. James Dickson ; w. Thomas Laidlaw, Wm. Thynne.

,, ,, Adam Lothian and Alison Raith, a.s.n. William Lothian ; w. Thomas Laidlaw, Wm. Thynne.

,, ,, Thomas Litle and Margaret Darling, a.d.n. Mary Litle ; w. John and Wm. Thynnes.

,, ,, Emanuel Man and Margaret Paterson, a.d.n. Jennet Man ; w. John and Wm. Thynnes.

,, 27. James Laidlaw and Agnes Pearson in Ladopmuire, a.s.n. James Laidlaw ; w. Thomas Laidlaw, Thomas Darling.

Nov. 8. James Bowie and Isabell Jacque in Melrose, a.s.n. Thomas Bowie ; w. James Bowie, Robert Bunzie, there.

,, 15. John Moodie and Isabell Mercer in Darnick, a.s.n. William Moodie and a.d.n. Isabell Moodie ; w. William Chisholme, William Rennaldson, there.

Dec. 22. Thomas Fairbairn of Broadwoodshiell and Grizell Karr, a.s.n. Thomas Fairbairn ; w. Wm. Karr, Thomas Laidlaw.

,, ,, Wm. Darling and Isabell Moffet in Blainslie, a.s.n. Andrew Darling ; w. Thomas Turner, Thomas Laidlaw.

1702.

Dec. 22. Thomas Turner and Alison Murray in Mosshouses, a.s.n. George
Turner ; w. Wm. Darling, Thomas Laidlaw.

,, ,, John Notman and Margaret Irwin in Kedzlidoors, a.s.n. Alexander
Notman ; w. Thomas Laidlaw, Thomas Turner.

,, ,, John Turner and Agnes Mercer in Colmsliehill, a.d.n. Jean Turner ;
w. John Moodie, Thomas Turner.

,, ,, Thomas Laidlaw and Eupham Matthie in Longshaw Milne, a.d.n.
Elisabeth Laidlaw ; w. Thomas Turner, Thomas Laidlaw.

,, 27. John Shiell and Isabell Purvis in Melrose, a.d.n. Isabell Shiell ; w.
George Shiell, Mungo Purvis.

1703

Jan. 10. Henry Cochran and Jennet Riddell in Newtoun, a.d.n. Jennet
Cochran ; w. James Mein, James Laidlaw.

,, ,, James Laidlaw and Christian Milne in Newtoun, a.d.n. Margaret
Laidlaw ; w. John Milne, Henry Cochran.

,, 17. Andrew Turnbull and Elisabeth Sclater in Bridgend, a.s.n. Andrew
Turnbull ; w. James Blaikie, Robert Hislop.

,, 31. John Mabon and Jennet Mabon in Melrose, a.s.n. Thomas Mabon ;
w. Robert Hervie, Charles Blaikie.

Feb. 7. George Mercer and Jean Marre in Darnick, a.d.n. Isabell Mercer ;
w. Andrew Rennaldson, John Usher.

,, 11. James Fisher of Bearfauld and Margaret Karr, a.s.n. Andrew
Fisher ; w. Andrew Aiton, David Rutherfoord.

,, 21. Andrew Mercer and Margaret Hervie in Westerlanglie, a.d.n.
Margaret Mercer, baptized at Gallashiells ; w. ——.

,, 28. John Milne and Isabell Milne in Newtoun, a.s.n. Mungo Milne ; w.
John Milne, Nicoll Cochran.

Mar. 14. William Dickson and Margaret Kylle in Darnick, a.s.n. James
Dickson ; w. John Mercer, John Drummond.

,, ,, Thomas Walker and Jean Blaikie in Melrose, a.s.n. Thomas Walker ;
w. Charles Blaikie, Nicoll Milne.

,, 31. John Haitlie and Jennet Watson in Mosshouses, a.d.n. Elisabeth
Haitlie ; w. John Brown, Wm. Romainhouse.

,, ,, John Wallace and Elspeth Marjoribanks in Blainslie, a.s.n. John
Wallace ; w. James Grieve, Andrew Mein.

,, ,, Wm. Swanstoun and Christian Brotherstone in Blainslie, a.s.n.
William Swanstoun ; w. James Grieve, Andrew Mein.

,, ,, Robert Wadderston in Housbyre and Jennet Duncan, a.s.n. Thomas
Wadderston ; w. James Grieve, Andrew Mein.

April 11. Alexr. Mein and Jennet Milne in Eildon, a.d.n. Agnes Mein, w.
Richard Mein, John Milne, there.

,, ,, James Fisher and Isabell Moss in Darnick, a.s.n. John Fisher ;
w. John Mercer, Andrew Moss, there.

,, 18. Andrew Mein and Agnes Mein in Newsteid, a.d.n. Elisabeth Mein ;
w. Wm. Mein, Wm. Hopkirk.

,, ,, George Grahamslie and Jennet Alley in Melrose, a.d.n. Christian
Grahamslie ; w. John Mercer, James Hunter.

,, ,, Thomas Cochran and Isabell Milne in Newtoun, a.s.n. Thomas
Cochran ; w. John Milne, Nicoll Cochran.

May. 9. William Karr and Elisabeth Brown in Newtoun, a.s.n. William Karr ;
w. John Riddell, Nicoll Cochran.

,, ,, Wm. Darling and Margaret Mattheson in Westhouses, a.d.n.
Margaret Darling ; w. Thomas Mattheson, James Hunter.

,, 16. John Hislop and Christian Cruikshank in Longhaugh, a.d.n. Isabell
Hislop ; w. George Chisholme, Andrew Martine.

,, ,, John Blaikie and Marion Lythgow in Housbyre ; a.d.n. Alison
Blaikie ; w. Thomas Turner, Andrew Lythgow.

,, ,, James Dauson and Agnes Mein in Eildon, a.s.n. Andrew Dauson ;
w. Alexr. Mein, John Sibbald.

,, ,, William Turner and Jennet Wright in Galtonside, a.d.n Isabell
Turner ; w. James Marre, Robert Bowstone.

1703.

May 18. Alexr. Thomson in Longshaw and Margaret Hall, a.s.n. Alexander Thomson ; w. John Moodie, Robert Moffet.

„ „ John Moodie and Elisabeth Moffet in Threepwood, a.d.n. —— Moodie ; w. Alexr. Thomson, John Brown.

„ „ John Brown and Jennet Owens in Threepwood, a.d.n. —— Brown ; w. John Moodie, Alexr. Thomson.

„ 23. Wm. Hunter in Netherbarns deceased, and Elisabeth Findlator, now in Melrose, a.s.n. William Hunter, presented by John Hunter in Rink ; w. Mr. Mark Duncanson of Greatlaws, James Hunter in Netherbarns.

June 13. Alexr. Fisher of Claikmae and Mary Simson, a.s.n. James Fisher, baptized at Earlstoun ; w. George Pringle, John Shiell, there.

„ 20. James Wallace and Agnes Hall in Melrose, a.d.n. Agnes Wallace ; w. John Mabon, Charles Blaikie.

July 2. James Sandilands and —— in Hagburn, a.s.n. Walter Sandilands ; w. George Chisholme, Thomas Thynne.

„ 4. John Grierson and Jean Ramsey in Darnick, a.d.n. Jennet Grierson ; w. John Mercer, James Usher.

„ „ Wm. Wight and Agnes Atchison in Sorrowlesfield, a.d.n. Isabell Wight ; w. James Atchison, Thomas Mattheson.

„ 6. William Nicolsone, bailie, and Lilias Pringle, a.s.n. George Nicolson ; w. ——.

„ 25. Thomas Martine and Jennet Runchiman in Galtonside, a.d.n. Jennet Martine ; w. Wm. Martine, John Sommervaill.

Aug. 15. James Hunter and Margaret Edgar in Melrose a.s.n. William Hunter ; w. James and Alexr. Edgars.

„ „ James Bowie and Marion Bell in Melrose, a.d.n. Helen Bowie ; w. James Hunter, Alexr. Bell.

„ 31. James Turner and Jean Hunter in Hagburn, a.s.n. Thomas Turner ; w. Thomas Turner, Wm. Welch.

„ „ Wm. Welch and Agnes Dewar in Colmeslie, —— Welch , w. Thomas and James Turners.

Sept. 2. John Mercer and Mary Mein in Newsteid, —— Mercer ; w. John and Wm. Meins.

„ 12. Robert Mein and Beatrice Hunter in Newsteid, a.s.n. William Mein ; w. Robert Eliot, John Mein.

„ 19. George Loury and Margaret Gill in Danieltoun, a.s.n. William Loury ; w. Wm. Gill, Robert Loury.

Oct. 10. Thomas Lookup and Agnes Milner in Melrose, a.d.n. Isabell Lookup ; w. Patrick and Wm. Lookups.

„ 17. John Gibson and Elspeth Philip in Melrose, a.s.n. Henry Gibson ; w. Henry Gibson, Robert Philp.

„ „ John Bartleman and Mary Bunzie in Newsteid, a.s.n. Andrew Bartleman ; w. James Hunter, James Ellies.

„ „ James Ellies and Isabell Usher in Melrose, a.d.n. Margaret Ellies ; w. James Hunter, John Bartleman.

„ 26. Richard Robson and Jennet Pringle in Blainslie, a.s.n. William Robson ; w. Thomas Laidlaw, Thomas Darling.

„ „ William Corser and Margaret Hardie, a.d.n. Anne Corser ; w. Thomas Laidlaw, Thomas Darling.

„ 31. Robert Bunzie and Isabell Bowie in Melrose, a.d.n. Marion Bunzie ; w. Andrew Lythgow, Thomas Williamson.

„ „ James Bowstone and Margaret Chisholme in Galtonside, a.s.n. Alexander Bowstone ; w. James and Andrew Marres.

Nov. 7. Robert Pringle and Jennet Mein in Newsteid, a.d.n. Violet Pringle ; w. George and James Pringles.

„ „ Andrew Haliday and Jennet Bain in Eildon, a.s.n. William Haliday ; w. John Sibbald, Nicoll Bower, there.

Dec. 5. Robert Hervie and Helen Manderson in Melrose, a.d.n. Jennet Hervie ; w. John Mabon, Robert Scott.

1703.
Dec. 14. James Fisher of Beartaulds and Margaret Karre, twins n. Marrion and Elisabeth Fishers ; w. ——.

,, 19. Henry Gibson and Isabell Fisher in Melrose, a.s.n. Henry Gibson ; w. William Chisholme, James Fisher.

,, 26. John Milne and Helen Glendinning in Eildon, a.d.n. Isabell Milne ; w. Thomas Cochran, Alexr. Mein.

,, 30 .James Stirling and Margaret Sommervaill in St. Leonards, a.d.n. Elisabeth Stirling ; w. John and Wm. Stirlings.

,, ,, George Brown and Isabell Laing in Blainslie, a.d.n. Marion Brown ; w. John and Wm. Stirlings.

,, ,, —— in Lauder ; w. John and Wm. Stirlings.

1704.
Jan. 2. Andrew Moss and Margaret Waugh in Darnick, a.d.n. Helen Moss ; w. James Fisher, James Waugh.

,, ,, Walter Tait and Alison Neill in Darnick, a.d.n. Elisabeth Tait ; w. John Usher, Hugh Bowstone.

,, ,, James Wallace and Anne Waugh in Melrose, a.d.n. Helen Wallace ; w. Andrew Paterson, Wm. Gill.

,, 16. Thomas Milne and Jennet Milne in Newtoun, a.d.n. Jennet Milne ; w. Nicoll Cochran, Mr. Andrew Patersone.

,, ,, Andrew Drummond and Mary Brown in Darnick, a.s.n. George Drummond ; w. John Drummond, John Hitoun.

,, ,, James White and Isabell Lumsden in Newsteid, a.d.n. Agnes White ; w. Robert Eliot, Thomas Milne.

,, 23. James Rennaldson and Isabell Leidhouse in Darnick, a.s.n. George Rennaldson ; w. John Mercer, Robert Hislop.

,, ,, John Mercer and Helen Sibbald in Darnick, a.s.n. George Mercer ; w. James Rennaldson, Robert Hislop.

Feb. 13. John Sibbald and Beatrice Rutherfoord in Eildon, a.s.n. Andrew Sibbald ; w. John Milne, Wm. Sibbald.

,, ,, James Mein and Jennet Coat in Newsteid, a.s.n. Robert Mein ; w. Andrew Mein, John Sibbald.

,, 17. John Steill and Isabell Thomson in Blainslie, a.d.n. Agnes Steill ; w. Thomas Laidlaw, George Darling.

,, ,, George Turner and Marion Pringle in Colmsliehill, a.d.n. Elisabeth Turner ; w. Thomas Laidlaw, Thomas Thynne.

,, 20. Robert Walker and Elspeth Bennet in Melrose, a.d.n. Mary Walker ; w. James Hunter, Nicoll Cochran.

Mar. 5. John Martine and Elisabeth Wood in Melrose, a.s.n. Robert Martine ; w. Andrew Martine, Robert Hislop.

,, ,, Wm. Laidlaw and Margaret Fouler in Newtoun, a.d.n. Margaret Laidlaw ; w. Andrew Martine, Robert Hislop.

,, ,, James Simson and Christian Penman in Melrose, a.d.n. Isabell Simson ; w. Mr. Andrew Paterson, Robert Hislop.

,, ,, Mungo Purvis and Margaret Ellies in Melrose, —— Purvis ; w. Mr. Andrew Paterson, Robert Hislop.

,, 19. William Ellies and Agnes Murray in Melrose, a.d.n. Agnes Ellies ; w. James Ellies, Thomas Gill.

,, ,, Thomas Gill and Isabell Ellies in Melrose, a.s.n. John Gill ; w. James and Wm. Ellies.

,, ,, Thomas Scott and Jean Frier in Melrose, a.s.n. Adam Scott ; w. Mr. Andrew Paterson, Robert Hislop.

,, 20. Thomas Laidlaw and Eupham Matthie in Longshaw milne, a.d.n. Margaret Laidlaw ; w. Thomas Turner, Thomas Laidlaw.

,, ,, John Thurbrand and Elisabeth Forsyth in Longshaw milne, a.s.n. Andrew Thurbrand ; w. Thomas Turner, Thomas Laidlaw.

April 2. John Scott and Jennet Robison in Laudergateside, a.d.n. Francis Scott ; w. George Pringle, Thomas Mattheson.

,, ,, Wm. Milne and Isabell Riddell in Newsteid, a.s.n. William Milne ; w. John Riddell, Nicoll Milne.

1704.

April 2. Robert Scott and Elisabeth Patersone in Danieltoun, a.d.n. **Isabell** Scott ; w. James Paterson, Robert Hervie.

,, 14. Robert Patersone of Old Melrose and Annie Eliot, a.d.n. **Elisabeth** Paterson ; w. Robert Eliot of Midlinn milne, Alexr. Lythgow of Drygrainge, James Ellies of Huntliewood and James Edgar.

,, 16. Robert Wight and Agnes Martine in Darnick, a.d.n. **Isabell Wight** ; w. Stephen Martin, James Blaikie.

,, 30. Thomas Bowston and Helen Cairncroce in Galtonside, a.d.n. **Isabell** Bowston : w. John Cairncroce, James Gardner.

,, ,, Thomas Leithan and Isabell Tait in Galtonside, a.s.n. **John Leithan** ; w. James Leithan, Robert Martin.

,, ,, Thomas Davidson and Isabell Bowston in Galtonside, a.s.n. **Thomas** Davidson ; w. Andrew and James Marres.

May 7. Wm. Martine and Isabell Marr in Galtonside, a.s.n. **William** Martine ; w. Robert Martine, elder and younger, there.

,, 21. James Young and Isabell Bartoun in Galtonside, a.s.n. **James Young** ; w. John and Thomas Bartouns.

,, ,, James Blaikie and Margaret Turnbull in Melrose, a.s.n. **James** Blaikie ; w. Robert Hervie, Mr. Andrew Patersone.

June 4. Wm. Mercer and Mary Dalgleish in Colmsliehill ; a.s.n. **Andrew** Mercer : w. John Mercer, James Usher.

,, 18. Andrew Hownam and Anna Cochran in Darnick, a.s.n. **George** Hownam : w. James Fisher, John Smith.

July 2. James Mein and Jennet Pursill in Newsteid, a.d.n. **Jean Mein** ; w. Andrw Mein, Robert Hislop.

,, ,, Andrew Mein and Elisabeth Richardson in Eildon, a.s.n. **Thomas** Mein ; w. James and Alexr. Meins.

,, 4. Thomas Thynne and Jean Montgomery in Whitlie, a.d.n. **Jean** Thynne ; w. William Turner, David Ballantine.

,, 16. Wm. Hoy and Isabell Hoy in Galtonside, a.s.n. **William Hoy** ; w. James Hoy, Alexr. Knox.

,, ,, Andrew Turnbull and Elisabeth Sclater in Bridgend, a.d.n. **Margaret** Turnbull ; w. James Blaikie, Mr. Andrew Patersone.

,, 23. George Vair and Jennet Drummond in Danieltoun, a.s.n. **George** Vair ; w. Thomas Drummond, George Loury.

,, 30. Walter Scott and Agnes Moffet in Galtonside, a.d.n. **Agnes Scott** ; w. John Bartoun, Robert Scott.

,, ,, Robert Patersone and Helen Muirhead in Hagburn, a.s.n. **Robert** Patersone ; w. Mr. Andrew Patersone, Robert Hislop.

Aug. 13. Thomas Bowstone and Isabell Mabon in Galtonside, a.d.n. **Isabell** Bowstone ; w. Robert Bowstone, John Mabon.

,, 21. Thomas Fairbairn of Broadwoodshiell and Grizell Karr, a.d.n. **Grizell Fairbairn** ; w. Thomas Laidlaw, John Wallace.

Sept. 3. James Hunter and Margaret Edgar in Melrose, a.d.n. **Isabell** Hunter ; w. James Edgar, James Bowie.

,, ,, Wm. Fisher and Agnes Drummond in Galtonside, a.s.n. **William** Fisher ; w. George and James Friers.

,, 19. Wm. Moffet and Isabell Moffet in Threepwood, a.d.n. **Jennet Moffet** ; w. Peter Moffet, John Moodie.

,, ,, Thomas Turner, a.s.n. **Jezreel Turner**, begotten in adultery with Alison Paterson ; w. Peter Moffet, John Moodie.

Oct. 1. James Hoy and Isabell Wright in Galtonside, a.s.n. —— **Hoy** ; w. William Hoy, John Wright.

,, ,, Thomas Thomson and Margaret Thomson in Galtonside, a.s.n. **Thomas Thomson** ; w. George Pringle, Wm. Thomson.

,, ,, George Mein and Isabell Frier in Galtonside, a.s.n. **Robert Mein** ; w. Wm. Mein, Robert Frier.

,, 8. John Mercer and Mary Mein in Newsteid, a.d.n. **Mary Mercer** ; w. James and William Meins.

,, ,, John Chisholme and Margaret Laing, a.d.n. **Margaret Chisholme** ; w. James and Joseph Laings.

1704.

Oct. 10. John Moffet and Helen Lidderdale in Ouplaw, twins n. Adam and Robert Moffet ; w. Edward Lythgow and John Moodie.

,, ,, Edward Lythgow and Margaret Hall in Newhouses, a.d.n. Mary Lythgow ; w. John Moodie, John Moffet.

,, 15. Thomas Stenhouse and Helen Sibbald in Newtoun, a.s.n. Thomas Stenhouse ; w. Wm. Karr, Henry Gibson.

,, 22. Thomas Gardner and Mary Scott in Melrose, a.s.n. James Gardner ; w. Robert Hislope, Thomas Scott.

,, 29. Nicoll Milne and Christian Blaikie in Melrose, a.d.n. Christian Milne ; w. Thomas Gardner, Robert Hislop.

,, ,, Walter Bryden and Margaret Mercer, a.d.n. Elizabeth Bryden, by fornication ; w. Thomas Gardner, Nicoll Milne.

,, ,, George Pringle and Ruth Clunie in Redpath, a.s.n. George Pringle ; w. James Pringle, Nicoll Milne.

Nov. 1. Robert Bowstone and Jennet Russell in Galtonside, a.s.n. Robert Bowstone ; w. James Marre, Thomas Bowstone.

,, 5. William Bell and Helen Haithe in Galtonsyde, a.d.n. Agnes Bell ; w. James and Andrew Marres.

,, 12. John Gill and Alison King in Newtoun, a.d.n. Jennet Gill ; w. John Milne, Nicoll Cochran.

,, 19. Nicoll Mercer and Mary Rennaldson in Bridgend, a.d.n. Jennet Mercer ; w. James Blaikie, David Speeding.

,, 23. James Grieve and Jean Allan in Blainslie, —— Grieve ; w.——.

,, ,, James Hitoun and —— in Hawicksheill, —— Hitoun ; w. ——.

,, 26. Alexr. Lyall and Margaret Bower in Melrose, a.d.n. Anne Lyall ; w. John Mabon, James Blaikie.

,, ,, William Gill and Margaret Turnbull in Danieltoun, a.s.n. Robert Gill ; w. James and Andro Patersones.

Dec. 5. James Laidlaw and Agnes Pearson in Ladopmuire, —— Laidlaw ; w. ——.

,, 10. John Bunzie and Marion Mein in Eildon, a.d.n. Isabell Bunzie ; w. James Hunter, John Sibbald.

,, ,, Nicoll Mercer and Margaret Drummond in Darnick, a.d.n. Isabell Mercer ; w. James Fisher, John Mercer.

,, 31. Wm. Milne and Agnes Sclater in Eildon, a.d.n. Isabell Milne ; w. James Hunter, Robert Fairbairn.

1705.

Jan. 10. Wm. Nicolson, baillie, and Lilias Pringle, a.d.n. Elisabeth Nicolson ; w. Mr. John Graham, James Hunter, Mr. Andrew Patersone.

,, 14. James Karr and Isabell Allan in Colmslie, —— Karr ; w. Robert Hislope, Andrew Martine.

,, 18. James Turner and Jean Hunter in Hagburn, —— Turner ; w. Thomas Turner, John Hislop.

,, ,, John Hislop and Christian Cruickshanks in Colmslie, —— Hislop ; w. Thomas and James Turners.

,, 21. George Pringle and Margaret Newton, —— Pringle ; w. Robert Hislop, Andrew Martine.

Feb. 4. James Mein and Elizabeth Hitoun in Newton, a.s.n. Andrew Mein ; w. Nicoll Cochran, John Milne.

Mar. 11. James Dauson and Agnes Mein in Eildon, a.d.n. Alison Dauson ; w. Alexr. Mein, John Sibbald.

April 8. Wm. Chisholme and Isabell Usher in Darnick, a.d.n. Isabell Chisholme ; w. James Blaikie, James Patersone.

,, ,, Robert Blaikie and Isabell Robertson in Darnick, a.d.n. Isabell Blaikie ; w. James Blaikie, Thomas Laidlaw.

,, 11. Thomas Litle and Margaret Darling in Blainslie, a.d.n. Grizell Litle ; w. Thomas Laidlaw, John Wallace.

,, 15. John Mabon and Jennet Mabon in Melrose, a.d.n. Margaret Mabon ; w. Robert Hervie, John Martine.

,, ,, Thomas Wight and Jennet Sword in Galtonside, a.s.n. William Wight ; w. James Marre, Alexr. Knox.

1705.

April 22. John Drummond and Jennet Dickson in Galtonside, a.d.n. Isabell Drummond ; w. James Hunter, James Bowie.

,, ,, James Mattheson and Jennet Haliwell in Galtonside, a.d.n. Margaret Mattheson ; w. John Dinnand, John Frier.

May 6. Thomas Ormiston and Jennet Pringle in Melrose, a.d.n. Anne Ormiston ; w. David Cook, Alexr. Lyall.

,, 9. Andrew Hog and Katherin Lees in Williamlaw, a.s.n. Robert Hog ; w. Thomas Laidlaw, John Wallace.

,, ,, —— Kirkhop and —— in Blainslie, a.d.n. —— Kirkhop ; w. Thomas Laidlaw, John Wallace.

,, ,, John Darling and Isabell Lythgow in Blainslie, a.d.n. —— Darling ; w. John Wallace, Thomas Laidlaw.

June 10. Robert Wadderston and Jennet Duncan in Housbyre, a.s.n. William Wadderston ; w. John Brown, Thomas Black.

,, 14. William Rennaldson and Agnes Mein in Newsteid, a.d.n. Margaret Rennaldson ; w. Andrew Rennaldson, Wm. Mein.

,, 24. William Bower and Margaret Mercer in Melrose, a.s.n. James Bower ; w. James Mercer, Wm. Brown.

,, ,, George Drummond and Jennet M'Nair in Darnick, a.s.n. Walter Drummond ; w. Wm. Chisholme, Andrew Drummond.

July 8. James Mercer and Margaret Vair in Darnick, a.s.n. George Mercer ; w. George Mercer, Wm. Chisholme.

,, ,, John Henderson and Christian Mein, a.s.n. Robert Henderson, by fornication ; w. James Marre, Robert Hislop.

,, ,, Robert Hervie and Helen Manderson in Melrose, a.d.n. Isabell Hervie ; w. John Mabon, Robert Scott.

,, 15. John Brown and Jennet Owens in Colmsliehill, a.d.n. Margaret Brown ; w. George Turner, Andrew Owens.

Aug. 5. Robert Mein and Beatrice Hunter in Newsteid, a.d.n. Margaret Mein ; w. Robert Elliot, James Hunter.

,, ,, George Romainhouse and Alison Fogo in Blainslie, a.d.n. Agnes Romainhouse ; w. James Grieve, James Scott.

,, ,, Andrew Mein and Agnes Mein in Newsteid, a.d.n. Agnes Mein ; w. Robert Eliot, Wm. Mein.

,, ,, Wm. Mertoun, deceased, and Jennet Hislop, a.d.n. Isabell Mertoun, presented by John Wilson ; w. Robert and Andrew Meins.

,, 7. Thomas Thynne and Jean Montgomery in Whitlie, a.s.n. George Thynne ; w. George Fraiter, Adam Ballantine.

,, 9. James Lythgow of Drygrainge and Elisabeth Lauder, a.s.n. James Lythgow ; w. Mr. James Daes of Coldenknows, John Brown of Park, James Ellies of Huntliwood and Andrew Lythgow.

,, 26. James Bowie and Marion Bell in Melrose, a.s.n. John Bowie ; w. James Hunter, Alexr. Bell.

Sept. 2. John Milne and Isabell Milne in Newtoun, a.s.n. Nicoll Milne ; w. John Milne, Nicoll Cochrane.

,, 9. Henry Cochrane and Jennet Riddell in Newtoun, —— Cochrane ; w. John Riddell, John Milne.

,, 23. George Frier and Elisabeth Tweedie in Galtonside, a.s.n. Alexander Frier ; w. John Frier, James Clerk.

,, ,, James Rennaldson and Isabell Leidhouse in Darnick, a.d.n. Isabell Rennaldson ; w. John Mercer, Wm. Rennaldson.

,, ,, James Kyll and Isabell Sword in Westhouses boathouse, a.s.n. John Kyll ; w. John and James Fiddess.

,, 28. Adam Ballantine and Katharin Pringle, a.s.n. George Ballantine ; w. David Ballantine, Wm. Firsyth.

Oct. 14. William Darling and Alison Lees in Colmslie, a.d.n. Jennet Darling ; w. James Laidlaw, James Law.

,, ,, James Carribbes and——Crosbie in Sorrowlessfield, a.s.n. John Carribbes ; w. James Laidlaw, Wm. Darling.

,, 24. Richard Sclater and Alison Dauson in Blainslie, a.s.n. —— Sclater ; w. Thomas Laidlaw, John Wallace.

1705.

Oct. 24. **Andrew Mein** and Jennet Gray in Blainslie, —— Mein ; w. Thomas Laidlaw, John Wallace.

,, 28. **Robert Philip** and Margaret Sclater in Galtonside, a.s.n. Thomas Philip ; w. Robert and John Bowstones.

,, ,, **William Darling** and Margaret Mattheson in Westhouses, a.s.n. Thomas Darling ; w. Thomas Mattheson, elder and younger.

,, ,, **James Fisher** and Isabell Moss in Darnick, a.s.n. James Fisher ; w. James Usher, John Mercer.

Nov. 4. **John Grierson** and Jean Ramsey in Darnick, a.d.n. Katharin Grierson ; w. John Mercer, James Usher.

Dec. 2. **John Mercer** and Helen Sibbald in Darnick, a.s.n. William Mercer ; w. John Sibbald, Charles Mercer.

,, ,, **Robert Pringle** and Jennet Mein in Newsteid, a.s.n. Robert Pringle ; w. John Sibbald, Charles Mercer.

,, 9. **William Mein** and Margaret Mein in Eildon, a.s.n. Andrew Mein ; w. Richard Mein, John Bunzie.

,, ,, **Wm. Milne** and Isabell Riddell in Newsteid, a.s.n. Robert Milne ; w. John and Andrew Riddells.

,, 16. **Robert Bowstone** and Jennet Russell in Galtonside, a.d.n. Mary Bowstone ; w. James Marre, Wm. Hoy, presented by Thomas Bowstone in the father's absence.

,, 23. **Andrew Drummond** and Mary Brown in Darnick, a.s.n. Andrew Drummond ; w. John Mercer, James Usher.

,, 30. **Andrew Mercer** and Margaret Hervie in Westerlanglie, a.s.n. Thomas Mercer ; w. James Hunter, John Mercer.

1706.

Jan. 13. **John Moodie** and Isabell Mercer in Darnick, a.d.n. Jennet Moodie ; w. Wm. Chisholme, John Usher.

,, ,, **Robert Bunzie** and Isabell Bowie in Melrose, a.d.n. Margaret Bunzie ; w. James Hunter, Robert Hislop.

,, ,, **Robert Fairbairn** and Alison Sclater in Eildon, a.s.n. John Fairbairn ; w. John Sibbald, Robert Hislop.

,, ,, **George Grahamslie** and Jennet Allie in Melrose, a.d.n. Elizabeth Grahamslie ; w. James Hunter, James Blaikie.

,, 20. **Robert Bunzie** and Marion Hopkirk in Newsteid, a.s.n. William Bunzie ; w. Wm. Hopkirk, Robert Hislop.

,, 22. **Thomas Laidlaw** and Eupham Matthie in Longshaw Milne, a.s.n. Andrew Laidlaw ; w. John Turner, Wm. Darling.

,, 27. **George Loury** and Margaret Gill in Danieltoun, a.s.n. Robert Loury ; w. James and Andrew Patersones.

Feb. 10. **David Henderson** and Christian Milne in Melrose, a.d.n. Jennet Henderson, presented by Thomas Gill in the father's absence ; w. John Maban, Robert Wallace.

,, ,, **Thomas Learmont** and Marion Wilson in Langhaugh, a.s.n. Robert Learmont ; w. Robert Wilson, Robert Hislop.

,, ,, **James Wight** and Agnes Hardie in Drygrainge, a.d.n. Elisabeth Wight ; w. James Atchison, Robert Wadderstone.

,, 12. **John Haitlie** and Jennet Watson in Mosshouses, a.s.n. William Haitlie ; w. Thomas Hardie, Adam Shiell.

Mar. 10. **James Blaikie** and Agnes Hitoun in Danieltoun, a.s.n. John Blaikie ; w. James and Andrew Patersones.

,, 12. **John Wallace** and Elspeth Marjoribanks in Blainslie, a.s.n. John Wallace ; w. Thomas Laidlaw, Edward Darling.

,, 17. **Cornelius Mein** and Isabell Mein in Eildon, a.d.n. Alison Mein ; w. Wm. and Richard Meins.

,, 24. **Thomas Vint** and Elisabeth Fairage, a.s.n. Alexander Vint ; w. James Hunter, Wm. Mein.

,, ,, **Wm. Hoy** and Isabell Hoy in Galtonside, a.d.n. Isabell Hoy ; w. James Marre, Robert Bowstone.

,, ,, **Henry Gibson** and Isabell Fisher in Melrose, a.d.n. Isabell Fisher ; w. John Mabon, John Loury.

1706.

Mar. 25. Thomas Stenhouse and Helen Sibbald in Newtoun, a.s.n. John Stenhouse ; w. John Milne, Nicoll Cochran.

„ 28. John Moodie and Elisabeth Moffat in Threepwood, two daughters n. Jennet and Isabell Moodies : w. Robert and Andrew Moffets.

April 4. William Nicolson, law baillie, and Lilias Pringle in Melrose, a.s.n. Francis Pringle ; w. George Keith, present baillie, James Wilkieson.

„ 7. Wm. Bell and Helen Haitlie in Galtonside, a.d.n. Helen Bell ; w. James Marre, James Blaikie.

„ „ John Bunzie and Isabell Atchison in Melrose. a.d.n. Jennet Bunzie ; w. Mr. Andrew Patersone, John Martine.

„ 9. James Stirling and Margaret Sommervaill in Blainslie, a.s.n. George Stirling ; w. John and William Stirlings.

„ „ James Corser and ——, a.d.n. —— Corser ; w. John Wallace, Thomas Laidlaw.

„ 28. Thomas Leithan and Isabell Tait in Galtonside, a.d.n. Isabell Leithan ; w. Robert Martine, James Leithan.

May 5. James Stodhart and Isabell Moss in Darnick, a.s.n. George Stodhart ; w. Wm. Moss, Robert Scott.

„ „ Robert Scott and Elisabeth Patersone in Danieltoun, a.s.n. Robert Scott ; w. James and Andrew Patersones.

„ „ Andrew Turnbull and Elisabeth Sclater in Bridgend, a.s.n. Robert Turnbull ; w. James Blaikie, Mr. Andrew Patersone.

June 2. George Turner and Marion Pringle in Colmesliehill, a.d.n. Margaret Turner ; w. Thomas Turner, Robert Moffet.

„ 13. Thomas Laidlaw and Helen Darling in Blainslie. a.d.n. Isabell Laidlaw ; John Wallace, James Darling.

„ 30. Richard Fraiter and Isabell Mercer in Darnick, a.s.n. Andrew Fraiter : w. Andrew Mercer, John Martine.

„ 16. William Wilson and Rachell Mitchell in Melrose. a.s.n. Robert Wilson ; w. James Hunter, John Martine.

July 14. John Milne and Helen Glendinning in Eildon, a.s.n. John Milne ; w. James Hunter, Wm. Milne.

„ „ Wm. Brown and Alison Young in Melrose, a.s.n. William Brown ; w. James Blaikie, John Mabon

„ 16. John Gibson and Elspeth Philip in Melrose, a.s.n. Michael Gibson, presented by Henry Gibson in the father's absence ; w. John Mabon, Robert Hervie.

„ 28. Wm. Turner and Jennet Wright in Galtonside, a.s.n. William Turner ; w. James Marr, Wm. Hoy.

Aug. 4. William Gill and Margaret Turnbull in Danieltoun, a.s.n. William Gill ; w. James and Andrew Patersones.

„ „ Andrew Mein and Elisabeth Richardson in Eildon, a.d.n. Elisabeth Mein ; w Alexr. Mein, Wm. Milne.

„ 11. Thomas Bowstone and Isabell Mabon in Galtonside, a.s.n. Robert Bowstone ; w. James and Andrew Bowstone.

„ „ John Hownam and Isabell Patersone in Bridgend, a.s.n. George Hownam : w. Andrew Turnbull, Nicoll Mercer.

„ 12. James Mein and Margaret Cairncroce in Newtoun, a.s.n. William Mein ; w. Nicoll Cochran, John Riddell.

„ 18. James Mein and Jennet Coat in Newsteid, a.d.n. Agnes Mein : w. John and Wm. Meins.

Sept. 1. James Wallace and Anne Waugh in Melrose, a.d.n. Margaret Wallace ; w. Andrew Patersone, Wm. Gill.

„ 29. John Chisholme and Margaret Laing in Newsteid, a.s.n. John Chisholme ; w. Robert Eliot, Wm. Mein.

Oct. 2. John Steill and Isabell Thomsone in Blainslie, a.d.n. Jean Steill ; w. John Wallace, Thomas Laidlaw.

„ 13. Robert Simontoun and Marion Wilson in Drygrainge, a.s.n. John Simontoun : w. Adam and David Ballantines.

„ „ Robert Wallace and Jennet Milne in Melrose. a.s.n. Thomas Wallace ; w. John Mabon, James Wallace.

1706.

Nov. 3. Robert Hervie and Helen Manderson in Melrose, a.s.n. John Hervie ; w. James Blaikie, John Mabon.

Dec. 1. John Bowstone and Isabell Mein in Galtonside, a.s.n. Robert Bowstone ; w. Robert Bowstone, Robert Philip.

,, ,, Thomas Gill and Isabell Ellies in Melrose, a.s.n. George Gill ; w. James Ellies, Wm. Rennaldson.

,, 8. Nicoll Milne and Christian Blaikie in Melrose, a.s.n. James Milne ; w James Blaikie, John Moodie.

,, 22. George Frier and Elisabeth Tweedie in Galtonsyde, a.d.n. Mary Frier ; w. John Frier, Wm. Fisher.

,, 23. James Fisher of Bearfaulds and Margaret Karre, a.d.n. Marion Fisher ; w. Robert Fisher of Easterlanglie, John Mercer.

1707.

Jan. 15. Adam Balantine and Katharin Pringle in Drygrainge, a.d.n. —— Ballantine ; w. Alexr. Fisher, James Marre.

,, 15. John Thurbrand and Elisabeth Forsyth in Langshaw Milne, a.d.n. —— Thurbrand : w. Alexr. Fisher, James Marre.

,, 19. Nicoll Mercer and Mary Rennaldson in Bridgend, a.s.n. William Mercer ; w. Andrew Mercer, Andrew Drummond.

,, 26. Thomas Foster and Elisabeth Hope in Melrose, a.d.n. Elisabeth Foster ; w. Robert Hunter, John Martine.

,, ,, John Martine and Elisabeth Wood in Melrose, a.d.n. Helen Martine ; w. Andrew Martine, elder and younger.

Feb. 2. Robert Bunzie and Alison Bowston in Newsteid, a.s.n. John Bunzie and a.d.n. Jennet Bunzie ; w. James Mercer, Robert Bunzie.

,, 4. Andrew Haliday and Jennet Bain, a.s.n. Thomas Haliday ; w. James Dickson, Thomas Laidlaw.

,, 17. James Lythgow of Drygrainge and Elisabeth Lauder, a.s.n. John Lythgow ; w. James Ellies of Huntliwood, James Lythgow, Mr. Andrew Mein, Mr. Andrew Tait.

,, 23. Thomas Steill and Margaret Eliot in Melrose, a.s.n. William Steill ; w. William Steill, John Martine.

,, ,, Wm. Martine and Isabell Marre in Galtonside, a.d.n. Isabell Martine ; w. James Marr, Robert Martine.

Mar. 2. Thomas Bowstone and Helen Cairncroce in Galtonside, a s.n. Thomas Bowstone ; w. John Bartoun, Thomas Frier.

,, ,, James Hunter and Margaret Edgar in Melrose, a.s.n. Thomas Hunter ; w. James Lythgow, James Bowie.

,, 9. John Hoy and Isabell Bartoun in Galtonside, a.s.n. John Hoy ; w. John and William Hoys there.

,, ,, James Mein and Jennet Pursill in Newsteid, a.s.n. Mark Mein ; w. John Mein, Mark Pursill.

,, 16. Thomas Wight and Jennet Sword in Galtonsyde, a.s.n. John Wight ; w. James Marre, John Martine.

,, ,, William Dickson and Margaret Kyll in Darnick, a.s.n. Thomas Dickson ; w. John Mercer, James Usher.

,, ,, James Thynne and Marion Hunter in Sorrowlessfield, a.s.n. Philip Thynne ; w. John and William Thynnes.

,, 23. Walter Scott and Agnes Moffet in Galtonside, a.s.n. Walter Scott ; w. Thomas Martine, Robert Scott.

,, 30. Henry Gibsone and Isabell Fisher in Melrose, a.d.n. Margaret Gibson ; w. John Mabon, James Hunter.

April 2. James Mein and Elisabeth Hitoun, a.s.n. John Mein ; w. Nicoll Cochrane, Thomas Milne.

,, ,, Thomas Milne and Jennet Milne in Newtoun, a.s.n. Thomas Milne ; w. Nicoll Cochran, James Mein.

,, 6. Thomas Usher and Jennet Murray in Melrose, a.s.n. James Usher ; w. John Usher, James Murray.

,, ,, William Rennaldson and Agnes Mein, a.d.n. Agnes Rennaldson ; w. Robert and Wm. Meins.

1707

April 20. Thomas Thomson and Margaret Thomson in Galtonside, a.s.n. William Thomson ; w. James Marre, John Martine.

,,   27. Wm. Atchison and Margaret Notman in Appletreeleaves, a.s.n. James Atchison ; w. James Atchison, John Martine.

,,   30. James Turner and Jean Hunter in Langshaw, a.d.n. Elisabeth Turner ; w. James Thynne, Robert Moffet.

May   4. Wm. Chisholme and Isabell Ushar in Darnick, a.s.n. John Chisholme ; w. James Usher, Hugh Bowstone.

,,   4. Hugh Bowstone and Sarah Renwick in Darnick, a.d.n. Sarah Bowstone ; w. Wm. Chisholme, Robert Marre.

,,   11. James Young and Isabell Bartoun in Galtonside, a.d.n. Elizabeth Young ; w. John and Thomas Bartouns.

,,   ,, John Sibbald and Beatrice Rutherfoord in Eildon, two daughters n. Isabell and Beatrice ; w. Wm. Sibbald, Thomas Stenhouse, Andrew and Mr. Andrew Patersones.

,,   ,, David Speeding and Elizabeth Govan in Easterlanglie, a.s.n. Robert Speeding ; w. Robert Fisher thereof and James Napier.

,,   18. James Scott and Agnes Blaikie in Blainslie, a.s.n. Alexander Scott ; w. Thomas Laidlaw, George Romainhouse.

,,   ,, George Vair and Jennet Drummond in Danieltoun, a.s.n. Alexander Vair ; w. Thomas Drummond, George Loury.

,,   25. Thomas Stenhouse and Helen Sibbald in Newtoun, a.d.n. Christian Stenhouse ; w. Wm. Cook, Wm. Sibbald.

,,   ,, Wm. Milne and Isobel Riddell in Newsteid, a.s.n. Robert Milne ; w. Thomas Stenhouse, Nicoll Milne.

,,   27. Alexr. Fisher of Claikmae and Mary Simson, a.d.n. Margaret Fisher ; w. Robert Moffet, Edward Darling.

June   8. Alexr. Lyall and Margaret Bower in Melrose, a.s.n. John Lyall ; w. Thomas Gardner, John Martine.

,,   ,, Thomas Gardner and Mary Scott in Melrose, a.d.n. Jean Gardner ; w. Alexr. Lyall, John Martine.

,,   15. James Mercer and Margaret Vair in Darnick, a.s.n. Andrew Mercer ; w. John Mercer, James Usher.

,,   ,, John Milne and Isabell Milne in Newtoun, a.d.n. Alison Milne ; w. John Milne, Nicoll Cochran.

,,   22. James Jameson and Christian Hope in Welmeadow, a.s.n. John Jameson ; w. John Mercer, John Martine.

,,   ,, John Gill and Alison King in Newtoun, a.d.n. Jennet Gill ; w. Nicoll Cochran, Thomas Gill.

,,   ,, Andrew Scott and Margaret Chisholme in Langshaw, a.s.n. James Scott ; w. Nicoll Cochran, Thomas Gill.

July   1. Robert Mein and Jean Weir in Newsteid, a.s.n. John Mein ; w. Nicoll Cochran, Wm. Mein.

,,   10. Alexr. Peter and Jennet M'Main in Blainslie, a.s.n. John Peter ; w. Thomas Laidlaw, John Wallace.

,,   ,, Richard Sclatter and Alison Dauson in Blainslie, a.s.n. John Sclater ; w. Thomas Laidlaw, John Wallace.

,,   ,, John Thynne and Agnes Milne in Blainslie, a.d.n. Katharin Thynne ; w. Thomas Laidlaw, John Wallace.

,,   13. Adam Davidson and Christian Forsan in Melrose, a.s.n. Adam Davidson ; w. John Mabon, John Martine.

,,   20. John Drummond and Jennet Dickson in Galtonside, a.d.n. Margaret Drummond ; w. Robert Bowstone, Wm. Dickson.

,,   21. James Ellies and Isabell Usher in Melrose, a.s.n. George Ellies ; w. Wm. Ellies, James Martine.

,,   24. Wm. Milne and Agnes Sclater in Eildon, a.d.n. Marion ; w. Alexr. Mein, James Hunter.

Aug.   10. John Mercer and Helen Sibbald in Darnick, a.s.n. John Mercer ; w. John Sibbald, James Usher.

,,   31. Andrew M'Fadzean and Elizabeth Martine in Melrose, a.d.n. Christian M'Fadzean ; w. Andrew and John Martines.

1707.

Aug. 31. Robert Bunzie and Isabell Bowie in Melrose, a.d.n. Jean Bunzie ; w. James Bowie, John Martine.

Sept. 14. Robert Mein and Beatrice Hunter in Newsteid, a.s.n. Robert Mein ; w. Robert Elliot, James Thynne.

„ „ John Sheill and Isabell Purvis in Melrose, a.s.n. John Sheill ; w. George Sheill, Mungo Purvis.

„ 16. Thomas Thynne and Jean Montgomery in Whitlie, a.d.n. Margaret Thynne ; w. Georg Hog, John Martine.

„ 21. George Pringle and Margaret Newton, a.d.n. Margaret Pringle ; w. James Pringle, James Marre.

„ 28. James Carribbes and Isabell Crosbie in Sorrowlessfield, a.d.n. Elisabeth Carribbes ; w. James Crosbie, James Thynne.

Oct. 7. James Grieve and Jean Allan in Blainslie, a.s.n. George Grieve ; w. Hugh Allan, John Wallace.

„ „ Richard Robson and Elizabeth Pringle in Blainslie, a.s.n. John Robson ; w. Hugh Allan, John Wallace.

„ „ Andrew Darling and Helen Lythgow in Threepwood, a.d.n. Marion Darling ; w. John Wallace, Hugh Allan.

„ „ James Karr and Isabell Allan in Colmeslie, a.s.n. Hugh Karr ; w. Hugh Allan, John Wallace.

„ „ John Sclater and Isabell Litle, a.d.n. Marion Sclater ; w. Hugh Allan, John Wallace.

Nov. 2. John Karr and Anna M'Fadzean in Westhouses, a.s.n. John Karr ; w. Wm. Sandilands, Alexr. M'Fadzean.

„ „ Alexr. Mein and Jennet Milne in Eildon, a.d.n. Isabell Mein ; w. John Sibbald, Wm. Milne

„ „ George Loury and Margaret Gill in Danieltoun, a.s.n. George Loury ; w. Robert Loury, Wm. Gill.

„ 9. William Mein and Isabell Wright in Galtonside, a.s.n. Robert Mein ; w. George Mein, John Martine.

„ „ Robert Bunzie and Marion Hopkirk in Melrose, a.d.n. Isabel Bunzie ; w. Wm. Hopkirk, elder and younger.

„ 10. John Brown and Jennet Owens in Colmesliehill, a.d.n. Margaret Brown ; w. Robert Moffet, John Martine.

„ 23. Wm. Gill and Margaret Turnbull in Danieltoun, a.s.n. William Gill ; w. James and Andrew Patersone.

„ „ Robert Philip and Margaret Sclater in Galtonside, a.d.n. Isabell Philip ; w. John Gibson, John Bowstone.

Dec. 7. James Wallace and Anne Waugh in Melrose, a.d.n. Helen Wallace ; w. Andrew Patersone, Wm. Cook.

„ 14. Robert Pringle and Jennet Mein in Newsteid, a.s.n. James Pringle ; w. James Pringle, Andrew Mein.

„ 17. James Stirling and Margaret Sommervail in Blainslie, a.s.n. James Stirling ; w. Edward Darling, James Pringle.

„ „ Robert Pride and —— in Whitlie, a.s.n. James Pride ; w. Edward Darling, James Pringle.

„ „ Alexander Thomson in Blainslie, and Margaret Hall, a.d.n. Marion Thomson ; w. Edward Darling, James Pringle.

„ 21. James Stodhart and Isabell Moss in Darnick, a.s.n. William Stodhart ; w. John Mercer, Wm. Dickson.

„ „ George Mein and Isabell Frier in Galtonside, a.d.n. Margaret Mein ; w. Robert Frier, Wm. Mein.

„ „ Robert Wallace, deceased, and Jennet Milne in Melrose, a.s.n. Robert Wallace, presented by Thomas Gill ; w. John Mabon, John Martine.

„ 28. John Mabon and Jennet Mabon in Melrose, a.s.n. Adam Mabon ; w. James Blackie, John Martine.

1708.

Jan. 11. George Mercer and Jennet Waters in Danieltoun, a.d.n. Isabell Mercer ; w. Robert Scott, John Martine.

F

1708.

Feb. 1. James Blaikie and Margaret Turnbull in Melrose, a.s.n. William
        Blaikie ; w. Andrew Turnbull, Mr. Andrew Patersone.

,, 16. Wm. Brown and Jean —— in Mosshouses, a.s.n. Thomas Brown ; w.
        Mr. Rot. Marre, John Frier.

,, ,, John Lauder and Elisabeth Henderson in Kedzlidoors, a.d.n. Eliza-
        beth Lauder ; w. Mr. Robert Marre, John Frier.

,, ,, Robert Wadderstone and Jennet Duncan in Housbyre, a.s n.
        Patrick Wadderstone ; w. Mr. Robert Marre, John Frier.

Mar. 7. Thomas Martine and Jennet Runchiman in Galtonside, a.d.n. Isabell
        Martine ; w. John Sommervaill, Wm. Martine.

,, 14. Wm. Bell and Helen Haitlie in Galtonside, a.d.n. Isabell Bell ; w.
        Robert Bowstone, Wm. Hoy.

,, 28. Thomas Hervie and Margaret Scott in Westhouses, a.s.n. William
        Hervie ; w. Robert Hervie, Andrew Mercer.

,, ,, Thomas Bowstone and Elisabeth Rutherfoord in Galtonside, a.s.n.
        Thomas Bowstone ; w. Mr. Robert Marre, John Frier.

,, ,, Henry Gibsone and Isabell Fisher in Melrose, a.d.n. Isabell Gibson ;
        w. John Mabon, John Gibson.

April 11. Robert Wight and Agnes Martine in Darnick, a.s.n. William Wight ;
        w. James Blaikie, John Martine.

,, 18. Nicoll Mercer and Mary Rennaldson in Bridgend, a.s.n. Nicoll
        Mercer ; w. James Rennaldson, Andrew Mercer.

,, 18. George Grahamslie and Jennet Alley in Melrose, a.s.n. Alexander
        Grahamslie ; w. Andrew Bryden, Nicoll Mercer.

,, ,, Andrew Bryden and Jennet Brown in Easterlanglie, a.d.n. Margaret
        Bryden ; w. Robert Fisher thereof, James Bowie.

,, 29. John Pearson and —— Crosbie in Allanshaws, —— Pearson ; w.
        Andrew Wood, John Moffet.

May 6. John Pratsell and Elspeth Christie in Bentmill, a.s.n. John Pratsell ;
        w. John Darling, Andrew Simontoun.

,, 9. Cornelius Mein and Isabel Mein in Eildon, a.s.n. Richard Mein : w.
        Richard Mein, William Mein.

,, ,, John Riddell and Jennet Pursell in Melrose, a.d.n. Barbara Riddell ;
        w. James Hunter, John Martine.

,, ,, Robert Simontoun and Marion Wilson in Dryrgrainge, a.d.n.
        Katharin Simontoun ; w. John Riddell, John Martine.

,, ,, James Bowie and Marion Bell in Melrose, a.s.n. James Bowie ; w.
        Alexr. Bell, Robert Bunzie.

,, ,, Andrew Turnbull and Elisabeth Sclater in Brigend, a.d.n. Elisabeth
        Turnbull ; w. James Blaikie, John Martine.

June 13. John Moodie and Elisabeth Moffet in Melrose, a.d.n. Grizell Moodie ;
        w. Robert Bunzie, Wm. Williamson.

July 4. James Mein and Margaret Cairncroce in Newtoun, a.d.n. Elisabeth
        Mein ; w. Robert Mein, John Martine.

,, ,, Bernard Ellies and Isabell Tait in Newsteid, a.s.n. John Ellies ; w.
        John and William Meins.

,, ,, Andrew Mein and Marion Fairgrieve in Galtonside. —— Mein ; w.
        James Marre, elder and younger.

,, 6. George Brown and —— Laing in Blainslie, a.d.n. Anne Brown ; w.
        John Wallace, Thomas Laidlaw.

,, 11. Thomas Darling and Isabell Notman in Buckholme, a.d.n. Margaret
        Darling ; w. George and Edward Darlings.

,, ,, James Watson and Margaret Bunzie in Newsteid, a.d.n. Helen
        Watson ; w. Wm. Mein, Andrew Bunzie.

,, ,, John Blaikie in Hagburn and Marion Lythgow, a.s.n. John Blaikje ;
        w. George Hog, Robert Moffat.

,, ,, Andrew Wood and Margaret Pringle in Allanshaws, a.s.n. David
        Wood : w. George Hog, Robert Moffet.

,, 25. James Rennaldson and Isabell Leidhouse in Darnick, a.d.n. Mary
        Rennaldson ; w. John Mercer, John Martine.

1708.
Aug.   1. John Hoy and Isabell Bartoun in Galtonside. a.d.n. Isabell Hoy ; w. John and Wm. Hoys.
  „   8. John Grierson and Jean Ramsey in Darnick, a.s.n. John Grierson ; w. Wm. Grierson, John Martine.
  „   „ Robert Mein and Jean Weir in Newsteid, a.d.n. Margaret Mein ; w. John and Wm. Meins.
  „   22. James Waugh and Jennet Mein in Eildon, a.d.n. Margaret Waugh ; w. Andrew Moss, John Sibbald.
Sept. 12. Robert Hervie and Helen Manderson in Melrose, a.d.n. Agnes Hervie ; w. Robert Scott, John Mabon
  „   19. Henry Cochran and Jennet Riddell in Newtoun, a.s.n. Nicoll Cochran ; w. John and Andrew Riddell.
  „   28. James Darling and Helen Pringle in Blainslie, —— Darling ; w. —— .
  „   „ Alexr. Horsburgh and Jennet Lauder in Threepwood, —— ; w. —— .
Oct. 10. Alexr. Pringle and Marion Pringle in Langshaw, a.d.n. Jennet Pringle ; w. James Turner, John Hardie.
  „   „ David Speeding and Elisabeth Gavan in Easterlanghlie, a.s.n. David Speeding ; w. Robert Fisher thereof, Andrew Bryden.
  „   17. Wm. Wilson and Rachell Mitchell in Melrose, a.s.n. Andrew Wilson ; w. Andrew Douglas, bailie, Robert Wilson.
  „   24. John Martine and Elisabeth Wood in Melrose, a.d.n. Marion Martine ; w. Andrew Martine, John Mabon.
  „   „ James Sandilands and —— in Bentmill, —— Sandilands ; w. Andrew and John Martines.
Nov.   7. James Kin and Marion Pringle in Galtonside, —— Kin ; w. James and Mr. Robert Marres.
  „   14. Thomas Leithan and Isabell Tait in Galtonside, a.d.n. Isabell Leithan ; w. James Leithan, Robert Martine.
  „   21. Andrew Karr and Elisabeth Loury, —— Karr : w. John Martine, Wm. Aitchison.
  „   28. Andrew Moss and Margaret Waugh in Darnick, a.s.n. Andrew Moss ; w. James Rennaldson, John Mercer.
  „   „ Thomas Thomsone and Margaret Thomsone in Galtonside, a.s.n. William Thomsone ; w. Wm. Thomsone, Wm. Hoy.
Dec.   5. Wm. Hoy and Isabell Hoy in Galtonside, a.s.n. William Hoy ; w. James and Mr. Robert Marres.
  „   26. John Scott and Jean Robison in Westhouses, a.d.n. Margaret Scott ; w. Thomas Mattheson, Wm. Darling.
  „   „ George Mercer and Jean Marre in Darnick, a.d.n. Margaret Mercer ; w. John and Charles Mercers.
1709.
Jan. 16. James Laing and Christian Mein in Melrose, a.s.n. William Laing ; w. Richard Sclater, John Chisholme.
Feb.   6. Andrew Mein and Elisabeth Richardson in Eildon, a.d.n. Margaret Mein ; w. Alexr. Mein, John Sibbald.
  „   8. Alexr. Fisher of Claikmae and Mary Simson, a.s.n. Alexander Fisher ; w. James Thynne, James Crosbie.
  „   13. Wm. Martine and Isabell Marre in Galtonside, a.s.n. David Martine ; w. Robert Martine, James Tait.
  „   „ James Jamisone and Christian Hope in Melrose, a.s.n. John Jamisone ; w. George Loury, John Martine.
  „   15. John Thynne and Agnes Milne in Blainslie, a.s.n. John Thynne ; w. John Wallace, Edward Darling.
  „   „ James Scott and Agnes Blaikie in Blainslie, a.d.n. Agnes Scott ; w. John Wallace, Edward Darling.
  „   „ George Hog and Jennet Tait in Hagburn, a.s.n. William Hog ; w. John Wallace, Edward Darling.
  „   27. Thomas Stenhouse and Helen Sibbald in Newtoun, a.s.n. John Stenhouse ; w. Nicoll Milne, John Riddell.

1709.

Feb. 27. Thomas Foster and Elisabeth Hope in Melrose, a.s.n. Archbald Foster ; w. James Jamison, Robert Hunter.

,, ,, John Hownam and Isabell Paterson in Bridgend, a.d.n. Jennet Hownam ; w. Andrew Turnbull, John Martine.

,, ,, Thomas Usher and Jennet Murray in Melrose, a.d.n. Jennet Usher ; w. James Murray, John Martine.

Mar. 20. Thomas Bowstone and Isabell Mabon in Galtonside, a.s.n. Robert Bowstone ; w. James Marre, John Mabon.

,, ,, James Fisher and Isabell Moss in Darnick, a.d.n. Margaret Fisher ; w. Michael Fisher, James Mercer.

,, ,, Wm. Fisher and Agnes Drummond in Galtonside, a.d.n. Isabell Fisher ; w. James Marre, Thomas Bowstone.

,, 23. Thomas Laidlaw and Helen Darling in Blainslie, a.s.n. John Laidlaw, baptized at Ligertwood ; w. Edward and John Darlings.

,, 27. Robert Scott and Elisabeth Patersone in Danieltoun, a.d.n. Jean Scott ; w. Robert Hervie, Mr. Andrew Patersone.

April 3. Thomas Milne and Jennet Milne in Newtoun, a.s.n. Thomas Milne ; w. John Riddell, Nicoll Milne.

,, ,, James Mein and Agnes Milne in Newsteid, a.s.n. John Mein ; w. James Laing, John Martine.

,, ,, George Penman and Agnes Sandilands in Melrose, a.d.n. Elisabeth Penman ; w. James and Robert Penmans.

,, 4. Andrew Douglas, baillie, and Jean More in Melrose, a.d.n. Helen Douglas ; w. James Hunter, Robert Bunzie and Mr. Andrew Patersone.

,, 5. Wm. Mercer and Mary Dalgleish in Colmesliehill, a.s.n. Walter Mercer ; w. John and Robert Moffets.

,, ,, James Karr and Agnes Allan in Colmeslie, a.d.n. Agnes Karr ; w. John and Robert Moffets.

,, ,, George Turner, deceased, and Marion Pringle in Colmsliehill, a.s.n. George Turner ; w. John and Robert Moffets.

,, ,, Alexr. —— and Elisabeth Ramsey in Longhaugh, a.d.n. Elisabeth —— ; w. John and Robert Moffets.

,, 24. Robert Hilson and Agnes Bower in Melrose, a.s.n. John Hilson ; w. James Blaikie, John Mabon.

,, ,, Alexr. Lyall and Margaret Bower in Melrose, a.d.n. Mary Lyall ; w. James Hunter, James Blaikie.

May 8. James Thynne and Marion Hunter in Sorrowlessfield, a.s.n. Thomas Thynne ; w. Robert Purvis, Wm. Thynne.

,, 27. Nicoll Milne and Elisabeth Vair in Newtoun, a.d.n. Isabell Milne ; w. William Dickson, Wm. Rennaldson.

,, ,, Wm. Dickson and Margaret Kyll in Darnick, a.d.n. Jennet Dickson ; w. Nicoll Milne, Wm. Rennaldson.

,, ,, Wm. Rennaldson and Agnes Mein in Newsteid, a.d.n. Jennet Rennaldson ; w. Nicoll Milne, Wm. Dickson.

June 12. James Turner and Jean Hunter in Langshaw, a.s.n. Thomas Turner ; w. Wm. Turner, John Martine.

,, ,, Wm. Turner and Jennet Wright in Galtonside, a.s.n. James Turner ; w. James Turner, John Martine.

,, 26. John Thurbrand and Elisabeth Forsyth in Langshaw, —— Thurbrand ; w. John and George Martines.

July 3. Robert Philip and Margaret Sclater in Galtonside, a.s.n. Robert Philip ; w. James Hoy, John Bowstone.

,, ,, Wm. Milne and Isabell Riddell in Newsteid, a.d.n. Jennet Milne ; w. Nicoll Milne, John Mein.

,, 24. Andrew Haliday and Jennet Bain, a.d.n. —— Haliday ; w. Andrew and John Martines.

Aug. 19. James Fisher of Bearfaulds and Margaret Karr, a.d.n. Jean Fisher ; w. Nicoll Milne, John Martine.

1709.

Aug. 21. John Glendinning and Margaret Mein in Eildon, a.s.n. Robert
Glendinning ; w. Richard Mein, John Sclater.

" 28. —— and Margaret Turnbull in Mosshouses, —— ; w. John and
George Martines.

Sept. 4. Andrew Mercer and Margaret Hervie in Westerlanglie, a.d.n. Isabell
Mercer ; w. John and Wm. Mercers.

" " Andrew Mercer and Margaret Frier in Darnick, a.s.n. George
Mercer ; w. James Mercer, Charles Frier.

" 28. John Smith and Margaret Phaup in Darnick, a.d.n. Jennet Smith ;
w. Nicoll Milne, John Martine.

Oct. 9. John Mercer and Helen Sibbald in Darnick, a.s.n. John Mercer ; w.
John Sibbald, John Hitoun.

" 25. Wm. Brown and —— in Blainslie, a.s.n. John Brown ; w. Robert
Moffet, Nicoll Milne.

Nov. 6. John Hitoun and Jennet Mercer in Darnick, a.s.n. Andrew Hitoun ;
w. James Ushar, John Mercer.

" " Wm. Gill and Margaret Turnbull in Danieltoun, a.d.n. Margaret
Gill : w. Andrew Patersone, George Loury.

" 13. James Kin and Marion Pringle in Galtonside, a.s.n. Patrick Kin ; w.
James and Mr. Robert Marres.

" 20. Andrew Hownam and Agnes Hitoun in Darnick, a.d.n. Margaret
Hownam ; w. Andrew Hownam, Andrew Hitoun.

" " Adam Davidson and Christian Forsan in Melrose, —— Davidson ;
w. James Gray, David Hendersone.

" 22. Mr. Andrew Patersone, schoolmaster, and Jean Cowan in Melrose,
a.d.n. Jennet Patersone : w. Andrew Douglass, bailie, Robert
Patersone of Drygrainge, John Duncansone.

" 30. Walter Thomson and Margaret Hardie in Ladhopmuir, a.d.n. Isabell
Thomson ; w. Alexr. Horsburgh, John Martine.

" " Alexr. Horsburgh and Jennet Lauder in Threepwood, a.d.n. Margaret
Horsburgh ; w. Walter Thomson, John Martine.

" " Wm. Turner and Marion Notman in Colmeslichill, a.s.n. John
Turner ; w. Walter Thomson, Alexr. Horsburgh.

Dec. 11. George Frier and Elisabeth Tweedie in Galtonside, a.d.n. Isabell
Frier ; w. John Frier, James Young.

" " Thomas Gill and Isabell Ellies in Melrose, a.s.n. George Gill ; w.
James Ellies, David Henderson.

" 18. —— Atchison and —— Notman in Sorrowlessfield, a.s.n. Robert
Atchison : w. John and Andrew Martines.

" 27. Archibald Frier and Isabel Mattheson in Galtonside, a.d.n. Margaret
Frier ; w. Robert Fisher of Easterlanglie, John Martine.

" " William Henry and Margaret Douglass, a.s.n. William Henry ; w.
Robert Fisher of Easterlanglie, John Martine.

1710.

Jan. 1. David Lidderdale of Tores and Helen Dumbar in Melrose, a.s.n.
Thomas Lidderdale ; w. James Pringle of Buckholme, Mr. Andrew
Douglass, baillie.

" 15. John Notman and Jennet Moodie, a.d.n. Isabell Notman, by fornication ; w. Andrew and John Martines.

" " Nicoll Milne and Christian Blaikie, a.s.n. Robert Milne ; w. Charles
Blaikie, Alexr. Bell, in Melrose.

" " John Chisholme and Mary Laing in Galtonside, a.d.n. Elisabeth
Chisholme ; w. Nicoll Milne, John Martine.

" 22. Robert Mein and Beatrice Hunter in Newsteid, a.s.n. William Mein ·
w. James Thynne, Andrew Mein.

" 31. Adam Ballantine and Katharin Pringle in Drygrainge, a.d.n. Elisabeth
Ballantine ; w. David and Robert Ballantines.

" " James Ainsley and Jean Watson in Langshaw milne, a.d.n. Mary
Ainsley ; w. David and Robert Ballantine.

Feb. 5. Andrew Mein and Helen Mein in Newsteid, a.s.n. John Mein ; w.
Andrew and Robert Meins.

1710.

Feb. 12. James Richardson and Isabell Gray, a.s.n. George Richardson ; w. James Marre, Andrew Turnbull.

,, 19. Andrew Bryden and Jennet Brown in Easterlanglie, a.s.n John Bryden ; w. Robert Fisher thereof, David Speeding.

,, 26. Thomas Laidlaw and Elisabeth Simontoun in Mosshouses, a.d.n. Jean Laidlaw ; w. James Turner, John Martine.

,, ,, Thomas Wight and Jennet Sword in Galtonside, a.d.n. Margaret Wight ; w. James and Mr. Robert Marre.

,, ,, George Loury and Margaret Gill in Danieltoun, a.d.n. Margaret Loury ; w. Wm. Gill, Andrew Patersone.

Mar. 12. James Ushar and Isabell Mercer in Darnick, a.s.n. John Ushar ; w. John Ushar, John Mercer.

,, ,, John Milne and Isabell Milne in Newtoun, a.d.n. Christian Milne ; w. Johne Milne, John Riddell.

,, 28. James Laidlaw and Agnes Pearson in Buckholme, —— Laidlaw ; w. David Brown, Wm. Atchison.

,, 29. Cornelius Mein and Isabell Mein in Eildon, a.d.n. Isabell Mein ; w. Richard and Wm. Meins.

,, 31. John Mercer and Elisabeth Scott in Darnick, a.d.n. Agnes Mercer ; w. ——.

April 2. Robert Bowstone and Jennet Russell in Galtonside, a.d.n. Elisabeth Bowstone ; w. Thomas Bowstone, Mr. Robert Marre.

,, 5. James Grieve and Jean Allan in Blainslie, a.d.n. Agnes Grieve ; w. John and James Stirlings.

,, ,, John Steill and Isabell Thomsone in Blainslie, a.d.n. Agnes Steill ; w. John and Wm. Thynnes.

,, 23. James Mercer and Margaret Vair in Darnick, a.d.n. Margaret Mercer ; w. James Usher, John Mercer.

,, 30. Wm. Hislop and —— in Darnick, a.d.n. Margaret Hislop : w. John Mercer, John Mercer.

May 14. Robert Simontoun and Marion Wilson in Drygrainge, a.s.n. Robert Simontoun ; w. Adam Ballantine, John Hardie.

,, ,, John Hardie and —— in Langshaw, —— Hardie ; w. Robert Simontoun, John Martine.

,, 21. John Brown and Elisabeth Trotter in Mosshouses, a.d.n. Christian Brown ; w. Wm. Brown, John Haitlie.

,, ,, Adam Shiell, deceased, and Isabell Henderson in Colmeslie, a.d.n. Agnes Shiell ; w. Wm. and John Browns.

,, 28. Robert Bunzie and Isabell Bowie in Melrose, a.s.n. John Bunzie : w. James Bowie, Alexr. Bell.

June 4. James Mercer and Jennet Craig in Newsteid, a.d.n. Jennet Mercer ; w. James Mercer, Robert Mein, John Bunzie.

,, ,, Walter Nicoll and Isabell Purvis, a.s.n. Alexander Nicoll : w. James Karr, Wm. Turner.

,, 6. Richard Sclater and Alison Dauson in Blainslie, a.s.n. William Sclater ; w. Thomas Sclater, James Dauson.

,, ,, Richard Robson and Elisabeth Pringle in Blainslie, a.d.n. Helen Robson ; w. Thomas Laidlaw, Richard Sclater.

,, 25. Wm. Chisholme and Margaret Hobkirk in Darnick, a.d.n. Helen Chisholme : w. Andrew and John Martines.

July 2. Wm. Milne and Agnes Sclater in Eildon, a.d.n. Agnes Milne ; w. Alexr. Mein, Wm. Sclater.

,, ,, Wm. Darling and Margaret Mattheson in Westhouses, a.d.n. Margaret Darling ; w. Thomas Mattheson, Thomas Williamson.

,, ,, Wm. Mein and Isabell Wright in Galtonside, a.s.n. John Mein ; w. William Hoy, George Mein.

,, ,, John Hownam and Isabell Patersone in Galtonside ; w. Andrew Drummond, Nicoll Mercer.

,, 16. John Mabon and Jennet Mabon in Melrose, a.d.n Isabell Mabon ; w. Thomas Bowstone, John Martine.

1710.

July 23. James Bowie and Marion Bell in Melrose, a d.n. Jennet Bowie ; w. Robert Bowie, Alexr. Bell.

  ,, 30. William Brown and —— in Mosshouses, a.s.n. Robert Brown : w. John and Andrew Martines.

Aug. 6. James Stirling and Margaret Sommerville in Rone of Blainslie ; w. John and Wm. Stirlings.

  ,, ,, Robert Bunzie and Marion Hopkirk in Newsteid, a.d.n. Elisabeth Bunzie ; w. Wm. Hopkirk, John Bunzie.

Sept. 10. Robert Pringle and Jennet Mein in Newsteid, a.d.n. Mary Pringle ; w. James Pringle, Wm. Wallace.

  ,, 17. James Hoy and Margaret Vetch in Galtonside, a.s.n. George Hoy ; w. William Hoy, James Hoy.

Oct. 29. Alexr. Knox and Jennet Frier in Galtonsyde, a.s.n. William Knox ; w. John and Charles Friers.

  ,, ,, John Lauder and Elisabeth Henderson in Kedzliedoors, a.d.n. Marion Lauder ; w. Alexr. Knox, John Martine.

Nov. 5. James Wilson and Elisabeth Rutherfoord in Newsteid, a.s.n. Andrew Wilson ; w. Andrew Wilson, John Sibbald.

  ,, 12. John Patersone and Margaret Riddel in Galtonside, a.d.n. Agnes Patersone : w. James Oliver, Andrew Scott.

  ,, ,, Alexr. Mein and Marion Fairgrieve in Galtonside, a.s.n. John Mein ; w. John Sommervaill, Wm. Martine.

  ,, 19. John Hoy and Isabell Bartoun in Melrose, a.s.n. George Hoy ; w. George Bartoun and George Hoy.

  ,, 26. Robert Bunzie and Katharin Thomson in Newsteid, a.d.n. Margaret Bunzie : w. Andrew and James Bunzies.

  ,, ,, James Stodhart and Isabell Moss in Darnick, a.d.n. Jennet Stodhart ; w. Wm. Dickson, Robert Spotwood.

Dec. 10. Wm. Bell and Helen Haitlie in Galtonside, a.s.n. William Bell ; w. Alexr. Knox, James Marre.

  ,, ,, James Moodie and Jean Smith in Drygrainge, a.s.n. Robert Moodie ; w. Robert Patersone thereof, John Moodie.

  ,, 21. William Wallace and Mary Scott in Melrose, a.d.n. Helen Wallace ; w. John Martine, Nicoll Milne.

  ,, 24. John Mercer and Margaret Jamison in Williamlaw, a.s.n. John Mercer ; w. Thomas Hervie, Thomas Purvis.

1711.

Jan. 7. Wm. Milne and Isabell Riddell in Newsteid, a.d.n. Margaret Milne ; w. John Riddell, Nicoll Milne.

  ,, 21. James Mein and Margaret Cairncroce in Newtoun, a.s.n. John Mein w. Wm. and Robert Meins.

  ,, 28. John Johnstoun and —— in Threepwood, a.d.n. Jean Johnstoun ; w. John and George Martines.

Feb. 3. Thomas Darling and —— Leidhouse in Blainslie, a.d.n. Barbara Darling ; w. Thomas Darling, John Thynne.

  ,, 11. Nicoll Milne and Elisabeth Vair in Newtoun : a.s.n. John Milne ; w. Nicoll Milne, John Milne.

  ,, ,, Andrew Turnbull and Elisabeth Sclater in Bridgend, a.d.n. Marion Turnbull ; w. James Blaikie, John Martine.

  ,, 18. Thomas Stenhouse and Helen Sibbald in Newtoun, —— Stenhouse ; w. Nicoll Milne, Wm. Sibbald.

Mar. 11. James Laing and Christian Mein in Melrose, a.d.n. Agnes Laing ; w. Mungo Purvis, James Ellies.

  ,, 17. David Brown and Isabell Williamson in Melrose, a.s.n. Thomas Brown ; w. Alexr. Bell, John Martine.

  ,, 18. Robert Hilson and Agnes Bower in Melrose, a.s.n. James Hilson : w. James Blaikie, James Laing.

  ,, ,, Andrew Mein and Elisabeth Richardson, a.d.n. Marion Mein ; w. John Sibbald, Alexr. Mein.

April 8. James Mein and Agnes Milne in Newsteid, a.s.n. James Mein ; w. James Laing, James Blaikie.

1711.

April 8. Andrew Scott and Isabell Patersone in Old Melrose, —— Scott ; w. James Blaikie, James Laing.

" 9. John Walker and Jennet Mercer in Darnick, a.d.n. Isabell Walker ; w. James Blaikie, Robert Spotwood.

" " George Penman and Agnes Sandilands in Melrose, a.s.n. Andrew Penman : w. James and Robert Penmans.

" 15. James Sandilands and —— in Langshaw, a.d.n. Beatrice Sandilands ; w. John and George Martines.

" 22. John Bunzie and Agnes Turner in Melrose, a.s.n. Alexander Bunzie ; w. James Mercer, John Martine.

" 29. James Mercer and Jennet Craig in Newsteid, a.s.n. James Mercer ; w. James Mercer, Robert Bunzie.

" " John Haitlie, deceased, and Jennet Watson, a.d.n. Jean Haitlie, presented by James Watson ; w. James Mercer, Robert Bunzie.

May 6. John Darling and Jennet Bowstone in Appletreeleaves, a.s.n. Robert Darling ; w. George Mercer, James Mein.

" " James Mein and Jennet Pursell in Newsteid, a.s.n. David Mein ; w. John Darling, George Mercer.

" " George Mercer and Katharin Ramsey in Danieltoun, a.s.n. John Mercer ; w. James Mein, John Darling.

" 13. Thomas Wight and Jennet Sword in Galtonside, a.d.n. Agnes Wight ; w. John Hoy, John Martine.

" " Andrew Douglas, baillie, and Jean More in Melrose, a.d.n. Anne Douglas ; w. —— Douglas of Bonjedburgh, David Lidderdale of Tores, James Ellies of Huntliwood.

" 27. David Lidderdale of Tores and Helen Dumbar, a.s.n. Alexander Lidderdale ; w. Robert Patersone of Drygrainge, James Ellies of Huntliwood, John Duncansone.

June 4. Mr. William Hunter and Jennet Bowstone in Buckholme, a.d.n. Alison Hunter ; w. John Darling, John Martine.

" 20. William Simson and Jennet Murray in Langshaw, —— Simson : w. Thomas Laidlaw, John Martine.

" 29 Robert Patersone of Drygrainge and Anne Eliot, a.d.n. Margaret Patersone ; w. Robert Patersone of Midlim mill, John and David Browns, elder and younger of Park, Robert Fisher of Easterlanglie.

July 1. James Kyll and Isabell Sword, a.s.n. William Kyll : w. Wm. Sandilands, John Martine.

" 15. Andrew Mercer and Margaret Frier in Darnick, —— Mercer ; w. John and George Martines.

" 22. James Stobo and —— Stobo in Hewishaugh.

" 25. James Ainslie and Jean Watson in Langshaw mill, a.d.n. Margaret Ainslie ; w. James Turner, John Gray.

" " John Gray and Jennet Thynne in Mosshouses, a.d.n. Agnes Gray ; w. James Turner, James Ainslie.

" " James Turner and Jean Hunter in Mosshouses, a.s.n. John Turner ; w. John Gray, James Ainslie.

Aug. 5. Thomas Leithan and Isabell Tait in Galtonside, a.d.n. Elisabeth Leithan ; w. James Leithan, Wm. Hoy.

" 12. Andrew Moss and Margaret Waugh in Darnick, a.s.n. James Moss ; w. James Fisher, James Waugh.

" " Thomas Lookup and Jean Martine in Melrose, a.s.n. Andrew Lookup : w. Patrick and Andrew Lookups.

" 19. Andrew Hownam and Agnes Hitoun in Darnick, a.d.n. Isabell Hownam ; w. Andrew Hownam, Andrew Hitoun.

" " John Gill and Alison King in Newtoun, a.d.n. Alison King ; w Thomas Stenhouse, John Milne.

" " Robert Simontoun and Marion Wilson in Drygrainge, a.d.n. Margaret Simontoun ; w. Robert Paterson thereof, John Martine.

Sept. 16. Thomas Steill and Margaret Eliot in Melrose, a.d.n. Margaret Steill ; w. Wm. Steill, John Bell.

1711.

Sept. 16. Richard Fraiter and Isabell Mercer in Darnick, —— Fraiter ; w. Wm. Steill, John Bell.

„ 30. William Sandilands and Katharin Marre in the Boathouse, a.d.n. Alison Sandilands ; w. James and Mr. Robert Marres.

Oct. 4. John Notman and Jennet Moodie in Threepwood, a.s.n. Andrew Notman ; w. Peter and Archibald Moffets.

„ „ Richard Sclater and Margaret Mein in Blainslie, a.d.n. Margaret Sclater ; w. Thomas Sclater, John Bartoun.

„ 7. Wm. Sclater and Helen Bunzie in Newsteid, a.d n. Margaret Sclater ; w. Wm. Milne, Wm. Cook.

„ 28. Alexr. Dickson and Isabell Park in Gateside, a s.n. Francis Dickson ; w. John Park, Wm. Sandilands.

Nov. 4. David Speeding and Elisabeth Govan in Easterlanglie, a.s.n. William Speeding ; w. Robert Fisher thereof, Andrew Bryden.

„ „ George Mein and Isabell Frier in Galtonside, a.d.n. Isabell Mein ; w. Wm. Mein, Robert Frier.

„ „ Alexr. Lyall and Margaret Bower in Melrose, a.d.n. Margaret Lyall ; w. James Blaikie, James Hunter.

„ „ John Fiddes and Jennet Pringle in Drygrainge, a.s.n. Andrew Fiddes ; w. John and George Martines.

„ 7. John Blaikie and Marion Lythgow in Hagburn, a.s.n. William Blaikie ; w. George Hog, Thomas Thynne.

„ „ Edward Lythgow and Marion Remainhouse, a.d.n. Katherin Lythgow by fornication ; w. George Hog, Thomas Thynne.

„ 11. Wm. Young and Isabell Ormistoun in Galtonside, a.d.n. Isabell Young ; w. James Marre, John Martine.

Dec. 2. John Mercer and Helen Sibbald in Darnick ; a.d.n. Isabell Mercer ; w. John Hitoun, John Sibbald.

„ „ Andrew Mercer and Margaret Maxwell in Melrose, a.d.n. Jennet Mercer ; w. Thomas Drummond, Andrew Patersone.

„ „ John Wood and Marion Blaikie in Melrose, a.d.n. Christian Wood ; w. James Bowie, James Blaikie.

„ 9. Thomas Martine and Jennet Runchiman in Galtonside, a.d.n. Margaret Martine ; w. Wm. Martine, John Sommervaill.

„ 16. John Mercer and Elisabeth Scott in Darnick, a.s.n. Andrew Mercer ; w. James Fisher, Mr. Robert Marre.

„ 23. Thomas Bowstone and Elisabeth Rutherfoord in Galtonside, a.s n. Thomas Bowston ; w. John and George Martines.

1712.

Jan. 6. John Hitoun and Jennet Mercer in Darnick, a.s.n. John Hitoun ; w. James Usher, John Mercer.

„ „ James Rennaldson and Isabell Leidhouse in Darnick, a.s.n. James Rennaldson ; w. John Mercer, James Usher.

„ „ John Chisholme and Margaret Laing in Galtonside, a.d.n. Katharin Chisholme ; w. James Laing, John Martine.

„ 9. Mr. Andrew Patersone, schoolmaster, and Jean Cowan in Melrose, a.d.n. Isabell Patersone ; w. Mr. Robert Wilson, James Blaikie.

„ 16. James Karr and Jennet Allan in Bentmill, a.s.n. Hugh Karr ; w. George Hog, Robert Moffet.

„ „ John Brown and Jennet Owens in Colmesliehill, a.d.n. Jennet Brown ; w. George Hog, Robert Moffet.

„ „ Thomas Darling and Mary Dods in Blainslie, a.d.n. Elspeth Darling ; w. Edward and John Darlings.

Feb. 3. Wm. Milne and Isabell Riddell in Newsteid, a.s.n. John Milne ; w. John Riddell, Nicoll Milne.

„ „ Thomas Williamson and Mary Mein in Newsteid, a.s.n. James Williamson ; w. Wm. and Robert Williamsons.

„ „ James Thynne and Marion Hunter in Sorrowlessfield, a.s.n. George Thynne ; w. John and Wm. Thynnes.

1712.

Feb. 5. James Stirling and Margaret Somervail in the Rone, a.d.n. Agnes
Stirling ; w. John Stirling, John Thynne.

„ „ George Brown and Isabell Laing in Blainslie, —— Brown ; w.
John Thynne, John Stirling.

„ 10. Archibald Frier and Isabell Mattheson in Galtonside, a.d.n. Jennet
Frier ; w. Thomas Mattheson, Wm. Darling.

„ „ Wm. Martine and Isabell Marre in Galtonside, a.d.n. Elisabeth
Martine ; w. Archibald Frier, John Martine.

„ 17. Thomas Thomson and Margaret Thomson in Galtonside a.s.n.
Alexander Thomson ; w. John and George Martines.

„ 19. Wm. Turner and Jennet Wright in Galtonside, a.d.n. Margaret
Turner ; w. Thomas Mattheson, Thomas Hervie.

„ „ Thomas Foster and Elisabeth Hope in Galtonside, a.d.n. Jennet
Foster ; w. Thomas Hervie, Thomas Mattheson.

Mar. 2. James Mein and Elisabeth Hitoun in Newtoun, a.s.n Thomas Mein ;
w. John Mein, John Riddell.

„ 4. James Dickson and Isabell Hitoun in Blainslie, a.s.n. James Dickson ;
w. Robert Moffet, Thomas Laidlaw.

„ „ Walter Thomson and Margaret Hardie in Ladhopmuire, a.s.n. John
Thomson ; w. Thomas Laidlaw, Robert Moffet.

„ „ Thomas Laidlaw and Elisabeth Simontoun in Colmeslie, a.s.n
William Laidlaw ; w. Thomas Laidlaw, Thomas Turner.

„ 9. Robert Mein and Jean Simontoun in Newsteid, a.s.n. William Mein ;
w. Thomas Tait, Wm. Rennaldson.

„ 16. Andrew Bryden and Jennet Brown in Easterlanglie, a.s.n. William
Bryden ; w. James Hunter, James Bowie.

„ 17. John Wallace and Margaret Dick in Blainslie, a.s.n. John Wallace ;
w. Wm. Thynne, Mungo Dick.

„ „ John Tait and Agnes Pringle in Blainslie, a.d.n. Jean Tait ; w. Wm.
Thynne, Mungo Dick.

„ 18. Wm. Turner and Marion Notman in Colmeslie, a.s.n. James Turner ;
w. John Darling, John Martine.

April 9. Andrew Scott and Margaret Sheriff, a.s.n. Andrew Scott ; w. Thomas
Thynne, John Hardie.

„ „ Thomas Thynne and Jean Montgomery in Whitlie, a.d.n. Mary
Thynne ; w. Andrew Scott, John Hardie.

„ „ John Hardie and Christian Dewar, a.d.n. Margaret Hardie ; w.
Thomas Thynne, Andrew Scott.

„ 20. Andrew Mein and Helen Mein in Newsteid, a.s.n. Andrew Mein ;
w. Andrew and Robert Meins there.

„ 27. James Waugh and Jennet Mein in Eildon a.d.n. Isabell Waugh ; w.
Cornelius Mein, Andrew Moss.

„ „ Cornelius Mein and Isabell Mein in Eildon, a.s.n. Cornelius Mein ;
w. Richard Mein, James Waugh.

„ „ Wm. Chisholme and Margaret Hopkirk, a.s.n. William Chisholme,
presented by Wm. Hopkirk in Melrose, in the father's absence ;
w. John Mein, John Mabon.

May 18. James Brown and Agnes Mein in Newsteid, a.d.n. Alison Brown ; w.
Wm. Brown, John Martine.

„ „ James Wilsone and Elisabeth Napier in Bridgend, a.d.n. Jennet
Wilsone ; w. James Napier, John Martine.

„ 27. John Pearson and Isabell Crosbie in Appletreeleaves, a.s.n. Robert
Pearson ; w. John Darling, James Laidlaw.

„ „ James Laidlaw and —— Pearson in Appletreeleaves, a.d.n. Jennet
Laidlaw ; w John Darling, John Pearson.

June 1. William Mein and Isabell Wright in Galtonside, a.d.n Isabell Mein ;
w. George Mein, Robert Wright.

„ 15. Philip Douglass and Agnes Hall in Melrose, a.s.n. James Douglass ;
w. James Hunter, Alexr. Bell.

„ 22. Thomas Hervie and Margaret Scott in Westhouses, a.d.n. Elisa-

1712.

beth Hervie ; w. Robert Fisher of Easterlanglie, Thomas Matthesone.

June 22. James Mercer and Margaret Vair in Darnick, a.d.n. Helen Mercer ; w. John Haliwell, John Martine.

July 6. George Vair and Jennet Drummond in Danieltoun, a.s.n. George Vair ; w. Thomas Drummond, William Mabon.

" " David Lidderdale of Tores and Helen Dumbar, a.d.n. Margaret Lidderdale ; w. Andrew Douglass, baillie, John Duncanson.

" 17. James Hunter and —— in Blainslie ——.

" " Andrew Hitoun and Agnes Linton in Darnick, —— ; w. John Mercer, John Hitoun.

" 27. Robert Scott and Agnes Bunzie in Newsteid, a.s.n. Alexander Scott ; w. Alexander Trotter, Robert Bunzie.

Aug. 17. Mr. Gideon Rutherfurd and Jean Karr in Westerlanglie, a.s.n. John Rutherfurd and a.d.n. Jennet Rutherfurd ; w. Robert Fisher of Easterlanglie, Mr. William Hunter.

" " Thomas Milne and Jennet Milne in Newtoun, a.d.n. Alison Milne ; w. John Riddell, Nicoll Milne.

" 22. James Watson and Isabell Henderson in Langshaw, a.d.n. Elizabeth Watson ; w. James Ainslie, John Boe.

" 24. Richard Robson and —— in Blainslie, a.s.n. John Robson ; w. James Blaikie, John Martine.

Sept. 7. Thomas Usher and Jennet Murray in Melrose, a.d.n. Marion Usher ; w. James Murray, John Martine.

" 21. Robert Pringle and Jennet Mein in Newsteid, a.d.n. Katharin Pringle ; w. George Hoy, John Martine.

Oct. 5. Andrew Douglass, baillie, and Jean More, in Melrose a.d.n. Helen Douglas ; w. James Ellies of Huntlywood, James Wilkieson, clerk.

" 25. George Shiell and Isabell Kyle in Melrose, a.d.n Jennet Shiell ; w. ——.

" 26. John Mercer and Mary Mein in Newsteid, a.s.n. William Mercer ; w. Robert Bunzie, John Martine.

" " Robert Bunzie and Marion Hopkirk in Newsteid, a.s.n. James Bunzie ; w. John Mercer, John Martine.

Nov. 16. Wm Sclater and Helen Bunzie in Newsteid, a.s.n. William Sclater ; w. Thomas and Robert Bunzie.

" 19. William Milne and Agnes Sclater in Eildon, a.s.n. John Milne ; w. John Sibbald, Nicol Bower.

" 30. James Anderson and Jean Balantine in Faldonside, a s.n. Thomas Anderson ; w. Wm. Dickson, Alexr. Knox.

" " Alexr. Knox and Jennet Frier in Galtonside, a.s.n. James Knox ; w. James Anderson, Wm. Dickson.

Dec. 4. Robert Mein and Jean Wier in Newsteid, a.d.n. Isabell Mein ; w. John and George Martines.

" 5. James Bowie and Marion Bell in Melrose, a.d.n. Marion Bowie ; w. Alexr. Bell, Robert Bunzie.

1713.

Jan. 4. James Pringle and Helen Mein in Newsteid, a s.n. Andrew Pringle ; w. Robert Pringle, Andrew Mein.

" " Walter Vetch and Helen Marshall in Galtonside, a.s.n. James Vetch ; w. James Mar, Wm. Williamson.

" " James Kyle and Beatrix Miller in Drygrainge, a.d.n. Jennet Kyle ; w. Robert Paterson of Drygrainge, George Martine.

" 11. Walter Mabon and Elizabeth Gill in Danieltoun, a.d.n. Elizabeth Gill ; w. Andrew Paterson, George Loury.

Feb. 1. William Mein and Margaret Mein in Eildon, a.d.n. Agnes Mein ; w. Richard Mein, John Bunzie.

" " John Hoy and Isabell Bartoun in Melrose, a.s.n. John Hoy ; w. George Hoy, George Bartoun.

1713.

Feb. 15. Nicoll Bower and Alison Riddell in Eildon, a.s.n. Nicoll Bower ; w.
              Richard Bower, John Riddell.

  „   24. William Lees and Jennet Jackson in Stow, a.s.n. Robert Lees : w.
              Thomas Thyn, George Hog.

  „   „ John Tait and Helen Rutherfurd in Stow, a.d.n. Margaret Tait ; w.
              Thomas Thyn, George Hog.

  „   „ James Grieve and Jean Allan in Blainslie, a.d.n. Jean Grieve ; w.
              Thomas Thynne, George Hog.

Mar. 15. James Stodhart and Isabell Moss in Darnick, a.s.n. James Stodhart ;
              w. John Walker, William Dickson, there.

  „   „ James Laing and Christian Mein in Melrose, a.s.n. James Laing ; w.
              James Blaikie, Robert Hilsone.

  „   „ William Wallace and Mary Scott in Melrose, a.d.n. Jennet Wallace ;
              w. James Blaikie, Robert Hilsone.

April 5. John Paterson and Margaret Riddell in Galtonside, a.d.n. Margaret
              Paterson ; w. Andrew Scott, James Oliver.

  „   „ James Usher and Isabell Mercer in Darnick, a.s.n. George Usher ; w.
              John Hitoun, John Usher there.

  „   14. Edward Lythgow and Marion Romanus in Threepwood, a.s.n. William
              Lythgow ; w. Robert Moffet, Edward Darling.

  „   „ James Kedzie and Helen Haitlie in Langshaw, a.d.n. Elizabeth
              Kedzie ; w. Edward Darling, Robert Moffet.

May   3. John Milne and Helen Glendinning in Eildon, a s.n. John Milne ; w.
              James Blaikie, James Laing.

  „   „ The deceased Patrick Watson and Jennet Mercer in Boldside, a.s.n.
              Patrick Watson, presented by Thomas Thurbrand in Galashiells ;
              w. John Donaldson, John Darling.

  „   10. Thomas Stenhouse and Helen Sibbald in Newton, a.s.n. William
              Stenhouse ; w. John Riddell, John Sibbald.

  „   17. John Milne and Isabell Milne in Newton, a.d.n. Jennet Milne ; w.
              Nicol Milne, Thomas Milne.

  „   „ Andrew Fisher and Helen Armstrong in Melrose, a.d.n. Jean Fisher ;
              w. John Mabon, William Bower.

June   7. John Smith and Margaret Phaup in Darnick, a.s.n. James Smith ; w.
              John Smith, younger, George Loury.

  „   „ George Loury and Margaret Gill in Danieltoun, a.d.n. Helen Loury ;
              w. Andrew Paterson, William Gill.

  „   „ Andrew Drummond and Helen Mathison in Bridgend, a.d.n.
              Margaret Drummond ; w. Thomas Mathison, Nicol Mercer.

  „   „ John Sprott and Margaret Hitoun in Darnick, a.s.n. Robert Sprott ;
              w. James Laing, Robert Wight.

  „   „ The deceased John Martine and Elizabeth Wood in Melrose, a.d.n.
              Elizabeth Martine, presented by John Mabon in Melrose ;
              w. Andrew Martine, Andrew M'Faden.

  „   14. Robert Patersone of Drygrainge and Anne Eliot, his lady, a.s.n. Robert
              Patersone ; w. Robert Eliott, elder, and Robert Eliott of Midlim
              mill, Robert Fisher of Easterlangie, and John Brown of Park.

  „   16. Mungo Park and Margaret Cranstoun in Westhouses Boathouse, a.d.n.
              Helen Park ; w. Thomas Hervie, Thomas Mathison.

July.   David Lidderdale of Tores, collector of excise, and Helen Dumbar,
              his lady, a.s.n. John Lidderdale ; w. Andrew Douglass, baillie,
              James Wilkieson, clerk, John Duncanson.

Aug.   2. Henry Cochran and Jennet Vair in Newtoun, a.s.n. Henry Cochran ;
              w. James Mein, Thomas Milne.

  „   „ Andrew Moss and Margaret Wauch in Darnick, a.d.n. Margaret
              Moss ; w. James Wauch, George Martine.

  „   9. James Wilson and Elisabeth Rutherfurd in Eildon, a.d.n. Beatrix
              Wilson ; w. John Sibbald, George Martine.

  „   „ John Bell and Jennet Mabon in Melrose, a.d.n. Helen Bell ; w.
              Alexander Bell, Robert Bunzie.

1713.

Aug. 17. William Henry and Elisabeth Douglass in Williamlaw, a.s.n. William Henry ; w. John Mercer, Thomas Purvis.

„ „ Thomas Darling and Isabell Notman in Calfhill, a.d.n. Marion Darling ; w. William Darling, George Darling.

„ 30. James Mein and Agnes Milne in Newsteid, a.s.n. Andrew Mein ; w. James Laing, Andrew Patersone.

„ „ James Wallace and Anne Wauch in Melrose, a.s.n. James Wallace ; w. Andrew Patersone, William Gill.

Sept. 10. David Grieve and Helen Pringle in Blainslie, —— ; w. James Grieve, Edward Darling.

„ 19. The deceased Andrew Turnbull and Elisabeth Sclater in Bridgend, a.s.n. William Turnbull, and a.s.n. James Turnbull ; w. Andrew Drummond, Andrew Baittie.

„ „ Thomas Gill and Isabell Ellies in Melrose, a.d.n. Margaret Gill ; w. John Mabon, James Ellies.

Oct. 11. William Young and Isabell Ormiston in Galtonside, a.s.n. John Young ; w. Robert Martine, George Martine.

„ „ Robert Martine and Elisabeth Purvis in Galtonside, a.d.n. Grizell Martine ; w. William Young, George Martine.

„ 18. Robert Simontoun and Marion Wilson in Drygrainge, a.s.n. Archibald Simontoun ; w. William Dicksone, George Martine.

„ „ William Dickson and Margaret Kyle in Darnick, a.s.n. William Dickson ; w. Robert Simontoun, James Stodhart.

Blank till January 1714.

1714.

Jan. 3. Robert Philp and Margaret Sclater in Galtonside, a.s.n. Thomas Philp ; w. Thomas Sclater, Robert Haliwall.

„ „ Andrew Patersone and Alison Milne in Danieltoun, a.d.n. Helen Patersone ; w. William Gill, George Loury.

„ 17. William Hislope and Margaret Murray in Darnick ; w. John Mercer, James Usher.

„ 20. James Hunter and Jean Speeding in Blainslie, a.s.n. Robert Hunter ; w. Edward Darling, John Thynne.

„ „ Thomas Laidlaw and Elisabeth Simontoun in Langshaw mill, a.d.n. Jean Laidlaw ; w. John Thynne, Edward Darling.

„ 24. Andrew Mercer and Margaret Frier in Darnick, a.s.n. James Mercer ; w. John Mercer, John Walker.

„ „ Mr. Andrew Patersone, schoolmaster, and Jean Cowan in Melrose, a.s.n. James Patersone ; w. Andrew Patersone, Robert Scott.

„ 31. John Mercer and Helen Sibbald in Darnick, a.d.n. Isabell Mercer ; w. John Hitoun, James Usher.

Feb. 7. Alexander Johnston and Elisabeth Laing in Melrose, a.s.n. James Johnston ; w. William Cook, Alexander Cook.

. 9. Alexander Fisher of Sorrowlessfield and Mary Simson, a.s.n. Robert Fisher ; w. George Martine and ——.

„ 10. Thomas Marshell and Eupham Moffet in Easterhousbyre, a.s.n. Thomas Marshell ; w. William Pearson, Walter Haliburton.

„ „ William Turner and Marion Notman, a.s.n. Thomas Turner ; w. William Pearson, Walter Haliburton.

„ 14. James Rennaldson and Isabell Leadhouse in Darnick, a.s.n. William Rennaldson ; w. William Rennaldson, Nicoll Mercer.

„ „ John Bunzie and Agnes Turner in Melrose, a.s.n. James Bunzie ; w. Robert Bunzie, George Martine.

„ 18. John Purvis and Jean Martine in Langhaugh, a.d.n. Jean Purvis ; w. John Darling, William Wilson.

„ „ Andrew Thomson and —— Blaikie in Galashiells, a.s.n. James Thomson ; w. William Wilson, John Darling.

„ „ James Laidlaw and Agnes Pearson in Netherbarns, a.d.n. Agnes Laidlaw ; w. John Darling, William Wilson.

1714.

Feb. 28. William Darling and Margaret Mathison in Westhouses, a.d.n. Agnes Darling ; w. Thomas Mathison, John Hervie.

Mar. 2. Edward Lythgow of Newhouses and Marion Romanus, a.d.n. Helen Lythgow ; w. ——.

„ 7. Andrew Mercer and Margaret Maxwell in Melrose, a.s.n. Andrew Mercer ; w. Thomas Drummond, Robert Hunter.

„ 14. Thomas Lookup and Jean Martine in Melrose, a.s.n Robert Lookup ; w. Andrew Lookup, William Lookup.

„ 21. Thomas Williamson and Mary Mein in Newsteid, a.s.n. Thomas Williamson ; w. William Williamson, Robert Williamson.

„ 28. Robert Scott and Agnes Bunzie in Newsteid, a.s.n. Walter Scott ; w. John Bunzie, Robert Bunzie.

„ 30. John M'Henry and Margaret Caribbes in Whitlie, a.s.n. James M'Henry ; w. Thomas Thynne, George Hog.

April 4. Cornelius Mein and Isabell Mein in Eildon, a.d.n. Marion Mein ; w. Richard Mein, William Mein.

„ 11. William Milne and Isabell Riddell in Newsteid, a.d.n. Agnes Milne ; w. John Riddell, Nicoll Milne.

„ „ William Mabon and Marion Sclater in Danieltoun, a.d.n. Margaret Mabon ; w. Thomas Drummond, Walter Mabon.

„ 25. John Mein and Mary Mein in Newsteid, a.s.n. John Mein ; w. James Hunter, Andrew Mein.

„ „ Nicoll Mercer and Mary Rennaldson in Bridgend, a.s.n. John Mercer ; w. Andrew Drummond, Andrew Mercer.

„ „ Thomas Wilson and Alison Hoy in Langhaugh, a.s.n. William Wilson ; w. Nicoll Mercer, George Mercer.

„ „ George Mercer and Katharin Ramsay in Danieltoun, a.s.n. Thomas Mercer ; w. Thomas Wilson, Nicoll Mercer.

„ „ William Sandilands and Katharin Mar, a.s.n. William Sandilands ; w. Mr. Robert Marr, John Mein.

May 9. Nicoll Milne and Isabell Turnbull in Newtoun, a.d.n. Agnes Milne ; w. Thomas Stenhouse, John Riddell.

„ „ Nicoll Mercer and Christian Mein in Darnick, a.s.n. George Mercer ; w. John Mercer, James Fisher.

„ „ Andrew Red and Jennet Pearson in Appletreeleaves, a.d.n. Jean Red ; w. John Darling, John Pearson.

„ „ John Usher in Darnick and Christian Bower in Eildon, a.s.n. John Ushar by fornication ; w. Nicoll Milne, Nicoll Mercer.

„ 23. James Wauch and Jennet Mein in Melrose, a.d.n. Isabella Waugh ; w. Robert Hilsone, George Martine.

„ 25. John Boyd and —— Paterson in Langshaw, a.s.n. James Boyd ; w. James Park, George Martine.

„ 31. James Chisholme —— in Buckholme, a.s.n. John Chisholme ; w. George Martine, Andrew Martine.

June 13. James Mein and Elisabeth Hitoun in Newtoun, a.d.n. Elisabeth Mein ; w. John Riddell, Philip Douglass.

„ „ Robert Bunzie and Marion Hopkirk in Newsteid, a.s.n. Alexander Bunzie ; w. John Bunzie, Robert Bunzie.

„ „ William Craig and —— Donaldsone in Galashiells, a.s.n. James Craig ; w. John Donaldson, James Blaikie.

„ 14. Thomas Turner and Alison Murray in Colmeslie, a.d.n. Mary Turner ; w. James Turner, Thomas Laidlaw.

„ „ John Hardie and Christian Dewar in Langshaw, a.d.n. Helen Hardie ; w. Edward Darling, James Park.

„ 20. James Heriot, excise officer, and Helen Hume in Melrose, a.s.n. James Heriot ; w. James Blaikie, Mr. Andrew Patersone.

„ „ George Penman and Agnes Sandilands in Melrose, a.d.n. Margaret Penman ; w. James Penman, Andrew Dauson.

„ 27. John Gill and Alison King in Newtoun, a.s.n. John Gill ; w. Thomas Gill, George Martine.

1714.

July   4. Andrew Douglass, baillie, and Jean More in Melrose, a.s.n. Charles
           Douglas ; w. David Lidderdale of Tores, James Ellies of Huntli-
           wood, James Wilkieson, clerk.

  ,,   18. John Chisholme and Margaret Ritchie in Bentmill, a.d.n. Mary
           Chisholme ; w. George Martine, Andrew Martine.

Aug.   8. John Curry and Alison Dods in Blainslie, a.d.n. Alison Curry ; w.
           George Martine Andrew Martine.

  ,,   15. Andrew Bryden and Jennet Brown in Easterlanglie, a.s.n. Robert
           Bryden ; w. Robert Fisher, James Hunter.

  ,,   17. Philip Douglass and Agnes Hall in Melrose, a.d.n. Elisabeth Douglass ;
           w. George Martine, Andrew Martine.

  ,,   19. William Simson and Jennet Murray in Langshaw, a.d.n. Jennet
           Simson ; w. Hugh Cairncross of Hislope, Thomas Turner.

  ,,   ,, Alexander Wood and Jennet Young in Appletreeleaves, a.d.n. Marion
           Wood ; w. James Ainslie, Thomas Turner.

  ,,   22. William Rennaldson and Agnes Mein in Newsteid, a.d.n. Elisabeth
           Rennaldson ; w. Andrew Bunzie, John Wilson.

  ..   29. James Bunzie and Jean Wilson in Newsteid, a.s.n. Andrew Bunzie ;
           w. Andrew Bunzie, John Wilson.

  ,,   ,, William Mein and Jennet Wright in Galtonside, a.s.n. Robert Mein ;
           w. William Hoy, George Hoy.

Sept.   5. James Kyle and Isabell Swoord in Westhouses, a.d.n. Mary Kyle ;
           w. William Mabon, John Mabon.

  ..   ,, Andrew Mein and Helen Mein in Newsteid, a.s.n. John Mein ; w.
           Andrew Mein, Robert Pringle.

  ..   10. John Chisholme and Margaret Laing in Galtonside, a.s.n. William
           Chisholme and a.d.n. Katharin Chisholme ; w. ——.

  ..   12. David Lidderdale of Tores, collector of excise, and Eleanor Dumbar,
           a.d.n. Eleanor ; w. Captain Dumbar, younger of Mochrum, Andrew
           Douglas, baillie, James Ellies of Huntliwood, James Wilkieson, clerk.

  ,,   16. Andrew Shillinglaw and Jennet Grieve in Blainslie, a.s.n. Robert
           Shillinglaw ; w. Edward Darling, Robert Stirling.

  ..   .. James Kerr and Isabell Allan in Bentmill, a.s.n. William Kerr ; w.
           Edward Darling, Robert Stirling.

  ,,   .. Thomas Darling and Mary Dods in Blainslie, a.d.n. Agnes Darling ;
           w. Edward Darling, Robert Stirling.

  ..   19. Thomas Wight and Jennet Swoord in Galtonside, a.d.n. Jennet
           Wight ; w. Andrew Mar, Mr. Robert Mar.

  .,   .. Andrew Hounam and Agnes Hitoun in Darnick, a.s.n. Andrew
           Hounam ; w. James Usher, Andrew Hitoun.

  ..   26. John Welch and Bessie Scott in Langhaugh, a.d.n. Helen Welch ; w.
           John Darling, George Martine.

  ..   ,, Nicoll Milne and Elspeth Vair in Newtoun, a.d.n. Agnes Milne ; w.
           Nicoll Milne, John Riddell.

  ,,   30. Thomas Foster and Elisabeth Hope in Melrose, a.d.n. Helen Foster ;
           w. Andrew Dauson, John Hoy.

Oct.   17. John Haitlie and —— in Drygrainge boathouse, a.d.n. Anne Haitlie ;
           w. William Marshell, George Martine.

  ..   31. John Bowston and Agnes Thomson in Galtonside, a.s.n. John
           Bowston ; w. Archibald Frier, Robert Philip.

Nov.   7. John Frier and Jennet Turner in Galtonside, a.d.n. Isabell Frier ; w.
           Robert Frier, Robert Balantine.

  ..   ,, William Hopkirk and Isabell Hunter in Kilnow, a.s.n. William
           Hopkirk ; w. William Hopkirk, John Frier.

  ..   21. John Mercer and Mary Mein in Newsteid, a.d.n. Mary Mercer; w.
           Robert Mein, Andrew Mein.

  ..   28. Mungo Laidlaw and Margaret Cochran in Newtoun, a.d.n. Christian
           Laidlaw ; w. James Laidlaw, Nicoll Milne

Dec.   5. William Stodhart and Jennet Smith in Darnick, a.d.n. Isabell
           Stodhart ; w. James Stodhart, John Smith.

1714.

Dec.   7. George Shiell and Christian Cook in Melrose, a.d.n. Margaret Shiell ;
           w. Alexr. Cook, William Cook.

  „   15. James Stirling and —— in Blainslie, —— Stirling ; w. Richard
           Robson, Andrew Haliday.

  „   „ Richard Robson and —— in Blainslie, —— Robson ; w. James
           Stirling, Andrew Haliday.

  „   „ Andrew Haliday and Jennet Bain in Blainslie, —— Haliday ; w.
           Richard Robson, James Stirling.

  „   19. James Wilson and Elisabeth Napier in Bridgend, a.d.n. Elisabeth
           Wilson ; w. Andrew Drummond, James Napier.

  „   „ Robert Bunzie and Katharin Thomson in Newsteid, a.s.n. Andrew
           Bunzie ; w. William Atchison, Robert Mein.

  „   26. William Hoy and Isabell Hoy in Galtonside, a.s.n. John Hoy ; w.
           Andrew Mar, Mr. Robert Mar.

  „   „ Nicoll Milne and Christian Blaikie in Melrose, a.d.n. Margaret
           Milne ; w. Alexander Bell, William Milne.

  „   „ George Mein and Isabell Frier in Galtonside, a.d.n. Jennet Mein ; w.
           William Mein, Robert Frier.

1715.

Jan.   2. John Gibson and Agnes Sclater in Melrose, a.s.n. David Gibson ; w.
           Henry Gibson, William Sclater.

  „   „ James Laing and Christian Mein in Melrose, a.s.n. David Laing ; w.
           Richard Sclater, Alexander M'Faden.

  „   10. Mr. Gideon Rutherfurd and Jean Kar in Westerlanglie, a.s.n.
           Gideon Rutherfurd ; w. James Fisher of Bearfaulds, George
           Martin.

  „   20. William Young and Isabell Ormiston in Galtonside, a.d.n. Margaret
           Young ; w. Robert Ormiston, William Cook.

  „   25. Alexander Thomson and Agnes Hall in Blainslie, a.s.n. James
           Thomson ; w. Thomas Laidlaw, William Thynne.

  „   „ James Houden and Elisabeth Hog in Hagburn, a.s.n. George
           Houden ; w. Thomas Laidlaw, William Thynne.

  „   26. Robert Balantine and Jennet Frier in Galtonside, a.s.n. John
           Balantine ; w. Adam Balantine, John Frier.

  „   29. John Mabon and Jennet Mabon in Melrose, a.d.n. Jennet Mabon ; w.
           William Mabon, Thomas Mabon.

Feb.   6. James Mercer and Margaret Vair in Darnick, a.d.n. Jennet Mercer ; w.
           James Stodhart, John Mercer.

  „   „ Walter Mabon and Elisabeth Gill in Danieltoun, a.d.n. Isabell
           Mabon ; w. Thomas Drummond, William Mabon.

  „   8. John Brown and Elisabeth Trotter in Mosshouses, a.s.n. Alexander
           Brown ; w. Alexander Trotter, George Martine.

  „   14. John Wallace and Margaret Dick in Blainslie, a.s.n. Mungo Wallace ;
           w. Edward Darling, William Thynne.

  „   20. Nicoll Bower and Alison Riddell in Newtoun, a.s.n. Andrew Bower ;
           w. Richard Bower, John Riddell.

  „   „ Robert Mein, smith, and Jean Simontoun in Newsteid, a.d.n. Agnes
           Mein ; w. John Mercer, William Rennaldsoun.

Mar.   1. Richard Sclater and Margaret Mein in Blainslie, a.d.n. Marion
           Sclater ; w. Thomas Darling, Robert Moffet.

  „   6. John Hoy and Isabell Bartoun in Melrose, two sons n. Andrew
           and William Hoy : w. William and George Hoy.

  „   15. Thomas Purvis and Isabell Lamb in Williamlaw, —— Purvis ;
           w. ——.

  „   „ John Notman and Isabell Martine in Colmeslie, —— Notman ;
           w. ——.

  „   20. Andrew Drummond and Helen Mathison in Bridgend, a.s.n. William
           Drummond ; w. Thomas Mathison, John Napier.

  „   „ Thomas Bowston and Elisabeth Rutherfurd in Galtonside, a.s.n.
           Andrew Bowston : w. Mr. Robert Mar, Thomas Bowston.

1715.

April 4. James Scott and Agnes Blaikie in Blainslie, —— Scott ; w. Edward Darling, William Thynne.

,, 10. Andrew Stewart and Agnes Mein in Galtonside, a.s.n. Andrew Stewart ; w. George Bartoun, Robert Ormiston.

,, ,, Thomas Stenhouse and Helen Sibbald in Newtoun, a.s.n. Nicoll Stenhouse ; w. Nicoll Milne, John Riddell.

,, 17. Thomas Wilson and Alison Hoy in Langhaugh, a.s.n. John Wilson ; w. William Hoy, John Hoy.

,, ,, James Mercer and Jennet Craig in Melrose, a.d.n. Jean Mercer ; w. James Mercer, George Martine.

,, 24. Thomas Martine and Jennet Runchiman in Galtonside, a.s.n. William Martine ; w. William Martine, John Sommervaill.

,, ,, Walter Vetch and Helen Marshell in Galtonside, a.d.n. Helen Vetch ; w. Thomas Martine, Walter Thomson.

,, ,, Walter Thomson and Margaret Hardie in Ladhopmuir, a.d.n. Margaret Thomson ; w. Walter Vetch, Thomas Martine.

May 6. John Wood and Jennet Notman in Mosshouses, a.d.n. —— Wood ; w. John Notman, John Forrest.

,, 22. William Turner and Jennet Wright in Galtonside, a.d.n. Jennet Turner ; w. George Wright, Charles Frier.

,, ,, Robert Mein and Jean Weir in Newsteid, a.d.n. Jennet Mein ; w. William Mein, James Brown.

,, ,, John Usher and Christian Bower in Eildon, a.s.n. Thomas Usher ; w. James Usher, John Sibbald.

,, 27. Richard Thomson and Isabell Moffet in Williamlaw, a.s.n. James Thomson ; w. Mr. William Hunter, James Laidlaw.

,, ,, Andrew Scott and Isabell Paterson in Buckholme, a.d.n. Isabell Scott ; w. James Laidlaw, Mr. William Hunter.

,, ,, James Laidlaw and Christian Brunton in Buckholme, a.d.n. Jean Laidlaw ; w. Mr. William Hunter, Andrew Scott.

June 12. James Loury and Isabell Brown in Newtoun, a.s.n. Thomas Loury ; w. Nicoll Milne, John Riddell.

,, ,, John Mercer and Helen Sibbald in Darnick, a.s.n. Andrew Mercer ; w. James Usher, John Hitoun.

,, ,, Thomas Usher and Jennet Murray in Melrose, a.s.n. John Usher ; w. James Ellies, Thomas Gardiner.

,, 26. James Brown and Agnes Mein in Newsteid, a.s.n. James Brown ; w. James Hunter, William Brown.

,, ,, James Mein and Jennet Pursell in Newsteid, a.s.n. John Mein ; w. David Pursell, Mark Pursell.

,, 29. James Watson and —— in Langshaw mill, —— Watson ; w. Edward Darling, John Thynne.

July 15. John Gordon and Katharin Grieston in Darnick, —— Gordon ; w. ——.

,, 24. John Milne and Helen Glendinning in Eildon, a.d.n. Agnes Milne ; w. John Sibbald, Alexander Mein.

,, ,, James Stodhart and Isabell Moss in Darnick, a.d.n. Isabell Stodhart ; w. William Dickson, John Mercer.

Aug. 7. William Mein and Margaret Mein in Eildon, a.d.n. Marion Mein ; w. Richard Mein, Cornelius Mein.

,, ,, John Wilson and Elisabeth Pursell in Newsteid, a.d.n. Agnes Wilson ; w. John Mein, Robert Wilson.

,, 14. Robert Martine and Elisabeth Purvis in Galtonside, a.d.n. Isabell Martine ; w. Robert Purvis, William Martine.

,, 21. Adam Hislope and Elisabeth Mercer in Darnick, a.s.n. John Hislope ; w. John Walker, John Hounam.

Sept. 4. John Smith and Margaret Phaup in Darnick, a.s.n. Andrew Smith ; w. John Smith, John Hounam.

,, 11. Andrew Patersone and Alison Milne in Danieltoun, a.s.n. James Patersone ; w. William Gill, George Loury.

G

1715.

Sept. 21. Robert Paterson of Drygrainge, and Anne Eliott, his lady, a.s.n. John Patersone ; w. Robert Fisher of Easterlanglie, David Brown of Park.

,, 25. James Sandilands and Margaret Lorn in Blainslie, a.s.n. William Sandilands ; w. Thomas Darling, Edward Darling.

Oct. 9. The deceased Robert French and Elisabeth Hopkirk in Melrose, a.d.n. Margaret French, presented by William Hopkirk there ; w James Blaikie, James Hunter.

,, 16. John Bell and Jennet Mabon in Melrose, a.s.n. Thomas Bell ; w Alexander Bell, James Bowie.

,, ,, David Lidderdale of Tores, collector of excise, and Elenor Dumbar his lady, a.s.n. David Lidderdale ; w. Andrew Douglass, baillie John Christian, supervisor of excise.

,, 23. William Wallace and Mary Scott in Melrose, a.d.n. Agnes Wallace ; w. James Wallace, George Martine.

,, ,, John Notman and Agnes Davie in Melrose, a.s.n. John Notman ; w. John Mabon, Richard Sclater.

Nov. 6. James Wilson and Elisabeth Rutherfurd in Eildon, a.s.n. Robert Wilson ; w. George Martine, John Wilson.

,, ,, William Bunzie and Jennet Fairbairn in Newsteid, a.s.n. Robert Bunzie ; w. Robert Fairbairn, Robert Bunzie.

,, ,, James Moodie and Jennet Mercer in Darnick, a.s.n. John Moodie ; w. John Mercer, James Blaikie.

,, 13. John Napier and Jennet Drummond in Bridgend, a.s.n. James Napier ; w. Andrew Drummond, James Wilson.

,, ,, George Vair and Jennet Drummond in Danieltoun, a.d.n. Jennet Vair ; w. Thomas Drummond, William Mabon.

,, ,, Robert Hilson and Agnes Bower in Melrose, a.s.n. John Hilson ; w. John Bell, George Hoy.

,, 20. Henry Cochran and Jennet Vair in Newtoun, a.s.n. Andrew Cochran ; w. Thomas Milne, James Mein.

,, ,, George Loury and Margaret Gill in Danieltoun, a.d.n. Helen Loury ; w. Andrew Patersone, William Gill.

Dec. 4. John Fiddes and Jennet Pringle in Galtonside, a.s.n. James Fiddes ; w. Robert Pringle, George Martine.

,, 25. Peter Moffet and Agnes Smith in Threepwood, a.s.n. William Moffet ; w. Robert Moffet, Peter Moffet.

,, 28. Andrew Douglass, baillie, and Jean More in Melrose, a.s.n. William Douglass ; w. Mr. Walter Douglass, minister at Linton, David Lidderdale of Torres, collector of excise.

1716.

Jan 1. Andrew Moss and Margaret Wauch in Darnick, a.d.n. Isabell Moss ; w. James Wauch, John Mercers.

,, 8. Mr. Andrew Patersone, schoolmaster, and Jean Cowan in Melrose, a.d.n. Elisabeth Patersone ; w. James Heriot, Robert Scott.

,, 15. James Heriot, officer of excise, and Helen Hume in Melrose, a.d.n. Helen Heriot ; w. James Hunter, James Blaikie.

,, ,, James Martine and Jennet Dickson in Darnick, a.d.n. Elisabeth Martine ; w. Michael Fisher, Michael Fisher, younger.

,, 22. Andrew Hitoun and Agnes Linton in Darnick, a.d.n. Agnes Hitoun ; w. James Usher, James Mar.

,, 29. Richard Fraiter and Isabell Mercer, a.s.n. Thomas Fraiter ; w. Thomas Drummond, Andrew Mercer.

Feb. 5. James Bowie and Marion Bell in Melrose, a.d.n. Isabell Bowie ; w. Alexander Bell, Robert Bunzie.

,, 8. William Brown and Jean Thurbrand in Colmesliehill, a.d.n. Jean Brown ; w. Thomas Brown, John Thynne.

,, ,, James Hunter and Margaret Speeding in Blainslie, a.s.n. John Hunter ; w. John Thynne, William Thynne.

,, ,, David Grieve and Helen Pringle in Blainslie, a.d.n. Agnes Greive ; w. John Thynne, William Thynne.

1716.

Feb. 19. Nicoll Milne and Isabell Turnbull in Newtoun, a.d.n. Elisabeth Milne ; w. John Riddell, Thomas Stenhouse.

„ 22. Thomas Marshell and Eupham Moffet in Easterhousbyre, a.s.n. John Marshell ; w. Robert Huntly, John Mercer.

„ 23. William Henry and Elisabeth Douglass in Williamlaw, a.s.n. Michael Henry ; w. William Darling, Andrew Bryden.

„ 26. John Bunzie and Agnes Turner in Melrose, a.d.n. Mary Bunzie ; w. James Mercer, James Gray.

Mar. 4. William Sclater and Helen Bunzie in Newsteid, a.d.n. Jennet Sclater ; w. Thomas Bunzie, Robert Bunzie.

„ 8. John Mercer and Helen Patersone in Colmeslie, a.s.n. William Mercer ; w. James Laidlaw, William Atchison.

„ 11. Nicoll Mercer and Mary Rennaldson in Bridgend, a.d.n. Margaret Mercer ; w. Andrew Drummond, Andrew Mercer.

„ 18. Andrew Mercer and Margaret Maxwell in Danieltoun, a.s.n. Robert Mercer ; w. Thomas Drummond, George Vair.

„ „ Andrew Pringle and Margaret Pringle in Galtonside, a.d.n. Katharin Pringle ; w. Andrew Mar, Mr. Robert Mar.

„ 19. Richard Sclater and Margaret Mein in Blainslie, a.s.n. Richard Sclater ; w. John Thynne, Edward Darling.

„ „ John M'Henry and Margaret Caribbes in Blainslie, a.s.n. George M'Henry ; w. Edward Darling, John Thynne.

„ 25. James Caribbes and Isabell Crosbie in Sorrowlessfield, a.s.n. William Caribbes ; w. Robert Crosbie, John Pearson.

April 8. Andrew Mercer and Margaret Frier in Darnick, a.s.n. Andrew Mercer ; w. John Mercer, John Hounam.

„ 22. Andrew Mar and Susanna Lythgow in Galtonside, a.d.n. Elisabeth Mar ; w. James Hunter, George Martine.

„ „ Robert Scott and Agnes Bunzie in Newsteid, a.d.n. Jennet Scott ; w. Robert Bunzie, William Bunzie.

May 1. Mungo Park and Margaret Cranstoun in Westhouses Boathouse, a.s.n. John Park ; w. Thomas Mathison, John Park.

„ 20. Andrew Mercer and Katharin Mercer in Bridgend, a.d.n. Isabell Mercer ; w. John Mercer, Nicoll Mercer.

„ „ Robert Bunzie and Marion Hopkirk in Newsteid, a.s.n. Robert Bunzie ; w. William Hopkirk, John Bunzie.

„ „ James Mein and Elisabeth Hitoun in Newtoun, a.d.n. Mary Mein ; w. Nicoll Milne, Thomas Stenhouse.

„ „ Andrew Bryden and Jennet Brown in Easterlanglie, a.s.n. James Bryden ; w. Robert Fisher, David Speeding.

„ „ William Dickson and Margaret Kyle in Darnick, a.d.n. Isabell Dickson ; w. James Mein, Andrew Mercer.

„ 22. John Tait and —— in Blainslie, a.s.n. Robert Tait ; w. John Thynne, Thomas Darling.

„ 25. Thomas Williamson and Mary Mein in Newsteid, a.s.n. William Williamson ; w. ——.

June 3. Robert Philip and Margaret Sclater in Galtonside, a.s.n. John Philip ; w. Robert Balantine, Robert Haliwell.

„ 7. John Mercer, Beatshiell, and —— Scott in Darnick, a.s.n. William Mercer, w. John Mercer, James Usher.

„ 10. John Pearson and Margaret Crosbie in Old Melrose, a.d.n. Isabell Pearson ; w. Robert Crosbie, James Caribbes.

„ 14. James Fisher, Bearfaulds, and Margaret Kar in Darnick, a.s.n. James Fisher ; w. John Walker, John Grieston.

„ 17. John Cochran and Jennet Rutherfurd in Newtoun, a.d.n. Isabell Cochran ; w. Nicoll Milne, John Riddell.

„ 25. William Hutchison and Jennet Speeding in Langhaugh, a.s.n. Alexander Hutchison ; w. Robert Fisher and ——.

July 12. John Mercer and Elisabeth Hitoun in Bridgend, a.d.n. Isabell Mercer ; w. John Mercer, Andrew Drummond.

1716.

July 17. James Ainslie and Jean Watson in Langshaw mill, a.d.n. Jean Ainslie ; w. Edward Darling, Robert Frier.

" " John Frier and Jennet Turner in Mosshouses, a.d.n. Alison Frier ; w. Robert Frier, Edward Darling.

Aug. 5. James Loury and Isabell Brown in Newtoun, a.s.n. John Loury ; w. George Martine, Andrew Martine.

" 19. Richard Robson and Bessie Pringle in Blainslie, a.s.n. Richard Robson ; w. Edward Darling, William Thynne.

" " John Rae and Mary Park in Housbyre, a.d.n. Isabell Rae ; w. John Mercer, George Martine.

Sept. 2. James Bunzie and Jean Wilson in Newsteid, a.s.n. James Bunzie ; w. Andrew Bunzie, John Mercer.

" 23. Andrew Mein and Helen Mein in Newsteid, a.s.n. Robert Mein ; w. Andrew Mein, Robert Mein.

" " Walter Mabon and Elisabeth Gill in Danieltoun, a.d.n. Jennet Mabon ; w. Thomas Drummond, William Mabon.

" " Robert Bunzie and Beatrix Frame in Newsteid, a.d.n. Agnes Bunzie ; w. Robert Bunzie, Thomas Bunzie.

" 30. Thomas Gill and Alison Gill in Danieltoun, a.d.n. Helen Gill ; w. Andrew Paterson, George Loury.

Oct. 7. William Mabon and Marion Sclater in Newsteid, a.s.n. John Mabon ; w. William Sclater, John Wilson.

" 13. John Hitoun and Jennet Mercer in Darnick, a.s.n. John Hitoun ; w. John Mercer, George Martine.

" 14. John Paterson and Margaret Riddell in Galtonside, a.s.n. John Patersone ; w. Andrew Scott, William Young.

" " James Vair and Margaret Kerr in Newtoun, a.d.n. Isabell Vair ; w. William Kerr, John Riddell.

Nov. 4. Thomas Mathison and Margaret Bonniton in Westhouses, a.d.n. Agnes Mathison ; w. Thomas Mathison, Alexander Mathison.

" 11. Robert Balantine and Jennet Frier in Galtonside, a.d.n. Isabell Balantine ; w. Robert Frier, John Frier.

" " Robert Crosbie and Elisabeth Crosbie in Sorrowlessfield, a.d.n. Helen Crosbie ; w. James Caribbes, John Pearson.

" 18. William Milne and Isabell Milne in Newsteid, a.d.n. Isabell Milne ; w. John Riddell, Nicoll Milne.

" 25. Andrew Stewart and Agnes Mein in Galtonside, a.s.n. Robert Stewart ; w. George Stewart, George Bartoun.

" " James Laing and Christian Mein in Melrose, a.d.n. Margaret Laing ; w. Richard Sclater, James Ellies.

" " George Bartoun and Alison Mercer in Galtonside, a.d.n. Helen Bartoun ; w. John Hoy, Andrew Mercer.

Dec. 2. Walter Ker and Jennet Moffat in Galtonside, a.d.n. Jennet Ker ; w. John Moffet, William Mathison.

" " William Mathison and Jennet Livingston in Galtonside, a.d.n. Isabell Mathison ; w. James Mathison, James Miles.

" " James Mar and Margaret Mercer in Darnick, a.d.n. Isabell Mar ; w. James Wauch, William Lookup.

" " Philip Douglass and Agnes Hall in Melrose, a.d.n. Christian Douglass ; w. James Phaup, Thomas Gardiner.

" " Joseph Cuninghame, soldier in Preston's Regiment, and Katharin Waldie, a.d.n. Katharin Cuninghame ; w. George Martine, Andrew Martine.

" 4. Edward Lithgow and Marion Rommanus in Appletreeleaves, a.s.n. John Lithgow ; w. Andrew Darling, Thomas Laidlaw.

" " Andrew Darling and Helen Lithgow in Threepwood, a.d.n. Christian Darling ; w. Walter Thomson, George Thomson.

" " Thomas Laidlaw and Elisabeth Simontoun in Colmeslie, a.d.n. Elisabeth Laidlaw ; w. James Ainslie, John Rae.

1716.

Dec. 4. Robert Walker and Jennet Curry in Langhaugh, a.s.n. George
Walker ; w. Walter Thomson, George Thomson.

,, 9. Andrew Mein and Elisabeth Richardson in Eildon, a.d.n. Katharin
Mein ; w. John Sibbald, Alexander Mein.

,, ,, Thomas Steel and Margaret Elliot in Melrose, a.s.n. Thomas Steel ;
w. John Moodie, Andrew Dauson.

,, 16. Robert Wilson and Margaret Pearson in Drygrainge, a.s.n. John
Wilson ; w. John Pearson, George Martine.

,, 23. James Mercer and Jennet Craig in Newsteid, a.d.n. Jennet Mercer ;
w. George Martine, William Mercer.

1717.

Jan. 6. John Sprotts and Margaret Hitoun in Darnick, a.s.n. John Sprotts :
w. Robert Scott, Mark Blaikie.

,, 8. Robert Pringle and Jean Gilry, a.d.n. Jean Pringle, by fornication :
w. Robert Fisher, George Martine.

,, 13. Thomas Sclater and Jennet Vair in Eildon, a.s.n. Robert Sclater ; w.
John Bunzie, Robert Sclater.

,, 15. Alexander Wood and —— in Buckholme, a.s.n. Alexander Wood ; w.
Edward Lithgow, John Fraiter.

,, ,, James Chisholme and Isabell Patersone in Langhaugh, a.d.n. Isabell
Chisholme ; w. John Fraiter, Edward Lithgow.

,, 20. John Gibson and Agnes Sclater in Melrose, a.d.n. Mary Gibson ; w.
Mr. Andrew Patersone, Robert Sclater.

,, 27. John Mercer and Mary Mein in Newsteid, a.s.n. Robert Mercer ; w.
John Mein, Andrew Mein.

,, ,, Andrew Mein and Jennet Mercer in Newsteid, a.d.n. Agnes Mein ;
w. John Mein, John Mercer.

,, 30. John Hoy and Isabell Bartoun in Melrose, a.d.n. Alison Hoy ; w.
Robert Bunzie, Thomas Martine.

Feb. 3. John Usher and Christian Bower in Eildon, a.s.n. James Usher ; w.
James Usher, John Bunzie.

,, ,, Thomas Lookup and Jean Martine in Melrose, a.s.n. Thomas
Lookup ; w. Andrew Lookup, William Lookup.

,, 5. John Boyd and Isabell Coatts in Langshaw, a.s.n. Adam Boyd ; w.
John Gray, George Martine.

Mar. 3. John Mein and Mary Mein in Newsteid, a.s.n. Robert Mein ; w.
Andrew Mein, James Hunter.

,, ,, Mungo Laidlaw and Margaret Cochran in Newtoun, a.s.n. Nicoll
Laidlaw ; w. James Laidlaw, Nicoll Milne.

,, ,, Walter Brodie and Margaret Bunzie in Melrose, a.s.n. Robert
Brodie ; w. John Bunzie, George Atchison.

,, 4. Richard Thomson and Isabell Moffet in Appletreeleaves, a.d.n.
Isabell Thomson ; w. John Darling, Edward Lithgow.

,, 13. Andrew Shillinglaw and Jennet Grieve in Blainslie, a.d.n. Isabell
Shillinglaw ; w. David Grieve, William Thynne.

,, 17. Alexander M'Faden and Agnes Napier in Melrose, a.d.n. Helen
M'Faden ; w. Andrew M'Faden, James M'Faden.

,, 24. Andrew Moss and Margaret Wauch in Darnick, a.s.n. James Moss ;
w. James Wauch, John Mercer.

,, ,, Andrew Drummond and Helen Mathison in Bridgend, a.s.n. Thomas
Drummond ; w. Thomas Mathison, William Darling.

,, 25. Thomas Turner and Alison Murray in Colmeslie, a.s.n. William
Turner ; w. Andrew Scott, George Martine.

Mar. 25. Andrew Scott and Isabell Patersone in Langshaw, a.s.n. John Scott :
w. Thomas Turner, George Martine.

,, 31. William Stodhart and Jennet Smith in Darnick, a.s.n. George
Stodhart ; w. James Stodhart, John Smith.

April 9. James Houden and —— in Hagburn, a.s.n. James Houden ; w. John
Thynne, James Grieve.

,, ,, Walter Thomson and Margaret Hardie in Ladhopmuir, a.d.n. Marion
Thomson ; w. John Thynne, James Grieve.

1717.

April 10. Thomas Purvis and Isabell Lamb in Drygrainge, a.d.n. Anne Purvis ; w. Robert Paterson thereof, James Purvis.

„ 14. Robert Hunter and Jean Brock in Melrose, a.d.n. Helen Hunter ; w. Andrew Martine, James Hunter.

„ 21. John Milne and Helen Glendinning in Eildon, a.s.n. William Milne ; w. John Sibbald, Alexander Mein.

„ „ John Smith and Helen Mercer in Darnick, a.s.n William Smith ; w. James Moodie, John Smith.

„ 28. John Wilson and Elisabeth Pursell in Newsteid, a.d.n. Jennet Wilson ; w. Andrew Mein, Bernard Mercer.

May 2. John Chisholme and Margaret Ritchie in Bentmill, a.s.n. John Chisholme : w. John Thynne, James Grieve.

„ „ James Mitchell and Jennet Fraiter in Blainslie, a.d.n. Marion Mitchell : w. James Grieve, John Thynne.

„ „ Thomas Sandilands and Marion Swanston in Colmeslie, a.d.n. Jennet Sandilands : w. John Thynne, James Grieve.

„ 26. Robert Mein and Jean Simontoun in Newsteid, a.s.n. Andrew Mein ; w. Robert Mein, George Martine.

„ „ Robert Mein and Jean Weir in Newsteid, a.s.n. Robert Mein ; w. Robert Mein, George Martine.

„ „ Francis Pringle and Elspeth Trotter, a.s.n. Alexander Pringle, by fornication ; w. Robert Mein, George Martine.

„ 28. George Kirkhope and Jennet Knight in Buckholme, a.d.n. Jennet Kirkhope : w. James Laidlaw, William Napier.

June 2. John Gill and Alison King in Newtoun, a.d.n. Jennet Gill ; w. Nicoll Milne, Thomas Stenhouse.

„ 15. Robert Ormiston and Agnes Smith in Galtonside, a.d.n. Jennet Ormiston ; w. James Young, William Martine.

„ 16. Gilbert Welch in Melrose and Marion Corser, a.s.n. William Welch : w. Robert Bunzie, George Martine.

„ „ Robert Bunzie and Marion Hopkirk in Newsteid, a.d.n. Marion Bunzie ; w. Gilbert Welch, George Martine.

„ 23. Mr. Andrew Paterson, schoolmaster in Melrose, and Jean Cowan, a.d.n. Elisabeth Paterson ; w. Andrew Paterson, Robert Scott.

„ 30. James Lauder and Mary Brounlees in Housbyre, a.s.n. Thomas Lauder : w. George Martine, Andrew Martine.

July 11. John Haliwell and Helen Nicoll in Galtonside, a.d.n. Margaret Haliwell ; w. William Bell, William Hoy.

„ 21. John Bower and Agnes Dalgliesh in Eildon : a.d.n. Jennet Bower ; w. John Sibbald, Mungo Dalgliesh.

„ 28. James Bowston and Marion Blaikie in Galtonside, a.s.n. Thomas Bowston : w. James Blaikie, Thomas Bowstone.

Aug. 2. James Ker and Isabell Allan in Colmeslie, a.s.n. John Kerr ; w. ——.

„ 3. Nicoll Bower and Alison Riddell in Newtoun, —— Bower ; w. ——.

„ 4. William Sandilands and Katharin Mar in Galtonside, a.s.n. James Sandilands : w. Andrew Mar, William Hoy.

„ „ George Mein and Isabell Frier in Galtonside, a.d.n. Agnes Mein ; w. William Mein, William Hoy.

„ „ John Notman and Isabell Martine in Sorrowlessfield, a.d.n. Elisabeth Notman ; w. William Sandilands, George Mein.

„ 5. James Laidlaw and Christian Brunton in Buckholme, a.s.n. Rober Laidlaw : w. William Napier, George Martine.

„ 9. William Bunzie and Jennet Fairbairn in Newsteid, a.d.n. Helen Bunzie ; w. Robert Bunzie, William Sclater.

„ 19. Adam Hislope and Elisabeth Mercer in Darnick, a.d.n. Isabell Hislope : w. William Hislope, George Martine.

„ 25. William Mein and Margaret Mein in Eildon, a.s.n. Richard Mein ; w. John Bunzie, Cornelius Mein.

„ 26. George Wight and Jennet Carmichell in Williamlaw, a.d.n. Isabell Wight ; w. John Frater, Walter Watsone.

1717.

Sept. 8. Thomas Williamson and Mary Mein in Newsteid, a.s.n. William Williamson ; w. William Williamson, Robert Williamson.

,, ,, William Young and Isabell Ormiston in Galtonside, a.d.n. Jennet Young ; w. Thomas Wight, Robert Balantine.

,, ,, William Napier and Helen Mathison in Buckholme, a.s.n. James Napier ; w. James Napier, John Napier.

,, 15. John Notman and Agnes Davie in Melrose, a.d.n. Helen Notman ; w. John Mabon, Thomas Gill.

,, ,, John Dauson and Margaret Fairbairn, a.d.n. Alison Dauson, by fornication ; w. Alexander Mein, Thomas Mein.

,, 22. Thomas Martine and Jennet Runchiman in Galtonside, a.d.n. Christian Martine ; w. William Martine, George Martine.

,, ,, George Herd and —— in Blainslie, a.d.n. Christian Herd ; w. Thomas Martine, George Martine.

,, 29. Alexander Bell and Jennet Bell in Melrose, a.s.n. John Bell ; w. John Bell, James Bowie.

Oct. 6. John Bell and Jennet Mabon in Melrose, a.s.n. John Bell ; w. Alexander Bell, George Atchison.

,, ,, George Atchison and Elisabeth Hopkirk in Melrose, a.d.n. Elisabeth Atchison ; w. William Hopkirk, John Bell.

,, ,, William Mein and —— Wright in Galtonside, a.d.n. Jennet Mein ; w. James Mein, John Bell.

,, 8. John Hardie and Christian Dewar in Langshaw, a.d.n. Christian Hardie ; w. ——.

,, 27. James Mein and Elisabeth Hitoun in Newtoun, a.s.n. David Mein ; w. Nicoll Milne, John Riddell.

,, ,, Walter Vetch and Helen Marshell in Galtonside, a.d.n. Christian Vetch ; w. Andrew Mar, Mr. Robert Mar.

Nov. 3. James Usher and Agnes Frier in Darnick, a.s.n. James Usher ; w. John Usher, Charles Frier.

,, 11. William Swanston and Jennet Davidson in Mosshouses, a.s.n. David Swanston ; w. George Martine and ——.

,, 17. James Mercer and Margaret Vair in Darnick, a.s.n. Robert Mercer ; w. Andrew Moss, James Stodhart.

,, ,, John Chisholme and Margaret Laing in Galtonside, a.d.n. Mary Chisholme ; w. James Laing, James Mercer.

,, ,, Thomas Stavert and Marion Williamson in Langhaugh, a.s.n. James Stavert ; w. James Williamson, Hugh Young.

,, 24. William Turner and Jennet Wright in Galtonside, a.s.n. George Turner ; w. George Wright, George Martine.

Dec. 8. John Smith and Margaret Phaup in Darnick, a.d.n. Agnes Smith ; w. James Phaup, John Smith.

,, 22. James Wilson and Elisabeth Napier in Bauchlin, a.d.n. Jean Wilson ; w. James Napier, George Martine.

,, ,, Andrew Mercer and Katharin Mercer in Bridgend, a.s.n. John Mercer ; w. Mr. Andrew Patersone, George Martine.

,, 24. William Wilson and Helen Lauder in Blainslie, a.d.n. Helen Wilson ; w. John Stirling, James Stirling.

,, 29. John Bunzie and Anne Davidson in Newsteid, a.s.n. Thomas Bunzie ; w. John Mercer, Robert Bunzie.

,, ,, Robert Mein and Agnes Chisholme in Newsteid, a.d.n. Jean Mein ; w. John Mercer, Robert Bunzie.

1718.

Jan. 23. James Stirling and —— Sommervaill in Blainslie, a.s.n. Robert Stirling ; w. James Grieve, William Thynne.

,, 26. William Morison and Margaret Bowie in Melrose, a.s.n. James Morison ; w. James Bowie, William Hopkirk.

Feb. 2. Robert Balantine and Jennet Frier in Galtonside, a.s.n. William Balantine ; w. Robert Frier, John Frier.

1718.

Feb. 2. Thomas Gill and Alison Gill in Danieltoun, a.d.n. Jean Gill ; w.
Andrew Patersone, George Loury.

,,   6. Thomas Thynne and Jean Montgomery in Whitlie, a.s.n. Robert
Thynne ; w. Mr William Hunter, George Hog.

,,   9. Nicoll Milne and Isabell Turnbull in Newtoun, a.d.n. Christian
Milne ; w. Thomas Stenhouse, Thomas Milne.

,,   ,, Thomas Stenhouse and Helen Sibbald in Newtoun, a.d.n. Agnes
Stenhouse ; w. Nicol Milne, Thomas Milne.

,,   ,, Thomas Milne and Jennet Milne in Newtoun, a.d.n. Alison Milne ;
w. Nicol Milne, Thomas Stenhouse.

,,   ,, Andrew Mercer and Margaret Maxwell in Melrose, a.d.n. Margaret
Mercer ; w. Thomas Drummond, George Mercer.

,,   ,, Robert Edgar and Jean Young in Melrose, a.d.n. Mary Edgar ;
w. John Mabon, David Henderson.

,, 11. James Grieve and —— Allan in Blainslie, a.d.n. Margaret Grieve ;
w. Hugh Allan, William Thynne.

,, 26. John Darling and Jennet Bowston in Appletreeleaves, a.s.n. John
Darling and a.d.n. Jennet Darling ; w. ——.

,,   ,, Peter Moffet and Agnes Smith in Threepwood, —— Moffet ;
w. ——.

Mar. 3. John Haitlie and Cecill Gladstones in Drygrainge Boathouse,——
Haitlie ; w. Andrew Pringle and ——

,,   9. Charles Frier and Agnes Thurbrand in Galtonside, a.s.n. James Frier ;
w. Alexander Knox, Robert Huntlie.

,,   ,, William Hoy and Isabell Hoy in Galtonside, a.d.n. Christian Hoy ,
w. Alexander Knox, Robert Huntlie.

,, 16. John Moffet and Christain Ker in Galtonside, a.s.n. John Moffet ;
w. Thomas Bowstone, Thomas Haliwell.

,,   ,, Thomas Foster and Elisabeth Hope in Galtonside, a.s.n. Andrew
Foster ; w. Andrew Mar, Mr. Robert Marre.

,, 23. James Moodie and Jennet Mercer in Darnick, a.s.n. William
Moodie ; w. John Mercer, George Martine.

,,   ,, Andrew Bryden and Jennet Brown in Easterlanglie, a.s.n. Adam
Bryden ; w. David Speeding, George Mercer.

,,   ,, James Martine and Jennet Dickson in Darnick, a.d.n Margaret
Martine ; w. Michael Fisher, John Hownam.

,,   ,, William Wallace and Mary Scott in Melrose, a.s.n. James Wallace ;
w. Thomas Gardiner, William Lookup.

,,   ,, Robert Hilson and Agnes Bower in Melrose, a.s.n. Robert Hilson ;
w. George Hoy, Alexander M'Faden.

,, 26. James Watson and Jennet Henderson in Langshaw Mill, a.d.n.
Jean Watson ; w. James Ainslie, John Hardie.

,,   ,, John Wallace and Margaret Dick in Blainslie, a.s.n. James Wallace ;
w. John Stirling, James Grieve.

,,   ,, James Raith and Agnes Shillinglaw in Blainslie, a.s.n. James Raith ;
w. James Grieve, John Stirling.

,, 30. John Wadderston and Jean Ramsay in Newsteid, a.d.n. Elisabeth
Wadderston ; w. Andrew Lindsay, George Martine.

April 6. James Caribbes and Isabell Crosbie in Sorrowlessfield, a.d.n. Jean
Caribbes ; w. John Pearson, James Purves.

,,   8. Robert Patersone of Drygrainge and Anne Eliot, his lady, a.s.n.
William Patersone ; w. David Brown of Park, James Purves.

,, 21. John Frier and Jennet Turner in Housbyre, a.s.n. John Frier ; w.
Thomas Turner, Robert Frier.

,,   ,, Mungo Park and Isabell Hervie in Westhouses boathouse, a.s.n.
Thomas Park ; w. John Hervie, George Martine.

May 18. John Notman and Jennet Waddell in Gledswood, a.d.n. Alison
Notman ; w. John Waddell, William Waddell.

,,   ,, James Wilson and Elisabeth Rutherford in Eildon, a.d.n. Jean
Wilson ; w. Alexander Mein, John Sibbald.

1718.

May 25. James Mein and Margaret Mein in Newsteid, a.s.n. John Mein; w. Andrew Mein, John Mercer.

June 8. John Purvis and Jean Martine in Langhaugh, —— Purvis; w. George Martine, Andrew Martine.

,, 20. James Boyd and Elisabeth Raith in Blainslie, a.d.n. Agnes Boyd; w. Alexander Fisher, James Sandilands.

,, ,, James Sandilands and Agnes Lorimer in Colmeslichill, a.d.n. Jean Sandilands; w. Alexander Fisher, James Boyd.

July 7. John Tait and Jennet Pringle in Blainslie, a.d.n. Elisabeth Tait; w. Robert Purvis, James Purvis.

,, ,, Walter Watson and Jennet Lauder in Kedzliedoors, a.d.n. Agnes Watson; w. Robert Purvis, James Purvis.

,, 13. Andrew Usher and Isabell Thomson in Darnick, a.d.n. Marion Usher; w. James Ellies, George Martine.

,, 20. William Sclater and Helen Bunzie in Newsteid, a.d.n. Agnes Sclater; w. Robert Bunzie, John Bunzie.

,, 24. James Mar and Margaret Mercer in Darnick, a.d.n. Margaret Mar; w. Andrew Mar, Robert Mar.

,, 28. Robert Scott and Agnes Bunzie in Newsteid, —— Scott; w. Andrew Martine, George Martine.

Aug. 24. James Bunzie and Jean Wilson in Newsteid, a.s.n. James Bunzie; w. Andrew and Robert Bunzies.

,, 31. George Mercer and Agnes Knox in Easterlanglie, a.s.n. George Mercer; w. Robert Fisher, Andrew Bryden.

,, ,, Alexander Pringle and Marion Pringle in Galtonside, —— Pringle; w. Mr. Robert Mar, Andrew Linsday.

Sept. 3. John Mercer and Helen Sibbald in Darnick, a.d.n. Jennet Mercer; w. John Hitoun, James Usher.

,, 7. John Pearson and —— Caribbes in Old Melrose, a.s.n. George Pearson and a.d.n. Elisabeth Pearson; w. James Caribbes, Adam Balantine.

,, 10. George Bartoun and Alison Mercer in Galtonside, a.s.n. George Bartoun; w. George Bartoun, James Bowston.

,, 14. Andrew Hitoun and Agnes Linton in Darnick, a.s.n. John Hitoun; w. James Usher, James Mar.

,, ,, James Vair and Margaret Ker in Newtoun, a.s.n. William Vair; w. Nicoll Milne, William Ker.

,, ,, George Geddes and Christian Spear in Langshaw, a.s.n. John Geddes; w. Thomas Thymne, John Wood.

,, 28. Thomas Milne and Christian Walker in Newtoun, a.s.n. John Milne; w. Nicoll Milne, John Milne.

Oct. 26. James Rennaldson and Isabell Leadhouse in Darnick, a.s.n. James Rennaldson; w. John Mercer, John Smith.

,, ,, Robert Ormiston and Agnes Smith in Galtonside, a.d.n. Isabell Ormiston; w. John Smith, John Mercer.

Nov. 23. Thomas Wilson and Alison Hoy in Langhaugh, a.s.n. George Wilson; w. George Hoy, John Hoy.

Dec. 14. Walter Rae and Anne Eccles in Newtoun, —— Rae; w. Nicoll Milne, John Riddell.

,, 21. James Sibbald and —— Moss in Darnick, a.s.n. George Stodhart; w. John Mercer, William Stodhart.

,, 22. William Mein and Margaret Mein in Newtoun, a.d.n. Margaret Mein; w. Nicoll Milne, John Bunzie.

1719.

Jan. 4. Nicoll Milne and Elspeth Vair in Newtoun, a.s.n. William Milne; w. Nicoll Milne, Thomas Stenhouse.

,, ,, Nicoll Milne and Agnes Turnbull in Newtoun, a.d.n. Jennet Milne; w. Nicoll Milne, Thomas Stenhouse.

,, ,, John Sibbald and Agnes Stenhouse in Eildon, a.d.n. Christian Sibbald; w. Nicoll Milne, Thomas Stenhouse.

1719.

Jan.　4. Walter Mabon and Elisabeth Gill in Danieltoun, a.d.n. Katharin Mabon ; w. John Sibbald, Nicoll Milne.

　,,　7. James Purvis and Agnes Knox in Sorrowlessfield, a.s.n. Andrew Purvis ; w. Robert Purvis, William Wilsone.

　,,　8. John Mercer and Helen Patersone in Westhouses, a.s.n. Andrew Mercer ; w. Andrew Mar, Mr. Robert Mar.

　,,　11. John Gibson and Agnes Sclater in Melrose, a.s.n. William Gibson ; w. Henry Gibson, John Mabon.

　,,　18. John Bell and Jennet Mabon in Melrose, a.d.n. Jean Bell ; w. James Bowie, Alexander Bell.

　,,　25. Richard Bower and Isabell Simson in Eildon, a.d.n. Jean Bower ; w. John Sibbald, John Bunzie.

　,,　31. Andrew Mein and Jennet Mein in Newsteid, a.s.n. John Mein ; w. William Milne, John Milne.

Feb.　1. Thomas Mein and Isabell Hoy in Eildon, a.s.n. Alexander Mein ; w. George Hoy, John Hoy.

　,,　8. Andrew Bunzie and Margaret Robertson in Newsteid, a.s.n. Andrew Bunzie ; w. Robert Bunzie, James Bunzie.

　,,　10. William Hutchison and Jennet Speeding in Westhouses, a.s.n. Andrew Hutchison ; w. John Fraiter, John Darling.

Mar. 10. George Thomson and —— Hardie in Ladhopmuir, a.s.n. John Thomson ; w. Walter Thomson, Andrew Martine.

　,,　11. Mr. Andrew Patersone, schoolmaster, and Jean Cowan in Melrose, two daughters named Jean and Margaret Patersone ; w. ——.

　,,　22. James Bowie and Marion Bell in Melrose, a.s.n. Alexander Bowie ; w. Alexander Bell, Robert Bunzie.

　,,　,, James Loury and Isabell Brown in Newtoun, a.s.n. John Loury ; w. Nicoll Milne, John Riddell.

　,,　25. James Laidlaw and Christian Brunton in Buckholme, a.d.n. Eupham Laidlaw ; w. Andrew Darling, James Davidson.

　,,　,, Andrew Darling and Helen Lithgow in Threepwood, —— Darling ; w. James Laidlaw, James Davidson.

April　5. Robert Hunter and Jean Brock in Melrose, a.s.n. James Hunter ; w. James Hunter, Andrew Martine.

　,,　19. Mungo Laidlaw and Margaret Cochran in Newtoun, a.s.n. James Laidlaw ; w. James Laidlaw, Nicoll Milne.

May　3. John Napier and —— Drummond, a.s.n. William Napier ; w. Andrew Drummond, Andrew Mercer.

　,,　,, Philip Douglass and Agnes Hall in Melrose, a.d.n. Emilia Douglass ; w. James Phaup, Alexander Bell.

　,,　,, Alexander Bell and Jennet Bell in Melrose, a.d.n. Anne Bell ; w. James Bowie, Robert Bunzie.

　,,　10. William Mathison and Jennet Livingston in Galtonside, a.s.n. James Mathison ; w. James Mathison, Andrew Mar.

　,,　12. Robert Stirling and Isabell Stewart in Blainslie, a.s.n. John Stirling ; w. John Stirling, James Stirling.

　,,　,, James White and Jennet Turnbull in Hawicksheill, a.d.n. Jane White ; w. John Stirling, James Stirling.

　,,　,, John Spotwood and Agnes Wilsone in Langhaugh, a.s.n. Helen Spotwood ; w. John Fisher, Robert Fisher.

May 25. James Bowston and Marion Blaikie in Galtonside, a.s.n. James Bowston ; w. Andrew Bowston, James Blaikie.

　,,　,, John Fiddes and Jennet Pringle in Galtonside, —— Fiddes ; w. James Blaikie, Andrew Bowston.

June　4. Richard Thomson and Isabell Moffet in Williamlaw, a.d.n. Isabell Thomson ; w. Mr. William Hunter, Thomas Thynne.

　,,　,, John Herd and Agnes Small in Whitliedykes, a.d.n. Helen Herd ; w. Mr. William Hunter, Thomas Thynne.

　,,　7. George Atchison and Elisabeth Hopkirk in Melrose, a.d.n. Jennet Atchison ; w. William Hopkirk, Thomas Atchison.

1719.

June 28. Nicoll Mercer and Christian Mein in Darnick. a.s.n. William Mercer ; w. James Mein, William Grieston.

,, ,, John Hoy and Isabell Bartoun in Melrose, a.s.n. John Hoy ; w. George Hoy, George Bartoun.

July 3. Richard Robson and Elisabeth Pringle in Blainslie, a.s.n. James Robson ; w. John Thynne, Hugh Allan.

, ,, William Thynne and Marion Fairbairn in Blainslie, a.d.n. Margaret Thynne ; w. John Thynne, Hugh Allan.

,, 20. John Lawson of Colmeslie and Sarah Gunter, his lady, a.d.n. Margaret Lawson ; w. Mr. Gideon Rutherfurd, George Martine.

Aug. 2. William Bunzie and Jennet Fairbairn in Newsteid, a.s.n. William Bunzie ; w. Robert Fairbairn, Robert Bunzie.

,, ,, Robert Bunzie and Marion Hopkirk in Newsteid, a.d.n. Mary Bunzie ; w. William Hopkirk, William Bunzie.

,, 9. Andrew Stewart and Agnes Mein in Galtonside, a.s.n. Robert Stewart : w. George Stewart, Robert Ormiston.

,, ,, John Chisholme and Margaret Ritchie in Langshaw, —— Chisholme : w. George Martine, Andrew Martine.

,, 23. John Cochran and Jennet Rutherfurd in Newtoun, a.s.n. John Cochran ; w. Nicoll Milne, Thomas Stenhouse.

Sept. — David Grieve and Helen Pringle in Blainslie, a.s.n. James Grieve : w. James Grieve, William Thynne.

,, — John Hardie and Christian Dewar in Langshaw, a.d.n. Christian Hardie ; w. James Grieve, William Thynne.

,, 13. James Usher and Agnes Frier in Darnick, a.s.n. Thomas Usher ; w. Charles Frier, John Usher.

,, 27. Robert Huntlie and Isabell Frier in Galtonside, a.s.n. Robert Huntlie ; w. Charles Frier, Andrew Mercer.

,, ,, Andrew Mein and Helen Mein in Newsteid, a.s.n. James Mein ; w. Andrew Mein, Thomas Williamson.

,, ,, Andrew Mercer and Margaret Frier in Darnick, a.d.n. Agnes Mercer ; w. James Usher, Robert Huntlie.

Oct. 14. Robert Balantine and Jennet Frier in Galtonside, a.d.n. Jennet Balantine ; w. John Frier, Robert Frier.

,, 18. John Bunzie and Anne Davidson in Newsteid, a.s.n. James Bunzie ; w. Robert Bunzie, William Sclater.

,, ,, John Gill and Alison King in Melrose, a.s.n. Thomas Gill ; w. Thomas Gill, George Martine.

Nov. 1. Andrew Drummond and Helen Mathison in Bridgend, a.s.n. George Drummond ; w. George Drummond, Thomas Mathison.

,, 16. James Ker and Isabell Allan in Housbyre, a.d.n. Christian Ker ; w. Alexander Knox, George Stewart.

,, ,, John Laing and Elisabeth Purvis, a.s.n. William Laing, by fornication, presented by William Martin in Galtonside : w. Alexr. Knox, George Stewart.

,, 22. John Notman and Agnes Davie in Melrose, a.s n. Alexander Notman ; w. John Mabon, Thomas Gill.

,, ,, Thomas Gill and Alison Gill in Danieltoun, a.d.n. Helen Gill ; w. Alexander Patersone, George Loury.

,, ,, Robert Patersone of Drygrainge and Anne Eliott his lady, a.s.n. Robert Patersone ; w. Robert Fisher of Easterlanglie, David Broun of Park, James Wilkieson, clerk.

,, 26. Peter Moffet and Agnes Smith in Threepwood, a.d.n. Agnes Moffet ; w. James Stirling, William Thynne.

Dec. 2. John Usher and Christian Bower in Eildon, a.s.n. John Usher ; w. Thomas Stenhouse, James Mein.

,, ,, William Rutherfurd and Isabell Telfer, a.s.n. George Rutherfurd ; w. James Mein, Thomas Stenhouse.

,, 17. Charles Frier and Agnes Thurbrand in Galtonside, a.d.n. Christian Frier ; w. James Mathison, William Mathison.

1719.

Dec. 26. Robert Mein and Jean Wier in Newtoun, a.d.n. Mary Mein ; w. Andrew Mein, James Broun.

,, 23. Mr. Gideon Rutherfurd and Jean Kar in Langshaw, a.s.n. Robert and a.d.n. Jean Rutherfurd ; w. Robert Fisher of Easterlanglie, Thomas Fairbairn of Broadwoodshiell.

,, ,, Thomas Waddell and Eupham Moffet, a.s.n. John Waddell ; w. the said Robert Fisher and Thomas Fairbairn.

1720.

Jan. 17. John Mein and Mary Mein in Newsteid, a.s.n. Thomas Mein ; w. Andrew Mein and Andrew Mein.

,, ,, Adam Hislope and Elisabeth Mercer in Darnick, a.s.n. James Hislope ; w. John Mercer, James Stodhart.

,, 19. Thomas Young and Margaret Thomson in Appletreeleaves, a.s.n. George Young ; w. John Fraiter, John Darling.

    24. Andrew Mercer and Katharin Mercer in Bridgend, a.d.n. Alison Mercer : w. John Mercer, William Mercer.

,, ,, Andrew Moss and Margaret Wauch in Darnick : a.d.n. Isabell Moss ; w. James Wauch, John Mercer.

Feb. 7. Andrew Mar and Susanna Lithgow in Galtonside, a.d.n. Alison Mar ; w. James Mar, John Mar.

,, ,, John Sibbald and Agnes Stenhouse in Eildon, —— Sibbald ; w. ——.

,, 14. John Smith and Helen Mercer in Darnick, a.s.n. Andrew Smith ; w. John Smith, Patrick Thomson.

,, ,, Thomas Martine and Jennet Runchiman in Galtonside, a.d.n. —— Martine ; w. George Martine, Andrew Martine.

,, 17. Nicoll Milne and Isabell Turnbull in Newtoun, a.d.n. Christian Milne ; w. Thomas Stenhouse, John Stenhouse.

,, 21. Henry Cochran and Jennet Vair in Newtoun, a.d.n. Isabell Cochran ; w. Nicoll Milne, John Riddell.

,, ,, Robert Mein and Agnes Chisholme in Newsteid, a.d.n. Mary Mein ; w. Andrew Mein, John Mein.

Mar. 6. Mr. Andrew Patersone, schoolmaster, and Jean Cowan, a.d.n. Jean Paterson ; w. Andrew Patersone, Robert Scott.

,, 14. George Wight and Jean Carmichell in Whitlie, a.s.n. James Wight ; w. Thomas Thynne, George Thynne.

,, 20. Mungo Park and Isabell Hervie in Westhouses, a.s.n. Mungo Park ; w. Andrew M'Faden, James Bunzie.

,, 28. John Welch and Elisabeth Scott in Buckholme, a.d.n. Margaret Welch ; w. James Laidlaw, William Atchison.

April 3. James Gardiner and Margaret Bowston in Galtonside, a.d.n. Helen Gardiner ; w. Thomas Bowston, James Gardiner.

,, 17. John Anderson and Elisabeth Pearson in Drygrainge, a.s.n. Robert Anderson : w. Robert Wilsone, Robert Martine.

,, ,, Robert Wilsone and Margaret Pearson in Drygrainge, a.d.n. Isabell Wilsone ; w. John Anderson, Robert Martine.

,, 24. John Bower and Agnes Dalgliesh, a.d.n Katharin Bower ; w. John Bunzie and John Bunzie.

,, 26. Thomas Wood and Margaret Currie in Blainslie, a.d.n. Jennet Wood ; w. John Thynne, William Thynne.

(Blank till 29th May, when handwriting changes.)

May 29. James Mar in Dernick and Isobel Mercer, a.d.n. Helen : w. John Mercer, John Stoddart.

,, ,, At Galashiels, George, son to James Williamson and Elspeth Scot in Hugh Darlings in Langliehaugh ; w. Wm. Williamson, John Donaldson.

June 4. George Mercer and Agnes Knox in Easterlanglie, a.s.n. Robert ; w. Robert Fisher in Easterlanglie ; Andrew Bryden, his servant.

1720.

June 12. Richard Frater and Isobel Mercer in Danzieltoun, a.d.n. Isobel ; w. Andrew and Thomas Mercers.

„ 19. John Friar, tennent in Calfhill, and Jennet Turner, his wife ; w. John Mercer, James Usher in Darnick.

„ 26. James Mein in Newtoun and Bessie Heatoun, his wife, a.s.n. William ; w. Nicol Milns, elder and younger.

July 3. James Smaill, weaver in Melrose, and Elizabeth Ellies, his wife, a.d.n Isobel ; w. Thomas Guill, William Elleis.

„ „ Robert Williamson, wright in Gatonside and Agnes Scott, a.d.n. Margaret ; w. William and Thomas Williamsons.

„ 14. Alexander M'Fadkin, taylor in Melross, and Agnes Napier, his wife, a.s.n. Alexander ; w. Andrew and James M'Fadkins.

„ 18. Andrew Hounam, weaver in Darnick, and Margaret Moodie, a.d.n. Alison ; w. James Moodie, Andrew Henderson.

, „ James Mercer, taylor in Newsteed and Jennet Craig, his wife, a.s.n. William ; w. William and John Mercers.

„ 22. John Fisher of Westerhousbyre and Margaret Rutherford, a.s.n. Andrew ; w. Robert Fisher of Easterlanglie, Mr. Thomas Rutherford, schoolmaster in Earlstoun.

„ 31. Walter Leithhead in Longnewtoun and Joan Walker in Darnick, a.d.n. Jennet ; w. John Walker, James Stoddart.

Aug. 12. ——.

„ 23. John Wallace in Blainslie and Margaret Dick, his wife, a.s.n. Adam ; w. John and William Thynnes.

„ „ William Wilson, weaver in Blainslie, and Helen Lauder, a.d.n. Margaret ; w. William Thyne, John Wallace.

„ 30. George Aillie in Westerlanglie and Marion Frater, a.d.n. Grizzal ; w. Robert Frater, Alexander Melross.

Sept. 4. Thomas Stenhouse and Helen Sibbald, his wife, a.s.n. James ; w. Nicol Miln, John Sibbald.

„ „ George Maxwell in Gatonside and Isobel Paterson, a.d.n. Isobel ; w. Alexander and Andrew M'Fadkins.

„ „ Robert Rutherford in Bridgend and Elizabeth Heatoun, his wife, a.d.n. Jennet ; w. Andrew and George Beatties.

„ 11. Robert Bunzie, mason in Newsteed, and Beatrix Frame, a.s.n. Thomas ; w. Thomas Bunzie, Andrew Mein.

„ „ John Kemp in Westhouses and ——, a.d.n. Jennet ; w. George Martine, George Moodie.

„ 18. Richard Bower in Eildoun and Isobel Simson, a.s.n. John ; w. John Sibbald, John Bunzie.

, 25. Thomas Mein in Eildoun and Isobel Hoy, a.s.n. William ; w. Alexander Mein, his father, James Hunter.

„ „ William Morison and Margaret Bowie, a.s.n. William ; w. James Bowie, James Bunzie.

„ 27. John Corsbie in Clakmae and Elizabeth Hardie, a.d.n. Agnes ; w. Alexander Sanderson, Alexander Lindsay.

„ „ James Martine in Newhouses and Jennet Dickson, a.s.n. John ; w. Thomas Laidla, James Scott.

„ „ James Stirling and Margaret Stirling in the Rhone, a.d.n. Margaret ; w. Robert and John Stirlings.

„ „ William Robson in Gatonside and Elizabeth Scott, a.d.n. Isobel ; w. Robert Halywell, Robert Philp.

Oct. 2. John Bunzie and Jean Sibbald in Newtoun, a.s.n. John ; w. Nicol Milne, Thomas Stenhouse.

„ „ Robert Walker in Langhaugh and Jennet Currie at Galashields, a.d.n. Margart.

„ 9. John Bunzie and Marion Wallace in Eildoun, a.d.n. Marion ; w. George Martine, bedal ; John Frater in Langhaugh.

„ 16. Thomas Mathison and Margaret Bonningtoun in Westhouses, a.s.n. Alexander ; w. William Darlings, elder and younger.

1720.

Oct. 18. John Fairbairn and Jean Trotter in Colmslie, a.s.n. John ; w. John
Fisher, portioner in Housebyre ; John Mercer.

    23. William Mebon in Newsteid and Jennet Simson, a.s.n. John ; w.
Walter Mebon, William Sclater.

.. 23. James Mein in Newsteid and Margaret Bunzie, a.d.n. Agnes ; w.
Robert and Andrew Bunzies there.

.. ,, James Hart in Galtonside and Agnes Thomson, a.d.n. Agnes ; w.
William Hart, his brother ; George Martine, bedal.

.. ,, John Darling and Jennet Lees in Blainslie, a.s.n. George ; w. John
and Thomas Darlings.

.. ,, James Scott and Helen Lauder in Blainslie, a.d.n. Isobel ; w. James
Edgar, George Darling.

.. 30. John Smith, taylor in Darnick, and Margaret Phaap, a.s.n. John ; w.
James Phaap, his father-in-law ; John Smith, younger.

Nov. 5. James Purvis in Drygrange and Agnes Knox, a.d.n. Grizzal : w.
James Hunter, procurator in Melrose, George Martine.

., ,, Robert Wilson and Agnes Bower, a.d.n. Alison ; w. Alexander Bell,
James Hunter.

,, 13. Andrew Crawford in Newsteid and Mary Mein, a.d.n. Elizabeth ; w.
John Mein, portioner there, James Pringle.

,, ., Robert Scott and Agnes Bunzie in Newsteid, a.s.n. Andrew ; w.
Robert Bunzie, James Scott.

,, 15. Robert Brown and Isobel Brunton in Blainslie, a.d.n. Isobel ; w.
John and William Thynne.

., 20. Patrick Thomson, sclatter in Galtonside, and Isobel Moffett, a.d.n.
Margaret ; w. John Smith, Robert Halywell.

,, ,. George Bartone in Galtonside and Alison Mercer, a.d.n. Isobel ; w.
John and George Hoys.

.. 27. James Mein, taylour in Newsteid, and Margaret Mein, a.d.n. Agnes ;
w. James Broun, James Mein.

,, ,. —— Halywell in Galtonside and —— Nicol, —— ; w. Andrew
Marr, Thomas Boustoun.

Dec. 4. Robert Mein in Newsteid and Jean Symmingtoun, a.d.n. Jennet ; w.
John Mercer, William Rennaldson.

.. ., James Vair in Newtoun and Margaret Ker, a.d.n. Elizabeth ; w.
Nicol Miln, John Gill.

,, 15. James Raith and Agnes Shillinglaw in Blainsly, a.s.n. William : w.
Thomas Darling, David Grieve.

.. 23. John Moffett in Galtonside and Christian Ker, a.d.n. Jean ; w.
Patrick Thomson, Andrew Marr.

1721.

Jan. 1. Robert Fairbairn, weaver in Danieltoun, a.s.n. John ; w. Margaret
Davidson, Andrew Paterson, George Lawrie.

,, 14. Robert Ballantyne and Jennet Friar in Galtonside, a.d.n. Jennet ; w.
John Friar, her father, Robert Friar.

, 22. George Drummond, weaver in Bridgend, and —— Scot, his wife,
a.s.n. William : w. Andrew Drummond there, John Mercer elder,
in Darnick.

    26. Nicol Bower and Jennet Riddell in Newtoun a.s.n. William ; w.
John Riddell, Thomas Mein.

Feb. 5. Walter Murray, cowper in Melrose, and Isobel Mathison, a.s.n.
Thomas : w. John and William Mebons.

,, ,, William Mercer in Galtonside and Elizabeth Lumsdale, a.d.n. Jennet ;
w. Andrew Mercer, James Waugh.

    12. Andrew Smith in Galtonside and Helen Boustoun, a.s.n. James ; w.
Thomas Bouston, James Gardiner there.

.. ,, Andrew Henderson in Darnick and Margaret Hounam, a.s.n.
Andrew ; w. Andrew Hounam, John Smith.

    27. John Taite in Blainsly and Margaret Pringle, a.s.n. John ; w. William
Thynne, James Grieve.

1721.

Mar. 6. William Thynne in Blainsly and Marion Fairbairn, a.d.n. Katharine : w. John Thynne, James Stirling.

,, 12. Andrew Mein in Newsteid and Jennet Mein, a.s.n. John ; w. John Mercer, John Mein.

,, ,, Thomas Wight in Galtonside and Alison Moss, a.d.n. Jennet : w. Robert Ballantyne, James Stoddart.

,, 18. Alexander Bell and Jennet Bell, a.s.n. William ; w. James Bowie, merchant in Melrose, Robert Bunzie.

,, 28. James Wood in Housbyre and Jean Fortune, a.s.n. Gilbert : w. John Wood, his brother, John Mercer there.

,, ,, Robert Mercer and Jennet Little, a.d.n. Jennet ; w. as before.

April 2. James Wilson in Bauchline and Elizebath Napier, a.s.n. Alexander : w. John Napier, George Martine.

,, ,, John Wood in Hagburn and —— Notman, a.d.n. Margaret ; w. James Hoge.

,, 16. Andrew Usher, weaver in Darnick, and Isobel Thomson, a.d.n. Jennet ; w. John Heaton, John Mercer there.

,, ,, John Pearson in Old Melrose and Margaret Crosbie, a.s.n. Michael ; w. John Anderson, John Mein, in Newsteid.

,, ,, Andrew Bunzie in Newsteid and Margaret Robertson, a.s.n. Andrew ; w. Robert and James Bunzies in Melrose.

,, 18. James Laidla in Buckholm and Christian Brunton, a.s.n. Walter ; w. James Laidla, Alexr. Wood.

,, ,, James Clapperton and Jean Haddon in Appletreeleaves, a.s.n. Alexander ; w. as before.

,, 23. Nicol Miln in Newtoun and Isobel Turnbull, a.d.n. Isobel ; w. Thomas Stenhouse, Nicoll Bower.

,, ,, William Rennaldson and —— , a.s.n. Andrew ; w. as before.

,, 28. Walter Watson and Jennet Lauder in Kedzliedoors, a.d.n. Isobel ; w. William Marshal, Andrew Pringle.

,, ,, John Napier and Jennet Drummond, a.s.n. John ; w. Andrew and George Drummond in Bridgend.

May 7. James Bouston in Galtonside and Marion Blaikie, a.d.n. Margaret ; w. James Blaikie, messenger in Melrose, Thomas Boustoun.

,, 19. John Paterson in Galtonside and Margaret Riddel, a.s.n. George ; w. Andrew Marr, portioner, Robert Ballantyne.

June 4. George Aitchison, smith in Melrose, and Elizebath Hopkirk, a.d.n. —— : w. William Hopkirk, Andrew M'Fadzeon.

,, 18. John Riddel of Muselie, and Margaret Riddel, a.s.n. James ; w. Robert Paterson of Drygrange, James Ellies of Huntliewood.

,, 25. Patrick Bulman and Isobel Ker in Newtoun, a.d.n. Helen ; w. John Riddel, Nicol Miln.

July 23. John Gill, miller in Melrose, and Alison King, a.s.n. George ; w. Thomas Gill, Archibald Wallace.

,, ,, John Cossar and Margaret Purvis, a.d.n. Margaret : w. Mungo Purvis, James Smail.

Aug. 8. Mr. Gideon Rutherfoord and Jean Ker in Langshaw, a.d.n. Christian : w. Robert Fisher of Langlie, John Fisher of Housebyre.

,, 13. Andrew Heaton and Agnes Linthill in Darnick, a.s.n. Andrew : w. John Moodie, James Usher.

,, ,, Robert Friar and Mary Fisher in Galtonside, a.d.n. Mary : w. John Friar, his father, William Winter.

,, ,, Walter Rae, weaver in Newtoun, and Anna Ecklis, a.s.n. Walter : w. John Riddel, Nicol Miln.

,, 19. William Bunzie and Jennet Fairbairn, a.d.n. Jennet : w. Robert Bunzie, weaver, Robert Bunzie, mason.

,, ,, Robert Bunzie and Marion Hopkirk, a.d.n. Elizabeth ; w. William Bunzie, William Hopkirke.

,, 27. Robert Paterson of Drygrange and Anna Elliot, a.d.n. Marion : w. John Riddel of Muselie, James Wilkison.

1721.

Aug. 27. John Mein and Mary Mein, a.s.n. William ; w. William Hopkirk, William Williamson.

,, ,, James Mein and Katharine Shiel, a.d.n. Jennet ; w. Robert Bunzie, James King.

Sept. 10. Robert Hunter and Jean Broke, a.d.n. Christian ; w. James Blaikie, Andrew Martine.

,, 14. James Hog and Isobel Sandilands in Hagburn, a.d.n. Agnes ; w. James Howden, George Hog.

,, 17. Thomas and Allison Gills, a.d.n. Margaret ; w. Andrew Paterson, George Lawrie.

,, ,, John Turnbul and Elizabeth Familton, a.s.n. William ; w. Thomas Bowstoun, Andrew Smith.

,, 23. John Bunzie, weaver in Newsteid, and Ann Davidson, a.s.n. John ; w. Robert and Thomas Bunzies.

Oct. 8. James Leithan and Margaret Sclatter, a s.n. Robert ; w. John Sibbald, John Bunzie.

,, ,, John Rae, gardiner in Melrose, a.d.n. Margaret ; w. Alexander Bell, Robert Ormistoun.

,, 10. Thomas Waddal and Euphan Moffet, a.d.n. Isobel ; w. Mr. Gideon Rutherferd, John Friar.

,, ,, James Watson and Isobel Henderson in Langshawmiln, a.s.n. Gideon ; w. as before.

,, ,, James Grieve and Jean Watson, a.d.n. Jennet ; w. William and John Thynnes.

,, 22. John Stenhouse and Helen Kyle, a.d.n. Christian ; w. Thomas Stenhouse, Nicol Miln.

,, ,, John Sibbald in Eildoun, and Agnes Stenhouse, a.d.n. Helen; w. John and Thomas Stenhouse.

,, 28. George Beatty and Marion Wright, a.s.n. Andrew ; w. Andrew Drummond, Andrew Beatty.

,, ,, Thomas Williamson, wright in Newsteid, and Mary Mein, a.d.n. Mary ; w. John Mein, portioner in Newsteid, William Williamson, his brother.

Nov. 7. Andrew Mein, Wyndfoot in Newsteid, and Helen Mein, a.s.n. Thomas ; w. Andrew Mein, Robert Bunzie.

,, 13. George Alley in Westerlanglie and Marion Frater, a.s.n. George ; w. George Alley, his father, John Frater.

,, ,, John Hall in Calfhill and Margaret Hope, a.d.n. Elizabeth ; w. James Broun, Thomas Young.

,, 19 Robert Ormstoun in Galtonside and Agnes Smith, a.s.n. Andrew ; w. John Smith, elder, William Young.

,, ,, William Stoddart in Darnick and Jennet Smith, a.d.n. Jennet ; w. James Stoddart, weaver in Darnick, John Smith, there.

,, 25. John Mercer, mason in Newsteid, and Agnes Mein, a.d.n. Agnes ; w. John Mercer, his son, Robert Mein, smith there.

Dec. 6. James Heatoun and Jean Darling, a.d.n. Agnes ; w. Mr. Andrew Darling, John Frater.

,, 10. Robert Mein in Newsteid and Jean Wier, a.d.n. Jean ; w. Andrew Mein, his brother, Andrew Mein, elder.

,, 20. John Fisher of Westerhousebyre, and Margaret Rutherford, his lady, a.s.n. Robert ; w. William Darling, George Martine, bedal.

,, 25. George Heard and Agnes Small in Whitlaw, a.d.n. Elisabeth ; w. George Wright, John Pringle.

,, 31. Robert Mein in Newsteid and Agnes Chisholm, a.d.n. Jean ; w. John Mein, portioner there, Andrew Mein.

1722.

Jan. 7. Robert Sclatter and Jennet Eliot, a.s.n. Richard ; w. John Sibbald, John Bunzie.

,, ,, John Mercer and Margaret Davidson, a.d.n. Elspeth : w. Robert Bunzie, Andrew Mein.

1722.

Jan. 19. William Miln and Isobel Riddel in Newsteid, a.s.n. Adam ; w. John Mercer, Andrew Mein.

,, ,, Mungo Park and Isobel Harvie, a.s.n. John ; w. John Harvie, James Niel.

,, ,, Thomas Bunzie and Jean Wilson in Newsteid, a.s.n. Robert ; w. Robert Bunzie, Robert Wilson.

,, 28. William Mien and Margaret Mien in Eildoun, a.d.n. Marion ; w. John Sibbald, John Bunzie.

Feb. 4. John Marr and Isobel Lithgow in Galtonside, a.s.n. James ; w. Robert Mar, Edward Lithgow.

,, ,, James Smaill and Elizebath Ellice, a.d.n. Helen ; w. John Mebon, William Ellice.

,, 5. Richard Thomson and Isobel Moffet in Williamlaw, a.s.n. William ; w. James Hog, John Wallace.

,, 19. Thomas Darling and Mary Dods in Blainslie, a.s.n. Hugh ; w. William and John Thynnes.

,, ,, James Wallace and Euphan Darling there, a.d.n. Euphan ; w. John and Michael Wallaces.

,, 25. John Mercer in Galtonside and Helen Paterson, a.d.n. Agnes ; w. John and Nicol Mercers.

,, 26. James Davidson in Buckholm and Jennet Henrie, a.s.n. Michael ; w. James Laidla, William Aitchison.

Mar. 4. James Mar and Margaret Mercer in Dernick, a.s.n. Robert ; w. Robert and Andrew Mars.

,, ,, John Fiddes and Jennet Pringle in Galtonside, a.s.n. Walter ; w. Robert and James Pringles.

,, 11. John Mien in Newtoun and Elizabeth Heatoun, a.s.n. Walter ; w. James Mien, Nicol Miln.

,, 18. Andrew Drummond, weaver in Bridgend, and Helen Mathison, a.d.n. Isobel ; w. Mr. John Cranstoun, writer hereof, George Martine, bedal.

,, ,, Robert Rutherford and Elizabeth Heatoun in Bridgend, a.d.n. Elizabeth ; w. Andrew Drummond aforesaid, Andrew Heatoun in Dernick.

April 8. John Waite and Jennet Purvis in Drygrange, a.d.n. Marion ; w. James Purvis, William Riddel.

,, ,, Robert Turnbull, gardiner in Newstoun, and Elizabeth Gibson, a.s.n. John ; w. Nicol Miln, Henrie Cochran.

,, ,, Andrew Mercer and Margaret Friar in Dernick, a.s.n. George ; w. James Usher, Charles Friar.

,, 12. James Scott and Helen Lauder in Blainslie, a.s.n. George ; w. Thomas Thynne, James Hunter.

,, ,, Thomas Young and Isobel Thomson in Appletreeleaves, a.d.n. Elizabeth ; w. John Darling, James Clappertoun.

,, 21. John Vogan and Isobel Hunter in Danieltoun, a.d.n. Christian ; w. Andrew Paterson, George Lawrie.

May 3. Peter Moffet in Threepwood and Agnes Smith, a.s.n. Thomas ; w. George Moffet, John Chisholm.

,, ,, William Broun and Jean Dickson in Colmsliehill, a.d.n. Janet ; w. as before.

,, 14. William Sibbald and Jannet Martine, a.s.n. Alexander ; w. Thomas Boustoun, George Stuart.

,, ,, James Gardiner and Margaret Bouston in Galtonside, a.s.n. James ; w. Thomas Bouston, William Oliver.

,, ,, James Stoddart and Elizabeth Moss in Dernick, a.d.n. —— ; w. John Mercer, John Smith.

,, 27. Alexander and Marion Pringles in Melrose, a.s.n. Thomas ; w. Alexr. Bell, James Hunter.

,, 28. Nicol Milne and Jennet Vair in Newtoun, a.d.n. Jennet ; w. Nicoll Milne, Thomas Stenhouse.

1722.

June   3. John Kemp in Galtonside and Helen Grant, a.s.n. John ; w. Thomas
Boustoun, William Hoy.

„   10. Richard Bower in Eildoun and Isobel Simpson, a.s.n. Richard ; w.
John Bunzie, John Sibbald.

„   17. John Miln, portioner, in Newtoun, and Isobel Aird, a.s.n. John ; w.
Nicol Miln, elder and younger, there.

„   „ James Fisher of Bearfolds and Margaret Ker, a.s.n. Robert ; w. Mr.
Gideon Rutherford in Langshaw, Robert Fisher of Langlie.

„   „ John Thomson and Margaret Martine in Galtonside, a.d.n. Isobel ;
w. William Sibbald, Patrick Thomson.

„   „ Robert Chisholm and Bessie Pringle in Galtonside, a.s.n. William ;
w. Andrew Marr, Andrew Lindsay.

„   18. John Fairbairn and Jean Trotter in Colmslie, a.s.n. Thomas ; w.
Andrew Lithgow, Richard Frater.

„   „ Andrew Darling and Helen Lithgow in Threepwood, a.s.n. Adam ;
w. Andrew Lithgow, Peter Moffet.

July   1. William Aitchison, mason in Newsteid, and Jennet Shiel, a.s.n. John ;
w. George Shiel, John Mien.

„   „ George Penmans and Margaret Sandilands, a.d.n. Anna ; w. Robert
Penmans, elder and younger.

„   „ John Bell, weaver in Melrose, and Jennet Mabone, a.s.n. George ; w.
Thomas Mabon, Robert Speedin.

„   8. Thomas Draquhill, in the paroch of Bouden, upon bringing a line
from the elders, had his child, a.s.n. Thomas, baptised here ; w.
Andrew Paterson, George Lawrie.

„   „ Walter Thomson in Mosshouses and Margaret Harvie, a.d.n. Jennet ;
w. as above.

„   „ John Anderson in Drygrange and Elizabeth Pearson, a.s.n. Alexander ; w. James Purvis, John Pearson.

„   12. Andrew Mercer in Bridgend and Katharine Mercer, a.s.n. Andrew ;
w. John and William Mercers.

„   16. Robert Ormistoun and Helen Hopkirke, a.d.n. Jennet ; w. William
Hopkirke, George Aitchison.

Aug.   15. William Oliver in Melrose and Mary Pringle, a.d.n. Isobel ; w.
Andrew and William Lukeups.

[Blank till 7th October.]

Oct   7. Robert Paterson of Drygrange and Anna Elliot, a.s.n. William ;
w. John Riddel of Muselie, James Ellies of Huntlie.

„   „ Walter Murray and Isobel Mathison, a.s.n. Andrew ; w. Archibald
Wallace, John Mebon.

„   20. —— To John Bunzie ——.

Nov.   18. William Morison and Margaret Bowie, a.s.n. Thomas ; w. James
Bowies, elder and younger.

„   „ John Usher and Christian Bower in Eildoun, a.d.n. Christian ; w.
James Usher in Dernick, Richard Bower.

„   20. William Cairncross and Jennet Williamson in Ha Rae, a.s.n. Thomas.

„   „ John Purvis and Jean Martine in Langhaugh, a.s.n. Robert.

„   25. Andrew Shillinglaw in Blainslie, a.s.n. Robert ; w. William and
John Thynnes.

„   30. Patrick Thomson and Isobel Moffett in Galtonside, —— ; w. Andrew
Mien, Thomas Boustoun.

Dec.   5. Thomas Stenhouse and Helen Sibbald, a.s.n. James ; w. James
Mein, Thomas Miln.

„   16. Andrew Hownam and Margaret Moodie, a.d.n. Agnes ; w. John
Hounam, Andrew Henderson.

„   „ George Grahamslie and Margaret Caldcleugh, a.d.n. Jennet ; w.
George Grahamslie, Andrew Paterson.

„   24. Andrew Broun and Margaret Gowanlock in Langhaugh, a.d.n.
Grizzal ; w. John Darling, John Frater.

1722.
Dec. 26. Robert Mercer and Jennet Little in Housebyre, a.s.n. Robert ; w. John and Robert Mercers.

,, 28. George Rolmainzies and Agnes Grieve in Blainslie, a.d.n. Agnes ; w. John Grieve, Thomas Darling.

,, 30. John Cossar and Margaret Purvis in Melrose, a.d.n. Agnes ; w. Mungo and John Purvis.

,, ,, James Edgar and Helen Laidla in Eildoun, a.s.n. John ; w. Thomas Laidla, John Sibbald.

1723.
Jan. 8. James Martine and —— Dickson in Blainslie, —— ; w. James Dickson, elder and younger.

,, 15. James Hunter and Agnes Burnlie in Housebyre, ——.

,, 20. John Mien and Mary Mien of Old Melrose, a.d.n. Margaret ; w. Mr. Robert Mein, procurator, John Mein, chirurgeon.

,, ,, James Dods and Anna Riddel, gardiner in Newsteid, a.d.n. Margaret ; w. John Dods, William Riddel.

,, ,, James Mercer in Newsteid and Jennet Craig, a.d.n. Mary ; w. William and John Mercers.

,, 27. Thomas Wight and Alison Moss in Galtonside, a.d.n. Anna ; w. James Stoddart, Robert Ballantyne.

,, ,, Andrew M'Fadzeon and Christian Cook, a.d.n. Elizabeth ; w. Andrew Martine, chirurgeon, Alexr. M'Fadzeon.

Feb. 1. Nicol Miln and Agnes Turnbull, a.d.n. Alison ; w. Patrick Bullman, George Martine.

,, 3. Alexander M'Fadzeon and Agnes Napier, a.d.n. Margaret ; w. Andrew M'Fadzeon, George Hoy.

,, 19. Walter Watson and Jennet Lauder in Keadzliedoors, a.d.n. Jennet ; w. Robert and Peter Moffets.

,, ,, Andrew Allan, tinker, and Marion Henderson in Colmslie, a.s.n. Andrew ; w. as before.

,, 24. William Rennaldson and Agnes Mien in Newsteid, a.d.n. Mary ; w. John Mercer, elder, Robert Mein, smith.

,, 27. John Riddel of Muselie and Margaret Riddel, a.d.n. Mary ; w. James Wilkison, James Lythgow.

Mar. 3. Patrick Bulman and Isobel Ker in Newtoun, a.d.n. Elizabeth ; w. Nicol Miln, John Miln of Brae.

,, ,, James Rae, gardiner in Melrose, and Alison Lyal, a.s.n. Andrew ; w. Andrew Martine, George Martine.

,, ,, Philip Douglass and Agnes Hall, a.s.n. George ; w. James Phaap, John Gill.

,, 10. James Mien and Margaret Mien in Newsteid, a.s.n. Andrew ; w. Robert Mien, James Broun.

,, ,, George Aitchison and Elizabeth Hopkirke, a.d.n Helen ; w. William Hopkirke, Robert Ormistoun.

,, 17. John Hope in Newtoun, and Christian Bonningtoun, a.s.n. William ; w. Archibald and Michael Wallaces.

,, ,, Andrew Usher, weaver in Darnick, and Isobel Thomson, a.d.n. Isobel ; w. James Smaill, John Mien.

,, ,, Robert Bunzie and Rachel Forson in Newsteid, a.d.n. Agnes ; w. Robert Forsons, elder and younger.

,, 24. Mr. John Cranstoun, schoolmaster at Melrose, and Mary Skelly, a.s.n. Robert ; w. Mr. Gideon Rutherford, George Cranstoun.

April 14. John Gill, moulterer of ye mills in Melrose, and Alison King, a.d.n. Margaret ; w. James Phaap, Thomas Gill.

,, 21. Andrew Bunzie in Newsteid, and Margaret Robertson, a.s.n. John ; w. Robert and James Bunzies.

,, ,, James Purvis in Drygrange and Agnes Knox, a.d.n. Alison ; w. John Pearson, George Martine.

,, ,, James Small in Langhaugh and Jennet Broun, a.s.n. Alexander ; w. John Darling, William Shiell.

1723.

April 21. Michael Vetch and —— Sandilands, ——; w. same witnesses.

,, ,, James Hart in Langlie and Agnes Thomson, a.d.n. Elizabeth ; w. William Hart, David Speedin.

May 5. Robert Ballantyne and Jennet Fryar, a.s.n. Robert ; w. Thomas Boustoun, Robert Fryar.

,, ,, William Mebon, weaver in Newsteid, and Jennet Simpson, a.s.n. William : w. William Sclatter, James Scott.

,, 19. Robert Williamson and Agnes Scot, a.s.n. Thomas ; w. Thomas and William Williamsons.

,, 26. John Moffet and Christian Ker in Galtonside, a.d.n. Jennet ; w. Patrick Thomson, Robert Myles.

,, ,, Robert Fairbairn and Margaret Davidson in Danieltoun, a.d.n. Isobel ; w. Andrew Paterson, Robert Scott.

,, ,, Walter Rae and Jennet Eccles in Newtoun, a.d.n. Jennet ; w. John and Thomas Stenhouse.

June 2. William Bower and Isobel Paterson, a.s.n. William ; w. William Ellies, John Bell.

,, 15. James Mein and Margaret Bunzie in Newsteid, a.d.n. Mary ; w. James Pringle, Andrew Martine.

,, 16. David Grieve, deceased, and Helen Pringle, a.s n. David ; w. James Grieve, his brother, germain to the said David being sponsor, Thomas and John Darlings.

,, 22. John Haliwell and Helen Nicol in Galtonside, a.d.n. Jennet ; w. Robert and Thomas Haliwell.

,, 30. James Boustoun and Marion Blackie in Galtonside, a.d.n. Jennet ; w. James and Marke Blackies.

,, ,, James Deuar and Marion Hardie (being gotten in fornication), a.d.n. Isobel ; w. James Blackie, George Hoy.

July 1. John Wallace and Margaret Dick in Blainslie, a.d.n. Helen ; w. James and Adam Wallaces.

,, 15. Robert Bunzie and Marion Hopkirke in Newsteid, a.d.n. Agnes ; w. William Hopkirke, elder and younger.

,, ,, William Pringle in Blainslie and ——, a.d.n. Helen : w. ——.

,, 21. Thomas Lukeup, weaver in Melrose, and Jean Martine, a.d.n. Jean ; w. Andrew and William Lukeups.

,, ,, James Liethan in Aeildoun and Margaret Sclatter, a.d.n. Helen : w. John Gibson, Robert Sclatter.

,, 29. James Mein in Newsteid and Katharine Shiel, a.d.n. Katharine ; w. James Laing, George Martine.

,, 30. James Laidla in Buckholm and Christian Bruntoun, a.d.n. Margaret ; w. William and James Aitchison.

Aug. 18. George Drummond and Isobel Scot in Bridgend, a.d.n. Isobel ; w. Andrew Beaty, Thomas Dixon.

,, 21. George Alley in Westerlanglie and Marion Frater, a.d.n. Margaret ; w. John Frater, James Lumsdale.

,, 26. Andrew Smith in Galtonside and Helen Bouston, a.d.n Helen ; w. Thomas Bouston, James Gardiner.

,, ,, John Pearson in Drygrange and Margaret Crosbie, a.d.n. Margaret ; w. James Cribbes, John Aird.

,, ,, John Taite and Isobel Pringle in Blainslie, a.d.n. Isobel ; w. Andrew Mein, John Mercer.

Sept. 8. Thomas Gill in Danieltoun, and Alison Gill, a.s.n. John ; w. Andrew Paterson, Robert Scot.

,, ,, Andrew Heaton in Darnick and Isobel Young, a.s.n. George ; w. George Young, John Fortune.

,, ,, John Mercer in Newsteid and Mary Mien, a.d.n. Alison ; w. John Mercer, Thomas Williamson.

(*No date*) William S. to William Bower and Isobel Paterson ; w. John Bell and Robert Hillson.

[The above entry on first page of 2nd volume of the Record.]

II.—Baptisms, Marriages, and Discipline

in the parish of Melrose since November 1723, att which time
Mr. Gavin Eliot was admitted School-master and Session-clerk.

1723.

Nov. 24. John Smith and Helen Mercer in Darnick, a.s.n. William ; w. John Smith, James Moodie, there.

This day granted testimonials to Jannet Pringle.

„ 26. James Wood and Jean Fortune in Appletreeleaves, a.s.n. William ; w. John Fortune and John Thin in Blainslie.

„ „ William Brown and Jannet Dicksone in Colmslie, a.s.n. James ; w. *ut supra.*

„ „ William Wilson and Helen Lauder in Blainslie, a.d.n. Helen ; w. *ut supra.*

„ „ William Lauder and Helen Rolmanhouse in Blainslie, a.d.n. Catharine ; w. *ut supra.*

Dec. 10. John Milne and Isobel Aird in Newtoun, a.s.n. Alexander ; w. Mungo and Nichol Milnes there

„ 14. This day booked in order for marriage, Robert and Mary Mein, both in this parish : Robert Mein in Newsteid cautioner for the said parties. w.

„ 19. John Sibbald and Agnes Stenhouse in Eildon, a.s.n. John ; William and Andrew Sibbalds there.

„ 22. George Martin and Jannet Haliburtone in Melrose, a.s.n. John ; w. Andrew and Robert Martines there.

„ 29. William Simpson and Bessie Moffat in Newtown, a.s.n. William ; w. Nichol Milne, Thomas Stenhouse, there.

„ 30. James Cribbas and Isobel Crosbie in Sorrowlessfield, a.s.n. Alexander ; w. James Purves, John Pearson in Drygrainge.

„ 31. Mungo Park and Isobel Harvie in Westerboathouse, a.d.n. Isobel : w. Andrew Marr, William Hoy.

1724.

Jan. 5. Andrew Mercer and Catharine Mercer in Bridgend, a.s.n. Andrew ; w. John Moodie, Robert Bunzie in Melrose.

„ 11. This day booked in order for marriage, Robert Myles and Jannet Mathisone, both in this parish ; Nichol Mercer in Melrose cautioner.

„ 19. John Bunzie and Anna Davidson in Newsteid, a.s.n. Thomas ; w. Robert and Thomas Bunzies there.

„ 26. John Thomson and Margaret Martine in Gattonside, a.s.n. John : w. Patrick Thomson, William Sibbett, there.

„ „ William Bunzie and Jannet Fairbairn in Newsteid, a.s.n. John ; w. *ut supra.*

Feb. 9. John Gordon and Isobel Dalgleish in Darnick, a.s.n. John ; w. Robert Gibson, John Dalgleish, there.

„ 23. George Beatie and Marion Wright in Bridgend, a.d.n. Elizabeth ; w. Andrew Beatie, George Wright.

„ „ After prayer sederunt, the minister, Drygrainge, James Blaikie, John Mercer, Andrew Drummond, Andrew Paterson, Nichol Milne, &c., elders. Case against Isobel Bunzie, daughter to Robert Bunzie in Melrose, now residing in the parish of Mertown, and Andrew Tait, son to John Tait, gardner in Melrose.

Mar. 1. Alexander Bell and Janet Bell in Melrose, a.d.n. Mary ; w. John Bowie, Robert Bunzie, there.

„ „ After prayer sederunt, the Minister, Drygrainge, James Blaikie, Andrew Patersone, &c., elders.

The session appoints Drygrainge, John Mabane, George Hoy, Andrew Patersone, to meet with the minister and clerk to-morrow eight days to visit the treasurer's accompts.

Case against Isobel Bunzie and Andrew Tait continued.

1724.

Mar. 4. John Wood and Agnas Noteman in Mosshouses, **a.s.n.** Alexander ; w. Thomas Laidlay, Robert Moffatt.

„ „ George Geddes and Jean Spear in Longshaw, **a.s.n.** George ; w. *ut supra.*

„ 8. After prayer sederunt, Minister, Drygrainge, Longlee, John Mabane, Laird Marr, Nichol Milne, &c., elders. Case against Andrew Tait and Isobel Bunzie continued.

„ 9. This day the Minister, Drygrainge, John Mabane, George Hoy, and Andrew Paterson mett according to appointment, and examined and approved the treasurer's accompts., and put into the box £18 : 16s. stg., and left remaining in his hand £103 : 7s. Scotts money.

„ 11. James Darling and Margaret Fairbairn in Blainslies, **a.d.n.** Margaret ; w. Thomas Darling, William Thin, there.

„ „ James Hislop and Marion Laidlay in Colmslie, **a.d.n.** Agnes ; w. *ut supra.*

„ 15. Isobel Bunzie, compeared for the first time, was exhorted.

„ 22. Richard Bower and Isobel Simpson in Eildon, **a.s.n.** William ; w. Andrew and Robert Martins in Melrose.

„ „ This day Isobel Bunzie appeared for the 2nd time.

„ 27. This day booked in order for marriage John Laidlay and Agnes Mein, both in this parish ; John Mein, portioner of Newsteid, cautioner.

„ 29. This day Isobel Bunzie was dismissed and gave in half a crown as ordinary in such cases.

April 2. Andrew Martine and Catharine Shillinglaw in Blainslie, **a.s.n.** William ; w. George Rolmanhouse, John Grieve, there.

„ 9. The deceased John Anderson and Bessie Pearson in Drygrainge, **a.s.n.** John ; w. Thomas Anderson, James Purves, there.

„ 12. Thomas Gray and Margaret Fisher in Darnick, **a.d.n.** Elizabeth ; w. James Stoddart, Wm. Dicksone, there.

„ 19. John Turnbull and Bessie Familtown in Gattonside, **a.s.n.** Patrick ; w. Thomas Bowstone, James Gardner, there.

„ „ James Lawrie and Janet Brown in Old Melrose, **a.s.n.** James ; w. John Mein, George Martine.

„ 26. After prayer sederunt. the Minister, Drygrainge, Longlee, Andrew Mar, Nichol Milne, James Blaikie, &c., elders. Case against George Wright, married, weaver in Gattonside, and Janet Nisbet, there.

„ 29. John Stirling and Isobel Wilson in Blainslie, **a.d.n.** Helen ; w. John and Robert Stirlings there.

May 3. After prayer sederunt, the Minister, Drygrainge, Longlee. Andrew Patersone, John Mabane, &c., the elders. The officer reports that he had according to appointment cited George Wright and Janet Nisbet. The witnesses to be summoned are Isobel Mein, Janet Frier, Isobel Frier, Robert Scott, William Bell and Margaret Simpson.

Drygrainge proposed that there should be a meeting of the heretors and all others concerned against the 2nd of June next, for repairing the kirk and schoolhouse, which was cordially gone in with. The sederunt closed with prayer.

„ 10. After prayer sederunt, the Minister, Drygrainge, Longlee, Andrew Patersone, Laird Mar, James Blaikie, &c., elders. In the affair of George Wright and Janet Nisbet, there were examined (1) Robert Scott, unmarried, aged nineteen years ; (2) Isobel Frier, *soluta,* aged five and twenty years ; (3) Margaret Simpson. married, aged twenty-four years. Other witnesses to be summoned, James Young, Wm. Bell, Robert Huntly, and Janet Wright. The session closed with prayer.

„ 11. James Davidson and Jennet Henry in Buckholme, **a.s.n.** James ; w. James Laidlay, James Atchison, there.

1724.

May 11. James Clapperton and Jean Hadden in Appletreeleaves, a.d.n. Elizabeth ; w. *ut supra.*

  ,, ,, James Watson and Isobel Hendersone in Langshawmilne ; w. *ut supra.*

  ,, 15. This day booked in order for marriage, Robert Forsan in this parish and Margaret Brokie in the parish of Stow ; John Gill, miller in Melrose, cautioner.

  ,, ,, Was booked in order for marriage, Michael Boustown and Isobel Fairbairn, both in this parish ; John Fairbairn, cautioner.

  ,, 17. After prayer sederunt, the Minister, Drygrainge, Longlee, James Blaikie, Thomas Thin, John Mabane, &c., elders. This day the minister intimated a meeting of the heritors against the 2nd June next.

In the case against George Wright and Janet Nisbet the following parties were examined :—Robert Huntlie, widower, aged thirty-six years ; Janet Wright, aged about fifty years, and William Bell, unmarried, aged about fourteen years.

This day Andrew Tait, having appeared for the 3d time, was rebuked and dismissed, and paid in his fine.

  ,, 23. David Walker and Janet Wilson, both in this parish, were booked in order for marriage ; James Bunzie, stationer in Melrose, cautioner.

  ,, 24. James Moodie and Janet Mercer in Darnick, a.d.n. Alison ; w. John Mercer, John Smith, there.

  ,, ,, John Bunzie and Mary Wallace in Eildon, a.s.n. John ; w. *ut supra.*

  ,, ,, After prayer sederunt, the Minister, Langlee, Andrew Marr, James Blaikie, John Mabane, &c., elders.

After James Young, aged fifty-six, was examined, the case against George Wright was remitted to the Presbytery of Selkirk.

  ,, 29. This day William Mershall and Jean Sunderland were booked in order for marriage ; James Mercer in Newsteid, cautioner.

  ,, 30. Thomas Sclatter and Eupham Robson in Eildon, a.s.n. Robert ; w. George and Robert Martines.

  ,, 31. No sermon, the Minister assisting at Nenthorn sacrament.

June 7. William Hog and Agnes Hardie in Melrose, a.s.n. James : w. George Martine, John Mabane, there.

  ,, 11. James Scott and Helen Lauder in Blainslie, a.d.n. Jannet ; w.

  ,, 13. This day booked in order for marriage, John Sclatter and Jannet Little, both in this parish ; Jacob Darling, cautioner.

  ,, 20. Booked in order for marriage, Thomas Thin in this parish, and Mary Bell in the parish of Earlestown ; Alexr. Bell in Melrose, cautioner.

  ,, 21. Charles Frier and Agnes Thorburn in Gattonside, a.s.n. George ; w. Alexr. Fisher, John Frier.

  ,, ,, Robert Frier and Mary Fisher in Gattonside, two sons named John and Alexander ; w. *ut supra.*

  ,, ,, Richard Thomson and Agnes Moffat in Williamlaw, a.d.n. Jannet ; w. *ut supra.*

  ,, ,, John Fairbairn and Jean Troter in Colmslie, a.d.n. Margaret , w.

  ,, ,, The Minister intimated the Sacrament of the Supper against this day fourteen days.

  ,, 28. After prayer sederunt, the Minister, Drygrainge, Longlee, Thomas Thin, Nicol Milne, James Stoddart, Thomas Laidlay, Andrew Paterson, &c., elders.

This day the session in regard of Galashiels Fair Tuesday next, thought fit to proceed to their privy censures, and accordingly the elders were removed two by two and severally tryd, and nothing being censurable, they were encouraged to go on in the Lord's work.

1724.

The Humiliation day before the sacrament is appointed Thursday next.

July   2. Being the fast before the sacrament there was collected £10 : 14s.

 ..   .. James Noteman and Isobel Martine in Colinslie. a.s.n. James : w. James Laidlay, John Frater.

 ..   4. The preparation day collected £14 : 3s.

 ..   5. Sabbath day's collection, £28 : 15s.

 ..   6. James Mar and Mary Mercer in Darnick. a.s.n. James.

 ..   .. Andrew Mercer and Margaret Frier in Darnick. a.d.n. Helen : James Usher, Charles Frier, witnesses for both baptisms.

Munday's collection, £14 : 6s.

Sum of collections on this occasion extending to	£67	18	0
Debursed of the said sum to poor of the parish poor by recommendation, and common poor, to presentor and beadle.	54	11	0
	£13	7	0

 ..   12. After prayer sederunt, the Minister, Longlee, Thomas Thin, Nicol Milne, James Blaikie, &c., elders. The sum remaining of the sacrament money is ordered to be given in to the treasurer, wherewith he is to charge himself. The sederunt closed with prayer.

 ..   17. This day booked in order for marriage. Robert Peman in this parish, and Margaret Peacock in the parish of Galashiels : Robert Penman, portioner of Melrose, cautioner.

 ..   19. Andrew Lindsay and Margaret Simpson in Gattonside. a.s.n. James : w. ———.

 ..   .. John Runchaman and Elizabeth Chisholm there. a.s.n. John : w. Andrew Mar, William Hoy there.

 ..   26. Robert Lethen and Mary Nisbet in Gattonside. a.d.n. Jannet : w. James Lethan, Charles Frier, there.

After prayer sederunt, the Minister, Drygrainge, Longlee, Thomas Thin, John Sibbald, William Hoy, &c., elders.

Case against Andrew Tait and Isobel Bunzie again mentioned.

Andrew Paterson, George Hoy, John Sibbald, with the clerk, are appointed to meet Tuesday first to examine the treasurer's accompts.

 ..   28. This day according to appointment Andrew Paterson, John Sibbald, George Hoy meet with the clerk and treasurer, and examined and approved his accompts, and left in his hand £100 : 11s. Scots, wherewith he is to charge himself.

Aug.   2. No sermon, the minister being att Moffatt well.

 ..   4. This day booked in order for marriage. Richard Robertson and Christian Davidson, both in this parish : George Ormiston, cautioner.

 ..   .. Robert Rutherford and Elizabeth Heiton in Bridgend. a.s.n. John.

 ..   .. Thomas Williamson and Mary Mein in Newsteid. a.d.n. Violet.

 ..   .. The deceased George Bertown and Alison Mercer in Gattonside. a.s.n. George.

 ..   .. James Usher and Agnes Frier in Darnick. a.d.n. Agnes : w. John Hoy, Charles Frier, for above four entries.

After prayer the minister, Drygrainge, Longlee, John Mabane, Nicol Milne, James Blaikie, &c., elders. The clerk reports he wrote Mr. Goudie, and there was accordingly produced an execution against Andrew Tait, pro. 2do., and the session resolved that the affair should be referred to the presbytery of Selkirk, and accordingly they did, and hereby do refer the same for decision, which is to meet at Selkirk the first Tuesday of September. The clerk

1724.

is appointed to extract the process. He was called in and summoned *apud acta* to the said meeting.

Aug. 23. John Mercer and Margaret Davidson in Newsteid, a.d.n. Mary: w. John Mercer, Robert Mein, there.

.. 27. James Heiton and Jean Darling in Langhaugh, a.s.n. Thomas: w. ————.

.. 30. Robert Patersone and Anna Eliot of Drygrainge, a.d.n. Catharine: w. Alexr. Cunningham of Hyndhope, David Brown of Park, Mr. Eliot, schoolmaster.

.. 31. To the deceased William Oliver and Mary Pringle in Melrose, a.s.n. William: w. ————.

Sept. 6. John Napier and Janet Drummond in Bridgend, a.d.n. Isobel: w. William Napier, Andrew Drummond, there.

.. 13. After prayer sederunt, the Minister, Drygrainge, Langlee, Thomas Thin, John Mabane, Nicol Milne, William Thine, &c., elders. This day Andrew Tait professed his sorrow.

.. 14. John Darling and Janet Lees in Blainslies, a.s.n. John.

.. .. James Wallace and Euphan Darling in Blainslies, a.d.n. Agnes.

.. .. George Herd and Janet Simpson in Whitlaw, a.d.n. Mary: the Laird of West Housebyres and Thomas Turner for above three entries.

.. 15. John Fisher and Margaret Rutherford of Housebyres, a.d.n. Helen: w. Mr. John Shiel in Earlstown, George Martine.

.. 20. Robert Mercer and Mary Mein in Newsteid, a.s.n. James: w. James and John Mercers there.

.. 27. Richard Jerdain and Bettie Forrest, a.d.n. Annabella.

.. 27. William Sibbett and ———— in Gattonside, a.s.n. William: w. Henry Forrest, George Martine, for above two entries.

Oct. 4. This day the Minister read the petition of the Presbyterians in New York, America, and the General Assembly's recommendation for a collection, which is appointed this day eight days.

.. .. Andrew Tait and Isobel Bunzie, a.s.n. Robert, by fornication.

.. .. John Bunzie and Jean Schbold in Newtown, a.d.n. Elizabeth: w. Thomas Sterlings, Nicol Milne, there, for two above entries.

.. 11. There was collected this day, as appointed, £36 Scotts, which was delivered to the Minister to be transmitted.

.. 18. John Bunzie and Janet White in Newsteid, a.s.n. John.

.. .. John Marr and Isobel Lythgow in Gattonside, a.d.n. Alison: w. Andrew and William Marrs for the above two entries.

.. 25. This day booked in order for marriage, Andrew Riddell and Marry Hallwall, both in this parish: Robert Hallwall, cautioner.
Item, James Pearson and Margaret Troter, both in this parish: James Myles in Gattonside, cautioner.

.. 26. William Bowar and Isobel Paterson in Melrose, a.s.n. Robert.

.. .. William Milne and Isobel Riddell in Newsteid, a.d.n. Margaret: w. John Mercer, Andrew Mein.

Nov. 1. George Grahamslie and Margaret Coldcleugh in Danieltown, a.s.n John.

.. .. William Atchison and Janet Shiel in Newsteid, a.s.n. William.

.. .. Robert Bunzie and Beatrix Farme in Newsteid, a.d.n. Beatrix: w. George Scott, Andrew Paterson, for above entries.

.. 6. Booked in order for marriage, John Wallace and Sarah Purves, both in this parish: Thomas Darling in Blainslie, cautioner.

.. 7. Booked in order for marriage, George Chisholm and Margaret Welsh, both in this parish: William Welsh, cautioner.

.. 15. Andrew Drummond and Helen Mathison in Bridgend, a.d.n. Helen: w. Walter Murray, James Mathison.

.. 18. John and Margaret Riddells of Muselee, a.s.n. Thomas: w. Mr. Robert Scott, brother to the late Whitstead, Patrick Riddell, Muselee's son.

1724.

Nov. 23. Peter Moffat and Agnes Smith in Threepwood, a.s.n. Peter.

"   " James Dewar and Marion Hardie in Overlangshaw, a.d.n. Catherine :
w. Robert Moffat, John Wood.

"   24. Walter Milstone and Christian Sadler in Gattonside : w. William
Hoy, Thomas Bowstone.

"   26. Nicol Milne and Isobel Turnbull in Newtown, a.d.n. Janet ; w. John
Bunzie, Patrick Bulman.

Dec. 5. This day William Wilkie in the parish of Bowden and Alison
Dawson were booked in order for marriage ; William Mabane,
cautioner.

      Item, Robert Grierson and Marion Wilson, both in this parish ;
John Pearson in Drygrainge, cautioner.

"   13. James Dods and Anna Riddell in Newsteid, a.d.n. Agnes ; w.
Andrew Mein, Robert Forsan, there.

"   16. James Small and Janet Brown in Longhaugh, a.s.n. John ; w. John
Frater, James Brown, there.

"   20. George Atchison and Bessie Hopkirk in Melrose, a.s.n. Thomas ; w.
Wm. Hopkirk, older and younger, there.

"   20. John Mercer and Isabel Speeding in Newsteid, a.d.n. Elizabeth ; w.
ut supra.

"   27. Thomas Mercer and Margaret Atchison in Melrose, a.s.n. Thomas ;
w. Nichol Mercer, Wm. Williamson there.

      After prayer sederunt, the Minister, James Blaikie, William
Thin, Andrew Mar, John Mabane, &c., elders.

      This day the session orders that all who have failed in
solemnizing marriage give in two dollars, according to obligation.
The sederunt closed with prayer.

"   29. Alexr. Laing and Agnes Grieve in Laudhopemure, a.s.n. John ; w.
John Brown, William Murray.

1725.

Jan. 2. This day booked in order for marriage, John Somervail and Janet
Nisbet, both in this parish ; Thomas Nisbet, cautioner.

"   3. After prayer sederunt, the Minister, Drygrainge, James Blaikie,
Nichol Milne, John Mabane, William Dickson, &c., elders. Case
against Christian Bunzie about the time Barbara Stirling was
buried on 21st May 1724.

"   7. This day booked in order for marriage, James Laing and Margaret
Far in the parish of Gallashiels : John Corsar, cautioner.

"   10. Robert Myles and Janet Mathison in Gattonside, a.d.n. Janet ; w.
John Marr, James Myles, there.

      After prayer sederunt, the Minister, Drygrainge, Langlea,
James Stoddart, Wm. Hoy, James Blaikie, &c., elders.

      Christian Bunzie being called, compeared not. The session
order her to be summoned pro 2do. The sederunt closed with
prayer.

"   17. After prayer sederunt, the Minister, Drygrainge, Langlee, Andrew
Paterson, George Hoy, &c., elders.

      This day the minister, conform to appointment of the Presbytery,
tendered the oath of purgation to George Wright, which he had
refused to take after he had repeated some part of it and then
pulled down his hand. He was this day convened before the
session and seriously exhorted to confess, but he still persisted in
his denyal, upon which he was cited *apud acta* to compear before
the Presbytery the first Tuesday next moneth. The sederunt
closed with prayer.

"   18. George Allay and Marion Frater in Westerlanglee, a.d.n. Mary ; w.
John Frater, George Allay.

"   30. John Laidlay and Agnes Mein in Newtown, a.d.n. Janet.

"   " Robert Turnbull and Elizabeth Gibson in Newtown, a.d.n. Janet ; w.
Nichol Milne and Nichol Milne there, for both entries.

1725.

Feb. 4. Thomas Stenhouse and Helen Sibbald in Newtown, a.s.n. George ; w. Nichol and Thomas Milne there.

,, 6. This day booked in order for marriage, James Bell and Elizabeth Laing, both in this parish ; cautioner, James Laing, weaver in Melrose.

,, 7. John Cossar and Margaret Purves in Melrose, a.s.n. James.

,, ,, James Smail and Elizabeth Ellies in Melrose, a.d.n. Elizabeth ; w. Wm. Ellies, James Blaikie in Melrose, for both entries.

,, 8. Thomas Young and Isabel Thomsone in Colmslie, a.d.n. Marion.

,, ,, Thomas Waddell and Janet Brown in Overlongshaw, a.d.n. Elizabeth ; w. Robert and Peter Moffatt, for both entries.

,, 14. Andrew Mein and Janet Mein in Newsteid, a.s.n. Andrew ; w. John Mein, William Milne.

This day the Minister read the recommendation of the General Assembly for a collection to make new erections in Durness, which is to be gathered Wednesday next, a day appointed as a fast through the Presbytery's bounds.

,, 17. Collected for the end above mentioned, £29 : 10s. Scotts.

,, 24. William Thine and Marion Fairbairn in Blainslie, a.d.n. Alison : w. William Thine, Thomas Darling, there.

,, 27. This day booked in order for marriage, Mr. Adam Milne, our minister, and Mrs. Alison Hunter, daughter to Mr. William Hunter, minister of the gospell at Lilisleaf.

,, 28. Alexr. M'Fadden and Agnes Napier in Melrose, a.d.n. Anne.

,, ,, Walter Murray and Isobel Mathison in Melrose, a.s.n. Walter ; w. Andrew M'Fadden, George Hoy there.

Mar. 7. After prayer sederunt, the Minister, Drygrainge, Langlee, Robert Moffatt, elders.

Upon a representation of the straitening circumstances of Walter Mabane's family and at his request the session conde-scended to let him have out of the box £15 Scotts upon his son's security, as also to give him by way of charity £3 Scotts.

The session appoints Drygrainge, Andrew Paterson, John Mabane and George Hoy, to meet with the minister and clerk and examine the treasurer's accounts Friday first, the twelveth instant. The sederunt closed with prayer.

,, 12. The committee appointed to examine the treasurer's accounts did not meet.

,, 20. William Mein and Margaret Mein in Eildon, a.s.n. William ; w. ——.

,, ,, James Mein and —— Mein in Newsteid, a.s.n. James : w. Thomas Williamson, John Mercer, there.

,, 24. Robert Stirling and Isobel Stuart in the Rhone, a.d.n. Isabel ; w. James Stirling, John Thin in Blainslies.

April 4. Walter Rae and Anne Eccles in Newtown, a.s.n. Walter ; w. Nichol Milne, Thomas Stenhouse.

,, 12. Thomas Thine and —— Gibsone in Blainslies, —— ; w. John and Wm. Thines there.

,, 18. After prayer sederunt, the Minister, Drygrainge, Langlee, Thomas Thine, John Sibbald, John Mabane, &c., elders.

Upon a flagrant report against Beatrix Wallace, daughter to James Wallace in Melrose, she is ordered to be cited to this day eight days session. The sederunt closed with prayer.

,, 25. Here you have account of the severall collections in this our parish, and for debursements they are to be seen in another volume of this size.

Collected by Nichol Milne and John Sibbald, £3 : 3s. Scotts.

,, ,, James Vair and Margaret Kerr in Newtown, a.s.n. Thomas : w. Nichol Milns, elder and younger.

After prayer sederunt, the Minister, Drygrainge, John Sibbald, James Stoddart, &c., elders.

1725.

Beatrix Wallace was this day called but compeared not. She is appointed to be cited pro 2do., and in regard it is reported that George Edgar is gone off with her to marriage. He is also appointed to be summoned to the session this day eight days.

The appointment on Drygrainge, Andrew Paterson, John Mabane and George Hoy to revise James Blaikie's accounts is renewed because they did not meet as per appointment on March 7th, and they are appointed to meet Tuesday next. The sederunt closed with prayer.

April 26. Thomas Little and Isobel Knox in Blainslie, a.s.n. George.

,,   ,,   Michael Bostone and Isobel Fairbairn in Blainslie, a.d.n. Catharine.

,,   ,,   James Laidlay and Christian Brunton in Buckholme, a.d.n. Isobell ; w. John Kirkwood, Wm. Atchison, for the above three entries.

,,   30. This day booked in order for marriage, John Frater in this parish, and Mary Gray in the parish of Ancrum ; John Riddell of Musely, cautioner.

This day the Minister, John Mabane, George Hoy, with their clerk, met and examined James Blaikie's accounts, and after compearing charge and discharge there is remaining in his hand, £88 : 13s. Scotts.

May   2. After prayer sederunt, the Minister, Drygrainge, Langlee, Andrew Paterson, Andrew Marr, &c., elders.

Collected by John Mabane and George Hoy, £2 Scotts.

George Edgar and Beatrix Wallace being summoned were called but compeared not. They are appointed to be cited to this day eight days session. The sederunt closed with prayer.

,,   9. Thomas Thin and Mary Bell in Whitlaw, a.s.n. James ; w. Thomas Jackson, Thomas Laidlay.

After prayer sederunt, the Minister, Drygrainge, Langlee, Thomas Thin, Andrew Paterson, James Blaikie, elders.

Collected by Andrew Paterson and Wm. Hoy, £2 : 10s. Scotts.

Case against George Edgar and Beatrix Wallace, who acknowledged their marriage, and produced a testimonial, dated at Edinr. April 24th, 1725, subscribed by William Wallace, minister ; Alexr. Guthrie and David Muschet, witnesses. They were removed, and the session came to this resolution that they should compear Sabbath first and be rebuked for their clandestine marriage. They were called in and gravely rebuked and seriously admonished, and ordered to compear in the place of publick repentance Sabbath first. The sederunt closed with prayer.

,,   14. This day booked in order for marriage, Henry Forrest in this parish, and Isobel Robertson in the parish of Galashiels : John Hownam in Darnick, cautioner.

,,   ,,   James Phaup and Alison Cook bound in order for marriage, both in this parish ; John Smith in Darnick, cautioner.

Item, Patrick Bulman and Isobel Vair, both in this parish : Nichol Milne in Newtown, cautioner.

,,   16. George Edgar and Beatrix Wallace compeared according to appointment and were rebuked.

Collected by Andrew Marr, Wm. Hoy and John Mercer, £3 : 7s.

,,   19. This day booked in order for marriage, Andrew Meather in the parish of Roxburgh, and Janet Pringle in this ; Alexr. Fisher of Sorrowlessfield, cautioner.

,,   23. George Edgar and Beatrix Wallace compeared the 2nd time.

Collected by John Bunzie and William Dickson, £2 : 17s.

,,   28. This day William Thin and Janet Wallace, both in this parish, were booked in order for marriage ; Wm. Thin in Blainslie, cautioner.

1725.

May 30. After prayer sederunt, the Minister, Drygrainge, Wm. Hoy, John
Sibbald, John Mabane, James Blaikie, &c., elders.

Collected by Andrew Mar and John Sibbald, £2 : 9s.

This day Janet Bell in Melrose compeared and complained
upon George Ormistone, weaver in Melrose, and upon Anne
Ormiston his sister, that whereas upon Munday and Tuesday last,
the 24th and 25th of this current moneth of May, they uttered
and spoke many fowl and approbrious words tending to ruin my
reputation and to take away my good name, such as that I and
my consorts took his coals and burnt them in my fire, and that I
would do well not to awaken sleeping dogs, else they would tell
me more of their minds, and would waken up what had not been
heard these seven years, with much more to this purpose. The
lybell being read Janet Bell owned the same, and having consigned
her half-crown, George and Anne Ormiston being summoned,
were called, compeared and confessed in the terms of the lybell.
They were removed, and after the affair was duly considered, it
was put to the vote whether they should be publickly or privately
rebuked. Rolls being called and votes marked, it carried that
they should be immediately rebuked in presence of the session.
They were called in and gravely rebuked. They expressed their
sorrow for such expressions, and begged forgiveness of God and
Janet Bell's pardon. They were admissed with certification.

A charge against John Young and Isobel Dalgleish being
made, the session has ordered them to be cited to this day fourteen
days session. The sederunt closed with prayer.

June 6. Thomas Anderson and Mary Dickson in Drygrainge, a.s.n. Alexander.

„ „ John Bell and Janet Mabane in Melrose, a.s.n. James.

„ „ Robert Forsan and Margaret Brockie in Newsteid, a.d.n. Agnes : w.
John Bowie and Alexr. Bell in Melrose, for above three entries.

Collected by John Mabane, George Hoy and Andrew Mein,
£4 : 13s. Scotts.

„ 13. Robert Fairbairn and Margaret Davidson in Danieltown, a.s.n.
James ; w. Andrew Paterson, Robert Scott, there.

„ „ After prayer sederunt, the Minister, Drygrainge, Langlee, Andrew
Marr, George Hoy, Andrew Drummond, &c., the elders.

Collected by James Stoddart, John Mercer, Robert Moffatt,
£2 : 3s.

John Young and Isobel Dalgleish being summoned, were
called and compeared. They were charged for their too familiar
correspondence and discharged converse for the future.

James Kennedy and Margaret Riddell in Darnick are appointed
to be summoned to this day eight days session.

This day the Minister produced a discharge for the collection
of this parish for New York, subscribed by the collector thereof,
extending to £36 Scotts ; as also another discharge for Durness
extending to £29 : 12s. Scotts. The sederunt closed with prayer.

„ 20. James Leithen and Margaret Sclatter in Eildon, a.s.n. Andrew ; w.
John Sibbald, John Gibson.

After prayer sederunt, the Minister, Drygrainge, Langlee, John
Sibbald, Nicol Milne, &c., elders.

Collected by Andrew Paterson and John Sibbald, £2 Scotts.

The session resolve that the session shall meet Tuesday, the
sixth of July next, to consider the state of the poor, and intimation
to be made this day eight days

James Kennedy being called, compeared and discharged to
stay any longer in the house with Margaret Riddel. The sederunt
closed with prayer.

„ 21. James Martin and Janet Dickson in Blainslie, a.s.n. Thomas : w.
John Thin, John Wallace there.

1725.

June 23. This day booked in order for marriage, John Lukup in the parish of Selkirk, and Anne Gastown in this parish ; Robert Ormistone, merchant in Melrose, cautioner.

„ 27. John and Mary Mein of Old Melrose, a.s.n. Charles ; w. The Lairds of Drygrainge and Muselee.

After prayer sederunt, the Minister, Drygrainge, Thomas Thin, Andrew Paterson, James Blaikie, &c., elders.

Collected by Andrew Paterson and Andrew Drummond, £1 : 7s.

The Minister read the act of the commission of the General Assembly for the observation of a fast, Thursday next.

Compeared this day Mary Pringle in Melrose and complained on Robert Ormistown, merchant there, that the 21st of this instant he spoke many foul and infamous words tending to ruin her reputation, such as that she had not seen his cow in her skaith, &c. James Ormistone was called, and compeared and offered to prove the lybell. He is ordered to give in a list of the witnesses to the clerk. The sederunt closed with prayer.

July 1. This being the fast day as appointed. The Minister appointed the elders to meet Tuesday next, in order to list the poor of the parish.

Collected by John Bunzie and Wm. Hoy, £4 : 7s.

„ 4. This day the Minister intimated his purpose to administer the Sacrament of the Supper this day fourteen days.

Collected by Andrew Marr and George Mercer, £4 Scotts.

„ 6. After prayer sederunt, the Minister, Drygrainge, Langlee, James Blaikie, Andrew Marr, John Mabane, George Hoy, Robert Moffatt, John Bunzie, John Sibbald, Thomas Laidlay and Nicol Milne, elders. The session considering the approach of the tryals, thought fit to enter on their privy tryals, so accordingly the elders present were removed severally two by two, were tryed and approven, and encouraged to go on in the Lord's work.

After reading of the act of the Justices of the Peace of the shire, the following list of poor was given in by the elders in whose bounds they resided, viz. :—

In Melrose.

James Murray.
Robert Hilsone and his weak child.
Thomas Blaikie.
Isobel Jack.
Jannet Rutherford.
Margaret Maxwell.
Christian Bunzie.

In Newsteid.

Agnes Mein.
Christian Forsan.
Andrew Pringle.

In Westhouses.

Helen Lauder.
Isobel Ormiston.

In Darnick.

Leonard Hownam.
Robert Charters.

In Gattonside.

Helen Nichol.
Janet Henderson.
Thomas Leithan.

In Langhaugh.

John Purves and his wife.
Isobel Paterson and her son.
John Sandilands and his daughter.

In Blainslie.

Janet Lees and two father- less children.
William Swanstone.
Janet Hislop.
Neil Campbell.
James Turner.

The session appoints intimation to be made for the heretors to meet the 2d Wednesday of August next, in order to stent them-

1725.

selves for the maintenance of the said poor. The sederunt closed with prayer.

July   7. Richard Robertson and Christian Davidson in Blainslie, a.d.n. Marion ; w. Laird Grieve, Robert Martin, there.

„   11. This day the minister appointed Thursday next as a day of fasting and humiliation before the Sacrament.

„   „ Robert Balientyne and Janet Frier in Gattonside, a.s.n. Robert : w. William Williamson, George Martine in Melrose.

Collected by William Dickson, Andrew Drummond and James Stoddart, £5 : 5s.

„ 15. Fast day's collection,	-	-	-	-	-	£8	17	0
„ 17. Saturday's collection,	-	-	-	-	-	12	9	0
„ 18. Sabbath day's collection,	-	-	-	-	27	7	0
„ 19. Munday's collection,	-	-	-	-	13	10	0

Sum of collections,   -   -   -   -   -   £62   3   0
Debursed to poor of the parish, common poor and others with recommendations, precentor and beadle,   54 16   0

£7   7   0

Which £7 : 7s. is ordered to be given to the treasurer, with which he is to charge himself.

„   „ Andrew Bunzie and Margaret Robertson in Newsteid, a.d.n. Margaret : w. James and Robert Bunzies there.

„   25. After prayer sederunt, the Minister, Drygrainge, Langlee, Thomas Thin, James Blaikie, &c., elders.

Collected by George Hoy, John Mabane, Robert Moffatt, £4 : 1s.

This day the Minister intimated a meeting of the heritors the 11th of August next.

Michael Wallace and Isobel Blaikie irregularly married are appointed to be cited to the session this day eight days. The sederunt closed with prayer.

„   27. Walter Thomson and Margaret Hardie in Mosshouses, a.s.n. George.

„   „ James Purves and Agnes Knox in Colmslie, a.d.n. Elizabeth ; w. James Ainslie, Robert Moffatt, for above three entries.

Ult :— Andrew Usher and Isobel Thomson in Darnick, a.d.n. Janet ; w. James and William Stoddarts there.

Aug.   1. John Kemp and Helen Grant in Gattonside, a.s.n. James.

„   „ Robert Johnstone and Jean Gillas in Melrose, a.d.n. Helen.

„   „ Andrew Smith and Helen Bowstone in Gattonside, a.d.n. Euphan ; w. Thomas Bowstone, James Gardner, there, for three above entries.

Collected by John Sibbald and John Bunzie, £2 : 12s.

Michael Wallace and Isobel Blaikie being cited were called, compeared and interrogate if married, answered affirmative and produced a testimonial of the same dated att Carham, July 8th, 1725, subscribed by Thomas Ogle, minister De Carham. They were gravely rebuked, admonished, and dismissed. The sederunt closed with prayer.

Aug.   8. Collected by Andrew Drummond, William Hoy, Robert Moffatt, £2 : 12s.

„   11. This day being appointed for the heritors to meet and consider the state of the poor, the list formerly given in was read and considered, but in regard none of the heritors save Drygrainge were present, nothing was done. They appoint intimation for another meeting the first Wednesday of September next. The sederunt began and ended with prayer.

„   15. John Bunzie and Anne Davidson in Newsteid, a.s.n. Robert : w. Robert Bunzie, William Sclater, there.

1725.

Collected by ——, £1 : 16s. Scotts.

Aug. 22. John Moffat and Christian Kerr in Gattonside, a.d.n. Jannet.

,,   ,,   George Beatie and Marion Wright in Bridgend, a.d.n. Margaret ; w. Andrew Beatie, Andrew Drummond.

After prayer sederunt, the Minister, Drygrainge, Langlee. James Blaikie, Nichol Milne, Andrew Drummond, &c., elders.

Collected by George Hoy and Andrew Drummond, £2 : 8s.

This day a petition was given by George Mercer, portioner of Danieltown, concerning his son John, craving assistance to make him a scholar, because he inclines much that way. The session after hearing the said petition, allowed a crown to the school-master as a part of his wages till further consideration.

This day Andrew Drummond addressed the session for the loan of fifty merks from the box, which the session granted upon sufficient cautionary.

The session orders their officer to cite Robert Ormistone, James Bunzie and Mary Pringle to the session this day eight days. The sederunt closed with prayer.

,,   29. After prayer sederunt, the Minister, Drygrainge, Langlee, Andrew Marr, Nichol Mercer, &c., elders.

Collected by James Stoddart and Wm. Dickson, £2 : 17s.

Robert Ormistone, James Bunzie and Mary Pringle being cited, Robert Ormistone was called and compeared, and to prove what he had undertaken as per sederunt, June 27th, gave in the following list of witnesses, viz. :—Alexr. Laing and his wife, Margaret Walker, servetrix to the said Mary Pringle ; William Wilkie and his wife, Alison Young, Elizabeth Walker, servitrix to the said Robert Ormistown. In regard Alexr. Laing and his wife are now residing in Oxnam parish, the session appoints their clerk to write Mr. Colden to cause cite them to the session this day fourteen days. Mary Pringle and James Bunzie are appointed to get a copy of the witnesses that are to be examined in their affair. The sederunt closed with prayer.

Sept. 2. This day booked in order for marriage, John Pringle in this parish, and Margaret Young in the parish of Yetholm ; John Pringle in Blainslie, cautioner.

,,   5. Collected by Wm. Hoy and Andrew Drummond, £2 : 4s.

,,   12. James Mein and Catharine Shiel in Newsteid, a.d.n. Margaret.

,,   ,,   Robert Mein and Mary Mein in Newsteid, a.d.n. Agnes ; w. John Mercer, Andrew Mein there, for two above entries.

After prayer sederunt, the Minister, Langlee, Nicol Milne, Andrew Mar, John Mabane, Andrew Patersone, &c., elders.

Collected by Andrew Marr. Nichol Milne, John Bunzie. £3 : 3s.

James Bunzie and Mary Pringle compeared. All the witnesses also compeared except Alexr. Laing and his wife. James Bunzie and Mary Pringle declared they had nothing to say why they might not be examined in their affair. Then the minister gravely administered the oath, they were removed except Alison Young, *soluta,* aged fifty-four years, solemnly sworn. purged of malice and partial counsel, deponed *nihil novit.*

William Wilkie married, aged twenty-four years, solemnly sworn, &c., deponed *ut supra.*

The following other witnesses were examined :—Alison Dawson, married, aged twenty years.

Margaret Walker, aged twenty years, unmarried.

Elizabeth Walker, aged nineteen years.

James Bunzie and Mary Pringle were summoned *apud acta* to the session this day eight days. The sederunt closed with prayer.

1725.

Sept. 19. William Brown and Jean Dickson in Colmsliehill, a.d.n. Margaret.

" " Robert Bunzie and Marion Hopkirk in Newsteid, a.d.n. Isobel ; w. Wm. Hopkirks, elder and younger, in Melrose, for above two entries.

After prayer sederunt, the Minister, Drygrainge, James Blaikie, Andrew Paterson, John Mercer, &c., elders.

Collected by John Mabane and John Mercer, £2 : 5s.

This day the depositions of Alison Dawson and Margaret Walker were read, and after serious consideration the session came to this resolution, that Mary Pringle and James Bunzie shall both appear three several Lord's days in the place of publick repentance, and to enter to the pillar Sabbath first and be rebuked. They were called in and this intimate to them. The sederunt closed with prayer.

" 26. William Robertson and Bessie Scott in Gattonside, a.s.n. Walter ; w. John Robertson, Walter Riddell.

After prayer sederunt, the Minister, Drygrainge, Langlee, Nichol Milne, Andrew Mein, &c., elders.

Collected by Andrew Paterson and James Hoy, £3 Scotts.

Mary Pringle appointed to compear before the congregation this day did not compear, the appointment is continued on her to compear this day eight days. The sederunt closed with prayer.

Oct. 3. Mary Pringle compeared for the first time, and was rebuked and ordered to continue there two Sabbaths.

Collected by James Stoddart, Wm. Dicksone, Andrew Mein, £1 : 18s.

" 10. Mary Pringle compeared for the second time.

" " Andrew Marr and Susanna Lythgow in Gattonside, a.s.n. Andrew.

" " John Dalgleish and Margaret Darling in Darnick, a.s.n. Alexander.

" " James Helin and Marion Thomson in Housebyres, a.s.n. James ; w. Thomas Darling, James Wallace, for above three entries.

Collected by Nicol Milne, John Bunzie and Wm. Hoy, £2 : 2s.

" 17. Mary Pringle compeared for the 3d time, was rebuked and dismissed.

Collected by George Hoy and John Mabane, £1 : 12s.

" 18. James Wilkieson and Isobel Rodger in Appletreeleaves, a.s.n. James ; w. James Darling, James Clapperton, there.

" 23. This day booked in order for marriage, Nichol Miln and Mary Mein, both in this parish : Andrew Bartleman in Newsteid, cautioner.

" 24. Robert Penman and Margaret Peacock in Melrose, a.s.n. James.

" " John Wood and Agnes Noteman in Mosshouses, a.d.n. Agnes ; w. Robert Penman, James Smail in Melrose, for above two entries.

After prayer sederunt, the Minister, Drygrainge, Langlee, John Sibbald, Nichol Milne, &c., elders.

Collected by John Mercer and Andrew Drummond, £1 : 17s.

Wednesday come twenty days the seventeen of November is appointed for revising the treasurer's accompts : John Mabane, Andrew Patersone, George Hoy are appointed with the minister and clerk. The sederunt closed with prayer.

" 31. John Mercer and Mary Mein in Newsteid, a.s.n. —— ; w. Andrew Mein and Robert Bunzie there.

Collected by Andrew Paterson and John Mercer, £2 : 10s.

Nov. 7. John Sclatter and Janet Little in Eildon, a.d.n. Margaret : w. John Sibbald, John Usher, there.

Collected by James Stoddart and John Bunzie, £2 : 2s.

" 14. This day George Edgar and Beatrice Wallace compeared for the third time and were rebuked, and were dismissed.

" " John Somervail and Janet Nisbet in Gattonside, a.d.n. Janet.

" " Wm. Mabane and Janet Simpson in Newsteid, a.d.n. Margaret.

" " George Edgar and Beatrix Wallace in Melrose, a.d.n. Anne : w. James Wallace, Robert Edgar.

I

1725.

Collected by Andrew Mein and Wm. Hoy, £3 : 4s.

Nov. 16. Booked in order for marriage, George Stewart and Janet Halliwall, both in this parish ; Robert Halliwall in Gattonside, cautioner ; as also John Coats and Janet Purves, both in this parish ; Robert Coatts, cautioner.

Item. James Fisher in this parish and Isobel Wright in the parish of Earlestone : Alexr. Fisher, cautioner.

,, 17. This day the Minister, John Mabane, George Hoy, mett with their treasurer and clerk and revised his accompts and approved the same, and left remaining in his hand £83 : 1s. Scotts.

,, 21. James Bunzie and Jean Wilson in Newsteid, a.s.n. Joseph ; w. Robert and Andrew Bunzies there.

Collected by John Mabane and George Hoy, £2 : 14s.

,, 28. Robert Hunter and Jean Brock in Melrose, a.s.n. Andrew ; w. Wm. Hunter, James Blaikie, there.

Collected by Wm. Hoy and John Mercer, £2 : 9s.

Dec. 5. Collected by James Stoddart and Andrew Drummond, £1 : 18s.
,, 12. Collected by —— £2 : 16s.
,, 16. John Wallace and Sarah Purves in Blainslie, a.s.n. John.
,, ,, John M'Dougal and Janet Suanstone in Blainslie, a.d.n. Margaret ; w. Thomas Darling, John Wallace, there, for above two entries.
,, 19. Collected by John Sibbald and John Bunzie, £2 : 6s.
,, 20. John Crosbie and Elizabeth Hardie in Clackmae, a.d.n. Elizabeth ; w. Alexr. Fisher, James Cribbas.
,, 26. Thomas Marr and Jean Craig in Melrose, a.s.n. James.
,, ,, James Stoddart and Isobel Moss in Darnick, a.s.n. John ; w. Andrew and James Marrs.

Collected by John Mabane, George Hoy and John Mercer, £2 : 2s.

1726.

Jan. 1. This day booked in order for marriage, Mungo Dalgleish and Jannet Glendinning, both in this parish : James Dods in Newsteid, cautioner.

,, 2. After prayer sederunt, the Minister, Drygrainge, Langlee, John Mabane, George Hoy, &c., elders.

Collected by Andrew Paterson and John Mabane, £2 : 18s.

Henry Forrest was gravely rebuked and admonished and ordered to compear with his wife in the place of publick repentance, so soon as his wife can come out. The sederunt closed with prayer.

,, 9. Thomas Pinkertone and Margaret Grieve in Melrose, a.s.n. Thomas.
,, ,, Robert Bunzie and Rachel Forsan in Newsteid, a.d.n. Alison ; w. Robert and Andrew Forsan, for above two entries.

Collected by Andrew Mein and Andrew Drummond, £1 : 10s.

,, 12. Henry Forrest and Isobel Robertson in Westhouses, a.s.n. John.
,, ,, Robert Williamson and Agnes Scott in Westhouses, a.d.n. Isobel ; w. George Mein, George Martine.
,, 16. Collected by James Stoddart and John Mercer, £1 : 18s.
,, 18. John Milne and Isobel Aird in Newtown, a.s.n. George : w. Nichol and Mungo Milne.
,, 23. Collected by Andrew Mar and Andrew Mein, £2 : 7s.
,, 26. Nicol Milne and Agnes Turnbull in Newtown, a.s.n. John ; w. John Cochram, James Laidlay.
,, 30. Collected by John Sibbald, Wm. Hoy, John Mabane, £1 : 18s.

Feb 2. James Boid and Elizabeth Raith in Blainslie, a.s.n. George ; w. James Ainslie, John Coats.
,, 6. Collected by George and Wm. Hoy, £2.
,, 10. John Usher and Christian Bower in Eildon, a.s.n. James ; w. John and Andrew Sibbalds.
,, 13. James Mein and Margaret Bunzie in Newsteid, a.s.n. James.

1726.

Feb. 13. William Laidlay and Margaret Atchison in Melrose, a.s.n. George ;
w. George Martine, John Tait, there, for both above entries.
After prayer sederunt, the Minister, Drygrainge, Langlee,
Nichol Milne, George and Wm. Hoys, &c., elders.
Collected by —— £2 : 2s.
The minister desired the elders to consider if there were any
in their several quarters whom they would recommend for the
office of elders. The sederunt closed in prayer.

,, 20. Collected by James Stoddart and John Mercer, £2 : 6s.

,, 25. This day booked in order for marriage, Alexr. Borthwick in the
parish of Lauder, and Margaret Darling in this ; Thomas Darling,
portioner of Blainslie, cautioner.

,, 27. Collected by Andrew Paterson and John Sibbald, £2 : 6s.
This day Henry Forrest and Isobel Robertson, his wife, compeared for the 1st time and were rebuked.

,, 28. John Chisholm and Margaret Rilchie in Calfhil, a.s.n. George ; w.
George Martine, Andrew Haliday.

Mar. 6. Collected by George Mercer —— £2 : 6s.
Henry Forrest and his spouse compeared for the 2nd time.

,, 7. Booked in order for marriage, David Murray, in the parish of Selkirk,
and Agnes Darling in this parish ; Thomas Darling, cautioner.

,, 12. Booked in order for marriage, Mr. Gavin Eliot, schoolmaster, and
Margaret Angus, in the parish of Selkirk.

,, 13. Collected by James Stoddart and Andrew Drummond, £3 : 7s.
Henry Forrest and his wife dismissed.

,, 20. Andrew M'Fadden and Christian Cook in Melrose, a.d.n. Anne.

,, ,, Andrew and Catharine Mercer in Bridgend, a.d.n. Janet ; w. George
Martine, Alexr. M'Fadden, for above two entries.
Collected by John Mabane and William Dickson, £2 : 16s.

,, 27. Collected by John Sibbald, Andrew Mar and Nichol Milne,
£2 : 14s.

April 3. Alexr. and Jannet Bell in Melrose, a.d.n. Helen.

,, ,, George Martine and Isobel Haliburton in Melrose, a.d.n. Isobel ; w.
John Bowie, Andrew Martine.
Collected by Andrew Drummond and John Mercer, £3 : 19s.

,, 17. William Bunzie and Janet Fairbairn in Newsteid, a.d.n. Isobel ; w.
Robert and Robert Bunzies.
Collected by Wm. and George Hoys, £2 : 1s.

,, 24. John Marr and Isobel Lythgow in Gattonside, a s.n. Robert.

,, ,, Richard Burnet and Agnes Eliot in Drygrange, a.d.n. Grissel.
Collected by James Stoddart, John Sibbald, Nichol Milne,
£2 : 10s.

May 1. Collected by Wm. Dicksone and Andrew Mein, £3 : 5s.

,, 4. Mr. Adam Milne, minister, and Alison Hunter, a.d.n. Margaret,
baptised by Mr. John Goudie ; w. the laird of Muselee, James
Blaikie.

,, 7. This day booked in order for marriage, Gilbert Bourlee and Barbara
Moodie, both in this parish ; Wm. Bourlee, cautioner.

,, 8. James Boustone and Marion Blaikie in Gattonside, a.d.n. Margaret.

,, ,, Michael Wallace and Isobel Blaikie in Melrose, a.d.n. Margaret ; w.
James and Mark Blaikies, for above two entries.
Collected by Robert Moffat and Andrew Drummond, £4.

,, 15. Robert Ormistown and Agnes Smith in Gattonside, a.s.n. Robert ;
w. John Smith, Wm. Cook.
Collected by Wm. Hoy and Andrew Paterson, £3 : 3s.

,, 18. James and Agnes Lauder, a.s.n. Andrew.

,, ,, Alexr. Laing and Agnes Grieve in Blainslie, a.s.n. Alexander.

,, ,, Andrew and Jannet Shillinglaw in Blainslie, a.d.n. Janet.

,, ,, John Tait and Agnes Pringle in Blainslie, a.d.n. Helen. w. John and
James Wallace for above four entries.

1726.

May 22. James Pearson and Margaret Troter in East Housebyres, a.s.n.
Robert.

„   „ John Turnbull and Elizabeth Hamiltone in Gattonside, a.d.n.
Elizabeth.
Collected by John Mercer and Thomas Laidlay, £2 : 9s.

„   29. Wm. Wilkie and Alison Dawson in Melrose, a.s.n. James ; w. James
Blaikie, John Mabane.
After prayer sederunt, the Minister, Drygrainge, Langlee,
James Blaikie, George Hoy, Andrew Paterson, &c., elders.
Collected by John Sibbald and John Mabane, £2 : 10s.
George Hoy, Andrew Paterson, John Mabane are appointed
to meet with the minister and clerk to-morrow fourteen days to
inspect the treasurer's accounts. The sederunt closed with
prayer.

June 5. After prayer sederunt, the Minister, Drygrainge, Langlee, George
Hoy, James Blaikie, John Mabane, &c., elders.
Collected by Thomas Laidlay and Andrew Patersone, £2 : 13s.
This day the minister and elders resolved that the Sacrament
of the supper shall be given in this place, the 17th day of next
month, being the third Sabbath. The sederunt closed with
prayer.

„   12. —— in ——, a.s.n. Martine.

„   „ James Phaup and Alison Cook in Melrose, a.d.n. Elizabeth ; w.
William and Alexr. Cooks there.
Collected by John Sibbald and William Dickson, £2 : 18s.

„   13. This day the minister, John Mabane, George Hoy and Andrew
Paterson, with the clerk, mett with the treasurer and his accompts,
which being revised and approven, there was left in his hand
£101 : 19s. Scotts.

„   16. Booked in order for marriage, George Frater in this parish and
Elizabeth Dalgleish in the parish of Yarrow ; Peter Frater,
cautioner.

„   19. Collected by Andrew Paterson, Andrew Mein, £2 : 5s.

„   26. Collected by Andrew Mar and George Hoy, £2 : 3s.

July 1. Booked in order for marriage, Thomas Faniltone in the parish of
Stitchill and Agnes Hoy in this parish ; Wm. Hoy in Gattonside,
cautioner.

„   3. This day the minister read the Assembly's act appointing a fast, and
the King's proclamation directing it to be Thursday next the 7th
instant. As also he intimated his design of administering the
Sacrament of the supper this day fourteen days, being the 17th
instant.
Collected by John Mercer, £2 : 2s.

„   7. Being the fast day, collected by Nichol Milne and William Dickson,
£4 : 10s.

„   10. John Thomsone and Margaret Martine in Gattonside, a.d.n.
Margaret ; w. James and Andrew Boustones there.
This day the minister intimated Thursday next as the fast
before the Sacrament.
After prayer sederunt, the Minister, Drygrainge, Langlee,
James Blaikie, John Mabane, &c., elders.
Collected by Andrew Marr and John Mercer, £3 : 1s.
The session appoints Tuesday next for the private tryals of
the elders.
Received testimonials for Thomas Pinkertone, officer of excise,
and his wife and servant, from Kelso.
Received from Stow for James Blaikie and his family, testi-
monials. The sederunt closed with prayer.

„   12. This day appointed for privy tryals.
After prayer sederunt, the Minister, Drygrainge, Wm. and

1726.

George Hoy, Wm. Dickson, James Blaikie, Andrew Paterson, Nichol Milne, John Sibbald, John Mabane, James Stoddart, John Mercer, Thomas Laidlay, Robert Moffatt, Andrew Marr, elders.

The elders present were this day severally removed, tryed, approved and encouraged to go on in the Lord's work. The sederunt closed with prayer.

July	14.	Fast day's collection,	-	-	-	-	-	£10	18	00
,,	16.	Saturday's collection,	-	-	-	-	-	13	18	00
,,	17.	Sabbath Day's collection,	-	-	-	-	-	26	06	00
,,	18.	Munday's collection,	-	-	-	-	-	15	00	00

Sum of collections, - - -	£66	02	00
Debursed to the poor of the parish, common poor, and poor with recommendations, precentor and beadle, - - - - - -	45	02	00
	£21	00	00

Which sum of ballance of £21 Scotts, is appointed to be given in to the treasurer wherewith he is to charge himself.

,, 18. Patrick Thomson and Isobel Moffat in Gattonside, a.s.n. Patrick ; w. Robert Sibbald, Robert Halliwall, there.

,, 19. John Chisholm and —— Blaikie in Whitlaw, a.s.n. William ; w. James Blaikie, George Martine.

,, 23. This day booked in order for marriage, William and Helen Fisher both in this parish ; Alexr. Fisher of Sorrowlessfield, cautioner.

,, 24. Collected by John Mabane, Andrew Drummond, and Andrew Mein, £3 : 6s.

Aug. 1. John Davidson and Agnes Mein in Newsteid, a.s.n. John.

,, ,, John Sibbald and Agnes Stenhouse in Eildon, a.d.n. Agnes ; w. Thomas Stenhouse, Nichol Milne in Newtown.

,, ,, After prayer sederunt, the Minister, Drygrainge, Langlee, James Blaikie, John Mabane, George Hoy, &c., elders.
Collected by Nichol Milne and John Sibbald, £2 : 7s.
Christian Rutherford, servetrix to Mary Pringle in Melrose, is ordered to get testimonials twixt and this day fourteen days, else she will not be allowed residence in this parish. The sederunt closed with prayer.

,, 4. Nichol Milne and Mary Mein in Newtown, a.s.n. Nichol.

,, ,, James Usford and Jannet Marr, a.d.n. Helen ; w. Thomas Stenhouse, Nichol Milne, there.

,, 5. John Fisher and Mary Rutherford of Westerhousebyres, a.d.n. Elizabeth.

,, ,, George Alley and Marion Frater in West Langlee, a.s.n. Robert : w. Robert Fisher of Langlee, John Frater.

,, 7. Patrick Bulman and Isobel Vair in Newtown, a.s.n. Andrew ; w. Nichol Milne, George Martine.

,, 14. Collected by Robert Moffat and Wm. Dickson, £1 : 19s.
Collected by George Hoy and Andrew Drummond, £1 : 15s.

,, 21. After prayer sederunt, the Minister, Drygrainge, Langlee, Andrew Paterson, James Blaikie, &c., elders.
Collected by Wm. Hoy and John Mercer, £2 : 8s.
John Mabane reported that he spoke to Christian Rutherford that she might have her testimonials ready within fourteen days, but in regard she is at her harvest the affair is delayed. The sederunt closed with prayer.

,, 28. James Lumsdean and Agnes Mabane in Colmslie, a.s.n. James.

,, ,, David Thomson and Margaret Ker in Calfhill, a.d.n. Jannet ; w. James Hog, James Young, there.

1726.

Collected by John Sibbald, Andrew Drummond and John
Mercer, £4 : 4s.

Sept. 4. Nichol Milne and Mary Mein in Newtown, a.d.n. Mary ; w. Thomas
and Nichol Milnes there.

Collected by Andrew Marr and John Mercer, £2 : 16s.

,, 11. Collected by John Mabane and George Hoy, £2 : 9s.

,, 18. Andrew Lindsey and Margaret Simpson in Gattonside, a.s.n. George ;
w. James Phaup, John Mabane in Melrose.

Collected by James Stoddart and William Dicksone, £1 : 16s.

,, 25. Thomas Miln and Christian Walker in Newtown, a.s.n. Andrew ; w.
Nichol and John Milns there.

Collected by Andrew Paterson, John Mabane and Andrew
Mein, £1 : 14s.

Oct. 2. John Smith, younger, and Helen Mercer in Darnick, a.d.n. Helen ; w.
John Smith, elder, George Mercer, there.

Collected by Wm. Hoy, Andrew Marr and Nichol Milne,
£2 : 9s.

,, 6. Wm. Lauder and Helen Rolmanhouse in Blainslie, a.d.n. Helen ; w.
James Lauder, George Rolmanhouse, there.

,, 9. After prayer sederunt, the Minister, Drygrainge, Langlee, Wm. Hoy,
Andrew Mar, John Mabane, &c., elders.

Collected by John Mercer and William Dickson, £2 : 5s.

Christian Rutherford not producing testimonials according to
the session's appointment, application was made to Drygrainge,
the magistrate, for a warrant to apprehend her if she produced
them not against this day eight days.

John Mabane and James Blaikie are appointed to acquaint
John Young and Isobel Dalgleish that unless they forbear one
another's company, the session will proceed in censures against
them. Also Wm. Dickson and John Mercer are appointed to
acquaint James Kennedy and —— Riddell, that they forbear
living together else the session will also proceed in censures
against them. The sederunt closed with prayer.

,, 15. This day booked in order for marriage, James Henderson in the
parish of Longnewtown and Isabel Halliwall in this parish ;
Richard Slatter in Blainslie, cautioner.

,, 16. After prayer sederunt, the Minister, Drygrainge, Langlee, Nicol
Milne, Wm. Dickson, John Mercer, &c., elders.

Collected by John Sibbald and John Mercer, £2 : 10s.

James Blaikie's appointed to attend the synod at Kelso,
Tuesday next.

£8 Scotts are appointed to be given for the highland and
lowland bursars. The sederunt closed with prayer.

,, 20. This day booked in order for marriage, Thomas Bunzie in this parish,
and Helen Bryden in the parish of Stow : John Bunzie in Eildon,
cautioner.

,, 22. Booked in order for marriage, Walter Scott and Janet Mein, both in
this parish : Robert Scott in Danieltown, cautioner.

,, ,, Booked in order for marriage, Robert Gibson and Isobel Dinnand,
both in this parish : John Gibson in Melrose, cautioner.

,, 23. This day the minister read an act of the Presbytery, appointing a
collection for several families in Selkirk that had lately suffered
by fire, against this day eight days.

,, ,, John Pearson and Mary Crosbie in Old Melrose, a.s.n. Alexander.

,, ,, Wm. Telfair and Helen Lindsay (begot in fornication) in Gattonside,
a.d.n. Helen : w. Wm. Wilson, James Cribbas.

Collected by Mabane, Andrew Mein, Andrew Paterson, £2 : 7s.

,, 28. This day booked in order for marriage, Walter Rae and Christian
Richie, both in this parish ; Andrew M'Fadden in Melrose,
cautioner.

1726.

Oct. 30. Robert Grierson and Margaret Wilson in Darnick, a.s.n. John : w. John Grierson, William Wilson.

Collected by James Stoddart, William Dickson, Andrew Drummond, for the cause as narrated, £34 : 2s. Scotts.

Nov. 6. Robert Leithen and Mary Nisbet in Gattonside, a.d.n. Elizabeth : w. Thomas Nisbet, James Leithen there.

After prayer sederunt, the Minister, Drygrainge, Langlee, Wm. Hoy, Wm. Dickson, Andrew Paterson, &c., elders.

Collected by Andrew Mar and John Mercer, £2 : 10s.

This day the minister informed the session that Robert Pringle, mason in Newsteid, waited on the Presbytry at their last meeting and craved that he might be purged by oath of the scandal. The Presbytry ordered him a copy of the oath. He is to attend the session this day eight days when a copy of it is to be ready.

The session being informed that Margaret Pringle, banished from Selkirk for her wickedness, is come to this parish, they appoint James Blaikie to speak to her and to charge her to leave the parish.

This day the minister gave in a discharge for £34 : 2s. for the relief of these who suffered by fire in Selkirk. The sederunt closed with prayer.

,, 13. Thomas Sclatter and Euphan Robertson in Newsteid, a.s.n. James : w. Andrew Mein, John Mercer, there.

After prayer sederunt, the Minister, Drygrainge, Langlee, James Stoddart, John Mercer, John Mabane, &c., elders.

Collected by Andrew Mein, John Sibbald and John Mercer, £2 : 7s.

A copy of the oath of purgation was given in, but Robert Pringle being away from home it remains in the minister's hand.

This day was read a petition from John Sclater, portioner of Eildon, craving that Drygrainge, as baillie, and the session, would allow him to build a seat at the north side of the east door, which petition being considered and the place viewed, they granted his petition, provided always it do prejudice to no body. The sederunt closed with prayer.

,, 16. James Fisher and Isobel Wight in Sorrowlessfield, a.s.n. Alexander ; w. George Wight, John Fisher.

,, 17. John Frater and Mary Gray, portioner of Langhaugh, a.s.n. George ; w. James and George Alleys in Galabridge.

,, 19. This day booked in order for marriage, William Milne and Elizabeth Mein, both in this parish : John Bowie, cautioner.

,, 20. Wm. Pringle and —— Tait in Blainslie, a.s.n. Andrew : baptized att Ligertwood.

After prayer sederunt, the Minister, Drygrainge, Langlee, James Blaikie, George Hoy, &c., elders.

Collected by Andrew Paterson, Wm. Hoy, John Mabane, £2 : 8s.

Robert Pringle this day waited on the session, whereat the minister with suitable exhortations gave him the oath of purgation to advise upon.

The session being informed that Christian Bunzie, who was sometime out of the parish, is now returned, they are resolved she shall be summoned to the session this day eight days, that she may be dealt with, and therefore appoints the beadle accordingly.

The session appoints Drygrainge, Andrew Paterson, John Mabane and George Hoy, with the minister and clerk, to meet Tuesday next with James Blaikie their treasurer, to take in his accompts. The sederunt closed with prayer.

,, 25. This day booked in order for marriage, Andrew Lythgow in this

1726.

parish and Euphan Smith in the parish of Channelkirk ; George Martine, cautioner.

Nov. 25. Booked Thomas Speeding in the parish of Galashiels and Margaret Myles in this parish ; James Myles in Gattonside, cautioner.

„ 27. James Vair and Margaret Ker in Newtown, a.s.n. ——.

„ „ Thomas Mercer and Margaret Atchison in Melrose ; w. Nichol Mercer, James Laing.

After prayer, sederunt, the Minister, Drygrainge, Langlee, James Stoddart, Nichol Milne, &c., elders.

Collected by Andrew Mar and John Sibbald. £2 : 10s.

Christian Bunzie being summoned was called and compeared, and after serious and suitable exhortations to bring her to a confession, she being a person wicked to the last degree and not sound in judgment. She being removed, the session plainly perceived that all they could say would have no influence to bring her to a confession, and also considering that it is a relapse, and that the former scandal is not altogether purged, resolved to refer the same to the Presbytry of Selkirk for decision. And therefore they did and hereby do refer the same to the Reverend Presbytry of Selkirk that's to meet within the Kirk hereof Tuesday, the sixth next moneth. She was called in and summoned *apud acta* to compear the said day.

In regard these appointed to revise the treasurer's accompts not meet conform to appointment, the same is continued on them to meet to-morrow. The sederunt closed with prayer.

„ 28. This day the Minister, John Mabane, George Hoy and Andrew Paterson mett according to appointment and revised the treasurer's accompts, and approved and found correct, and find in his hand £123 : 7s.

Dec. 3. This day booked in order for marriage, William Darling in this parish and Janet Hislop in the parish of Bowden ; Walter Murray, cautioner.

„ 4. Collected by Andrew Paterson and George Hoy, £2 : 6s.

„ 11. After prayer sederunt, the Minister, Drygrainge, Langlee, Wm. Dickson, James Stoddart, John Mabane, &c., elders.

Collected by James Stoddart and John Mercer, £1 : 18s.

This day the minister acquainted the session that Christian Bunzie waited on the Presbytry Tuesday last, and in everything adhered to her former confession, and that the Presbytry had past upon her the lesser excommunication, but he forbore to pronounce and execute the same in regard he heard that the said Christian was desirous to speak with the session and was waiting on for that effect. The session was of the mind she should be called in, which was accordingly done, and being asked what she had to say to the session, answered rather than be excommunicate she would make a confession against William Swain, weaver in Hawick, a single unmarried man, landlord of the house wherein Henry Gibson's relict lives. She said that she had seen him playing at the kails in her father's garden, and being asked what moved her to emit such a confession at this time, answered as above, that she was afraid of being excommunicated. She was removed, and the session upon consideration thought fitt to call her in. Several questions were put to her to which no satisfying answer was returned. The session appointed an extract of this confession to be drawn out and laid before the Presbytry. The first Tuesday of January next. And she is summoned *apud acta* to attend the Presbytry the said day att Selkirk. The sederunt closed with prayer.

„ 18. Richard Park and Margaret Pringle in Allanshaws, a.s.n. —— baptised att Stow.

1726.

Dec. 18. Robert Sclatter and Janet Elliot in Eildon, a.s.n. James ; w. Thomas Sclatter, James Leithen, there.

   „   „ John Bunzie and Mary Wallace in Eildon, two sons named James and Thomas ; w. *ut supra.*
        Collected by Wm. Hoy, Wm. Dickson and Andrew Drummond, £2 : 2s.

   „ 19. John Coats and Janet Purves in Langshaw, a.s.n. John ; w. Langlee and Charles Ainslie.

   „ 25. Collected by John Mercer and Andrew Mein, £2 : 8s.

   „ 26. James Little and Janet Litherdale in Buckholme, a.d.n. Isobel ; w. John Frater, James Small.

1727.

Jan. 1. Andrew Mein and Janet Mein in Newsteid, a.s.n. Robert.

   „   „ John Corsar and Margaret Purves in Melrose, a.s.n. John ; w. George and Andrew Martines there.
        This day the minister, after many necesary cautions against rash swearing, tendered the oath of purgation to Robert Pringle.
        Collected by Nichol Milne, John Sibbald and Andrew Paterson, £2 : 14s.

   „   8. Robert Ormistown and Helen Hopkirk in Melrose, a.s.n. Robert ; w. Wm. Hopkirk, George Ormistown, there.
        After prayer sederunt, the Minister, Drygrainge, Langlee, James Blaikie, Nichol Milne, Wm. Hoy, &c., elders.
        Collected by George Hoy and John Mabane, £2 : 5s.
        This day the minister pronounced the sentence of the lesser excommunication against Christian Bunzie ; and also absolve Robert Pringle from the same, who purged himself by oath last Lord's day.
        Christian Bunzie was called in and much dealt with. The session appointed her to appear in sackcloath before the congregation Sabbath next. The session appoints their clerk to extract her last confession and convey it to Mr. Charles Telfair, minister of Hawick. The sederunt closed with prayer.

   „ 15. George Beatie and Marion Wright in Bridgend, a.d.n. Janet ; w. George Hoy, Andrew Beatie.
        This day Christian Bunzie appeared in the sackcloath and was spoke with in order to bring her to a sense of her sin.
        Collected by Wm. Dickson, James Stoddart and John Mercer, £2 : 5s.

   „ 22. Christian Bunzie compeared and was spoke with *ut supra.*
        After prayer sederunt, the Minister, Drygrainge, Langlee, James Stoddart, John Sibbald, &c , elders.
        Collected by Andrew Paterson, £1 : 9s.
        This day the session required there might be a meeting of the heretors called for repairing the kirk, that is in an extraordinary bad state. But in regard Farnilee is at Edinr., the session appoints their clerk to write to him about it, and that of a necessity there must be a meeting for that effect about the beginning of March next.
        Margaret Pringle discharged the town and parish of Selkirk, now residing in Melrose, is appointed to bring testimonials, else to leave this place.
        The clerk reports he sent an extract of Christian Bunzie's affair to the minister of Hawick. The sederunt closed with prayer.

   „ 29. Christian Bunzie compeared this day *ut supra* and was admonished.

   „   „ Alexr. and Helen Young in Gattonside, a.d.n. Isobel : w. James and John Young there.
        Collected by ——, £1 : 18s.

Feb. 4. This day booked in order for marriage. James Martine and Margaret Ellies, both in this parish : James Smail in Melrose, cautioner.

1727.

Feb. 5. Christian Bunzie compeared and was spoken with *ut supra*.

        Collected by John Sibbald and Andrew Mein, £2 : 5s.

  ,, 8. William Thine and Margaret Fairbairn in Blainslie, —— ; w. John and William Thins there.

  ,, 12. Robert Rutherford and Elizabeth Heiton in Bridgend, a.d.n. Agnes ; w. George and Robert Martines in Melrose.

        After prayer sederunt, the Minister, Drygrainge, Langlee, Laird Marr, James Blaikie, &c., elders.

        Collected by George Hoy and John Mabane, £2 : 10s.

        This day the session, upon the reading of a minute from Galashiels session about taking some course with one Isobel Smal of scandalous behaviour in Langhaugh, applied to the civil magistrate to have her removed the place, and the magistrate is to grant warrant to his officers to cause her remove within such a time.

        The beadle is ordered to summon Grissal Little in Langhaugh to compear before the session of Galashiels against the 19th instant. The sederunt closed with prayer.

  ,, 19. Collected by Andrew Paterson and William Dickson, £1 : 14s.

        John Sclatter in Eildon having sett down a seat in the kirk, gave in to the poor 12s.

  ,, 26. Collected by Wm. Hoy, James Stoddart and John Mercer, £2 : 9s.

        Christian Bunzie compeared this day *ut supra*, and was dealt with to bring her to a sense of her sin.

Mar. 2. Thomas Thin and —— Simpson in Blainslie, a.d.n. Isobel ; w. John and William Thins there.

  ,, 4. This day Andrew Bartleman and Janet Cochran, both in this parish, were booked in order for marriage ; James Mein in Newsteid, cautioner.

  ,, 5. This day Christian Bunzie compeared *ut supra* and spoke with, she was dismissed from further attendance for some time, but not absolved till she should give some signs of repentance and sorrow, nor till such time could she be relaxed from the sentence of excommunication.

  ,, ,, James Lowrie and Isobel Brown in Newtown, a.s.n. Walter.

  ,, ,, William Bowar and Isobel Paterson in Melrose, a.s.n. John ; w. John Bell, William Steel.

        Collected by Nichol Milne and John Sibbald, £2 : 10s. Scotts.

  ,, 11. This day booked in order for marriage, Andrew Turnbull in this parish and Mary Lamb in Wiltown parish ; Robert Rutherford, cautioner.

  ,, 12. James Dewar and Marion Hardie in Housebyres, a.d.n. Mary ; w. John Turner, Walter Thomson.

        Collected by John Mabane and John Mercer, £2 : 10s.

  ,, 17. This day booked in order for marriage Michael Vetch and Elizabeth Saidler, both in this parish ; John Tait in Melrose, cautioner.

  ,, 19. This day the minister intimated from the pulpit a meeting of the heretors against Wednesday, the 12th of Aprill, about the reparation of the kirk.

  ,, ,, William Mercer and Elizabeth Lumsdain in Gattonside, a.d.n. Margaret ; w. James Marr, Robert Martine, there.

        Collected by Andrew Marr and William Dickson, £2 : 6s.

  ,, 23. James Martin and Jannet Dickson in Blainslie, a.d.n. Isobel.

  ,, ,, James Scott and Helen Lauder in Blainslie, a.d.n. Isobel : w. James Dickson, John Wallace, thereat, for above two entries.

  ,, 26. Nichol Milne and Agnes Turnbull in Newtown, a.s.n. James.

  ,, ,, John Bunzie and —— Sibbald in Newtown, a.d.n. Isobel.

  ,, ,, James Hart and Agnes Thomson in Gattonside, a.d.n. Elizabeth ; w. Thomas Stenhouse, John Milne, for above three entries.

        Collected by Andrew Drummond and John Mercer, £2 : 6s.

1727.

April. 2. Collected by Wm. and George Hoys and Andrew Mar, £2 : 11s.

" 6. James Laidlay and Christian Brunton in Buckholm, a.s.n. James ; w. Robert Moffatt, Wm. Atchison.

" 7. Robert Paterson and Anna Eliot of Drygrainge, a.s.n. Gilbert ; w. John Riddell of Muselee, David Brown of Park.

" 8. This day Peter Grieve and Elizabeth Tait, both in this parish, intending marriage, were booked ; John Tait, cautioner.

" 9. Mr. Gavin Eliot, schoolmaster, and Margaret Angus, a.d.n. Margaret ; w. Alexr. Paterson, younger, of Drygrainge, Patrick Angus.

Collected by Andrew Drummond and Thomas Laidlay, £2 : 12s.

" 16. John Mein and Mary Mein of Old Melrose, a.d.n. Mary ; w. Andrew Mein and Andrew Mein.

After prayer sederunt, the Minister, Drygrainge, Thomas Laidlay, Robert Moffat, George Hoy, &c., elders.

Collected by John Sibbald, and John Mercer elder, £2 : 12s.

Nichol Milne is appointed to attend the Synod at Kelso, Tuesday next. The sederunt closed with prayer.

" 23. Collected by John Mabane and George Hoy, £2 : 4s.

" 30. After prayer sederunt, the Minister, Drygrainge, Langlee, George Hoy, Wm. Dickson, Wm. Hoy, &c., elders.

Collected by Wm. Thin, Robert Moffatt, £2 : 19s.

There was this day a petition from Robert Edgar, indweller in Melrose, craving that the session would take an house to him for the ensuing year. The session having considered the same, condescended to allow him a crown to help him to take an house.

This day the minister intimated to the session his purpose of augmenting the number of elders, and accordingly named John Wallace, John Stirling, George Rolmanhouse and John Pringle in Blainslies, Andrew Lythgow in Threepwood, James Laidlay in Buckholm, John Frater in Langhaugh, Thomas Stenhouse in Newtown, and Robert Scott in Danieltown. 'Tis recommended to the several elders to enquire into and enform themselves of their walk and conversation and converse with the above named persons, and to report to their next meeting.

Being informed that Margaret Pringle banished the town of Selkirk, is lurking in Melrose, the session did unanimously apply to Drygrainge, as bailie of the regality, to have her expelled the said regality till she bring in testimonials of her behaviour from other parishes. The bailie is to grant warrant to his officers for that end.

Peter Grieve and Elizabeth Tait, who had a penny wedding last week, are appointed to be cited before the Presbytry of Selkirk against Tuesday next. As also John Tait and Isobel Wauch in Melrose, in whose house the wedding was held. The sederunt closed with prayer.

May 3. James Wallace and Eupham Darling in Blainslie, a.s.n. John.

" " William Wilson and Margaret Shillinglaw in Blainslie, a.s.n. John.

" " Robert Mercer and Jannet Little in Easterhousebyre, a.s.n. Alison ; w. Robert and Andrew Pringles.

" 7. John Inglis and Jannet Hadden in Langhaugh : —— baptized at Galashiels.

After prayer sederunt, the Minister, Drygrainge, Langlee, Wm. Dickson, John Sibbald, &c., elders.

Collected by Thomas Laidlay and John Mercer, £2 : 14s.

In case of the minister's absence Nichol Milne and John Sibbald, elders, are to distribute the tokens att Lessudain this day eight days to such of the parish as are inclined to join them in the Sacrament of the Supper. The sederunt closed with prayer.

" 12. This day booked in order for marriage, Adam Wallace in this parish and Janet Hislop in the parish of Ligertwood ; James Wallace in Blainslie, cautioner.

1727.

May 14. No sermon this day, the minister being att the General Assembly.

,, 16. This day booked in order for marriage, Wm. Hart and Margaret Mein, both in this parish ; Cornelius Mein in Eildon, cautioner.

,, ,, Booked in order for marriage, James Brown in this and Agnes Wauch in the parish of Ligertwood ; Mr. William Hunter in Williamlaw, cautioner.

,, ,, Booked also in order for marriage. John Hog and Helen Pearson, both in this parish : Wm. Pearson in Hagburn, cautioner.

,, 20. This day booked in order for marriage, Wm. Sibbald and Isobel Boustone, both in this parish ; Thomas Boustone in Gattonside, cautioner.

,, ,, Booked, Robert Rolmanhouse and Alison Laidlay, both in this parish ; Wm. Lauder in Blainslie, cautioner.

,, 21. Collected by Wm. Hoy and John Mercer, younger, £2 : 15s.

,, 22. John Wallace and Margaret Dick in Blainslies, a.s.n. George ; w. James Martine, George Scott, there.

,, 26. Booked in order for marriage, Thomas Dalgliesh in the parish of Galashiels, and Janet Brown in this parish ; Mark Blaikie in Melrose, cautioner.

,, 28. George Edgar and Beatrix Wallace in Melrose, a.d.n. Helen.

,, ,, Thomas Anderson and Margaret Dickson in Drygrainge Boathouse, a.d.n. Jean ; w. Michael Wallace, William Wilkie.

After prayer sederunt, the Minister, Drygrainge, Nichol Milne, Thomas Laidlay, John Sibbald, elders.

Collected by Nichol Milne and Andrew Paterson, £3 Scotts.

This day the affair of the elders was resumed, and the minister named the following persons whom he has spoke with, and does not find them averse from that office, viz. :—John Wallace in Blainslies, Andrew Lythgow in Threepwood, James Laidlay in Buckholm, John Frater in Langhaugh, William Milne in Newsteid, and Robert Scott in Danieltown. It was asked if the session knew anything why these persons might not be taken into the number of elders, and nothing offering, they appoint intimation of their resign to be made Sabbath first from the pulpit. As also of the session meeting, Thursday, the 15th of June, to receive what objections made be made by the parish against the said persons.

Upon the report of Margaret Pringle's still skulking in the town of Melrose, the session appoints their officer to summon her to the session against this day eight days. The sederunt closed with prayer.

June 2. This day booked in order for marriage, Alexr. Familtone in the parish of Stitchill and Isobel Hoy in this parish ; William Hoy, portioner of Gattonside, cautioner.

,, 4. This day the minister intimated to the congregation the session's purpose of admitting the persons named in their last sederunt to the office of elders, that if any in the parish had anything to object against the said persons, they might attend the session Thursday come eight days, where they will be heard.

,, ,, James Dods and Annie Riddell in Newsteid, a.d.n. Anne ; w. George and Andrew Martines.

After prayer sederunt, the Minister, Drygrainge, Langlee, Wm. Hoy, John Mabane, &c., elders.

Collected by John and John Mercers, £2 : 6s.

Case against Margaret Pringle and Walter Rae, carrier in Selkirk, in James Rickleton's house in Selkirk.

The session is of the mind that this her confession be extracted and transmitted to the session of Selkirk, whereupon the clerk is appointed accordingly, and she's dismissed till further orders. The sederunt closed with prayer.

1727.

June 10. This day booked in order for marriage, George Walker in this parish and Isobel Hoggart in the parish of Stitchill; Robert Penman in Melrose, cautioner.

„ 11. Wm. Atchison and Jannet Shiel in Newsteid, a.s.n. George; w. George Shiel, Andrew Mein.

Collected by John Mabane and George Hoy, £3 : 5s.

„ 15. After prayer sederunt, the Minister, Drygrainge, James Blaikie, John Mabane, George Hoy, Andrew Marr, Wm. Hoy, Andrew Mein, Andrew Paterson, Thomas Laidlay.

This day being appointed for hearing objections against the persons intended to be admitted elders, the beadle was sent to the several doors to intimate if any had anything to object why the above named persons may be admitted to the office of elders, they might lay the same before the session now sitting in the kirk for that end. None appearing, the session appoints Sabbath come eight days for their admission, and the beadle is ordered to acquaint them herewith that they may be present in order there, &c.

This day was read the petition of Andrew Lookup, portioner of Melrose, craving that a bond of cautionary he had given in to the session to present Francis Pringle to them, might be given up to him in regard he did present the said Francis.

The session do grant his petition.

Upon application from James Blaikie, treasurer, the session do appoint Drygrainge, Andrew Paterson, Nichol Milne, John Sibbald and George Hoy, with the minister and clerk, to meet at the said James Blaikie's house this same day, and revise his accompts. The sederunt closed with prayer.

„ „ *Quo supra*, sederunt, the Minister, Drygrainge, Nichol Milne, John Sibbald, Andrew Paterson and George Hoy, and revised and approved the treasurer's accompts, and do find remaining in his hand, £110 : 14s.

„ 16. This day booked in order for marriage, James Brotherstone and Eupham Dickson, both in this parish; James Ainslie, cautioner.

„ 18. Thomas and Alison Gill in Danieltown, a.s.n. William.

„ „ Andrew Drummond and Helen Mathesone in Bridgend, a.d.n. Jannet; w. Andrew Paterson, Walter Murray.

Collected by John Sibbald and Wm. Dicksone, £5 : 1s.

„ 25. John Sclatter and Jannet Little in Eildon, a.d.n. Agnes; w. James Wauch, George Martine in Melrose.

This day being appointed for admitting the elders, there compeared John Frater, Robert Scott, Wm. Milne, Andrew Lythgow, James Lindsay and John Wallace, who were gravely admitted to the office of elders in common form.

After prayer sederunt, the Minister, Drygrainge, John Mabane, John Mercer and Wm. Hoy, &c., elders.

Collected by Andrew Marr and Wm. Hoy, £2 : 1s.

The elders admitted in the forenoon were exhorted to their duty, and enjoined to keep the secrets of the session. The sederunt closed with prayer.

„ 26. Wm. Pringle and ——— in Blainslie, a.d.n. Jean; w. Thomas Darling, George Martine.

July 2. Collected by James Laidlay and George Hoy, £3 : 2s.

„ 9. Collected by Robert Scott and Andrew Mein, £2 : 16s.

„ 11. George Mercer and Agnes Knox in Blainslie, a.s.n. George; w. Langlee and Andrew Bryden.

„ „ Mr. Adam Milne, minister, and Alison Hunter, a.d.n. Elizabeth; w. Drygrainge and John Duncansone.

„ 14. This day booked in order for marriage, Robert Blaikie in the parish of Stow and Barbara Ainslie in this; James Ainslie, cautioner;

1727.

> also John Usher and Agnes Leithen, both in this parish ; James Leithen, cautioner : also John Fisher and Isobel Scott, both in this parish : Alexr. Fisher, cautioner.

July 16. James Wauch and Mary Duncan in Melrose, a.d.n. Mary.

„ „ John Laidlay and Alison Mein in Newtown, a.s.n. —— ; w. John Gill, George Ormistown, for both above entries.

> After prayer sederunt, the Minister, Drygrainge, Langlee, James Blaikie, Andrew Lythgow, Robert Moffat, &c., elders.
> Collected by Wm. Milne, Andrew Drummond, Andrew Paterson, £2 : 13s.
> The minister acquainted the session that he, twixt sermons, had called several of the elders, and pitched upon the 6th day of August next for the celebration of the Sacrament of the Supper, and that he accordingly had intimated the same from the pulpit. The session was very well pleased with the time. The sederunt closed with prayer.

„ 22. This day booked in order for marriage, Walter and Margaret Grays, both in this parish ; James Smail in Melrose, cautioner.

„ 23. After prayer sederunt, the Minister, Drygrainge, Langlee, Wm. Milne, Robert Scott, John Frater, &c., elders.
> Collected by John Frater and Wm. Dicksone, £2 : 15s.
> The session appoints Munday come eight days for privy censures and ordering other affairs. The sederunt closed with prayer.

„ 27. Wm. Pearson and Isobel Stirling in Hagburn, —— .

„ „ Richard Thomson and Isobel Moffat in Williamlaw, —— : w. Langlee and Robert Martine.

„ 29. James Darling and Margaret Fairbairn in Blainslies, a.s n. Thomas ; w. James Fisher, Thomas Darling.
> This day booked in order for marriage, Robert Mercer in the parish and Anaple Ovens in the parish of St. Boswals ; Wm. Bunzie, cautioner.

„ 30. This day the minister appointed Thursday next as a day of fasting and humiliation before the sacrament of the supper.
> Collected by James Lindsay, John Wallace, and John Mabane, £3 : 5s.

„ 31. After prayer sederunt, the Minister, Drygrainge, Langlee, James Blaikie, John Mabane, George and Wm. Hoy, Andrew Paterson, Robert Scott, Wm. Dickson, John Mercer, Nicol Milne, Andrew Mein, Andrew Drummond, John Sibbald, John Frater, &c., elders.
> This day appointed for privy tryals the elders as named were by pairs severally removed, approven and encouraged to go on in the Lord's work.
> The way the collection is to be gathered the several days of the Sacrament.

Thursday.

Andrew Paterson and Andrew Drummond at the south door ; John Mercer at the west : Wm. Dickson at the north.

Saturday.

Robert Moffat at the east stile : Andrew Mar at the minister's entry to be continued : Andrew Mein at the south door : Andrew Lythgow and Thomas Laidlay at the south stile : James Laidlay and John Frater at the west stile.

Lord's Day.

John Mabane at the north door : Nicol Milne and Robert

1727.

Scott at the west stile ; William Milne and Andrew Mein at the south stile ; John Wallace at the east stile.

Munday.

William Hoy at the east stile ; George Hoy at the south stile ; Andrew Mein for the south entry thro' the kirk ; John Mercer for the west stile.

The order of keeping the doors the Lord's Day.

John Sibbald and John Mercer for the east door till eleven of the clock ; Robert Scott, William Thin, and Robert Moffat, till one. Then John Wallace and Andrew Lythgow till the action be over.

For the West Door.

James Blaikie and George Hoy till eleven.
Wm. Dickson, Andrew Drummond, and James Laidlay till one.
Then Andrew Mein and Wm. Milne to the end.
The elders were enjoined caution in distributing the tokens.
The sederunt closed with prayer.

Aug. 3. Henry Forrest and Isobel Robison in Westhouses, a.d.n. Anaple ; w. George and Andrew Martines.
Collected by the person as appointed, £10 : 8s.

„	„	Fast day's collection,	-	-	-	-	£10	8	0
„	5.	Saturday's collection,	-	-	-	-	12	11	0
„	6.	Sabbath day's collection,	-	-	-	-	26	8	0
„	7.	Munday's collection,	-	-	-	-	12	6	0

Sum of collections,	-	-	-	-	-	£61	13	0
Debursed to poor of the parish, common poor and poor with recommendations, precentor and beadle,					39	5	0
						£22	8	0

Which sum of £22 : 8s. Scotts of ballance is appointed to be given to the treasurer wherewith he is to charge himself.

„ 13. James Henderson and Isobel Halliwall in Gattonside, a.s.n. Robert ; w. Robert Halliwall, George Stuart, there.
After prayer sederunt, the Minister, Drygrainge, Langlee, James Blaikie, Wm. Dicksone, &c., elders.
Collected by John Mabane and Robert Scott, £2 : 5s.
The minister acquainted the session that being importuned to baptise a child to one William Dewar come to reside in Newsteid, he had no freedom to do it, in regard that they were married irregularly, &c. That he had write to Mr. Henry Hume, minister in Channelkirk, where the said William gave in his marriage lines, and had got Mr. Hume's return, which cleared the session as to the marriage in general, and that they were rebuked before their session, but does not satisfy as to the date of their marriage. Whereupon the session is of the mind that a more special account of the time of their marriage is to be given before the child was to be baptised.
The minister is appointed to write to Mr. Hume for a more particular account of the date of their testimonials. The sederunt closed with prayer.

„ 20. After prayer sederunt, the Minister, Drygrainge, James Blaikie, William Milne, George Hoy, Robert Scott, &c., elders.
Collected by Thomas Laidlay and William Hoy, £3 : 11s.
The minister reports that he wrote to Mr. Hume but had got

1727.

no return ; it is recommended to James Blaikie to desire James Robson, carrier, to call for the answer this week.

Case against Jean Lindsay, servitrix to James Lythgow, portioner of Melrose ; the beadle is ordered to summon her to the session this day eight days. The sederunt closed with prayer.

Aug. 27. After prayer sederunt, the Minister, Drygrainge, Wm. Dickson, John Sibbald, &c., elders.

Collected by John Mercer, elder, and Wm. Milne, £2 : 18s.

The minister reported that there was no word come from Mr. Hume.

Case against Jean Lindsay and George Smith, now in Lesudain, formerly servant to Mr. Ellies of Huntliewood. The sederunt closed with prayer.

Sept. 3. Thomas Marr and Jean Craig in Melrose, a.d.n. Agnes ; w. Andrew and James Marrs.

After prayer sederunt, the Minister, Langlee, Wm. Thin, Thomas Laidlay and Robert Moffat, &c., elders.

Collected by John Sibbald and John Mercer, younger, £3 : 5s.

The clerk reports that he wrote to Mr. Byres according to appointment, and there was produced in execution of the summons against George Smith, he was called but compeared not. He's appointed to be summoned pro 2do.

The session appoints plush to be bought for a Mortcloath for children. The sederunt closed with prayer.

„ 10. After prayer sederunt, the Minister, Drygrainge, Langlee, John Wallace, John Mabane, Andrew Paterson, &c., elders.

Collected by Robert Scott and Andrew Drummond, £2 : 15s.

The session being informed that George Smith is gone to reside in Sandieknow in Smailholm parish, they appoint their clerk to write to Mr. Cunninghame, to cause cite him to our session this day eight days pro 2do. The sederunt closed with prayer.

„ 17. Thomas Bunzie and Helen Bryden in Eildon, a.s.n. John.

„ „ Thomas Waddell and Jannet Brown in Westerhousebyres, a.d.n. Jannet.

„ „ Wm. Stuart and Euphan Gray in Gattonside, a.d.n. Janet ; w. John Bunzie, John Bowie.

After prayer sederunt, the Minister, Drygrainge, Langlee, James Laidlay, Wm. Milne and John Mabane, &c., elders.

Collected by John Frater and William Dickson, £2 : 15s.

The clerk reports that according to appointment he wrote to the minister of Smailholm to cause cite George Smith in Sandieknow to this day's session. There was accordingly produced an execution against the said George, which being read, he was called and compeared and interrogate, was admonished and then removed. The session, on consideration that he seemed to have no fixed residence, was of the mind that he should compear before the congregation Sabbath first. He was called in and this intimate to him and seriously exhorted to repentance, then dismissed. The sederunt closed with prayer.

„ 19. Archibald Robson and Christian Davidson in Blainslies, a.d.n. Margaret.

„ „ Andrew Mar and Susanna Lythgow in Gattonside, a.d.n. Susanna ; w. Wm. Mar, Thomas Speeding, there.

„ 24. This day George Smith compeared before the congregation.

Collected by Wm. Hoy and Andrew Patersone, £2 : 13s.

Oct. 1. Thomas Mathisone and Margaret Bonningtone in Westhouses, a.s.n. Robert ; w. Walter Murray, George Hoy.

George Smith compeared for the second time.

Collected by Andrew Mein and Wm. Milne, £2 : 9s.

1727.

Oct. 8. After prayer sederunt, the Minister, Drygrainge, Langlee, James Blaikie, George Hoy, &c., elders.

This day was produced a testimonial of Wm. Dewar and Elizabeth Mein's marriage, dated Lowick, Nov. 18, 1726, subscribed James Miller, minister. It is recorded that they had previously resided at Kaimes, Eccles parish. The sederunt closed with prayer.

" " After prayer sederunt, the Minister, Drygrainge, John Mabane, Wm. Milne, John Mercer, &c., elders.

George Smith compeared, was rebuked and dismissed.

Collected by John Mercer and Andrew Marr, £2 : 9s.

William Dewar and Elizabeth Mein, his wife, being summoned were called and compeared, and dismissed till further orders. The session appoints their clerk to extract their confessions and transmit them to Mr. John Lauder, minister of Eccles.

The session being certainly informed that George Atchison, smith, shoed some rakish profane gentlemen's horses Sabbath last, they appoint their beadle to summon the said George to this day eight day's session.

Jean Lindsay is ordered to compear before the congregation Sabbath next. The sederunt closed with prayer.

" 14. This day booked in order for marriage, James Speeding and Jannet Mercer, both in this parish : Nicol Mercer, portioner of Bridgend, cautioner.

" 15. Robert Gibson and Isobel Dinnand in Gattonside, a.d.n. Margaret.

" " John Dalgleish and Agnes Darling in Daernick, a.s.n. John.

" " Wm. Robertson and Bessie Scott in Gattonside, a.d.n. Elizabeth ; w. John Gibson, Robert Boustone.

Jean Linsday compeared for the first time and was rebuked.

After prayer sederunt, the Minister, Drygrainge, James Blaikie, James Linsday, Wm. Hoy, &c., elders.

Collected by John Mabane and George Hoy, £2 : 11s.

George Atchison being summoned was called and compeared. He testifyed his sorrow for prophaning the Lord's day in shoeing these gentlemen's horses. He was called in, and the minister did accordingly gravely rebuke him and took his promise never to be guilty of any such things for the future. Then he was dismissed with certification.

Drygrainge is appointed to attend the synod at Kelso. Tuesday next. The sederunt closed with prayer.

" 21. This day booked in order for marriage John Milne in the parish of Bowden and Isobel Sibbald in this parish : Wm. Sibbald, portioner of Eildon, cautioner.

Also Robert Welsh in the parish of Bowden and Margaret Glendinning in this parish : John Usher in Eildon, cautioner.

Item, James Welsh in the parish of Bowden and Alison Blaikie in this parish : Gilbert Welsh in Gattonside, cautioner.

Item, Robert Boustone and Alison Mein, both in this parish : Cornelius Mein, portioner of Eildon, cautioner.

" 22. Robert Bunzie and Marion Hopkirk in Newsteid, a.s.n. James ; w. Wm. Hopkirks, elder and younger.

Jean Lindsay compeared pro 2 'o.

Collected by Andrew Paterson, Wm. Dickson and Robert Scott, £2 : 17s.

" 29. Jean Linsday was rebuked and dismissed.

Collected by Andrew Marr and Wm. Hoy, £2 : 5s.

" 30. Alexr. Tait and Isobel Shiel in Mosshouses, a.d.n. Margaret ; w. Westerhousbyres and John Turner.

Nov. 3. This day booked in order for marriage Andrew Hislop in the

K

1727.

parish of Earlestoun and Mary Burnet in this ; John Fisher of Westerhousebyres, cautioner.

Nov. 3. This day James Laing and Agnes Ritchie. both in this parish, were booked in order for marriage ; James Smail, cautioner.

  ,,   4. This day John Hoy in this parish and Alison Cunningham in the parish of Martine were booked in order for marriage ; Alexr. Familtown in Eildon, cautioner.

  ,,   5. Collected by John Sibbald and Andrew Lythgow, £2 : 17s.

  ,,   8. This day James Small in this parish and Grissal M'Clain in the parish of Galashiels were booked in order for marriage ; John Tait in Melrose, cautioner.

  ,, 12. Andrew Usher and Isobel Thomson in Darnick, a.d.n. Helen ; w. James Smail, John Mercer.

         After prayer sederunt, the Minister, Drygrainge, Langlee, Andrew Lythgow, Wm. Milne, &c., elders.

         Collected by John Mercer and Wm. Milne, £2 : 7s.

         'Twas this day recommended to the elders to enquire carefully for testimonials of those that come into their several quarters.

         This day received a testimonial for Violet M'Clain, and the session grants her another. The sederunt closed with prayer.

  ,, 14. Granted testimonials to Grissal Eliot for half an year, as also to Elizabeth Pursall for upwards of twelve years.

  ,, 19. This day the minister read a recommendation of the General Assembly for repairing the harbour of Bamf, which collection is to be gathered this day eight days.

  ,, ,, James Leithan and Margaret Sclater in Eildon, a.d.n. Agnes ; w. John Gibson. John Mabane.

         Collected by John Frater and Nicol Milne, £2 : 10s.

         Allowed testimonials to Elizabeth Rolmanhouse for one year, and received testimonials for John Murray from Lauder.

  ,, 24. This day booked in order for marriage John Murray in this parish and Isobel Hutton in the parish of Lauder : Thomas Fairbairn of Broadwoodshiels, cautioner.

  ,, 25. Booked in order for marriage James Pringle and Margaret Brown, both in this parish ; Robert Bunzie, cautioner.

  ,, 26. John Gordon and Isobel Ellies in Darnick, a.d.n. Margaret.

  ,, ,, John Milne and Isobel Aird in Newtown, a.d.n. Margaret ; w. John Dalgleish, John Griersone.

         Collected by John Mabane, William Dickson and George Hoy, for repairing the harbour of Bamf, £12 Scotts.

  ,, 27. Robert Henry and Elizabeth Blaikie in Appletreeleaves, a.d.n. Elizabeth ; w. John Frater, George Scott.

Dec. 1. This day booked in order for marriage John Douglas and Alison Riddell, both in this parish ; James Kennedy, cautioner.

  ,, 3. After prayer sederunt, the Minister, Drygrainge, Langlee, John Frater, William Dickson, James Blaikie, &c., elders.

         Collected by Andrew Paterson and Robert Scott, £3 : 7s.

         The session having some time ago appointed the elder of Bridgend to enquire for testimonials of —— Tunter, residing in Bridgend, there was this day produced a letter from Mr. Gilchrist, minister of Bedrule, to our minister that was no way satisfying, and it being nottourly known that the said Tunter was judicially convicted of horse stealing at one of the quarter's sessions in Jedburgh, and that he had signed an act of banishment, and over and above that he is of a scandalous and offensive behaviour in the neighbourhood. The session unanimously agreed that application should be made to Drygrainge, magistrate of this place, and one of the Justices of Peace of the shire, to have the said Tunter removed from their bounds, and all persons

1727.

whatsomever discharged to harbour or lodge him, accordingly they did and hereby do apply.

Testimonials granted to Elizabeth Hopkirk and Jannet Henderson from their infancy. To Elizabeth Haliburtone for two years preceding Martinmas 1726.

The session appoints that each using the plush Mortcloath pay in ten pence to the box.

Dec. 9. This day booked in order for marriage William Stoddart and Isobel Young, both in this parish ; George Young, cautioner.

„ 10. After prayer sederunt, the Minister, Drygrainge, Langlee, Wm. Milne, James Blaikie, &c., elders.

Collected by John Mercer, elder and younger, £2 : 3s.

Case against Alison Riddell in Darnick, and John Douglass, servant to the minister.

„ 17. Walter Scott and Margaret Mein in Danieltown, a.s.n. James.

„ „ Andrew Crawford and —— Mein in Newsteid, a.d.n. Isobel : w. Andrew Paterson, George Laury there.

Collected by William Dickson, £1 : 11s.

„ 24. William and Helen Fisher in Darnick, a.d.n. Agnes.

„ „ Walter Rae and Christian Ritchie in Newtown, a.d.n. Margaret.

„ „ Thomas Speeding and Margaret Myles in Gattonside, a.d.n. Isobel : w. John Mercer, William Dickson.

Collected by William Milne and Andrew Mein, £2 : 6s.

„ 31. William Hog and Agnes Hardie in Darnick ; w. James Blaikie, John Mabane.

Collected by John Mercer, younger, Andrew Drummond, £2 : 5s.

1728.

Jan. 7. This day John Douglass and Alison Riddell compeared before the congregation for the first time and were rebuked.

Collected by John Sibbald and William Hoy, £2.

„ 12. This day booked in order for marriage George Mercer and Christian Tait, both in this parish : Nichol Mercer in Melrose, cautioner.

„ 14. Andrew Bartleman and Janet Cochran in Newtown, a.d.n. Isobel ; w. Henry Cochran, James Mein there.

John Douglass and Alison Riddell compeared for the second time.

Collected by Robert Scott and Andrew Patersone, £1 : 16s.

„ 20. This day booked in order for marriage Wm. Welsh in the parish of Bowden and Isobel Simpson in this parish : James Fisher in Darnick, cautioner.

„ 21. Alison Riddell compeared for the third time.

Collected by George Hoy and John Mabane, £2 : 1s.

„ 22. Peter Grieve and Elizabeth Tait in Longshawmilne, a.s.n. John ; w. John Tait, George Martine.

„ 28. Collected by John Frater, Wm. Dickson and Andrew Drummond, £2 : 16s.

Alison Riddell compeared for the fourth time.

Feb. 4. Alexr. M'Fadden and Agnes Napier in Melrose, a.d.n. Isobel : w. Andrew M'Fadden, Thomas Gardiner.

After prayer sederunt, the Minister, Drygrainge, Langlee, Nicol Milne, John Sibbald, &c., elders.

Collected by Wm. Hoy, Andrew Marr, James Laidlay, £2 : 15s.

Drygrainge, John Mabane, George Hoy, Andrew Paterson, with the Minister and clerk, are appointed to meet to-morrow with the treasurer to inspect his accompts. The sederunt closed with prayer.

„ 5. Alison Riddell compeared for the fifth time.

This day the Minister, John Mabane, Andrew Paterson, George Hoy and Robert Scott, according to appointment met

1728.

with their treasurer and clerk, and revised their treasurer's accompts and approved the same, and do find in his hand £119 : 8s. Scotts.

Feb. 11. Wm. Milne and Lizie Mein in Darnick, a.d.n. Agnes : w. John Mercer, John Heiton there.

John Douglass and Alison Riddell compeared before the congregation, were rebuked, exhorted and dismissed.

After prayer sederunt, the Minister, Drygrainge, John Mabane, George Hoy, Wm. Dickson, &c., elders.

Collected by Nicol Milne and Andrew Drummond, £2 : 10s.

This day the session resolved that there should be intimation made for a collection to build a bridge over Darnick burn and to repair Elwand bridge, as also for some people that have suffered by fire in the parish of Robertown and to a minister's relict in Orkney in great distress, and the elders to gather this from house to house in their several quarters.

Testimonials allowed to John Douglass and Alison Riddell for half year preceding Martinmas. The sederunt closed with prayer.

" 14. Andrew Smith and Helen Boustone in Gattonside, a.d.n. Margaret ; w. Thomas and James Boustone's there.

" 17. This day booked in order for marriage Thomas Darling in this parish and Helen Thomson in the parish of Lauder ; James Heiton, cautioner ; as also John Tait and Margaret Martine, both in this parish : Wm. Martine in Melrose, cautioner.

" 18. This day the minister according to the Presbytry's appointment intimated a fast to be observed Wednesday next.

" " Robert Bunzie and Rachel Forsan in Newsteid, a.d.n. Janet : w. William and James Bunzies there.

Allowed testimonials to Agnes Bouston from her infancy to Martinmas last.

Collected by John Sibbald and Wm. Milne, £2 : 2s.

" 21. This day the minister intimated that the elders would gather through their several quarters what they would willingly contribute for the relief of these that suffered by fire in the parish of Robertown, and a distressed minister's relict, as also for making a bridge over Darnick burn and repairing that on Elwand.

Collected by Andrew Mein and Andrew Paterson, £2 : 17s.

" 25. Collected by John Mabane and George Hoy, £2 : 4s.

Mar. 3. Andrew Turnbull and Mary Turnbull in Bridgend, a.d.n. Isobel : w. James Blaikie, Andrew Drummond.

After prayer sederunt, the Minister, Drygrainge, John Sibbald, Andrew Paterson, Robert Scott, &c., elders.

Collected by Robert Scott, Andrew Marr and Wm. Hoy, £2 : 11s.

This day was presented a petition from Robert Bunzie, mason in Newsteid, complaining that James Smail, weaver in Melrose, hath lately set down a seat holding two or three persons, whereas his authors never had any but a chair for one person, so that his furm is put out of its place to his injury and the inconveniency of people having their seats thereabouts and withall craving the session would have his right restored. The session do appoint James Blaikie and John Mabane to meet with the persons concerned to consider the affair and report to the session. The sederunt closed with prayer.

" 4. James Purves and Agnes Knox in Colmslie, a.s.n. Robert ; w. Robert Moffatt, Thomas Laidlay.

" 7. This day these appointed Sabbath last mett, and after enquiry into the affair of Robert Bunzie and James Smail's seat, they order James Smail to reduce his seat to what will only contain one, and Robert Bunzie to take a foot of his furm.

1728.

Mar. 10. James Smail and Lizie Elies in Melrose, a.s.n. John ; w. John Mabane, Thomas Gill there.

Collected by John Frater, Andrew Lythgow, £2 : 9s.

There was also this day given in by the several elders for the purpose mentioned Feb. 21 last—

					Scotts.		
Collected by Andrew Lythgow from his quarter,					£8	17	0
From Melrose,	-	-	-	-	20	13	3
Darnick,	-	-	-	-	2	15	0
Blainslies,	-	-	-	-	5	0	0
Danieltown,	-	-	-	-	2	10	6
Housbyres,	-	-	-	-	3	19	0
Bridgend,	-	-	-	-	1	10	6
Gattonside,	-	-	-	-	9	16	0
Newtown,	-	-	-	-	4	8	0
Newsteid,	-	-	-	-	2	7	0
Clakmae and Sorrowlessfield,		-	-	-	1	15	6
Eildon,	-	-	-	-	2	12	0
Langhaugh,	-	-	-	-	1	10	0
By the elder of Buckholm,	-	-	-	5	13	6
Whitstead,	-	-	-	-	3	0	0
					£76	7	3

The total sum, extending to £76 : 7 : 3d. Scotts, lodged with the minister.

,, 11. William Brown and Jean Dickson in Langshaw, a.s.n. Thomas.

,, ,, Andrew Lythgow and Euphan Smith in Threepwood, a.d.n. Elizabeth ; w. John and William Thin.

,, 13. John Frater and Mary Gray in Langhaugh, a.d.n. Janet ; w. Wm. Brown, George Martine.

,, 17. John Thomson and Margaret Martine in Gattonside, a.s.n. Robert ; w. James and Andrew Boustones there.

Collected by John Wallace and Andrew Drummond, £2 : 5s.

This day the minister gave in a receipt for £7 : 4s. Scotts, given for the relief of those that suffered by fire at Robertown.

,, 24. Wm. Hart and Margaret Mein in Newsteid, a.s.n. William ; w. Andrew Mein, John Mercer.

Collected by Andrew Paterson and Andrew Marr, £2 : 2s.

Testimonials allowed John Scott from his infancy till Martinmas 1720.

,, 31. Collected by Andrew Drummond and William Hoy, £2 : 11s.

April 7. Collected by Nicol Milne and John Sibbald, £2 : 4s.

,, 9. James Brotherstone and Euphan Dickson in Mosshouses, a.d.n. Isobel ; w. James Burnet, John Thomson.

,, 14. William Mabane and Jannet Simpson in Newsteid, a.d.n. Isobel ; w. Wm. Bunzie, Wm. Sclater.

Collected by John Mercer, elder, and Andrew Mein, £2 : 3s.

,, 21. Collected by John Mabane and George Hoy, £2 : 4s.

,, 22. John Hog and Helen Pearson in Williamlaw, a.s.n. Andrew ; w. Michaell and William Pearson's there.

,, 26. This day booked in order for marriage Thomas Watson in the parish of Lauder and Isobel Cochran in this parish : w. John Cochran in Newtoun, cautioner.

,, 28. John Mercer and Mary Mein in Newsteid, a.s.n. John.

,, ,, —— Mein and —— Mein, Newsteid, a.d.n. Catharine ; w. ——

Collected by Robert Scott and John Wallace, £2 : 8s.

May 5. Collected by Andrew Paterson and John Mercer, £2 : 4s.

Testimonials granted Alexr. Hislope for one year, preceeding this present time.

1728.

May 10. This day booked in order for marriage Timothy West in the parish of Lauder and Elizabeth Darling in this parish ; John Darling in Blainslie, cautioner.

„ 12. John Moffat and Christian Ker in Gattonside, a.d.n. Mary ; w. Robert Scott, Patrick Thomsone there.

Collected by John Wallace and Andrew Lythgow, £2 : 17s.

Testimonials granted to Thomas Thin and his wife for four years.

To John Tait and his wife for sixteen years preceding the present time, and to John Lythgow from his infancy preceeding Whitsunday 1724.

„ 16. Nichol Milne and Mary Mein in Newtown ; a.s.n. Nichol.

„ 16. James Cesford and Janet Mar there, a.d.n. Helen ; w. Thomas Stenhouse and Nichol Milne there.

„ 19. Collected by John Sibbald and Andrew Drummond, £2 : 7s.

Received testimonials from Wm. Kincard and allowed him one for the last half year.

„ 24. This day booked in order for marriage John Darling and Margaret Bunzie, both in this parish ; Thomas Darling, cautioner.

„ 26. After prayer sederunt, the Minister, Drygrainge, Wm. Milne, Robert Scott, &c., elders.

Collected by Wm. Thin, John Frater, £3 : 2s.

The session being certainly informed that Archibald Cleuch, tennent in Appletreeleaves has certainly no regard for the Lord's day, but goes unnecessary journies to the great profanation of the Sabbath and offense of God. Therefore they order their officer to cite him to the session this day eight days.

Testimonials granted Helen Wallace from her infancy till Martinmas 1726. The sederunt closed with prayer.

„ 30. This day booked in order for marriage Alexr. Purves in the parish of Cranshaws and Mary Little in this ; Jacob Darling, cautioner.

Item, Robert Halliwall and Margaret Nisbet, both in this parish ; Thomas Halliwall in Gattonside, cautioner.

„ 31. After prayer sederunt, *pro renata*, the Minister, Drygrainge, John Mabane, James Blaikie, &c., elders, Wm. Dickson also.

Case against Janet Walker in Darnick and John Sproat there.

This day the minister intimated a meeting of the heretors against Thursday come eight days the 13th instant.

After prayer sederunt, the Minister, Drygrainge, John Mercer, Wm. Dickson, John Sibbald, &c., elders.

Collected by Wm. Milne and John Mabane, £3 : 3s.

Archibald Cleuch being summoned was called, and compeared and charged with profaning the Lord's day, which he could not altogether deny, but endeavoured to extenuate his fault. He was removed, and the session resolved, in regard it was the first time he had been charged with such a crime, that he should be rebuked immediately. He was called in and accordingly he was gravely rebuked. He's ordered to have testimonials to the session which he has undertaken to produce.

John Sprots being summoned was called and compeared not.

Janet Walker was also called and compeared. Her confession was read, to which she adhered.

The officer is ordered to cite the said John *pro* 2do to the said diet.

The clerk is appointed to write to the non residing heretors anent the meeting the 13th instant. The sederunt closed with prayer.

June 9. This day the minister read the King's proclamation for the encouragement of piety and virtue, and for the preventing and punishing of vice, profaneness and immorality.

1728.

After prayer sederunt, the Minister, Drygrainge, Andrew Marr, Wm. Hoy, Andrew Lythgow, &c., elders.

Collected by Robert Scott and Andrew Mein, £1 : 16s.

John Sprots being cited *pro* 2do, was called but compeared not. Janet Walker being summoned was called and compeared. She was seriously exhorted to repentance. She declared she knew nothing where the said John was. She is dismissed till further orders. The officer is ordered to summon the said John *pro* 3tio.

The minister with the session have unanimously condescended that the sacrament of the supper shall be celebrate in this place the second Sabbath next moneth, being the 14th thereof. The sederunt closed with prayer.

June 16. After prayer sederunt, the Minister, Drygrainge, John Sibbald, Wm. Dickson, Robert Scott, &c., elders.

Collected by James Laidlay and Wm. Dickson, £2 : 12s.

John Sprots being summoned *pro* 3tio was called but compeared not. The affair is delayed till the Sabbath immediately preceding the presbytery in regard the said John is gone out of this place. The sederunt closed with prayer.

„ 23. Wm. Haliday and Margaret Atchison in Melrose, a.d.n. Catharine : w. Robert Johnstone, George Martine there.

Collected by Andrew Lythgow and John Mercer, younger, £2 : 19s.

„ 30. This day the minister intimated to the congregation his purpose of celebrating the sacrament of the supper this day fourteen days, and gave directions suitable to that purpose. Then baptised.

„ 3. Walter and Margaret Gray in Melrose, a.d.n. Margaret : w. James Smail, James Gray.

After prayer sederunt, the Minister, Drygrainge, Nichol Milne, William Hoy and John Sibbald, &c., elders.

Collected by Andrew Drummond and John Wallace, £3 : 5s.

The session appoints Tuesday come eight days for privy censures.

In regard there is no report of John Sprots his return who had absented himself and whose affair was delayed till this day, the woman was called in and interrogate if she knew anything about him. Answered negative. She was duely exhorted to repentance. The session unanimously thought fit to referr the whole affair to the presbytry of Selkirk, and accordingly did and hereby do referr the same to be laid before them Tuesday first. Janet was summoned *apud acta* thereto, and the clerk is appointed to extract the said process for that end. The sederunt closed with prayer.

July 2. Andrew Darling and Helen Lythgow in Threepwood, a.s.n. Adam.

„ „ Adam Wallace and Janet Hislop in Blainslie, a.s.n. John.

„ „ John Stirling and Isobel Wilson in Blainslie, a.d.n. Marion.

„ „ Michael Bostone and Isobel Fairbairn, a.d.n Margaret ; w. Thomas Laidlay, John Wallace, for above four entries.

„ 7. This day the minister intimated Thursday next as the humiliation day before the sacrament, and gave suitable and serious exhortations to humility and contrition for sin.

After prayer sederunt the Minister, Drygrainge, James Laidlay, Wm. Milne, James Blaikie, &c., elders.

Collected by Andrew Marr and John Frater, £4 : 19s.

The minister acquainted the session that upon the hearing of John Sprots, his return, he had caused him to be summoned to this diet. He was accordingly called and compeared to the session Tuesday next, and the officer is ordered to cite the woman thereto.

Tuesday next is appointed for privy tryals.

1728.

July 9. After prayer sederunt, the Minister, Drygrainge, James Blaikie, George and Wm. Hoys, Thomas and James Laidlays, Andrew Marr, John Mercer younger, Andrew Drummond, Robert Scott, Wm. Dickson, Nicol Milne, John Frater, Andrew Mein, John Wallace and John Mabane, elders.

The elders present were severally removed by pairs, tryed and approven and encouraged to go on in the Lord's work.

„ 11. Being the fast day, collected by the persons appointed, £11 Scotts.

Collection, Fast day,	-	-	-	-	£11 0 0
Collection, Saturday,	-	-	-	-	10 2 0
Collection, Lord's day,	-	-	-	-	24 0 0
Collection, Munday,	-	-	-	-	11 13 0
Sum of collections,	-	-	-	£56 15 0
Debursed to poor of the parish, common poor, poor recommended, to precentor and beadle,	-	-	-	-	33 6 0
					£23 9 0

Which sum is appointed to be given into the Treasurer, wherewith he is to charge himself.

„ 20. This day booked in order for marriage Cornelius Mein and Elizabeth Darling, both in this parish : John Sclatter in Eildon, cautioner.

„ 21. After prayer sederunt, the Minister, Drygrainge, John Sibbald, George Hoy, Wm. Dickson, &c., elders.

Collected by James Laidlay and Andrew Lythgow, £4 : 2s. Scots.

Granted testimonials to Alexr. Sandilands from his infancy, to David M'Clearn from Whitsunday 1726 to 1727.

„ 28. Collected by Robert Scott and John Mabane, £2 : 8s. Scots.

Aug. 4. Alex. Familtone and Isobel Hoy in Eildon, ——— ; w. John Sibbald and Alexr. Mein there.

„ 9. This day booked in order for marriage Andrew Marr and Mary Fisher, both in this parish ; Alexr. Fisher, cautioner.

„ 11. Robert Williamson and Agnes Scott in Westhouses ———.

After prayer sederunt, the Minister, Drygrainge, James Laidlay, Robert Scott, Wm. Hoy, &c., elders.

Collected by Wm. Hoy and John Wallace, £3 : 7s. Scots.

Drygrainge, John Mabane, George Hoy, Robert Scott are appointed to meet Thursday next with the minister and clerk to revise the treasurer's accompts.

„ 12. James Brown and Jannet Wauch in Williamlaw.

„ „ James Fisher and Isobel Wright in Sorrowlessfield, a.d.n. Janet ; w. Alexr. and John Fishers.

„ 15. Mett conform to appointment, the Minister, John Mabane, George Hoy, Robert Scott, with their treasurer and clerk, and revised their said treasurer his accompts and approved the same, and left in his hand £141 : 14s. Scots.

„ 18. Robert Grierson and ——— Wilson in Darnick, a.s.n. Robert ; w. Wm. Dickson, John Mercer there.

Collected by John Frater and Wm. Hoy, £4 : 17s. Scots.

„ 25. Collected by Wm. Milne and John Sibbald, £3 : 3s. Scots.

„ 26. John Ingles and Mary Blaikie in Langshaw, a.d.n. Mary ; w. ———.

Sept 1. Wm. Sibbald and Isobel Bostone in Eildone, a.s.n. John ; w. John Sibbald, John Mabane.

Collected by John Mercer and Robert Moffat, £3 Scots.

„ 8. Collected by Robert Scott and Wm. Milne, £3 : 9s. Scots.

„ 15. George Stuart and Margaret Halliwall in Gattonside, a.s.n. Robert.

1728.

Sept. 15. James Laing and Agnes Richie in Melrose, a.d.n. Agnes ; w. Wm. Hopkirk, Walter Gray.

Collected by John Mabane and George Hoy, £2 : 17s. Scots.

„ 22. This day the minister intimated a meeting of the heritors against the 8th next moneth about the reparation of the kirk.

Collected by Andrew Mein and William Dickson, £3 Scots.

„ 28. This day booked John Cochran and Margaret Mein, both in this parish ; Henry Cochrane in Newtown, cautioner.

„ 29. Wm. Wilkie, deceased, and Alison Dawson in Melrose, a.s.n. William ; w. Robert Scott, George Lawrie.

Collected by Wm. Milne, James Laidlay and Andrew Drummond, £3 : 4s. Scots.

Oct. 6. Collected by Nichol Milne, Wm. Hoy and John Mercer, younger, £2 : 18s. Scots.

„ 13. The precentor read as directed by the heritors, and sederunt Tuesday last.

Collected by John Sibbald and William Hoy, £2 : 13s. Scots.

„ 19. This day booked, John Young and Isobel Mein, both in this parish ; James Young, cautioner.

„ 20. George Walker and Isobel Hogarth in Melrose, two sons named Robert and Adam.

„ „ John Turnbull and Bessie Familtone in Gattonside, a.d.n. Isobel.

„ „ Robert Fairbairn and Margaret Davidson in Danieltown, a.d.n. Elizabeth ; w. Robert Walker, James Smail.

After prayer sederunt, the Minister, Drygrainge, Wm. Milne, Robert Scott, John Mabane, &c., elders.

Collected by Andrew Marr and Andrew Drummond, £3 : 3s. Scots.

This day Thomas Stenhouse, portioner, of Newtown, gave in a petition craving that the session would appoint a day, and try if room could be got for him to build a seat in the kirk, conform to a grant he had from the heritors at their meeting the 8th of this instant. The session having heard and considered the petition, appoint a meeting Monday come fourteen days to see what can be done in that affair, and they ordain all wanting seats and that pay kirk stent to attend that day, as also all concerned in these pews be south the pulpet to be present, in regard it is alledged that room may be win among these pews for moe seats.

This they appoint the precentor to intimate from his desk this day eight days that none may pretend ignorance.

The session likeways appoint their Moderator, Drygrainge and Robert Scott to meet with Huntliewood and deal with him to break out a window and give light to the pews beneath his loft according to promise at building the said loft, and to report to the said meeting. Robert Bunzie's heirs are ordered to be cited to the said meeting to tell by what authority they have built seats in that said corner.

„ 24. This day booked John Noteman and Margaret Purves, both in this parish ; Thomas Darling, chirurgeon in Lanhaugh, cautioner.

Item, John Couper and Agnes Waugh, both in this parish ; James Purves in Colmslie, cautioner.

„ 25. This day booked John Simpson in the parish of Earlestown, and Helen Dickson in this parish ; James Brotherston in Mosshouses, cautioner.

„ 27. George Atcheson and Bessie Hopkirk in Melrose, a.d.n. Isobel ; w. Robert Bunzie, Wm. Hopkirk.

The precentor read as appointed above.

Collected by Robert Scott, John Mabane, and Wm. Milne, £3 : 7s.

Nov. 2. This day booked Wm. Richardson in this parish and Janet

1728.

Ormistown in the parish of Earlestown ; Andrew **Dawson** in Melrose, cautioner.

Nov. 3. Robert Forsan and Margaret Brokie in Newstead, a.s.n. Robert ; w. John and Andrew Forsans there.

Collected by George Hoy and Wm. Dickson, £3 Scots.

,, 4. After prayer sederunt the minister, Drygrainge, Wm. and Nichol Milne's, John Mercer's, elder and younger, James Blaikie, John Sibbald, Andrew Mein, Robert Scott, Andrew Drummond, and William Dickson, elders.

The session upon tryal find that twixt Wm. Hunter's seat and James Blaikie's there's sufficient room for Thomas Stenhouse to build a seat upon, Wm. Hunter being ordered to remove his furm and allowed to place a deal of four inches and an half breadth in place thereof, which is large as much as the old seat was conform to a declaration of the wright who altered the seat. The session also orders James Ellies and James Phaup their seats to be brought to the measure of two feet, and sixteen inches of entry to be left access to James Wilkison and George Laurie their seats.

Here Thomas Stenhouse is allowed to build his seat, and orders him to take an extract of this from the clerk for his warrant.

John Mein was called and interrogate why he had brought his seat so much to the eastward to prejudice the entry. The said John made it appear that Laird Marr had brought his so much east of the place, Laird Mar is appointed to reduce his seat to its former stent, and John promises to do the same.

Drygrainge and the minister report that Mr. Ellies promised to them with all expedition to break out a window and glass it.

None compearing for the Bunzies save John in Eildon, who has pretentions to one of these seats, the sessions and bailie reserve to themselves the disposal of the other room, and do confirm the said John his right to the seat he possesses. The people of Blainslie compeared and repeated the petition they made to the heretors to this session. Whereupon the session read to them the two last deliverances of the heretors to their petitions, and being very sensible to the loss the people of Blainslie sustain for want of a room in the church, recommended to the next meeting of the heretors to consider their case, and if they will accept of the place betwixt her Grace's loft and build a loft upon it themselves as a part of their share, they think it proper it be assigned to them.

The petitions of Wm. Cook, Robert Hunter and John Usher were read and delayed till the meeting.

,, 10. George Martine and Janet Haliburton in Melrose, a.s.n. Andrew.

,, ,, Michael Wallace and Isobel Blaikie in Melrose, a.s.n. James.

,, ,, Mr. Gavin Elliot, schoolmaster, and Margaret Angus, in Melrose, a.d.n. Jean ; w. Drygrainge and James Angus, writer in Edinburgh.

Collected by Wm. Hoy and Andrew Drummond, £2 : 11s. Scots.

,, 12. This day booked James Clappertone and Grissel Little, both in this parish ; Thomas Little, cautioner.

,, 17. Thomas Mercer and Margaret Atchison in Melrose, a.d.n. Janet ; w. James Laing, Nichol Mercer, there.

Collected by John Wallace, Nichol Milne and Robert Scott, £3 : 5s. Scots.

,, 23. This day booked Robert Haliday and Margaret Hownam, both in this parish ; Andrew Hownam, cautioner.

,, 24. John Bunzie and Jean Sibbald in Newtown, a.s.n. John ; w. Nichol Milne, James Milne, there.

Collected by Andrew Marr and John Sibbald, £2 : 13s. Scots.

1728.

Nov. 29. This day booked Wm. Steel and Elizabeth Walker, both in this parish ; William Mabane, cautioner.

Dec. 1. Collected by Wm. Milne and Andrew Mein, £2 : 17s. Scots.

„ 8. Collected by Robert Scott, Andrew Mar and John Mabane, £3 : 2s. Scots.

„ 11. John Fisher and Margaret Rutherford of Westerhousebyres, a.s.n. John ; w. ——.

„ 15. James Martin and Margaret Ellies in Gattonside, a.s.n. William.

„ „ John and Mary Meins, portioner in Newsteid, a.s.n. Thomas ; w. James Smail, Wm. Martine.

After prayer sederunt, the Minister, Wm. Dickson, Robert Scott, &c., elders.

Collected by George and William Hoys, £2 : 15s. Scots.

The session being informed that William Lukup in Melrose, about the 4th or 5th of this instant moneth, drank from house to house to great excess and profaned the blessed name of God by horrid oaths. They order him to be cited to the session this day eight days. And James Blaikie, treasurer, is ordered to pursue the said William for ten merks he borrowed of the session when his father was buried for which they have his bill. George Atchison in whose house he drank is ordered to be cited.

There was this day a petition presented by Robert Hunter, portioner of Melrose and Newsteid, and read mentioning that since the session and bailie, per session November 4th, had at their disposing room for a pew beneath Huntliewood's loft, and that that very room did formerly belong to the land he now possesses, craved that the session with her Grace's bailie would assign and destine the said room to his use according to justice. The session having heard the petition delayed the consideration thereof in regard Drygrainge, our bailie, is absent.

„ 16. James Beattie and —— in Drygrainge, two daughters named Anne and —— ; w. ——.

„ 22. After prayer sederunt, the Minister, Drygrainge, James Blaikie, John Mabane, &c., elders.

Collected by Nichol Milne, Andrew Drummond and John Mercer £2 : 14s.

William Lukup being summoned was called and did compear, and being charged with the sin of drunkenness and swearing did not disown the same. He professed his sorrow for these hainous sins, and declared he resolved through grace to walk circumspectly for the future. He was removed, and the session considering the sorrow he had just now professed, and that a private rebuke before the session might tend more to reclaim him, in regard he has been more than once already rebuked before the congregation, resolved he should be instantly rebuked before the session with certification. He was called in and gravely rebuked and certified that if ever given that way in time coming they would proceed to the highest censure against him.

George Atchison being called, compeared and declared his sorrow in giving entertainment to the said Wm. Lukup. He promised he should never give him or any like him drink in time coming.

The session is informed that Thomas Gardner was with Wm. Lukup when he drank from house to house, as also that Robert Ormistown entertained them after they were the worse of drink. The session orders them both to be cited to their diet Sabbath next.

As to Robert Hunter's petition, it appearing plain to the baillie and session that the said Robert is in possession of the Bunzie's land in Newsteid, to whom that room he is craving did belong.

1728.

They unanimously did and hereby do assign and destine the said room to the said Robert Hunter to be possessed by him and his, and that they build a pew there when they please, and they order him to take an extract of this their distination from the clerk of session.

George Martine craving of the bailie and session that he may be allowed to build a seat be north Boatshiel's seat, where he has been in possession of the room these many years. The bailie and session allowed his request provided none be enjured thereby.

Dec. 29. After prayer sederunt, the Minister, Drygrainge, Wm. Dicksone, Jane Blaikie, Robert Scott, Wm. Milne, &c., elders.

Collected by Andrew Mein and John Mercer, £2 : 4s. Scots.

Thomas Gardner being called, compeared and acknowledged he was in company with the said Wm. Lukup, and was heartily sorry for the same, and promised to associate no more with him.

Robert Ormistone also compeared, and promised to give no liquor to Wm. Lukup or any such.

1729.

Jan. 3. This day booked John Donaldson in the parish of Galashiels, and Isobel Frier in this ; Robert Ballantine, cautioner.

,, 5. John Fairbairn and Bessie Flint in Drygraingemilne, a.s.n. Robert ; w. Thomas Anderson, Robert Pringle.

Collected by John Mabane and Andrew Drummond, £2 : 19s. Scots.

,, 12. Robert Penman and Margaret Peacock in Melrose ; a.s.n. Robert.

,, ,, Robert Gibsone and Isobel Dinning in Gattonside, a.d.n. Elizabeth ; w. Andrew and John Dawson.

Collected by John Sibbald and Thomas Laidlay, £3 : 7s. Scots.

,, 22. Robert Rolmainhouse and —— Laidlay in Blainslie, a.d.n. Alison.

,, ,, John Coats and —— Purves in Langshaw, a.d.n. Anne ; w. John and James Wallaces.

,, 26. James Haliwall and Helen Nicol in Gattonside, a.d.n. Isobel ; w. James and Andrew Bowstones there.

Collected by Robert Scott and James Laidlay, £3 : 4s. Scots.

Feb. 2. After prayer sederunt, the Minister, Drygrainge, James Blaikie, Wm. Hoy, John Mabane, Robert Scott, &c., elders.

Collected by John Sibbald, Wm. Dicksone, £3 : 1s. Scots.

This day Mungo Park, having lately made a choise of a burying place in the kirkyard, gave into the poor £3 Scots.

The session appoints Drygrainge, George Hoy, John Mabane, Robert Scott, with their moderator and clerk, to meet with their treasurer, James Blaikie, Wednesday come eight days, att ten of the clock forenoon, and examine his accompts, and consider the session's bonds and bills.

(Case of discipline against Jean Ormistown in Melrose and Broadmeadows.)

,, 9. James Beatie and Marion Wright in Bridgend, a.s.n. John.

,, ,, Robert Mercer and Anaple Ovens in Newsteid, a.d.n. Isobel ; w. John and Andrew Meins.

After prayer sederunt, the Minister, Drygrainge, Wm. Hoy, John Mabane, James Blaikie, &c., elders.

Collected by John Mercer, Wm. and Nichol Milns, £2 : 18s. Scots.

Received for the use of the poor from Robert Hunter, who lately sett up a seat in the kirk, 1s. 6d.

,, 12. After prayer sederunt, the Minister, Drygrainge, James Blaikie, John Mabane, George Hoy, Robert Scott, John Sibbald, N. and Wm. Milne, John Mercers. elder and younger, Andrew Drummond and Wm. Dickson, &c., elders.

1729.

This day the session, considering that their clerk has no fee from them for that office, and that he has many minutes to record and much business of theirs to manage at present, as also considering that formerly before the heritors repaired the school and schoolhouse, the session clerk had always from them twenty merks for taking an house, whereupon they did for the encouragement of Mr Gavin Eliot, their present session clerk, and hereby do allow him out of their box twenty shillings sterling yearly, to be paid about the Candlemass time for the future, and appoint their treasurer instantly to pay him the foresaid sum for the year by past.

Allowed testimonials to Wm. Thine and Janet Wallace, his spouse, from their infancy, preceeding Whitsunday last.

Feb. 12. Mett to conform a former appointment, the Minister, Drygrainge, John Mabane, George Hoy, Robert Scott, with James Blaikie, their treasurer, and revised his accompts, and after comparing charge with discharge, together with £27 : 13s. Scots, of Mortcloath and marriage money given in by George Martine, find remaining in his hand, £178 : 2s. Scots, wherewith he is to charge himself at next accompting.

As also the bonds and bills were this day viewed and considered, and instructions given to the treasurer what to do in that affair, and to report.

„ 16. James Speeding and Janet Mercer in Bridgend, a.d.n. Mary ; w. Andrew Drummond, George Beatie, there.

After prayer sederunt, the Minister, Drygrainge, James Blaikie, George Hoy, Robert Scott, &c., elders.

Collected by John Mabane and William Hoy, £3 : 11s.

James Blaikie is allowed to take bills from these due the session, who are not able to renew their bonds on stampt paper.

„ 19. Alexr. Gray and Margaret Thin in Blainslies, a.d.n. Agnes ; w. John and Wm. Thin there.

„ 22. This day booked Robert Ballentine and Janet Bowstone, both in this parish ; Thomas Bowstone, cautioner.

„ 23. This day the minister read an act of the Synod against charms and scoring above the breath, which the minister followed with suitable admonitions.

„ „ Thomas Williamson and Mary Mein in Newsteid, a.d.n. Mary ; w. Wm. and Robert Williamsons.

After prayer sederunt, the Minister, Drygrainge, Wm. Hoy, Robert Scott, James Blaikie, &c., elders.

Collected by James Laidlay and Wm. Dicksone, £2 : 18s. Scots.

„ 25. After prayer sederunt, the Minister, Drygrainge, James Blaikie, George Hoy, John Mabane, John Mercer, Robert Scott, &c., elders. (Case of discipline continued against Jean Ormistoun and Broadmeadows.)

„ 28. This day booked in order for marriage Thomas Alison in the parish of Lauder and Ann Grieve in this ; William Wilsone, cautioner.

Mar. 2. Collected by John Sibbald and Andrew Drummond, £3 : 6s.

Witnesses cited for Jean Ormistown : Margaret Edgar, Alison Cook, Agnes Napier, Margaret Bowar and Alison Cunningham.

A petition from Elizabeth Sclater and Andrew Turnbull, her son, was read craving they would remit the interest of his bond for several reasons contained in the petition.

The session upon consideration do grant the said petition, provided he pay up the principal against Martinmas next.

„ 15. This day booked Wm. Hastie and Elizabeth Govenlock, both in this parish ; Thomas Anderson, cautioner.

„ 16. After prayer sederunt, the Minister, Drygrainge, Robert Scott, Wm. and George Hoy, John Mabane, &c., elders.

1729.

Collected by Robert Scott, George Hoy and John Mabane, £2 : 19s. Scots.

(Case of discipline continued, Jean Ormistone and Broadmeadows.)

Witnesses cited for Broadmeadows : Isobel Ballentine, Christian Riddell, Marion Bunzie, Elizabeth Martine, John Tait and his wife, and John Tait, his son, John Young.

Case of discipline against Elizabeth Gowanlock, servant to Thomas Anderson in Drygrainge, boathouse, and William Hastie, servant to the said Thomas.

Mar. 19. After prayer sederunt, the Minister, Drygrainge, John Mabane, George Hoy, Robert Scott and Andrew Mein, elders.

„   23. This day the minister intimated a meeting of the heritors Wednesday come fourteen days, the ninth of April next, to consider what is further to be done in the reparation of the kirk.

„   „ Thomas Williamson and Mary Mein in Newsteid, a.d.n. Mary ; w. Wm. and Robert Williamsons.

After prayer sederunt, the Minister, Drygrainge, Wm. Milne, Robert Scott, John Mabane, &c., elders.

Collected by Nichol Milne, Andrew Marr and Andrew Mein, £3 : 2s.

(Cases of discipline continued.)

„   29. This day booked Thomas Mein and Margaret Jerdain, both in this parish ; Alexr. Mein in Eildon, cautioner.

„   30. John Davidson and —— in Newsteid, a.s.n. John.

„   „ Thomas Bunzie and —— in Eildon, a.s.n. John ; w. Andrew Mein, James Bunzie both two above entries).

After prayer sederunt, the Minister, Drygrainge, John Sibbald, James Laidley, Robert Scott, &c., elders.

Collected by John Mercer, Wm. Dickson, £2 : 18s. Scots.

(Cases of discipline continued.)

April 6. The minister read a recommendation of the general assembly for a contribution to the settling a fund, building a kirk and manse att Enzie in the highlands of Scotland, where popery prevails through the want of such necessary accomodations, which collection is appointed to be gathered this day eight days in common form.

After prayer sederunt, the Minister, Drygrainge, Andrew Lythgow, Andrew Marr, Wm. Hoy, &c., elders.

Collected by John Wallace and John Sibbald, £3 : 1s.

(Jean Ormistown's case of discipline continued. Further witnesses cited : Elizabeth Gardner, her late fellow servant in Broadmeadow's family, Anna Lyall, Elizabeth Moodie, Janet Murray and Isobell Gill.) . . . In regard the said Elizabeth Gardner is living att Bunkle beyond Duns, the session resolve to dispatch one tomorrow or Tuesday to bring her here, that the affair may be inquired into with all expedition, and it is recommended to the minister to write Mr. William Hart, minister at Bunkle, to cause cite the said Elizabeth Gardner to this session Thursday next, and to send an execution of summons along with the said Elizabeth.

„   10. After prayer sederunt, the minister, Drygrainge, John Mabane, Robert Scott, elders.

(Jean Ormistown and Broadmeadow's case continued.)

„   13. After prayer sederunt, the Minister, Drygrainge, Wm. Hoy, Robert Scott, Laird Mar, &c., elders.

Collected by Robert Moffatt and Andrew Lythgow, £24 Scots.

(Case of discipline continued, examination of witnesses).

The session appoint their clerk to extract what was done this day eight days, Thursday last, and this day, that the brethren of the synod's advice may be got on that head.

1729.

April 18. Nichol Milne, laird, and Isobel Turnbull in Newtown, a.s.n. Nichol.

„ „ John Laidlay and Agnes Mein in Newtown, a.s.n. Alexr. ; w. Thomas Stenhouse, Nichol Milne (for above two entries).

„ 20. Thomas Sclater and Euphan Robson in Newsteid, a.s.n. Thomas ; w. [——].

This day the minister intimated a fast to be observed Thursday next by appointment of the synod.

Collected by Andrew Mein and Marr, and Robert Scott, £2 : 16s. Scots.

„ 24. John Pearson and Margaret Crosbee in Drygrainge, a.d.n. Marion : w. John Crossbee, Thomas Anderson.

Collected by James Laidlay and John Wallace, £8 : 9s. Scots.

„ 27. After prayer sederunt, the Minister, Drygrainge, John Mabane, Wm. Hoy, Robert Scott, &c., elders.

Collected by John Mercer and Wm. Dickson, £3 : 2s. Scots.

The minister acquainted the session that Wm. Hastie had been with him about the baptism of his child, but in regard he had not made satisfaction, he delayed the same till he heard the session's mind about it. The session is of the mind that the said William provide a sponsor, and then he may have baptism for his child.

Allowed testimonials to James Lauder and his wife and two servants.

May 4. Collected by Wm. Hoy and Andrew Drummond, £2 : 18s. Scots.

„ 5. Wm. Brown and Jean Dickson in Overlangshaw, a.s.n. John.

„ „ John Darling and Margaret Bunzie in Blainslies, a.d.n. Marion ; w. Thomas and Andrew Darlings.

„ 10. This day booked Robert Speeding in the parish of Bowdain, and Christian M'Fadden in this parish ; Doctor Martine in Melrose, cautioner.

„ 11. Collected by Andrew Mar and Robert Scott, £3 : 15s. Scots.

„ 16. This day booked Wm. Moffat in this and Elizabeth Moffatt in the parish of Stow ; John Tait in Melrose, cautioner.

„ 18. Collected by Nichol Milne and Andrew Marr, £3 : 8s. Scots.

Allowed testimonials to Wm. Teugh and his wife for thirty years by past.

„ 23. This day booked John Cochran and Helen Bartleman, both in this parish ; John Milne in Newtown, cautioner.

„ 25. Collected by Wm. Milne and John Mabane, £3 : 4s. Scots.

June 1. Collected by Andrew Lythgow and John Wallace, £3 : 11s. Scots.

„ „ David Jamison and Margaret Ker in Bent milne, a.s.n. William ; w. George and Robert Martines in Melrose.

Wm. Hastie and Elizabeth Gowanlock compeared (before the congregation) for the first time.

„ 8. Robert Williamson and Agnes Scot in Westhouses, a.s.n. Robert ; w. ——.

Wm. Hastie and his spouse compeared for the 2d time.

After prayer sederunt, the Minister, Drygrainge, James Blaikie, John Mabane, John Hoy, &c., elders.

Collected by James Laidlay and Wm. Hoy, £4 : 9s. Scots.

It was this day represented to the session that Robert Penman, elder in Melrose, last week for some days together had a very scandalous behaviour through drunkenness. The session appoint him to be cited to the session this day fourteen days.

Allowed testimonials to John Chisholm and Margaret Blaikie for three years preceeding Whitsunday last.

„ 15. Wm. Hastie and his spouse compeared, rebuked and were dismissed.

„ „ James Vair and Margaret Kerr in Newtown, a.s.n. James ; w. Nicol and Nicol Milne's in Newtown.

1729.

Collected by Wm. Milne and Andrew Drummond, £2 : 11s. Scots.

June 22. After prayer sederunt, the minister, Drygrainge, James Blaikie, Nicol Milne, Wm. Hoy, &c. elders.

Collected by Andrew Lythgow and Robert Moffat, £3 : 2s. Scots.

Robert Penman being cited was called and compeared. He was charged with drunkenness and exhorted to confess the same, which he stiffly disowned. The session resolve to lead a probation against him, and for that end appoint John Moody, Wm. Andrew and Alexr. Cooks, Robert and George Walkers, James Smail and Andrew Martine, all in Melrose, to the session against this day fourteen days.

„ 29. Wm. Hastie and Elizabeth Gowanlock in Drygrainge, a.s.n. Alexr.

„ „ James Waugh and Mary Duncan in Melrose, a.d.n. Anne ; w. John Mabane, James Blaikie.

Collected by James Laidlay and Wm. Hoy, £2 : 1s. Scots.

July 5. This day booked John Clappertone in the parish of Stow and Janet Mercer in this ; Wm. Hopkirk in Melrose, cautioner.

„ 6. John Hoy and Alison Cunningham in Melrose, a.d.n. Barbara ; w. George Hoy, John Bowie, there.

After prayer sederunt, the Minister, Drygrainge, Robert Scott, James Laidlay, Andrew Lythgow, &c., elders.

Collected by John Mabane and John Mercer, £3 : 12s. Scots.

Robert Penman being cited was called and compeared, and at last owned he was the worse of drink, and was sorry that he had given offence by his unseemly behaviour. He was gravely rebuked, exhorted and admonished, and having promised to guard against such behaviour in time coming, he was dismissed.

„ 13. This day the minister intimated an exercise this evening about eight of the clock.

After prayer sederunt, the Minister, Drygrainge, John Mercer John Mabane, George Hoy, &c., elders.

Collected by Andrew Lythgow and Wm. Milne, £3 : 5s. Scots.

The minister and elders condescended to give the sacrament of the supper in this place the 3rd Sabbath of August next, if not prevented by the harvest.

This night about five of the clock Mr. Hunter of Liliesleaf baptised to Mr. Adam Milne, minister, and Alison Hunter, a.s.n. William ; w. Drygrainge, Doctor Hunter.

„ 17. This day David Umpherstone in the parish of Haddingtone and Janet Nisbet in this were booked ; Robert Haliwall in Gattonside, cautioner.

„ 20. Collected by Nicol Milne and Wm. Hoy, £1 : 19s. Scots.

„ 24. James Blaikie, kirk treasurer, by reason of his weakness and indisposition having applied to the minister and elders for to meet and take his accompts, papers and everything else relating to his office off his hand, accordingly there mett this 20th and 4th day, the Minister, Drygrainge, George Hoy, John Mabane and Robert Scott, elders, who having examined and approven the said treasurer's accompts, they received the money in his hand extending to £363 : 13s. Scotts, whereof they gave to Mark Blaikie, son to the said James, £12 : 12s. Scotts for making up some of their register, as also the said committee received from the said treasurer all papers and everything else relating to his office as kirk treasurer, and discharged him of the said sum instantly received and of all his intromissions whatsomever, as the discharge in itself more fully bears, which money and papers were lodged with Mr. Elliot, session clerk, till the session shall be fully advised who shall be chosen for the office of treasurer.

1729.

July 25. This day booked John Pringle in this and Margaret Scott in the parish of Stow ; John Fisher in Easterlanglee, cautioner.

,, 27. Robert Halliwall and Margaret Nisbet in Gattonside, a.s.n. John.

,, 27. Adam Torburn and Susanna Rutherford in Melrose, a.d.n. Agnes : w. Andrew and Robert Martines in Melrose.

After prayer sederunt, the Minister, Drygrainge, John Mabane, George Hoy, &c., elders.

Collected by James Laidlay and Andrew Drummond, £3 : 9s. Scots.

The minister and elders resolve that intimation of the sacrament of the supper shall be made this day eight days.

It was represented that William Robson in Gattonside did come home from a journey this day eight days about the middle of the day very drunk. The session order him to be cited to the session this day eight days.

Aug. 2. Case of discipline against Jean Gilroy in Westhouses and Adam Harvie in the boathouse.

,, 3. This day the minister intimated the celebration of the Lord's supper in this place this day fourteen days.

After prayer sederunt, the Minister, Drygrainge, Robert Scott, Wm. Hoy, Nicol Milne, &c., elders.

Collected by Andrew Lythgow, John Sibbald and Marr, £3 : 16s. Scots.

William Robson being called, compeared and charged with drunkenness and breach of the Sabbath, disowned that he was drunk, but that he travelled on the Sabbath day and carried home wool along with him, and that though he came to the parish about seven of the morning, yet he came not to his own house till two of the afternoon. Nor was he waiting on ordinances. He professed his sorrow for the offence he had given and promised never to be guilty of the like again. He was removed, and the session was of the mind that he should be instantly rebuked with certification. He was called in and accordingly gravely rebuked and dismissed with certification.

,, 4. [Jean Gilroy and Adam Harvie's case of discipline continued.]

,, 7. James Martine and Jannet Dicksone in Blainslie, a.d.n. Jannet : w. John Wallace, Wm. Thine there.

,, 10. The minister intimated Thursday next as the humiliation day before the sacrament of the supper.

,, ,, James Phaup and Alison Cook in Melrose, a.s.n. James ; w. Alexr. and Wm. Cooks.

After prayer sederunt, the Minister, Drygrainge, John Mabane, Wm. Hoy, Nicol Milne, &c., elders.

Collected by Andrew Marr, George Hoy, John Mabane, £4 : 19s. Scots.

Case of discipline continued. Jean Gilroy ("*now in eternity*") and Adam Harvie.

The session appoint their meeting for privy tryals Tuesday next.

,, 12. After prayer sederunt, the Minister, Drygrainge, James Laidlay, Robert Scott, John Sibbald, Andrew Marr, Andrew Drummond, John Mabane, George Hoy, Andrew Lythgow, John Wallace, Wm. Dickson, Wm. Hoy, Nicol Myle, John Mercer, Andrew Mein, elders.

The elders present were severally removed by pairs, tryed and approven to go on in the Lord's work.

,, 14. On the humiliation day were baptised to Andrew Mein and Jannet Mein in Newsteid, a.s.n. George.

,, ,, Robert Ormistown and Helen Hopkirk in Melrose, a.d.n. Elizabeth.

,, ,, Henry Forrest and Isobel Robertson in Westhouses, a.d.n. Mar on w. Robert Williamson, Thomas Mathison.

L

1729.

Collected by elders as specially appointed, £13 : 15s. Scots.
Sum of collections time of the sacrament—

Collection, Fast Day,	-	-	-	£13	15	0
Collection, Saturday,	-	-	-	15	10	0
Collection, Lord's Day.	-	-	-	33	9	0
Collection, Munday,	-	-	-	15	0	0
Sum of collections,	-	-	-	£77	14	0
Debursed to poor of the parish, common poor, and poor recommended, &c.	-			52	14	0
				£25	0	0

Which sum is appointed to be given in to the treasurer wherewith he is to charge himself.

Aug. 18. Robert Lindsay and Jean Bruntown in Williamlaw, a.d.n. Isobel : w. James Brown, Richard Thomson there.

„ 24. After prayer sederunt, the minister, Drygrainge, John Wallace, Robert Scott, John Mabane, &c., elders.
Collected by Andrew Marr, John Mabane, £5 : 3s. Scots.
(Case of discipline, Adam Harvie, continued).

„ 25. George Forsyth and Jannet Blaikie in Whitlaw, a.s.n. George : w. James Laidlaw, Thomas Darling.

„ 31. Collected by John Mercer, Wm. Milne and Andrew Mein, £3 : 4s. Scots.

Sept. 7. The minister intimated the baptism of some children to-morrow at Blainslie.
Collected by Robert Scott, Wm. Dickson, Andrew Drummond, £3 : 12s. Scots.

„ 8. David Brown and Marion Deepman, a.s.n. Alexr.

„ „ William Pringle and Margaret Tait, a.d.n. Agnes.

„ „ William Lauder and Helen Rolmainhouse, a.d.n. Alison : w. John and Wm. Thines.

„ 14. This day the minister read the King's brieve with the General Assembly's recommendation for a collection which is to be collected at the kirk door against this day eight days.
Collected by Andrew Mein, Nicol Milne, £3 : 7s. Scots.

„ 21. Collected as intimated above by Andrew Marr, Wm. Milne and John Sibbald, £17 Scots.

„ 28. The minister intimated the baptism of a child at Blainslies, Wednesday next.

„ „ John Kemp and —— Grant in Gattonside, a.d.n. Grisal : w. Thomas Thomson, Robert Myles.

„ 30. John Sibbald and Agnes Stenhouse in Eildon, —— ; w. Wm. and Andrew Sibbalds.

Oct. 1. Wm. Thine and Marion Fairbairn in Blainslies, a.d.n. Agnes ; w. John Thin, Alexr. Gray.

„ 5. Wm. Hog and Agnes Hardie in Darnick, a.s.n. George.

„ „ John Cochran and Margaret Mein in Eildon, a.d.n. Janet.

„ „ John Cribbas and —— in Sorrowlessfield, a.d.n. Margaret ; w. George Martine, John Tait in Melrose.
The minister intimated the baptism of some children at Langhaugh, Tuesday.
Collected by Andrew Drummond and John Mabane, £3 : 10s.

„ 7. Thomas Darling and Helen Thomson in Langhaugh, a.s.n. Andrew.

„ „ Thomas Gordon and Agnes Blaikie, a.s.n. John : w. Mr. Darling, John Noteman.

„ 12. Wm. Steel and Elizabeth Walker in Melrose, a.s.n. Thomas ; w. Robert and George Walkers.

1729.

Collected by George and Wm. Hoy, £3 : 5s. Scots.

Oct. 19. James Hart and Agnes Thomson in Gattonside, a.s.n. James.

„ „ John Bunzie and Marion Wallace in Eildon, a.d.n. Elizabeth ; w. John and William Sibbalds.

Collected by Robert Scott and John Wallace, £2 : 15s. Scots.

„ 24. Booked James Burnet in the parish of Earlestown and Margaret Seirven in this ; George Seirven, cautioner.

„ 26. Collected by Wm. Milne and John Wallace, £3 : 3s. Scots.

Nov. 2. James Cessford and Janet Mather in Newtown, a.s.n. James : w. Nicol Milne, Thomas Stenhouse.

Collected by Andrew Drummond and Andrew Marr, £3 : 1s. Scots.

„ 9. This day the minister gave suitable admonitions before the fair.

Intimated the baptism of a child at Langlee, Tuesday next.

After prayer sederunt, the Minister, Drygrainge, John Mabane, George Hay, &c., elders.

Collected by Andrew Mein and John Mercer, £2 : 11s.

(Case of discipline against Violet Pringle in Newsteid and John Hatton, servant to Cornet Gottard in Captain Jerdain's troop.)

The minister gave in two lowland bursar's discharges, viz. : from Martinmas 1727 to Martinmas 1729, for £8 Scots, subscribed by James Henderson.

The appoint Drygrainge, George Hoy, John Mabane and Robert Scott to met with the minister and clerk the first Munday of Decr. to inspect George Martine's accompts, who was appointed to receive the poor's money.

Allowed testimonials to Wm. Hoy from his infancy.

„ 11. John Couper and Agnes Waugh in Mosshouses, a.d.n. Isobel ; w. Andrew Bryden, Robert Hog.

„ 16. This day the minister intimated the baptism of a child at Clackmae, Wednesday next.

Collected by John Mabane and George Hoy, £2 : 15s. Scots.

„ 19. Michael Boustone and Agnes Fairbairn in Blainslies, a.s.n. James ; w. Alexr. Fisher, George Martine.

„ 22. This day booked George Pringle and Jean Hunter, both in this parish ; James Ainslie in Langhaw, cautioner.

„ 23. The minister intimated a thanksgiving to be observed Wednesday next appointed by the presbytry for the causes therein contained.

Collected by Robert Scott, £2 : 2s. Scots.

„ 26. Collected by Nicol Milne, John Mercer, Andrew Drummond, £4 : 2s. Scots.

„ 30. Walter Scott and Janet Mein in Danieltown, a.s.n. William : w. Robert Fairbairn, George Lawrie.

Collected by William Milne, £2 : 13s. Scots.

Dec. 1. This day mett the minister, Drygrainge, John Mabane, George Hoy and Robert Scott, they examined George Martine's accompts, who has been employed since March 2d last by past, because of James Blaikie, late treasurer, his infirmity in taking in the collections and debursing the same to the several poor in the parish, and having compared charge and discharge, they find of ballance with Mortcloath money and the remains of the sacrament money, £99 : 11s. Scots, whereof there is £10 : 8s., due by Andrew M'Fadden, and six shillings due by himself, which with £21 : 1s. Scots, he is to charge himself with at next clearing, £63 : 18s., as the rest of the ballance with twenty shillings sterling of John Moodie's bill is added to the £351 : 1s. Scots in the box makes £426 : 19s. Scots. The meeting continue George Martine till they be ripe for choosing a treasurer. The minister reports that he has received the remains of Wm. Hoy's bond.

„ 7. Collected by John Sibbald and Andrew Marr, £2 : 15s. Scots.

1729.

Dec. 11. John Thomson and Margaret Martine in Gattonside, a.d.n. Isobel ; w. Andrew Mar, James Thomson.

,, 13. This day booked John Hownam and Isobel Usher, both in this parish : James Usher. cautioner.

,, 14. Walter Gray and Margaret Gray in Melrose, a.s.n. John ; w. James Smail, James Laing, there.

Collected by Andrew Drummond, John Mercer and William Hoy, £2 : 13s. Scots.

,, 21. John Dalgleish and Margaret Darling in Darnick, a.d.n. Margaret ; w. John and George Mercers there.

Collected by John Mabane, Robert Scott, £2 : 15s. Scots.

,, 28. Collected by Andrew Mein and George Hoy, £2 : 9s.

1730.

Jan. 2. Booked John Embers in Galashiels parish and Agnes Blaikie in this ; James Blaikie in Appletreeleaves, cautioner.

,, 4. Collected by James Laidlay and John Wallace, £3 : 4s. Scots.

,, 7. Robert Henry and Catharine Blaikie in Appletreeleaves, a.s.n. Robert.

,, 7. John Wylie and Janet Waugh in Langhaugh, a.s.n. Adam ; w. Thomas Darling, John Noteman.

,, 10. Booked Wm. Martin and Isobel Drummond, both in this parish ; Wm. Martine in Gattonside, cautioner.

,, 11. Thomas Marr and Jean Craig in Melrose, a.d.n. Alison ; w. Andrew Marr, James Smail.

After prayer sederunt, the Minister, Drygrainge, Robert Scott, George Hoy, &c., elders.

Collected by Andrew Lythgow and Wm. Dickson, £2 : 16s. Scots.

The minister read a letter from the session of Maxtown, desiring that Mary Mein in this our parish may be cited before their session for excessive drinking in their parish.

The session ordered accordingly.

Adam Nisbet and —— Scott, journey men to John Cochran in Newtown, are ordered to bring in testimonials or to remove from the parish.

,, 14. Thomas Anderson and Margaret Dickson in Drygrainge, boathouse, a.d.n. Helen ; w. James Beatie, Thomas Atcheson, there.

,, 18. After prayer sederunt, the Minister, Drygrainge, George Hoy, Wm. Hoy, John Mercer, &c., elders.

Collected by Wm. Milne and Andrew Drummond, £2 : 14s. Scots.

It is reported that these by the former sederunt were appointed to bring in testimonials, have promised to do so.

This day the session proceeding to the choise of a treasurer, George Hoy was chosen by the plurality of voices, and the session appoints the first Munday of March for giving up money and papers into his hand.

,, 25. After prayer sederunt, the Minister, Drygrainge, John Mabane, Robert Scott, &c., elders.

Collected by Andrew Marr, Andrew Mein, £2 : 18s. Scots.

(Case of discipline against Charles Wilkieson and Isobel Haliburtone, servitrix to Mungo Park in the Westerboathouse.)

Feb. 1. This day the minister dehorted the people from giving in spurious coin which abounds amongst us.

After prayer sederunt, the Minister, Drygrainge, John Mabane, John Wallace, &c., elders.

Collected by Wm. Hoy and John Mercer, £2 : 12s.

(Case of discipline against Charles Wilkieson and Isobel Haliburtone continued.)

The sederunt closed with prayer.

1730.

Feb. 8. This day Isobel Haliburtone appeared and was admonished.

„ „ James Bunzie and Jean Wilson in Newsteid, a.d.n. Jean ; w. Thomas Williamson, Robert Mein, there.

>Collected by Andrew Marr and Andrew Drummond, £2 : 13s. Scots.

>This day the minister gave in for this parish's collection towards the building a place for publick worship in Enzie a discharge for 40s. sterling, signed att Edinburgh, January 17th, 1730. As also a receipt signed by Henry Erskine at Selkirk for £1 : 18 : 4 sterling, as this parish's collection for the harbour of St. Andrews.

„ 15. Collected by Andrew Drummond and John Mercer, £2 : 2s. Scots.

>Isobel Haliburtone appeared for the 2d time.

„ 22. Thomas and Alison Gills in Danieltown, a.d.n. Margaret.

„ „ James Smail and Elizabeth Ellies in Melrose, a.d.n. Janet ; w. John Mabane, Thomas Gill.

>Isobel Haliburtone rebuked and dismissed.

>Collected by Robert Scott and Andrew Mein, £2 : 15s.

Mar. 1. After prayer sederunt, the Minister, Drygrainge, George Hoy, John Mabane, Wm. Hoy, &c., elders.

>Collected by John Mabane and John Sibbald, £3 : 5s.

>The session adjourns their meeting that was appointed to meet to-morrow, till to-morrow eight days for delivering up to George Hoy, treasurer, the poor's money and papers.

„ 5. George Rutherford and Jean Chisholm in Hagburn, a.s.n. Thomas ; w. Wm. Pearson, Robert Mercer there.

„ 8. Collected by John Mabane, £1 : 18s. Scots.

„ 9. Mett this day, the Minister, Drygrainge, John Mabane, Robert Scott and George Hoy. They revised and examined George Martine's accompts, charge and discharge compared, the Committee find the balance, £52 : 12s. Scots ; £10 : 18s. due by Andrew M'Faden, and £3 : 12s. Scotts due by the said George Martine as per sederunt December 1st last by past being included in the charge, all which he has paid down and is hereby discharged of the same. As also there was given in this day £26 : 14s., due by Andrew Turnbull per bond, which with the foresaid sum of £52 : 12s. and £426 : 17s. Scots, makes £506 : 3s. Scots, with the session box and papers were all delivered to George Hoy, treasurer, wherewith he is to charge himself and be accountable to the session, as he shall be charged.

>The minister is to give in the remains of Wm. Hoy's bond.

„ 15. After prayer sederunt, the Minister, Drygrainge, John Mabane, John Mercer, &c., elders.

>Collected by Wm. Milne and James Laidlay, £3 : 6s. Scots.

>The minister reported the acts of the synod came only to hand last presbytry day, whereby George Wright is ordered to be excommunicated any time the session of Melrose shall judge convenient. The session does appoint this day fourteen days, and it is recommended to the minister to speak to the said George before that time.

„ 22. Collected by Andrew Mein and Andrew Marr, £2 : 13s. Scots.

„ 24. Nicol Milne and Isobel Turnbull in Newtown, a.d.n. Alison ; w. Thomas Stenhouse, Nicol Milne there.

„ 29. This day the minister read the sentence of the lesser excommunication pronounced by the synod against George Wright with suitable exhortations and admonitions to the people.

>Collected by Andrew Lythgow and Robert Scott, £4 Scots.

April 5. Collected by Andrew Marr and Nicol Milne, £2 : 13s. Scots.

„ 12. Collected by John Sibbald and Wm. Dickson, £2 : 12s. Scots.

„ 19. Robert Paterson of Drygrainge and Anne Eliot his lady, a.s.n. Thomas

1730.

April 19. James Mein and Margaret Bunzie in Newsteid, a.s.n. **Andrew.**

,,   ,,   Thomas Mein and Margaret Jerdain in Eildon, a.d.n. Janet.

,,   ,,   Wm. Mein and Isobel Lumsdain in Gattonside, a.d.n. Christian ; w. The lairds of Park and Hyndhope, and Mr. Elliot, schoolmaster.
Collected by Andrew Drummond and John Mercer, £3 : 7s. Scots.

,,   26. This day the minister intimated a meeting of the heretors, May 7th next, about repairing the kirk.
Collected by Andrew Lythgow and James Laidlay, £3 : 7s. Scots.

May   3. James Laing and Agnes Richie in Melrose, a.s.n. James ; w. William Hopkirk, Walter Gray there.
Collected by John Wallace and William Milne, £3 : 8s. Scots.

,,   10. Robert Hunter and Jean Broke in Melrose, a.d.n. Jannet ; w. Doctor Martine, Wm. Hunter.
Collected by Robert Scott, Wm. Hoy and John Sibbald, £6 : 1s. Scots.

,,   14. John Murray and Isobel Heiton in Broadwoodsheil, a.s.n. John ; w. John and Wm. Thine.

,,   17. Collected by Andrew Drummond and John Mercer, £2 : 6s. Scots.

,,   19. James Brown and Janet Waugh in Williamlaw, a.d.n. Mary ; w. James Laidlay, Wm. Atchison.

,,   24. Walter Rae and Christian Richie in Newtown, a.d.n. Isobel ; w. Thomas Stenhouse, Nicol Milne.
Collected by Andrew Mein and Andrew Lythgow, £3 : 1s.

,,   27. Booked James Thomson in the parish of Stow, and Isobel Alley in this parish ; George Alley in Westerlanglee, cautioner.

,,   31. Collected by Wm. Milne and Robert Moffatt, £4 : 3s. Scots.

June   3. James Watherstone and Margaret Bailie of Newhouses, a.s.n. Alexr. ; w. Robert and Peter Moffatts.

,,   5. Booked Thomas Rutherford in this and Janet Eckford in the parish of Stow ; Richard Park in Allanshaws, cautioner.
Also Wm. Darling in this and Magdalene Allan in the parish of Westruther ; Thomas Darling, cautioner.
Andrew Haitly in the parish of Earlstone and Alison Dawson in this ; Andrew Dawson, cautioner.

,,   7. After prayer sederunt, the Minister, Drygrainge, John Mabane, Wm. Hoy, John Mercer, &c., elders.
Collected by Andrew Marr and Andrew Drummond, £3 : 15s. Scots.
This day the session unanimously agreed that the sacrament of the supper should be administered here, the third Sabbath of July next.
The session also resolve that four silver cups be purchased for the use of the sacrament, and that they be got ready against the forsaid third Sabbath of July next.
Allowed a certificate to Thomas Fairbairn from his infancy.

,,   12. Booked Nicol Milne in this parish and Janet Fiddes in the parish of Maxtown ; Thomas Milne, cautioner.

,,   14. After prayer sederunt, the Minister, Drygrainge, Wm. Hoy, Robert Scott, &c., elders.
Collected by Robert Scott and George Mabane, £2 : 9s. Scots.
Upon the report of Wm. Noble, servant to Mr. Ellies of Huntliewood in Melrose, his being clandestinely married to Margaret Pringle in Melrose, the minister ordered him to be cited to this day's session. He was called and compeared and interrogate if married to the said Margaret. Owned he was married to her in Huntliewood's house, his present master. He said he could not produce the lines because his wife, who is now at Edinburgh, had them a keeping. He was admonished and rebuked, and summoned *apud acta* to this day fourteen days' session.

1730.

The treasurer appointed to pursue for the poor's money of such as have married irregularly.

June 21. Collected by John Mabane and Andrew Marr, £2 : 4s.

,, 28. John and Mary Meins in Newsteid, a.d.n. Elizabeth ; w. Adam Ainslie, Andrew Mein there.

After prayer sederunt, the Minister, Drygrainge, Wm. Hoy, John Mercer, &c., elders.

Collected by John Wallace and Wm. Dickson, £3 : 11s. Scots.

This day the minister intimated the celebration of the sacrament of the supper this day three weeks, and gave suitable admonitions and exhortations to the people.

Wm. Noble and Mary Pringle being summoned were called, compeared and interrogate if married, answered they were, and produced their marriage lines, datted at Melrose the 16th day of April 1730, signed James Maccubine, minister.

Because the session do suspect forgery of witnesses they intend to examine into that affair, and they are dismissed till further orders.

July 5. Collected by John Sibbald and John Wallace, £2 : 18s. Scots.

,, 11. James Fisher and Isobel Wight of Sorrowlessfield, a.s.n. John ; w. Alexr. and John Fishers.

,, 12. The minister intimated Thursday as the humiliation before the sacrament.

,, ,, Alexr. M'Fadden and Agnes Napier in Melrose, a.s.n. Alexr. ; w. Andrew M'Fadden, Thomas Gardner.

After prayer sederunt, the Minister, Drygrainge, Andrew Mar, Wm. Dickson, John Sibbald, Wm. and George Hoys, Andrew Lythgow, John Mercer, Nicol and Wm. Milne, Robert Scot, Andrew Mein, Andrew Drummond, Robert Moffatt and John Wallace.

The elders present were severally removed by pairs, tryed, approven and encouraged to go on in the Lord's work. Then ordered the way of the collections and the keeping of the doors.

,, 16. George Mercer and Agnes Knox in Kaidsliedoors, a.d.n. Isobel : w. Alexr. and James Fishers.

,, 20. Alexr. and Helen Young in Gattonside, a.d.n. Margaret.

,, ,, Michael Wallace and Isobel Blaikie in Melrose, a.d.n. Isobel.

,, ,, John Bunzie and —— Wallace in Eildon, a.d.n. Jean : w. Laird Marr, William Hunter.

Collection, Fast day,	-	-	-	-	£13 13 0
Collection, Saturday,	-	-	-	-	14 6 0
Collection, Sabbath day,	-	-	-		35 14 0
Collection, Munday,	-	-	-	-	15 13 0
Sum of collections,		-	-	-	£79 16 0
Debursed to the poor of the parish, common poor and upon recommendations, precentor and beadle, &c.	-	-	-	-	44 14 0
					£35 2 0

Which sum is appointed to be given to the treasurer, wherewith he is to charge himself.

,, 22. This day the minister and Drygrainge took out of the box £30 sterling to send to Edinburgh for cups, &c., for which particular receipts are to come out in order to be recorded.

,, 26. Wm. Haliday and Margaret Atcheson in Newsteid, a.s.n. ——

,, ,, Andrew and Catharine Mercer in Bridgend, a.s.n. —— : w. John and Andrew Meins.

1730.

After prayer sederunt, the Minister, Drygrainge, Wm. Hoy, John Mabane, &c., elders.

Collected by Andrew Marr and John Mercer, £4 : 12s.

Drygrainge reports that the discharges for the cups and flaggons and velvet are in his hand, which he is to give in to be recorded, with three shillings sterling, given to the poor by the goldsmith, as also £2 : 4s. Scotts for the old peuther.

The session allows Agnes Sclatter £12 Scots upon producing James Leithen, her brother-in-law, cautioner.

Allowed the schoolmaster of Blainslies a crown for teaching poor scholars.

Aug.   2. After prayer sederunt, the Minister, Drygrainge, Robert Scott, Wm. Dickson, &c., elders.

Collected by Nicol and Wm. Milne, John Sibbald, £4 : 10s. Scots.

Charles Wilkison and Isabel Haliburton's case continued ; witnesses cited, Mr. Lythgow, Christian Millar.

The session condescended to lend John Lawrie thirty shillings sterling, on his bond to the treasurer.

  „   9. David Umpherstone and Janet Nisbet in Gattonside, a.s.n. George ; w. Laird Marr, Wm. Hoy there.

After prayer sederunt, the Minister, Drygrainge, John Mabane, George Hoy, &c., elders.

Collected by Andrew Mein and John Mercer, £2 : 18s. Scots. (Case of discipline continued.)

  „   16. John Noteman and Margaret Purves in Langhaugh, a.d.n. Anne ; w. Thomas Darling, George Martine.

  „   23. Collected by Wm. and Nicol Milne, £3 : 3s. Scots.

Wm. Noble and Margaret Pringle appointed to be cited to the session this day eight days.

  „   30. After prayer, the Minister, Drygrainge, Wm. Hoy, John Mabane, &c., elders.

Collected by Andrew Marr and Mein and John Mercer, £3 : 13s. Scots.

Wm. Noble and Margaret Pringle, being called, compeared.

They were dealt with to tell ingeniously if married, when and who were the witnesses, in regard their testimonials seem very suspicious. They alledged they were genuine, and moreover said Alexr. Ellies knew of it. They are summoned to this day eight days' session.

  „   31. Alexr. Gray and Margaret Thine in Blainslies, a.d.n. Agnes ; w. Thomas Darling, John Thine.

Sept. 6. Thomas Waddell and ——— Brown in Drygrainge Milne, a.s.n. George.

  „   „   Andrew Turnbull and Mary Lamb in Bridgend, a.d.n. Elizabeth ; w. Mark Blaikie, Robert Turnbull.

After prayer sederunt, the Minister, Drygrainge, Andrew Marr, Wm. Milne, John Wallace, &c., elders.

Collected by John Mabane and James Laidlay, £3 : 14s. Scots.

Wm. Noble and Margaret Pringle being called, compeared and interrogate who these men were who signed witnesses to their marriage lines, answered they knew them not, nor did they ever speak with them. He was asked whether or not they were married at the time my Lord Justice-Clerk was in Melrose. He said he could not say but it was so, which is nottourly known to have been the 9th day of May last, whereas their testimonials bear the date of the 16th of April preceding. She owned she went to Edinburgh to get their marriage lines altered, pretending there was some ommission in their first lines. They were ordered to attend as they should be called for. As they were going off he, the said Wm., in a rude, unmannerly way and in passion, said he would

1730.

rather go to Flanders than be harrassed with sessions at this rate, and that he knew no fault he was guilty of, and some very insolent things he uttered. He was called back and gravely rebuked and admonished by the minister, then dismissed. The session unanimously agreed to refer this affair for advice to the Reverend presbytry of Selkirk, to meet there Tuesday next, and appoints their clerk to extract the same in order to be sent thereunto.

Sept. 13. James Leithen and ―― Sclatter in Eildon, a.s.n. James.

" " Robert Grierson and Marion Wilson in Darnick, a.s.n. William ; w. Wm. Wilson, John Mercer.

Collected by Robert Scott and Andrew Drummond, £3 : 10s. Scots.

The accounts of the silver cups, the flaggons and velvet being come to hand, the clerk is appointed to insert them *verbatim* into their minutes as follows :—

Edinburgh, July 5th, 1730. Accompt the session of Melrose Dr. to James Anderson.

To repair communion cups w. : 70 ounces 8 drop at five shillings and 10 pence, silver and duty is. - - -	£20	11	3 sterling
To making at 18 pence per ounce, -	5	5	9
To engraving 18 pence per piece, -	0	6	0
	£26	3	0

Edinburgh, July 22nd, 1730, received by the hands of John Brown in name of the session of Melrose full and compleat payment of the account of twenty-six pounds, three shillings sterling, and discharges the same, and all proceedings the date hereof. As witnesses my hand sic subscribitur, James Anderson, July 17th, 1730. Accompt the session of Melrose to John Brown for 3 yards of fine block velvet at 16 shillings and 6 per yard.

Inde -	£2	9	6
For a box of wood, - - - - -	0	1	2
	£2	10	8

Edinburgh, July 24th, 1730, received the accompts, two pounds ten shillings and eight pence sterling, and discharges the same by me, sic subsribitur, John Brown, July 15th, 1730. The session of Melrose Dr. to Mrs. Ingles.

To 4 Chopin flagons at 5s. 6d. per piece, - -	£1	2	0
Discompt for old peuther, - - - -	0	3	8
	£0	18	4

Edinburgh, July 22nd, 1730, received by the hands of John Brown in name of the session of Melrose full and compleat payment of the ballance of eighteen shillings and four pence sterling, and hereby discharges the same and all preceeding the date hereof as witness my hand sic subs. Isobel Hume.

" 20. Collected by John Sibbald and Andrew Mar, £3 Scots.

" 26. Booked George Scott in this and Isobel Tailor in the parish of Minto : Wm. Lawrie, cautioner.

" 27. Collected by Wm. Dickson and Andrew Drummond, £2 : 18s. Scots.

Oct. 4. After prayer sederunt, the Minister, Drygrainge, Wm. Hoy, John Sibbald, Andrew Marr, &c., elders.

Collected by Nicol Milne and Andrew Marr, £3 Scots.

The minister informed the session that it was the mind of the presbytry that Mr. Ellies's servants should be cited to declare what they know of that marriage twixt Wm. Noble and Margaret

1730.

Pringle, accordingly appoints Alexr. Ellies and Elizabeth Fiddes to be cited to this day eight days session.

Oct. 7. James Purves and Agnes Knox in Colmslie, a.s.n. John ; w. Thomas Laidlay, Andrew Lythgow.

„ 11. George Martine and Agnes Wilson in Gattonside, a.d.n. Margaret ; w. Laird Marr, Wm. Hoy there,

After prayer sederunt, the Minister, Drygrainge, John Mabane, &c., elders.

Collected by Robert Scott and Andrew Marr, £3 : 17s. Scots.

Elizabeth Fiddes compeared and declared that she was not witness to Wm. Noble and Margaret Pringle's marriage, but that she saw the minister as she was coming by the cross but not in their house, and that it was the forenoon of that day the Lord Justice-Clerk was in Melrose in his way to the circuit at Jedburgh. Alexr. Ellies is appointed to be summoned pro 2do.

Adam Harvie being ordered to attend was called and compeared and dealt with to confess if guilty with Jean Gilroy, refused the charge. The clerk is appointed to give him a copy of the oath of purgation.

Drygrainge is appointed to attend the synod att Kelso, Tuesday come eight days.

„ 17. Booked Alexr. Brodie in this and Marion Wood in the parish of Westruther ; Alexr. Fisher, cautioner.

„ 18. John Cochran and Helen Bartleman in Newtown, a.s.n. John ; w. Nicol and John Milns.

After prayer sederunt, the Minister and Drygrainge, John Wallace, John Mercer, &c., elders.

Collected by John Sibbald and Andrew Lythgow, £3 : 4s. Scots.

Alexr. Ellies being called, compeared and interrogate if present when Wm. Noble and Margaret Pringle were married answered he was when they were presented, but then retired for some time and returned when they were married. He declared that the minister employed him to write the marriage lines, directed him what to write, and to put down as witnesses, —— Ferguson and Campbell, though no such was there. He owned he did so, and that this was done the 9th of May last. He was rebuked and dismissed.

(Case of discipline against Elizabeth Moodie and Mr. Walter Scott in Humbleknows.)

Isobel Leithen and Thomas Darling in Westhouses are appointed to be summoned for a scandalous behaviour.

„ 23. Booked John Mercer and Elizabeth Cook, both in this parish ; Wm. Cook, cautioner.

„ 25. After prayer sederunt, the Minister, Drygrainge, George Hoy, Nicol Milne, &c., elders.

Collected by Andrew Drummond and Wm. Hoy, £3 : 5s. Scots.

Wm. Noble appeared and gave in the testimony of ——, mason in Jedburgh, emitted before James Robson and Thomas Lockie in Jedburgh, shewing that he saw the said Noble married the 9th of May last by past.

Isobel Leithen and Thomas Darling being called, he only appeared. She is appointed to be summoned pro 2do to the session next Sabbath. The said Thomas is appointed to attend. Janet Moodie and Janet Shiel are appointed to be summoned to the said diet. The sederunt closed with prayer.

„ 27. Thomas Stenhouse and Helen Sibbald in Newtown, a.s.n. George : w. Nicol and Nicol Milns.

„ 29. Booked John Crawmond in the parish of Smailholm and Janet Turnbull in this ; Andrew Turnbull, cautioner.

1730.

Oct. 31. Booked James Scott and Janet Sandilands, both in this parish ; John Fisher, cautioner.

Nov. 1. After prayer sederunt, the Minister, Drygrainge, John Sibbald, Wm. Hoy, &c., elders.

Collected by Wm. Milne, Wm. Dickson, and John Mercer, £3 : 6s. Scots.

Case of discipline against Isobel Leithen and Thomas Darling continued ; witnesses cited, Jannet Moodie, Janet Shiel.

Drygrainge, John Mabane, Robert Scott, with the minister and clerk, are appointed to meet as a committee to-morrow, and examine George Hoy, their treasurer, his accompts.

Allowed testimonials to Jannet Rennaldson from her infancy till Whitsunday 1728.

,, 2. This day the Minister, Drygrainge, John Mabane and Robert Scott, with the clerk, revised the treasurer's accompts, and having compared charge with discharge, mortcloath, marriage and sacrament money, and the remains of Wm. Hoy's bond being ten pounds Scotts, do find in his hand, £235 : 5 : 6 Scots. They also allow the said George Hoy, their treasurer, one penny per pound of collections and deburs ements, whereof he is to discharge himself at his several countings.

,, 4. John Fisher and Margaret Rutherford of Housebyres, a.d.n. Christian ; w. D. Elliot, Mr. Trotter.

,, 6. Booked John Goven in this and Jannet Jamieson in the parish of Selkirk ; George Allie, cautioner.

,, 7. Booked James Gray and Margaret Moffat, both in this parish ; Robert Penman, cautioner. As also Robert Huntlie and Margaret Young, both in this parish ; James Young, cautioner.

,, 8. After prayer sederunt, the Minister, Drygrainge, Wm. Hoy, Robert Scott, &c., elders.

Collected by Andrew Marr and John Mabane, £2 : 11s. Scots.

Case of discipline against Isobel Leithen and Thomas Darling continued.

,, 11. Booked George Blaikie in the parish of Stow and Mary Gray in this parish ; George Rutherford, cautioner.

,, 13. Booked Robert Trotter and Margaret Mabane, both in this parish ; Wm. Mabane, cautioner.

,, 15. John Davidson and —— Mein in Newsteid, a.s.n. Andrew ; w. Andrew Mein, Wm. Milne.

After suitable admonitions and cautions, the oath of purgation was tendered to Adam Harvie.

Isobel Leithen compeared and was rebuked.

,, 17. Wm. Martine and Isobel Drummond in Gattonside, a.d.n. Jannet ; w. Wm. and David Martines there.

After prayer sederunt, the Minister, Drygrainge, John Mabane, Wm. Hoy, &c., elders.

Collected by John Sibbald and John Mercer, £3 : 7s. Scots.

Case of discipline against Alexr. Strachan, lately come from Jedburgh. The session resolve to enquire into the said affair, and for that end appoint the said Alexr. Strachan to be summoned, as also Alexr. and Andrew Cooks, and Michael Wallace to the session this day eight days.

,, 21. Booked Thomas Vair and Jean Mein, both in this parish ; James Vair, cautioner.

,, 22. Robert Bunzie and Rachel Forsan in Newsteid, a.s.n. Robert ; w. Wm. and John Bunzies there.

Isobel Leithen compeared for the second time.

After prayer sederunt, the Minister, Drygrainge, John Sibbald, Wm. Hoy, &c., elders.

Collected by Andrew Drummond, Nicol Mylne, £2 : 16s. Scots.

1730.

Granted testimonials to Robert Forsan and his wife. As also to John Gill and his family.

Alexr. Strachen compeared and charged as per last sederunt. He is appointed to be summoned to the session this day eight days, and Christian M'Millan is appointed to be summoned to the said diet.

Nov 28. Booked Wm. Bunzie and Jannet Little, both in this parish ; Thomas Little, cautioner, likeways Andrew Forsan and Janet Mabane, both in this parish ; Wm. Lawrie, cautioner ; Thomas Vair and Margaret Wilson, both in this parish ; Wm. Lawrie, cautioner.

29. Isobel Leithan compeared, rebuked and dismissed.

After prayer sederunt, the Minister, Drygrainge, Laird Mar, John Mercer, &c., elders.

Collected by Andrew Mein and Wm. Dickson, £3 Scots.

(Alexr. Strachan and Christian M'Millan's case continued.)

Dec. 6. Wm. Stodart and Isobel Young in Darnick, a.d.n. Anne ; w. John Mercer and William Dickson there.

Thomas Darling appeared for the first time and was rebuked.

After prayer sederunt, the Minister, Drygrainge, Wm. Milne and Nicol Milne, &c., elders.

Collected by John Mabane and James Laidlay, £3 : 3s. Scots.

The minister gave in a discharge for £4 Scotts as an year of the lowland burse, viz., from Martinmas 1729 to Martinmas 1730, subscribed by John Cranstone.

In the affair of Alexr. Strachan, the session appointed Alison Young, Wm. Brown, Robert Penman and his servant woman, and Jannet Glendinning to be cited as witnesses, . . . as also the said Strachan to be present.

„ 13. James Martine and Margaret Ellies in Gattonside, a.s.n. James.

„ „ Adam Moffat and Isobel Howieson in Gattonside, a.d.n. Jannet ; w. Wm. Martine, James Smail.

After prayer sederunt, the Minister, Drygrainge, Nicol Milne, John Wallace, George Hoy, &c., elders.

Collected by Andrew Mein and Wm. Hoy, £2 : 16s. Scots.

(Case of discipline against Alexr. Strachan continued.)

„ 14. James Watson and Isobel Cochran in Blainslies, a.s.n. James ; w. John Wallace, Thomas Darling, there.

„ 16. James Hunter and Marion Pringle in Whitlaw, a.s n. James ; w. George Scott, Wm. Pearson, there.

„ 20. Collected by Andrew Marr and Nicol Milne, £3 : 14s. Scots.

„ „ John Fisher and Isobel Scott in Easterlanglie, a.s.n. Alexr. ; Andrew Bryden, John Chisholm.

„ 23. Robert Ormistown and Helen Hopkirk in Melrose, a.s.n. Robert ; w. John Mabane, Wm. Hopkirk.

„ 27. Wm. Hart and Margaret Mein in Newsteid, a.s.n. John : w. James Mein, James Hart.

Collected by Robert Scott and Andrew Drummond, £3 : 2s.

Allowed testimonials for Christian M'Millan.

1731.

Jan. 2. Booked Wm. Brown and Catharine Little, both in this parish ; Thomas Darling, cautioner.

„ 3. James and Margaret Mein in Newsteid, a.d.n. Mary ; w. James Brown.

„ 10. Andrew Bartleman and Janet Cochran in Newtown, a.s.n. Henry.

„ „ Wm. Sandilands and Catharine Marr in Gattonside, a.s.n. Andrew : w. Laird Marr, Thomas Stenhouse.

After prayer sederunt, the Minister, Drygrainge, Wm. Hoy, John Mercer, &c., elders.

Collected by James Laidlay and John Mabane, £2 : 16s. Scots.

1730.

Case of discipline against Gavin Tweedie, servant to Robert Johnstone, shoemaker in Melrose, and Anne Ormistone.

The session resolve to examine witnesses in this affair and for that end order their beadle to summoned John Fairbairn, miller, and his wife Bessie Flint, Bessie Hog, their woman, John Lyal, John Dawson and James Wilson to the session this day eight days.

A petition was presented from Isobel Haliburton desiring that Charles Wilkison may take with the child she brought furth the sixth day of April last, and not retard the baptism of the child. The consideration of this is delayed. The sederunt closed with prayer.

Jan. 17. John Fiddes and Jannet Pringle in Gattonside, a.s.n. Walter.

„ „ John Cochran and Isobel Mein in Eildon, a.d.n. Isobel; w. Henry Cochran, Andrew Bartleman in Newtown.

The minister intimated a collection for the French and German protestant congregation in Copenhagen against this day eight days.

After prayer sederunt, the Minister, Drygrainge, Laird Marr, John Mabane, George Hoy, &c., elders.

Collected by Robert Scott, John Mercer, £3 : 16s. Scots.

Received testimonials from George Anderson till Whitsunday 1730.

„ 24. Robert Mercer and Anaple Ovens in Newsteid, a.s.n. William.

„ „ John Hoy and Alison Cuningham in Melrose, a.s.n. Henry; w. Henry Cuningham, George Hoy.

After prayer sederunt, the Minister, Drygrainge, John Mercer, John Mabane, &c., elders.

Collected by Robert Scott and Andrew Drummond, £18 : 10s. Scots.

Received testimonials from Wm. Douglass till Martinmas 1730.

Anne Ormistown not compearing, the beadle is appointed to charge her to compear next Sabbath, as also the miller and his wife.

The petition given in by Isobel Haliburton was this day considered, and the minister is appointed to converse with Mr. Wilkisone.

„ 31. This day Anne Ormistown compeared for the first time and was rebuked.

John Fairbairn and Bessie Flint compeared, but as the minister was rebuking him he charged the session with partiality, and spoke very impertinently, and so was not dismissed.

After prayer sederunt, the Minister, Drygrainge, John Mabane, George Hoy, &c., elders.

Collected by Andrew Mein, £2 : 9s. Scots.

On account of John Fairbairn's unmannerly behaviour the time the minister was rebuking him he is appointed to be summoned to the session against this day eight days.

The clerk is appointed to extract some of the material oaths emitted against Alexr. Strachen.

It is appointed to Drygrainge to speak to Mr. Wilkison.

Feb. 7. Anne Ormistown compeared for the second time.

„ „ After prayer sederunt, the Minister, Drygrainge, Robert Scott, Andrew Mein, &c., elders.

Collected by Nicol Milne, Wm. Dickson and John Sibbald, £3 : 18s. Scots.

John Fairbairn being called, compeared. He was asked the reason of his rude and unmannerly behaviour last Sabbath. Did this day rather make his fault worse, and alledged the session was partial in their dealings in conniving at faults. He was charged

1731.

to condescend upon them, and the session allows him this day eight days to make good his assertion. He is summoned *apud acta* to that diet.

Charles Wilkison is also appointed to be summoned thereto. William Noble and Margaret Pringle are appointed to be cited.

It is reported Gavin Tweedie is gone from this bounds.

Feb. 14. Anne Ormistown appeared, was rebuked and dismissed.

After prayer sederunt, the Minister, Drygrainge, Nicol Milne, John Mabane, &c., elders.

Collected by Wm. Milne and Andrew Drummond, £3 : 1s. Scots.

John Fairbairn was called and compeared and interrogate if he was ripe and ready to make good his charge he had alledged on the session. Answered he could do nothing in it, but that he was sorry for the offence given. He was removed, and it being put to the vote, rebuke in public or private, it carried public. So he was called in and appointed to appear Sabbath first for that effect.

Charles Wilkison was called and compeared, and Isobel Haliburton's petition was read to him. He required an extract of the said petition, which the session condescended to. He is summoned to this session this day eight days.

She is ordered to attend.

(Wm. Noble and Margaret Pringle's case continued.)

„ 21. John Fairbairn compeared, was rebuked and dismissed.

After prayer sederunt, the Minister, Drygrainge, William Milne, Laird Marr, &c., elders.

Collected by Robert Scott and John Mercer, £2 : 17s. Scots.

Charles Wilkison was called, compeared and interrogate if he had got the extract of Isobel Haliburton's petition. He answered he had. She was called in, and owned that it was the petition given in by her. He desired this day eight days that he might further consider the same, which the session allowed.

„ 22. George Forsyth and Jannet Blaikie in Whitlaw, a.s.n. Robert.

„ „ Robert Mercer and Jannet Little in Bentmilne, a.d.n. Catharine.

„ „ Andrew Lythgow and Eupham Smith in Threepwood, a.d.n. Janet ; w. Robert and Wm. Moffatts.

„ 28. Wm. and Helen Fishers of Langlee, a.s.n. Robert.

„ „ Wm. Sibbald and Helen Boston in Eildon, a.s.n. Robert ; w. James Lythgow, Doctor Martine.

After prayer sederunt, the Minister, Drygrainge, John Mabane, George Hoy, Nicol Milne, &c., elders.

Collected by Andrew Marr and Andrew Drummond, £3 Scots.

Charles Wilkison was called and compeared, and asked what he had to answer to Isobel Haliburton's petition, said he would prove by witnesses the said Isobel's scandalous behaviour with others. The session appoint him to meet with their clerk, and has the charge ready to give in against this day eight days' session, to which he is summoned.

Mar. 7. After prayer sederunt, the Minister, Drygrainge, John Mercer, John Wallace, Nicol Milne, Andrew Mein, &c., elders.

Collected by John Mercer and Wm. Hoy, £3 : 8s. Scots.

Alexr. Strachan compeared in the place of publick repentance, and was rebuked, conform to directions from the presbytry of Selkirk, as having confessed to what was proven against him.

The minister gave in a discharge for three years of the Lithuanian burse.

Received testimonials for Alison Hume.

Case of discipline against Charles Wilkison and Isobel Haliburton continued ; witnesses cited, Mungo Park, Isobel

1731.

Harvie, Margaret and Helen Parks. As also John Thomson and Adam Harvie to the session this day eight days.

Mar. 14. Alexr. Strachan compeared for the second time.

After prayer sederunt, the Minister, Drygrainge, Wm. Milne, John Sibbald, Andrew Mein, &c., elders.

Collected by Nicol Milne and Laird Marr, £2 : 17s. Scots.

Charles Wilkison compeared. The charge he gave in last day was this day read to him. He was required to subscribe it which he refused to do, but said he owned it as his, and having consigned half-a-crown he was removed, and the persons impeached, viz., John Thomson and Adam Harvie, were called in, and the charge read to them, and they seriously exhorted to confess if guilty and prevent the taking of oaths.

They refused guilt, whereupon Mungo Park, Isobel Harvie, Margaret and Helen Parks were called in. Charles Wilkison and Isobel Haliburtone were also called in, the parties concerned declared they had no objection against the witnesses.

After the minister had held out to them the nature of an oath, the said Mungo Park, Isobel Harvie, Margaret and Helen Parks were solemnly sworn, and severally examined in the terms of the charge, and all of them deponed they knew nothing of the affair. The witnesses were dismissed, and parties removed. The session finding nothing proven against John Thomson and Adam Harvie were of opinion that they should be instantly called in and assoilzied. Charles Wilkison was also called in and sharply rebuked for his groundless charge of calumney against John Thomson and Adam Harvie, and the session was to consider what further censure he was to undergo for the same. then he was dismissed, and the sederunt closed with prayer.

,, 21. Alexr. Strachan compeared for the third time and was rebuked.

,, ,, John Fairbairn and Bessie Flint in Melrose, a.s.n. —— ; w. George Martine, John Tait, there.

After prayer sederunt, the Minister, Drygrainge, Wm. Milne, John Sibbald, Andrew Marr, &c., elders.

Collected by Wm. Hoy and Andrew Lythgow, £3 : 10s.

Alexr. Strachan being cited, compeared and testified his sorrow for his sin. He was exhorted, admonished and dismissed. The minister is to report the same to the presbytry.

The session appoint Charles Wilkison to be cited to the session this day eight days.

,, 24. John Pringle and Margaret Scott in Blainslies, a.d.n. Margaret ; w. John Fisher, Wm. Thine.

,, 28. After prayer sederunt, the Minister, Drygrainge, John Wallace, John Mabane and Wm. Hoy, &c., elders.

Collected by James Laidlay, John Mercer and Andrew Drummond, £4 : 7s. Scots.

This day Charles Wilkison was called and compeared and required to satisfy for the guilt confest by him in common form, which he refused to do. He was then dismissed, and the session considering the affair and the many delays he had occasioned and the aggravation of his crime by slandering the innocent, they thought fit to referr this whole business to the rev. presbytry of Selkirk. Whereupon they did and hereby do referr this affair to the said presbytry to meet att Selkirk the first Tuesday of next month, and the clerk is appointed to extract the whole process for that effect.

April 2. Booked Thomas Darling and Isobel Martine, both in this parish ; Thomas Martine, portioner of Gattonside, cautioner.

,, 4. John Laidlay and Margaret Mein in Newtown, a.d.n. Christian ; w. Nicol Milne, Thomas Stenhouse there.

1731.

Collected by John Mabane and Andrew Drummond, £2 : 18s. Scots.

April 5. John Stirling and Isobel Wilson in Blainslies, a.d.n. Marion ; w. John Thine, James Wallace there.

„ 11. This day the minister relaxed Alexr. Strachan from the lesser excommunication by the appointment of the presbytry.

After prayer sederunt, the Minister, Drygrainge, Wm. Hoy, Laird Marr, John Mabane, &c., elders.

Collected by Robert Scott and John Mercer, £4 : 12s. Scots.

(Case against Charles Wilkison and Isobel Haliburtone continued.)

William Noble and Margaret Pringle appointed to compear in the publick place of repentance.

„ 18. William Noble and Margaret Pringle compeared for the first time, and were rebuked.

Collected by Wm. Milne, James Laidlay and Andrew Mein, £4 : 17s. Scots.

„ 25. Andrew Drummond and Helen Mathison in Bridgend, a.s.n. Andrew.

„ „ Robert Fairbairn and Margaret Davidson in Danieltown, a.d.n. Marion.

„ „ Andrew Haitly and Alison Dawson in Danieltown, a.d.n. Agnes ; w. Robert Scott, George Lawrie there.

William Noble and Margaret Pringle compeared the second time.

Collected by Andrew Marr, Wm. Hoy and John Sibbald, £3 : 3s. Scots.

„ 30. Booked James Dalgleish in the parish of Lauder and Marion Brown in this ; John Brown in Blainslies, cautioner.

May 1. Booked James Darling and Janet Shiel, both in this parish ; Alexr. Fisher in Clackmae, cautioner.

„ 2. William Noble and Margaret Pringle compeared and were rebuked.

„ 5. —— and Isobel Haliburtone, a.s.n. Charles ; w. John Mein, John Bunzie.

„ 9. The minister intimated a meeting of the heritors to meet the 26th instant about the reparation of the kirk.

„ „ Margaret Pringle compeared for the fourth time.

„ „ Robert Williamson and Agnes Scott in Westhouses, a.s.n., William ; w. Wm. and Thomas Williamsons.

Collected by Nicol and Wm. Milnes and Andrew Drummond, £3 : 3s. Scots.

„ 10. William Darling and Magdalene Allan in Blainslies, a.d.n. Margaret ; w. Thomas Darling, John Thine.

„ 14. Booked Michael Andison in the parish of Yarrow and Margaret Hownam in this ; Robert Marr in Darnick, cautioner.

„ 15. Booked John Smith and Margaret Wight, both in this parish ; John Smith, elder in Darnick, cautioner.

„ 16. Margaret Pringle compeared for the fifth time and was rebuked.

Collected by John Mabane and John Mercer, £3 : 17s. Scots.

„ 21. Booked in order for marriage William Mercer in the parish of Galashiels and Margaret Allie in this ; George Allie in Westerlanglee, cautioner.

„ 23. Wm. Noble and Margaret Pringle in Melrose, a.s.n. John.

„ „ Thomas Williamson and Mary Mein in Newsteid, a.d n. Catharine.

„ „ Thomas Crosbie and Margaret Brown in Drygrainge, a.d.n. Margaret ; w. William Williamson, George Hoy.

After prayer sederunt, the Minister, Drygrainge, John Mercer, John Mabane, Wm. Dickson, &c., elders.

Collected by Wm. Hoy, Andrew Marr, £3 : 12s. Scots.

Received testimonials from Grissel Nicolson, as also from John Spears and his wife.

1731.

Allowed testimonials to William Laidlay and to Alexr. Strachan, contained that he satisfied for a scandal he was guilty of here. It is recommended to Drygrainge and John Mabane to speak with Charles Wilkison and report.

May 30. After prayer sederunt, the Minister, Drygrainge, John Mabane, John Mercer, Wm. Dickson, &c., elders.

Collected by Andrew Lythgow, Nicol Milne, John Sibbald £3 : 8s. Scots.

Drygrainge reports that Charles Wilkison seemed to wave him when he spoke to him of his affair, and John Mabane reports that the said Charles said he would wait on the minister Munday next.

June 4. Booked Andrew Sibbald in the parish of Earlestown and Elizabeth Pringle in this ; Wm. Bain in Melrose, cautioner.

,, 6. Thomas Bunzie and Helen Bryden in Eildon, a.d.n. Francis.

,, ,, James Boustone and Marion Blaikie in Gattonside, a.d.n. Marion ; w. Thomas and John Boustone's there.

Collected by Andrew Marr and Andrew Mein, £4 Scots.

,, 13. Thomas Darling, portioner of Langhaugh and —— Thomson, a.d.n. —— ; w. Mr. Andrew Darling, James Heiton, there

After prayer sederunt, the Minister, Drygrainge, Wm. Milne, Andrew Mein, Nicol Milne, George Hoy, &c., elders.

Collected by Robert Scott and Andrew Marr, £4 : 6s. Scots.

The session have resolved that the sacrament of the supper shall be celebrated in this place the 3rd Sabbath next moneth.

Allowed testimonials to Jannet Hog from her infancy except two half years in the parish of Stow. The sederunt closed with prayer.

,, 19. Booked James Edgar and Elizabeth Pringle, both in this parish ; John Pringle, portioner of Blainslie, cautioner.

,, 20. Collected by Andrew Drummond and Wm. Milne, £1 : 18s. Scots.

,, 27. Robert Hog and Isobel Drummond in Colmslie, a.d.n. Isobel.

,, ,, Wm. Brown and Jean Dickson in Overlangshaw, a.d.n. Isobel ; w. George Brown, George Martine.

Collected by Robert Scott and James Laidlay, £2 : 5s. Scots.

July 1. James Brotherstone and Euphan Dixon in Mosshouses, a.d.n. Agnes ; w. Walter Thomson, Wm. Brown.

,, 4. This day the minister intimated the celebration of the supper in this place, this day fourteen days.

Collected by John Wallace and John Mabane, £3 : 9s. Scots.

,, 11. The minister intimated Thursday next as the humiliation day before the sacrament.

,, ,, John Turnbull and Bessie Familtown in Gattonside, a.d.n. Christian ; w. Wm. Hoy, Laird Marr.

After prayer sederunt, the Minister, Drygrainge, Robert Scott, William Dickson, Milne, &c., elders.

Collected by James Laidlay and Andrew Lythgow, £5 Scots.

Tuesday next is appointed for privy censures.

,, 13. After prayer sederunt, the Minister, Drygrainge, John Mabane, Robert Scott, James Laidlay, John Sibbald, Andrew Lythgow, Andrew Drummond, Nicol Milne, Andrew Mein, Andrew Marr, Wm. Hoy, Wm. Dixon, John Mercer, John Wallace, and Wm. Thine, elders.

The elders present were this day removed by pairs, tryed and approven, and exhorted to go on in the Lord's work. Then ordered the collections and the keeping of the doors.

Collected, Fast day,	-	-	-	-	£13 12 0
Collected Saturday,	-	-	-	-	18 0 0
			Carry forward,	-	£31 12 0

1731.

	Brought forward,	-	£31	12	0
Collected Lord's day,	-	-	-	37	7	0
Collected Munday,	-	-	-	16	18	0
Summ of collections,	-	-	£85	17	0

Debursed to the poor of the parish, common
poor, and poor recommended, &c.   -   -   52   0   0
                                              ————————
                                                  £33 17   0

Ballance is appointed to be given in to the treasurer wherewith
he is to charge himself.

July   15. Robert Trotter and Margaret Mabane in Melrose, a.s.n. Robert ; w.
John and William Mabans there.

,,   23. Booked William Brown and Christian M'Millian, both in this parish ;
Michael Wallace in Melrose, cautioner.

,,   25. After prayer sederunt, the Minister, Drygrainge, Wm. Hoy, Wm.
Milne, George Hoy, John Mabane, &c., elders.

Collected by Andrew Drummond and John Mercer, £3 : 18s.
Scots.

The session appoint Drygrainge, John Mabane and Robert
Scott to meet with the minister and clerk to examine their
treasurer's accompts against Wednesday the 11th next moneth.

(Case of discipline against James Darling and Jannet Shiel in
Kaidslie, his wife.)

The session being informed of Alexr. Strachen, his rude and
scandalous behaviour in forcing into Margaret Heron's house,
they are appointed to be cited to the forsaid diet.

Aug.   1. After prayer sederunt, the Minister, Drygrainge, Wm. Hoy, John
Mabane, Robert Scott, &c., elders.

Collected by Andrew Marr and Wm. Milne, £2 : 8s. Scots.

(Jannet Shiel and James Darling's case continued.)

The affair of Alexr. Strachen delayed, because the woman was
not at home and so not cited. They are appointed to be cited to
the next day's session.

The minister and some of the elders signed testimonials to
get Margaret Steel, who is feared has a cancer in her breast, into
the Infirmary.

,,   8. Henry Forrest and —— Robson in Westhouses, a.d.n. Anaple ; w.
John Forrest, Robert Williamson, there.

After prayer sederunt, the Minister, Drygrainge, Andrew
Lythgow, Andrew Mein, Wm. Hoy, &c., elders.

Collected by Andrew Drummond and John Mercer, £3 Scots.

Case against Alexr. Strachen and Margaret Heron continued ;
witnesses cited, Wm. Hog's wife and Wm. Brown.

,,   11. This day the Minister, Drygrainge, Robert Scott, with their clerk,
mett and examined their treasurer's accompts and having compared
charge with discharge, they find remaining in his hand
£343 : 5 : 6 Scots, wherewith he is to charge himself att next
accompting.

,,   15. Collected by John Sibbald, John Mercer, Nicol Milne, £3 : 13s.
Scots.

After prayer sederunt, the Minister, Drygrainge, John Wallace,
Wm. Hoy, &c., elders.

Case against Margaret Heron and Alexr. Strachen continued.

In regard a child was exposed at the east end of this town
Friday morning last and the mother cannot be heard tell of, the
session appoint a committee of their number to meet to-morrow at
eight of the clock morning and examine these persons who was at
the taking up of the child.

1731.

Aug. 16. After prayer sederunt, the Minister, Nicol, Andrew Marr, Robert Scott, George Hoy, &c., elders.

Thomas Trotter being cited was called and compeared and interrogate what he knew about the child found at the east end of the town Friday morning, declared that about four of the clock of the said morning a man came and told him as he was opening the door that there was a child lying at the east end of the town, and that he saw the same man go east immediately before who returned and told him of the same : that he Wm. Mabane and Wm. Hopkirk went out to see about it, but by that time Isobel Williamson had the child in her arm, and this is all he knows of the affair.

Isobel Williamson cited, compeared and declared that she knew nothing who were the parents to the forsaid child or who laid it down, that she was the first came to the child, that she and others thought could not be above fourteen days' old, that the child had a day and night busken with it, some hippings, but no writ, that the men in Oxnam water were present at her taking up the child, who also alarmed the rest of the neighbourhood. This is all she knows of the affair.

„ 22. George Atchison and Elizabeth Hopkirk in Melrose, a.s.n. George.

„ „ Robert Gibson and Isobel Dinning in Gattonside, a.d.n. Isobel.

„ „ Wm. Fleck and Helen Black in Williamlaw, a.d.n. Lilias ; w. John Young, Robert Philp.

James Darling and Jannet Shiel compeared, were rebuked and dismissed, and gave in the penalty of £4 Scots.

Collected by Andrew Marr and Andrew Mein, £3 Scots.

„ 29. After prayer sederunt, the Minister, Drygrainge, Wm. Hoy, John Wallace, Andrew Lythgow, &c., elders.

Collected by Robert Scott and John Mabane, £3 : 1s. Scots.

Isobel Haliburtone this day required an extract of her process with Charles Wilkison, which the session thought reasonable and ordered accordingly.

Allowed testimonials to Nicol Bowar and Wm. Robson from their infancy.

Sept. 5. After prayer sederunt the Minister, Drygrainge, John Mercer, Nicol and Wm. Miln's, &c., elders.

Collected by John Sibbald and John Wallace, £2 : 11s. Scots.

The mother of the exposed child being after much search and great expences found, being apprehended in Jedburgh, confesses her name Elspeth Philp, a Lothian woman, that the child was begot at Lustruther in Southdean parish by one ——— Gibb, a Kelso man, and brought furth in Belford in Moorbattle parish in the house of one ——— Gray, an elder of the church. The session thought fit to send her to Moorbattle parish under a guard that they may enquire more punctually into the scandal.

„ 12. Robert Halliwall and Margaret Nisbet in Gattonside, a.s.n. Thomas.

„ „ James Pringle and Margaret Brown in Newsteid, a.d.n. Jannet.

„ „ James Waugh and Mary Duncan in Melrose, a.d.n. Helen ; w. James Waugh, junior, Alexr. Bell.

Collected by Andrew Marr, John Mercer, and Wm. Milne, £2 : 19s. Scots.

Allowed testimonials to George Rutherford and his wife.

„ 16. Booked Wm. Frier and Isobel Bain, both in this parish : Thomas Martine, portioner of Gattonside, cautioner.

„ 18. Booked John Young in this and Margaret Gill in the parish of Earlestown ; James Young weaver in Gattonside, cautioner.

„ 19. John Marr and ——— Lythgow in Gattonside, a.s.n. John.

„ „ Adam Thorburn and Susanna Rutherford in Melrose, a.s.n. Robert.

1731.

Sept. 19. George Scott and Isobel Tailor in Danieltown, a.d.n. Helen; w. Robert Scott, Wm. Laurie in Danieltown.

Collected by Andrew Drummond and Robert Scott, £3 : 3s. Scots.

,, 23. Booked Alexr. Pringle in the parish of Lauder and Isobel Stobo in this ; Andrew Shillinglaw in Blainslies, cautioner.

,, 26. James Laing and Agnes Richie in Melrose, two daughters named Margaret and Christian ; w. Wm. Hopkirk, Walter Gray.

Collected by John Mabane and Andrew Mein, £3 Scots.

Oct. 3. Thomas Vair and Margaret Wilson in Danieltown, a.d.n. Margaret ; w. George and Robert Lauries there.

,, ,, Andrew and Catharine Mercers in Bridgend, a.d.n. Margaret ; w. *ut supra.*

Collected by John Sibbald, Nicol Milne and John Mercer, £3 Scots.

,, 10. After prayer sederunt, the Minister, Drygrainge, Nicol Mylne, John Mabane, Laird Marr, &c., elders.

Collected by Wm. Milne and John Wallace, £3 : 3s. Scots.

The minister represented that Jannet Nisbet had waited on the presbytry Tuesday last and was dealt with in order to bring her to a sense of her sin of adultery confest by her. She was remitted to the session that they may order her censure. She was accordingly cited to this day's session, who considering the affair appoint her to appear in sackcloath this day fourteen days. She was called in and this intimate to her. The sederunt closed with prayer.

,, 17. Collected by Andrew Drummond and Andrew Mein, £2 : 2s. Scots.

,, 20. Mett att Langhaugh this day. After prayer the Minister, Drygrainge and Robert Scott, elders, as a committee of the session upon a report. . . .

(Case of discipline against Jannet Darling and John Leech, servant to James Lees in Overshiels in the parish of Stow.)

,, 21. Alexr. Bell and Margaret Dodds in Drygrainge, a.d.n. Margaret ; w. Andrew and John Meins in Newsteid.

,, 23. Booked Andrew Mein and Jannet Renaldson both in this parish, John Milne portioner in Newtown, cautioner.

Item. Booked James Purves and Margaret Scott, both in this parish ; Mark Purves in Old Melrose, cautioner.

,, 24. Jannet Nisbet appeared in sackcloath for the first time and was admonished.

,, ,, Robert Johnstone and Jean Gillas in Melrose, a.s.n. Andrew.

,, ,, Wm. Bunzie and Jannet Little in Newsteid, a.d.n. Mary ; w. John Tait, George Martine.

Collected by Wm. Hoy, John Mercer and Wm. Milne, £3 : 18s. Scots.

,, 29. Booked Robert Shiel in the parish of Earlestown, and Elizabeth Shiel in this ; John Tait in Melrose, cautioner.

Booked Adam Harvie and Isobel Leithen, both in this parish : Wm. Sandilands in Gattonside, cautioner.

,, 31. Jannet Nisbet appeared for the second time.

Collected by Robert Scott and Andrew Marr, £2 : 12s. Scots.

Nov. 6. Booked Thomas Hoy and Jannet Smith, both in this parish : James Thaup in Melrose, cautioner.

Booked Robert Scott and Alison Laidlay, both in this parish ; James Scott, portioner of Blainslie, cautioner.

,, 7. Jannet Nisbet compeared for the third time and was admonished.

Collected by Wm. Hoy and Andrew Drummond, £2 : 17s. Scots.

,, 11. Booked in order for marriage James Middlemist in the parish of Galashiels, and Helen Beatie in this ; George Beatie in Bridgend, cautioner.

,, 13. Booked Nicol Mercer and Agnes Steel, both in this parish ; John Bowie in Melrose, cautioner.

1731.

Nov. 14. Jannet Nisbet compeared for the fourth time and was admonished.

After prayer sederunt, the Minister, Drygrainge, Wm. Hoy and Nicol Milne, &c., elders.

Collected by Robert Scott and Andrew Mein, £3 Scots.

The session order their beadle to cite Janet Darling before the session of Stow against the first Sabbath of December next.

The session agreed to lend John Laurie 30s. sterling, for which he is to renew the bond he gave formerly for the like sum and grant one for £3 sterling.

It was thought fitt that Jannet Nisbet should appear before the presbytry next presbytry day to receive further orders.

,, 20. Booked Thomas Bunzie and Agnes Mein, both in this parish ; Wm. Mein in Eildon, cautioner.

Booked Wm. Cook and Margaret Lawrie, both in this parish ; Alexr. Cook, portioner of Melrose, cautioner.

,, 21. Jannet Nisbet compeared the fifth time.

The minister intimated a synodical fast to be observed Wednesday next.

,, ,, George Stewart and Jannet Haliwall in Gattonside, a.s.n. —— ; w. Laird Marr, Wm. Hoy.

Collected by John Mabane and John Mercer, £3 : 9s. Scots.

,, 24. Collected by John Sibbald, Wm. Dickson and Andrew Mein, £6 : 7s. Scots.

,, 26. Booked James Wight in the parish of Bouden and Elizabeth Ainslie in this ; James Ainslie in Langshaw milne, cautioner.

Booked Andrew Grierson in the parish of Ancrum and Jannet Couper in this ; Walter Rae in Newtown, cautioner.

,, 28. Jannet Nisbet compeared the sixth time.

Collected by Wm. Hoy, John Mercer and Robert Scott, £2 : 9s. Scots.

Dec. 2. Wm. Bailie and Isobel Park in Hackburn, a.s.n. Thomas ; w. James Laidlay, Wm. Atchison in Buckholm.

,, 4. Booked George Penman in this parish and Jannet Wood in the parish of Mackerstone ; Andrew Dawson, cautioner.

,, 5. Nicol Milne and Isobel Turnbull in Newtown, a.s.n. John ; w. Thomas Stenhouse, elder and younger.

Jannet Nisbet compeared the seventh time.

Collected by Wm. Milne, £2 : 10s. Scots.

,, 8. John Coats and Jannet Purves in Langshaw milne, a.s.n. Thomas ; w. Walter Thomson, James Combie.

,, 11. Booked James Wight and Jannet Skirven, both in this parish ; John Smith in Darnick, cautioner.

,, 12. Robert Hunthe and Margaret Young in Gattonside, a.s.n. James.

,, ,, Robert Myles and Jannet Mathison in Gattonside, a.d.n. Anaple ; w. John Young, James Mathison.

Jannet Nisbet compeared for the eighth time and was dismissed having appeared before the presbytry Tuesday last.

After prayer sederunt, the Minister, Drygrainge, Wm. Dickson, James Laidlay, George Hoy, &c., elders.

Collected by Andrew Marr, John Mercer and Andrew Drummond, £2 : 10s. Scots.

Received Jannet Nisbet's fine, £3 Scots.

The beadle is appointed to cite Jannet Walker to compear before the congregation in sackcloath Sabbath next, and in the meantime to speak with the minister sometime this week.

,, 19. Jannet Walker compeared in sackcloath the first time and was admonished.

After prayer sederunt, the Minister, Drygrainge, Wm. Hoy, Andrew Mein, John Mabane, &c., elders.

Collected by John Wallace, £2 : 1s. Scots.

1731.

It was recommended to the minister to enquire after testimonials of Mr. Gibson and Mrs. Jannet Carncross, their marriage.

Dec. 26. Jannet Walker compeared the second time.

After prayer sederunt, the Minister, Drygrainge, John Mabane, Wm. Hoy, &c., elders.

Collected by Wm. Milne and Andrew Mein, £2 : 2s. Scots.

John Sprotts being cited was called and compeared and seriously exhorted to confess the adultery alledged upon him by Jannet Walker, but all in vain. He declared he was ready to purge himself by oath before the congregation. The session order him to wait on their clerk and get a copy of the said oath. The sederunt closed with prayer.

1732.

Jan. 1. Booked Mark Shillinglaw and Jannet Wilson, both in this parish ; James Bunzie, portioner of Newsteid, cautioner.

„ 2. Jannet Walker compeared the third time and was admonished.

Collected by Robert Scott, Wm. Dickson and Andrew Mein, £3 : 1s. Scots.

„ 9. Wm. Steel and Elizabeth Walker in Melrose, a.d.n. Isobel ; w. George Walker, Nicol Mercer in Melrose.

Jannet Walker compeared the fourth time.

Collected by Andrew Mein and Wm. Hoy, £1 : 18s. Scots.

„ 16. Jannet Walker compeared the fifth time and was admonished.

Collected by John Sibbald and Andrew Drummond, £1 : 11s. Scots.

„ 23. Jannet Walker compeared the sixth time.

John Sprotts was this day called before the congregation in order to purge himself by oath. He compeared and was seriously dealt with to prevent his adding sin to sin. The minister tendered so much of the oath to him, but because of pregnant presumptions of guilt, he stopped.

„ „ Wm. Hog and Agnes Hardie in Darnick, a.d.n. Jean.

„ „ Walter Scot and Margaret Mein in Danieltown, a.d n. Elizabeth : w. George Lawrie, Robert Scott, there.

Collected by Andrew Marr and Robert Scott, £2 : 3s. Scots.

„ 24. George Blaikie and Marion Gray in Langhaugh, a.s.n. James.

„ „ Wm. Brown and Catharine Little in Langhaugh, a.d.n. Margaret ; w. John Fisher, David Speeding.

„ 30. After prayer sederunt, the Minister, Drygrainge, Wm. Milne, John Mabane, Robert Scott, &c., elders.

Collected by John Mercer, Wm. Hoy and Andrew Mein, £2 : 15s. Scots.

Jannet Walker having compeared the seventh time before the congregation, she was ordered to attend the session. She being called was seriously admonished and exhorted and told she was not to compear till she was warned to compear before the presbytry.

The session appoint Jean Ormistown to appear Sabbath next in sackcloath.

James Thomson allowed testimonials from his infancy.

„ 31. James Brown and Jannet Waugh in Bentmilne, a.s.n. John.

„ „ John Fisher and Isobel Scott in Langlee, a.s.n. Alexander ; w. Andrew Marr, Alexr. Fisher.

Feb. 6. Jean Ormistown appeared in sackcloath for the first time.

Collected by John Wallace and Andrew Drummond, £2 : 1s. Scots.

„ „ William Milne and Elizabeth Mein in Darnick, a.s.n. Nicol.

„ „ Walter Rae and Christian Richie in Newtown, a.d.n. Christian ; w. John and George Mercers in Darnick.

„ 13. Jean Ormistown compeared the second time.

„ „ Thomas Marr and Jean Craig in Melrose, a.s.n. Andrew ; w. Andrew and John Marrs in Gattonside.

1732.

Collected by James Laidlay, John Mabane and Robert Scott, £3 : 14s. Scots.

Feb. 20. Jean Ormistone appeared the third time and was spoke with.

After prayer sederunt, the Minister, Drygrainge, Wm. Dickson, John Wallace, &c., elders.

Collected by Wm. Hoy and Wm. Milne, £2 Scots.

The session appoints Drygrainge, Robert Scott, John Mabane, to meet with the minister and clerk as a committee to examine the treasurer's accompts to-morrow. Given in a discharge of the lowland bursary preceeding Martinmas 1731.

,, 21. This day the Minister, Drygrainge, John Mabane and Robert Scott mett with the treasurer and revised his accompts and with mortcloath and marriage money included, there remains in his hand, £367 : 1s. : 6d. Scotts, wherewith he is to charge himself at compting.

,, 27. Jean Ormistone compeared the fourth time.

Collected by Nicol Milne and Wm. Dickson, £2 : 17s. Scots.

Mar. 5. Jean Ormistone compeared the fifth time.

,, ,, John Spear and Alison Gibson in Newsteid —— ; w. Andrew Mein, George Martine.

Collected by Wm. Hoy, John Mercer and John Wallace, £3 Scots.

,, 12. Jean Ormistone appeared the sixth time.

,, ,, John Dalgliesh and Agnes Darling in Darnick, a.s.n. George ; w. John and George Mercers there.

Collected by John Mercer and Andrew Drummond, £2 : 17s. Scots.

,, 19. Jean Ormistown appeared the seventh time.

,, ,, Alexr. M'Fadden and Agnes Napier in Melrose, a.d.n. Christian.

,, ,, John Cochran and Elizabeth Bartleman in Newtown, a.s.n. John.

,, ,, Thomas Simpson and Janet Mein in Eildon, a.s.n. John ; w. George and Alexr. Martines.

After prayer sederunt, the Minister, Drygrainge, Andrew Mein. Wm. Dickson, &c., elders.

Collected by Andrew Marr, John Mercer, Wm. Hoy, £3 : 4s. Scots.

Jean Ormiston compeared before the session and was admonished and exhorted, and was appointed to appear before the presbytry the first Tuesday of April next.

Jannet Walker is also to appear that day.

The session order their beadle to summond George Gibson and Mrs. Jannet Carncross, Hugh Grieve and Margaret Darling for their irregular marriages.

,, 26. Thomas Darling and Isobel Martine in Gattonside, a.s.n. William ; w. Thomas Mathison, William Darling.

Collected by William and Nicol Milne, £2 : 1s. Scots.

,, 27. William Smail and Jannet Sandilands, a.d.n. Jannet ; w. James Hunter, George Martine.

April 1. Booked John Gordon in this, and Margaret Walker in this parish : Andrew Renaldson, portioner of Darnick, cautioner.

,, 2. John Sibbald and Agnes Stenhouse in Eildon, a.d.n. Isobel ; w Thomas Stenhouse, Nicol Milne in Newtown.

After prayer sederunt, the Minister, Drygrainge, John Mabane. George Hoy, &c., elders.

Collected by John Sibbald, £2 : 13s. Scots.

A letter of excuse was produced and read from Mrs Jannet Carncross, which was sustained, and the beadle appointed to summon them to the session this day eight days.

Hugh Grieve and Margaret Darling compeared, and produced their marriage lines datted at Edinr. the 28th day of February

1732.

1732, subscribed James Wingate minister. They were rebuked for the same, and their fine reserved.

April 6. This day Hugh Grieve came and paid 15s. as his fine.

Received a receipt of collection that was levied for the German and French protestants in Copenhagen as collected here, January 24th, 1731, extending to £18 : 10s., discharged by Robert Brown for Gavin Hamiltone.

„ 9. After prayer sederunt, the Minister, Drygrainge, James Laidlay, John Wallace, Robert Moffatt, &c., elders.

Collected by Robert Scott and Andrew Drummond, £3 : 10s. Scots.

Mr. Gibson and Mrs. Jannet Carncross, being cited, were called, but not compearing, the beadle is ordered to summon them pro 2ⁿᵈᵒ. to the session this day eight days.

The minister represented that the presbytry's opinion concerning Jannet Walker and Jean Ormistown is that they should not yet be absolved in regard the process is still depending.

„ 16. George Beatie and Marion Waugh in Bridgend, a.d.n. Helen ; w. Andrew Turnbull and Drummond.

After prayer sederunt, the Minister, Drygrainge, Wm. Milne, James Laidlay, &c., elders.

Collected by John Mabane and William Milne, £3 : 4s. Scots.

Mr. George Gibson and Jannet Carncross being called, compeared not. Drygrainge represented that Mrs. Jannet is in a bad state of health, and that they are both content to come before a committee of the session if they would appoint one for that end, the other side of the water. The session condescended, and they do appoint Drygrainge, Andrew Mar, Wm. Hoy, to meet with the minister and clerk as a committee at Gattonside, Wednesday come eight days. Drygrainge is to acquaint them of the said meeting.

„ 23. John Grieve and Margaret Thomson in Galabridge, a.s.n. William ; w. George Alley, John Goven.

Collected by James Laidlay and Wm. Thine, £2 : 17s. Scots.

„ 25. David Brown and Jannet Dick, a.s.n. William.

„ „ James Edgar and Elizabeth Pringle in Blainslies, a.d.n. Barbara ; w. John Pringle, Alexr. Gray.

„ 26. This day, according to appointment, after prayer, the minister, Drygrainge, Andrew Marr and George Hoy, elders, att Gattonside. George Gibson compeared, and presented to the said committee a testimonial of his marriage, subscribed by Patrick Midleton, minister, dated Aug. 25th, 1731, which was sustained. A letter was received from Mrs. Gibson of her indisposition, which was sustained. He was rebuked, and as his modified fine has instantly paid 15s. sterling, for which the clerk is appointed to give him a discharge.

„ 30. Collected by Wm. Milne and Andrew Marr, £2 : 17s. Scots.

May 3. Andrew Forsan and ——— in Drygrainge, a.d.n. ——— ; w. George and Andrew Martines.

„ 7. Collected by James Laidlay and John Mercer, £3 : 10s. Scots.

„ 11. Booked James Cesford and Isobel Cochran, both in this parish ; Nicol Bowar, cautioner.

„ 13. Booked Patrick Bulman and Agnes Cochran, both in this parish ; John Cochran, cautioner.

„ 14. Collected by John Mabane, Robert Scott and John Sibbald, £3 : 5s. Scots.

„ 16. James Dalgleish and Marion Brown, a.s.n. Adam.

„ „ Wm. Thin and Marion Fairbairn in Blainslies, a.s.n. William ; w. John Thine, Alexr. Gray.

„ 20. Booked William Mabane and Isobel Ballentyne, both in this parish ; Robert Trotter, merchant, cautioner.

1732.

May 21. Thomas and Alison Gills in Danieltown, a.s.n. John ; w. Robert Scott, George Laurie.

This day the minister intimated his purpose of administring the sacrament of the supper in this place this day fourteen days.

Collected by Andrew Marr and John Wallace, £3 : 15s. Scots.

,, 26. Booked Thomas Waugh in the parish of Lauder, and Agnes Forsan in this ; John Fisher of Westerhousebyres, cautioner.

,, 28. The minister intimated Thursday next to be observed as the humiliation day before the sacrament. The people were suitable exhorted to their duty on this solemn occasion.

After prayer sederunt, the Minister, Drygrainge, Wm. Hoy, John Mabane, &c., elders.

Collected by Andrew Marr and Drummond, £3 : 6s. Scots.

Tuesday next is appointed for privy tryals.

,, 30. After prayer sederunt, the Minister, Drygrainge, James Laidlay, George Hoy, John Sibbald, Robert Scott, John Mabane, Andrew Marr, Andrew Drummond, Wm. Milne, John Mercers, elders.

The elders present were severally removed by pairs, tryed, and approven, and encouraged to go on in the Lord's work.

The collection to be gathered the several days as follows :—

Thursday.

Andrew Mein, Andrew Drummond, at the east door. John Mercer at the west. Wm. Dickson at the north.

Saturday.

Robert Moffat at the east stile. Andrew Mein at the south door. Andrew Marr to be continued at the minister's entry. Andrew Lythgow and Robert Scott at the south stile. James Laidlay and John Wallace at the west stile.

Lord's Day.

John Mabane at the north door. John Wallace at the east stile. Nicol Milne and Robert Scott at the west stile. Wm. Milne and Andrew Mein at the south stile.

Munday.

Wm. Hoy at the east stile. George Hoy at the south stile. Andrew Mein at the entry through the kirk. John Mercer at the west stile.

Order of keeping the doors the Lord's Day.

John Sibbald and John Mercer for the east door till eleventh.
Robert Scott, Wm. Thine and Robert Moffatt till one.
John Wallace and Andrew Lythgow till the action be over.

For the West Door.

Walter Murray and George Hoy till eleventh.
William Dickson, Andrew Drummond and James Laidlay till one.
Andrew Mein and William Milne from that to the end.
The elders are enjoined to be circumspect in distributing the tokens.

1732.

Collected, Fast Day,	-		-	-	£13	10	0
Collected, Saturday,	-		-	-	15	18	0
Collected, Lord's Day,	-		-	-	37	14	0
Collected, Munday,	-		-	-	16	5	0

Sum of collections, -   -   -   -   £83 7 0
Debursed to poor of the parish, common
poor, and poor recommended, &c.,   -   45 18 0

£37 9 0

Which sum is appointed to be given in to the treasurer wherewith he is to charge himself.

June 5. Charles Frier and Agnes Thorburn, a.d.n. Agnes.

,, ,, Thomas Gordon and Agnes Blaikie in Easterlanglie, a.d.n. Marion ; w. Andrew Marr, John Fisher.

,, 8. James Fisher and Agnes Wight of Sorrowlessfield, a.d.n. Mary ; w Andrew Marr, Alexr. Fisher.

,, 9. Booked John Murray in the parish of Bowden, and Isobel Young in this ; James Young, cautioner.

Wm. Cook and Helen Hopkirk both in this parish ; Wm. Hopkirk in Melrose, cautioner.

Mr. Charles Wilkiesone in this, and Mrs. Anna Paterson in one of the parishes of Edinburgh : James Lythgow of Kirklands, cautioner.

,, 11. David Umpherstone and Jannet Nisbet in Gattonside, a.d.n. Mary ; w. Robert Halliwall, Wm. Mathisone there.

After prayer sederunt, the Minister, Drygrainge, Wm. Milne, Robert Scott, &c., elders.

Collected by John Mabane and John Wallace, £4 : 12s. Scots.

The vagrant beggars, Munday last, being many of them beastly drunk, and, as it is said, Bessie, Helen and William Hopkirks aforded them drink, the session order the said persons to be cited to the session this day eight days.

,, 17. Booked George Livingstone in this parish, and Mary Dewar in the parish of Ligerwood : James Ainslie, cautioner.

,, 18. After prayer sederunt, the Minister, Drygrainge, John Mabane, Wm. Hoy, &c., elders.

Collected by Nicol Milne, John Mercer and Andrew Drummond, £3 : 6s. Scots.

The persons mentioned in the former sederunt compeared this day, and in regard the crime could not be particularly fixed, they were instantly rebuked and dismissed.

Andrew Pringle in Blainslies, tincker, being married irregularly, he is ordered to be cited to the session this day eight days.

,, 23. After prayer sederunt, the Minister, Drygrainge, Andrew Lythgow, John Wallace, Robert Moffatt, &c., elders.

Collected by Nicol Milne and John Sibbald, £2 : 13s. Scots.

Andrew Pringle being summoned compeared and acknowledged he was married to Sarah Murray, and produced their marriage lines, subscribed att Edinburgh, April 6th, by David Strange, minister. They having expressed their sorrow for breaking the order of the church were rebuked, and he was ordered to wait on the session clerk and grant his bill for 15s. sterling, as his fine for the use of the poor of this parish.

July 2. Thomas Mein and Margaret Jerdain in Eildon, a.d.n. Elizabeth ; w. John Sibbald, John Cochran there.

Collected by Andrew Mein and Andrew Marr, £6 : 3s. Scots.

,, 9. Mr. Gavin Elliot, schoolmaster, and Margaret Angus, a.s.n. William ; w. Robert Paterson of Drygrainge, and the Laird of Whitstead.

1732.

Collected by Wm. Milne and John Mercer, £2 : 17s. Scots.

July 14. Wm. Brown and Christian M'Millian in Melrose, a.s.n. William ; John Mabane and Wm. Steel there.

Booked David Speeding in the parish of Galashiels, and Agnes Bell in this parish ; Charles Frier in Gattonside, cautioner.

,, 16. Collected by Wm. Hoy and Andrew Mein, £2 : 12s. Scots.

,, 20. Wm. Mabane and —— Simpson in Newsteid, a.d.n. Jannet ; w. John Spears, Andrew Mein there.

,, 22. Booked David Tait in the parish of Smailholm, and Isobel Fisher in this ; James Fisher in Byrend, cautioner.

,, ,, John Smith and —— Wight in Darnick, a.d.n. Agnes ; w. James and Wm. Wights there.

,, 23. Collected by John Mabane and Andrew Marr, £2 : 5s. Scots.

,, 31. Collected by John Mercer, Andrew Mein and Wm. Hoy, £2 : 5s. Scots.

Aug. 6. After prayer sederunt, the Minister, Drygrainge, John Mabane, Wm. Hoy, Robert Scott, &c., elders.

Collected by Nicol Milne and John Sibbald, £2 : 17s. Scott. (Case of descipline against Adam Harvie and his wife.)

,, 13. John Young and Margaret Gill in Gattonside, a.d.n. —— ; w. Alexr. Young, Robert Huntlie, there.

After prayer sederunt, the Minister, Drygrainge, Nicol Milne, Andrew Mein, Wm. Milne, &c., elders.

Collected by Wm. Hoy and Wm. Dickson, £3 Scots.

The session appoint their beadle to cite Adam Harvie and his wife, and two women that were present at the child's bearing, to the session against this day eight days.

,, 20. After prayer sederunt, the Minister, Drygrainge, Wm. Hoy, Andrew Marr, Robert Moffatt, &c., elders.

Collected by John Sibbald and John Wallace, £2 : 14s. Scots. (Case of discipline against Adam Harvie and his wife continued and dismissed ; witnesses cited, Margaret Thomson, Margaret Bonington.

,, 27. Collected by Andrew Mein and Wm. Milne, £3 : 6s. Scots.

,, 29. James Watherstone and ——, Bailie of Newhouses, a.s.n. James.

,, ,, Alexr. Gray and Margaret Thin in Blainslies, a.d.n. Mary.

,, ,, James Wallace and Euphan Darling in Blainslies, a.d.n. Elizabeth ; w. John Thin, John Wallace there.

Sept. 3. Collected by Robert Scott and Wm. Hoy, £5 : 4s. Scots.

,, 10. Collected by John Sibbald and Andrew Drummond, £3 : 3s. Scots.

,, 17. Collected by John Mercer, Andrew Mein and Wm. Milne, £3 : 2s. Scots.

,, 21. James Leithen and —— Sclatter in Eildon, —— ; w. John Sibbald, John Cochrane there.

,, 24. Collected by Nicol Milne and Andrew Marr, £3: 1s. Scots.

Oct. 1. John Cochrane and Margaret Mein in Eildon, a.d.n. Margaret.

,, 1. Thomas Speeding and Margaret Miles in Gattonside, a.d.n. Isobel.

,, 1. James Murray and Elizabeth Gavinlock in Westerlanglee, a.d.n. Helen ; w. John Laidlay, Andrew Bartleman.

Collected by Andrew Mein and James Laidlay, £3 : 18s. Scots.

,, 4. John Edgar and Jean Grieve in Blainslies, a.d.n. Marion ; w. Hugh and John Grieves there.

,, 7. Booked George Scott in the parish of Hopkirk and Margaret Scott in this ; Alexr. Scott in Whitlaw, cautioner.

Item. Thomas Cochran and Janet Dickson, both in this parish ; John Cochran in Eildon, cautioner.

,, 8. After prayer sederunt, the Minister, Drygrainge, Wm. Dickson, Andrew Lythgow, John Mabane, &c., elders.

Collected by John Sibbald and Robert Scott, £3 : 1s. Scots.

The minister produced an extract of the presbytery in Charles

1732.

Wilkieson's affair bearing that the presbytery's mind is that the minister call the said Charles Wilkisone and rebuke him wheresoever he appears in the church, and, withal, to intimate to him that he must ly under the scandal always and till he remove the same in common form as others have done.

Oct. 14. Booked Wm. M'Caul and Helen Moss, both in this parish; James Fisher, portioner of Darnick, cautioner.

,, 15. Collected by Andrew Drummond, John Mercer, and Wm. Milne, £3 : 2s. Scots.

,, 22. Thomas Bunzie and Agnes Mein in Newsteid, a.s.n. Andrew.

,, ,, Nicol Mercer and Agnes Steel in Melrose, a.s.n. Thomas.

,, ,, Alexr. Young and Helen Young in Gattonside ; a.s.n. Walter ; w. John Young, Robert Huntlie.
Collected by James Laidlay and Andrew Drummond, £2 : 10s. Scots.

,, 29. Collected by Wm. and Nicol Milne, £2 : 18s. Scots.

Nov. 5. Collected by Andrew Marr and Robert Scott, £2 : 16s. Scots.

,, 9. Adam Wallace and Jean Stewart in Blainslies, a.s.n. John.

,, ,, Wm Pringle and Margaret Tait in Blainslies, a.s.n. Robert ; w. John and James Wallace there.

,, 12. Collected by Andrew Drummond and Andrew Mein, £3 : 2s. Scots.

,, 14. Booked John Milne in this and Helen Brown in the parish of Crailing ; Nicol Milne, cautioner.
Item, Andrew Ormistown in this parish and Marion Ormistown in the parish of Smailholm ; Robert Ormistown in Melrose, cautioner.
Item, Andrew Pringle in this parish and Anna Brock in the parish of Earlestown ; Wm. Brown, portioner of Melrose, cautioner.

,, 18. Booked Wm. and Helen Hunters, both in this parish ; John Bowie, merchant, cautioner.
Item, Wm. Cook and Helen Hopkirk, both in this parish ; John Mein in Newsteid, cautioner.

,, 19. The minister intimated the sentence of the presbytry, concerning Mr Wilkisone.
Collected by Robert Scott and Wm. Hoy, £2 : 7s. Scots.

,, 26. George Martine and Agnes Wilson in Gattonside, a.d.n. Elizabeth ; w. John Young, Robert Gibsone, there.
Collected by Wm. Milne and Wm. Hoy, £2 : 8s. Scots.

,, 27. James Darling and Margaret Fairbairn in Blainslies, a.d.n.——; w. John Thin, Thomas Darling.

,, 29. Booked Robert Hog in the parish of Maxtone and Margaret Gillas in this ; Robert Johnstone, cautioner.

,, 30. Thomas Vair and Jean Mein in Newsteid, two sons named James and William ; w. James Mein, Robert Bunzie, there.

Dec. 2. Booked John Mein and Elizabeth Haliburtone, both in this parish ; James Mein, portioner of Newtown, cautioner.

,, 3. Collected by John Mabane and John Mercer, £3 : 8s. Scots.

,, 9. Booked George Mercer and Isobel Hunter, both in this parish ; Wm. Hunter, cautioner.
Wm. Morison and Margaret Atchison, both in this parish ; James Bowie in Melrose, cautioner.

,, 10. Collected by John Mabane, Wm. Dickson, and Andrew Mein, £5 : 2s. Scots.

,, 17. James Martine and Isobel Ellies in Gattonside, a.d.n. Isobel ; w. Wm. Martine, James Smail.
Collected by Wm. Milne and Wm. Hoy, £2 : 12s. Scots.

,, 19. Thomas Gray and Isobel Barry in Appletreeleaves, a.d.n. Marion ; w. John Fisher, Thomas Darling.

,, 24. Wm. Sandilands and Catharine Marr in Gattonside, a.d.n.——.

1732.

Dec. 24. James Purves and Margaret Scott in Old Melrose, a.d.n. Elizabeth ;
w. James Scott, Andrew Mein.

Collected by John Sibbald, £3 : 11s. Scots.

„ 31. Andrew and Catharine Mercer in Bridgend, a.s.n. Robert ; w. George
and Andrew Martines.

Collected by Andrew Mein and Robert Scott, £2 : 16s. Scots.

1733.

Jan. 7. Wm. Martine and —— Drummond in Gattonside, a.s.n. William.

„ „ John Bunzie and —— Wallace in Eildon, a.d.n. Margaret : w. Laird
Marr, Wm. Hoy.

Collected by Wm. Dickson, Andrew Drummond, and John
Mercer, £2 : 14s. Scots.

„ 14. Collected by John Sibbald, £1 : 18s. Scots.

„ 21. Collected by Wm. Milne, £2 : 3s. Scots.

„ 28. Wm. Mercer and Elizabeth Lumsdale in Gattonside, a.d.n. Agnes ;
w. George Martine, Wm. Mathison.

After prayer sederunt, the Minister, Drygrainge, John Mabane,
Wm. Hoy, &c., elders.

Collected by Andrew Drummond, £2 : 7s. Scots.

(Case of discipline against Alexr. Sandilands, who came from
the parish of Stow to this, att Martinmass last, and Margaret Ker,
his wife. The clerk is appointed to write to the session of Stow
anent this affair.

The session appoint Drygrainge, John Mabane, Robert Scott,
John Mercer to meet with the minister and clerk to inspect the
treasurer's accompts the 8th of next month.

Feb. 4. Collected by Robert Scott and Andrew Mein, £2 : 4s. Scots.

„ 8. This day Drygrainge, John Mabane, Robert Scott mett with the
minister and clerk and revised and approved the treasurer's
accompts, and they leave in his hand £546 : 1s. 6d. Scots, with
which he is to charge himself.

The minister this day gave in discharges for the high lowland
burses, as also an accompt of what he has disposed of the collection levied February 21st, 1728, extending to £76 : 5s. Scots, of
which sum was disposed of by the minister for necessary uses
narrated in the intimation, £39 : 10s. Scots, which the elders
appoint their clerk to attest under his hand.

„ 10. Booked Robert Penman and Christian Grahamslie, both in this
parish ; Robert Penman, elder, cautioner.

„ 11. This day the minister intimated a fast to be observed Wednesday
next, as appointed by the presbytry on account of an universal
sickness that rages.

Then baptised to ——

Robert Trotter and Margaret Mabane in Melrose, a.s.n. John.

„ „ Robert Grierson and Marion Wilson in Darnick, a.s.n. James.

„ „ John Haig and Margaret Duncan in Drygrainge, a.d.n. Jean : w.
John and Wm. Mabane.

Collected by Andrew Drummond and Wm. Hoy, £2 : 7s.
Scots.

„ 14. The fast day, collected by Wm. Milne and John Sibbald, £6 : 12s.
Scots.

„ 15. John Noteman and Margaret Purves in Langhaugh, a.d.n. Margaret.

„ „ James Crosbee and Agnes Haitlie in Housebyres, a.d.n. Helen ; w.
George Blaikie, Robert Williamson.

„ 18. Wm. Cook and Margaret Lawrie in Melrose, a.d.n. Elizabeth ; w.
George Lawrie, Alexr. Cook.

Collected by Nicol Milne and Andrew Mein, £2 : 7s. Scots.

„ 24. After prayer sederunt *pro re nata* the Minister, Drygrainge, John
Mabane, George Hoy, &c., elders.

(Case of discipline against James Dickson, miller of Melrose

1733.

milne and his wife.) Witnesses cited, Mary Keil, midwife, Mary Mein and Alison Gibson.

The Session considering the affair found that it could not inferr any censure and therefore ordered baptism to the child.

Feb. 25. James Dickson and —— Blaikie in Newsteid, a.d.n. Isobel ; w. John Mein, Andrew Mein, there.

Collected by John Mabane and Robert Scott, £2 : 6s. Scots.

Mar. 3. James Purves and Agnes Knox in Colmslie, a.d.n. Barbara ; w. Robert and John Laidlays.

,, 4. James Cessford and Isobel Cochran in Newtown, a.s.n. James.

,, ,, John Gordon and Margaret Walker in Darnick, a.d.n. Jannet ; w. Nicol Milne, Thomas Stenhouse.

Collected by Andrew Drummond and Andrew Mein, £2 : 16s. Scots.

,, 10. Booked in order for marriage John Brown and Agnes Spear, both in this parish ; John Spear in Newsteid, cautioner.

,, 11. Andrew Smith and Helen Boston in Gattonside, a.d.n. Margaret ; w. James Smith, Thomas Bostone.

After prayer sederunt, the Minister, Laird Marr, Wm. Hoy, John Wallace, Robert Scott, &c., elders.

Collected by John Mabane and Wm. Hoy, £2 : 9s. Scots.

This day the minister represented to the session that he was last week with George Wright in Gattonside who seems to be dying, and that the said George emitted the following declaration signed under his hand as follows—"I, George Wright, portioner of Gattonside, do hereby declare that whereas I have been often charged as being guilty of that hainous sin of adultery with Jannet Nisbet now married to David Umpherstone and have obstinately denyed the same for which I am heartily sorry, I do now for the easing of my conscience declare that I was guilty and this is my declaration. I subscribe without any constraint and in the full exercise of my judgment and reason, at Gattonside the 7th of March 1733, before these witnesses—Wm. Hoy, portioner of Gattonside, and George Beatie, portioner of Bridgend, and Andrew Marr, writer hereof *sic* subscribitur, George Wright, Wm. Hoy, witness, Andrew Marr, witness, George Beatie, witness."

,, 12. Alexr. Sandilands and —— in Buckholm, a.s.n. James ; w. George and Alexr. Scotts in Whitlaw.

Received from Walter Murray in Melrose, who has taken possession of a burial place, 12s. Scotts.

,, 17. Booked James and Agnes Mein, both in this parish ; James Mein in Newtown, cautioner.

,, 18. John Hoy and Alison Cunningham in Melrose, a.s.n. James.

,, ,, Thomas Hoy and Jannet Smith in Gattonside, a.s.n. William ; w. George Hoy, John Smith.

Collected by John Sibbald and Nicol Milne. £1 : 19s. Scots.

,, 25. Wm. Mabane and Isobel Ballentine in Melrose, a.d.n. Anne ; w. John and Thomas Mabane.

Received from Mungo Glendinning for the priviledge of a new burial place, 12s. Scotts.

Collected by Robert Scott, £2 : 1s. Scots.

,, 31. Booked Andrew Shillinglaw and Isobel Stuart ; Alexr. Gray, cautioner.

April 1. John Cochran and Helen Bartleman in Newtown, a.d.n. Mary.

,, ,, John Laidlay and Agnes Mein in Newtown, a.d.n. Isobel.

,, ,, Wm. Haliday and Margaret Atchison in Newsteid, a.d.n. Catharine.

,, ,, John Pringle and Margaret Young in Blainslies, a.d.n. Agnes ; w. Nicol Milne, Laird Marr.

,, ,, After prayer sederunt, the Minister, Drygrainge, Nicol Milne, Wm. Dickson, John Mabane, &c., elders.

Collected by John Wallace and Andrew Drummond, £2 : 18s. Scots.

1733.

This day Mr. Gavin Elliot, session clerk, gave in a lybel against Nicol Bowar, portioner of Newtown, the tenor whereof follows, complains Mr Gavin Elliot, schoolmaster and session clerk of Melrose, on Nicol Bowar, portioner of Newtown, that whereas the said Nicol sent yesterday to the complainer a pacquet of letters dated 30th of March last with a scrape of a letter therein inclosed which the said Nicol alleges reflects on him and averrs was sent by the complainer, which pacquet being directed to the complainer is stufft with the most inhumane, stupid, brutal, nonsensical, foolish, venomous and scurrilous expressions. As that the complainer is void of all virtue and everything that is good, filled with everything that is hatefull and abominable, giddy brained, below an ass, camel, jackmidding, montebank, merry Andrew, &c., and that it is not at all consistent he should serve this Court in the capacity of clerk, which the complainer conceives reflects very much on the session in general, as well as upon the complainer in particular; and though the substance of this pacquet is competent for the civil magistrate, yet the complainer judges, what so directly levels against the wisdom and prudence of the session in choosing and continuing him as clerk is specially to be reprehended by them; and further, that the drift of such foul opprobrious language is to be adverted to as tending to weaken the authority and credite of a teacher who should form and mould youth to the hopes of succeeding ages. The complainer cannot but take notice of the epethets given him upon the back of one of the said Nicol's letters; such as reverend, wise philosopher, learned Grecian and none such for arithmetick, with an hotch potch of nonsensical ribaldry, more like the product of a distracted brain, that ought to be hissed to Bedlam, or some other place competent for such, than of one who enjoys the conversation of sober and serious persons. Mr. Elliot having consigned 2s. 6d. was removed. Laird Marr chosen clerk *pro tempore*. Nicol Bowar being cited was called and compeared and owns the letters whereupon the lybel is founded to be his. The session finds the said lybel proven by the said letters. Mr. Elliot was called in and interrogate if the said scrape sent to him within Nicol's pacquet was his, denyed the same, which the defender offers to prove by witnesses, viz., Wm. Tutup, servant to John Cochran, shoemaker in Newtown, and Wm. Dickson, son to Wm. Dickson, smith in Darnick. The session adjourns this affair till to-morrow eight days.

The beadle is ordered to cite the two foresaid witnesses to the said session and parties are summoned *apud acta* to the said diet. The sederunt closed with prayer.

April 4. John Fisher and Isobel Scott in Langlee, a.d.n. May; w. Andrew Bryden, Laird Marr.

„ 8. Andrew Mein and Jannet Renaldson in Newtown, a.d.n. Elizabeth; w. Walter Scott, James Mein.

Collected by Wm. Dickson and John Mercer, £2 : 11s. Scots.

„ 9. This day after prayer sederunt, the Minister, Drygrainge, George Hoy, Nicol Milne, Robert Scott, Wm. Dickson, &c., elders.

This day appointed for enquiring into that affair of Nicol Bowar and Mr. Elliot. The said Mr. Elliot compeared and Nicol being called on, compeared not. An excuse was offered for him, to wit, this his grandmother lying a corpse he could not wait on the session this day. The session sustain this excuse. Mr. Elliot was removed and the session after some thought called Wm. Dickson, who compearing declared that he wrote that letter sent to Nicol Bowar, and that nobody else whatsomever advised him to it or had an hand in it, that he was very sorry he should have

1733.

delivered the same on the Sabbath day, and that no other is chargeable with the said letter. He was dismissed. The session also dismissed Wm. Tutup as wanting no evidence further than the said William Dickson had made. Mr. Elliot was called in and this intimate to him, and the session appoint Sabbath first as their next meeting, whereunto the said Nicol Bowar is ordered to be cited. The Sederunt closed with prayer.

April 15. After prayer sederunt, the Minister, Drygrainge, Andrew Mar, Wm. Dickson, John Wallace, &c., elders.

Collected by James Laidlay and Andrew Mein, £2 : 17s. Scots.

Nicol Bowar being called, compeared and being informed of William Dickson's declaration as above, was asked if he was sorry for his offence to Mr. Elliot. Answered he could not say he was, since he believed the letter he received had come from him. After much pains taken by the minister, he said he was sorry, but in such an indifferent, unpleasant way, as was not at all satisfying to the session. He is however dismissed for the time, and the sederunt closed with prayer.

„ 22. After prayer sederunt, the Minister, Drygrainge, Wm. Hoy, George Hoy, John Mabane, Robert Scott, &c., elders.

Collected by John Sibbald and John Mabane, £3 : 6s. Scots.

This day the session considering Nicol Bowar's behaviour last day, order him to be cited to the session this day eight days. The sederunt closed with prayer.

„ 23. John Sterling and Isobel Wilson in Blainslies, a.s.n. Robert.

„ „ John Lauder and Bessie Dickson in Mosshouses, a.d.n. Agnes ; w. John Wallace, Alexr. Gray.

„ 29. John Tait and Margaret Martine in Melrose, a.s.n. Robert.

„ „ Andrew Bartleman and Jannet Cochran in Newtown, **a.s.n.** John ; w. George and Andrew Martines.

After prayer sederunt, the Minister, Drygrainge, James Laidlay, John Wallace, Andrew Mein, &c., elders.

Collected by Robert Scott and Andrew Drummond, £3 : 9s. Scots.

Nicol Bowar was this day called, and compeared, and professed his sorrow for giving such an offensive letter to Mr. Elliot, and promised that he should do no such thing in time coming. He was sharply rebuked and dismissed.

May 6. Collected by William Milne and Andrew Mein, £2 : 14s. Scots.

„ 12. Booked Wm. Robson and Margaret Scott, both in this parish ; Thomas Bostone in Gattonside, cautioner.

„ 13. Michael Wallace and Isobel Blaikie in Melrose ; a.s.n. William.

„ „ Ad. Moffat and Isobel Howistown in Gattonside, a.d.n. Catharine : w. James Wallace, Laird Marr.

Collected by Nicol Milne and John Sibbald, £3 : 18s. Scots.

„ 15. Booked Archibald Fairbairn in the parish of Coldstream, and Elizabeth Davidson in this parish : John Brown in Melrose, cautioner.

„ 19. Booked Michael Andison and Isobel Deans, both in this parish ; James Speeding in Bridgend, cautioner.

„ 20. Collected by Robert Moffatt and Andrew Marr, £2 : 8s. Scots.

„ 27. Collected by James Laidlay and Andrew Drummond, £4 : 1s. Scots.

„ 30. Booked John Henry in the parish of Stow, and Elizabeth Walker in this ; John Gordon in Darnick, cautioner.

Alexr. Broomfield in the parish of Stitchill, and Isobel Mein in this parish ; Charles Frier in Gattonside, cautioner.

June 3. After prayer sederunt, the Minister, Drygrainge, Robert Moffatt, John Wallace, John Mabane, &c., elders.

Collected by Wm. Hoy and John Sibbald, £4 : 1s. Scots.

This day the minister and elders unanimously resolved that the sacrament of the supper shall be celebrated in this

1733.   place the second Sabbath next month, being the fifteenth day thereof.

June 8. Booked John Purves and Agnes Thin, both in this parish : George Shiel in Melrose, cautioner.

  „ 10. Thomas Williamson and Mary Mein in Newsteid, a.s.n. Robert ; w. John Mein, John Mercer, there.

          Collected by Robert Moffat and Andrew Mein, £2 : 10s. Scots.

  „ 17. Collected by John Sibbald and Andrew Marr, £1 : 5s. Scots.

  „ 24. Wm. Bunzie and Jannet Little in Newsteid, a.s.n. Thomas.

  „   „ George Scott and Isobel Tailor in Danieltown, a.s.n. Robert.

  „   „ George Mercer and ——— Knox Clackmae, a.d.n. Jannet ; w. Robert Scott, John Mein.

          Collected by Robert Moffatt and Robert Scott, £2 : 6s. Scots.

  „ 25. Thomas Hunter and Mary Martine in Melrose, a.s.n. William.

  „   „ ——— Frier and ——— in Buckholm, a.s.n. George ; w. Doctor Martine, George Martine.

July 1. The minister intimated the celebration of the supper in this place against this day fourteen days.

  „   „ After prayer sederunt, the Minister, Drygrainge, John Mabane, Wm. Hoy, &c., elders.

          Collected by Andrew Drummond and Wm. Hoy, £3 : 5s. Scots.

          (Case of discipline against Andrew Shillinglaw and his wife.)

  „   7. Booked George Frier and Jannet Ballentyne, both in this parish ; Robert Myles, portioner of Gattonside, cautioner.

  „   8. George Martine and Jannet Haliburtone in Melrose, a.s.n. Andrew.

  „   „ George Walker and Isobel Hogart in Melrose, a.d.n. Elizabeth : w. John Tait, James Smail.

          This day the minister intimated Thursday next as a day of fasting and humiliation before the sacrament.

          After prayer sederunt, the Minister, Drygrainge, James Laidlay, John Mabane, George Hoy, &c., elders.

          Collected by Andrew Drummond and James Laidlay, £4 : 6s. Scots.

          The session appointed Tuesday next for privy tryals and ordering things about the sacrament.

  „ 10. After prayer sederunt, the Minister, Drygrainge, John Mabane, Robert Scott, George and Wm. Hoys, John Sibbald, Nicol Milne, Andrew Marr, Andrew Drummond, John Mercer, John Wallace, elders.

          The elders present were severally removed by pairs, tryed, and approven, and encouraged to go on in the Lord's Work.

          The way of collecting and keeping the doors continued as last year.

          The elders were enjoined caution in distributing of tokens.

  „ 12. David Brown and ——— Dick in Blainslies, a.d.n. Agnes ; w. John Wallace, Wm. Darling, there.

Collected, Fast day,	-	-	-	£13 13 0
Collected, Saturday,	-	-	-	17 8 0
Collected, Lord's day,	-	-	-	34 6 0
Collected, Munday,	-	-	-	16 8 0
Sum of collections,	-	-	-	£81 15 0
Debursed to the poor of the parish, and poor recommended, &c.	-	-	-	44 2 0
				£37 13 0

          Which sum is appointed to be given in to the treasurer, wherewith he is to charge himself.

  „ 16. James Brotherstone and Euphan Dickson in Mosshouses, a.s.n. Thomas.

  „   „ Wm. Brown and Jean Dixon in Langshaw, Thomas : w. a.n s. Walter Thomson, James Purves.

N

1733.

July 21. Booked Nicol Bowar in this parish and Margaret Mein in the parish of Roxburgh ; John Milne, Brae, cautioner.

Item, Adam Tait and Margaret Mathison both in this parish ; Wm. Mathison in Gattonside, cautioner.

,, 22. Collected by Wm. Dickson, Nicol Milne and John Sibbald, £4 : 10s. Scots.

,, 29. Collected by Robert Scott, Wm. Hoy and Andrew Marr, £4 : 10s. Scots.

Aug. 5. Thomas Bunzie and Helen Bryden in Eildon, a.d.n. Margaret ; w. John Bunzie, John Sibbald.

Collected by Andrew Drummond and William Milne, £3 : 3s. Scots.

,, 12. Collected by John Sibbald and James Laidlay.

,, 15. Thomas Darling and Helen Thomson in Langhaugh, a.s.n. Alexr. ; w. Mr. Andrew Darling, George Blaikie.

,, 19. Adam Harvie and —— Leithen in Westhouses, a.s.n. Thomas.

,, ,, John Fairbairn and Bessie Flint in Melrose, a.d.n. Elizabeth ; w. John Bowie, Thomas Lukup.

Collected by Andrew Drummond and John Mercer, £2 : 6s. Scots.

,, 26. George and Jean Turners in Calfhill, a.s.n. Thomas.

,, ,, John Thomson and Margaret Martine in Gattonside, a.s.n. John ; w. George and Andrew Martines.

Collected by John Mabane and John Wallace, £2 : 11s. Scots.

Sept. 2. James Speeding and Margaret Mercer in Bridgend, a.d.n. Margaret ; w. Nicol Mercer, Andrew Drummond.

Collected by Wm. Milne and John Mercer, £2 : 9s. Scots.

,, 9. Collected by Nicol Milne and Andrew Mein, £3 : 4s. Scots.

,, 16. Robert Williamson and Agnes Scott in Westhouses, a.d.n. Anne.

,, ,, —— Darling and —— in Langlee, a.d.n. Marion : w. Wm. and Thomas Williamsons.

After prayer sederunt, the Minister, Drygrainge, Robert Scott, Wm. Milne, George Hoy, &c., elders.

Collected by John Sibbald and Andrew Marr, £3 : 5s. Scots.

In regard, Andrew Shillinglaw and his wife have not compeared they are appointed to be summoned to the session against this day fourteen days.

,, 21. Booked James Hunter and Isobel Gray, both in this parish ; Wm. Hopkirk in Melrose, cautioner.

,, 23. Collected by John Sibbald, Nicol Milne and John Mercer, £2 · 18s. Scots.

,, 30. After prayer sederunt, the Minister, Drygrainge, Wm. Milne, John Wallace, James Laidlay, &c., elders.

Collected by John Mabane, Andrew Mein, £2 : 2s. Scots.

Andrew Shillinglaw being cited, compeared, the session ordered him and his wife to compear Sabbath first and continue three days.

Oct. 3. John Scott and Mary Adamson in Darnick, a.s.n. George : w. John Smith, Wm. Stoddart, there

,, 4. George Forsyth and Jannet Blaikie in Colmslie, a.s.n. George ; w. John Coat, George Martine.

,, 7. Wm. Morison and Margaret Atchison in Danieltown, a.s.n. John.

,, ,, Thomas Darling and —— in Gattonside, a.s.n. Thomas ; w. Laird Marr, Robert Scott.

Collected by Laird Marr and Robert Scott, £3 : 5s. Scots.

,, 10. Booked Mr John Huggan in the parish of Langholm, and Mrs Jannet Paterson in this parish.

,, 14. After prayer sederunt, the Minister, Drygrainge, John Mabane, John Sibbald, &c., elders.

Collected by Wm. Hoy and Wm. Milne, £2 : 6s. Scots.

The session appoint Andrew Shillinglaw and his wife to be cited to the session this day eight days.

,, 21. Walter Gray and Margaret Gray in Melrose, a.s.n. James.

1733.

Oct. 21. George Atchison and Bessie Hopkirk in Melrose, a.d.n. Susanna.

„ „ George Chisholm and Margaret Welsh in Darnick, a.d.n. Anne ; w. John Mabane, Deacon Smail.

This day compeared Andrew Shillinglaw and Isobel Stuart for the first time and were admonished.

Collected by Andrew Drummond and John Sibbald, £2 : 8s. Scots.

„ 24. Richard Park and Margaret Pringle in Allanshaws, a.s.n. Thomas ; w. Robert Moffat, Thomas Park.

„ 28. This day Andrew Shillinglaw and his wife compeared for the second time.

„ „ Walter Rae and Christian Richie in Newtown, a.s.n. Walter : w. Nicol Milne, Thomas Stenhouse.

Collected by Wm. Milne and Andrew Marr, £2 : 13s. Scots.

Nov. 1. Robert Myles and Jannet Mathison in Gattonside, a.s.n. James ; w. Wm. Mathison, Charles Frier.

„ 4. After prayer sederunt, the Minister, Drygrainge, James Laidlay, John Mabane, &c., elders.

Collected by Andrew Drummond and Andrew Mein, £3 Scots.

Upon the report of Mrs Agnes Ellies, her marrying irregularly, the session appoint her and Mr Wright, to whom it is said she is married, to be summoned to the session against this day eight days.

„ 9. Booked George Grieve in this parish and Margaret Somervail in the parish of Ligerwood ; Hugh Grieve, cautioner.

„ 11. This day Andrew Shillinglaw and his wife compeared the third time, and were admonished and rebuked and paid their fine, £4 Scotts.

„ „ Andrew Pringle and Anne Broke in Melrose, a.s.n. William.

„ „ Thomas Vair and —— Wilson in Danieltown, a.s.n. George ; w. George and Robert Lawries.

The minister reported that Mr Wright came to him and promised him that within twenty days he and his wife should wait on the session.

Collected by Andrew Marr and Wm. Hoy, £2 : 7s. Scots.

„ 13. Booked Thomas Ormistown in this and Jannet Hay in the parish of Nenthorn ; Robert Ormistone in Melrose, cautioner.

Booked John Brown and Isobel Hunter, both in this parish ; Robert Johnstone in Melrose, cautioner.

„ 14. Andrew Shillinglaw and Isobel Steuart in Blainslies, a.d.n. Isobel ; w. James and John Stirlings there.

„ 18. Collected by Andrew Drummond and Wm. Hoy, £2 : 3s. Scots.

„ 25. George Mercer and Isobel Hunter in Darnick, a.d.n. Margaret : w. John Mercer, Wm. Hunter.

Collected by Wm. Milne and John Mercer, £8 : 17s. Scots.

„ 26. The minister yesterday, having informed the elders that Mr Wright had sent to acquaint him that he was willing to wait on the session when they pleased, he and his wife being summoned to the session this day, so, after prayer sederunt, the minister, George Hoy, John Mabane, Robert Scott, elders.

Mr Wright and Mrs Agnes Ellies being called, compeared. They were interrogate if married. Answered they were and produced their marriage lines, dated at Lauder the 31st of July last, signed James Strange, minister, before George Gibson and Walter Morison, witnesses. They were gravely rebuked, and Mr Wright gave in for the use of the poor of this parish £12 : 12s. Scotts.

„ 28. Henry Forrest and —— Robson in Westhouses, a.d.n. Isobel ; w. John Forrest, John Fisher.

„ 30. Booked James Lythgow in this parish and Isobel Riddell in the parish of Liliesleaf ; Thomas Marr, cautioner.

Dec. 2. This day the minister intimated a collection from house to house for encouraging the search for coal at Redpath.

After prayer sederunt, the Minister, Wm. Milne, Robert Moffat, John Sibbald, &c., elders.

Collected by John Mabane and Andrew Drummond, £1 : 16s. Scots.

The elders are appointed to go through their several quarters twixt and the end of this moneth.

The session considering that there are elders wanting in several places of the parish, the minister recommended to the several elders to consider whom in their respective quarters they can have the freedom to recommend for that office.

This day a petition from Robert Williamson, portioner of Gattonside, and Henry Forrest, portioner of Westhouses, was presented and read, craving that they may be allowed to mount a loft twixt the end of the mason's loft and the window in the Silverless isle, the consideration whereof was delayed.

Received testimonials from John Hislop, barber, as also from Helen Familtown.

Dec. 9. John Milne and —— Brown in Newtown, a.d.n. Isobel ; w. Nicol Milne, Thomas Stenhouse.

Collected by Wm. Hoy and Robert Scott, £2 : 15s. Scots.

„ 13. This day John Kirkwood and —— Tait in the parish of Stow, were married here and paid the dues.

„ 16. Robert Johnstone and Jean Gillas in Melrose, a.d.n. Jean ; w. Doctor Martine, John Tait.

Collected by Andrew Marr and John Mabane, £1 : 19s. Scots.

„ 23. James and Margaret Mein in Newsteid, a.d.n. Mary : w. Andrew Mein, Wm. Milne.

Collected by Andrew Mein and Wm. Milne. £2 : 12s. Scots.

„ 30. After prayer sederunt, the Minister, Drygrainge, John Mabane, Andrew Marr, &c., elders.

Collected by Wm. Hoy and Andrew Drummond, £2 : 6s. Scots.

The session appoint their moderator, John Mabane, Robert Scott to meet with their treasurer and clerk to-morrow and examine his accompts.

There was this day presented a petition from Thomas Marr, James Wadderstone of Newhouses, James Bowie, John Gill, Michael Wallace, Wm. Steel, James Williamson, Andrew Cook, Philip Fair, Wm. Brown, Nicol Bowar, Wm. Milne and Thomas Bunzie, fewars and tradsmen in the parish of Melrose, craving liberty to build a loft in the kirk above the weaver's loft or any other place most convenient for them and least prejudicial to others, the consideration whereof was delayed.

The session this day allowed one Christian Faudy, formerly Machometan, now Christian, recommended to the several synods by the commission of the General Assembly, a crown.

„ 31. This day mett conform to appointment, the minister, John Mabane, Robert Scott, with their treasurer and clerk.

There was this day produced by the minister £12 Scotts, given in by Wm. Henderson in the parish of Birnie, who fell heir to his sister in this parish.

The treasurer brought out the sum of collections at the sacrament, extending to £37 : 13s. Scotts.

The mortcloath and marriage money extends to £42 : 6s. Scotts. The balance of the charge exceeds the discharge since last clearance, £46 : 9s. Scotts.

Which sums laid together, viz. :—

Given in by Wm. Henderson,	-	-	£12	0	0
Communion money to be charged,	-	-	37	13	0
Carry forward.	-		£49	13	0

1733.

Brought forward,	£49	13	0
Mortcloath and marriage money, -	42	6	0
Balance of charge and discharge,	46	9	0
	£138	8	0

The treasurer having disposed of £32 : 17s. Scotts of bad copper coin at five pence per pound weight, which came only to £4 : 5s. Scotts. Which balance being defaulked from the added sum of £138 : 8s., there remaineth £108 : 3s. Scotts, which added to £546 : 1 : 6, formerly his charge, makes £654 : 4s. Scotts wherewith he is to charge himself, all proceedings being discharged.

The minister produced discharges of mason and wright work and barrowman work, as also of materials for the bridge of Darnick burn, extending to £32 : 19s. Scotts, which with £39 : 10s. Scotts formerly expended makes £72 : 9s. Scotts, which deduced from £76 lodged in the minister's hand for building the bridge of Darnick burn, and other things mentioned in the intimation, Feb. 21st, 1728, there remains in Mr. Miln's hand £3 : 11s. Scotts.

1734.

Jan. 2. Robert Hog and Isobel Drummond in Colmslie, a.s.n. Andrew.

„ „ James Brown and Jannet Waugh in Bentmilne, a.s.n. James ; w. James Purves, John Laidlay.

„ 5. This day mett att Eildon pro re nata. After prayer sederunt, the Minister, John Mabane, Nicol Milne and John Sibbald, elders.

Case of discipline against Elizabeth Mein, William Dryden (alleged), and Robert Speeding, taxman of Burnbraemilne of Bowden. . . . She was seriously admonished and exhorted, and gravely rebuked for accusing the innocent. The clerk is appointed to send an extract of this to Bowden.

„ 6. Collected by Nicol and Wm. Milns and Robert Scott, £3 : 2s. Scots.

„ 9. For best mortcloath to Isobel Sclatter, £2 : 4s. Scots.

„ „ For ditto to Jannet Wallace, £2 : 4s. Scots.

„ 12. James Dalgleish and Margaret Brown in Blainslie, a.s.n. James.

„ „ James Darling and Jannet Shiel in Clackmae, a.d.n. Margaret ; w. Alexr. Fisher, George Martine.

„ 13. Collected by Wm. Dickson and John Sibbald, £2 : 2s. Scots.

„ 14. Mortcloath for a child, 8s. Scotts.

„ 17. For ditto to a child, 8s. Scotts.

„ 19. For plush mortcloath to John Dods, £1 : 4s. Scots.

„ 20. William Hart and Margaret Mein in Newsteid, a.s.n. James ; w. John and Andrew Meins.

Collected by Andrew Mein and Wm. Mein and Wm. Hoy, £2 : 12s. Scots.

„ 27. Robert Halliwall and —— Nisbet in Gattonside, a.d.n. Elizabeth ; w. Andrew Marr, John Thomson.

Collected by Andrew Drummond and Wm. Milne, £2 : 10s. Scots.

Feb. 3. John Dalgliesh and Mary Darling in Darnick, a.s.n. George ; w. John and James Wallaces.

Collected by John Mabane and Andrew Mein, £2 : 12s. Scots.

„ 4. Best mortcloath to Jannet Fiddes, £2 : 4s. Scots.

„ 10. This day the minister read a recommendation of the General Assembly for a collection for building a bridge over the river Stincher in the parish of Colmonel which is to be levied in this parish Sabbath next.

Collected by John Wallace and Andrew Drummond, £2 : 0s. Scots.

Received a discharge from Christian Faudie for a crown formerly allowed him.

„ 11. Andrew and Marion Ormistones in Blainslies, a.s.n. Thomas ; w. Alexr. Gray, Thomas Ormistones.

1734.

Feb. 17. Robert Hog and Margaret Gillas in Melrose, a.d.n. Agnes ; w. Robert
          Johnstone, John Tait, there.
                Collected by Robert Scott, John Sibbald and John Mercer,
          £9 : 10s. Scots., to be disposed of as above.

  „   24. John Young and Margaret Gill in Gattonside, a.s.n James.

  „   „ Andrew Haitly and Alison Dawson in Danieltown, a.d.n. Isobel ; w.
          Andrew Dawson, elder and younger.
                Collected by Wm. Hoy and Andrew Drummond, £3 : 9s. Scots.

Mar. 3. Collected by John Mabane, Andrew Marr and Nicol Milne, £2 : 12s.
          Scots.

  „   10. Collected by John Sibbald and John Mercer, £3 : 10s. Scots.

  „   11. Little mortcloath to Agnes Hoy, 8s. Scots.

  „   13.   Ditto   to Mr Fisher's son, 12s. Scots.

  „   17. Collected by John Sibbald and Andrew Marr, £2 : 8s. Scots.

  „   24. James Cessford and Isobel Cochran in Newtown, a.d.n. Margaret ; w.
          Nicol Milne, Thomas Stenhouse.
                Collected by Robert Scott and William Hoy, £2 : 9s. Scots.

  „   27. Plush mortcloath to John Dods, elder, £1 : 4s. Scots.

  „   28.   Ditto   to Jean Leithhead, £1 : 4s. Scots.

  „   29. Booked Wm. Forson in the parish of Martown and Jannet Bunzie in
          this ; Wm. Bunzie in Newtown, cautioner.

  „   30. Booked Andrew Martine and Margaret Alexander, both in this parish ;
          John Tait in Melrose, cautioner.

  „   31. After prayer sederunt, the Minister, Drygrainge, Wm. Hoy, Andrew
          Marr, &c., elders.
                Collected by John Wallace and Andrew Drummond, £2 : 12s.
          Scots.
                Case of descipline against George Frier and his wife.
                The session appoints their meeting against Munday come
          eight days to inspect the bonds and bills due the poor, and to con-
          sider two petitions formerly given in.

April 1. Wm. Bailie and —— in Hagburn, a.s.n. Andrew ; w. James Hunter
          Alexr. Scott in Whitlaw.
                After prayer sederunt, the Minister, Drygrainge, John Mabane,
          Wm. Hoy, &c., elders,
                Collected by James Laidlay and Robert Moffatt, £2 : 11s. Scots.
                Upon information of Jannet Smail, present servant the Lady
          Whithaugh in Melrose, her scandalous behaviour upon Thursday
          night last. She is ordered to be summoned to the session
          to-morrow.

  „   8. After prayer sederunt, the Minister, Drygrainge, John Mabane,
          George Hoy, Robert Scott, John Wallace, John Mercer, Nicol
          Milne, John Sibbald, Andrew Mein, elders.
                The petitions above mentioned were this day considered, and
          the session, with consent of Drygrainge, Lady Isabella's bailie, did
          allow Robert Williamson and Henry Forrest to build and erect a
          loft in the place condescended upon in the petition, which loft is
          to be possessed by their two families in common, the session allways
          granting this, but prejudice of any having seats already, or of the
          window where they are to enter from without, and this the session
          orders to be recorded and extracts to be taken by the persons
          concerned.
                In the affair of the fewars and tradsmen, their petition,
          Drygrainge, Lady Isabella's bailie having some time ago acquainted
          the above petitioners that in case the fewars of Blainslies should
          choose the places they pitched on to build a loft for themselves,
          the said fewars were to be preferred. The people of Blainslies
          being informed of this, and of the session's meeting for that effect
          this day, there appeared none save Alexr. Gray and John Wallace,
          and that only for themselves. The above petitioners almost all
          appearing, insisted for a grant to their petition, representing the

1734.

inconvenience they were put to for want of accommodation this way. The session with the said bailie considering the affair, do allow them to build a loft, either above the weaver's loft, or in that space twixt the pulpit and the Lady's loft, if the people of Blainslies do not before the 1st of June next sett about the building in either of these rooms, and in case the said fewars of Blainslies should neglect to do the same, the above mentioned Alexr. Gray craves he may be allowed to join with the said tradsmen in building their loft in either of the said rooms, which desire was granted by the session and accepted of by the said tradsmen, whom the session do hereby allow to build a loft in either of these rooms, as the choise of the fewars of Blainslies shall determine, and that to be possessed by them and theirs in all time coming still but prejudice of such as already have seats. This, their act, they ordain to be recorded and extracts to be given.

Alexr. Gray, forsaid, alleging a pew might be got for him as part of his room amongst these pews beneath Huntliwood's loft, and tradsmen being called in to measure the same, found that room for one pew might be win if all the rest were adjusted to an uniform breadth, whereupon the session, with consent of the baihe, appoint and ordain these concerned in the forsaid seats to reduce and contract the forsaid pews to two foots breadth, whereby room will be got for one to Alexr. Gray, portioner of Blainslies, and that he is to fix and plant the said pew immediately behind Nicol Milne's, portioner of Newtown, to be possessed by him and his in all time coming. The session appoint this to be recorded and extracts to be given. The forsaid John Wallace, also alleged that room might be win at the east end of the area of the kirk for him to set down a furm in. The session, with the bailie and some tradsmen, went and viewed the place, and upon examination found that room might be had if the furms there stood a little closer, and if —— Martin's furm was reduced four inches of its breadth and its back stood straight up. The session therefore appoint accordingly, and appoint and ordain John Wallace, portioner of Blainslies, to plant a furm as the fourth from the passage of Mr. Wilkison's seat, to be possessed by him and his in all time coming, and appoints this their act to be recorded, and extracts to be given.

Case of discipline against Jannet Smail and Alexr. Brown continued. She was removed, and the session considering the affair, appointed that she should appear three several Lord's days in the publick place of repentance, and be rebuked but not dismissed till the session should be informed about the man whether married or unmarried. She was called in, admonished, and exhorted, and this intimate to her, and appointed to appear Sabbath first in manner forsaid.

The session have inventaried the bonds and bills due the poor's box, and the copy thereof under the clerk's hand given in to the treasurer. The method for recovering the money is to be considered next meeting of the session.

Plush Mortcloath for Wm. Sclatter, £1 : 4s. Scots.

April 8. George Frier and Jannet Ballentyne in Gattonside, a.d.n. Jannet ; sponsor, James Crosbie in Westerhousebyres ; w. John Marr, John Mercer.

,, 14. Wm. Steel and Elizabeth Walker, baxtor in Melrose, a.s.n. Robert.

,, ,, Thomas Trotter and Marion Henderson, baxtor in Melrose, a.d.n. Marion ; w. John Mabane, George Walker.

Collected by Robert Scott and John Wallace, £3 : 4s. Scots.
Jannet Smail compeared for the first time and was admonished.

,, 18. John Edgar and —— Grieve in Blainslies, a.s.n. William ; w. Alexr. Gray, William Thine, there.

1734.

April 21. Alexr. Broomfield and —— Mein in Gattonside, a.d.n. Isobel ; w. Laird Marr, Wm. Hoy.

      Jannet Smail compeared for the second time.

      After prayer sederunt, the Minister, Drygrainge, Wm. Hoy, John Mabane, &c., elders.

      Collected by Andrew Drummond and Andrew Marr, £2 : 15s. Scots.

      Case of discipline against Bessie Dickman, servant to Robert Laidlay in Colmsliehill, and John Laidlay in Colmsliehill.

      The session resolve that George Martine should go to everyone that is due the session money by bill or bond, and desire them to pay up their money else diligence will be used against them.

   ,, 28. Jannet Smail compeared the third time, and was rebuked but not dismissed.

      After prayer sederunt, the Minister, Drygrainge, Wm. Hoy, John Mabane, James Laidlay, &c., elders.

      Collected by Robert Moffatt, John Mercer, and Andrew Mein, £3 : 1s. Scots.

      John Laidlay and Bessie Dickman ordered to compear next day in the common place to be rebuked.

May   4. This day booked Andrew Renaldson in this parish and Jannet Scott in the parish of Ancrum ; Wm. Renaldson, cautioner.

      Booked John Anderson in the parish of Dalkeith and Elizabeth Fiddes in this ; Andrew Dawson, cautioner.

   ,, 5. Elizabeth Dickman compeared for the first time and was rebuked.

      Collected by Andrew Marr and John Sibbald, £2 : 15s. Scots.

   ,, 6. Thomas Watson and Isobel Cochran in Blainslies, a.d.n. Catharine.

   ,, ,, Thomas Dalgleish and Jannet Brown in Langshawmilne, a.d.n. Elizabeth.

   ,, ,, Thomas Young and Isobel Thomson in Mosshouses, a.s.n. Thomas ; w. Alexr. Gray, Wm. Thine.

   ,, 7. Plush Mortcloath to Mungo Glendinning, £1 : 4s. Scots.

   ,, 10. Booked James Wilson in this parish and Jannet Hislop in the parish of Galashiels ; John Hownam, cautioner.

   ,, 11. Booked Andrew Darling and Helen Fleeming, both in this parish ; Alexr. Cook, cautioner.

   ,, 12. Elizabeth Dickman compeared the second time.

   ,, ,, Nicol Mercer and Agnes Steel in Melrose, a.s.n. John.

   ,, ,, Walter Scott and Jannet Mein in Danieltown, a.s.n. Robert : w. Robert Scott, George Lawrie, there.

      Collected by James Laidlay and Andrew Drummond, £3 : 6s. Scots.

   ,, 19. Elizabeth Dickman compeared for the third time, and was rebuked and dismissed and gave in £1 : 10s. Scots.

      Collected by Robert Scott, John Mercer and Wm. Hoy, £2 : 8s. Scots.

   ,, 26. Robert Mercer and Anaple Ovens in Newsteid, a.s.n. Andrew.

   ,, . Adam Tait and Margaret Mathison in Darnick, a.s.n. Walter : w. Wm. Mathison, John Smith.

      After prayer sederunt, the Minister, Drygrainge, Wm. Hoy, John Mabane, Robert Scott, &c., elders.

      Collected by Andrew Marr and Andrew Drummond, £3 Scots.

      The session appoints Munday come eight days as a meeting for the elders, proposing whom they shall think fitt for being elders in their several quarters.

      The session resolves the sacrament of the supper shall be celebrate in this place the 14th of July next.

      Jannet Walker is ordered when called to make her publick appearance, and the minister is to baptise the child if he thinks fitt.

June 2. This day John Laidlay compeared in the forenoon for the first time and was rebuked.

1734.

    Jannet Walker, adulteress, compeared in sack cloath in the afternoon and was rebuked. She is ordered to give in £12 Scotts, or a bill for the same, and her child to be baptised.

    Collected by John Mercer, Robert Moffatt and John Sibbald, £2 : 9s. Scots.

June 3. After prayer sederunt, conform to a former appointment, the Minister, John Mabane, Nicol Milne, George Hoy, Robert Scott, elders.

    James Smail, Wm. Stoddart, Thomas Bowstone, Thomas Stenhouse, John Mercer, George Blaikie, Robert Laidlay, George Kolmainhouse, and James Fisher being proposed as elders, the minister is to speak with them.

,, 7. Booked Thomas Stenhouse in the parish of Lesudain and Agnes Milne in this ; Thomas Stenhouse, cautioner.

,, 9. Thomas Marr and Jean Craig in Melrose, a.s.n. John.

,, ,, William Brown and Christian M'Millian in Melrose, a.d.n. Jean ; w. John Mabane, Robert Trotter, there.

    Collected by Robert Scott, £2 : 4s. Scots.

    John Laidlay compeared for the second time.

,, 12. John Purves and Agnes Thin in Melrose, a.d.n. Margaret ; w. James Smail, George Martine.

,, 16. John Laidlay compeared the third time, was rebuked and dismissed and paid his fine, £2 : 10s. Scots.

,, ,, John and Mary Mein in Newsteid, a.d.n. Elizabeth ; w. Andrew Mein, James Williamson.

    Collected by Andrew Drummond and Wm. Hoy, £2 : 11s. Scots.

,, 17. James Edgar and Elizabeth Pringle in Blainslie, a.d.n. Anne ; w. Alexr. Gray, John Wallace.

,, 20. Plush mortcloath for Isobel Moffatt, £1 : 4s. Scots.

,, 22. John Laidlay and Elizabeth Dickman by fornication in Colmslichill, a.d.n. Anne ; w. David Wight, Andrew Martine.

,, 23. Thomas Speeding and Margaret Miles in Gattonside, a.d.n. Margaret ; w. Laird Marr, Robert Myles.

    Collected by John Sibbald and John Wallace, £4 : 5s. Scots.

,, 29. Mortcloath for Margaret Myles, £1 : 4s. Scots.

,, 30. David Tait and Isobel Speeding in Darnick, a.s.n. James.

,, ,, Robert Penman and Christian Grahamslie in Melrose, a.d.n. Jannet ; w. Robert Penman, James Fisher.

    This day the minister intimated the celebration of the sacrament of the supper in this place Sabbath come fourteen days, and gave suitable exhortations.

    Collected by John Sibbald and Andrew Marr, £3 : 3s Scots.

July 4. John Fisher and Isobel Scott in Langlee, a.s.n. John ; w. Andrew Bryden, George Martine.

,, 7. This day the minister intimated Thursday next as the humiliation day before the sacrament and gave proper directions.

,, ,, Robert Scott and Jannet Glendinning in Melrose, a.d.n. Anne.

,, ,, Thomas Vallance and Jean Waugh in Blainslies, a.d.n. Mary ; w. Alexr. Gray, John Wallace.

    After prayer sederunt, the Minister, Drygrainge, Wm. Hoy, Wm. Milne, &c., elders.

    Collected by James Laidlay, John Mercer and John Wallace, £4 : 14s. Scots.

    This day the session appointed Tuesday next for privy tryals and ordering other affairs.

,, 9. This day being appointed for privy tryals, after prayer sederunt, the Minister, Drygrainge, John Mabane, John Sibbald, Wm. Milne, Robert Scott, John Wallace, Andrew Drummond, Wm. Hoy, Nicol Milne, John Mercer, Andrew Mein, James Laidlay, Andrew Marr, George Hoy, elders.

    The elders present were severally removed by pairs, tryed and approven and encouraged to go on in the Lord's work.

1734.

The collections are to be gathered and doors kept as preceeding year. The minister adjoined caution in distributing the tokens.

July 11. James and Euphan Chisholm in Blainslies, a.d.n. Agnes; w. Alexr. Gray, Hugh Grieve.

„ 12. Best mortcloath to Jannet Runchiman, £2 : 4s. Scots.

Collected Fast day,	-	-	-	£10	4	0
Collected Saturday,	-	-	-	13	2	0
Collected Sabbath day,	-	-	-	26	2	0
Collected Munday,	-	-	-	13	0	0
Sum of collections,	-	-	-	£62	8	0
Debursed to the poor of the parish, poor recommended, &c.		-	-	45	18	0
				£16	10	0

Which sum is appointed to be given in to the treasurer, wherewith he is to charge himself.

„ 20. Booked Robert Lumsdain in the parish of Lauder and Elizabeth Grierson in this parish; Robert Grierson, cautioner.

„ 21. Collected by James Laidlay, John Sibbald and Andrew Marr, £3 : 11s. Scots.

„ 22. Alexr. Gray and Margaret Thin, portioner of Blainslies, a.d.n. Eupham; w. William Thin, G. Romanus.

„ 27. Booked Simon Haitlie and Marion Bunzie, both in this parish.

„ 28. Nicol Bowar and Margaret Mein in Newtown, a.s.n. Nicol; w. Thomas Stenhouse, Nicol Milne, there.

After prayer sederunt, the Minister, Drygrainge, John Mabane Nicol Milne, Andrew Marr, Robert Scott, &c., elders.

Collected by Andrew Marr and Andrew Drummond, £1 : 12s. Scots.

Case of discipline against Marion Bunzie and Simon Haitlie.

Aug. 4. Mr Gavin Elliot, schoolmaster, and Margaret Angus. a.d.n. Anne; w. Dr John Rutherford, Mr Paterson of Drygrainge.

This day the minister intimated a fast to be observed Wednesday next, appointed by the Commission of the General Assembly.

Collected by Andrew Marr and Robert Scott, £2 : 13s. Scots.

„ 7. The fast day collection by James Laidlay and Andrew Drummond, £5. Scots.

Mortcloath for William Dickson, £2 : 4s. Scots.

„ 8. Ditto to John Bunzie's child, 8d.

„ 11. William Mabane and —— Simpson in Newsteid, a.s.n. Walter; w. Wm. Slater, Wm. Renaldson, there.

After prayer sederunt, the Minister, Drygrainge, Nicol Milne, Robert Scott, Andrew Marr, &c., elders.

Collected by Robert Scott and Andrew Marr, £11 : 5s. Scots.

This day the session resolved that whoever erects seat or loft in the kirk shall give an acknowledgment to the poor of the parish.

Upon the report of Mr. Fisher of Westerhousbyres being married clandestinely with Mrs. Hannah Haig, daughter to the deceased Mr. Haig of Beemersyde, the session orders their beadle to cite Housebyres, and the said Mrs. Haig to the session this day eight days.

„ 13. Mortcloath for John Sibbald. a child, 8s. Scots.

„ 15. Ditto for William Steel's child, 8s. Scots.

„ 18. This day the minister read the abbreviate of the laws against vice and profaneness.

„ „ John Cochran and Helen Bartleman in Newtown, a.s.n. William; w. Thomas Stenhouse. Nicol Milne, there.

After prayer sederunt, the Minister, Drygrainge, John Mabane, Andrew Mein, Andrew Marr, Robert Scott, &c., elders.

Collected by James Laidlay and Andrew Mein, £4 : 3s. Scots.

1734.

Housebyres and Mrs. Haig being summoned sent word that he could not wait on the session, but that he would against this day eight days.

The sederunt closed with prayer.

Aug. 25. John Gordon and Margaret Walker in Darnick, a.s.n. James.

" " William and Helen Hunters in Melrose, a.d.n. Jean.

" " John Mack and —— Tudhope in Gattonside, a.d.n. Isobel : w. Dr. Martine, Robert Hunter in Melrose.

Collected by Robert Scott, £2 : 10s. Scots.

Sept. 1. After prayer sederunt, the Minister, Drygrainge, John Mabane, Andrew Mein, Nicol Milne, &c., elders.

Collected by Andrew Marr and John Wallace, £2 : 1s. Scots.

No excuse being offered for Housebyres' noncompearance the session order him to be summoned pro 2ndo to the session this day eight days.

" 7. Mortcloath for Marion Turnbull, £1 : 4s. Scots.

" 8. John Spear and Alison Gibson in Newsteid, a.d.n. Janet ; w. John and Andrew Meins there.

After prayer sederunt, the Minister, Drygrainge, Robert Scott, John Wallace, Andrew Drummond, &c., elders.

Collected by Andrew Drummond and Nicol Milne, £2 : 4s. Scots.

Housebyres not being summoned as appointed last session the officer not being well, and not compearing this day, the appointment to cite him pro 2ndo is continued.

" 10. Mortcloath to Agnes Rutherfurd, £1 : 4s. Scots.

" 15. John Lauder and Elizabeth Dickson in Kedzliedoors, a.d.n. Catharine ; w. Mungo Park, Laird Marr.

After prayer sederunt, the Minister, Drygrainge, Andrew Marr, James Laidlay, Nicol Milne, Robert Scott, &c., elders.

Collected by William Hoy and William Milne, £3 : 6s. Scots.

Housebyres and Mrs. Haig being summoned pro 2ndo were called but compeared not. The minister informs the session that he conversed with them, but found them altogether against compearing before the session. The session orders them to be summoned against this day eight days pro 3tio.

" 22. James Laing and Agnes Richie in Melrose, a.d.n. Agnes ; w. William Hopkirk, John Corsar.

Simon Haitlie and Marion Bunzie compeared for the first time and were rebuked.

After prayer sederunt, the Minister, Drygrainge, John Mabane, William Milne, William Hoy, Andrew Mein, &c., elders.

Collected by Andrew Drummond, £1 : 6s. Scots.

Housebyres and Mrs. Haig being cited pro 3tio to this day's session were called, but compeared not. The session resolve to give them a month's time to advise of the affair before they extract the same, in order to lay it before the presbytry.

" 27. Booked Alexr. Vair and Janet Wilson, both in this parish : Thomas Vair, cautioner.

" 29. Simon Haitlie and Marion Bunzie, compeared for the second time.

" " Collected by Robert Scott, £2 : 5s. Scots.

Mortcloath to Isobel Leadhouse, £2 : 4s. Scots.

Oct. 5. Booked Peter Legg in the parish of Selkirk and Margaret Frier in this parish ; Walter Murray, cautioner.

" 6. William Blyth and Helen Tailor in Gattonside, a.s.n. Walter.

" " James Henderson and Isobel Halliwall in Gattonside, a.s.n. James : w. Andrew Marr, Robert Halliwall there.

Collected by John Sibbald and Andrew Drummond, £2 : 8s. Scots.

" 7. John Johnstone and Isobel Ballentyne in Williamlaw, a.s.n. Thomas ; w. John Fisher, George Chisholm.

1734.

Mortcloath to Isobel Hoy, £2 : 4s. Scots.
Mortcloath to Francis Bunzie, a child, 8s. Scots.
Best mortcloath for John Wallace, £2 : 4s. Scots.

Oct.   12. Booked John Moss and Mary Mein, both in this parish ; William
Milne, cautioner.
Mortcloath to Isobel Haliburtone's child, 8s. Scots.

„   13. William Hog and Agnes Hardie in Darnick, a.d n. Agnes ; w. William
Stoddart, James Dickson, there.
Simon Haitlie and Marion Bunzie appeared the third time,
were rebuked and dismissed.
Collected by Andrew Mein and William Milne, £2 Scots.

„   14. Simon Haitlie and Marion Bunzie in Melrose, a.s.n. Andrew ; w.
Andrew Mein, George Martine.

„   19. Booked in order for marriage Philip Fair in this parish and Alison
Stevenstone in the parish of Smalholm : John Young cautioner.

„   20. After prayer sederunt, the Minister, Drygrainge, Wm. Hoy, John
Mabane, Nicol Milne, &c., elders.
Collected by William Milne, £3 : 6s. Scots.
The minister delivered in £3 Scots he received at the synod,
as arrears due Mr. Duncansone.
The session appoints Munday come fourteen days for clearing
their accounts, and do appoint Drygrainge, Robert Scott and John
Mabane to meet with the minister and clerk for that end.

„   25. Booked John Romanus in the parish of Lauder and Marion Darling
in this parish James Darling, cautioner.

„   „ Booked James Paterson in the parish of Earlestown, and Isobel Bell
in this ; William Bell, cautioner.
Item, booked George Martine and Agnes Fair, both in this
parish ; John Young, cautioner.
Mortcloath to George Wallace, a child, 8s. Scots.

„   27. John Grieve and Margaret Thomson in Westerlanglee, a.s.n.
Thomas ; w. John Fisher, G. Martine.
Collected by Andrew Drummond, £2 : 3s. Scots.

Nov.   3. After prayer sederunt, the Minister, Drygrainge, John Mabane,
Robert Scot, Andrew Mein, &c., elders.
Collected by Andrew Mein and John Sibbald, £3 : 3s. Scots.
Thomas Darling, portioner of Appletreeleaves, in name of the
rest of the fewars of Appletreeleaves and Langhaugh applyed to
the session for their consent to build a loft for themselves above
the new loft bewest the ladies' loft, they having her Ladyship's
bailie's consent thereto. The session does go in with the same,
only if James Fisher of Sorrowlessfield apply to them for a
share of the same within a month, they are to take him in as a
sharer.
Received testimonials for Margaret White, Jean Lawrie and
Agnes Gray.

„   4. This day mett conform to appointment, Drygrainge, John Mabane,
Robert Scot, the minister and clerk, and revised the treasurer's
accompts. They find the charge exceed the discharge £45 : 9s.
Scots. There was given in of the remains of the sacrament money
£16 : 10s. There was also given in of mortcloath and marriage
money, £34 : 1 : 6, which in all makes £96 : 1 : 6. This added to
£654 : 4s. makes £750 : 5 : 6, wherewith the treasurer is to
charge himself.
The minister gave in a discharge for £9 Scots collected for the
bridge of Stauchar.

„   7. James Hunter and Isobel Gray in Whitlaw, a.s.n. James ; w. Robert
Lees, Wm. Bailie, there.

„   8. Patrick Bulman and Agnes Cochran in Newtown, a.s.n. Andrew ; w.
Nicol Milne, Thomas Stenhouse, there.

„   10. Collected by Andrew Marr and Wm. Milne, £2 : 14s. Scots.

1734.

Nov. 12. Booked Edward Turner and Margaret Wilson, both in this parish ; George Blaikie, cautioner.

„ 13. Mortcloath for Janet Haliburtone, £2 : 4s. Scots.

„ 15. Booked George Stirling in this parish and Grisal Runchaman in the parish of Ligerwood : John Stirling, cautioner.

„ 17. Collected by Robert Scot and Wm. Hoy, £2 : 15s. Scots.

„ 21. Thomas Hoy and Jannet Smith in Gattonside, a.d.n. Margaret : w. Andrew Marr, Wm. Hoy.

„ 23. Mortcloath for John Fairbairn's child, 8s. Scots.

„ 24. Collected by Andrew Drummond, £1 : 17s. Scots.

Dec. 1. John Brown and Isobel Hunter in Melrose, a.s.n. David ; w. Robert Johnstone, Andrew Martine.

Collected by Robert Scot and Andrew Drummond, £2 Scots.

„ 7. Booked Andrew Henderson in this parish and Janet Mack in the parish of Gordon : John Thomson, cautioner.

„ 8. James Dickson and Janet Blaikie in Newsteid, a.d.n. Helen ; w. John Mein, John Spear.

After prayer sederunt, the Minister, Drygrainge, Andrew Mein, Andrew Marr, John Mabane, Robert Scot, &c., elders.

Collected by William Milne, £2 : 12s. Scots.

The beadle is appointed to order George Frier and his wife to appear for their antenuptial fornication this day eight days.

It was represented for James Fisher of Sorrowlessfield that he craved the session's concurrence to have a share of the loft to be built by the fewars of Appletreeleaves. The session appoint him this day eight days to appear for the said suit himself.

„ 9. Andrew Pringle and —— in Blainslies, a.d.n. Janet : w. John Fisher, John Forrest.

„ 10. Mortcloath for John Purves, child, 8s. Scots.

„ 15. This day the minister intimated a recommendation of the synod for a collection to assist in building a meeting house for the dissenting congregation of Falstone on North Tyne which is to be gathered this day eight days, as also for relieving a poor man in Faldonside that had his house burnt.

After prayer sederunt, the Minister, Drygrainge, Wm. Hoy, Nicol Milne, John Sibbald, John Mercer, Andrew Mein, &c., elders.

Collected by John Sibbald, £2 : 12s. Scots.

James Fisher of Sorrowlessfield compeared and craved the session's concurrence for a share of that loft to be built by the fewars of Appletreeleaves, which the session complyed with, and granted that he should come in as a partner with them.

George Frier is appointed to be summoned pro 2[nd]o to appear with his wife for their antenuptial fornication.

„ 16. This day mett at the desire of George Hoy, treasurer, in a weak state of body to take in his accompts, the minister, John Mabane, Robert Scot, with their clerk, and having compeared charge with discharge since last clearance, they find he has debursed £13 : 1s. Scots more than he has received, which deduced from £750 : 5s., that was to be accompted for by him, makes remaining in his hand £737 : 4s., which money being told over by the minister and elders in the presence of John Hoy, brother to the said George, amounted to £670 : 13s., which with £48 lent by the session's consent by the said treasurer makes £718 : 13s., this coming short of the sum chargeable upon the treasurer, £18 : 11s. was intimate to the said George by the minister. There was £9 : 6s. of white money and £10 : 13s. of brass coin lodged in George Martine's hand for the present exigeness of the parish ; the rest, consisting of 24 guineas and £29 sterling, was put up in bags till the session consider what way it is to be disposed of. All other papers belonging to the session were also received.

„ 21. Mortcloath for Margaret Pearson, £2 : 4s. Scots.

1734.
Dec. 22. George Frier and his wife appeared for the first time and were
          rebuked.
                Collected by John Mabane and Andrew Marr, for the purposes
                intimated day eighth days, £21 : 10s. Scots.
  „   23. George Blaikie and Mary Gray in Langhaugh, a.d.n. Janet ; w.
          Thomas Darling, James Blaikie.
  „   26. James Fisher and Isobel Wight of Sorrowlessfield, a.d.n. Isobel ; w.
          Andrew Marr, Alexr. Fisher.
  „   27. Mortcloath to John Mart's child, 8s. Scots.
  „   29. George Frier and his wife appeared for the second time.
                Collected by William Milne and Laird Marr, £2 : 6s. Scots.

1735.
Jan. 4. Mortcloath for Alison Hog, £2 : 4s. Scots.
  „   5. George Frier and his wife appeared for the third time and were
          dismissed.
                After prayer sederunt, the Minister, Drygrainge, John Mabane,
                William Hoy, John Mercer, John Sibbald, Andrew Mein, &c.,
                elders.
                Collected by Robert Scot and John Mercer, £2 : 10s. Scots.
                The minister reports that he has conversed with Housebyres,
                who says he cannot get the testificate of his marriage from Mr.
                Robison who married them.
                The session referrs this division of the collection gathered
                22nd ult. to the minister's direction.
  „   10. Alexr. and Janet Bells in Melrose, a.s.n. James ; w. Robert Ormistone,
          Andrew Martine, there.
  „   11. Mortcloath to Helen Mathison, 12s. Scots.
  „   12. John Laidlay and Agnes Mein in Eildon, a.d.n. Agnes ; w. Mungo
          Laidlay, Nicol Milne.
                Collected by Andrew Mein, £2 : 6s. Scots.
  „   19. John Smith and Margaret Wight in Darnick, a.s.n. John ; w. John
          Smith, James Wight, there.
                After prayer sederunt, the minister, Drygrainge, William Hoy,
                William Milne, John Mercer, &c., elders.
                Collected by Wm. Hoy and Wm. Milne, £2 : 8s. Scots.
                The minister gave in a receipt for 13s. sterling, given to Blyth
                in Faldonside, and another for 2s. 6d. to one in Robertone parish.
                The session have this day resolved to lend to Andrew Marr,
                portioner of Gattonside, what money they can spare belonging to
                the poor upon heretable security.
  „   24. This day Andrew Marr, portioner of Gattonside, gave in an heretable
          bond to the session for £54 sterling, which exhausts the sum
          lodged in the box, except 4s. sterling, which with the said bond
          was laid up in the box.
  „   26. Robert Trotter and Margaret Mabane in Melrose, a.d.n. Barbara.
  „   „ James Lythgow and Margaret Riddell, there, a.s.n. James ; w. John
          and William Mabanes.
                Collected by Andrew Marr and Andrew Drummond, £2 : 2s.
                Scots.
Feb. 1. Booked Robert Turnbull and Isobel Shiel, both in this parish :
          William Atchison, cautioner.
                Mortcloath to Jean Hunter, a child, 10s. Scots.
  „   2. Andrew Mein and Janet Renaldson in Newtown, a.d.n. Agnes ; w.
          Thomas Stenhouse, James Mein, there.
                Collected by Nicol Milne and John Mercer, £2 : 9s Scots.
  „   3. William Moffatt and Elizabeth Moffatt in Ouplaw, a.s.n. John.
  „   „ John Murray and Grisel Alley in Williamlaw, a.s.n. John.
  „   „ William Smail and Janet Sandilands in Langhaugh, a.s.n. James.
  „   „ John Mann and Agnes Ruth in Williamlaw, a.d.n. Barbara ; w. James
          Purves, Robert Moffatt.
  „   9. Collected by John Sibbald and Andrew Drummond, £2 : 9s. Scots.

1735.

Feb. 12. George Martine and Agnes Wilson in Gattonside, a.s.n. James ; w. John Marr, Alexr. Young, there.

,, 16. Collected by Andrew Marr and James Laidlay, £2 : 9s. Scots.
Mortcloath for John Moody ——.

,, 23. Andrew Forsan and —— Mabane in Drygrangemiln, a.d.n. Margaret ; w. John and Andrew Mein.

After prayer sederunt, the Minister, Drygrainge, John Mabane, Andrew Mein, John Sibbald, Nicol Milne, Robert Scot, &c., elders.

Collected by Andrew Marr, £1 : 12s. Scots.

Margaret Tait in Melrose having brought forth a child as is reported to Thomas Mabane, son to John Mabane in Melrose, the beadle is appointed to cite them both to the session against this day fourteen days.

Mr. Fisher of Housebyres having given no satisfaction to the session about the irregular marriage, the session referrs the whole affair to the presbytry of Selkirk that is to meet at Selkirk the 4th of March next, and the clerk is appointed to extract the same for that end.

,, 28. Booked George Walker in this and Anne Pringle in the parish of Earlestown ; Andrew Pringle, cautioner.

Mar. 2. John Cochran and Margaret Mein in Eildon, a.d.n. Agnes.

,, ,, John Haig and Margaret Duncan in Newsteid, a.d.n. Margaret ; w. John Sibbald, John Mein.

After prayer sederunt, the Minister, Drygrainge, John Mercer, John Sibbald, John Mabane, Robert Scot, &c., elders.

Collected by Robert Scot and Andrew Drummond, £2 : 11s. Scots.

Case of discipline against Robert Mercer in Newsteid and Agnes Yorkstone there.

Drygrainge appointed to wait on the session, Tuesday next.

,, 5. John Pringle and Margaret Young in Blainslies, a.s.n. John : w. John Wallace, William Thine.

,, 9. After prayer sederunt, the Minister, Drygrainge, Andrew Mein, William Milne, William Hoy, Andrew Marr, Nicol Milne, &c. elders.

Collected by John Sibbald and Andrew Mein, £2 : 8s. Scots.

Case of discipline against Margaret Tait and Thomas Mabane continued.

Case of discipline against Agnes Yorkstone and Robert Mercer continued.

,, 10. Mortcloath to Agnes Napier, £1 : 4s. Scots.

,, 16. Thomas Bunzie and Agnes Mein in Newsteid, a.s.n. Robert.

,, ,, Walter Rae and Christian Richie in Newtown, a.d.n. Margaret.

,, ,, James Crosbie and Agnes Haitlie in Housebyres, a.d.n. Hanna ; w. Thomas Stenhouse, Nicol Milne.

Mary Tait appeared for the first time and was rebuked.

After prayer sederunt, the Minister, Drygrainge, John Mabane, John Sibbald, James Laidlay, Robert Moffatt, &c., elders.

Collected by John Mercer and Andrew Drummond, £1 : 18s. Scots.

Case of discipline against Agnes Yorkstone and Robert Mercer continued.

,, 23. Margaret Tait appeared the second time.

After prayer sederunt, the Minister, Drygrainge, William Hoy, John Sibbald, John Mabane, Robert Scot, &c., elders.

Collected by Robert Scot and Andrew Marr, £2 : 8s. Scots.

In the affair of Robert Mercer and Agnes Yorkstone, nothing having cast up but that she accuses him, and he accuses her, the session was of the mind that they should be called and rebuked and discharged converse with one another. She was accordingly

1735.

called in, seriously admonished, gravely rebuked, and discharged converse with the said Robert with certification. Robert was also called, admonished, rebuked, and discharged with the said Agnes, then dismissed.

Mar. 26. Best Mortcloath to James Bostone, Wynd, £2 : 4s. Scots.

,, 29. Booked Alexander Strachan and Mary Mein, both in this parish ; William Mein, cautioner.

,, 30. Walter and Margaret Grays in Melrose, a.s.n. James.

,, ,, William Milne and Elizabeth Mein in Darnick, a.d.n. Isobel ; w. John Mercer, Robert Milne.

Margaret Tait compeared for the third time, was rebuked and dismissed. She paid in £1 : 10s. Scots.

Collected by William Milne, £2 : 8s. Scots.

,, 31. John Coat and Agnes Purves in Langshaw, a.s.n. Robert ; w. James Laidlay, Wm. Atchison.

April 6. Mortcloath to John Milne's child, 8d.

,, ,, Robert Grierson and Marion Wilson in Darnick, a.s.n. George ; w. Wm. Wilson, Thomas Vair.

Thomas Mabane appeared for the first time, and was rebuked for his sin of fornication with Margaret Tait.

This day the minister gave in a discharge for 20s. sterling for the dissenting congregation of Falstone, collected December 22nd last.

Collected by Andrew Drummond and Andrew Mein, £1 : 4s. Scots.

,, 13. James Craig and Helen Peper in Melrose, a.d.n. Isobel ; w. Wm. Bain, Wm. Steel.

Thomas Mabane compeared for the second time.

Collected by John Sibbald and Wm. Milne, £2 Scots.

,, 17. Mortcloath to Eupham Leadhouse, £1 : 4s. Scots.

,, 18. Mortcloath to Isobel Milne, a child, 8s. Scots.

,, ,, Adam Harvie and Isobel Leithen in Westhouses, a.s.n. Mungo ; w. George and Andrew Martines.

,, 20. Andrew Renaldson and Janet Scot in Darnick, a.s.n. James.

,, ,, Thomas Mabane in fornication with Margaret Tait in Melrose, a.d.n. Isobel ; w. John Mercer, William Renaldson.

Thomas Mabane compeared the third time, and was rebuked and dismissed, and paid in £2 : 10s. Scots.

Collected by Robert Scot, Andrew Drummond, £1 : 15s. Scots.

Mortcloath to John Hog's child, 8s. Scots, by ditto for a burial place, 12s. Scots.

Mortcloath to Alexr. Ellie's child, 8s. Scots.

,, 24. Alexr. Strachan and Mary Mein, married in the manse, 12s. Scots.

,, ,, James Martine and Margaret Ellies in Gattonside, a.d.n. Elizabeth ; w. Wm. Blyth, Wm. Martine.

,, 27. William Mabane and Isobel Bannatyne in Melrose, a.s.n. Adam.

,, ,, Andrew Martine and Margaret Alexander in Melrose, a.s.n. Andrew.

,, ,, Robert Waddell and Agnes Turner in Buckholm, a.s.n. William ; w. John Mabane, George Martine.

Collected by John Wallace and John Mercer, £2 : 12s. Scots.

May 4. Collected by William Hoy and Robert Moffat, £2 : 5s. Scots.

,, 6. Mortcloath to Isobel Milne, £2 : 4s. Scots.

,, ,, Ditto to Anne Scot, a child, 8d.

,, 9. Booked James Atchison in this and Janet Davidson in the parish of Earlestown ; William Mein, cautioner.

,, 10. Mortcloath to George Hoy, £2 : 4s. Scots.

,, ,, Ditto to Alexr. Fisher, £2 : 4s. Scots.

,, 11. Collected by James Laidlay and John Mabane, £3 : 19s. Scots.

,, 16. Booked John Mitchelhill in this and Mary Chisholm in the parish of Galashiels ; Richard Park, cautioner.

Item, William Thin in the parish of Lauder and Eupham Smith in this parish ; John Tait, cautioner.

1735.

May 18. Collected by Andrew Drummond and William Milne, £5 : 1s. Scots.

" 23. Booked John Mein in the parish of Galashiels and Isobel Familtone in this parish ; James Mein, cautioner.

" 24. Booked William Martine and Jean Grieve, both in this parish ; Thomas Darling, cautioner.

Item, William Haliday in this parish and Elizabeth Dickman in the parish of Earlestown ; William Bailie, cautioner.

Mortcloath to Elizabeth Martine, a child, 8d.

" 25. Collected by Andrew Mein and John Sibbald, £2 : 9s. Scots.

" 28. Booked John and Elizabeth Stirling, both in this parish ; James Stirling, cautioner.

" 30. Mortcloath to William Elliot, Mr. Elliot's child, 12s. Scots.

" 31. Ditto to Nicol Mercer's child, 8s. Scots.

June 1. After prayer sederunt, the Minister, Drygrainge, John Wallace, William Hoy, William Milne, Robert Moffatt, &c., elders.

Collected by Andrew Marr and John Mercer, £2 : 14s. Scots.

John Hoy, John Bell, and James Sandilands are ordered to be cited to the session this day fourteen days, as having profaned the Lord's day.

" 3. Thomas Thomson and Margaret Hog from Stow, married here, gave in 12s. Scots.

" 6. James Burnet and Margaret Skirven in Darnick, a.s.n. Andrew ; w. James Wight, James Stoddart.

" 8. Robert Thomson and Magdalene Hope in Drygrainge boathouse, a.s.n. John.

" " Andrew Pringle and Anne Brock in Melrose, a.d.n. Janet ; w. Walter Murray, Alexr. Cook.

Collected by John Mercer and Andrew Drummond, £2 : 8s. Scots.

" 15. John Hoy and Alison Cunningham in Melrose, a.s.n. Andrew.

" " James Hart and Agnes Thomson in Gattonside, a.s.n. John ; w. Andrew Marr, William Hoy.

After prayer sederunt, the Minister, Drygrainge, John Mercer, William Hoy, Andrew Marr, Andrew Drummond, &c. elders.

Collected by James Laidlay and Robert Scot, £3 : 1s. Scots.

James Sandilands and John Bell being summoned were called and compeared, and interrogate if present when John Hoy turned over an hay stack in the minister's yard about three weeks ago in the time of Divine Worship, answered they were, and that they frequently forbad him, but he would do it, and said it was the last ill turn he was to do about the town. They were exhorted to a strict observance of the Lord's Day, and dismissed. Then John Hoy was called and compeared with what is above emitted and and did not deny the same. He was removed, and the session considering the affair, thought proper he should be called in and rebuked instantly with certification. He was called in and the same accordingly done.

The session have agreed that the sacrament of the supper shall be given here the 13th next moneth.

" 17. Andrew Darling and Margaret Fleeming in Blainslies, a.d.n. Mary ; w. Alexr. Gray, William Thin.

" 20. Mortcloath for William Thin's daughter, £1 : 4s. Scots.

" 22. Collected by Nicol Milne and John Sibbald, £3 : 1s. Scots.

" 29. The minister intimated the celebration of the sacrament of the supper in this place, this day fifteen days, the 13th next moneth.

Collected by Wm. Hoy and Andrew Mein, £2 Scots.

July 6. John Anderson and Elizabeth Fiddes in Melrose, a.d.n. Janet ; w. John Fiddes, Andrew Dawson.

The minister intimated Thursday next, the fast before the sacrament.

1735.

After prayer sederunt, the Minister, Drygrainge, John Mabane, Robert Scot, Andrew Mein, &c., elders.

Collected by John Mabane and Andrew Marr, £3 : 6s. Scots.

The session appointed Thursday next for privy tryals and ordering about the distribution of tokens.

Mortcloath for Marion Wright, £1 : 4s. Scots.

July   8. This day being appointed for privy tryals, after prayer sederunt, the Minister, Drygrainge, John Mabane, Robert Scott, William Hoy, Andrew Marr, Andrew Drummond, Nicol Milne, James Laidlay, and John Sibbald, elders.

The elders present were removed by pairs, tryed and approven, and encouraged to go on in the Lord's work.

Collections to be gathered on Thursday by Andrew Marr and Andrew Drummond at the south door ; John Mercer and Andrew Mein at the west door ; James Laidlay at the north door.

Saturday.

Robert Moffat at the east stile.

Andrew Marr at the minister's entry to be continued.   Andrew Mein at the south door.   Robert Scot at the south stile.   James Laidlay and John Wallace at the west stile.

The collections Lord's Day and Monday to be gathered as formerly, and doors kept as preceeding years.

The elders were enjoined circumspection in the distribution of tokens.

The sederunt closed with prayer.

Collection, Fast Day,	-	-	-	-	£10 4 0
Collection, Saturday,	-	-	-	-	11 8 0
Collection, Sabbath Day,	-	-	-	-	19 0 0
Collection, Monday,	-	-	-	-	11 0 0
Sum of collections,	-	-	-	-	£51 12 0
Debursed to the poor of the parish to poor recommended, &c.	-	-	-	-	34 16 0
					£16 16 0

Which is appointed to be given in to the treasurer, wherewith he is to charge himself.

,,   16. Mortcloath to Thomas Trotter's child, 8d.

,,   20. Thomas Hunter and Mary Martine in Melrose, a.s.n. Thomas :   w. Doctor and George Martine.

Collected by John Sibbald and John Mercer, £4 : 2s. Scots.

,,   27. Collected by Robert Moffat and John Mabane, £1 : 4s. Scots.

Aug.   1. John Noteman and Mary Purves in Langhaugh, a.d.n. Janet ;   w. Thomas Darling, Gilbert Welsh.

Mortcloath to Elizabeth Mein, a child, 8d.

,,   3. The minister intimated a fast to be observed Thursday next appointed by the General Assembly.

After prayer sederunt, the Minister, Drygrainge, Wm. Milne, Andrew Marr, John Mabane, &c., elders.

Collected by Wm. Hoy and Andrew Drummond, £2 : 14s. Scots.

It was represented for Charles Wilkieson that he is willing to submit this affair to the session, and it being put to the vote whether the rebuke he got before should stand for one day's appearance, it carried that it should.   Then it was condescended upon that he should appear Thursday next, being the fast day, and the Sabbath thereafter.

,,   5. Charles Wilkieson and Anne Paterson, a.d.n. Margaret :   sponsor, Drygrainge ;   w. Mr Gavin Elliot, Wm. Pomphray.

,,   6. Mortcloath to James Stirling's wife, £2 : 4s. Scots.

1735.

Aug. 7. James Leithen and —— Sclatter in Eildon, a.d.n. Margaret ; w. John Sibbald, John Cochran.

    Collected by John Mabane and Robert Scott. £5 : 15s. Scots.

  ,, 10. Collected by John Sibbald and William Milne, £3 Scots.

  ,, 12. Mortcloath to George Sibbald's child, 8s. Scots.

  ,, ,, Ditto   to Helen Clark, £1 : 4s. Scots.

  ,, 14. Ditto   to Helen Sibbald, £2 : 4s. Scots.

  ,, 17. Collected by Nicol Milne and Andrew Mein, £2 : 18s. Scots.

  ,, 24. Collected by John Sibbald, £2 : 3s. Scots.

  ,, 25. Mortcloath for John Heiton, £2 : 4s. Scots.

  ,, 27. John Fisher and Isobel Scot in Easter Langlee, a.s.n. Alexander : w. Walter and George Thomson.

  ,, 28. Mortcloath to Isobel Mercer, £1 : 4s. Scots.

  ,, 29. Mortcloath to John Waddell, 14s. Scots.

  ,, 31. Collected by Wm. Hoy and Andrew Drummond, £2 : 7s. Scots.

Sept. 7. William Morison and Margaret Atchison in Melrose, a.d.n. Margaret ; w. George and William Lawries.

    Collected by Robert Scot and Wm. Milne, £2 : 13s. Scots.

  ,, 14. The minister intimated the sentence of the lesser excommunication against Mr Walter Scott, late of Whitstead.

    Collected by Andrew Drummond, £2 : 2s. Scots.

  ,, 21. Itimated a collection for the Orphans' Hospital at Edinburgh to be gathered against this day 8th days.

  ,, ,, William Cook and Margaret Lawrie in Melrose, a.s.n. George ; w. Alexr. Cook, George Lawrie.

    Collected by William Milne, £2 : 1s. Scots.

  ,, 28. Robert Steel and Elizabeth Walker in Melrose, a.s n. Robert ; w. George Walker, Nicol Mercer.

    After prayer sederunt, the Minister, Drygrainge, John Mabane, Wm. Hoy, Andrew Mein, &c., elders.

    Collected as intimated last day, by Robert Scott and Andrew Mar, and Andrew Drummond, £28 : 12s. Scots.

    A report of Mrs Jean Elliot, niece to Lady Whithaugh, her being with child, the session appoints their meeting Thursday next to enquire into that affair, and the said Mrs Elliot, and Mr John Lythgow to whom it is said she is married, are ordered to be cited to the same diet.

  ,, 29. Mortcloath to John Anderson's child, 8d.

Oct. 2. After prayer sederunt, the Minister, Drygrainge, John Mabane, Andrew Marr, elders.

    Mr John Lythgow being called, compeared, and being required if married to Mrs Jean Elliot, to produce his marriage lines, which he did, bearing date March 6th, 1732, subscribed by William Willie, minister, John Law and James Wilson, witnesses. Though this was of the date before his residence in this place, yet he was rebuked and gave in to the poor of this place £12 : 12s. Scots.

  ,, 3. Booked Thomas Plenderleith in the parish of Earlstone and Margaret Welsh in this ; Gilbert Welsh, cautioner.

  ,, 5. George Martine and Agnes Fair in Westhouses, a.d.n. Agnes.

  ,, ,, John Anderson and Janet Mack in Gattonside, a.d.n. Margaret : w. Andrew Marr, Andrew Stuart.

    Collected by William Hoy and Andrew Drummond, £2 : 8s. Scots.

  ,, 7. Alexr. Sandilands and Margaret Ker in Bentmilne, a.d.n. Eupham.

  ,, ,, George Grieve and —— Somervail in Blainslies, a.d.n. Janet ; w. Alexr. Gray, John Wallace.

    John Anderson, skiner in Melrose, gave in for a new burial place, 10s. Scots.

  ,, 12. James Lockie and Marion Lockie in Eildon, a.d.n. Helen.

  ,, ,, Philip Fair and Margaret Stevenstone in Gattonside, a.d.n. Janet ; w. Andrew Marr, Andrew Stuart.

1735.

Collected by Robert Scot and John Sibbald, £1 : 4s. Scots.

Mortcloath to Margaret Frier, £1 : 4s. Scots.

Oct. 12. Alexr. Ellies and Margaret Wilson in Danieltown, a.d.n. Agnes ; w. Henry Cook, George Martine.

,, 18. Booked John Dawson in the parish of Smalholm, and Helen Hog in this parish ; Robert Hog, cautioner.

Item, booked Robert Bunzie and Margaret Mein, both in this parish ; John Bunzie, cautioner.

,, 19. Collected by William Milne, £2 : 8s. Scots.

,, 24. John Milne and —— Brown in Newtown, a.s.n. Alexr. ; w. Thomas Stenhouse, Nicol Milne.

Booked Gilbert Bourlees in the parish of Stow and Helen Mark in this parish ; Richard Park, cautioner.

Booked Thomas Speeding in the parish of Bowden and Margaret Bunzie in this parish ; Andrew Bunzie, cautioner.

,, 26. Collected by Nicol Milne, £2 : 9s. Scots.

Nov. 1. Booked Richard Allan in the parish of Lauder and Jean Allan in this parish ; Hugh Grieve, cautioner.

,, 2. Mortcloath to John Milne, a child, 8d.

,, ,, John Purves and Agnes Thin in Melrose, a.s.n. William.

,, ,, Wm. Haliday and Margaret Atchison, a.d.n. Agnes ; w. Andrew Marr, James Smail.

Collected by Andrew Marr and Andrew Drummond, £2 : 7s. Scots.

,, 6. Andrew Smith and —— Boustone in Gattonside, a.s.n. Thomas ; w. Thomas and John Boustones.

,, 7. Booked John Edmund in the parish of Selkirk and Agnes Eastone in this : William Bain, cautioner.

Booked George Martine and Margaret White, both in this parish ; Dr. John Rutherfurd, cautioner.

,, 8. Booked John Gill and Helen Paterson, both in this parish ; James Smail, cautioner.

Mortcloath to James Stirling's son, £1 : 4s. Scots.

,, 9. Thomas Marr and Jean Craig in Melrose, a.s.n. Robert.

,, ,, George Scot and Isobel Tailor in Danieltone, a.s.n. Thomas ; w. Robert Scot, Andrew Marr.

After prayer sederunt, the Minister, Drygrainge, William Hoy, John Mabane, Robert Scot, Andrew Mein, &c., elders.

Collected by Andrew Mein and Andrew Drummond, £2 : 8s. Scots.

The session appoints first Monday next month for revising the accompts, and other affairs.

,, 16. James Speeding and Janet Mercer in Bridgend, a.s.n. David ; w. Andrew Drummond, Robert Rutherfurd, there.

,, ,, George Atchison and Bessie Hopkirk in Melrose, a.s.n. Thomas ; w. William Hopkirk, William Cook, there.

Collected by Robert Scot, £1 : 16s. Scots.

,, 19. Booked in order for marriage Adam Dods and Elizabeth Gill, both in this parish ; George Lawrie, cautioner.

,, 20. Mortcloath to John Haliwall, £1 : 4s. Scots.

,, 23. George Mack and Janet Tudhope in Gattonside, a.s.n. John.

,, ,, Thomas Trotter and Marion Henderson in Melrose, a.d.n. Margaret ; w. John Mabane, Laird Marr.

Collected by John Sibbald and Andrew Mein, £2 : 10s. Scots.

,, 29. Mortcloath to Janet Redpath, £2 : 4s. Scots.

,, 30. Collected by William Milne and Andrew Drummond, £2 : 16s. Scots.

Dec. 1. After prayer sederunt, conform to former appointment the minister, John Mabane, Andrew Marr, Robert Scott, Andrew Mein, elders,

The session considering the smallness of their number by reason of the badness of the weather, delayed every thing they intended in this session till a new meeting, save that they remove

1735.

hence for the receiving the account of the poor's money, in the meantime, the sederunt closed with prayer.

Same day the minister, John Mabane, Robert Scott, Andrew Marr and Nicol Milne mett with their clerk, and examined the accounts of the poor's money since December 16th, 1734, and after comparing charge with discharge, they find the charge exceeds the discharge £140 : 14s. Scots, wherewith George Martine, whom the session continues to take in the poor's money, is to charge himself with at next meeting, £140 : 14s. Scots.

Dec. 5. Booked John Walker in the parish of Ancrum and Elizabeth Martine in this parish, John Tait, cautioner.

,, 5. John Cochrane and Helen Bartleman in Newtown, a.d.n. Helen ; w. Nicol Milne, Thomas Stenhouse.

,, 6. Booked William Bunzie in this parish and Barbara Trotter in the parish of Ancrum ; Robert Bunzie, cautioner.

,, 7. Collected by John Sibbald and William Hoy, £2 : 8s. Scots.

,, 10. Mortcloath to George Turner, £2 : 4s. Scots

,, 13. Michael Wallace and Isobel Blaikie, a.d n. Marion : w. George and Andrew Martines.

,, 14. Charles Wilkieson compeared before the congregation for his guilt with Isobel Haliburtone.

Collected by Andrew Drummond and Andrew Marr, £2 : 9s. Scots.

,, 15. Mortcloath for Marion Wallace, a child, 8d.

,, 16. Thomas Darling, surgeon, and —— Thomson in Langhaugh, a.d.n. Agnes : w. James Heiton, John Noteman.

,, 21. Charles Wilkieson compeared, was rebuked and dismissed.

Collected by James Laidlay and John Sibbald, £2 : 2s. Scots.

,, 22. Thomas Watson and —— Cochran in Blainslies, a.s.n. Thomas ; w. Alexr. Gray, John Wallace.

,, 26. Mortcloath to Alexr. Bell's child, 8d.

,, 28. George Walker and Anne Pringle in Melrose, a.s.n. George.

,, ,, William and Helen Hunters in Melrose, a.d.n. Margaret ; w. Doctor Martine, Robert Hunter.

After prayer sederunt, the Minister, Drygrainge, John Mabane, Andrew Mein and William Milne, &c., elders.

Collected by Andrew Mein and Andrew Drummond, £2 : 2s. Scots.

The session appoints the 22nd day next month for considering what is necessary concerning the poor's money.

1736.

Jan. 3. Mortcloath to a child, 8d.

,, 4. Collected by Robert Scot and William Milne, £2 : 3s. Scots.

,, 9. Booked George Hoy in the parish of Earlstone, and Isobel Hoy in this parish ; Thomas Hoy, cautioner.

,, 11. Collected by Andrew Mein and Andrew Marr, £2 : 3s. Scots.

,, 12. Mortcloath to Margaret Henderson, £1 : 4s. Scots.

,, 18. John Laidlay and Agnes Mein in Eildon, a.s.n. Thomas.

,, ,, William Martin and Margaret Drummond in Gattonside, a.s.n. John : w. John Sibbald, Wm. Sandilands.

Collected by William Milne, £1 : 19s. Scots.

,, 22. After prayer sederunt, the Minister, John Mabane, William Milne, Robert Scott, elders.

This day the elders because of the paucity of their number could do no business, but adjourned their meeting till this day eighth days, and George Martine is to acquaint the several elders.

,, 25. Collected by Andrew Marr and Wm. Milne, £1 : 18s. Scots.

,, ,, Received from —— Pearson for a new burial place, 10d.

,, 28. Mortcloath to Margaret Mein, £2 : 4s. Scots.

,, 29. After prayer sederunt, the Minister, Drygrainge, Andrew Marr, Robert Scott, Andrew Drummond, John Sibbald, William Hoy, John Mabane, John Mercer, elders.

1736.

The session considering the state of the debts due the poor, and they having sold by way of roup John Bowar's house belonging to them to John Mein in Newsteid, and the said John having sold the same to William Williamson, present possessor of the said house, the money being unpaid and the rights undelivered, the session orders a disposition to be drawn for the said house and subscribed by the Minister, Drygrainge, Robert Scot and John Mabane in the name of the session, and given the said William Williamson, and he to pay or give security for the money.

The session is to give in a list of debts to Wm. Hunter Monday next, that he pursue for and recover them.

Application being made by Robert Mercer, weaver, portioner of Newsteid, for the loan of £5 sterling, the session condescends to allow him the same upon heretable security.

Thomas Williamson, representing that he made John Dods and his wife coffins, and is still unpaid, nor is there anything to pay him with, the session allow him 10s. sterling for the two ; as also 5s. sterling to Thomas Gill for John Waddell's coffin.

John Hoy was called and charged to pay £18 : 11s. Scots, the sum his brother George came short off during his treasurership, which the said John though succeeding to all refuses to do.

This day, Drygrainge, Mr. Gavin Elliot, schoolmaster, and Thomas Boustone, Burnbraehead, gave in a crown to the poor as an acknowledgement for their liberty of building a loft to the west of Lady Isabella's, which loft Drygrainge is to possess the just half to the eastward, Mr. Elliot and Thomas Boustone the other half equally twixt them, that is, by turns, and the said Thomas with his brother John, who has the equall half of his half, having possessed the west side last year, is to take the east side this, after Candlemas next, and so on *per vices* twixt Mr. Elliot and them in all time coming.

Jan. 31. The two best mortcloaths to Helen Sibbald, £3 : 8s. Scots.

Feb. 1. James Watt and Margaret Darling in Melrose, a.s.n. Andrew.

„ „ Alexr. and Helen Youngs in Gattonside, a.s.n. James ; w. Robert Penman, John Young.

Collected by John Mercer, £2 : 3s. Scots.

„ 3. This day mett the Minister, Drygrainge, John Mabane, Robert Scott, and according to their resolution the 29th last, gave in to William Hunter a list of debts due the poor, which he is to pursue for and recover, as also a power to pursue John Hoy, portioner of Melrose, for the £18 : 11s. his brother George came short in during his treasurership.

They likeways in name of the session signed a disposition to William Williamson and delivered the same with other evidents relative thereto, from whom they received as the price of the house he possesses conform to the roup of the same March 1720, £46 Scots, and his bill for £20 Scots, as an acknowledgement for possessing the said house since that time, of which £46 there was delivered to Mr. Wilkison, clerk, for his pains about the papers £5 : 4s. Scots.

Given in by Charles Wilkieson as his penalty, £2 : 10s. Scots.

Mortcloath for Helen Scott, £1 : 4s., a new burial place for ditto, 10d.

„ 8. George Mercer and Isobel Hunter in Darnick, a.d.n Helen.

„ „ Andrew Wood and Jean Mack in Gattonside, a.d.n. Margaret ; w. John Mercer, William Hunter.

Collected by Andrew Drummond, £1 : 12s. Scots.

„ 15 Andrew and Catharine Mercers in Bridgend, a.s.n. William ; w. William Hude, James Speeding.

Collected by Nicol Milne and Andrew Mein, £2 : 6s. Scots.

1736.

After sermon the minister baptised to Mr. John Lythgow and Jean Elliot, a.s.n. James ; w. John Fisher, John Bowie.

Collected at said baptism, 15s. Scots.

Feb. 16. Mortcloath for Bessie Moffatt, £1 : 4s. Scots.

,, 17. James Ker and Margaret Park, married here, 12s. Scots.

,, 18. Mortcloath for Christian Laidlay, £2 : 4s. Scots.

,, 22. Collected by Andrew Mein, £1 : 5s. Scots.

,, 24. Mortcloath for Margaret Jerdain, £1 : 4s. Scots.

,, 29. John Fairbairn and Bessie Flint in Melrose, a.d.n. Isobel ; w. Thomas and Wm. Lookup.

Collected by Andrew Drummond and Andrew Marr, £1 : 9s. Scots.

Mar. 2. The two best mortcloaths to Elizabeth Heiton, £3 : 8s. Scots.

Item, mortcloath to Margaret Skirven, £2 : 4s. Scots.

,, 3. James Lambert and Margaret Turnbull in Buckholm, a.s.n. James.

,, ,, Richard Park and Marion Pringle in Allanshaws, a.d.n. Marion ; w. —— Hilslop, James Purves.

,, 4. Mortcloath to Isobel Laidlay, a child, 8s. Scots.

For a new burial place, 10s. Scots.

,, 7. John Bunzie and —— Wallace in Eildon, a.s.n. James.

,, ,, Alexr. Strachan and Mary Mein in Melrose, a.d.n. Susanna.

,, ,, Robert Myles and Janet Mathison in Gattonside, a.d.n. Annabella ; w. John Sibbald, Richard Bowar.

Collected by John Sibbald, £2 : 19s. Scots.

Mortcloath to Nicol Stenhouse, £2 : 4s. Scots.

,, 13. Booked in order for marriage, James Blyth and Margaret Fisher, both in this parish ; John Moss, cautioner.

,, 14. Collected by Andrew Marr and John Mabane, £2 : 7s. Scots.

,, 15. Thomas Dalgliesh and Janet Brown in Langshawmiln, a.s.n. Adam ; w. Alexr. Gray, William Thin.

,, 19. Mortcloath for Catharine Paterson, £2 : 4s. Scots.

,, 21. Robert Hog and Margaret Gillas in Melrose, a.s.n. John ; w. Robert Johnstone, John Mabane.

Collected by Andrew Drummond and Andrew Mein, £1 : 19s. Scots.

,, 24. Mortcloath for John Cochran, £2 : 4s. Scots.

,, 26. Mortcloath to Charles Bowie, surgeon, £2 : 4s. Scots.

,, 27. Booked in order for marriage, James M'Dougal and Janet Heiton, both in this parish ; John Smith, cautioner.

,, 28. James Henderson and Isobel Haliwell, in Gattonside, a.s.n. John.

,, ,, Walter Scot and Janet Mein in Danieltown, a.d.n. Mary ; w. Robert Scot, George Lawrie.

Collected by Andrew Mein and Robert Scot, £2 : 8s. Scots.

,, 30. Booked Thomas Hog in the parish of Abbotrule and Elizabeth Martine in this ; Dr. Martin, cautioner.

April 4. Nicol Mercer and Agnes Steel in Melrose, a.d.n. Margaret.

,, ,, James Atchison and Janet Davidson in Newtown, a.d.n. Agnes ; w. William Steel, John Bowie.

Collected by John Wallace and Andrew Drummond, £2 : 9s. Scots.

,, 8. John Lawder and Elizabeth Dickson in Mosshouses, a.d.n. Janet.

,, ,, John and Elizabeth Stirlings in Blainslies, a.d.n. Margaret ; w. Alexr. Gray, John Wallace.

,, 9. Mortcloath to a poor man, 10d.

,, 11. Collected by Andrew Drummond and John Sibbald, £2 : 5s. Scots.

Mortcloath to John Pringle, £2 : 4s. Scots.

,, 13. Ditto to Robert Forsan, a child, 8d.

,, 18. Collected by Robert Scot and Andrew Mein, £2 : 6s. Scots.

Mortcloath for Agnes Wight, £1 : 4s. Scots.

,, 19. Nicol Bowar and Margaret Mein in Newtown, a.s.n. William ; w. Wm. Stenhouse, Richard Bowar.

1730.

April 23. Mortcloath for Agnes Milne, £2 : 4s. Scots.

,,　25. Henry Forrest and Isobel Robison in Westhouses, a.s.n. John.

,,　,, James Wight and Mary Skirven in Darnick, a.s.n. Robert ; w. John Forrest, Andrew Usher.

　　　Collected by Wm. Milne and John Wallace, £2 : 2s. Scots.

,,　30. Mortcloath for Andrew Crawford, £1 : 4s. Scots.

May　2. Andrew Renaldson and Janet Scott in Darnick, a.s.n. James ; w. George and Wm. Renaldson.

　　　Collected by Robert Scot and John Sibbald, £2 : 7s. Scots.

,,　7. Booked James Hunter and Helen Romanus, both in this parish ; John Edgar, cautioner.

,,　8. Mortcloath to William Morison, £1 : 4s. Scots.

,,　9. Ditto to Edward Darling, £2 : 4s. Scots.

,,　,, Mr. Gavin Elliot, schoolmaster, and Margaret Angus, a.s.n. William ; w. Dr. Rutherfurd, Drygrainge, elder and younger.

　　　After prayer sederunt, the Minister, Drygrainge, William Hoy, William Milne, John Mabane, &c., elders.

　　　Collected by Andrew Mein and John Mercer, £2 : 5s. Scots.

　　　The session being informed that John Corsar, indweller in Melrose, did lately on a Sabbath morning cast divots on the hill-side, do appoint their officer to cite him to the session this day eighth days.

　　　Upon the report of Janet Moodie's being with child, the session appoint her to be cited to the said diet.

,,　10. James Williamson and Elizabeth Shiel in Langhaugh, a.s.n. James.

,,　,, James Brown and Janet Waugh in Mosshouses, a.d.n. Janet ; w. James Blaikie, Andrew Bryden.

,,　14. Booked William Atchison and Christian Wilson, both in this parish ; George Blaikie, cautioner.

,,　15. Booked Robert Mein and Mrs. Marion Fisher, both in this parish : James Fisher of Bearfaulds, cautioner.

,,　16. Thomas Bunzie and Helen Bryden in Eildon, a.s.n. Francis.

,,　,, John Brown and Isobel Hunter in Melrose, a.d.n. Janet ; w. John and William Mabane.

　　　After prayer sederunt, the Minister, Drygrainge, Andrew Marr, Robert Scott, John Mercer, Wm. Milne, &c., elders.

　　　Collected by John Mabane and Wm. Milne, £2 : 5s. Scots.

　　　John Corsar being cited was called, compeared, and charged with casting divots on the Lord's day, which he denyed.

　　　The session resolve to enquire into that affair, and accordingly order their officer to cite Thomas Simpson and Agnes Robson, servants to William Bain, maltster in Melrose, to the session against this day eighth days. John is summoned to the said diet.

　　　Janet Moodie was called, compeared, and acknowledged she was with child ; that Alexr. Thomson in Henderleithen is the father ; that they were married two years past in October : that he, the said Alexr., had got the marriage lines in order, as he said, to show them to Mr. Brown, minister of Selkirk, but that, as she hears, he hath not shown them. She was cited to compear before the session of Selkirk this last Sabbath of this month, where he is to be brought in order to confront them, because as it is reported he refuses the marriage. The clerk is appointed to transmitt an extract of this to the said session.

　　　Mortcloath to Thomas Stenhouse, a child, 8d.

,,　17. Ditto, George Dalgliesh, a child, 8d.

　　　Ditto to John Bunzie, a child, 8d.

,,　28. Ditto to John Hart, a child, 8d.

,,　12. Booked James Darling in this parish and Agnes Moffatt in the parish of Earlestown : Andrew Darling, cautioner.

　　　Item, booked John Moodie and Agnes Wright, both in this parish ; John Tait, cautioner.

1736.

May 23. After prayer sederunt, the minister, Drygrainge, John Mabane, James
Laidlay, William Milne, &c., elders.

Collected by John Wallace and Andrew Mein, £2 : 9s. Scots.

John Corsar being called, compeared, and being dealt with to
confess his sin, denyed the same. The witnesses, Thomas
Simpson and Agnes Robson were called. The nature of an
oath was held out to them. John declared he had nothing to
say against them. They were solemnly sworn and Agnes
removed.

Thomas Simpson, married, aged about 45 years, purged
of malice and partial counsel, deponed that about a month ago, as
he was going out in the morning, twixt five and six, he saw a man
on the hillside casting divots : that he cryed to him at the same
time he was casting off the divots. The person answered, " What
do you say " ; that the deponent said, " Do you not know that this
is the Lord's day," at which word the person went away, but by
the voice he perceived it was John Corsar ; and that sun
shining, and at a great distance, he could not discover him by any
thing else. This is the truth as he shall answer. He declares he
cannot write.

Agnes Robson, aged about seventeen years, purged of malice
and partial counsel deponed that upon the day forsaid, as she was
going in the morning to Dryburgh, Thomas Simpson was setting
her away. He went off the road and cryed to a man he said was
casting divots, but she did not see him. This is the truth as she
shall answer.

John was much dealt with to confess, but all in vain. He is
summoned to the session against this day twenty days.

The minister gave in to the session the deliverance concerning
Elizabeth Moody, viz., that she is to be rebuked in this parish, as
residing in the same.

Case of discipline against Elizabeth Marjoribanks, formerly in
this parish, now in Stitchill, and Robert Wilson, servant to Robert
Johnstone, shoemaker in Melrose.

The session appoints their clerk to write to Mr. Alexr. Home,
minister of Stitchill, to cite the said Elizabeth Marjoribanks before
them, and take her particular confession, and transmitt the same,
and summon the said Elizabeth to this session against Sabbath
come fourteen days, that they may be confronted.

Received testimonials from Mungo Glendinning.

  ,, 28. Mortcloath to Isobel Wright, £1 : 4s. Scots.

  ,, 30. Thomas Yule and Esther Forsan in Drygrainge, a.s.n. Patrick ; w.
Robert Thomson, Adam Wilson.

After prayer sederunt, the Minister, Drygrainge, John Mabane,
Robert Scott, John Wallace, Andrew Marr, &c., elders.

Collected by Robert Moffat and Andrew Drummond, £2 : 3s.
Scots.

The session being informed that John Young and Isobel
Dalgliesh are cohabiting together, though formerly discharged by
the session. The session appoint the minister and John Mabane
to speak to them to part houses.

Mortcloath for Janet Wilson, £1 : 4s. Scots.

June 2. Booked in order for marriage, George Beatie and Margaret Haig,
both in this parish ; John Tait, cautioner.

  ,, 6. Collected by James Laidlay and John Mercer, £2 : 10s. Scots.

  ,, ,, Mortcloath to James Dickson's child, 8s. Scots.

Ditto to a child, 8s. Scots.

  ,, 7. Francis Paisley and Margaret Wilson from Stow, married here,
1s. sterling.

  ,, 11. Mortcloath for Nicol Bowar, a child, 8s. Scots.

  ,, 13. After prayer sederunt, the Minister, Drygrainge, John Wallace,

Robert Scot, John Mabane, William Hoy, James Laidlay, &c., elders.

Collected by John Sibbald and Andrew Mein, £2 : 7s. Scots.

John Corsar was called and much dealt with if guilty of the breach of the Sabbath as is alledged ; still denyed the same. The proof being lame, but the presumptions strong against him, he was instantly rebuked and dismissed with certification.

Case of discipline against Elizabeth Marjoribanks and Robert Wilson, continued. They were both admonished and seriously exhorted, and she appointed Sabbath first to appear before the congregation.

The minister reports that he conversed with John Young and Isobel Dalgliesh, but was not satisfied with the answer he had from them. They are ordered to be cited to the session this day eighth days.

June 20. George Mercer and Margaret Knox in Housebyres, a.s.n. Andrew.

„   „ John Gordon and Margaret Walker in Darnick, a.s.n. Thomas ; w. John Mercer, John Walker.

After prayer sederunt, the Minister, Drygrainge, John Mabane, John Mercer, Nicol Milne, William Milne, Robert Scott, &c., elders.

Collected by Nicol Milne and William Milne, £2 : 13s. Scots.

John Young and Isobel Dalgliesh being summoned, were called, but compeared not. They are ordered to be cited pro 2^{ndo} to this day eighth days session.

The minister and session resolve that the sacrament of the supper shall be celebrated in this place the 3rd Sabbath next moneth. The sederunt closed with prayer.

„ 22. Mortcloath for Margaret Grieve. £2 : 4s. Scots.

„ 23. William Haliday and Margaret Dickman in Hagburn, a.s.n. Thomas : w. Thomas Mathison, John Bunzie.

Mortcloath to George Atchison's child, 8d.

„ 27. William Wood and Elizabeth Brown in Sorrowlessfield, a.d.n. Janet.

„   „ Adam Tait and Margaret Mathison in Darnick, a.d.n. Janet ; w. John Smith, William Mathison.

Elizabeth Marjoribanks appeared for the second time.

After prayer sederunt, the Minister, Drygrainge, William Mabane, James Laidlay, John Wallace, Andrew Mein, &c., elders.

Collected by John Wallace and Andrew Marr, £2 : 6s. Scots.

John Young and Isobel Dalgliesh being summoned, were called, but compeared not. They are appointed to be cited to the session against this day eighth days pro 3$^{tio.}$

July 2. This day booked William Turner and Mary Purves, both in this parish : James Turner, cautioner.

„ 3. Mortcloath to Jean Turnbull, a child, 8s. Scots.

„ 4. Ditto to Agnes Mein, £1 : 4s. Scots.

This day the minister intimated the celebration of the sacrament in this place, this day fourteen days.

Elizabeth Marjoribanks compeared for the 3rd time, was rebuked and dismissed. Gave in a penalty, £1 : 10s. Scots.

„   „ After prayer sederunt, the Minister, Drygrainge, Nicol Milne, John Mabane, Robert Scott, Andrew Marr, John Wallace, &c., elders.

Collected by James Laidlay and Andrew Drummond, £2 : 5s. Scots.

John Young, who was neglected to be summoned pro 3^{tio} is appointed to be cited to the session against this day eighth days. The sederunt closed with prayer.

„ 11. The minister intimated Wednesday next as the humiliation day before the sacrament, being the day the presbytry appointed to be kept as a fast through their bounds, on account of the great drought

1736.

Then baptised to Thomas Vair and Janet Mein in Newstead, a.d.n. Janet ; w. John and James Mein.

After prayer sederunt, the Minister, Drygrainge, John Mabane, William Milne, Nicol Milne, Robert Scot, Andrew Marr, &c., elders.

Collected by Andrew Mein and John Wallace, £2 : 19s. Scots.

The session appointed Tuesday next for privy tryals. The minister gave in a discharge for £3 sterling, as the collection of this parish for the Orphans' Hospital, signed Thomas Gairdner.

July 13. After prayer sederunt, the Minister, Drygrainge, James Laidlay, John Mabane, Robert Scott, Andrew Mein, Andrew Marr, Nicol Milne, Andrew Drummond, William Hoy, John Mercer, elders

The elders present were severally removed by pairs, tryed and approven, and encouraged to go on in the Lord's work. The order of collecting and keeping the doors as formerly.

„ 14. Humiliation day. The minister intimated that all the tokens were to be distributed sessionally, and for that end the session is to meet at ten o'clock, Saturday.

Collected Fast day,	-	-	-	£7	17	0
Collected Saturday,	-	-	-	13	16	0
Collected Sabbath day,	-	-	-	25	15	0
Collected Munday,	-	-	-	12	13	0
				£60	01	0
Debursed of the above collections, to the poor of the parish, to poor recommended, &c.	-			40	18	0
				£19	3	0

Which sum is appointed to be given in to the treasurer, wherewith he is to charge himself.

„ 21. Robert Williamson and the deceased Agnes Scot in Gattonside, a.d.n. Agnes ; w. George and Andrew Martines.

Mortcloath to Agnes Scot, £1 : 4s. Scots.

„ 25. Booked Thomas Familtone in the parish of Earlestown and Agnes Smith in this ; John Smith, cautioner.

„ 26. William Brown and Christian M'Millian in Melrose, a.s.n. Robert ; w. Robert Trotter, John Anderson.

Robert Wilson compeared for the first time and was admonished.

Collected by John Wallace and James Laidlay, £3 Scots.

Aug. 1. After prayer sederunt, the Minister, Drygrainge, John Sibbald, James Lindsay, Robert Scot, Andrew Marr, John Mabane, &c., elders.

Collected by Andrew Drummond, £2 : 3s. Scots.

John Young and Isobel Dalgliesh being cited were called, compeared and produced their marriage lines signed at Edinburgh, July 9th, 1736, by John Strange, minister. They were rebuked and the session resolved to pursue for the fine according to law.

The minister proposed that the session should consider whether the 20s. sterling formerly allowed the session clerk should be continued, the consideration whereof was delayed, and the sederunt closed with prayer.

„ 2. John Edgar and Elizabeth Pringle in Blainslies, a.s.n. Thomas.

„ „ Adam Wallace and Janet Stuart in Blainslies, a.d.n. Isobel ; w. James Brother-stones, Thomas Coldcleugh.

„ 4. John Mein, portioner of Newstied, paid in to the session, £93 : 12s. Scots, as the contents of John and Andrew Mein's bonds, principally as rents and expences.

„ 5. Mortcloath for Isobel Mein, £1 : 4s. Scots.

„ 8. Collected by William Hoy and Robert Moffat, £2 : 4s. Scots.

1736.

Aug. 9. Alexr. Gray and Margaret Thin in Blainslies, a.s.n. Alexr. ; w. William Thin, John Wallace.

„   15. Collected by Andrew Drummond and Andrew Marr, £3 : 9s. Scots.

„   20. Mortcloath for Jean Wilson, £2 : 4s. Scots.

„   22. After prayer sederunt, the Minister, Drygrainge, William Milne, Nicol Milne, John Sibbald, William Hoy, John Sibbald, &c., elders.
    Collected by William Hoy and John Sibbald, £2 : 11s. Scots.
    The session being informed that Jean Fisher, daughter to James Fisher of Bearfaules, is clandestinely married to John Cunningham, glover in Edinburgh, and as he is for the present in the place, the session appoint them to be cited before the session against this day eighth days.

„   27. Mortcloath for Margaret Bunzie, a child, 8d.

„   29. Thomas Vair and Margaret Wilson in Danieltown, a.s.n. Robert.

„   29. William Bailie and Isobel Park, a.s.n. John ; w. Wm. Wilson, George Lawrie.
    After prayer sederunt, the Minister, Drygrainge, William Hoy, John Wallace, Robert Scott, &c., elders.
    Collected by John Mabane and Wm. Hoy, £2 : 7s. Scots.
    The minister informed the session that Mrs. Jean Fisher desired the session would delay their affair till Mr. Cunningham, her husband, should come to the country, which the session complyed with.

Sept. 5. John Spears and Alison Gibson in Newsteid, a.d.n. Margaret ; w. John Mein, Thomas Williamson.
    Collected by Andrew Mein, £1 : 15s. Scots.

„   12. Collected by Robert Scott, £1 : 15s. Scots.

„   19. Collected by John Sibbald and William Milne, £2 Scots.
    Mortcloath for William Moodie, £1 : 4s. Scots.

„   25. Ditto for Robert Williamson's child, 8d.

„   „ Ditto for John Darling, £1 : 4s. Scots.

„   26. Robert Bunzie and Margaret Mein in Newsteid, a.d.n. Jean.

„   „ Wm. Bunzie and Barbara Trotter in Newsteid, a.d.n. Janet ; w. Robert and Wm. Bunzies.
    After prayer sederunt, the Minister, Drygrainge, John Mabane, William Milne, Nicol Milne, &c., elders.
    Collected by Robert Scott, £2 : 6s. Scots.
    The session orders Mr. Cunningham to be cited before them with Mrs. Jean Fisher for their irregular marriage. As also to require testimonials from Grisal Nicolson and her sister Janet.

„   27. Mortcloath for Wm. Thin, £1 : 4s. Scots.

„   28. Ditto for Margaret Mercer, £1 : 4s. Scots.

Oct. 1. Ditto for Elizabeth Darling, £2 : 4s. Scots.

„   3. Adam Dods and Bettie Gill in Danieltown. a.s.n. William.

„   „ John Tait and Margaret Martin in Melrose, a.d.n. Helen ; w. Dr. Martine, George Martine.
    Collected, £2 : 5s. Scots.

„   9. Booked in order for marriage James Grieve in this parish and Helen Tait in the parish of Traquair ; George Howden, cautioner.

„   10. Wm. Bunzie and Janet Little in Eildon, a.d.n. Margaret ; w. Robert and John Bunzies.
    Collected by William Milne and William Hoy, £2 : 16s. Scots.

„   12. John Fisher and Isobel Scot in Colmslie, a.s.n. Adam ; w. Robert Fisher, George Alley.

„   13. Mortcloath to Gilbert Paterson, £2 : 4s. Scots.

„   16. Booked James Burnet and Mary Renaldson, both in this parish ; Andrew Renaldson, cautioner.

„   17. After prayer sederunt, the Minister, Drygrainge, Robert Scott, Wm. Hoy, John Sibbald, &c., elders.
    Collected by Andrew Marr, John Mabane, £2 : 3s. Scots.

1736.

The session appoint their officer to cite Violet Pringle before the session of Kelso, Sabbath next.

Oct. 18. Mortcloath for John Young, £2 : 4s. Scots.

,, 24. After prayer sederunt, the Minister, Drygrainge, John Wallace, William Hoy, James Laidlay, Robert Scott, &c., elders.
Collected by Robert Scot and Wm. Hoy, £2 : 8s. Scots.
James Blyth being cited, compeared and acknowledged antenuptial fornication with —— Fisher, his present spouse. He was admonished and exhorted, and appointed to appear when his wife is recovered.

29. Booked Andrew Ainslie in the parish of Stow and Helen Darling in this parish ; James Watt, cautioner.

,, 30. Booked George Henderson in the parish of Stow and Christian Wight in this parish ; Thomas Blaikie, cautioner.

31. John Anderson and Elizabeth Fiddes in Melrose, a.s.n. John.

,, ,, Alexr. Vair and Jannet Wilson in Danieltown, a.d.n. Elizabeth ; w. Robert Trotter, George Lawrie.
Mortcloath to Bessie Wood, £2 : 4s. Scots.

Nov. 5. Booked John Hope in the parish of Bowden and Isobel Haliburtone in this parish ; George Atchison, cautioner.

,, 7. John Gill and Helen Paterson in Melrose, a.s.n. Thomas.

,, ,, John Young and Margaret Gill in Gattonside, a.s.n. John ; w. Thomas Gill, George Lawrie.
James Blyth and Margaret Fisher appeared for the first time and were exhorted.
Collected by Andrew Mein and Andrew Drummond, £1 : 16s. Scots.

,, 11. Booked James Aitchison in the parish of Stow and Janet Turner in this parish ; Edward Turner, cautioner.

,, 12. Booked George Henry and Marion Thomson, both in this parish ; Robert Scott, cautioner.

,, 14. James Blyth and his spouse appeared for the second time.
Collected by John Sibbald and Wm. Hoy, £2 : 3s. Scots.

,, 21. Collected by Robert Scott, £2 : 4s. Scots.

,, 24. James Dickson and Marion Blaikie in Newsteid, a.d.n. Marion ; w. George Martine, John Tait.

,, 28. William Martin and Jean Grieve in Gattonside. a.s.n. William ; w. Hugh Grieve, John Edgar.
Collected by John Wallace, £1 : 14s. Scots.
Mortcloath to a child, 8s. Scots.

Dec. 3. Booked Thomas Speeding in the parish of Mertown and Margaret Brown in this ; William Bell, cautioner.

,, 4. Booked Nicol Milne and Janet Frater, both in this parish ; Thomas Milne, cautioner.
Booked John Mercer and Helen Scirven, both in this parish ; George Mercer, cautioner.
Booked Andrew Marr and Helen Mercer, both in this parish ; James Waugh, cautioner.

,, 5. James Blyth and Margaret Fisher, compeared for the third time, were rebuked and dismissed.

,, ,, Robert Trotter and Margaret Mabane in Melrose, a.s.n. Adam.

,, ,, James Speeding and Janet Mercer in Bridgend, a.d.n. Janet.

,, ,, Thomas Darling and Isobel Martine in Gattonside, a.d.n. Janet.

,, ,, James Blyth and Margaret Fisher in Darnick, a.s.n. Francis ; w. John and William Mabanes.
Collected by Wm. Hoy and Andrew Drummond, £1 : 18s. Scots.
James Blyth and Margaret Fisher's penalty, £4 Scots.

,, 12. Adam Thorburn and Susanna Rutherfurd in Melrose, a.d.n. Janet ; w. James Laing, John Corsar.
Collected by William Milne, £1 : 13s. Scots.

1736.

Dec. 15. John Edgar and Agnes Grieve in Blainslies, a.d.n. Margaret; w. John and James Wallaces.

„ 16. John Lawrie paid in the contents of his bond, extending to £45 Scots.

„ 17. William Mabane and Elizabeth Mein in Darnick, a.s.n. John; w. John and George Mercers.

„ 18. Mortcloath to John Bowar, £1 : 4s. Scots.

„ 19. Collected by Robert Scot, £1 : 7s. Scots.

„ 24. Mortcloath for James Dickson's child, 8s. Scots.

„ 26. Michael Wallace and Isobel Blaikie in Melrose, a.s.n. George.

„ „ Robert Mercer and Anaple Ovens in Newsteid, a.d.n. Mary; w. John Mein, Thomas Williamson.

Collected by Andrew Mein, £1 : 11s. Scots.

„ 28. Mortcloath to Elizabeth Wilson, £2 : 4s. Scots.

„ 31. Ditto to William Marr, £2 : 4s. Scots.

Item, Mortcloath for a child, 8d.

1737.

Jan. 2. After prayer sederunt, the Minister, John Mabane, Robert Scot, Wm. Hoy, John Wallace, &c., elders.

Collected by Andrew Drummond and John Sibbald, £3 : 14s. Scots.

The session being informed that Andrew Burnet, innkeeper in this town is married irregularly, they order him and his wife to be cited to the session Wednesday next that is appointed to meet for that end, and taking in.

„ 5. After prayer sederunt, the Minister, Nicol Milne, Andrew Marr, Robert Scott, John Mabane, John Mercer, William Milne, Andrew Mein, elders.

Andrew Burnet and Eleoner Turnbull being cited, were called. They compeared, and interrogate if married, answered they were, and produced the lines of their marriage dated at Carham, Dec. 30th, 1736, and signed Thomas Ogle, de Carham. They were rebuked for their disorder, and paid down as their modified fine £12 : 12s. Scots.

The session mett, revised the poor's money, and having compeared charge with discharge, they find chargeable on George Martine, whom they continue some time to take in the poor's money, £371 : 7 : 6. Scots, all former intromissions being discharged.

This day John Hog granted his bill for £18 : 11s. Scots, due by his deceased brother George.

„ 9. Thomas Hoy and Janet Smith in Gattonside, a.d.n. Isobell.

„ „ James Blyth and Christian Taylor in Gattonside, a.d.n. Mary; w. William Hoy, Laird Marr.

After prayer sederunt, the Minister, Wm. Hoy, Andrew Marr, Robert Scott, Andrew Mein, &c., elders.

Collected by Robert Scott and Wm. Hoy, £2 : 18s. Scots.

Mr. John Cunningham, glover in Edinr., married to Mrs. Jean Fisher, waited on the session and owned that he had clandestinely married the said Jean Fisher and that he had not the lines along with him, but that he should send them to satisfie the session with the first occasion, for which disorderly course he was rebuked, and promised before he should leave the country to give his bill for a guinea to the use of the poor.

The session upon application from Alexr. M'Fadzean condescended to lend him £7 Scots, if he should find sufficient caution.

„ 11. Mortcloath for Jean Lawrie, £1 : 4s. Scots.

After prayer sederunt, the Minister, Andrew Marr, Nicol Milne, John Mercer, John Mabane, &c., elders.

Collected by William Hoy and Andrew Drummond, £2 : 16s. Scots.

This day Mr. Cunningham's bill for a guinea was lodged in George Martine's hand.

1737.

The session condescended to lend William Milne 20s. sterling upon bill.

Jan. 19. Mortcloath to John Lumsdale, £1 : 4s. Scots.
  ,, 20. Ditto to William Elliot, Mr. Gavin Elliot's child, 12s. Scots.
  ,, 23. Peter Legg and Margaret Frier in Melrose, a.s.n. James ; w. Walter Murray, Andrew Dawson.
      Collected by Andrew Mein and William Milne, £1 : 1s. Scots.
  ,, 29. Mortcloath to Hugh Darling, £1 : 4s. Scots.
  ,, 30. Andrew Hart and Janet Davidson in Newsteid, a.s.n. Robert ; w. Thomas and James Williamsons.
      Collected by Andrew Drummond, £1 : 9s. Scots.
Feb. 3. Mortcloath for Elizabeth Dods, £2 : 4s. Scots.
  ,, 6. James Craig and Helen Peper in Melrose, a.d.n. Christian ; w. Wm. Steel, Wm. Williamson.
      Collected by John Sibbald, £1 : 7s. Scots.
  ,, 13. After prayer sederunt, the Minister, John Sibbald, John Mercer, John Mabane, William Hoy, &c. elders.
      Collected by Andrew Mein and Wm. Milne, £1 : 13s. Scots.
      The session appoint their officer to cite Violet Pringle before the session of Kelso, Sabbath first, pro 2do.
      James Craig's wife being brought to bed of a living child and in no ways in a condition to nurse the child, the session have allowed 10s. 6d. to help the nursing of the said child out of the house.
  ,, 15. John Carter and Isabel Purves in Clackmae, a.s.n. John.
  ,, ,, Thomas and Marion Pringle in Blainslies, a.s.n. William.
  ,, ,, James Wallace and Eupham Darling, a.d.n. Janet ; w. John Wallace, William Pringle.
  ,, 16. Mortcloath to James Stirling, £2 : 4s. Scots.
      Ditto to George Mercer, £1 : 4s. Scots.
  ,, 19 Booked in order for marriage, William Wilson in this and Mary Wright in the parish of Earlestown ; Thomas Vair, cautioner.
  ,, 20. John Turnbull and Bessie Familtone in Gattonside, a.s.n. Thomas ; w. Andrew Marr, John Marr.
      After prayer sederunt, the Minister, John Mabane, Andrew Mein, John Sibbald, &c., elders.
      Collected by Robert Scot and Andrew Mein, £1 : 7s. Scots.
      Case of discipline against Mary Wright, late servitrix to Drygrainge, and William Wilson, present servant to Mr. Paterson, bailie. They were both admonished and exhorted, and in regard they are about to be married their compearance is delayed till married.
  ,, 27. Patrick Bulman and Agnes Cochran in Newtown, a.d.n. Isobel ; w. Nicol Milne, Thomas Stenhouse.
      Collected by John Sibbald and Andrew Mein, £1 : 18s. Scots.
Mar. 3. Mortcloath to Robert Wight, a child, 8d.
  ,, 6. William Forsan and Janet Bunzie in Drygrainge, a.d.n. Isobel ; w. William and John Bunzies.
      Collected by Nicol Milne and James Laidlay, £2 : 3s. Scots.
  ,, 7. Mortcloath to Patrick Thomson, £1 : 4s. Scots.
  ,, 8. Booked William Thomson and Janet Gray, both in this parish ; John Tait, cautioner.
  ,, 9. Mortcloath to Janet Lawrie, £2 : 4s. Scots.
  ,, 13. Collected by William Milne and Andrew Marr, £1 : 12s. Scots.
  ,, 15. Alexander Thomson and Margaret Hog in Buckholm, a.s.n. George ; w. Andrew Bryden, Thomas Gordon.
  ,, 18. Mortcloath to Robert Marr, £1 : 4s. Scots.
      Ditto to Janet Fairbairn, a child, 8d.
  ,, 20. Andrew Mein and Janet Renaldson in Newtown, a.s.n. James ; w. James Mein, Nicol Milne.
      William Wilson and Mary Wright compeared in the forenoon

1737.

for the first time for their antenuptial fornication and were rebuked.

Marion Bunzie compeared in the afternoon for the third time, was exhorted and dismissed.

Collected by Robert Scott and Andrew Drummond, £2 : 13s. Scots.

Mar. 25. Mortcloath for Isobel Mercer, £1 : 4s. Scots.

„ 26. Ditto to Elizabeth Rutherford, £1 : 4s. Scots.

„ 27. Walter Horsburgh and Margaret Bain in Danieltown, a.s.n. John ; w. William Bain, Walter Scot.

William Wilson and Mary Wright compeared the second time. Collected by Andrew Drummond, £1 : 7s. Scots.

„ 28. James Moffatt and Mary Pringle in Overlangshaw, a.d.n. Agnes ; w. Robert Fairbairn, George Martine.

„ 29. Mortcloath to Charles Grieve, a child, 8d.

April 3. William Wilson and Mary Wright compeared the third time, were dismissed and paid in £4 Scotts of penalty.

Collected by Wm. Hoy and Andrew Marr, £1 : 13s. Scots.

„ 7. Booked in order for marriage John Gill in the parish of Lauder and Elizabeth Romanes in this parish ; John Gill, cautioner.

„ 8. Booked Gilbert Smith in the parish of Prestonpans and Margaret Fairbairn in this parish ; Thomas Fairbairn, cautioner.

„ 9. Booked Alexr. Lockie and Grisal Nicolson, both in this parish ; Andrew Dawson, senior, cautioner.

Mortcloath for Richard Mein, £2 : 4s. Scots.

„ 10. William Mabane and Isobel Ballentyne in Melrose, a.d.n. Janet ; w. John Mabane, Robert Fratter.

Collected by Andrew Mein and Drummond, £1 : 15s. Scots.

„ 14. Received for a poor man's cloaths that were rouped, whom the session buried.

„ 16. Booked John Brotherstones in the parish of Earlstown and Isobel Laidlay in this parish ; Robert Scott, cautioner.

„ 17. Collected by William Mabane and William Hoy, £2 Scots.

„ 19. Mortcloath for Marion Milne, £2 : 4s. Scots.

„ 24. Collected by Nicol Milne and Robert Scott, £1 : 12s. Scots.

Mortcloath for a child, 8d.

„ 29. Mortcloath for Jean Balfour, 10d.

May 1. After prayer sederunt, the Minister, Nicol Milne, Robert Scot, John Mabane, &c., elders.

Collected by John Sibbald and Andrew Marr, £2 : 1s. Scots.

Upon the report of Robert Scott and Janet Darling in Blainslies, their irregular marriage, the minister caused cite them to this day's session. They being called, compeared, and produced their marriage lines, dated att Edinr. April 22nd, 1737, and signed James Strange, minister. They were gravely rebuked and ordered to pay as their modified fine to the poor £9 Scotts.

„ 8. George Martine and Margaret White in Melrose, a.d.n. Margaret : w. John Tait, Andrew Martine.

Collected by Robert Scott and Andrew Drummond, £1 : 12s. Scots.

Mortcloath to James Welsh, £1 : 4s. Scots.

„ 14. Booked in order for marriage, John Bunzie and Isobel Wilson, both in this parish ; William Rutherfurd, cautioner.

Booked William Mathison and Janet Frier, both in this parish ; Walter Murray, cautioner.

Booked James Bunzie in this parish and Isobel Moodie in the parish of Roxburgh ; Andrew Bunzie, cautioner.

„ „ John Milne and Eupham Brown in Newtown, a.s.n. John ; w. Nicol Milne, James Mein.

„ 15. Robert Penman and Christian Grahamslie in Melrose, a.s.n. Andrew ; w. Robert Penman, Andrew Dawson.

1737.

Collected by Andrew Marr and John Sibbald, £2 : 6s. Scots.

May 19. Mortcloath for John Brown, £2 : 4s. Scots.

„ 22. Collected by James Laidlay and William Hoy, £2 : 2s. Scots.

„ 28. Booked John Usher in this parish and Janet White in the parish of Ancrum ; John Hownam, cautioner.

„ 29. Nicol Bowar and —— Mein in Newtown, a.d.n. Janet.

„ „ Adam Harvie and Isobel Leithen in Westhouses, a.d.n. Isobel ; w. Mungo Park, Nicol Milne.

Collected by William Hoy and John Sibbald, £2 : 11s. Scots.

June 1. George Blaikie and Mary Gray in Langhaugh, a.s.n. George ; w. James Dickson, George Martine.

„ 3. Booked Robert Lees in this parish and Bettie Mertle in the parish of Ligerwood ; John Tait, cautioner.

„ 5. William Wilson and Mary Wright in Danieltown, a.s.n. Robert ; w. Thomas Vair, Robert Grierson.

After prayer sederunt, the Minister, John Mabane, Nicol Milne, Andrew Mein, &c., elders.

Collected by Andrew Drummond and William Milne, £1 : 9s. Scots.

This day the session agreed that the sacrament of the supper shall be celebrated in this place the third Sabbath of July next. The sederunt closed with prayer.

„ 6. Alexr. Cuningham of Hindhope and Elizabeth Paterson, a.d.n. Elizabeth ; w. Alexr. Paterson, Charles Wilkieson.

„ 7. Mortcloath for Isobel Blaikie, £2 : 4s. Scots.

„ 8. Mortcloath for a child, 8d.

„ 12. Collected by Robert Moffatt and Wm. Hoy, £2 : 9s. Scots.

„ 13. Mortcloath to Adam Fisher, a child, 8d.

„ 14. Ditto to George Wallace, a child, 8d.

„ 17. Booked in order for marriage Nicol Mercer and Margaret Chisholm, both in this parish ; James Speeding, cautioner.

„ 19. John Hoy and Alison Cunningham in Melrose, a.s.n. William.

„ „ Thomas Plenderleith and Margaret Welsh in Langhaugh, a.s.n. James ; w. John Bowie, Andrew Lookup.

This day read an act of the sherriff and justices of the peace anent the poor.

After prayer sederunt, the Minister, Robert Scott, Andrew Marr, James Laidlay, &c., elders.

Collected by John Wallace and John Mabane, £2 : 4s. Scots.

Case of discipline against Margaret Foord, formerly in Blainslies, now in Lauder, and John Martine, deceased, son to Andrew Martine, portioner of Blainslies. The session resolve to delay the affair for some time.

„ 25. Booked in order for marriage John Cochran and Margaret Drummond, both in this parish ; William Martine, cautioner.

This day intimated a meeting concerning the poor Thursday next.

Collected by Andrew Mein, £1 : 1s. Scots.

„ 27. John Darling and —— Bunzie in Eildon, a.s.n. Thomas.

„ „ John Laidlay and —— Mein in Eildon, a.d.n. Isobel ; w. John Sibbald, John Cochran.

„ 30. This day several of the heretors mett with the session and gave in a list of the poor, and ordered something concerning their subsistance till Tuesday next, when heretors and session have appointed their meeting.

July 3. This day the minister intimated the administration of the Lord's supper in this place this day fourteen days.

„ „ George Martine and Agnes Wilson in Gattonside, a.d.n. Isobel ; w. Andrew and John Marrs.

The precentor this day intimated a meeting of the heretors and kirk session in this place Tuesday first for settling provisions

1737.

to the poor of the parish, and the poor are ordered to attend the said meeting.

After prayer sederunt, the Minister, John Mercer, Nicol Milne, Robert Scott, Andrew Marr, &c., elders.

Collected by Robert Moffatt and Andrew Drummond, £3 : 13s. Scots.

The session appoints their meeting to-morrow to inspect the bills and bonds due the poor, and to see what money is in the box.

The session being informed of a great profanation of the Lord's day Sabbath last, by drinking, fighting and other abuses in the house of Alexr. Lockie in Melrose, the session appoints him and Grizal Nicolson, his wife, to be cited to the session this day eight days.

July 4. This day the minister and elders mett conform to appointment, and inspected the bills and bonds due the poor.

" 5. This day the heretors and kirk session mett and considered the state of the poor, and have ordered subsistance for ensuing quarter, as per sederunt of the heretors of this day's date.

" 8. Mortcloath money, James Moodie, £1 : 4s. Scots.

" 9. Ditto for a child, 8d.

" 10. The minister intimated Thursday first as the humiliation day before the sacrament.

The precentor intimated concerning the poor as per sederunt of the heretors the 5th instant.

After prayer sederunt, the Minister, John Mercer, Nicol Milne, Robert Scot, Andrew Marr, &c., elders.

Collected by James Laidlaw and John Wallace, £2 : 8s. Scots.

Alexr. Lockie and his wife being summoned were called. He compeared, and charged with profaning the Lord's day by drinking and fighting this day fourteen days, he said he saw no fighting, nor any drinking to excess. He was summoned to the session this day fourteen days, and the beadle is ordered to cite his wife to the same diet.

The session appoint Tuesday next for privy tryals, and ordering other things about the sacrament.

" 12. This day being appointed for privy tryals, after prayer sederunt, the Minister, James Laidlaw, John Mabane, Nicol Milne, Andrew Mein, Andrew Drummond, Andrew Marr, John Wallace, Robert Scott, John Sibbald, John Mercer, Wm. Hoy, elders.

The elders present were severally removed by pairs, tryed, approven and encouraged to go on in the Lord's work.

The collections to be gathered, and doors kept as formerly.

The sederunt closed with prayer.

Collected, Fast Day,	-	-	-	-	£8	0	0
Collected, Saturday,	-	-	-	-	11	8	0
Collected, Sunday,	-	-	-	-	18	10	0
Collected, Monday, -	-	-	-	-	10	8	0
Sum of collections,	-	-	-	-	£48	6	0
Debursed to the precentor, beadle, the poor of							
the parish and poor recommended,	-	-	-	22	0	0

The half of this £26 6 0 was given in to the heretors, as also the half of all collections, &c. to assist them in the maintenance of the poor, conform to the several acts thereanent.

" 17. Mortcloath to John Paterson, £1 : 4s. Scots.

" 18. Best ditto to George Bannatyne, £2 : 4s. Scots.

1737.
July 24. After prayer sederunt, the Minister, Andrew Marr, Robert Scott, John Mercer, Wm. Hoy, &c., elders.
  Collected by John Sibbald, Andrew Marr, £2 : 10s. Scots.
  Alexr. Lockie and Grizal Nicolson, his spouse, compeared. They declared they were not accessary to either fighting or drinking, and they were sorry any such thing should have happened in their house. They were exhorted and admonished, and dismissed.
  „ 29. Booked Thomas Hardie in the parish of Lauder and Agnes Grieve in this parish ; William Darling in Blainslies, cautioner.
  „ 31. Thomas Marr and Jean Craig in Melrose, a.d.n. Jean : w. Andrew Dawson, William Steel.
  Collected by Andrew Mein and John Mercer, £1 : 5s. Scots.
Aug. 6. Mortcloth to a child, 8d.
  „ 7. Collected by John Sibbald and Nicol Milne, £2 : 6s. Scots.
  To the little mortcloath, 8d.
  „ 14. Collected by William Milne and Andrew Drummond, £3 : 19s. Scots.
  „ 16. Plush mortcloath to Margaret Watson, £1 : 4s. Scots.
  „ 21. After prayer sederunt, the Minister, John Mabane, Nicol Milne, Robert Scott, John Mercer, &c., elders.
  Collected by Robert Scott and Andrew Drummond, £2 Scots.
  Upon the report of William Mathison's wife being brought to bed long before the time, he was summoned and compeared this day, and confessed. He was seriously exhorted and gravely rebuked, and dismissed till his wife's recovery.
  „ 23. Mortcloath for Janet Blackwell, £1 : 4s. Scots.
  „ 28. Thomas Bunzie and —— Mein in Newsteid, a.d.n. Jean : w. James and Andrew Bunzies.
  Collected by John Sibbald and Andrew Marr, £2 : 1s. Scots.
  Mortcloath to Wm. Atchison, £1 : 4s. Scots.
Sept. 4. Andrew Pringle and Anne Brock in Newsteid, a.s.n. Andrew ; w. Walter Murray, James Rutherfurd.
  Collected by William Hoy and Nicol Milne, £2 : 18s. Scots.
  „ 11. After prayer sederunt, the Minister, Andrew Marr, John Mabane, Robert Scot, Andrew Mein, &c., elders.
  Collected by Robert Scot, Andrew Drummond, £2 : 1s. Scots.
  (Case of discipline against Marion Usher.)
  „ 13. William Mathison and Janet Frier, a.s.n. Archibald ; w. Andrew and John Dawsons.
  „ 16. Booked John Gill in the parish of Galashiels and Elizabeth Moffat in this parish : John Gill in Melrose, cautioner.
  Item, booked John Fiddes and Elizabeth Martine, both in this parish ; John Anderson, cautioner.
  „ 18. John Smith and Margaret Wight in Darnick, a.d.n. Isobel ; w. John Smith, James Wight, there.
  After prayer sederunt, the Minister, John Mabane, John Mercer, Robert Scott, Wm. Hoy, &c., elders.
  Collected by Nicol Milne and John Sibbald, £1 : 13s. Scots.
  (Case of discipline against Marion Usher continued.)
  „ 25. Charles Wilkieson and Anne Paterson in Melrose, a.d.n. Margaret.
  „ „ James Watt and Margaret Darling in Melrose, a.d.n. Margaret ; w. Dr. John Rutherfurd, Alexr. Paterson.
  This day the minister intimated a meeting of the heretors, &c. here, Thursday next, to consider the state of the poor, and a committee of the session to meet to-morrow to clear counts with George Martine, who is continued treasurer.
  Collected by Robert Scott and Andrew Mein, £1 : 14s. Scots.
  „ 26. This day mett the minister, John Mabane, Robert Scott and John Mercer. They inspected what was collected and brought in by marriages and mortcloaths since July last, and do find £35 : 9s.

1737.

Scots., the half whereof is to be accounted for to the heretors Thursday next, at which time George Martine is ordered to have ready an account of the deburesments he has made. £26 : 6s. Scots of sacrament money was also told by.

Sept. 29. The heritors mett this day and provided for the poor ensuing quarter.

Oct. 2. After prayer sederunt, the Minister, Nicol Milne, John Mabane, John Mercer, Andrew Marr, &c., elders.

Collected by William Milne and Andrew Drummond, £1 : 14s. Scots.

Best mortcloath for Isobel Cochran, £2 : 16s. Scots.

(Case against Marion Usher continued.)

(Case of discipline against Jean Rae, daughter to Walter Rae, weaver in Newtown, and William Rae, her father's apprentice.)

,, 7. This day booked William Bartleman in this parish and Jean Pringle in the parish of Earlestown ; Andrew Bartleman, cautioner.

Mortcloath to Janet Pursel, £1 : 4s. Scots.

,, 8. Booked Wm. and Janet Raes, both in this parish ; George Rae, cautioner.

Also Walter Haitley in this parish and Margaret Moffat in the parish of Earlestown ; John Fairbairn, cautioner.

,, 9. Philip Fair and Alison Stephenson in Gattonside, a.s.n. John ; w. Andrew Marr, Thomson Bostone.

After prayer sederunt, the Minister, William Hoy, John Mercer, John Mabane, &c., elders.

Collected by William Hoy and Andrew Mein, £1 : 15s. Scots.

(Case against Jean and Wm. Rae continued.)

Marion Usher was this day called and dealt with, but to no purpose. She is summoned to the session this day fourteen days.

,, 11. The little mortcloath to a child, 8d.

This day the heretors mett with the session and took up an account of the last quarter's weekly collections, sacrament collections included ; as also saw the applications of the £19 sterling given up by the session to the heretors at their meeting July last, and have ordered the 40s. sterling of bad brass money, mentioned in the said sederunt, to be disposed upon and applyed to the payment of the enrolled poor this quarter.

,, 16. Collected by John Sibbald and Andrew Drummond, £2 : 1s. Scots.

,, 17. James Brotherstone and Eupham Dickson in Drygrainge, a.d.n. Eupham ; w. Robert Philp, Robert Ormistown.

,, 18. Booked James Stirling and Agnes Scot, both in this parish ; Robert Scott, cautioner.

,, 23. Andrew Burnet and Eleanor Turnbull in Melrose, a.s.n. William ; w. Dr. Martine, James Lythgow.

After prayer sederunt, the Minister, John Mabane, Andrew Mein, William Hoy, Andrew Marr, &c., elders.

Collected by Robert Scot and Andrew Drummond, £2 : 14s. Scots.

(Case against Marion Usher continued.)

,, ,, The session statute and appoint every one that calls for the new velvet mortcloath pay 5s. sterling within the parish, and 7s. sterling out of the parish.

For the 2nd velvet one half a crown, and for the best plush one half a crown ; and that the old plush one be dyed, and to bring in 18d. from every one who uses it.

Best velvet mortcloath, £3 Scots.

,, 25. Testimonials produced of the marriage of William Thistletown, soldier, and Margaret Jones, dated Dec. 22nd, 1728, by John Road, vicar of St. Peter parish, in the city of Hareford, whereupon was baptised Elizabeth, daughter to the forsaid persons ; w. Robert Scot, George Martine.

1737.

Oct. 27. Second plush mortcloath to Robert Pringle, 16d.

Booked Robert Speeding in the parish of Galashiels and Janet Glendinning in this parish ; John Forrest, cautioner.

,, 29. Booked Robert Hog in this parish and Alison Trotter in the parish of Westruther ; John Fisher, cautioner.

Item, booked Andrew Mein and Helen Lawrie, both in this parish ; Robert Lawrie, cautioner.

,, 30. Intimated a collection against this day eight days for William Bowar in Melrose, who had his house burnt.

Collected by William Hoy and Andrew Mein, £2 Scots.

Nov. 2. Received testimonials for Thomas Blaikie and Agnes Wight, and baptised Elizabeth, daughter to them, living in Westhouses ; w. George Martine.

,, 6. Booked John Scott and Agnes Renaldson, both in this parish ; John Mein, younger, cautioner.

Collected by John Sibbald and Robert Scott, £12 : 16s. Scots, which was delivered to William Bowar, as above appointed.

,, 11. Booked George Wight and Christian Pringle, both in this parish ; George Walker, cautioner.

James Smith and Catharine Pringle, both in this parish ; James Williamson, cautioner.

,, 13. Andrew Wood and Jean Mack in Gattonside, a.d.n. Agnes ; w. Laird Mar, William Hoy.

Collected by Wm. Hoy and Wm. Milne, £1 : 12s. Scots.

,, 15. Thomas Henderson and Elizabeth Pringle in Sorrowlessfield, a.d.n. Janet ; w. James Fisher, John Mertown.

,, 16. To the mortcloath, 12d.

Item, ditto, 16d.

,, 19. Booked John Mercer and Isobel Mabane, both in this parish ; James Mabane, cautioner.

,, 20. Jean and William Raes appeared before the congregation for the first time, and were rebuked.

Collected by Andrew Drummond and Nicol Milne, £1 : 5s. Scots.

(Case of discipline against Agnes Gray, servitrix to Alexr. Paterson, bailie.)

,, 21. After prayer sederunt, the Minister, John Mabane, Robert Scot, Andrew Melders.

(Case against Agnes Gray continued.)

Item, best mortcloath for Dr. Martine, £2 : 16s. Scots.

,, 27. William Hart and Margaret Mein in Newstead, a.s.n. Robert ; w James and Andrew Meins.

Wm. and Jean Raes compeared the second time.

After prayer sederunt, the Minister, James Laidley, Robert Moffat, John Wallace, Andrew Mein, elders.

Collected by William Milne and Andrew Mein, £1 : 6s. Scots.

(Case against Marion Usher continued.)

(Case against Agnes Gray continued.) She was called, but compeared not, nay, it was represented that she told the officer that though she had come last day at the minister's desire, yet she would not come this day, and the session being also informed that she is to go off to-morrow resolved forthwith to apply to the magistrate of the place to have her secured that she may answer the session when they may have occasion for her. The session immediately dispatched their officer to Mr. Paterson, the magistrate, to see whether he would wait on the session or the session should wait on him. The officer reported that the said Mr Paterson would be with them immediately. Accordingly, the ministers and elders, with the clerk, mett the bailie in the valley, where the minister told him of the flagrant report of Agnes Gray, his servant, her being with child, and of her intention to go off to-morrow, and required him as magistrate to secure her till she answer the session, that they may make a narrow scrutiny into this matter, which he peremptorily refused to do, upon which the minister took instruments in the clerk's hand and craved an extract thereof. This was done twixt eighth and nine of the morning, in presence of several of the elders and George Martin, beadle. It is the mind of the session that application should be made to some justice of the peace, viz., to Mr. Riddell of Riddell, for his warrant to secure the said Agnes Gray, which the minister undertook to do. The said Agnes is ordered to be cited pro 3tio to the session to-morrow at nine in the morning, Nov. 29th. The session constitute, Mr. Paterson, bailie, compeared and craved an extract of the instrument taken against him yesterday, which the session granted, and appointed their clerk accordingly. Mr. Milne, minister, did, in presence of the session, require the said Mr. Paterson to secure the said Agnes Gray by virtue of a warrant from Mr. Riddell of Riddell, one of his Majestie's justices of the peace in the shire, which the said Mr. Paterson refusing, the minister took instruments in the clerk's hand. There were cited Mary Kyle, midwife, Isobel Ellies, Margaret Bowar and Isobel Hunter to make tryal of the said Agnes Gray, her being with child, in case she should compear and deny she was with child. Agnes Gray being cited was called but compeared not, and in regard she was delivered to James Wallace, as constable and jailor, yesternight upon instrument by virtue of the forsaid justices' warrant the session sent of their officer to the said James Wallace to demand that he present his prisoner in terms of the instrument. James Wallace compeared and told the session that he sat with her till it was late yesternight, and that she said all the men in Melrose should not take her to prison. So he left her, and this morning he went to the bailies to find her out and present her to the session, but though in quest of her he could not find her, whereupon the minister took instruments that he had not secured her in the terms of the warrant. The session appoints their meeting to-morrow morning at nine of the clock, Nov. 30th. The session sitting in judgment were certainly informed that Agnes Gray went off yesterday with up sun upon an horse of the bailie's, and his servant Thomas Fife riding before her. The session gave orders that the said Thomas Fife, Margaret Borthwick and Isobel Forrest, servants to Bailie Paterson, Thomas Williamson, wright in Newstead, Thomas Bunzie, weaver there, and Andrew Fife, father to the said Thomas, and James Bowie in Melrose, be cited to the session to-morrow at ten of the clock, Dec. 1st. The session mett and constitute, Thomas Fife being cited was called but compeared not, yea, told the officer he would not attend the session. Margaret Borthwick and Isobel Forrest were also called, but compeared not. Thomas Williamson, wright in Newstead, cited and called, compeared and declared that on Tuesday last twixt three and four afternoon he met Agnes Gray riding behind Thomas Fife, the bailie's servant, at the brae going down to the boat ; and that he shook hands with her, and that she said she was going to her mother's. This he is ready to declare upon oath when required. Thomas Bunzie, weaver there, declared *in omnibus ut in priori*, and further added that it was the bailie's black horse. Andrew Fife cited, called, compeared and declared that yesterday morning as his son was returning he called at his house, and that he said he had got a cold morning, for he had ridden a long way, to wit, from Bown, where he had left Agnes Gray with her mother, and this he is ready to declare upon oath if required.

1737.

Dec. 2. Booked William Waugh in the parish of Lauder and Agnes Lees in this parish; James Wallace, cautioner.

Married here Ninian Black and Marion Williamson, not proclaimed here, paid in 12d.

4. Wm. and Jean Raes appeared for the third time, were rebuked and dismissed. Paid in £4 Scots.

After prayer sederunt, the Minister, John Mabane, Robert Scott, John Mercer, &c., elders.

Collected by Andrew Marr and Andrew Drummond, £1 : 0 : 9 Scots.

This day the minister reported to the session that as Mr. Paterson's servants were absent Thursday last when cited to be examined, the said Mr. Paterson came to him when the session was risen and offered that his servants should appear when called to be examined in the affair of Agnes Gray. This day the clerk read over the proceedings of the several session last week, and they considering the affair were unanimously of the mind that the whole matter should be extracted and laid before the Rev. presbytry of Selkirk Tuesday next, and they appoint their clerk accordingly. Moreover the session recommended to the minister to write to the presbytry of Earlstown concerning the said Agnes Gray residing at Bown within their bounds, in regard there is no minister at Ligerwood.

11. Wm. Mathison and Janet Frier appeared for the first time and were rebuked.

13. William Frier and Isobel Bain in Isle Rae, a.d.n. Isobel.

,, James Hunter and Isobel Gray in Westerlanglee, a.d.n. Mary : w. Thomas Darling, George Blaikie.

18. Nicol Milne and —— Frater in Newtown, a.s.n. Thomas ; w. Nicol and John Milnes.

,, William Mathison and Janet Frier compeared the second time.

The minister intimated the sentence of the greater excommunication pronounced by the presbytry of Edinburgh against Mr. William Strang according to appointment.

Collected by Robert Scott, John Mercer, £1 : 11s. Scots.

19. William Darling and —— Allan in Blainslies, a.s.n. Robert ; w. John Grieve, Alexr. Gray.

21. After prayer sederunt, *pro re nata*, the Minister, John Mabane, Andrew Mein, Robert Scot, elders.

(Case against Marion Usher continued). She now involved James M'Gie, gardener at Ford, Northumberland.

22. Mortcloath money for two children, 16s. Scots.

24. Andrew Renaldson and Janet Scot in Darnick, a.s.n. Andrew.

,, William Bunzie and Barbara Trotter in Newsteid, a.s.n. Robert : w. Robert and Alexr. Bunzies in Newsteid.

Wm. Mathison and Janet Frier compeared for the third time, were rebuked and dismissed, and paid in £4 Scots of penalty.

The minister intimated Thursday next for the heretors and fewars to meet for considering the state of the poor for ensuing quarter.

After prayer sederunt, the Minister, Nicol Milne, Andrew Marr, John Mercer, &c., elders.

Collected by John Sibbald and Andrew Marr, £1 : 8s. Scots.

(Case of discipline against Elizabeth Moodie and Mr. Walter Scot, late of Whitslead, continued.)

29. This day being appointed for a meeting of the heretors, there mett for revising the session's accompts, the Minister, John Mabane, James Laidlaw and Robert Scot.

An accompt of the collections, mortcloath and marriage money with penalties was produced extending to £49 : 16s. Scots, the half whereof was given in to the heretors their collection for Melrose

1737.

district. There was also produced an account of deburseiments by George Martine, amounting to £19 : 6s. Scots, which deduced from £24 : 18s. Scots, there remains £5 : 12s. Scots, wherewith he is to charge himself.

The minister gave in £3 Scots, an year's rent of Robert Mercer's bond, which is also lodged with George Martine.

The minister reported that he received 7s. sterling as John Brown's penalty, which he distributed to several the time of the sacrament.

The heretors mett and provided for the poor for ensuing quarter.

Dec. 30. Thomas Vallance and Jean Waugh in Blainslies, a.d.n. Janet ; w. Alexr. Gray, John Wallace.

Booked Charles Ormistown and Jean Lockie, both in this parish ; Robert Ormistown, cautioner.

1738.

Jan. 1. George Martine and —— Fair in Westhouses, a.d.n. Isobel ; w. John and Henry Forests.

Elizabeth Moodie appeared for the first time and was admonished.

Collected by Wm. Milne, Andrew Drummond and Andrew Marr, £1 : 13s. Scots.

,, 8. Collected by Robert Scot and William Milne, £1 : 9s. Scots.

Elizabeth Moodie appeared for the second time.

,, 14. James Waugh and Marion Duncan in Melrose, a.d.n. Isobel : w. George and Andrew Martines.

,, 15. William Steele and Elizabeth Walker in Melrose, a.s.n. William ; w. George Walker, Nicol Mercer.

Elizabeth Moodie, appeared the third time.

After prayer sederunt, the Minister, John Mabane, Robert Scot, Andrew Mein, &c., elders.

Collected by John Mabane and Andrew Marr, £2 : 16s. Scots.

(Case against Agnes Gray continued.)

,, 18. Best mortcloath to Alison Murray, £3 Scots.

,, 19. John Fisher and Isobel Scot in Colmslie, a.d.n. Isobel ; w. Robert Laidlaw, Peter Moffat.

,, 22. James Wight and Janet Skirven in Darnick, a s.n. George ; w. James Burnet, John Mercer.

Elizabeth Moodie appeared the fourth time and was dealt with.

After prayer sederunt, the Minister, John Mercer, John Sibbald, Nicol Milne, &c., elders.

Collected by Nicol and William Milne, £2 : 2s. Scots.

(Case against Agnes Gray continued.)

,, 25. For the second plush mortcloath, 16d.

,, 29. James Mercer and Anne Tailor in Darnick, a.d.n. Janet.

,, ,, Wm. Martine and Jean Grieve in Gattonside, a.d.n. Jean.

,, ,, Thomas Speeding and Margaret Brown in Gattonside, a.d.n. Margaret ; w. Andrew Marr, Thomas Boustone.

Elizabeth Moodie appeared for the fifth time.

After prayer sederunt, the Minister, John Wallace, John Sibbald, Andrew Marr, &c., elders.

Collected by Andrew Marr and Nicol Milne, £1 : 14s. Scots.

(Case against Agnes Gray continued).

Feb. 1. Mortcloath for a child, 8d.

,, 5. George Walker and Anne Pringle in Melrose, a.s.n. John.

,, ,, John Hope and Isobel Haliburtone in Gattonside, a.s.n. Andrew.

,, ,, Andrew Dickson and —— Haliburtone in Drygrainge, a.s.n. George.

,, ,, Alexr. Strachan and Mary Mein in Melrose, a.d.n. Jean ; w. Andrew Marr, John Tait (for four above entries).

Elizabeth Moodie was rebuked and dismissed.

1738.

After prayer sederunt, the Minister, John Sibbald, John Mercer, Nicol Milne, &c., elders.

Collected by Andrew Drummond and Andrew Mein, £1 : 14s. Scots.

Elizabeth Moodie's penalty, £1 : 10s. Scots.

(Case against Agnes Gray continued.)

Feb. 8. George Grieve and —— Somervel in Blainslies, a.d.n. Jean ; w. Hugh Grieve, James Wallace.

,, 10. Mortcloath for Margaret Phaup, £1 : 10s. Scots.

,, 12. After prayer sederunt, the Minister, Robert Scot, John Mabane, Andrew Mein, &c., elders.

Collected by John Wallace, £1 : 13s. Scots.

There was produced an execution of summons against Agnes Gray pro 3 tio. She was called but compeared not, nay, she told the officer that summoned her, though he should summon her till the day of his death, she would not answer, besides, there was a letter produced dated the 10th instant from Bown, directed to the minister, acknowledging her being with child to Mr. Paterson, bailie here. The session do for the time delay this affair.

,, 19. Collected by Andrew Drummond, £1 : 6s. Scots.

The mortcloath to a child, 8d.

,, 26. Walter Scot and Janet Mein in Danieltown, a.s.n. Walter ; w. Robert Scot, George Lawrie.

Collected by Robert Scot and Andrew Drummond, £1 : 11s. Scots.

Mar. 5. Alexr. Lockie and Grissal Nicolson in Melrose, a.d.n. Elizabeth ; w. Andrew Dawsons, elder and younger.

After prayer sederunt, the Minister, Andrew Mein, John Sibbald, Nicol Milne, &c., elders.

Collected by James Laidlaw and Wm. Milne, £1 : 3s. Scots.

(Case against Agnes Gray and Mr. Paterson continued.)

,, 11. Mortcloath for Isobel Williamson, £1 : 10s. Scots.

,, 12. James Lythgow and Isobel Riddell in Gattonside, a d.n. Margaret ; w. Andrew Marr, Andrew Mein.

After prayer sederunt, the Minister, Andrew Mein, John Sibbald, Nicol Milne, &c., elders.

Collected by Andrew Drummond and Andrew Marr, £1 : 3s. Scots.

(Case against Mr. Paterson and Agnes Gray continued.)

,, 18. Booked John Pearson and Janet Moodie, both in this parish ; James Mercer, cautioner.

,, 19. Collected by Drummond, 19d.

,, 20. Mortcloath money, £1 : 16s. Scots.

,, 23. Mortcloath, £3 Scots.

,, 26. John Haliburtone and Alison Rae in Drygrainge, a.d.n. Helen ; w. Andrew Dickson, Wm. Forsan.

Collected by John Mabane and Andrew Marr, £1 : 14s. Scots.

Mortcloath money, 16s. Scots.

This day the minister intimated a meeting of the heretors, Tuesday next, to consider the state of the poor.

William Mathison and Janet Frier, for antenuptial fornication, gave in the penalty £4 Scots.

,, 28. This day the Minister, John Mabane, Robert Scott, &c. mett and gave up the half of the collections, &c. to the heretors. (Same day).— The heretors mett and provided for the poor for ensuing quarter.

,, ,, John Noteman and —— Purves in Hewieshaugh, a.s.n. Thomas ; w. George Martine.

,, 30. Mortcloath money, 16s. Scots.

April 2. After prayer sederunt, the Minister, John Mercer, John Sibbald, Andrew Marr, &c., elders.

1738.

             Collected by William Milne and Andrew Drummond, £1 : 8s. Scots.

             (Case against Mr. Paterson and Agnes Gray continued.)

April 3. Mr. Russel and Jean Boston in Langshaw, a.s.n. William ; w. George Alley, Robert Laidlay.

  ,,   ,, Thomas Darling and —— Thomson in Langhaugh, a.s.n. Robert ; w. George Alley, George Martin.

  ,, 4. Mortcloath money, £3 Scots.

  ,, 9. After prayer sederunt, the Minister, Andrew Marr, John Sibbald, Nicol Milne, &c., elders.

             Collected by Andrew Mein and Robert Scott, £1 : 19s. Scots.

             (Case against Marion Usher, continued.)

  ,, 16. John Fairbairn and Bessie Flint in Melrose, a.d.n. Mary ; w. Thomas Lookup, John Hoy.

             Collected by Andrew Mein and Andrew Drummond, £1 : 14s. Scots.

  ,, 17. Thomas Young and Isobel Thomson in Langshaw, a.d.n. Janet.

  ,,   ,, Thomas Dalgliesh and Janet Brown, a.d.n. Isobel ; w. Alexr. Scot. John Laidlaw.

             Mortcloath money, 8d.

  ,, 23. Collected by John Sibbald and Robert Scot, £1 : 6s. Scots.

             Item, to mortcloath money, 8d.

  , 30. Collected by Wm. Milne and Andrew Marr, £1 : 10s. Scots.

May 5. Booked Thomas Kennedy in the parish of Galashiels and Helen Laidlaw in this parish , John Thomson, cautioner.

             Mortcloath money, 8d.

  ,, 7. Robert Bunzie and Margaret Mein in Newsteid, a.d.n. Isobel ; w. William and John Bunzies.

             Collected by John Mercer and Andrew Drummond, £1 : 19s, Scots.

  ,, 14. Collected by Andrew Mein, £1 : 7s. Scots.

  ,, 19. Wm. and Helen Hunters in Melrose, a.s.n. James ; w. Robert and James Hunters.

  ,, 21. Collected by Robert Scott. £2 : 11s. Scots.

             Mortcloath money, 8d.

  ,, 28. Thomas Bunzie and Helen Bryden in Eildon, a.d.n. Marion ; w. John Sibbald, John Bunzie.

             Collected by Robert Moffat and Andrew Drummond, £1 : 10s. Scots.

  ,, 31. Booked John Lyal in the parish of Ligerwood and Margaret Turner in this parish ; Thomas Turner, cautioner.

June 4. John Lauder and —— in Housebyres, a.s.n. James ; w. Laird Marr, Thomas Boston.

             After prayer sederunt, the Minister, John Mercer, Andrew Mein, John Mabane, &c., elders.

             Collected by Robert Scott, £1 : 8s. Scots.

             The session unanimously resolve that the sacrament shall be celebrate in this place the 3rd Sabbath of July next. The sederunt closed with prayer.

             Mortcloath money, £1 : 10s. Scots.

  ,, 10. Booked John Chisholm in this parish and Elizabeth Lauder in the parish of Earlestown ; John Fisher, cautioner.

  ,, 11. Andrew Martin and Margaret Alexander in Melrose. a.d.n. Catharine.

  ,, ,, James Burnet and —— Renaldson in Darnick, a.d.n. Isobel.

  ,, ,, Robert Huntlie and Margaret Young in Gattonside, a.d.n. Isobel.

  ,, ,, Wm. Pringle and —— Tait in Blainslies, a.d.n. Christian ; w. George Martin, Robert Johnstone (for four preceding entries).

             Collected by John Sibbald, £1 : 7s. Scots.

  ,, 18. Margaret Redfurd, fornicatrix, compeared for the first time.

             Collected by Andrew Mein and Andrew Drummond, £1 : 6s. Scots.

1738.

June 21. Robert Lees and Eupham Mertle in Whitlaw, a.d.n. Janet ; w. ——

„ 25. The minister intimated a meeting of the heretors Tuesday next, concerning the poor.

After prayer sederunt, the Minister, John Mercer, Andrew Marr, John Sibbald, &c., elders.

Collected by John Sibbald and Andrew Marr, £1 : 10s. Scots.

(Case of discipline against Susanna Wanlees Gatesyde, Newcastle, and Wm. Hopkirk, younger.)

„ 27. The Minister, John Mabane, Robert Scott, &c., mett and gave up the half of the collections to the heretors.

Same day.—The heretors mett and provided for the poor for ensuing quarter, as per their sederunt of this date.

July 1. Booked for marriage Wm. Mein and Margaret Mercer, both in this parish : Nicol Bowar, cautioner.

„ 2. Andrew Riddell and Margaret Haliwall in Gattonside : w. John Thomson, Thomas Boston.

Margaret Redfurd compeared the third time, was rebuked and dismissed. Paid in her penalty, £1 : 10s. Scots.

This day the minister intimated the celebration of the sacrament of the supper in this place against this day fourteen days, and gave suitable exhortations.

After prayer sederunt, the Minister, John Sibbald, Robert Scott, Andrew Mein, &c., elders.

Collected by James Laidlay and Andrew Drummond, £1 : 12s. Scots.

It was this day represented that Henry Dalaway, dancing master in this place, did upon this day eighth days transport his wife, children and effects the time of divine service, to the great offence of the people. The session order him to be cited to the session against this day eight days.

„ 8. Booked David Brown and Janet Carter, both in this parish : John Tait, cautioner.

„ 9. The minister appointed Thursday next as the humiliation day before the sacrament.

After prayer sederunt, the Minister, Andrew Marr, Andrew Mein, Robert Scott, &c., elders.

Collected by John Mabane, £1 : 13s. Scots.

Henry Dalaway being cited, was called and compeared. He was charged with profaning the Lord's day in transporting himself, family and effects in time of Divine worship. He acknowledged his fault and expressed his sorrow for so doing, and promised never to be guilty for any such thing in time coming.

The session appoint Tuesday next for privy tryals and ordering other things about the sacrament.

„ 11. This day being appointed for privy tryals, after prayer sederunt, James Laidlaw, Nicol Milne, John Sibbald, John Wallace, John Mercer, Andrew Drummond, Robert Scott, John Mabane, Andrew Marr, elders.

The elders present were severally removed by pairs, tryed, approven and encouraged to go on in the Lord's work.

The collections are to be gathered and doors kept as formerly.

„ 13. Robert Grierson and Marion Wilson in Darnick, a.s.n. Gabriel.

„ „ Alexr. Vair and —— Wilson in Danieltown, a.s.n. George.

„ „ —— and —— in Blainslies, a.s.n. John.

„ „ Nicol Mercer and —— Chisholm in Bridgend, a.d.n. Margaret ; w. Thomas Vair, William Wilson.

„ 17. John Usher and Janet White in Darnick, a.s.n. James ; w. James Usher, John Hownam.

1738.

Collected, Fast day,	-	-	-	-	£7 4 0
Collected, Saturday,	-	-	-	-	11 3 0
Collected, Sabbath day,	-	-	-	-	21 14 0
Collected, Monday,	-	-	-	-	10 4 0
					£50 5 0
Given to the precentor, within and without doors,					6 12 0
To the beadle,	-	-	-	-	3 0 0

July 18. Mett Blainslies, after prayer sederunt, *pro re nata*, the Minister, Robert Moffat, John Wallace, Robert Scot, elders.
    (Case of discipline against Jean Steel in Blainslies and George Kirkwood, clerk of Lauder.)

,, 21. For the mortcloath, £3 Scots.

,, 23. After prayer sederunt, the Minister, John Sibbald, Robert Scott, Andrew Mein, &c. elders.
    Collected by Andrew Drummond and Andrew Marr, £2 : 6s. Scots.
    Received testimonials for Robert Laidlaw and family.
    The confession of Jean Steel taken at Blainslies the 18th instant was read to the session, and as the guilt was committed in Lauder and the scandal most nottour there, the session appoint their clerk to send the said confession to the minister of Lauder, that they may enquire into it.

,, 28. Booked William Wilson in this and Margaret Ford in the parish of Lauder; Robert Scot, cautioner.
    Mortcloath to a child, 8d.
    To a new burial place, 10d.

,, 30. Collected by Andrew Drummond, £1 : 9s. Scots.

Aug. 6. Collected by Robert Scott, £1 : 19s. Scots.

,, 13. Walter Rae and Christian Richie in Newtown, a.d.n. Agnes.

,, ,, Wm. Turner and Mary Purves in Gattonside, a.d.n. Isabel; w. Laird Marr, Thomas Boston.
    Collected by Wm. Milne and Andrew Marr, £1 : 14s. Scots.

,, 16. Little mortcloath to two children, 16d.

,, 20. Robert Hog and —— Gillas in Melrose, a.s.n. George.

,, ,, Wm. Wilson and Mary Wright in Danieltown, a.d.n. Helen; w. Robert Johnstone, Robert Penman.
    Collected by Andrew Drummond, £1 : 10s. Scots.

,, 21. Alexr. Gray and Margaret Thinne in Blainslies, a.s.n. William; w. Wm. Darling, Robert Scot.

,, 27. Collected by Robert Scott and John Wallace, £1 : 14s. Scots.
    Mortcloath money, £1 : 10s. Scots.
    Ditto to a child, 8d.

,, 29. James Edgar and Bessie Pringle in Blainslies, a.s.n. James : w. John Fisher.

Sept. 3. Collected by William Milne and Andrew Mein, £1 : 7s. Scots.

,, 10. Wm. Bartleman and Jean Pringle in Newsteid, a.s.n. William.

,, ,, John Purves and Agnes Thinne in Melrose, a.d.n. Helen : w. Thomas Marr, James Smail.
    Collected by John Mabane, £1 : 7s. Scots.

,, 17. Collected by Robert Scott and Andrew Marr, £1 : 8s. Scots.
    Mortcloath money, 16s. Scots.

,, 22. Booked James Waugh in the parish of Ligerwood and Jean Grahamslie in this parish; Robert Penman, cautioner.

,, 23. Booked Thomas Anderson in the parish of Earlstown and Agnes Brown in this parish; James Fisher, cautioner.

,, 24. John Gill and Helen Paterson in Melrose, a.d.n. Alison.

,, ,, John Fiddes and Elizabeth Martine in Gattonside, a.d.n. Isobel; w. Thomas Gill, George Lawrie.
    This day the minister intimated a meeting of the heretors Friday first.

1738.

Collected by Andrew Mein and John Mercer, £1 : 9s. Scots.

Sept. 25. Best mortcloath, £3 Scots.

,, 29. This day was given in the half of the collections &c., to the heretors, who as none of the principal heretors mett, the meeting is continued till Thursday next, and intimation is to be made Sabbath next.

,, 30. Booked Alexr. Cook, senior, and Isobel Moodie, both in this parish ; Alexr. Cook, cautioner.

Oct. 1. Robert Trotter and Margaret Mabane in Melrose, a.d.n. Janet ; w. John and William Mabanes.
Collected by Robert Scot, 15d.
Intimation was made conform to appointment Friday last.

,, 5. The heritors mett and provided for the poor for ensuing quarter, as per their sederunt.

, 7. Booked Robert Lawrie in this parish and Alison Wight in the parish of Bowden ; Wm. Cook, cautioner.

,, 8. Andrew Marr and —— Mercer in Darnick, a.s.n. Robert ; w. John Dalgliesh, John Hownam, there.

,, 9. Martcloath money, £4 : 10s. Scots.

,, 12. Ditto £3 Scots.

,, 14. Booked John Hoy and Helen Bartown, both in this parish ; Thomas Hoy, cautioner.

,, 15. John Mercer and —— Mabane in Newsteid, a.s.n. John ; w. John Mein, elder and younger.
Collected by Robert Scott, £1 : 2s. Scots.

,, 18. Mortcloath, 8d.

,, 20. Booked James Henry in the parish of Galashiels and Margaret Ellies in this parish ; Wm. Alley, cautioner.

,, 21. Booked Alexr. M'Faddzean and Janet Sked, both in this parish ; John Lyal, cautioner.
Mortcloath money, £1 Scots.

,, 22. Collected by Andrew Drummond, £1 : 11s. Scots.

,, 27. George Scott and Isobel Tailor in Danieltown, two daughters named Elizabeth and Isobel ; w. Walter Scots, George Lawrie.

,, 29. John Bunzie and Isobel Wilson in Newtown, a s.n. Robert ; w. Nicol Milne, John Sibbald.
After prayer sederunt the Minister, Andrew Mein, Robert Scot, John Mercer, &c., elders.
Collected by Andrew Marr, £1 : 12s. Scots.
Michael Wallace having married irregularly was with his wife cited to this day's session. Michael compeared and produced the lines of his marriage, dated at Edinburgh the 12th of October 1738, signed —— Robertsone, minister. Produced also testimonials for his wife from Hawick, proceeding Whitsunday last. He was rebuked for the same, and his wife not compearing she is ordered to be cited to the session this day eight day, and the said Michael to pay his fine due to the poor of the parish.
(Case against Mr. Paterson and Agnes Gray continued.)

Nov. 1. Booked James Peacock in the parish of Galashiels and Isobel Elliot in this ; William Wallace, cautioner.

,, 5. John Scot and Agnes Renaldson in Newsteid, a.s.n. John ; w. Andrew Mein, Robert Bunzie.
After prayer sederunt the Minister, Wm. Milne, Nicol Milne, Andrew Mein, elders.
Collected by Andrew Drummond and Andrew Marr, £1 : 6s. Scots.
Agnes Wright, spouse to Michael Wallace, being cited to this session was called but compeared not. She is ordered to be cited *pro secundo* to the session against this day eight days.

,, 7. Mortcloath to Janet Bunzie, £3 Scots.

1738.

Nov. 9. William Martin and Isobel Drummond in Gattonside, a.s.n. William ; w. Andrew Marr.

„ 12. James Speeding and Janet Mercer in Bridgend, a.d n. Jean ; w. Nicol Mercer, William Hud.

After prayer sederunt the Minister, John Mercer, Andrew Mein, &c., elders.

Collected by John Sibbald and Andrew Marr, £1 : 16s. Scots.

Agnes Wright being summoned, was called but compeared not. The session appoint her to be cited pro 3tio to the session against this day eight days. The sederunt closed with prayer.

„ 17. James Dickson and —— Blaikie in Westhouses, a.d.n. Isobel ; w. Mungo and John Parks.

„ 18. Booked Nicol Laidlaw and Elizabeth Milne, both in this parish ; Mungo Laidlaw, cautioner.

„ „ Andrew Darling in this parish and Margaret Somervel in the parish of Lauder : Alexr. Scott, cautioner.

Mortcloath to a child, 8d.

„ 19. After prayer sederunt, the Minister, John Mabane, Andrew Marr, &c., elders.

Collected by Nicol Milne and Robert Scot, £1 : 15s. Scots.

Agnes Wright being called, compeared not. The affair is delayed for the time.

The session has condescended to take a crown as Janet Glendinning's penalty in not compleating marriage with —— Speeding, in Galashiels parish.

Mortcloath to a child, 8d.

Robert Scot's penalty for irregular marriage, £9 Scots.

„ 25. Booked Thomas Gill and Isobel Riddell, both in this parish ; John Gill, cautioner.

Andrew Mein and Alison Mein, both in this parish ; Cornelius Mein, cautioner.

John Park in this parish and Margaret Henderson in the parish of Gordon ; Mungo Park, cautioner.

„ 26. James M'Dougal and Janet Heiton in Darnick, a.s.n. Andrew.

„ „ Andrew and Helen Bunzies in Newsteid, a.d.n. Christian ; w. John and Andrew Meins.

Collected by Wm. Milne, £1 : 8s. Scots.

„ 29. Peter Legg and Margaret Frier in Melrose, a.s.n. Peter ; w. Thomas and Andrew Murrays.

Dec. 1. Booked William Tait in the parish of Stow, and Isobel Turner in this parish ; John Hoy, cautioner.

„ „ Thomas Slatter in this parish, and Janet Darling in the parish of Ligerwood ; Alexr. Scott, cautioner.

„ 2. Booked William Scot in this parish and Elizabeth Cochran in the parish of Lesuden : John Gill, cautioner.

Collected by Andrew Drummond, £1 : 5s. Scots.

„ 4. Charles Ormistoun and Jean Lockie in Melrose, two daughters named Elizabeth and Margaret ; w. John Mabane.

„ 5. Richard Park and Margaret Pringle in Allanshaws, a.s.n. Richard.

„ „ John Edgar and Agnes Grieve in Blainslies, a.d.n. Agnes ; w. John Fisher, John Wallace.

„ 7. Booked William Brown in this and Janet Scot in the parish of Ashkirk ; Andrew Pringle, cautioner.

„ 8. John Brown and Marion Fairbairn, both in this parish ; John Robertson, cautioner.

John Mein and Christian Hunter, both in this parish ; James Hunter, cautioner.

„ 10. After prayer sederunt, the Minister, Andrew Marr, John Mabane, John Mercer, &c., elders.

Collected by William Milne, £1 : 16s. Scots.

1738.

(Case of discipline against Margaret Walker and James Hopkirk.)

Dec 17. After prayer sederunt, the Minister, James Laidlaw, Robert Scott Andrew Mein, &c., elders.

        Collected by Andrew Drummond and Andrew Marr, £1 : 18s Scots.

        William Hopkirk, guilty with Susanna Wanlees in Newcastle, having applied that he may make satisfaction before this congregation, appeared this day before the session and testified his sorrow for his sin, and appointed to appear Sabbath first in common form.

        (Case against James Hopkirk and Margaret Walker continued.)

"   " The best mortcloath, £3 Scots.

        To a new burial place, 10d.

"   18. Wm. Wood and Elizabeth Brown in ——, a.d.n. Isobel ; w. John Fisher, Alexr. Scot.

"   19. Best mortcloath, £3 Scots.

"   24. This day the minister intimated a meeting for the poor, Tuesday next.

"   " George Mercer, and Isobel Hunter in Darnick, a.s.n. John ; w. John Mercer. Wm. Hunter.

        Collected by Andrew Marr, and John Sibbald, £2 : 1s. Scots.

        Wm. Hopkirk compeared for the first time and was admonished.

"   26. This day the heretors and session mett and provided for the poor for ensuing quarter, as per their sederunt of this date.

        Andrew Bartleman, tailor, indweller in Newtown, presented a petition craving the heretors and kirk session would allow him liberty to build a seat for his family in the Silverless isle at the end of James Pringles. The heretors and session viewed the place and granted his petition, provided he prejudice none that have seats already.

"   28. Robert Hog and Alison Trotter in Bentmilne, a.s.n. John ; w. Mungo Park, John Park.

        Best mortcloath to Peter Legg, £3 Scots.

        Do. to Robert Fisher, £3 Scots.

"   31. Charles Wilkieson and Anne Paterson in Melrose, a.s.n. Thomas.

"   " Wm. Bunzie and Janet Little in Newstead, a.s.n. Thomas.

"   " George Wight and Christian Pringle in Darnick, a.s.n. George ; w. Dr. Rutherfurd, Bailie Paterson.

        Collected by Andrew Mein and Wm. Milne, £2 : 15s. Scots.

        (Baptisms and other bookings are to be found separately in another book.)

1739.

Jan. 5. Mortcloath money £1 : 10s. Scots.

"   7. Wm. Hopkirk compeared the third time, was rebuked, dismissed, and paid in £2 : 10s. Scots.

        Collected by John Mercer and Andrew Marr, £1 : 7s. Scots.

        The session appoints their clerk to speak to Mr. Paterson and see if he will compear before a committee of the session any time that is most convenient for him, and own his guilt with Agnes Gray.

"   28. James Hopkirk compeared the first time, and was admonished.

        After prayer sederunt, the Minister, John Wallace, Andrew Mein, &c., elders.

        (Case against Mr. Paterson continued.) The session is of the mind that affair should be again laid before the presbytry.

        The session appointed their clerk to speak to Michael Wallace that he would cause his wife compear before the session and acknowledge her marriage, and give in their penalty due the poor for such irregular marriage, and in case he refuse to acquaint him the session will prosecute him before the Justices of the Peace.

Feb. 4. James Hopkirk compeared the second time.

1739.

Collected by Robert Scott, 17½d.

The minister indisposed.

Feb. 11. James Hopkirk compeared the third time, was rebuked and dismissed. Paid his penalty, £2 : 10s. Scots.

Collected by Andrew Drummond, £1 : 6s. Scots.

„ 18. Collected by Robert Scott and Andrew Marr, £1 : 10s. Scots.

„ 25. After prayer sederunt, the Minister, John Mercer, Andrew Mein, Robert Scott, &c., elders.

Collected by Andrew Marr, Nicol Milne, £1 : 6s. Scots.

(Case of discipline against Wm. Scot and Elizabeth Cochran, his wife, also the case against Michael Wallace and Agnes Wright, continued.)

Mar. 4. After prayer sederunt, the Minister, James Laidlaw, Nicol Milne, Andrew Marr, &c., elders.

Collected by Andrew Drummond and Andrew Mein, £1 : 11s. Scots.

(Case against William Scot and Elizabeth Cochran continued.)

Agnes Wright, spouse to Michael Wallace, compeared, and testified her sorrow for their irregular marriage. It is recommended to the clerk to speak to Michael to pay his fine as others have done in like cases.

„ 11. About nine of the clock morning. After prayer sederunt, the Minister, Nicol Milne, Robert Scott, John Mabane, &c., elders.

(Case of discipline against Bearfawld's servant maid.)

Collected by John Mabane, £1 : 1s. Scots.

For the little mortcloath, 8d.

„ 18. After prayer sederunt, the Minister, John Wallace, Robert Scott, John Mercer, &c., elders.

Collected by William Milne, £1 : 17s. Scots.

(Case against Isobel Wilson, servitrix to Mr. Fisher, Bearfawld, and young Mr. Fisher.)

„ 19. Mortcloath money, 8d.

„ 25. The minister intimated a meeting of the heretors, &c. Thursday next concerning the poor.

After prayer sederunt, the Minister, William Milne, Andrew Mein, &c., elders.

Collected by Robert Scott, £1 : 14s. Scots.

(Case against Isobel Wilson and Andrew Fisher continued.)

„ 29. The heretors mett and provided for the poor for ensuing quarter, as per their sederunt of this date.

„ 30. Mortcloath money, 20d.

April 1. After prayer sederunt, Minister, John Mabane, John Mercer, Andrew Marr, elders.

Collected by Andrew Drummond, £1 : 6s. Scots.

The session appoints to-morrow fourteen days for inspecting George Martin's accompts, and they ordain him to have them ready against that time.

As Isobel Wilson compeared not according to appointment, it is recommended to the elder in Darnick to speak to her.

„ 5. The little mortcloath, 8d.

„ 8. Collected by William Milne, £1 Scots.

„ 15. Collected by Robert Scott, £1 : 11s. Scots.

„ 16. This day met, conform to a former appointment.

After prayer, the Minister, John Mabane, Nicol and William Milns, Andrew Mein, Andrew Mar, Robert Scott, elders.

The session having looked into George Martin's accompts, charge and discharge since July 1737, and the same being in several separate papers. The session appoint him to make them out in some sheets of paper bookways against the 7th of May next, at

1739.

which time the session appoints their meeting to revise and approve the same.

The minister acquainted the session that he has a demand on these, in whose hands the poor's money and papers are lodged, for certain sums which he claims to be returned to him, and the session, to be disposed of by them only for pious uses, as they shall think proper. *Imprimis*, Whereas it is the general practise of the ministers of the kingdom to pay the synod clerk's fees out of their collections, Mr. Milne, considering that their stock was but smal, and for other reasons, has paid it out of his own pocket these twenty-eight years, amounting to £84 Scots, at a crown per annum. *Secundo*, Whereas the allowance for the communion elements was only £20 Scots till anno 1724, this £20 Scots used to be given in to the session, and they defrayed all expences relative thereto out of the collections. This Mr. Milne paid out of his own pocket which a modest calcul will amount to £200 Scots. This the minister desired might be recorded and affixed to George Martin's accompts to be given in to the heretors.

April 22. Collected by William Milne, £1 : 7s. Scots.

(Case against Isobel Wilson and Andrew Fisher continued.)

Received testimonials for the said Isobel Wilson preceeding Whitsunday 1736.

    29. Collected by John Mabane, £1 : 5s. Scots.

May 5. Mortcloath money, £1 : 16s. Scots.

    6. After prayer sederunt, the Minister, Robert Scott, Andrew Mein, Andrew Drummond, elders.

Collected by Andrew Marr, £1 : 4s. Scots.

Isobel Wilson, servitrix to Mr. Fisher, having been cited pro 3^{tio} to compear before the congregation appears not. The session is to consider the affair at their next meeting.

    7. After prayer sederunt, the Minister, Nicol Milne, John Mabane, Robert Scott, Andrew Drummond, elders.

The session this day saw an accompt of the collections for four quarters preceeding April last, given in by George Martin. They approved the same, and appointed them to be given in to the bailie, with what Mr. Milne represented the 16th of April adjected thereto.

    13. Collected by Robert Scott, £1 : 11s. Scots.

For the little mortcloath, 8d.

    20. The minister intimated a meeting of the heretors, &c. Thursday come eight days about repairing the kirk.

After prayer sederunt, the Minister, John Mabane, Robert Scott, John Mercer, Andrew Marr, &c., elders.

Collected by Andrew Drummond, £1 : 6s. Scots.

(Case of discipline against Mary Lauder, servitrix to Alexr. Scott in Housebyres, and George Scott, son to the said Alexr.

Isobel Wilson, still living in the family with Andrew Fisher, notwithstanding he has once and again been charged to put her away. The session do unanimously referr that affair to the presbytry of Selkirk to meet at Liliesleaf last Tuesday of this moneth, and the beadle is ordered to cite the said Andrew and Isobel to the said diet of the presbytry.

    27. After prayer sederunt, the Minister, Robert Scott, James Laidlaw, Nicol Milne, &c., elders.

Collected by Andrew Mein, £2 : 2s. Scots.

(Case against George Scott and Mary Lauder continued.)

Received testimonials for James Kyle, his wife, and Mary Bourlees, preceeding Whitsunday 1728.

June 3. The minister intimated a meeting of the heretors Thursday next for repairing the kirk.

Q

1739.

Mary Lauder appeared for the first time, and was rebuked.

Collected by Andrew Drummond, £1 : 9s. Scots.

June   5. The little mortcloath, 8d.

William Keddie and Isobel Brown from the parishes of Selkirk and Liliesleaf, married here, 12d.

„   9 The plush mortcloath, £1 Scots.

„   5. Mary Lauder appeared the second time.

After prayer sederunt, the Minister, John Mabane, John Mercer, Robert Scott, &c., elders.

Collected by William Milne, £1 : 9s. Scots.

This day the session unanimously agreed that the sacrament of the supper shall be celebrated in this place the 3rd Sabbath of July next.

Walter Thompson in Laudhopemuire is ordered to be cited to the session against this day eight days for some indecent behaviour on the Sabbath day.

(Case against Mary Lauder continued.)

July 17. After prayer sederunt, the Minister, Nicol Milne, Andrew Mein, Andrew Marr, &c., elders.

Collected by Robert Moffatt, £1 : 11s. Scots.

Walter Thomson being cited was called and did compear, and acknowledged his sorrow for giving offence by any indecent behaviour on the Sabbath day.   He was rebuked and admonished and dismissed.

„ 24. The minister intimated a meeting about the kirk and poor, Wednesday first.

Collected by Andrew Drummond, 18d. sterling.

„ 27. This day the session gave up the half of the collections, viz., £12 : 19 : 6 Scots.

„   „ The heretors mett and provided for the poor for ensuing quarter, conform to their sederunt of this date.

July   1. The minister intimated the celebration of the supper in this place this day fourteen days, with suitable exhortations and cautions.

Collected by Robert Scott, £1 : 10s. Scots.

„   2. Best velvet and best plush mortcloath for John Sibbald, £4 : 10s. Scots.

„   8. The minister intimated Thursday next as a day of humiliation before the sacrament of the supper.

After prayer, the Minister, John Mabane, Robert Scott, William Milne, &c., elders.

Collected by Robert Moffatt, £2 : 16s. Scots.

The session appointed their meeting for privy tryals and regulating other things about the sacrament Tuesday next.

„ 10. This day appointed for privy tryals. After prayer sederunt, the Minister, James Laidlaw, Robert Scott, John Mabane, Andrew Marr, Andrew Drummond, John Mercer, Nicol Milne, elders.

The elders present were severally removed, tryed and approven and encouraged to go on in the Lord's work.

The collection to be gathered and doors kept as formerly.

„ 11. Mortcloath for a child, 8d.

„ 15. The minister administered the sacrament of the supper in common form, ten tables and a broken one.

Collections the several days of the communion.

On the Fast day,	-	-	-	-	£5 8 0
Saturday's collection,	-	-	-	-	13 0 0
Sabbath day's collection,	-	-	-	-	20 12 0
Monday's collection,	-	-	-	-	12 0 0
		Carry forward,	-		£51 0 0

1739.

	Brought forward,	£51	0	0
Debursed the precentor, within and without doors,		6	12	0
To the beadle,		3	0	0
To John Gill for mending the furms, and mounting the tent,		3	8	0
		£13	0	0
	Ballance,	£38	0	0

July 19. This day the seat possessed by Robert Scott, weaver in Danieltown, and Robert Hunter, flesher in Melrose, was, at their mutual desire and consent, recorded in the session register to be possessed by them and theirs in all time coming, whereof the said Robert Scott has two-thirds and the said Robert Hunter the other third, which they are to occupy without any preference, which seat is bounded with the seat of Robert Penman, Junior, immediately before it to the west, and the passage before Hagburn seat behind it to the east.

„ 22. After prayer sederunt, the Minister, John Mercer, John Moffatt, Andrew Mein, elders.

The session appoint Tuesday next for taking in the collections at the sacrament, and considering the state of the poor.

„ 24. After prayer sederunt, the Minister, John Mabane, Robert Scott, &c., elders.

The session gave in the half of the sacrament money to the clerk for the use of the heretors, extending to £19 Scots. The session disposed of a good part of the other half as will appear by George Martin's accompts.

„ 29. Collected by John Mabane, £1 : 3s. Scots.

Mortcloath money, £1 Scots.

Aug. 4. Best mortcloath for James Wilkieson, £3 Scots.

„ 5. Collected by Robert Scott, £2 : 2s. Scots.

Little mortcloath, 8d.

„ 12. Collected by Andrew Drummond, £1 : 8s. Scots.

Mortcloath to Robert Penman, £3 Scots.

„ 19. Collected by William Milne, £1 : 15s. Scots.

„ 26. Collected by Andrew Drummond, £1 : 8s. Scots.

Sept. 2. Collected by John Mabane, £1 : 8s. Scots.

Mortcloath money, £3 Scots.

„ 9. Collected by Andrew Drummond, £1 : 5s. Scots.

„ 15. Best velvet mortcloath to Alexr. Paterson, bailie, £3 Scots.

„ 16 George Scott, guilty with Mary Lauder, compeared the first time, and was admonished.

(Case of discipline against Jean Carter, late servitrix to James Watt, merchant in Melrose, and George Watt, smith.)

(Case against Marion Usher continued.)

„ 23. George Scott compeared the second time.

A meeting of the heretors, &c., anent the poor, appointed Thursday next.

After prayer sederunt, the Minister, John Mercer, James Laidlaw, John Mabane, Andrew Marr, &c., elders.

(Case against George Watt and Jean Carter continued.)

„ 27. This day the session mett and gave up the half of the collections, £10 : 4s. Scots.

„ „ The heretors mett and provided the poor for ensuing quarter as per their sederunt of this date.

„ 30. After prayer sederunt, the Minister, Andrew Mein, Robert Scott, Andrew Marr, &c., elders.

Collected by Andrew Drummond, £1 : 10s. Scots.

1739.

(Case against George Watt and Jean Carter continued.)

Oct. 3. Mortcloath money, £1 Scots.

,, 7. The minister intimated a fast to be kept to-morrow on account of the unseasonableness of the weather, and at the same time intimated two collections recommended by the synod, viz., one for Long-framlingtown and another for repairing Killendrige Chapel, to be gathered to-morrow.

After prayer sederunt, the Minister, James Laidlaw, Robert Moffatt, Robert Scott, &c., elders.

Collected by Andrew Mein, £1 : 3s. Scots.

(Case against George Watt and Jean Carter continued.)

To the little mortcloath, 8d.

,, 8. Collected by John Mercer and Robert Scott, £13 : 10s. Scots, which was given in to the minister for the purposes as mentioned.

,, 14 George Scott compeared for the third time, was rebuked and dismissed. Paid in for his penalty, £1 : 10s. Scots.

After prayer sederunt, the Minister, John Mabane, Robert Scott, Robert Moffatt, &c., elders.

Collected by William Milne, £1 : 3s. Scots.

(Case against George Watt and Jean Carter continued.)

Mortcloath money, £1 : 10s. Scots.

,, 21. Collected by Nicol Milne, £1 : 5s. Scots.

,, 28. Collected by William Milne, £1 : 9s. Scots.

Committee of the session to meet Tuesday first.

,, 30. After prayer sederunt, the Minister, Nicol Milne, John Mercer, Robert Scott and Andrew Drummond, elders, as a committee of the session for considering the act of mortification intended by Andrew Martine, surgeon in Melrose, which deed was read, and the above committee having considered the same, they concluded that if they empowered to judge of the proper objects of this charity and freed and exonerated from all omissions, and accountable only for intromissions and the power of application lodged jointly with them and the mortifier and his heirs, they cannot in safety accept of the mortification, leaving the mortifier the intention of Mr. Martine in the way and manner he thinks most agreeable thereto.

Nov. 4. Collected by Andrew Drummond £1 : 11s. Scots.

,, 10 Best mortcloath, £3 Scots.

,, 11. Collected by Robert Scott, £1 : 9s. Scots.

,, 16. Mortcloath money, £1 : 10s. Scots.

,, 18. Collected by William Milne, £1 : 12s. Scots.

,, 25. Collected by Andrew Mein, £1 : 13s. Scots.

Dec. 2. Collected by John Wallace, £1 : 9s. Scots.

Mortcloath money, £1 : 10s. Scots.

,, 9. Collected by Andrew Drummond, £1 : 8s. Scots.

Mortcloath money, £1 : 10s. Scots.

,, 13. William Sandilands and Margaret Fife in Mertown parish, married here, 12s. Scots.

,, 16. Collected by William Milne, £1 : 1s Scots.

,, 23. Collected by John Mabane, £1 : 12s. Scots.

On the report of Andrew Mein, apprentice to George Watt, smith in Melrose, his being clandestinely married to Janet Atchison, servitrix to Charles Wilkieson, the officer is appointed to cite them to the session this day eight days.

,, 26. This day the session gave up the half of the collections, &c., £10 : 16s. Scots.

,, 26. The heritors mett and provided for the poor for ensuing quarter as per their sederunt of this date.

,, 27. Mortcloath money, £1 Scots.

,, 28. Received Agnes Scott's marriage penalty, £6 Scots.

1739.

Dec. 30. After prayer sederunt, the Minister, Andrew Mein, John Mercer, Robert Scott, &c., elders.

Collected by Andrew Drummond, 9s. Scots.

Andrew Mein and Janet Atchison being cited, were called and compeared. They produced their marriage lines, dated att Edinburgh 17th December 1739, signed J. Robertson, minister, but as there is but only one witness insert, the session resolves to enquire into it. They were rebuked and dismissed for the time.

1740.

Jan. 1. Mortcloath for James Usher, £1 : 10s. Scots.

,, 6. This day the minister read an act of the late commission of the assembly for a general fast, and the King's proclamation for observing the same through all Scotland, Wednesday next, the ninth instant, as also he read an act of the general assembly appointing a collection for the distressed protestants in Bobie and Villar, in Piedmont, to be levied here the foresaid ninth instant with suitable exhortations.

,, 9. Collected by Robert Scott and Andrew Marr, £15 : 12s. Scots for the purposes above mentioned.

,, 10. Best mortcloath for Janet Mabane, £3 Scots.

,, 13. Collected by Andrew Mein, 13s. Scots.

,, 14. Best Mortcloath for Janet Boston, £3 Scots.

,, 20. Collected by William Milne and James Laidlay, 17d.

,, 25. Plush mortcloath to Helen Beinstone, £1 : 10s. Scots.

,, 27. Collected by Robert Scott, £1 : 4s. Scots.

The season being so extraordinary straitening, the minister and elders condescended to take 20s. sterling and distribute among the poor, besides what has been formerly given among them.

Feb. 3. Collected by William Milne, £1 : 6s. Scots.

The minister intimated that he was to go from family to family within Melrose to receive their charity for the relief of the poor in this straitening season. The elders are desired to do the same within their bounds.

,, 4. There was this day collected from the town of Melrose £25 : 8s. Scots, which, with what came in from Newtown, Eildon, Newstead, Gattonside, Darnick and Bridgend, extended to £54 : 6s. Scots. The elders with the minister and clerk mett and distributed to the necessituous persons and families £41 : 5s. Scots. What remains undisposed of is reserved till next week, in regard the storm seems still to continue.

There was also levied from the town of Melrose Dec. 31, £18 Scots, which was that same day divided among the poor householders in Melrose.

,, 8. Plush mortcloath to James Vair, £1 : 10s. Scots.

,, 10. Collected by Andrew Mein, £1 : 7s. Scots.

The elders to meet to morrow to consider the state of the poor.

,, 11. After prayer sederunt, the Minister, Robert Scott, John Mabane, Nicol Milne, Andrew Drummond, Andrew Marr and Andrew Mein, elders.

There was added to the £13 : 1s. Scots that was not disposed of this day eight days, £3 : 16s. Scotts brought in by the elders from householders that had not contributed before, which with £5 : 8s. Scots. remaining of the 20s. sterling formerly allowed by the session to be distribute makes £21 : 15s. Scots, whereof the session this day distributed to the indigent £12 : 2s. Scots, so there remains undisposed £9 : 13s. Scots till next week.

Received testimonials for Agnes Wight preceeding Martinmas last. The sederunt closed with prayer.

,, 17. Collected by Andrew Drummond, £1 : 8s. Scots.

1740.

The elders meet to-morrow to consider the state of the poor.

Feb. 18. The elders mett, and of the £9 : 13s. Scots that remained undisposed of last week, they distribute this day £7 : 10s. Scots, and the £2 : 3s. Scots remained was delivered to the minister to be distribute to the poor of the highlands.

„   20. Mortcloath for Margaret Young, £1 Scots.

„   24. Collected by Andrew Mein, £1 : 13s. Scots.
Mortcloath for Isobel Lamb, £3 Scots.

Mar.   1. James Donaldson and Janet Harvie in Bouden parish, married here 12s. Scots.

„   2. After prayer sederunt, the Minister, John Mabane, John Mercer, Robert Scott, &c., elders.
Collected by John Wallace, £1 : 12s. Scots.
(Case against George Watt and Jean Carter continued).
Mortcloath for Alison Dawson, £1 Scots.

„   9. Collected by Andrew Drummond, £1 : 5s. Scots.

„   16. Collected by Andrew Mein, £1 : 9s. Scots.
Mortcloath to Margaret Kyle, £1 : 10s. Scots.

„   23. Collected by Robert Moffatt, £1 : 15s. Scots.
Intimated a meeting anent the poor Thursday next.

„   26. Mortcloath to James Creightone, £1 Scots.

„   27. The heretors mett this day and provided the poor for ensuing quarter as per their sederunt of this date.

„   30. Collected by Robert Scott, £1 : 4s. Scots.
Mortcloath for Mrs. Bannatyne, £3 Scots.

„   31. Mortcloath for John Laidlaw, £1 : 10s. Scots.

April 6. Agnes Gray guilty with the deceased Mr. Alexr. Paterson, appeared for the first time and was admonished.
Collected by John Mabane, £1 : 8s. Scots.

„   7. Mortcloath for Bessie Gill, £1 Scots.

„   13. Collected by Andrew Drummond, £1 : 11s. Scots.
Agnes Gray appeared the second time.
Mortcloath to Agnes Alley, £1 : 10s. Scots.

„   19. Ditto. to Andrew Moss, £1 : 10s. Scots.

„   20. Intimated a meeting of the heretors for repairing the kirk.
Collected by Robert Moffatt, £1 : 4s. Scots.

„   27. Collected by Robert Scott, £1 : 7s. Scots.

„   29. The minister produced a discharge from William Alexander, collector for the protestant inhabitants of Babi and Villars, in Piedmont, of this parishes, moiety extending to £15 : 6s. Scots, levied the 9th of January last.

May   4. Collected by Andrew Drummond, 19s. Scots.

„   11. Collected by Robert Scott, £1 : 16s. Scots.
The minister produced a discharge from the collector for rebuilding the meeting house att Longframlington, for £6 Scots, as also another for that at Killendridge Chapel for £4 Scots. To Helen Nicol who had her house burnt £3 Scots, which sum compleats the sum levied Oct. 8th, 1739.

May 18. Margaret Walker guilty with James Hopkirk, compeared for the first time and was rebuked.
Collected by Andrew Drummond, £1 : 7s. Scots.

„   25. Margaret Walker compeared for the second time.
After prayer sederunt, the minister. Andrew Marr, John Wallace, Robert Scott, elders.
Collected by Andrew Mein, £1 : 5s. Scots.
The session being informed that one Peter Strachan, residing in Melrose, and Anne Ormistown, also in Melrose, have married irregularly, order them to be sited to the session against this day eight days.

1740.

June 1. After prayer sederunt, the Minister, John Mercer, John Mabane, Andrew Marr, &c., elders.

    Margaret Walker compeared for the third time and was rebuked and dismissed, and paid in £1 : 10s. Scots.

    This day Peter Strachan and Anne Ormistone being cited for their irregular marriage compeared, who owned they were married and produced lines, dated att Edinburgh May 21st. 1740 signed David Strang, minister. They were rebuked and ordered to pay their penalty incurred according to law.

,, 8. Collected by John Mabane, 17d.

,, 15. After prayer sederunt, the Minister, John Wallace, Robert Scott, Andrew Marr.

    Collected by Robert Scott, £1 : 13.

    The minister and session unanimously agreed that the sacrament of the supper shall be administered in this place the 20th of July next.

,, 22. Collected by Nicol Milne, £2 : 12s. Scots.

    Intimated a meeting of the heretors, &c. concerning the poor Wednesday next.

,, 25. The heretors mett and provided for the poor as per their sederunt.

,, 29. This morning the minister called the elders and proposed on account of the barren and threatening weather there should be a day of fasting aud humiliation kept here some day this week. They unanimously condescended on Wednesday next.

    The minister intimated Wednesday next to be observed as an humiliation day, accordingly gave suitable exhortations.

    Collected by Andrew Drummond, £1 : 14s. Scots.

July 2. There was this day collected £11 : 15s Scots, whereof was instantly distributed £7 : 12s. Scots, so £4 : 3s. Scots was lodged with George Martine.

,, 6. This day the minister intimated the celebration of the supper in this place this day fourteen days.

    Agnes Gray appeared for the third time and was dismissed.

    After prayer sederunt, the Minister, John Mercer. Robert Scott, James Laidlaw, &c., elders.

    Collected by Andrew Mein, £1 : 18s. Scots.

    Agnes Gray's penalty, £1 : 10s. Scots.

    (Case of discipline against John Kemp and his wife.)

,, 13. After prayer sederunt, the Minister. William Milne, Nicol Milne, Andrew Mein, &c., elders.

    The minister this day intimated Thursday next as the day of humiliation before the sacrament of the supper.

    Application was made this day by Jean Lamb, spouse to Andrew Dawson, Junior (who has shown a manifest contempt of the sacrament of baptism), that the minister and session would allow her baptism to her child. The session considering the case agree that she holding the child and taking the vows, the minister should baptize her child.

    (Case against John Kemp and his wife continued.)

    The session appoint Tuesday for privy censures.

,, 15. After prayer sederunt, the Minister, James Laidlaw, Andrew Marr, Andrew Mein, Andrew Drummond, and Robert Scott, elders. The elders present were severally removed, tryed and approven, and encouraged to go on in the Lord's work.

    Collections to be gathered and doors kept as formerly.

,	17. Fast day, collected,	-	-	-	-	-	£6	4	0
,,	19. Saturday, collected,	-	-	-	-	-	11	18	0
,,	20. Sabbath day, collected,	-	-	-	-	-	20	8	0

Carry forward, - £38 10 0

1740.

		Brought forward,	£38	10	0
July	21. Monday, collected,		12	18	0

		£51	8	0
There was distribute of this,	- - -			
To the precentor and beadle and several poor, -		26	16	0

	£24	12	0

„   22. The day in a constitute session, the session distribute to the several poor within the parish.

„   24. Mortcloath money £1 Scots.
       To the remains of Alison Dawson's do., 10d.

„   27. Collected by Andrew Mein, £1 : 15s. Scots.

Aug.   3. After prayer sederunt, the Minister, John Mercer, James Laidlaw, &c., elders.
       Collected by William Milne, 12d.
       (Case against George Watt and Jean Carter, continued.)
       (Case of discipline against Andrew Mein and Janet Atchison, his spouse.)

„   10. After prayer sederunt, the Minister, Andrew Mein, Robert Scott, Andrew Marr, elders.
       Collected by Nicol Milne, £1 : 17s. Scots.
       (Case against Andrew Mein continued.)

„   17. Collected by Andrew Drummond, £1 : 14s. Scots.
       Andrew Mein and Janet Atchison compeared for the first time and were admonished.

„   24. Collected by Andrew Marr, £1 : 14s. Scots.
       Andrew Mein and Janet Atchison compeared the second time.

„   31. Collected by James Laidlaw, £1 : 7s. Scots.

Sept.   7. Collected by Robert Scott, £1 : 13s. Scots.

„   14. Collected by John Wallace, £1 : 14s. Scots.

„   21. Collected by Andrew Mein, £1 : 11s. Scots.
       Andrew Mein and Janet Atchison compeared for the third time, were exhorted, rebuked and dismissed.
       Then the minister intimated a meeting for considering the state of the poor Friday next.

„   26. The heretors met and adjourned their meeting till Friday the 10th of October next.

„   28. Collected by William Milne, £1 : 10s. Scots.

Oct.   5. After prayer sederunt, the Minister, John Mabane, Andrew Mein, Andrew Marr, &c., elders.
       Collected by Andrew Drummond, £1 : 13s. Scots.
       It was moved to the session that conform to the sederunt of the heretors the 26th last, an information should be laid before the justices of the peace, anent such as are deficient in their payments of the poor's money. The session unanimously agreed that an information and representation signed by their clerk should be laid before them by Nicol Milne, portioner of Newtown, Tuesday next.

„   10. The heretors mett and provided for the poor as per their sederunt.

„   12. Collected by Robert Scott, £2 Scots.

„   19. Collected by Nicol Milne, £2 : 10s. Scots.
       Mortcloath money, 8d.

„   26. Collected by Robert Scott, £1 : 13s. Scots.

Nov.   2. Collected by Robert Scott, £1 : 3s. Scots.

„   9. Collected by John Mercer, £1 : 11s. Scots.

„   16. Collected by Andrew Drummond, £1 : 16s. Scots.

„   18. Mortcloath to Andrew Boston, £3 Scots.

„   23. Collected by William Milne, £1 : 11s. Scots.

„   30. Collected by Robert Scott, £1 : 19s. Scots.

1740.

John Kemp and Anne Christie compeared for their antenuptial fornication and were rebuked.

Dec. 7. Collected by Andrew Marr, £1 : 15s. Scots.

John Kemp and spouse compeared the second time.

„ 14. Collected by Andrew Mein, £1 : 6s. Scots.

John Kemp and spouse compeared the third time, were rebuked and dismissed.

The minister intimated a meeting of the heretors Thursday next.

Mortcloath for Katharine Pringle, £1 : 10s. Scots.

„ 18. The heretors mett and provided the poor for ensuing quarter, as per their sederunt.

„ 21. Collected by Andrew Drummond, £1 : 6s. Scots.

„ 28. Collected by James Laidlaw, £1 : 8s. Scots.

1741.

Jan. 1. Collected by William Milne, £1 : 15s. Scots.

Jean Carter guilty of fornication with George Watt compeared for the first time.

Mortcloath money, £1 Scots.

„ 11. Jean Carter compeared the second time.

Collected by Robert Scott, £1 : 16s. Scots.

John Laidlaw and Margaret Burnet, clandestinely married, are ordered to be cited to the session against this day eight days.

Dec. 17. Mortcloath money, 8d.

„ 18. Jean Carter compeared the third time, was rebuked and dismissed. She paid in of her penalty £1 : 4s. Scots.

After prayer sederunt, the Minister, John Mercer, John Mabane, Andrew Drummond, &c., elders.

Collected by Robert Scott, £1 : 9s. Scots.

John Laidlaw and Margaret Burnet, being cited, were called. John compeared, but Margaret did not, the day being bad. He was asked if married to Margaret Burnet. Answered he was and produced lines thereof, dated at Edinr. Dec. 8th, 1740, signed George Aytone. John was removed, and the session considering the said lines, they are of the mind they are not genuine, because they are neither good sense nor are there one word of them right spelled; besides the said John and asked about them prevaricated before the session, saying at first that the said George Aytone wrote them. Then that one in the company wrote them and he signed them, as both the testificate looks suspicious, and he alters in telling the affair. John owns guilt with the said Margaret before the said marriage. The session have allowed him till this day two weeks to produce a more satisfying testificate from the said George Aytone, which diet of the session he and the said Margaret Burnet is ordered to attend.

Mortcloath to Christian Milne, £3 Scots.

Jan. 25. Collected by Andrew Mein, 18d.

„ 26. Received John Laidlaw's penalty for not compleating marriage with Jean Brown, delivered to the minister 9s : 6d. sterling.

John Bruce, officer, got 6d.

„ 29. Mortcloath money, £1 Scots.

Feb. 1. The minister intimated Wednesday next as a day of fasting and humiliation, according to the late commission and King's proclamation.

After prayer sederunt, the Minister, Andrew Marr, John Mabane, &c., elders.

Collected by Robert Scott, £1 : 10s. Scots.

John Laidlaw being cited to this diet compeared, and Margaret Burnet. He was asked if he had got any other attestation of his marriage. Answered no. He was seriously talked with about

1741.

the irregular course he had taken, and as the lines produced seem very suspicious, the session resolve to enquire farther into it. They were dismissed till further orders and the sederunt closed with prayer.

Feb. 4. Collected £6 : 18s., which was delivered to the minister.

  ,, 8. Collected by Andrew Drummond, £1 : 1s. Scots

  ,, 15. After prayer, the Minister, Andrew Mein, William Milne, John Mercer, elders.

          Collected by Robert Scott, £1 : 12s. Scots.

          The minister produced documents for John Laidlaw's marriage with which the session is satisfied.

          Case of discipline against Mr. Fisher of Bearfauld's servant.

  ,, 22. Isobel Wilson, guilty with Andrew Fisher, compeared the first time and was exhorted.

          After prayer sederunt, the Minister, Robert Scott, Andrew Mein, Andrew Marr, &c., elders.

          Collected by William Milne, £1 : 11s. Scots.

          (Case against Hannah Jamieson, servitrix to Mr. Fisher, and Andrew Fisher, his son, continued.)

          By a letter from the kirk session of Bowden ; a case of discipline against Margaret Aird, who left this parish at Martinmas, and Mungo Glendinning, servant to Mr. Wilkieson.

Mar. 1. The precentor read an advertisement concerning beans being to be got at Berwick.

          After prayer sederunt, the Minister, Andrew Mein, John Mercer, elders.

          Collected by Robert Scott, £1 : 13s. Scots.

          The beadle reports he could not get Andrew Fisher to cite him to this diet, he living at Kippielaw. He is appointed to go to the kirk officer at Bowden and cause him cite Andrew Fisher, who at present is staying at Kippielaw, to our session this day eight days.

The records of session are to be found in the beginning of another volume like this.

N.B.—Andrew Henderson's children are marked after July 30th, 1769. (The above is written on a separate page, beginning of volume.)

1739.

Jan. 8. Hugh Grieve and Margaret Darling in Blainslies, a.d.n. Margaret ; w. John Fisher, John Darling.

  ,, 14. Nicol Bowar and Margaret Mein in Newtown, a.d.n. Alison ; w. Nicol Miln, John Miln, there.

  ,, 29. Andrew Darling and —— Fleeming in Blainslies, a.s.n. Thomas ; w. James and Alexr. Scotts there.

Feb. 4. John Milne and Helen Brown in Newtown, a.s.n. Nicol ; w. Thomas Stenhouse, Nicol Milne, there.

  ,, 8. Nicol Milne and Janet Frater in Newtown, a.s.n. Nicol ; w. John Milne, Nicol Bowar, there.

  ,, 11. Alexr. Ellis and Margaret Wilson in Danieltown, a.s.n. James ; w. John Bowie, Robert Trotter.

  ,, 26. Robert Mercer and Annabella Ovens in Newstead, a.s.n. Robert.

  ,, ,, William Cook and Margaret Lawrie in Melrose, a.d.n. Margaret ; w. George and Robert Lawries.

  ,, 28. George Dalgliesh and Agnes Hoy in Overlangshaw, a.s.n. James

  ,, ,, James Brown and Janet Waugh in Netherlangshaw, a.s.n. Thomas ; w. Robert Moffat, John Wallace.

Mar. 4. James Hopkirk and Margaret Walker in Melrose, by fornication, a.s.n. James ; w. William and Thomas Steel.

  ,, 8. George Blaikie and Mary Gray in Langhaugh, a.s.n. Robert ; w. James Blaikie, Andrew Bryden.

1739.

Mar. 18. John Young and Margaret Gill in Gattonside, a.s.n. Thomas.

,, ,, Robert Myles and Janet Mathison in Gattonside, a.s.n. Robert ; w. John Gill, William Mathison, there.

,, 25. Alexr. Broomfield and Isobel Mein in Gattonside, a.s.n. Robert.

,, ,, Andrew Hart and Janet Davidson in Newsteid, a.d.n. Margaret ; w. John Mein, elder and younger.

April 8. George Martine and Margaret White in Melrose, a.d.n. Agnes ; w. John Tait, Andrew Martine.

,, 29. Robert Penman and Christian Grahamslie in Melrose, a.s.n. Robert.

,, ,, Simon Haitley and Marion Bunzie in Melrose, a.s.n. Thomas.

,, ,, John Tait and Margaret Martine in Melrose, a.d.n. Elizabeth ; w. Robert Penman, Andrew Dawson.

,, 30. John Chisholm and Elizabeth Lauder in Colmslie, a.s.n. John.

,, ,, James Moffat and Mary Pringle in Overlangshaw, a.d.n. Alison ; w. James Dickson, Thomas Mathison.

May 16. Robert Scott and Janet Darling in Blainslies, a.s.n. James ; w. James and Alexr. Scots there.

,, 20. Thomas Hoy and Janet Smith in Gattonside, a.d.n. Agnes ; w. John Smith, John Hoy.

June 5. John Givan and Janet Jamieson in Overlangshaw, a.d.n. Agnes ; w. John Park, Thomas Watson.

,, 10. Thomas Bunzie and Agnes Mein in Newstead, a s.n. Robert.

,, ,, John Pringle and Margaret Young in Blainslies, a.d.n. Margaret ; w. James and Andrew Bunzies.

,, 14. James Wallace and Eupham Darling in Blainslies, a.d.n. Janet.

,, ,, John Carter and Isobel Purves in Clackmae, a.d.n. Elizabeth ; w. Thomas Purves, Mungo Park.

,, 17. William Mein and Margaret Mercer in Newtown, a.d.n. Mary ; w. Hugh Mein, Nicol Mercer.

,, 24. Andrew Burnet and Eleanor Turnbull in Melrose, a.s.n. Robert ; w. James Watt, William Steel.

July 22. Alexr. Cunningham of Hyndhope and Elizabeth Paterson, his lady ; w. Alexr. Paterson, Charles Wilkieson.

,, 29. Adam Dods and Bettie Gill in Danieltown, a.s.n. Robert.

,, ,, Alexr. M'Fadzean and Janet Sked in Melrose, a.d.n. Janet.

,, ,, David Shiel and Isobel Tailor in Easterlanglee, a.d.n. Helen.

,, ,, Robert Speeding and Christian M'Fadzean in Bowden milne, a.d.n. Helen ; w. John Mabane, Robert Scott.

Aug. 2. James Fisher and Isobel Wight in Clackmae, a s.n. James.

,, ,, John and Elizabeth Stirlings in Blainslies, a.s.n. Robert.

,, ,, William Darling and —— Allan in Blainslies, a.d.n. Mary ; w. Thomas Purves, Robert Knox.

,, 5. Philip Fair and —— Simpson in Gattonside, a.s.n. George.

,, ,, Andrew Martine and Margaret Alexander in Melrose, a.d.n. Elizabeth.

,, ,, John Anderson and Elizabeth Fiddes in Melrose, a.d.n. Elizabeth ; w. John Tait, George Martine.

,, 12. John Hope and Isobel Haliburtone in Darnick, a.d.n. Catharine ; w. George Martine, John Tait.

,, 26. James Watt and Margaret Darling in Melrose, a.d.n. Agnes ; w. James Smail, Thomas Marr.

Sept. 9. William Wilson and —— in Blainslies, a.s.n. William ; w. Alexr. Gray, Robert Scott.

,, 16. Thomas Speeding and Margaret Brown in Gattonside, a.s.n. Thomas.

,, ,, James Wight and Margaret Skirven in Darnick, a.d.n. Agnes ; w. Andrew Marr, James Bouston.

Oct. 4. Michael Wallace and Agnes Wright in Melrose, a.d.n. Jean ; w. James Richardson, Andrew Mein.

,, 7. Thomas Vair and —— Wilson in Danieltown, a.d.n. Janet ; w. Alexr. Vair, George Lawrie.

,, 21. Thomas Gill and —— Riddell in Danieltown, a.s.n. James.

1739.

Oct. 21. William Martine and Jean Grieve in Gattonside, a.d.n. Margaret ;
w. George Lawrie, Andrew Marr.

„ 28. William and Helen Hunters in Melrose, a.s.n. Andrew ; w. Charles
Wilkieson, Henry Cook.

Nov. 18. William Brown and —— Scott in Gattonside, a.s.n. John ; w. Andrew
Marr, John Boston.

„ 25. Thomas Vair and Jean Mein in Newstead, a.d.n. Agnes ; w. John
Mein, Andrew Mein.

Dec. 2. Thomas Marr and Jean Craig in Melrose, a.s.n. William ; w. Andrew
Marr, James Marr.

„ 16. William Mathison and Janet Frier in Melrose, a.s.n. William ; w.
Andrew Marr, James Marr.

„ „ Nicol Mercer and Margaret Chisholm in Bridgend, a.d n. Mary : w.
Thomas Mathison, Walter Murray.

„ 23. Mungo Laidlaw and Elizabeth Milne in Newtown, a.d.n. Isabel.

„ „ Robert Lawrie and Alison Wight in Danieltown, a.d.n. Isabel ; w.
Nicol Milne, George Lawrie.

„ 30. John Hoy and Alison Cunningham in Melrose, a.s.n. Samuel ; w.
Alexr. and William Meins.

1740.

Jan. 26. Andrew Haitley and Alison Dawson in Danieltown, two sons named
Alexander and Andrew ; w. Robert and Walter Scotts.

„ 28. Alexr. Sandilands and Margaret Hog in Buckholm, a.s.n. James ; w.
George Alley, George Blaikie.

Feb. 7. Andrew Darling and Margaret Somervel in Newhouses, a.s.n.
Andrew ; w. Robert and William Moffatt.

„ 22 George Grieve and —— Somervel in Blainslies, a s.n. James ; w.
Alexr. Gray, James Wallace.

„ 24. Walter Rae and Christian Richie in Newtown, a.s.n. Robert.

„ „ Robert Bunzie and Margaret Mein in Newstead, a.s.n. Andrew ; w.
Nicol Milne, William Bunzie.

Mar. 2. George Speeding and Helen Wilson in Bowden, a.s.n. Thomas : w.
Andrew Marr, Thomas Boston.

„ 11. James Russel of Ashiesteel and Jean Boston, his lady, a.d.n.
Catharine : w. Alexr. Russel, Alexr. Baptie.

„ 23. John Milne and Eupham Brown in Newtown, a.d.n. Elizabeth ; w.
Thomas Stenhouse, Nicol Milne.

April 2. Thomas Watson and Isobel Cochran in Blainslies, ——.

„ „ George Henry and Janet Thomson in Bentmilne, —— : w. John
Fisher, James Russell.

„ 3. John Boston and —— Hunter in Gattonside, a.s.n. Robert ; w.
Robert Philp, Thomas Boston.

„ 13. John Fairbairn and Elizabeth Flint in Melrose, a.d.n. Elizabeth ; w.
George and Andrew Martines.

„ 21. Robert Lees and —— Mertle in Whitlaw, a.s.n. William ; w. William
Mertle, William Lees.

„ 22. Thomas Henderson and Isobel Pringle in Sorrowlessfield, a.s.n.
William : w. James Fisher, James Henderson.

„ 27. Robert Trotter and Margaret Mabane in Melrose, a.s.n. James.

„ „ John Mein, junior, and Christian Hunter in Newsteid, a.d.n. Helen.

„ „ John Bunzie and Isobel Wilson in Newtown, a.d.n. Agnes ; w. John
Mein, Robert Hunter.

May 4. John Darling and —— Bunzie in Melrose, a.s.n. William.

„ „ Thomas Darling and Margaret Martin in Gattonside, a.d.n.
Margaret ; w. Andrew Marr, John Tait.

„ 19. William Wallace and Marion Brown in Blainslies, a.s.n. William ; w.
Alexr. and John Grays.

„ 25. Alexr. Lockie and Grissal Nicolson in Melrose, a.s.n. William.

„ „ George Martine and Agnes Fair in Westhouses, a.d.n. Mary : w. John
and William Mabanes.

1740.

June   1. William M'Caul and Margaret Mercer in Darnick, a.d.n. Margaret.

,,   ,, John Frier and Isobel Scott in Colmslie, a.s.n. Adam ; w. James Dixon, Henry Forrest.

,,   15. James Bunzie and Isobel Moodie in Newsteid, a.s.n. George ; w. Andrew and Thomas Bunzies.

,,   29. George Walker and Anne Pringle in Melrose, a.d.n. Anne.

,,   ,, James Martine and Margaret Ellies in Gattonside, a.d.n. Margaret ; w. Andrew Marr, William Steel.

July   3. Robert Tait and Jean Gordon in Blainslies, a.s.n. John.

,,   ,, James Stirling and Agnes Scott in Rhone, a.d.n. Agnes ; w. James and Alexr. Scotts

,,   6. William Milne and —— Mein in Darnick, a.d.n. Isobel ; w. John and George Mercers.

,,   13. Andrew Dawson and Jean Lamb in Melrose, a.d.n. Margaret ; w. Andrew Martine, Adam Thorburn.

,,   27. The deceased John Laidlaw and Agnes Mein in Eildon, a.d.n. Christian ; w. Alexr. Mein, Nicol Milne.

Aug.   3. John Mein and Elizabeth Familtown in Lindean, a.s.n. John ; w. James Mein, George Martine.

,,   24. George Wigh and Christian Pringle in Melrose, a.d.n. Ruth.

,,   ,, John Scott and Agnes Renaldson in Newstead, a.d.n. Agnes ; w. John and Andrew Meins.

Sept.   7. Thomas Mabane and Margaret Tait in Melrose, a.d.n. Janet ; w. John and William Mabanes.

,,   14. William Steel and Elizabeth Walker in Melrose, a.d.n. Elizabeth ; w. Thomas Steel, George Walker.

,,   21. Andrew Mein and Janet Atchison in Newsteid, by antenuptial fornication, a.d.n. Alison ; w. George Martine, John Tait.

Oct.   1. Alexr. Cuningham of Hyndhope and Elizabeth Paterson, his lady, in Old Melrose, a.s.n. Charles ; w. Charles Wilkieson, George Martine.

,,   2. Alexr. Gray and Margaret Thyne in Blainslies, a.s.n. George ; w. John Gray, Robert Scott.

,,   12. Andrew Renaldson and Janet Scott in Darnick, a.s.n. Walter ; w. William and George Renaldsons.

,,   19. James Fisher and Janet Glendinning in Darnick, a.s.n. John.

,,   ,, David Martine and Helen Bell in Gattonside, a.s.n. William ; w. William Martine, John Mercer.

,,   20. Charles Wilkieson and Anne Paterson in Melrose, a.d.n. Elizabeth ; w. Alexander Cunningham, William Hunter.

Nov.   2. John Bruce and Christian Forsan in Melrose, a.s.n. George.

,,   ,, Andrew Pringle and Anne Brock in Newsteid, a.s.n. Robert ; w. Thomas and James Williamsons.

,,   4. Andrew Bowar and Margaret Stenhouse in Newtown, a s.n. Nicol ; w. Nicol Bowar, Nicol Milne.

,,   9. James Wight and ——- Skirven in Darnick, a.s.n. George ; w. John and George Mercer.

,,   10. John Coats and Janet Purves in Langshaw, a.d.n. Margaret ; w. Henry Forest, Thomas Mathison.

,,   23. John Gill and Helen Paterson in Melrose, a.d.n. Isobel ; w. Thomas Gill, George Lawrie.

,,   27. Robert Laidlaw and Agnes Gray in Colmsliehill, a.d.n. Helen.

,,   ,, James Dickson and Margaret Blaikie in Westhouses, a.d.n. Helen ; w. Alexr. Gray, Adam Harvie.

Dec.   7. William Hopkirk and Isobel Tait in Melrose, a.d.n. Isobel ; w. William Hopkirk, John Tait.

,,   19. Nicol Bowar and —— Mein in Newton, a.s.n. John ; w. Thomas and Nicol Milnes.

,,   28. Robert Grierson and Marion Wilson in Darnick, a.d.n. Margaret ; w. Thomas Vair, James Wilson.

,,   29. Alexr. Broomfield and Margaret Mein in Gattonside, a.d.n. Margaret.

1740.
Dec. 29. Thomas Hoy and Janet Smith in Gattonside, a.d.n. Christian ; w.
Andrew and John Marrs.

1741.
Jan.   4. Robert Blaikie and Margaret Pepdin in Bridgend, a.d.n. Elizabeth ;
w. Andrew Drummond, William Hudd.

„   6. Mungo Park and Janet Blaikie in Westhouses, two sons named John
and James.

„   „ George Mercer and Isobel Hunter in Darnick, a.d.n. Isobel.

„   „ John Kemp and Anne Christie by antenuptial fornication, a.d.n.
Helen ; w. John Mercer, John Heiton.

„   11. Walter Scott and Janet Mein in Danieltown, a.s.n. Walter ; w. George
Lawrie, Robert Scott.

„   12. Richard Park and Margaret Pringle in Allanshaws, a.s.n. William ; w.
John Fisher, Walter Thomson.

„   18. Andrew Hart and Margaret Davidson in Newsteid, a.s.n. Andrew.

„   „ Andrew Burnet and Eleanor Turnbull in Melrose, a.d.n. Helen ; w.
John Scott, Robert Bunzie.

Mar.   1. William Turner and Mary Purves in Gattonside, a.d.n. Elizabeth ; w.
Andrew Marr, Thomas Boston.

„   15. James Welsh and Agnes Gibson in Gattonside, a.d.n. Isobel ; w.
Gilbert Welsh, James Boston.

„   22. William Martine and Margaret Drummond in Gattonside, a.s.n.
William : w. David Martine, John Cochran.

„   25. William Thyne and Marion Forsyth in Blainslies, a.s.n. James.

„   „ William Pringle and —— Tait in Blainslies, a.s.n. Hugh ; w. John
and Alexr. Gray.

„   29. Alexr. Vair and Janet Wilson in Danieltown, a.d.n. Janet ; w. Thomas
Vair, James Wilson.

April   2. Thomas Darling and —— Thomson in Langhaugh, a.d.n. Agnes.

„   „ William Tait and Janet Atchison in Williamlaw, a.d.n. Agnes ; w.
Thomas Inglis, George Blaikie.

„   8. James Anderson and Alison Boston in Easterlanglee, a.s.n. Thomas ;
w. James Dickson, George Martine.

„   12. James Speeding and Janet Mercer in Bridgend, a.s.n. James.

„   „ John Lyal and Isobel Gill in Melrose, a.s.n. Alexander ; w. Nicol
Mercer, John Gill.

„   19. Andrew Martine and Margaret Alexander in Melrose, a.s.n. John ;
w. George Martine, John Tait.

May   1. Henry Forest and —— in Westhouses, a.s.n. Henry ; w. John Forest,
James Dixon.

„   10. William Martine and Jean Grieve in Gattonside, a.s.n. James ; w.
Andrew Marr, John Boston.

„   20. Simon Haitley and Marion Bunzie in Melrose, a.s.n. Robert ; w. John
Bowie, George Martine.

„   24. Walter Rae and Christian Richie in Newtown, a.s.n. James.

„   „ James Brown and Janet Waugh in ——, a.d.n. Elizabeth ; w. Nicol
Milne, Thomas Stenhouse.

June   3. Andrew Chisholm and Marion Turner, a.s.n. James ; w. James
Laidlaw, John Gordon.

July   12. Alexr. Strachan and Mary Mein in Melrose, a.s.n. James.

„   „ William Bunzie and Janet Mabane in Newsteid, a.d.n. Janet ; w.
John Mein, James Bunzie.

„   21. John Fisher and Isobel Scott in Colmslie, a.d.n. Isobel.

„   „ Zerub. Forsan and Agnes Purves in Langshaw milne, a.d.n. Margaret :
w. Walter Thomson, Gideon Watson.

Aug.   16. William Mabane and Isobel Bannatyne in Melrose, a.s.n. John.

„   „ Adam Dods and Bettie Gill in Danieltown, a.s.n. Thomas : w. Robert
and Thomas Trotters.

„   23. George Scott and Isobel Tailor in Danieltown, a.s.n. Andrew ; w.
Robert and Walter Scotts.

1741.

Sept. 6. John Givan and —— in Gattonside, a.d.n. Beatrix; w. James Speeding, Thomas Hoy.

„ 8. The deceased James M'Dougal and Agnes Heiton in Darnick, a.s.n. James; w. John Anderson, Robert Tait.

„ 20. John Boston and Helen Hunter in Gatttonside, a.s.n. Robert; w. Robert Philp, James Boston.

Oct. 11. Andrew Dawson and Jean Lamb in Melrose, a.s.n. Andrew.

„ „ Nicol Laidlaw and Elizabeth Milne in Newton, a.d.n. Margaret.

„ „ William Mein and —— Mercer in Newtown, a.d.n. Elizabeth; w. Nicol Milne, Mungo Laidlaw.

„ 15. James Atchison and Janet Turner in Langshaw, a.s.n. James.

„ „ James Russel and Jean Boston in Langshaw, two daughters named Elizabeth and Catharine.

„ „ John Chisholm and Elizabeth Lawder, a.d.n. Elizabeth; w. Wm. Russel of Ashiesteel, Walter Thomson.

„ 25. John Fairbairn and Margaret Young in Newtoun, a.d.n. Isobel; w. William and Robert Bunzies.

Nov. 1. Nicol Mercer and Agnes Steel in Melrose, a.s.n. Nicol; w. William and Thomas Steels.

„ 12. William Wilson and Margaret Ford in Blainslies, a.s.n. James.

„ „ Robert Scott and Janet Darling in Blainslies, a.d.n. Agnes; w. John and Alexr. Grays.

Dec. 7. Robert Mein and the deceased Marion Fisher in Newstead, a s.n. Robert; w. John Meins, elder and younger, there.

„ 13. James Watt and Margaret Darling in Melrose, a.s.n. James; w. Thomas Marr, James Smail.

1742.

Jan. 10. George Dickson and Janet Turner in Drygraingemilne, a.d.n. Margaret; w. James Dickson, William Riddell.

„ 24. Cornelius Mein and Helen Sibbald in Eildon, a.s.n. Richard; w. Cornelius Mein, John Sibbald.

Feb. 1. Andrew Darling and Margaret Somervell in Newhouses, a.d.n. Annabella; w. Mr. Russell, John Fisher.

„ 11. Robert Waddell and Agnes Turner in Williamlaw, a.s.n. Thomas; w. George and James Blaikies.

„ 13. Robert Mercer and Annabella Ovens in Newsteid, a.d.n. Annabella; w. James and Andrew Pringles.

Mar. 8. John Carter and Agnes Purves in Clackmae, a.d.n. Janet; w. James and Charles Ainslies.

„ 9. George Blaikie and Mary Gray in Langhaugh, a.d.n. Janet; w. Thomas Welsh, George Martine.

„ 14. Andrew Hart and —— in Newsteid, a.d.n. Elizabeth; w. John and Andrew Meins.

„ 20. John Speirs and Alison Gibson in Newsteid, a.s.n. John; w. James Mein, George Martine.

„ 28. William Bartleman and Jean Pringle in Newsteid, a.s.n. John.

„ „ Mungo Glendinning and Margaret Shiel, by fornication, a.s.n. John; w. Thomas and James Bunzies.

„ 29. Robert Lees and Bettie Mertle in Whitelaw, a.d.n. Barbara; w. William Mertle, William Lees.

April 4. John Lyal and Isobell Gill in Melrose, a.d.n. Isobell; w. Thomas and John Gills.

„ 7. John Laidlaw and Margaret Burnet in Overlangshaw, by antenuptial fornication, a.d.n. Margaret; w. Robert Laidlaw, George Martine.

„ 11. Andrew Mein and Janet Renaldson in Newtown, a.d.n. Agnes; w. James Mein, John Scott.

„ 12. William Brown and Janet Scott in Gattonside, a.s.n. Robert and a.d.n. Agnes.

„ „ James Lythgow and Isobel Riddell in Gattonside, a.d.n. Alison; w. Andrew Marr, James Boston.

1742.

May   9. Nicol Milne and Janet Frater in Newtown, a.s.n. Richard.
  "   " John Hoy and Alison Cunninghame in Melrose, a.d.n. Alison ; w. Alexr. Mein, George Martine.
  " 12. Alexr. Cunningham of Hyndhope and Elizabeth Paterson, his lady, in Old Melrose, a.s.n. Adam : w. Charles Wilkieson, George Martine.
  " 18. Thomas Slatter and Janet Darling in Blainslies, a.s.n. Richard ; w. Alexr. and John Grays.
  " 31. John Mein and Christian Hunter in Newsteid, a.d.n. Jean ; w. John Mein, William Hunter.
June 27. George Martine and Margaret White in Melrose, a.s.n. George ; w. John Tait, Andrew Martine.
July 4. William Mathison and Janet Frier in Melrose, a.d.n. Isobel : w. Walter Murray, Thomas Mathison.
  " 18. William Martine and Jean Grieve in Gattonside, a.s.n. William.
  "   " John Cochran and Margaret Drummond in Newtown, a.s.n. Henry ; w. Henry Cochran, Andrew Marr.
  " 20. Andrew Bartleman and —— Cochran in Newtown, a.d.n. Mary ; w. Nicol Milne, James Mein.
  " 25. James Fisher and Janet Glendinning in Darnick, a.s.n. James.
  "   " James Welsh and Agnes Gibson in Gattonside, a.s.n. William ; w. William Bell, James Boston.
  " 31. John Milne and Eupham Brown in Newtown, a.d.n. Isobel.
  "   " Andrew Bowar and Margaret Stenhouse in Newtoun, a.d.n. Helen ; w. Nicol Milne, William Stenhouse.
Aug. 1. Adam Thorburn and Susanna Rutherfurd in Melrose, a.d.n. Susanna ; w. Andrew Martine, Robert Tait.
  " 15. David Martine and Helen Bell in Gattonside, a.s.n. William ; w. Thomas Hoy, William Bell.
  " 22. John Gill and Helen Paterson in Melrose, a.d.n. Helen : w. Thomas Gill, James Smail.
Sept. 5. John Bruce and Christian Forsan in Melrose, a.s.n. John : w. William Williamson, Thomas Marr.
  " 19. Henry Forest and —— Henderson in Westhouses, a.s.n. Henry.
  "   " Alexr. Lockie and Grizzal Nicolson in Melrose, a.s.n. Alexander.
  "   " James Burnet and —— Renaldson in Darnick, a.d.n. Margaret ; w. John Mein, William Steel.
  " 30. Robert Myles and Janet Mathison in Gattonside, a.d.n. Elizabeth ; w. Andrew Marr, George Martine.
Oct. 1. James Wauch and Isobel Smail in Melrose, a.s.n. James ; w. James Smail, James Waugh.
  " 12. Robert Trotter and Margaret Mabane in Melrose, a.s.n. Thomas ; w. John and William Mabans.
  " 17. Thomas Bunzie and Janet Mein in Newsteid, a.d.n. Agnes ; w. James and Andrew Bunzies.
  " 27. John Edgar and Margaret Grieve in Blainslies, a.s.n. John.
  "   " John Wood and Alison Bourlees in Threepwood, a.d.n. Margaret : w. —— .
Nov. 7. George Wright and Christian Pringle in Melrose, a.s.n. William.
  "   " Andrew Mein and Janet Atchison in Newsteid, a.d.n. Agnes : w. John Mein, Andrew Mein.
  " 17. Richard Park and ——.Pringle in Allanshaws, a.s.n. John.
  "   " Alexr. Gray and Margaret Thyne in Blainslies, a.d.n. Agnes ; w. John Gray, Thomas Moffat.
  " 28. William Wright and Agnes Brown in Darnick, a.d.n. Agnes ; w. James Wight, George Mercer.
Dec. 5. Philip Fair and —— in Gattonside, a.s.n. Philip.
  "   " Thomas Vair and Margaret Mein in Newsteid, a.s.n. Thomas ; w. Andrew Marr, John Mein.
  " 19. Nicol Bowar and Margaret Mein in Newtown, a.d.n. Barbara.

1742.

Dec. 19 James Speeding and Janet Mercer in Bridgend, a.d.n. Christian ; w. Nicol Milne, Thomas Stenhouse.

„ 26. John Scott and —— Renaldson in Newsteid, a.d.n. Jean ; w. John Mein, Robert Bunzie.

„ 27. James Anderson and Alison Boston in Easterlanglee, a.d.n. Catharine ; w. Mr. John Boston, Ebenezer Currie.

1743.

Jan. 9. William Govan and Isobel Willson in Lindean, a.s.n. William.

„ „ Michael Wallace and Agnes Wright in Melrose, a.d.n. Agnes ; w. Andrew and John Dawsons.

„ 10. William Waugh and Agnes Lees in Blainslies, a.s.n. John.

„ „ George Henry and Marion Thomson there, a.d.n. Elizabeth ; w. James and Charles Ainslie.

„ 16. William Bunzie and Barbara Trotter in Newsteid, a.s.n. James.

„ „ George Mercer and Isobel Hunter in Darnick, a.d.n. Isobel ; w. William Hunter, John Mercer.

„ 23. Andrew Burnet and Eleanor Turnbull in Melrose, a.d.n. Margaret ; w. James Watt, Andrew Dawson.

Feb. 13. Thomas Hoy and Janet Smith in Gattonside, a.s.n. William.

„ „ George Walker and Anne Pringle in Melrose, a.s.n. William.

„ „ Alexander M'Faddzean and —— Sked in Melrose, a.s.n. Andrew ; w. William Steel, Andrew Marr.

Mar. 6. John Anderson and Elizabeth Fiddes in Melrose, a.d.n. Margaret ; w. James Smail, George Walker.

„ 9. Charles Wilkieson and Anne Paterson in Melrose, a.s.n. Alexr. ; w. Dr. Rutherfurd, Henry Cook.

„ 17. William Thyne and —— Forsyth in Blainslies, a.d.n. Helen ; w. Alexr. Gray, Robert Scott.

„ 19. John Haliburton and —— Rae in Drygrainge boathouse, a.s.n. Andrew ; w. Thomas Atchison, George Martine.

April 3. Thomas Stenhouse and Agnes Milne in Newtoun, a.s.n. John.

„ „ Andrew Renaldson and Janet Scott in Darnick, a.d.n. Elizabeth ; w. Nicol Milne, James Mein.

„ 10. Alexr. Broomfield and Isobel Mein in Gattonside, a.s.n. George.

„ „ William Steel and Elizabeth Walker in Melrose, a.d.n. Margaret ; w. Andrew Marr, George Walker.

„ 14. William Tait and Janet Atchison in Buckholm, a.d.n. Helen ; w. John Turner, George Henderson.

„ 17. Patrick Bulman and —— in Newtown, a.s.n. James.

„ „ George Martine and Agnes Fair in Westhouses, a.d.n. Jean ; w. Nicol Milne, Thomas Stenhouse.

„ 18. James Dixon and —— Blaikie in Old Melrose, a.d.n. Agnes.

„ „ William Gray and —— in Drygrainge milne, a.d.n. Susanna ; w. William Hunter, John Mein.

„ 24. Nicol Laidlaw and Elizabeth Milne in Newtown, a.s.n. Nicol.

„ „ John Kemp and —— Christie in Gattonside, a.s.n. Samuel ; w. Nicol Milne, Mungo Laidlaw.

„ 27. Thomas Henderson and Isobel Pringle in Sorrowlessfield, a.s.n. Thomas ; w. James Fisher, George Martine.

May 1. William Milne and Elizabeth Mein in Darnick, a.s.n. —— : w. George and John Mercers.

„ 15. John Purves and Agnes Thyne in Melrose, a.s.n. James.

„ „ John Atchison and Janet Turner in Buckholm, a.s.n. John : w. John and Mungo Parks.

„ 29. William M'Caul and Margaret Mercer in Darnick, a.d.n. Elizabeth.

„ „ James Atchison and Janet Frater in Langlee, a.d.n. Alison ; w. Andrew and George Martines.

June 5. Robert Lawrie and —— Wight in Danieltown, a.d.n. Margaret : w. Robert Scot, George Lawrie.

„ 6. James Fisher and Isobel Wight in Clackmae, a.s.n. George.

R

1743.

June 6. Robert Tait and Jean Gordon in Blainslies, a.d.n. Agnes.
  „   „   William Darling and Magdaline Allan in Blainslies, a.d.n. Magdaline ;
             w. James and Robert Scots.
  „   19. John Tait and Margaret Martine in Melrose, a.s.n. John ; w. George
             and Andrew Martines.
July 3. Robert Dods and Marion Usher in Darnick, a.d.n. Isobel.
  „   „   Robert Hog and —— Frater in ——, a.d.n. Margaret ; w. Andrew
             Renaldson, William Stoddart.
  „   10. James Henry and —— Ellies in Westerhousebyre, a.s.n. John.
  „   „   Andrew Cook and Anne Stedman in Melrose, a.d.n. Elizabeth ; w.
             Alexr. and William Cooks.
  „   28. William Turner and Mary Purves in Gattonside, a.s.n. William ;
             w. Andrew and James Marrs.
  „   29. John Fairbairn and Margaret Young in Newtown, a.s.n. Robert ; w.
             Henry Cochran, John Simpson.
Aug. 11. Mungo Park and Janet Blaikie in Westhouses, a.s.n. James ; w.
             Mungo Park, George Martine.
  „   13. John Laidlaw and Margaret Burnet in Langshaw, a.s.n. Thomas ; w.
             George and Andrew Martines.
  „   14. William Martine and Isobel Drummond in Gattonside, a.d.n. Margaret.
  „   „   John Boston and Helen Hunter in Gattonside, a.d.n. Helen ; w.
             George and John Martines.
  „   21. Thomas Darling and Helen Thomson in Langhaugh, a.s.n. John.
  „   „   William Bryden and Janet Haliday in Langhaugh, a.d.n. Janet.
  „   „   William Mathison and Janet Frier in Melrose, a.d.n. Isobel ; w.
             George Blaikie, Andrew Bryden.
Oct.   9. Cornelius Mein and Helen Sibbald in Eildon, a.s.n. John ; w. John
             Sibbald, John Bunzie.
  „   30. Thomas Vair and Margaret Wilson in Danieltown, a.s.n. Thomas.
  „   „   John Sprots and Lilias Leslie in Darnick, by fornication, a.d.n.
             Margaret ; w. John Tait, George Martine.
Nov. 3. John Frater and Alison Turner in Colmslie, a.s.n. Thomas.
  „   „   Robert Laidlaw and Agnes Gray in Colmslie, a.s.n. Thomas ; w.
             George Elliot, John Fisher.
  „   13. John Dawson and Elizabeth Marr in Melrose, a.s.n. Andrew.
  „   „   William Slatter and —— Gardener in Newsteid, a.s.n. William.
  „   „   Thomas Dixon and Isabel Mercer in Bridgend, a.d.n. Margaret ; w.
             Andrew and Thomas Marrs.
  „   14. George Blaikie and Mary Gray in Langhaugh, a.s.n. John.
  „   „   Thomas Welsh and Agnes Fair in Langhaugh, a.s.n. John ; w. John
             Tait, George Alley.
  „   20. Simon Haitley and Marion Bunzie in Melrose, a.d.n. Margaret ; w.
             John Bowie, Andrew Haitley.
Dec.   4. Robert Lookup and Christian Lockie in Melrose, a.d.n. Margaret.
  „   „   Robert Mercer and Annabella Ovens in Newsteid, a.d.n. Margaret ;
             w. Thomas and Andrew Lookup.

1744.

Jan.   1. Walter Rae and Christian Richie in Newtown, a.d.n. Mary.
  „   „   Andrew Mein and Isobel Renaldson in Newtown, a.d.n. Margaret.
  „   1. Nicol Mercer and Agnes Steel in Melrose, a.d.n. Janet ; w. William
             Steel, George Walker.
Feb.   5. James Wallace and Helen Familtown in Blainslies, a.d.n. Elizabeth ;
             w. Adam and James Wallaces.
  „   26. Andrew Dawson and Jean Lamb in Melrose, a.s.n. George.
  „   „   Robert Mein and Helen Scott in Newsteid, a.s.n. Robert ; w. John
             Mein, Robert Bunzie.
Mar.   8. Andrew Darling and —— in Overlangshaw, a.d.n. Janet ; w. Robert
             and William Moffats.
  „   12. John Mein and Christian Hunter in Newsteid, a.s.n. John ; w. John
             and Robert Meins.

1744.

Mar. 30. John Sibbald and Agnes Stenhouse in Eildon, a.d.n. Christian ; w. Thomas Stenhouse, Cornelius Mein.

April 1. John Mercer and —— Skirven in Darnick, a.d.n Helen ; w. John and George Mercers.

„ 8. William Martine and Jean Grieve in Gattonside, a.s.n. Hugh ; w. Andrew Marr, John Boston.

„ 12. John Anderson, deceased, and Margaret Waugh in Melrose, a.s.n. John ; w. James Waugh, James Smail.

„ 15. James Welsh and —— Gibson in Gattonside, a.d.n. Marion ; w. James Boston, Andrew Marr.

„ 20. The deceased Robert Cavers and Janet Wright in Melrose, a.d.n. Robina ; w. Thomas Lookup, George Martine.

„ 29. John and Isobel Bostons in Gattonside, a.d.n. Marion ; w. Thomas and James Bostons.

„ 30. James Brown and Janet Waugh in Housebyres, a.s.n. John ; w. George Mercer, George Martine.

May 6. William Brown and —— Scott in Gattonside, a.d.n. Janet ; w. Thomas and John Bostons.

„ 14. John Noteman and Margaret Purves in Hewieshaugh, a.d.n. Christian.

„ „ Thomas Rutherfurd and —— in Butterhole, a.d.n. Janet ; w. Walter and George Thomsons.

„ 31. Andrew Darling and Margaret Somervel in Newhouses, a.d.n. Helen ; w. George Romanus, John Darling.

June 12. John Haliburtone and —— Rae in Drygrainge, a.d.n. Agnes ; w. John Mein, George Martine.

„ 17. John Givan and —— in Gattonside, a.s.n. John.

„ „ Andrew Martine and Margaret Alexander in Melrose, a.d.n. Margaret ; w. John Tait, George Martine.

„ 23. David Martine and Helen Bell in Gattonside, a.d.n. Helen ; w. Andrew Marr, William Martine.

„ 24. John Cochran and —— Drummond in Newtown, a.d.n. Mary.

„ „ Nicol Milne and —— Mercer in Newtown, a.d.n. Mary.

„ „ William Bunzie and Barbara Trotter in Newsteid, a.d.n. Agnes ; w. Robert Bunzie, John Mein.

July 1. James Waugh and Isobel Smail in Melrose, a.d.n. Elizabeth ; w. James Smail, James Waugh, Senior.

„ 8. John Bowar and Margaret Mercer in Melrose, a.s.n. James.

„ „ William Fair and Catharine Wilson in Gattonside, a.d.n. Margaret ; w. Thomas Boston, William Steel.

„ 22. James Crosbie and Agnes Haitley in Drygrainge, a.s.n. James ; w. Thomas Marr, Robert Crosbie.

Aug. 12. James Fisher and Janet Glendining in Darnick, a.d.n. Isobel ; w. John Mercer, John Usher.

„ 16. James Stirling and Agnes Scott in Rhone, a.s.n. James ; w. James and Robert Scots.

„ 19. John Gill and Helen Paterson in Melrose, a.s.n. John.

„ „ George Scott and Isobel Tailor in Danieltown, a.s.n. James ; w. Thomas Gill, Robert Scott.

Sept. 2. Henry Forest and —— in Westhouses, a.s.n. Alexander ; w. William Steel, George Martine.

„ 16. John Kemp and —— Christie in Gattonside, a.s.n. Alexander.

„ „ William Wight and —— Brown in Darnick, a.d.n. Jean.

„ „ Andrew Smith and Alison Hownam in Darnick, a.d.n. Margaret ; w. James Wight, Andrew Hownam.

„ 23. Alexr. M'Faddzean and Janet Sked in Melrose, a.s.n. Andrew.

„ „ Robert Williamson and —— in Gattonside, a.d.n. Eupham.

„ „ James Hunter and Isobel Milne in Newsteid, a.d.n. Isobel ; w. Nicol Milne, Robert Hunter.

Oct. 16. James Atchison and Janet Turner in Buckholm, a.s.n. James ; w. Mungo Park, Thomas Mathison.

1744.

Oct. 21. John Lyal and Isobel Gill in Melrose, a.s.n. Thomas; w. Thomas and John Gills.

.. 24. Alexr. Broomfield and Isobel Mein in Gattonside, a.d.n. Jean; w. Thomas Hoy, Thomas Boston.

.. 28. Robert Dods and —— Usher in Darnick, a.d.n. Elizabeth; w. Robert and George Scots.

Nov. 11. Andrew Burnet and Eleanor Turnbull in Melrose, a.d.n. Jean; w. William Bain, William Hunter.

., 18. James Hudd and Janet Mercer, by fornication, in Bridgend, a.d.n. Janet; w. John Mercer, Walter Scott.

.. 21. Alexr. Gray and Margaret Thine in Blainslies, a.s.n. James.

,, ,, James Atchison and Janet Frater in Langshaw, a.s.n. Andrew; w. John Gray, William Wilson.

Dec. 9. James White and Janet Ker in Gattonside, a.d.n. Elizabeth; w Andrew Dawson, Andrew Martine.

,, 11. James Anderson and Alison Boston in Easterlanglie, a.s.n. James; w. William Alley, Mungo Park.

,, ,, John Chisholm and——Lauder in Colmslie, a.d.n. Isobel; w. *ut supra.*

., 16. Nicol Bowar and —— Mein in Newtown, a.d.n. Mary; w. Nicol and John Milns.

.. 23. Mungo Park and Anne Purves in Westhouses, a.d.n. Isobel.

,, ,, Robert Trotter and Margaret Mabane in Melrose, a.d.n. Christian; w. William Mabane, Andrew Martine.

,, 30. John Bruce and Christian Forsen in Melrose. a.s.n. Robert.

,, ,, Thomas Bunzie and —— Bryden in Eildon, a.s.n. Thomas.

,, ,, John Dawson and Elizabeth Marr in Melrose, a.d.n. Susanna.

,, ,, Andrew Pringle and Anne Brock in Newsteid, a.s.n. John and a.d.n. Anne; w. John Mein, William Bartleman.

1745.

Jan. 6. Alexr. Vair and —— Wilson in Danieltown, a.s.n. James.

,, ,, Andrew Hart and —— Davidson in Newsteid, a.s.n. Andrew; w. John Mein, Robert Bunzie.

.. 13. James Blaikie and Elizabeth Purves in Drygrainge, a.s.n. Robert.

.. ,, William M'Caul and Margaret Mercer in Darnick, a.d.n. Catharine.

,, ,, Philip Fair and Alison Stephenstone in Gattonside, a.d.n. Anne; w. John Usher, John Mercer.

,, 27. Nicol Mercer and——Chisholm in Bridgend, a.d.n. Janet; w. James Speeding, William Mein.

Feb. 3. William Cook and Margaret Lawrie in Melrose, a.s.n. William.

,, ,, James Lythgow and Isobel Riddell in Gattonside, a.s.n. Edward; w. George and Robert Lawries.

,, 4. Nicol Laidlaw, deceased, and Elizabeth Milne in Newtown, a.s.n. William; w. Nicol Milne, Mungo Laidlaw.

., 10. John Hoy and Alison Cunningham in Melrose, a.s.n. Francis; w. John Bowie, Thomas Lookup.

., 21. Alexr. Bowie and Elizabeth Atchison, by fornication, a.s.n. George.

Mar. 10. Thomas Vair and Jean Mein in Newsteid, a.s.n. John.

.. .. Andrew Cook and Anne Stedman in Melrose, a.s.n. William; w. Alexr. and William Cooks.

.. 17. William Hopkirk and Isobel Tait in Melrose, a.s.n. William.

,, ., Walter Tait and Janet Story in Melrose, a.d.n. Anne; w. John Tait, William Hopkirk.

.. 19. John Laidlay and Margaret Burnet, presented by the said Margaret, as John is under scandal, a.s.n. John.

,, ,, William Tait and Janet Atchison in Buckholm, a.d.n. Anne; w. Robert and William Moffatts.

.. 24. George Wight and Christian Pringle in Darnick, a.d.n. Christian; w. John and George Mercers.

,, 27. Thomas Hart and Barbara Ainslie, by fornication, a.d.n. Elizabeth; w. Robert and William Moffatts.

1745.

April 7. James Mein and Janet Mercer in Newtown, a.d.n. Janet.

,, ,, John Heiton and Janet Mein in Darnick, a.d.n. Janet ; w. John and George Mercers.

,, 22. John Edgar and Agnes Grieve in Blainslies, a.s.n. James ; w. Hugh Grieve, Alexr. Gray.

May 5. William Mein and Helen Lockie in Eildon, a.s.n. Thomas.

,, ,, John Turnbull and Janet Usher in Gattonside, a.s.n. John.

,, ,, Thomas Bunzie and —— Mein in Newsteid, a.s.n. Thomas ; w. John Turnbull, John Sibbald.

,, 9. William Thine and Helen Forsyth in Blainslies, a.d.n. Janet ; w. Alexr. Gray, Robert Scott.

,, 12. William Lawrie and Agnes Wilson in Melrose, a.s.n. John.

,, ,, George Martin and Margaret White in Melrose, a.s.n. Gavin.

,, ,, John Scott and Margaret Renaldson in Newsteid, a.d.n. Elizabeth ; w. John Tait, Andrew Martine.

,, 16. James Dalgliesh and Janet Waugh in Melrose, a.s.n. John ; w. John Bowie, George Martine.

,, 26. James Williamson and Elizabeth Mercer in Newsteid, a.d.n. Margaret ; w. John Mein, Robert Bunzie.

June 16. William Bell and Janet Bell in Gattonside, a.s.n. William ; w. Thomas and John Bostons.

,, 19. William Ruthven and Agnes Tait in Blainslies, a.d.n. Elizabeth ; w. John Thomson, Alexr. Gray.

,, 30. John Mein and Christian Hunter in Newsteid, a.d.n. Mary ; w. John Mein, James Hunter.

July 15. John Dickson and —— Lees in Westerboathouses, a.s.n. James.

,, ,, James Welsh and Agnes Gibson in Gattonside, a.s.n. James ; w. James Dickson, Thomas Boston.

,, 21. Andrew Bowar and Margaret Stenhouse in Newtown, a.d.n. Alison ; w. Nicol Milne, Thomas Stenhouse

,, 28. Adam Thorburn and Susanna Rutherford in Melrose, a.d.n. Margaret ; w. William and Thomas Mabans.

Aug. 4. Thomas Dixon and Isobel Mercer in Bridgend, a.d.n. Alison ; w. James Dixon, William Stoddart.

,, 25. William Bryden and Janet Halliwell in Langhaugh, a.s.n. Andrew.

,, ,, George Walker and Anne Pringle in Melrose, a.d.n. Jean ; w. Thomas Marr, William Steel.

Sept. 3. John Grahamslie and —— Henderson in Danieltown, a s.n. George ; w. Andrew Martine, Thomas Davidson.

,, 8. Wm. Martine and Jean Grieve in Gattonside, a.s.n. James.

, ,, Walter Horseburgh and Margaret Bain in Housebyres, a.s.n. William.

,, ,, John Haliburton and Alison Rae in Melrose, a.d.n. Alison ; w. William Bain, William Steel.

,, 29. Alexr. Strachan and Mary Mein in Melrose, a.s.n. Charles ; w. Alexr. and Andrew Cooks.

Oct. 7. George Blaikie and Mary Gray in Langhaugh, a.s.n. George ; w. Mungo Park, George Martine.

,, 8. Adam Dods and Elizabeth Gill in Danieltown, a.d.n. Elizabeth ; w. George and Robert Lawries.

,, 13. James Waugh and Isobel Smail in Melrose, a.s.n. John.

,, ,, John Mercer and Helen Skirven in Darnick, a.s.n. John ; w. John and George Mercers.

,, 23. Cornelius Mein and Helen Sibbald in Eildon, a.s.n. Cornelius ; w. Cornelius Mein, John Sibbald.

Nov. 10. William Slatter and Jean Gardener in Newsteid, a.s.n. James.

,, ,, Walter Rae and —— Richie in Newtown, a.d.n. Alison.

,, ,, James Inglis and Isobel Haliburton in Drygrainge, a.d.n. Isobel ; w. John Mein, Robert Mein.

,, 24. John Anderson and Lizie Fiddes in Melrose, a.d.n. Alison ; w. Alexr. and Andrew Cooks.

1745.

Nov. 28. Thomas Hoy and Janet Smith in Gattonside a.s.n. John ; w. Thomas Boston, Robert Philp.

Dec. 1. James Wilson and —— in Bridgend, a.s.n. Robert : w. John Mercer, Andrew Drummond.

„ 8. Alexr. Cook and Margaret Deans in Melrose, a.s.n. William ; w. Andrew and William Cooks.

1746.

Jan. 7. John Wallace and Helen Familtown in Blainslies, a.s.n. John ; w. James and Alexr. Fishers.

„ 12. Robert Lookup and Christian Lockie in Melrose, a.s.n. John ; w. Thomas and Andrew Lookup.

„ 27. William Hunter and Margaret Moffatt in Newstead, a.s.n. Thomas ; w. John Meins, elder and younger.

„ 28. John and Isobel Bostons in Gattonside, a.s.n. Thomas.

„ „ Alexr. Black and Margaret M'Dougal in Westerboathouse, a.s.n. John ; w. James and Thomas Bostons.

„ 29. Gilbert Welsh and Rachel Welsh in Langhaugh, a.s.n. Thomas.

„ „ James Williamson and Elizabeth Shiel in Blainslies, a.d.n. Margaret ; w. Robert and William Moffatts.

Feb. 23. George Henry and Marion Horseburgh in Easterlanglee, a.d.n. Marion ; w. Mungo Park, elder and younger.

Mar. 2. David Thomson and Margaret Mein in Melrose, a.s.n. Robert ; w. William Mabane, William Cook.

„ 3. James Moffat and Marion Laidlaw in Langshaw, a.s.n. John.

„ „ Thomas Welsh and Mary Fair in Langhaugh, a.s.n. Thomas.

„ „ John Frater and Alison Turner in Colmslie, a.d.n. Janet ; w. Walter Thomson, George Elliot.

„ 9. Adam Harvie and Isobel Leithen in Westhouses, a.s.n. Mungo ; w. William Steel, George Martine.

„ 16. Robert Mein and Helen Scott in Newsteid, a.s.n. William ; w. John Meins, elder and younger.

„ 17. William Brown, soldier, and Christian M'Millian in Melrose, a.s.n. Hugh : w. Andrew Martine, George Tait.

„ 19. Andrew Darling and —— in Blainslies, a.s.n. Andrew ; w. Alexr. and John Grays.

April 1. Alexr. Scott and —— Mowat in Blainslies, a.s.n. William ; w. Robert Scott, Alexr. Gray.

„ 6. Robert Bunzie and Margaret Blaikie in Newsteid, a.s.n. James.

„ „ Mungo Park and Anne Purves in Westhouses, a.d.n. Helen.

„ „ Nicol Milne and —— Mercer in Newtown, a.d.n. Isobel : w. Thomas Stenhouse, John Mein.

„ 20. John Hoy, soldier, and Esther Martine in Melrose, a.s.n. John ; w. John Hoy, George Martine.

May 1. William Moffatt and Marion Somervel in Threepwood, a.d.n. Jean ; w. Robert Moffatt, George Elliot.

„ 11. William Hopkirk and Isobel Tait in Melrose, a.s.n. William.

„ „ William Brown and —— Scott in Gattonside, a.d.n. Agnes ; w. William Hopkirk, John Tait.

„ 18. Robert Grierson and Marion Wilson in Darnick, a.d.n. Elizabeth ; w. William Stoddart, James Wight.

„ 25. William Turner and Mary Purves in Gattonside, a.d.n. Margaret ; w. Thomas and James Bostons.

July 31. John Gill and Helen Paterson in Melrose, a.d.n. Helen ; w. Thomas Gill, George Lawrie.

Aug. 1. Thomas Darling and —— Thomson in Langhaugh, a.d.n. Elizabeth.

„ „ John Coldwalls and Jean Currer in Blainslies, a.s.n. Alexr.

„ „ Andrew Darling and Helen Fleeming in Blainslies, a.s.n. James.

„ „ George Mercer and Isobel Hunter in Westerhousebyres, a.s.n. James : w. Alexr. Gray, George Darling.

1746.

Aug. 4. Charles Wilkison and Anna Paterson in Melrose, a.s.n. Charles ; w.

,,   10. John Turnbull and Janet Usher in Gattonside, a.d.n. Christian : w. John Turnbull, James Boston.

,,   17. James White and Janet Ker in Gattonside, a.s.n. Andrew ; w. Thomas and James Bostons.

,,   24. Andrew Smith and —— Hownam in Darnick, a.d.n. Helen ; w. John and George Mercers.

,,   31. John Young and Margaret Gill in Gattonside, a.s.n. Alexander.

,,   ,, John Bowar and Janet Mercer in Melrose, a.d.n. Margaret : w. Thomas and John Bostons.

Sept. 7. George Buttler and Janet Watson in ——, a.d.n. Janet ; w. George Elliot, Walter Thomson.

,,   21 James Atchison and Janet Turner in Buckholm, a.s.n. Edward ; w. John Dixon, Adam Harvie.

,,   28. John Kemp and —— in Gattonside, a.s.n. Adam ; w. John Thomson, William Bell.

,,   30. James Inglis and Janet Ormistown, by fornication, a.d.n. Jean : w. Walter Scott, William Mein.

Oct. 23. Thomas Paterson and Janet Paterson in Mosshouses, a.s.n. James.

,,   ,, Robert Cribbas and Agnes Mathison in Sorrowlessfield, a.d.n. Janet ; w. Thomas and John Bostons.

,,   26. James Mercer and Margaret Pearson in Darnick, a.d.n. Margaret ; w. Andrew Mercer, John Pearson.

Nov. 2. Henry Forest and Margaret Henderson in Westhouses, a.d.n. Margaret.

,,   ,, Robert Waddell and Agnes Turner in Williamlaw, a.d.n. Margaret : w. Mungo Park, Walter Thomson.

,,   4. George Atchison and Isobel Haliburton, by fornication, a.s.n. Thomas ; w. Andrew Burnet, Robert Scott.

,,   9. Andrew Cook and Anne Stedman in Melrose, a.s.n. Andrew ; w. Alexr. and William Cooks.

,,   16. Andrew Burnet and Eleanor Turnbull in Melrose, a.s.n. Dunbar.

,,   ,, Walter Tait and Janet Story in Melrose, a.s.n. Rutherfurd : w. John Tait, William Bain.

,,   23. William Bunzie and Barbara Trotter in Newsteid, a.d.n. Margaret : w Robert Bunzie, John Mein.

,,   30. The deceased George Pringle and Alison Haitley in Danieltown, a.d.n. Alison ; w. Andrew Martine, Thomas Davidson.

Dec. 14. Alexr. Broomfield and Agnes Mein in Gattonside, a.s.n. Alexr.

,,   ,, John Heiton and Janet Mein in Darnick, a.s.n. Andrew ; w. Thomas Boston, George Mercer.

,,   21. George Wright and Christian Pringle in Darnick, a.d.n. Margaret ; w. George and John Mercers.

,,   22. James Mein and —— Nesten in Newsteid, two daughters named Janet and Isobel ; w. Andrew and Thomas Bunzies.

,,   28. Nicol Mercer and —— Chisholm in Bridgend, a.d.n. Elizabeth ; w. Andrew Drummond, Andrew Mercer.

1747.

Jan. 11. John Dawson and Elizabeth Marr in Melrose, a.s.n. Andrew.

,,   ,, Nicol Milne and Janet Frater in Newtown, a.s.n. Andrew ; w. John Milne, Andrew Dawson.

,,   25. John Boston and Helen Hunter in Gattonside, a.s.n. John.

,,   ,, Robert Dods and —— Usher in Darnick, a.d.n. Jean ; w. William Stoddart, John Usher.

Feb. 8. Robert Trotter and Margaret Mabane in Melrose, a.d.n. Christian ; w. William and Thomas Mabanes.

,,   9. William Mercer and Agnes Dalgliesh in Housebyres, a.s.n. James.

,,   ,, William Coldcleugh and Elizabeth Wadderstone in Mosshouses, a.d.n. Isobel ; w. George Elliot, Robert Laidlaw.

1747.

Mar. 1. James Williamson and Lizie Mercer in Newsteid, a.s.n. Thomas.

,, ,, Robert Williamson and Eupham Anderson in Gattonside, a.d.n. Agnes ; w. John Mein, Andrew Mein.

,, 8. James Fisher and Janet Glendinning in Darnick, a.s.n. Robert.

,, ,, George Scott and Isobel Tailor in Danieltown, a.d.n. Elizabeth ; w. Walter Scott, Robert Lawrie.

,, 22. William Fair and Catharine Wilson in ——, a.s.n. John ; w. Philip Fair, George Martine.

,, 23. John Mein and Christian Hunter in Newsteid, a.s.n. Robert ; w. Robert and Andrew Meins.

,, 29. John Sprots and Lilias Leslie in Darnick, a.s.n. John ; w. Andrew Martine, Thomas Davidson.

,, 30. William Bryden and Janet Haliday in Langhaugh, a.d.n. Margaret ; w. James Laidlaw, William Tait.

April 18. William Redford and Margaret Neil in Threepwood, a.s.n. John and a.d.n. Mary ; w. William Moffatt, Richard Park.

,, 19. Andrew Black and —— Service in Taff-field, a.d.n. Helen ; w. George and Andrew Martines.

,, 26. William Martine and Jean Grieve in Gattonside, a.d.n. Margaret ; w. Thomas and John Bostons.

May. 3. James Lythgow and Isobel Riddell in Gattonside, a.d.n. Isobel ; w. Thomas Hoy, John Bannatyne.

,, 24. John Dickson and —— Lees in Westhouses boathouse, a.s.n. William ; w. James Dickson, William Mabane.

,, 31. Andrew Mein and Janet Renaldson in Newtown, a.s.n. William ; w. Thomas Stenhouse, James Mein.

June 2. John Laidlaw and —— Burnet in Langshaw, a.d.n. Helen ; w. Thomas Davidson, George Martine.

,, 7. James Waugh and Isobel Smail in Melrose, a.d.n. Janet ; w. George and Andrew Martines.

,, 16. Alexr. Bowar and Agnes Murray in Melrose, a.s.n. James ; w. ——.

,, 17. John Haliburton and Alison Rae in Melrose, a.d.n. Alison ; w. James Hilson, George Martine.

,, 21. William Lawrie and Agnes Wilson in Melrose, a.d.n. Jean.

,, ,, William Sibbet and Janet Ferquartson in Gattonside, a.d.n. Janet ; w. Thomas Hoy, John Thomson.

July 5. John Hoy and Alison Cunningham in Melrose, a.s.n. Walter.

,, ,, John Grahamslie and Margaret Henderson in Danieltown, a.s.n George ; w. George Grahamslie, George Scott.

,, 24. George Martine and Margaret White in Melrose, a.d.n. Milne ; w. James Waugh, Robert Scott.

Aug. 2. Alexr. Vair and —— Wilson in Danieltown, a.s.n. Alexr. ; w. George and Robert Lawries.

,, 16. William Wight and Agnes Brown in Darnick, a.s.n. Robert.

,, ,, Nicol Bowar and Margaret Mein in Newtown, a.d.n. Janet.

,, ,, Alexr. Laing and Agnes Sprate in Gattonside, a.d.n. Jean ; w. James Wight, Thomas Hoy.

,, 23. James Hunter and Isobel Milne in Melrose, a.s.n. Robert ; w. Nicol Milne, Robert Hunter.

,, 24. James Cleugh and Isobel Purves in Colmslie ; a.d.n. Isobel.

,, ,, Thomas Coldcleugh and —— in Mosshouses, —— ; w. George Elliot, John Coats.

,, 30. James Fiddes and Marion Anderson in Westboathouse, a.d.n. Margaret ; w. James and John Bostons.

Sept. 11. William Moffatt and Marion Somervell in Threepwood, a.s.n. Peter.

,, ,, Andrew Darling and —— in Newhouses, a.d.n. Margaret ; w. Robert Laidlaw, Robert Moffatt.

,, 14. William Mein and —— Mercer in Newtown, a.s.n. James ; w. Nicol and John Milns.

1747.

Sept. 20. William Mein and —— Lockie in Eildon, a.d.n. Margaret ; w. John Sibbald, John Bunzie.

,, 27. George Watt and Margaret Craig in Melrose, a.s.n. James ; w. James Smail, James Waugh.

Oct. 4. James Dickson and —— Blaikie in Newsteid, a.s.n. —— ; w. Robert Bunzie, Andrew Hart.

,, 14. William Bartleman and Jean Pringle in Newsteid, a.d.n. Isobel ; w. John Scott, John Mein.

Nov. 1. Alexr. Sibbett and Janet Bannatyne in Gattonside, a.s.n. William ; w. William Sibbett, John Bannatyne.

,, 13. John Mabane and Janet Jack in Newsteid, a.s.n. James.

,, ,, George Renaldson and —— Mein in Darnick, a.s.n. James ; w. John Mein, Andrew Renaldson.

Dec. 13. Thomas Dixon and —— Mercer in Bridgend, a.s.n. William.

,, ,, Andrew Stuart and —— Bertown in Gattonside, a.d.n. Agnes.

,, ,, James Wight and Jean Mein in Newsteid, a.d.n. Jean ; w. Andrew Mein, Thomas Hoy.

,, 20. Andrew Moss and Agnes Wight in Darnick, a.d.n. Margaret.

,, ,, Mungo Park and Anne Purves in Drygrainge boathouse, a.s.n. Archibald ; w. John Mercer, John Usher.

1748.

Jan. 11. John and Isobel Boston in Gattonside, a.d.n. Isobel ; w. James Boston, William Sibbet, there.

,, 15. Alexr. Strachen and Mary Mein in Melrose, a.d.n. Margaret ; w. George Martine, James Waugh.

,, 27. James Millar and Jean Gladstains in Drygrainge, a.s.n. John.

Feb. 10. James Williamson and Elizabeth Mercer in Newsteid, a.s.n. John : w. ——.

,, 14. Walter Rae and —— Ritchie in Newtown, a.s.n. Brown ; w. Nicol Milne, Thomas Stenhouse.

,, ,, John Sibbald and Agnes Stenhouse in Eildon, a.d.n. Helen ; w. as above.

,, 21. Adam Dods and Bettie Gill in Danieltown, a.d.n. Margaret ; w. Robert Scott, George Lawrie.

,, 28. John Anderson and Lizie Fiddes in Melrose, a.s.n. Adam ; w. James Smail, James Waugh.

Mar. 6. Alexr. Cook and —— Deans in Melrose, a.d.n. Margaret ; w. Andrew and William Cooks.

,, 13. Thomas Welsh and Margaret Fair in Appletrecleaves, a.d.n. Elizabeth; w. George Martin, George Chisholm.

,, 20. Andrew Mein and Janet Atchison in Newsteid, a.d.n. Jean ; w. John Scott, George Martine.

,, 27. David Thomson and Margaret Mein in Melrose, a.s.n. Andrew ; w. Thomas and Andrew Lookups.

April 6. William Brown and —— Scott in Gattonside, a.s.n. James and a.d.n. Margaret ; w. John Thomson, John Bannatyne.

,, 7. Andrew Bowar and Margaret Stenhouse in Newtown, a.d.n. Margaret ; w. Nicol Milne, Thomas Stenhouse.

,, 10. Robert Bunzie and Margaret Blaikie in Newsteid, a.d.n. Janet.

,, ,, John Sprots and Lilias Leslie in Darnick, a.d.n. Catharine : w. John Usher, John Mein.

,, 17. William and Janet Bells in Gattonside, a.s.n. Hugh.

,, ,, William Slater and —— Gardner in Newsteid, a.s.n. Thomas.

,, ,, William Mabane and Margaret Harroway, by fornication, a.s.n. James ; Thomas Boston, Robert Bunzie.

,, 24. Alexr. Forest and Jean Colquhon in Melrose, a.d.n. Dalrumple ; w. Thomas Lookup, John Hoy.

May 1. William Buttler and Agnes Watson in Housebyres, a.d.n. Margaret.

,, ,, Andrew Smith and Alison Hownam in Darnick, a.d.n. Isobel ; w. Andrew Hownam, William Milne.

1748.

May   29. Nicol Mercer and Agnes Steel in Melrose, a.d.n. Agnes ; w. William and Thomas Steels.

June   5. Robert Tait and —— in Blainslies, a.s.n. Jacob, baptised at Ligerwood.

,,   12. James Welsh and —— Gibson in Gattonside, a.s.n. John.

,,   ,, William Sibbet and Mary Ferquartson in Gattonside, a.d.n. Margaret ; w. John Young, William Martine.

,,   19. William Turner and Mary Purves in Gattonside, a.d.n. Janet ; w. James Marr, William Mathison.

July   3. William Hislop and Mary Currie in Westerlanglee, a.d.n. Janet ; w. John Tait, William Stenhouse.

,,   24. Robert Lawrie and Alison Wight in Danieltown, a.s.n. George ; w. George Lawrie, William Cook.

Aug.   7. Thomas Ovens and Janet Mercer in Newsteid, a.d.n. Isobel ; w. John Mein, elder and younger.

,,   14. James Mercer and —— Pearson in Darnick, a.d.n. Agnes ; w. John Usher, James Wight.

,,   19. John Simpson and Margaret Dixon in Blainslies, a.s.n. John and a.d.n. Agnes ; w. Alexr. Gray, Robert Laidlaw.

,,   21. Walter Tait and Janet Storie in Melrose, a.d.n. Jean Cokeburn ; w. John Tait, George Martine.

Sept.   4. —— Skirven and —— Mercer in Newsteid, —— ; w. ——.

,,   ,, John Cochran and Margaret Drummond in Newtown, a.s.n. John ; w. Nicol Milne, James Mein.

,,   11. Thomas Bunzie and —— Mein in Newsteid, a.d.n. Janet.

,,   ,, John Mercer and —— Familtone in Bridgend, a.d.n. Bessie ; w. Andrew Mein, Andrew Drummond.

,,   19. Alexr. Bowie and Agnes Murray in Melrose, a.d.n. Eleonora ; w. ——.

,,   25. Thomas Usher and Janet Mercer in Gattonside, a.s.n. John.

,,   ,, James Fisher and Janet Glendinning in Darnick, a.d.n. Agnes ; w. John and Thomas Bostons.

Nov.   4. Philip Thine and —— in Clackmae, a.d.n. Margaret, baptized at Earlston.

,,   6. John Turnbull and Janet Usher in Gattonside, a.s.n. William.

,,   ,, Philip Fair and —— Stephenstone in Gattonside, a.s.n. James.

,,   ,, James Hudd and Isobel Spotswood in Melrose, a.s.n. William.

,,   ,, John Bowar and —— Mercer in Melrose, a.s.n. John.

,,   ,, William Hopkirk and Isobel Tait in Melrose, a.d.n. Margaret ; w. John Tait, William Bell.

,,   13. Patrick Graham and Margaret Thomson in Easterlanglee, a.s.n. William ; w. William Stenhouse, Thomas Hoy.

,,   27. John Kemp and —— Christie in Gattonside, a.s.n. Hugh ; w. William Sibbet, John Turnbull.

Dec.   14. Thomas Boston and Isobel Bannatyne in Gattonside, a.d.n. Janet ; w. John and James Bostons.

,,   18. John Heiton and Janet Mein in Darnick, a.s.n. James ; w. George and John Mercers.

1749.

Jan.   1. John Dawson and Elizabeth Marr in Melrose, a.d.n. Jean ; w. Thomas Marr, William Steel.

,,   4. James Millar and Jean Gladstains in Drygrainge, a.s.n. William ; w. Mungo Park, George Martine.

,,   10. James Wilson and Catharine Maban in Housebyres, a.d.n. Isobel ; w. Thomas Hoy, Thomas Boston.

,,   13. Andrew Dawson and Jean Lamb in Melrose, a.d.n. Jean w. John Dawson, William Steel.

Feb.   5. Robert Trotter and Margaret Mabane in Melrose, a.d.n. Margaret ; w. William and Thomas Mabans.

,,   13. Thomas and —— Patersons in Mosshouses, a.d.n. Janet ; w. George Elliot, George Martine.

,,   19. John Mabane and Janet Jack in Newsteid, a.s.n. William.

1749.

Feb. 19. Adam Thorburn and Susanna Rutherfurd in Melrose, a.d.n. Helen ; w. William Steel, Walter Murray.

,, 26. William Cavers and —— Currer in Melrose, a.s.n. John ; w. William Steel, Alexr. Lockie.

Mar. 5. William Mercer and Anne M'Faddzean in Melrose, a.s.n. Nicol.

,, ,, Robert Dods and —— Usher in Darnick, a.s.n. Andrew.

,, ,, William Martin and Jean Grieve in Gattonside, a.d.n. Janet ; w. James Wight, John Usher.

,, 17. Alexr. Broomfield and —— Mein in Gattonside, —— ; w. Thomas Hoy, Thomas Bostone.

April 2. John Gill and Helen Paterson in Melrose, a.s.n. Andrew.

,, ,, John Forsan and Janet Winterup in Drygrainge, a.d.n. Janet ; w. George and Robert Lawries.

,, 9. Mr. James Brown, minister, and Helen Drummond, a.s.n. John ; w. Dr. Rutherfurd, Mr. Charles Wilkieson, and Mr. Elliot.

,, 13. William Wood and Marion Little in Blainslies, a.d.n. Agnes.

,, ,, William Coldcleugh and Elizabeth Wadderstone in Housebyres, a.s.n. Thomas.

,, ,, William Mercer and Agnes Dalgliesh there, a.d.n. Catharine ; w. William Butler, William Hopkirk.

,, 16. Alexr. Scott and Alison Mowat in Blainslies, a.d.n. Alison ; w. Robert Scott, James Scot.

,, 28. Nicol Alley and Mary Forrest in Langshawmiln, a.s.n. George ; w. George Elliot, Robert Laidlaw.

May 7. Mungo Park and Janet Blaikie in Gattonside, a.s.n. George.

,, ,, John Heiton and Elizabeth Eastown in Darnick, a.d.n. Agnes ; w. John Heiton, William Stoddart.

,, 9. The deceased John Purves and Agnes Thynne in Melrose, a.s.n. John ; w. James Smail, George Martine.

,, 14. James Hunter and Isobel Milne in Melrose, a.s.n. Nicol.

,, ,, Andrew Mein and —— Renaldson in Newtown, a.d.n. Alison ; w. Nicol Miln, James Mein.

,, 21. Henry Forest and —— Anderson in Westhouses, a.s.n. William ; w. William Stenhouse, William Alley.

June 4. George Wight and Christian Pringle in Darnick, a.s.n. Andrew ; w. James Wight, William Stoddart.

,, 18. James Wight and Janet Mein in Newsteid, a.d.n. Janet ; w. John Mein, James Williamson.

,, 28. George Winter and Margaret Robson in Blainslies, a.d.n. Janet.

,, ,, Wm. Redford and Margaret Neil in Threepwood, a.s.n. Walter ; w. Hugh Grieve, Andrew Hardie.

,, ,, James White and Janet Ker in Housebyres, a.s.n. Rutherfurd ; w. William and James Mercers.

July 24. James Forsyth and —— Simpson in Buckholm, a.d.n. Jean ; w. James and James Laidlaws.

,, 30. James Williamson and Elizabeth Mercer in Newsteid, a.s.n. James ; w. John Mein, James Dickson.

Aug. 6. Alexr. Henderson and Agnes Cranstoun in Newtown, a.d.n. Margaret ; w. Thomas Stenhouse, James Smail.

,, 13. Andrew Moss and Agnes Wight in Darnick, a.d.n. Janet ; w. John Mercer, James Wight.

,, 16. Janet Haliwell, in fornication to —— Turnbull in the Army, —— ; w. George Martine, Thomas Davidson.

,, 20. John Mein and Christian Hunter in Newsteid, a.s.n. John ; w. John Mein, Robert Hunter.

,, 22. Mungo Park and Anne Purves in Drygrainge a.d.n. Anne ; w. ——.

,, 27. John Grierson and Agnes Mercer in Darnick, a.s.n. Robert ; w. Robert Grierson, William Stoddart.

Sept. 3. James Mein and —— Weston in Newsteid, a.s.n. David ; w. John Mein and John Mein

1749.

Sept.   10. George Watt and Margaret Craig in Melrose, a.d.n. Sophia ; w.
            William Steel, Alexr. Lockie.

Nov.   3. Thomas Frier and Bettie Thomson in Calfhill, a.s.n. Robert.

,,   ,, William Henry and Christian Kirkwood in Whitlaw, a.d.n. Jean ;
            w. George Elliot, John Turner.

,,   29. John Govan and Janet Jamison in Gattonside, a.s.n. James ; w.
            Thomas Boston, Thomas Hoy.

Dec.   10. William Mein and —— Mercer in Newtown, a.d.n. Margaret ; w.
            Nicol Miln, Thomas Stenhouse.

,,   13. Thomas Usher and Jenet Mercer in Gattonside, a.s.n. James ; w.
            Thomas and James Bostons.

,,   15. William Maban and Isobel Bannatine in Melrose, a.s.n. George : w.
            James Waugh, James Smail.

,,   24. —— and Janet Waugh in Melrose, a.s.n. James ; w. Andrew
            Thomson, Andrew Martin.

,,   31. Bailie Scot and Christian Bunzie in Newsteid, a.d.n. Jean : w. Robert
            and William Bunzies.

1750.

Jan.   7. James Waugh and Isobel Smail in Melrose, a.s.n. James ; w James
            Smail, James Hilson.

Feb.   4. George Drummond and —— Dickson in Newtown, a.s.n. Andrew ;
            w. Thomas Stenhouse, John Miln, there.

,,   25. Thomas Vair and —— Wilson in Danieltown ; w. George and Robert
            Lawries there.

Mar.   4. Alexr. Sibbald and Janet Bannatyne in Gattonside, a.s.n. Robert ; w.
            John Bannatyne, John Boston.

,,   11. John Boston and Helen Hunter in Gattonside, a.s.n. Thomas ; w.
            Thomas and James Bostons there.

,,   18. John Grahamslie and —— Henderson in Danieltown, a.d.n. Janet ;
            w. George Grahamslie, George Scot, there.

,,   25. John Bunzie and Mary Miln in Newsteid, a.s.n. Nicol ; w. John
            Meins, elder and younger.

,,   28. Andrew Hilson and Margaret Richardson in Blainslies, a.d.n. Isobel ;
            w. George Darling, James Scott.

April   8. James Fiddes and —— Anderson in Gattonside, a.s.n. James.

,,   ,, Andrew Stuart and —— Bartone in Gattonside, a.s.n. George ; w.
            Thomas and James Bostons.

,,   15. Adam Dods and Bettie Gill in Danieltone, a.d.n. Helen.

,,   ,, William Ormiston and Margaret Scot in Melrose, a.d.n. Janet.

,,   ,, John Dickson and —— Lees in Bolside, a.d.n. Catharine.

,,   ,, Wm. Williamson and Mary Bunzie, by fornication, in Newsteid, a.s.n.
            William ; w. John Mein, George Scott and Robert Lawrie.

,,   22. Mr. James Brown, minister, and Helen Drummond, a.d.n. Catharine ;
            w. Robert Rutherfurd of Farnilee, Dr. Rutherfurd, Messrs. Charles
            Wilkieson and Gavin Elliot.

,,   26. George Wilson and Isobel Hastie in Langhaugh, a.s.n. John ; w.
            Andrew Walker, George Blaikie.

May   6. William Brown and —— Scot in Gattonside, a.s.n. William ; w.
            Thomas and John Bostons.

,,   14. William Butler and Agnes Watson in Westerhousebyres, a.d.n.
            Agnes ; w. Thomas Hoy, Thomas Boston.

June   3. John Anderson and Lizie Fiddes in Melrose, a.s.n. Robert.

,,   ,, William Mein and Jean Lockie in Eildon, a.d.n. Isobel : w. John
            Mein, John Bunzie.

,,   10. William Turner and Mary Purves in Gattonside, a.d.n. Mary ; w.
            Thomas Hoy, James Boston.

,,   12. William Moffat and Margaret Somervel in Threepwood, a.d.n. Agnes :
            w. Richard Park, Robert Moffat.

,,   24. John Mercer and —— in Bridgend, a.d.n. Agnes ; w. Andrew
            Drummond, John Mercer.

1750.

July 22. John Dawson and Elizabeth Marr in Melrose, a.s.n. Thomas ; w. Thomas and James Marrs.

Aug. 5. John Mercer and Helen Skirven in Darnick, a.s.n. George.

,, ,, Alexr. Bowie and Agnes Murray in Melrose, a.d.n. Marion Murray ; w. George Mercer, Alexr. Bell.

,, 12. James Boston and Janet Hunter in Gattonside, a.s.n. James ; w. John Mein, James Hunter.

,, ,, John Frater and —— in Colmslie, a.d.n. Alison.

,, 13. William Wood and —— in Blainslies, a.d.n. Marion ; w. George Ainslie, Thomas Pringle.

,, 19. —— Skirven and —— Mercer in Newsteid, a.s.n. John : w. John Meins, senior and junior.

Sept. 9. John Turnbull and Janet Usher in Gattonside, a.d.n. Elizabeth ; w. John Turnbull, Thomas Usher.

,, 10. Andrew Shiel and Bettie Purves in Hagburn, a.s.n. James ; w. James Knox, George Henderson.

,, 16. James Mercer and —— Pearson in Darnick, a.s.n. Andrew.

,, ,, Andrew Smith and Alison Hownam in Darnick, a.d.n. Janet ; w. Andrew and John Hownams.

,, 23 James Hudd and Isobel Spotswood in Melrose, a.d.n. Elizabeth ; w. Walter Murrays, elder and younger.

Oct. 7. Mungo Park and Margaret Boston in Westerboathouse, a.d.n. Marion ; w. Mungo Park, James Boston.

,, 12. Andrew Darling and —— Fleeming in Blainslie, a.s.n. Andrew ; w. Hugh Grieve, James Wallace.

,, 14. William Sibbat and —— in Gattonside, a.d.n. Mary.

,, ,, John Usher and Janet Paterson in Darnick, a.d.n. Janet ; w. John Hownam, John Heiton.

,, 21. John Heiton and Janet Mein in Darnick, a.d.n. Janet ; w. George Mercer, John Usher.

,, 30. Robert Scot and Janet Darling in Blainslies, a.s.n. Alexr. : w. James Scot, George Darling.

,, ,, William Roger and Agnes Tait in Threepwood, a.s.n. John.

Nov. 20. Robert Tait and Jean Gordon in Blainslies, a.d.n. Elizabeth : w. Robert and William Moffats.

Dec. 2. James Hilson and Jean Lookup in Melrose, a.s.n. Robert ; w. John Lyal, Robert Lookup.

,, 9. James Wallace and Alison Phawp in Melrose, a.s n. James ; w. James Phawp, James Hilson.

,, 14. George Brown and Margaret Lees in Langhaugh, a.s.n. James.

,, ,, Gilbert Welsh and Mary Graham in Langhaugh, a.d.n. Catharine ; w. George Blaikie, John Hardie.

,, 24. William Coldcleugh and Elizabeth Wadderston in Housebyres, a.s.n. Thomas ; w. William Mercer, William Pearson.

,, 30. John Mabane and Janet Jack in Newsteid, a.s.n. James ; w. William Maban, John Mein.

1751.

Jan. 14. Nicol Bowar and Margaret Mein in Newtown, a.d.n. Margaret : w. Nicol and John Milns.

,, ,, William Slater and Jean Gardener in Newsteid, a.s.n. John.

,, 20. Alexr. Vair and —— Wilson in Danieltown, a.s.n. George.

,, ,, William Mercer and Elizabeth M'Fadzean in Melrose, a.d.n. Agnes.

,, ,, David Thomson and Margaret Mein in Newtown, a.d.n. Margaret ; w. John Cochran, James Mein.

Feb. 2. William Wight and Agnes Brown in Darnick, a.d.n. Isobel ; w. James Wight, William Stoddart.

,, 3. Alexr. Strachan and Mary Mein in Melrose, a.d.n. Catharine Grant ; w. John Gill, William Maban.

,, 7. Alexr. Broomfield and —— Mein in Gattonside, a.d.n. Mein.

1751.

Feb. 7. Thomas Welsh and —— in Langhaugh —— ; w. John Boston, William Martin.

,, 10. Andrew Mein and Janet Atchison in Newsteid, a.s.n. John.

,, ,, James Hunter and Isobel Miln in Melrose, a.d.n. Christian ; w. Robert Hunter, Nicol Miln.

,, 22. George Williamson and —— Wood in Langhaugh, a.d.n. Helen ; w. John and Robert Laidlaws.

Mar. 3. Andrew Dawson and Jean Lamb in Melrose, a.s.n. William.

,, ,, William Hopkirk and Isobel Tait in Melrose, a.d.n Isobel ; w. John Dawson, Thomas Marr.

,, 7. William Martin and Isobel Shillinglaw in Blainslies, a.d.n. Catharine ; w. Robert Scott, Thomas Slatter.

,, 10. Alexr. Sibbat and Janet Bannatyne in Gattonside, a.d n. Isobel ; w. John Bannatyne, James Boston.

,, 13. Robert and Agnes Mein, by fornication, in Newsteid, a.s.n. Benjamin.

,, 21. The deceased Thomas Boston and Isobel Bannatyne in Gattonside, a.d.n. Isobel ; w. John and James Bostons.

,, 23. Patrick Graham and Margaret Thomson in Easterlanglee, a.d.n. Anne ; w. William Stenhouse, William Alley.

,, 24. Alexr. Cook and —— Deans in Melrose, a.s.n. Alexander ; w. Andrew and William Cooks.

April 7. John Sprots and Lilias Leslie in Darnick, a.s.n. Andrew ; w. William and George Stoddarts.

,, 14. George Watt and Margaret Craig in Melrose, a.s.n. John ; w. Thomas and James Marrs.

,, 21. James Welsh and Agnes Gibson in Gattonside, a.s.n. James ; w. John and James Bostons.

,, 23. James Millar and Jean Gladstains in Drygrainge, a.s.n. Thomas ; w. James Fiddes, George Martin.

May 5. John Gill and Helen Paterson in Melrose, a.s.n. Thomas.

,, ,, John Grierson and Agnes Mercer in Darnick, a.d.n. Margaret ; w. John Usher, John Lyal.

,, 12. James Williamson and Elizabeth Mercer in Newsteid, a.s.n. Thomas.

,, ,, Charles Ainslie and Janet Brown in Mosshouses, a.s.n. David.

,, ,, Nicol Alley and —— Forest in Blainslies, a.d.n. Isobel ; w. John Mein, James Moffat.

,, 19. John Kemp and —— in Gattonside, a.s.n. David ; w. Thomas Hoy, Robert Myles.

,, 30. James Hardie and Jean Baptie, by fornication, a.s.n. James ; w. Andrew Martin, Thomas Davidson.

June 9. John and Janet Boston in Gattonside, a.s.n. James.

,, ,, James Mercer and Elizabeth Rutherfurd in Easterhousebyre, a.d.n. Elizabeth ; w. James Boston, James Hunter.

,, 23. Robert Bunzie and Margaret Blaikie in Newsteid, a.s.n. James ; w. John Bunzie, John Mein.

,, 26. John Caldwalls and —— Currer in Blainslies, a.s.n. Alexr. ; w. William Martin, James Scott.

July 7. Philip Fair and Alison Stephenson in Gattonside, a.d.n. Margaret ; w. Robert Myles, William Martin.

,, 28. John Bannatyne and Alison Hunter in Gattonside, a.d.n. Janet ; w. James and John Bostons.

Aug. 11. Thomas Bunzie and Agnes Mein in Newsteid, a.d.n. Isobel ; w. Andrew Bunzies, elder and younger.

,, 18. Henry Forest and —— in Westhouses, a.s.n. Henry ; w. Mungo Park, William Alley.

,, 21. William Mercer and Agnes Dalgliesh in Easterhousebyres, a.s.n. Gustavus.

,, ,, Thomas and Janet Patersons in Mosshouses, a.s.n. Thomas.

,, ,, James Cribbas and Agnes Mathison in Kedzliedoors, a.s.n. James ; w. George Martin, William Mercer.

1751.

Aug. 25. Andrew Mein and Janet Renaldson in Newtown, a.d.n. Janet ; w. John and Nicol Milns.

Sept. 1. Mungo Park and Anne Purves in Westhouses, a.s.n. Robert.

,, ,, James Wight and —— Mein in Newsteid, a.d.n. Margaret : w. James Boston, John Mein.

,, 9. Alexr. Reid and Isobel Martin in Melrose, a.s.n. Walter ; w. James Smail, James Waugh.

,, 29. Andrew Moss and Agnes Wight in Darnick, a.s.n. John.

,, ,, Mr. James Brown, minister, and Helen Drummond, a.d.n. Elizabeth ; w. Doctor John Rutherfurd, Bailie Grant and Mr. Elliot, schoolmaster.

Oct. 6. Thomas Rae and Helen Gardener in Gattonside, a.s.n. James : w. James Gardener, Andrew Smith.

,, 20. William Ormiston and Margaret Scot in Melrose, a.s.n. Robert ; w. John Gill, Robert Trotter.

Nov. 24. William Drummond and Janet Myles in Bridgend, a.d.n. Janet.

,, ,, James Marr and Janet Mercer in Darnick, a.d.n. Alison : w. Andrew Drummond, John Usher.

,, 27. Nicol Bowar and Margaret Mein in Newtown, a.d.n. Margaret ; w. Andrew Bowar, John Miln.

Dec. 15. George Wright and Christian Pringle in Darnick, a.s.n. James ; w. John Usher, George Mercer.

,, 29. Thomas Davidson and Janet Brown in Melrose, a.d.n. Helen ; w. George and Andrew Martins.

1752.

Jan. 27. James Blaikie and Elizabeth Purves in Kedsliedoors, a.s.n. Thomas : w. James and Alexr. Fishers.

Feb. 2. William Cook and Margaret Lawrie in Melrose, a.d.n. Helen : w. George and Robert Lawries.

,, 7. William Martin and Jean Grieve in Gattonside, a.s.n. Robert ; w. William Alley, Mungo Park.

,, 16. Robert Dods and Marion Usher in Darnick, a.s.n. Robert ; w. Adam Dods, James Wight.

,, 21. William Redford and Margaret Neal in Blainslies, a.s.n. John ; w. Robert Scot, William Moffat.

Mar. 8. Andrew Bowar and —— Cochran in Newtown, a.d.n. Martha ; w. Thomas Stenhouse, John Cochran.

,, 10. John Mercer and —— Mabane in Newsteid, a.s.n. James ; w. William and Alexr. Bunzies.

,, 22. Mungo Park and Margaret Boston in Westerboathouse, a.s.n. John ; w. John and James Bostons.

,, 29. Bailie Scot and Christian Bunzie in Newsteid, a.s.n. Alexr. ; w. Robert and William Bunzies.

April 3. Robert Bulman and Janet Wood in Danieltown, a.d.n. Margaret ; w. George and Robert Lawries.

,, 11. William Wood and Margaret Waugh in Blainslies, a.d.n. Margaret : w. Robert Scot, Hugh Grieve.

,, 17. Adam Hoswel and Jean Elliot in Melrose, a.d.n. Elliot ; w. Thomas and James Marrs.

,, 19. James Boston and Janet Hunter in Gattonside, a.d.n. Jean : w. James Hunter, John Boston.

,, 26. John Scot and Jean Wilson in Newsteid, a.s.n. Robert.

,, ,, James Waugh and Isobel Smail in Melrose, a.d.n. Elizabeth.

,, ,, John Forsan and Janet Chisholm in Drygraingemiln, a.d.n. Elizabeth : w. James Smail, John Mein.

May 27. Alexr. Henderson and Agnes Cranston in Newtown, a.d.n. Isobel ; w. Andrew Mein, Andrew Bartleman.

,, 28. William Mercer and Elizabeth M'Fadzean in Housebyres, a.d.n. Christian.

,, ,, George Thomson and Isobel Wadderston in Hilslop, a.s.n. Walter : w. William Pearson, William Coldcleugh.

1752.

May 31. John Wilkieson and Elizabeth Dalgliesh in Melrose, a.d.n. Margaret ; w. John Dalgliesh, William Mabane.

June 7. George Scot and Isobel Tailor in Danieltown, a.s.n. Joseph.

,, ,, John Skirven and —— Mercer in Newsteid, a.d.n. Anne ; w. Robert Scot, George Lawrie.

,, 14. James Hilson and Jean Lookup in Melrose, a.s.n. Thomas.

,, ,, William Riven and Agnes Tait in Blainslies, a.s.n. Robert ; w. Robert Lookup, James Waugh.

,, 22. John Sibbald and Agnes Stenhouse in Eildon, a.d.n. Agnes ; w. Thomas Stenhouse, William Redford.

July 3. George Paterson and —— in Ladhopemure, a.d.n. Marion ; w. ——.

,, 12. William Hog and Helen Johnstone in Melrose, a.s.n. John.

,, ,, James Fisher and Janet Glendinning in Darnick, a.d.n. Janet ; w. John Mercer, Robert Johnstone.

,, 13. William Henry and Christian Kirkwood in Whitlaw, a.d.n. Elizabeth.

,, ,, The deceased John Bannatyne and Alison Hunter in Gattonside, a.d.n. Joan ; w. Mr. William Hunter, James Boston.

,, 15. John Turnbull and Janet Usher in Gattonside, a.s.n. William.

,, ,, James Millar and —— Gladstains in Drygrainge, a.s.n. Thomas ; w. John Forsan, James Williamson.

,, 20. John Mercer and Janet Familton in Bridgend, a.d.n. Janet.

,, ,, James Fiddes and Marion Anderson in Drygrainge boathouse, a.d.n. Margaret ; w. James Hudd, John Forsan.

Aug. 9. John Usher and Janet Paterson in Darnick, a.s.n. John ; w. Andrew Fisher, Thomas Usher.

,, 14. William Sprot and Christian Haliday in Galabridge, a.s.n. William ; w. John Tait, George Sprot.

,, 16. Walter Tait and Janet Story in Melrose, a.s.n. Robert ; w. Doctor Rutherfurd, Charles Wilkieson.

,, 23. William Mein and —— Lockie in Eildon, a.s.n. William.

,, ,, James Hunter and Isobel Miln in Melrose, a.s.n. Andrew.

,, ,, —— Hart and Anne Stoddart in Darnick, a.d.n. Isobel ; w. Robert Hunter, William Stoddart.

Sept. 17. John Dawson and Elizabeth Marr in Melrose, a.d.n. Isobel ; w. Thomas and James Marrs.

Oct. 1. William Turner and Mary Purves in Gattonside, a.s.n. William ; w. Robert Myles, William Matthison.

,, 8. John Mein and Agnes Marr in Newsteid, a.s.n. Thomas.

,, ,, Andrew Smith and Alison Hownam in Darnick, a.s.n. John ; w. John Mein, senior, and Thomas Marr.

,, 18. Charles Ainslie and Janet Brown in Mosshouses, a.s.n. James ; w. George Martin, George Henry.

,, 22. Andrew and Elizabeth Lauders in Broadwoodshiels, a.d.n. Agnes ; w. Hugh Grieve, William Martin.

Nov. 5. George Watt and Margaret Craig in Melrose, a.d.n. Elizabeth ; w. Alexr. Lockie, James Hunter.

,, 12. James Hudd and Isobel Spotswood in Melrose, a.s.n. Henry.

,, ,, John Martin and Elizabeth Bannatyne in Melrose, a.s.n. John ; w. Thomas Mar, George Martin.

,, ,, John Spratwell and Agnes Bathgate in Blainslies, a.s.n. James.

,, 20. William Moffat and Margaret Somervell in Threepwood, a.d.n. Margaret.

,, ,, John Lees and Agnes Gray, a.d.n. Euphan ; w. Robert Moffat, Robert Paterson.

,, 26. James Mercer and —— Pearson in Darnick, a.d.n. Helen : w. John Usher, James Wight.

,, 27. George Brown and Margaret Lees in Langhaugh, a.s.n. Robert ; w. George Blaikie, Andrew Walker.

1753.

Jan. 7. John Beinstone and Janet Maxwell in Melrose, a.s.n. George ; w. Thomas Marr, James Hilson.

1753.

Jan. 21. Adam Dods and Bettie Gill in Danieltown, a.d.n. Jean ; w. Robert Lawrie, George Scott.

Feb. 4. William Wight and Janet Brown in Darnick, a.d.n. Mary ; w. James Wight, John Usher.

,, 11. Mr. James Brown, minister, and Helen Drummond, a.d.n. Helen ; w. Bailie Grant, Messrs Charles Wilkieson and Gavin Elliot.

,, 25. James Wallace and Alison Phaup in Melrose, a.s.n. George ; w. James Phaup, Andrew Cook.

Mar. 4. John Clark and Jean Bruce in Drygrainge, a.d.n. Janet ; w. George and Andrew Martins.

,, 18. Thomas Usher and —— Mercer in Eildon, a.s.n. Robert ; w. John and Thomas Bunzies.

,, 25. James Williamson and Elizabeth Mercer in Newsteid, a.d.n. Mary ; w. John Meins.

April 15. William Scott and Elizabeth Cochran in Melrose, a.d.n. Anne ; w. Walter Murray, James Wallace.

May 20. William Stuart and —— Berton in Gattonside, a.s.n. John.

,, ,, Robert Bunzie and Margaret Blaikie in Newsteid, a.d.n. Margaret ; w. John Mein, Andrew Bunzie.

,, 26. John Gill and Helen Paterson in Melrose, a.d.n. Margaret ; w. John Lyal, James Smail.

,, 27. James Wight and Jean Mein in Newsteid, a.s.n. George.

,, ,, William Ormiston and Margaret Scot in Melrose, a.d.n. Helen ; w. Robert Penman, Robert Bunzie.

June 28. James Hislop and Eupham Burnet in Darnick, a.d.n. Jean.

July 1. John Grahamslie and Margaret Henderson in Danieltown, a s.n. John ; w. George Scot, George Grahamslie.

,, 22. John Heiton and Elizabeth Eastown in Darnick, a.d.n. Helen ; w John Usher, William Stoddart.

,, 24. Robert Scot and Janet Darling in Blainslies, a.d.n. Helen ; w. Hugh Grieve, James Wallace.

,, 30. James Marr and Janet Mercer in Darnick, a.d.n. Margaret ; w. John Usher, William Stoddart.

Aug. 19. Andrew Lookup and Margaret Shiel in Melrose, a.d.n. Jean ; w. John Bowie, John Bruce.

,, 26. Edward Amos and Elizabeth Turnbul, by fornication, a.s.n. James : w. John Tait, Andrew Martin.

Sept. 2. John Forsan and —— in Drygraingemiln, a.s.n. James.

,, ,, John Grierson and Agnes Mercer in Darnick, a.d.n. Agnes ; w. Robert Grierson, George Mercer.

,, 16. Alexr. Reid and Isobel Martin in Melrose, a.d.n. Janet ; w. George and Andrew Martins.

Oct. 14. John Darling and Agnes Bryden in Gattonside, a.d.n. Janet ; w. Thomas Hoy, James Boston.

,, 18. Thomas Haliday and Isobel Laidlaw, a.s.n. James.

,, ,, William Redford and Margaret Neal in Threepwood, a.d.n. Margaret ; w. Robert Moffat, James Laidlaw.

,, 21. John Turnbull and Janet Usher in Gattonside, a.s.n. John : w. James and John Bostons.

Nov. 4. William Brown and —— Scot in Gattonside, a.d.n. Jean.

,, ,, William Drummond and Janet Myles in Bridgend, a.d.n. Helen.

,, ,, Adam Nicol and Alison Bunzie in Melrose, a.d.n. Margaret : w. Robert Myles, John Bruce.

Dec. 7. James Wallace and Marion Symontone in Blainslies, a.d.n. Marion ; w. Hugh Grieve, Robert Scott.

,, 23. David Thomson and Agnes Mein in Newtown, a.s.n. David ; w. John and Robert Milns.

,, 30. Thomas Rae and Helen Gardener there, a.s.n. James ; w. James Marr, James Boston.

s

1754.

Jan. 4. Thomas Frier and Bettie Thomson in Calfhill, a.d.n. **Agnes**.

,, ,, Andrew Shiel and Bettie Purves in Hagburn, a.d.n. **Agnes**; w. Robert Moffat, George Ainslie.

,, 6. John Mein and Agnes Marr in Newsteid, a.s.n. **Thomas**; w. John Mein, senior, and Thomas Marr.

,, 8. Robert Miln and Isobel Redford in Newtown, a.s.n. **Thomas**; w. John Miln, Thomas Stenhouse.

,, 13. John Mercer and Margaret Lauder in Bridgend, a.s.n. **Andrew**.

,, ,, Thomas Dickson and Isabell Mercer in Bridgend, a.d.n. **Margaret**; w. Nicol Mercer, William Drummond.

,, 31. John Laidlaw and Margaret Burnet in Langshaw, a.d.n. **Alison**; w. Robert and William Moffatt.

Feb. 5. James Wilson and Catharine Mabane, a.s.n. **William**.

,, ,, Nicol Alley and Mary Forest, a.s.n. **William**; w. William Mercer, William Alley.

,, 15. William Sprot and Christian Harvie in Westerlanglee, a.s n. **William**; w. John Tait, Henry Sprot.

,, 17. James Boston and Janet Hunter in Gattonside, a.d.n. **Marion**; w. Robert and James Hunters.

,, 24. Mungo Park and Margaret Boston in Westerboathouse, a.d.n. **Margaret**; w. Mungo Park, senior, James Boston.

Mar. 8. William Mercer and Elizabeth M'Faddzean in Melrose, a.s.n. **William**; w. James and Alexr. Fishers.

,, 17. Thomas Davidson and Janet Brown in Melrose, a.d.n. **Jean**; w. George and Andrew Martins.

,, 25. George Thomson and Isobel Wadderstone in Ladhopmure, a.s.n. **John**.

,, ,, William Moffat and Marion Somervel in Threepwood, a.d.n. **Anne**; w. Robert Moffat, Robert Laidlaw.

April 7. John Wilkieson and —— Dalgliesh in Melrose, a.d.n. **Isobel**; w. William Mabane, William Cook.

,, 16. George Wight and Christian Pringle in Westhouses, a.s.n. **John**; w. William Stenhouse, William Alley.

,, 28. John Hatton and Margaret Tait in Melrose, a.s.n. **John**; w. George and Andrew Martins.

May 5. Alexr. Sibbat and Jannet Bannatyne in Gattonside, a.s.n. **John**; w. John and James Bostons.

,, 12. Mr. James Brown, minister, and Helen Drummond, a.d.n. **Mary**; w. Mr. Grant, bailie, Mr. Elliot, schoolmaster.

,, ,, James Hunter and Isobel Miln in Melrose, a.s.n. **John**.

,, ,, Andrew Moss and Agnes Wight in Darnick, a.s.n. **George**.

,, ,, —— Skirven and —— Mercer in Newsteid, a.s.n. **James**; w. Thomas Stenhouse, Thomas Marr.

,, 16. John Dawson and Elizabeth Marr in Melrose, a.s.n. **James**; w. George Martine, William Bowar.

,, 26. George Coldcleugh and Margaret Thomson in Gattonside, a.d.n. **Margaret**; w. Alexr. Sibbat, John Boston.

June 2. John Bell and Janet Rae in Melrose, a.d.n. **Janet**; w. John Bowie, James Hilson.

,, 12. Thomas Brown and Helen Wilkie in Melrose, a.s.n. **Peter**; w. George Martin, Robert Lookup.

,, 16. James Fiddes and Mary Anderson in Drygraingeboathouse, a.d.n. **Mary**; w. John Mein, Robert Bunzie.

July 14. Andrew Mein and Janet Atchison in Newsteid, a.d.n. **Janet**; w. John Mein, Robert Forsan.

,, 21. William Mercer and Anne M'Fadzean in Melrose, a.s.n. **Andrew**; w. George and Andrew Martins.

Aug. 4. James Millar and Jean Gladstains in Drygrainge, a.s.n. **Isaac**.

,, ,, John Mercer and —— Familton in Bridgend, a.d.n. **Janet**; w Andrew and William Drummonds.

1754.

Aug. 11. James Wallace aud Alison Phaup in Melrose, a.d.n. Alison ; w. Andrew and William Cooks.

  ,,   25. Alexr. Vair and Janet Wilson in Danieltown, a.d.n. Margaret.

  ,,   ,, James Laidlaw and Jean Redford in Eildon, a.d.n. Jean ; w. William Redford, Walter Scot.

Sept. 1. Robert —— and Mary Lothian in Gattonside, a.s.n. James ; w. Thomas Hoy, James Boston.

  ,,   8. Bailie Scot and Christian Bunzie in Newsteid, a.s.n. Thomas : w. Robert and Alexr. Bunzies.

  ,, 13. William Wood and Elspeth Waugh in Blainslies, a.d.n. Marion : w. Robert Scot, James Wallace.

  ,, 15. —— Stevenson and Helen Drummond in Bridgend, a.s.n. William ; w. Andrew and William Drummond.

  ,, 20. The deceased James Hog and Isobel Wilson in Old Melrose, a.d.n. Mary ; w. ——.

  ,, 29. John Boston and Janet Boston in Gattonside, a.s.n. Robert.

  ,,   ,, William Williamson and —— in Newsteid, a.d.n. Catharine ; w. James Boston, James Williamson.

Oct. 10. Robert Grierson and Isobel Stoddart in Darnick, a.d.n. Janet : w. Robert Grierson, senior, Wm. Hart.

Nov. 15. James Mercer and Elizabeth Rutherfurd in Easterhousebyres, a.s.n. William.

  ,,   ,, George Paterson and Margaret Little in Ladhopemure, a.s.n. George.

  ,,   ,, Wm. Tait and Eupham Laidlaw in Buckholm, a.d.n. Elizabeth ; w. William Turner, George Mercer.

  ,, 26. Andrew and Margaret Lauders in Broadwoodshiel, a.d.n. —— .

  ,,   ,, Philip Thyn and Margaret Pearson in Clackmae, a.d.n. Isobel ; w. James Fisher, Robert Penman.

  ,, 30. John Smal and Margaret Sanderson in Mosshouses, a.s.n. James ; w. Robert Scott, William Moffat.

Dec. 8. George Watt and Margaret Craig in Melrose, a.d.n. Agnes : w. Alexr. Lockie, William Steel.

1755.

Jan. 7. James Riddell and Alison Kyle in Overlangshaw, a.s.n. John ; w. Robert and William Moffats.

  ,, 26. Thomas Welsh and Mary Fair in Gattonside. a.s.n. Robert ; w. Thomas Hoy, John Boston.

Feb. 2. James Hilson and Jean Lookup in Melrose, a.s.n. James : w. John Lyal, Andrew Lookup.

  ,, 14. William Martin and Isobel Shillinglaw in Blainslies, a.s.n. Andrew ; w. Robert Scot, Hugh Grieve.

  ,, 16. John Heiton and Bessie Eastown in Darnick, a.d.n. Bettie ; w. John Usher, John Heiton.

Mar. 9. Robert Dods and Isobel Usher in Darnick, a.d.n. Agnes ; w. John Usher, James Wight.

  ,, 10. Andrew Thomson and Agnes Burnet in Overlangshaw, a.s.n. James.

  ,,   ,, Robert Carns and Anne Hope in Westhouses, a.s.n. James ; w. George Ainslie, William Alley.

  ,, 24. John Sprotwell and Agnes Bathgate in Blainslies, a.s.n. Andrew : w. Robert Scot, Robert Laidlaw.

  ,, 30. John Usher and Janet Paterson in Taff-field, a.s.n. Thomas.

  ,,   ,, Walter Murray and Elizabeth Smail in Melrose, a.d.n. Elizabeth ; w. James Smail, Walter Murray, senior.

April 13. John Wight and Alison Thyne in Melrose, a.d.n. Anne : w. James Waugh, James Hilson.

  ,, 20. John Coats and Elizabeth Thomson in Williamlaw, a.s.n. John : w. William Moffat, George Ainslie.

  ,,   ,, James Williamson and Elizabeth Mercer in Newsteid, a.s.n. John.

  ,,   ,, Wm. Hart and Anne Stoddart in Darnick, a.s.n. John ; w. John Heiton, John Mein.

1755.

May   4. John Grahamslie and —— Henderson in Danieltoun, a.s.n. James.

,,   ,,   William Ormistown and Margaret Scot in Melrose, a.d.n. Margaret ; w. James Smail, Robert Penman.

,,   11. Robert Richardson and Isobel Riddel in Eildon, a.s.n. William ; w. John Bunzie, William Redford.

,,   18. Alexr. Cook and Isobel Deans in Melrose, a.s.n. Andrew ; w. Andrew and William Cooks.

,,   19. John Lees and Agnes Gray in Colmsliehill, a.d.n. Alison ; w. Robert Laidlaw, William Mitchell.

June 15. James Wight and Janet Mein in Newsteid, a.s.n. James ; w. John Meins, elder and younger.

,,   17. Andrew Smith and Alison Hownam in Darnick, a.s.n. Andrew ; w. James Wight, Andrew Hownam.

,,   20. William Wight and Anne Noteman in Buckholm, a.d.n. Margaret ; w. James and James Laidlaws.

,,   29. William Rutherfurd and Janet Young in Halidean, a.s.n. William ; w. George and John Martins.

July   7. Robert Mitchelson and Anne Robison in Gattonside, a.d.n. Margaret ; w. William Mathison, Thomas Turnbull.

,,   11. John Scot and Janet Wilson in Newtown, a.s.n. William ; w. John Bunzie, William Redford.

Aug.   5. Gilbert Bourlees and Helen Knight in Langhaugh, a.s.n. Gilbert ; w. George and James Blaikies.

,,   ,, George Brown and Margaret Lees there, a.d.n. Jean ; the same witnesses.

,,   24. Wm. Hog and Helen Johnstone in Melrose, a.s.n. Andrew ; w. Robert Johnstown, Robert Martin.

Sept. 14. George Stoddart and Janet Ker in Darnick, a.d.n. Jean.

,,   ,, William Scot and Margaret Jamison in Danieltown, a.d.n. Janet ; w. Walter and Robert Scotts.

,,   21. John Brown and Barbara Hoy in Melrose, a.s.n. John ; w. John and Henry Hoy.

,,   28. Thomas Waugh and Christian Fisher in Westerhousebyre, a.s.n. Andrew ; w. Mr David Johnstone, student, and Wm. Pearson.

Oct.   5. Alexr. Sibbat and Janet Banantyne in Gattonside, a.d.n. Janet.

,,   ,, —— Handieside and Christian Usher in Drygrainge, a.d.n. Janet ; w. Thomas Hoy, John Boston.

,,   19. Robert Sibbat and Agnes Harvie in Gattonside, a.s.n. William ; w. John and James Bostons.

,,   26. Thomas Bunzie and Agnes Mein in Newsteid, a.s.n. James ; w. James and Andrew Bunzies.

Nov.   2. John Turnbull and Jean Johnstown in Melrose, a.d.n. Jean ; w. Robert and Andrew Johnstones.

,,   3. Walter Scot and Helen Fogo in Threepwood, a.s.n. James.

,,   ,, William Turner and Anne Laidlaw in Overlangshaw, a.d.n. Alison.

,,   ,, James M'Dougal by adultery confessed in Blainslies, a.s.n. James ; w. John Laidlaw, George Ainslie.

,,   16. Philip Fair and Alison Stephenson in Gattonside, a.d.n. Margaret ; w. John and James Bostons.

,,   30. William Turner and Mary Purves in Gattonside, a.s.n. James.

,,   ,, Andrew Lookup and Margaret Shiel in Melrose, a.d.n. Christian : w. Robert Lookup, John Bruce.

Dec.   3. Andrew Hilson and Margaret Richardson in Blainslies, a.d.n. Janet.

,,   ,, Thomas and Janet Patersons in Mosshouses, a.d.n. Margaret ; w. Robert Scot, Wm. Martin.

,,   19. Andrew Bowar and Isobel Cochran in Newtown, a.d.n. Janet ; w. John Milne, John Cochran.

,,   21. John Hatton and Margaret Tait in Melrose, a.s.n. John ; w. Walter Tait, George Matin.

,,   28. Wm. Mathison and Margaret Fiddes in Gattonside, a.s.n. William ; w. Wm. and James Mathisons.

1756.

Feb. 15. John Wilkieson and Bettie Dalgliesh in Melrose, a.d.n. Janet; w. John Dalgliesh, William Mabane.

,, 22. James Orr and Janet Waugh in Melrose, a.d.n. Anne; w. James Hilson, James Waugh.

,, 29. James Edgar and Jean Robison in Melrose, a.d.n. Beatrix.

,, ,, George Coldcleugh and Margaret Thomson in Gattonside, a.d.n. Margaret; w. Robert Lawrie, Thomas Hoy.

Mar 4. Robert Cribbas and Agnes Mathison in Drygrainge, a.d.n. Mary; w. James Millar, James Hay.

,, 7. Robert Miln and Isobel Redford in Newtown, a.d.n. Jean.

,, ,, John Grierson and Agnes Mercer in Darnick, a.d.n. Marion; w. Nicol Miln, Robert Grierson.

,, 21. John Bell and Janet Rae in Melrose, a.d.n. Anne; w. John Bowie, James Hilson.

,, 22. James Blaikie and Elizabeth Purves in Clackmae, a.d.n. Isobel; w. James and John Fishers.

April 2. Thomas Rae and Helen Gardner in Gattonside, a.s.n. Thomas.

,, ,, James Hay and Elizabeth Turnbul in Drygrainge, a.s.n. John; w. James Millar, John Neil.

,, 11. John Gill and Helen Paterson in Melrose, a.s.n. James.

,, ,, James Mercer and —— Pearson in Darnick, a.s.n. John; w. James Smail, James Wight.

,, 18. Andrew and Elizabeth Lauders in Broadwoodshiels, a.d.n. Margaret; w. Hugh Grieve, Robert Scot.

,, 20. William Sprots and Christian Harvie in Westerlanglee, a.s.n. John; w. John Tait, George Blaikie.

May 2. John Mein and Agnes Marr in Newsteid, a.s.n. Andrew; w. John Mein, senior, Thomas Marr.

,, 6. Andrew Thomson and Helen Burnet in Colmslie, a.d.n. Elizabeth; w. William Moffat, Robert Laidlaw.

,, 9. Robert Bunzie and Janet Blaikie in Newsteid, a.s.n. William.

,, ,, James Fiddes and Marion Anderson at Melrose, Bridgend, a.d.n. Marion; w. John Fiddes, Andrew Pringle.

,, 16. William Hopkirk and Margaret Lawrie in Melrose, a.s.n. James.

,, ,, James Hislop and Eupham Burnet in Darnick, a.s.n. Percival.

,, ,, James Marr and Jean Scot in Melrose, a.d.n. Marion; w. Thomas Marr, John Mein.

,, 23. James Hudd and Isobel Spotswood in Melrose, a.s.n. James.

,, ,, John and Janet Bostons in Gattonside, a.d.n. Janet,; w. James Boston, Thomas Marr.

,, 30. James Boston and Janet Hunter in Gattonside, a.d.n. Helen; w. John Mein, James Hunter.

June 27. Walter Murray and Elizabeth Smail in Melrose, a.s.n. Thomas.

,, ,, William Drummond and Janet Myles in Bridgend, a.s.n. Andrew; w. Walter Murray, senior, James Smail.

July 11. John Skirven and —— Mercer in Newsteid, a.d.n. Margaret.

,, ,, James Mercer and Elizabeth Rutherford in Easterhousebyre, a.d.n. Janet; w. William Pearson, John Mein.

,, 15. John Smail and Margaret —— in Newhouses; —— w. Robert Scot, Hugh Grieve.

Aug. 2. John Coat and Elizabeth Thomson in Threepwood, a.d.n. Janet; w. Robert and William Moffatts.

,, 14. Thomas Haliday and Isobel Laidlaw in Appletreeleaves, a.s.n. William; w. William Sprot, John Tod.

,, 19. Robert Scot and Janet Darling in Blainslie, a.s.n. John.

,, ,, George Thomson and Isobel Wadderston in Hilslop, a.d.n. Margaret; w. Alexr. Scott, William Mercer.

,, 22. James Hunter and Isobel Miln in Melrose, a.s.n. James; w. Robert and Andrew Hunters.

,, 29. William Mercer and Anne M'Fadzean in Melrose, a.s.n. William; w. James Waugh, George Martin.

1756.

Aug. 30. James Millar and Jean Gladstains in Drygrainge, a.s.n. Halbert ; w. John Forsan, George Martin.

  ,, 31. Thomas Frier and ——— Thomson in Calfhill, a.d.n. Bettie ; w. Robert Mercer, George Martin.

Sept. 12. David Musgrave and Margaret Watson in Melrose, a.d.n. Isobel ; w. Robert Penman, William Ormistown.

Oct.   3. Adam Nicol and Alison Bunzie in Melrose, a.s.n. George.

  ,, ,, William Williamson and Jean Dickson in Newsteid, a.s.n. Thomas.

  ,, ,, Rev. Mr. James Brown, minister, and May Tod, his spouse, a.d.n. Janet ; w. Bailie George Grant, Mr. Gavin Elliot, schoolmaster.

  ,, 4. William Ker and Isobel Cairns in Old Melrose, a.d.n. Agnes ; w. George Martin.

  ,, 17. Nicol Miln and Margaret Roger in Newtown, a.s.n. Nicol.

  ,, ,, John Mercer and Isobel Faniltown in Bridgend, a.s.n. Robert ; w. Thomas Stenhouse, James Hunter.

  ,, 24. Andrew Moss and Agnes Wight in Darnick, a.d.n. Helen ; w. John Usher, James Wight.

Nov.   7. William Leaden and Margaret Hoy in Eildon, a.d.n. Margaret ; w. Thomas Stenhouse, Nicol Miln.

  ,, 28. Nicol Alley and Margaret Forest in Gattonside, a.s.n. Henry ; w. Henry Forest, William Alley.

Dec.   5. William Scot and Eppie Cochran in Melrose, a.s.n. William.

  ,, ,, William Stephenson and Helen Drummond in Bridgend, a.d.n. Margaret.

  ,, ,, John Mercer and ——— Lauder there, a.d.n. Elizabeth ; w. William Drummond, Alexr. Cook.

  ,, 10. William Mercer and Elizabeth M'Fadzean in Housebyre, a.s.n. James ; w. John Tait, George Mercer.

  ,, 12. James Penman and Christian Tully in Melrose, a.d.n. ——— ; w. Robert Penman, James Hunter.

  ,, 16. George Williamson and Bettie Wood in Colmslie, a.s.n. John ; w. Robert Laidlaw, William Moffat.

  ,, 19. William Sibbat and Margaret Ferguson in Gattonside, a.s.n. Thomas ; w. Robert and Alexr. Sibbats.

  ,, 24. John Dawson and Elizabeth Marr in Melrose, a.d.n. Agnes ; w. George Martin, Thomas Marr.

  ,, 26. William Tait and Elizabeth Laidlaw in Buckholm, a.s.n. John ; w. James and James Laidlaws.

1757.

Feb.   6. James Matthison and Agnes Young in Gattonside, a.s.n. William.

  ,, ,, William Graham and Isobel Hunter in Newstead, a.d.n. Christian : w. James Boston, John Mein.

  ,, 11. William Wood and Elizabeth Waugh in Blainslies, a.d.n. Elizabeth.

  ,, ,, James Shiel and Elizabeth Grieve in Gattonside, a.d.n. Margaret ; w. William Thyne, William Stenhouse.

  ,, 28. David Thomson and Agnes Mein in Newtown, a.s.n. William ; w. John Miln, Andrew Mein.

Mar.   6. William Ormistown and Peggy Scott in Melrose, a.d.n. Bettie.

  ,, ,, George Hog and Peggy Ramsay in Melrose, a.d.n. Agnes.

  ,, ,, James Crosbie and Janet Learmond in Danieltown, a.d.n. Margaret ; w. Robert Penman, James Smail.

  ,, 22. William Mein and ——— Lockie in Eildon, a.d.n. Jean ; w. John Bunzie, William Redford.

April   3. George Stoddart and Janet Ker in Darnick, a.s.n. James.

  ,, ,, William Scott and Margaret Jamieson in Danieltown, a.d.n. Catharine ; w. Walter Scott, John Usher.

  ,, 7. William Rae and Isobel Robson in Gattonside, a.d.n. Isobel ; w. George and Andrew Martins.

  ,, 15. George Brown and Margaret Lees in Langhaugh, a.s.n. Robert ; w. John Tait, William Sprot.

1757.

April 17. James Laidlaw and Jean Redford in Eildon, a.s.n. John ; w. Robert Miln, William Redford.

May 1. James Marr and Jean Scott in Melrose, a.s.n. Thomas ; w. Thomas Marr, John Mein.

,, 6. James Brown and Isobel Ker in Blainslies, a.d.n. Elizabeth ; w. Hugh Grieve, William Moffat.

,, 8. William Redford and Bettie Bahner in Eildon, a.s.n. Wilham ; w. William Redford, William Mein.

,, 15. John Grahamslie and Peggie Henderson in Danieltown, a.s.n. Robert : w. George and Robert Lawries.

,, 29. John Trotter and Alison Marr in Melrose, a.d.n. Jean : w. Thomas Marr, Robert Trotter.

June 12. John Thomson and Margaret Ballentyne in Gattonside, a.d.n. Margaret ; w. John Martin, William Maban.

,, 13. George Ainslie and Isobel Donaldson in Langshawmiln, a.s.n. James : w. David Johnstone, John Coats.

,, 26. James Williamson and Lizie Mercer in Newsteid, a.s.n. Robert : w. John Meins, senior and junior.

July 3. David Tailor and Helen Elliot in Melrose, a.s.n. Thomas.

,, ,, James Wallace and Alison Phaup in Melrose, a.d.n. Elizabeth : w. Walter Murrays, senior and junior.

,, 5. Philip Thyne and Margaret Pearson in Clackmae, a.s.n. James ; w. James Fisher, David Johnstone.

,, 21. John Brown and Jean Dickson in Newsteid, a.d.n. Agnes : w. John Mein, James Dickson.

Aug. 7. John Turnbul and Jean Stuart in Gattonside, a.d.n. Jean : w. James Boston, James Marr.

,, 21. Richard Dogherty and May M'Ewen in Darnick, a.d.n. Jean ; w. James Williamson, John Usher.

,, 23. David Pile and Agnes Thyne in Blainslie, a.s.n. John ; w. Alexr. and Robert Scots.

Sept. 11. John Forsan and —— Chisholm in Drygrainge, a.d.n. Mary.

,, ,, Andrew Mein and Janet Atchison in Newsteid, a.d.n. Isobel ; w. James Dixon, John Mein.

,, 25. Charles Baxter and Janet Grieve at Bleachfield, a.s.n. Thomas.

,, ,, James Edgar and Jean Robson in Melrose, a.s.n. William : w. William and James Hunters

Oct. 2. Thomas Cochran and Bettie Scot in Newtown, a.d.n. Helen ; w. John and Nicol Milns.

,, 9. Mr. James Brown, our minister, and May Tod, his spouse, a.d.n. Margaret ; w. Mr. M'Lawrin of Drygrainge and Mr. Gavin Elliot, schoolmaster.

,, 12. Nicol Miln and Margaret Roger in Newtown, a.s.n. George : w. Thomas Stenhouse, John Miln.

,, 16. James Hilson and Jean Lookup in Melrose, a.d.n. Jean ; w. Andrew and Robert Lookups.

,, 30. William Matthison and Margaret Fiddes in Gattonside, a.d.n. Janet.

,, ,, George Paterson and Margaret Little in Housebyres, a.d.n. Isobel ; w. George Mercer, Robert Myles.

Nov. 20. Robert Grierson and Isobel Stoddart in Darnick, a.d.n. Janet ; w. Robert and John Griersons there.

,, 23. John Laidlaw and Margaret Burnet in Overlangshaw, a.d.n. Marion ; w. George Ainslie, William Moffat.

Dec. 4. James Scott and —— Gillas in Danieltown, a.s.n. Walter : w. George Scott, Walter Scott, there.

,, 11. John Mein, junior, and Agnes Marr in Newstead, a.d.n. Mary ; w. Thomas Marr, John Mein, senior.

,, 18. Walter Murray, junior, and Lizie Smail in Melrose, a.s.n. John : w. James Smail, Walter Murray, senior, there.

1758.

Jan. 23. Andrew and Bessie Lauders in Broadwoodshiels, a.d.n. Barbara ; w.
James and Robert Scots.

Feb. 5. James Matthison and Agnes Young in Gattonside, a.s.n. John ; w.
John Young, Wm. Matthison, there.

„ 10. William Ogilvie of Hartwoodmyre, bailie, and Elizabeth Elliot, his
spouse, a.d.n. Jean ; w. Mr. David Johnstone, probationer, Wm.
Scott.

„ 12. George Wight and Christian Pringle in Easterlanglee, a.s.n. Thomas.

„ „ James Orr and Janet Waugh in Melrose, a.s.n. James ; w. James
Waugh, William Stenhouse.

„ 19. Thomas Martin and Christian Thomson in Gattonside, a.d.n. Jean ;
w. George and Andrew Martines.

„ 21. Robert Richardson and —— in Eildon, a.d.n. Margaret ; w. John and
Thomas Bunzies.

„ 26. James Pinkerton and Janet Cunningham in Melrose, a.s.n. Robert ;
w. Robert and Andrew Johnstones.

April 2. Alexr. Sibbat and Janet Bannatyne in Gattonside, a.d.n. Marion ; w.
John and James Marrs there.

„ 9. John Usher and Janet Drummond in Eildon, a.d.n. Helen ; w. John
and Thomas Bunzies there.

„ 17. John Richardson and —— in Drygrainge, a.s.n. Robert ; w. John
Nicol, George Martin.

„ 30. John Grierson and Agnes Mercer in Darnick, a.s.n. John ; w. Robert
Griersons, senior and junior.

May 3. James Wilson and Catharine Mabane in Easterhousebyre, a.s.n. Alexander ; w. Thomas Frier, George Martine.

„ 16. The deceased Wm. Hart, and Ann Stoddart in Darnick, a.s.n.
William ; w. John and Robert Griersons there.

„ 21. James Boston and Janet Hunter in Gattonside, a.d.n. Christian ; w.
James and Andrew Hunters.

„ 28. Andrew Bowar and —— Cochrane in Newtown, a.s.n. Andrew.

„ „ Adam Nicol and Alison Bunzie in Drygrainge, a.d.n. Isobel.

„ „ John Hatton and Margaret Tait in Melrose, a.d.n. Margaret : w.
Walter Tait, George Martine.

June 4. John and Janet Bostons in Gattonside, a.s.n. John ; w. James Boston,
James Marr, there.

„ 29. Thomas Frier and Bettie Thomson in Westerhousebyre, a.s.n.
Robert.

„ „ Wm. Turner and Anne Laidlaw in Overlangshaw, a.d.n. Bettie ; w.
Wm. Pearson, George Martin.

July 14. Robert Scot and Margaret Darling in Blainslies, a.d.n. Margaret ; w.
James Scot, Hugh Grieve, there.

„ 23. William Mercer and Anne M'Fadzean in Melrose ; w. George and
Andrew Martins.

„ 26. Robert Dods and Margaret Usher in Darnick, a.d.n. Jean ; w. Adam
Dods, John Usher.

„ 31. James Hislop and Effie Burnet in Darnick, a.d.n. Alison ; w. John
Usher, James Wight.

Aug. 6. John Skirven and —— Mercer in Newsteid, a.d.n. Isobel ; w. John
Mein, James Dixon.

„ 13. James Fiddes and Marion Anderson at Bridgend, a.s.n. Walter ; w.
John and James Bostons.

„ 20. Wm. Sprots and —— in Westerlanglee, a.d.n. Isobel ; w. George and
Andrew Martins.

„ 27. Mr. James Brown, minister, and May Tod, his spouse, two sons
named Robert and James.

„ „ George Hart and —— Chisholm in Newsteid, a.s.n. Andrew ; w.
Mr. Ogilvie, bailie, Mr. Hunter, writer, and Mr. Elliot, schoolmaster.

Sept. 17. Nicol Miln and Isobel Thomson in Newtown, a.s.n. John ; w. John
and Nicol Milns there.

1758.

Oct. 1. James Hunter and Isobel Milne in Melrose, a.d.n. Jean.

,, ,, John Sprots and Agnes Haitlie in Appletreeleaves, a.d.n. Alison ; w. Thomas Stenhouse, Nicol Miln.

,, 15. —— Blaikie and Marion Purves in Housebyres, a.s.n. John.

,, ,, Andrew Bunzie and Janet Hart in Newsteid, a.d.n. Margaret.

,, ,, John Mercer and —— Lauder in Bridgend, a.d.n. Isobel ; w. Andrew Hart, Andrew Bunzie.

,, 23. William Martin and Isobel Shillinglaw in Blainslies, a.s.n. John.

,, ,, Robert Crosbie and Agnes Matthison, a.s.n. Robert.

,, ,, George Ainslie and Isobel Donaldson in Langshawmiln, a.s.n. John.

,, ,, John Simpson and Catharine Carter, a.d.n. Agnes ; w. Charles Ainslie, George Martin.

Nov. 5. Bailie Scott and Christian Bunzie in Newsteid, a.s.n, Andrew ; w. Alexr. and Andrew Bunzies.

,, 7. John Stuart and Christian Harvie in Blainslie, a.s.n. James.

,, ,, Thomas Paterson and Janet Paterson in Mosshouses, a.d.n. Agnes ; w. John Laidlaw, Robert Scott.

,, 12. Wm. Rae, and —— Moffat in Gattonside, a.s.n John ; w. James and John Marrs.

Dec. 3. James Marr and Jean Scott in Melrose, a.s.n. John ; w. Thomas Marr, James Smail.

,, 8. George Henderson and Helen Mack in Whitlaw, a.s.n. George ; w. Thomas Davidson, Robert Waddell.

1759.

Jan. 21. James Rutherford and Isobel M'Dowgall, a.s.n. James.

,, ,, James Wallace and Alison Phaup, a.d.n. Ann.

,, ,, Wm. Graham and Isobel Hunter, a.d.n. Jean, all in Melrose ; w. James Rutherford, Thomas Marr.

Feb. 4. James Handieside and Christian Usher in Eildon, a.s.n. James.

,, ,, Alexr. Mitchel, by fornication in Galashiels parish, a.s.n. Benoni ; w. Thomas Hoy, John Usher.

,, 5. Wm. Mercer and —— M'Fadzean in Appletreeleaves, a.s.n. Andrew ; w. George Blaikie, Wm. Sprots.

,, 18. Wm. Hopkirk and Margaret Lawrie, a.s.n. Alexander.

,, ,, James Hudd and Isobel Spotswood, a.d.n. Agnes.

,, ,, David Musgrave and Margaret Watson, a.s.n. John, all in Melrose ; w. Thomas Marr, John Dawson.

,, 25. Wm. Redford and Bettie Balmer in Eildon, a.s.n. Alexander.

,, ,, John Usher and Isobel Paterson in Darnick, a.d.n. Isobel ; w. Thomas Usher, John Bunzie.

Mar. 4. James Penman and Christian Tully in Melrose, a.d.n. Margaret ; w. Robert Penman, senior and junior.

,, 11. Charles Baxter and Janet Grieve in the Bleachfield, a.s.n. John ; w. Thomas and James Marrs.

,, 18. John Bell and —— Rae in Melrose, a.d.n. Helen ; w. John Bowie, Andrew Martin.

,, ,, Andrew Thomson and Helen Burnet in Threepwood, a.d.n. Janet, baptised at Lauder.

,, 25. John Trotter and Alison Marr in Melrose, a.s.n. Robert ; w. Thomas Marr, Robert Trotter.

April 15. Andrew Darling and Lizie Armstrong in Melrose, a.s.n. Thomas.

,, ,, James Elliot and Isobel Smail in Eildon, two sons named Andrew and James.

,, ,, Robert Bunzie and —— Blaikie in Newstead, a.s.n. Isobel ; w. Wm. Ormistown, James Smail.

,, 22. James Laidlaw and Jean Redford in Eildon, a.s.n. Nicol ; w. Wm. Redford, Robert Miln.

,, 29. John Fairbairn and Agnes Harvie in Westhouses, a.d.n. Agnes ; w. John Harvie, Wm. Stenhouse.

1759.

May　6. Wm. Ormistown and Margaret Scot in Melrose, a.s.n. Robert ; w. James Smail, Robert Penman.

June　3. Alexr. Cook and Isobel Deans in Melrose, a.s.n. George.

,,　,, Andrew Pringle and Nellie Carncross in Newsteid, a.s.n. James ; w. Andrew Cook, James Pringle.

,,　5. Robert Sibbat and —— Harvie in Gattonside, a.s.n. James and a.d.n. Isobel ; w. Wm. Bell, Alexr. Sibbat.

,,　7. Nicol Miln and Margaret Roger in Newtown, a.s.n. John ; w. Thomas Stenhouse, John Miln.

,,　17. David Tailor and Helen Elliot in Melrose, a.s.n. John ; w. George Scot, Robert Lawrie.

,,　24. John Mein and Agnes Marr in Newstead, a.d.n. Janet ; w. John Mein, senior, Thomas Marr.

,,　27. David Murray and Elspeth Harvie in Drygrainge, a.d.n. Jean ; w. John Richardson, John Forsan.

July　15. William Scot and —— Jamison in Danieltown, a.s.n. Walter.

,,　,, James Mercer and Bettie Rutherford in Newsteid, a.d.n. Agnes.

,,　,, John Heiton and —— Burnet in Darnick, a.d.n. Margaret ; w. Walter and James Scots.

,,　30. Walter Murray and Lizie Smail in Melrose, a.s.n. Andrew ; w. Walter Murray, senior, James Smail.

Aug.　5. Thomas Usher and —— Mercer in Eildon, a.s.n. Thomas.

,,　,, John Turnbul and Margaret Stuart in Gattonside, a.d n. Margaret ; w. James Marr, James Boston.

,,　6. George Thomson and Isobel Wadderstone in Ladhopemure, a.s.n. Walter.

,,　,, John Richardson, senior, and Janet Sudden in Drygrainge, a.s.n. Thomas ; w. John Frater, John Jamison.

,,　12. James Edgar and Jean Robison in Melrose, a.d.n. Anne ; w. Alexr. and Andrew Cooks.

,,　13. William Ogilvie of Hartwoodmyres and Elizabeth Elliot, his lady, a.s.n. William Elliot ; w. John Martin, Robert Dalgliesh.

,,　17. David Pyle and Lizie Mercer in Newstead, a.d.n. Elizabeth ; w. John Mein, William Williamson.

Sept.　2. Robert Scot and Christian Craig in Danieltown, a.s.n. Thomas.

,,　,, John Forsan and —— Chisholm in Drygrainge, a.d.n. Mary ; w. George Scot, Robert Lawrie.

,,　16. Thomas Cochran and Bettie Scot in Newtown, a.s.n. Thomas ; w. Nicol and Robert Milns.

,,　23. William Williamson and Jean Dickson in Newstead, a.d.n. Mary ; w. James Williamson, John Mein.

Oct.　7. Thomas Bunzie and Margaret Sibbald in Eildon, a.d.n. Agnes ; w. John Bunzie, Nicol Miln.

,,　21. James Scot and Isobel Gillas in Danieltown, a.d.n. Bettie ; w. Walter and George Scot.

,,　,, George Plenderleth and Janet Scot in Old Melrose, a.d.n. Jean ; w. as above.

Dec.　9. George Lothian and Marion Mitchelhill in Gattonside, a.s.n. John ; w. Thomas Hoy, James Marr.

,,　16. James Mathison and Agnes Young in Gattonside, a.s.n. James ; w. John and James Bostons.

,,　23. John Grahamslie and Margaret Henderson in Danieltown, a.s.n. Robert ; w. George Grahamslie, Robert Scot.

1760.

Jan.　15. Robert Miln and Isobel Redford in Eildon, a.d.n. Christian.

,,　,, John Richardson and Ann Adamson in Drygrainge, a.d.n. Jean.

,,　,, George Brown and Anne Turnbull, by fornication, a.d.n. Bettie ; w. John Miln, Thomas Davidson.

,,　20. Robert Paterson and Margaret Lorain in Melrose, a.s.n. John ; w. David Thomson, James [*torn*].

1760.

Jan. 22. William Forsan and Margaret Young in Gattonside, by fornication, a.s.n. William ; w. Thomas Hoy, James Marr.

  ,, 30. Nicol Miln and Isobel Thomson in Newtown, a.s.n. Nicol ; w. John Miln, John Martin.

Feb. 8. Walter Scot and Helen Fogo in Langshaw, a.s.n. George ; w. William Moffat, John Sibbald.

  ,, 10. Andrew Mein and Isobel Maban in Newstead, a.d.n. Janet ; w. William and John Mabans.

  ,, 22. William Moffat and Marion Somervel in Threepwood, a.s.n. George ; w. William Moffat, John Laidlaw.

Mar. 16. George Renaldson and Christian Fisher in Melrose, a.d.n. Christian ; w. James and Walter Renaldson.

  ,, 30. James Orr and Janet Waugh in Melrose, a.s.n. John ; w. James Small, James Hilson.

April 28. John Laidlaw and Margaret Burnet in Langshaw, a.s.n. George ; w. William Moffat, George Sibbald.

May 8. Andrew and Elizabeth Lauders in Broadwoodshiel, a.d.n. Christian ; w. Hugh Grieve, Robert Scot.

  ,, 11. James Graham and Helen Scott in Melrose, a.s.n. Robert.

  ,, ,, James Lindsay and Janet Lockie in Gattonside, a.d.n. Margaret ; w. George Scot, James Marr.

  ,, 18. Robert Tacket and Janet Penman in Melrose, a.s.n. John.

  ,, ,, John Skirven and Isobel Mercer in Newstead, a.s.n. William ; w. Robert and James Penmans.

  ,, 19. James Fiddes and Marion Anderson at Bridgend, a.s.n. Walter ; w. John Fiddes, John Martin.

June 1. George Hog and Margaret Ramsey in Melrose, a.d.n. Agnes ; w. James Smail, James Ramsey.

  ,, 15. James Hunter and Isobel Miln in Melrose, a.d.n. Agnes.

  ,, ,, James Marr and Margaret Mein in Gattonside, a.d.n. Isobel ; w. Nicol Miln, John Marr.

July 6. James Boston and Janet Hunter in Gattonside, a.d.n. Janet ; w. James Hunter, James Marr.

  ,, 20. John Hatton and Margaret Tait in Melrose, a.s.n. George.

  ,, ,, Wm. Winter and Helen Hardie in Blainslie, a.s.n. George ; w. Andrew and John Martins.

Aug. 3. John Trotter and Alison Marr in Melrose, a.s.n. Thomas.

  ,, ,, John Mercer and Margaret Lawder in Bridgend, a.d.n. Margaret ; w. Thomas Marr, Robert Trotter.

  ,, 24. John Usher and Janet Drummond in Eildon, a.s.n. John ; w. John and Thomas Ushers.

  ,, 25. George Ainslie and Isobel Donaldson in Langshawmiln, a.d.n. Isobel ; w. John Laidlaw, George Sibbald.

Sept. 7. Adam Nicol and Alison Bunzie in Drygrainge, a.s.n. Robert ; w. Robert Forsan, John Bruce.

  ,, 16. John Mark and Elspeth Elliot in Hagburn, a.s.n. George ; w. James Tod.

  ,, 21. Charles Baxter and Janet Grieve at Bleachfield, a.s.n. Charles.

  ,, ,, Wm. Rae and —— Moffat in Gattonside, a.s.n. Thomas.

  ,, ,, Andrew Drummond and Isobel Martin in Darnick, a.s.n. Andrew ; w. John Usher, Thomas Hoy.

  ,, 28. James Marr and Jean Scott in Melrose, a.d.n. Jean ; w. Thomas Marr, John Mein.

Oct. 17. George Henderson and Helen Mack in Whitlaw, a.s.n. Andrew ; w. Thomas Waddell, Wm. Forsyth.

  ,, 26. Wm. Stevenson and Helen Drummond in Bridgend, a.s.n. John ; w. Andrew and William Drummonds.

Nov. 2. John Heiton and Marion Burnet in Darnick, a.s.n. John ; w. James Burnet, James Wight.

  ,, 3. Robert Pringle and Mary Lawson in Blainslies, a.s.n. William.

1760.

Nov. 3. John Stuart and Christian Harvie in Blainslies, a.s.n. John ; w. Robert Scot, William Martin.

Dec. 7. William Hart and —— Marr in Newstead, a.s.n. James ; w. John Mein, Andrew Hart.

,, 21. James Hilson and Jean Lookup in Melrose, a.d.n. Agnes ; w. Andrew Lookup, John Lyal.

,, 24. George Boid and Isobel Blaikie in Mosshouses, a.s.n. James ; w. George Sibbald, Wm. Moffat.

,, 27. James Blaikie and Elizabeth Purves in Drygrainge, a.s.n. William ; w. Adam Nicol, John Forsan.

1761.

Jan. 29. Andrew Bowar and Isobel Cochran, two daughters named Isobel and Henrietta ; w. Thomas Stenhouse, John Cochran.

Feb. 8. Robert Scot and Christian Craig in Danieltown, a.s.n. James ; w. George Scott, Robert Lawrie.

Mar. 1. James Wilson and Catharine Maban in Bridgend, a.d.n. Elizabeth.

,, ,, James Laidlaw and Janet Redford in Eildon, a.d.n. Agnes ; w. Wm. Redford, Robert Miln.

,, 13. Thomas Harvie and Isobel Speeding in Darnick, a.s.n. James : w. John Martin, Robert Penman.

,, 22. Walter Murray in Melrose, a.d.n. Isobel ; w. James Smail, Walter Murray, senior.

,, 25. John Morrison and Elspeth Fleck in Colmslie, a.d.n. Anne ; w. John Jamieson William Moffat.

,, 29. John Mein and Agnes Marr in Newstead, a.s.n. James.

,, ,, James Huntlie and —— Mercer in Gattonside, a.d.n. Margaret ; w. Thomas and James Marrs.

April 12. Robert Stuart and Janet Tait in Gattonside, a.d.n. Janet ; w. James Marr, James Boston.

,, 17. Andrew Fisher of Westerhousebyres and Isobel Howden, a.s.n. James ; w. Colonel Edmonstoun and Mr. Gideon Rutherfurd.

,, 17. George Mein and —— Dods in Newstead, a.s.n. James ; w. Andrew and John Martines.

,, 26. George Renaldson and Christian Fisher, a.d.n. Isobel ; w. Mr. Fisher, Thomas Marr.

May 7. William Sprot and Christian Harvie in Westerlanglee, a.d.n. Christian ; w. George Blaikie, John Wyllie.

,, 10. Andrew Pringle and Nellie Carncross in Newstead, a.d.n. Margaret ; w. James Pringle, John Mein.

,, 24. Mr. James Brown, our minister, and Mrs. May Tod, a.s.n. John ; w. Mr. William Ogilvie, bailie, Mr. Elliot, schoolmaster.

,, ,, William Ormistown and Margaret Scot in Melrose, a.s.n. Adam ; w. as above.

,, 31. James Wallace and Alison Phaup in Melrose, a.s.n. George.

,, ,, William Scot and —— Jamieson in Danieltown, a.s.n. James.

,, ,, Nicol Miln of Whitehill and Margaret Roger, a.s.n. Robert ; w. Thomas Stenhouse, John Miln.

June 24. Bailie Scot and Christian Bunzie, a.d.n. Agnes.

,, ,, Robert Sibbat and Isobel Harvie in Gattonside, a.d.n. Janet ; w. James Marr, William Mathison.

July 5. James Penman and Christian Tully, a.d.n. Isobel.

,, ,, James Rutherford and Isobel M'Dowgal in Melrose, a.d.n. Margaret ; w. Robert Penman, James Rutherford, senior.

,, 17. Philip Thyne and Margaret Pearson in Clackmae, a.d.n. Agnes ; w. James Fisher, senior and junior.

,, 27. John Bell and Janet Rae in Melrose, a.s.n. Alexander ; w. Andrew and John Martins.

Aug. 16. Andrew Dalgleish and Janet Walker in Darnick, a.d.n. Margaret ; w. James and John Ushers.

,, 23. James Fisher and Janet Glendinning in Darnick, a.d.n. Helen ; w. John Heiton, John Mercer.

1761.

Aug. 30. John Skirven and Margaret Mercer in Melrose, a.s.n. John ; w. James Hilson, William Wallace.

Sept. 6. William Matthison and Margaret Fiddes in Gattonside, a.s.n. John.

,, ,, John Mure and Catharine Hope in Melrose, a.d.n. Isobel ; w. James Marr, George Hog.

,, 20. John and Janet Bostons in Gattonside, a.s.n. John.

,, ,, James Lindsay and Janet Lockie in Gattonside, a.d.n. Janet : w. James Boston, John Thomson.

Oct. 4. Walter Tait and Margaret Haliburton in Darnick, a.s.n. Adam.

,, ,, George Hart and Isobel Chisholm in Newstead, a.d.n. Margaret ; w. Andrew Hart, James Burnet.

,, 11. David Murray and Elspeth Harvie in Drygrainge, a.s.n. David ; w. Adam Nicol, Alexr. Paterson.

,, 20. Charles Baxter and Janet Grieve in Bleachfield, a.s.n. Charles.

,, 25. Archibald Stuart and Bettie Cook in Gattonside, a.d.n. Margaret.

,, ,, John Henderson and Bettie Beatie in Easterlanglee, a.d.n. Agnes ; w. James Marr, James Boston.

,, ,, John Cleugh and —— Hardie, a.d.n. Elizabeth ; baptised at Lauder.

Nov. 8. Thomas Bunzie and Isobel Sibbald in Eildon, a.s.n. John.

,, ,, Andrew Mein and Isobel Maban in Newstead, a.d.n., Margaret ; w. John Bunzie, John Mein.

,, 15. David Burton and Jean Grahamslie in Danieltown, a.s.n. George.

,, ,, William Drummond and Janet Myles in Gattonside, a.d.n. Margaret ; w. George and John Grahamslies.

Dec. 6. Robert Bunzie and Margaret Blaikie in Newstead, a.d.n. Isobel ; w. John Mein, John Dixon.

,, 8. George Thomson and Janet Wadderston in Ladhopemure, a.d.n. Isobel.

,, 8. William Turner and Anne Laidlaw in Overlangshaw, a.d.n. Janet ; w. John Fairbairn, John Martin.

,, 13. Nicol Miln and Margaret Thomson in Newtown, a.s.n. James ; w. John and Nicol Milns.

,, 20. John Turnbull and Jean Stuart in Gattonside, a.s.n. Thomas ; w. John Boston, John Marr.

,, 27. Robert Paterson and Margaret Lorain in Melrose, a.s.n. Simon ; w. James Smail, David Thomson.

1762.

Jan. 10. Robert Mercer and Janet Blaikie in Newstead, a.d.n. Janet.

,, ,, James Graham and Helen Scott in Melrose, a.d.n. Isobel ; w. George Scot, William Graham.

Feb. 7. William Dods and Isobel Burnet in Danieltown, a.s.n. Adam ; w. Adam and Robert Dods.

,, 17. John Grahamslie and Margaret Henderson in Danieltown, two daughters named Margaret and Jean ; w. John Martin, Thomas Davidson.

,, 28. John Usher and Janet Paterson in Taffield, a.d.n. Agnes : w. Thomas Usher, John Heiton.

Mar. 21. James Hudd and Isobel Spoteswood in Melrose, a.s.n. Adam.

,, ,, Robert Tacket and Janet Penman in Melrose, a.s.n. Robert.

,, ,, Andrew Martin and Agnes Dods, by fornication, a.s.n. James ; w. Robert Penman, George Skirvin.

April 4. James Boston and Janet Hunter in Gattonside, a.s.n. Robert ; w. John Mein, John Boston.

,, 18. —— Williamson and Jean Dickson in Newstead, a.d.n. Margaret ; w. Robert Bunzie, Wm. Mabane.

,, 19. James Laidlaw and Isobel Welsh in Buckholm, a.s.n. James ; w. James Laidlaw, senior, Mr. Welsh.

May 2. Thomas Cochran and Bettie Scott in Newtown, a.s.n. John.

,, ,, John Heiton and Marion Burnet in Darnick, a.s.n. George.

1762.

May 2. Adam Yule and Janet Black in Gattonside, a.s.n. George ; w. Robert Myles, Thomas Stenhouse.

,, 9. James Ore and Janet Waugh in Melrose, a.d.n. Margaret.

,, ,, Wm. Brown and Janet Nicol in Drygrainge, a.d.n. Isobel ; w. James Smail, James Hilson.

,, 16. William Hog and Helen Johnston in Melrose, a.d.n. Helen ; w. Robert and Andrew Johnstones.

,, 23. William Wood and Elspeth Waugh in Blainslies, a.d.n. Margaret ; w. Alexr. and Robert Scots.

,, 30. Alexr. Cook and Margaret Deans in Melrose, a.d.n. Elizabeth ; w. Andrew and Wm. Cooks.

June 13. James Marr and Jean Scot in Melrose, a.s.n. Henry ; w. Thomas Marr, John Mein.

July 7. John Mein and Agnes Marr in Newstead, a.s.n. William ; w. Thomas and James Marrs.

,, 18. James Renaldson and Isobel Knox in Darnick, a.s.n. Andrew ; w. George and Andrew Renaldsons.

,, 21. James Edgar and Jean Robison in Melrose, a.s.n. George ; w. James Hilson, James Rutherford.

Aug. 22. William Nicol and Margaret Smith in Melrose, a.d.n. Jean ; w. Alexr. and Andrew Cooks.

,, 29. James Blaikie and Alison Williamson in Melrose, a.d.n. Catharine.

,, ,, Thomas Harvie and Isobel Speeding in Darnick, a.d.n. Isobel ; w. John Usher, William Mabane.

Sept. 12. Wm. Mercer and Anne M'Faddzean, a.d.n. Christian ; w. Alexr. Fadie, John Hoy.

,, 19. George Hog and Margaret Ramsay, a.s.n. James ; w. Alexr. and Andrew Cooks.

Oct. 3. Robert Dods and —— Usher in Darnick, a.s.n. Thomas ; w. John and Thomas Ushers.

,, 19. Alexr. Stephen and Bettie Thomson, a.s.n. Thomas.

,, ,, John Trotter and Alison Marr, a.s.n. Robert.

,, ,, William Darling and Alison Gibson, a.s.n. John ; w. Thomas Marr, James Smail.

,, 24. George Mien and Margaret Dods in Newstead, a s.n. John ; w. John and Andrew Mien.

,, 29. Andrew Fisher and Isobel Houden in Darnick, a.d.n. Marion ; w. John Mercer, Gideon Rutherford.

,, 31. David Fairbairn and Ma. Mercer in Melrose, a.s.n. Nicoll ; w. Thomas Mercer, Wm. Steel.

,, ,, John Mercer and Ma. Lauder, a.d.n. Alison ; w. as above.

Nov. 1. George Ainslie and Isobel Donaldson, a.s.n. George.

,, ,, Andrew Wallace and Elspeth Wallace, a.s.n. John.

,, ,, Thomas Wallace and Janet Carter, a.s.n. Adam ; w. Wm. Moffat, George Sibbald.

,, 14. Walter Murray and Elizabeth Smail in Melrose, a.d.n. Janet.

,, ,, Robert Mercer and Elspeth Shiel in Westhouses, a.d.n. Agnes ; w. Thomas Marr, James Smael.

,, 21. James Mar and Janet Mercer in Darnick, a.d.n. Isobel ; w. Thomas and James Marrs.

Dec. 9. Robert Ormiston and Janet Riddle in Gattonside, a.d.n. Agnes ; w. John Young, Thomas Vair.

,, ,, Thomas Park and Mary Darling Elinshaws, a.s.n. Joseph ; w. Wm. Moffat, George Sibbald.

1763.

Jan. 2. George Renaldson and Christian Fisher, a.s.n. Andrew ; w. Andrew Fisher, Andrew Renaldson.

,, 17. —— Vair and Janet Speidon in Newtown, a.d.n. Janet.

,, ,, Andrew Murray and Margaret Liethen, a.s.n. Andrew ; w. Thomas Stenhouse, John Mill.

1763.

Jan. 23. James Fiddes and Marion Anderson, a.s.n. Andrew ; w. Thomas and James Marr.

,, 26. George Henderson and Helen Mack in Whitlay, a.d.n. Isobel ; w. Robert and Thomas Waddel.

Feb. 25. George Boid and Isobel Blackie in Mosshouses, a.d.n. Janet ; w. Thomas Frier, William Stenhouse.

,, 27. Andrew Pringle and Helen Cairncross in Newstead, a.d.n. Helen ; w. Thomas and James Marr.

April 7. Nicoll Mill and Margaret Roger in Newtown, a.s.n. James ; w. John Mill, Nicoll Stenhouse.

,, 17. James Mathison and Agnes Young in Gattonside, a.d.n. Margaret ; w. Thomas and James Marr.

,, ,, John Skirven and Isobel Mercer in Melrose, a.s.n. Alexander.

,, 18. William Moffat and Marion Somervel, a.d.n. Janet ; w. William Moffat, John Jamieson.

,, 24. William Redford and Bettie Balmer, a.s.n. Robert.

,, ,, James Grahme and Helen Scott in Melrose, a.s.n. George ; w. George and Robert Scott.

May 8. John Usher and Janet Drummond in Yeildon, a.s.n. Andrew.

,, ,, James Penman and Christian Tully in Melrose, a.s.n. Robert ; w. Thomas and James Marr.

,, 9. Edom Nicoll and Alison Bunzie in Drygrange, a.d.n. Rachael ; w. David Murray, William Shiel.

,, 15. William Scott and Margaret Jamieson in Danieltoun, a.s.n. William ; w. Walter and James Scotts.

,, 22. John Muir and Catharine Hopp in Melrose, a.s.n. Alexander.

,, ,, William Stevenson and Helen Drummond in Bridgend, a.d.n. Elizabeth ; w. Thomas Marr, James Marr.

,, 25. John Stewart and Christian Harvie in Blainslie, a.s.n. William.

,, ,, William Stenhouse and William Sandilands in Housebyres, a.d.n. Catharine ; w. John Stenhouse, Thomas Frier.

June 5. John Helliwill and Janet Helliwill at Gattonside, a.s.n. Robert ; w. James Hood, Thomas Marr.

,, 12. David Taylor and Helen Eliot at Melrose, a.s.n. John ; w. Thomas Marr, James Hood.

,, 26. George Heart and Anne Chisholm at Newstead, a.s.n. Robert ; w. James Hilson, James Marr.

,, ,, John Young and Margaret Mercer at Gattonside, a.s.n. John ; w. Thomas Marr, John Mein.

,, ,, James Scott and Isobel Gillis at Danieltoun, a.s.n. Andrew ; w. George Scott, Robert Scott.

,, ,, Walter Taitt and Margaret Helliburton at Darnick, a.d.n. Helen ; w. Robert Scott, James Hilson.

,, 28. *Vide* July 30, 1769.

July 3. Thomas Young and Elspath Smith at Gattonside, a.s.n. John ; w. James Marr, William Moffit.

,, 13. Charles Lauder and Janet Gibson at Blainslies, a.d.n. Isabel ; w. Hugh Grieve, William Moffit.

,, 31. Andrew Drummond and Isabel Martin at Darnick, a.s.n. George ; w. John Hitton, James Williamson.

Aug. 14. William Ormiston and Peggy Scott at Melrose, a.d.n. Isabel.

,, ,, John Heitton and Margaret Taitt at Melrose, a.d.n. Margaret ; w. Thomas Frier, James Hilson.

,, 15. Nicol Miln and Isobel Thomson at Newtown, a.s.n. William ; w. Andrew and James Meins.

Sept. 4. Thomas Laidlaw and Margaret Thomson at Newtown, a.d.n. Isabel ; w. Robert Lawrie, James Hilson.

,, 18. James Marr and Margaret Mein at Gattonside, a.s.n. John ; w. James Marr, George Skirven.

,, 25. Andrew Mercer and Helen Wight at Bridgend, a.s.n. George ; w. Thomas Marr, James Hudd.

1763.

Oct.   2. David Burton and Jean Grahamslie at Danielton, a.d.n. Margaret :
        w. Robert Lawrie, Robert Scott.

 ,,   9. James Hilson and Jean Lookup at Melrose, a.s.n. Thomas ; w. James
        Vair, Robert Grierson.

 ,,   ,, Robert Steuart and Janet Taitt at Gattonside, a.s.n. George ; w.
        James Vair, Robert Grierson.

 ,,   10. John Jamison and Helen Lockie at Colmslie, a.d.n. Margaret ; w.
        James Moffat, George Williamson.

 ,,   16. John Laidlaw and Jean Rutherford at Eildon, a.s.n. Thomas ; w.
        John Jamison, James Marr.

 ,,   25. John Cleugh and Margaret Hardie at Blainslie, a.d.n. Mary ; w.
        Alexr. and Robert Scotts.

Nov.   8. James Wilson and Catharine Maban at Appletreeleaves, a.s.n. James :
        w. George Bleakie, George Brown.

 ,,   13. William Dods and Isabel Burnet at Danieltoun, a.s.n. James ; w.
        Thomas Marr, John Jamison.

 ,,   14. Robert Marr and Janet Mercer at Gattonside, a.s.n. John ; w. John
        Martine, John Marr.

Dec.   4. Thomas Bunzie and Isabel Sibbald at Eildon, a.d.n. Mary ; w.
        James Marr, George Skirvine.

 ,,   5. John Murray and Catharine Gray at Threepwood, a.s.n. George ; w.
        William Moffat, George Sibbald.

 ,,   9. James Huntly and Margaret Mercer at Gattonside, a.s.n. George ; w.
        Alexr. Brownfield, Thomas Hoy.

 ,,   11. Andrew Mein and Isabel Maben at Newstead, a.s.n. John ; w. John
        Hitton, John Usher.

 ,,   12. John Rutherfurd and Margaret Dalglesh at Bridgend, a.s.n. Robert ;
        w. John Dalglesh, John Mercer.

 ,,   26. David Murray and Elspeth ―――― at Drygrange boathouse, a.s.n.
        George ; w. Adam Nicoll, William Brown.

    1764.

Feb.   3. James Laidlaw and Isabel Welsh at Buckholm, a.s.n. John ; w.
        William Aitchison, Alexr. Sandilands.

 ,,   6. William Turner and Anne Laidlaw at Overlangshaw, a.d.n. Peggy ;
        w. William Moffit, John Laidlaw.

 ,,   12. Robert Vair and Nelly Dickson at the Bleachfield, a.d.n. Betty ; w.
        Thomas Marr, George Skirven.

 ,,   19. Thomas Boston and Janet Hunter in Gattonside, a.s.n. Thomas ; w.
        to both, James Marr, James Hilson.

 ,,   23. John Wallace and Helen Henry in Blainslie Roan, a.d.n. Simmerval ;
        w. Robert and Alexr. Scotts.

Mar.   18. John Mien and Agnes Marr at Newstead, a.s.n. Andrew.

 ,,   ,, Robert Taket and Janet Penman in Melrose, a.s.n. Andrew.

 ,,   ,, Charles Baxter and Janet Grieve at Bleachfield, a.d.n. Christian ; w.
        to all the three, Thomas Marr, James Williamson.

 ,,   25. Archibald Steuart and Betty Cook at Gattonside, a.s.n. George ; w.
        James Hilson, William Moffit.

April   1. John Hitton and Marion Burnet at Darnick, a.d.n. Marion ; w. James
        Marr, Robert Lourie.

 ,,   15. John Mercer and Margaret Lauder at Gallafoot, south of Tweed,
        a.s.n. John ; w. James Marr, John Hitton.

 ,,   21. Thomas Frier and Bettie Thomson at Westerhousebyre, a.s.n. James ;
        w. Henry Fretor, John Frier.

 ,,   22. George Mein and Margaret Dods at Newstead, a.s.n. Thomas ; w.
        John Hitton, James Marr.

June   10. Thomas Hervey and Isabel Speiden at Bridgend, a.d.n. Janet ; w.
        Thomas Marr, James Hilson.

 ,,   19. George Williamson and Mary Wood at Blainslie, a.s.n. James ; w.
        William Bleakie, James Clapperton.

 ,,   ,, William Anderson and Christian Lauder at Blainslie, a.s.n. John ; w.
        George Henderson, Robert Waddel.

1764

July 15. John Usher and Janet Paterson of Toftfield, a.d.n. Christian ; w. William Moffit, John Mein.

,, 23. Henry Fraiter and Marion Mercer at Easterhousebyre, a.s.n. Robert ; w. Thomas Marr, James Hilson.

Aug. 5. John Young and Margaret Mercer at Gattonside haugh, a.d.n. Margaret ; w. James Marr, James Williamson.

,, 26. Thomas Cochran and Betty Scott at Newtown, a.s.n. William ; w. Walter Scott, John Lyal.

Sept. 2. William Elliot and Bettie Renaldson at Easterlanglee, a.s.n. William ; w. John Trotter, James Pringle.

,, 13. Robert Mercer and Elspeth Shiel at Drygrange, a.s.n. William ; w. John Merton, Adam Nicoll.

,, 16. George Hart and Ann Chisholm at Newsteid, a.s.n. George ; w. Thomas Marr, John Hitton.

,, 23. Andrew Bunzie and Janet Haistie at Newsteid, a.s.n. Andrew ; w. James Hilson, Alexr. Bromfield.

Oct. 21. Walter Murray and Elizabeth Smail at Melrose, a.s.n. John ; w. John Mien, James Williamson.

Nov. 4. James Bleakie and Alison Williamson in Melrose, a.s.n. Robert ; w. Thomas Marr, James Hilson.

,, ,, John Trotter and Alison Marr in Melrose, a.s.n. Andrew ; w. Thomas Marr, James Hilson.

,, 11. James Wallace and Alison Phaup at Melrose, a.s.n. William ; w. John Hitton, James Marr.

,, ,, James Hunter and Isabel Miln in Melrose, a.d.n. Elizabeth ; w. John Hitton, James Marr.

,, 18. James Scott and Agnes Martine at Eildon, a.s.n. Walter ; w. Robert Lukup, James Pringle.

Dec. 2. William Dods and Isabel Burnet at Danieltown, a.d.n. Mary ; w. John Hitton, Thomas Marr.

,, 16. James Marr and Janet Mercer at Darnick, a.d.n. Katharine ; w. John Mein, William Moffat.

,, 23. John Turnbul and Jean Stewart at Gattonside, a.s.n. Alexander ; w. Thomas Marr, John Hitton.

,, ,, David Fairbairn and Peggy Mercer in Melrose, a.d.n. Agnes ; w. James Hilson, Adam Mill.

1765.

Jan. 13. Samuel Gilles and Nelly Laidlaw at Melrose, a.s.n. William ; w. Thomas Marr, James Marr.

,, 20. William Nicoll and Peggy Smith at Melrose, a.d.n. Helen ; w. George Bleakie, James Hilson.

,, 25. John Gibson and Margaret Ballantine at the Isle of Rea, a.d.n. Janet ; w. Alexr. Baptie, John Mertain.

Feb. 3. William Vair and Janet Speeden at Newton mill, a.s.n. James ; w. Robert Lukup, Robert Lawrie.

,, ,, John Mercer and Helen Johnston at Newstead, a.s.n. William ; w. Robert Lukup, William Vair.

,, 17. William Williamson and Jean Dickson at Newstead, a.s.n. James ; w. James Williamson, John Gill.

,, ,, Andrew Mercer and Helen Wight at Bridgend, a.s.n. Andrew ; w. James Williamson, John Mein.

,, ,, Andrew Pringle and Nellie Cairncross at Newstead, a.d.n. Janet ; w. James Hilson, John Mein.

,, ,, George Hogg and Peggy Ramsay at Melrose, a.d.n. Jean ; w. Thomas Marr, Andrew Pringle.

,, 24. William Drummond and Janet Meyls at Bridgend, a.s.n. William ; w. John Mein, James Marr.

Mar. 14. Nicol Milne and Margaret Roger of Whitehill, a.s.n. Thomas ; w. Thomas and John Stenhouses.

T

1765.

Mar. 21. Robert Ormiston and Janet Riddle at Gattonside, a.d.n. Marion ; w. Henry Forrester, John Welsh.

„ 31. William Scott and Pegy Jamison at Danieltown, a.s.n. Robert : w. Robert Lawrie, James Hilson.

April 7. Nicol Milne and Isabel Thomson at Newtoun, a.d.n. Isabel ; w. John Hitton, James Hilson.

„ 12. Andrew Wallace and Elspath Wallace at Blainslie, a.s.n. James ; w. Hugh Grieve, Robert Scott.

„ „ George Thomson and Isabel Waderston at Ladhopmuir, a.s.n. George ; w. William Moffat, George Sibbald.

May 26. John Grahamslie and Margaret Henderson in Danieltown, a.s.n. David ; w. James Marr, Robert Lawrie.

„ „ Thomas Young and Elspath Smith in Gattonside, a.s.n. James ; w. Thomas Marr, Robert Lukup.

„ „ Walter Taitt and Peggy Halliburton in Darnick, a.d.n. Margaret ; w. John Mein, Walter Scott.

June 10. The deceased Thomas Gray at Faunsloanhead and Jean Murray at Drygrange boathouse, a.d.n. Jean ; w. John Martin, Andrew Bell.

„ 16. Thomas Laidlaw and Pegie Thomson at Newtown, a.s.n. William ; w. Thomas Marr, John Hitton.

„ „ John Lunn and Bettie Leyden at Darnick, a.s.n. Thomas ; w. Thomas Marr, John Hitton.

„ „ James Marr and Jean Scott at Melrose, a.s.n. Andrew ; w. Thomas Marr, John Hitton.

„ „ Robert Marr and Peggie Williamson at Melrose, a.d.n. Elizabeth ; w. Thomas Marr, John Hitton.

„ 20. Thomas Dods and Catharine Thomson at Williamlaw, a.d.n. Elizabeth ; w. Robert Scott, Robert Waddel.

„ 23. Robert Laidlaw and Jean Rutherfoord at Eildon, a.s.n. James ; w. John Mein, George Scott.

„ 30. James Scott and Isabel Gilles at Danieltown, a.d.n. Isabel ; w. Walter Scott, John Boston.

July 3. John Cleugh and Margaret Hardie at Blainslie, a.s.n. Archibald ; w. Robert Scot, William Moffet.

„ 14. John Muir and Catharin Hope in Melrose, a.s.n. Andrew ; w. James Marr, John Mein.

„ 21. [*Vide* 30 July 1769.]

Aug. 2. William Moffat and Marion Sommervel at Threepwood, a.s.n. William ; w. George Sommervel, Peter Moffat.

„ 11. James Mein and Margaret Mercer at Newtown, a.s.n. Andrew ; w. John Mein, Robert Lawrie.

„ 18. Robert Paterson and Margaret Lorain at Melrose, a.d.n. Janet ; w. Thomas Marr, John Boston.

„ 27. George Boyd and Isabel Blaikie at Overlangshaw, a.s.n. Robert ; w. John Laidlaw, Charles Tod.

Sept. 22. William Redfoord and Bettie Burnet in Eildon, a.d.n. Margaret ; w. George Skirven, John Hitton.

Oct. 6. James Williamson and Elizabeth Mercer in Newstead, a.d.n. Joanna ; w. John Mein, James Hilson.

„ 13. Robert Steuart and Janet Taitt in Gattonside, a.s.n. Adam ; w. John Hitton, William Maben.

„ „ Andrew Lumsdale and Betty Baxter in Newstead, a.d.n. Jean ; w. John Hitton, William Maben.

Nov. 3. Andrew Drummond and Isabel Mertain at Bridgend, a.s.n. Andrew ; w. James Hilson, John Layel.

„ 14. William Glen and Isabel Fiddes, she living in Gattonside and he abroad, a.s.n. John ; w. Andrew Merton, Nicol Mercer.

„ 24. David Burton and Jean Grahamslie at Danieltown, a.s.n. John ; w. George Skirven, James Hunter.

Dec. 8. Charles Hardie and Jean Brown in Melrose, a.s.n. John ; w. Thomas Marr, John Usher.

1765.

Dec. 8. James Orr and Ann Bartoman in Melrose, a.d.n. Margaret ; w. Thomas Marr, John Usher.

,, ,, John Rutherford and Margaret Dalglesh in Bridgend, a.d.n. Mary : w. Thomas Marr, John Usher.

,, 20. John Murray and Katharine Gray at Colmslee, a.s.n. James ; w. William Moffat, John Laidlaw.

,, 15. Andrew Mein and Isobel Maben at Newstead, a.d.n. Isabel ; w. John Martine, James Marr.

,, 22. William Pringle and Mary Scot at Newstead, a.s.n. Andrew : w. James Hilson, David Thomson.

,, 30. John Forest and Peggy Mason at Westhouses, a.d.n. Anne ; w. Andrew Pringle, John Martin.

1766.

Jan. 12. George Ronaldson and Christian Fisher in Melrose, a.d.n. Janet ; w John Boston, James Matheson.

,, 21. George Ainslie and Isabel Donaldson at Langshaw mill, a.s.n. Charles ; w. William Moffat, George Sibbald.

,, 27. John Wilson and Isabel Keadie at Blainslie, a.s.n. William and a d.n. Isabel ; w. William Moffat, Hugh Grieve.

Feb. 2. John Skirven and Isabel Mercer in Melrose, a.s.n. John : w. James Hilson, John Mein.

,, 10. Robert Vair and Nelly Dickson at the Bleachfield, a.d.n. Margaret : w. John Martin, Andrew Lumsdale.

,, 25. Robert Williamson and Mary Stuart in Gattonside, a.d.n. Mary ; w. Alexr. Brownfield, John Boston.

Mar. 9. John Hatton and Margaret Taitt in Melrose, a.s.n. George ; w. Thomas Marr, John Hitton.

,, 16. James Boston and Janet Hunter in Gattonside, a.s.n. James : w. John Boston, John Mein.

,, ,, John Hitton and Maron Burnet in Darnick, a.d.n. Isabel ; w. John Boston, John Mein.

,, 30. William Mercer and Anne Faddie in Melrose, a.s.n. Alexander ; w. William Moffat, James Hilson.

,, ,, John Young and Peggy Mercer in Gattonside Haugh, a.s n. James : w. James Williamson, John Gill.

April 6. George Mein and Margaret Dodds in Newstead, a.s.n. John : w. John Mein, James Williamson.

,, ,, Robert Tacket and Janet Penman in Melrose, a.s.n. George ; w. John Hitton, Thomas Marr.

,, ,, Alexander Corsbie and Ann Ridford in Drygrange, a.s.n. Robert ; w. John Hitton, Thomas Marr.

,, ,, David Murray and Elspath Harvie at Drygrange boathouse, a.s.n. John ; w. John Hitton, Thomas Marr.

,, 20. James Usher and Margaret Grieve at Topfield, a.s.n. John : w. Hugh Grieve, George Skirven.

,, ,, Andrew Mercer and Betty Scott in Gattonside, a.s.n. James ; w. John Mein, James Marr.

May 11. John Mercer and Margaret Lauder at Galafoot, south side of Tweed, a.d.n. Beatrix ; w. Thomas Marr, James Marr.

,, 25. Charles Baxter and Janet Grieve at the Bleachfield, a.s.n. John ; w. James Hilson, John Layel.

,, ,, William Darling and Peggy Gibson in Gattonside, a.s.n. Robert ; w. John Mein, James Hilson.

,, 28. George Smith and Janet Wallace in Blainslie, a d.n. Margaret ; w. Hugh Grieve, Robert Scott.

June 8. Robert Millne and Janet Cochran in Newtown, a.d.n. Margaret ; w. James Hilson, Thomas Marr.

,, 15. Walter Robson and Elizabeth Gibson in Gattonside, a.s.n. Robert : w. Andrew Lookup, George Scott.

1766.

July 2. Harry Frater and Marion Mercer in Housebyres, a s.n. William ; w. William Turner, Alexr. Brownfield.

„ 6. Robert Ballyntine in Melrose and Christian Turnbull, by fornication, a.s.n. Robert ; w. Thomas and James Marrs.

„ 13. Mr. James Brown, minister of the Gospel at Melrose, and Mrs. May Tod, a.s.n. Thomas ; w. John Mein, James Hilson.

Aug. 1. John Cleugh and Margaret Hardie in Blainslie, a.s.n. George ; w. William Moffat, Robert Scott.

„ 17. John Usher and Janet Drummond in Eildon, a.s.n. Thomas ; w. Jonn Hitton, James Marr.

Sept. 5. Andrew Fisher of Westerhousebyres and Isabel Howden, a.d.n. Janet ; w. John Mercer, Charles Baxter.

„ 12. Thomas Hervie and Isabel Speden in Bridgend, a.d.n. Marion ; w. James Hilson, Robert Lawrie.

„ 21. James Duncan and Agnes Marten in Melrose, a.d.n. Elizabeth ; w. James Hilson, Robert Lawrie.

„ 28. Robert Ormiston and Margaret Riddel in Gattonside, a.d.n. Janet ; w. John Hitton, Thomas Marr.

Oct. 5. James Huntly and Peggy Mercer in Gattonside, a.s.n. Robert ; w. David Thomson, Robert Grierson.

„ „ George Darling and Janet Mercer in Bridgend, a.d.n. Janet ; w. David Thomson, Robert Grierson.

„ 12. Robert Ballyntine and Betty Scot in Melrose, a.s.n. Walter ; w. Thomas Marr, John Hitton.

„ „ James Marr and Margaret Mein in Gattonside, a.d.n. Margaret ; w. Thomas Marr, John Hitton.

„ „ William Shiel and Helen Haig in Newstead, a.s.n. David ; w. Thomas Marr, John Hitton.

„ „ Archibald Stewart and Betty Cook in Gattonside, a.d.n. Janet ; w. Thomas Marr, John Hitton.

„ 13. William Turner and Anne Laidlaw in Overlangshaw, a.d.n. Jean ; w. John Merton, John Laidlaw.

„ 18. Charles Lauder and Janet Gibson in Blainslie, a.s.n. John ; w. James Thomson, William Robson.

„ 26. James Marr and Jean Scott in Melrose, a.s.n. Robert ; w. Thomas Marr, John Mein.

Nov. 16. Robert Marr and Peggy Williamson in Melrose, a.d.n. Jean ; w. James Hilson, James Marr.

„ „ Robert Heart and Margaret Marjoribanks in Newstead, a.d.n. Margaret ; w. James Hilson, James Marr.

„ 23. James Graham and Nelly Scott in Melrose, a.s.n. Patrick ; w. George Scott, Robert Lawrie.

Dec. 3. Thomas Cochran and Betty Scott in Newtown, a.s.n. Andrew ; w. Thomas Bunzie, William Rutherford.

„ 30. James Fiddes and Marion Anderson at Westhouse boathouse, a.s.n. Adam ; w. Henry Forrest, David Brown.

1767.

Jan. 19. Thomas Bunzie and Isabel Sibbald in Eildon, a.s.n. Thomas ; w. Thomas and Nicol Stenhouses.

„ „ Nicol Milne and Isabel Thomson in Newtown, a.s.n. Thomas ; w. Thomas and Nicol Stenhouses.

„ „ Nicol Milne and Margaret Rodger in Whitehill, a.d.n. Jean ; w. Thomas and Nicol Stenhouses.

Mar. 22. Mr. Peter Williamson and Mrs. Peggy Wilson in Melrose, a.s.n. James ; w. Thomas Marr, James Hilson.

„ „ Robert Mercer and Elspeth Shiel at Drygrange, a.d.n. Helen ; w. Thomas Marr, James Hilson.

„ 29. Andrew Drummond and Isabel Merton in Bridgend, a.s.n. William ; James Marr, John Hitton.

1767.

April 5. Robert Bunzie and Margaret Blaikie in Newstead, a.s.n. Robert ; w. Robert Lawrie, John Gill.

„ 12. Adam Nicoll and Ailly Bunzie at Drygrange, a.s.n. Adam ; w. Thomas Marr, Adam Milne.

„ „ James Matheson and Agnes Young in Gattonside, a.s.n. Saunders ; w. Adam Milne, Robert Lawrie.

„ „ Thomas Turnbull and Peggy Forsan in Gattonside, a.d.n. Agnes ; w. Adam Milne, Robert Lawrie.

„ 19. Thomas Romainnis and Margaret Dykes in Colmslie, a.d.n. Mary ; w. Mr. James Blaikie, William Moffet.

„ 26. [*Vide* 30 July 1769.]

May 3. James Scott and Agnes Merton in Eildon, a.s.n. George ; w. James Hilson, William Maben.

„ 10. Thomas Young and Elspath Smith in Gattonside, a.s.n. Thomas ; w. Robert Grierson, Robert Lawrie.

„ „ John Muir and Katharine Hop in Melrose, a.d.n. Agnes ; w. Robert Grierson, Robert Lawrie.

„ 13. Richard Robson and Isabel Sclaiter in Blainslie, a.s.n. John ; w. Hugh Grieve, Robert Scott.

„ 24. James Mein and Mary Mercer in Newtown, a.s.n. Nicoll ; w. Robert Grierson, Adam Milne.

„ „ George Heart and Anne Chisholm in Newstead, a.d.n. Janet ; w. George Scott, David Thomson.

June 14. James Scott and Isabel Gillis in Danieltown, a.s.n. James ; w. Walter and George Scotts.

„ 28. William Dodds and Isabel Burnet in Danieltown, a.d.n. Betty ; w. Thomas Marr, John Hitton.

„ 30. James Penman and Christian Tully in Melrose, a.d.n. Christian ; w. John Merton, John Layen.

July 12. Andrew Pringle and Nelly Cairncross in Newstead, a.d.n. Margaret.

„ „ Thomas Laidlaw and Peggy Thomson in Newtown, a.d.n. Margaret ; w. James Hilson, John Hitton, to both.

„ 26. Charles Hardie and Jean Brown in Melrose, a.s.n. Charles ; w. George and James Scotts.

„ „ James Wallace and Alison Phaup in Melrose, a.s.n. Robert ; w. George and James Scotts.

Aug. 9. David Burton and Jean Grahamslie in Danieltown, a.s.n. Robert ; w. James Hilson, William Moffat.

[*Vide*, 2 Sept. 1770.]

Sept. 6. George Ronaldson and Christian Fisher in Melrose, a.s.n. James ; w. John Mein, Andrew Murray.

„ „ Andrew Hope and Isabel Hunter in Melrose, a.s.n. James ; w. James Hilson, David Thomson.

„ „ Nicol Stenhouse and Agnes Sibbald at Whitelees, a.s.n. Thomas ; w. George Scott, James Taitt.

„ 13. William Scott and Margaret Jamieson at Danieltown, a.d.n. Margaret ; w. Walter Scott, Robert Grierson.

Oct. 6. George Wight and Mary Sclaiter in Darnick, a.s.n. James ; w. James Wight, John Usher.

„ 18. William Pringle and Mary Scott in Newstead, a.d.n. Anne ; w. Adam Milne, David Thomson.

„ „ John Barklay and Isabel Cochran in Newtoun, a.d.n. Margaret ; w. Adam Milne, David Thomson.

Nov. 8. James Vair and Nelly Hunter in Melrose, a.s.n. James ; w. Thomas Marr, John Boston.

„ 15. Samuel Gilles and Nelly Laidlaw in Melrose, a.s.n. Joseph ; w. Robert Paterson, Adam Milne.

Dec. 6. James Williamson and Elizabeth Mercer in Newstead, a.s.n. Robert ; w. John Mein, John Gill.

„ „ John Leyden and Isabel Smith in Darnick, a.s.n. John ; w. John Mein, John Gill.

1767.

Dec. 6. John Young and Margaret Mercer in Gattonside haugh, a.d.n. Elizabeth ; w. John Mein, John Gill.

,, 13. Walter Murray and Elizabeth Smail in Melrose, a.s.n. Andrew ; w. Andrew Murray, John Merton.

,, ,, John Turnbull and Jean Steuart in Gattonside, a.d.n. Janet ; w. James Hilson, Adam Milne.

,, ,, James Boston and Janet Hunter in Gattonside, a.d.n. Christian ; w. James Hunter, John Mein.

,, ,, Alexander Cuthel and Peggie Haitlie in Melrose, a.d.n. Marion ; w. David Thomson, George Scott.

1768.

Jan. 24. James Usher and Peggy Grieve at Topfield, a.d.n. Margaret ; w. John Usher, Hugh Grieve.

,, 28. Robert Marr and Peggy Williamson in Melrose, a.s.n. Thomas ; w. Thomas Marr, James Williamson.

,, ,, John Little and Nelly Park in Krukhimin in Canabie parish, a.d.n. Janet ; w. Thomas Marr, James Williamson.

Feb. 21. John Heitton and Marion Burnet at Darnick, a.s.n. Robert ; w. Adam Milne, James Hilson.

,, ,, John Henderson and Janet Mercer in Melrose, a.s.n. James ; w. Adam Milne, James Hilson.

Mar. 6. Andrew Lumsdale and Betty Baxter in Newstead, a.s.n. James ; w. Charles Baxter, James Williamson.

,, ,, Andrew Mein and Isobel Maben in Newstead, a.d.n. Christian ; w. Thomas Marr, John Heitton.

,, 27. Walter Taitt and Margaret Halliburton in Darnick, a.d.n. Alison ; w. Robert and Andrew Lukups.

April 9. James Vair and Peggy Cochran in Newstead, a.s.n. Thomas and a.d.n. Margaret ; w. Andrew Bunzie, John Vair.

,, 17. David Fairbairn and Margaret Mercer in Melrose, a.d.n. Margaret ; w. James Hilson, John Heitton.

,, ,, John Skirven and Isabel Mercer at the Bleachfield, a.d.n. Christian ; w. Robert Lukup, Thomas Marr.

,, ,, Robert Taket and Janet Penman in Melrose, a.d.n. Isabel ; w. Thomas Marr, George Scott.

,, 18. John Cleugh and Margaret Hardie in Blainslie, a.d.n. Isabel ; w. William Moffat, Robert Scott.

,, ,, George Smith and Janet Wallace in Blainslie, a.s.n. Robert ; w. William Moffat, Robert Scott.

,, ,, Hugh Pringle and Janet Brown in Blainslie, a.d.n. Agnes ; w. William Moffat, Robert Scott.

,, ,, George Boid and Isabel Blaikie in Langshaw, a.d.n. Barbara ; w. William Moffat, John Laidlaw.

,, ,, Thomas Frier and Betty Thomson at Westerhousebyres, a.d.n. Janet ; w. John Frier.

,, 24. Robert Williamson and Mary Steuart in Gattonside, a.s.n. Thomas ; w. Adam Milne, James Hilson.

,, ,, Andrew Bell and Janet Pringle at Broomfield of the Newstead, a.d.n. Jean ; w. George Bell, James Pringle.

May 15. James Ronaldson and Isabel Knox at Darnick, a.d.n. Margaret ; w. John Mein, Andrew Lookup.

June 20. John Murray and Katharine Gray in Colmslie, a.s.n. William ; w. William Moffat, John Jamison.

,, 26. John Mein and Agnes Marr in Newstead, a.s.n. Samuel ; w. Thomas Marr, James Marr.

,, ,, Robert Vair and Nelly Dickson at the Bleachfield, a.s.n. Thomas ; w. John Heitton, James Hilson.

July 17. Mr. Frederick Maclagan, minister, and Mrs. Christian Turnbull, his spouse, a.s.n. Hector ; w. James Hilson, Robert Lawrie.

1768.

July 30. George Darling and Isabel Mercer in Mosshouses, a.d.n. Margaret ; w. William Moffat, George Ainslie.

,, 31. John Lunn and Bettie Leyden in Darnick, a.s.n. Frederick ; w. John Boston, Andrew Lukup.

Aug. 14. Robert Paterson and Peggy Lorain in Melrose, a.d.n. Agnes ; w. John Mein, James Marr.

,, 19. James Kirkwood and Isabel Pringle in Langshaw, a.d.n. Isabel ; w. John Laidlaw, Thomas Scott.

,, 28. James Marr and Jean Scott in Melrose, a.s.n. William ; w. John Mein, John Heitton.

,, ,, Robert Bunzie and Isabel Hoy in Newstead, a.d.n. Nelly ; w. Robert Grierson, James Pringle.

Sept. 4. James Orr and Anne Borrowman in Melrose, a.s.n. William ; w. Andrew Lukup, Adam Milne.

,, 25. Nicol Milne and Isabel Thomson in Newtown, a.s.n. Robert ; w. William Moffat, John Merton.

Oct. 9. John Pringle and Isabel Fisher in Darnick, a.s.n. William ; w. Adam Milne, James Hunter.

,, 16. Andrew Bunzie and Janet Haistie in Newstead, a.s.n. James ; w. Adam Milne, Robert Grierson.

Nov. 13. ohn Barklay and Peggy Hart in Newstead, a.s.n. William ; w. John Mein, Andrew Pringle.

,, 14. John Rutherford and Margaret Dalglesh in Bridgend, a.s.n. John ; w. John Dalglesh, John Mercer.

,, 19. Thomas Haig and Janet Sandlans, at Bridgend, who being of age took the vows upon himself, a.s.n. Andrew ; w. Andrew Haitlie, John Merton.

,, 20. James Mein and Mary Darling in Newstead, a.d.n. Janet ; w. James Thynn, James Marr.

,, ,, Walter Robson and Elspath Gibson in Gattonside. a.d.n. Isabel ; w. James Thynn.

,, 23. James Thynn and Margaret Dods in Blainslie. a.s.n. William ; w. Robert Scott, Richard Robson.

,, ,, Richard Robson and Isabel Sclaiter in Blainslie. a.d.n. Janet ; w. Robert Scott, James Usher.

,, 29. Nicoll Stenhouse and Agnes Sibbald at Whitelees. a.d.n. Agnes ; w. Thomas Stenhouse, Nicol Milne.

Dec. 4. Thomas Hervie and Isabel Speden at the Bleachfield, a.d.n. Christian ; w. James Hilson, Adam Milne.

,, ,, Robert Ballantine and Betty Scott in Melrose, a.s.n. James ; w. John Mein, James Marr.

,, ,, William Shiel and Helen Haig in Newstead, a.s.n. Anthony ; w. John Layel, Thomas Hervie.

,, 23. William Blaikie and Elizabeth Scott at Hilslop. a.d.n. Agnes ; w. George Ainslie, John Jamison.

1769.

Jan. 1. Andrew Hope and Isabel Hunter in Melrose, a.s.n. John ; w. John Heitton, Thomas Marr.

,, 18. John Wilson and Isabel Kedy in Blainslie, a.d.n. Janet ; w. Robert Scott, James Usher.

,, ,, Thomas Wallace and Janet Kerter in Blainslie, a.d.n. Katharine ; w. Robert Scott, James Usher.

,, ,, Thomas Darling and Betty Bathgate in Blainslie, a.d.n. Isabel ; w. Robert Scott, James Usher.

,, 29. Adam Nicol and Alison Bunzie in Drygrange, a.s.n. Thomas ; w. John Mein, James Hilson.

,, ,, George Mein and Margaret Dods in Newstead, a.d.n. Katharine ; w. John Mein, James Hilson.

1769.

Feb. 5. John Hatton and Margaret Taitt in Melrose, a.d.n. Elizabeth ; w. Robert Lukup, William Moffat.

Mar. 5. Charles Lauder and Janet Gibson in Blainslie, a.d.n. Margaret ; w. Hugh Grieve, James Wilson.

,, 12. Robert Scot and Christian Craig in Danieltown, a.s.n. William ; w. Alexr. Lokie, George Scott.

,, ,, James Mein and Mary Mercer in Newtown, a.s.n. James ; w. Alexr. Lokie, George Scott.

,, 19. Charles Hardie and Jean Brown in Melrose, a.s.n. Edward ; w. James Hilson, Robert Grierson.

,, ,, Thomas Turnbull and Peggy Phorsan in Gattonside, a.s.n. John ; w. James Hilson, Robert Grierson.

,, ,, Henry Freator and Marion Mercer in Easterhousebyres, a.s.n. George ; w. Charles Hardie, Thomas Turnbull.

April 2. David Burton and Jean Grahamslie in Danieltoun, a.s.n. David ; w. James Hilson, William Moffat.

,, 5. John Beattie and Isabel Ballantine in Melrose, a.d.n. Margaret ; w. William Vair.

,, 16. George Ronaldson and Christian Fisher in Melrose, a.s.n. Walter ; w. James Scott, William Darling.

,, ,, James Penman and Christian Tully in Melrose, a.s.n. James ; w. William Darling, George Ronaldson.

,, ,, James Scott and Isabel Gillis in Danieltown, a.s.n. William ; w. William Darling, George Ronaldson.

,, ,, William Darling and Margaret Gibson in Gattonside, a.d.n. Margaret ; w. James Scott, George Ronaldson.

,, 17. Thomas Scott and Janet Blaikie in Langshawmill, a.d.n. Margaret ; w. William Moffat, George Ainslie.

,, 23. John Bell and Janet Rea in Melrose, a.d.n. Jean ; w. James Marr, John Heitton.

April 27. James Usher and Peggy Grieve in Blainslie, a.s.n. James ; w. George Scott, James Stirling.

May 7. Thomas Young and Elspath Smith in Gattonside, a.d.n. Margaret ; w. Robert Lukup, John Heitton.

June 19. George Ainslie and Isabel Donaldson in Langshaw mill, a.s.n. William ; w. William Moffat, Thomas Frier.

,, 22. Andrew Cribbes and Agnes Mercer in Blainslie, two daughters named Elizabeth and Margaret ; w. Peter Hardie, Robert Scott.

,, 25. William Dods and Isabel Burnet in Danieltown, a.d.n. Peggy ; w. James Hilson, Robert Lawrie.

July 16. James Graham and Nelly Scott in Melrose, a.s.n. James ; w. Robert Lawrie, George Scott.

,, 24. John Young and Margaret Mercer in Gattonside haugh, a.s.n. John ; w. George Blaikie, Thomas Marr.

,, ,, John Fisher and Elizabeth Gilles in Darnick, a.d.n. Elizabeth ; w. James Blaikie, James Marr.

,, 30. James Vair and Nelly Hunter in Melrose, a.s.n. Robert ; w. James Hunter, Nicoll Milne.

1763.

June 28. Andrew Henderson and Mary Inglis in Easterlanglee, a.s.n. John ; w. Thomas Wilson, Thomas Mein.

1765.

July 21. Andrew Henderson and Mary Inglis in Easterlanglee, a.d.n. Agnes ; w. Thomas Wilson, Thomas Mein.

1767.

April 26. Andrew Henderson and Mary Inglis in Easterlanglee, a.s.n. Andrew ; w. Thomas Mein, John Familtown.

1769.

June 22. Andrew Henderson and Mary Inglis at Highcross, a.s.n. Charles ; w. John Familtown, Thomas Mein.

1769.

Aug. 13. Thomas Romanes and Peggy Dykes in Hilslop, a.s.n. William ; w. William Moffat, James Pringle.

,, ,, John Barklay and Isabel Cochran in Newtown, a.s.n. Andrew ; w. James Pringle, William Moffat.

,, 16. Ned ——, being a native of Africa and come to the age of manhood took the vows upon himself ; w. Mr. Robert Mein, John Mein.

,, 20. George Wight and Mary Sclaiter in Darnick, a.s.n. Thomas : w. James Wight, John Heitton.

Sept. 3. Thomas Cochran and Betty Scott in Newtown, a.s.n. Francis ; w. James Hilson, John Boston.

,, 4. Mr. Andrew Fisher and Miss Isabel Howden in Darnick, a.d.n. Margaret ; w. John Mercer, Charles Baxter.

,, ,, Andrew Drumond and Isabel Mertain in Darnick, a.s.n. Andrew ; w. John Mercer, Charles Baxter.

,, 13. [*Vide* Feb. 17, 1771.]

,, 25. Robert Marr and Peggy Williamson in Melrose, a.s.n. Andrew ; w. James Williamson, Thomas Marr.

Oct. 6. Nicol Milne and Margaret Rodger in Whitehill, a.s.n. William ; w. Thomas Stenhouse, John Scott.

,, 8. William Rutherford and Betty Bamuir in Eildon, a.d.n. Jean ; w. John Henderson, Andrew Bell.

,, ,, Andrew Bell and Janet Pringle at Brumhill, a.d.n. Margaret ; w. John Henderson, William Rutherford.

,, ,, John Henderson and Janet Mercer in Melrose, a.d.n. Agnes ; w. Andrew Bell, William Rutherford.

,, 21. James Brown and Christian Lauder in Coumsliehill, a.s.n. William ; w. William Moffat, James Boyd.

,, 22. William Pringle and Mary Scott in Newstead, a.d.n. Janet ; w. James Pringle, Robert Grierson.

,, 29. Alexander Cuthel and Peggy Haitlie in Melrose, a.d.n. Agnes ; w. James Hilson, James Marr.

Nov. 12. James Blaikie and Alison Williamson in Melrose, a.s.n. Thomas ; w. Robert Lawrie, Adam Milne.

,, ,, David Murray and Agnes Gray in Drygrange mill, a.d.n. Mary ; w. Robert Lawrie, George Scott.

,, 19. Henry Hope and Margaret Mercer at Highcross, a.s.n. Andrew ; w. James Hunter, Nicol Milne.

Dec. 3. William Mercer and Ann Fadie in Melrose, a.d.n. Jean : w. Robert Lukup, David Taylor.

,, ,, Robert Scott and Isabel Ronaldson in Melrose, a.d.n. Janet : w. Andrew Pringle, James Hunter.

,, 6. William Blaikie and Elizabeth Scott in Hilslop, a.s.n. Thomas ; w. William Moffat, George Ainslie.

,, ,, William Turner and Ann Laidlaw in Langshaw, a.d.n. Marion ; w. John Laidlaw, William Moffat.

,, 15. Robert Mercer and Elspath Shiel in Drygrange, a.s.n. George ; w. George Mercer, Adam Nicoll.

,, 26. Thomas Proctor and Mary Forsan in Westhouses boathouse, a.d.n. Agnes ; w. John Boston, James Marr.

,, 31. John Pecoak and Agnes Waitt in Darnick, a.d.n. Margaret ; w. David Taylor, Robert Grierson.

1770.

Jan. 19. Andrew Mein and Isabel Maben in Newstead, a.s.n. James : w. James Pringle.

Feb. 11. James Boston and Janet Hunter in Gattonside, a.d.n. Margaret : w. Thomas Marr, Walter Murray.

,, 25. Walter Taitt and Margaret Helliburton in Darnick, a.s.n. John ; w. Robert Bunzie, Andrew Heitton.

Mar. 11. Thomas Laidlaw and Peggy Thomson in Newtown, a.s.n. James ; w. James Hunter, Andrew Lumsdale.

1770.

Mar. 11. Mr. Frederick Maclagan and Mrs. Christian Turnbull in Melrose, a.d.n. Janet ; w. James Hunter, John Heitton.

" 22. John Johnston and Isabel Laing in Old Melrose, a.s.n. William ; w. Nicol Milne, Robert Mein.

" 25. George Hogg and Peggy Ramsay in Melrose, a.s.n. Andrew ; w. James Hunter, Andrew Heitton.

" 27. John Cleugh and Margaret Hardie in Blainslie, a.d.n. Margaret ; w. James Usher, Robert Scott.

April 8. James Marr and Jean Scott in Melrose, a.d.n. Janet ; w. Thomas Marr, James Taitt.

" 15. John Thorburn and Margaret Watherstone in Easterlanglee, a.d.n. Margaret ; w. John Mein, John Boston.

" " James Huntlie and Margaret Mercer in Gattonside, a.d.n. Agnes ; w. John Boston, John Heitton.

" 17. John Murray and Katharine Gray in Colnslie, a d.n. Marion ; w. Robert Lees, David Keil.

" 29. Andrew Pringle and Nelly Cairncrose in Newstead, a.s.n. Hugh ; w. Hugh Cairncrose, Thomas Marr.

May 6. Thomas Bunzie and Isabel Sibbald in Eildon, a.s.n. Andrew ; w. John Boston, Alexander Brownfield.

" 11. —— and Nelly Cook, in fornication, in Melrose, a.s.n. William ; w. John Layel, John Merton.

" 27. Peter Williamson and Peggy Wilson in Melrose, a.s.n. Thomas ; w. Thomas Marr, David Fairbairn.

" " Nicol Stenhouse and Agnes Sibbald in Whitelees, a.s.n. Andrew ; w. Peter Williamson, David Fairbairn.

" " James Aird and Betty Robson in Newtown, a.s.n. Adam ; w. James Marr, Nicol Stenhouse.

" " David Fairbairn and Peggy Mercer in Melrose, a.s.n. Thomas ; w. James Marr, Nicol Stenhouse.

June 10. Samuel Gilles and Nelly Laidlaw, a.d.n. Williebetty ; w. Robert Lukup, James Rutherford.

" 17. Robert Taket and James Penman in Melrose, a.s.n. William ; w. Robert Bunzie, George Ronaldson.

" 23. George Darling and Isabel Mercer in Mosshouses, a.d.n. Agnes ; w. Robert Laidlaw.

" 24. James Frier and Isabel Dalglish in Gattonside, a.s.n. Charles ; w. James Hilson, Adam Meben.

July 1. James Jamison and Margaret Burn in Melrose, a.s.n. James ; w. John Hatton, John Usher.

" " Robert Phorsan and Isabel Unns in Newstead, a.s.n. Robert ; w. John Mein, Robert Bunyan.

" 10. James Thomson and Elizabeth Henry in Threepwood, a.d.n. Margaret ; w. Wm. and Peter Moffats.

" 15. Archibald Stewart and Betty Cook in Gattonside, a.s.n. William ; w. Alexander Brownfield, Robert Grierson.

" " James Marr and Margaret Mein in Gattonside, a.d.n. Margaret ; w. Thomas Marr, George Blaikie.

" 30. Andrew Ronaldson and Mary Lee in Darnick, a.s.n. Andrew ; w. Robert Lawrie, John Heitton.

Aug. 13. Nicol Milne and Isabel Thomson in Newtown, a.s.n. Robert ; w. Andrew Mein, John Barklay.

Sept. 1. Henry Cochran and Peggy Mein in Newtown, two sons named John and Alexander ; w. John Cochran and John Cochran.

" 2. Robert Williamson and Mary Stewart in Gattonside, a.s.n. Thomas ; w. Thomas Marr, Thomas Boston.

" " John Muir and Katharine Hope in Melrose, a.s.n. William ; James Pringle, Robert Williamson.

" " Robert Fairbairn and Jean Menton in Eildon, a.s.n. John ; w. George Ronaldson, John Boston.

1770.
Sept. 2. James Pringle and Isabel Layel in Melrose, a.s.n. James ; w. John
              Layel, Andrew Pringle.
  ,,   ,, James Orr and Anne Barroman in Melrose, a.d.n. Anne ; w. James
              Hilson, James Pringle.

1767.
Aug. 9. William Paton and Janet Brown in Drygrange, a.d.n. Jean ; w.
              Robert Mercer, David Murray.

1770.
Feb. 11. William Paton and Janet Brown in Gattonside, a.d.n. Isabel ; w.
              Thomas Marr, Walter Murray.
Sept. 30. Andrew Lumsdale and Bettie Baxter in Newstead, a.d.n. Margaret ;
              w. Charles Baxter, Andrew Fisher.
  ,,   ,, John Barcklay and Peggy Heart in Newstead, a.d.n. Janet ; w.
              Robert Hunter, George Ronaldson.
Oct. 15. Thomas Darling and Betty Bathgate in Blainslie, a.s.n. Andrew ; w.
              Hugh Grieve, Robert Scott.
  ,,   21. John Young and Margaret Mercer in Melrose, a.d.n. Margaret ; w.
              Walter Murray, James Heitton.
Nov. 26. John Snedden and Isabel Bunzie in Melrose. a.d.n. Joanna ; w.
              Robert Lukup, Andrew Mairton.
Dec.   1. Thomas Young and Elspath Smith in Gattonside. a.s.n. Thomas ; w.
              James Brown, James Pringle.
  ,,   24. George Moffat and Mary Mercer in Hagburn, a.s.n. James ; w.
              James Kerr, William Moffat.
  ,,   30. Thomas Mercer and Janet Haitlie in Melrose, a.s.n. William ; w.
              James Taitt, John Heitton.

1771.
Jan. 20. William Bell and Mary Speede, in fornication, in Gattonside, a.s.n.
              Thomas ; w. Robert Boston, George Ronaldson.
  ,,   27. George Ronaldson and Katharine Fisher in Melrose, a.d.n. Marion ;
              w. John Usher, John Heitton.
Feb.   6. Robert Mercer and Elspath Shiel in Drygrange, a.s.n, George ; w.
              James Brown, George Mercer.
  ,,   17. William Dods and Isabel Burnet in Melrose, a.s.n. James ; w. John
              Gill, John Mein.

1769.
Sept. 13. George Smith and Janet Wallace in Blainslie, a.s.n. John ; w.
              Thomas Hardie.

1771.
Mar.   4. John Henderson and Margaret Paterson in Colmslie, a.d n. Euphan ;
              w. James Kirkwood, George Boid.
  ,,   ,, James Kirkwood and Isabel Pringle in Langshaw, a.d.n. Anne ; w.
              John Henderson, George Boid.
  ,,   ,, George Boid and Isabel Blaikie in Langshaw, a.d.n. Betty ; w. John
              Henderson, James Kirkwood.
  ,,   17. Thomas Hervey and Isabel Speeden at the Bleachfield, a.s.n.
              Thomas ; w. John Layel, Robert Mein.
  ,,   22. James Brown and Mary Gray in Drygrange, a.d.n. Mary ; w. David
              Murray.
  ,,   24. James Mein and Mary Mercer in Newtown, a.s.n. William ; w.
              James Hilson, John Layel.
April 21. George Mein and Margaret Dods in Newstead, two sons named
              George and William ; w. John Grant, James Vair.
  ,,   ,, James Vair and Nelly Hunter in Melrose, a.s.n. James ; w. George
              Mein, John Grant.
  ,,   ,, John Skirven and Isabel Mercer at the Bleachfield, a.s.n. Thomas ;
              w. James Vair, John Grant.
  ,,   ,, Robert Stewart and Janet Taitt in Gattonside, a.d.n. Margaret ; w.
              James Vair, John Grant.

1771

April 21. John Grant and Nelly Mein in Newtown, a.d.n. Margaret ; w. James Taitt, John Skirven.

,, ,, James Taitt and Jean Young in Darnick, a.d.n. Mary ; w. John Skirven, Robert Stewart.

May 5. William Vair and Janet Speden in Newtown, a.s.n. William ; w. James Pringle, Robert Mein.

,, ,, James Reid and Janet Shiel at Holmes, a.d.n. Helen ; w. James Blaikie, William Vair.

June 9. Robert Vair and Nelly Dickson at Highcross, a.s.n. John ; w. Robert Lawrie, John Leyden.

,, ,, John Leyden and Isabel Dods in Darnick, a.s.n. John ; w. Robert Lawrie, Robert Vair.

,, 26. John Moffat and Alison Louden in Ouplaw, a.d.n. Maron ; w. William Moffat, Thomas Currer.

July 2. John Waugh and Alison Moffat in Blainslie, a.s.n. James ; w. James Wilson, William Smith.

,, 7. James Scott and Isabel Gilles in Danieltown, a.s.n. Robert ; w. James Dalgleish, Thomas Marr.

,, ,, James Dalgleish and Alison Mercer in Gattonside, a.d.n. Agnes ; w. James Scott, John Heitton.

,, 14. James Mein and Mary Darling in Eildon, a.d.n. Helen ; w. Andrew Lumsdale, Walter Murray.

,, 21. John Fair and Nelly Smith in Gattonside, a.s.n. Philip ; w. George Wight, Henry Hope.

,, ,, George Wight and Mary Slaiter in Darnick, a.d.n. Janet ; w. John Fair, Henry Hope.

,, ,, Henry Hope and Peggy Mercer in Darnick, a.d.n. Margaret ; w. George Wight, John Hatton.

,, ,, John Hatton and Margaret Taitt in Melrose, a.d.n. Anne ; w. James Hilson, Robert Lawrie.

,, 29. Andrew Henderson and Mary Ingles in Westhouses, a.d.n. Mary ; w. Thomas Wilson, Thomas Mein.

,, 31. Nicol Milne and Margaret Rodger of Whitehill, a.d.n. Isabel ; w. James Aird, Thomas Stenhouse.

,, ,, James Aird and Betty Robson in Newtown, a.s.n. Gideon ; w. Nicol Milne, Thomas Stenhouse.

Aug. 4. Andrew Mein and Isabel Maben in Newstead, a.d.n. Agnes ; w. James Heitton, Robert Boston.

Sept. 1. Robert Scott and Isabel Ronaldson in Newstead, a.s.n. Alexander ; w. George Ronaldson, Thomas Breadie.

,, ,, David Burton and Jean Grahamslie in Danieltown, a.s.n. John ; w. Robert Scott, Thomas Breadie.

,, 8. Andrew Bunnie and Janet Haistie in Newstead, a.s.n. Robert ; w. Adam Milne, James Hilson.

,, 22. John Fisher and Elizabeth Gilles in Darnick, a.s.n. James ; w. Walter Murray, John Boston.

Oct. 6. James Hog and Susanna Dawson in Melrose, a.s.n. John : w. Thomas Marr, George Blaikie.

,, 13. Robert Ormiston and Mary Darling in Gattonside, a.d.n. Jean ; w. Robert Lawrie, Robert Bunzie.

,, 20. Robert Ballantine and Betty Scott in Melrose, a.s.n. John ; w. Robert Lawrie, Andrew Heitton.

,, ,, Mr. Frederick Maclagan and Mrs. Christian Turnbul in Melrose, a.d.n. Jean ; w. Robert Lawrie, John Heitton.

,, 27. John Heitton and Maron Burnet in Darnick, a.s.n. Thomas : w. James Heitton, George Mercer.

,, 27. George Mercer and Janet Heitton in Darnick, a.s.n. John ; w. John and James Heittons.

Nov. 4. James Usher and Peggy Grieve in Blainslie, a.s.n. Hugh ; w. Hugh Grieve, John Cleugh.

1771.

Nov. 4. John Cleugh and Margaret Hardie in Blainslie, a.d.n. Janet; w. Hugh Grieve, James Usher.

„ 24. Andrew Ronaldson and Mary Lee in Darnick, a.s.n. William; w. John Heitton, Andrew Lumsdale.

Dec. 22. William Pringle and Mary Scott in Newstead, a.s.n. William; w. Andrew Pringle, James Pringle.

„ 26. Thomas Turnbull and Margaret Forsan in Gattonside, a.s.n. Thomas; w. Alexr. Brownfield, John Turnbull.

1772.

Jan. 5. Alexander Cuthel and Pegg Haitlie in Melrose, a.s.n. John; w. James Brownfield, James Hunter.

„ „ James Brownfield and Isabel Hunter in Melrose, a.d.n. Isabel; w. James Hunter, John Heitton.

Feb. 2. John Milne and Alison Helliburton in Darnick, a.s.n. William; w. John Boston, James Hilson.

„ 18. James Matheson and Agnes Young in Gattonside, a.d.n. Janet; w. Robert Meyls, James Marr.

„ „ Nicol Stenhouse and Agnes Sibbald in Whitelees, a.s.n. John; w. Thomas Stenhouse, Nicoll Milne.

Mar. 1. Robert Phorson and Isabel Unns in Newstead, a.d.n. Janet; w. John Mein, Robert Bunnie.

„ 5. John Barklay and Isabel Cochran in Newtown, three sons named John, Henry and Robert; w. ——.

„ 22. Walter Taitt and Margaret Helliburton in Darnick, a.d.n. Janet: w. James Taitt, John Heitton.

„ 29. Andrew Pringle and Nelly Cairncrose in Newstead, a.s.n. Andrew; w. James Brown, James Marr.

„ „ James Brown and Christian Lauder in Gattonside haugh, a.s.n. James; w. Andrew Pringle, James Marr.

„ „ Robert Marr and Janet Mercer in Gattonside, a.s.n. James; w. Andrew Pringle, James Brown.

April 12. Robert Hilson and Susanna Ballantine in Melrose, a.s.n. James; w. James Hilson, Walter Ballantine.

„ 19. James Pringle and Isabel Layel in Melrose, a.d.n. Isable; w. John Layel, Andrew Pringle.

„ 25. John Murray and Katharine Gray in Colmslie, a.s.n. John; w. William Moffat, William Wight.

„ „ William Wight and Margaret Loch in Threepwood, a.d.n. Margaret; w. William Moffat, John Murray.

May 3. David Fairbairn and Peggy Mercer in Melrose, a.s.n. David; w. Andrew Lumsden, Robert Ballantine.

„ „ Robert Taket and Janet Penman in Melrose, a.d.n. Christian; w. David Fairbairn, Andrew Lumsden.

„ 10. Andrew Lumsden and Peggy Baxter in Newstead, a.s.n. James; w. John Layel, Robert Lukup.

„ 17. Thomas Cochran and Betty Scott in Newtown, a.s.n. Robert; w. Robert Taket. James Wight.

„ 21. John Muir and Katharine Hope in Melrose, a.s.n. John; w. John Merten, David Taylor.

„ 31. James Boston and Janet Hunter in Gattonside, a.s.n. Andrew: w. Thomas Marr, Robert Fairbairn.

„ „ Robert Fairbairn and Jean Martin in Newtown, a.s.n. George; w. James Boston, Robert Lawrie.

June 7. Thomas Laidlaw and Peggy Thomson in Newtown, a.s.n. Robert; w. James Pringle, John Mein.

„ 14. James Amos and Helen Hoy in Gateside, a.d.n. Alison; w. Robert Bunnie, Walter Murray.

„ 21. James Marr and Jean Scott in Melrose, a.s.n. James; w. Andrew Murray, Andrew Heitton.

1772.

June 28. James Vair and Nelly Hunter in Melrose, a.s.n. William ; w. Robert Boston, Walter Murray.

July 19. James Pecoack and Agnes Waitt in Darnick, a.d.n. Maron ; w. James Blaikie, Andrew Heitton.

,, 27. James Frier and Isabel Dalgleish in Gattonside, a.d.n. Margaret ; w. William Shiell, Robert Scott.

,, ,, William Shiell and Helen Haig in Newstead, a.d.n. Margaret ; w. James Frier, James Blaikie.

Aug. 23. James Graham and Nelly Scott in Melrose, a.d.n. Agnes ; w. James Taitt, George Scott.

Sept. 20. Thomas Young and Elspath Smith in Gattonside, a.s.n. Taylor ; w. John Sibbald, Thomas Marr.

,, ,, John Sibbald and Marion Brown in Eildon, a.s.n. Thomas ; w. James Hilson, David Thomson.

,, 21. William Turner and Anne Laidlaw at Bentmill, a.s.n. James ; w. John and Robert Laidlaws.

,, ,, Hugh Pringle and Janet Brown in Blainslie, a.d.n. Margaret ; w. Robert Scott, Hugh Grieve

,, 27. George Ronaldson and Katharine Fisher in Melrose ; a.d.n. Elizabeth ; w. Robert Taket, James Pringle.

Oct. 11. Nicol Miln and Isobel Thomson in Newtown, a.s.n. George ; w. Robert Marr, Henry Cochran.

,, ,, Henry Cochran and Janet Lokie in Newtown, a.d.n. Janet ; w. Nicol Milne, Robert Marr.

,, ,, Robert Marr and Peggy Williamson in Drygrange boathouse, a.d.n. Elizabeth ; w. Nicol Milne, Henry Cochran.

,, 18. Thomas Haig and Janet Bunnie in Newstead, a.s.n. Thomas ; w. Robert Bunnie, John Heitton.

,, ,, William Brown and Margaret Henry in Blainslie, a.s.n. David ; w. James Aitchison, Andrew Waddel.

,, 25. John Barklay and Margaret Heart in Newstead, a.s.n. Andrew ; w. James Taitt, John Usher.

,, ,, Robert Fraizer and Betty Shiell in Newtown, a.d.n. Helen ; w. John Barklay, Thomas Marr.

Nov. 20. George Pecoa and Grizel Murray in Threepwood, a.s.n. Walter ; w. William Moffat, John Moffat.

,, 22. John Welch and Marion Spence in Drygrange, a.d.n. Agnes ; w. Thomas Marr, Andrew Murray.

,, 27. George Moffat and Mary Mercer in Hagburn, a.s.n. William ; w. James Kerr, William Moffat.

Dec. 13. Peter Caruthers and Janet Fisher in Melrose, a.s.n. Robert; w. Robert Lawrie, John Cochran.

,, ,, John Cochran and Janet Vair in Eildon, a.s.n. John ; w. Adam Milne, James Hilson.

,, 26. Robert Stewart and Janet Taitt in Gattonside, a.d.n. Isabel : w. Alexander Brownfield, Robert Henderson.

1773.

Jan. 10. James Taitt and Jean Young in Darnick, a.d.n. Isabel ; w. Andrew Heitton, James Marr.

,, 24. William Dods and Isabel Burnet in Melrose, a.d.n. Peggy ; w. James Hilson, Walter Murray.

Feb. 14. Henry Freator and Marion Mercer in Easterhousebyre, a.d.n. Alison ; w. John Layal, David Thomson.

Mar. 21. Andrew Ronaldson and Mary Lee in Darnick, a.s.n. Walter ; w. John Layel, James Hilson.

,, 30. John Gibson and Elizabeth Bulman in Blainslie, a.d.n. Mary : w. John Waugh, James Wilson.

,, ,, John Waugh and Alison Moffat in Blainslie, a.d.n. Alison : w. James Wilson, John Gibson.

1773.

April 4. John Barklay and Isabel Cochran in Newtown, a.d.n. Janet ; w. James Taitt, Robert Mein.

,, 9. Henry Hope and Peggy Mercer in Darnick, a.d.n. Isabel ; w. Robert Grierson, John Pecoa.

,, 18. Robert Scott and Isabel Ronaldson in Newstead, a.d.n. Christian ; w. Robert Lukup, John Heitton.

,, 25. James Scott and Isabel Gilles in Danieltown, a.d.n. Mary ; w. James Hilson, John Layel.

,, ,, John Fair and Nelly Smith in Gattonside, a.d.n. Agnes ; w. John Mein, John Smith.

May 9. James Marr and Peggy Mein in Gattonside, a.s.n. James ; w. Robert Mein, Walter Murray.

,, ,, William Darling and Margaret Gibson in Gattonside, a.s.n. William ; w. James Marr, Robert Heart.

,, ,, Robert Heart and Peggy Marjorybanks in Newstead, a.d.n. Betty ; w. William Darling, James Marr.

,, 16. John Leyden and Isabel Dods in Darnick, a.s.n. Robert ; w. Andrew Heitton, Walter Murray.

July 4. Walter Taitt and Margaret Helliburton in Darnick, a.d.n. Janet ; w. Robert Laurie, Walter Murray.

,, ,, James Jamison and Margaret Burn in Darnick, a.d.n Margaret ; w. Walter Taitt, Thomas Marr.

,, 18. James Dalglesh and Alison Mercer in Gattonside, a.s.n. George ; w. James Pringle, Andrew Nicoll.

,, ,, Andrew Nicoll and Mary Mein in Newtown, a.d.n. Mary ; w. James Dalgliesh, James Pringle.

,, 21. James Usher and Margaret Grieve in Blainslie, a.d.n. Janet ; w. Hugh Grieve, John Usher.

Aug. 1. John Mein and Nelly Stonhouse in Eildon, a.s.n. Cornelius ; w. Adam Milne, Nicol Milne.

,, 15. Mr. Frederic Maclagan, minister, and Mrs. Christian Turnbul in Melrose, a.s.n. George ; w. Thomas Marr, John Mein.

,, ,, James Reid and Janet Shiel in Newtown, a.s.n. Thomas ; w. James Hilson, Thomas Marr.

,, 22. Alexander Bell and Jean Neill in Drygrange, a.d.n. Peggy ; w. Robert Bunnie, John Heitton.

Sept. 12. Robert Williamson and Mary Stewart in Gattonside, a.d.n. Agnes ; w. Thomas Marr, Thomas Broadie.

,, 26. Robert Bunnie and Isabel Hoy in Newstead, a.s.n. William ; w. James Purves, Walter Murray.

Oct. 10. Andrew Bell and Janet Pringle in Broomhill, a.s.n. George ; w. James Marr, Andrew Murray.

,, 17. David Mein and Agnes Bunnie in Newstead, a.s.n. James ; w. Robert Bunnie, John Heitton.

,, 24. Nicol Stonhouse and Agnes Sibbald in Whitelees, a.s.n. William ; w. Thomas Stonhouse, Charles Baxter.

Nov. 7. Samuel Gilles and Nelly Laidlaw in Melrose, a.s.n. John ; w. John Usher, John Heitton.

,, ,, David Burton and Jean Grahamslie in Danieltown, a.d.n. Janet ; w. Andrew Heitton, Samuel Gilles.

,, 12. George Darling and Helen Crosbie in Mosshouses, a.d.n. Helen ; w. William Moffat, Thomas Laidlaw.

,, 14. Robert Mercer and Elspath Shiel in Gattonside, a.d.n. Margaret ; w. Andrew Heitton, James Blaikie.

,, 21. Mr. Archibald Dick and Mrs. Isabel Nickel in Melrose, a.d.n. Isabel ; w. James Hilson, Robert Laurie.

Dec. 12. John Martin and Janet Boston in Melrose, a.d.n. Isabel ; w. James Hilson, John Heitton.

,, 15. Robert Fraizer and Betty Shiel in ——, a.d.n. Agnes ; w. Nicol Milne, John Cochran.

1773.

Dec 17. Thomas Turnbul and Margaret Forsan in Gattonside, a.s.n. Zerubbabel : w Alexr. Brownfield, John Boston.

1774.

Jan. 2. James Corsbie and Janet Dalgleish in Eildon, a.d.n. Agnes ; w.
Thomas Brodie, James Scott.

„ 9. John Fisher and Betty Gilles in Darnick, **a.s.n. Andrew** ; w. Thomas
Marr, John Mein.

„ 25. James Blaikie and Betty Turnbull in Langhaugh, **a.d.n.** Agnes ; w.
John Dalgliesh, Alexr. Wilson.

„ 30. Mr. John Mercer and Mrs. Betty Wilkison in Melrose, a.s.n. George ;
w. James Sanderson, James Pringle.

„ „ James Pringle and Isabel Layel in Melrose, a.s.n. Alexander.

„ „ John Barcklay and Margaret Heart in Newstead, a.d.n. Jean ; w. for
both the last, John Layel, John Gill.

Feb. 13. John Mercer and Elizabeth Leyden in Darnick, a.s.n. John ; w.
James Hilson, Robert Grierson.

„ 27. George Wight and Mary Slaiter in Darnick, a.d.n. Mary ; w. John
Heitton, Robert Boston.

„ „ John Pecoack and Agnes Waitt in Darnick, a.d.n. Agnes ; w. James
Purves, George Wight.

Mar. 13. Robert Phorson and Isabel Unns in Drygrange, a.s.n. Thomas ; w.
Andrew Lumsden, James Amos.

„ „ Andrew Drummond and Isabel Martin in Darnick, a.s.n. George ; w.
Robert Phorson, James Amos.

„ „ Andrew Lumsden and Betty Baxter in Newstead, a.s.n. Thomas ; w.
Andrew Drummond, James Marr.

„ „ James Amos and Nelly Hoy in Gateside, a.s.n. Adam ; w. Robert
Phorsan, Andrew Drummond.

April 10. John Milne and Alison Helliburton in Darnick, a.s.n. John ; w.
Thomas Boston, Robert Mein.

„ 24. William Gibson and Nelly Gill in Melrose, a.s.n. James ; w. John
Gill, John Layel.

„ „ William Pringle and Mary Scott in Newstead, a.d.n. Janet ; w.
William Gibson, John Layel.

May 15. Alexander Cuthel and Peggy Thomson in Melrose, a.d.n. Isabel ; w.
James Hilson, Alexander Gibson.

June 3. Thomas Laidlaw and Peggy Thomson in Newtown, a.d.n. Janet ; w.
Nicol Milne, John Barklay.

„ 12. Richard Mein and Elizabeth Oliver in Eildon, a.s.n. Cornelius ; w.
John Heitton, Robert Mein.

July 13. Nicoll Milne and Margaret Rodger of Whitehill, a.s.n. Andrew ; w.
William Clarke.

„ 17. David Murray and Agnes Gray in Eildon, a.s.n. Alexander ; w.
Thomas Marr, Andrew Heitton.

„ 25. Robert Taket and Janet Penman in Melrose, a.s.n. John ; w. James
Hilson, James Pringle.

„ 31. Thomas Young and Elspath Smith in Gattonside, a.s.n. John ; w.
Andrew Heitton, John Cochran.

„ „ John Cochran and Janet Vair in Newtown, a.d.n. Janet ; w. Thomas
Young, Andrew Heitton.

Aug. 17. John Walker and Peggy Ingles in Langhaugh, a.s.n. James ; w. John
Dalgliesh, James Liddel.

„ 21. Andrew Bunnie and Janet Haistie in Newstead, a.s.n. William ; w.
John Layel, Walter Murray.

Sept. 11. George Ronaldson and Catharine Fisher in Melrose, a.d.n. Marion :
w. Andrew Heitton, Walter Murray.

„ 13. John Gibson and Elizabeth Bulman in Blainslie, a.s.n. Thomas ; w.
George Smith.

„ 19. John Sibbald and Marion Brown in Eildon, a.d.n. Agnes ; w. George
Mercer, James Hilson.

1774.

Sept. 19. George Mercer and Janet Heitton in Darnick, a.d.n. Janet ; w. John Heitton, Andrew Heitton.

Oct. 9. Robert Marr and Peggy Williamson in Melrose, a.s.n. Thomas ; w. Thomas Marr, James Wight.

,, 23. Henry Cochran and Janet Lokie in Newtown, a.d.n. Margaret ; w. Thomas Marr, John Heitton.

Nov. 20. Thomas Mercer and Janet Haitlie in Melrose, a.s.n. Nicol ; w. David Fairbairn, Andrew Murray.

,, ,, David Fairbairn and Peggy Mercer in Melrose, a.d.n. Isabel ; w. Thomas Mercer, John Layel.

,, 23. George Boyd and Isabel Blaikie in Colmslie, a.d.n. Jean ; w. Thomas Laidlaw, George Thomson.

Dec. 11. Andrew Nicol and Mary Mein in Newtown, a.d.n. Christian ; w. John Heitton, Robert Bunyie.

,, 18. James Taitt and Jean Young in Darnick, a.d.n. Margaret ; w. Andrew Murray, William Moffat.

,, 23. James Usher and Peggy Grieve in Blainslie, a.s.n. Thomas ; w. Hugh Grieve, Robert Kirkwood.

,, ,, Robert Kirkwood and Peggy Spittle in Blainslie, a.d.n. Mary ; w. James Usher, Hugh Grieve.

,, ,, Charles Ormiston and Agnes Karter in Blainslie, a.d.n. Agnes ; w. James Usher, Robert Kirkwood.

1775.

Jan. — Thomas Proctor and Mary Forsan in Melrose, a.s.n. Hart ; w. Thomas Broadie, Andrew Murray.

,, 8. Mr. Frederic Maclagan, minister, aud Mrs. Christian Turnbul, a.s.n. Frederick ; w. James Hilson, John Layel.

,, 15. Mr. John Mercer and Mrs. Betty Wilkison in Melrose, a.s.n. Thomas ; w. John Heitton, John Layel.

,, 29. James Ronaldson and Elspath Gray in Darnick, a.s.n. George ; w. Thomas Marr, Robert Bunnie.

Feb. 12. Andrew Ronaldson and Mary Lee in Darnick, a.s.n. George ; w. James Boston, Robert Bunnie.

,, ,, James Boston and Janet Hunter in Gattonside, a.d.n. Isabel ; w. Andrew Ronaldson, Walter Murray.

,, 15. Nicol Milne and Isabel Thomson in Newtown, a.d.n. Helen ; w. Richard Mein, John Usher.

Mar. 12. Alexander Bell and Jean Neill in Drygrange, a.s.n. Alexander ; w. John Layel, James Hilson.

,, ,, Robert Hilson and Suzanna Ballantine in Melrose, a.s.n. Walter ; w. John Layel, James Hilson.

,, 24. John Moffat and Alison Louden in Ouplaw, a.d.n. Betty ; w. George Moffat, John Louden.

,, ,, George Moffat and Mary Mercer in Hagburn, a.d.n. Margaret ; w. John Moffat, John Louden.

1743.

Aug. 6. Richard Park and Betty Louden in Hagburn, a.s.n. John ; w. ——.

1775.

Mar. 30. John Waugh and Alison Moffat in Blainslie, a.d.n. Mary ; w. James Stirling, James Scott.

,, ,, James Stirling and Nelly Kirkwood in Blainslie, a.d.n. Agnes ; w. John Waugh, James Scott.

,, ,, James Scott and Agnes Kirkwood in Blainslie, a.d.n. Margaret : w. John Waugh, James Stirling.

1771 (?).

Sept. 30. James Moffat and Agnes Dickson in Blainslie, a.s.n. James ; w. James Aitcheson, Simon Watherston.

1772.

Jan. 12. James Moffat and Agnes Dickson in Blainslie, a.d.n. Janet ; w. William Moffat, John Wilson.

U

1775.

April 28. James Moffat and Agnes Dickson in Blainslie, a.d.n. Isabel ; w.

„   30. James Dalgliesh and Alison Mercer in Gattonside, a.d.n. Alison ; w. James Purves, Robert Taket.

„   „   John Muir and Katharine Hope in Melrose, a d.n. Agnes ; w. David Thomson, Henry Hope.

May 14. Colline Fairfowl and Christian Trotter in Melrose, by fornication, a.s.n. Robert ; w. Robert Bunnie, Walter Murray.

„   28. David Milne in the parish of Eckells and Agnes Fairbairn in Newstead, a.s.n. John, in fornication, born June 12th, 1772 ; w. Andrew Pringle, William Barcklay.

June 4. John Fair and Nelly Smith in Gattonside, a.s.n. Andrew ; w. Andrew Heitton, Thomas Haig.

„   „   Thomas Haig and Janet Bunnie in Old Melrose, a.s.n. Robert ; w. John Fair, Andrew Heitton.

„   „   Andrew Heitton and Janet Usher in Darnick, a.d.n. Janet ; w. Andrew Cook, William Vair.

„   „   William Vair and Janet Speden in Bridgend, a.d.n. Christian ; w. Andrew Cook, John Fair.

„   „   Andrew Cook and Beatrix Porteus in Melrose, a.d.n. Elizabeth ; w. William Vair, John Fair.

„   „   Nicol Stonhouse and Agnes Sibbald in Whitelees, a.d.n. Agnes ; w. Thomas Stonhouse, Nicol Milne.

„   11. John Forsyth and Peggy Mason in Westhouses, a.s.n. William ; w. John Layel, John Heitton.

July 24. Robert Fairbairn and Jean Martin in Newtown, a.s.n. Robert ; w. Adam Milne, James Hilson.

Aug. 20. John Mein and Nelly Stonhouse in Newstead, a.s.n. Thomas ; w. Thomas Stonhouse, James Purves.

Sept. 3. James Pringle and Isabel Layel in Melrose, a.s.n. James ; w. James Hilson, John Layel.

„   „   Thomas Laidlaw and Peggy Thomson in Newtown, a.d.n. Christian ; w. James Pringle, Thomas Marr.

„   10. John Smith and Mary Williamson in Darnick, a.d.n. Elizabeth ; w. James Williamson, James Wight.

„   17. Robert Stewart and Janet Taitt in Gattonside, a.d.n. Mary ; w. Robert Bunnie, Andrew Heitton.

„   24. Michael Paterson and Nelly Stevenson in Darnick mains, two sons named John and William ; w. James Knox, John Burnet.

Oct. 15. George Hog and Peggy Ramsay in Melrose, a.s.n. Andrew ; w. Robert Scott, Andrew Heitton.

„   „   Robert Scot and Isabel Ronaldson in Newsteid, a.s.n. Andrew ; w. George Hoy, Andrew Heitton.

Nov. 5. Andrew Bell and Janet Pringle in Broomhill, a.s.n. James ; w. Andrew Pringle, James Hilson.

„   12. John Heitton and Marion Burnet in Darnick, a.s.n. Thomas ; w. John Layel, John Boston.

„   26. William Chisholm and Agnes Heitton in Darnick, a.s.n. John ; w. John Heitton, Walter Murray.

Dec. 10. George Bell and Peggy Martin in Melrose, a.s.n. George ; w. Robert Ballantine, James Pringle.

„   „   Robert Ballantine and Betty Scott in Melrose, a.s.n. Thomas ; w. George Bell, William Ballantine.

1776.

Jan. 7. David Burton and Jean Grahamslie in Danieltown, a.d.n. Jean ; w. Thomas Broadie, William Hoy.

„   21. Gideon Coilart and Margaret Stewart in Darnick, a.s.n. Robert ; w. Andrew Heitton, Adam Maben.

„   „   John Martin and Janet Boston in Melrose, a.d.n. Margaret ; w. James Hilson, John Layel.

1776.

Jan. 26. Thomas Young and Elspath Smith in Gattonside, a.s.n. Taylor ; w. John Boston, James Marr.

Feb. 4. William Stoddart and Agnes Fisher in Newtoun, a.s n. Robert ; w. ——

,, 11. John Burnet and Isabel Cribbes in Darnick mains, a.d.n. Janet ; w. William Turner, John Heitton.

,, ,, William Turner and Katharine Marr in Gattonside, a.d.n. Isabel ; w. John Burnet, John Layel.

,, 18. Andrew Pringle and Nelly Cairncross in Newsteid, a.s.n. James ; w. James Pringle, James Hilson.

Mar. 3. Robert Scott and Christian Craig in Danielton, a.s.n. Robert ; w. George Scott, Thomas Marr.

,, 10. William Gibson and Nelly Gill in Melrose, a.s.n. John ; w. John Gill, Robert Bunnyie.

,, 24. Andrew Bunnie and Janet Haistie in Newsteid, a.d.n. Janet ; w. James Hilson, Robert Mein.

April 7. James Amos and Nelly Hoy in Gattonside, a.d.n. Helen ; John Elliot, Adam Maben.

,, ,, John Elliot and Isabel Bunnie in Newsteid, a.d.n. Margaret ; w. James Amos, John Heitton.

,, 14. William Pringle and Mary Scott in Newsteid, a.s.n. Robert ; w. James Crosbie, Thomas Vair.

,, ,, James Crosbie and Janet Dalgliesh in Eildon, a.s.n. Robert ; w. William Pringle, John Layel.

,, ,, Thomas Vair and Peggy Burnet in Darnick, a.d.n. Mary ; w. James Crosbie, William Pringle.

,, 15. John Dalgliesh and Margaret Renwick in Langhaugh, a.d.n. Isabel.

,, 21. George Mein and Margaret Dods in Newsteid, a.d.n. Elizabeth ; w. James Wight, Robert Mein.

May 5. John Barcklay and Isabel Cochrane in Newtoun, a.s.n. John ; w. Robert Bunnie, Andrew Heitton.

,, ,, Andrew Weddel and Janet Summervil in Langshaw, a.s.n. John ; w. Adam Meban, John Layel.

,, 28. John Laurie and Joanna Ballantine in Drygrange, a.d.n. Alison ; w. John and Thomas Slaiters.

June 2. James Reid and Janet Shiel in Newtown, a.s.n. William ; w. James Hilson, George Laurie.

,, 9. George Wight and Mary Slaiter in Darnick, a.s.n. George ; w. John Heitton, Thomas Boston.

,, ,, Richard Park and Elizabeth Louden in Hagburn, a.s.n. Andrew ; w. ——

,, 16. John Heitton and Margaret Taitt in Melrose, .s.n. John ; w. Robert Marr, John Walker.

,, ,, Robert Marr and Peggy Williamson in Melrose, a.s.n. Adam ; w. James and Thomas Williamsons.

,, ,, John Walker and Margaret Ingles in Eildon, a.s.n. Alexander ; w. James Williamsone, James Wight.

,, ,, James Kirkwood and Isabel Pringle in Langshaw, a.d.n. Mary ; w John Hatton, John Walker.

,, 21. John Sibbald and Marion Brown in Eildon, a.d.n. Elizabeth ; James Marr, Robert Mein.

July 25. Robert Bunnie and Isabel Hoy in Newstead, a.s.n. John ; w. George Scott, John Heitton.

,, 29. Mr. Frederic Maclagan, minister, and Mrs. Christian Turnbul, a.s.n. William ; w. John Layel, John Usher.

Aug. 25. James Bulman and Nelly Lunn in Darnick, a.d.n. Betty ; w. John Heitton, Thomas Stonhouse.

Sept. 6. Richard Mein and Elizabeth Oliver in Eildon, a.s.n. Abraham ; w. James Laidlaw, John Mein.

1776.

Sept. 8. James Graham and Nelly Scott in Newhouses, a.d.n. Nelly ; w. George Scott, William Maben.

,, 9. The deceased Robert Forsan and Isabel Unns in Newstead, a.s.n. Andrew ; w. John Mein, Captain Robert Mein.

,, 15. John Muir and Catharine Hop in Melrose, a.s.n. Thomas ; w. John Henderson, George Scott.

,, ,, John Henderson and Janet Mercer in Gattonside, two sons named Nicol and Robert ; w. John Muir, George Scott.

,, 22. John Brack and Barbara Bower in Newtown, a.s.n. John ; w. James Scott, Robert Mein.

,, ,, James Scott and Isabel Gilles in Danieltown, a.d.n. Anne ; w. John Layel, Adam Maben.

,, 29. John Barcklay and Peggy Heart in Newstead, a.s.n. Andrew ; w. Robert Heart, Andrew Heitton.

,, ,, Robert Heart and Peggy Marjoribanks in Newsteid ; a.d.n. Janet ; w. Andrew Pringle, James Hilson.

Oct. 13. John Fisher and Betty Gilles in Darnick, a.s.n. John ; w. John Heitton, James Purves.

,, 18. John Frier and Peggy Bathgate in Allanshaws, a.d.n. Janet ; w. Thomas Frier.

,, 27. Robert Fairbairn and Jean Martin in Newtown, a.s.n. Robert ; w. Andrew Murray, Thomas Brodie.

,, ,, Andrew Lumsden and Betty Baxter in Newstead, a.s n. Andrew ; w. James Blaikie, David Kyle.

1774.

April 4. John Dalgleish and Peggy Renwick in Langhaugh, a.s.n. William ; w. George and James Browns.

Nov. 14. Thomas Turnbul and Margaret Forson in Gattonside, a.d.n. Betty ; w. Alexr. Brownfield, James Marr.

,, 18. Thomas Proctor and Mary Forsan in Gattonside, a.s.n. —— ; w. Alexr. Brownfield, James Marr.

Dec. 15. John Goven and Jean Brownfield in Gattonside, a.s.n. James ; w. Alexander Brownfield, Robert Williamson.

,, ,, Alexr. Brownfield and Isabel Beanston in Gattonside, a.s.n. Alexander ; w. John Goven, Robert Williamson.

,, ,, Robert Williamson and Mary Stewart in Gattonside, a.s.n. James ; w. Alexr. Brownfield, James Wight.

,, 24. John Idington and Elspath Wilkison in Drygrange, a.d.n. Joanna ; w. John Laurie, Adam Nicol.

1777.

Jan. 5. James Ronaldson and Euphan Gray in Darnick, a.d.n. Margaret ; w. Andrew Heitton, James Hilson.

,, 12. George Laurie and Jean Stoddart in Danielton, a.s.n. Robert ; w. George Stoddart, Robert Grierson.

,, ,, John Milne and Alison Helliburton in Darnick, a.d.n. Alison ; w. George Laurie, John Layel.

,, 19. George Bell and Peggy Martin in Melrose, a.s.n. Andrew ; w. William Moffat, Robert Mercer.

,, ,, Robert Mercer and Elspath Shiel in Gattonside, a.s.n. James ; w. William Moffat, George Bell.

,, 26. John Cochran and Janet Vair in Eildon, a.s.n. Alexander ; w. Adam Milne, Adam Maben.

Feb. 7. James Usher and Peggy Grieve in Blainslie, a.s.n. George ; w. Hugh Grieve, James Usher.

1776.

Jan. 15. George Scott and Agnes Kirkwood in Blainslie, a.s.n. Robert ; w. Robert Scott, James Wilson.

1777.

Feb. 16. James Pringle and Isabel Layel in Melrose, a.s.n. John ; w. John Layel, John Gill.

1777.

Feb. 16. Alexander Bell and Jean Neill in Drygrange, a.s.n. John ; w. John Lawrie, Andrew Lourie.

Mar. 2. Robert Hilson and Susann Ballantine in Darnick, a.d.n. Jean ; w. James Hilson, John Layel.

„ 8. James Blaikie and Betty Turnbull in Langhaugh, a.d.n. Mary ; w.

„ 9. George Brownfield and Janet Waugh in Gattonside, a.d.n. Isabel ; w. Walter Murray, William Sibbald.

„ 16. James Cochran and Isabel Shearp in Newstead, a.s.n. John ; w. Andrew Heitton, Andrew Murray.

„ 23. John Murray and Peggy Sclaiter in Melrose, a.s.n. William ; w. Thomas Grieve, Walter Murray.

„ „ Thomas Grieve and Christian Deans in Melrose, a.d.n. Mary ; w. John Murray, Robert Bunnie.

April 6. William Ailly and Agnes Darling in fornication, a.d.n. Mary ; Adam Maben, James Hilson.

„ 20. William Shiel and Nelly Haig in Newstead, a.s.n. John ; w. Robert Bunie, David Keil.

„ 27. Andrew Heitton and Janet Usher in Darnick ; a.s.n. John ; w. John Heitton, James Hilson.

„ „ William Chisholm and Agnes Heitton in Darnick a.s.n. Walter, and a.d.n. Betty ; w. John Heitton, James Hilson.

May 4. John Learmont and Agnes Bunnie in Drygrange mill, a.d.n. Agnes ; w. John Smith, David Kyle.

„ „ John Smith and Mary Williamson in Darnick, a.d.n. Agnes ; w. James Williamson, Thomas Williamson.

„ „ George Nicol and Agnes Dickson in Gattonside, a.s.n. John ; w. John Martin, John Forsyth.

„ „ Alexander Grieve and Helen Symenton in Mosshouses, a.s.n. John ; w. William Moffat, Thomas Laidlaw.

„ „ William Campbell and Janet Waitt in Langshaw, a.d.n. Elspath ; w. William Moffat, Thomas Laidlaw.

„ 11. Nicol Stonhouse and Agnes Sibbalt in Whitelees, a.s.n. Nicol ; w. Thomas Stonhouse, Andrew Sibbalt.

„ 18. John Forrest and Peggy Mason in Westhouses, a.s.n. Henry ; w. John Heitton, John Boston.

June 8. James Vair and Nelly Hunter in Melrose, a.d.n. Christian ; w. Thomas Stonhouse, James Scott.

July 14. George Scott and Agnes Kirkwood in Blainslie, a.s.n. John ; w. James Brown, James Easton.

„ 20. Michael Paterson and Nelly Stevenson in Darnick mains, a.s.n. Alexander ; w. Andrew Ronaldson, Thomas Stonhouse.

„ „ Andrew Ronaldson and Mary Lees in Darnick, a.d.n. Isabel ; w. Michael Paterson, Thomas Stonhouse.

„ 23. John Mein and Helen Stonhouse in Newstead, two sons named Richard and John ; w. Thomas Stonhouse, Richard Mein.

„ 28. Andrew Cook and Beatrice Porteous in Melrose, a.d.n. Mary ; w. John Layel, James Pringle.

Aug. 17. William Dickson and Isabel Fairbairn in Darnick, a.d.n. Elspath , w. George Scott, John Layel.

„ 24. Thomas Vair and Peggy Burnet in Darnick, a.s.n. James ; w. John Heitton, Walter Murray.

Sept. 2. Mr. John Mercer and Mrs. Betty Wilkieson in Melrose, a.s.n. Charles Wilkieson ; w. Mr. William Hunter, Thomas Usher.

„ 21. Francis Elliot and Isabel Barklay in Newstead, a.d.n. Jean ; w. William Mabon, James Hilson.

Oct. 5. David Kyle and Betty Kedzie in Melrose, a.s.n. William ; w. James Marr, George Scott.

„ „ Thomas Scott and Margaret Dunn in Danielton, a.s.n. George , w. John Layel, Robert Bunnie.

1777.

Oct.   5. Henry Freator and Marion Mercer in Easterhousebyre, a.d.n. Katharine ; w. John Heitton, Walter Murray.

,,   19. James Jamieson and Margaret Burn in Darnick, a.d.n. Jean ; w. George Skirven, Adam Milne.

Nov. 13. John Moffat and Alison Louden in Ouplaw, a.s.n. John ; w. William Moffat, John Frier.

,,   ,, John Frier and Peggy Bathgate in Threepwood, a.d.n. Betty ; w. William Moffat, John Moffat.

,,   23. John Thomson and Betty Park in Melrose, a.d.n. Alison ; w. James Wight, Thomas Broadie.

Dec. 22. Thomas Haig and Janet Bunnie in Drygrange, a.s.n. Thomas ; w. Adam Nicol, Alexander Bell.

,,   30. Charles Hislop and Katharine Thynn in Gattonside, a.d.n. Margaret ; w. Alexander Brownfield, John Boston.

    1778.

Jan.   5. John Laurie and Joanna Ballantine in Drygrange, a.d.n. Margaret ; w. John Tod, Adam Laidlaw.

,,   18. John Martin and Janet Boston in Melrose, a.d.n. Janet ; w. Robert Grierson, James Hilson.

Feb.   1. George Laurie and Jean Stoddart in Danieltown, a.s.n. James ; w. George Stoddart, William Gibson.

,,   ,, William Gibson and Nelly Gill in Melrose, a.d.n. Helen ; w. John Gill, George Laurie.

,,   8. George Ronaldson and Katharine Fisher in Melrose, a.s.n. George ; w. Andrew Fisher, James Hilson.

,,   21. John Thomson and Margaret Haig in Drygrange boathouse, a.d.n. Isabel ; w. William Sibbald, John Pringle.

Mar. 15. James Bulman and Nelly Lunn in Darnick, a.s.n. Patrick ; w. Andrew Murray, Robert Bunnie.

,,   ,, Robert Marr and Peggy Williamson in Melrose, a.d.n. Mary ; w. Thomas Williamson, George Wight.

,,   16. Andrew Pringle and Peggy Familton in Newstead, a.d.n. Nelly ; w. Andrew Pringle, John Atchison.

,,   22. John Fair and Nelly Smith in Gattonside, a.d.n. Anne ; w. John Smith, Adam Mabon.

April 21. James Hopkirk and Agnes Wright in Melrose, a.d.n. Agnes ; w. James Hilson, John Heitton.

,,   26. John Forsyth and Jean Mein in Newstead, a.d.n. Mary ; w. James Marr, George Grahamslie.

May   3. George Mercer and Janet Heitton in Darnick, a.s.n. James ; w. John Heitton, Andrew Heitton.

,,   10. George Mein and Margaret Dods in Newstead, a.d.n. Margaret ; w. John Mein, John Laurie.

,,   21. James Scott and Anne Scott in Westhouses, procreate in fornication, a.s.n. William ; w. John Martin.
        N.B.—See Thomas Reas age marked in the year 1789, April 11th.

,,   24. Robert Williamson and Mary Stewart in Gattonside, a.s.n. John ; w. Robert Ballantyne, Andrew Murray.

,,   ,, Robert Ballantyne and Betty Scott in Darnick, a.d.n. Nelly ; w. Robert Williamson, John Layel.

,,   31. John Brack and Barbara Bower in Newtown, a.d.n. Margaret ; w. Adam Mabon, Robert Myles.

June 14. Andrew Pringle and Nellie Cairncross in Newstead, a.d.n. Nelly ; w. Robert Heart, George Grahamslie.

,,   ,, Robert Heart and Peggy Marjoribanks in Newstead, a.d.n. Isabel ; w. Andrew Pringle, Andrew Heitton.

,,   21. Richard Mein and Elizabeth Oliver in Melrose, a.s.n. Richard ; w. John Heitton, John Muir.

,,   ,, John Muir and Katharine Hope in Melrose, a.d.n. Agnes ; w. Adam Mabon, Thomas Boston.

1778.

July 12. John Gill and Christian Hunter in Melrose, a.s.n. John ; w. John Gill, John Hunter.

,, ,, John Elliot and Isabel Bunnie in Newstead, a.d.n. Alison ; w. John Gill, John Hunter.

,, 27. Alexander Brownfield and Isabel Beanston in Gattonside, a.d.n. Janet ; w. John Heitton, John Layel.

,, 28. David Murray and Agnes Gray in Eildon, a.s.n. Thomas ; w. James Hilson, William Mabon.

Aug. 9. David Fairnbairn and Peggy Mercer in Melrose, a.d.n. Margaret ; w. James Hilson, Charles Baxter.

,, 23. John Wight in Melrose in fornication with Peggy Bathgate, a.d.n. Katharine ; w. Wm. Smith, George Hume

Sept. 6. Alexander Skirven and Peggy Cook in Melrose, a.s.n. James ; w. George Skirven, Robert Paterson.

,, 21. William Wilson and Betty Mercer in Bridgend, a.d.n. Janet ; w. John Mercer, James Speeden.

,, 27. Thomas Young and Elspath Smith in Gattonside. a.s.n. Robert Taylor ; w. Thomas Usher, David Taylor.

Oct. 18. Thomas Laidlaw and Isabel Thomson in Newtown, a.s.n. William ; w. John Goven, John Sinclair.

,, ,, John Goven and Jean Brownfield in Gattonside, a.d.n. Isabel ; w. John Sinclair, Thomas Laidlaw.

,, ,, John Paterson and Peggy Bower in Darnick, a.d.n. Janet ; w. John Sinclair, John Goven.

,, ,, John Sinclair and Agnes Bunnie in Newtown, a.d.n. Janet ; w. John Paterson, John Layel.

,, 25. John Walker and Peggy Ingles in Darnick. a.s.n. Andrew ; w. Alexander Skirven, David Kyle.

,, ,, David Kyle and Betty Kedzie in Melrose, a.d.n. Betty ; w. John Walker, Andrew Heitton.

Nov. 22. William Turner and Katharine Marr in Gattonside, a.d.n. Mary ; w. George Grahamslie, Andrew Heitton.

,, 29. Robert Bulman and Peggy Leithen in Danielton, a.s.n. William ; w. John Murray, Andrew Murray.

Dec. 6. John Mein and Betty Kersel in Newstead, a.d.n. Betty ; w. George Scott, Thomas Broadie.

,, 28. John Wight and Janet Freeman in Melrose, a.d.n. Peggy ; w. John Barcklay, Frances Elliot.

,, ,, John Barcklay and Peggy Heart in Newstead, a.d.n. Jean ; w. John Wright, Frances Elliot.

,, ,, Frances Elliot and Isabel Barcklay in Newstead, a.d.n. Margaret ; w. John Barcklay, John Wight.

1779.

Jan. 3. Robert Taket and Janet Penman in Melrose, a.s.n. William ; w. George Skirven, Robert Bunnie.

,, 15. George Brownfield and Janet Wauch in Gattonside, a.d.n. Elizabeth ; w. Alexander Brownfield, Walter Murray.

,, ,, Thomas Proctor and Mary Forson in Gattonside, a.s.n. Zerobabel ; w. John Boston, Walter Murray.

,, 24. James Usher and Peggy Grieve in Topfield, a.s.n. William ; w. Hugh Grieve, Thomas Usher.

,, ,, George Wight and Mary Sclaiter in Darnick, a.d.n. Agnes ; w. James Usher, Robert Paterson.

,, 31. Mr. John Mercer and Mrs. Betty Wilkieson in Melrose, a.d.n. Anne ; w. Messrs. David Brown and William Moffat.

Feb. 7. William Mabon and Peggy Brown in Newstead, a.s.n. John ; w. William Mabon, John Heitton.

,, ,, William Mabon and Peggy Brown in Newstead, a.s.n. John ; w. John Layel, George Bell.

1779.

Mar. 8. John Moffat and Alison Loudain in Ouplaw, a.d.n. Alison ; w. George Moffat, John Swanston.

,, ,, George Moffat and Mary Mercer in Hagburn, a.d.n. Isabel ; w. John Moffat, John Swanston.

,, ,, John Swanson and Isabel Loudain in Whitelay, a.s.n. William ; w. John Moffat, George Moffat.

,, 14. Andrew Bunnie and Janet Haistie in Newstead, a.s.n. William ; w. James Hilson, Robert Bunnie.

April 6. Alexander Cuthel and Peggy Haitlie in Melrose, a.s.n. Alexander ; w. John Layel.

,, 11. Andrew Heitton and Janet Usher in Darnick, a.s.n. James ; w. John Heitton, John Layel.

,, ,, William Dickson and Isabel Fairbairn in Darnick, a.s.n. Thomas ; w. Andrew Heitton, George Scott.

,, 18. Michael Paterson and Nelly Stevenson in Abbatslee, a.s.n. Michael ; w. Thomas Turnbull, Andrew Murray.

,, ,, Thomas Turnbull and Peggy Forsan in Gattonside, a.d.n. Margaret ; w. John Boston, Andrew Heitton.

,, 24. Thomas Lillie and Helen Laidlaw in Langshaw mill, a.s.n. Alexander ; w. Robert Laidlaw, James Kirkwood.

,, 25. James Hopkirk and Anne Wright in Melrose, a.d.n. Anne ; w. Robert Bunnie, John Smith.

,, ,, John Idinton and Elspeth Wilkieson in Drygrange, a.d.n. Isabel ; w. William Ailly.

May 2. James Pringle and Isabel Layel in Melrose, a.d.n. Margaret ; w. John Layel, James Hilson.

,, 16. James Cochran and Isabel Sharp in Newtead, a.s.n. Robert ; w. Adam Milne, Andrew Murray.

,, 30. Robert Fairbairn and Jean Martin in Newtown. a.s.n. John ; w. James Hilson, Robert Lukup.

June 26. James Dalgliesh and Alison Mercer in Gattonside, a.d.n. Mary ; w. Nicol Stonhouse, James Stirling.

,, 27. Edward Waddle and Marion Carter in Darnick, a.s.n. Francis ; w. Charles Baxter, John Heitton.

,, ,, James Bower and Agnes Miller in Melrose, a.s.n. John ; w. Edward Waddle, George Scott.

July 11. William Pringle and Mary Scott in Newstead, a.d.n. Anne ; w. John Gill, James Pringle.

,, 18. Gideon Coilart and Margaret Stewart in Darnick, a.d.n. Agnes ; w. Adam Milne, Adam Mabon.

,, 26. Nicol Stonhouse and Agnes Sibbald in Whitelees, a.s.n. George ; w. James Stirling, James Wilson.

Aug. 22. Robert Bunzie and Isabel Hoy in Newstead, a.s.n. Robert ; w. Robert Mein and Robert Mein, senior.

Sept. 23. John Forrest and Margaret Mason in Westhouses, a.s.n. Joseph ; w. John Scott, John Hunter.

Oct. 3. John Smith and Mary Williamson in Darnick, a.s.n. James ; w. James Williamson, George Lawrie.

,, ,, George Lawrie and Jean Stoddart in Danieltown, a.s.n. George ; w. John Smith, George Moss.

,, 31. William Gibson and Nellie Gill in Melrose, a.s.n. William ; w. John Gill, Andrew Cook.

,, ,, Charles Hislop and Katharine Thynn in Gattonside, —— ; w. ——.

Nov. 23. John Church and Peggy Thomson in Gattonside, a.d.n. Margaret ; w. George Laurie, James Church.

Dec. 2. James Stirling and Nelly Kirkwood in Blainslie, a.d.n. Margaret ; w. James Stirling, James Wilson.

1780.

Jan. 6. John Frier and Peggy Bathgate in Threepwood, a.d.n. Alison ; w. James Kirkwood, John Moffat.

1780.

Jan. 6. Thomas Swan and Helen Dudgen, a.s.n. James ; w. John Frier
James Kirkwood.

 ,, 9. John Cochran and Janet Vair in Eildon, a.s.n. James ; w. Andrew
Heitton, Robert Bunnie.

Feb. 3. David Kyle and Betty Kedzie in Melrose, a.d.n. Margaret ; w. John
Boston, Andrew Heitton.

 ,, 11. John Brack and Barbara Bower in Newton, a.s.n. Nicol ; w. Nicol
Milne, Henry Cochran.

 ,, 13. Andrew Riddel and Betty Knox in Darnick, a.s.n. Robert ; w. John
Layel, James Pringle.

 ,, ,, William Shiel and Nellie Hague in Newstead, a.d.n. Isabel ; w.
Andrew Riddel, John Heitton.

 ,, 27. Robert Marr and Peggy Williamson in Melrose, a.d.n. Agnes ; w.
David Kyle, John Dickson.

Mar. 5. James Bulman and Nelly Lunn in Darnick, a.s.n. John ; w. John
Heitton, Andrew Murray.

 ,, 6. John Fair and Nelly Smith in Gattonside, a.s.n. George ; w. John
Boston, Alexander Brownfield.

 ,, 12. James Ronaldson and Eupham Gray in Darnick, a.s.n. James : w.
Adam Milne, Adam Mabon.

 ,, ,, James Muir and Jean Ross in the Bleachfield, a.s.n. John ; w. James
Ronaldson, John Heitton.

 ,, 24. John Laurie and Joanna Ballintine in Drygrange, a.s.n. George ; w.
Messrs. John Tod and William Gillan.

 ,, ,, Robert Hunter and Euphan Berry in ——, a.s.n. John ; w. John
Laurie, Mr. William Gillan.

April 2. William Ailly and Agnes Darling in Gattonside, a.s.n. Nicol ; w.
James Notman, Andrew Murray.

 ,, ,, James Notman and Bettrice Elliot in Melrose, a.d.n. Bettrice ; w.
William Ailly, John Boston.

 ,, 9. Robert Brown and Elizabeth Henderson in Eildon, a.d.n. Margaret ;
w. John Cochran, John Grahamslie.

 ,, 16. Andrew Pringle and Peggy Familton in Newstead, a.d.n. Anne ; w.
George Wight, George Stoddart.

 ,, 23. James Orr, soldier, and Agnes Mercer in Darnick, a.d.n. Janet ; w.
John Martin, John Mein.

 ,, 30. John Gill and Christian Hunter in Melrose, a.s.n. James ; w. John
Gill, Robert Hunter.

May 7. John Barcklay and Isabel Cochran in Newtown, a.d.n. Isabel ; w.
Andrew Murray, George Skirven.

 ,, 28. Thomas Boston and Isabel Boston in Gattonside, a.s.n. Thomas ; w.
John Boston, James Brown.

 ,, ,, James Brown and Peggy Butler in Darnick, a.d.n. Janet ; w. Thomas
Boston, Robert Grierson.

 ,, ,, William Haig and ——, a.s.n. William ; w. Thomas Boston, James
Brown.

June 11. Robert Wight and Janet Brack in Darnick, a.s.n. William ; w. John
Mein, John Forsyth.

 ,, ,, John Forsyth and Jean Mein in Newsteid, a.s.n. James ; w. John
Mein, Robert Wight.

 ,, ,, John Mein and Betty Kersel in Newsteid, a.d.n. Janet ; w. John
Forsyth, Robert Wight.

 ,, ,, William Paterson and Janet Drummond in Westhouses, a.d.n.
Margaret ; w. John Mein, John Forsyth.

July 2. John Grahamslie and Mary Ormiston in Melrose, a.s.n. John ; w.
John Martin, Robert Grierson.

 ,, ,, James Jamieson and Margaret Burn in Darnick, a.d.n. Mary ; w.
John Martin, John Grahamslie.

 ,, ,, John Martin and Janet Boston in Melrose, a.d.n. Betty ; w. James
Hilson, John Layel.

1780.

July   9. Alexander Skirven and Peggy Cook in Melrose, a.s.n. Alexander ; w. John Martin, Andrew Heitton.

„   „   Andrew Heitton and Janet Usher in Darnick, a.s.n. Thomas ; w. John Heitton, Alexander Skirven.

„   16. Andrew Cook and Bettrice Porteous in Melrose, a.d.n. Anne; w. James Stirling, James Wilson.

„   20. Thomas Scott and Margaret Dunn in Danielton, a.s.n. James ; w. James Scott, George Scott.

„   30. John Thomson and Betty Park in Melrose, a.s.n. John ; w. Andrew Murray, Robert Bunnie.

Aug.   6. William Chisholm and Agnes Heitton in Darnick, a.s.n. John ; w. John Heitton, George Wight.

„   13. Alexander Brownfield and Isabel Beanston in Gattonside, a.d.n. Isabel ; w. Alexander Brownfield, Robert Paterson.

„   20. Thomas Vair and Peggy Burnet in Darnick, two daughters named Janet and Christian ; w. William Cook, John Heitton.

„   „   William Cook and Elizabeth Murray in Melrose, a.d.n. Elizabeth ; w. George Laurie, Andrew Murray.

Sept.   3. William Maben and Peggy Brown in Newstead, a.s.n. George ; w. Robert Grierson, James Hilson.

„   10. Thomas Cleghorn and Peggy Bower in Newstead, a.d.n. Margaret ; w. George Laurie, Robert Lookup.

Oct.   1. John Sibbald and Jean Laidlaw in Eildon, a.d.n. Jean ; w. James Laidlaw, George Laurie.

„   8. Thomas Hague and Janet Bunny in Drygrange, a.d.n. Margaret ; w. Robert Bunny, John Laurie.

Nov.   5. John Henderson and Janet Mercer in Melrose, a.s.n. John ; w. John Walker, John Layel.

„   „   John Walker and Peggy Ingles in Abbatslee, a.s.n. George ; w. John Henderson, George Laurie.

„   „   James Sanderson and Grizel Thorburn at Melrose wakmill, a.d.n Mary ; w. John Henderson, John Walker.

„   26. Thomas Young and Elspath Smith in Gattonside. a.d.n. Nelly ; w. Andrew Lumsden, Robert Bunnie.

1781.

Jan. 12. Frances Elliot and Isabel Barklay in Newstead, a.d.n. Jean ; w.
————.

„   21. Robert Hilson and Susanna Ballantine in Melrose, a.d.n. Margaret ; w. William Mabon, Adam Milne.

„   28. John Mack and Bettrice Edgar, both unmarried, a.d.n. Jean. The father is in England and the mother in Melrose ; w. James Hilson, William Ailly.

Feb.   4. George Ronaldson and Katharine Fisher in Melrose, a.s.n. James ; w. John Layel, Robert Grierson.

„   „   James Chochran and Isabel Sharp in Newstead, a.d.n. Janet ; w. Andrew Murray, Robert Bunney.

„   20. Robert Mercer and Elspath Shiel in Easterhousebyre, a.s.n. Robert ; w. William Cockburn.

„   „   James Kirkwood and Jean Fairbairn in Langshaw, a.d.n. Betty ; w. Thomas Swan, William Turner.

„   25. George Stoddart and Katharine Makall in Darnick, a.s.n. George ; w. Walter Scott, George Dickson.

„   „   George Dickson and Elizabeth Fairbairn in Newstead, a.s.n. John ; w. George Laurie, Walter Scott.

Mar. 11. David Kyle and Bettie Kedzie in Melrose, a.d.n. Margaret ; w. Andrew Lumsden, Thomas Baxter.

„   18. Robert Fairbairn and Janet Mertin in Newtown, a.s.n. George ; w. John Gill, George Grahamslie.

„   „   William Dickson and Betty Frier in Drygrange mill, a.s.n. William ; w. John Laurie, Robert Fairbairn.

1781.

Mar. 25. John Wilson and Betty Mercer in Bridgend, a.s.n. John ; w. William Maben, George Stoddart.

„ „ James Bower and Agnes Miller in Melrose. a.d.n. Janet ; w. George Laurie, John Boston.

April 6. John Swenston and Isabel Lethain in Hagburn, a.s.n. John ; w. Andrew Gibson, Thomas Gibson.

„ 8. George Bell and Peggy Mertin in Melrose, a.s.n. John ; w. John Mertin, Thomas Boston.

„ 28. Charles Hislop and Katharine Thynn in Gattonside, a.s.n. William ; w. John Boston, William Darling.

„ 29. William Dickson and Isabel Fairbairn in Darnick, a.d.n. Isabel ; w. John Heitton, Robert Grierson.

May 6. William Stevenson and Janet Mein in Newstead, a.s.n. William ; w. John Dickson, Alexander Sibbald.

1780.

Oct. 22. James Orr and Grizel Man in Melrose, a.s.n. Andrew ; w. James Mein, James Habkirk.

1781.

May 20. John Hunter and Janet Waddel in Westhouses, a.s.n. Robert ; w. George Laurie, George Stoddart.

„ 20. George Laurie and Jean Stoddart in Danielton, a.d.n. Janet ; w. George Stoddart, John Hunter.

„ 27. William Drummond and Isabel Martin in Darnick, a.d.n. Isabel ; w. Andrew Murray, Andrew Heitton.

June 10. Thomas Lillie and Nelly Laidlaw in Langshaw, a.s.n. Robert ; w. Robert Kirkwood, William Blaikie.

July 14. James Hill and Jean Davidson in Melrose, a.s.n. James ; w. Thomas Davidson, James Hilson.

„ 15. David Ballantine and Janet Dabson in Galashiels, a.d.n. Mary ; w. Andrew Lumsden, Andrew Heitton.

„ 26. Mr. John Mercer and Mrs. Betty Wilkieson in Melrose, a.d.n. Isabel ; w. James Hilson, George Laurie.

„ 30. Nicol Stonhouse and Agnes Sibbald in Whitelees, a.s.n. James ; w. Thomas Stonhouse, Nicol Milne.

„ „ James Pringle and Isabel Layel in Melrose, a.s.n. Andrew ; w. John Layel, Thomas Brown.

„ „ Andrew Brown and Janet Wilson in Melrose, a.d.n. Margaret ; w. James Wilson, John Layel.

Aug. 19. John Smith and Mary Williamson in Darnick, a.d.n. Agnes ; w. James Williamson, Andrew Murray.

Sept. 9. Thomas Turnbull and Peggy Forsan in Gattonside, a.s.n. William ; w. William Mabon, James Hilson.

„ „ George Brownfield and Janet Waugh in Gattonside, a.d.n. Janet ; w. Thomas Turnbull, Robert Bunnie.

„ 23. Gideon Coaler and Margaret Stewart in Darnick, a.s.n. James ; w. John Layel, James Hilson.

Oct. 6. James Williamson and Agnes Pringle in Newsteid, a.d.n. ——.

„ 14. Thomas Boston and Isabel Boston in Gattonside, a.s.n. John ; w. John Boston, James Usher.

Nov. 5. William Shiel and Christian Paterson in Sunnyside, a.d.n. Isabel ; w. James Scott, Robert Paterson.

„ 8. William Gibson and Nelly Gill in Melrose. a.s.n. Alexander ; w. John Gill, senior, John Gill, junior.

„ 24. William Cook and Elizabeth Murray in Melrose, a.s.n. William ; w. Robert Trotter, John Martin.

„ 25. William Matheson and Janet Linsay in Gattonside, a.d.n. Janet ; w. George Laurie, William Mabon.

Dec. 2. John Elliot and Isabel Bunny in Newsteid, a.s.n. James ; w. Andrew Heitton, John Paterson.

„ „ John Paterson and Peggy Bower in Darnick, a.d.n. Margaret ; w. Andrew Heitton, James Usher.

1782.

Jan. 6. George Mercer and Janet Heitton in Darnick, a.s.n. George ; w. John Mercer, Andrew Heitton.

„ 10. Robert Marr and Peggy Williamson in Melrose, a.d.n. Joanna ; w. George Scott, Alexander Skirven.

„ „ George Skirven and Katharine Vogan in Melrose, a.d.n. Janet ; w. Alexander Skirven, George Scott.

„ 20. John Wright and Janet Freeman in Melrose, a.s.n. James ; w. Andrew Murray, George Scott.

„ 31. John Mein and Nelly Riddel in Newstead, a.d.n. Isabel ; w. Thomas Mein, William Ailly.

Feb. 1. William Baptie and Janet Stoddart in Williamlaw, a.d.n. Barbara ; w. George Mercer, James Sanderson.

„ 7. Robert Davidson and Katharine Williamson in Melrose, a.d.n. Jean ; w. Thomas Williamson, Thomas Boston.

„ 17. John Gill and Christian Hunter in Melrose, a.s.n. Thomas ; w. James Vair, James Stirling.

Mar. 3. Thomas Scott and Marion Grierson in Darnick, a.d.n. Agnes ; w. Robert Grierson, Andrew Lumesden.

April 4. John Moffat and Alison Loudain in Ouplaw, a.s.n. John ; w. Andrew Helliday, William Blaikie.

„ 7. James Usher and Peggy Grieve in Topfield, a.s.n. Andrew ; w. Robert Grierson, Andrew Murray.

„ „ Francis Elliot and Isabel Barcklay in Newstead, a.s.n. James ; w. James Usher, Robert Bunnie.

„ „ Henry Hope and Peggy Thomson at the Bleachfield, a.d.n. Agnes ; w. David Taylor, Robert Paterson.

„ 14. Mr. Frederic Maclagan and Mrs. Christian Turnbull in Melrose, a.s.n. William ; w. James Usher, Robert Paterson.

„ „ George Grahamslie and Janet Young in Melrose, a.d.n. Margaret ; . w. John Layel, James Pringle.

„ „ William Ailly and Agnes Darling in Melrose, a.d.n. Agnes ; w. John Layel, Andrew Heitton.

„ 28. Alexander Brownfield and Isabel Beanston in Gattonside, a.s.n. John : w. Alexander Brownfield, William Mabon.

„ „ Alexander Laing and Agnes Anderson in Melrose, a.s.n. George ; w. Andrew Heitton, Robert Grierson.

May 12. William Pringle and Mary Scott in Newstead, a.d.n. Agnes ; w. John Layel, Andrew Murray.

„ „ William Mabon and Peggy Brown in Newstead, a.d.n. Agnes ; w. John Layel, Andrew Murray.

„ „ Andrew Riddel and Betty Knox in Darnick, a.d.n. Betty ; w. John Laurie, Robert Grierson.

„ 19. Hugh Fairful and Agnes Maclechan in Melrose, a.d.n. Jean ; w. Adam Mabon, Robert Ballantine.

1781.

Sept. 15. James Walker and Jean Walker in Gattonside, a.s.n. Peter ; w. Alexander Mein, Andrew Morton.

1782.

June 2. David Kyle and Betty Kedzie in Melrose, a.d.n. Jean ; w. Alexander Lokie, Robert Penman.

„ 16. John Mein and Betty Kersel in Newstead, a.s.n. Andrew ; w. George Scott, James Hilson.

„ „ John Fisher and Betty Gilles in Darnick, a.d.n. Janet ; w. Andrew Murray, George Scott.

„ 23. John Fair and Nelly Smith in Gattonside, a.s.n. John ; w. John Sibbald, Thomas Boston.

„ „ Thomas Vair and Peggy Burnet in Darnick, a.d.n. Margaret ; w. John Boston, Robert Bunnie.

„ „ John Sibbald and Jean Laidlaw in Eildon, a.d.n. Marion ; w. John Fair, George Wight.

1782.

July 3. John Dickison and Agnes Frier in Gattonside, a.d.n. Betty; w. Robert Myles, James Marr.

,, 7. John Currie and Janet Fox in Newtown, a.s.n. Thomas; w. Andrew Lookup, James Hilson.

,, ,, John Dickson and Janet Sibbald in Gattonside, a.s.n. James; w. George Burton, Adam Mabon.

,, 21. John Martin and Janet Boston in Melrose, a.d.n. Jean; w. John Laurie, William Mabon.

,, ,, Thomas Hoyl and Peggy Gill in Melrose, a.d.n. Betty; w. John Gill, James Pringle.

,, 29. John Thomson and Betty Park in Melrose, a.d.n. Elizabeth; w. John Gill, James Stirling.

Aug. 11. George Laurie and Jean Stoddart in Danieltown, a.s.n. William; w. Robert Paterson, James Usher.

,, ,, James Ronaldson and Euphan Gray in Darnick, a.s.n. James; w. John Layel, George Laurie.

,, 25. Thomas Cleghorn and Peggy Bower in Westhouses, a.s.n. Thomas; w. Andrew Pringle, George Wight.

,, ,, Andrew Pringle and Peggy Familton in Newstead, a.s.n. Andrew; w. Thomas Cleghorn, Andrew Heitton.

,, ,, Robert Wight and Janet Brack in Darnick, a.s.n. John; w. George Wight, Robert Ballantine.

Sept. 6. Thomas Pringle and Agnes Hardie in Blainslie, a.d.n. Isabel; w. James Stirling, John Cleugh.

,, 8. William Paterson and Janet Drummond in Westhouses, a.s.n. John; w. William Mabon, James Usher.

,, ,, William Haitlie and Peggy Jamieson in Darnick, a.s.n. Thomas; w. William Paterson, Adam Ormiston.

,, 22. John Grahamslie and Mary Ormiston in Melrose, a.d.n. Janet; w. George Grahamslie, Adam Ormiston.

Oct. 6. John Miln and Alison Helliburton in Darnick, a.d.n. Elizabeth; w. James Stirling, John Layel.

,, ,, William Miller and Janet Mein in Newstead, a.d.n. Janet; w. John Miln, Robert Grierson.

,, 20. Thomas Scott and Isabel Martin in Gattonside, a.s.n. Thomas; w. John Layel, James Hilson.

,, 27. Mr. James Riddel and Betty Rutherford, a.d.n. Jean; w. Andrew Bell, William Mabon.

Nov. 3. Alexander Skirven and Peggy Cook in Melrose, a.s.n. William; w. Robert Bunnie, Andrew Heitton.

,, 17. Alexander Hobkirk and Barbara Amos in Melrose, a.d.n. Betty; w. James Laidlaw, Andrew Lumesden.

,, 24. Andrew Bunnie and Janet Haistie in Newstead, a.s.n. John; w. William Mabon, James Scott.

Dec. 1. Robert Ormiston and Nelly Cook in Melrose, a.s.n. James; w. James Slater, Robert Bunnie.

,, 8. James Notman and Beatrice Elliot in Melrose, a.s.n. James; w. Robert Grierson, William Mabon.

,, 12. George Wight and Mary Sclater in Darnick, a.s.n. John; w. James Wight, William Mercer.

,, 13. James Kirkwood and Jean Fairbairn in Langshaw, a.d.n. Janet; w. William Turner, William Blaikie.

,, 29. James Brown and Peggy Butler in Darnick, a.d.n. Margaret; w Robert Grierson, Robert Bunnie.

1783.

Jan. 19. John Walker and Peggy Ingles in Abbatslee, a.s.n. Thomas; w. James Scott, William Mabon.

,, 26. Robert Bunnie and Isabel Hoy in Newstead, a.s.n. Alexander; w. John Layel, William Mabon.

1783.

Mar. 9. Andrew Brown and Janet Wilson in Melrose, a.d.n. Agnes ; w. John Layel, James Pringle.

„ 9. William Cook and Elizabeth Murray in Melrose, a.d.n. Peggy ; w. Robert Trotter, Andrew Murray.

„ 16. John Forsyth and Jean Mein in Newstead, a.d.n. Janet ; w. Andrew Lumesdean, William Mabon.

„ 20. George Smith and Janet Wallace in Drygrange, Bridgend, a.d.n. Janet ; w. Andrew Bell, John Wedderlie.

„ „ John Wedderlie and Isabel Fiddes in Drygrange, a.d.n. Isabel ; w. George Smith, Andrew Bell.

„ 25. George Stoddart and Katharine Mackeal in Darnick, a.d.n. Margaret ; w. Robert Grierson, Thomas Vair.

„ 30. William Smith and Peggy Bunnie in Newstead, a.s.n. James ; w. Andrew Murray, James Hilson.

„ „ James Sclaiter and Ann Mein in Newstead, a.s.n. William ; w. George Scott, Walter Scott.

May 4. James Bower and Agnes Miller in Melrose, a.d.n. Ann ; w. Walter Scott, Andrew Murray.

„ „ Thomas Gray and Peggy Dunlop in Melrose, a.d.n. Jean ; w. Andrew Murray, Walter Scott.

„ „ William Wilson and Betty Mercer in Bridgend, a.s.n. James ; w. Robert Grierson, John Smith.

„ 26. Thomas Lillie and Nelly Laidlaw in Langshaw mill, a.s.n. George ; w. ——.

„ 28. John Smith and Mary Williamson in Darnick, a.s.n. John ; w. Thomas Williamson, John Gill.
N.B.—See Robert Bunzie's age, 28th June 1789.

June 1. George Pringle and Janet Blaikie in Newstead, a.d.n. Janet ; w. William Mabon, James Laidlaw.

„ „ Andrew Drummond and Peggy Heitton in Bridgend, a.d.n. Marion ; w. George Pringle, Andrew Heitton.

„ 22. Andrew Brown and Janet Smith in Westhouses, a.s.n. Andrew ; w. James Usher, Andrew Murray.

„ „ William Thomson and Agnes Oliver in Melrose, a.s.n. Robert ; w. John Martin and John Martin.
N.B.—John Stevenson's children are marked at the year 1789, June 8.

July 6. George Brownfield and Janet Waugh in Gattonside, a.s.n. John ; w. Alexander Brownfield, Alexander Laing.

„ „ William Matheson and Janet Linsay in Gattonside, a.d.n. Agnes ; w. George Brownfield, John Boston.

„ „ Alexander Laing and Agnes Anderson in Melrose, a.d.n. Jean ; w. James Pringle, George Laurie.

„ 20. William Melrose and Elizabeth Reppath in the Bleachfield, a.s.n William ; w. Andrew Murray, George Wight.

Aug. 10. —— and Isabel Ailly in Melrose, a.d.n. Isabel ; w. John Martin, John Maclagan.

„ 28. Andrew Brown and Janet Mather in Melrose, a.d.n. Agnes ; w. John Layel, James Pringle.

Oct. 20. John Dickison and Agnes Frier in Gattonside, a.s.n. Robert ; w. Thomas Purves, Robert Myles.

„ 23. Thomas Haig and Janet Bunnie in Drygrange, a.d.n. Jean ; w. Mr. John Hunter, William Bunnie.

1784.

Feb. 2. Mr. Frederick Maclagan and Mrs. Christian Turnbul in Melrose, a.d.n. Christian ; w. ——.

Mar. 27. John Turnbull and Isabel Brydon in Hagburn, a.s.n. John ; w. Thomas Gibson, John Dickson.

May 23. John Gill and Christian Hunter in Melrose, a.s.n. Robert ; w. John Layel, James Pringle.

1784.

May 23. William Chisholm and Agnes Heitton in Melrose, a.s.n James ; w. Andrew Murray, William Smith.

,, ,, Andrew Heitton and Janet Usher in Darnick, a.s.n. Andrew ; w. James Usher, John Paterson.

,, ,, Thomas Vair and Peggy Burnet in Darnick, a.s.n. Thomas ; w. David Taylor, John Layel.

,, ,, William Mabon and Peggy Brown in Newstead, a.s.n. John ; w. George Lawrie, George Skirven.

,, ,, Henry Hope and Peggy Thomson in Melrose Bleachfield, a.s.n. John ; w. James Usher, James Pringle.

,, ,, James Vair and Nellie Hunter in Melrose, a.s.n. Andrew ; w. Andrew Murray, William Smith.
(Examined Dan. M'Lain.)

,, ,, John Forest and Margaret Mason in Westhouses. a.d.n. Margaret : w. William Mabon, John Layel.

,, ,, James Usher and Peggy Grieve in Topfield, a.d.n. Janet ; w. James Pringle, James Hilson.

,, ,, John Wright and Janet Freeman in Melrose, a.d.n. Ann ; w. Robert Hilson, Henry Hope.

,, ,, Robert Marr and Peggy Williamson in Melrose, a.d.n. Mary ; w. Thomas Williamson, William Sibbald.

,, ,, George Hutcheson and Jean Goldie in Melrose, a.d.n. Isabel ; w. John Layel, James Hilson.

,, ,, James Pringle and Isabel Layel in Melrose, a.d.n. Janet ; w. John Layel, James Hilson.

,, ,, Robert Hilson and Susanna Ballantine in Melrose, a.d.n. Isabel ; w. Robert Ballantine, Andrew Murray.

,, ,, James Hog and Ann Shiel in Melrose, a.d.n. Sophia ; w. George Bell, John Layel.

,, ,, John Paterson and Isabel Henderson in Melrose, a.d.n. Margaret ; w. James Pringle, John Layel.

,, ,, George Skirven and Katherine Vogan in Melrose, a.s.n. George Skirven, was born on the 21st day of October last, and baptised this day ; w. John Layel, James Hilson.

,, 30. George Dickson and Elizabeth Fairbairn in Newstead, a.d.n. Agnes ; w. James Pringle, William Mabon.

July 18. James Johnston and Peggy Cowan in Melrose, a.s.n. William ; w. William Shiel, John Layel.

,, ,, John Cochrane and Janet Vair in Eildon, a.d.n. Peggy ; w. William Shiel, James Johnston.

,, ,, William Shiel and Christian Paterson in Darnick, a.s.n. Andrew ; w. John Cochran, James Pringle.

,, ,, Robert Fairbairn and Jean Martin in Newtown, a.d.n. Agnes ; w. Robert Grierson, James Scott.

,, 20. Mr. David Brown and Mrs. Anne Hepburn, his spouse, a.s.n. David, was born on the 7th day of July 1784 and baptised the 20th day thereof ; witnesses at the baptism are Mr. John Mercer, John Martin.

Aug. 22. William Stevenson and Janet Mein in Newsteid, a.s.n. Andrew ; w. Andrew Murray, Andrew Heitton.
(The last child, son to William Stevenson, was born on the 19th day of July last.)

,, ,, John Dickson and Janet Sibbald in Gattonside, a.s.n. Alexander ; w. Thomas Scott, Thomas Turnbull.

,, ,, Thomas Turnbull and Peggy Forsan in Gattonside, a.s.n. Andrew ; w. John Layel, William Mabon.

,, ,, Thomas Scott and Isabel Martin in Melrose, a.d.n. Christian ; w. Thomas Martin, John Dickson.

Sept. 19. Thomas Boston and Isobel Boston in Gattonside, a.s.n. Robert ; w. John Boston, John Martin.

1784.

Sept. 19. William Bunnie and Janet Mein in Newsteid, a.s.n. Robert ; w. John Layel, Andrew Heitton.

,, ,, James Dawson and Jean Simson in Melrose, a.s.n. John ; w. Robert Bunnie, William Mabon.

,, ,, William Anderson and Mary Scott in Gattonside, a.s.n. John ; w. Thomas Boston, William Millar.

,, ,, William Millar and Janet Mein in Newsteid, a.s.n. William ; w. John Boston, Robert Grierson.

,, ,, William Blaikie and Mary Aitchison in Colmslie, a.d.n. Mary ; w. John Smith, James Pringle.

,, ,, John Dunwoody and Isabel Mitchel in Gattonside, a.s.n. John ; w. John Boston, John Layel.

,, ,, William Edgar and Katharine Ronaldson in Melrose, a.d.n. Christian ; w. James Pringle, Alexander Brownfield.

,, ,, William Farmer and Isabel Fairbairn in Newtown, a.d.n. Isabel ; w. Thomas Boston Miller. This last child was born Jan. 8th, 1784.

Oct. 29. Thomas Bartrum and Jean Allan in Sorrowlessfield, a.d.n. Mary ; w. Mr. Laurance Johnston, Mr. John Martin.

Dec. 5. William Heart and Isabel Hutton in Darnock, a.d.n. Helen ; w. George Stoddart, Robert Grierson.

,, ,, George Stoddart and Katharine Makal in Darnick, a.d.n. Isabel ; w. James Hilson, George Laurie.

,, ,, George Laurie and Jean Stoddart in Danielton, ad.n. Janet ; w. George Stoddart, John Layel.

,, ,, William Smith and Peggy Bunnie in Newstead, a.d.n. Janet ; w. John Dickson, Andrew Murray.

,, 26. John Bower and Nelly Davidson in Melrose, a.s.n. John ; w. Thomas Boston, George Wight.

,, ,, Robert Boston and Katharine Graham in Darnick, a.d.n. Isabel ; w. William Smith, Robert Paterson.

1785.

Feb. 27. Robert Scott and Anne Sherrow in Gattonside, a.s.n. Andrew ; w. John Gill, Thomas Boston.

1784.

June 27. John Sibbald and Jean Laidlaw in Eildon, a.s.n. James ; w. William Rutherford, Robert Rutherford.

1785.

Mar. 1. John Wetherly and Isabel Fiddes in Drygrange mill, a.d.n. May was born on the 27th day of January last and baptised this day ; w. Adam Nicol, James Fiddes.

April 8. James Kirkwood and Jean Fairbairn in Langshaw mill, a.d.n. Helen, was born on the 21st day of October 1784, and baptized this day ; w. William Blaikie, William Thomson.

,, 17. Alexander Laing and Agnes Anderson in Melrose, a.s.n. Thomas ; w. James Sclaiter, John Paterson.

,, ,, Alexander Hobkirk and Barbara Amos in Melrose, a.d.n. Jean ; w. John Mein, George Pringle.

,, ,, Alexander Brockie and Violey Colleyr in Bamerside, a.d.n. Peggy ; w. Andrew Heitton, Andrew Murray.
    N. B. – See Jane Bunzie's age, 28th June 1789.

,, ,, John Paterson and Peggy Bower in Darnick, a.d.n. Janet ; w. John Layel, John Boston.

,, ,, James Sclaitter and Anne Mein in Newsteid, a.s.n. Robert ; w. John Mein, John Layel.

,, ,, George Pringle and Janet Blaikie in Newsteid, a.d.n. Isabel ; w. William Mabon, John Paterson.

,, ,, William Bunnie and Janet Mein in Newsteid, a.d.n. Jean ; w. John, Mein, George Pringle.

,, ,, John Fair and Nellie Smith in Gattonside, a.s.n. James ; w. James Sclaiter, Andrew Heitton.

1785.
May 1. George Wight and Mary Slaiter in Darnick, a.s.n. Robert ; w. William Mabon, John Layel.

,, ,, John Gramslie and Mary Ormiston, a.s.n. James, was born March 13th, 1785, in Melrose, and baptised this day ; w. George Wight, John Layel.

,, ,, George Mercer and Janet Heitton in Darnick, a.d.n. Helen ; w. Robert Grierson, James Hilson.

,, ,, Andrew Lees and Martha Lorain in Williamlaw, a.d.n. Betty, was born June 8th, 1784, and baptised this day ; w. ——.

July 24. James Williamson and Agnes Pringle in Newsteid, a.s.n. James ; w. Thomas Williamson, John Layel.

,, ,, John Smith and Mary Williamson in Darnick, a.s.n. Thomas ; w. James Williamson, Thomas Williamson.

,, ,, William Matheson and Janet Linsay in Gattonside, a.s.n. James ; w. John Layel, Andrew Murray.

,, ,, James Brown and Peggy Butler in Darnick, a.s.n. George ; w. Robert Grierson, John Layel.

,, ,, Andrew Hog and Agnes Fairbairn in Newsteid, a.s.n. William ; w. James Brown, John Smith.

,, ,, Thomas Gray and Peggy Dunlop in Melrose, a.d.n. Isabel ; w. James Hilson, John Gill.

Aug. 21. William Edgar and Katharine Ronaldson in Melrose, a.d.n. Isabel ; w. Andrew Murray, John Gill.

,, 28. John Laidlaw and Jamina Grant in Eildon peasehill, a.d.n. Nelly ; w. James Laidlaw, William Rutherford.

Nov. 27. Thomas Welsh and Betty Lunn in Westhouses, a.s.n. Thomas ; w. George Wight, John Moodie.

1786.
Feb. 4. This day was born James, son to Mr. David Brown and Mrs. Anne Hepburn, his spouse, and was baptised an the 23rd day of March 1786 years ; w. Mr. William Riddel, Mr. Andrew Murray.

May 7. William Ailly and Agnes Darling in Sorrowlessfield, a.d.n. Alison was baptised this day, and who was born May 6th, 1785 ; w. John Trotter, James Notman.

June 12. William Bathgate, see Register 1789, page 2.

Aug. 14. David Kyle and Agnes Scoon in Melrose, a.s.n. David, and born on the 29th day of December 1785 ; w. John Heiddon, James Pringle.

,, 21. Robert Brown and Elizabeth Henderson in Gattonside, a.s.n. Robert : w. Mr. John Gray.

Sept. 3. Andrew Heitton and Janet Usher in Darnick, a.s.n. George ; w. Mr. Andrew Fisher, Thomas Usher.

Oct. 22. John Laidlaw and Jamina Grant in Eildon, a.d.n. Janet ; w. George Scott, Robert Usher.

Dec. 17. John Pringle and Jean Grahmslie, in fornication, a.d.n. Margaret ; w John Layel, George Vair.

,, 27. James Usher and Peggy Grieve in Topfield, a.s.n. James, and was born June 1786 ; w. Thomas Usher, John Smith.

1787.
Jan. 7. Thomas Scot and Isabel Martin in Melrose, a.s.n. William ; w. Andrew Murray, Andrew Heitton.

,, ,, Andrew Riddell and Betty Knox in Darnick, a.d.n. Isabel ; w. Andrew Murray, Andrew Heitton.

,, ,, George Brownfield and Janet Waugh in Gattonside, a.d.n. Jean ; w. Andrew Murray, John Frier.

,, 12. John Walker and Margaret Ingles, a.s.n. Charles, was born this day and baptised the 2nd of February 1787 ; w. John Burn, Abbatslee.

,, 21. John Frier and Peggy Bathgate in Uperlangshaw, a.d.n. Agnes ; w. James Hilson, John Layel.

, ,, John Mein and Betty Kersal in Newsteid, a.d.n. Biggy ; w. John Frier, John Layel.

x

1787.

Feb. 22. Andrew Brown and Janet Maither in Melrose, a.d.n. Joanna ; w. Nicol Milne, Robert Paterson.

1785

Oct. 10. John Dickison and Agnes Frier in Gattonside, a.s.n. Thomas, was born on the 10th day October 1785, and baptised on the 16th day of January 1787 ; w. Robert Miels, James Marr.

1787.

Mar. 4. John Forsyth and Jean Mein in Drygrange, a.s.n. James ; w. Andrew Heitton, Andrew Murray.

„ „ George Pringle and Janet Blaikie in Newstead, a.d.n. Jean ; w. James Hilson, John Park.

„ 18. James Dawson and Jean Simpson in Melrose, a.s.n. Andrew ; w. James Hilson, John Layel.

„ „ George Vair and Katharine Ballantine in Danielton, a.s.n. Thomas ; w. James Dawson, William Stevenson.

„ „ James Sanderson and Mary Haldane in Melrose, a.s.n. James ; w. William Stevenson, George Vair.

„ „ William Stevenson and Janet Mein in Newstead, a.d.n. Nelly, born December 11th, 1786 ; w. John Layel, John Paterson.

„ „ Andrew Drumond and Peggy Heitton in Bridgend, a.s.n. William ; w. John Paterson, Robert Ballantine.

„ „ William Paterson and Janet Drummond in Westhouses, a.d.n. Nelly ; w. John Layel, Robert Grierson.

„ 25. John Paterson and Isabel Henderson, deceased, in Melrose, a.s.n. Robert ; w. John Bower, Alexander Laing.

„ „ Alexander Laing and Agnes Anderson in Melrose, a.s.n. Alexander ; w. John Martin, William Chisholm.

„ „ William Chisholm and Agnes Heitton in Melrose, a.s.n. James ; w. John Paterson, John Bower.

„ „ John Mertin and Marion Heitton in Melrose, a.d.n. Elizabeth ; w. James Wilson, Andrew Martin.

„ „ John Bower and Nelly Davidson in Melrose, a.d.n. Janet ; w. John Paterson, James Wilson.

„ „ Adam Bryden and Margaret Lockie in Newtown, a.d.n. Janet ; w. John Bower, James Wilson.

The last six children were baptised in Lauder Kirk by Mr. James Ford, minister there.

1785.

Aug. 16. Thomas Milne and Mary Shiels in Newtown, a.d.n. Anne ; w. John Shiel, Alexander Mein.

1787.

April 29. John Smith and Mary Williamson in Darnick, a.s.n. Andrew, was born March 13th, 1787, and baptised April 29th, 1787.

„ „ John Dickson and Christian Johnston in Gattonside, a.d.n. Isabel ; w. John Smith, Andrew Murrow.

1786.

Nov. 13. John Common and Margaret Common in Friarshall, a.d.n. Anne, and was born Nov. 3rd, 1786.

1787.

June 21. Jesse Maither and Isabel Matheson in Newtown, a.d.n. Isabel ; w. John Bertle, Andrew Mein.

„ „ Henry Hope and Peggy Thomson in Melrose, a.d.n. Meina ; w. John Layel, John Trotter.

„ „ James Hopkirk and Anne Wright in Melrose, a.s.n. David ; w. John Layel, John Trotter.

July 2. James Pringle and Isabel Layel in Melrose, a.d.n. Elizabeth, who was born in the 23rd day of October 1785, and baptised July 2nd, 1787 ; w. John Layel, David Burton.

Oct. 20. Andrew Brown and Janet Mather in Melrose, a.d.n. Jean ; w. Alexander Lockie, Nicol Mill.

Nov. 17. Thomas Scott and Isabel Martin in Melrose, a.d.n. Isabel ; w. ——.

1787.

Dec. 27. Thomas Williamson and Peggy Watson in Newstead, a.s.n. Jeames : w. James Williamson, George Mercer.

,, ,, James Williamson and Agnes Pringle in Newstead, a.d.n. Mary ; w. Thomas Williamson, George Mercer.

,, ,, John Musgrave and Katharine Jamieson in Melrose, a.d.n. Isabel : w. James Dawson, David Kyle.

,, ,, William Edgar and Katharine Ronaldson in Newstead, a.s.n. Andrew ; w. George Ronaldson, George Mercer.

,, ,, James Johnston and Peggy Cowan in Melrose, a.s.n. John ; w. James Williamson, John Musgrave.

,, ,, George Mercer and Janet Heitton in Darnick, a.d.n. Elizabeth ; w. Robert Grierson, James Williamson.

1788.

Jan. 3. John Laidlaw and Jamina Grant in the Peasehill of Eildon, a.s.n. James ; w. George Scott, James Rutherford.

1787.

June 24. William Chapman and Janet Riddell in Melrose, a.d.n. Peggy ; w. Andrew Merton, David Thomson.

1788.

Feb. 1. Mr. David Brown and Mrs. Anne Hepburn, his spouse, in Melrose, a.s.n. John, being born on the 15th day January last 1788 ; w. Joseph Gillon, Charles Erskine.

,, ,, John Gill and Christian Hunter in Melrose, a.d.n. Isabella ; w. Robert Hunter, James Johnston.

,, 3. John Middlton and Mary Bunzie in Newstead, a.s.n. George : w. William Millar, Andrew Heitton.

,, ,, James Sanderson and Mary Haldane in Melrose, a.s.n. John ; w. John Middlton, Andrew Heitton.

,, ,, Andrew Heitton and Janet Usher in Darnick, a.s.n. Robert ; w. John Heitton, Robert Grierson.

,, ,, John Paterson and Peggy Bower in Darnick, a.s.n. John ; w. John Layel, Andrew Murray.

,, ,, Mr. William Hoy and the deceased Janet Sibbald, his spouse, in Gattonside, a.d.n. Janet ; w. Andrew Heitton, Robert Grierson.

,, ,, John Bell and Peggy Turnbull in Newstead, a.d.n. Jean ; w. John Layel, John Boston.

,, ,, William Millar and Janet Mein in Newstead, a.d.n. Mary ; w. John Middlton, John Bell.

,, 6. William Smith and Peggie Bunzie in Newstead, a.s.n. William ; w. Andrew Bunzie, John Martin.

,, 7. George Laurie and Jean Stoddart in Danieltown, a.s.n. Andrew, was born on the 9th day of November 1786, and baptised on the 7th day of February 1788.

,, 20. William Hart and Isabell Heitton in Melrose, a.d.n. Anne ; w. Robert Grierson, George Stoddart.

,, 28. Thomas Haig and Janet Bunzie in Drygrange, a.d.n. Janet, who was born June 30th, 1786 ; w. James Notman, Thomas Learmont.

,, ,, Robert Boston and Katharine Graham in Darnick, a.s.n. John, was born in January 22nd, and baptised March 6th, 1787 : w. Robert Myles, James Rutherford.

Mar. 16. Thomas Stevenson and Janet Ormiston in Darnick, a.s.n. Adam ; w. Robert Grierson, James Slaiter.

,, ,, Thomas Scott and Euphan Smith in Melrose, a.s.n. Robert : w. William Matheson, Robert Ballantin.

,, ,, William Matheson and Janet Lindsay in Gattonside, a d.n. Janet ; w. Thomas Stevenson, Andrew Scott.

,, ,, Andrew Scott and Grissel Sawrs in Newstead, a.d.n. Agnes ; w. James Slaiter, William Matheson.

,, ,, William Shiel and Christian Paterson in Sunniside of Darnick, a.s.n. John ; w. John Gill Andrew Murray.

1788.

April 13. Thomas Taylor and Jean Trotter in Melrose, a.s.n. David ; w. David Taylor, John Trotter.

  „ 22. William Mabon and Margaret Brown in Newstead, a.s.n. James, was born July 21st, 1787 ; w. James Ramsay, Andrew Bunzie.

  „   „ Walter Thomson and Mary Blek in Westhouses, a.d.n. Mary, was born on the 23rd day of April 1782, and baptised on the 10th day of June 1787.

  „   „ John Dickieson and Agnes Frier, a.d.n. Janet, was born on the 9th day of April 1788, and baptised on the 6th day of June 1788 ; w. James Frier, James Marr.

  „   „ William Stevenson and Anne Gray in Newtown, a.d.n. Jean ; w. Thomas Laidlaw, Jesse Mather.

  „   „ Jesse Mather and Isabel Matheson in Newtown, a.s.n. Andrew ; w. William Stevenson, Thomas Laidlaw.

June 8. John Burn and Grissel Ingles in Melrose, a.d.n. Grissel ; w. Andrew Murray, James Usher.

  „   „ John Burn and Grissel Ingles in Melrose, a.s.n. William, was baptised at Blainslie by Mr. James Ford, minister at Lauder ; w. John Walker, February 2nd, 1787.

  „ 22. James Wilkie and Jean Stonhouse in Gattonside, a.s.n. John ; w. John Boston, John Musgrave.

(Beginning of W. Turnbull's Entries.)

July 13. William Cook and Elizabeth Murray in Melrose, a.d.n. Elizabeth ; w. George Laurie, Adam Mill.

  „ 30. Doctor Samuel Davidson and Christian Anderson in Melrose, a.d.n. Jean ; w. Archibald Anderson, Archibald Mitchell.

Sept. 7. William Chisholm and Agnes Heiton in Melrose, a.d.n. Helen ; w. John Martin, James Boston.

  „ 21. James Binning and Betty Ker in Katefield, a.d.n. Isobel ; w. John Martine and John Martine.

Nov. 2. William Edgar and Christian Ronaldson in Newstead, a.s.n. George ; w. James Blaikie, Robert Paterson.

  „   „ James Brown and Peggy Buttler in Darnick, a.s.n. John ; w. James Blaikie, Robert Paterson.

  „   9. George Pringle and Jannet Blaikie in Newstead, a.d.n. Elizabeth, born 3rd October ; w. James Blaikie, David Kyle.

  „ 10. John Swanston and Isabel Lothian in Threepwood, two daughters named Marion and Margaret, baptised 22nd May 1783 ; w. John Graham, John Lothian.

  „   „ Dr. John Swanston and Isabel Lothian in Threepwood, a.s.n. Andrew, baptised 22nd March 1785 ; w. John Moffat, James Mitchel.

  „ 23. John Dickson and Jannet Sibbald in Gattonside, a.s.n. John, born 2nd August ; w. James Laidlaw, John Martin.

  „   „ John Sibbald and Jean Laidlaw in Eildon, a.d.n. Agnes, born 28th August 1788 ; w. James and Thomas Laidlaws.

Dec. 9. Robert Kirkwood and Isabel Sibbald in Blainslie, two sons named Alexander and William ; w. James Stirling, James Wilson.

  „ 25. David Kyle and Agnes Scoon in Melrose, a.d.n. Isabella Kyle, born 14th April 1787, and baptised 25th Dec. 1788 : w. Robert Hunter, Mr. Aitchieson.

  „   „ Alexander Laing and Agnes Anderson in Melrose, a.d.n. Margaret Laing, born Nov. 7th, 1788, and baptised 21st Dec. 1788 ; w. Robert Paterson, James Brown.

  „ 28. George Heitton and Janet Scott, a.d.n. Betty ; w. Walter Turnbull, John Martin.

1789.

Jan. 4. Alexander Bell and Margaret Stewart in Melrose, a.d.n. Elizabeth, born 21st June 1788 and baptised this day : w. Walter Turnbull, John Martin.

1789.

Jan. 18. John Bell and Margaret Turnbull in Melrose, a.s.n. James ; w. Walter Turnbull, John Martin.

1786.

June 12. George Bathgate, wright at Darlingshaugh, and Alison Purves, a 1st son, named William, baptised 28th June 1786 ; w. John Bathgate, William Thomson.

1788.

Nov. 20. George Bathgate and Alison Purves in Darlingshaugh, a 2nd son, named Simon, baptised 9th December 1788 ; w. John Bathgate, Robert Dickson.

1789.

Feb. 10. Thomas Boston and Isabel Boston in Gattonside, a.d.n. Nelly, born 17th January 1789 and baptised 8th February 1789 ; w. Mr. John Mill, William Buttler.

" 13. Alexander Hobkirk and Barbara Amos in Melrose, a.s.n. William : w. Walter Turnbull, John Martin.

" 22. Andrew Hogg and Agnes Fairbairn in Melrose, a.d.n. Elizabeth ; w. David Kyle, Andrew Ronaldson.

" " James Turner and Janet Horsbrugh in Calfhill, a.d.n. Janet ; w. David Kyle, Andrew Ronaldson

" " James Sclater and Anne Mien in Newstead, a.s.n. Andrew, born 10th Dec. 1788 ; w. David Kyle, Andrew Ronaldson.
N.B.—See John Sclaiter, marked in the year 1799.

Mar. 12. John Lothian and Anne Welsh in Westhouses, a.s.n. James, baptised by Mr. Elder, minister in Newtown ; w. James Clapperton, John Scott.

" 29. Henry Hope and Margaret Thomson in Melrose, a.d.n. Agnes ; w. David Kyle, John Haldean.
N.B.—Agnes Hope was born the 11th November 1788.

April 5. John Common and Margaret Common in Friarshall, below Gattonside, a.s.n. John, born 15th January 1789 ; w. David Kyle, John Haldean.

" " John Laidlaw and Jemima Grant in Eildon, a.s.n. John, baptised 19th March 1789 ; w. James Marr, James Rutherford.

" 11. George Rea and Jannet Vair in Newton, a.s.n. Thomas, born 19th May 1778 ; w. Robert Easton, William Bichet.

" 12. Andrew Riddle and Elizabeth Knox in Darnick, a.s.n. Andrew ; w. David Kyle, Andrew Ronaldson.

" 14. George Laurie and Jean Stoddart in Danzielton, a.d.n. Alison ; w. William Cook, William Donaldson.

" 23. Andrew Scot and Grizel Sawers in Newstead, a.s.n. Alexander, born 1st March last 1789 ; w. David Kyle, John Haldean.

" 26. Andrew Lambart and Agnes Mason in Newstead, a.s.n. George, born 14th Nov. 1787 ; w. George Scot, John Martin.

" " George Wyllie and Margaret Wyllie in Newstead, a.s.n. James, born 5th March 1789 ; w. David Kyle, John Haldean.

" " Alexander Muir and Janet Hymers in Melrose, a.s.n. John, born 2nd Oct. last ; w. David Kyle, John Haldean.

" " George Brownfield and Janet Waugh in Gattonside, a.d.n. Mein, born 2nd Feb. 1789 ; w. David Kyle, John Haldean.

" " James Kemp and Christian Skirvan in Melrose Bleachfield, a.s.n. William, born 9th June 1788 ; w. David Kyle, John Haldane.

May 10. Robert Crawford and Jean Hogg, a.d.n. Jean, born 7th September 1786, Melrose.

" " Robert Crawford and Jean Hogg, a.s.n. John, born 21st September 1788 ; w. George Scott, John Martin.

" 24. William Mathison and Janet Lindsay in Gattonside, a.s.n. William ; w. John Haldean, Alexander Bell.

" " John Smith and Mary Williamson in Darnick, a.d.n. Mary ; w. John Haldean Alexander Bell.

1789.

May 31. William Burns and Alison Fait in Housebyre, a.s.n. William, born 2nd June 1788 ; w. John Haldane, Alexander Bell.

June 7. Robert Boston and Katharine Graham, a.s.n. William ; w. Robert Grierson, Thomas Vair.

,, 14. John Jamieson and Agnes Hay in Newtoun, a.s.n. William ; w. John Haldean, James Scott.

,, ,, William Chapman and Janet Riddel in Melrose, a.d.n. Janet ; w. David Thomson, John Scott.

,, 28. Robert Anderson and Jean Wilson in Newstead, a.d.n. Margaret ; w. John Martin, Walter Turnbull. This child was born 27th March last, O.S.

,, ,, William Bunzie and Janet Mein in Newstead, a.s.n. Robert, born October 24th, 1783.

,, ,, The above William Bunzie and Janet Mein, a.d.n. Jane, born 26th January 1785.

,, ,, The above William Bunzie and Janet Mein, a.s.n. John, born 26th May 1789 ; w. James Blaikie, James Mein.

,, ,, Adam Bryden and Margaret Lockie in Newton, a.d.n. Peggy ; w. Walter Turnbull, David Kyle.

1783.

Dec. 28. John Stevenson and Isabel Waugh in Bridgend, a.s.n. William ; w. James Slater, William Stevenson.

1785.

June 8. John Stevenson and Isabel Waugh in Darnick, a.s.n. Thomas ; w. Thomas Wilson, William Martin.

1787.

June 26. John Stevenson and Isabel Waugh in Darnick, a.s.n. John ; w. Thomas Wilson, William Martin.

1789.

July 5. James Hobkirk and Agnes Wright in Melrose, a.s.n. John ; w. Robert Paterson, James Blaikie.

,, 19. John Grieve and Isabel Marr in Gattonside, a.d.n. Margaret, born 16th Sept. 1788 ; w. John Martin, Andrew Ronaldson.

,, ,, George Stewart and Isabel Dickson in Gattonside, a.s.n. Archibald, born 27th February 1788 ; w. John Martin, John Martin, junior.

,, ,, Lieut. Robert Aitchison, Royal Navy, and Mrs. Mary Scott in Melrose, a.s.n. Robert Scott, born 7th July, baptised 17th ditto ; w. Robert Aitchison, William Turnbull.

Aug. 2. James Dawson and Jean Simpson in Melrose, a.s.n. James ; w. James Scott, Robert Heymer.

,, 8. James Stirling and Nelly Kirkwood in Blainslies, a.s.n. Thomas, born 16th Oct. 1786.

,, ,, James Stirling and Nelly Kirkwood in Blainslies, a.s.n. Robert, born 5th March 1789 ; w. Robert Stirling, Thomas Laidlaw.

,, 9. John Fair and Nelly Smith in Gattonside, a.s.n. Andrew ; w. James Blaikie, Robert Paterson.

,, ,, Alexander Sanderson and Helen Philips in Melrose, a.s.n. Robert ; w. James Blaikie, Robert Paterson.

,, ,, Thomas Williamson and Margaret Watson, a.d.n. Christian, baptised 19th July 1789 ; w. John Martin, Andrew Ronaldson.

,, 16. George Graham and Joan Riddell in Colinslies, a.d.n. Martha ; w. James Blaikie, Robert Paterson.

1784.

July 21. Andrew Sanderson and Jane Scott in Kersfield, a.s.n. Thomas.

1786.

Mar. 28 Andrew Sanderson and Jane Scot in Kersfield, a.s.n. John.

1788.

May 31. Andrew Sanderson and Jane Scot in Kersefield, a.d.n. Janet ; w. John Watson, John Cochron.

1789.
Oct. 18. Thomas Haig and Janet Bunzie in Drygrange, a.d.n. Agnes.
,, ,, William Edgar and Christian Ronaldson in Newstead, a.d.n. Agnes ;
w. John Haldane, John Martin.
Nov. 8. Andrew Drummond and Margaret Heaton in Bridgend, a.s.n. John ;
w. Andrew Heaton, John Heaton.
,, 15. James Johnstone and Margaret Cowans in Melrose, a.d.n. Jean.
,, ,, George Kay and Catharine Phillips in Darnick, a.d.n. Mary Kay.
born 15th October 1789 ; w. James Blaikie, Robert Paterson.
1786.
Nov. 10. The above George Kay and Catharine Phillips, a.s.n. James, born
6th October 1786 ; w. James Usher, John Smith.
1789 (?)
Nov. 29. William Smith and Margaret Bunzie in Newstead, a.s.n. Andrew ; w.
Andrew Heiton, Andrew Riddell.
Dec. 13. Alexander Bell and Margaret Stewart in Melrose, a.d.n. Janet, born
28th October 1789 ; witnesses to the baptism, Walter Turnbull,
John Martin.
1790.
Jan. 10. David Kyle and Agnes Scoon in Melrose, a.d.n. Janet, born 12th
January 1789 ; w. to the baptism, Andrew Mabon, David
Haldane.
,, 13. John Cochran and Agnes Leeden in Newtown, a.s.n. John, born 3rd
September 1789 ; w. to the baptism, Nicol Milne, James Laidlaw.
,, 17. James Kemp and Christian Skirvan in Melrose Bleechfield, a.s.n.
John, born on the 4th January 1790 ; w. to the baptism, John
Haldane, David Kyle.
,, 19. John Gill and Christian Hunter in Melrose, a.s.n. Hunter Gill, born
17th December 1789 ; w. Robert Hunter, John Hogg.
,, 24. Thomas Scott and Isabel Martin in Melrose, a.d.n. Jean ; w. David
Kyle, John Haldane.
,, ,, Alexander Laing and Agnes Anderson in Melrose, a.s.n. John ; w.
Robert Paterson, James Blaikie.
,, 27. George Johnstone in Darlingshaugh and Agnes Watt, a.s.n. Ebenezer,
born 5th Dec. 1789 ; w. to the baptism, James Blaikie, Alexander
Kyle.
Feb. 14. Andrew Grierson and Isobell Adamson in Danielton, a.d.n. Nelly ; w.
Robert Heymers, John Knox.
Mar. 4. William Mabon and Margaret Brown in Newstead, a.s.n. William ;
w. David Kyle, James Kemp.
,, 25. John Neil and Jean Milne in Westerhousebyres, a.s.n. Andrew ; w.
Walter Turnbull, John Knox.
,, 29. John Moffat and Alison Lowden in Bent miln, a.s.n. George ; w.
John Cleugh, John Friar.
April 11. Robert Darling and Sarah Riddell in Melrose, a.d.n. Isoble ; w.
John Haldane, John Martine.
,, ,, William Hart and Isoble Heitton in Melrose, a.s.n. George ; w. John
Haldane, John Martine.
,, 18. James Bell and Janet Bruce in Drygrange, a.d.n. Jean ; w. Robert
Heymers, John Martin.
May 9. John Mossgrave and Grizel, say Katharine, Jamieson in Melrose, a.d.n.
Margaret ; w. William Cook, John Martine.
1785.
Mar. 1. James Martine and Margaret Ewans in Melrose, a.s.n. Andrew, born
1st March 1785.
1786.
April 7. Ditto James Martine and Margaret Ewans in Melrose, a.d.n. Agnes,
born 1st April 1786.
1789.
Dec. 5. Ditto James Martine and Margaret Ewans, a.s.n. John, born 5th
Dec. 1789.

1790.

June 13. George Pringle and Janet Blaikie in Newstead, a.d.n. Margaret, born
    16th May 1790.

„   „   William Burns and Alison Tait in Easterhousebyre, a.d.n. Margaret.

„   „   George Stewart and Isabel Dickson in Gattonside, a.d.n. Isabel ; w.
    John Haldane, Andrew Bell.

„   14. Jesse Mather and Isabel Mathison in Newtoun, a.s.n. James, born
    26th May 1790 ; w. to the baptism, Nicol Milne, John Cochran.

„   28. Thomas Stark and Margaret Carter in Blainslies, a.s.n. William.

„   „   John Lowdon and Janet Waddie in Blainslies, a.d.n. Janet Lowdon ;
    w. James Stirling, James Wilson.

„   „   Andrew Sanderson and Jane Scot in Kersfield, a.d.n. Agnes, born 1st
    July ; w. John Watson, John Cochran.

July 15. Mr. David Brown and Mrs. Ann Hepburn, his spouse, in Melrose,
    a.d.n. Mary Ann, born 24th June and baptised 15th July 1790 ; w.
    Charles Erskine, William Scot.

„   18. James Inglis and Margaret Dun in Greenwalls, a.d.n. Elizabeth ; w.
    John Martin, Andrew Bell.

„   22. Robert Bunzie and Isabel Hoy in Newstead, a.d.n. Barbara, born
    28th July 1789 and baptised 22nd July 1790 ; w. John Haldane,
    Andrew Bell.

„   26. John Grieve and Isabel Mar in Gattonside, a.s.n. James, born 17th
    June and baptised 26th July 1790 ; w. John Martin, John Mar.

Aug. 1. William Paterson and Janet Drummond in Westhouses, a.s.n.
    William ; w. John Martin, Robert Paterson.

„   „   William Ker and Nelly Laidlaw in Newstead, a.s.n. Alexander, born
    24th April and baptised 23rd May 1790 ; w. James Laidlaw, Nicol
    Milne.

„   31. William Haig and Janet Anderson in Danielton, a.s.n. William, born
    11th April 1789 and baptised nine weeks after in Newtown meeting
    house.

Sept. 26. William Millar and Janet Mein in Newstead, a.s.n. Andrew ; w.
    Robert Paterson, James Lindsay.

Oct.   3. John Forsyth and Jean Mein in Drygrange, a.d.n. Jean ; w. Robert
    Paterson, James Blaikie.

„   24. John Middlemas and Mary Bunzie in Newstead, a.s.n. James ; w.
    Robert Bunzie, George Pringle.

„   31. William Galloway and Euphan Scott in Melrose, a.s.n. William ; w.
    Robert Paterson, John Martine.

Nov.   5. John Milne and Alison Haliburton in Darnick, a.d.n. Isabel ; w.
    Robert Grierson, Andrew Heiton.

„   21. Robert Crawford and Jean Hog in Melrose, a.s.n. George ; w.
    Robert Paterson, John Martine.

„ (Dec.?) 5. John Burns and Grizel Inglis in Melrose, a.s.n. James ; w.
    John Martine, Robert Paterson.

1791.

Jan.   2. John Marr and Janet Helliwell in Gattonside, a.s.n. Robert ; w.
    Thomas Boston, Alexander Sibbet.

„   „   James Slater and Anne Mein in Newstead, a.d.n. Mary ; w. John
    Mein, George Pringle.

„   9. Robert Anderson and Jean Wilson in Newstead, a.d.n. Elizabeth ; w.
    George Pringle, James Fettes.

„   12. George Bathgate, wright, and Alison Purves, his spouse, in Darlings-
    haugh, a 1st daughter named Alison, born 29th Dec. 1790 and
    baptised this day ; w. John Bathgate, Robert Dickson.

„   23. George Hatton and Janet Scott in Melrose, a.s.n. John ; w. John
    Bower, John Hatton.

„   30. George Vair and Katharine Ballantyne in Danieltone, a.d.n. Nelly ;
    w. George Laurie, Thomas Scott.

Feb. 13. William Cessford and Nelly Turnbull in Gattonside, a.d.n. Christian ;
    w. Thomas Boston, John Cessford.

1791.
Feb. 13 David Kyle and Agnes Scoon in Melrose, a.d.n. Elizabeth, born 24th Dec. 1790 ; w. to the baptism, John Haldane, Thomas Scoon.

Mar. 6. James Scot and Isabel Martine in Melrose, a.d.n. Isabel.

  ,,   ,, Alexander Hobkirk and Barbara Amos in Melrose, a.d.n. Christian ; w. James Hobkirk, Robert Paterson.

  ,,   9. James Millar and Mary Sibbald in Wooplaw, a.d.n. Jean.

  ,,   ,, James Turner and Janet Horsburgh in Coomsliehill, a.s.n. James.

  ,,   ,, William Blaikie and Mary Aitchison in Ladhopmoor, a.d.n. Agnes.

  ,,   ,, Walter Chisholm and Jean Cowan in Langshawmill, a.s.n. James : w. John Cleugh, James Scott.

  ,, 27. John Smith and Margaret Oliver in Darnick, a.d.n. Isabel.

  ,,   ,, James Brown and Margaret Buttler in Darnick, a.d.n. Jean ; w. Robert Grierson, Andrew Heitton.

April 2. William Cook and Elizabeth Murray in Melrose, a.d.n. Elizabeth, born 15th March and baptised 21st March 1791 ; w. Andrew Murray, Charles Erskine.

  ,,   ,, Andrew Ronaldson, writer, and Mrs. Margaret Smith, his spouse, in Melrose, a.s.n. James Smith Ronaldson, born on the 19th February and baptised 8th March 1791 ; w. Captain Gillon, Robert Taket.

  ,, 17. Robert Nicol and Margaret Heart in Drygrange Tollbarr, a.s.n. Adam, born 24th February and baptised 17th April 1791.

  ,,   ,, John Heiton and Jannet Elliot in Darnick, a.d.n. Elizabeth, born 12th March, and baptised 17th April 1791 ; w. Francis Burnet, Andrew Heiton.

  ,, 24. Andrew Hog and Agnes Fairbairn in Melrose, a.d.n. Agnes.

  ,,   ,, Thomas Welsh and Betty Lun in Danielton, a.d.n. Mary ; w. William Cook, John Martine.

May 1. William Stevenson and Anne Gray in Newtown, a.s.n. John.

  ,,   ,, John Jamieson and Agnes Hay in Newtown, a.d.n. Christian ; w. Nicol Milne, Thomas Laidlaw.

  ,,   ,, Alexander Bell and Margaret Steuart in Melrose, a.d.n. Margaret, born 20th April.

  ,,   8. John Martine and Marrion Heiton in Melrose, a.s.n. George.

  ,,   ,, George Mercer and Janet Heiton in Darnick, a.s.n. John ; w. Andrew Heiton, John Heiton.

  ,, 11. Thomas Boston and Elizabeth Boston in Gattonside, a.s.n. James ; w. John Boston, George Stewart.

  ,, 22. James Chambers and Mary Fowler in Galashiels Toll-bar, a.d.n. Janet : w. William Oliver, William Craig.

  ,,   ,, James Hobkirk and Anne Wright in Melrose, a.d.n. Margaret ; w. Robert Paterson, Andrew Bell.

  ,,   ,, John Common and Margaret Common in Friarshall, a.d.n. Margaret, born 23rd January 1791.

  ,, 31. John Dickison and Agnes Friar in Cattonside, a.s.n. John ; w. Robert Miles, George Mercer.

  ,,   ,, John Laidlaw and Jemima Grant in Peasehill, a.s.n. Nicol, baptised 27th March 1791 and born 31st October 1790 ; w. William Wallace, William Reid.

  ,,   ,, James Friar and Elizabeth White in Darlingshaugh, a.s.n. Edward, born 3rd October 1790 ; w. to the baptism, Robert Gill, Hugh Sanderson.

1789.
July 24. John Stevenson and Isabel Waugh in Bridgend, a.s.n. George ; w. Andrew Mercer, John Leech.

1791.
May 16. Lieut. Robert Aitchison, Royal Navy, and Mrs. Mary Scot, his spouse, in Melrose, a.s.n. William Oliver Aitchison, born 22nd April 1791, and baptised this day ; w. Messrs. Thomas Gillon, Charles Erskine.

1791.

June 5. Robert Boston and Catharine Graham in Darnick, a.s.n. William.

,, ,, George Moss and Janet Kennedy in Brigend, a.d.n. Nancy.

,, ,, James Jamieson and Margaret Ormistone in Melrose, a.d.n. Isabel.

,, ,, George Cook and Margaret Sanderson in Melrose, a.d.n. Margaret ; w. William Cook, Robert Taket.

,, ,, Francis Burnet and Joan Williamson in Newstead, a.d.n. Elizabeth, baptised 17th April 1791 ; w. John Mein, George Pringle.

,, ,, William Stevenson and Janet Mein in Newstead, a.s.n. John, born 21st December 1790, and baptised 10th April 1791 ; w. Andrew Bunzie, William Mabon.

July 3. John Sibbald and Jean Laidlaw in Eildon, a.d.n. Nelly, born 26th May 1791, and baptised this day ; w. James Laidlaw, Thomas Laidlaw.

,, 17. William Cowan and Nelly Fisher in Whitehill, a.s.n. Robert.

,, ,, Robert Kemp and Jean Graham in Darnick, a.s.n. William ; w. James Kemp, William Graham.

,, 24. Alexander Sanderson and Hellen Phillips in Melrose, a.s.n. James ; w. William Cook, Robert Taket.

,, ,, William Wilson and Beety Richardson in Bridgend, a.d.n. Nelly, born 2nd February 1786 ; and

,, ,, William Willson and Beety Richardson in Bridgend, a.s.n. William, born 4th Dec. 1790, and both baptised 29th October 1790 ; w. James Usher, Andrew Heiton.

Aug. 11. John Renwick and Janet Kennedy in Buckholm, a.d.n. Isabel ; w. John Murray, Andrew Bell.

,, 21. Robert Jamieson and Agnes Mercer in Melrose, a.d.n. Elizabeth ; w. Robert Taket, William Cook.

,, 28. Adam Anderson and Violet Cranstone in Melrose, a.s.n. James.

,, ,, James Rutherford and Agnes Hog in Melrose, a.s.n. James ; w. Nicol Milne, William Cook.

Sept. 4. Robert Scot and Jannet Cochran in Newtoun, a.s.n. Thomas ; w. Nicol Milne, William Cook.

1779. James Clapperton and Mary Boston in Westerlanglee, a.s.n. John, born 18th February 1779.

1780. James Clapperton and Mary Boston in Westerlanglee, a.d.n. Janet, born 6th October 1780.

1782. James Clapperton and Mary Boston in Westerlanglee, a.d.n. Isabel, born 4th January 1782 ; these three baptised at Westerlanglee ; w. Simon Bathgate, James Ketchen.

1783. James Clapperton and Mary Boston in Westerhousebyre, a.d.n. Mary, born 12th November 1783.

1785. James Clapperton and Mary Boston in Westerhousebyre, a.d.n. Jane, born 28th June 1785.

1787. James Clapperton and Mary Boston in Westerhousebyre, a.s.n. James, born 20th November 1787.

1788. James Clapperton and Mary Boston in Westerhousebyre, a.d.n. Christian, born 20th November 1788 ; these four baptised at Westerhousebyre ; w. John Bathgate, James Ketchen.

1791.

Sept. 12. James Stirling and Hellen Kirkwood in Blainslies, a.d.n. Isabel ; w. James Wilson, Thomas Pringle.

,, 18. James Nicol and Alison Mein in Drygrange, a.d.n. Agnes ; w. John Mein, Robert Nicol.

,, 25. Robert Ormistone and Hellen Cook in Melrose, a.s.n. George ; w. Robert Taket, William Cook.

,, ,, Frances Elliot and Isabel Bartleman in Maxpople, parish of Lessuden, a.d.n. Sina ; w. Robert Ormistone, William Cook.

Oct. 16. Thomas Usher and Elizabeth Stevenson in Newstead, a.d.n. Helen ; w. William Mabon, George Pringle.

1791.
Oct. 23. George Kay and Katharine Phillips in Darnick, a.s.n. John ; w. Andrew Phillips, **Andrew Riddell.**

1789. William Sanderson and Margaret Walker in Darlingshaugh, a.d.n. Elizabeth, born 16th November 1789.

1791. William Sanderson and Margaret Walker in Darlingshaugh, a.d.n. Christian, born 2nd July 1791 ; w. Adam Young, Thomas Pringle.

1787. Robert Scot and Isabel Lang in Darlingshaugh, a.s.n. James, born 19th May 1787.

1789. Robert Scot and Isabel Lang in Darlingshaugh, a.s.n. Robert, born 29th December 1789.

1791. Robert Scot and Isabel Lang in Darlingshaugh, a.d.n. Isabel, born 18th August 1791 ; w. Adam Young, Thomas Pringle.

1784. Robert Walker, dyer, and Janet Lang in Darlingshaugh, a.s.n. Robert, born 17th September 1784.

1787. Robert Walker and Janet Lang in Darlingshaugh, a.s.n. James, born 27th April 1787.

1789. Robert Walker and Janet Lang in Darlingshaugh, a.d.n. Mary, born 15th May 1789.

1791. Robert Walker and Janet Lang in Darlingshaugh, a.s.n. John, born 25th July 1791 ; w. George Litster, Adam Young.

1791. Adam Paterson and Elizabeth Tait in Darlingshaugh, a.s.n. William, born 8th Feb. 1791 ; w. George Litster, Adam Young.

1788. Thomas Pringle and Mary Inglis in Darlingshaugh, a.d.n. Jean, born 29th May 1788 ; w. John Leech, William Wilkie.

1791. Thomas Pringle and Mary Inglis in Darlingshaugh, a.d.n. Margaret, born 10th June 1791 ; w. William and John Renwick.

1789. George Mercer and Elizabeth Thorburn in Wilderthaugh, a.d.n. Isabel, born 3rd Aug. 1789 ; w. William and Adam Wilson.

1790. Adam Wilson and Agnes Douglas in Willderthaugh, a.s.n. Thomas, born 12th Sept. 1790 : w. John Watson, Richard Lees.

1791.
May 31. James Kemp and Christian Skirvan in Bleechfield, a.d.n. Georgina : w. James Rutherfurd, Alexander Skirvan.

Oct. 23. Thomas Williamson and Margaret Watson in Newsteid, a.d.n. Elizabeth ; w. George Pringle, William Bunzie.

1780. John Murray and Elizabeth Laidlaw in Bucholm, a.s.n. Robert, born 2nd Aug. 1780.

1782. John Murray and Elizabeth Laidlaw in Buckholm, a.s.n. Alexander, born 7th March 1782.

1783. John Murray and Elizabeth Laidlaw in Buckholm, a.d.n. Elizabeth, born 1st April 1783.

1784. John Murray and Elizabeth Laidlaw in Buckholm, a.s.n. Walter, born 29th April 1584.

1785. John Murray and Elizabeth Laidlaw in Buckholm, a.d.n. Margaret, born 18th September 1785.

1787. John Murray and Elizabeth Laidlaw in Buckholm, a.d.n. Jean, born 30th May 1787.

1789. John Murray and Elizabeth Laidlaw in Buckholm, a.s.n. Thomas, born 21st February 1789.

1791. John Murray and Elizabeth Laidlaw in Buckholm, a.s.n. Adam, born 30th July 1791 ; w. to their baptisms, William Craig, William Laidlaw.

1791.
Nov. 13. Robert Pringle and Agnes Burnet in Newstead, a.s.n. George, born 19th August 1787.

,,   ,,   Robert Pringle and Agnes Burnet in Newstead, a.d.n. Janet, born 24th August 1789.

,,   ,,   Robert Pringle and Agnes Burnet in Newstead, a.d.n. Hannah, born 10th October 1791 ; w. to their baptism, Robert Bunzie, George Pringle.

1791.

Nov. 20. Thomas Stevenson and Janet Ormistone in Darnick, a.d.n. Margaret, born 26th May 1790.

„ „ Thomas Stevenson and Janet Ormiston in Darnick, a.d.n. Elizabeth, born 20th November 1791.

„ „ John Dickson and Christian Jonson in Gattonside, a.s.n. William.

„ „ William Paterson and Janet Drummond in Westhouses, a.d.n. Isabel.

„ „ William Wallace and Agnes Bell in Melrose, a.d.n. Alison.

„ „ James Johnson and Margaret Cowan in Melrose, a.s.n. Andrew ; w. William Cook, Robert Taket.

1792.

Jan. 22. William Smith and Margaret Bunzie in Newstead, a.d.n. Elizabeth.

„ „ George Lawrie and Jean Stoddart in Danielton, a.s.n. John ; w. William Cook, Robert Taket.

Feb. 2. Andrew Moffat and Vilet Hatton in Melrose, a.s.n. John ; w. William Cook, Robert Taket.

„ 6. George Graham and Joan Riddell in Colmslee, a.d.n. Elizabeth ; w. William Blaikie, James Millar.

„ 12. William Mabon and Ann Easton, a.d.n. Ann ; w. John Forrest, Andrew Brown.

„ „ Robert Biggar and Jean Thomson in Sunnyside, a.d.n. Agnes ; w. George Wight, John Moss.

„ 19. John Mathison and Ann Scot in Gattonside, a.d.n. Elizabeth ; w. George Stuart, Thomas Boston.

Mar. 18. William Mabon and Margaret Brown in Newstead, a.s.n. Thomas ; w. John Mean, James Sclater.

„ 30. James Martin and Margaret Ewans in Melrose, a.d.n. Janet, born 12th February 1791.

„ „ James Martin and Margaret Ewans in Melrose, a.s.n. William, born 3rd March 1792, both baptised 30th March 1792 ; w. Andrew Martine, George Graham.

April 8. Mr. George Thomson, minister in Melrose, and Margaret Gillon, his spouse, a.s.n. George, born 7th March, and baptised 8th April 1792 ; w. Thomas Gillon, Joseph Gillon.

„ 15. William Turnbull and Mary Donaldson in Darlingshaugh, a.s.n. John, born 26th February 1792, and baptised 15th April 1792 ; w. William Young, Robert Hymers.

„ „ Peter Sanderson and Elizabeth Henderson in Melrose, a.s.n. Peter, born 23rd July 1791 and baptised 6th April 1792 ; w. Robert Taket, William Cook.

„ 18. Andrew Ronaldson, writer, and Mrs. Margaret Smith, his spouse, in Melrose, a.s.n. John ; w. Thomas Gillon, Walter Turnbull.

1791. David Murray and Christian Buchan in Greenwells, a.d.n. Elizabeth Ellioty Murray, born 10th April 1791 ; w. James and Andrew Buchan.

1792.

May 20. James Bell and Janet Bruce in Drygrange, a.d.n. Isabel ; w. James and Robert Nicol.

„ 21. Thomas Laidlaw and Janet Davidson in Eildon, a.d.n. Agnes ; w. John Usher, David Kedie.

„ „ Andrew Sanderson and Jane Scott in Kersfield, a.s.n. James, born 22nd February 1792 ; w. John Watson, Robert Lees.

„ 27. Andrew Pringle and Rachel Easton in Newstead, a.s.n. William.

„ „ Adam Young and Rachel Lun in Darnick, a.d.n. Elizabeth.

„ „ Robert Thomson and Agnes Turnbull in Gattonside, a.d.n. Margaret.

„ „ John Mein and Elizabeth Kersell in Newstead, a.s.n. Robert ; w. Robert Taket, George Pringle.

June 24. Andrew Heart and Margaret Pringle in Newstead, a.s.n. George.

„ „ Andrew Drummond and Margaret Heiton in Bridgend, a.s.n. Andrew ; w. Andrew Heiton, John Martine.

1792.
July 19. John Neil and Jean Milne in Drygrainge, a.s.n. James and a.d.n. Elspeth ; w. James Nicol, Robert Nicol.

,, 23. William Cochran and Nelly Thorburn in Coomslie, a.d.n. Joan.

,, ,, James Turner and Janet Horsburgh in Coomsliehill, a.s.n. Alexander ; w. William Cook, Robert Taket.

,, 29. John Cochran and Agnes Leeden in Newtoun, a.s.n. Alexander ; w. Nicol Milne, James Laidlaw.

,, ,, Alexander Bell and Margaret Stewart in Melrose, a.d.n. Ann ; w. William Cook, George Stewart.
This child was born 13th June 1792.

1786. John Turnbull and Isabel Brydon in Williamlaw, a.s.n. James, born 11th September and baptized 11th December 1786 ; w. Robert Young, Henry Gill.

1792.
May 15. John Turnbull and Isabel Brydon in Williamlaw, a.s.n. William, born 14th April and baptised 15th May 1792 ; w. John Pringle, John Renwick.

1782. Henry Watson and Isabel Lees in Darlingshaugh, a.s.n. John, born 4th June 1782.

1785. Henry Watson and Isabel Lees in Darlingshaugh, a.s.n. Richard, born 12th June 1785.

1789. Henry Watson and Isabel Lees in Darlingshaugh, a.d.n. Janet, born at Jedburgh 28th August 1789.

1792. Henry Watson and Isabel Lees in Darlingshaugh, a.d.n. Alison, born 22nd February 1792 ; w. Thomas Lunn, John Watson.

1791. George Johnson and Agnes Watt in Darlingshaugh, a.d.n. Mary, born 12th September 1791 ; w. Mr. James Blaikie, Henry Watson.

1792.
June 28. William Haig and Janet Anderson in Danieltoun, a.s.n. John, born 20th May 1792, and baptised in Newtoun meeting house 28th June 1792 ; w. James Scot, William Scot.

1784. James Millar and Mary Sibbald in Wooplaw, a.d.n. Nelly, born 21st July 1784.

1786. James Millar and Mary Sibbald in Wooplaw, a.s.n. Gabriel, born 1st July 1786, baptised in the Stow Kirk ; w. James Mitchell, Andrew Henderson.

1792.
April 6. James Clapperton and Mary Boston in Westerhousebyre, a.d.n. Margaret, born 6th April 1792.

Aug. 5. William Scot and Margaret Huntley in Gattonside. a.d.n. Margaret ; w. Thomas Boston, John Dickson.

,, 18. John Bower and Helen Davidson in Melrose, a.d.n. Janet.

,, ,, William Heart and Isabel Hutton in Melrose, a.d.n. Isabel ; w. John Haddon, John Martine.

1785. William M'Gill and Isabel Fiddes in Darlingshaugh, a.s.n. William, born 3rd August 1785.

1791. William M'Gill and Isabel Fiddes in Darlingshaugh, a.s.n. Robert, born 9th September 1791.

1783. Alexander Brownfield and Isabel Beanstown in Kedslee, a.s.n. Robert, born 3rd December 1783.

1786. Alexander Brownfield and Isabel Beanston in Kedslee, a.s.n. George, born 28th March 1786.

1788. Alexander Brownfield and Isabel Beanston in Kedslee, a.s.n. Andrew, born 16th August 1788.

1790. Alexander Brownfield and Isabel Beanston in Kedslee, a.d.n. Isabel, born 2nd April 1790 ; w. to all their baptisms, William Martin, Alexander Hamilton.

1791. John Stevenson and Isabel Waugh in Bridgend, a.d.n. Agnes, born 17th July 1791 ; w. to the baptism, Andrew Mercer, William Martin.

1792.

Aug. 31. James Wight and Marrion Ronaldson in Darnick, a.d.n. Christian ; w. George Wight, Robert Vair.

,,   ,,   John Gill and Christian Hunter in Melrose, a.s.n. Andrew and a.d.n. Jean, born 30th July and baptised 5th Aug. 1792 ; w. Robert Hunter, Nicol Henderson.

1773.   John Cuthbertson and Margaret White in Melrose, a.d.n. Jean, born 21st June and baptised 29th June 1773.

1775.   John Cuthbertson and Margaret White in Melrose, a.d.n. Isabel, born 17th February and baptised 20th February 1775.

1777.   John Cuthbertson and Margaret White in Melrose, a.s.n. John, born 8th July and baptised 12th July 1777.

1779.   John Cuthbertson and Margaret White in Melrose, a.d.n. Rachel, born 12th April and baptised 14th April 1779.

1781.   John Cuthbertson and Margaret White in Melrose, a.s.n. Thomas, born 11th April and baptised 15th April 1781.

1783.   John Cuthbertson and Margaret White in Melrose, a.d.n. Margaret, born 20th June and baptised 28th June 1783.

1787.   John Cuthbertson and Margaret White in Melrose, a.d.n. Elizabeth, born 17th September and baptised 22nd September 1787 ; w. to all, William White, James Craw.

1783.   John Anderson and Mary Cumming in Gattonside, a.s.n. John, born 9th June 1783.

1786.   John Anderson and Mary Cumming in Gattonside, a.s.n. James, born 6th April 1786.

1790.   John Anderson and Mary Cumming in Gattonside, a.d.n. Helen, born 19th August 1790 ; w. to their baptism, William Martin, Alexander Hamilton.

1792.

Sept. 2. Robert Anderson and Jean Wilson in Newstead, a.s.n. John ; w. John Martin, George Pringle.

1775.   James Blaikie and Elizabeth Turnbull in Langhaugh, a.s.n. George, born 5th August 1775.

1777.   James Blaikie and Elizabeth Turnbull in Langhaugh, a.d.n. Mary, born 19th February 1777.

1778.   James Blaikie and Elizabeth Turnbull in Langhaugh, a.d.n. Agnes, born 25th December 1778.

1780.   James Blaikie and Elizabeth Turnbull in Langhaugh, a.s.n. John, born 18th July 1780.

1782.   James Blaikie and Elizabeth Turnbull in Langhaugh, a.d.n. Elizabeth, born 4th April 1782.

1784.   James Blaikie and Elizabeth Turnbull in Langhaugh, a.d.n. Janet, born 5th April 1784.

1785.   James Blaikie and Elizabeth Turnbull in Langhaugh, a.d.n. Isabel, born 7th November 1785.

1787.   James Blaikie and Elizabeth Turnbull in Langhaugh, a.s.n. Robert, born 6th June 1787.

1789.   James Blaikie and Elizabeth Turnbull in Langhaugh, a.s.n. James, born 26th February 1789.

1790.   James Blaikie and Elizabeth Turnbull in Langhaugh, a.s.n. Thomas, born 4th July 1790.

1792.   James Blaikie and Elizabeth Turnbull in Langhaugh, a.s.n. Walter, born 5th January 1792 ; w. William Gray, Robert Turnbull.

1789.   John Nicol and Isabell Murray, a.s.n. John, born 10th July 1789.

1781.   Thomas Pringle and Agnes Hardy in Blainslie, a.d.n. Isabel, born 25th August 1781.

1784.   Thomas Pringle and Agnes Hardy in Blainslie, a.s.n. George, born 28th March 1784.

1785.   Thomas Pringle and Agnes Hardy in Blainslie, a.s.n. John, born 1st September 1785.

1787. Thomas Pringle and Agnes Hardy in Blainslie, a.d.n. Margaret, born 3rd June 1787.

1790. Thomas Pringle and Agnes Hardy in Blainslie, a.d.n. Agnes, born 8th April 1790.

1792. Thomas Pringle and Agnes Hardy in Blainslie, a.d.n. Jean, born 8th April 1792 ; w. James Stirling, James Wilson.

1792. William Kerr, schoolmaster in Newstead, a.d.n. Nelly, born 1st October 1792.

Oct. 4. Adam Aitchison and Isabel Mein in Galabridge, a.s.n. James ; w. Eben. Thomas, William Heitly.

,, 7. Thomas Boston and Isabel Boston in Gattonside, a.s.n. William.

,, ,, John Marr and Janet Halliday in Gattonside, a.d.n. Margaret.

,, ,, James Wilkie and Jean Stenhouse in Gattonside, a.d.n. Jean ; w. Robert Paterson, John Martin.

,, 26. Francis Burnet and Joan Williamson in Newstead, a.s.n. George.

Dec. 30. Robert Nicol and Margaret Hart in Fly-Bridge, a.d.n. Jean.

,, ,, John Pringle and Janet Murray in Newstead, a.s.n. Robert.

1793.
Jan. 6. Andrew Drummond and Janet Clapperton in Gattonside, a.s.n. Andrew, baptised January 6th, 1793 ; w. Thomas Boston, Andrew Drummond.

,, 27. John Martin and Marion Heiton in Melrose, a.s.n. George ; w. James Blaikie, Robert Paterson.

,, ,, William Burns and Alison Tait in Langhaugh, a.d.n. Janet ; w. Walter Tait, and son, Adam Tait.

Feb. 3. Thomas Taylor and Jean Trotter in Melrose, a.d.n. Alison Elliot : w. Robert Grierson, Adam Milne.

1792.
Aug. 12. John Laidlaw and Jemima Grant in Peasehill, a.s.n. William; w. Robert Myles, Robert Kiddie.

Nov. 10. Alexander Laing and Agnes Anderson in Melrose, a.s.n. James, baptised 10th November 1792; w. James Bromfield, George Ronaldson.

1793.
Feb. 19. James Moffat, surgeon, and Margaret Usher in Melrose, a.d.n. Margaret, born 19th December 1792 and baptised 19th February 1793 ; w. James Usher, John Martin.

,, 25. John Lile and Nelly Haw in Melrose, a.s.n. John, baptised 25th February 1793 ; w. James Blaikie, Robert Paterson.

Mar. 13. David Murray and Christian Buchan in Greenwells, a.s.n. Andrew, born 27th January and baptised 13th March 1793 : w. Captain Gillon, Nicol Milne.

,, 24. Alexander Muir and Janet Aymers in Melrose, a.s.n. William, baptised 24th March 1793 ; w. John Muir, R. Paterson.

,, ,, James Nicol and Alison Mein in Drygrange, a.d.n. Alison.

,, 31. James Jameson and Margaret Ormiston in Melrose, a.d.n. Janet : w. John Martine, John Bower.

April 7. William Smith and Margaret Bunzie in Newstead, a.d.n. Betty.

,, ,, Robert Crawfurd and Jane Hog in Melrose, a.d.n. Margaret.

,, ,, John Mosgrove and Katharine Jamieson in Melrose, a.s.n. David.

,, 21. Walter Ronaldson and Janet Wight in Melrose, a.d.n. Mary.

,, ,, David Sinclair and Margaret Hart in Newstead, a.d.n. Grisel.

,, 28. Robert Scott and Janet Cochrane in Newton, a.s.n. James.

,, ,, William Cowan and Helen Fisher in Newton, a.s.n. George.

,, ,, Thomas Haig and Janet Bunzie in Drygrange, a.d.n. Helen.

May 5. Robert Kemp and James Graham in Darnick, a.s.n. David.

,, ,, James Sclater and Ann Mein in Newstead, a.s.n. James.

,, 12. James Scott and Agnes Dalgliesh in Gattonside, a.d.n. Grisel.

,, 21. John Murray and Elizabeth Laidlaw in Buckholm, a.d.n. Mary, born 30th April and baptised 21st May ; w. Thomas Paterson William Laidlaw, Galashiels.

1793.

June   2. John Moss and Betty Dunlap in Kayside, a.s.n. Andrew ; w. George Brodie, John Martin.

"   "   James Hopkirk and Anne Wright in Melrose, a.s.n. Alexander.

1765.   Thomas Miln and Ann Aitchison in Newtown, a.s.n. John, born 10th November 1765.

1767.   Thomas Miln and Ann Aitchison in Newtown, a.s.n. Thomas.

1775.   Thomas Miln and Mary Shields in Newtown, a.s.n. Richard, born 1st January 1775.

1777.   Thomas Miln and Mary Shields in Newtown, a.s.n. James, born 18th November 1777.

1779.   Thomas Miln and Mary Shields in Newtown, a.s.n. Nicol, born 4th August 1779.

1783.   Thomas Miln and Mary Shields, a.d.n. Isabel, born in Newtown 12th May 1783.

1793.

May   26. Thomas Steinson and Janet Ormiston in Darnick, a.s.n. Robert, baptised 26th May 1793.

June   1 John Nicol and Isabel Murray, a.s.n. Robert, born 1st June 1793.

"   9. Lieut. Robert Aitchison, Royal Navy, and Mrs. Mary Scot, his spouse, in Melrose, a.d.n. Mary Anne Aitchison, born 12th May and baptised 9th June 1793 ; w. Messrs. Anderson, supervisor, David Kyle, vintner.

"   16. Thomas Usher and Betty Steinson in Newstead, a.s.n. John, baptised 16th June 1793.

"   30. George Moss and Jane Kennedy in Berryhall, a.d.n. Mary, born 9th June and baptised 30th same month 1793.

"   "   George Laurie and Jane Stoddart in Danieltown, a.s.n. John, baptised 30th June 1793.

"   "   Alexander Hopkirk and Barbara Amos in Melrose, a.d.n. Margaret.

"   "   George Cook and Margaret Sanderson in Melrose, a.d.n. Alison.

July   7. Andrew Scot and Grizel Sawers in Newstead, a.d.n. Mary Anne, baptised 7th July 1793.

"   21. William Nicol and Betty Kiddie in Darnick, a.s.n. John, baptised 21st July 1793.

"   29. George Pringle and Janet Blaikie in Newstead, a.s.n. Robert, baptised 29th July 1793.

"   "   Andrew Brown and Janet Mather in Melrose, a.d.n. Janet : w. John Paterson, John Martin.

Aug.   18. John Paterson and Margaret Stuart in Melrose, a.s.n. Thomas, born 5th July and baptised 18th August 1793.

"   25. Alexander Saunderson and Nelly Phillips in Melrose, a.d.n. Jane, baptised 25th August 1793.

Sept.   3. Andrew Heiton and Isabel Govin in Darnick, a.s.n. Andrew ; w. James Usher, Jean Mein.

"   29. George Hatton and Janet Scott in Melrose, a.d.n. Margaret.

Oct.   2. Thomas Dickson and Elizabeth Vair in Darnick, a.s.n. Thomas, born 20th September and baptised 2nd October 1793 ; w. Thomas Vair, Robert Vair.

"   6. James Rutherford and Anne Hog in Melrose, a.d.n. Margaret Edgar.

"   8. William Cook and Elizabeth Murray in Melrose, a.s.n. Walter : w. George Laurie, John Martin.

"   13. Robert Boston and Katharine Graham in Darnick, a.d.n. Janet.

"   "   Rev. Mr. George Thomson, minister in Melrose, and Margaret Gillon, his spouse, a.d.n. Mary Anne, born 16th September and baptised 13th October 1793.

"   "   John Smith and Mary Williamson in Darnick, a.d.n. Violet.

"   21. Richard Lees and Mary Paterson in Buckholm side, a.s.n. John.

"   27. William Wallace and Agnes Bell in Melrose, a.s.n. James ; w. David Brown, Thomas Gillon.

1793.
Oct. 27. William Edgar and Christian Waugh in Melrose, a.s.n. George.
Nov. 10. John Vair and Isabel Lunn in Darnick, a.d.n. Elizabeth.
  ,, 19. John Rutherford and Katharine Turnbull in Bridgend, a.d.n. Margaret.
Dec. 1. John Smith and Margaret Oliver in Darnick, a.s.n. James.
  ,, ,, Thomas Williamson and Margaret Watson in Newstead, a.s.n. Thomas ; w. George Pringle, Thomas Mather.
  ,, 26. John Laidlaw and Jemima Grant in Peasehill, a.d.n. Agnes ; w. Robert Myles, Andrew Bell.
  ,, 29. Adam Anderson and Violet Cranston in Melrose, a.d.n. Violet.
  ,, 30. Thomas Bell, Esq., of Langlee, and Mrs. Janet Liddell, his spouse, a.s.n. James Liddell Bell, born 13th December and baptised the 30th ; w. Mr. Blaikie, Mr. Thomson.

1794.
Jan. 5. John Heiton and Janet Elliott in Darnick, a.s.n. John.
Feb. 4. James Moffat, surgeon, and Margaret Usher in Melrose, a.d.n. Mary, born 28th November 1793 and baptised 4th February 1794 ; w. James Usher, John Martin.
  ,, 9. Robert Heymer and Elizabeth Miller in Melrose, a.s.n. Robert, born 8th January 1794.
  ,, ,, Alexander Bell and Margaret Stuart in Melrose, a.d.n. Nelly, born 31st December 1793.
Mar. 5. John Turnbull and Jane Currie in Gattonside, a.d.n. Janet, born 17th February and baptised 5th March ; w. Thomas Boston, James Marr.
  ,, 23. John Middleton and Mary Bunzie in Newstead, a.d.n. Mary.
  ,, ,, John Matthieson and Anne Scott in Gattonside, a.s.n. William.
  ,, 30. William Turnbull and Mary Donaldson in Darlingshaugh, a.s.n. Walter, born 14th January 1794.
  ,, ,, William Turnbull and Mary Donaldson in Darlingshaugh, a.d.n. Jane, born 14th January 1794 ; w. William Young, Robert Heymers.
April 6. Alexander Scott and Margaret Mathieson in Newstead, a.s.n. Alexander, born 9th February 1794.
  ,, 13. Andrew Hart and Margaret Pringle in Newstead, a.s.n. Andrew.
  ,, ,, John Lile and Nelly Haw in Melrose, a.d.n. Jane ; w. David Kyle, James Blaikie.
April 19. William Galloway and Euphan Scott in Melrose, a.d.n. Jean, born 16th and baptised 19th April 1794 ; w. to the baptism, William Cook, John Trotter.
  ,, 20. Thomas Biggar and Isabel Taket in Gingle, a.s.n. John, born 29th January 1794.
  ,, ,, Alexander Denholm and Margaret Thorburn in Langlee, a.s.n. John, born 18th March 1794 and baptised 20th April ; w. Robert Taket, George Brodie.
  ,, ,, James Inglis and Margaret Dunn in Greenwells, a.s.n. Andrew.
  ,, ,, Robert Pringle and Agnes Burnet in Newstead, a.d.n. Margaret ; w. Robert Taket, George Brodie.
May 11. James Ballantyne and Janet Scott in Darnick, a.d.n. Nelly.
  ,, ,, James Wight and Marion Ronaldson in Darnick, a.d.n. Mary ; w. R. Paterson, J. Martin.
  ,, 18. Adam Fiddes and Margaret Harriot in Drygrange, a.d.n. Nelly ; w. Robert Taket, James Usher.
June 1. William Mathieson and Janet Henderson in Gattonside, a.s.n. David.
  ,, ,, William Scott and Margaret Huntly in Gattonside, a.s.n. David.
  ,, 15. William Steinson and Agnes Gray in Newtown, a.d.n. Anne.
  ,, 29. George Waddie and Margaret Waddie in Drygrange Bridge, a.d.n. Isabel.
Sept. 4. Andrew Brown and Janet Mather in Melrose, a.d.n. Janet ; w. John Martin, Robert Taket.

Y

1794.
Sept. 8. Andrew Heiton and Isabel Goven in Darnick, a.d.n. Margaret; w. James Usher, John Heiton.

„ 21. John Sibbald and Jane Laidlaw in Eildon, a.s.n. Andrew; w. James Laidlaw, Nicol Milne.

Oct. 5. Andrew Bartlie and Barbara Robison in Newtown, a.d.n. Isabel; w. William Cook, Nicol Milne.

„ 26. James Hobkirk and Ann Wright in Melrose, a.s.n. Walter.

„ „ William Miller and Janet Mein in Newstead, a.d.n. Margaret; w. William Cook, Robert Bunzie.

Nov. 9. James Burnet and Isabel Forrest in Westhouses, a.d.n. Margaret.

„ „ Robert Anderson and Jean Wilson in Newstead, a.s.n. Robert.

„ „ John Turnbull and Alison Noble in Gattonside, a.s.n. Thomas; w. Robert Bunzie, Thomas Boston.

„ 16. Thomas Taylor and Jean Trotter in Melrose, a.s.n. Thomas; w. William Cook, Robert Taket.

1793. William Sessford and Helen Turnbull in Gattonside, a.d.n. Joan, born 23rd November 1793 and baptised 10th December 1793; w. James Blaikie, Thomas Boston.

1794.
Nov. 30. Andrew Drummond and Elizabeth Clapperton in Gattonside, a.d.n. Elizabeth; w. Thomas Boston, Robert Taket.

Dec. 7. John Martine, wright, and Marrion Heiton in Melrose, a.d.n. Marrion.

„ „ Alexander Laing and Agnes Anderson in Melrose, a.s.n. William; w. William Cook, Robert Taket.

1795.
Jan. 4. Walter Ronaldson and Janet Wight in Melrose, a.d.n. Catharine.

„ „ James Johnston and Margaret Cowan in Melrose, a.d.n. Margaret; w. William Cook, Robert Taket.

1793. James Scott and Janet Pringle in Calfhill, a.d.n. Agnes, born 1st November 1793.

1794. James Scott and Janet Pringle in Calfhill, a.s.n. Thomas, born 30th December 1794.

„ Francis Burnet and Joan Williamson in Newstead, a.s.n. James, born 18th October and baptised 30th November 1794; w. Robert Bunzie, William Cook.

„ David Murray and Christian Buchan in Greenwells, a.s.n. David, born 9th September and baptised 16th December 1794; w. James Laidlaw, Nicol Milne.

„ John Grieve and Elizabeth Reid in Melrose, a.s.n. Adam, born 7th April and baptised 9th June 1794; w. Archibald Anderson, John Elliot.

„ James Clapperton and Mary Boston in Gattonside, a.s.n. Robert, born 22nd August 1794.

„ Lieut. Robert Aitchison, Royal Navy, and Mrs. Mary Scot, his spouse, in Melrose, a.s.n. Edward, born 15th October 1794 and baptised 5th January 1795; w. James Moffat, David Kyle.

„ John Elliot and Agnes Inglis in Melrose, a.d.n. Joan, born 20th October 1794 and baptised 19th March 1795; w. William Cook, John Grieve.

1795.
Jan. 11. Robert Burnet and Janet Burnet in Melrose, a.s.n. William; w. William Cook, Robert Taket.

Mar. 10. Richard Lees, manufacturer in Buckholmside, and Mary Paterson, his spouse, a.d.n. Mary, born 12th February 1795; w. George Bathgate, Robert Walker.

„ 12. Robert Nicol and Margaret Hart at Drygrange Flybridge, a.s.n. William, born 10th January and baptised 12th March; w. James Bell, James Nicol.

„ „ James Nicol and Alison Mein in Drygrange, a.s.n. Adam, born 25th February and baptised 12th March; w. James Bell, Robert Nicol.

1795.

Mar. 15. John Musgrove and Katharine Jamieson in Melrose, a.d.n. Helen ; w. Robert Taket, Alexander Cook.

1792. David Kyle and Agnes Scoon in Melrose, a.s.n. Thomas, born 23rd October 1792, and

1795.

Mar. 2. David Kyle and Agnes Scoon in Melrose, a.s.n. James, born 21st January 1795 and both baptised 2nd March 1795 ; w. John Haldane, Robert Taket.

April 5. James Jamieson and Margaret Ormistone in Melrose, a.d.n. Helen.

,, ,, Andrew Pringle and Rachel Easton in Newstead, a.s.n. Robert ; w. Robert Taket, William Cook.

,, 12. James Scott and Agnes Dalgliesh in Gattonside, a.d.n. Mary ; w. Robert Taket, William Cook.

,, 15. James Millar and Mary Sibbald in Calfhill, a.d.n. Mary, born 15th December 1794.

,, ,, James Boyd and Elizabeth Chisholme in Coomslies, a.d.n. Jean, born March 1794.

,, ,, William Henderson and Janet Fall in Calfhill, a.s.n. George, born 24th March 1794 ; w. John Cleugh, Walter Chisholme.

May 3. William Stevenson and Janet Mein in Newstead, a.d.n. Janet.

,, ,, Robert Hart and Elisabeth Scott in Newstead, a.s.n. William.

,, ,, John Grieve and Isobel Marr in Gattonside, a.d.n. Elizabeth ; w. Robert Bunzie, Thomas Boston.

,, 10. The Rev. Mr. George Thomson and Mrs. Margaret Gillon, a.s.n. Robert Gillon, born 27th March and baptised 10th May 1795 ; w. David Brown, John Mercer.

,, ,, Andrew Moffat and Violet Hatton in Melrose, a.d.n. Margaret ; w. George Brodie, Walter Tait.

,, 14. Andrew Martin and Helen Thin in Blainslie, a.d.n. Margaret, born 4th May 1794, and

,, ,, Robert Laidlaw and Agnes Fairbairn in Blainslie, a.d.n. Agnes, born March 1794, both baptised 14th May 1795 ; w. John Simpson, James Wilson.

,, ,, George Bathgate and Alison Purves in Darlingshaugh, a.s.n. George, born 10th April and baptised 14th May 1795 ; w. Simon and John Bathgate.

June 14. Robert Kirkwood and Isabel Sibbald in Gattonside, a.s.n. John, born 21st April 1795.

,, ,, John Kyle and Christian Thomson in Melrose, a.d.n. Agnes.

,, ,, Robert Kemp and Jean Graham in Darnick, a.s.n. James, born in May : w. Thomas Boston, Robert Taket.

July 5. John Moss and Betty Dunlap in Kayside, a.d.n. Alison.

,, ,, James Rutherford and Agnes Hog in Melrose, a.s.n. Andrew ; w. Robert Taket, William Cook.

,, 19. William Burns and Alison Tait in Kittyfield, a.s.n. Walter.

,, ,, James Henderson and Isabel Aitken in Melrose, a.s.n. John ; w. George Brodie, Robert Taket.

,, 23. Robert Crawford and Jean Hog in Melrose, a.d.n. Agnes ; w. Robert Taket, William Cook.

Aug. 2. George Hatton and Janet Scot in Melrose, a.d.n. Elizabeth.

,, ,, Alexander Muir and Janet Heymers in Melrose, twins named James and Andrew ; w. Robert Taket, Robert Heymers.

1794.

Feb. 5. John Anderson and Mary Cumming in Gattonside, a.s.n. Robert, born February and baptised April 1794 ; w. Alexander Familton, William Turner.

1795.

Aug. 16. William Ker and Helen Laidlaw in Newstead, a.d.n. Christian ; w. Robert Bunzie, William Cook.

1795.

Aug. 16. Andrew Young and Mary Bell in Melrose, a.d.n. Beatrix ; w. Robert Taket, William Cook.

„   18. William Smith and Margaret Bunzie in Drygrange, a.s.n. James.

„   „   Thomas Haig and Janet Bunzie in Drygrange, a.d.n. Jane ; w. James and Robert Nicol.

„   23. Alexander Bell and Margaret Stewart in Melrose, a.d.n. Jane, born 8th July and baptised 23rd August 1795 ; w. Robert Taket, William Cook.

„   „   Adam Tait and Margaret Harper in Darnick, a.s.n. Walter, born 13th July and baptised 23rd August 1795.

„   „   Adam Tait and Margaret Harper in Darnick, a.d.n. Mary, born 3rd May and baptised 16th June 1793 : w. Andrew Heiton, Robert Grierson.

Oct. 11. Adam Dalgliesh and Agnes Wilson in Hilslop, a.s.n. William, born 15th September and baptised 11th October 1795 ; w. James Scot, Robert Paterson.

„   25. John Lyall and Helen Hall in Melrose, a.s.n. William.

„   „   John Rutherfurd and Katharine Turnbull in Bridgend, a.d.n. Isabel ; w. James Wight, John Martine.

Nov. 1. Alexander Hobkirk and Barbara Amos, a.d.n. Anne Mercer Hobkirk ; w. Mr. John Mercer, Mr. David Brown.

„   15. Mr. David Brown and Mrs. Anne Hepburn, his spouse, in Melrose, a.s.n. William, born 7th October and baptised 15th November 1795 ; w. John Martine, Alexander Wormall.

„   „   Robert Boston and Katharine Graham in Darnick, a.s.n. Thomas : w. John Smith, Robert Grierson.

„   22. John Loudon and Anne Welsh in Darnick, a.s.n. Thomas ; w. John Smith, John Harper.

„   „   John Stevenson and Isabel Waugh in Bridgend, a.s.n. Henry, born 14th October 1793 ; w. John Rutherford, John Martine.

„   „   Henry Watson and Isabel Lees in Darlingshaugh, a.s.n. James, born 8th March 1795 ; w. Thomas Lunn, John Watson.

Dec. 6. William Wallace and Agnes Bell in Melrose, a.s.n. George ; w. John Martine, William Cook.

„   7. George Laurie and Jean Stoddart in Danieltown, a.s.n. Adam ; w. Robert Taket, William Cook.

„   10. Andrew Heitton and Isabel Govan in Darnick, a.d.n. Isabel ; w. James Usher, John Smith.

1796.

Jan. 21. John Dickison and Agnes Friar in Gattonside, a.d.n. Agnes, born 3rd January 1795 and baptised 23rd January 1795 ; Robert Miles, John Anderson.

Feb. 7. James Wight and Mary Ronaldson in Darnick, a.d.n. Elizabeth.

„   „   George Moss and Jane Kennedy in Berryhall, a.s.n. James, born 9th January and baptised 7th February ; w. George Wight, John Mercer.

„   14. William Edgar and Christian Waugh in Melrose, a.s.n. William.

„   „   Alexander Sanderson and Helen Phillips in Melrose waulkmill ; w. James Brownfield, James Hobkirk.

Mar. 2. Major John Bull and Mrs. Ann Kentish, his spouse, a.d.n. Ann Louisa Frances, born 21st May 1795 and christened 21st November following ; w. Mr. John Mercer, Walter Turnbull.

„   13. Adam Young and Helen Lunn in Darnick, a.d.n. Helen ; w. John Smith, Andrew Ronaldson.

„   20. Robert Heymers and Elizabeth Millar in Melrose, a.d.n. Sarah, born 26th November 1795 and baptised 20th March 1796 ; w. Andrew Brown, Walter Turnbull.

„   „   Alexander Ross and Sarah Currie in Westhouses, a.s.n. Daniel ; w. Andrew Brown, Thomas Wilson.

„   31. James Bunzie and Jean Moffat in Newstead, a.d.n. Jean ; w. James Ramsey, John Martine.

1796.

April 3. William Turnbull and Mary Donaldson in Darlingshaugh, a.s.n. William, born 19th February and baptised 3rd April ; w. Robert Heymers, William Young.

,, ,, Robert Pringle and Agnes Burnet in Newstead, a.d.n. Agnes.

,, ,, William Nicol and Elizabeth Kedzie in Darnick, a.d.n. Margaret ; w. Thomas Williamson, John Smith.

,, 10. John Stevenson and Isabel Waugh in Bridgend, a.d.n. Janet ; w. Andrew Mercer, John Rutherfurd.

,, 17. William Heart and Isabel Hutton in Melrose, a.d.n. Elizabeth.

,, ,, Alexander Scot and Margaret Mathison in Newstead, a.s.n. James.

,, ,, William Sessford and Helen Turnbull in Gattonside, a.s.n. James ; w. Thomas Boston, William Cook.

,, ,, James Bell and Janet Bruce in Drygrange, a.d.n. Helen, born 9th September 1794 and christened about five weeks thereafter ; w. James and Robert Nicol.

,, ,, James Chalmers and Mary Fowler in Galashiels, a.d.n. Mary, born 10th April 1794 and baptised a month thereafter : w. William Craig, Thomas Sanderson.

,, ,, James Chalmers and Mary Fowler in Galashiels, a.s.n. James, born 28th January 1796 and baptised 28th February 1796 ; w. James Blaikie, George Bathgate.

May 1. Alexander Denholm and Margaret Thorburn in Easterlanglee, a.d.n. Mary : w. John Easton, Thomas Wilson.

,, 8. Thomas Wilson and Joan Pentland in Westhouses, a.d.n. Margaret.

,, ,, William Mitchell and Margaret Burnet in Newstead, a.d.n. Janet.

,, ,, William Wilson and Beatrix Richardson in Danielton, a.d.n. Elizabeth : w. Alexander Denholm, George Laurie.

,, 15. James Thomson and Margaret Stewart in Gattonside, a.d.n. Janet, born 12th March and baptised 16th same month 1794 : w. James Marr, Robert Stewart.

,, , James Thomson and Margaret Stewart in Gattonside, a.s.n. John, born 23rd April and baptised 15th May 1796 : w. Robert Stewart, Alexander Sibbald.

,, 22. John Martin and Marrion Heitton in Melrose, a.d.n. Mary.

,, ,, John Paterson and Margaret Stewart in Melrose, a.d.n. Anne ; w. Robert Taket, John Martine.

,, 28. John Winter and Helen Hog in Melrose, a.d.n. Helen ; w. John Hog, Andrew Brown.

,, ,, Thomas Usher and Elizabeth Stevenson in Newstead, a.d.n. Janet ; w. Robert Taket, Thomas Williamson.

June 5. John Turnbull and Jean Currie in Gattonside, a.s.n. John.

,, ,, Andrew Heart and Margaret Pringle in Newstead, a.s.n. Robert ; w. Thomas Boston, Thomas Williamson.

,, 26. Archibald Campbell and Elizabeth Kennedy in Westhouses, a.s.n. Steven Stewart Campbell.

,, ,, Robert Burnet and Janet Burnet in Melrose, a.s.n. John, born 20th April last ; w. John Easton, William Cook.

,, ,, John Nichol and Isabel Murray in Melrose, a.s.n. Walter, born 5th December 1790.

,, ,, John Nicol and Isabel Murray in Melrose, a.s.n Andrew, born 28th December 1795 ; w. William Cook, Robert Taket.

July 3. William Stevenson and Anne Gray in Newtoun, a.d.n. Agnes ; w. Nicol Milne, George Brodie.

,, ,, James Bower and Agnes Millar in Melrose, a.d.n. Mary ; w. Nicol Milne, William Cook.

,, 16. William Paterson and Janet Drummond in Darnick, a.s.n. Andrew w. William Cook, Robert Taket.

,, 25. William Scot and Margaret Dickson in Blainslie, a.d.n. Agnes, born 12th July 1796 ; w. James Wilson, Robert Laidlaw.

1796.

Aug. 7. James Ronaldson, mason in Darnick, and Euphan Gray, a.s.n. Robert, born 12th July 1796 ; w. John Smith, Robert Grierson.

" " John Milne, labourer, and Allison Haliburton in Darnick, a.s.n. William, born 12th July 1796; w. John Smith, Robert Grierson.

" " John Leech and Isabel Robison in Newstead, a.s.n. James ; w. Thomas Williamson, John Moffat.

" 31. John Clark and Janet Ivly in Darlingshaugh, a.s.n. William, born 28th June 1796 ; w. William Cook, Robert Taket.

1788. Robert Hilson, weaver, and Susanna Ballantyne in Melrose, a.s.n. Thomas, born in the year 1788.

1793. James Kemp, bleecher, and Christian Skirven in Melrose Bleechfield, a.s.n. Andrew, born 7th August 1793 ; w. Andrew Brown, David Kyle.

1796.

Sept. 4. Andrew Bartlie and Barbara Robertson in Newtoun, a.d.n. Alison ; w. Nicol Milne, James Laidlaw.

" 25. Alexander Tudhope and Isabel Turner in Melrose, a.d.n. Katharine ; w. John Trotter, William Cook.

" " John Grieve and Elizabeth Reid in Melrose, a.d.n. Elizabeth Turnbull, born 12th June and christened 11th September 1796 ; w. Archibald Anderson, John Elliot.

" " John Elliot and Agnes Inglis in Melrose, a.s.n. Robert, born 23rd June and christened 4th September 1796 ; w. Archibald Anderson, John Grieve.

1793. Andrew Sanderson and Jane Scot in Kersfield, a.d.n. Agnes, born 9th November 1793.

1796. Andrew Sanderson and Jane Scot in Kersfield, a.d.n. Isabel, born 8th May 1796 ; w. John Watson, Robert Lees.

" Robert Walker, weaver, and Elizabeth Stenhouse in Darlingshaugh, a.d.n. Janet, born 14th December 1785.

" Robert Walker, weaver, and Elizabeth Stenhouse in Darlingshaugh, a.s.n. William, born 12th May 1786.

" Robert Walker, weaver, and Elizabeth Stenhouse in Darlingshaugh, a.d.n. Helen, born 6th March 1788.

" Robert Walker, weaver, and Elizabeth Stenhouse in Darlingshaugh, a.d.n. Isabel, born 4th July 1791.

" Robert Walker, weaver, and Elizabeth Stenhouse in Darlingshaugh, a.s.n. James, born 10th August 1793.

" Robert Walker, weaver, and Elizabeth Stenhouse in Darlingshaugh, a.d.n. Elizabeth, born 19th September 1795 ; w. George Litster, George Bathgate.

" William Haldane and Jean Richardson in Darlingshaugh, a s.n. John, born 21st August 1796 ; w. George Bathgate, George Litster.

1790. James Friar, mason, and Elizabeth White in Darlingshaugh, a.s.n. Edward, born 3rd October 1790 ; w. Robert Gill, Hugh Sanderson. (This entered last register May 1791.)

1793. James Friar, mason, and Elizabeth White in Darlingshaugh, a.s.n. Walter, born 22nd February 1793.

1796. James Friar, mason, and Elizabeth White in Darlingshaugh, a.s.n. James, born 30th April 1796 ; w. George Litster, George Bathgate. *N.B.*--This name should be Frier.—W. T.

1795. James Sym, manufacturer, and Margaret Clapperton in Darlingshaugh, a.s.n. James, born 2nd April 1795 ; w. George Bathgate, George Litster.

1793. George Litster, wright, and Agnes Sibbald in Darlingshaugh, a.s.n. Alexander, born 18th May 1793; w. William Haldane, George Bathgate.

1794. George Litster, wright, and Agnes Sibbald in Darlingshaugh, a.d.n. Elizabeth, born 3rd October 1794 ; w. George Bathgate, William Haldane.

1795. James Melrose, smith, and Mary Brown in Darlingshaugh, a.s.n. Thomas, born 31st January 1795 ; w. George Bathgate, George Litster.

1796. Robert Walker, manufacturer, and Janet Lang in Buckhamside, a.d.n. Janet, born 29th March 1796 ; w. Richard Lees, John Watson.

,, William Wintrup, farmer in Broadwoodshiell, and Dorothy Robison, his spouse, a.s.n. John, born 24th September 1796 ; w. Alexander Stevenson, James Stirling.

1796.
Oct. 2. Thomas Taylor, merchant, and Jean Trotter in Melrose, a.s.n. John ; w. Andrew Brown, John Trotter.

,, ,, Richard Lees, manufactuer in Buckhamside, and Mary Paterson, his spouse, a.d.n. Agnes, born 26th September 1796 ; w. George Bathgate, Robert Walker.

,, 9. William Mathison, cooper, and Janet Henderson in Gattonside, a.d.n. Elizabeth.

,, ,, Thomas Dickson, weaver, and Elizabeth Vair in Darnick, a.d.n. Helen ; w. Thomas Boston, Andrew Heiton.

,, ,, William Dickson and Alison Dickson in Blainslie, a.s.n. William, born 30th September last ; w. James Stirling, James Wilson.

,, 16. John Gibson, baker, and Isabel Martine in Melrose, a.s.n. James.

,, ,, James Grieve, labourer, and Janet Brydon in Melrose, a.s.n. Walter ; w. John Martine, William Cook.

Nov. 5. John Smith, wright, and Margaret Oliver in Darnick, a.d.n. Margaret ; w. Andrew Heiton, Thomas Stevenson.

1788. Peter Clark and Anne Scott in Newstead, a.d.n. Janet, born 5th July 1788 ; w. John Cuthbertson, Robert Vair.

1796.
Oct. 20. James Scott and Janet Pringle in Calfhill, a.s.n. George ; w. Mr. Hewit, James Boyd.

,, ,, James Boyd and Elizabeth Chisholme in Calfhill, a.d.n. Elizabeth ; w. James Scott, Mr. Hewit.

,, 25. Robert Robson, mason, and Jean Harper in Gattonside, a.d.n. Susanna ; w. Thomas Boston, John Dickson.

,, ,, David Sinclair and Margaret Rutherford in Melrose, a.s.n. James.

,, ,, Andrew Drummond and Janet Clapperton in Darnick, a.d.n. Isabel ; w. Andrew Heiton, Thomas Boston.

,, 26. David Murray and Christian Buchan in Greenwells, a.s.n. John, born 21st November 1796 ; w. William Balfour, Robert Speeding.

,, ,, John Forrest and Christian Bouston in Westerlanglee, a.s.n. John, born 9th September and christened 20th October 1796 ; w. Mr. George Bruce, John Easton.

Dec. 18. William Beattie, soldier in the 31st Regiment of foot, in Melrose, and Mary Beattie, his spouse, a.s.n. Samuel, born 8th December 1796 ; w. Robert Taket, Adam Brydon.

1797.
Feb. 10. Mr. William Spence, surgeon, and Mrs. Janet Park, his spouse, in Melrose, a.d.n. Elizabeth, born 26th August and baptised 12th October 1796 ; w. the Rev. Mr. Andrew Spence, Mr. John Park.

,, 15. Walter Turnbull, schoolmaster in Melrose, and Euphan Dickson, his spouse, a.d.n. Isabel, born 3rd January 1797 ; w. Robert Heymers, John Turnbull.

,, 25. Rev. Mr. George Thomson, minister of the Gospel in Melrose, and Mrs. Margaret Gillon, his spouse, a.s.n. Joseph, born 17th January and baptised 25th February 1797 ; w. the Rev. Messrs. Robert Douglas and William Balfour.

Mar. 5. Robert Hart and Elizabeth Scot in Newstead, a.s.n. Robert.

,, ,, John Turnbull and Alison Noble in Newstead, a.d.n. Isabel.

,, ,, Andrew Bunzie and Margaret Williamson in Newstead, a.d.n. Margaret ; w. Thomas Williamson, David Kyle.

1797.

Mar. 12. Adam Fiddes and Margaret Herriot in Newstead, a.d.n. Meney ; w. Thomas Williamson, James Nicol.

,, 19. George Laurie and Jean Stoddart in Danielton, a.s.n. David, born 17th December 1796.

,, ,, James Johnstone and Margaret Cowan in Melrose, a.d.n. Helen ; w. Robert Taket, Thomas Scott.

,, ,, John Moss and Elizabeth Dunlop in Keaside, a.d.n. Agnes, born 20th January and baptised 11th February 1797 : w. Walter Tait, Peter Anderson.

April 2. John Sibbald and Jean Laidlaw in Eildon, a.s.n. Nicol ; w. Andrew Bell, Nicol Milne.

,, 7. Alexander Adamson and Elizabeth Gilles, a.s.n. Peter, born 28th February and christened 7th April 1797 ; w. John Gill, Alexander Hobkirk.

,, ,, James Sanderson, wright, and Helen Martine at Galashiells toll-bar, a.d.n. Isabel, born 14th November 1796 ; w. Mr. James Blaikie, Mr. John Graham.

,, ,, James Nicol and Alison Mein in Drygrange, a.s.n. John, born 16th February and christened 29th March 1797 ; w. Robert Nicol, James Bell.

,, ,, Walter Purves and Helen Porteous in Blainslie, a.s.n. Alexander, baptised 10th April 1797 ; w. James Wilson, Robert Romanos.

,, ,, William Stirling and Margaret Campbell, a.s.n. Robert, born 7th July 1796 and christened three weeks after ; w. James Stirling, Robert Henry.

,, 16. William Write and Mary Tait in Darnick, a.d.n. Margaret, baptised 16th April 1797 ; w. James Tait, John Martine.

,, 30. James Hobkirk and Anne Wright in Melrose, a.s.n. Robert ; w. Alexander Hobkirk, William Cook.

May 14. John Musgrave and Katharine Jamieson in Melrose, a.s.n. John ; w. Robert Heymers, James Jamieson.

1792.

May 16. John Wilson and Mary Scot in Westerlanglee, a.d.n. Isabel, born October 1792.

1797.

May 16. James Wilson and Mary Scot in Westerlanglee, a.s.n. James, born 1st January 1797 ; w. John Forrest, John Easton.

,, 21. George Waldie and Margaret Waldie in Drygrange, a.s.n. Archibald, born 4th March and christened 21st May 1797 ; w. James Bell, James Nicol.

,, 28. James Hislop and Isabel Jamison in Darnick, a.s.n. John ; w. John Smith, Robert Grierson.

,, ,, James Henderson and Isabel Aitken in Melrose, a.d.n. Isabel, born 3rd March 1797 ; w. William Cook, Robert Taket.

June 9. James Walker and Janet Sclater in Darnick, a.s.n. William ; w. James Usher, Robert Grierson.

,, 18. James Scot and Agnes Dalgliesh in Gattonside, a.s.n. William ; w. William Cook, Robert Taket.

July 9. Alexander Bell and Margaret Stewart in Melrose, a.d.n. Mary, born 5th May 1797 ; w. George Stewart, William Cook.

,, ,, James Bunzie and Ann Thomson in Newstead, a.s.n. Andrew ; w. William Cook, Robert Taket.

,, 23. George Muir and Isabel Dickson in Mosshouses, a.d.n. Jane, born 29th May last ; w. William Cook, Robert Taket.

,, 31. John Mathison and Ann Scot in Gattonside, a.s.n. Henry ; w. William Cook, Robert Tacket.

Aug. 6. Andrew Young and Mary Bell in Melrose, a.s.n. William ; w. William Cook, Robert Ormistone.

1787. William Johnstone and Isabel Cochrane in Darlingshaugh, a.s.n. Andrew, born 1st October 1787.

1787. William Johnstone and Isabel Cochrane in Darlingshaugh, a.s.n. William, born 17th October 1789; w. Archibald Cochran, Richard Cochran.

1797.
Aug. 13. John Rutherfurd and Katharine Turnbull in Bridgend, a.s.n. John, born 11th July 1797; w. Andrew Martine, Andrew Drummond.

   „   „ John Swanston and Isabel Lothian in Colmslee, a.d.n. Elizabeth, born 11th August 1793; w. Walter Chisholme, James Millar.

1795.
Aug. 13. Robert Laidlaw and Agnes Fairbairn in Blainslie, a.s.n. Thomas, born 22nd July 1795.

1797.
Aug. 13. Robert Laidlaw and Agnes Fairbairn in Blainslie, a.s.n. John, born 22nd January 1797; w. William Thin, Andrew Martine.

   1795. Andrew Martine and Helen Thin in Blainslie, a.d.n. Isabel, born 28th July 1795.

   1797. Andrew Martine and Helen Thin in Blainslie, a.s.n. William, born 7th January 1797; w. Robert Laidlaw, William Thin.

1796.
July 28. Alexander Broomfield and Isabel Beinstoun in Blue Cairn, a.d.n. Beinstoun Broomfield, born 16th July 1796; w. Nicol and William Scot.

1797.
Aug. 27. John Grieve and Isabel Marr in Gattonside, a.s.n. Gideon; w. William Scot, George Stewart.

   „   „ William Scot and Margaret Huntley in Gattonside, a.d.n. Janet; w. John Grieve, George Stewart.

   „   „ George Leitster and Agnes Sibbald in Darlingshaugh, a.d.n. Mary, born 19th February 1797; w. James Melrose, William Haldane.

   „   „ James Melrose and Mary Brown in Darlingshaugh, a.d.n. Mary, born 6th July 1797; w. George Leitster, William Haldane.

Sept. 23. Walter Ronaldson, mason, and Janet Wight in Darnick, a.d.n. Agnes.

   „   „ William Mercer, shoemaker, and Janet Heart in Melrose, a.s.n. Thomas; w. John Smith, William Cook.

Oct. 1. James Jamison and Margaret Ormistone in Melrose, a.s.n. Archibald.

   „   „ Andrew Moffat and Violet Hatton in Melrose, a.s.n. Andrew; w. Andrew Brown, William Cook.

   1785. John Watson, skinner, and Katharine Lees in Buckholmside, a.s.n. George, born 5th June 1785.

   1787. John Watson, skinner, and Katharine Lees in Buckholmside, a.d.n. Mary, born 9th November 1787.

   1790. John Watson, skinner, and Katharine Lees in Buckholmside, a.s.n. Henry, born 26th May 1790.

   1792. John Watson, skinner, and Katharine Lees in Buckholmside, a.s.n. John, born 30th November 1792.

   1794. John Watson, skinner, and Katharine Lees in Buckholmside, a.d.n. Agnes, born 19th July 1794; w. Henry Watson, John Lees.

1797.
Nov. 17. George Mathison and Isabel Campbell in Melrose, a.d.n. Isabel, born 14th June last; w. George Skirven, Robert Taket.

Dec. 16. Alexander Laing, soldier and serjeant in the 31st regiment of foot, and Margery Blacketer, his spouse, a.d.n. Elizabeth, born 9th and christened 15th December 1797; w. John Bower, William Chisholme.

   „ 21. William Wallace, labourer, and Agnes Bell in Melrose, a.d.n. Beatrix.

   „   „ Francis Burnet and Joan Williamson in Newstead, a.s.n. John.

   „   „ James Rutherfurd, labourer, and Agnes Hogg in Melrose, a.s.n. Thomas; w. William Cook, Robert Taket.

   „   „ Robert Crawford, shoemaker, and Jean Hogg in Melrose, a.d.n. Joan, born 12th November 1797; w. Robert Taket, George Hogg.

1797.

Dec. 24. George Hatton and Janet Scot in Melrose, a.d.n. Mary ; w. William Cook, Robert Taket.

" " George Mabon and Elizabeth Young in Melrose, a.s.n. William, born in September 1790.

" " George Mabon and Elizabeth Young in Melrose, a.d.n. Isabel, born in July 1789 ; w. John Martine, John Bower.

" " John Wright and Margaret Oliver in Melrose, a.d.n. Janet, born 5th November 1790 ; w. William Cook, Robert Taket.

1798.

Jan. 17. Mr. John Simpson and Elizabeth Somerville in Blainslie, a.s.n. John, born 12th December 1797 and baptised 17th January 1798 ; w. Messrs. John Simpson, senior, John Sommerville.

" 21. Robert Heymer and Elizabeth Millar in Melrose, a.s.n. John, born 4th November 1797 and baptised this day.

" " Andrew Heiton and Isabel Govan in Darnick, a.d.n. Margaret.

" " Adam Tait and Margaret Harper in Darnick, a.d.n. Margaret.

" " Alexander Turnbull and Elizabeth Mitchell in Darnick, a.d.n. Janet ; w. John Smith, William Cook.

" 23. James Millar and Elizabeth Heart in Newstead, a.s.n. Andrew, born December 31st, 1797, and baptised 23rd January 1798 ; w. William Mitchell, Andrew Morton.

" " James Thomson and Mary Buttler in Newstead, a.s.n. Thomas, born 19th December 1797 and baptised 23rd January 1798 ; w. William Mitchell, Andrew Morton.

" 24. Archibald Pitilla and Janet Wright in Newtown, a.d.n. Janet.

" " Robert Reid and Margaret Turnbull in Newtown, a.d.n. Jean ; w. Nicol Milne, John Bower.

" 25. William Coats and Grizel Burnet in Craigsford Mains, a.d.n. Jean ; w. Thomas Grieve, Joan Coats.

" 28. Thomas Elliot, schoolmaster, and Mary Scot in Newstead, a.s.n. Robert ; w. Thomas Williamson, James Nicol.

Feb. 4. James Wight, poortioner in Broomilees, and Marrion Ronaldson, his spouse, a.d.n. Janet ; w. John Smith, George Mercer.

" " James Bunzie and Helen Bruce in Newstead, a.d.n. Janet ; w. Thomas Williamson, James Nicol.

1797. Thomas Rutherford and Helen Oliver in Westerlanglee, a.s.n. George, born 25th April and christened 10th May 1797 ; w. James Wilson, James Thomson.

1798.

Feb. 11. John Gibson and Isabel Martine in Melrose, a.s.n. John.

" " David Sinclair and Margaret Rutherfurd in Melrose, a.s.n. John ; w. Williamn Cook, Robert Taket.

Mar. 4. Walter Davidson and Edgar Hislop in Westlanglee, a.s.n. Andrew, born 23rd January ; w. Thomas Boston, Robert Taket.

1797. Robert Nicol and Peggy Hart in Drygrange, a.d.n. Alison, born 20th October 1797 ; w. James Nicol, James Bell.

1793. George Graham and Joan Riddell in Bentmill, a.s.n. George, baptised in December 1797.

1798.

April 16. John Friar, tenant in Overlangshaw, and Margaret Bathgate, his spouse, a.d.n. Mary ; w. James Scot, Walter Chisholm.

1797. William Sessford and Helen Turnbull in Gattonside, a.s.n. James, born 10th March 1797, baptised 25th April 1797 ; w. Thomas Boston, Alexander Sibbald.

1798.

April 25. James Chalmers and Mary Fowler in Galashiels toll-bar, a.d.n. Jean, born 15th November 1797 ; w. Thomas Sanderson, John Scott.

" " Thomas Sanderson and Helen Martine at Galabridgeend, a.d.n. Agnes, born 18th February 1798 ; w. James Chalmers, John Scott.

1798.
April 25. Thomas Hislop and Elizabeth Watson in Darlingshaugh, a.s.n. Andrew, born 3rd January 1798.

,, ,, William Haldane and Jean Richardson in Darlingshaugh, a.s.n. Robert, born 17th March 1798 ; w. James Blaikie, Andrew Sanderson.

,, ,, James Sime and Margaret Clapperton in Darlingshaugh, a.d.n. Margaret, born 29th September 1797 ; w. William Haldane, Thomas Lun.

May 20. George Moss and Jean Kennedy in Berrymoss, a.s.n. Thomas ; w. John Smith, John Moss.

,, ,, John Leech and Isabel Robertson in Newstead, a.s.n. Andrew ; w. John Martine, Robert Taket.

1786. Jesse Mather and Isabel Mathison in Newtoun, a.d.n. Isabel, born 11th June 1786.

1788. Jesse Mather and Isabel Mathison in Newtown, a.s.n. Andrew, born 13th March 1788 ; w. Nicol Milne, Thomas Laidlaw.

1798.
June 3. William Smith and Margaret Bunzie in Drygrange, a.d.n. Margaret, born 7th March 1790 ; w. James Nicol, Thomas Haig.

,, ,, Alexander Denholm and Margaret Thorburn in Easterlanglee, a.d.n. Janet, born 12th April 1798 ; w. John and James Easton.

,, 10. James Grieve and Janet Brydon in Melrose, a.s.n. Robert ; w. William Cook, Robert Taket.

,, 17. John Cochran and Margaret Vair in Newstead, a.d.n. Margaret ; w. Thomas Vair, Robert Taket.

July 1. John Turnbull and Jean Currie in Gattonside, a.s.n. George, born 3rd June 1798 ; w. Thomas Boston, John Dickson.

,, ,, James Ballantyne and Janet Scott in Darnick, a.s.n. James ; w. John Smith, James Wight.

,, ,, Alexander Hobkirk and Barbara Amos in Melrose, a.d.n. Elizabeth ; w. James Hobkirk, Robert Taket.

,, ,, Thomas Heggie and Margaret Graham in Melrose, a.d.n. Margaret, born 27th May last ; w. William Cook, Robert Taket.

,, 26. Thomas Allan, baker, and Janet Scot in Melrose, a.d.n. Agnes.

,, ,, Robert Pringle, labourer, and Agnes Burnet in Newstead, a.s.n. John ; w. William Cook, Robert Taket.

,, ,, —— and Elizabeth Mein in Darnick, a.s.n. John Mein, born 18th July 1778 ; w. Thomas Vair, John Smith.

,, 30. Robert Walker, manufacturer in Buckholmside, and Janet Lang, his spouse, a.s.n. George, born 30th July 1798 ; w. George Bathgate, Richard Lees.

1797. James Bell and Janet Bruce in Drygrange, a.d.n. Margaret, born 26th January 1797 ; w. James and Robert Nicol.

1798.
Aug. —. Andrew Martine and Helen Thin in Blainslie, a.d.n. Helen, born 1st August 1798 ; w. William Thin, Andrew Shillinglaw.

,, ,, William Thin and Janet Broomfield in Blainslie, a.s.n. James, born 12th August 1798 ; w. Andrew Martine, Andrew Shillinglaw.

,, 26. John Martine, wright, and Mary Heiton in Melrose, a.s.n. John, born 30th July 1798 ; w. Robert Taket, Andrew Heiton.

,, 27. James Scott and Janet Pringle in Calfhill, a.d.n. Margaret, born 17th August 1798 ; w. John Pringle, John Dalziel.

,, ,, Mr. David Kyle and Agnes Scoon in Melrose, a.s.n. Alexander, born 24th June 1798 ; w. William Cook, Walter Turnbull.

,, ,, Thomas Cleghorn and Janet Kyle in Melrose, a.s.n. James, born 18th February 1798 and baptised 12th April 1798 ; w. Robert Taket, John Kyle.

Sept. 30. John Winter, labourer in Melrose, and Helen Hogg, his spouse, a.d.n. Agnes, born 20th August and baptised 30th September 1798 ; w. John Hogg, Andrew Brown.

1798.

Sept. 30. John Kyle, baker in Melrose, and Christian Thomson, his spouse, a.s.n. George, born 9th day of December 1796, and baptised 19th day of December 1797 ; w. Robert Taket, Alexander Hobkirk.

Oct. 14. Robert Anderson, labourer in Newstead, and Jean Wilson, his spouse, a.s.n. Thomas ; w. Adam Anderson, Robert Taket.

Nov. 11. Christian Thomson in Gattonside, a.s.n. John Thomson, born 15th May 1797 ; w. James Usher, Robert Taket.

„ 29. Archibald Campbell, gardener in Westerlanglee, and Elizabeth Kennedy. his spouse, a.d.n. Jean, born 9th November 1798 ; w. Robert Taket, William Cook.

„ 30. George Mathison, servant in Melrose, and Isabel Kennedy, his spouse, a.d.n. Jean, born 17th November 1798 ; w. Robert Taket, John Martine.

Dec. 23. Thomas Stevenson, smith in Darnick, and Janet Ormiston, his spouse, a.s.n. Alexander, born 20th October 1798 ; w. Adam Ormistone, Robert Taket.

„ „ Walter Turnbull, schoolmaster in Melrose, and Euphan Dickson, his spouse, a.s.n. James, born 23rd November 1798 ; w. Robert Taket, William Cook.

1799.

Jan. 6. Robert Turnbull, wright in Darnick, and Janet Elliot, his spouse a.s.n. Robert : w. John Smith, Andrew Heiton.

„ „ Robert Scott, labourer in Westerlanglee, and Betty Renwick, his spouse, a.s.n. Michael ; w. John Smith, Andrew Heiton.

„ 13. William Coats and Grizel Burnet in Craigsford, a.s.n. John, born 25th December 1798 ; w. Thomas Grieve, John Coats.

„ „ Robert Heart and Betty Scott in Newstead, a.d.n. Isabel, born 8th November 1798 ; w. James Nicol, James Bell.

„ „ James Nicol and Alison Mein in Drygrange, a.d.n. Agnes, born October 1798 : w. Robert Heart, James Bell.

Mar. 10. William Cook, merchant and portioner in Melrose, and Elizabeth Murray, his spouse, a.d.n. Helen, born 16th February 1799 ; w. Robert Taket, Robert Waugh.

„ 17. James Thomson, baker in Gattonside, and Margaret Stewart, his spouse, a.s.n. Robert, born January 1799 ; w. Thomas Boston, George Broomfield.

„ 24. William Burns, labourer in Kittyfield, and Alison Tait, his spouse, a.d.n. Mary, born 8th November 1798 ; w. Thomas Boston, Robert Taket.

„ „ John Turnbull, weaver, and Alison Noble in Newstead, a.d.n. Margaret, baptised 10th February 1799 ; w. Robert Heart, George Noble.

„ „ John Laidlaw, farmer, and Jemima Grant in Peashill, a.s.n. Thomas, baptised 14th July 1795 ; w. John Usher, John Sibbald.

„ „ John Laidlaw, farmer, and Jemima Grant in Peashill, a.s.n. Alexander, baptised 6th November 1796 : w. Thomas and Thomas Hardie.

„ „ John Laidlaw, farmer, and Jemima Grant in Peashill, a.s.n. Robert, baptised 26th February 1798 ; w. John Grant, James Bunzie.

„ „ Alexander Tudhope, flesher, and Isabel Hunter in Melrose, twins, a.s.n. Robert and a.d.n. Margaret, born 28th April 1798 and baptised 31st January 1799 ; w. Robert Myles, Robert Keddie.

„ „ John Paterson, weaver, and Margaret Stewart in Melrose, twins named Betty and Jean, born 5th January and baptised 19th January 1799 : w. Robert Taket, Robert Heymer.

„ „ John Elliot, candlemaker, and Agnes Inglis in Melrose, a.s.n. James, born 15th December 1798 ; w. Archibald Anderson, Robert Taket.

„ „ John Grieve, excise officer, and Elizabeth Reid in Melrose, a.d.n. Anne Agnes, born 21st March 1798 ; w. Archibald Anderson, Robert Taket.

1799.

April 14. Andrew Heart and Margaret Pringle in Newstead, a.s.n. James, born 24th January 1799 ; w. Andrew Pringle, Thomas Williamson.

,, ,, Andrew Pringle and Rachel Easton in Newstead, a.d.n. Helen, born 30th January 1799 ; w. Andrew Heart, Thomas Williamson.

,, ,, George Yorston, soldier in the Earl of Hopeton's Fencibles, and Isabel Anderson, a.s.n. Alexander, born at Aberdeen 13th April 1797 ; and

May 5. The same George Yorston, non-labourer at Darnick, and Isabel Anderson, a.s.n. George, born 18th April 1799 ; w. Andrew Heiton, John Smith.

,, ,, George Purves and Betty Spiers in Newtown, a.s.n. James, born 3rd May 1796.

,, ,, George Purves and Betty Spiers in Newtown, a.d.n. Janet, born 10th May 1798 ; w. Gideon Scott, Thomas Laidlaw.

,, ,, John Gibson and Betty Millar in Blainslie, a.s.n. Peter, born 8th April 1799 ; w. Robert Salmon, John Ford.

,, 26. Archibald Pitilla and Janet Wright, a.s.n. Gideon, born 29th April 1799 ; w. William Vair, Robert Taket.

,, ,, Thomas Wilson and Joan Pentland in Harlaburn, a.d.n. Alison, born 26th March 1799 ; w. Thomas Usher, John Smith.

,, 30. Thomas Haig, gardener, and Mary Sibbald in Drygrange, a.s.n. Archibald ; w. James Bell, James Nicol.

June 2. Andrew Bunzie, weaver, and Peggy Williamson in Newstead, a.s.n. Andrew ; w. Thomas Williamson, James Ramsay.

,, 6. John Cleugh and Janet Tait in Threepwood, a.d.n. Margaret, born 13th April 1799.

,, ,, Walter Chisholm and Jean Cowan in Langshawmiln, a.s.n. James, born 1st May 1799 ; w. John Cleugh, James Millar.

,, ,, William Mitchell and Peggy Burnet in Newstead, a.d.n. Jean, baptised 2nd June 1799 ; w. James Ramsay, Thomas Williamson.

,, ,, Robert Boston and Christian Graham in Darnick, twins, a.s.n. Robert and a.d.n. Mary, born 8th May 1799 and baptised 19th May 1799 ; w. Thomas Dickson, John Duncan.

,, 9. James Johnstone and Peggy Cowan in Melrose, a.d.n. Janet ; w. Robert Taket, William Cook.

,, 23. Andrew Heiton and Isabel Govan in Darnick, a.s.n. William, born 1st May 1799 ; w. John Heiton, John Smith.

July 7. Andrew Young and Mary Bell in Melrose, a.s.n. James ; w. William Cook, Robert Taket.

1798. William Sessford and Helen Turnbull in Gattonside, a.s.n. William, born 10th October 1798 and baptised 10th November 1798 ; w. Thomas Boston, John Robson.

1799.

July 21. John Rutherfurd and Katharine Turnbull in Bridgend, a.d.n. Mary, born 18th June 1799 ; w. William Cook, John Smith.

,, 25. Betty Cook, born 22nd December 1779 ; w. Nicol Milne, James Laidlaw.

Aug. 4. Adam Dalgliesh and Agnes Wilson in Calfhill, a.s.n. Adam, born 19th June 1799.

,, ,, James Boyd and Betty Chisholm in Calfhill, a.s.n. George, born 22nd March 1799 ; w. Thomas Chisholm, James Millar.

,, ,, Thomas Usher and Elizabeth Stevenson in Newstead, a.d.n. Christian ; w. Thomas Williamson, James Ramsay.

,, ,, David Sinclair, shoemaker, and Margaret Rutherfurd in Melrose, a.d.n. Isabel, born 9th July 1799 ; w. James Rutherfurd, Robert Taket.

,, ,, George Waldie and Margaret Waldie in Drygrange, a.d.n. Janet, born 1st April 1799 ; w. James Nicol, James Bell.

,, ,, James Hopkirk, shoemaker, and Anne Wright, a.d.n. Mary, born 17th April 1799 ; w. William Cook, Robert Taket Melrose.

1799.

Aug.   4. James Henderson, shoemaker, and Isabel Aitken in Melrose, a.d.n. Janet, born 17th January 1799 ; w. William Cook, Robert Taket.

,,   ,, John Drummond, labourer, and Agnes Walker in Newtown, a.d.n. Isabel, born 21st May 1799 ; w. Nicol Milne, James Laidlaw.

,,   ,, James Henderson, labourer, and Jean Young in Eildon, a.d.n. Agnes, born 23rd April 1797 ; w. James Laidlaw, Nicol Milne.

,,   ,, James Henderson, labourer, and Jean Young in Eildon, a.s.n. James, born 19th January 1799 ; w. James Laidlaw, Nicol Milne.

,,   ,, William Mercer, shoemaker, and Janet Heart in Melrose, a.d.n. Margaret, born 30th May 1799 ; w. Nicol Mercer, John Hatton.

,,   ,, Thomas Sanderson, wright, and Helen Martine at Galashiels toll-bar, a.s.n. Thomas, born 24th March 1799 ; w. James Blaikie, John Graham.

,,   8. James Bunzie and Anne Thomson in Newstead, a.s.n. William ; w James Ramsay, Thomas Williamson.

,,   11. Andrew Cunninghame and Mary Turner in Gattonside, a.s.n. Henry, born 29th May 1799 ; w. John Cessford, Thomas Bell.

,,   13. Mr. William Spence, surgeon, and Mrs. Janet Park, his spouse, in the Haugh, a.d.n. Margaret, born 2nd July 1799 ; w. John Park, James Millar.

,,   ,, Alexander Pringle, merchant, and Barbara Millar in Melrose, born 10th March 1799 ; w. James Pringle, Robert Penman.

,,   ,, Alexander Pringle, merchant, and Barbara Millar in Melrose, a.d.n. Sarah, born 10th March 1799 ; w. James Pringle, Robert Penman.

,,   ,, John Clark, weaver, and Janet Ivly in Darlingshaugh, a.s.n. James, born 6th December 1798 and christened 17th January 1799 ; w. James Lees, John Roberts.

,,   ,, William Turnbull, stocking weaver, and Mary Donaldson in Darlingshaugh, a.s.n. George, born 13th November 1798 ; w. Thomas Sanderson, Thomas Hislop.

,,   ,, Robert Walker, weaver, and Elizabeth Stenhouse in Darlingshaugh, a.s.n. John, born 3rd August 1798 ; w. Archibald and Richard Cochrans.

,,   ,, James Sime, manufacturer, and Margaret Clapperton in Darlingshaugh, a.d.n. Janet, born 27th January 1799 ; w. William Haldane, Thomas Lun.

,,   16. Andrew Drummond, smith, and Janet Clapperton in Darnick, a.s.n. Robert, born 14th January 1799 ; w. Andrew Heiton, Robert Boston.

,,   ,, John Moss, portioner, and Betty Dunlop in Keaside, a.s.n. John, born 28th June 1799 ; w. George Moss, George Wight.

,,   31. John Sanderson, mason, and Joan Murray in Kersfield, a.s.n. Thomas, born 18th July 1798 ; w. Thomas and Andrew Sandersons.

,,   ,, Richard Lees, manufacturer, and Mary Paterson in Buckholmside, a.d.n. Isabel, born 2nd June 1798 ; w. John Lees and John Lees.

Sept. 8. William Heart, labourer, and Isabel Hatton in Melrose, a.s.n. William, born 27th July 1799 ; w. William Cook, John Easton.

,,   ,, George Muir, shepherd, and Isabel Dickson in Mosshouses, a.d.n. Isabel, born 27th May 1794 ; w. John Frier, Walter Chisholm.

,,   ,, George Muir, shepherd, and Isabel Dickson in Mosshouses, a.d.n. Janet, born 23rd June 1799 ; w. John Frier, Walter Chisholm.

,,   ,, Thomas Taylor, merchant, and Jean Trotter in Melrose, a.d.n. Helen, born 4th September 1799 ; w. William Cook, Andrew Brown.

,,   ,, Andrew Sanderson, mason, and Jean Scott in Kersfield, twins, a.s.n. William and a.d.n. Mary, born 9th September 1799 ; w. Thomas and John Sandersons.

,,   ,, William Hume, farmer, and Isabel Gibson in Gateside, a.s.n. Alexander, born 27th December 1793 : w. William Scot, James Hay.

1799.

Sept. 8. William Hume, farmer, and Isabel Gibson in Gateside, a.d.n. Beatrix, born 18th July 1794 ; w. William Scot, James Hay.

,, ,, William Hume, farmer, and Isabel Gibson in Gateside, a.s.n. John, born 3rd May 1796 ; w. William Scot, James Hay.

,, ,, William Hume, farmer, and Isabel Gibson in Gateside, a.s.n. William, born 1st March 1798 : w. William Scot, James Hay.

,, 29. Francis Burnet, labourer, and Joan Williamson in Newstead, a.s.n. John, born 12th August 1799; w. Thomas Williamson, James Ramsay.

,, ,, Robert Scott, weaver, and Martha Smaill in Danieltown, a.s.n. William, born 8th June 1799 and baptised 30th June 1799 at Newtown by Mr. Elder, minister ; w. William Scott, Walter Balmer.

,, ,, John Kyle, baker, and Christian Thomson in Melrose, a.s.n. David, born 18th February 1799 ; w. William Cook, Robert Taket, elders in Melrose.

Oct. 20. William Scott, weaver, and Margaret Huntley in Gattonside, a.d.n. Mary, born 21st August 1799 ; w. George Stewart, Thomas Boston.

,, 27. John Easton, wright, and Margaret Watson in Melrose, a.s.n. George, born 13th September 1799 ; w. Robert Taket, William Cook.

Nov. 17. John Taket, merchant, and Janet Martin in Melrose, a.s.n. Robert, born 25th October 1799 ; w. Robert Taket, John Martin.

,, ,, Robert Heiton, weaver, and Elizabeth Fisher in Darnick, a.d.n. Elizabeth, born 21st October 1799 : w. James Wilson, John Graham.

,, 22. Robert Thomson, shepherd, and Agnes Brownlees in Ouplaw, a.s.n. Alexander, born 3rd September 1799 ; w. James Wilson, John Graham.

,, ,, John Lees, farmer, and Isabel Paterson in Whitlaw, a.s.n. William, born 16th June 1788.

,, ,, John Lees, farmer, and Isabel Paterson in Whitlaw, a.s.n. Robert born 6th September 1791.

,, ,, John Lees, farmer, and Isabel Paterson in Whitlaw, a.d.n. Margaret, born 10th May 1797 : w. James Blaikie, John Murray.

,, ,, John Lees, farmer, and Isabel Paterson in Whitlaw, a.d.n. Elizabeth, born 14th July 1794.

,, 24. William Nicol, labourer, and Elizabeth Keddie in Darnick, a.s.n. Robert, born 1st September 1799 ; w. James Usher, John Smith.

,, 27. Mr. John Simpson and Elizabeth Sommerville in Blainslie, a.d.n. Janet, born 19th October 1799 : w. George Sommerville, George Henderson.

,, ,, Adam Spiers and Mary Scott in Blainslie, a.s.n. George, born 26th October 1799 ; w. George Sommerville, George Henderson.

Dec. 1. John Lindsay, wright, and Eliza Smith in Gattonside, a.s.n. James, born 22nd July 1798 ; w. Thomas Boston, John Dickson.

,, ,, John Lindsay, wright, and Eliza Smith in Gattonside, a.d.n. Margaret, born 1st November 1799 ; w. Thomas Boston, John Dickson.

,, ,, William Mathison, portioner, and Janet Henderson in Gattonside, a.d.n. Isabel, born 16th October 1799 ; w. Thomas Boston, John Lindsay.

,, ,, James Sclaiter and Ann Mein in Newstead, a.s.n. John, born 2nd January 1787 ; w. William Mabon, James Ramsay.

,, ,, James Sclaiter and Ann Mein in Newstead, a.d.n. Nelly, born 1st October 1790 ; w. William Mabon, James Ramsay.

,, 15. Adam Fiddes, mason, and Margaret Herriot in Newstead, a.s.n. James, born 27th September 1799 ; w. James Ramsay, Thomas Williamson.

1799.

Dec. 15. John Laidlaw and Jemima Grant in Peasehill, a.d.n. Margaret, born 13th November 1799 and baptised 18th December 1799 ; w. John Grant, Robert Myles.

  ,, ,, James Tait, portioner, and Margaret Stoddart, Berry-Loch, a.s.n. James, born at Greenhead in Galashiels parish 8th December 1785 ; w. George Wight, George Moss.

  ,, ,, James Tait, portioner, and Margaret Stoddart, Berry-Loch, a.s.n. William, born 12th July 1787 ; w. George Wight, George Moss.

  ,, ,, James Tait, portioner, and Margaret Stoddart, Berry-Loch, a.d.n. Mary, born 15th March 1790 ; w. George Wight, George Moss.

  ,, ,, John Gray, labourer, and Mary Hall in Blainslie, a.d.n. Rebekah, bord 3rd December 1799, christened 19th January 1800 ; w. Thomas Laurie, William Thynne.

1800.

Jan. 26. Rev. Mr. George Thomson and Mrs. Margaret Gillon, his spouse, a.s.n. Thomas, born in Melrose Manse 2nd January 1800 and christened this day ; w. William Cook, Robert Taket.

1797. Thomas Laurie, ploughman, and Jean Turnbull in Broomhill, a.s.n. Andrew, born 3rd March 1797 ; w. James Mercer, George Cranstone.

1799. Thomas Laurie, ploughman, and Jean Turnbull in Broomhill, a.d.n. Helen, born 11th September 1799 ; w. James Mercer, George Cranstone.

1800.

Feb. 16. James Bunzie, labourer, and Nelly Bruce in Newstead, a.s.n. Thomas, born 28th December 1799 ; w. Thomas Williamson, James Ramsay.

  ,, ,, Andrew Brown, merchant, and Janet Mather in Melrose, a.d.n. Mary, born 18th January 1800 ; w. Robert Taket, William Cook.

  ,, ,, Alexander Hopkirk, tailor, and Barbara Amos in Melrose, a.s.n. David Erskine, born 27th November 1799 ; w. Robert Taket, William Cook.

  ,, ,, John Elliot, candlemaker, and Agnes Inglis in Melrose, a.d.n. Isabel, born 13th September 1799 ; w. Robert Taket, William Cook.

  ,, ,, Thomas Hislop and Elizabeth Watson in Darlingshaugh, a.s.n. James, born 9th December 1799 ; w. Thomas Sanderson, William Johnstone.

  ,, 23. Robert Heymer and Elisabeth Millar in Melrose, a.s.n. James, born 12th November 1799 ; w. Andrew Brown, William Cook.

1784. Andrew Maither, smith in Blainslie, and Agnes Hamilton, a.s.n. John, born 20th and baptised 30th April 1784.

1785. Andrew Maither, smith in Blainslie, and Agnes Hamilton, a.d.n. Elspeth, born 15th and baptised 25th January 1785.

1787. Andrew Maither, smith in Blainslie, and Agnes Hamilton, a.d.n. Mary, born 28th December 1787 and baptised 3rd January 1788 ; w. Andrew Martin, Robert Laidlaw.

1800. James Chalmers and Mary Fowler at Galashiels toll-bar, a.d.n. Margaret, born 23rd January 1800 ; w. Thomas Sanderson, Thomas Hislop.

Mar. 23. Andrew Moffat and Violet Hatton in Melrose, a.s.n. William, born 15th February 1800, a.s.n. William ; w. Robert Hymer, George Hatton.

April 6. John Hatton, taylor, and Isabel Brown in Melrose, a.d.n. Agnes, born 12th February 1800 ; w. Andrew Moffat, Andrew Brown.

  ,, ,, James Jamison, miller, and Margaret Ormistone in Melrose, a.s.n. Andrew, born 25th February 1800 ; w. Andrew Brown, William Cook.

  ,, ,, James Jamison, smith, and Agnes Veitch in Newtown, a.s.n. Thomas born 13th December 1799 ; w. Nicol Milne, William Stevenson.

  ,, 20. William Wallace, labourer, and Agnes Bell in Melrose, a.s.n. William ; w. William Cook, Robert Taket.

1800.

April 27. James Melrose, smith, and Mary Brown in Darlingshaugh, a.d.n. Bina, born 4th March 1800 ; w. Adam Young, James Syme.

May 4. James Nicol, miller, and Alison Mein in Drygrange, a.d.n. Jean, born 24th February 1800 ; w. James Bell, Andrew Brown.

„ „ William Easton, labourer, and Elizabeth Robertson in Hagburn, a.s.n. Samuel, born 7th February 1800 : w. John Lees, Robert Inglis.

„ 11. Walter Ronaldson, mason, and Janet Wight in Darnick, a.s.n. George, born 11th March 1800 : w. George Ronaldson, George Wight.

„ 25. John Stevenson, weaver, and Isabel Waugh in Bridgend, a.d.n. Mary, born 17th April 1800 ; w. John Rutherfurd, John Mercer.

„ „ Thomas Dickson and Betty Vair in Darnick, a.s.n. Robert, born 11th April 1800 : w. John Smith, James Usher.

„ „ Robert Scott, labourer, and Betty Renwick in Westerlanglee, a.s.n. Robert, born 30th April 1800 ; w. William Ainslie, James Ainslie.

„ „ James Millar, labourer, and Betty Hart in Newstead, a.s.n. Robert, born 5th January 1800 : w. Thomas Williamson, James Ramsay.

June 8. Thomas Inglis, gardener, and Margaret Allan in Darnick, a.d.n. Christian, born 10th May 1800 ; w. John Smith, Andrew Heiton.

„ „ Robert Crawfurd, shoemaker, and Jean Hogg in Melrose, a.d.n. Agnes, born 1st March 1800 ; w. George Hogg, David Kyle.

„ 11. James Scott, tenant, and Janet Pringle in Calfhill, a.d.n. Elizabeth, born 31st May 1800 : w. James and George Hewit.

„ 21. George Moss and Jean Kennedy in Berryloch, a.s.n. George, born 21st May ; w. Andrew Heiton, John Smith.

„ 29. John Musgrave, shoemaker, and Katharine Jamison in Melrose, a.d.n. Elisabeth, born 18th May 1800 : w. James Jamison, Robert Taket.

July 24. Thomas Cook and Elizabeth Dobson in Stow parish, a.s.n. John Cook, born 25th February 1782 ; w. Thomas Boston, John Dickson.

„ „ John Mack and Beatrice Edgar in Newstead, a.s.n. William, born 2nd April 1782 : w. Thomas Williamson, James Ramsay.

Aug. 10. Robert Anderson and Jean Wilson in Newstead, a.d.n. Alice ; w. James Ramsay, Thomas Williamson.

„ „ William Mein and Janet Millar in Haxlaws, a.d.n. Isabel, born 5th April 1800 ; w. Nicol Milne, Robert Taket.

„ 24. Walter Turnbull, schoolmaster, and Euphemia Dickson in Melrose, a.d.n. Euphemia, born 23rd July 1800 ; w. William Cook, Robert Taket.

Sept. 14. George Drummond, weaver, and Helen Frame in Darnick, a.s.n. Andrew ; w. Andrew Drummond, John Smith.

„ „ Robert Heart, weaver, and Betty Scot in Newstead, a.s.n. John, born 15th July 1800 ; w. Robert Taket, William Cook.

„ „ Robert Robson, mason, and Jean Harper in Gattonside, a.d.n. Susan. [See this entered 25th December 1796].

„ „ James Wight, portioner, and Mary Ronaldson in Darnick, a.d.n. Isabel : w. George Wight, George Ronaldson.

Oct. 5. William Edgar and Christian Waugh in Melrose, a.s.n. Robert, born 18th May 1800 ; w. William Cook, Robert Taket.

„ „ John Martin, wright, and Marrion Heiton in Melrose, a.d.n. Margaret, born 24th September 1800 ; w. John Taket, William Cook.

„ 26. John Paterson, weaver, and Margaret Stewart in Melrose, a.s.n. Simon, born 29th June 1800 ; w. William Cook, Robert Taket.

Nov. 17. William Sessford and Nelly Turnbull in Gattonside, a.s.n. Robert, born 22nd September 1800 ; w. George Broomfield, John Dickson.

„ „ Alexander Bell and Peggy Stewart in Melrose, a.s.n. John, born 30th July 1800 : w. William Cook, Robert Taket.

z

1800.

Nov. 17. Andrew Pringle, merchant, and Barbara Millar in Melrose, a.s.n.
James, born 27th July 1800, and baptized 4th November ; w.
Robert Penman, James Pringle.

.,   ,, Archibald Pitilla and Janet Wright in Newtown, a.d.n. Janet, born
8th November 1800 ; w. Nicol Milne, John Bowar.

Dec. 28. John Winter, labourer, and Nelly Hogg in Melrose, a.d.n. Mary,
born December 1800 ; w. John Hogg, John Easton.

.,   ,, Andrew Harkness and Janet Mathison in Gattonside, a.s.n. William,
born 1st September 1800 ; w. William and John Mathison.

,,   ,, William Thynne and Janet Brownfield in Blainslie, a.d.n. Isabel,
born 29th June 1800 ; w. Andrew Martine, James Thynne.

1801.

Feb. 8. Andrew Anderson, labourer, and Violet Cranston in Melrose, a.s n.
Adam, born 31st December 1800 ; w. John Martine, Robert
Ormistone.

,,   ,, James Henderson, shoemaker, and Isabel Aitken in Melrose, a.d.n.
Jean, born 16th December 1800 ; w. John Martin, Alexander
Bell.

., 12. Robert Pringle, labourer, and Margaret Burnet in Newstead, a.s.n.
James, born 16th January 1801 ; w. Thomas Williamson, James
Ramsay.

.,   ,, John Sanderson and Joan Murray in Kersfield, a.s.n. David, born
13th October 1800 ; w. Thomas and Andrew Sanderson.

,,   ,, Thomas Sanderson and Helen Martin in Gala-bridgend, a.s.n.
William, born 14th January 1801 ; w. James Blaikie, John
Graham.

,,   ,, Andrew Martin, portioner in Blainslie, and Nelly Thynne, his spouse,
a.s.n. James, born 27th November 1800 ; w. William Thynne,
Robert Laidlaw.

Mar. 6. John Goodsman, residing in Darlingshaugh, near Galashiels, and
Ann Darling, his spouse, a.s.n. John, born 4th January 1801, and
baptized 6th March instant 1801.

,,   ,, Robert Laidlaw, soldier in his Majesty's 22nd light dragoons, and
Dorothy Evans, his spouse, a.s.n. Thomas, born 5th April 1798.

.,   ,, The above Robert Laidlaw and Dorothy Evans, a.s.n. William, born
28th June 1800 ; w. Nicol Milne, Nicol Stenhouse.

April 4. Thomas Vair and Janet Burnet in Darnick, a.s.n. James, born
4th January 1801 ; w. John Smith, James Usher.

,,   ,, Robert Fairbairn and Peggy Elliot in Newtown, a.s.n. Robert, born
January 1801 ; w. Nicol Milne, James Milne.

,, 19. William Mercer, shoemaker, and Janet Heart in Melrose, a.d.n.
Margaret, born 21st February 1801 ; w. John Taket, Nicol
Mercer.

.,   ,, James Henderson and Jean Young in Eildon, a.s.n. Robert, born
8th October 1800.

., 26. John Drummond and Agnes Walker in Newtown, a.d.n. Isabel,
born 14th March 1801.

,,   ,, John Graham, mason, and Mary Ormiston in Melrose, a.s.n. Thomas ;
w. William Cook, Robert Taket.

May 10. John Turnbull and Jean Currie in Gattonside, a.d.n. Jean, born
1st April 1801 ; w. Thomas Turnbull, Robert Taket.

,,   ,, William Hume and Margaret Hume in Gattonside, a.s.n. Alexander,
born 29th June 1800.

,,   ,, Robert Robson, mason, and Jean Harper in Gattonside, a.d.n.
Euphan, born 2nd December 1799 ; w. Thomas Boston, George
Stewart.

,,   ,, William Turnbull, stockingweaver, and Mary Donaldson in
Darlingshaugh, a.s.n. Robert, born 22nd April 1801 ; w. Thomas
Sanderson, James Blaikie.

1801.

May 10. Richard Cochran, weaver, and Anne Sanderson, a.d.n. Anne, born 17th January 1801 ; w. Thomas Sanderson, James Blaikie.

,, ,, William Haldane and Jean Richardson in Darlingshaugh, a.d.n. Mary, born 11th October 1799 ; w. Thomas Sanderson, James Blaikie.

,, ,, Robert Walker, weaver, and Betty Stenhouse in Darlingshaugh, a.s.n. Thomas, born 6th April 1801 ; w. Thomas Sanderson, James Blaikie.

,, ,, James Syme, manufacturer, and Margaret Clapperton in Darlings-haugh, a.d.n. Elizabeth, born 12th February 1801 ; w. James Blaikie, Thomas Sanderson.

June 7. Robert Aitken and Janet Fisher in Caseside, a.d.n. Janet, born 1st May 1801 ; w. Robert Taket, William Cook.

,, ,, Robert Anderson, mason, and Peggy Thomson in Melrose, a.s.n James, born 11th May 1801 ; w. James Graham, William Cook.

,, ,, James Fish and Isabel Tait in Darnick, a.s.n. John ; w. James Usher, John Smith.

,, 28. Adam Tait, portioner, and Margaret Harper in Darnick, a.s.n. John, born 22nd May 1801.

,, ,, James Johnstone, labourer, and Margaret Cowan in Melrose, a.d.n. Isabel, born May 1801 ; w. Robert Taket, John Smith.

July 5. Andrew Pringle, mason, and Rachael Easton in Newstead, a.s.n. Andrew ; w. John Martin, Thomas Williamson.

,, ,, William Thomson and Isabel Marr in Newstead, a.d.n. Margaret, born 15th April 1787 ; w. James Marr, John Mein.

,, 29. Mr. John Simson and Elizabeth Sommerville in Blainslie, a.d.n. Euphemia, born 29th June 1801 ; w. Mr. James Sommerville, Mr. Donald Cameron.

,, ,, Andrew Aitchison and Isabel Fairbairn in Blainesly, a.d.n. Mary ; w. as above.

,, ,, Thomas Hay, tenant in Keaside, and Janet Smail, a.s.n. James, born 18th June 1801 ; w. James Hay, James Mercer.

,, ,, James Mercer, portioner, Coatgreen, and Alison Hay, a.d.n. Elizabeth, born 17th April 1801 ; w. James and Thomas Hay.

,, ,, Thomas Haig, gardener, and Mary Sibbald in Drygrange, a.d.n. Janet, born 22nd July 1801 ; w. James Bell, James Nicol.

,, ,, William Haldane, carrier, and Jean Richardson in Darlingshaugh, a.s.n. Adam, born 11th July 1801 ; w. Thomas Sanderson, James Blaikie.

,, ,, George Murray, dyer, and Agnes Sanderson in Darlingshaugh, a.d.n. Mary, born 28th February 1801 ; w. Thomas Sanderson, James Blaikie.

,, ,, John Clark, weaver, and Janet Ivly in Darlingshaugh, a.s.n. John, born 29th August 1801 ; w. John and William Watson.

,, ,, Robert Scott, weaver, and Martha Smaill in Danielton, a.s.n. Thomas, born 19th April 1801 ; w. William Scott, George Lawrie.

Sept. 27. John Lindsay, wright, and Elizabeth Smith in Gattonside, a.s.n. John, born 25th June 1801 ; w. Thomas Boston, William Cook.

,, ,, Robert Murray, burgess in Lauder, and Isabel Pringle, his spouse, a.s.n. William, born at Blainslie 1st April 1801 ; w. James Weatherstone, Thomas Wight.

,, ,, Andrew Bunzie, weaver, and Peggy Williamson in Newstead, a.d.n. Mary, born 8th July 1801 ; w. Thomas Williamson, James Ramsay.

Oct. 4. James Rutherford, labourer, and Agnes Hogg in Melrose, a.d.n. Janet, born 20th August 1801 ; w. William Cook, Robert Taket.

,, ,, Alexander Tudhope, flesher, and Isabella Turner in Melrose, a.s.n. William, born 19th November 1800 ; w. William Cook, Robert Taket.

1801.

Oct.   4. John Grieve, excise officer, and Elizabeth Reid in Melrose, a.d.n. Janet, born 23rd November 1800 ; w. William Cook, Robert Taket.

„   18. William Mathison, portioner, and Janet Henderson in Gattonside, a.s.n. Alexander, born July 1801 ; w. Thomas Boston, George Broomfield.

„   „ Rev. Mr. George Thomson and Mrs. Margaret Gillon, his spouse, a.d.n. Margaret, born in Melrose Manse, 21st September 1801 ; w. William Cook, Robert Taket.

Nov.   1. Andrew Cunningham and Mary Turner in Gattonside, a.d.n. Mary, born 28th August 1801 ; w. Alexander Tudhope, Thomas Boston.

„   „ John Rutherford, portioner, and Catharine Turnbull in Bridgend, a.d.n. Catharine, born 29th August 1801 ; w. John Mercer, Walter Turnbull.

„   11. George Mathison, servant, and Isabel Campbell, his spouse, in Melrose, a.s.n. John, born 31st October 1801 ; w. William Cook, Robert Taket.

„   „ William Coats, farmer, and Grizel Burnet in Craigsford, a.d.n. Margaret, born 14th October 1801 ; w. Thomas Grieve, Thomas Williamson.

Dec.   6. Thomas Allan, baker, and Janet Scott, his wife, in Melrose, twins named Helen and Elisabeth, born 5th October 1801 ; w. Andrew Brown, Robert Allan.

„   „ James Millar, labourer, and Betty Heart in Newstead, a.s.n. James, born 5th January 1800 ; w. James Ramsay, Thomas Williamson.

„   „ John Laidlaw, portioner, and Jemima Grant in Peashill, twins named Andrew and Walter, born 28th September 1801 ; w. John Sibbald, Robert Myles.

„   „ George Cook, labourer, and Peggy Sanderson in Melrose, a.d.n. Betty, born 18th October 1801 ; Robert Taket, William Cook.

1802.

Jan.   2. George Nobel, weaver, and Jean Laurie in Melrose, a.d.n. Jean, born ——— ; w. George Laurie, William Cook.

„   „ John Paton, portioner, and Isabel Cochran in Melrose, a.s n. John, born 4th March 1784 ; w. Helen Gill, Katharine Vogan.

„   24. Hardie, say to George Hardie and Anne Purves in Newstead, a.s.n. John, born 24th November 1801 ; w. Thomas Hardie, Francis Burnet.

Feb.   7. Francis Burnet and Joan Williamson in Newstead, a.d.n. Jenny, born 15th November 1801.

„   „ Robert Collier and Jean Dods in Gattonside, a.d.n. Margaret, born 10th November 1801 ; w. Thomas Williamson, Thomas Bostone.

„   „ Thomas Laidlaw, mason in Blainslie, and Peggy Scott, a.s.n. Thomas, born July 30th, 1799.

„   „ Thomas Laidlaw, mason in Blainslie, and Peggy Scott, a.d.n. Agnes, born January 7th, 1802 ; w. James Scott, Robert Laidlaw.

„   „ Adam Spiers, smith in Blainslie, and Mary Tait, a.d.n. Agnes, born 10th January 1802 ; w. John Simson, James Wilson.

„   11. John Grieve and Isabel Marr in Gattonside, a.s.n. Gideon, born 15th December 1801 ; w. Thomas Boston, John Dickson.

„   16. James Scott, farmer, and Janet Pringle in Calfhill, a.s.n. James, born 3rd February 1802.

„   „ Adam Dalgliesh and Agnes Wilson, a.d.n. Elisabeth, born 27th November 1801 ; w. George Pringle, George Hewit.

„   21. Andrew Heart, mason, and Peggy Pringle in Newstead, a.d.n. Helen ; w. James Ramsay, James Pringle.

Mar.   7. William Douglas, dyer, and Janet Lees in Darlingshaugh, a.s.n. Robert, born 26th January 1802 ; w. Thomas Sanderson, James Blaikie.

„   „ Thomas Hislop, labourer, and Betty Watson in Darnick, a.s.n. Thomas : w. Andrew Heiton, James Usher.

1802.

Mar. 7. John Hatton, tailor, and Isabel Brown in Melrose, a.s.n. John, born 24th January 1802 ; w. George Hatton, Andrew Brown.

" " John Easton, wright, and Peggy Watson in Melrose, a.s.n. Robert, born 26th January 1802 ; w. Robert Taket, William Cook.

April 11. Andrew Muir, teacher, and Margaret Fairbairn in Melrose, a.d.n. Margaret, born 7th March 1802 ; w. John Martin, Thomas Fairbairn.

" 18. Thomas Usher and Betty Stevenson in Newstead, a.s.n. William ; w. Robert Pringle, James Ramsay.

May 2. John Taket, merchant, and Janet Martine in Melrose, a.s.n. John, born 10th April 1802 ; w. Robert Taket, John Martine.

" " John Lees, clothier, and Jean Young in Channel, a.s.n. John, born 14th January 1802 ; w. James Blaikie, Thomas Sanderson.

" " James Sime, clothier, and Margaret Clapperton, Darlingshaugh, a.d.n. Isabel, born 23rd February 1802 ; w. same as above.

" " James Chalmers and Mary Fowler at Galashiels toll-bar, a.s.n. William, born 5th March 1802 ; same witnesses.

" " John Sanderson, wright, and Anne Shortreid, a.d.n. Anne, born 31st March 1802 ; same witnesses.

" " Robert Walker, clothier, and Janet Lang in Buckholmside, a.s.n. Andrew, born 2nd February 1802 ; same witnesses.

" " Joshua Wood, clothier, and Isabel Walker in Buckholmside, a.s.n. John, born 22nd July 1801 ; w. James Blaikie, Thomas Sanderson.

" " John Sandilands, weaver, and Agnes Murray in Channel, a.d.n. Esther, born 10th February 1802 ; same witnesses.

" 9. Robert Crawford, shoemaker, and Jean Hogg, a.s.n. Robert ; w. William Cook, Robert Taket in Melros e.

" " Andrew Drummond, smith, and Janet Clapperton in Darnick, a.s.n. James ; w. Andrew Heiton, John Smith.

" " Alexander Mitchell and Janet Hunter in Clackmae, a.d.n. Mary, born 13th January 1801 ; w. John and James Fisher.

" " George Armstrong, farmer, and Margaret Bell in Broadwoodshiell, a.s.n. William, born 1st April 1802 ; w. James Stirling, William Houlistone.

" 23. William Law, shepherd, and Betty Linton in Ouplaw, a.d.n. Elizabeth ; w. John Frier, Walter Chisholm.

June 10. Thomas Nisbet and Agnes Gavenlock in Darlingshaugh, a.s.n. Robert ; w. James Blaikie, Thomas Sanderson.

" 20. James Wight and Mary Ronaldson in Darnick, a.s.n. George, born 16th May 1802 ; w. John Smith, Andrew Heiton.

July 10. Andrew Heiton, portioner, and Isabel Govan in Darnick, a.s.n. James, born 1802 ; w. John Smith, George Mercer.

" " Walter Ronaldson, mason, and Janet Wight in Darnick, a.d.n. Janet, born 1802 ; w. John Smith, George Wight.

" " Walter Davidson, labourer, and Edgar Hislop in Cartleehole, a.s.n. John, born 4th April 1802 ; w. John Rutherford, George Wight.

" " Walter Davidson, labourer, and Edgar Hislop in Cartleehole, a.d.n. Janet, born 12th September 1799 ; w. John Smith, George Wight.

" 22. Thomas Bell, weaver, and Nelly Turner in Gattonside, a.s.n. William ; w. Thomas Boston, John Dickson.

Aug. 15. James Bunzie and Nelly Bruce in Newstead, a.d.n. Agnes ; w. Thomas Williamson, James Ramsay.

" 22. Alexander Hopkirk, taylor, and Barbara Amos, a.d.n. Jean, born in Melrose, June 17th, 1802.

" " George Moss and Jean Kennedy at Berryloch, a.s.n. Andrew, born 21st July 1802.

" " Walter Turnbull, schoolmaster in Melrose, and Euphan Dickson, a.d.n. Nelly, born 19th July 1802 ; w. Robert Taket, George Brodie.

" " James Mercer, portioner, and Alice Hay in Coatgreen, a.s.n. George, born 6th April 1802 ; w. James Hay, George Mercer.

1802.

Aug. 22. James Scott, weaver, and Agnes Lindsay in Gattonside, a.d.n. Janet, born 11th January 1800.

„ 29. James Scott, weaver, and Agnes Lindsay in Gattonside, a.s.n. James, born 17th July 1802 ; w. Thomas Boston, John Lindsay.

„ „ John Mercer, portioner, and Euphan Scott in Bridgend, a.d.n. Isabel, born 6th November 1801 ; w. Andrew Mercer, John Rutherford.

„ „ John Darling, portioner, and Isabel Williamson, his spouse, in Langhaugh, a.d.n. Janet, born 8th February 1792.

„ „ John Darling, portioner, and Isabel Williamson in Langhaugh, a.d.n. Helen, born 13th April 1794.

„ „ John Darling, portioner, and Isabel Williamson in Langhaugh, a.d.n. Margaret, born 20th October 1796.

„ „ John Darling, portioner, and Isabel Williamson in Langhaugh, a.d.n. Isabel, born 26th November 1798.

„ „ John Darling, portioner, and Isabel Williamson in Langhaugh, a.s.n. Thomas, born 8th February 1801 ; w. Alexander Darling, James Blaikie.

„ „ Robert Walker, junior, clothier, and Elizabeth Nisbet, in fornication, in Buckholmside, a.s.n. Thomas, born June 1802.

„ „ Andrew Sanderson, mason, and Jean Scott in Kersfield, a.d.n. Jean, born 3rd September 1801 ; w. Thomas Sanderson, John Graham.

„ „ Adam Wilson, dyer, and Agnes Douglas in Buckholmside, a.d.n. Agnes, born 24th April 1795.

„ „ Adam Wilson, dyer, and Agnes Douglas in Buckholmside, a.d.n. Mary, born 20th July 1797 ; w. Robert Walker, James Walker.

„ „ James Litster, wright, and Betty Bathgate in Buckholmside, a.d.n. Mary, born 16th February 1800.

„ „ James Litster, wright, and Betty Bathgate in Buckholmside, a.d.n. Anne, born 4th May 1802 ; w. George Bathgate, James Blaikie.

„ „ James Scott, hynd, and Margaret Weatherstone in Blainslie, a.s.n. James, born 15th August 1800.

„ „ James Scott, hynd, and Margaret Weatherstone in Blainslie, a.s.n. John, born 4th March 1802 ; w. William and George Scott.

Oct. 2. Andrew Moffat, servant, and Violet Hatton in Flybridge, a.s.n. Andrew, born 31st July 1802.

„ „ William Smith, smith, and Peggy Bunzie, in Flybridge, a.d.n. Jean, born also 31st July 1802 ; w. James Nicoll, James Bell.

„ „ William Mitchel, servant, and Peggy Burnet in Flybridge, a.s.n. James, born 30th July 1802 ; w. John Burnet, Francis Burnet.

„ 12. Alexander Tudhope, flesher, and Isabel Turner in Melrose, a.d.n. Anne, born 4th September 1802 ; w. Robert Myles, William Spence.

„ „ William Thomson, clothier, and Margaret Young in Darlingshaugh, a.s.n. Hugh, born 25th May 1802 ; w. James Sime, Gilbert Thomson.

„ „ William Leithhead and Janet Thomson in Abbotslee, a.s.n. John, born 23rd June 1798.

„ „ William Leithhead and Janet Thomson in Abbotslee, a.d.n. Esther, born 23rd February 1800.

„ „ William Leithhead and Janet Thomson in Abbotslee, a.s.n. George, born 26th October 1801 ; w. John Leithhead, Robert Murray.

„ „ Andrew Martine, portioner of Blainslee and Nelly Thin, a.d.n. Catharine, born 9th September 1802 ; w. William Thin, Robert Laidlaw.

Nov. 14. David Sinclair, shoemaker in Melrose, and Margaret Rutherford, a.d.n. Margaret, born 21st October 1802 ; w. John Taket, Alexander Bell.

„ „ Thomas Sanderson, wright, and Helen Martin in Galabridge, a.s.n. Andrew, born 15th September 1802 ; w. Andrew Sanderson, John Graham.

1802.

Nov. 14. Alexander Broomfield, farmer, and Mary Nicol in Bluecairn, a.sn. Alexander, born 20th November 1802 ; w. James Thin, James Nicol.

" " James Scott, weaver, and Margaret Grant in Danielton, a.s.n. James, born 8th August 1802 ; w. James Scott, Robert Scott.

" " James Henderson, farmer, and Jean Young in Eildon, a.d.n. Alice, born 19th October 1802 ; w. John Sibbald, Andrew Bell.

Dec. 5. Alexander Bell, stockingweaver, and Margaret Stewart in Melrose, a.s.n. Archibald, born 10th October 1802.

" " Andrew Young, labourer, and Mary Bell in Melrose, a.s.n. Robert, born 11th October 1802.

" " James Jamison, miller, and Margaret Ormistone in Melrose, a.d.n. Margaret, born 3rd October ; w. William Cook, Robert Taket.

" " James Bunzie, weaver, and Anne Thomson in Newstead, a.s.n. Robert, born 13th June 1802 ; w. James Ramsay, Thomas Usher.

" 26. George Brodie, smith, and Mary Stewart in Melrose, a.d.n. Mary Robertson Brodie, born 20th November 1802 ; w. Walter Turnbull, William Cooke.

" " Thomas Dickson, weaver, and Betty Vair in Darnick, a.s.n. John, born 26th October 1802 ; w. James Usher, John Smith.

" " William Mein, younger, of Haxlaws, and Janet Millar in Newtown, a.d.n. Janet, born 7th January 1803 ; w. James Mein, Nicol Milne.

" " John Martin, wright, and Marion Heiton in Melrose, a.d.n. Isabel, born 26th October 1802.

" " William Wallace, labourer, and Agnes Bell in Melrose, a.s.n. Robert, born 13th November 1802 ; w. John Taket, Andrew Young.

" " Alexander Muir and Janet Heymer in Newstead, a.s.n. Alexander, born 12th September 1802.

" " John Paterson and Peggy Stewart in Melrose, a.s.n. John, born 23rd November 1802.

1803.

Jan. 23. Thomas Vair, weaver, and Janet Burnet in Newstead, a.s.n. George, born 7th November 1802.

" " Robert Hart, weaver, and Betty Scott in Newstead, a.s.n. Adam, born 5th December 1802.

" " William Edgar, taylor, and Christian Waugh in Melrose, a.s.n. Archibald Tod Edgar, born 3rd December 1802 ; w. John Taket, John Martin.

" " Thomas Inglis, gardener, and Margaret Allan in Westhouses, a.s.n. Charles, born 16th December 1802 ; w. James Usher, Andrew Heiton.

" " Alexander Mitchell, servant in Clackmae, and Janet Hunter, a.s.n. John, born 23rd July 1802 ; w. John and James Fisher.

Mar. 20. Robert Fairbairn and Margaret Elliot in Broomhill, a.d.n. Isabel ; w. John and James Mercer.

April 9. Robert Anderson, mason, and Margaret Thomson in Melrose, a.d.n. Helen, born 28th February 1803 : w. James Graham, Robert Taket.

" 10. James Hopkirk, shoemaker, and Anne Wright in Melrose, a.s.n. Thomas, born 21st January 1803 ; w. Alexander Hopkirk, William Cook.

" 17. James Goodfellow, cooper, and Helen Newlands in Melrose, a.s.n. James, born 9th February 1803 ; w. John Bower, William Edgar.

May 1. William Mathison, weaver, and Elizabeth Anderson in Gattonside, a.s.n. William, born 6th April 1803 ; w. John Mathison, John Grieve.

" 4. Andrew Bertram in Sorrowlessfield, and Alice Brown, a.d.n. Alice, born 30th September 1802 ; w. John Martin, Walter Turnbull.

1803.

May   8. John Winter and Nelly Hogg in Melrose, a.d.n. Abigail, born 23rd March 1803 ; w. John Hogg, John Easton.

"   " William Mercer, shoemaker, and Janet Heart in Melrose, a.d.n. Mary, born 2nd March 1803.

"   " William Roger, labourer, and Anne Bower in Melrose, a.d.n. Isabel, born 16th April 1803 ; w. Nicol Mercer, John Taket.

"   " William Tait, shepherd, and Isabel More in Williamlaw, a.s.n. Thomas, born 25th January 1801 ; w. John Murray, Thomas Robertson.

"   " Thomas Cleghorn and Janet Kyle in Newtown, a.d.n. Agnes, born 25th March 1802 ; w. John Bower, Nicol Milne.

"   " James Lambert, servant, and Isabel Dalgliesh in Langhaugh, a.s.n. John, born 17th December 1801 ; w. James Blaikie, Thomas Sanderson.

"   " Mr. John Goodsman, tenant, and Anne Darling in the Roan, a.d.n. Mary, born 27th February 1803 ; w. John Simson, William Brokie.

"   " William Thin, tenant, and Janet Broomfield in Blainslie, a.d.n. Margaret, born 31st January 1803.

"   " Robert Laidlaw, portioner, and Agnes Fairbairn in Blainslies, a.s.n. Robert, born 5th September 1802 ; w. Thomas Laidlaw, Andrew Martin.

"   " George Muir and Isabel Dickson in Mosshouses, a.d.n. Margaret, born 18th October 1802 ; w. John Frier, Walter Chisholm.

"   " Robert Henderson, shoemaker, and Janet Broomfield in Melrose, a.s.n. John, born 20th March 1803 ; w. Robert Waugh, William Cook.

"   22. John Moss, portioner, and Betty Dunlop in Darnick, a.d.n. Isabel, born 31st January 1803 ; w. John Smith, Andrew Heiton.

"   " John Usher, portioner, and Agnes Blaikie in Toftfield, a.d.n. Isabel, born 30th November 1802 ; w. James Usher, Andrew Heiton.

"   29. William Wilson, weaver, and Beatrice Richardson in Danielton, a.d.n. Elisabeth, born 3rd May 1802 ; w. George Laurie, Thomas Scott.

"   " John Laidlaw, portioner, and Jemima Grant in Peasehill, a.s.n. Archibald, born 10th February 1803 ; w. John Grant, Andrew Bell.

"   " Alexander Pringle, merchant, and Barbara Millar in Melrose, a.s.n. John, born 10th February 1803 ; w. John and James Pringle.

"   " John Smith, labourer, and Janet Watson in Darnick, a.d.n. Janet, born 20th November 1802 ; w. Adam Tait, James Thomson.

"   " Richard Cochran, weaver, and Anne Sanderson, a.d.n. Janet, born 30th May 1803 ; w. James Blaikie, John Sanderson, living in Darlingshaugh.

"   " James Millar, labourer, and Betty Hart in Newstead, a.s.n. William, born 25th January 1802 ; w. Thomas Williamson, James Ramsay.

"   " William Sanderson, hynd, and Mary Veitch in Langhaugh, a.s.n. James, born 30th August 1802.

"   " Alexander Robertson, hynd, and Margaret Blithe in Langhaugh, a.d.n. Elisabeth, born 19th March 1803 ; w. James Blaikie, James Sime.

June 19. William Mack, shoemaker, and Betty Laurie in Melrose, a.s.n. John, born 28th May 1803 ; w. John Martin, William Cook.

"   22. Robert Scott, weaver, and Margaret Smail in Danielton, a.d.n. Elisabeth, born 3rd May 1803 ; w. George Laurie, James Scott.

"   " Adam Wilson, dyer, and Agnes Douglas in Buckholmside, a.s.n. Robert, born 13th October 1787 ; w. John and Richard Lees.

1786. William Elder, dissenting minister in Newtown, and Isabel Mein, a.s.n. David, born 5th October 1786.

1788. William Elder, dissenting minister in Newtown, and Isabel Mein, a.d.n. Jean, born 5th April 1788.

1795. William Elder, dissenting minister in Newtown, and Margaret Rodger, a.d.n. Isabel, born 2nd July 1795.

1796. William Elder, dissenting minister in Newtown, and Margaret Rodger, a.s.n. James, born 20th December 1796.

1799. William Elder, dissenting minister in Newtown, and Margaret Rodger, a.d.n. Janet, born 26th May 1799.

1803.
July 27. George Mathison, servant, and Isabel Campbel in Melrose, a.s.n. George, born 8th July 1803; w. James Johnstone, John Paterson.

1798. William Scott, wright, and Margaret Dickson in Blainslie, a.s.n. James, born 9th October 1798.

1800. William Scott, wright, and Margaret Dickson in Blainslie, a.d.n. Nelly, born 16th July 1800.

1802. William Scott, wright, and Margaret Dickson in Blainslie, a.s.n. George, born 27th September 1802; w. John Simson, James Wilson.

1787. Hugh Hall and Mary Goodfellow, servants in Gattonside, a.s.n. James, born 28th September 1787.

1789. Hugh Hall and Mary Goodfellow, servants in Gattonside, a.s.n. David, born 24th September 1789.

1793. Hugh Hall and Mary Goodfellow, servants in Gattonside, a.s.n. William, born 12th August 1793.

1795. Hugh Hall and Mary Goodfellow, servants in Gattonside, a.s.n. Hugh, born 12th June 1795.

1797. Hugh Hall and Mary Goodfellow, servants in Gattonside, a.d.n. Isabel, born 15th March 1797.

1799. Hugh Hall and Mary Goodfellow, servants in Gattonside, a.s.n. George, born 16th January 1799.

1800. Hugh Hall and Mary Goodfellow, servants in Gattonside, a.d.n. Jean; w. George Bruce, William Ainslie.

1787. Andrew Mercer, portioner, and Elizabeth Thomson in Bridgend, a.s.n. Andrew, born 23rd November 1787; w. John Mercer, John Rutherford.
  Attested by Mr. Riddell, Justice of Peace.

1803. John Hardie and Janet Blyth in Blainslie, a.d.n. Nelly, born 3rd January 1803: w. Thomas Hardie, George Burnet.

1796. Thomas Laurie, labourer, and Mary Drummond in Blainslie, a.s.n. John, born 7th July 1796; w. Robert Laidlaw, William Scott.

1803. John Simson and Elisabeth Sommerville in Blainslie, a.s.n. Thomas, born 3rd July 1803; w. James Wilson, William Brokie.

,, William Brokie, farmer, and Isabel Cunningham in Blainslie, a.s.n. William, born 21st June 1803: w. John Simson, James Wilson.

,, Andrew Hogarth, hynd, and Mary Lyal in Blainslie, a.s.n. William' born 24th June 1803; w. William Brokie, Thomas Douglas.

,, James Thin, farmer, and Peggy Nicol in Blainslie, a.s.n. James, born 10th March 1803: w. James Thin, senior, William Thin.

,, William Easton, herd, and Elisabeth Robertson in Hawkburn, a.s.n. John, born 7th April 1803; w. John Lees, Alexander Clapperton.

Aug. 14. John Chisholm, shoemaker, and Alice Elliot in Melrose, a.s.n. William, born 25th July 1803; w. William Chisholm, James Broomfield.

,, 15. John Rutherford, portioner, and Catharine Turnbull in Bridgend, a.s.n. Robert, born 16th July 1803; w. Andrew Drummond, James Hardie.

Sept. 4. Robert Pringle, labourer, and Agnes Burnet in Newstead, a.d.n. Isabel, born 10th July 1803; w. Francis Burnet, Andrew Bunzie.

,, ,, John Lees, clothier, and Jean Young in Channel, a.d.n. Janet, born 8th August 1803; w. James Blaikie, James Sime.

,, ,, Richard Lees, clothier, and Mary Paterson in Buckholmside, a.s.n. George, born 31st May 1803; w. George Bathgate, John Lees.

1803.

Sept. 4. John Sanderson and Joan Murray in Kersfield, a.s.n. John, born 1st
              January 1803 ; w. Andrew Sanderson, John Graham.

„   „   Walter Ballantine, spinner, and Sarah Donald in Darlingshaugh,
              a.s.n. James, born 17th April 1802.

„   „   Walter Ballantine, spinner, and Sarah Donald in Darlingshaugh,
              a.s.n. John, born 18th August 1803 ; w. William Turnbull, James
              Sime.

„   „   James Clark and Nelly Henry in Blainslie, a.d.n. Peggy, born 24th
              July 1796.

„   „   James Clark and Nelly Henry in Blainslie, a.d.n. Elizabeth, born 2nd
              October 1797.

„   „   James Clark and Nelly Henry in Blainslie, a.s.n. Robert, born 27th
              April 1799 ; w. William Scott, John Henry.

Oct. 2. George Drummond, weaver, and Nelly Frame in Darnick, a.s.n. John,
              born 25th August 1803 ; w. John Smith, James Usher.

„   „   Robert Burnet and Janet Burnet in Melrose, a.d.n. Mary, born 3rd
              September 1803 ; w. Walter Turnbull, Robert Taket.

„   16. George Noble, weaver, and Jean Laurie in Melrose, a.s.n. Robert ; w.
              George Laurie, William Cook.

„   23. James Henderson, labourer, and Isabel Aitken in Melrose, a.d.n.
              Agnes, born 20th August 1803 ; w. John Martine, Robert
              Henderson.

„   „   Andrew Drummond, weaver and portioner, and Margaret Heiton in
              Bridgend, born 29th June 1803 ; w. John Mercer, John Rutherford.

„   30. William Heart, labourer, and Isabel Hutton in Melrose, a.s.n. James,
              born 28th September 1803 ; w. John Martin, John Taket.

„   „   William Leithead, farmer, and Janet Thomson in Abbotslee, a.d.n.
              Jean, ; w. James Usher, John Thomson.

„   „   George Mabon, weaver, and Elizabeth Young in Melrose, a.s.n. John,
              born 31st December 1803 ; w. John Bower, John Martin.

„   „   Robert Penman, weaver, and Isabel Pringle in Melrose, a.d.n. Isabel,
              born 17th August 1792 ; w. Alexander Pringle, James Martin.

„   „   Robert Penman, weaver, and Isabel Pringle in Melrose, a.d.n.
              Christian, born 8th May 1794.

„   „   Robert Penman, weaver, and Isabel Pringle in Melrose, a.d.n.
              Margaret, born 17th April 1796.

„   „   Robert Penman, weaver, and Isabel Pringle in Melrose, a.s.n. James,
              born 17th January 1798.

„   „   Robert Penman, weaver, and Isabel Pringle in Melrose, a.d.n. Janet,
              born 29th October 1799.

„   „   Robert Penman, weaver, and Isabel Pringle in Melrose, a.s.n. Robert,
              born 2nd October 1801.

„   „   Robert Penman, weaver, and Isabel Pringle in Melrose, a.d.n.
              Elizabeth, born 25th November 1803 ; same witnesses.

„   „   James Martin, carrier, and Margaret Ewans in Melrose, a.s.n. Robert,
              born 28th October 1793 ; w. Robert Penman, Alexander Pringle.

„   „   James Martin, carrier, and Margaret Ewans in Melrose, a.s.n. James,
              born 1st April 1796.

„   „   James Martin, carrier, and Margaret Ewans in Melrose, a.s.n. George,
              born 4th August 1799.

„   „   James Martin, carrier, and Margaret Ewans in Melrose, a.s.n. David
              born 23rd May 1803 ; same witnesses.

„   „   William Veitch, millwright, and Alison Bell in Darlingshaugh, a.s.n.
              William, born 15th November 1803 ; w. George Bathgate, John
              Sanderson.

1804.

Jan. 1. John Mathison and Ann Scot in Gattonside, a.d.n. Margaret, born
              21st August 1803.

„   „   James Jamison, smith, and Agnes Veitch in Newtown, a.d.n. Jean,
              born 26th September 1803 ; w. Nicol Milne, Thomas Boston.

1804.

Jan.   1. Adam Tait, portioner, and Margaret Harper in Darnick, a.s.n. Adam, born 30th December 1803 ; w. John Smith, Thomas Stevenson.

Feb.   8. William Spence, surgeon, and Catharine Swanston, his spouse, in Gattonside-haugh, a.d.n. Janet, born 28th December 1803 ; w. Walter Turnbull, Adam Ormistone.

„   18. John Scouffield, hynd, and Elizabeth Hardie in Blainslie, a.d.n. Isabel, born 19th January 1804 ; w. John Simson, Robert Laidlaw.

„   „   George Armstrong, farmer, and Margaret Bell in Broadwoodshiel, a.s.n. George, born 16th December 1803 ; w. James Stirling, William Brokie.

April 1. Andrew Muir and Margaret Fairbairn in Melrose, a.s.n. John, born 22nd February 1804 ; w. John Martin, John Bower.

„   15. Francis Burnet, labourer, and Joan Williamson in Newstead, a.s.n. Francis, born 7th February 1804 ; w. Thomas Williamson, Robert Burnet.

„   „   Walter Turnbull, schoolmaster, and Euphan Dickson in Melrose, a.s.n. William, born 2nd March 1804 ; w. William Cook, Robert Taket.

„   „   George Stoddart, portioner, and Agnes Brown in Darnick, a.d.n. Agnes, born 31st October 1803 ; w. John Smith, Andrew Heiton.

„   „   George Hardie, labourer, and Anne Purves in Newstead, a.s.n. Robert, born 5th March 1804 ; w. Thomas Hardie, Robert Haig.

„   „   Robert Haig, weaver, and Beatrice Scott in Newstead, a.d.n. Margaret, born 9th March 1804 ; w. Thomas and George Hardie.

„   20. David Davidson, gardener, and Janet M‘Nicol in Westerlanglee, a.d.n. Marianne, born 30th April 1804 ; w. William Ainslie, John Lees.

„   „   James Scott, farmer, and Janet Pringle in Calfhill, a.s.n. Robert, born 3rd April 1804 ; w. John Frier, Walter Chisholme.

„   „   Andrew Heiton, portioner, and Isabella Govan in Darnick, a.s.n. Thomas, born 14th May 1804 ; w. John Smith, James Usher.

„   „   Andrew Heart, mason, and Margaret Pringle in Newstead, a.s.n. Hugh, born 1st April 1804 ; w. Andrew Bunzie, Robert Heart.

July   1. Thomas Usher, weaver, and Betty Stevenson in Newstead, a.s.n. Thomas, born 28th April 1804.

„   „   Andrew Bunzie, weaver, and Peggy Williamson in Newstead, a.s.n. William, born 17th April 1804 ; w. Thomas Williamson, James Ramsay.

„   „   Thomas Vair, weaver, and Margaret Tait in Darnick, a.d.n. Margaret, born 20th May 1804 ; w. Andrew Heiton, John Smith.

„   „   Andrew Cunningham, portioner, and Mary Turner in Gattonside, a.d.n. Margaret, born 1st May 1804 ; w. Thomas Boston, John Dickieson.

„   8. Andrew Young, labourer, and Mary Bell in Melrose, a.d.n. Mary, born 28th May 1804 ; w. William Wallace, James Johnston.

„   „   John Clark, weaver, and Janet Ivly in Darlingshaugh, a.d.n. Mary, born 24th May 1804 ; w. James Blaikie, William Watson.

„   15. Walter Davidson, ploughman in Cartleehole, and Edgar Wesler, a.s.n. William, born 19th April 1804 ; w. John Rutherfurd, Andrew Mercer.

„   22. Adam Fiddes, mason, and Margaret Herriot in Newstead, a.d.n. Margaret, born 14th June 1804.

„   „   John Hatton, tailor, and Isabel Brown in Melrose, a.d.n. Agnes, born 10th June 1804.

„   „   Andrew Brown, merchant, and Janet Mather in Melrose, a.s.n Andrew, born 23rd June 1804 ; w. William Cook, Robert Taket.

„   „   John Usher, portioner, and Agnes Blaikie in Toftfield, a.d.n. Janet, born 17th March 1804 ; w. James Usher, Andrew Heiton.

1804.

July 22. Thomas Smail and Agnes Hunter in Melrose, a.s.n. Robert, born
24th February 1804, and baptised 6th March 1804 by the Rev.
John Hunter of Oxnam.

,,   ,, James Clapperton, shoemaker, and Joan Cunningham in Gattonside,
a.d.n. Margaret, born 8th April 1802.

,,   ,, James Clapperton, shoemaker, and Joan Cunningham in Gattonside, a.d.n. Elisabeth, born 16th December 1803 ; w. Robert
Clapperton, Henry Cunningham.

,,   ,, James Millar, labourer, and Betty Hart in Newstead, a.d.n. Margaret,
born 3rd May 1804 ; w. Thomas Hardie, James Ramsay.

Aug. 19. James Elliot and Agnes White in Newstead, a.d.n. Jean, born 14th
August 1804 ; w. James Ramsay, Thomas Vair.

,,   ,, Jame Sime, clothier, and Margaret Clapperton in Darlingshaugh,
a.d.n. Helen, born 9th December 1803.

,,   — William Thomson, clothier, and Margaret Young in Darlingshaugh,
a.d.n. Mary, born 23rd August 1804.

,,   — James Allan, weaver, and Jacobina Ballantine in Darlingshaugh,
a.s.n. John, born 10th June 1804.

,,   — James Chalmers and Mary Fowler at Galabridge toll barr, a.d.n.
Agnes, born 17th June 1804 ; w. James Blaikie, John Sanderson.

,,   — John Kinlee, labourer, and Alice Gill in Threepwood, a.s.n. John,
born 9th April 1803 ; w. Charles Simpson, William Millar.

Sept.   9. William Mathison, weaver, and Elizabeth Anderson in Gattonside,
a.d.n. Isabel, born 12th August 1804 ; w. J. Dickieson, J.
Boston.

,,   ,, David Sinclair, shoemaker, and Margaret Rutherford in Melrose,
a.s.n. James, born 16th August 1804 ; w. John Taket, Andrew
Brown.

,,   ,, John Grieve, labourer, and Isabel Marr in Easterlanglee, a.s.n.
George, born 29th August 1804 ; w. Alexander Stewart, John
White.

,,   ,, Alexander Broomfield, farmer, and Mary Nicol in Bluecairn, a.d.n.
Elizabeth, born 18th July 1804.

Sept. 16. William Hopkirk, shoemaker, and Isabella Horne in Gattonside,
a.d.n. Elisabeth, born 28th July 1804.

,,   ,, Thomas Allan, baker, and Janet Scott in Melrose, a.d.n. Janet, born
12th May 1804.

,,   ,, John Scott, labourer, and Janet Mercer in Newstead, a.s.n. Walter,
born 23rd August 1804.

,,   ,, Andrew Mercer, portioner, and Elisabeth Thomson in Bridgend,
a.d.n. Isabel, born 5th April 1785 ; w. George Wight, John
Rutherford.

,,   ,, Andrew Bertram, farmer, and Alice Brown in Sorrowlessfield, a.d.n.
Beatrice, born 2nd August 1804 ; w. James Nicol, James
Ramsay.

Oct. 21. James Bunzie, labourer in Newstead, and Nelly Bruce, his wife, a.s.n.
James, born 7th September 1804.

,,   ,, William Tait, labourer, and Margaret Hilson, his wife, in Darnick,
a.d.n. Susanna, born 8th July 1804.

,,   ,, John Easton, wright in Melrose, and Margaret Watson, his wife,
a.d.n. Jean Riddell, born 21st September 1804.

,,   ,, James Vair, gardener at Greenwells, and Elizabeth Hatton, his wife,
a.d.n. Margaret, born at Melrose 12th July 1789 ; w. John
Hatton, Andrew Moffat.

Nov.   4. James Johnstone, carter in Melrose, and Margaret Cowan, his wife,
a.s.n. Samuel, born 20th September 1804.

,,   18. Robert Anderson, mason in Melrose, and Margaret Thomson, his
wife, a.s.n. Alexander, born 28th October 1804.

1804.

Nov. — James Vair, gardener at Greenwells, and Elizabeth Hatton, his wife, a.d.n. Margaret, born at Melrose, 12th July 1789, and baptised there ; w. John Hatton, Andrew Moffat.

" — James Vair, gardener, and Elizabeth Hatton, his wife, a.d.n. Anne, born at Carterhaugh, in the parish of Selkirk, 17th April 1793, and baptised by the Rev. Mr. Robertson ; w. Peter Tait, John Vair.

" — James Vair, gardener, and Elizabeth Hatton, his wife, a.d.n. Jean, born at Kelso 20th September 1797, and baptised by the Rev. Mr. Hall ; w. Jame Yuile, Andrew Stavert.

" — James Vair, gardener, and Elizabeth Hatton, his wife, a.s.n. James, born at Kelso, 26th August 1799, and baptised by Rev. Mr. Hall ; w. James Yuile, Andrew Stavert.

" — James Vair, gardener, and Elizabeth Hatton, his wife, a.d.n. Elizabeth, born at Kelso 13th June 1801, and baptised by Rev. Mr. Hall ; w. James Yuile, Andrew Stavert.

" — James Vair, gardener, and Elizabeth Hatton, his wife, a.s.n. Thomas, born at Greenwells 15th October 1803, and baptised by Rev. Mr. Elder ; w. John Cochran, William Grierson.

" — James Turner and Janet Horseburgh in Colmsliehill, a.s.n. Robert, born 5th May 1794 ; w. William Cook, Robert Taket.

Dec. 23. Thomas Wilson and Helen Tait, a.d.n. Margaret ; w. Robert Taket, George Broadie.

" " Thomas Forsythe and Agnes Chisholm, a.s.n. Alexander, born 10th September 1802.

" " Thomas Forsythe and Agnes Chisholm, a.d.n. Christian, born 3rd December ; w. John Bower, Robert Tacket.

" — John Turnbull, clothier, and Elizabeth Hamilton in Darlingshaugh, a.s.n. Richard, born 5th June.

" — William Reed, farmer, South Midleton, and Isabel Hamilton in Darlingshaugh, a.d.n. Isabella, in fornication, born 16th June.

" -- Alexander Stewart, Langlee, and Helen Ballentine, a.s.n. Thomas, in fornication, born 11th August ; w. John Bower, Margaret Beattie.

" — Alexander Johnston and Margaret Thinn, a.s.n. Alexander, born 28th November 1804 ; w. John Bower, George Brodie.

" — John Chisholm and Alison Elliot, a.d.n. Isabella, born 5th December, and baptised ; w. the congregation.

1805.

George Broadie and Marione Stewart in Melrose, a.s.n. William, born 3rd January 1805, and baptised : w. John Bower, Robert Tacket.

1797.

Robert Gray and Janet Sanderson in Blainslie, a.s.n. Robert, born 29th December 1797, and baptised first Sunday of February 1798.

Mar. 10. George Stoddart and Agnes Brown in Darnick, a.s.n. George, born 18th January : w. Robert Heiton, Thomas Vair.

" " David Tait and Barbary Vair in Darnick, a.d.n. Nelly, born 17th February 1805 ; w. Robert Taket, George Broadie.

" 17. Robert Heart and Betty Scott in Newstead, a.s.n. Andrew, born 3rd January : w. Thomas Williamson, James Ramsay.

1802.

Thomas Hay, farmer, and Janet Smail in Kaeside, a.d.n. Betty, born 18th December 1802, and baptised at an examine in Sunnyside ; w. James Hay, Alexander Hay.

The above Thomas Hay and Janet Smail, a.d.n. Peggy, born likewise on 18th December 1802, and baptised at the same time with the other, being twins.

1805.

The above Thomas Hay and Janet Smail, a.d.n. Martha, born 4th January, and baptised 21st March 1805, at an examine in Dingleton ; w. James Scott. Robert Scott.

1804.

Mar. 31. Rev. Mr. Thomson and Mrs. Margaret Gillon in Melrose, a.d.n. Jean, born 14th February, and baptised before the congregation.

,,   ,,   Robert Henderson, shoemaker, and Janet Broomfield in Melrose, a.d.n. Janet, born 5th March, and baptised on 31st before the congregation.

,,   ,,   William Chisholm and Ratchel Blair in Melrose, a.d.n. Margaret, born 6th March, and baptised in public 31st March 1805.

April 14. Robert Crawford, shoemaker, and Jean Hogg in Melrose, a.s.n. John, born 12th January, and baptised 14th April 1805 before the congregation.

,,   ,,   David Webster and Helen Smith in Westerlanglee, a.d.n. Margaret, born 17th March, and baptised 14th April before the congregation.

,,   ,,   James Mercer and Alison Hay in Coatgreen, a.d.n. Janet, born in November 1804, and baptised at that place by Mr. Elder; w. George Mercer, John Hay.

,,   28. John Musgrave, shoemaker, and Catharine Jamieson in Melrose, a.s.n. Andrew, born 3rd March, and baptised 28th April 1805 before the congregation.

May   5. James Wilson and Sarah Lees in Westerlanglee, a.s.n. James, born 3rd April, and baptised 5th May 1805 before the congregation.

Jan. 10. William Wallace, labourer, and Agnes Bell in Melrose, a.d.n. Agnes, born 10th January, and baptised 16th February 1805; w. Robert Taket, Andrew Young.

,,   ,,   Robert Allan and Agnes Paterson in Melrose, a.d.n. Lorrain, born 2nd October 1803 and baptised 9th day same year; w. Thomas Allan, Adam Ormiston.

,,   ,,   Robert Stevenson and Margaret Dodds, a.s.n. John, born 10th September 1804, and baptised at Newtown about a month after; w. William Govan, John Boyd.

,,   ,,   Alexander Turnbull, wright, and Betty Mitchell in Darnick, twins named Isabel and Betty, born 23rd September 1804.

1805.

June 9. William Mercer, shoemaker, and Betty Heart in Melrose, a.s.n. Robert, born 11th April, and baptised 9th June 1805 before the congregation.

,,   16. James Goodfellow, cooper, and Helen Newlands in Melrose, a.d.n. Elisabeth, born 25th May, and baptised 16th June 1805 before the congregation.

,,   17. John Rutherford and Catharine Turnbull in Bridgend, a.s.n. George, born 2nd May and baptised 17th June 1805; w. James Usher, elder.

,,   ,,   John Kinlay and Alison Gill, a.d.n. Mary, born 28th February, and baptised 31st March before the congregation.

Aug. 1. Simon Aitchison, weaver, and Elspeth Dalgliesh in Darlingshaugh, a.d.n. Elspeth, born 26th June, and baptised at Galashiels 4th August 1805.

Sept. 1. Robert Heiton, weaver, and Betty Fisher in Darnick, a.d.n. Marrion, born 29th July, and baptised 1st September 1805 before the congregation.

,,   ,,   John Simpson and Elizabeth Sommerville in Blainslie, a.d.n. Eliza, born 19th March, and baptised 19th April 1805; w. Robert Romanes, James Wilson.

,,   ,,   William Scott, wright, and Margaret Dickson in Blainslie, a.s.n. William, born 4th December 1804, and baptised about a fortnight after.

,,   ,,   Alexander Mitchell and Janet Hunter in Clackmae, a.s.n. Alexander, born 6th May 1804, and baptised about a month after; w. Gilbert Elliot, William Mercer.

1805

Sept. 1. Thomas Robertson, shepherd, and Isabel Wood in Ouplaw, a.d.n. Marion, born 29th January 1803, and baptised about six weeks after in Stowe Kirk.

„ „ Thomas Robertson, shepherd, and Isabel Wood in Ouplaw, a.s.n. John, born 19th March 1804, and baptised about a month after in Stowe meeting-house.

„ „ John Lees, clothier, and Jean Young in Darlingshaugh, a.s.n. William, born 3rd July 1805.

Oct. 6. Adam Anderson, labourer, and Violet Cranston, a.d.n. Elizabeth, born 7th September, and baptised publicly this day.

„ 9. James Ballantyne and Janet Scott in Darnick, a.s.n. Hugh John, born 12th September and baptised 9th October 1805 ; w. James Usher, Thomas Stevenson.

„ „ James Scott and Margaret Weatherston in Blainslie, a.s.n. William, born 6th October 1803.

„ „ William Fox, miller, and Margaret Hog in Newtown, a.d.n. Margaret, baptised publicly this day—three weeks old.

, „ John Henderson, weaver, and Isabel Linton in Melrose, a.d.n. Betty, baptised publicly this day—five weeks old.

„ „ George Armstrong and Margaret Bell in Broadwoodshiel, a.d.n. Hannah, born 4th and baptised 17th July 1805 ; w. William Bell, James Allan.

Nov. 23. George Mathison and Isabel Campbell in Melrose, a.d.n. Janet, born 19th October and baptised 23rd November 1805.

Dec. 8. Andrew Henderson, taylor, and Jane Henderson in Melrose, a.d.n. Elizabeth, baptised 8th December 1805—eight weeks old.

„ 29. Francis Burnet and Joan Williamson in Newstead, a.d.n. Marion, born 5th October 1805, and baptised before the congregation 29th December same year.

„ „ David Kyle, vintner, and Agnes Scoon in Melrose, a.s.n. Alexander, born 24th June 1798, and baptised in Spring 1805.

„ „ Robert Scott, weaver, and Martha Smail in Dingleton, a.d.n. Margaret, born 3rd August 1805, and baptised 31st by Rev. Mr. Hay at Newtown.

1806.

Feb. 16. Robert Pringle, labourer, and Agnes Burnet in Newstead, a.d.n. Grisel, born 6th December 1805, and baptised this day.

„ 23. James Hopkirk, shoemaker, and Jean Turnbull in Melrose, a.s.n. James, born about the latter end of January 1806, and baptised publicly this day.

„ „ William Mitchell, hostler, and Mary Burnet in Melrose, a.d.n. Agnes, born about the latter end of November 1805, and baptised publicly this day.

„ 24. John Turnbull and Jean Currie in Gattonside, a.d.n. Joan, born 21st December 1805, and baptised at an examine 24th February 1806.

Mar. 16. James Henderson, labourer, and Isabel Aitken in Melrose, a.d.n. Isabel, born 12th December 1805, and baptised this day before the congregation.

April 13. James Fish, joiner, and Isabel Tait in Newstead, a.d.n. Jean, born 23rd February 1806, and baptised publicly this day.

„ 20. Alexander Muir, labourer, and Janet Hymers in Melrose, a.s.n. William, born 12th February, and baptised this day before the congregation.

„ 27. Michael Mercer, labourer, and Isabel Milne, a.s.n. Alexander, born 21st March last, and baptised this day before the congregation. The parents reside at Westerlanglee.

„ „ Mr. Richard Lees, clothier, and Mary Paterson in Buckholmside, a.s.n. Thomas, born 21st February 1800.

„ „ Mr. Richard Lees, clothier, and Mary Paterson, in Buckholmside, a.s.n. Robert, born 26th September 1801.

1806.

April — Thomas Tait, hind, and Jeany Dobson in Langhaugh, a.d.n. Betty, born 18th March, and to be baptised by Dr. Douglas in Galashiels within eight days, 4th May 1806.

,, — Robert Penman and Isabel Pringle in Melrose, a.d.n. Christian, born 1st July 1805. Parents are Methodists.

June 1. Robert Pringle, mason, and Jean Laing in Newstead, a.s.n. William, born 7th April last, and baptised this day before the congregation.

,, 15. Thomas Adams, labourer, and Margaret Mein in Newstead, a.s.n. William, born 25th March 1806.

,, ,, Andrew Hogg, mason, and Margaret Pringle in Melrose, a.d.n. Mary, born 16th March 1806.

,, ,, John Thomson, mason, and Isabel Common in Newstead, a.d.n. Margaret, born about nine weeks ago, and baptised this day, with the two preceding, before the congregation.

,, ,, James Black, weaver, and Margaret Thomson in Darnick, a.s.n. Robert, born 6th April 1806, and baptised this day before the congregation.

,, 22. William Edgar, tailor, and Christian Waugh in Melrose, a.d.n. Betty, born 10th April 1806, and baptised this day before the congregation.

,, ,, William Turnbull, merchant, and Mary Donaldson in Darlingshaugh, twins, a.s.n. Thomas, and a.d.n. Mary, born 13th October 1805 and baptised 16th May 1806 ; w. James Chalmers, John Scott.

July 24. John Martin, wright, and Marion Heiton in Melrose, a.s.n. Robert, born 19th May 1806, and baptised this day before the congregation.

,, ,, Isabel Brown, aged 20 years, appeared this day before the session and was baptised ; w. James Ramsay, Thomas Williamson.

,, ,, Alexander Broomfield and Mary Nicol in Colmsleehill, a.s.n. Walter, born 26th November 1805, and baptised about six weeks after.

,, ,, Alexander Pringle, merchant, and Barbara Millar in Melrose, a.d.n. Margaret, born 14th May 1804.

,, ,, Alexander Pringle, merchant, and Barbara Millar in Melrose, a.s.n. James, born 23rd February 1806, and baptised 21st June same year.

Aug. 24. Robert Turnbull, wright, and Janet Elliot, a.s.n. Alexander, born 25th June 1806, and baptised this day before the congregation.

,, ,, John Mein and Elizabeth Mein in Darnick, a.d.n. Marrion, born 21st June 1806, and baptised this day before the congregation.

,, ,, Adam Tait, farmer, and Margaret Harper in Darnick, a.s.n. James, born 28th May 1806, and baptised this day before the congregation.

,, ,, John Chisholm, shoemaker, and Alison Elliot in Melrose, a.s.n. John, born 1st August 1806, and baptised this day before the congregation.

,, ,, Robert Allan, baker, and Agnes Paterson in Melrose, a.d.n. Elizabeth, born 3rd July 1806, and baptised this day before the congregation.

,, ,, James Wight and Marion Ronaldson in Darnick, a.s.n. George, baptised this day before the congregation, and born about five weeks before.

,, ,, George Turnbull and Helen Oliver in Melrose, a.d.n. Christian, baptised this day before the congregation, and born about seven weeks before.

,, ,, John Scott and Janet Mercer in Gattonsidehaugh, a.s.n. George, baptised this day before the congregation, with the seven preceding, and born about seven weeks before.

,, — Richard Laidlaw, farmer, and Margaret Hislop in Nether Blainslie, a.s.n. William, born 25th February 1806.

Sept. 7. Andrew Bertram and Alison Brown in Gattonside, a.s.n. Thomas, born 16th June last, and baptised this day before the congregation.

1806.

Sept. 14. Andrew Cunningham and Mary Turner in Gattonside, a.s.n. William, baptised this day before the congregation,—seven weeks old.

„ — Thomas Hogarth, hind, and Janet Rae in Ouplaw, a.d.n. Isabel, born 31st May 1802, and baptised about seven weeks after.

„ — Thomas Hogarth, hind, and Janet Rae in Ouplaw, a.d.n. Jean, born 7th February 1805, and baptised about three weeks after.

„ — Joshua Wood, clothier, and Isabel Walker in Buckholmside, a.s.n. William, born 13th September 1803, not baptised.

„ — Joshua Wood, clothier, and Isabel Walker in Buckholmside, a.s.n. Robert, born 4th July 1806, not baptised.

„ — Andrew Martin, portioner, and Nelly Thin in Blainslie, a.s.n. Andrew, born 29th July 1804.

„ — Andrew Martin, portioner, and Nelly Thin in Blainslie, a.s.n. Robert, born 14th June 1806.

„ — Richard Dickson, farmer, and Margaret Simson in Blainslie, a.s.n. George, born 5th July, and baptised 24th August 1806 in Lauder Church.

„ — Thomas Robertson, herd, and Isabel Wood in Ouplaw, a.s.n. James, born 4th March, and baptised 10th April 1806.

„ — Richard Dickson in Bluecairn, a.s.n. George, see year 1826.

„ — Richard Lees, clothier, and Mary Paterson in Buckholmside, a.s.n. Richard, born 16th June 1805, unbaptised.

„ — John Sanderson, wright, and Ann Shortreid in Buckholmside, a.d.n. Betty, born 26th April 1804.

„ — John Sanderson, wright, and Ann Shortreid in Buckholmside, a.s.n. William, born 21st February 1806.

Oct. 5. George Short, miller, and Janet Scott in Melrose, a.s.n. John, born 2nd September 1806, and baptised this day before the congregation.

„ „ Thomas Elliot, teacher, and Mary Scott in Newsteid, a.s.n. Thomas, born 8th October 1794.

„ „ Thomas Elliot, teacher, and Mary Scott in Newsteid, a.s.n. Robert, born 24th October 1797, both above baptised ; w. Thomas Williamson, James Ramsay.

„ 19. John Chisholm, mason, and Elizabeth Callender in Langshawmill, a.d.n. Margaret, born 23rd September 1806, and baptised this day before the congregation.

Nov. 2. Robert Anderson, mason, and Margaret Thomson in Melrose, a.d.n. Agnes, born 2nd October 1806, and baptised this day before the congregation.

„ 9. David Webster and Helen Smith in Westerlanglee, a.d.n. Elizabeth, born 12th October 1806, and baptised this day before the congregation.

„ 23. Andrew Young and Mary Bell in Melrose, a.s.n. Andrew, born about the 26th October 1806, and baptised this day before the congregation.

„ „ John Hatton, tailor, and Isabel Brown in Melrose, a.d.n. Margaret, born 8th October 1806, and baptised this day before the congregation.

„ „ James Crawford, Excise officer, and Elizabeth Paterson in Melrose, a.s.n. James, born 14th December 1806.

„ „ John Turnbull, dyer, and Elizabeth Ambleton in Darlingshaugh, a.s.n. William, born 25th October 1806, and to be baptised by Dr. Douglas, minister in Galashiels.

1807.

Jan. 2. Walter Ronaldson, mason, and Janet Wight in Darnick, a.d.n. Betty, born 15th December 1805 and baptised this day ; w. William Linton, John Bowar, senior.

„ „ James Walker and Margaret Beattie in Buckholmside, a.d.n. Isabel, baptised this day,—two months old ; w. same as above.

2 A

1807.

Jan. 14. John M'Caul, gardener, and Jean Anderson in Melrose, a.s.n. William
         Riddell M'Caul, born 4th January 1807 and baptised this day ; w.
         William Riddell, Esq., John Bowar.

  ,,   18. Alexander Mathison, cooper, and Ann Davidson in Newstead, a.d.n.
         Barbara, born 15th December 1806, and baptised this day in the
         church.

  ,,   ,, George Dun, farmer, and Euphan Ellis, a.s.n. John, born 5th January
         1802, baptised by Mr. Dalziel in Earlston.

  ,,   ,, George Dun, farmer, and Euphan Ellis, a.d.n. Janet, born 2nd
         August 1804, and baptised at Earlston by Rev. Mr. Lauder.

  ,,   ,, Robert Millar, plowman, and Margaret Rutherford in Appletree-
         leaves, a.s.n. Robert, born 9th January 1807, and to be baptised
         by Rev. Dr. Douglas in Galashiels.

  ,,   ,, Thomas Cleghorn, millwright, and Mary Inglis in Buckholmside,
         a.s.n. Thomas, born 28th January 1807, and to be baptised by
         Rev. Dr. Douglas in Galashiels.

Mar.   8. William Chisholm, shoemaker, and Rachel Blair in Melrose, a.s.n.
         William, born 8th February 1807, and baptised this day before the
         congregation.

  ,,   ,, Robert Burns, watchmaker, and Betty Dewar in Melrose, a.s.n.
         James, born 3rd February 1807, and baptised this day before the
         congregation.

  ,,   ,, James Henderson and Margaret Stevenson, a.d.n. Margaret, in
         fornication, born 1st January 1805, and baptised 1st March before
         the session,—the child's grandfather, William Stevenson, being
         sponsor.

  ,,   ,, William Hopkirk, shoemaker, and Isabel Hume in Gattonside, a.s.n.
         James, born 14th December 1806.

  ,,   15. Andrew Anderson, tailor, and Jean Henderson in Melrose, a.d.n.
         Helen, born 21st January 1807, and baptised this day before the
         congregation.

April 12. Thomas Wilson and Helen Tait, a.s.n. James, born 9th March 1807,
         and baptised this day in the church.

  ,,   ,, Adam Sanderson, clothier, and Jean Edgar in Darlingshaugh, a.s.n.
         James, born 8th February 1807, and baptised 29th March by Rev.
         Dr. Douglas in Galashiels.

  ,,   ,, John Scott, plowman, and Jean Brown in Bridgend, a.s.n. John, in
         fornication, born 12th August 1806, and baptised by Rev. Mr.
         Elder, Newtown.

  ,,   ,, William Leithhead, farmer, and Janet Thomson in Abbotslee, a.s.n.
         James, born 19th October 1806, and baptised 16th December
         same year by Rev. Mr. Lauder in Earlston.

  ,,   15. James Bunzie, labourer, and Ann Thomson in Newstead, a.d.n. Ann,
         born 25th January 1807, and baptised this day before the congre-
         gation.

  ,,   ,, Thomas Hogarth, hynd, and Janet Rae in Ouplaw, a.d.n. Mary, born
         5th March 1807, and baptised 15th April following ; w. John
         Freer, William Chisholm.

  ,,   18. Mr. Charles Erskine, writer, and Mrs. Barbara Pott in Melrose, a.d.n.
         Barbara, born 24th March 1807, and baptised 18th April following ;
         w. Messrs. James Grieve, William Knox.

  ,,   26. Thomas Allan, baker, and Janet Scott in Melrose, a.d.n. Jean, born
         5th February 1807, and baptised this day before the congregation.

June   7. George Moss and Jean Kennedy in Berrymoss, a.d.n. Janet, born
         20th April 1807, and baptised this day before the congregation.

  ,,   ,, James Goodfellow, cooper, and Helen Newlands in Melrose, a.d.n.
         Isabel, born 8th April 1807, and baptised this day before the
         congregation.

  ,,   ,, Andrew Drummond, smith, and Janet Clapperton in Darnick, a.s.n.
         John, born 16th April 1807, and baptised this day before the
         congregation.

1807.

June 7. Thomas Vair, weaver, and Margaret Tait, a.d.n. Nelly, baptised this day before the congregation, and born about seven weeks before.

„ 21. Robert Henderson and Janet Broomfield, a.d.n. Jean, born 19th May 1807, and baptised this day before the congregation.

„ 28. Robert Heart, weaver, and Betty Scott in Newstead, a.s.n. John, born 17th April 1807, and baptised this day before the congregation.

„ „ Andrew Heart, mason, and Margaret Pringle in Newstead, a.d.n. Ann, born 2nd May 1807, and baptised this day before the congregation.

July 5. Andrew Mercer, labourer, and Janet Pringle in Newstead, a.d.n. Mary, born 15th May last, and baptised this day ; w. Andrew Pringle, Robert Pringle.

Aug. 1. Andrew Bunzie, weaver, and Peggy Williamson in Newstead, a.s.n. James, born 1st August 1807, and baptised 13th September same year.

„ 2. William Grant, shoemaker, and Agnes Blaikie in Melrose, a.d.n. Jean, born 2nd July 1807, and baptised this day before the congregation.

„ „ George Armstrong, farmer, and Margaret Bell in Broadwoodshiel, a.d.n. Margaret, born 28th June, and baptised 6th July same year.

„ „ John Rutherford, portioner, and Catharine Turnbull in Bridgend, a.d.n. Janet, born 9th July 1807, and baptised 3rd August same year : w. James Usher, &c.

Sept. 13. George Brodie, smith, and Mary Stuart in Melrose, a.s.n. Alexander, born 1st August 1807, and baptised this day before the congregation.

„ — James Syme, clothier, and Margaret Clapperton in Darlingshaugh, a.s.n. John, born 12th, and baptised 28th July 1807.

„ — David Thomson, clothier, and Helen Young in Darlingshaugh, a.s.n. Gilbert, born 26th May 1806, unbaptised.

„ — Daniel Taylor, farmer, and Mary Grieve in Blainslie, a.d.n. Helen, born 10th September 1807, and baptised 10th October same year ; w. George Taylor, Archibald Boyd.

„ — Thomas Riddell, Esq., younger of Camiestown, and Mrs. Jane Ferrier, *alias* Riddell, a.s.n. William, born 4th August and baptised the 16th September 1807 ; w. William Riddell, Esq. of Camiestown, Alexander Carre, Esq. of Caverse, and John Mercer, Esq., Melrose.

1806. James Millar in Newsted and Betty Heart, his wife, a.s.n. Andrew, born 20th October 1806. and baptised at Newtown about six weeks after : w. Andrew Morton, Walter Balmer.

1807.

Oct. 22. Robert Scott, weaver, and Martha Smaill in Danieltown, a.d.n. Janet, born 13th September, and baptised 22nd October 1807 : w. David Burton, George Laurie.

„ „ Adam Fiddes, mason, and Margaret Harriet in Newstead, a.d.n. Joan, born 21st November 1807, and baptised 13th March 1808 before the congregation.

Dec. 27. James Hopkirk, shoemaker, and Jean Turnbull in Melrose, a.s.n. William, baptised this day,—seven weeks old.

„ „ John Easton, wright, and Margaret Watson in Melrose, a.d.n. Elizabeth, born 20th November 1807, and baptised this day before the congregation.

„ „ Andrew Scott, farmer, and Joan Hope in Gattonside, a.s.n. Alexander, born 16th November 1803, and baptised 24th December same year.

„ „ Andrew Scott, farmer, and Joan Hope in Gattonside, a.s.n. James, born 9th September 1805 and baptised 19th October that year.

„ „ Andrew Scott, farmer, and Joan Hope in Gattonside, a.s.n. Robert, born 14th October 1807. and baptised 2nd December following.

1808.

Jan. 2. George Mathieson and Isabel Campbell in Melrose, a.d.n. Isabel born 3rd December 1807, and baptised this day ; w. Robert Taket, George Skirven.

„ 3. William Mercer, shoemaker, and Janet Heart in Melrose, a.s.n. William, born 9th November 1807, and baptised this day before the congregation.

„ 10. John Young, weaver, and Jean Blythe in Melrose, a.s.n. John, born 20th November 1807, and baptised this day before the congregation.

„ 17. Robert Jaffrey, servant, and Ann Duncan in Melrose, a.d.n. Jane, baptised before the congregation this day,—about five weeks old.

„ „ Alexander Mitchell, hynd, and Janet Hunter in Sorrowlessfield, a.s.n. James, born 19th March 1806, and baptised 20th April following ; w. John Douglas, Robert Redford.

Feb. 13. Robert Pringle, labourer, and Agnes Burnet in Newstead, a.s.n. Robert, born 3rd February 1808, and baptised this day ; w. George Burnet, senior and junior.

„ 21. James Fowler, hynd, and Agnes Bowar in Broomlees, a.d.n. Joan, born 14th December 1807, and baptised this day before the congregation.

Mar. 1. William Linton, flesher, and Agnes Wight in Melrose, a.s.n. John, born 1st July 1807, and baptised this day ; w. John Henderson, John Bowar.

„ „ Walter Ronaldson, mason, and Janet Wight in Darnick, a.s.n. Walter, born 1st September 1807, and baptised this day ; same witnesses.

„ „ John Henderson, weaver, and Isabel Linton in Melrose, a.s.n. Nicol, born 18th January 1808, and baptised this day ; same witnesses.

„ „ Thomas Vair, weaver, and Janet Burnet in Newstead, a.d.n. Janet, born 18th January 1808, and baptised 20th February following ; w. Robert Pringle, J. Ramsay.

„ „ George Stoddart, weaver, and Agnes Brown in Darnick, a.d.n. Catharine, born 7th August 1808, and baptised the February following.

„ „ George Ronaldson, mason, and Margaret Brown in Melrose, a.s.n. George, born 27th September 1807, and baptised 27th December following before the congregation.

„ 13. John Thomson, mason, and Isabel Common in Newstead, a.d.n. Isabel, born 27th January 1808, and baptised this day before the congregation.

„ „ John Lees, clothier, and Jean Young in Channel, a.d.n. Agnes, born 23rd December 1807.

„ „ David Thomson, clothier, and Helen Young in Darlingshaugh, a.s.n. William, born 2nd October 1807.

„ 20. Thomas Thomson, servant, and Isabel Turnbull in Melrose, a.s.n. Thomas, born 14th February last, and baptised this day before the congregation.

April 17. Robert Pringle, mason, and Jean Laing in Newstead, a.s.n. Alexander, born 10th March 1808, and baptised this day before the congregation.

„ „ Robert Collier, hynd, and Jean Dodds in Gattonside, a.s.n. Gideon born 8th March 1808, and baptised this day before the congregation.

„ „ John Grieve, hedger, and Isabel Marr in Langlee, a.d.n. Isabel, born 1st April 1808, and baptised same month ; w. Alexander Stuart, etc.

„ „ John Wilson, hynd, and Isabel Wilson in Ouplaw, a.d.n. Margaret, born 9th February 1808, and baptised 4th March following ; w. Thomas Robertson, James Hutchison.

May 1. John Taket, grocer, and Janet Martin in Melrose, a.d.n. Janet, born 30th March 1808, and baptised this day before the congregation.

1808.

May 1. Richard Laidlaw, farmer, and Margaret Hyslop in Blainslie, a.d.n. Christian, born 7th March 1808, and baptised 27th of same month ; w. George Wilson, Andrew Shillinglaw.

,, — John Mein, weaver, and Elizabeth Mein in Darnick, a.d.n. Elizabeth, born 16th March 1808, and baptised 5th June following before the congregation.

,, — William Govan, wright, and Betty Cuthbertson, a.s.n. William, born 4th May 1807, and baptised 31st of same month and year by the Rev. Mr. Elder.

,, — James Scott, weaver, and Peggy Grant in Danielton, a.d.n. Nelly, born 25th March 1805, and baptised about a month after.

,, — James Scott, weaver, and Peggy Grant in Danielton, a.s.n. John, born 10th January 1808, and baptised about two months after by the Rev. Mr. Elder ; w. to both above, Robert Scott, Robert Carruthers.

,, — Robert Dickson, shoemaker, and Agnes Ballantyne in Buckholmside, a.s.n. James, born 29th November 1807, and baptised 17th January 1808 ; w. James and Andrew Ballantyne.

June 12. John Chisholm, shoemaker, and Alison Elliot in Melrose, a.s.n. James, born 13th May 1808, and baptised this day before the congregation.

,, ,, Robert Crease, hynd, and Christian Wight in Bluecairn, a.d.n. Margaret, born 9th June 1808, and to be baptised at Lauder first opportunity.

July 3. Andrew Pringle, mason, and Rachael Easton, a.s.n. Thomas, born 1st April 1808, and baptised this day before the congregation. (Newstead).

,, ,, John Scott, labourer, and Beatrice Notman in Melrose, a.s.n. William, born 18th May 1808, and baptised this day before the congregation.

,, 17. James Wilson, wright, and Helen Mercer in Darnick, a.s.n. John, born 29th May 1808, and baptised this day before the congregation.

,, ,, Archibald Tod, Esq. of Drygrange, and Mrs. Eliza Pringle, his spouse, a d.n. Eliza Margaret, born 21st March 1804.

, ,, Archibald Tod, Esq. of Drygrange, and Mrs. Eliza Pringle, his spouse, a.d.n. Jane, born 2nd November 1806.

,, ,, Archibald Tod, Esq. of Drygrange, and Mrs. Eliza Pringle, a.d.n. Jemima, born 30th March 1808, and all baptised by the Rev. Mr. Thomson.

,, 21. Andrew Hogg, mason, and Margaret Pringle in Melrose, a.s.n. George, born 18th May 1808, and baptised this day ; w. John Bowar, James Henderson.

,, ,, James Henderson, labourer, and Isabel Aitken in Melrose, a.d.n. Elizabeth, born 17th December 1807, and baptised this day ; w. John Bowar, Andrew Hogg.

,, 31. William Armstrong, labourer, and Margaret Easton in Newstead, a.s.n. Andrew, born 23rd June 1808, and baptised this day before the congregation.

,, ,, Andrew Bertram and Alison Brown in Gattonside, a.s.n. George, born 10th July 1808, and baptised this day before the congregation.

,, ,, Adam Tait, portioner in Darnick, and Margaret Harper, a.s.n. Alexander, born 27th May 1808, and baptised 17th July following before the congregation.

Aug. 21. James Borroman and Margaret Cook in Melrose, a.s.n. William, born 10th August 1808, and baptised this day before the congregation.

,, ,, Robert Walker, junior, and Betty Davidson in Buckholmside, a.s.n. Robert, born 14th October 1807.

,, 28. Andrew Rutherford and Agnes Sibbald in Eildon, a.d.n. Jean, born 1st August 1808, and baptised this day before the congregation.

1808.

Sept. 18. Thomas Atkin, mason, and Margaret Jamieson in Darnick, a.s.n. George, baptised this day before the congregation—seven weeks old.

„ „ William Thynne, farmer, and Janet Broomfield in Gattonside, a.s.n. Alexander, born 4th September 1808, and baptised.

„ „ Thomas Laidlaw, mason, and Margaret Scott in Blainslie, a.s.n. James, born 18th June 1808.

„ 25. Andrew Common, labourer, and Agnes Curle in Gattonside, a.s.n. John, born 28th July 1808, and baptised this day before the congregation.

„ „ George Henderson, labourer, and Ann Mitchell in Buckholmside, a.s.n. John, born 12th September 1808, and to be baptised in Galashiels.

„ „ David Webster, gardener, and Helen Smith in Westerlanglee, a.s.n. William, born 5th October 1808, and baptised 20th same month.

„ „ John Salton, weaver, and Jean Murray in Darlingshaugh, a.d.n. Isabel, born 15th August 1808.

„ „ Isabella, daughter of Richard Dickson in Bluecairn. *See* years 1809 and 1826.

Oct. 9. Charles Erskine, Esq., writer, and Mrs. Barbara Pott in Melrose, a.d.n. Henrietta, born 25th September 1808, and baptised 9th October following ; w. Messrs. James Curle, Colin Stalker.

„ „ Mr. Richard Dickson, farmer, and Margaret Simson in Bluecairn, a.d.n. Isabel, born 11th August 1808, and baptised by the Rev. Mr. Cozens at Lauder.

Nov. 6. John Scott, farm servant, and Janet Mercer in Newstead, a.d.n. Helen, born 16th September 1808, and baptised this day before the congregation.

„ 13. Andrew Drummond, smith, and Janet Clapperton in Darnick, a.s.n. John, born 16th September 1808, and baptised this day before the congregation.

„ „ John Turnbull, slater, and Isabel Henderson in Buckholmside, a.s.n, Robert, born 25th October 1804, and baptised the 29th same month ; w. Robert Turnbull, William Aitkin.

„ „ John Turnbull, slater, and Isabel Henderson in Buckholmside, a.s.n. Thomas, born 17th September 1806, and baptised 17th October same year : w. William Fairbairn, John Rob.

„ „ John Turnbull, slater, and Isabel Henderson in Buckholmside, a.d.n. Elizabeth, born 2nd October 1808, and to be baptised in Galashiels Church next Sunday.

„ 20. William Mitchell, servant, and Peggy Burnet in Melrose, a.s.n. George, born 23rd October 1808, and baptised this day before the congregation.

„ „ John Freer, dyer, and Elizabeth Mein in Newtown, a.s.n. John, in fornication, born 10th July 1804, and baptised by Rev. Mr. Elder in Newtown two years after ; w. William Milne, William Scott.

„ „ Robert Millar, hynd, and Margaret Rutherford in Appletreeleaves. a.d.n. Janet, born 6th August last, and to be baptised by the Rev. Dr. Douglas at Galashiels first opportunity.

„ 27. Alexander Gibson and Marrion Gibson, a.s.n. Henry, born 22nd November 1808, and baptised this day before the congregation. The parents are hawkers of japanned goods.

Dec. 4. John Hatton, tailor, and Isabel Brown in Melrose, a.s.n. George, born 23rd September 1808, and baptised this day before the congregation.

„ „ William Anderson, hynd, and Hannah Wilson in Friarshaugh, a.s.n. Robert, born 13th April 1808.

„ „ William Leithhead, farmer, and Janet Thomson in Abbotslee, a.s.n. William, born 17th April 1808, and baptised 21st August following ; w. Robert Murray, James Scott.

1808.

Dec. 4. William Grierson, hynd, and Agnes Smail in Whitehill, a.d.n. Margaret, born 9th November 1808 and baptised.

1809.

Feb. 9. Ann Dickson in Melrose, a.s.n. Thomas, born 2nd June 1790, in fornication, and baptised this day before the session.

" " John Chisholm, hynd, and Barbara Young in Uplaw, a.s.n. Peter, born 26th December 1808, and to be baptised at Stowe 26th February 1809.

" 26. William Grant, shoemaker, and Agnes Blaikie in Melrose, a.d.n. Helen, born 18th January 1809, and baptised this day before the congregation.

" " Thomas Cleghorn, millwright, and Mary Inglis, a.d.n. Margaret, born 7th January 1809, and to be baptised on 5th March at Galashiels.

" — James Bunzie, labourer, and Nelly Bruce in Newstead, a.s.n. George, born 22nd March 1808, and baptised about three weeks after ; w. William Millar, James Ramsay.

" — George Fergrieve, weaver, and Alison Robson in Darlingshaugh, a.s.n. John, born 16th November 1805.

" — George Fergrieve, weaver, and Alison Robson in Darlingshaugh, a.s.n. James, born 12th December 1807.

" — William Lang, weaver, and Isabel Potts in Buckholmside, a.s.n. George, born 20th February 1809.

" — William Hogg, labourer, and Isabel Bruce in Melrose, a.s.n. Andrew, born 15th October 1808, and baptised about the end of the same year.

" — Thomas Aldcorn, smith, and Grace Fraiter in Newtown, a.s.n. John, born 17th January 1809, and baptised about a month after.

May 21. William Hopkirk, shoemaker, and Isabel Hume in Gattonside, a.s.n. John, born 1st April 1809, and baptised this day.

" " James Walker and Margaret Beattie in Buckholmside, a.s.n. George, born 12th November 1808, and baptised 20th May 1809.

" 27. John M'Caul, gardener, and Jean Anderson, a.d.n. Margaret Riddell, born 30th March 1809, and baptised 27th May following ; w. William Kennedy, John Bowar.

" " William Kennedy, coachman, and Mary Davidson in Melrose, a.s.n. Thomas, born 2nd April 1809, and baptised 27th May following ; w. John M'Caul, John Bowar.

" 28. Robert Pringle, labourer, and Agnes Burnet in Newstead, a.s.n. Robert, born 21st April 1809, and baptised this day before the congregation.

" " Robert Hart, weaver, and Betty Scot in Newstead, a.s.n. Thomas born 9th April 1809, and baptised this day before the congregation.

" " George Watson, skinner, and Ann Wheale in Buckholmside, a.s.n. John, born 21st January 1809.

1807.

Aug. 11. James Smith, blacksmith in Blainslie, and Margaret Kennedy, his wife, a.s.n. William, born 27th July 1807 ; w. J. Hardie, R. Crease.

1809.

June 11. William Edgar, tailor, and Christian Waugh in Melrose, a.s.n. Andrew, born 6th March 1809, and baptised this day before the congregation.

" " George Turnbull, carter, and Helen Oliver in Melrose, a.d.n. Helen, born 31st April 1809, and baptised this day before the congregation.

" " Mr. John Simson and Mrs. Elizabeth Sommerville, his spouse, in Blainslie, a d.n. Agnes, born 4th March 1809, and baptised on the 27th following ; w. Messrs. Robert Romanes, James Somerville.

1809.

June 25. John Chisholm, mason, and Elizabeth Callender in Langshawmill, a.s.n. Walter, born 20th May 1809, and baptised this day before the congregation.

„   „   Mr. John Rutherford and Catherine Turnbull in Bridgend, a.d.n. Betty, born 27th May 1809, and baptised 7th July following ; w. John and James Rutherford.

July   9. Thomas Vair, weaver, and Margaret Tait in Darnick, a.s.n. Robert, born 6th June 1809, and baptised this day before the congregation.

„   „   William Moffat, farmer, and Joan Easton in Newstead, a.s.n. John, born 25th May 1809, and baptised this day before the congregation.

„   „   Robert Anderson, mason, and Peggy Thomson in Melrose, a.d.n. Agnes, born 6th June 1809, and baptised this day before the congregation.

„   „   Robert Burns, watchmaker, and Betty Dewar in Melrose, a.d.n. Margaret, born 23rd May 1809, and baptised this day before the congregation.

„   „   John Lees, clothier, and Jean Young in the Channel, a.d.n. Mary, born 9th March 1809.

„   „   Adam Sanderson, clothier, and Jean Edgar in Darlingshaugh, a.s.n. John, born 14th June, and to be baptised at Galashiels.

Aug. 20. Mr. David Spence at Fenwick, a.d.n. Elizabeth, unlawfully begotten in fornication, baptised at Melrose ; w. Mrs. and Miss Spence ; sponsor, Andrew Young.

Sept. 8. Michael Mercer, labourer, and Isabel Millne in Bridgend, a.d.n. Betty, born 4th August 1809, and baptised this day.

„   „   William Rodgers, private in Dumfriesshire Militia, and Ann Bowar, a.s.n. James, born 24th January 1805, and baptised about a fortnight after.

„   „   William Rodgers, private in Dumfriesshire, Militia, a.s.n. William, born 21st September 1808 (?), and baptised about a fortnight after.

Oct.   8. John Bowar, tailor, and Alison Dove in Melrose, a.d.n. Helen, born 16th August 1809, and baptised this day before the congregation.

„   „   Andrew Brown, labourer, and Margaret Bennet in Darnick, a.s.n. Andrew, born 8th August 1809.

„   „   Robert Crawford, shoemaker, and Jean Hogg in Melrose, a.s.n. James, born 12th July 1809, and baptised 6th October 1809.

„   „   Richard Dickson, farmer, and Margaret Simson in Blainslie, a.d.n. Isabella, born 11th August 1808, and baptised 25th September following by Rev. Dr. Ford.

„   „   Thomas Wilson, wright, and Mary Scott in Darlingshaugh, a.d.n. Janet, born 24th April 1807, and baptised 7th June following by Rev. Mr. Lawson.

„   „   Thomas Wilson, wright, and Mary Scott in Darlingshaugh, a.s.n. John, born 17th November 1808, and baptised 18th December following by Rev. Mr. Lawson.

„   8. Alexander Gibson, baker, and Margaret Paterson in Melrose, a.d.n. Isabel, baptised 14th August 1809, and born in fornication about a year and a half before ; w. Mrs. Spence, Andrew Young.

Nov. 26. John Pringle, hynd, and Margaret Riddell in Leaderfoot, a.d.n. Janet, baptised this day before the congregation,—about seven weeks old.

Dec. 10. James Goodfellow, cooper, and Helen Newlands in Melrose, a.d.n. Janet, born 13th October 1809, and baptised this day ; w. John Bowar, senior and junior.

„   24. George Brodie, smith, and Mary Stuart in Melrose, a.d.n. Margaret, born 1st November 1809, and baptised this day before the congregation.

„   28. Thomas Adams, labourer, and Margaret Mein in Newstead, a.d.n. Margaret, born 10th October 1809, and baptised this day ; w. James Ramsay, T. Williamson.

1809.

Dec. 28. James Bunzie, labourer, and Ann Thomson in Newstead, a.d.n. Janet, born 30th October 1809, and baptised this day ; w. as above.

  ,,   ,, Robert Dickson, shoemaker, and Agnes Ballantyne in Buckholmside, a.s.n. Robert, born 18th November 1809, and to be baptised at Galashiels 7th January 1810.

1810.

Jan. 26. Archibald Tod, Esq. of Drygrange, and Mrs. Eliza Pringle, his spouse, a.s.n. Thomas, born —— and baptised this day ; w. George Baillie, Esq. of Jerriswood, Colonel Robertson.

Feb. 11. John Henderson, weaver, and Isabel Linton in Melrose, a.d.n. Janet, baptised this day before the congregation, being about eleven weeks old.

  ,,   ,, Alexander Mitchel, hind, and Janet Hunter in Sorrowlessfield, a.d.n. Betty, born 8th February 1809, and baptised 12th March following ; w. Robert Redford, John Douglas.

  ,,   ,, James Roughhead and Margaret Bell in Melrose, a.d.n. Margaret, born 10th October 1809, and baptised 21st January 1810 ; w. Alexander Bell, John Bowar.

  ,, 28. Charles Erskine, Esq., writer, and Mrs. Barbara Pott, his spouse, in Melrose, a.s.n. James, born 22nd January 1810, and baptised this day ; w. Col. Erskine, Col. M'Murdo, and Mr. Knox.

Mar. 1. Mr. James Crawford, officer of Excise, and Margaret Oliver in Melrose, a.d.n. Margaret Warwick, born 26th January 1810, and baptised this day before the congregation.

  ,,   ,, Archibald Vallance, hynd, and Jean Thomson in Broadwoodshiel, a.s.n. Archibald, born 17th March 1808, and baptised about a month after ; w. Mr. Smith, Mr. Armstrong.

  ,,   ,, Archibald Vallance, hynd, and Jean Thomson in Broadwoodshiel, a.s.n. William, born 21st June 1809, and baptised about a month after ; w. same as above.

  ,, 29. Thomas Hay and Janet Smail, a.d.n. Jessy, born 23rd March at Kaeside.

  ,,   ,, John Kenly and Alison Gill, a.d.n. Christian.

April 1. James Borroman, teacher of dancing, and Margaret Cook in Melrose, a.d.n. Elizabeth, born 11th February 18—, and baptised this day before the congregation.

  ,,   ,, James Henderson, labourer, and Isabel Aitken in Melrose, a.s.n. William, baptised this day before the congregation, – about eleven weeks old.

  ,, 8. James Hopkirk, shoemaker, and Jean Turnbull in Melrose, a.d.n. Marrion, born about five weeks ago, and baptised this day before the congregation.

  ,,   ,, Thomas Thomson, plowman, and Isabel Turnbull in Melrose, a.s.n. William, born 11th March 1810, and baptised this day before the congregation.

  ,,   ,, Thomas Allan, baker, and Janet Scott in Melrose, a.s.n. Thomas, born 6th February 1810, and baptised this day before the congregation.

  ,,   ,, John Kinlayside, fisher, and Helen Thomson in Cobleheugh, a.d.n. Betty, born 5th January 1809, and baptised 12th day same month : w. Hugh Hall, Thomas Tait.

  ,, 14. William Anderson, hind, and Hannah Wilson, Friershaw, a.s.n. James, born 2nd April 1810, and baptised before the congregation at Newtown.

  ,, 29. John Taket, merchant, and Janet Martin in Melrose, a.s.n. Robert, born 21st March 1810, and baptised this day before the congregation.

  ,,   ,, Thomas Symington, wright, and Isabel Somers in Darlingshaugh, a.s.n. John, born 10th January 1810, and to be baptised at Galashiels by Rev. Dr. Douglas.

1810.

April 29. James Mercer, farmer, and Alison Hay in Coatgreen, a.d.n. Margaret, born 2nd April 1808, and baptised there by Rev. Mr. Lawson about three weeks after; w. Thomas Hay, George Mercer.

May 27. Alexander Adamson, hostler, and Betty Gillies in Melrose, a.d.n. Mary, born 14th March 1810, and baptised this day before the congregation.

„ „ William Linton, flesher, and Agnes Wight in Melrose, a.d.n. Mary, born 8th June 1810, and baptised 25th May same year.

„ „ Walter Ronaldson, mason, and Janet Wight in Darnick, a.s.n. Andrew, born 7th April 1810, and baptised 25th May same year.

June 17. John Chisholm, shoemaker, and Alison Elliot in Melrose, a.s.n. John, born 2nd May 1810, and baptised this day before the congregation.

„ „ William Mercer, shoemaker, and Janet Hart in Melrose, a.s.n. Nicol, born 10th March 1810, and baptised this day before the. congregation.

„ „ Thomas Brown, baker, and Jean Stoddart in Buckholmside, a.d.n. Betty, born 24th May 1810, and to be baptised at Galashiels by Rev. Dr. Douglas.

July 15. Robert Pringle, mason, and Jean Laing in Newstead, a.s.n. Robert, born 16th June 1810, and baptised this day before the congregation.

„ 22. Robert Collier, servant, and Jane Dods in Darnick, a.s.n. Robert, born 14th May 1810, and baptised this day before the congregation.

„ 30. Robert Small and Jenny Glendinning, a.d.n. Betty, born 19th December 1809, and baptised before the congregation this day.

Aug. 2. John Easton, wright, and Margaret Watson in Melrose, a.s.n. Robert Riddell, born 18th June 1810, and baptised this day; w. William and Thomas Riddell, Priorbank.

„ 12. Thomas Hendry and Janet Ormiston in Whitehill, a.d.n. Janet, born 28th June 1810, and baptised this day before the congregation.

„ 19. John Thomson, mason, and Bell Common in Newstead, a.s.n. John, born 22nd July 1810, and baptised this day before the congregation.

„ „ John Kenly and Alison Gill, a.d.n. Margaret.

Oct. 8. James Wilson and Helen Mercer, a.d.n. Janet, born 16th August 1810.

„ „ William Hogg and Isabel Bruce, a.d.n. Helen, born 18th June 1810.

„ — Alexander Mitchell, hynd, and Janet Hunter in Sorrowlessfield, a.s.n. Samuel, born 7th, and baptised 31st October 1810; w. Messrs James Fisher, John Laidlaw.

„ — James Scott, weaver, and Agnes Lindsay in Gattonside, a d.n. Helen, born 25th February 1803, and baptised about a month after.

„ — James Scott, weaver, and Agnes Lindsay in Gattonside, a.s.n. John, born 29th September 1805, and baptised about a month after; w. Thomas Boston, John Dickson.

„ — Daniel Taylor, farmer, and Mary Grieve in Blainslie, a.s.n. George, born 16th June 1810, and baptised 14th July following; w. Mr. Boyd, Mr. George Taylor.

„ — Robert Scott, weaver, and Martha Smail in Danielton, a.s.n. Robert, born 28th June 1810, and baptised —— 1810; w. Walter Balmer, Robert Carruthers.

„ — William Kyle, baker, and Janet Fairbairn in Melrose, a.d.n. Jean, born 27th September 1807, and baptised about a month after.

Nov. 21. William Kyle, baker, and Janet Fairbairn in Melrose, a.s.n. William Riddell Kyle, born 29th October 1810, and baptised this day; William Riddell, Esq., Thomas Riddell, Esq.

„ „ Andrew Stevenson, servant, and Isabel Brown in Newtown, a.s.n. William, born 28th January 1810, and baptised 11th March following; w. Alexander Mitchell, Robert Clapperton.

1810.

Nov. 21. James Henderson and Jean Young in Newtown, a.s.n. Alexander, born 6th December 1807, and baptised 17th January 1808 before the congregation.

"   "   Andrew Young, plowman, and Mary Bell in Melrose, a.d.n. Helen, born 19th October 1810, and baptised 24th November following ; w. William Wallace, John Bowar.

"   "   George Paterson, mason, and Isabel Gray, a.s.n. George, born 5th November 1809, and baptised 19th same month ; w. Messrs William Paterson, John Sanderson.

"   "   Adam Paterson, mason, and Janet Sanderson in Buckholmside, a.s.n. Adam, born 27th February 1807.

"   —   Adam Paterson, mason, and Janet Sanderson in Buckholmside, a.s.n. William, born 16th January 1808.

"   —   Adam Paterson, mason, and Janet Sanderson in Buckholmside, a.s.n. James, born 29th May 1809 ; all unbaptised.

"   —   Richard Lees, servant, and Marrion Purves in Melrose Bleachfield, a.d.n. Janet, born 16th November 1810, and baptised 30th December 1810 ; w. James Usher, Thomas Boston.

1811.

Jan.   —   Thomas Cleghorn, millwright, and Mary Inglis in Buckholmside, a.s.n. James, born 23rd December 1810, and to be baptised at Galashiels 20th January 1811.

"   — —   Robert Lawrie, butler, and Helen Lockie at Eildon Hall, a.s.n. Robert, born 2nd January 1811, and baptised 28th same month.

"   —   Andrew Scott, farmer, and Joan Hope in Newtownmill, a.d.n. Margaret, born 6th March 1810, and baptised 29th April same year.

"   —   John Herbertson, gardener, and Ann Dodds in Drygrange, a.d.n. Mary, born 15th October 1810, and baptised 4th November following ; w. John Forsyth, George Waldie.

Feb.   3.   William Grant, shoemaker, and Agnes Blaikie in Melrose, a.s.n. John, born 7th January last, and baptised this day before the congregation.

"   "   Andrew Common and Agnes Curle in Gattonside, a.d.n. Grisel, born 22nd November 1810, and baptised this day before the congregation.

"   "   Robert Dickson, shoemaker, and Agnes Ballantyne in Buckholmside, a.d.n. Margaret, born 8th February 1811, and to be baptised at Galashiels.

"   24.   James Johnstone, shoemaker, and Elizabeth Martin in Melrose, a.s.n. James, born 20th January 1811, and baptised this day before the congregation.

"   "   William Chisholm and Ratchel Blair in Melrose, a.d.n. Agnes, born 27th January 1811, and baptised this day before the congregation.

"   "   Mr. John Mercer and —— in Bridgend, a.d.n. Margaret, born 20th December 1803, and baptised about six weeks after.

"   "   Mr. John Mercer and —— in Bridgend, a.d.n. Euphemia, born 12th March 1806, and baptised about a month after.

"   "   Mr. John Mercer and Euphan Scott in Bridgend, a.d.n. Maria, born 21st January 1808, and baptised about six weeks after.

"   "   Mr. John Mercer and Euphan Scott in Bridgend, a.d.n. Jean, born 20th October 1809, and baptised about two months after.

"   "   Alexander Tudhope and Isabel Turner, a.d.n. Mary, born 2nd June 1805.

"   "   Alexander Tudhope and Isabel Turner, a.d.n. Isabel, born 5th May 1807.

"   "   Alexander Tudhope and Isabel Turner, a.s.n. Alexander, born 2nd November 1809, and all baptised by the relief minister at Earlston ; w. Robert Tudhope, James Millar.

Mar.   1.   John Clephan and Mary Nielson, a.s.n. Thomas, born 21st November, and baptised this day by the Rev. Mr. Thomson ; w. Thomas Inglis, John Grieve.

1811.

Mar.   3. Charles and Charlotte, two children, surnamed Melrose, having been found exposed, the former about Whitsunday 1802 and the latter on the evening of 18th December 1810, were both baptised this day before the congregation, who were required to be their sponsors.

Mar. 17. Robert Fairbairn, hynd, and Margaret Elliot in Peasehill, a.d.n. Agnes, born 15th November 1810, and baptised this day before the congregation.

„   „ John Turnbull, slater, and Isabel Henderson in Buckholmside, a.d.n. Isabel, born 25th February 1811, and to be baptised 24th March at Galashiels.

„   21. John Bowar, tailor, and Alison Dove in Melrose, a.d.n. Janet, born 15th February 1811, and baptised this day before the congregation.

„   „ George Moss and Jean Kennedy in Berryloch, a.d.n. Margaret, born 1st January 1811, and baptised about three weeks after ; w. James Usher, George Wight.

„   „ William Dickson, mason and Isabel Aillie in Gattonside, a.d.n. Agnes, born 31st January 1811, and baptised 28th February following ; w. John Dickson, Thomas Boston.

„   „ William Mein and Janet Millar, a.s.n. James, born 19th April 1810, and baptised three weeks after.

April 14. James Henderson and Margaret Stevenson, a.s.n. James, born in fornication, August 1807, at Newstead, and baptised this day before the session ; sponsor, William Stevenson.

„   30. George Tinlin, wright, and Jean Crawford in Melrose, a.d.n. Jean, born in fornication 26th December 1808, and baptised this day ; w. Robert Crawford, John Bowar.

„   „ George Henderson, labourer, and Mary Curle in Gattonside, a.s.n. John, born 18th June 1809, and baptised about a month after.

„   „ Robert Crease, hynd, and Christian Wight in Bluecairn, a.d.n. Jean, born 31st March 1811, and baptised 28th April following ; w. George Smith, George Baillie.

„   „ Alexander Scott, labourer, and Janet Scott in Newstead, a.d.n. Isabel, born about Candlemas 1808, and baptised this day before the session.

„   „ Thomas Sanderson, shoemaker, and Mary Blaikie in Darlingshaugh, a.s.n. Thomas, born 20th February 1811.

„   „ David Thomson, clothier, and Helen Young in Darlingshaugh, a.d.n. Ann, born 11 August 1810.

„   „ James Vetch, steward, and Margaret Watson in Greenwells, a.d.n. Agnes, born 29th July 1807.

„   „ James Vetch, steward, and Margaret Watson in Greenwells, a.d.n. Frances, born 28th March 1809.

„   „ James Vetch, steward, and Margaret Watson in Greenwells, a.s.n. Thomas, born 31st December 1810, and all baptised at Newtown by Rev. Mr. Elder ; w. Henry Cochran, Walter Balmer.

June   6. Andrew Brown and Margaret Bennet in Darnick, a.s.n. Alexander, born 6th June 1811.

Robert Laurie and Janet Rait, a.s.n. John, born 7th September, and baptised this day : w. William Cooke, Thomas Scott.

Arthur Reid and Janet Govin, a.d.n. Agnes, born 25th September, and baptised this day before the congregation.

„   16. William Hopkirk, shoemaker, and Isabel Home in Gattonside, a.s.n. William, born 9th May 1811.

„   „ James Kennedy, coachman, and Margaret Oliver in Drygrange, a.s.n. Ralph, born 18th April 1811.

„   „ George Fair, weaver, and Isabel Christie in Gattonside, a.d.n. Helen, born 3rd April 1811, and all three baptised this day before the congregation.

„   „ Simeon Aitchison, dyer, and Elspeth Dalgliesh in Darlingshaugh, a.s.n. William, born 15th March 1809.

1811.
June 16. Simeon Aitchison, dyer, and Elspeth Dalgleish, a.s.n. Alexander, born 11th June 1811, and both to be baptised by Rev. Dr. Douglas, Galashiels.

„ 30. Robert Pringle, labourer, and Agnes Burnet in Newstead, a.s.n. William, born 23rd February 1811, and baptised this day before the congregation.

„ „ Richard Dickson in Bluecairn, a.d.n. Marrion. *See* year 1826.

„ „ Thomas Vair, weaver, and Jess Burnet in Newstead, a.d.n. Margaret, born 23rd March 1811, and baptised this day before the congregation.

„ „ William Moffat and Joan Easton in Newstead, a.d.n. Helen, born 13th May 1811, and baptised this day before the congregation.

Aug. 4. James Crawford, officer of Excise, and Margaret Oliver in Melrose, a.s.n. James, born 19th July 1811, and baptised this day before the congregation.

„ 18. William Blythe and Alison Tait in Darnick, a.s.n. William, born 8th July, and baptised this day before the congregation.

„ „ William Lesslie and Marion Stirton, a.s.n. Alexander, born 29th July, and baptised this day.

„ 29. John Simpson, a.s.n. Charles, born 6th June, and baptised 4th July 1811.

1799. (*A former omission.*)
John Anderson and Mary Cumming, a.s.n. Thomas, born 12th August 1799, and baptised at Earlstown.

1811.
Sept. 8. Adam Russel and Margaret Hall, a.s.n. Thomas, born 15th August 1811, and baptised this day before the congregation.

„ „ Robert Burns and Betty Dewer in Melrose, a.d.n. Barbara, born 28th July, and baptised this day before the congregation.

„ 9. Archibald Todd and Eliza Pringle in Drygrange, a.s.n. Archibald, born 31st July 1811, and baptised 24th August 1811.

1809.
James Vair, gardener in Greenwells, and Elizabeth Hatton, a.d.n. Mary, born 21st May 1809, and baptised 20th June 1809.

1811.
Sept. 12. James Vair and Elizabeth Hatton, a.s.n. John, born 10th August 1811.

1806.
James Vair and Elizabeth Hatton, a.s.n. Robert, born 14th March 1806, and baptised 15th April 1806.

1811.
Sept. 15. Thomas Wilson and Nelly Tait, a.d.n. Janet, born 25th August 1811, and baptised this day before the congregation.

„ 22. John Chisholm and Elizabeth Calender, a.s.n. Robert, born 10th August 1811, and baptised this day before the congregation.

Nov. 9. John Chisholm and Alison Elliot, a.d.n. Agnes, born 26th September, and baptised this day by Rev. Mr. Thomson.

„ „ John Dodds and Cecilia Elliot, a.d.n. Isabel, born 3rd October, and baptised this day by Mr. Thomson.

Dec. 15. Adam Sanderson, clothier, and Jean Edgar in Darlingshaugh, a.d.n. Margaret, born 9th November, and to be baptised in Galashiels.

„ 29. Robert Anderson and Margaret Thomson, a.d.n. Janet, born 1st December 1811, and baptised 29th current.

1812. James Gray and Margaret Shiel, a.s.n. Andrew, born 8th January, and baptised this day.

1811. Richard Lees and Mary Paterson in Buckholmside, a.s.n. Hugh, born 21st September 1811.

1800. Richard Lees and Mary Paterson in Buckholmside, a.s.n. Thomas born 21st February 1800.

1801.

Richard Lees and Mary Paterson in Buckholmside, a.s.n. Robert, born 26th September 1801.

William Leithhead and Janet Thomson, a.s.n. Andrew, born 29th March, and baptised 19th April.

1812.

Jan. 5. James Scott and Janet Knox in Greenwells, a.s.n. David, born 28th November, and baptised before the congregation.

" 6. Adam Dixon and his wife, Alison Mather, in Newstead, a.d.n. Jean, born 2nd December 1811, and baptised 6th January.

" 25. Andrew Stevenson and Isabel Brown, a.d.n. Margaret, born 1st January, and baptised.

Feb. 18. Michael Mercer and Isabel Milne, a.s.n. Nicol, born 30th December 1811.

April 5. Thomas Adams and Margaret Mien, a.s.n. Thomas, born 5th January, and baptised before the congregation.

" 7. George Haig and Jean Ramsay, a.s.n. Robert, born 4th February ; w. Nicol Milne, James Ramsay.

" 12. Thomas Aldcorn and Grice Frater, a.s.n. James, born 11th January : w. Nicol Milne, George Laurie.

" 26. James Mercer and Alison Hay in Coatgreen, a.s.n. James, born 24th March, and baptised.

May 3. George Mill and Margaret Cleland, a.s.n. William, born 31st March 1812.

David Hopkirk and Margaret Grieve, a.d.n. Janet, born 23rd February same year.

Walter Scott and his wife, Betty Robertson, a.s.n. George, born 26th August, and baptised 30th September 1811.

Alexander Stewart and Janet Patterson, a.d.n. Marion, born 27th June 1810.

Thomas Vair and his wife, Margaret Tait, a.s.n. James, born 23rd April.

July 19. Thomas Brown and his wife Jane Stoddart, in Buckholmside, a.s.n. Andrew, born 23rd June.

Thomas Renwick and his wife, Alison Brunton, a.s.n. John, born 13th November 1811, and baptised 25th December following.

James Swanston and Marion Purvis, his wife, a.d.n. Agnes, born 12th June, and baptised.

James Rutherford and Margaret Forsythe, a.s.n. Thomas, born 12th April 1811.

Thomas Wood's children in Uplaw are inserted year 1825.

John Watson. *See* year 1821.

Andrew Drummond and Janet Claperton, a.s.n. George, born 11th October 1811, and baptised.

George Turnbull and Helen Oliver, a.d.n. Mary, born 3rd April 1812.

George Hutchison and Margaret Hills, a.d.n. Betty, born 2nd July 1812.

Andrew Scott and Joan Hope, his wife, a.s.n. Andrew, born 20th July 1812, and baptised.

John Lees and Jean Young, a.s.n. Robert, born 19th October 1811.

David Thomson and Helen Young, a.d.n. Jessy, born 30th June 1812.

George Watson and Anne Wheale, a.s.n. James, born 14th February 1811, and baptised 14th March.

1812.

July 19. James Hardie and Janet Skiel, a.s.n. James, born 25th July 1811, and baptised.

" 23. Andrew Martin and Isabel Allie, a.s.n. William, born 1794, and baptised this day.

Aug. — William Dickson and Marion Smith, a.s.n. William, born 8th July, and baptised.

1812.
William Dickson and Marion Smith, a.s.n. Edward, born 14th November 1809, and baptised.

Sept. — John Brockie and Charlotte Wemys, a.s.n. Robert, born 3rd August 1812, and baptised.

" 5. Thomas Cleghorn and Mary Inglis, a.d.n. Margaret, born 5th September.

" 6. Alexander Pringle and Barbara Millar in Melrose, a.s.n. Alexander, born 6th February 1809 ; w. Mr. Robert Phin, John Pringle.

" " Alexander Pringle and Barbara Millar in Melrose, a.s.n. William Millar, born 15th November 1810 ; w. Mr. Robert Phin, Mr. George Thomson.

" 20. John Taket and Janet Martin, a.s.n. Andrew, born 26th July. Mary Tait. *See* year 1820.

" 27. Richard Lees and Marion Purves, a.s.n. James, born 31st August.

Oct. 4. William Dixon and Isabel Aillie, a.d.n. Janet, born 29th July.

" " Thomas Laing and Betty Wood, a.d.n. Betty, born 28th August.

" 11. John Henderson and Isabel Linton, a.s.n. John, born 6th September.

" 18. William Grant and Agnes Blaikie, a.s.n. Robert, born 14th September.

Nov. 22. James Hume and Jean Aitchison in Old Melrose, a.d.n. Marion, born 24th October.
John Mein and Elizabeth Mein, a.s.n. James, born 5th January 1811.

Dec. 27. Andrew Common and Agnes Curle, a d.n. Margaret, born 24th October.

" " George Brodie and Mary Steuart in Melrose, a.d.n. Elizabeth, born 29th November.

" " William Moffat and —— Easton in Newstead, a.d.n. Alison, born 3rd December.

1813.
William Mercer and Janet Hart, a.d n. Janet, born 13th December 1812.

Feb. 7. Thomas Thomson and Isabel Turnbull, a.d.n. Marion, born 27th December 1812.

" " James Crawford, officer of Excise, and Margaret Oliver, a.s.n. Andrew, born 19th December 1812.

" 14. David Storey and Janet Anderson, a.d.n. Isabel, born 9th January 1812.

" " George Stoddart and Agnes Brown, a.d.n. Isabel, born 27th November 1810.
Arther Read and Janet Given, a.s.n. James, born 26th December 1812.
George Fairgrieve and Alison Robson, a.d.n. Mary, born 16th September 1810.
William Hogg and Isabel Bruce, a.d.n. Agnes, born 10th June 1812.

Dec. 25. John Rutherford and Cathrane Turnbull, a.s.n. Alexander, born 30th November 1813 ; w. James Usher.

1810. James Simson and Helen Boston, a.s.n. James, born 7th November 1810.

—— 11. James Rutherford and Margaret Forsythe, a.s.n. John, born 15th March.

" " James Johnston and Elizabeth Martin, a.d.n. Mary, born 9th March.
1813.

May 9. David Laurence and Agnes Dixon, a.d.n. Janet, born 30th March 1813.

" " John Dixon and Elizabeth Scott, his wife, a.s.n. James, born 31st March 1813.
—— Smith and his wife, twins named James and Adam, born 16th April 1798.
Robert Dixon and Agnes Ballantyne, a.d.n. Janet, born 2nd March 1813.

Oct. 21. Alexander Robertson and Isabel Walker in Drygrange, a.d.n. Margaret, born 23rd September 1811, and baptised as per margin.

1813.

    William Young and Peggy Rutherford, a.s.n. James, born 27th February 1813.

    Robert Dixon and Agnes Ballantyne, a.d.n. Janet, born 2nd March 1813.

    Thomas Thomson in Darlingshaugh and Janet Walker, his wife, a.s.n. Thomas, born 13th September 1807.

    Thomas Thomson in Darlingshaugh and Janet Walker, a.d.n. Elizabeth, born 21st August 1809.

    Thomas Thomson in Darlingshaugh and Janet Walker, a.s.n. Robert, born 21st March 1812.

    John Dods and Jenny Elliot, his wife, a.d.n. Janet, born 24th March 1813.

April 9. Archibald Tod, Esq. of Drygrange, and Eliza Pringle, his wife, a.d.n. Katharine Mary, born 13th March 1813, and baptised by the Rev. Mr. Thomson.

    James Gibson and Elspeth Scott, his wife, a.s.n. William, born 26th April 1813.

    Walter Ronaldson and Janet Wight, a.d.n. Joan, born 1814.

    William Linton and Agnes Wight, a.s.n. George, born April 1814.

July 4. James Gray and Mary Robson, a.d.n. Margaret, born 25th May 1806.

„ „ Thomas Dickson and Margaret Paterson, a.s.n. Thomas, born 16th May 1813.

„ „ William Hardie and Alison Dalgliesh, a.d.n. Isabel, born 2nd June 1813.

1812. Thomas Sanderson and Mary Blaikie in Darlingshaugh, a.s.n. William, born 12th December 1812.

1787. Thomas Starke and Margaret Carter, his wife, in Blainslie, a.s.n. Thomas, born 16th December 1787.

1804. John Usher and Agnes Blaikie, his wife, a.d.n. Jess, born at Toftfield on 17th March 1804.

1806-7 (?) John Usher and Agnes Blaikie, twins named Agnes and Mary, born 19th October 1806-7 (?)

1809. John Usher and Agnes Blaikie, a.s.n. John, born 10th October 1809.

1811. John Usher and Agnes Blaikie, a.d.n. Betsy, born 10th June 1811.

1813.

Aug. 1. William Bathgate and Margaret Richardson, his wife, a.s.n. George, born 21st June 1813.

„ „ Adam Russel and Margaret Hall, a.d.n. Margaret, born 22nd July.

July 15. James Clapperton and Joan Cunninghame, a.s.n. Robert, born 15th May 1813.

Sept. 12. William Thomson and Margaret Scott, a.d.n. May, born 22nd July 1813.

„ „ George Tinline and Margaret Dickieson, a.d.n. Elizabeth, born 25th July 1813.

1810. James Brown and Jean Sanderson, a.s.n. John, born 7th August 1810.

    James Lees and Margaret Elliot, a.d.n. Helen, born 10th February, and baptised 14th March.

    John Lees and Jean Young, a.d.n. Isabel, born 15th June and baptised.

    Richard Dickson in Bleucairn, a.s.n. Richard. *See* year 1826.

1813. Alexander Laidlaw and Helen Cochran, a.s.n. Thomas, born 23rd September 1813.

1805. Thomas Scott and Betty Inglis, a.s.n. John, born 17th August and baptised.

1807. Thomas Scott and Betty Inglis, a.s.n. James, born in Whitelee, 28th August 1807.

1812. Thomas Scott and Betty Inglis, a.d.n. Elizabeth, born at Drygrange 16th January 1812.

1810. John Scott and Elizabeth Maclean, his wife, in Buckholmside, a.s.n. John, born 22nd November 1810.

    Walter Scott and Isabel Brown, a.d.n. Margaret, born November 1810.

1809. John Purvis and Jean Leithead, a.s.n. William, born 20th March 1809.

1812. John Thomson and Bell Common, a.d.n. Anne, born 25th December 1812.

„ John Muir and Barbara Lumsden, a.d.n. Margaret, born 25th November 1813.

1803. George Bell and Jean White, a.s.n. Andrew, born 16th July 1803.

1805. George Bell and Jean White, a.s.n. George, born 22nd April 1805.

1807. George Bell and Jean White, a.d.n. Isabel, born 10th August 1807.

1810. George Bell and Jean White, a.d.n. Jannet, born 13th April 1810.

1813. George Bell and Jean White, a.d.n. Margaret, born 9th May 1813.

William Blyth and Alison Tait, a.s.n. James, born 9th June 1813.

John Roberts and Mary Ovens, a.d.n. Jean, born 25th April 1813.

Thomas Scott and Christian Hopkirk, a.d.n. Margaret, born 22nd October 1813.

William Johnstone and Alison Cairns, a.s.n. James, born 7th October 1813.

1814.

Jan. 8. George Haig and Jane Ramsay, a.d.n. Elizabeth, born 8th January 1814.

„ 9. John Harper and Jean Hart, a.s.n. George, born 1st August 1813.

James Henderson and Jane Young, a.s.n. William, born 3rd January 1813.

James Henderson and Jane Young, a.s.n. Andrew, born 26th January 1814.

„ — John Robertson and Agnes Clerk, a.d.n. Elizabeth, born 31st January 1814.

Alexander Robertson and Isabella Walker, a.d.n. Isabella, born 10th September 1813.

Thomas Brown and Jean Stoddart, a.d.n. Isabella, born 17th March 1814.

George Stewart and Janet Sanderson, a.s.n. John, born 29th February 1814.

Mar. — Archibald Ormiston and Isabel Hart, a.s.n. Archibald, born 30th October 1813.

Thomas Laing and Betty Wood, a.s.n. Alexander, born 7th February 1814.

Robert Burns and Betty Dewars, a.d.n. Isabel, born 27th January 1814.

John Chisholm and Alice Elliot, a.s.n. Walter, born 31st December 1813.

Alexander Laing and Betty Dickson, a.s.n. Alexander, born 19th February 1814.

William Smith and Helen Scott, a.s.n. William, born 16th January 1814.

William Bartrem and Alison Brown, a.s.n. Thomas, born 25th March 1814.

Robert Colliard and Jane Dods, a.s.n. Robert, born 22nd January 1814.

May 18. William Paterson and Margaret Robson, a.d.n. Margaret, born 26th March 1814.

„ „ John Macferlin and Marrion Alexander, a.d.n. Marrion Smith, born 18th April 1814.

Thomas Murray and Anne Mercer, a.d.n. Elizabeth, born 28th September 1813.

William Hogg and Isabel Bruce in Melrose, a.d.n. Agnes, born 25th February 1814.

1812. William Dobson and Elizabeth Milne, a.d.n. Helen, born 6th June 1812.

1814. Alexander Stenhouse and Esther Riddell in Newtown, a.d.n. Agnes, born 30th January 1814.

June 14. William Chisholm and Ratchel Blair in Melrose, a.d.n. Marrion, born 11th April 1814.

1814.

Robert Anderson and Margaret Thomson in Melrose, a.s.n. Robert, born 23rd April 1814.

William Ovens and Christian Tait, a.s.n. Thomas, born 5th February 1814.

George Stoddart and Nancy Brown in Darnick, a.s.n. John, born 9th April 1814.

William Bathgate and Margaret Richardson, a.s.n. Simeon, born 22nd June 1814.

James Watson. *See* year 1821.

June 17. William Buckham and Janet Blaikie in Melrose, a.d.n. Catharine, born 24th May 1814.

John Taket and Janet Martin in Melrose, a.s.n. George, born 17th June 1814.

William Dickson and Isabel Allie in Gattonside, a.s.n. John, born 31st May 1814.

James Hume and Jane Aitchison, a.s.n. William, born 7th July 1814.

Robert Small and Janet Clendening, a.s.n. Alexander, born 13th June 1814.

July 3. Andrew Drummond and Janet Claperton in Darnick, a.s.n. George, born 12th May 1814.

,, 9. Thomas Adams and Margaret Milne, a.d.n. Agnes, born 4th March 1814.

,, ,, John Henderson and Isabel Lintin, a.s.n. John, born 17th May 1814.

Aug. 7. Charles Erskine, Esq., writer in Melrose, and Mrs. Barbara Pott, his spouse, a.s.n. George Pott Erskine, born 25th July 1814 ; w. Mr. James Curle, writer in Melrose, Mr. George Thomson, student of divinity.

Robert Laurie, Eildonhall, a.d.n. Helen, born 4th August 1814.

,, 21. James Leithead and Helen Walker, a.d.n. Agnes, born 27th July 1814.

1809. James Miller and Betty Hart in Newstead, a.s.n. James, born 11th June 1809.

1814. James Miller and Betty Hart, a.d.n. Janet, born 19th October 1813.

William Linton and Agnes Wight, a.d.n. Betty Linton, born 17th May 1814.

George Newtown and Margaret Weatherston, a.s.n. Peter, born 25th March 1814.

1806.

May 24. Nicol Mercer and Mary Jamieson, a.d.n. Margaret, born 18th September 1805.

1814.

June 9. Nicol Mercer and Mary Jamieson, a.s.n. Thomas, born 18th March 1808.

Thomas Whitehead and Jane Burton in Dingleton, a.d.n. Jannet, born 10th January 1810.

Thomas Whitehead and Jane Burton in Dingleton, a.s.n. George, born 19th February 1811.

Thomas Whitehead and Jane Burton in Dingleton, a.s.n. David, born 10th September 1812.

Thomas Whitehead and Jane Burton in Dingleton, a.s.n. Thomas, born 15th October 1813, all baptised on 9 June 1814 ; w. John Grahame, William Bishop.

John Jackson and Joan Marr, a.s.n. John, born 17th April 1814.

John Baptist Menard and Margaret Hopkirk, a.s.n. Alexander, born 10th September 1813.

Arthur Reid and Janet Given in Melrose, a.d.n. Isabel, born 8th July 1814.

William Armstrong and Margaret Easton, a.d.n. Helen, born 3rd August 1814.

Margaret Tait. *See* year 1820.

1814.

Richard Lees and Mary Purvis in Melrose, a.s.n. Richard, born 13th August 1814.

June 26. Andrew Stevenson and Isabel Brown in Melrose, a.s.n. Andrew, born 11th May 1814.

Oct. 9. John Stewart and Agnes Pringle in Newstead, a.d.n. Margaret, born 31st December 1811.

John Stewart and Agnes Pringle in Newstead, a.s.n. Andrew, born 2nd November 1813.

Alexander Blaikie and Isabel Henderson, a.s.n. William, born 8th September 1814.

Alexander Tudhope and Isabel Turner in Melrose, a.d.n. Helen, born 25th June 1812.

Alexander Tudhope and Isabel Turner in Melrose, a.d.n. Janet, born 19th May 1814.

" 23. Robert Laurie and Janet Rait in Dingleton, a.s.n. George, born 20th September 1814.

" " William Hopkirk and Bell Hume, a.s.n. David, born 18th August 1814.

" " Adam Dickson and Alison Mather, a.d.n. Alison, born 13th September 1814.

" 30. Thomas Ballintine and Jean Douglas, a.s.n. Robert, born 29th September 1814.

Nov. 17. Adam Aitchison and Jane Bonner, a.s.n. Alexander, born 1st August 1814.

" " James Gibson and Elspith Scott, a.d.n. Margaret, born 28th September 1814.

" 22. David Thomson and Helen Young, a.s.n. James, born 22nd February 1814, not baptised.

Dec. 18. Thomas Thomson and Isabell Turnbull, a.s.n. Charles, born 31st October 1814.

" " Thomas Wilson and Christian Linsay, a.s.n. Adam, born 18th December 1814.

1815.

Jan. 16. George Crawford and Elisabeth Hogg, a.s.n. George, born 5th May 1813.

" 17. Anthony Emelius Pool, a native of Holland, and Jean Bell in Melrose, a.s.n. George Alexander, born 5th November 1813.

" 18. James Scott, and Isabell Smith, a.s.n. James, born 10th August 1814.

" " Andrew Scott and Joan Hope, a.s n. George, born 15th July 1814.

" 24. Archibald Tod and Elisa Pringle, a.d.n. Susannah, born 24th November 1814, and baptised 13th December.

Feb. 5. John Dods and Seninnah Elliot, a s.n. Nichol, born 12th November 1814.

" .. Andrew Millar and Janet Easton, a.s.n. William, born 13th December 1814.

1812.

Mar. 6. Robert Scott and Elisabeth Scott, a.s.n. Walter, born 6th March 1815 (*sic*).

1814.

June — Robert Scott and Elisabeth Scott, a.s.n. James, born 21st June 1814.

1815.

Feb. 6. Robert Dickson and Agnes Balantyne in Darlingshaugh, twins named Ann and Agnes, born 28th November 1814.

" " James Crawford in Melrose and Margaret Oliver, a.d.n. Mary, born 9th January 1815.

Mar. 5. James Black and Margaret Thomson, a.d.n. Margaret, born 13th December 1813.

" " Thomas Acorn and Grace Frater, a.s.n. Robert, born 25th November 1814.

1815.

Mar. 26. John Chisholm and Elizabeth Ballander, a.d.n. Janet Chisholm, born 15th January 1815.

April 9. Alexander Gibson and Catharine Ross, a.s.n. William, born 2nd February 1815.

,, ,, John Laidlaw and Mary Nicholson, a.d.n. Ann, born 15th March 1815.

,, ,, Thomas Dickson and Margaret Paterson, a.s.n. William, born 18th February 1815.

,, 26. Adam Russell and Margaret Hall, a.s.n. David, born 23rd March 1815.

May 2. John Laidlaw and Beatrix Laidlaw, a.s.n. John, born 6th September 1814.

1813.

Mar. 9. George Pringle and Janet Elliot, a.s.n. Robert, born 9th March 1813.

1815.

Jan. 24. Samuel Rutherford and Elisabeth Moffat, a.s.n. John, born 14th October 1814.

,, — William Johnson and Alison Cairns, a.s.n. William, born 29th October 1814.

April 30. Alexander Keltie and Ann Fair, a.s.n. James, born 29th January 1815.

,, — George Brodie and Mary Stewart, a.d.n. Jane Brodie, born 10th March 1815.

May 7. George Pringle and Janet Elliot, a.s.n. Walter, born 25th Feb. 1815.

,, ,, Thomas Allen and Janet Scott, a.s.n. Robert, born 20th April 1815.

,, ,, George Burdon and Mary Brown, a.s.n. John Burdon, born 30th December 1814.

,, 28. George Tinline and Margaret Dickson, a.s.n. James, born 12th April 1815.

June 4. John Dickson and Elisabeth Scott, a.d.n. Hannah, born 14th April 1815.

,, — Alexander Laidlaw and Helen Cochrane, a.s.n. Adam, born 24th May 1815.

1811.

May — James Calcleugh and Jean Chisholm, a.s.n. Walter, born January 1812 [*sic*].

1812.

Nov. — Alexander Turnbull and Euphamia Davidson, a.d.n. Elizabeth, born 2nd November 1812.

1815.

June 20. Alexander Turnbull and Euphamia Davidson, a.s.n. William, born 22nd May 1815.

,, 22. Alexander Bold and Jean Brown, a.s.n. Alexander, born 12th December 1814.

1813.

Oct. 26. Thomas Hope and Agnes Knox, a.s.n. James, born 26th October 1813.

1815.

April 26. Thomas Hope and Agnes Knox, a.d.n. Agnes, born 29th March 1815.

July 2. William Blythe and Alison Tait, a.s.n. Robert, born 29th May 1815.

,, 16. Robert Collier and Jane Dods, a.s.n. Andrew, born 7th May 1815.

,, ,, David Spence and Margaret Goodfellow, a.s.n. Joseph, born August 1810.

,, 19. Thomas Vair and Margaret Tait, a.d.n. Mary Vair, born 14th June 1815.

,, — John Scott and —— Smith, a.s.n. John, born July 1815, liven only nine days.

Aug. 6. Barney Herken and Janet Thomson, a.s.n. John, born 13th July 1815.

,, — George Steward and Janet Sanderson in Darlingshaugh, a.s.n. Andrew, born 4th June 1815.

,, Walter Laidlaw and Isabell Scott in Bucchamside, a.d.n. Isabell, born 23rd June 1815.

1815.

Aug. 20. Andrew Common and Agnes Curle, a.s.n. Andrew, born 16th January 1815.

Sept. — George Turnbull and Helen Oliver, a.s.n. John, born 29th May 1814.

,, — George Turnbull and Helen Oliver, a.s.n. Thomas, born 8th July 1815.

,, — James Rutherford and Margaret Forsythe, a.d.n. Jean Rutherford, born 3rd September 1814.

,, — William Thomson and Margaret Scott, a.s.n. Alexander Thomson, born 30th July 1815.

Oct. 11. Walter Ronaldson and Janet Wight, a.d.n. Isabell, born 31st May 1815.

,, — Alexander Allen, Esq. in Lauder, and Elisa Jemima Moffat, a.s.n. Alexander Moffat, born 26th May 1815.

,, 16. Andrew Robertson and Elisabeth Thomson, a.s.n. Thomas, born 1st October 1815.

Richard Dickson in Bluecairn, a d.n. Jean. *See* year 1826.

Nov. 6. James Craig and Isabell Thorburn, a.d.n. Ann, born 1st October 1815.

William Smith and Helen Scott, a.d.n. Marrien, born 10th October 1815.

Feb. 1. Robert Scott and Martha Smail, a.s.n. James, born 1st February, and baptised 20th April 1815.

1810. John Turnbull and Alison Bathgate, a.d.n. Alison Turnbull, born 25th September 1810.

1812. John Turnbull, tanner, and Alison Bathgate in Buckhamside, a.s.n. John, born 19th August 1812.

1814. John Turnbull, tanner, and Alison Bathgate in Buckhamside, a.d.n. Jean, born 21st July 1814.

1816.

Jan. 7. James Bunzie and Helen Bruce, a.s.n. Robert, born 2nd December 1816 [*sic.*]

1815.

Dec. 9. Charles Hendry and Isabell Milne, a.d.n. Alison, born 20th November 1815.

1816.

Jan. 7. William Moffat and Joan Easton, a.d.n. Alison Moffat, born 2nd January 1816.

,, 16. William Buckham, brewer in Melrose, and —— Blaikie, a.s.n. Archibald Weatherston, born 16th January 1816, and baptised 7th February 1816.

Mar. 3. Andrew Bartram and Alison Brown, a.d.n. Mary Anne, born 26th January 1816.

,, 4. James Hume and Jean Aitchison, a.s.n. Robert Hume, born 26th January 1816.

Andrew Watson. *See* year 1821.

1815.

Aug. — Duncan Macdonald Church and Elisabeth Robertson, a.d.n. Elisabeth, born 10th July 1816.

Dec. 1. Thomas Scott and Alison Blyth, a.s.n. Thomas, born 1st December 1815.

1816.

April 26. William Moffat and Helen Rentoul in Williamlaw, a.d.n. Helen, born 30th December 1815.

,, ,, William Anderson and Hannah Wilson, twins, a.s.n. Thomas John and a.d.n. Helen, born 15th May 1815.

,, 28. John Somerville and Jean Miller, a.s.n. William Somerville, born 11th October 1815.

May 5. James Robertson and Jean Lockie in Blainslie, a.d.n. Fanny, born 17th April 1816.

1815.

Jan. 15. James Robertson and Jean Lockie in Blainslie, a.s.n. Richard Robertson, born 17th December 1814.

1816.
May 12. James Leithhead and Helen Walker, a.d.n. Janet, born 4th April 1816.
1815.
Jan.   5. Thomas Sanderson and Mary Blaikie in Darlingshaugh, a.d.n. Mary, born 5th January 1815.
1816.
April — James Gibson and Elspeth Scott, a.d.n. Helen, born 21st March 1816.
June   7. Robert Young and Isabell Slater, ——, born 27th May 1816.
1814.
July   16. John Gray and Isabell Weatherston in Blainslie, a.s.n. Robert, born 16th July 1814.
1816.
April 11. Arthur Reid and Janet Gavin, a.d.n. Janet Reid, born 11th April 1816.
  ,,   16. William Dickson and Isabel Aillie, a.d.n. Jean, born 16th April, and baptised 16th June 1816.
  ,,   29. George Haig and Jean Ramsay, a.s.n. John, born 29th April 1816.
May   16. Robert Laurie and Janet Rait in Danieltown, a.s.n. Robert, born 16th May 1816.
June   3. Thomas Ballantyne and Jane Douglas, a.s.n. Alexander Ballantyne, born 3rd June 1816.
  ,,   ,, Thomas Fairbairn and Margaret Smith in Melrose, a.s.n. David, born 25th June 1816.
  ,,   ,, John Gray and Isabel Weatherston in Blainslie, a.s.n. John, born 25th June 1816.
July   8. Adam Russel and Margaret Hall in Melrose, a.s.n. Robert, born 8th July 1816.
1815.
Dec.   13. John Dunence and Janet Pringle, a.d.n. Betty, born 13th December 1815.
1816.
July   9. William Ovens and Christian Tait in Darlingshaugh, a.d.n. Margaret.
  ,,   23. Adam Sanderson and Jean Edgar in Darlingshaugh, a.d.n. Agnes.
  ,,   ,, Andrew Scott and Joan Hope in Newtown, a.s.n. John, born 11th June 1816.
  ,,   ,, William Watson and Margaret Stevenson, a.d.n. Wilhelmina, born 29th September 1811.
  ,,   ,, Robert Henderson and Mary M'Keller in Galashiels, a.s.n. Thomas, born 29th September 1816.
Aug.   20. Robert Dickson and Agnes Ballantyne in Galashiels, a.d.n. Ann.
1812.
Feb.   28. Alexander Mackintosh and Elisabeth Bell, a.s.n. Alexander Macintosh, born 28th February 1812.
 1816.
May   25. Thomas Adams and Margaret Mein, a.d.n. Catharine, born 25th May 1816.
  ,,   ,, William Mercer and Janet Hart in Melrose, a.s.n. William, born 3rd March 1816.
  ,,   ,, William Chisholm and Rachael Blair in Melrose, a.s.n. George, born 5th January 1816.
  ,,   ,, George Turnbull and Helen Oliver, a.s.n. John Turnbull, born 29th May 1804.
  ,,   ,, George Turnbull and Helen Oliver, a.s.n. Thomas, born 8th July 1815.
  ,,   ,, James Rutherford and —— Forsythe, a.d.n. Jean Rutherford, born 3rd August 1814.
Nov.   3. Robert Anderson and Margaret Thomson, a.s.n. John, born 25th September 1816.
  ,,   ,, James Rutherford and Margaret Forsythe, a.s.n. James, born 4th September 1816.
  ,,   ,, William Mabin and Margaret Dickson, a.d.n. Alison, born 29th October 1814.

1816.
Nov. 9. John Bower and Margaret Scott in Melrose, a.d.n. Isabell Bower, born 2nd September 1816.

,, 10. Alexander Keltie and Ann Fair in Darnick, a.s.n. John, born 10th November 1816.

,, ,, Andrew Stevenson and Isabell Brown in Melrose, a.d.n. Ann, born 21st June 1816.

Dec. 1. James Clerk and Isabel Henderson, a.s.n. James, born 1st October 1816.

,, 12. Thomas Tait and Jean Dobson in Galabridge, a.s.n. Thomas, born 12th October 1816.

1817.
Jan. 22. Thomas Vair and Jessy Burnet in Newstead, a.s.n. Thomas, born 29th August 1816.

,, ,, John Watson and Janet Fairbairn in Clackmae, a.d.n. Anne, born 29th September 1814.

,, ,, John Watson and Janet Fairbairn in Clackmae, a.s.n. David, born 11th December 1816.

,, 29. William Quarry and Mary Lermont in Leaderfoot, a.d.n. Christian, born 10th January 1817.

Archibald Thomson and Mary Gray in Newtown, a.d.n. Mary, born 31st October 1816.

Feb. 2. William Johnson and Alison Cairns in Melrose, a.s.n. Thomas, born 12th November 1816.

,, 9. John Dickson and Margaret Gowanlock, a.s.n. Thomas Dickson, born 2nd December 1816.

,, ,, Thomas Sanderson and Mary Blaikie in Darlingshaugh, a.d.n. Alison, born 28th December 1816.

1816.
Aug. 30. Duncan Macdonald Church and Elisabeth Robertson in Langlee, a.s.n. James Robertson, born 30th August 1816.

Nov. 20. John Macdonald in Kettyfield, and Margaret Turnbull, a.s.n. Alexander, born 12th August 1816.

1817.
Mar. 2. William Drydon and Agnes Thomson in Buckhamside, a.s.n. James, born 17th February 1817.

,, 31. Michael Mercer and Isabell Milne in Darnick, a.d.n. Isabell, born 31st March 1817.

April James Sanderson and Elizabeth Walker, a.d.n. Elisabeth, born 20th November 1816.

,, Alexander Robertson and Isabella Walker in Leaderfoot, a.d.n. Mary Ann, born 1st January 1817.

,, 13. John Sinclair and Janet Wight, a.s.n. David, born 9th March 1817.

,, 20. Thomas Scott and Alison Blythe in Danieltown, a.s.n. William, born 20th March 1817.

,, 22. Thomas Wilson and Christian Linsay in Buckhamside, a.s.n. George, born 3rd April 1817.

,, ,, John Thomson and Isabell Common, a.d.n. Jean Thomson, born 12th August 1815.

May 18. Peter Maxwell and Agnes Lees in Darnick, a.s.n. Alexander, born 4th April 1817.

,, ,, John Drummond and Mary Lumsdan in Darnick, a.d.n. Margaret, born 23rd March 1817.

,, ,, John Hall and Mary Renaldson, a.d.n. Mary, born 12th April 1817.

,, 20. John Watson and Margaret Carruthers in Langlee, a.s.n. Alexander, born 18th May 1817.

,, ,, John Dickson and Elizabeth Scott, a.s.n. Alexander Dickson, born 20th April 1817.

June 10. Alexander Allen and Elisabeth Jemima Moffat, a.s.n. James Moffat, born 13th April 1817, and baptised on 26th May by Rev. Mr. Peter Cozens, Lawder.

1817.

June 23. George Stewart and Janet Sanderson, a.s.n. George, born 13th May 1817

,, ,, James Curle, writer in Melrose, and Isabella Romanes, a.d.n. **Agnes**, born 21st April, and baptised 20th May 1817.

July 13. Richard Lees and Mary Purves in Melrose, a.s.n. George, born 10th June 1817.

,, ,, Thomas Dickson and Lillie Gibson, a.s.n. Thomas, born 11th January 1817.

,, ,, James Watson and Janet White in Alenshaws, a.d.n. Margaret, born 13th November 1812.

,, ,, James Watson and Janet White in Alenshaws, a.s.n. Robert, born 1st November 1814.

Aug. 1. Andrew Millar and Janet Easton, a.s.n. Thomas, born 8th July 1817.

,, ,, John Dickson and Jean Smith, a.d.n. Isabella, born 27th June 1817.

,, ,, George Cochran and Jean Cramond, a.s.n. Thomas, born 11th June 1817.

,, ,, Robert Gill and Margaret Smith in Melrose, a.s.n. James, born 22nd July 1816.

,, ,, George Brodie and Mary Stewart, a.d.n. Agnes, born 9th June 1817.

,, 10. John Turnbull, slater, and Isabell Henderson in Darlingshaugh, a.d.n. Jane, born 16th June 1817.

,, 13. Oliver Young and Isabell Slater in Langlee, a.s.n. Robert, born 6th July 1817.

,, 14. James Black in Darnick and Margaret Thomson, his spouse, a.d.n. Isabella, born 14th December 1808.

James Black in Darnick and Margaret Thomson, his spouse, a.s.n. William, born 15th January 1810.

,, ,, James Black in Darnick and Margaret Thomson, his spouse, a.s.n. James, born 12th June 1812.

,, ,, James Black in Darnick and Margaret Thomson, his spouse, a.d.n. Janet, born 23rd June 1817.

,, 24. John Brokie and Charlotte——, his lawful wife, a.s.n. George, born 18th June 1817.

,, ,, James Oliver and Isabell Lumsdane in Newtown, a.s.n. Andrew, born 18th September 1794.

,, ,, James Oliver and Isabell Lumsdane in Newtown, a.s.n. John, born 7th March 1800.

Sept. 14. George Ronaldson and Margaret Brown, a.d.n. Janet, born 25th March 1809.

,, ,, David Thomson and Helen Young in Darlingshaugh, a.s.n. David, born 21st December 1816.

,, 21. Barney Harkan and Janet Thomson, a.d.n. Mary, born 2nd August 1817.

,, ,, Robert Morgan and Euphemia Simpson in Old Melrose, a.d.n. Jean, born 11th September 1817.

Oct. 19. William Bathgate, millwright in Buckholmside, and Margaret Richardson, his spouse, a.d.n. Mary, born 23rd September 1817.

,, ,, Simeon Bathgate, millwright in Buckholmside, and Euphamia Aitchison, his spouse, a.d.n. Alison, born 2nd October 1817.

,, ,, James Mathew and Margaret Mercer in Darlingshaugh, a.d.n. Isabella, born 9th July 1817.

,, ,, William Hogg and Isabell Bruce in Melrose, a.s.n. Alexander, born September 1816.

,, ,, Charles Stewart Hendry and Isabell Milne, a.d.n. Lillie, born 8th September 1817.

Nov. 16. Thomas Newtown and Agnes Rob, a.d.n. Elisabeth, born 7th November 1817.

,, 25. William Cleghorn, clothier in Darlingshaugh, and Agnes Rae, his lawful wife, a.s.n. Thomas, born 11th November 1817.

1817.

Nov. 25 James Anderson in Darlingshaugh and Christian Currie, a.s.n. Robert, born 2nd November 1817.

,, ,, William Hopkirk and Isabell Hume, a.s.n. Robert, born 30th December 1816.

,, ,, Alexander Paterson and Jean Sibbald in Newstead, a.d.n. Helen, born 23rd April 1817.

,, ,, George Stoddart and Nancy Brown, a.d.n. Janet, born 11th August 1817.

1818.

Jan. 11. John Bower, Junior, and Margaret Scott, a.d.n. Margaret, born 20th November 1817.

,, ,, —— Helen ——.

,, ,, Andrew Smith and Agnes Ketchen, a.s.n. John, born 13th December 1817.

,, 25. John Chisholm, shoemaker in Melrose, and Alison Elliot, his lawful wife, a.d.n. Alison Chisholm, born 3rd October 1817.

,, ,, James Crawford, Excise officer in Melrose, and Margaret Oliver, his lawful wife, a.d.n. Helen, born 19th December 1818 [*sic.*]

Feb. 4. James Lees and Margaret Elliot in Darlingshaugh, a.d.n. Elisabeth, born 27th November 1817.

1817.

Dec. 9. Captain James Steedman of Broomhill and Mrs. Sophia Mercer, his spouse, a.d.n. Elisabeth, born in Edinburgh 16th November 1817.

1818.

Feb. 22. John Duning and Janet Pringle, his spouse, in Eildon, a.d.n. Margaret, born 30th January 1818.

,, 25. Thomas Hopkirk and Christian Fraser in Melrose, a.s.n. David, born 30th January 1818.

,, ,, Thomas Laing and Elisabeth Wood, his spouse, in Gattonside, a.s.n. John, born 17th April 1816.

Mar. 1. Thomas Laing and Elisabeth Wood, his spouse, in Gattonside, a.s.n. Thomas, born 17th January 1818.

,, ,, Thomas Aldcorn and Grace Frater, his spouse, in Newtown, a.s.n. James, born 23rd January 1816.

,, ,, Alexander Tudhope and Isabell Turner, his spouse, in Melrose, a.d.n. Euphemia, born 18th January 1818.

April 5. William Blythe and Alison Tait, his lawful wife, in Darnick, a.s.n. David, born 7th February 1818.

,, 6. James Lothian, dyer, and Joan Armstrong, his lawful wife, in Buckamside, a.s.n. John, born 3rd March 1818.

,, ,, John Wood and Janet Drummond in Langlee, a.s.n. George, born 21st March 1818.

,, ,, William Thomson and Margaret Scott in Bridgend, a.d.n. Margaret, born 16th February 1818.

,, ,, Andrew Mercer and Mary Yellowlees in Lochend, a.d.n. Isabell, born 28th September 1818.

,, , William Henderson and Helen Leadbetter in Hawksnest, a.s.n. James, born 9th March 1818.

,, ,, Joshua Wood, clothier, and Isabell Walker in Buckhamside, a.s.n. William, born 13th September 1803.

,, ,, Joshua Wood, clothier, and Isabell Walker in Buckhamside, a.s.n. Robert, born 4th July 1806.

,, ,, Joshua Wood, clothier, and Isabell Walker in Buckhamside, a.s.n. Joshua, born 29th June 1809.

May — Joshua Wood, clothier, and Isabell Walker in Buckhamside, a.d.n. Isabell, born 24th February 1817.

,, — James Coldcleugh and Jean Chisholm in Colmsliehill, a.s.n. George Coldcleugh, born 11th March 1818.

,, — Walter Brown and Christian Thomson in Gattonside, a.s.n. James Thomson, born 11th April 1818.

1818.

May — James Dickson, mason in Gattonside, and Isabell Bosten, his wife,
a.s.n. Robert, born 9th April 1818.

,, — Arthur Reid and Janet Govan, a.d.n. Isabell, born 12th May 1818.

,, — Thomas Brydon in Keyside, and Alison Milne, his lawful wife, a.d.n.
Alison, born 17th April 1818.

,, — William Crosby and Isabella Brunton, his lawful wife, in Darnick,
a.s.n. David, born 26th March 1818.

,, — Leaver Legge, Esq., and Jane Bushby, his lawful wife, in Eildonhall,
a.d.n. Catharine, born 4th March 1818.

,, — James Robertson and Jean Lockie, his lawful wife, in Blainslie,
a.d.n. Isabella, born 14th December 1817, and baptised 25th March
1818.

June 17. Adam Aitchison and Jean Bonar in Drygrange Mains, a.d.n. Jean,
born 31st December 1818 [*sic*].

,, 23. Thomas Scott and Alison Blythe in Danieltoun, a.d.n. Mary, born
26th March 1818.

,, ,, Thomas Allen, baker in Melrose, and Janet Scott, his lawful wife,
a.s.n. John, born 6th April 1818.

,, ,, John Dods and Seninnah Elliot in Newstead, a.d.n. Mary, born 28th
February 1818.

,, 30. John Dods and Seninnah Elliot in Newstead, his lawful wife, a.s.n.
Francis, born 19th March 1816.

,, ,, Robert Hart and Betty Scott in Newstead, a.s.n. George, born 13th
April 1818.

July 2. James Park and Mary Middlemiss in Melrose, his lawful wife, a.s.n.
William, born 19th May 1818.

,, ,, Walter Ormiston, nurseryman in Melrose, and Agnes Brown, his lawful wife, a.s.n. Archibald, born 9th August 1815.

,, ,, Walter Ormiston, nurseryman in Melrose, and Agnes Brown, a.d.n.
Janet, born 30th December 1816.

,, 19. Gordon Wayness and Elspeth Young in Abbotslee, a.d.n. Elizabeth,
born 14th June 1818.

,, ,, Archibald Brodie and Mary Wight, a.d.n. Mary, born in February
1794.

,, ,, Archibald Brodie and Mary Wight, a.d.n. Isabell, born in April 1798.

,, ,, Walter Ronaldson and Janet Wight, a.s.n. Andrew Ronaldson, born
27th May 1818.

,, ,, Nichol Brack in Newtown, and Christian Lindsey, a.s.n. John, born
16th June 1818.

,, ,, Nichol Brack and Christian Lindsey, a.d.n. Margaret, born 19th October
1815.

,, — John Laidlaw, Gattonside House, and Mary Nicholson, his lawful wife,
a.d.n. Mary, born 19th March 1815.

,, — James Leithhead and Helen Walker in Toftfield, a.d.n. Jeanie, born
2nd July 1818.

,, — Thomas Davidson and Janet Syme, his lawful wife, in Darlingshaugh,
a.d.n. Margaret, born 30th March 1818.
Richard Watson. *See* year 1821.

1816. John Turnbull, skinner, and Alison Bathgate, his lawful wife, in Buckhamside, a.d.n. Agnes, born 9th April 1816.

1818. John Turnbull, skinner, and Alison Bathgate, a.s.n. George, born 10th
April 1818.

Adam Stewart and Margaret Coldcleugh in Gattonside, twins named
Robert and John, born 13th July 1818.

Thomas Stevenson and Agnes Brunton, his lawful wife, in Darnick,
a.d.n. Christian, born 11th July 1818.

1815. Thomas Stevenson and Agnes Brunton, a.s.n. Thomas, born 6th
December 1815.

1817. Thomas Stevenson and Agnes Brunton, a.s.n. Alexander, born 3rd
August 1817.

1817.

James Gibson, baker in Melrose, and Elspeth Scott, his lawful wife, a.s.n. John, born 12th August 1817.

1818. Thomas Dickson in Darnick and Margaret Paterson, his lawful wife, a.d.n. Isabell, born 2nd August 1818.

. Thomas Adams in Newstead and Margaret Mein, his lawful wife, a.d.n. Elisabeth, born 22nd August 1818.

Alexander Robertson, farmer in Leaderfoot, and Isabell Walker, his lawful wife, a.d.n. Agnes, born 17th August 1818, and baptised on 24th September following.

David Spence, writer in Melrose, and Helen Brodie, a.d.n. Agnes, born 2nd September 1818, and baptised 24th October following.

1815.

John Roberts and Mary Ovens in Darlingshaugh, a.d.n. Margaret, born 16th May 1815.

1817.

John Roberts and Mary Ovens in Darlingshaugh, a.d.n. Agnes, born 19th October 1817.

1818.

James Sanderson and Elisabeth Walker, his lawful wife in Darlingshaugh. a.d.n. Isabella, born 12th September 1818.

Dec. 12. John Dickson and Margaret Govanlock in Melrose, a.d.n. Janet, born 9th November 1818.

,, ,, John Laidlaw and Beatrix Laidlaw in Melrose, a.s.n. Adam, born 24th September 1818.

,, — Alexander Stenhouse and Esther Riddell, a.d.n. Margaret, born 25th January 1818.

,, — William Dickson, mason in Gattonside, and Isabell Aillie, a.s.n. William, born 17th October 1818.

,, — James Wallace, mason in Melrose, and Elisabeth Henderson, his lawful wife, a.d.n. Margaret, born 29th November 1818.

,, — Thomas Fairbairn, joiner in Melrose, and Margaret Smith, his lawful wife, a.d.n. Euphemia, born 15th December 1818.

,, — John Chisholm, shoemaker in Melrose, and Alison Elliot, his lawful wife, a.s.n. Adam, born 3rd December 1818.

,, — James Rutherford and Margaret Forsythe in Melrose, a.d.n. Agnes, born 28th November 1818.

1819.

Peter Maxwell, mason in Darnick, and Agnes Lees, his lawful wife, twins, a.s.n. Andrew and a.d.n. Matilda, born 21st December 1818.

Thomas Wight, ploughman in Kettyfield, and Margaret Beard, a.d.n. Christian, born 17th December 1818.

Thomas Smith, builder in Darnick, and Jean Turnbull, his lawful wife, a.d.n. Elisabeth, born 8th December 1818.

Thomas Ballantyne in Darnick, and Jean Douglas, his lawful wife, a.s.n. Thomas, born 11th December 1818.

Andrew Scott, millar in Newtown, and Joan Hope, his lawful wife, a.s.n. Robert, born 13th November 1818.

James Curle, Esq., writer in Melrose, and Isabella Romanes, his lawful wife, a.s.n. Alexander, born 2nd February 1819, and baptised 26th of same month.

Alexander Allen in New Blainslie and Elisabeth Jemima Moffat, his lawful wife, a.s.n. William Henry, born 10th September 1818, and baptised 10th November following.

James Sanderson and Violet Reed in Darlingshaugh, a.d.n. Agnes, born 1st October 1817.

Thomas Wilson and Christian Lindsay in Darlingshaugh, a.d.n. Grezal, born 20th February 1819.

Mar. 28. John Drummond and Mary Lumsdan in Darnick, a.s.n. Andrew, born 15th February 1819, and baptised this day.

1819.

Mar. 28. William Grant and Agnes Blaikie in Melrose, a.s.n. Robert, born 9th February 1819, and baptised this day.

,, ,, Adam Stevenson and Harriet Wilson in Darnick, a.d.n. Marion, born ——, and baptised this day.

April 10. Alexander Robertson and Isabell Berry in Danieltown, a.s.n. Alexander, born 1st April 1819.

,, 20. Walter Ormiston, nursery and seedsman in Melrose, and Nancy Brown, his lawful wife, a.s.n. Andrew, born 20th December 1818, and baptised 20th April 1819.

,, 27. George Tinline, shepherd in Broomylees, and Margaret Dickieson, a.s.n. John, born 1st March 1819.

1817.

Walter Laidlaw and Isabell Scott, his lawful wife in Darlingshaugh, a.d.n. Margaret, born 23rd April 1817.

1819.

May 12. Oliver Young, stewart at Easterlanglee, and Isabell Sclater, his lawful wife, a.d.n. Mary, born 6th April 1819.

,, ,, George Cochrane and Jean Crammond, Toll Bar of Melrose Bridge, twins, named Elspeth and Jean, born 8th May 1819, and baptised on 4th June.

,, ,, William Hunter and Margaret White in Threepwood, a.s.n. John, born 12th April 1819, and baptised 2nd May.

,, ,, Thomas Tait in Galabridge, and Jeanie Dobson, a.s.n. Ralph, born 5th April 1819.

,, 24. Archibald Thomson and Mary Gray in Newtown, a.d.n. Philis, born 30th April 1819.

July 4. John Hall in Toftfield and Mary Ronaldson, a.s.n. Walter, born 10th June 1819, and baptised this date.

,, ,, Andrew Hart, lately deceased, in Newstead and Jane Hardy, a.s.n. Andrew, born 7th May 1819.

,, ,, Robert Dickson, shoemaker in Darlingshaugh, and Agnes Ballantyne, his lawful wife, a.s.n. William, born 21st June 1819.

,, 18. John Mathieson and Jean Lyle in Gattonside, a.d.n. Janet, born 7th May 1819.

,, ,, James Burnet and Janet Thomson in Gattonside, a.d.n. Margaret, born 30th April 1819.

,, — John Lees, clothier in Channel, and Jean Young, his lawful wife, a.d.n. Jean, born 2nd October 1816.

,, — John Lees, clothier in Channel, and Jean Young, a.s.n. Richard, born 30th November 1817.

,, — Robert Redpath, shepherd in Appletreeleaves, and ——, his lawful wife, a.s.n. Walter, born 25th May 1819.

,, — Adam Russel, saddler in Melrose, and Margaret Hall, his lawful wife, a.s.n. William, born 22nd July 1819.

Sept. 9. Walter Cook in Melrose and Elisabeth Wight, a.s.n. William, born 21st June 1819.

,, ,, James Scott, flesher in Melrose, and Mary Wight, a.d.n. Mary, born 5th August 1819.

,, 12. George Mark and Marion Forrest in Melrose, a.s.n. Peter, born 27th August 1819.

Oct. 10. James Elliot and Margaret Graham in Newstead, a.d.n. Violet, born 13th May 1819.

,, 15. George Davidson and Catharine Cowie, a.s.n. William, born 19th September 1819.

Nov. 2. Robert Milne in Langlands, and Catharine Hunter, his lawful wife, a.s.n. Nicol, born 13th October 1819.

,, 25. Robert Morgan and Euphemia Simson, his lawful wife, a.d.n. Margaret, born 24th September 1819.

Dec. 2 William Brown in Newstead, and Margaret Weynas, a.s.n. William, born 7th October 1819.

1819.
Dec. 2. Charles Simson, Esq. of Threepwood, and Margaret Romanes, his
lawful wife, twins, named Janet and Jean, born 1st September 1819.
 „   „ James Crawford, Excise officer in Melrose, and Margaret Oliver, his
lawful wife, a.d.n. Janet, born 29th October 1819, and baptised 16th
December following.
1820.
Jan. 9. Barney Harken in Bridgend, and Janet Thomson, his lawful wife,
a.s.n. Barney, born 5th November 1819.
1819.
Sept. 28. John Macdonald, hynd, and Margaret Turnbull, a.d.n. Agnes, born
16th August 1819.

III.—The names of the persons proclaimed within the parish of Melros.

PROCLAMATIONE OF MARIAGE.

1642.
June 30. Compeared Robert Greisone and gave up his name to be proclaimed
upon Bessie Ard in Bowdowne.
Aug. 27. William Fairgreive in the parichone of Selkirk gave up his name to
be proclaimed upon Mary Tait in this parish and were married.
Sept. 11. George Boo with Jennet Wright in Galtonside and were married.
 „   25. William Tait and Janet Ealies in Melros.
 „   „ Andro Thomson in the parish of the Stow and Agnes Blakie.
Oct. 16. Jon. Cochran and Mergaret Falla.
 „   23. Mark Troumble and Mary Adamsone.
Dec. 15. Jon. Clerk in Drygrange and Helen Anderson in Redpeth.
 „   25. James Wayghtman in Gallosheillis and Elspeth Hage in Langhaugh.

MARRIAGES.

1645.
May 28. Robert Stirling married Jennet Scheill.
June 3. James Boustein m. Mary Broun.
 „   17. Thomas Sclatoure m. Agnes Hoy.
 „   27. George Messer m. Issobell Kennedie.
 „   „ James Tomeling m. Bessie Andersone.
July 22. Williame Sueit of the parosch of Lassudene m. Helene Donaldsone.
 „   25. John Waddell m. Marg. Carnecross.
 „   „ Edward Romanies m. Marrione Thinne.
 „   „ William Moffett m. Jennett Moffett.
Aug. 25. Johne Scheill in the parosch of Earslingtoune m. Heilene Fischer.
 „   29. Johne Pringill m. Margrett Hall.
Nov. 23. George Patersone m. Jennett Wilsone.
 „   25. George Dewar m. Margarett Thomson.
 „   „ William Spotswood m. Margrett Darling.
Dec. 2. Johne Smaill m. Eupha Quhirk.
 „   3. Johne Hall m. Issobell Fischer.
 „   4. James Pringill m. Agnes Hardie.

1645.
Dec. 20. Johne Griersone m. Issobell Laidlaw.
   ,,   27. Charles Clarke m. Jennet Drumant.
   ,,   28. Adame Trumbel m. Agnes Bouzie.
   ,,   30. Richart Sclaitter m. Jennett Mein.
1646.
Jan.   7. Adame Brunton m. Issobell Blaikie.
   ,,   27. Mark Turnbul m. Katherine Mylne.
Feb.   8. James Leithane m. Issobell Belle in Erslingtoune parosche.
May   26. Wm. Laidlaw m. Jennett Mark.
   ,,   28. Wm. Cochrane in Lassodene parosch m. Allysone Hounam.
   ,,   ,, James Carncross m. Jennett Helliwill.
June   4. David Thomsone m. Marrione Haddone.
   ,,   ,, Wm. Barrey m. Elizabeth Scott.
   ,,   ,, Barclay Wallace m. Marrione Dicksone.
   ,,   ,, Androw Drummond m. Elizabeth Jamisone.
   ,,   9. Androw Kennedie m. Margaret Mudie.
   ,,   25. Thomas Lyell m. Anna Romannis.
July   2. James Meine m. Agnes Meine.
   ,,   8. Wm. Suanstone m. Issobell Patersone.
   ,,   14. Thomas Mylnes m. Jeine Wallace.
Aug. 19. Thomas Hietoune m. Jennet Cowper.
Nov. 17. Thomas Darling m. Issobell Dausone.
   ,,   ,, John Rathay m. Issobell Blaikie.
   ,,   ,, Andrew Cuik m. Margaret Boustoune.
   ,,   ,, James Donaldsone in Galtonside paroch m. Bessie Darling.
   ,,   -- George Pringill m. Jennet Hietoune.
   ,,   19. Thomas Miller in Lauder parosh m. Isobell Adomsone.
1647.
Jan. 17. Alexr. Thomson m. Bessie Dauson.
   ,,   ,, Bernard Wilson m. Bessie Leithan.
Feb.   7. John Scot m. Jennet Williamson.
   ,,   ,, James Bowar m. Agnes Mein.
Mar. 20. William Redfurd m. Marion Wilson.
   ,,   ,, Alexr. Boudoune m. Jennet Walker.
April 1. John Anderson m. Christian Mare.
May   2. Thomas Hopkirk m. Annapel Andersone.
   ,,   ,, William Myln m. Jenet Macke.
   ,,   9. Thomas Caldcleugh m. Isabel Wilkieson.
   ,,   ,, James Davidson m. Christian Edgar.
   ,,   ,, Robert Marke m. Bessie Hastie.
   ,,   23. John Moffet m. Isabel Lyal.
   ,,   ,, Andro Hislop m. Margaret Smith.
   ,,   ,, William Mercer m. Jennet Mercer.
   ,,   28. Thomas Cochran m. Jennet Cokburn.
   ,,   ,, George Couper m. Isobel Williamsone.
June 25. Robert Mein m. Jennet Tunno.
   ,,   ,, William Laidlaw m. Margaret Ker.
   ,,   ,, William Wallace m. Jennet Mein.
July 10. John Mercer m. Jennet Chisholme.
   ,,   16. William Halywell m. Elizabeth Bowstone.
   ,,   ,, David Oliver, a testimonial from Andro Boustone, m. Bessie Bunzie.
   ,,   ,, Andro Hoi m. Margaret Heitton.
   ,,   ,, Alexr. Speeding in Galasheilds, a testimonial from the elders, m. Jennet Sandelands.
   ,,   ,, George Pringle in Galasheilds, a testimonial from the elders, m. Margret Friar.
   ,,   ,, Mungo Donaldson in Selkirk, a testimonial from Mr. John Schaw, m. Katharin Frater.
   ,,   ,, James Borthwick m. Lilias Porteous. A testimonial from her father the minister of Borthwick.

1647.

July 16. James Atchison m. Nicolas Gray. A testimonial from the minister of Legertwood.

" " William Anderson in Gallosheilds m. [*torn*].

Oct. 29. Robert Maban m. Katerne Scott.

" 30. George Dason m. Margrat Brown.

" 31. Olivar Meine m. Margrat Davison. A testimoniall from the minister of Libberton.

" " James Meine m. Elspethe Portise. A testimoniall from the minister of Libberton.

Nov. 28. Thomas Jak m. Janet Fisher.

Dec. 3. Richard Lithgow m. Bessie Kairter. A testimoniall from the minister of Ersilton.

" 17. Robert Myll m. Margrat Carfrie.

" " James Corsbie m. Margrat Hohne.

1648.

Jan. 9. Andro Tonno m. Bessie Meine.

" 21. James Lithane m. Margrat Bouston.

Feb. 19. George Hoi m. Isobell Merten.

Mar. 9. William Frissell m. Bessie Paterson. A testimoniall from the minister of Ersiltone.

April 8. John Helliburton in Merton m. Grizzell Ker. A testimoniall from the minister.

May 19. Andro Rutladge m. Bessie Trumll in Selkirk. A testimoniall from the minister.

June 18. James Waugh m. Bessie Sheill.

" 25. Peter Wallace in Salton m. Isobell Cesfard. A testimoniall from the minister.

July 9. Robert Cairncross m. Marion Cairter.

" 20. Robert Blaikie m. Janet Person, both in Gallowsheils. A testimoniall from John Freir.

" 22. Alexr. Mein m. Agnes Mar.

" " Nicoll Moss m. Alison Moss.

Aug. 5. William Bell m. Alison Bowston.

Sept. 22. William Ridfurd m. Marion Kedgey in Ersilton. A testimoniall from ye minister.

" " William Cowan in Selkirk m. Isobell Ellot. A testimoniall from the minister.

" last. James Burie in Gallowsheills m. Margrat Meban. A testimoniall from John Freir, elder.

" " Bartholomew Meine m. Margrat Bowar.

Oct. 22. James Bunzie m. Janet Meine.

" 29. George Bowston m. Helin Freter.

Nov. 3. Adam Trumbll m. Janet Messer.

" 19. James Meine m. Alison Bunzie.

" 26. James Romanous m. Bessie Pringll.

Dec. 31. Wm. Ormston m. Elspeth Waitch.

1649.

Jan. 6. Georg Moodie m. Margaret Blaikie.

" " Georg Ormston m. Margret Darling.

" — Andro Mein m. Helian Mein. A testimoniall from Mr. James Dais in Erslintoune.

" 16. Alexr. Claperton m. Jenet Saidler. A testimonial from Mr. Jon Kneilan.

" 17. Wm. Hadden m. Margot Feirgreive. A testimonial from Mr. John Schaw.

" 25. John Wilson m. Marion Paterson. A testimonial from the elders of Gallowsheils.

Mar. 4. Georg Baitie m. Marion Greirson. A testimonial from Mr. John Knox in Bowdain.

April 1. Archibald Ellot in Askirk m. Elspith Fischar. A testimonial from the presbitrie, no minister being there.

1649.

April 8. John Bunze m. Isobel Lidderdain. A testimonial from Mr. James
               Guthrie, minister at Lauder.
  ,,   ,,   John Bunze m. Margret ——.
  ,,   ,,   Hendrie Pringle m. Isabel Mein.
  ,,   22.   James Ridel m. Alison Mylne.
  ,,   ,,   Thomas Stenhous m. Malie Sclaitter.
  ,,   ,,   Patrick Blaikie m. Isobel Hewitson.
  ,,   29.   Thomas Young m. Helian Ker. A testimonial for his satisfaction
               from the minister of Minto.
  ,,   ,,   Mark Blaikie m. Margret Nicol.
  ,,   ,,   John Mersar m. Margret Blaikie.
May   6.   James Feirgreive m. —— Laidlaw. A testimonial from the minister ot
               Gallowsheils.
  ,,   ,,   Andro Whyt m. Isobel Houdain. A testimonial from the minister of
               Bowdain.
June 17.   John Escher m. Marien Hastie.
  ,,   ,,   John Escher m. Jenet Stenhous.
  ,,   ,,   Nicol Mersar m. Isobel Mein.
  ,,   24.   James Boustain m. Isobel Freir.
  ,,   ,,   Andro Heiton m. Helian Bulman. A testimonial from the minister
               of Langnewtoune.
July 23.   John Louthian in the parish of Lauder m. Jenet Sonnais in this. A
               testimoniall from the session of Lauder in the minister's absence.
Sept. 2.   John Stenhous in the paroch of Maxton m. Helian Merser in this
               paroch. A testimonial from the minister of Maxton.
  ,,   9.   Walter Waitch in this paroch m. Marion Tailfur in the paroch of
               Galowsheils. A testimonial from Mr. Mark Duncisone, minister
               in Gallowsheills.
Oct.   7.   George Pringall of Buckholme in this parish m. Margret Pringall in
               the parish of Stow. A testimoniall from the minister of Stow.
  ,,   21.   Thomas Heiton m. Margret Bowstain, parischoners.
  ,,   28.   George Freir m. Bessie Myls, parischoners.
  ,,   4.   Alexr. Escher m. Jenet Mein, parischoners.
Nov.   1.   John Pringal in this parischoner m. Agnes Howatson in the parish of
               Gallowsheils. A testimonial from the minister of Gallowsheils.
Dec.   4.   John Howatson m. Jenet Dods, parishoners.
  ,,   25.   John Wod in the parish of Merton m. Marion Symenton. A
               testimoniall from the elders of Merton in the minister's absence.
       1650.
Jan. 13.   John Frater in this parish m. Marion Blaikie in the parish of Stow.
Feb. 10.   Anton Whyt m. Jenet Symenton, parishoners, who caim from Edin-
               burgh and brought testimonials from Mr. Patrick Howyson.
  ,,   24.   Andro Tunno in this parish m. Marion Wilkie in the parish of
               Gallowsheills.
Mar.   3.   John M'Cubie in this parish and Jenet Maisson in the parish
               Lawder. A testimoniall from the clerk of the session and elders
               of the said toun, the minister being away.
  ,,   24.   Wm. Wallace in the parish of Ladiekirk m. Jenet Pringall, parishoner.
               A testimonial from the clerk and elders of Ladiekirk, the minister
               being dead.
  ,,   ,,   Wm. Trumble in the parish of Bowdain m. Jenet Merton, parishoner.
               A testimoniall from the minister of Bowdain.
April 28.   Thomas Thomson in the parish of Ersltoun m. Margret Chirnsyde,
               parishoner. A testimoniall from the minister of Ersltoune.
May   5.   Alexr. Heiton m Margret Mein, parishoners.
  ,,   12.   John Lees in the parish of Ersltoun and Marion Smith, parishoner.
               A testimoniall from the minister of Ersltoun.
  ,,   25.   John Notman m. Bessie Leus, parishoners.
June   2.   Wm. Lawder in the parish of Lawder m. Bessie Cairncroce. A
               testimoniall from the clerk of Lawder and elders of Lawder, they
               not having a minister.

1650.

June 2. John Flabern in the parish of Ersltoune m. Margret Wallace, parishioner. A testimonial from the minister of Erslton.

,, ,, John Howatson m. Helen Moffet, parishioners.

,, 9. Georg Uscher, parishioner, m. Bessie Tait in the parish of Gallowsheils. A testimonial from the minister.

,, 16. James Moffet in this parish m. Jenet William in the parish of Gallosheills. A testimonial from the minister.

,, ,, Thomas Steill in the parish of Belingem in England m. Agnes Notman in this parish. A testimoniall from the minister of Bellingem.

Aug. 4. Wm. Rutherfurd m. Margret Merton, parishioners.

Sept. 1. Alexr. Eiles m. Jenet Mein, parishioners.

,, ,, James Mein in this parish m. Margret Anderson in the parish of Ersltoun. A testimonial from the minister.

,, 22. Thomas Reidfurd m. Helen Mabon, parishioners.

Oct. 20. John Mabon m. Jenet Heliwall.

Dec. 15. Robert Clark m. Jenet Boustoun.

,, 22. James Wod m. Margret Notman, parishioners.

(*Blank till August* 1651.)

MELROSE.

The names of these persones following that entered into the band of marreage with uthers the particular dayes and yeirs of God underwritten, to witt :—

Upon the sevintein day of August 1651 marreage was perfytet betwixt Hew Wilsone and Jennett Wauch.

Sept. 14. Andro Messr m. Issobell Heitoun.

,, 21. Johne Messr m. Helene Dromond.

,, 28. John Edgar in Ledgertwood m. Issobell Moffitt.

Oct. 19. Robert Midlmest m. Aleson Schisholme.

,, 26. George Aird in Ersltoun m. Bessie Messer.

Nov. 8. Adam Darling m. ——.

,, ,, Johne Jonston in Selkirk m. Aleson Turneor.

,, 30. John Vaire m. Jonet Bowar.

Dec. 21. Wm. Renek m. Margaret Heslope.

,, 29. Andro Ridpeth m. Jocasta Watson in Vlar.

1652.

Jan. —— Thomas Wolsone m. Margret Lidos in Danzeltoun.

Feb. 2. John Frater m. Jonatt Claghorne in Gallosheills.

,, ,, Wm. Wilson in Gallosheills m. Agnus Law.

,, ,, James Greive m. Margaret Davidson.

April 21. Thomas Turneor m. Bessie Hardie in Legertwood.

May 9. George Messr m. Jonett Paterson.

,, 16. Wm. Reidfurd m. Agnes Moffit.

,, ,, John Bowston m. Issobell Olifar.

,, 23. John Rolmainhous m. Issobell Muray.

,, ,, James Eillies m. Jonatt Sheill.

,, ,, Wm. Jonston m. Agnus Sclaitter.

June 25. James Messr m. Jonett Mein, both in Gallosheills paroshin.

July 4. James Fisher m. Jonatt Mein.

,, 18. Wm. Greison in Bowdon m. Katharen Heiton.

,, ,, Robert Davidson m. Margaret Wood.

Aug. 1. Antton Muray m. Margaret Ker.

,, 14. Thomas Gray m. Agnus Forsan.

Oct. 17. Thomas Mar. m. Jonett Gay.

,, ,, Wm. Clerk m. Jonett Coatts.

,, — John Merton m. Jonett Browne.

,, 24. Thomas Jonston m. Issobell Merton.

Nov. 7. Nicoll Darling m. Jonett Henderson.

Dec. 5. James Jonston m. Jean Fischer.

2C

1653.
Jan.   — Wm. Donaldson m. Jonett Tamson.
  „   30. Williame Merton m. Margaret Williamsone.
Feb. 27. Alexr. Stodart in Gallosheills m. Bessie Turneor.
Mar. 13. Johne Milne m. Agnus Wood.
April 24. Robert Currie in the paroche of Lidgertwood m. Elspeth Swanne in
              this paroche.
May   1. Robert Wauche in this paroche m. Margaret Newreson in the parish
              of Dundie.
  „   29. William Mabon m. Helen Mein.
  „   „ Robert Lauder m. Bessie Rolmaines.
July 24. Robert Hislop m. Marion Broun.
Sept. 4. Robert Mein m. Jenet Spence.
Oct.   3. George Cairncross m. Bessie Breadie.
  „   „ Thomas Boustone m. Jenet Martine.
  „   „ John Tait m. Bessie Beatie.
  „   „ Robert Night m. Lusie Hall.
  „   „ Andrew Broune in the parish of Halierudhouse m. Jennet Tunno in
              this parish.
Nov.   — Robert Halliwell m. Isabell Halliwell.
1654.
Jan. 12. Andrew Drumand m. Jenet Mudie.
  „   18. Patrick Redfurd m. Margaret Lookup.
May   13. John Miln m. Isabell Moffet.
June   2. Alexr. Haitlie m. Agnes Eckford.
  „   6. John Riddell m. Jenet Cochran.
July   8. Thomas Milds m. Margaret Halliwell.
Aug. 15. George Sheill, a testimonial being received from Mr. Thomas Lemb
              for him, m. Jennet Henburne in this paroch.
  „   22. John Bell m. Issabell Bunzie (Bruce ?).
Oct. 24. John Bowar m. Helen Gibsone.
Dec.   1. Thomas Halliwell m. Christian Chisholme.
  „   19. Thomas Boustine m. Agnes Martenne.
  „   22. Robert Halliwell m. Isabell Halliwell.
  „   29. Andrew Patersone m. Bessie Patersone.
1655.
Feb. 13. Robert Bunzie m. Helen Meen.
  „   20. Andrew Chisholme m. Isabell Fishar.
May   20. George Lawrie m. Margaret Meen.
June 14. John Thomsone m. Jenet Fennick.
  „   19. Nicoll Messar m. Christian Forsan.
  „   24. John Penman, a testimonial received from Mr. Robert Knox, minister
              at Kelso for him, m. Jenet Meen in this parish.
  „   28. James Fischar m. Bessie Griersone.
  „ (July ?) 14. Robert Halliwell in this m. Jenet Haliwell in the parish of Geinl-
              kirk, a testimoniall being received from Mr. David Liddell.
  „ (July ?) 21. John Hall m. Margaret Alexander.
Aug.   7. John Pringle m. Margaret Stirling.
  „   22. James Frier m. Bessie Milds.
Oct.   — James Malcomtosh m. Marione Griersone.
Nov.   1. Robert Sheill m. Margaret Boustone.
  „   11. Thomas Blakie m. Margaret Darling.
1656.
——   6. Andrew Drummond m. Isabell Hounam.
April 13. Thomas Meen m. Margaret Bowar.
  „   22. James Lookup m. Margaret Martoune.
  „   24. John Breadie m. Jenet Peaco.
May   3. George Cleghorn m. Christian Heitoune.
  „   5. James Ridpeith in this parish m. Jenet Hardie in the parish of
              Bathens, a testimoniall being received from Mr. Lawrence Qharteis.
June 26. Michael Gibsone m. Jeane Summervaile.

1656.
Sept. 25. Wm. Brotherstones in the parish of Peebles m. Betrix Tunno in this parish.
Oct.   9. James Simpson m. Jenet Scot.
  „   26. John Browne in this parish m. Jenet Barr in the parish of Stichill, a
            testimoniall being received from Mr. David Stark, minister
            thairof, daited the 26th October 1656.
Nov. 20. Androw Penman m. Bessie Hoge.
  „   27. John Stobo m. Issobell Rennek.
                          (*Blank till April* 1657.)
1657.
Jan.   2. Robert Halliwell, a dtr. baptised namet Helen, witnesses John and
            Thomas Halliwell.   (Entry deleted.)
April 7. James Crawfurd m. Janet Mein.
  „   14. Jon Fiergreive m. Issobell Darling.
  „   26. James Muire m. Margaret Colinwood, parishioners in the Northwest
            Kirk of Edinburgh.
                          (*Blank till October.*)

Oct. 27. Andrew Olifer m. Janet Chisholme.
Nov.   5. John Messr m. Hellein Mosse.
  „   12. Jon Bavereach m. Issobell Donaldson at Lauder.
  „   12. Georg Ailey m. Janet Cleghorn at Gallowsheills.
                          (*Blank till May* 1659.)
1659.
May   8. James Huntar in Lessuden paroche m. Agnes Bowar in this paroch.
  „   15. Wm. Wallace m. Issobell Frater, both in this paroch.
  „   „ James Pecko in this paroch m. Issobell Blakie in the paroch of
            Gallascheills.
  „   20. James Thomsone in the Stow paroch m. Jean Mein in this paroch.
  „   „ James Bunzie m. Christian Forsan in this paroch.
  „   „ John Haitlie in Gorden paroch m. Marion Fennick in this parish.
  „   22. Wm. Laidlaw m. Elspeth Kar, in this paroch.
  „   „ John Penman in the paroch of Newcastle m. Issobell Scheill in this
            paroch.
June   3. Wm. Cockburne in the paroch of Polwarth m. Alison Spotswood in
            this paroch.
  „   10. Georg Mein m. Margaret Philip in this paroch.
July 14. Wm. Anderson m. Margaret Turner, both in this paroch.
Aug. 12. John Loukup m. Margaret Mertone in this paroche.
  „   16. John Sclaiter m. Jenet Sheill, both in this paroche.
  „   „ Stephen Merton m. Margaret Heiton, both in this paroche.
Nov.   4. John Messr m. Alison Mein, both in this paroch.
  „   „ James Bowie m. Jenet Uscher.
Dec. 15. John Maxwell m. Agnes Mein, both in this paroch.
  „   20. Wm. Merton in this paroch m. Jean Freir in the paroch of Gallasheill.
1660.
Jan.   4. John Lermont in this paroch m. Mart Wielsone in Lawder paroch.
  „   10. Wm. Wricht m. Issobell Bouston, both in this paroch.
  „   „ Thomas Anderson m. Alison Lidell in this paroch.
April 26. George Turner m. Bessie Lyell, both in paroch.
June   6. Thomas Watherston in Lawder paroch m. Jonet Trotter in this paroch.
            John Sterling m. —— Thin.
Nov.   5. John Winter m. Marion Scot.
  „   12. Andrew Darling m. Jennet Flatcher.
  „   15. James Eiles m. Agnas Sclaiter.
  „   22. John Pringle m. Isobel Darling.
  „   „ John Mein m. Isobel Mar.
  „   28. John Berton m. Isobel Berton.
Dec.   8. James Wallace m. Marion Edgar.
  „   14. Thomas Mil m. Jennet Cochran.
  „   27. Robert Loudin m. Margret Paterson.

1661.
Feb. 19. James Mertin m. Christian Maban.
May 7. George Blakie m. Christian Lees.
June 19. John Riddel m. Margrat Richardson.
„ 27. Hew Wallace m. Helen Wallace.
July 19. John Buy m. Jennet Myles.
„ 30. Wm. Fishar m. Agnes Mein.
„ „ Wm. Liviston m. Margrat Lyall.
Aug. 8. Michael Fisher m. Jean Edgar.
„ 14. John Mein m. Jennet Mein.
„ „ Andrew Hounim m. Margrat Hyton.
„ 16. Wm. Hud m. Agnes Hounim.
Sept. 3. George Darling m. Marion Tyler.
„ 17. Alexander Muray m. Margaret Cairncroce.
Nov. 6. Alexr. Hutton m. Helen Hair.
Dec. 3. Robert Riddell m. Margaret Holme.
„ „ Thomas Bouston m. Jennet Horsbrug.
„ 5. John Mein m. Mary Mein.
„ 24. John Fisher m. Agnes Hounim.
1662.
Feb. 23. James Mein m. Margrat Bredy.
June 3. Andrew Mein m. Agnus Cochrane.
„ 12. Robert Breddie m. Issobell Leithen
„ „ James Mille m. Isobell Thomsone.
„ 19. John Hadan m. Ketherin Mosse.
July 8. James Mille m. Marion Scheil.
„ 22. Thomas Mabone m. Isobell Boustone.
Aug. 14. Robert Hellwill m. Isobell Messer.
„ 22. James Gurlaw m. Bessie Couchrane.
„ 29. John Davidsone m. Barbarie Andersone.
Oct. 1. Robert Tutup m. Jennet Dicksone.
Nov. 20. George Moffet m. Issobell Darling.
Dec. 11. George Turnor m. Bessie Laidlaw.
„ 20. Andrew Rennelsone m. Jeanet Moss.
„ 23. Thomas Huntar m. Issobell Fischer.
„ „ Robert Meine m. Margret Meine.
1663.
Jan. 13. Patrick Loukup m. Jean Fischer.
April 1. Thomas Wolson m. Isobell Tomson.
June 2. John Gill m. Jennet Stenhouse.
„ 25. George Pringall m. Margaret Loukup.
„ 30. Thomas Hardie m. Issobell Hartsone.
July 2. James Pringall m. Bessie Lies.
„ 14. Johne Stevensone m. Jennet Ker.
Nov. 5. Johne Whick m. Issobell Boustone.
„ 19. Thomas Wilkiesone m. Margaret Eleis.
„ 24. Johne Mein m. Christian Mein.
„ 25. Johne Mill m. Agnes Scot.
Dec. 3. Walter Dalgleish m. Issobell Messr.
„ 10. George Eleis m. Issobell Mill.
„ 15. James Sympsone m. Margaret Haistie.
„ „ Thomas Gill m. Jennet Haistie.
„ 22. James Mar m. Issobell Boustoune.
„ 24. Wm. Boustoune m. Margaret Carter.
„ 29. Wm. Sclaitter m. Agnes Bowar.
1664.
Feb. 11. Edward Darling m. Jean Stoddart.
„ 16. Johne Messer m. Agnes Wright
„ 18. Andrew Fisher m. Marion Sympson.
June 23. Wm. Henderson m. Christian Broun.
July 12. Thomas Messer m. Jean Lawder.
„ 14. James Edgar m. Helen Wauch.

1664.
Aug. 9. Johne Hoy m. Alison Wright.
Oct. 13. Johne Thomsone m. Helen Drummond.
Nov. 15. Andrew Oliver m. Jenet Wrgick.
  ,, 17. Mungo Mill m. Agnes Fisher.
  ,, 22. Johne Howname m. Margaret Gray.
  ,, 24. Johne Hogg m. Elizabeth Brown
Dec. 6. Andrew Heitton m. Bessie Messer.
  ,, 12. George Pringall of Blinlie m. Violet Scot.
1665.
Jan. 24. George Merser m. Helen Uscher.
Feb. 1. James Edgar m. Issobell Eleis.
  ,, ,, Johne Ker m. Catharine Ker.
1666.
Feb. 21. Wm. Lukeup m. Margaret Adenstone.
  ,, 22. Wm. Maibbin m. Margaret Lithgow.
  ,, 27. George Howname m. Bessie Griersone.
April 28. Thomas Mairtine m. Mart Swanestone.
  ,, ,, George Wallace a son baptised namet James, witnesses James Ker
        and William Wallace. (*Entry deleted.*)
        (*The Record of Marriages is blank until 1690, but there follows a
        list of testimonials which include proclamations of bands and
        references to marriages.*)

A LIST of TESTIMONIALLS received from the ministers, and for the persons underwritten.

1652.
Oct. 4. A testimoniall received from Mr Robert Carsan, minister at New-
        toune for Rachell Turnbull.

1654.
June 4. A testimoniall received for Marion Watersone from the minister of
        Geinlkirk.
  ,, 12. A testimoniall received from the minister at Chrichtoune for Robert
        Rae and his familie.
        A testimoniall received from Mr. Thomas Louis for George Sheil to
        be proclaimed with Jennet Howburne in this parish, daited 15th
        July 1654.
        A testimoniall received from Mr. John Cleland for Margaret Louis,
        daited Apprile 1655.
        A testimoniall received from Mr. John Daes for Issabell Neil her
        proclamation with ——.
        A testimoniall received from Mr. Robert Cunninghame for Helen
        Murray, daited 22nd of Aprile 1655.
        A testimoniall received from Mr. William Johnstoune, minister at
        Lauder, for Elizabeth Brotherstones her proclamation with
        Alexander Paterson in this parish, dated 29th Aprile 1655.
        A testimoniall received from Mr. William Johnstoune for Isabell
        Wod her proclamation with John Laidlaw in this parish, dated
        the 25th of Aprile 1655.
        A testimonial received from Marie Blakie (from Mr. James Daes) for
        her proclamation with Alexr. Andersone in this parish, dated 12th
        of May 1655.
        A testimonial received from Mr. William Johnstoune for James
        Thomsone his proclamation with Jenet Cossar in this parish,
        dated the 3rd of May 1655.
        A testimonial received from Mr. William Calderwood, minister at
        Lidgertwood, for John Allane his proclamation with Isabell
        Fischar in this parish, dated 26th May 1655.
        A testimoniall received from Mr. Robert Knox, minister at Kelso, for
        John Penman his proclamation with Jennet Meen in this parish,
        dated the 16th May 1655.

1654.

A testimoniall received from Mr. James Daes for Isabell Lithgow her partaking of the sacrament of the Lord's supper, dated the 19th of August.

A testimoniall from Mr. James Daes likewise for Jennet Tullie for partaking of the sacrament.

A testimoniall received from Mr. Robert Cunninghame for James Tait his familie, dated the 7th of May 1655.

A testimoniall received from Mr. John Cleland for James Broune and his wyfe, dated the 5th of August 1655.

A testimoniall received from Mr. John Cleland for Robert Lies, dated the 23rd of January 1655.

A testimoniall received from Mr. Alexr. Vernar, minister at Pencaitland, for Andrew Litle, dated the last January 1655.

A testimoniall received from Mr. Thomas Louis, minister at Gallowshiels, for Agnes Maban for proclamation with James Gray in this parish, dated the 8th of November 1655.

A testimoniall received from Mr. John Cleland for John Lies, dated the 16th February 1656.

A testimoniall received from Mr. William Johnstoune for John Murray his proclamation with Catharine Hall in this parish, dated the 22nd February 1656.

A testimoniall received from Mr. John Cleland for Thomas Bald, his wyfe and his mother, dated the 10th February 1656.

A testimoniall received from Mr. Thomas Courtney, minister at Mertoune, for Isabell Robesone for satisfaction for the sin of adulterie committed with the Laird of Bemerside, dated 9th March 1655.

A testimonial received from Mr. Thomas Louis for Jenet Claghorn her proclamation with James Smily in this parish, dated 25th April 1656.

A testimoniall received from Mr. Laurence Charters, minister at Bathens, for Jennet Hardie for proclamation with James Ridpeth in this parish, dated the 22nd of April 1656.

A testimoniall received from Mr. Thomas Louis for Jennet Peaco, dated the 5th April 1656.

A testimoniall received from Mr. Williame Johnstoune for Elizabeth Barre for proclamation with Mr. John Dickson in this parish, dated the 19th Aprile 1656.

A testimoniall received from Mr. Thomas Louis for Margaret Barre for proclamation with Thomas Barr in this parish, dated the 3rd of May 1656.

A testimoniall received from Mr. James Nesmith, minister at Hammiltounne, for Mr. Maxwell for proclamation with Mr. Andrew Barre in this, dated the —— of —— 1656.

A testimoniall from Mr. Thomas Louis for Georg Cleghorn his proclamation with Christian Heitoune in this parish, dated the 3rd of May 1656.

A testimoniall received from Mr. John Cleland for Marione Turner her proclamation with George Turner in this parish.

A testimoniall received from Mr. Normand Leslie, minister at Gordoune, for Jenet Armstrang her proclamation with Mr. William Pringle in this parish, dated 18th May 1656.

A testimoniall received from Mr. John Cleland for Thomas Litle, dated 18th Aprile 1656.

A testimoniall received from Mr. John Cleland for James Tait his proclamation with Isabell Martoune, both in this parish, dated the 18th of May 1656.

A testimoniall received from Mr. William Johnstoune, minister at Lauder, for Jean Summervell her proclamation with Michael Gibsone in this parish, dated the 5th of June 1656.

1656.

A testimoniall received from Mr. David Stark, minister at Stitchill, for Jenet Barr her proclamation with John Browne in this parish, dated the 25th October 1656.

A testimoniall received fra Andrew Duncanson, minister at Bossills, for James Craufurd his proclamation with Jenet Mein in this parish, dated ——.

A testimoniall received fra Mr. George Hutcheson, minister of the West Kirk of Tolbuith at Edinburgh, for James Muire and Margaret Colinwood their proclamation in this kirk, dated the 10th April 1657.

A testimoniall received from Mr. William Calderwood for George Home, his wife and familie, dated the 10th of March 1657.

A testimoniall received from Mr. Andrew Kynnier, minister at Nenthorne, for James Adamson his proclamation with Hellein Murrow in this parish, dated 25th Aprill 1657.

A testimoniall received from Mr. Thomas Lowis, minister at Gallosheills for James Mercer his familie, dated —— May 1657.

A testimoniall received from Anick paroch in England for Robert Marre, his thrice proclamation with Bessie Andersone in this parish, dated the 23rd June 1657; subscribed by John Suinhouse.

A testimoniall received from Mr. Thomas Lowis, minister at Gallowsheills, for Margaret Mabon her behaviour, there dated 15th June 1657.

A testimoniall receavit from Mr. James Daes, minister at Ersilton, for Margaret Blaikie her proclamation with James Romanoies, 17th June 1657.

A testimoniall from Mr. James Daes, his elders, for Rachell Duncan her proclamation with Robert Forsan, dated 16th July 1657.

Ane absolviture of promise of mariadge of George Wilson from Mr. Barrie, obtained on his oath before the Sheriff, Androw Kar of Chatto, dated 10th day of July 1657.

A testmoniall received from Mr. Robert Cunninghame, minister at Eskirk, for Alexr. Fischars his behaviour there, dated 12th July 1657.

A testimoniall received from Mr. David Stark of Stichill for Jon Scot and his spouse, Jane Sterling, their behavior, there dated 26th January 1657.

A testimoniall received from Mr. John Shaw, minister at Selkirk, for Androw Olipher his behavior there ane year and half, dated 18th September 1657.

A testimonial receivit fra Mr. James Daes, Ersiltown, for Anna Sanderson, her proclamation with John Sunnais in our paroch, dated 16th October 1657.

A testimonial receivit fra Mr. Thom Lowis, minister at Gallowsheills, for Marion Sclater her proclamation with Robert Law in this parochin, dated 16th October 1657.

A testimoniall receivit fra Mr. John Shaw, minister at Selkirk, for George Ailye his proclamation with Janet Cleghorne in this parochin, dated 15th October 1657.

A testimonial receaved from the elders of Bowdon, viz., Wm. Rannaldson, for Andrew Olifers his behavior and the solemnization of his mariadge heer, dated 26th October 1657.

A testimonial receivit fra Mr. Wm. Jonstowne for Barbara Romainhouse her proclamation with Andrew Moffat, dated the 27th October 1657.

A testimonial receavet fra Mr. Thomas Lowes for Andrew Peacocks his proclamation with Margaret Thomson, dated 19th November 1657.

A testimonial received from Mr. John Shaw, minister at Selkirk, for Christian Wilkieson for proclamation with —— Niccoll heer, dated 10th December 1657.

1658.

A testimonial from Mr. James Kirkton, minister at Merton, for Agnes Richeson her proclamatione with Mr. Wm. Darling heer, dated 17th February 1658.

A testimonial receavit fra the elders of Bowdon for Robert Cairns his chyld's baptisme, subscribed and received the 24th day of March 1658.

A testimonial receavit fra Mr. James Kirktowne, minister at Merton, for Wm. Darling and Agnes Richeson her thrise proclamation, dated 5th April 1658.

A testimonial receivit fra Mr. Wm. Johnstowne, minister at Lauder, for Thomas Creibes his honest behavior there, dated 26th January 1658.

A testimonial from Mr. Wm. Calderwood, minister at Ligertwood, for John Sterling, Marion Watson, Margaret Darling, James Darling and Marion Purves for their behavior there, dated 3rd July 1658.

A testimoniall from Mr. Thomas Lowis for Janet Hastie, dated 18th July 1658.

A testimonial fra Bowdon elders for Helein Turnbull, dated 29th July 1658.

A testimonial fra Wm. Jonstowne, minister at Lauder, for Thomas Romainhouse his proclamation with Marion Symentowne, 5th November 1658.

A testimonial fra Mr. James Kirktowne for Marion Symentowne her behavior there, November 4th, 1658.

A testimonial fra Mr. Thomas Lowis for Isabel Blaikie her cariage in the parish of Gallowsheills, dated 24th April 1659.

A testimonial fra Mr. Wm. Cleland, minister at Stow for James Thomeson his cariage there, daitted the 22nd of May 1659.

A testimonial fra Mr. David Robertson, minister at Polwarth for, Wm. Cockburne his cariage, there daitted the 10th of June 1659.

A testimonial fra the southwest parish of Edinburgh for Margaret Turner her cariage, there daitted at Edinburgh the 12th day of July 1659.

A testimonial fra Mr. David Liddle, minister at Chinghillkirk for Robert Knycht and his wife their cariage, there daitted the 26th of May 1659.

A testimonial fra Mr. Wm. Calderwood, minister at Heriott church, for Wm. Borthwick and Bessie Hall thare cariage and marriage, and they were lawfully proclaimed, daitted at the 14th of July 1659.

A testimonial fra Mr. Johne Cleland, minister at Stow for Thomas Cruix and Christiane Williamsone, his wife, their cariage, there daitted at Stow 17th of July 1659.

A testimoniell resaued frome the elders of Lawder for James Edmistone his honest cariage, there daitted the 8th of October 1659.

A testimonial recaued from the elders of Bowden for Johne Hog his cariage, there dated the 23rd of October 1259.

A testimoniel recaued frome Sprewstone for Issobell Mewres her cariage, there daitted the last of July 1659.

A testimonial recaued fra Mertone for Johne Lermond his cariage, there daitted at Merton the 29th of October 1659.

A testimonial resaued fra the elders of Kelso for Wm. Scot and Mary Mow thair proclamation, there daitted at Kelso the 13th of November 1659.

A testimonial resaued fra Lawder fra Mr. David Forrester, minister there, for Margaret Neilsone her cairadge, there daitted the 11th of November 1659.

A testimonial resaued frome the elders of Kelso for Bessie Anderson her honest cariadge, there daitted 18th November 1659.

A testimonial resaued fra the elders of Bowden for Ro Fletcher his honest cariadge, there daitted at Bowden the 12th January 1660.

1660.

A testimonial resaued fra Mr. David Forrester, minister at Lawder for Thomas Watherstone his honest carradge, there dated at Lawder 3rd March 1660.

A testimonial resaued fra the elders of Bowden for Wm. Hog his honest cariadge, there daitted the 28th of Aprile 1660.

A testimonial resaued fra Mr. John Clelland, minister at Stow, for Margaret Pringle her cariadge, there daitted at Stow, the 22nd of June 1660.

A testimonial receaved from Mr. David Liddel, 8th August, for Patrick Haitlie and his familie their honest carriadge.

A testimonial receaved from Mr. Thomas Louis for Margaret Paterson her honest carriadge, daitted the 2nd November.

A testimonial receaved from Mr. James Kirton, minister at Merton, for Thomas Blaikie and his familie their honest carriadge, daitted 22nd January 1661.

A testimonial receaved from Mr. Robert Carson, minister at Newtoun, for Jennet Wauch her carriadge, daitted 13th November 1656.

A testimonial receaved from Mr. John Cleland, minister at Stow, for Christian Lees her honest carriadge, datted the 6th of April 1661.

A testimonial receaved from Mr. John Cleeland, minister at Stow, for Wm. Scot his honest carriadge, daitted at Stow 4th May 1661.

A testimonial receaved from Mr. John Cleland, minister at Stow, for Jennet Lukup her honest carriadge, daitted at Stow 4th May 1661.

A testimonial receaved from the elders of Lesuddin for Margaret Richardson her honest carriadge, daitted at Lesuddin the 17th of May 1661.

A testimonial receaved from Mr. Wm. Elliot, minister at Yara, for Margaret Tode her honest carriadg, their at the Kirk of Yara, daitted 26th June 1659.

A testimonial receaved from Mr. James Knox, minister at Boudon, for Mr. John Bug his honest carriadge, daitted their 21st June 1661.

A testimonial receaved from Mr. James Knox, minister at Boudon, for Wm. Hud his honest carriadge, there daitted 6th July 1661.

A testimonial receaved from Mr. David Liddell, minister at Chingilkirk, for Wm. Liviston his honest carriadge, daitted their 10th of July 1661.

A testimonial receaved from Mr. Thomas Louis, minister at Gallosheills, for Helen Halliwall her honest carriag, their daitted 3rd August 1661.

A testimonial receaved from Mr. James Daes, minister at Ersilton, for Georg Cairncrosse his honest carriag, daitted their 16th Jun 1661.

A testimonial receaved from Mr. John Somervell, minister at Lesuddin, for Jennet Dobson her honest carriag, daitted their 12th August 1661.

A testimonial receaved from Mr. Andro Duncanson, minister at Maxtoun for James Jameson his honest carriag, daitted their 11th August 1661.

A testimonial receaved from Mr. Patrick Purdie, minister at Newlands, for Alexr. Murray his honest carriag, daitted there 24th August 1661.

A testimonial receaved from Mr. James Nairn, minister at Cannogait, for Margrat Cairncroce her honest carriag, daitted their 26th June 1660.

A testimonial receaved from Mr. John Cleland, minister at Stow, for Robert Shiell his honest carriage, daitted their at Stow the 22nd day of August 1661.

A testimonial received from Mr. David Forrester, minister at Lauder, for Margrat Grieve her honest carriage, daitted their 18th October 1661.

1661.

A testimonial receaved from Mr. David Liddel, minister at Chingil-kirk, for Margrat Lyall for honest carriage, daitted 4th October 1661.

A testimonial from Mr. James Kirton, minister at Merton, for Margrat Baine her honest carriage, daitted their 30th October 1661.

A testimonial receaved from Mr. John Smith, minister in Edinburgh, for Jennet Douglas her honest carriag, daitted 8th September 1659.

A testimonial receaved from Mr. Andro Duncansone, minister at Maxtoun, for Jennet Henderson her honest carriag, daitted 17th November 1661.

A testimoniall receaved from Ancrum for Jennet Ker her good carriage, 3rd June 1663.

A testimonial receaved from Lidgertwood for Helen Grive her honest carriage, 26th June 1663.

A testimonial from Mertone, written be the clerk and subscribed be the elders thereof, for Johne Stevensone his proclamation with Jennet Ker within the kirk, 14th July 1663.

A testimonial from Mr. James Daes, minister at Erslton, for Margaret Purves her consent in marriadge with James Bower, 7th August 1663.

A testimonial receaved from the minister at Westruther for Christian Fortoun, 7th November.

Dec. —   A testimonial receaved from Mr. James Knox at Bowdon for Margaret Paterson for honest conversation.

1664.

Jan.   7. A testimonial receaved from the session of Mertoun for Thomas Eilies his honest conversation.

Feb.   4. A testimonie receaved from the Kirk session at Laswaid for Marion Symson her honest conversation.

  „   5. A testimonie receaved from the minister at Stitchel for Agnes Wright her honest conservation.

  „   14. A testimonial receaved from Mr. James Logan, minister at Laswade, for Marion Symson her honest conversation.

April 30. A testimonial receaved from Gallasheils under the clerks and elders hands for Johne Mertoun, his honest conversation.

June   2. A testimonial received from Mr. Thomas Wilkie, minister at Gallo-sheills, for Thomas Messer his honest conversation.

  „   4. A testimonial received from Erslingtoun for Jean Lawder her honest life and conversation.

1665.

May 13. A testimonial received from St. Boswell's for Bessie Watherston her honest life and conversation.

1666.

Ane testimonial received from Mr. James Daes, minister at Ersiltone, for Margaret Adenstone her consent of mariage with Wm. Luckope, 4th of January.

Ane testimonial received from Mr. James Knox, minister at Bowden, for Margaret Swanstone her consent of mariage with Thomas Martine, the 8th of March.

Ane testimonial from the paroche of Stow for Whalter Riddel and Marion Hendrie, his spows, their honest conversation, the 10th of March.

1690.

Nov.   7. John Wilkiesone m. Issobell Henrie in Gallosheills paroche ; John Short and Wm. Haddin their cautioners.

  „   „   Robert Halliwall m. Jennet Halliwall ; cautioner Andro Halliwall.

  „   11. Andro Bald m. Jennet Purvis in the paroche of Bowdon.

  „   18. Nicoll Milne m. Issobell Moss ; c. Andro Rennaldsone.

  „   25. George Rennaldsone m. Barbara Thomsone in Bowdone paroche.

  „   28. Henrie Myles m. Jennet Clark ; c. Thomas Myles, James Dicksone.

1690.
Nov. 28. James Mein m. Bessie Scott ; c. Georg Proffet.
„ 29. Thomas Duncane m. Jennet Cowan ; c. Georg Turner. Thomas Duncane likewise promised ane doller to the poor, and Buckholme was cautioner.
Dec. 1. Georg Grhame m. Jennet Allie ; c. John Mein.
„ 5. John Halliwall m. Bessie Gray ; c. Robert Halliwall.
„ „ Andro Turnbull m. Marion Laidlay ; c. James Mein.
„ 9. James Eillies m. Issobell Ushar ; c. Georg Ushar.
„ „ Wm. Feirgreive m. Alisone Caldwalls ; c. James Caldwalls.
„ „ John Gibsone m. Elspeth Philip ; c. Michael Gibsone, Robert Philip.
„ 12. James Sunhouse m. Anna Dicksone ; c. John Wallace.
„ 19. John Mercer m. Marie Mein ; c. Georg Mein, Townhead.
„ 29. John Symsone m. Elizabeth Swainston ; c. Wm. Greiston, Wm. Swainstone.
1691.
Jan 6. James Olivar m. Jean Leithhead ; c. Wm. Fishar, Andro Olivar.
„ 13. Thomas Ormstone m. Jennet Pringle ; c. John Bell, Georg Pringle.
„ 27. James Penman m. Agnes Thomsone ; c. Ballive Faa, Andro Penman.
Feb. 2. John Martine m. Issobell Lochlee ; c. Andro Turnbull, John Patersone.
„ 10. Andrew Kaidzie m. Margaret Rennaldsone ; c. John Moss, John Kaidzie.
Mar. 12. John Bunzie m. Agnes Milne ; c. Robert Bunzie, John Milne.
„ „ George Sheill m. Agnes Falla ; c. John and Thomas Sheills.
April 11. Andrew Mein m. Marie Bunzie ; c. Robert Bunzie, Georg Mein.
June 3. Thomas Cochrane m. Issobell Milne ; c. Thomas Stenhouse, John Milne.
„ 12. Mr. John Bitlestone m. Mistress Elizabeth Shafftie in the countie of Northumberland in England.
„ „ James Mark m. Elizabeth Watsone in Bowdone.
„ 15. John Wright m. Elizabeth Hoyie ; c. Georg Bartone, John Hoyie.
„ 18. James Fishar m. Margaret Smaill ; c. Wm. Fischar.
„ 24. James Sympsone m. Christian Penman ; c. John Penman.
July 3. Wm. Dicksone m. Christian Helme in the parish of Bowdone.
„ 17. Wm. Murray m. Margaret Patersone in Lindean in the paroche of Gallasheills.
„ 27. William Cairncroce of Westerlanglie m. Mistress Marie Gray.
„ 28. Michael Wallace m. Margaret Bowstone ; c. Thomas Bowstone, Wm. Guill.
„ 29. Adam Davidsone m. Christian Forsan ; c. John Bowie, wright.
Oct. 30. John Summervaill m. Margaret Mein ; c. Wm. Livingstone, Andrew Marr.
Nov. 3. Georg Fraiter m. Margaret Riddell ; c. Walter Riddell.
„ 12. John Mein m. Violet Halyburton ; c. Mr. Mark Duncansone.
„ 13. Thomas Laidlay m. Helen Darling ; c. John Darling, Andro Turnbull.
„ „ Wm. Walker m. Christian Fairbairn ; c. John Bell, Georg Fairbairn.
„ 27. John Blaikie m. Jean Dicksone ; c. Robert Halliwall.
„ „ Adam Wilsone m. Jean Guill in the paroche of Gallosheills.
„ „ James Myles m. Isabella Tait, Andro Marr, cautioner.
1692.
Jan. 7. Wm. Eilles m. Agnes Muray ; c. James Eilles.
„ 26. Andro Mercer m. Issobell Williamsone ; c. John Mercer.
„ „ James Pekah m. Issobell Wilsone ; c. Hugh Wilsone.
Feb. 23. James Vair m. Issobell Vair ; c. Thomas Vair.
Mar. 4. Andrew Tutop m. Jennet Dicksone ; c. Alexr. Dicksone.
„ 5. Robert Mein m. Margaret Karr ; c. John Mein.
„ 8. David Hendersone m. Christian Milne ; c. John Penman.
„ 10. John Turner m. Agnes Mercer ; c. Georg Turner.
April 5. Nicol Waithman m. Margaret Gibsone ; c. John Bell.

1692.

April the last. Robert Scott m. Margaret Bunzie ; c. John Moffatt.
June 2. Robert Stirling m. Marion Lythgow ; c. John Stirling.
  ,, ,, John Purvis m. Issobell Taitt ; w. Georg Hoge.
  ,, ,, Richard Clerk m. Issobell Hoyie ; c. George Chisholme.
  ,, 9. Thomas Watsone m. Issobell Laughler in the paroche of Gallosheills
  ,, 15. John Pekah m. Marion Dick ; c. Georg Chisholm.
July 5. Georg Pringle m. Margaret Hownam ; c. John Thomsone.
  ,, 8. Wm. Bowar m. Margaret Mercer ; c. John Mein.
Aug. 2. John Watsone m. Marione Grhame : c. Wm. Wilsone.
Dec. 1. John Milne m. Issobell Milne.
  ,, 16. Andro Mercer m. Jennet Turnbull.
  ,, 29. Hendry Gibsone m. Issobell Fischar.
  ,, 23. Robert Sheill m. Margaret Fairbairne.

1693.

Jan. 19. John Summervaill m. Margaret Thomsone.
Feb. 24. William Walker m. Alisone Fraiter.
June 22. John Blaikie m. Marion Lythgow.
  ,, ,, Edward Lythgow m. Margaret Hall.
  ,, ,, William Mabone m. Marion Watsone.
July 5. James Blaikie m. Margaret Turnbull.
  ,, 10. Robert Harvie m. Jennet Mabone.
  ,, ,, Thomas Gairner m. Mary Scot.
  ,, ,, Henry Miles m. Issobell Tait.
  ,, 14. Robert Edgar m. Helen Ridford.
  ,, 12. John Summervaill m. Issobell Mertine.
Aug. 9. William Stirling m. Elizabeth Mofatt.
  ,, ,, Alexr. Kirkwood m. Helen Scot.
  ,, ,, John Steel m. Issobell Thomsone.
Sept. 15. Robert Mein m. Issobell Bell.
Oct. 5. John Cranstone m. Margaret Mein.
Nov. 3. Thomas Patersone m. Elizabeth Welsh.
  ,, 17. John Halliwall m. Jean Ridpath.
  ,, 24. William Wallace m. Jennet Laidlay.
  ,, ,, At Minto, John Bunzie m. Agnes Melrose.
Dec. 1. William Darling m. Alisone Lees.
  ,, ,, Walter Dalgleish m. Margaret Gibsone.
  ,, 15. James Fischar m. Issobell Moss.
  ,, ,, At Bowdoun, Thomas Stenhouse m. Mary Davidsone.
  ,, 19. John Greistone m. Jean Ramsay.
  ,, ,, William Lees m. Helen Wilsone.
  ,, 22. William Martine m. Issobell Marr.
  ,, 29. William Atkinsone m. Elizabeth Wilsone.

1694.

Feb. 1. James Donaldsone m. Margaret Wilsone.
  ,, 15. At Bowdoun, Thomas Thomsone m. Margaret Thomsone.
  ,, 16. At Gallowsheils, Francis Braiden m. Elizabeth Stodhart.
  ,, ,, Alexr. Lyall m. Margaret Bowar.
  ,, 21. At Bowdoun, James Dawsone m. Agnes Mein.
Mar. 15. Hugh Wilsone m. Margaret Bowstone.
  ,, 22. John Peter m. Agnes Sheil.
April 11. William Mercer m. Helen Hittone.
July 13. At Bowdoun, Mungo Purvis m. Margaret Eiles.
June 14. At Earlestone, George Rodger m. Christian Litle.
  ,, 29. At Bowdoune, Robert Shortreed m. Elspeth Dalglish.
Aug. 3. Alexr. Horsebrugh m. Jennet Lawder.
  ,, 9. John Wright m. Issobell Turnbull.
Oct. 25. At Bassendean, William Hoyie m. Issobell Hoyie
  ,, 30. Mark Hoyie m. Issobell Blaikie.
Nov. 20. James Wedderstone m. Issobell Wedderstone.
  ,, ,, Patrick Lambert m. Marion Litle.

1694.
Nov. 30. Thomas Halliburtune m. Margaret Black.
Dec. 28. William Milne m. Agnes Sclaitter.
　1695.
April 16. William Welsh m. Agnes Dewar.
June 8. Georg Hall m. Elizabeth Bathgate.
　,,　,,　John Gray m. Katharine Thin.
　,,　,,　George Pringle m. Jennet Wilsone.
　,,　15. John Cuthbertsone m. Marion Trotter.
　,,　22. John Riddel m. Jennet Turnbull.
Aug. 1. John Inglish m. Margaret Hittone.
　,,　20. Robert Bunzie m. Issobell Bowie.
　,,　,,　Robert Hill m. Janet Lod.
Nov. 28. William Darling and Margaret Matheson.
Dec. 13. Thomas Lookup m. Agnes Maxwil.
　,,　,,　Robert Duns m. Margaret Moffatt.
　,,　15. Alexander Dalgleish m. Margaret Vair.
　,,　,,　John Lamberd m. Agnes Tait.
　,,　,,　Adam Sheil m. Mary Haitlay.
　1696.
Feb. 20. Thomas Martine m. Jennet Runchiman.
Mar. 1. James Greive m. Jean Allaine.
April last. James Young m. Issobell Bartine
June 5. Mungo Blaikie m. Christian Laidlay.
　,,　10. —— Tailzeor m. ——Watsone in Bowdoun.
　,,　12. James Hoyie m. Jean Turner.
　,,　,,　George Brown m. Issobell Laing.
　,,　16. Patrick Wallace m. Elizabeth Hardie.
　,,　,,　Robert Maither m. Issobell Scot.
　,,　17. Francis Braiden m. Margaret Bowar.
July 20. Stephen Hittone m. Issobell Mabone.
Aug. 12. John Halliwall m. Christian Dinant.
Sept. 18. James Thin m. Marion Huntar.
Dec. 18. Wm. Kirkwood m. Margaret Mertone.
　,,　22. At Earlestoune, George Tullie m. Isobell Fischar.
　,,　last. James Mein m. Jennet Pursil.
　,,　last. George Mercer m. Jean Marr.
　1697.
Jan. 3. Thomas Litle m. Margaret Thin.
　,,　,,　Thomas Williamsone m. Elizabeth Young.
Feb. 10. Robert Mein m. Marion Mein.
July 2. Wm. Chisholme m. Isobel Ushar.
　,,　8. Wm. Mercer m. Mary Dalgleish.
　,,　,,　John Mein m. Isobel Sybbald.
Aug. 13. Robert Wight m. Agnes Martine.
Nov. 19. Thomas Lucup m. Agnes Milner.
　,,　23. Richard Robertson m. Jennet Pringle.
　,,　,,　John Glendinning m. Janet Bowar.
　,,　25. Henry Cochran m. Janet Riddell.
　,,　26. James Rennaldson m. Isabell Leidhouse.
Dec. 14. John Penman m. Janet Rutherfoord.
　1698.
April 28. Robert Eliot m. Agnes Mein.
　,,　29. Walter Eliot m. Magdalen Lythgow.
June 23. Antony Moss m. Elizabeth Currie.
Aug. 26. William Sanderson m. Elizabeth Mein.
Sept. 6. John Sclater m. Agnes Mein.
Nov. 2. Lancelot Brown m. Margaret Adam.
　,,　25. John Mabon m. Jennet Mabon.
Dec. 14. James Mein m. Elizabeth Hiton.
　,,　22. James Lythgow of Drygrange m. Elizabeth Lauder.
　,,　29. Robert Pringle m. Jennet Mein.

1699.

Feb.　3. George Vair m. Jennet Drummond.
　,,　　,,　Thomas Simontoun m. Marion Notman.
Mar.　3. Walter Tait m. Alison Neel.
April 25. At St. Boswells, Alexander Maxwell m. Issabell Gray.
June　2. Andrew Drummond m. Mary Brown.
　,,　　,,　John Karr m. Isabell Wait.
　,,　16. Walter Haliburton m. Margaret Davidsone.
Sept. 26. Thomas Usher m. Jean Fisher.
Oct.　10. Thomas Laidlaw m. Eupham Matthie.
　,,　24. Robert Philip m. Margaret Sclater.
Nov. 22. Walter Hownam m. Alison Mein.
　,,　28. Emanuel Man m. Margaret Paterson.

1700.

Feb.　5. George Hoy m. Jennet Redpath.
April 23. Andrew Moss m. Margaret Waugh.
　,,　26. Thomas Ainsley m. Margaret Rutherfoord in Jedburgh
June　7. Stephen Hiton m. Margaret Bisset.
　,,　25. John Thynne m. Agnes Milne.
July　5. John Sommervaill m. Agnes Tait.
　,,　18. Thomas Walker m. Jean Blaikie.
Aug.　6. John Brown m. Jennet Owens.
　,,　9. Thomas Litle m. Margaret Darling.
Dec. 24. Andrew Mercer m. Margaret Hervie.

1701.

Jan.　7. Andrew Lookup m. Jean Dowglass.
Mar. 11. Thomas Drummond m. Jean Smith.
April 29. James Bowie m. Marion Bell.
June　— James Wight m. Agnes Hardie.
July　— John Bartleman m. Mary Bunzie.
Oct.　30. James Hunter m. Margaret Edgar.
Nov.　7. Alexander Knox m. Helen Hoy.
　,,　20. Nicoll Milne m. Christian Blaikie.
Dec.　4. Robert Scott m. Elizabeth Patersone.
　,,　5. Thomas Scott of Chappell m. Mary Grey.
　,,　,,　James Laidlaw m. Agnes Pearson.
　,,　,,　James Karr m. Isabell Allan.
　,,　— William Fisher m. Agnes Drummond.

1702.

Feb. 20. John Moodie m. Isabell Mercer.
June 12. William Dickson m. Margaret Kyll.
Aug.　7. John Milne m. Helen Glendinning.
　,,　13. John Hislop m. Christian Cruickshank.
Nov. 10. John Mein m. Margaret Sclater.
　,,　12. John Drummond m. Jennet Dickson.
　,,　,,　Richard Lothian m. Mary Scott.
　,,　27. William Gill m. Margaret Turnbull.
　,,　,,　George Loury m. Margaret Gill.
Dec. 15. Patrick Riddell m. Margaret Brown.
　,,　22. Adam Sadler m. Jean Blaikie.
　,,　31. James Brown m. Jean Wauch.
　,,　,,　James Blaikie m. Marion Sclater.

1703.

Jan. 27. John Hounam m. Elizabeth Dickson.
　,,　29. James Mein m. Jennet Coatt.
Feb. 11. Thomas Milne m. Jennet Milne.
　,,　26. William Milne m. Isabell Riddell.
April 23. Andrew Marr m. Alison Bell.
　,,　,,　John Mercer m. Helen Sibbald.
May 18. Andrew Mein m. Jennet Gray.
June　4. Nicoll Mercer m. Margaret Drummond.

1703.
July   2. Patrick Wadderston m. Jennet Chisholme.
  „   16. George Mein m. Isabell Frier.
Aug.   6. James Leithan m. Agnes Mein.
  „   „ Thomas Leithan m. Isabell Tait.
Nov.   18. George Wright m. Isabell Wright.
  „   „ William Bell m. Helen Haitly.
  „   19. John Halliwall m. Margaret Fairbairn.
  „   23. James Watson m. Margaret Bunzie.
Dec.   7. James Napier m. Jennet Hounam.
  „   10. James Hoy m. Isabell Wright.
  „   16. Nicoll Mercer m. Mary Rennaldson.
  „   17. James Mercer m. Margaret Waithman.
  „   31. Thomas Darling m. Mary Dods.
  „   „ Cornelius Mein m. Isabell Mein.
  „   „ William Mein m. Margaret Mein.
    1704.
Feb.   24. Andrew Mein m. Elizabeth Richardson.
June   2. John Park m. Jennet Graham.
  „   13. John Darling m. Isabell Lythgow.
  „   23. James Mercer m. Margaret Vair.
July   5. John Chisholme m. Margaret Laing.
  „   11. George Remainhouse m. Alison Fogo.
  „   21. William Rennaldson m. Agnes Mein.
Aug.   4. Richard Mein m. Jennet Mein.
Sept. 22. Robert Penman m. Isabell Lamb.
Nov.   2. Robert Bunzie m. Marion Hopkirk.
  „   3. William Mertoun m. Jennet Hislop.
  „   23. William Remainhouse m. Katharine Stuart.
  „   „ Richard Sclater m. Alison Dauson.
    1705.
Feb.   8. Thomas Young m. Jean Davidson.
  „   9. Thomas Thurbrand m. Jennet Marre.
Mar.   30. James Stodhart m. Isabell Moss.
April 20. James Usher m. Isabell Mercer.
  „   26. William Brown m. Alison Young.
June   5. James Blaikie m. Agnes Hitoun.
  „   28. Richard Fraiter m. Isabell Mercer.
July   13. John Hoy m. Isabell Bartoun.
Oct.   30. Robert Wallace m. Jennet Milne.
Nov.   29. Thomas Usher m. Jennet Murray.
Dec.   6. John Pratsell m. Elizabeth Christie.
  „   26. John Bowstone m. Isabell Mein.
  „   „ James Moodie m. Jean Smith.
    1706.
Feb.   22. William Mein m. Isabell Wright.
Mar.   20. Andrew M'Fadzean m. Elizabeth Martine.
April 25. John Wilson m. Jennet Stirling.
June   7. William Atchison m. Margaret Notman.
Oct.   17. John Laing m. Isabell Martine.
Nov.   8. Richard Robson m. Elizabeth Pringle.
  „   19. Andrew Darling m. Helen Lythgow.
  „   „ Willam Wilkieson m. Jennet Grierson.
  „   28. John Loury m. Esther Rutherfoord.
Dec.   4. James Hoy m. Margaret Vetch.
  „   „ John Karr m. Anne M'Fadzean.
    1707.
Mar.   7. Andrew Scott m. Margaret Sheriff.
April 30. Andrew Douglass, baillie, m. Jean More.
June   6. Thomas Bartoun m. Isabell Mercer.
  „   10. William Turner m. Marion Notman.

1707.

June 10. John Pearson m. Margaret Crosbie.
  „   13. Thomas Darling m. Isabell Notman.
  „   „ Andrew Mein m. Marion Fuirgrieve.
  „   20. Andrew Bryden m. Jennet Brown.
Oct. 14. Mr. Andrew Patersone m. Jean Cowan
Nov. 14. James Young m. Marion Fox.
  .,   „ Adam Shiell m. Isabell Henderson.
  ,, 21. Robert Hilson m. Agnes Bower.
Dec. 19. John Glendinning m. Margaret Mein.

1708.

Jan. 16. James Kin m. Marion Pringle.
Feb. — James Mein m. Agnes Milne.
  „   — James Laing m. Christian Mein.
June 4. Nicoll Milne m. Elizabeth Vair.
  „   25. Richard Sclater m. Katharin Laing.
  „   29. John Bunzie m. Agnes Turner.
Aug. 13. Andrew Mercer m. Margaret Frier.
Nov. 26. John Brown m. Elisabeth Trotter.
Dec. 3. John Hitoun m. Jennet Mercer.
  „   „ John Smith m. Margaret Phaup.
  ,, 24. Andrew Hownam m. Agnes Hitoun.

1709.

Feb. 11. William Martine m. Helen Thomsone.
  „   24. Thomas Laidlaw m. Elisabeth Simontoun.
Mar. 11. Archibald Frier m. Isabell Matthison.
April 8. William Sclater m. Helen Bunzie.
  „   22. Andrew Mein m. Helen Mein.
June 14. James Houden m. Elisabeth Hog.
  „   17. John Purvis m. Jean Martine.
  „   21. John Hardie m. Christian Dewar.
July 8. James Raith m. Agnes Shillinglaw.
Aug. 5. William Chisholme m. Margaret Hopkirk.
  „   19. Robert Davidson of Deanbrae m. Elisabeth Cairncroce.
Nov. 8. James Dickson m. Isabell Hitoun.
  „   18. Alexander Knox m. Jennet Frier.
  ,, 25. James Wilson m. Elisabeth Rutherfoord.
Dec. 2. John Patersone m. Margaret Riddell.

1710.

Mar. 28. Mr. William Hunter m. Jennet Bowstone.
June 13. John Notman m. Jennet Moodie.
  „   20. James Turner m. Christian Thynne.
July 21. John Bartoun m. Jennet Mein.
Aug. 4. George Mercer m. Katharin Ramsey.
  ., 15. Robert Mein m. Jean Simontoun.
  ., 18. William Wallace m. Mary Scott.
Oct. 27. Thomas Lookup m. Jean Martine.
Nov. 17. William Young m. Isabell Ormistoun.
  ,,   „ John Mercer m. Mary Mein.
  .,   ., James Gray m. Jennet Mercer.
Dec. 5. Richard Sclater m. Margaret Mein.
  ,. 19. Thomas Williamson m. Mary Mein.
  .. 21. William Sandilands m. Katharin Marre.
  ,, 29. John Walker m. Jennet Mercer.

1711.

Jan. 30. John Wood m. Marion Blaikie.
Feb. 14. Andrew Mercer m. Margaret Maxwell.
  ,, 29. James Pringle m. Helen Mein.
April 17. Philip Douglass m. Agnes Hall.
June 1. Nicoll Bower m. Alison Riddell.
  ., 19. William Stodhart m. Jennet Mercer.

1711.
June 22. James Wilson m. Elisabeth Napier.
July 13. James Hunter m. Margaret Speeding.
  ,, 26. James Watson m. Isabell Henderson.
Aug. 10. Andrew Hittoun m. Agnes Lintoun.
  ,, 14. George Scott m. Jennet Caldcleugh.
Oct. 19. Andrew Stuart m. Agnes Wright.
Nov. 6. Andrew Moodie m. Elisabeth Murray.
  ,, 22. George Shiell m. Isabell Kyll.
  ,, 23. William Hopkirk m. Isabell Hunter.
  1712.
Mar. 28. Walter Mabon m. Elisabeth Gill.
April 1. James Brown m. Agnes Mein.
May 15. Edward Lythgow m. Marion Remainhouse.
  ,, 17. John Chisholme m. Margaret Ritchie.
June 26. James Kedzie m. Helen Haitlie.
July 31. Andrew Patersone m. Alison Milne.
Aug. 4. John Sprotts m. Margaret Hitoun.
  ,, 15. Andrew Drummond m. Helen Mattheson.
  ,, 22. Thomas Purvis m. Isabell Lamb.
  ,, ,, John Bell m. Jennet Mabon.
Sept. 4. Robert Edgar m. Jean Young.
Oct. 10. Henry Cochran m. Jennet Vair.
Nov. 6. David Grieve m. Helen Pringle.
Dec. 18. James Bunzie m. Jean Wilson.
  ,, 19. Robert Martine m. Elisabeth Purvis.
  ,, 31. John Napier m. Helen Drummond.
  ,, ,, John Mercer m. Elisabeth Hitoun.
  1713.
Jan. — William Mabon m. Marion Sclater.
June 12. Thomas Wilson m. Alison Hoy.
July 3. Robert Wright m. Elizabeth Mein.
  ,, 7. John Boo m. Helen Matheson.
Aug. 7. Nicoll Mercer m. Christian Mein.
Sept. 8. John Frier m. Jennet Turner.
Nov. 20. George Shiell m. Christian Cook.
  ,, 27. John Bowston m Agnes Thomson.
  ,, ,, William Bunzie m. Jennet Fairbairn.
Dec. 4. Mungo Laidlaw m. Margaret Cochran.
  ,, 30. John Gibson m. Agnes Sclater.
  1714.
Feb. 12. Robert Balantine m. Jennet Frier.
  ,, 19. William Stodhart m. Jennet Smith.
Mar. 2. James Murray m. Beatrix Hunter.
June 8. Andrew Stuart m. Agnes Mein.
  ,, 15. Richard Thomson m. Isabell Moffet.
  ,, 18. Adam Hislope m. Elisabeth Mercer.
  ,, 25. John Halliwell m. Agnes Marshell.
July 2. John Hog m. Margaret Lindsay.
  ,, 15. James Park m. Helen Fisher.
Aug. 5. William Broun m. Jennet Logan.
  ,, 6. John Usher m. Christian Bower.
  ,, 11. Robert Crosbie m. Elspeth Crosbie.
Oct. 15. John Wilson m. Elisabeth Pursell.
Nov. 12. John Gordon m. Katharin Grieston.
  ,, 19. Thomas Coldcleugh m. Elisabeth Kar.
  ,, 25. Peter Moffet m. Agnes Smith.
Dec. 22. Andrew Lookup m. Margaret Newton.
  ,, 24. Robert French m. Elisabeth Hopkirk.
  ,, ,, James Moodie m. Jennet Mercer.
  1715.
Feb. 24. Colin Brodie m. Elspeth Miller.
2D

1715.

Feb. 24. Robert Murdoch m. Mary Haliburton.
June 17. John Cochran m. Jennet Rutherfurd.
  ,, 24. Andrew Mercer m. Katharin Mercer.
July 22. George Bartoun m. Alison Mercer.
Aug. 5. Walter Kerr m. Jennet Moffet.
Nov. 15. James Martine m. Jennet Dickson.
  ,, 25. George Maxwell m. Isabell Patersone.
Dec. 2. Thomas Sclater m. Jennet Vair.
  ,, 5. James Hutchison m. Elisabeth Darling.
  ,, 9. Thomas Gill m. Alison Gill.
  ,, 13. James Mar m. Margaret Mercer.
  ,, 20. Robert Ormiston m. Agnes Smith.
  ,, 23. James Vair m. Margaret Ker.
  ,, 24. John Wadderston m. Jean Ramsay.
  ,, 29. John Smith m. Hen Mercer.

1716.

Feb. 3. John Halliwell m. Helen Nicoll.
  ,, 10. James Mein m. Mary Bunzie.
Mar. 2. Thomas Blaikie m. Margaret Wood.
June 5. Alexander M'Faden m. Agnes Napier.
  ,, 8. William Napier m. Helen Mathison.
  ,, 21. Robert Hunter m. Jean Brock.
July 13. John Gordon m. Katharin Bower.
Aug. 16. James Bowston m. Marion Blaikie.
  ,, 17. Alexander Bell m. Jennet Bell.
  ,, 21. James Usher m. Agnes Frier.
Nov. 2. James Leithan m. Helen Clerk.
  ,, 12. James Thomson m. Isabell Forrest.
  ,, 17. Walter Brodie m. Margaret Bunzie.
  ,, 22. James Turner m. Agnes Hardie.
  ,, 23. John Bower m. Agnes Dalgleish.
  ,, 30. Thomas Gardiner m. Isabell M'Faden.
Dec. 4. William Wilson m. Helen Lauder.
  ,, 12. George Atchison m. Elisabeth Hopkirk.
  ,, 21. George Bell m. Jennet Oliver.
  ,, 27. James Edgar m. Isabell Mercer.
  ,, 28. William Morison m. Margaret Bowie.
  ,, ,, Robert Mein m. Agnes Chisholme.

1717.

April 26. John Vaugan m. Isabell Hunter.
June 7. John Notman m. Jennet Waddell.
  ,, 20. Mungo Park m. Isabell Hervie.
  ,, 21. George Darling m. Agnes Lauder.
July 2. James Mein m. Margaret Mein.
  ,, 5. Andrew Usher m. Isabell Thomson.
  ,, ,, George Frier m. Anne Stewart.
  ,, 9. James Swoord m. Jennet Fraiter.
Aug. 2. Robert Huntlie m. Isabell Frier.
  ,, 16. Robert Grieston m. Jennet Hislope.
Nov. 28. John Sibbald m. Agnes Stenhouse.
Dec. 3. Richard Bower m. Isabell Simson.
  ,, ,, George Mercer m. Agnes Knox.
  ,, 10. George Thomson m. Marion Hardie.
  ,, 13. Thomas Milne m. Christian Walker.
  ,, 19. William Robertson m. Elisabeth Scott.
  ,, 20. Andrew Bunzie m. Margaret Robertson.
  ,, ,, Nicoll Milne m. Agnes Turnbull.

1718.

Feb. 27. Thomas Mein m. Isabell Hoy.
June 20. William Thynne m. Marion Fairbairn.

1718.
June 20. Robert Stirling m. Isabell Stewart.
July 1. Thomas Simson m. Jennet Mein.
,, 4. John Hall m. Margaret Hope.
Aug. 19. Patrick Thomson m. Isabell Moffet.
Nov. 24. James Gardiner m. Margaret Bowston.
Dec. 11. Thomas Young m. Isabell Thomson.
,, ,, John Speeding m. Anne Corser.
,, 12. James Mein m. Margaret Bunzie.
,, 19. George Baittie m. Marion Wright.
,, 23. Andrew Bryden m. Margaret Mercer.
,, 26. Robert Williamson m. Agnes Scott.
1719.
Mar. 27. John Hervie m. Margaret Scott.
,, ,, Robert Manuall m. Agnes Gibson.
April 23. John Anderson m. Elisabeth Pearson.
June 2. Robert Fairbairn m. Margaret Davidson.
July 17. Andrew Hounam m. Margaret Moodie.
Sept. 18. James Smeall m. Elisabeth Ellies.
Nov. 17. George Allie m. Marion Fraiter.
,, ,, John Kemp m. Helen Grant.
,, 18. William Mercer m. Isabell Mein.
Dec. ― John Laing m. Elisabeth Purvis.
,, 10. James Hart m. Agnes Thomson.
,, 17. Walter Murray m. Isabell Mathison.
, 22. John Bunzie m. Jean Sibbald.
,, 30. Robert Rutherford m. Elisabeth Hitoun.
,, ,, William Mabon m. Jennet Simson.
,, 31. Patrick Bulman m. Isabell Ker.
,, ― Andrew Crawfurd m. Mary Mein.
1720.
(Blank till Nov.)
Nov. ― James Rae m. Alison Lyal.
Dec. 30. James Grieve m. Jean Watson.
,, ― James Liethan m. Margaret Sclatter.
1721.
Jan. 5. Robert Sclatter m. Jennet Elliot.
June 12. William Winter m. Isobell Friar.
,, 17. Robert Liethan m. Mary Nisbet.
,, 19. William Aitchison m. Jennet Shiel.
(Blank till 1722.)

1722.
Feb. 8. Thomas Bunzie m. Jennet White.
,, 15. James Edgar m. Helen Laidla.
,, 23. William Broun m. Jean Dickson.
Mar. 16. John Dods m. Anna Riddel.
,, 30. William Pringle m. Margaret Taite.
April 12. James Hunter m. Agnes Burnlie.
――― Andrew M'Fadzien m. Christian Cook.
April 26. Mr. John Cranstoun m. Mary Skelly.
June 8. Mr. Alexr. Cunninghame of Hindhope m. Mistress Elizabeth
Paterson, daughter to Robert Paterson of Drygrange.
,, 12. George Martine m. Jennet Haliburtoun.
Aug. 23. Walter Riddel m. Margaret Scot.
Oct. 30. Robert Bunzie m. Rachell Forsan.
Nov. 22. John Lawrie m. Isobel Miln.
,, 23. Robert Welsh m. Margaret Speedin.
,, ,, James Waugh m. Mary Duncan.
Dec. 14. Andrew Heaton m. Isobel Young.
,, 26. John Dalgliesh m. Mary Darling.
,, 28. Alexr. Gray m. Margaret Thynne.

1722.

Dec. 28. James Darling m. Margaret Fairbairn.

1723.

——— Alexr. Young m. Helen Young.

Feb.   1. Andrew Lindsay m. Margaret Simpson.

,,   19. James Duar m. Marion Hardie.

April   5. John Cochran m. Isobel Miln.

,,   ,, John Gordon m. Isobel Dalgliesh.

,,   18. John Davidson m. Agnes Mein.

,,   30. Thomas Sclatter m. Euphan Robertson.

June — John Stirling m. Isobel Wilson.

> NOTE.—*Marriages and proclamations between November* 1723 *and* 31*st December* 1738 *are to be found from pages* 117 *to* 239 *of this volume. The record from this point is kept in fairly good chronological order.*

1739.

Jan. 26. Booked in order for marriage John Comin in this parish and Margaret Fairbairn in the parish of Earlestown ; John Wallace, cautioner.

> [*To prevent repetition entries like the above are abbreviated. The contracting parties are all resident in Melrose parish except as otherwise stated. The words "in this parish" are omitted and "m." has been inserted to cover "bookings" as well as marriages.*]

Mar. 24. George Newtown in Ligerwood m. Isabel Boston ; c. Thomas Boston.

,,   28. Alexr. Dove in Kelso m. Isobel Hoy ; c. John Bowie.

April   6. Andrew Dawson m. Jean Lamb ; c. Robert Penman, senior.

,,   19. William Vallance m. Marion Bruce ; c. Alexr. Gray.

May 11. Simon Bathgate in Lauder m. Isobel Frier ; c. John Turner.

,,   12. William M'Cawl m. Margaret Mercer ; c. Adam Harvie.

,,   25. Robert Henry m. Janet Learmont in Earlestown ; c. Thomas Purves.

,,   ,, John Boston m. Helen Hunter in Ashkirk ; c. Robert Philp.

June   2. Andrew Bowar m. Margaret Stenhouse ; c. Mr. John Stenhouse.

,,   30. Thomas Maban m. Margaret Tait ; c. Robert Trotter.

Oct.   6. David Martine m. Helen Bell ; c. William Bell.

,,   13. William Hopkirk m. Isobel Tait ; c. John Tait.

,,   18. William Haitley m. Mary Gray in Ligerwood ; c. John Boston.

,,   20. Robert Laidlaw m. Agnes Gray ; c. John Laidlaw.

,,   ,, John Kemp m. Anne Christie ; c. John Hoy.

,,   ,, James Noble m. Margaret Dickson ; c. Robert Lawrie.

,,   ,, John Corsar m. Agnes Scott in Galashiels ; c. James Smail.

,,   27. Robert Wood in Ligerwood m. Isobel Stirling ; c. John Stirling.

Nov.   3. James Fisher m. Janet Glendinning ; c. John Mercer.

,,   9. George Dobson in Galashiels m. Margaret Chisholme ; c. John Chisholm.

,,   13. Mungo Park m. Janet Blaikie ; c. James Dixon.

1740.

Jan. 12. Adam Davidson m. Jean Roger in Hopkirk parish ; c. William Steel.

Feb. 16. John Lyal m. Isobel Gill ; c. John Gill.

April   3. James Welsh m. Agnes Gibson in Galashiels ; c. William Bain.

May   1. Zerubbabel Forsan m. Agnes Purves in Lauder ; c. John Tait.

,,   10. William Tait m. Janet Atchison in Earlestown ; c. Robert Laidlaw.

,,   17. Michael Audison m. Alison Haitley ; c. Andrew Haitley.

,,   24. Ebenezer Young in Ligerwood m. Elizabeth Darling ; c. John Gray.

,,   28. Henry Forrest m. Margaret Henryson in Galashiels ; c. James Ainslie.

,,   ,, William Bunzie m. Janet Mabane ; c. William Mabane.

,,   30. James Cook in Galashiels m. Elizabeth Wood ; c. William Aitchison.

,,   ,, Andrew Chisholm m. Marion Turner ; c. John Park.

June 21. John Laidlaw m. Jean Brown in Earlestown ; c. William Steel.

July 11. John Robson m. Helen Scott in Ancrum ; c. Hugh Grieve.

1740.
July 12. Walter Eastown in Maxtown m. Margaret Renaldson ; c. Andrew
        Mein.
Oct. 18. John Fairbairn m. Margaret Young in Bowden ; c. Cornelius Mein.
  ,,   ,, Andrew Cook m. Anne Stedman in Mertoun ; c. Alexr. Cook.
Nov. 7. Alexr. Scott m. Alison Mowat in Lauder ; c. Robert Scott.
  ,, 8. James Wilson m. Margaret Riddell ; c. John Moss.
  ,, ,, William Slatter m. Jean Gardner in Mertoun ; c. Alexr. Cook.
  ,, 11. Robert Williamson m. Eupham Anderson in Galashiels , c. Thomas
        Williamson.
  ,, 22. Cornelius Mein m. Helen Sibbald ; c. Cornelius Mein, senior.
  1741.
Aug. 22. John Martine in Earlestown m. Helen Martine ; c. William Martine.
Nov. 6. Robert Wood m. Agnes Hay in Earlston ; c. Hugh Grieve.
  ,, 11. William Bryden m. Janet Haliday ; c. John Bryden.
  ,, 27. Robert Thurburn in Galashiels m. Helen Park ; c. Mungo Park.
  ,, 28. Adam Johnstone in Lessuden m. Helen Martin ; c. William Martine.
  ,, ,, James Wauch m. Isobel Smail ; c. James Wauch, senior.
Dec. 12. Walter Milestone in Earlestown m. Jean Lindesay ; c. John
        Thomson.
  1742.
Feb. 6. James Turner m. Agnes Boustone ; c. John Boston.
April 10. Mungo Glendining and Margaret Aird ; c. John Fisher.
May 20. George Sprots in Galashiels m. Isobel Dalgliesh ; c. John Sprots.
July 10. John Mein m. Barbara Tullie in Earlestown ; c. Cornelius Mein.
  ,, 17. Robert Dods m. Marion Usher ; c. John Heiton.
Oct. 8. Thomas Ovens in St. Boswels m. Janet Mercer ; c. Nicol Laidlaw.
  ,, 9. Thomas Welsh m. Mary Fair ; c. Philip Fair.
Nov 27. John Boston m. Janet Boston ; c. James Boston.
  ,, ,, John Dawson m. Elizabeth Marr ; c. James Marr.
  ,, ,, John Bowar m. Janet Mercer ; c. John Dalgliesh.
  ,, ,, James Smith m. Agnes Hownam ; c. Andrew Smith
Dec. 3. John Anderson in Ashkirk m. Margaret Wauch ; c. James Wauch.
  ,, 4. William Mein m. Helen Lockie in Mertown ; c. John Sibbald.
  ,, 11. Thomas Dixon m. Isobel Mercer ; c. James Dickson.
  1743.
Jan. 22. William Kennedy in Bouden m. Isobel Renaldson ; c. Andrew
        Renaldson.
Feb. 25. James Wallace m. Helen Familtown in St. Boswells ; c. William
        Wallace.
Mar. 4. William Hamiltone in Selkirk m. Janet Heiton ; c. John Moodie.
  ,, 31. Andrew Darling m. Janet Cuthbertsone in Lauder ; c. Alexr. Gray.
April 1. Robert Mein m. Helen Scot in Yarrow ; c. John Mein.
May 13. John Lyal in Stow m. Mary Mein ; c. James Mein.
  ,, 21. John Sibbald m. Agnes Stenhouse ; c. Thomas Stenhouse.
June 3. James Moffat m. Marion Laidlaw ; c. William Laidlaw.
  ,, 4. James Hunter m. Isabel Milne ; c. William Hunter.
  ,, 10. William Fair m. Catharine Wilson ; c. Philip Fair.
  ,, ,, James Wilson in Liliesleaf m. Catharine Mabane ; c. Thomas Vair.
  ,, 11. Nicol Miln m. Mary Mercer ; c. John Milne.
July 23. Alexr. Mein m. Jean Smith in Stitchell ; c. John Mein.
Sept. 9. Robert Philp m. Margaret Bannatyne ; c. William Maban.
Nov. 5. Andrew Smith m. Alison Hownam ; c. Andrew Hownam.
  ,, 11. John Turnbull m. Janet Usher ; c. John Boston.
  ,, ,, David Thomson m. Margaret Mein ; c. William Steel.
  ,, ,, William Johnstown m. Margaret Brown ; c. George Henderson.
  ,, 12. Mungo Park m. Anne Purves ; c. William Steel.
  ,, 26. Robert Lawrie m. Isobel Mein ; c. Thomas Bunzie.
  ,, ,, John Heiton m. Janet Mein in Lesuden ; c. William Hunter.
Dec. 2. Andrew Pringle in Mertown m. Janet Walker ; c. John Mercer.
  ,, 3. Thomas Rutherford m. Margaret Turnbull in Cavers ; c. John Grant.

1743.
Dec. 14. James White m. Janet Ker in Morbottle ; c. James Marr.
1744.
Mar. 4. John Lothian m. Marion Scott ; c. Richard Park.
,, 11. John Watherstone in Stow m. Isobel Thomson ; c. William Moffatt.
June 1. George Pringle in Mertown m. Alison Haitley ; c. George Walker.
,, ,, Gilbert Welsh m. Rachel Welsh in Stow ; c. John Bryden.
,, 23. John Mabane m. Janet Jack in Earlestown ; c. William Slatter.
July 20. Thomas Bannatyne in Stow m. Margaret Park ; c. William Hunter.
,, 21. Thomas Boston m. Isobel Bannatyne ; c. John Bannatyne.
,, .. James Williamson m. Elizabeth Mercer ; c. James Dickson.
,, 28. John Smith in Stow m. Christian Laidlaw ; c. William Bain.
Aug. 1. Thomas Sanderson in Galashiels m. Agnes Walker ; c. Andrew
            Walker.
,, 4. George Beatie m. Isobel Hislop ; c. John Bowar.
,, 11. William Bell m. Janet Bell in Earlestown : c. James Boston.
Sept. 29. Robert Bunzie m. Margaret Blaikie in Galashiels ; c. John Mein.
Oct. 19. Nicol Mercer in Earlestown m. Lilias Wood ; c. William Bain.
Nov. 13. Robert Purves m. Margaret Speeding ; c. Thomas Frier.
,, 17. Thomas Fairbairn m. Jean Hope ; c. William Steel.
,, ,, James Mercer m. Margaret Pearson ; c. John Pearson.
Dec. 7. Alexr. Cook m. Margaret Deans in Bowden ; c. William Cook.
,, 26. William Crosbie m. Margaret Scott in Galashiels ; c. James Laidlaw.
1745.
Jan. 26. John Bryden m. Janet Fairbairn in Earlstoun ; c. William Bryden.
,, ,, George Watt m. Margaret Craig in Galashiels ; c. Andrew Burnet.
Feb. 9. James Wight m. Janet Mein ; c. James Mein.
April 13. William Hunter m. Margaret Moffatt in the New Kirk, Edinburgh ; c.
            Charles Wilkison.
May 11. William Moffatt m. Marion Somervel in Channelkirk ; c. George
            Moffatt.
,, 17. John Wightman m. Helen Bruce ; c. William Bain.
,, 23. William Coldcleugh m. Elizabeth Wadderstone in Stow ; c. George
            Grahamslie.
,, 25. Thomas Fair m. Janet Beinstown in Selkirk ; c. John Beinstown.
,, 31. Andrew Johnstown in Bowden m. Elizabeth Crawford ; c. James
            Scott.
,, ,, John Carns in Cavers m. Janet Atchison ; c. William Steel.
June 8. Thomas Purves m. Ann Clappertown ; c. Richard Park.
,, 14. Patrick Swinton in Westruther m. Agnes Gray ; c. Alexr. Gray.
July 3. William Buttler m. Agnes Watson ; c. William Steel.
,, 26. John Usher m. Janet Paterson in Bowden ; c. John Heiton.
Sept. 7. Robert Hope in Ancroft m. Isobel Redford ; c. William Redford.
Oct. 4. George Stobo in Galashiels m. Janet Mercer ; c. John Thomson.
,, 22. Walter Nisbet in Jedburgh m. Margaret Atchison ; c. George
            Atchison.
Nov. 2. James Mein m. Agnes Nesten ; c. Robert Mein.
,, 9. Thomas Paterson m. Janet Paterson ; c. William Bain.
,, 12. Robert Cribbas m. Agnes Mathison ; c. Thomas Mathison.
,, 30. Mungo Thomson m. Margaret Duncan in Bowden ; c. Alexr. Mein.
1746.
Mar. 8. Thomas Slater m. Isobel Young in Maxtown ; c. James Mein.
May 9. William Johnstone in Ligerwood m. Margaret Young ; c. Robert
            Ormistoun.
,, 24. Thomas Rae m. Helen Gardener ; c. Andrew Smith.
June 13. John Thomson in Lauder m. Agnes Romanus ; c. Thomas Darling.
,, ,, Thomas Atchison in Stow m. Margaret Cleugh ; c. Alexr. Gray.
,, 14. Jeremiah Smith in Neuthorn m. Isobel Mercer ; c. John Mercer.
,, ,, William Wood in Ligerwood m. Marion Little ; c. Hugh Grieve.
July 11. William Sibbett m. Helen Ferquartson in Traquair ; c. John
            Thomson.

1746.
Aug.   2. Andrew Stuart m. Isobel Bertown ; c. James Boston.
 „   9. Philip Thyne m. Margaret Pearson in Earlestown ; c. James Fisher.
Oct.   3. Walter Tait in Stow m. Annabella Atchison ; c. William Tait.
 „   18. George Drummond m. Isobel Dickson ; c. James Dixon.
Nov.   1. George Atchison and Margaret Gedd ; c. Robert Trotter.
 „   8. George Renaldson m. Catharine Mein ; c. Andrew Renaldson.
 „   27. James Lauder in Yarrow m. Janet Darling ; c. George Watt.
 „   29. Andrew Moss m. Agnes Wight : c. John Moss.
    1747.
Jan   3. Alexander Sibbett m. Janet Bannatyne ; c. John Bannatyne.
May   2. William Roger in Lauder m. Agnes Tait ; c. Thomas Pringle.
 „   22. James Telfair in Southdean m. Anne Maxwell ; c. John Young.
 „   30. John Darling m. Jean Watson ; c. Thomas Frier.
July   11. Robert Young in Stow m. Janet Thomson ; c. Walter Thomson.
Sept. 18. Thomas Rae in Stow m. Janet Brodie ; c. John Park.
Oct.   3. John Mercer m. Janet Familtown, Lessuden ; c. Robert Rutherfurd.
 „   „ Thomas Usher m. Janet Mercer : c. John Turnbull.
 „   10. John Fiddes m. Margaret Ainslie ; c. James Boston.
 „   24. John Skirven m. Isobel Mercer ; c. William Mercer.
 „   31. John Scott in Longnewtown m. Mary Mein ; c. James Mein.
Nov.   7. William Mercer m. Anne M'Fadzean ; c. Andrew Cook.
 „   11. William Henderson in Lauder m. Helen Pringle ; c. George Watt.
 „   21. John Eastown m. Elizabeth Allan in St. Boswalls ; c. John Mein,
           junior.
    1748.
Jan.   8. John Hall in Stow m. Alison Tait ; c. ——.
April   9. James Peacock m. Margaret Allan in Borthwick ; c. George
           Henderson.
 „   26. John Biggar in Yarrow m. Jean Currie ; c. Walter Tait.
May   12. Robert Cunningham in Kelso m. Helen Smail ; c. Thomas Marr.
 „   13. Mr. James Brown, our minister, m. Mrs. Helen Drummond in the
           parish of Carridden ; c. Mr. George Grant, bailie.
 „   21. James Stephenstone m. Esther Tully in Ednem ; c. Philip Fair.
 „   28. John Heiton m. Elizabeth Eastown ; c. John Heiton.
July   21. John Pringle m. Isobel Pringle ; c. Thomas Marr.
Sept. 24. John Grierson m. Agnes Mercer ; c. Robert Grierson.
Oct.   15. William Henry m. Christian Kirkwood in Stow ; c. Thomas Fair.
Nov.   11. Thomas Frier m. Elizabeth Thomson in Lauder ; c. John Turner.
 „   19. John Atchison m. Janet Sclatter ; c. William Atchison.
 „   „ Adam Harvie m. Elizabeth Finnie ; c. John Turnbull.
 „   26. Gilbert Welsh m. Elizabeth Dunn ; c. John Bryden.
Dec.   30. Andrew Pringle m. Alison Mortown in Earlestown ; c. George Wight.
    1749.
April 24. John Wybar m. Isobel Grieve ; c. Thomas Frier.
 „   29. William Mercer m. Elizabeth M'Faddzean ; c. William Butler.
May   5. William Kitching in Stow m. Christian Herd : c. George Herd.
 „   13. John Bunzie m. Mary Miln ; c. John Mein.
 „   19. Thomas Riddell m. Jean Henderson in Wiltown ; c. James Riddell.
 „   20. Patrick Nicolson in Ligerwood m. Jean Familtown ; c. Alexr.
           Lockie.
June   2. William Ormistown m. Margaret Scott in Bowden ; c. Walter Tait.
 „   16. William Martin m. Isobel Shillinglaw ; c. John Gray.
 „   24. William Bannatyne m. Nelly Pringle in Earlestown ; c. Walter
           Murray, junior.
July   6. William Stoddart in Selkirk m. Barbara Martin ; c. Walter Tait.
 „   22. Andrew Hownam m. Elizabeth Grahamslie in Bowden ; c. Andrew
           Smith.
 „   29. James Boston m. Janet Hunter ; c. John Bannatyne.
Oct.   7. George Wilson m. Isobel Haistie ; c. Robert Speeding.

1749.
Oct. 13. James Mercer m. Elizabeth Rutherfurd ; c. John Rutherfurd.
„ 26. Gilbert Welsh m. Mary Graham in Traquair ; c. Walter Tait.
Nov. 1. James Cribbas m. Eupham Smith ; c. Alexr. Fisher.
„ 14. Mungo Park m. Margaret Boston ; c. James Boston.
„ „ George Williamson m. Elizabeth Wood : c. John Laidlaw.
„ 25. George Brown m. Margaret Lees in Galashiels ; c. Thomas Trotter.
Dec. 2. James Hilson m. Jean Lookup ; c. Andrew Lookup.
„ „ Adam Haswell, surgeon in Jedburgh, m. Jean Elliot ; c. Mr. Gavin Elliot.

1750.
Jan. 6. James Wallace m. Alison Phawp ; c. James Phaup.
„ 13. James Rutherfurd m. Alison Fairbairn in Stitchell ; c. George Scott.
„ 20. Charles Ainslie m. Janet Brown in Mertown ; c. George Ainslie.
Mar. 16. William Laing m. Isobel Noteman in Earlestown ; c. Nicol Mercer.
„ 31. James Turner m. Margaret Beinstone ; c. John Beinstone.
April 28. John Bannatyne m. Alison Hunter ; c. William Mabane.
May 18. James Inglis in Galashiels m. Janet Ormistown ; c. William Hopkirk.
„ 25. James Stevenson in Lauder m. Isobel Mackelree ; c. George Watt.
June 15. William Frater in Westruther m. Margaret Darling ; c. George Darling.
„ 23. Robert Huntley m. Margaret Coldcleugh ; c. George Coldcleugh.
July 21. Jonathan Rodger in Selkirk m. Margaret Johnstone ; c. James Hunter.
Sept. 15. Walter Murray m. Elizabeth Smail ; c. James Marr.
„ 22. James Wallace m. Marion Symonton in Lauder ; c. Hugh Grieve.
„ 28. William Drummond m. Janet Myles ; c. William Matthison.
„ „ William Stephenson in Southdean m. Helen Drummond ; c. George Drummond.
Oct. 12. Thomas Davidson m. Janet Brown in Earlestown ; c. Nicol Miln.
„ 19. Robert Shillinglaw in Lauder m. Janet Thomson ; c. William Martin.
„ 20. Robert Miln m. Christian Miln ; c. Nicol Miln.
Nov. 13. Andrew Mercer m. Elizabeth Thomson in Selkirk ; c. John Mercer.
„ 16. John Hunter in Stow m. Helen Dickson ; c. George Henderson.
„ „ William Hog m. Helen Johnstone ; c. John Wilkieson.
„ 17. John Martin m. Elizabeth Bannatyne ; c. William Mabane.
„ 24. James Marr m. Janet Mercer ; c. John Mercer.
„ 30. James Lambert m. Margaret Tait ; c. John Park.
Dec. 1. John Scott m. Jean Wilson ; c. James Dixon.
„ „ James Walker m. Elizabeth Grieve ; c. Charles Ainslie.
„ „ William Hart m. Anne Stoddart ; c. George Stoddart.
„ „ Alexander Reid m. Isobel Martin ; c. John Martin.

1751.
Feb. 2. William Bold m. Elizabeth Lythgow ; c. James Hunter.
Mar. 7. Andrew Bowar m. Isobel Cochran in Selkirk ; c. William Stenhouse.
„ 30. James Anderson m. Catharine Shillinglaw ; c. George Anderson.
„ „ Robert Sandilands m. Marion Bunzie ; c. Nicol Miln.
April 4. John Forsan m. Janet Chisholm in Earlestown ; c William Bartleman.
May 4. John Tait in Stow m. Marion Fountain ; c. John Fountain.
„ 10. Robert Bulman m. Janet Wood in Galashiels ; c. James Hunter.
„ 11. George Paterson m. Margaret Little in Galashiels ; c. James Laidlaw.
„ 18. William Waddell in Lauder m. Janet Grieve ; c. Walter Tait.
„ 23. William Beatie in Southdean m. Agnes Rutherfurd ; c. John Rutherfurd.
„ 31. John Shillinglaw in Lauder m. Marion Waugh ; c. William Smith.
June 7. George Thomson m. Isobel Wadderstone in Kirknewton ; c. William Cavers.
„ 8. James Scot in Bedrule m. Janet Dalgliesh ; c. William Stenhouse.
July 5. James Knox m. Janet Lythgow in Lauder ; c. John Park.
Aug. 3. John Wilkieson m. Elizabeth Dalgliesh ; c. William Stenhouse.

1751.

Sept. 13. William Bryson in Lauder m. Agnes Hardie ; c. George Watt.
  ,,   25. Andrew Lauder m. Elizabeth Lauder in Lauder ; c. Robert Scot.
Oct. 10. John Waugh m. Janet Johnstone in Lauder ; c. John Wilkieson.
  ,,   19. John Clark in Martown m. Helen Atchison ; c. John Mein.
  ,,   ,, John Lees m. Agnes Gray ; c. John Laidlaw.
  ,,   26. John Mercer m. Margaret Lauder in Westruther ; c. Thomas Dixon.
Nov. 2. Alexr. Simpson m. Helen Wood ; c. Thomas Trotter.
  ,,   12. James Sanderson in Stow m. Margaret Hamilton ; c. John Hoy.
  ,,   15. James Edgar m. Margaret Wilkieson ; c. William Smith.
  ,,   30. John Mein m. Agnes Marr ; c. Robert Mein.
Dec. 6. James Edgar and Margaret Wilkieson married in a private house
            gave in 12 pence to the poor.
  ,,   19. John Mein and Agnes Marr, married in a private house, gave in 12
            pence to the poor.

1752.

Jan. 25. John Beinstone m. Janet Maxwell in Southdean ; c. Thomas Fair.
Feb. 14. George Howison in Earlestown m. Elizabeth Phawp ; c. James
            Phawp.
May   9. Thomas Fair m. Marion Lauder ; c. Andrew Mein.
June 6. Robert Milne m. Isobel Redford ; c. William Redford.
July 3. Thomas Spence in Lauder m. Helen Stirling ; c. James Stirling.
  ,,   7. Andrew Walker m. Margaret Brown ; c. William Walker.
Aug. 15. Andrew Thomson in Galashiels m. Helen Burnet ; c. John Laidlaw.
Oct. 21. Alexander Purves m. Margaret Brown ; c. Alexr. Fisher.
  ,,   27. John Bell m. Janet Rae ; c. James Phawp.
Nov. 22. John Coats m. Margaret Steel in Stow ; c. Robert Trotter.
Dec. 8. John Fife m. Janet Grierson in Jedburgh ; c. James Williamson.
  ,,   9. Adam Nicol m. Alison Bunzie ; c. George Simpson.
  ,,   30. William Hopkirk m. Margaret Lawrie ; c. John Dawson.

1753.

Mar. 23. George Hunter in Jedburgh m. Elizabeth Mercer ; c. James
            Williamson.
April 19. John Simpson m. Catharine Cartwright ; c. William Smith.
May 11. Robert Scot m. Elizabeth Welsh in Stow ; c. Thomas Trotter.
  ,,   17. William Bryson in Lauder m. Agnes Hardie ; c. George Watt.
  ,,   18. William Tait m. Elizabeth Laidlaw ; c. James Laidlaw.
  ,,   ,, James Tait in Stow m. Agnes Laidlaw ; c. William Tait.
  ,,   26. James Laidlaw m. Jean Redford ; c. William Redford.
June 2. George Coldcleugh m. Margaret Thomson ; c. Alexr. Sibbald.
  ,,   14. Alexander Lockie m. Jean Neil in Mertown ; c. William Hunter.
  ,,   ,, John Stuart and Elizabeth Brown from Yarrow parish married here.
July 13. James Riddell m. Alison Kyle ; c. John Laidlaw.
  ,,   20. John Keddoch in Earlestown m. Margaret Myles ; c. William
            Drummond.
Aug. 4. William Williamson m. Jean Dickson in Mertown ; c. James
            Williamson.
Oct. 13. Alexander Lockie m. Violet Colzier ; c. Robert Lookup.
Nov. 10. William Leaden m. Agnes Hog ; c. Thomas Stenhouse.
Dec. 1. Andrew Smith m. Janet Thomson ; c. John Turnbull.
  ,,   ,, James Scot m. Alison Thomson in Ancrum ; c. Thomas Stenhouse.
  ,,   8. Robert Grierson m. Isobel Stoddart ; c. George Stoddart.
  ,,   ,, John Hatton m. Margaret Tait ; Andrew Pringle.
  ,,   14. James Mathison m. Agnes Young ; c. William Matthison.
  ,,   28. Thomas Waugh in Ligerwood m. Janet Moore ; c. James Brown.

1754.

Jan. 2. John Coats m. Elizabeth Thomson ; c. George Ainslie.
May 30. William Smail in Lauder m. Alison Moffatt ; c. John Wilkieson.
June 1. John Thorburn in Lessuden m. Margaret Inglis ; c. James Hunter.
  ,,   ,, George Stoddart m. Janet Ker in Galashiels ; c. Robert Grierson.
  ,,   ,, Thomas Howetson m. Helen Howetson ; c. James Howetson.

1754.

June 13. William Wight m. Anne Noteman ; c. James Laidlaw.
,, 22. John Wight m. Alison Thyne ; c. Walter Scott.
July 12. Thomas Shiel in Lauder m. Janet Scot ; c. Robert Scot.
,, 19. James Shiel in Selkirk m. Janet Smail ; c. Walter Murray.
Oct. 10. James Anderson in Ennerleithen m. Christian Usher : c. John Turnbull.
Nov. 16. William Scot m. Margaret Jamieson in Bowden ; c. George Scott.
,, 29. John Thom in Kelso m. Isobel Forsan ; c. Robert Forsan.
,, 30. William Mathison m. Margaret Fiddes ; c. James Pringle.
,, ,, William Turner m. Anne Laidlaw ; c. George Ainslie.
Dec. 7. Andrew Wight in Bowden m. Jean Symonton ; c. John Laidlaw.
,, 14. Robert Sibbat m. Isobel Harvie ; c. John Thomson.

1755.

Jan. 10. James Marr m. Jean Scott in Hawick ; c. George Watt.
April 18. James Hopkirk m. Agnes Mercer ; c. Walter Murray, junior.
,, 19. John Thomson m. Margaret Banatyne ; c. William Mabane.
July 11. Alexander More in Galashiels m. Isobel Laidlaw ; c. Robert Laidlaw.
Aug. 30. William Martin m. Jean Scott ; c. William Bell.
Oct. 25. The Rev. Mr. James Brown, our minister, m. Mrs. May Tod in St. Cuthbert's parish ; c. Mr. Grant, our bailie.
Nov. 1. David Musgrave m. Margaret Watson in Mertown ; c. James Hunter.
Dec. 6. James Shiel m. Elizabeth Grieve ; c. William Martin.
,, 13. Nicol Miln m. Margaret Rogers in Ancrum ; c. William Stenhouse.

1756.

Jan. 17. George Kemp in Channelkirk m. Christian Pringle ; c. John Trotter.
Feb. 7. James Bryden in Galashiels m. Margaret Wilson ; c. George Wilson.
,, ,, George Hog m. Margaret Ramsey ; c. James Ramsey.
,, 21. Thomas M'Dougal in Maxtown m. Jean Martin ; c. Hugh Grieve.
Mar. 6. Thomas Ormistoun m. Bettie Hilson in Earlestown ; c. William Ormistown.
April 17. William Winter in Lauder m. Helen Hardie ; c. William Thinne.
,, ,, William Graham m. Isobel Hunter in Earlestown ; c. Alexr. Fisher.
May. 1. William Redford m. Bettie Balmer in Eckford ; c. Robert Miln.
,, 15. Robert Whitlaw m. Christian Trotter ; c. William Ormistown.
,, 20. Robert Laidlaw m. Alison Simpson ; c. William Smith.
,, 22. John Trotter m. Alison Marr ; c. John Mein.
,, 29. James Kitchen m. Christian Gibson in Lessuden ; c. William Stenhouse.
June 12. William Rae m. Isobel Robson ; c. James Marr.
,, ,, John Brown m. Jean Dickson in Earlestown ; c. Robert Bunzie.
,, 22. Robert Stirling m. Helen Lauder ; c. James Stirling.
July 9. Charles Baxter m. Janet Grieve in Hawick ; c. James Marr.
,, 30. George Ainslie m. Isobel Donaldson in Galashiels ; c. Charles Ainslie.
Aug. 4. David Tailor m. Helen Elliot in Jedburgh ; c. George Scott.
Oct. 2. James Penman m. Christian Tully in Earlestown ; c. Robert Penman.
,, 16. Thomas Miln m. Anne Atchison ; c. James Ramsey.
,, 23. John Usher m. Janet Drummond ; c. John Turnbull.
,, 29. John Turnbull m. Jean Stuart in Bowden ; c. John Young.
,, 30. Thomas Cochran m. Bettie Scot in Bowden ; c. William Bartleman.
Nov. 20. John Bryden m. Isobel Wilson ; c. William Stenhouse.
,, 27. James Scott m. Isobel Gillas in Bowden ; c. George Scott.

1757.

Mar. 5. John Pringle m. Mary Moffat in Lauder ; c. John Pringle.
May 21. Walter Paton in Lessuden m. Isobel Douglass : c. James Hudd.
June 4. James Marr m. Bettie Lethian in Lauder ; c. Thomas Marr.
July 1. William Thyne m. Elizabeth Murray in Galashiels ; c. Nicol Alley.
,, 9. Andrew Bunzie m. Janet Hart ; c. George Hart.
Sept. 10. William Rae m. Janet Moffat ; c. James Gardener.
,, 23. The Rev. Mr. Robert Gullan, minister of the Gospell at St. Boswells m. Miss Mary Ellies ; c. Mr. James Brown.

1757.
Oct. 28. James Rutherfurd m. Isobel M'Dougal in Maxtown ; c. Adam Miln.
Nov. 3. George Henderson m. Helen Mack in Gordon ; c. Walter Tait.
„ 5. George Hart m. Anne Chisholm ; c. Andrew Mein.
„ „ Nicol Miln m. Isobel Thomson ; c. William Alley.
„ 22. John Wallace m. Helen Henry ; c. James Wallace.
„ „ George Carter in Westruther m. Marion Thyne ; c. William Thyne.
Dec. 3. Andrew Beatie m. Andrew Thomson ; c. Adam Miln.
„ 10. Andrew Pringle m. Helen Carncross in Galashiels ; c. Andrew Pringle.
„ „ John Sprotts m. Agnes Haitlie ; c. Andrew Haitlie.
1758.
Jan. 28. William Rae in Smalholm m. Nellie Waugh ; c. John Bruce.
May 5. Thomas Darling m. Janet Riddell ; c. James Darling.
„ 26. William Porteous in Stow m. Isobel Darling ; c. William Thyne.
„ 27. Andrew Wallace in Stow m. Elizabeth Wallace ; c. James Wallace.
„ „ George Mercer in Stow m. Bettie Scott ; c. James Laidlaw.
„ „ Andrew Morison in Ligerwood m. Anne Vallance ; c. William Waugh.
„ „ Robert Wait in Mertown m. Isobel Carter ; c. Alexr. Fisher.
June 7. James Dixon in Galashiels m. Janet Harvie ; c. Robert Sibbat.
July 1. John Heiton m. Marion Burnet ; c. John Mercer.
„ 21. Andrew Kerr m. Janet Mercer in Selkirk ; c. James Elliot.
„ 31. John Murray in Borthwick m. Margaret Darling ; c. Hugh Grieve.
„ „ Robert Scott and Christian Craig married irregularly.
Oct. 7. John Pringle in Stow m. Janet Pringle ; c. William Martin.
„ 11. James Knox in Galashiels m. Margaret Mercer ; c. James Hunter.
„ 21. Andrew Mein m. Isobel Mabane ; c. Robert Bunzie.
„ 27. James Graham m. Helen Scott ; c. William Ormistown.
„ 28. John Brown m. Isobel Keddoch ; c. Alexander Scott.
„ „ William Jamieson in Roxburgh m. Helen Cochran ; c. William Barclay.
Nov. 11. George Boyd in Stow m. Isobel Blaikie ; c. Charles Ainslie.
„ „ Thomas Purves in Maxtown m. Janet Bowar ; c. John Usher.
„ 25. Robert Robison m. Marion Dickson ; c. John Mein.
Dec. 2. Thomas Bunzie m. Margaret Sibbald ; c. John Bunzie.
„ „ Thomas Mein m. Beatrix Thomson ; c. William Alley.
1759.
Mar. 24. Robert Paterson m. Margaret Lorain in Dunse ; c. Thomas Whale.
May 23. Thomas Murdie in Stow m. Isobel Gibson ; c. John Boston.
June 30. Robert Blaikie in Galashiels m. Janet Wight ; c. James Marr.
July 14. Walter Tait m. Margaret Haliburton in Earlestown ; c. James Tait.
„ 28. John Greenfield m. Isobel Ker in Stow ; c. Walter Tait.
Aug. 4. Robert Tacket m. Janet Penman ; c. Robert Penman, senior.
„ „ James Marr m. Margaret Mein ; c. Robert Marr.
„ „ William Hart, junior, m. Jean Robison ; c. Robert Robison.
Sept. 29. John Forsyth m. Isobel Scot in Stow ; c. Walter Tait.
Oct. 13. Nicol Miln m. Jean Bunzie ; c. Robert Bunzie.
Nov. 22. Robert Whitlaw m. Agnes Bunzie ; c. Alexr. Bunzie.
„ 24. Andrew Drummond m. Isobel Martin ; c. John Usher.
„ „ William Scot m. Janet Paton in Lessuden ; c. Nicol Miln.
„ 27. John Scot m. Agnes Thorburn, but not proclaimed here.
Dec. 8. Robert Pringle m. Margaret Lawson in Stow ; c. William Martin.
„ 22. Mark Rule in Earlestown m. Isobel Fisher ; c. John Fisher.
1760.
Jan. 2. A pair married here who paid the dues.
„ 5. William Hart, senior, m. Margaret Marr ; c. James Marr.
„ 26. George Renaldson m. Christian Fisher ; c. Thomas Lookup.
Feb. 9. Thomas Harvie m. Isobel Speeding ; c. William Drummond.
„ 16. Alexander Willie m. Agnes Martin ; c. George Brown.
April 12. George Mein m. Margaret Dods, both in Bowden ; c. Andrew Lumsden.

1760.

May   3. John Fiddes m. Ann Christie ; c. John Anderson.
 ,,   16. Henry Frater in Galashiels m. Mary Mercer ; c. William Mercer.
 ,,   24. James Huntlie m. Margaret Mercer ; c. John Young.
 ,,   ,,   Robert Coats m. Christian Dickson in Lauder ; c. James Usher.
 ,,   31. George Pringle m. Janet Swanstone in Bowden ; c. William Redford.
 ,,   ,,   Andrew Fisher of Housebyres m. Isobel Howden ; c. Thomas Marr.
June   7. Robert Stuart m. Janet Tait ; c. Archibald Stuart.
July   19. James Mein m. Isobel Dickson ; c. John Mein.
Aug.   9. Thomas Crosbie m. Agnes Darling ; c. James Fisher, junior.
Oct.   25. Robert Mercer m. Margaret Blaikie in Galashiels ; c. William Hopkirk.
 ,,   31. John Raith in Lauder m. Margaret Smith ; c. James Gardener.
Nov.   1. William Thomson in Gordon m. Marion Little ; c. Hugh Grieve.
 ,,   ,,   William Wallace m. Margaret Skirven in St. Boswals ; c. William Maban.
 ,,   ,,   Archibald Stuart m. Elizabeth Cook ; c. William Cook.
 ,,   8. John Dalgliesh m. Margaret Henry ; c. Robert Tacket.
 ,,   25. David Thomson m. Agnes Smith ; c. Adam Miln.
Dec.   6. David Burton m. Jean Grahamslie ; c. John Grahamslie.
 ,,   13. John Beinstone m. Alison Familtown ; c. Alexr. Familtown.

1761.

Feb.   4. James Forsyth in Lawder m. Janet Lees ; c. James Rutherfurd.
 ,,   14. Thomas Carter m. Margaret Burnet in Earlestown ; c. James Burnet.
 ,,   28. James Smail m. Anne Lyal ; c. John Lyal.
Mar.   7. William Dods m. Isobel Burnet ; c. James Burnet.
April   4. John Currer in Galashiels m. Helen Tait ; c. John Hatton.
 ,,   9. William Elliot in Minto m. Janet Symonton ; c. William Steel.
May   8. John Brotherstone m. Elizabeth Kellie in Lauder ; c. Walter Tait.
 ,,   23. William Cuthbertson in Lessuden m. Jean Bathgate ; c. John Trotter.
June   3. William Stenhouse m. Janet Sandilands ; c. Thomas Stenhouse.
 ,,   6. William Brown m. Janet Nicol in Cavers ; c. Adam Nicol.
 ,,   11. Andrew Henderson m. Mary Inglis in Selkirk ; c. David Tailor.
 ,,   20. James Laidlaw m. Isobel Welsh in Tweedsmure ; c. Walter Tait.
July   17. John Haliwell m. Janet Haliwell ; c. William Steel.
Aug.   1. William Nicol m. Margaret Smith in Liliesleaf ; c. Thomas Marr.
 ,,   8. John Darling m. Isobel Darling in Gordon ; c. Thomas Brodie.
Nov.   21. William Darling m. Margaret Gibson ; c. Archibald Stuart.
 ,,   24. Thomas Wallace m. Janet Carter ; c. Thomas Trotter.
 ,,   ,,   James Smith m. Helen Smith ; c. David Thomson.
 ,,   28. Robert Mercer m. Elizabeth Shiel ; c. George Mercer.
 ,,   ,,   John Rutherford m. Margaret Dalgliesh ; c. John Dalgliesh.
Dec.   5. Robert Miln m. Janet Cochran ; c. William Redford.

1762.

Jan.   16. Robert Ormistown m. Janet Riddell in Gordon ; c. Andrew Ormistown.
Feb.   12. Andrew Little in Stow m. Agnes Welsh ; c. John Trotter.
 ,,   20. William Vair m. Janet Speeding ; c. James Speeding.
April   28. James Roger in Earlestown m. Elizabeth Mercer ; c. Thomas Marr.
July   3. Andrew Mercer m. Helen Wight ; c. James Marr.
 ,,   10. John Mercer m. Helen Johnstone in Galashiels ; c. Robert Watson.
 ,,   20. James Pringle in Ligerwood m. Mary Dalgleish ; c. James Mein.
 ,,   30. James Mackerlee m. Margaret Pringle in Earlestown ; c. James Thine.
Oct.   9. John Wylie m. Bettie Rutherfurd ; c. George Brown.
Nov.   20. John Jamison m. Helen Lockie ; c. Alexr. Lockie.
 ,,   23. John Lumsden m. Helen Pringle ; c. Andrew Lauder.
Dec.   11. Thomas Laidlaw m. Margaret Thomson ; c. William Alley.
 ,,   18. Robert Marr m. Janet Mercer ; c. Robert Myles.

1763.

Jan.   1. Robert Vair m. Helen Dickson in Bouden ; c. Charles Baxter.

1763.
Jan.   1. Francis Boyd m. Mary Vietch ; c. Robert Watson.
Mar.   5. Andrew Darling m. Janet Hardie in Lauder ; c. John Dalgliesh.
June 24. William Goodfallow m. Katharine Lauder ; c. John Lauder.
Aug. 12. Robert Clapperton m. Elizabeth Weatherstone in Galashiels ; c.
            James Ingles.
Nov. 18. James Goodfallow in Bouden m. Isabel Turner ; c. Robert Myles.
  ,,   22. Andrew Bunizie m. Janet Haistie ; c. Adam Milne.
  ,,   ,, James Ramsay m. Aniple Myles ; c. Robert Myles.
Dec.   3. James Scott m. Agnes Martin ; c. John Fair.
    1764.
Jan. 14. Alexr. Hammilton m. Isabel Brownfield ; c. William Martine.
Mar.   9. Andrew Carter in Westruther m. Nelly Thinn ; c. James Thinn.
April 14. James Duncan m. Agnes Martine ; c. James Orr.
May   19. Robert Smail in Moxton m. Agnes Friar ; c. Robert Paterson.
  ,,   24. John Turner in Kelso m. Nelly Boston ; c. John Nicoll.
June   1. William Waddle m. Janet Caldwalls in Oxton ; c. Robert Wadal.
  ,,   2. George Dalglish in Stow m. Helen Taitt ; c. William Taitt.
July 27. Robert Marr m. Peggy Williamson ; c. John Marr.
Oct.   6. James Watson in Galashiels m. Agnes Wight ; c. George Stodart.
  ,,   13. George Fraiter m. Margaret Hamilton in St. Boswels ; c. James
            Macdowel.
Nov. 22. Thomas Smith in Lauder m. Janet Mertin ; c. William Mertine.
  ,,   ,, James Mein m. Mary Derling in Merton ; c. Andrew Mein.
  ,,   ,, Andrew Lumsdale m. Betty Baxter ; c. James Marr.
Dec. 28. Andrew Johnston m. Janet Cochran in Earlestown ; c. Robert
            Hunter.
    1765.
Jan.   5. William Pringle m. Mary Scott in Yarrow ; c. James Pringle.
  ,,   19. John Shiel m. Margaret Speden in Bowden ; c. Nicol Milne.
Feb. 16. John Forest m. Margaret Mason in Polwarth ; c. Andrew Mercer.
Mar.   2. John Wilson m. Isabel Kedie ; c. James Wilson.
  ,,   ,, James Orr m. Anne Barroman ; c. James Duncan.
May   10. Mr. Archibald Somervile in Lauder m. Margaret Laidlaw ; c. John
            Somervile.
  ,,   18. James Thomson in Channelkirk m. Agnes Smith ; c. Alexr. Thomson.
  ,,   25. James Usher m. Margaret Grieve ; c. Thomas Usher.
June   1. George Darling m. Janet Mercer ; c. James Mein.
  ,,   ,, Alexander Corsbie m. Anne Redfoord ; c. James Laidlaw.
  ,,   5. George Smith in Westruther m. Janet Wallace ; c. Andrew Wallace.
July   5. George Hogg in Galashiels m. Janet Lees ; c. George Hogg.
Aug. 10. Peter Thomson m. Janet Beatie ; c. George Caldcleugh.
Oct. 12. James Wallace m. Jean Mein in Earlestown ; c. John Mairtine.
  ,,   18. William Clark in Channelkirk m. Alison Hoy ; c. John Hoy.
Nov. 16. William Watterston in Lauder m. Betty Hardie ; c. Patrick Hardie.
  ,,   22. Robert Ballyntine m. Betty Scott ; c. Walter Scott.
  ,,   30. Thomas Mein in Mertown m. Agnes Vair ; c. Robert Bunizie.
Dec.   6. Robert Brown in Eckfoord m. Agnes Bell ; c. Andrew Bell.
  ,,   7. Robert Heart m. Margaret Marjoribanks in Mackertown ; c. William
            Heart.
  ,,   ,, Thomas Wilkie in Ancrum m. Elizabeth Riddel ; c. Robert Riddel.
  ,,   ,, John Leyden m. Isabel Smith ; c. James Leyden.
    1766.
Jan. 16. Thomas Henderson m. Betty Spiden in Bowden ; c. James Vair.
May   17. Andrew Oliver m. Janet Barclay ; c. John Barclay.
  ,,   ,, Thomas Turnbul m. Peggy Forsan ; c. Zerubbabel Forsan.
  ,,   23. James Dickson in Stow m. Margaret Haillyday ; c. Andrew Haillyday.
  ,,   ,, Thomas Romainis m. Peggy Dykes ; c. Andrew Purviss.
  ,,   31. George Wight m. Mary Sclaiter ; c. Robert Grieve.
  ,,   ,, Nicol Stenhouse m. Agnes Sibbald in Roxburgh ; c. Nicoll Milne.
June   7. James Wilson m. Elizabeth Bathgate in Ligerwood ; c. James Gray.

1766.

June 14. Robert Welsh m. Jean Lees in Stow ; c. Robert Lees.

" 21. Richard Robson m. Isabel Sclaiter ; c. Richard Sclaiter.

" " James Mein m. Christian Spiden ; c. William Vair.

July 5. William Given in Ashkirk m. Margaret Hervie ; c. Thomas Hervie.

Aug. 12. Thomas Laidlaw m. Isabel Henderson ; c. John Laidlaw.

Nov. 8. James Vair m. Nelly Hunter ; c. Robert Hunter.

" 22. John Barklay m. Isabel Cochran ; c. Hendry Cochran.

" 25. James Wight m. Mary Lees ; c. John Park.

" " Andrew Hog in Lauder m. Janet Smail ; c. James Mercer.

" " James Gordon m. Anne Rutherford in Bowden ; c. Nicol Milne.

1767.

Jan. 10. Robert Bunzie m. Isabel Hoy ; c. Alexander Grieve.

Jan. 17. John Thomson m. Isabel Brotherstone in Earlestown ; c. Charles Hardie.

Feb. 14. George Haldane in Galashiels m. Helen Laidlaw ; c. Thomas Laidlaw.

Mar. 20. John Tailor in Stow m. Bettie Baptie ; c. James Baptie.

May 1. James Amos m. Alison Frier ; c. James Hunter.

" 9. William Romanous in Lauder m. Janet Thomson ; c. Thomas Frier.

" 23. William Redpath m. Nelly Scott ; c. William Hunter.

June 13. James Vair m. Peggy Cochran ; c. Henry Cochran.

" " Andrew Bell m. Janet Pringle ; c. John Dickson.

July 11. James Dickson in Peebles m. Isabel Blaickie ; c. George Blaikie.

Aug. 20. Walter Mercer in Gallashiels m. Jean Moffat ; c. Thomas Trotter.

Oct. 17. John Haldon in Galashiels m. Janet Blaikie ; c. James Ballantine.

" 31. William Blaikie m. Elizabeth Scott ; c. Thomas Laidlaw.

" " John Pringle in Minto m. Isabel Fisher ; c. John Fisher.

Nov. 24. George Heard in Legerwood m. Margaret Fiddes ; c. Isaac Ketchen.

" " Andrew Dickson m. Peggy Clerk in Bowden ; c. Alexander Mein.

" 28. Thomas Darling m. Betty Bathgate in Lauder ; c. Hugh Grieve.

Dec. 12. John Barklay m. Margaret Hart ; c. James Sclaiter.

" 18. James Thynn m. Margaret Dodds in Westruther ; c. George Carter.

1768.

Jan. 13. William Smairt m. Agnes Pringle ; c. James Thynn.

May 12. Thomas Dudgeon in Cranshaws m. Margaret Laidlaw ; c. Thomas Laidlaw.

" 14. Robert Middlemis in Wilton m. Margaret Sprotts ; c. Andrew Sprotts.

" 20. John Waugh in Ligerwood m. Alison Moffat ; c. John Moffat.

" 22. Andrew Ormiston m. Peggy Brownfield ; c. John Martine.

" 28. John Baillie in Lauder m. Janet Forsan ; c. William Forsan.

June 1. John Fisher m. Elizabeth Gilles ; c. Walter Scott.

July 16. William Stoddart in Ancrum m. Agnes Fisher ; c. John Fisher.

" 29 Andrew Cribbes m. Agnes Mercer ; c. James Marr.

Oct. 15. Robert Noble in Bowden m. Isabel Lawrie ; c. George Lawrie.

Nov. 5. John Pecoack m. Agnes Wait ; c. Richard Sclaiter.

" 22. Michael Boston m. Katharine Wood ; c. James Wilson.

" " John Fowntain m. Janet Turnbul in Yarrow ; c. Robert Taket.

Dec. 3. James Houtson m. Betty Lees in Stow ; c. James Whitson.

" " Thomas Proctor m. Margaret Phorsan ; c. William Forsan.

" 15. David Murray m. Agnes Gray ; c. James Hunter.

1769.

Jan. 7. James Pringle m. Isabel Lavel ; c. George Bell.

Feb. 17. James Wilson m. Isabel Milne in Bowden ; c. James Taitt.

April 14. John Smart m. Katharine Govenlock in Lauder ; c. John Smart.

" 22. Walter Ronaldson m. Helen Shillinglaw in Ligertwood ; c. Andrew Murray.

" 29. Robert Lumsdale m. Margaret Skirven ; c. Robert Meyles.

May 12. Robert Crighton m. Isabel Louden ; c. George Moffat.

" 20. James Frier m. Isabel Dalglish ; c. William Bell.

" 26. William Baptie in Lessuden m. Margaret Mercer ; c. James Speeden.

1769.
May 31. Robert Ramsay m. Elizabet Gilray in Roxburgh ; c. John Mertine.
June 7. Thomas Blaikie in Gallashiels m. Isabel Scott ; c. James Clapperton.
,, 21. James Turnbull in Yarrow m. Agnes Blaikie ; c. Robert Taket.
,, 23. Charles Hislop in Minto m. Beatrice Goven ; c. John Goven.
July 8. Thomas Fair m. Agnes Lauder ; c. John Fair.
,, 29. Robert Phorsan m. Isabel Uns ; c. Thomas Williamson.
Aug. 5. Robert Fairbairn m. Jean Martin ; c. John Fair.
Sept. 8. Thomas Thomson m. Margaret Hogg ; c. Thomas Thomson.
Oct. 21. John Fair m. Nelly Smith ; c. John Smith.
Nov. 17. James Moffat m. Margaret Dickson ; c. George Moffat.
,, 22. William Forsyth in Stow m. Janet Thomson ; c. Alexr. Thomson.
,, ,, James Hoyd in Minto m. Margaret Pringle ; c. Andrew Haitlie.
,, ,, George Moffat m. Mary Mercer in Stow ; c. George Scott.
,, ,, James Dalgliesh m. Alison Mercer ; c. Robert Myles.
,, 25. Walter Scott m. Beatrice Scott in Morbattle ; c. James Scott.
,, 30. Thomas Mercer m. Janet Haitlie ; c. Andrew Morton.
Dec. 9. Henry Cochran m. Peggy Mein ; c. Robert Mein.
,, 16. James Taitt m. Jean Young in Greenlaw ; c. John Mercer.
1770.
April 19. John Gibson m. Elizabet Bulman ; c. George Lawrie.
May 12. Peter Wright m. Christian Hunter in Selkirk ; c. Alexander Mein.
,, 30. John Purves in Westruther m. Janet Brown : c. John Merton.
,, 30. James Reid m. Janet Shiel in Earlston ; c. William Ailly.
June 2. John Moffat m. Alison Louden ; c. Thomas Frier.
July 21. John Leyden m. Isabel Dods ; c. Andrew Dods.
Aug. 4. William Mitchel m. Betty Hollyday ; c. Charles Ainslie.
Oct. 13. Robert Ormiston m. Mary Darling ; c. Andrew Ormiston.
,, 20. George Mercer m. Janet Heitton ; c. Andrew Heitton.
,, ,, John Milne m. Alison Helliburton ; c. Adam Milne.
Nov. 17. Alexander Grieve in Galashiels m. Helen Symenton ; c. William
        Aillie.
,, 22. James Hog m. Susanna Dawson ; c. John Dawson.
Dec. 8. Peter Moffat m. Nelly Mack in Stow ; c. James Henderson.
,, ,, John Helliwall m. Agnes Christie ; c. John Turnbull.
,, 15. James Waters in Selkirk m. Janet Turnbull ; c. Thomas Mertine.
1771.
Jan. 12. James Brown m. Mary Gray ; c. David Murray.
,, 25. George Hay in Jedburgh m. Janet Grahamslie ; c. John Grahamslie.
Feb. 22. Thomas Lukup in Hawick m. Alison Gill ; c. John Gill.
Mar. 2. John Walker m. Margaret Ingles in Selkirk ; c. Alexr. Fisher.
April 13. Henry Cochran m. Janet Lokie in Mertown ; c. John Cochran.
,, 18. John Drydon in Jedburgh m. Helen Henderson ; c. John Grahamslie.
May 10. Archibald Vallance in Lauder m. Elspath Myles ; c. Robert Myles.
,, 11. John Mercer in Greenlaws m. Margaret Symonton ; c. Henry Freator.
,, 25. William Wight m. Margaret Loch in Lauder ; c James Dickson.
June 5. John Eckford m. Betty Dickson ; c. James Baptie.
July 6. Andrew Morton m. Janet Bathgate in Galashiels ; c. Thomas Mercer.
Aug. 13. William Chisholm in Stow m. Agnes Heitton ; c. John Rutherford.
,, 17. James Amos m. Helen Hoy ; c. James Sanderson.
Nov. 20. John Pursell in Dalkeith m. Agnes Ballantine ; c. Thomas Ballantine.
,, 22. Robert Fraizer m. Betty Shiel ; c. Nicol Milne.
Dec. 7. Andrew Heitton m. Janet Usher ; c. John Mercer.
,, 14. Richard Park in Stow m. Elizabeth Bathlouden [*sic*] (Betty Louden
        in birth entry) ; c. James Amos.
1772.
Jan. 18. John Cochran m. Janet Vair ; c. Henry Cochran.
April 9. James Hog in Hawick m. Jean Dawson ; c. James Dawson.
,, 11. Peter Caruthers m. Janet Fisher ; c. John Fisher.
May 30. John Mercer m. Elizabeth Leyden ; c. John Leyden.
June 27. John Mein m. Nelly Stonhouse ; c. Nicol Stonhouse.

1772.
July 10. Alexander Bell m. Jean Neil ; c. John Laurie.
  ,, 18. George Darling m. Helen Crosbie ; c. Thomas Laidlaw.
Oct. 17. Mr. John Mercer m. Miss Bettie Wilkison in Cranston ; c. James Sanderson.
Nov. 14. George Rea m. Janet Vair ; c. George Laurie.
  ,, 21. John Graham m. Jean Thomson in Traquair ; c. James Hunter.
  ,, 28. James Hog m. Nelly Drumond ; c. Robert Myles.
  ,, ,, James Crosbie m. Janet Dalgleish ; c. John Anderson.
  ,, ,, David Mein m. Agnes Bunnie ; c. William Maben.
Dec. 5. Robert Smail in St. Boswels m. Peggy Grierson ; c. Robert Grierson.
  ,, 11. James Chatto in Ladykirk m. Betty Cook ; c. Andrew Cook.
1773.
Jan. 15. Thomas Kerr in Kelso m. Marion Martin ; c. Robert Hunter.
  ,, 16. John Martin m. Janet Boston ; c. Andrew Martin.
Feb. 5. Mr. Alexander Fisher m. Miss Janet Kyle in St. Boswels ; c. James Fisher.
  ,, 20. James Taylor in Fala m. Betty Purves ; c. James Purves.
Mar. 13. James Blaikie m. Betty Turnbull in Innerleithen ; c. James Blaikie.
  ,, 20. William Rutherfurd in Earlston m. Peggy Gibson ; c. William Gibson.
May 20. William Caruthers in Galashiels m. Margaret Cochran ; c. John Cochran.
  ,, 23. Robert Hume m. Margaret Brown in Lauder ; c. John Martin.
  ,, 29. William Gibson m. Nelly Gill ; c. Walter Murray.
June 2. Robert Kirkwood m. Margaret Spittle ; c. James Usher.
  ,, 5. James Cairns in Earlston m. Katharine Phorsan ; c. William Phorsan.
  ,, 18. William Scott in Cavers m. Margaret Moss ; c. James Moss.
  ,, 26. John Waugh m. Isabel Scott ; c. Adam Scott.
July 9. Walter Pringle in Hawick m. Betty Heitton ; c. Andrew Riddel.
  ,, ,, John Brydon in Selkirk m. Alison Marr ; c. James Marr.
Nov. 6. Alexander Kennedy in Galashiels m. Isabel Brown ; c. David Taylor.
  ,, 20. John Brack m. Barbara Bower ; c. Nicol Milne.
  ,, 23. Robert Kelly m. Isabel Macqueen ; c. George Scott.
Dec. 4. John Millar in Ancrum m. Elizabeth Walker ; c. John Walker.
  ,, ,, Andrew Cook m. Beatrix Porteus ; c. William Cook.
  ,, 11. Charles Hardie m. Anne Fair ; c. John Fair.
  ,, 25. Robert Boston m. Isabel Douglas in Jedburgh ; c. Thomas Boston.
1774.
Feb. 6. James Ronaldson m. Euphan Gray in Selkirk ; c. Andrew Ronaldson.
  ,, 12. George Vair m. Christian Wight ; c. Thomas Scott.
  ,, 26. Thomas Milne m. Mary Shiel in Jedburgh ; c. Nicol Milne.
April 8. James Waddle in Borthwick m. Janet Scott ; c. John Trotter.
May 14. Peter Audison m. Isabel Mercer in Selkirk ; c. Alexr. Brownfield.
  ,, 28. James Cochran m. Isabel Sharp in Minto ; c. Adam Sharp.
July 30. John Elliot m. Isabel Bunnie ; c. Francis Elliot.
Aug. 12. William Forsan m. Margaret Mitchel ; c. Zerubbabel Forsan.
  ,, ,, Thomas Trotter in Smalholm m. Christian Mercer ; c. John Mercer.
Sept. 3. Rutherford Taitt m. Janet Trotter ; c. William Cook.
Nov. 22. John Horsburgh in Galashiels m. Peggy Riddel ; c. Andrew Riddel.
  ,, 26. John Smith m. Mary Williamson ; c. Adam Boyd.
Dec. 1. William Elliot in Eskdalemuir m. Rachel Grieve ; c. James Baptie.
1775.
Jan. 14. George Bell m. Peggy Martin ; c. Andrew Martin.
  ,, 21. Robert Simpson m. Margaret Clapperton ; c. Hugh Grieve.
  ,, 28. Thomas Lillie in Smalholm m. Nelly Laidlaw ; c. Thomas Laidlaw.
  ,, ,, Alexander Skaid m. Isabel Smith ; c. John Smith.
Feb. 4. John Mercer in Maxtown m. Elizabeth Wood ; c. John Grahmslie
Mar. 25. William Turner m. Katharin Marr ; c. James Purves.
April 15. Robert Kerr m. Janet Bulman ; c. George Laurie.
May 6. James Wallace m. Helen Burnet ; c. John Martin.

1775.
May 27. William Waddel in Lauder m. Maron Thyn : c. James Wilson.
,, ,, Thomas Vair m. Peggy Burnet ; c. Robert Vair.
June 3. John Ballantine m. Isabel Milne : c. Robert Ballantine.
,, 10. William Henderson m. Peggy Dickson ; c. William Dickson.
,, 17. Andrew Lockie in Merton m. Peggy Lukup ; c. Adam Boyd.
July 29. George Brownfield m. Janet Waugh ; c. Alexr. Brownfield.
,, ,, Thomas Smith m. Janet Purves in Lauder ; c. Andrew Waddel.
Sept. 2. John Frier m. Peggy Bathgate ; c. Robert Hunter.
Nov. 18. John Goven m. Jean Brownfield ; c. George Brownfield.
,, 22. William Keddie m. Margaret Waddel ; c. Thomas Waddel.
Dec. 2. James Bulman m. Nelly Lunn ; c. John Mercer.
,, ,, James Ballantine m. Margaret Lees in Galashiels ; c. Walter Ballantine.
,, ,, John Murray m. Peggy Sclaiter ; c. John Gill.
1776.
Jan. 13. Thomas Usher m. Jean Mein ; c. John Trotter.
,, 19. Charles Bunnie in Lauder m. Isabel Lillie ; c. William Bunnie.
,, 20. Alexander Brownfield m. Isabel Beanston ; c. George Brownfield.
Mar. 23. George Laurie m. Jean Stoddart ; c. William Cook.
May 11. David Piercie m. May Middlemas ; c. John Calderwood.
,, 16. Thomas Blair m. Agnes Cowper in Stow ; c. David Taylor.
,, 25. Frances Elliot m. Isabel Barcklay ; c. John Elliot.
,, 31. Isaac Wood in Jedburgh m. Jean Boston ; c. Robert Hunter.
June 1. John Learmont m. Agnes Bunnie ; c. Adam Nicol.
,, 5. Walter Ormiston m. Christian Oliver in Selkirk ; c. Robert Robertson.
,, 7. William Fletcher in Yarrow m. Janet Mercer ; c. James Ronaldson.
,, 8. William Dickson m. Isabel Fairbairn ; c. Robert Fairbairn.
,, 15. Andrew Pringle m. Peggy Fammilton ; c. William Pringle.
Aug. 10. John Taitt in Innerleithen m. Margaret Wood ; c. Robert Wood.
,, ,, Thomas Marshal in Ancrum m. Agnes Stirling ; c. James Stirling.
,, 13. John Vallance in Lauder m. Peggy Coats ; c. Andrew Carter.
Sept. 28. David Kyle m. Betty Kedzie in Hawick ; c. James Henderson.
Nov. 9. Thomas Scott m. Margaret Dunn in Ashkirk ; c. Robert Scott.
,, 29. John Robertson in Ancrum m. Christian Pertes ; c. John Robertson.
Dec. 14. James Butler m. Marion Grierson ; c. Robert Grierson.
,, ,, Colin Fairfowl in Selkirk m. Christian Trotter ; c. Robert Trotter.
,, 21. James Clapperton m. Mary Boston ; c. James Boston.
1777.
Feb. 22. Charles Hislop m. Katharine Thynn ; c. Andrew Hislop.
May 17. George Kemp in Bowden m. Janet Haitly ; c. George Kemp.
,, 31. John Forsyth m. Jean Mein ; c. John Mein.
,, ,, William Paterson in Galashiels m. Janet Drummond ; c. William Drummond.
June 6. Archibald Fairbairn in Kelso m. Grizel Fairbairn ; c. Robert Bunnie.
,, 14. Andrew Shillinglaw m. Elspath Mercer in Lauder ; c. William Merten.
,, 28. George Wilson m. Isabel Darling ; c. Adam Scott.
July 5. John Gill m. Christian Hunter in Lessuden ; c. Robert Hunter.
,, 29. Adam Scott m. Alison Brown in Lauder ; c. Andrew Scott.
Aug 1. William Burnat in Earlston m. Isabel Coldcleugh ; c. Thomas Coldcleugh.
Sept. 20. Alexander Skirven m. Peggy Cook ; c. George Skirven.
,, 25. William Wilson m. Betty Mercer ; c. George Laurie.
Nov. 22. Robert Myles m. Isabel Simpson in Earlston ; c. James Marr.
,, 25. John Paterson in Galashiels m. Peggy Bower ; c. James Bower.
Dec. 6. Robert Wight m. Janet Brack ; c. David Thomson.
,, 12. Francis Thomson in Selkirk m. Jean Mein ; c. Alexander Mein.
,, 18. John Sinclair m. Agnes Bunnie ; c. William Bunnie.
,, 20. Thomas Thomson in Galashiels m. Margaret Scott ; c. George White.

2E

1777.
Dec. 20. Robert Bulman m. Peggy Leithin ; c. George Laurie.
1778.
Mar. 21. William Mabon m. Peggy Brown in Lauder; c. William Mabon.
April 25. John Simpson m. Isabel Merchal in Lauder; c. George Scott.
May 16. Thomas Renwick m. Margaret Thynn in Lauder; c. Thomas Renwick.
  „ 23. John Brotherstons m. Jean Steel ; c. James Brown.
  „ „ James Bower m. Agnes Miller ; c. John Bower.
June 11. John Brown in Duns m. Isabel Donaldson ; c. David Kyle.
  „ 13. Robert Grieve m. Agnes Darling ; c. David Kyle.
  „ „ John Mein m. Betty Kersel in Cavers; c. John Forsyth.
July 9. James Fazer in Ednam m. Alison Lees ; c. James Lees.
Aug. 8. George Pringle m. Elizabeth Williamson ; c. James Williamson.
Oct. 17. Alexander Mackdonald in Inverleithen m. Jean Middlemass; c. David Kyle.
Nov. 7. John Swanston in Lauder m. Isabel Louden ; c. David Taylor.
  „ „ William Stevenson m. Janet Mein ; c. John Bower.
  „ 14. Bailie Dods m. Margaret Martin : c. Nicol Milne.
  „ „ Robert Brown m. Elizabeth Henderson ; c. Andrew Bell.
Dec. 5. Francis Corner in Bowden m. Janet Rea ; c. George Rea.
  „ 11. Andrew Lees m. Martha Lorran in Wilton ; c. Andrew Lees.
  „ 19. John Church in Eckford m. Peggy Thomson ; c. Adam Mabon.
1779.
Jan. 14. George Brown in Earlston m. Joanna Donaldson ; c. John Rule.
  „ 16. Robert Elliot m. Jean Scott in Jedburgh ; c. Thomas Clegharn.
  „ 28. William Ailly m. Agnes Darling ; c. William Aillie.
Feb. 18. Robert Bell in Oxnam m. Janet Scott ; c. David Kyle.
Mar. 7. James Brown m. Peggy Butler ; c. Robert Grierson.
  „ 12. William Dickson in Inverleithen m. Mary Turner ; c. William Turner.
April 17. Andrew Riddel m. Betty Knox ; c. Alexander Cook.
May 15. James Thynn m. Helen Wood in Westeruther ; c. James Thynn.
  „ 20. James Wilson in Galashiels m. Betty Aitkine ; c. William Aitkine.
  „ 26. Thomas Cleghorn m. Peggy Bower ; c. Nicol Milne.
June 12. Robert Ormiston m. Nelly Cook ; c. William Cook.
July 3. James Dunlap in Liliesleaf m. Isabel Usher ; c. James Usher.
  „ 31. John Grahamslie m. Mary Ormiston ; c. George Grahamslie.
Aug. 12. William Henderson in Lauder m. Katharine Wood ; c. Thomas Broadie.
Oct. 29. John Sibbald m. Jean Laidlaw ; c. James Laidlaw.
Nov. 20. James Kirkwood m. Jean Fairbairn ; c. Alexander Broomfield.
  „ „ William Cook m. Elizabeth Murray; c. George Laurie.
  „ 26. Richard Jack in Lessudden m. Elspath Williamson ; c. Robert Williamson.
Dec. 4. Walter Gray in Ancrum m. Jean Milne ; c. Thomas Milne.
  „ 10. Hugh Darling m. Margaret Hood in Galashiels ; c. James Ingles.
  „ 18. William Bichet in Bowden m. Jean Martin ; c. Thomas Martin.
1780.
Jan. 8. John Scott in Lauder m. Janet Smail ; c. Adam Smail.
  „ 29. Thomas Hope in Edrom m. Isabel Sanderson ; c. James Sanderson.
Feb. 13. Thomas Boston m. Isabel Boston ; c. John Boston.
  „ 19. John Gowenlock in Selkirk m. Isabel Scott ; c. John Scott.
Mar. 25. George Stoddart m. Katharine Mackall ; c. George Laurie.
April 29. George Herd m. Alison Kyle ; c. Thomas Turnbull.
May 19. William Jackson in Wilton m. Peggy Riddel ; c. Peter Dodds.
  „ 26. Adam Blake in Inverleithen m. Peggy Stevenson ; c. William Stevenson.
Aug. 12. John Lang in Earlston m. Margaret Pringle ; c. William Lang.
  „ „ John Mein m. Nelly Riddel : c. Andrew Riddel.
  „ 26. James Gibson in Smalholm m. Agnes Bunny : c. Robert Bunny.

1780.
Oct. 7. Thomas Purves in Earlston m. Nelly Boston : c. James Boston.
Nov. 3. George Skirven m. Katharine Vogan in Selkirk : c. Alexr. Skirven.
„ 8. George Gray in Stow m. Mary Ogilvie ; c. George Wight.
„ 30. James Scott in Stow m. Peggy Grierson ; c. John Trotter.
Dec. 2. John Young in Liliesleaf m. Janet Slaiter ; c. James Slaiter.
1781.
Jan. 27. Robert Davidson m. Katharine Williamson ; c. Thomas Williamson.
Feb. 17. James Riddel m. Marion Blaikie ; c. William Blaikie.
April 7. John Dickson m. Janet Sibbald ; c. Alexr. Sibbald.
„ 14. William Henderson m. Anne Waugh in Gordon : c. James Weir.
„ „ William Mathison m. Janet Linsay ; c. John Young.
„ 19. Robert Scott m. Elspath Williamson ; c. Peter Hordie.
„ 28. Andrew Taylor in Lauder m. Agnes Phaup ; c. James Usher.
May 5. Peter Cockburn m. Katharine Stewart in Kelso ; c. Robert Kirkwood.
„ 11. John Dickson m. Betty Sanderson in Galashiels ; c. John Dickson.
„ 12. Henry Hop m. Peggy Thomson ; c. John Layel.
„ 26. James Mein m. Isabel Lees in Mertoun ; c. Walter Scott.
June 1. Andrew Aitchison m. Isabel Fairbairn ; c. James Kirkwood.
„ 2. Alexander Laing m. Agnes Anderson in Kelso ; c. David Kyle.
„ 9. Charles Black in the west kirk parish of Edinburgh m. Isabel Nicol ;
c. Adam Nicol.
„ 30. James Williamson m. Agnes Pringle ; c. George Pringle.
July 7. James Lunn m. Nelly Scott in Ashkirk ; c. John Lunn.
„ 28. John Dickison m. Agnes Frier ; c. James Frier.
Aug. 3. Thomas Cossar in Ledgerwood m. Peggy Weir ; c. James Weir.
„ 4. James Shiel in Earlston m. Agnes Cochran ; c. Henry Cochran.
„ „ Thomas Pringle m. Agnes Hardie in Legerwood : c. James Usher.
„ „ John Neil m. Jean Milne in Mertown ; c. David Taylor.
Sept. 29. William Baptie m. Janet Stoddart : c. David Kyle.
Oct. 6. John Douglas m. Peggy Mein ; c. James Mein.
„ 20. William Haitlie m. Bettie Jamieson ; c. James Jamieson.
„ 27. James Stewart in Westruther m. Janet Hilson ; c. Robert Bunzie.
Nov. 22. James Wood m. Elspath Neil ; c. John Laurie.
„ 24. William Miller m. Janet Mein ; c. Andrew Mein.
1782.
Jan. 19. John Muir m. Anne Lyle ; c. John Martin.
„ 26. Andrew Brown m. Janet Smith ; c. Thomas Taylor.
Feb. 9. James Slaiter m. Anne Mein ; c. John Mein.
„ 16. George Pringle m. Janet Blaikie in Bowden ; c. James Williamson.
Mar. 2. John Nicol m. Isabel Mitchel ; c. Robert Stirling.
„ 16. James Ramsay m. Janet Bunnie ; c. George Hogg.
April 6. Andrew Drummond m. Peggy Hetton ; c. Andrew Hetton.
May 6. Joseph Archart m. Isabel Pringle ; c. William Stuart.
„ 24. William Smith m. Peggy Bunnie ; c. John Bell.
„ 25. William Anderson m. Mary Scott in Yarrow ; c. John Anderson.
„ „ Thomas Gray m. Peggy Dunlop ; c. Andrew Hunter.
June 15. John Anderson m. Mary Cuming ; c. George Brownfield.
„ 29. John Welch in Earlston m. Barbara Grierson : c. James Williamson.
Aug. 3. George Lithgow m. Peggy Neil ; c. James Slaiter.
„ 24. William Thomson in Stow m. Janet Purves ; c. Thomas Darling.
Oct. 10. Thomas Brown m. Agnes Laurie ; c. Thomas Brown.
Nov. 16. John Stevenson m. Isabel Waugh ; c. William Martin.
„ 29. Robert Kirkwood m. Isabel Sibbald ; c. James Usher.
„ 30. Alexander Curle in Stitchel m. Peggy Ormiston ; c. Adam Ormiston.
1783.
Jan. 11. Francis Corner m. Margaret Beatie in Bowden ; c. Nicol Milne.
„ „ Robert Watt in Earlston m. Alison Hamilton ; c. David Watt.
„ 17. James Mersel in Lessuden m. Margaret Bunnie ; c. Robert Bunnie.
„ 18. John Martin m. Marion Heitton ; c. John Martin.
May 17. John Paterson m. Isabel Henderson; c. Robert Brown.

1783.

May 23. Alexander Maillen m. Elizabeth Forsayth in Gordon; c. John Forsayth.

„ 24. John Lumisdon in Stow m. Betty Turner; c. David Taylor.

„ 28. John Cathie m. Mary Cairns in Borthwick; c. John Cathie.

June 14. Andrew Sanderson m. Jean Scott in Lauder; c. Alexander Scott.

July 5. Thomas Elliot in Selkirk m. Janet Scott; c. James Scott.

„ 26. David Pringle in Smalholm m. Elspath Thyn; c. David Pringle.

Sept. 5. George Buchan in Hunam m. Mary Williamson; c. James Williamson.

„ 25. Robert Walker m. Janet Lang in Lessuden; c. Robert Walker.

Oct. 17. John Rutherford in Westruther m. Janet Mein; c. James Slaiter.

„ 25. William Gray in Kelso m. Jean Turnbul; c. John Turnbull.

„ „ John Dabson in Gallashiels m. Margaret Skirven; c. Henry Hope.

Nov. 1. John Jack m. Agnes Jones in Earlston; c. John Elliot.

„ „ John Haldon m. Isabel Brown; c. David Kyle.

„ 8. Mr. Archibald Dickson in Minto m. Miss Marion Fisher; c. Mr. Andrew Fisher.

„ 21. Andrew Fairbairn m. Margaret Henderson in Jedburgh; c. Thomas Mairtin.

„ 22. Peter Clarke m. Anne Scott in Martin; c. Alexander Mein.

„ 25. William Vallance m. Peggy Cockburn; c. John Cockburn.

„ 28. John Bower m. Nelly Davidson; c. James Bower.

1784.

Jan. 3. Robert Boston m. Kathrane Graham; c. James Graham.

April 24. George Lees in Galashiels m. Mary Brownfield; c. Alexr. Brownfield.

Aug. 21. John Dunwoody in Cockpen m. Isabel Mitchel; c. John Dunwoody.

Dec. 19. Thomas Welsh m. Betty Lunn; c. James Usher.

„ 28. Alexander Brockie in Mertoun m. Violet Collyer; c. Gideon Collyer.

1785.

Jan. 1. David Kyle m. Anne Scoon in Selkirk; c. John Kyle.

Mar. 19. John Middleton m. Mary Bunzie; c. Robert Bunzie.

April 9. Andrew Ritchie m. Isabel Renwick in Selkirk; c. Andrew Bell.

„ 15. William Valance m. Elspath Brown in Westeruther; c. James Vair.

„ „ George Bathgate m. Alison Purves in Makerston c. George Bathgate.

May 14. George Bell m. Nelly Mercer; c. Andrew Bell.

„ 21. Robert Wilson m. Alison Hislop; c. George Huntly.

„ „ William Wilson m. Beatrice Richardson; c. William Wilson.

June 9. John Burn m. Grizel Ingles in Selkirk; c. John Walker.

Aug. 20. James Mitchel in Channelkirk m. Marion Darling; c. James Mitchel.

Oct. 15. Andrew Hoy m. Anne Fair; c. John Martin.

„ 22. William Dabson in Galashiels m. Betty Butler; c. Robert Grierson.

„ 29. George Vair m. Katharine Ballantine in Martown; c. John Martin.

Nov. 19. William Watson in Galashiels m. Janet Sanderson; c. John Sanderson.

„ 24. Peter Easton m. Anne Biggar in Eckford; c. Robert Easton.

Dec. 12. Mr. William Elder m. Miss Isabel Mein; c. John Shields.

„ 17. James Sanderson m. Mary Haldon; c. Alexander Sanderson.

1786.

Jan. 7. John Smith m. Margaret Oliver in Cavers; c. John Wright.

„ 28. John Musgrave m. Ketty Jamieson in Lessuden; c. John Jamieson.

Mar. 17. Robert Chisholm in Stow m. Nelly Tait; c. Walter Tait.

May 6. John Whillace in Ancrum m. Alison Mein; c. John Douglas.

„ 27. George Mercer m. Janet Fairbairn; c. George Brownfield.

June 3. William Mackintosh m. Peggy Haldon; c. James Sanderson.

„ 10. Thomas Lunn m. Alison Sanderson; c. John Sanderson.

„ 17. Mr. John Johnston in Lauder m. Peggy Gibson; c. Andrew Gibson.

„ „ Andrew Shiel in Lauder m. Betty Cleugh; c. John Cleugh.

„ 24. Mr. David Ovens m. Miss Anne Young in North Leith; c. John Martin.

July 1. William Hoy m. Janet Sibbald; c. John Smith.

1786.

July 22. Thomas Clodcleugh in Dalkeith m. Anne Speeden ; c. James Dalgliesh.

Aug. 15. William Thomson in Stow m. Betty Hunter ; c. John Hunter.

Oct. 28. William Laidlaw m. Nelly Cochran ; c. William Cochran.

Nov. 1. John Thomson m. Agnes Wilson in Westeruther ; c. John Thomson.

,, 4. Thomas Williamson m. Peggy Watson in Stow ; c. John Smith.

,, 22. John Louden m. Anne Welsh ; c. Thomas Welsh.

,, 28. George Graham m. Joanna Riddell in Yarrow ; c. John Graham.

Dec. 16. John Goven m. Agnes Matheson in Yarrow ; c. John Goven.

,, 23. William Johnston m. Isabel Cochran ; c. William Thomson.

1787.

Jan. 13. John Dickieson in Innerleithen m. Katharine Scott ; c. William Scott.

,, ,, Adam Wilson m. Agnes Douglass ; c. George Mercer.

,, 20. Andrew Thomson in Liliesleaf m. Christian Usher ; c. Andrew Heitton.

,, 27. George Lithgow in Earlston m. Alison Mercer ; c. Andrew Mercer.

Feb. 3. William Speeden in Bowden m. Peggy Bunzie ; c. William Bunzie.

,, ,, Robert Wilson m. Betty Moffat ; c. John Cutherston.

,, 17. John Sinclair m. Alison Mein ; c. David Sinclair.

April 17. William Brown m. Isabel Williamson ; c. Thomas Stark.

,, 21. Robert Pringle m. Agnes Burnet ; c. Frances Burnet.

July 14. Thomas Scott m. Isabel Scott ; c. James Scott.

Aug. 18. Alexander Bell m. Peggy Stewart ; c. George Stewart.

,, 25. Mr. Samuel Davidson m. Miss Christian Anderson ; c. Mr. Archibald Anderson.

Sept. 15. Thomas Macculoth m. Janet Murray ; c. William Cook.

Nov. 22. William Niel in Selkirk m. Anne Forrest ; c. John Forrest.

Dec. 1. George Heitton m. Janet Scott in Maxton ; c. Alexr. Stonhouse.

,, 8. James Frier in Merton m. Agness Usher ; c. John Dickieson.

,, 15. James Brown m. Isabel Hudson *alias* Scott in Alwinton ; c. James Brown.

,, 22. John Scott m. Betty Frier in Merton ; c. Andrew Ronaldson.

,, ,, James Kemp m. Christian Skirven ; c. Alexander Skirven.

1788.

Feb. 1. John Pile m. Janet Dickson in Westeruther ; c. James Wilson.

,, 23. Robert Robertson m. Isabel Hart ; c. Robert Hart.

April 5. James Telford in Liliesleaf m. Peggy Ramsay ; c. George Hogg.

May 24. John Nicol in Dalkeith m. Isabel Murray ; c. William Cook.

,, ,, Robert Smith m. Christian Dods in Merton ; c. Andrew Smith.

June 14. George Scott in Kelso m. Betty Butler ; c. Robert Grierson.

,, 28. John Grieve in Lessudden m. Isabel Marr ; c. James Marr.

Aug. 9. Alexander Sanderson m. Helen Philips ; c. Andrew Philips.

Oct. 11. John Coldcleugh m. Margaret Coldcleugh ; c. George Coldcleugh.

Nov. 15. James Mercer m. Margaret Scott ; c. James Mercer.

Dec. 13. John Marr m. Janet Hallady in Merton ; c. James May.

,, ,, Thomas Hardie in Ledgerwood m. Catharine Marr ; c. James Marr.

,, ,, Peter Wilson in Peebles m. Janet Lees ; c. John Lees.

1789.

Jan. 17. Walter Riddell in Selkirk m. Isabel Heiton ; c. John Heiton.

Mar. 6. John Pringle m. Mary Mather ; c. Richard Lieshman.

,, 28. William Martin m. Grizel Hall ; c. John Martin.

May 9. Andrew Ronaldson, writer in Melrose, m. Margaret Smith, only lawful daughter of the deceased John Smith, Esq., late of Philadelphia, N. America ; c. Andrew Riddle.

,, ,, John Haldean m. Beety Scott ; c. Walter Turnbull.

July 17. John Mitchel m. Christian Tinline in Crailing ; c. James Nicol.

Oct. 18. James Chrichton in Smailholme m. Helen Speeden ; c. John Dickison.

,, 31. William Walker in Stow m. Janet Coats ; c. Andrew Martin.

Nov. 14. John Hunter m. Jean Riddell ; c. Andrew Ronaldson.

,, 21. John Sanderson m. Isabel Grieve ; c. Richard Lees.

1789.

Nov. 21. Thomas Usher m. Betty Stevenson ; c. William Stevenson.
,, ,, William Galloway m. Euphans Scott ; c. William Cook, James Brownfield.
,, 24. John Young in Earlstone m. Dolly Burn ; c. John Haldean.
,, 28. John Heiton m. Janet Elliot in Lauder ; c. Robert Heiton.
,, ,, William Dunlop m. Margaret Vair ; c. John Usher.
,, ,, Andrew Morton m. Janet Lockie in Galashiels ; c. ——.
Dec. 5. Hugh Sanderson in Galashiels m. Mary Watson ; c. James Watson.

1790.

Jan. 5. Robert Kemp in Stow m. Jean Graham ; c. Robert Boston.
Feb. 20. David Sinclair m. Margaret Hart ; c. Robert Hart.
May 1. Robert Nicol m. Margaret Heart ; c. James Nicol.
,, 22. Peter Sanderson m. Betty Henderson ; c. Robert Hymers.
June 2. William Johnston in the West Kirk parish of Edinburgh m. Nelly Bunzie ; c. John Sibbald, Robert Bunzie.
,, 5. Francis Burnet m. Joan Williamson ; c. Andrew Bell.
,, 17. John Cairns in Hawick m. Isabel Fairbairn ; c. Robert Grierson.
,, 19. James Rutherford in Wilton m. Agnes Hog ; c. Andrew Hog.
,, ,, John Rule in St. Cuthberts, Portsburgh, m. Mary Cuningham ; c. Robert Purves.
,, ,, William Cochran m. Ann Sanderson ; c. Alexr. Bell, Robert Burnet.
July 9. Walter Tait m. Margaret Sanderson ; c. Hugh Sanderson.
Aug 7. Robert Morton in Holy Island m. Isabel Bower ; c. Andrew Morton, Nicol Milne.
Oct. 14. William Scot m. Janet Temple ; c. Robert Hymers.
,, 22. John Wright m. Isabel Crombie ; c. John Trotter.
Nov. 20. John Friar in Galashiels m. Elizabeth Welsh ; c. John Loudon.
,, 23. Charles Mitchelhill in St. Boswells m. Euphans Slater ; c. John Slater.
Dec. 18. James Nicol m. Alison Mein ; c. William Bunzie.
,, ,, William Wallace m. Agnes Bell in Morebattle ; c. George Burnet.

1791.

Jan. 1. Andrew Heart m. Margaret Pringle ; c. Andrew Bell.
,, 14. Thomas Kinimins in the parish of Selkirk m. Janet Stewart ; c. Alexr. Bell.
Feb. 5. George Hewit in Earlstone m. Elizabeth Scot ; c. James Scot.
Mar. 5. John Mathison m. Ann Scott in Lantown ; c. George Stewart.
,, 12. William Caldcleugh m. Ann Forrest ; c. John Forrest.
April 16. John Paterson m. Mary Turnbull ; c. William Paterson.
,, ,, William Scot m. Margaret Huntley ; c. George Brownfield.
May 14. John Paterson m. Agnes Cunningham ; c. John Lees.
,, 21. John Moss m. Elizabeth Dunlop in Ashkirk ; c. ——.
,, ,, Rev. Mr. George Thomson, minister, m. Miss Peggy Gillon ; c. Thomas Gillon.
,, 26. George Lugtown m. Janet Lawson in Humbie ; c. ——.
June 1. Adam Young m. Rachel Lun ; c. Thomas Lun.
,, — Booked Robert Heymer and Elizabeth Miller in Stitchel.
,, 11. Thomas Laidlaw m. Janet Davidson in Jedburgh parish.
,, 17. Andrew Pringle m. Rachel Easton ; c. William Pringle.
,, 25. Robert Thomson m. Agnes Turnbull ; c. John Turnbull.
July 2. Robert Usher m. Agnes Lorrain ; c. James Martine.
Aug. 5. John Hope m. Isabel Dickson in Legerwood ; c. Mr. John Gray.
,, 20. William Mathieson m. Janet Henderson.
,, ,, Robert Penman m. Isabel Pringle ; c. James Pringle.
Oct. 1. James Wilson m. Rabbina Stewart ; c. George Stewart.
,, 8. Richard Blaikie m. Mary Aitken in Wilton.
Nov. 5. James Thomson in Galashiels m. Mary Buttler ; c. James Hunter.
,, ,, Walter Ronaldson m. Janet Wight ; c. James Brownfield.
,, 24. James Rutherford in Ancrum m. Elizabeth Park ; c. John Park.
,, 26. James Scot m. Agnes Dalgliesh ; c. James Dalgliesh.
Dec. 3. James Wight m. Mary Ronaldson ; c. James Brownfield.

1792.
Feb. 3. James Wilson in Galashiells m. Mary Scot ; c. John Young.
„ 10. George Taket in Galashiels m. Mary Hall ; c. Robert Taket.
Mar. 24. James Moffat m. Margaret Usher ; c. John Usher.
April 28. George Litster m. Agnes Sibbald in Selkirk ; c. Thomas Cleghorn.
May 5. Robert Crosbie m. Margaret Walker ; c. James Crosbie.
„ 9. George Rea m. Mary Murray in Bowden ; c. David Murray.
„ 26. William Nicol m. Elizabeth Kedie ; c. James Usher.
June 9. Thomas Sibbald and Janet Wight in Ancrum ; c. Alexander Sibbald.
„ 30. John Watt in Earlstone m. Isabel Hamiltone ; c. Alexander Hamiltone.
Aug. 11. Andrew Heiton m. Isabel Govan ; c. John Martine.
„ „ William Edgar m. Christian Waugh in Yetholm ; c. Walter Ronaldson.

1791.
Aug. 1. John Paterson m. Margaret Stewart in Bowden ; c. William Cook.

1792.
Sept. 1. Alexander Scot m. Margaret Mathison ; c. William Mathison.
Oct. 13. James Ballantyne m. Janet Scott ; c Alexander Skirvan.
„ 27. Alexander Cook m. Janet Boston ; c. Alexander Skirvan.
Nov. 3. John Vair m. Isabel Lunn ; c. Thomas Dickson.
„ „ William Smith m. Margaret King.
„ 11. James Scott m. Janet Pringle in Earlston ; c. George Pringle.
„ „ James Brown m. Helen Forsyth ; c. William Hague.
„ 22. Andrew Lees in Stow m. Mary Lamert ; c. Thomas Fairgrieve.
Dec. 1. John Rutherford m. Catharine Turnbull ; c. James Bower.
„ „ Thomas Draughill m. Margaret Thomson ; c. John Buchan.
„ „ John Turnbull m. Alison Noble ; c. William Turnbull.
„ 8. Richard Lees m. Mary Paterson in Galashiels ; c. William Craig, writer in Galashiels.

1793.
Feb. 3. George Mercer m. Isabel Smith ; c. Mr. David Murray in Greenwells.
April 6. Robert Laidlaw m. Agnes Fairbairn in Legerwood : c. Andrew Martin.
„ 13. James Thomson m. Margaret Stewart ; c. John Turnbull.
May 5. John Lees in Galashiels m. Isabel Grieve in Melrose ; c. Mr. Blaikie.
„ 11. William Brown in Galashiels m. Isabel Watson ; c. John Lees.
June 1. Alexander Denholm m. Margaret Thorburn in Galashiels ; c. Andrew Ronaldson.
„ 2. Adam Loch m. Elizabeth Wallace in Westruther ; c. George Loch.
„ 5. James Stirling m. Beatrix Watherston in Gordon ; c. Thomas Scott.
„ „ James Friar in Stow m. Jane Annison ; c. John Lees.
„ „ Andrew Martin m. Nelly Thin ; c. Thomas Pringle.
„ 8. John Usher m. Janet Oliver in Chesters ; c. John Usher.
„ 22. William Watson m. Janet Gouvenlock in Galashiels ; c. John Dickison.
„ 29. John Darling m. Isabel Williamson ; c. John Martin.
July 19. James Melrose m. Mary Brown ; c. John Wright.
Aug. 2. James Lamert in Merton m. Mary Williamson ; c. Mr. Friar.
„ 10. William Chisholm m. Janet Sclater ; c. John Sclater.
Nov. 22. James Oliver and Isabel Lumsdain ; c. Walter Scott.
„ „ William Stirling in Bowden m. Margaret Campbell ; c. James Stirling.
„ „ Robert Burnet m. Janet Burnet in Galashiels ; c. Alexander Bell.
„ 29. Thomas Williamson m. Jessy Hall in Selkirk ; c. Robert Williamson.
„ 30. William Scott m. Margaret Dickson in Smaillholm ; c. George Scott.
Dec. 6. James Burnet in Robertown m. Isabel Forrest ; c. John Forrest.
„ 12. James Cochrane in St. Boswells m. Agnes Mein : c. Alexander Mein.

1794.
Jan. 11. James Walker m. Janet Sclater ; c. John Dickson.
„ 18. Thomas Scott m. Alison Home ; c. William Home.

1794.
Mar. 1. Walter Fletcher in Yetholm m. Agnes Laidlaw ; c. John Sibbald.
April 19. John Weir in Ashkirk m. Isabel Henderson ; c. James Ballantyne.
May 2. James Simm m. Margaret Clapperton in Galashiels ; c. Thomas Clapperton.
„ 23. Alexander Adamson in Wilton m. Betty Gillies ; c. David Kyle.
„ 25. Robert Peacock in Westeruther m. Isabel Jamieson ; c. John Martin.
„ „ John Watson m. Isabel Blake in Galashiels ; c. William Fairbairn.
June 1. John Leech m. Isabel Robinson in Sprouston ; c. David Sinclair.
„ 7. Thomas Kerr m. Janet Scott ; c. James Scott.
„ 14. George Cranston m. Dolly Easton ; c. John Bell, Robert Nicol.
July 19. William Haldane m. Jane Richardson in Galashiels ; c. John Haldane.
„ 26. Alexander Skirven m. Agnes Dickson in Galashiels ; c. Charles W. Mercer.
Aug. 9. Mr. William Elder, minister of Newtown, m. Miss Margaret Rodger in Selkirk ; c. Alexander Mein.
Sept. 6. John Lindsay in Dalkeith m. Alison Mein ; c. John Mein.
„ 13. James Watson in Kelso m. Elizabeth Sanderson ; c. William Brown.
Nov. 1. John Cochran m. Elizabeth Hogg ; c. John Gray.
„ 29. James Henderson m. Isabel Aitkin ; c. Henry Hope.
„ „ Andrew Young m. Mary Bett ; c. John Graham.
Dec. 30. John Winter m. Helen Hogg ; c. James Broomfield.
1795.
Jan. 17. Robert Gray m. Janet Sanderson in Earlstoun ; c. William Thinn.
Mar. 15. Thomas Grieve m. Elizabeth Mercer ; c. Andrew Mercer.
April 18. Walter Wilson m. Isabel Martine in Earlstoun ; c. John Mercer.
May 2. Walter Purves m. Helen Porteous ; c. John Simpson.
„ 5. Thomas Wilson m. Joan Pentland in South Leith : c. Walter Turnbull.
„ 16. David Sinclair m. Margaret Rutherfurd ; c. Alexander Pringle.
„ 27. Charles Kerr in Earlstoun m. Helen Easton ; c. Robert Easton.
May 23. John Shiel in Gordon m. Janet Scott.
June 3. John Dickson in Stow m. Isabel Cleugh ; c. John Cleugh.
July 10. Andrew Herkness in Bowden m. Janet Mathison ; c. William Herkness.
Aug. 8. Alexander Tudhope m. Isabel Turner : c. John Murray.
„ 22. John Scot in Ashkirk m. Janet Mercer ; c. Andrew Heiton.
„ „ Francis Smith in Glasgow m. Christian Taket ; c. Robert Taket.
„ 28. John Clark m. Janet Ivly in Lauder ; c. John Mercer.
Oct. 17. William Mitchell m. Margaret Burnet ; c. John Burnet.
„ 29. George Cunningham in Hawick m. Betty Cook ; c. Robert Heymers.
Nov. 4. John Forrest m. Christian Boston ; c. George Bruce, Esq.
„ 7. James Grieve m. Janet Brydon ; c. John Haldane.
„ 13. James Clark m. Helen Henry ; c. Robert Henry.
„ 29. Rev. Alexander Hunter, minister of Herriot, m. Janet Lees ; c. Richard Lees.
„ „ Alison Fairbairn in Ednam m. William Reidpath ; c. William Moffat.
1796.
Jan. 2. Walter Turnbull m. Euphemia Dickson in Hawick ; c. David Kyle.
Mar. 26. John Sanderson m. Joan Murray ; c. David Murray.
April 9. Alexander Hunter m. Janet Audison ; c. Andrew Bell, Thomas Usher.
May 20. James Millar in Earlstoun m. Elizabeth Heart : c. David Sinclair.
„ 28. James Henderson m. Jean Young in Maxtoun ; c. Alexander Mein.
Aug. 6. James Bunzie m. Anne Thomson in Bowden ; c. Andrew Bunzie.
Oct. 15. George Fairbairn in Neuthorn m. Jean Law ; c. Andrew Moffat.
Nov. 5. Thomas Sanderson m. Helen Martine.
„ „ William Coats m. Grizel Burnet in Merton.
„ „ James Bunzie m. Helen Bruce ; c. Andrew Bunzie.
„ „ Thomas Hislop m. Elizabeth Watson ; c. George Wight.
„ 12. John Simson m. Elizabeth Somervile in Channelkirk.

1796.

Nov. 18. Henry Purves in Channelkirk m. Alison Moffat.

" 22. Andrew Renwick in Smailholme m. Jean Hamilton ; c. William Hamilton.

Dec. 2. Thomas Elliot m. Mary Scot.

1797.

Feb. 17. Francis Scot m. Margaret Hislop ; c. James Scot.

Mar. 11. Serjeant Hugh M'Kay of His Majesty's 31st Regiment of foot m. Margaret Wright.

April 7. Robert Murray in Selkirk m. Helen Leithead ; c. John Leithead.

" 8. William Mercer m. Janet Heart ; c. John Wright.

May 14. James Lees m. Isabel Robb in Galashiels ; c. Thomas Sanderson.

June 7. William Leithead m. Janet Thomson in Liliesleaf ; c. John Leithead.

Aug. 19. William Thin m. Janet Broomfield ; c. Walter Turnbull.

" 26. Benjamin Tait in Dalkeith m. Agnes Stirling ; c. James Stirling.

Sept. 20. James Mather, serjeant in the 31st Regiment of foot, m. Jean Grieve ; c. John M'Laron.

Oct. 14. James Nicol in Earlstoun m. Agnes Lockie.

" " David Brown m. Margaret Shiell in Legertwood ; c. James Clark.

" 29. William Smart m. Janet Paterson ; c. James Wilson.

Dec. 2. Alexander Pringle m. Barbara Millar ; c. James Pringle.

1798.

Jan. 1. John Cochran m. Margaret Vair ; c. Thomas Vair.

" 6. John Bullman m. Christian Gibson ; c. William Wilkieson.

" 13. William Dickson in Earlstoun m. Margaret Goodfellow ; c. James Goodfellow.

" 20. William Wilkison m. Agnes Hay ; c. Walter Thomson.

Mar. 3. George Huntly m. Betty Speeden in Bowden ; c. George Broomfield.

" 8. David Ballantyne in Galashiells m. Margaret Watson ; c. William Brown.

" 31. Thomas Haig m. Mary Sibbald ; c. Thomas Boston.

May 5. William Turner m. Janet Keddie ; c. Robert Miles.

" 12. Robert Inglis m. Agnes Eckford in Stow ; c. James Blaikie.

" " William Millar m. Margaret Lambert : c. Robert Heymer.

" 20. James Fish m. Isabel Tait ; c. Nicol Milne.

" " John Blaikie m. Mary Stevenson ; c. George Brodie.

June 23. Thomas Currie in Eckford m. Agnes Hamilton ; c. George Brodie.

" " James Scot m. Agnes Lindsay ; c. George Brodie.

July 7. William Easton m. Elizabeth Robertson in Stow ; c. James Blaikie.

" 14. Robert Scot m. Martha Smail in Ancrum ; w. James Scot.

Aug. 27. Rev. Mr. William Balfour in Bowden m. Miss Mary Mein ; c. James Hume, Esq.

Nov. 4. William Matthews, soldier in His Majesty's 31st Regiment of foot, m. Grace Henderson ; c. Robert Thorp, serjeant.

" 8. Robert Carruthers m. Mary Scott ; c. Robert Scott.

" 24. Robert Taket m. Janet Martine ; c. William Taket.

" " James Nicol m. Elizabeth Harper ; c. John Harper, junior.

Dec. 8. Robert Heiton, weaver, m. Elizabeth Fisher ; c. Andrew Heiton.

" 29. George Henderson, militiaman, m. Isabel Fairbairn ; c. David Fairbairn.

1799.

Jan. 12. John Cleugh m. Janet Tait ; c. James Tait.

" 26. James Scot in Bowden m. Martha Leithead ; c. John Leithead.

" " John Laidlaw m. Christian Clapperton in Lauder ; c. Robert Laidlaw.

" " Robert Anderson m. Jean Burton ; c. David Burton.

" " Thomas Laidlaw m. Margaret Scot ; c. Robert Laidlaw.

April 13. Andrew Brown in Galashiells m. Elizabeth Anderson ; c. William Fairbairn.

May 25. Andrew Cunningham m. Mary Turner ; c. Thomas Bell.

" " Alexander Mitchel m. Janet Hunter ; c. John Martine.

June 1. William Weatherstone m. Agnes Forsythe.

1799.
June 1. Robert Tait m. Margaret Brown ; c. William Hume.
  ,, 8. William Tait m. Isabel More ; c. Thomas Sanderson.
  ,, 15. Thomas Henderson m. Agnes Young in Bowden ; c. Alexander
      Kinghorn.
Nov. 16. Robert Gladstones in Innerleithen m. Janet Law ; c. Archibald Law.
  ,, ,, John Hatton m. Isabel Brown in Maxton ; c. Andrew Brown.
  ,, 22. John Purdy in Eddlestone m. Elizabeth Leithead ; c. John Leithead.
  ,, 30. William Swanstone m. Agnes Rae ; c. Gilbert Rae.
Dec. 7. William Mein m. Janet Millar ; c. James Mein.
  1800.
Jan. 4. Robert Fairbairn m. Peggy Elliot ; c. Mr. James Milne.
Feb. 15. Thomas Vair m. Janet Burnet in Newstead ; c. George Burnet.
  ,, 22. Thomas Smaill in Lessuden m. Agnes Hunter ; c. John Gill.
Mar. 1. William Home m. Peggy Home ; c. David Kyle.
  ,, 3. Walter Thomson in Stow m. Agnes Hislop ; c. John Hall.
  ,, 28. Thomas Brydon in Ancrum m. Mary Tait ; c. Adam Brydon.
May 10. Robert Easton m. Euphan Lees in Earlston ; c. Andrew Bunzie.
  ,, ,, James Lambert m. Isabel Dalgliesh.
  ,, 17. George Monilaws m. Isabel Govan ; c. Alexander Broomfield.
June 7. Andrew Scot in Selkirk m. Elizabeth Scot ; c. Patrick Tait.
  ,, ,, Robert Davidson, gardener in Stow, m. Christian Laidlaw ; c. William
      Young.
  ,, 21. James Scot m. Margaret Weatherstone in Lauder ; c. John Kirkwood.
  ,, ,, Robert Stobs in the barony parish of Glasgow m. Margaret Turnbull ;
      c. John Turnbull.
  ,, 28. Andrew Gibson in Edrom m. Agnes Laidlaw ; c. Robert Laidlaw.
Aug. 2. Thomas Hay m. Janet Smail in Ancrum ; c. James Hay.
  ,, ,, James Mercer m. Alice Hay ; c. James Hay.
Oct. 25. Thomas Bell, weaver, m. Nelly Turner ; c. John Dickson.
Nov. 1. John Mercer m. Euphan Scott in Bowden ; c. Andrew Mercer.
  ,, ,, James Scott m. Flora Tait in Yarrow ; c. Robert Murray.
  ,, 8. George Carter m. Peggy Marr.
  ,, 29. George Noble m. Jean Laurie.
  1801.
Mar. 8. Joshuah Wood m. Isabel Walker
  ,, 21. Robert Murray in Lauder m. Isabel Pringle, who were married 14th
      November 1800.
  ,, 21. Nicol Mercer m. Elizabeth Martine, 15th January 1801.
April 18. William Law m. Betty Linton in Robertown.
May 30. James Turnbull m. Janet Easton.
  ,, ,, James Clapperton m. Joan Cunningham ; c. Hary Cunningham.
June 6. John Leich in Galashiels m. Janet Stevenson.
  ,, ,, Robert Collier m. Jean Dodds on 15th May last at Coldstream.
  ,, 13. James Johnstone m. Peggy Robert in Galashiels.
  ,, ,, Walter Ballantine m. Sally Donald in Bowden.
Sept. 26. Michael Mercer m. Isabel Milne.
Oct. 24. George Brodie m. Mary Stewart in Edinburgh.
  ,, 29. Andrew Livingstone in Lauder m. Jean Brown.
  ,, 31. Andrew Muir m. Peggy Fairbairn ; c. Thomas Fairbairn.
Dec. 12. William Roger m. Anne Boner.
  1802.
Jan. 2. James Scott m. Peggy Grant ; c. John Grant.
  ,, 9. Alexander Broomfield m. Mary Nicol.
Feb. 1. Archibald Tod, Esq. of Drygrange, m. Miss Elizabeth Pringle, second
      daughter to Sir James Pringle of Stitchell, Baronet.
  ,, 6. John Usher m. Agnes Blaikie.
  ,, 27. William Spence m. Katharine Swanstone in Haddockishole, Edin-
      burgh ; c. Adam Ormistone.
  ,, ,, James Goodfellow, cooper, m. Nelly Newlands in Kelso.
Mar. 6. John Thomson, wright, m. Agnes Murray in Cavers.

1802.
April 17. William Laing, labourer, m. Nelly Mabon in Earlstoun.
May 10. George Gray in Galashiels m. Margaret Sandilands in January last.
  „ „ John Lees, clothier, m. Jean Young last year.
  „ 29. William Mathison, weaver, m. Elizabeth Anderson.
Oct. 23. Thomas Houd in Minto m. Catharine Dalgliesh.
Nov. 6. William Runciman in Earlstoun m. Mary Forsythe.
  „ „ Thomas Dods m. Jean Watson.
  „ 13. James Thin m. Peggy Nicol.
  „ 23. John Learmonth m. Agnes Scot in Selkirk.
Dec. 6. George Bell m. Jean White in Lessuden.
  „ „ John Chisholm m. Alice Elliot.
  „ „ Robert Henderson m. Janet Broomfield on 17th November 1802.
  „ — James Pringle m. Margaret Cook on 21st December 1802.
  1803.
Jan. 1. George Stoddart, weaver, m. Agnes Brown in Maxton.
  „ 8. John Boston, wright, m. Janet Dickson.
  „ „ John Brokie in Merton m. Agnes Marshall.
  „ 22. James Rodger in Galashiels m. Nelly Heart.
Feb. 5. William Brokie m. Isabel Cunningham in Merton.
Mar. 12. Thomas Richardson in Smailholm m. Peggy Shortreid.
April 19. John Murray in Selkirk m. Ann Scott.
May 21. James Tait m. Betty Purves in Legertwood.
  „ 22. John Mein m. Isabel Lothian.
July 1. James Martin m. Mary Trotter.
  „ 24. George Scott in Lauder m. Janet Laidlaw.
Aug. 7. Thomas Vair m. Peggy Tait.
  „ „ David Tait m. Barbara Vair.
  „ 27. William Hopkirk, shoemaker, m. Isabel Hume.
  „ „ William Mercer, merchant, m. Elizabeth —— in Darlingshaugh.
Oct. 29. Richard Mitchell m. Betty Turnbull in Ancrum.
Nov. 4. Thomas Burnet m. Margaret M'Dougal in Earlstone.
  „ 5. William Winter m. Isabel Ballantine.
  „ „ Peter Walker m. Jean Lees.
  „ 11. William Purves in Legerwood m. Agnes Bell.
Dec. 2. Robert Brown in Selkirk m. Agnes Scot.
  „ 17. William Dunlop in the parish of St. Cuthberts m. Janet Usher.
  1804.
Jan. 21. James Hopkirk m. Jean Turnbull in Jedburgh.
  „ „ John Tait m. Margaret Sanderson in Duddingstone.
Mar. 17. James Hunter in Galashiels m. Mary Blaikie.
April 7. James Wilson m. Agnes Lees in Selkirk.
May 11. Thomas Brown m. Margaret Thomson in Stow.
  „ 17. James Scott m. Elspet Turnbull.
  „ 26. James Shiel m. Christian Scott.
  „ „ George Blaikie m. Elizabeth Brown in St. Cuthberts.
June 2. James Heatlie m. Margaret Sanderson.
Sept. 22. Andrew Bertram m. Alice Brown.
Oct. 19. Thomas Scot in Hobkirk m. Susanna Bell.
  „ 27. Robert Shillinglaw m. Mary Broomfield.
Nov. 3. Joan Grant m. Mary Scott.
  „ 29. John Turner m. Mary Laidlaw.
Dec. 1. William Chisholm m. Rachel Blair.
  „ 22. David Mills in Eccles m. Martha Scott.
  1805.
Jan. 23. Thomas Mair, mason, m. Janet Heiton.
Feb. 5. James Black m. Margaret Thomson.
Mar. 23. George Caruthers m. Betty Todd in Bowden.
May 11. Alexander Bunzie m. Janet Brown.
  „ „ John Thomson m. Isabel Common.
  „ 25. Thomas Adams m. Margaret Mein

1805.
June 15. John Henderson m. Isabel Linton.
July   7. John Williamson m. Isabel Dickson.
  „   14. John Chisholm in Galashiels m. Elizabeth Callender.
  „   20. John Mein m. Elizabeth Mein.
Aug.   3. William Turnbull m. Elizabeth Hoyle.
  „   17. Archibald Law in Stowe m. Ann Jerdan.
Nov. 16. Andrew Mercer m. Jenny Pringle.
  „   23. Nicol Mercer m. Mary Jamieson.
  „   „ Andrew Hogg m. Margaret Pringle.
Dec. 14. John Cleghorn in Stowe m. Isabel Lees.
  „   „ James Walker m. Margaret Beattie.
  „   „ Robert Pringle m. Jean Laing.
    1806.
Jan. 11. James Young in Merton m. Christian Nicol.
  „   „ James Fairbairn m. Anne Walker in Merton.
  „   18. John Wood m. Mary Dickson.
  „   „ James Turnbull in Bowden m. Janet M'Kenzie.
  „   „ Charles Erskine, Esq., writer in Melrose, m. Miss Barbara Pott,
         residing at Borthwick-sheels, parish of Roberton, daughter of the
         deceast George Pott, Esq. of Todrigg.
Feb. 22. Alexander Russel m. Mary Murray.
April 26. William Greaves m. Elizabeth Grinlay.
May   3. James Greig m. Agnes Watson.
  „   „ Robert Burns m. Betty Dewar.
  „   15. James Ramsay in Liliesleaf m. Barbara Morton.
  „   17. Gilbert Buckless in Swinton m. Margaret Henderson.
June   7. Thomas Cleghorn m. Mary Inglis in St. Boswells.
  „   11. William Scott, younger, of Redburn in this parish, m. Miss Susan
         Horsebrugh of Horsebrugh, in the parish of St. Cuthbert's, Edin-
         burgh.
  „   20. James Renton in Lauder m. Helen Lothian.
  „   21. William Govan m. Betty Cuthbertson in Ednam.
Aug.   3. Andrew Kerr in Selkirk m. Agnes Hilson.
  „   30. William Grant m. Agnes Blaikie.
Sept. 14. Henry Cochran m. Jess Laurie.
  „   15. Robert Walker m. Elizabeth Davidson.
  „   „ Andrew Fairbairn m. Mary Watson.
  „   „ Thomas Wilson m. Mary Scott.
Oct.   4. George Wilson m. Agnes Henry.
  „   „ Willison Glass m. Christian Bicket in Bowden.
  „   11. Thomas Thomson m. Janet Walker in Galashiels.
  „   18. James Vetch m. Peggy Watson.
  „   25. Thomas Scott m. Elizabeth Herbertson.
Nov. 15. John M'Gie m. Agnes Lockie.
  „   „ Thomas Newton m. Mary Elliot.
Dec.   6. George Anderson in Galashiels m. Janet Blaikie.
  „   „ William Kyle m. Janet Fairbairn.
  „   „ William Linton m. Agnes Wight.
  „   „ George Ronaldson m. Margaret Brown.
    1807.
Jan.   3. Andrew Riddell m. Mary Millar.
  „   17. John Young m. Jean Blythe.
Feb. 22. James Renwick m. Janet Freer.
Mar. 29. Thomas Thomson m. Isabel Turnbull.
April 18. William Armstrong m. Peggy Easton.
May   16. James Dodds in Abby St. Bathens m. Isabel More.
  „   23. James Millar m. Grizel Archibald in Bowden.
June   7. John Johnston m. Isabel Somerville in Channelkirk.
  „   14. James Wilson m. Helen Mercer.
  „   21. Thomas Whitehead in Dunse m. Jean Burton.

1807.

June 28. Andrew Lee in Salton m. Christian Edgar.
,, ,, Charles Wilson m. Margaret Mercer in Earlston.
July 4. Charles Turnbull m. Euphan Smith.
,, 11. Robert Walker in Galashiels m. Margaret Dobson.
,, ,, William Freer in Galashiels m. Agnes Murray.
,, ,, Alexander Hamilton m. Mary Steuart.
Aug. 1. James Dalgliesh m. Agnes Mercer.
,, ,, Thomas Gill in Galashiels m. Agnes Redford.
,, ,, At Edinburgh James Borrowman m. Margaret Cook, the certificate
whereof being laid before the session.
Oct. 3. William Allan in Humbie m. Betty Anderson.
,, 31. Thomas Martin m. Isabel Bathgate in Langton.
Nov. 3. James Coldcleugh m. Jean Chisholm.
,, ,, George Watson m. Ann Wheale in Earlston.
,, ,, William Hogg m. Mary Thomson.
,, 14. Andrew Rutherford m. Agnes Sibbald.
,, 28. Robert Geddes in Peebles m. Elizabeth Renwick.
Dec. 5. Lieut.-Col. William Sibbald of Pinnacle in Bowden m. Miss Susanna
Mein, daughter of Thomas Mein, Esq. of Greenwells in this parish.
,, 19. John Salton m. Jean Murray.

1808.

Jan. 2. James Graham m. Janet Shiel in Selkirk.
,, 8. John Gordon in Wilton m. Margaret Cochran.
,, 9. James Cranston in Smailholm m. Betty Moffat.
,, 10. This day Robert Jeffery and Ann Duncan were seriously exhorted
before the session for their irregular marriage and had it confirmed.
,, 15. James Ritchie in Traquair m. Charlotte Nicol.
,, 17. This day Andrew Common m. ———.
,, 23. John Kerr in Earlston m. Jean Nicol.
Mar. 18. John Robson in Dunse m. Elizabeth Douglas.
April 30. Thomas Purves in Smailholm m. Isabel Weatherston.
May 13. Thomas Thomson m. Janet Sibbald
,, 28. William Goodfellow m. Helen Martin.
June 18. George Henderson m. Mary Curle.
,, 25. Andrew Brown m. Margaret Bennet in Selkirk.
,, ,, William Small in Ancrum m. Margaret Walker.
July 2. Andrew Hardie m. Martha Blythe in Selkirk.
,, 23. James Hardie in Yarrow m. Nelly Hume.
,, 28. James Crawford m. Margaret Oliver.
Aug. 14. This day William Moffat and Joan Easton had their irregular
marriage confirmed.
Sept. 10. Robert Small m. Janet Glendenning in Legerwood.
,, 23. John Bowar m. Alison Dove.
,, 24. John Inglis m. Margaret Lockie.
Nov. 11. John Robson m. Helen Hall.
,, 25. Andrew Stevenson in St. Boswells m. Isabel Brown.
,, 26. William Wyllie in Ancrum m. Isabel Gray.
Dec. 31. Robert Stuart in Selkirk m. Agnes Leithhead.

1809.

—— At Edinburgh William Hogg m. Isabel Bruce.
May 7. Samuel Rutherford in Eccles m. Elizabeth Moffat.
,, 12. William Foster in Roberton m. Margaret Forest.
,, 13. John Laidlaw m. Mary Cleugh.
,, 24. Alexander Douglas m. Isabel Henderson in Cavers.
,, 27. James Mathieson m. Isabel Smith.
June 3. Mr. James Watson in Kelso m. Miss Janet Skirving.
,, 10. James Brown m. Jean Sanderson in Galashiels.
,, ,, James Roughead m. Margaret Bell.
,, ,, Robert Paterson m. Margaret Smith.

1809.

June 24. James Mein m. Mary Young in Maxton.

July 16. This day before the session John Skiel m. Margaret Waldie.

Aug. 19. John Turnbull m. Alison Bathgate.

Sept. 9. William Mathieson m. Elizabeth Elliot.

Nov. 11. James Currie m. Margaret Kirkwood in Lauder.

,, 22. Thomas Sanderson m. Margaret Blaikie.

Dec. 10. This day Thomas Park and Mary Redpath appeared before the session and had their marriage confirmed.

,, 23. Thomas Fergrieve in Galashiels m. Ann Mein.

,, 30. James Leadbetter in Stowe m. Dorothea Forman.

1810.

Jan. 20. William Anderson in Galashiels m. Mary Lang.

,, ,, James Murray in Peebles m. Janet Blaikie.

Feb. 24. Robert Lawrie m. Helen Lockie.

Mar. 17. William Dickson m. Isabel Aillie.

April 21. William Tait m. Janet Hume in Bowden.

,, 22. James Tinlin and Jean Johnston compeared before the session and produced a certificate of their marriage, dated at Edinburgh 3rd April 1810, and paid the dues.

May 9. David Crawford in Currie m. Margaret Wilson.

,, 18. William Mercer m. Margaret Haig in Earlston.

,, 25. James Richardson m. Mary Wright.

,, 26. William Blythe m. Alison Tait in Bowden.

June 2. John Noble, High Church parish, Edinburgh, m. Elizabeth Blaikie.

,, 10. This day George Tinlin and Janet Gibson presented to the session a certificate of their marriage.

,, 16. James Johnston m. Elizabeth Martin.

July 6. Alexander Hunter m. Janet Scott.

,, 7. Gilbert Douglas m. Jean Dobson.

Aug. 11. John Stewart m. Agnes Pringle.

,, ,, John Dickson m. Elizabeth Scott.

Sept. 2. James Watson m. Jannet White in St. Cuthberts.

,, 24. James Trotter m. Isabel Thomson.

Oct. 20. John Mercer m. Widow Sanderson in Galashiels.

Nov. 17. John Dodds in Smailholm m. Gulcini Elliot.

,, 22. William Johnston m. Janet Kellie in Gifford.

Dec. 15. John Dickson m. Isabel Boston.

1811.

Jan. 19. Charles Hutchison m. Elizabeth Clapperton.

Feb. 9. Andrew Napier in Stow m. Marrion Henderson.

,, ,, Andrew Mercer m. Elizabeth Brown in Ancrum.

April 6. Robert Penman m. Janet Ainslie in the parish of Grayfriars.

,, 20. Archibald Grieve in Yarrow m. Agnes Stevenson.

May 4. Adam Russell m. Margaret Hall.

,, 11. David Hopkirk m. Margaret Grieve in the High Church Parish, Edinburgh.

,, 18. William Chisholm m. Janet Forsythe in Biggar.

,, 25. Henry Watson m. Catharine Hume.

,, 29. William Welsh in Legerwood m. Helen Millar.

June 16. This day Arthur Reid and Janet Govan presented a certificate of their marriage at Edinburgh which was sustained.

,, 30. This day John Muir and Barbara Lumsden had their irregular marriage confirmed before the session.

Nov. 4. This day Thomas Dickson and Margaret Patterson in Darnick were married by the Rev. Mr. Thomson. 3s. 6d.

,, 7. At Melrose by the Rev. Mr. Thomson, James Rutherford m. Margaret Forsythe. 3s. 6d.

,, 22. Thomas Edmonds in Earlston m. Agnes Frazer. 3s. 6d.

,, ,, James Graham m. Isabel Renwick. 5s. 3d.

Dec. 27. Thomas Laing m. Betty Wood. 5s. 3d.

1812.
Jan.　20. Alexander Turnbull m. Euphan Davidson in St. Boswells.　5s. 3d.
　,,　29. James Gibson m. Elspeth Scott in Bowden.　3s. 6d.
Feb.　12. George Hamilton in St. Boswells m. Isabel Ormiston.　5s. 3d.
　,,　　,,　William Foggo m. Jean Allan.　7s.
May　3. George Pringle in St. Boswells m. Janet Elliot.　7s.
　,,　9. John Laidlaw m. Mary Nicholson.　7s.
　,,　22. Alexander M'Kenzie m. Elizabeth Turner in Stowe.　7s.
　,,　,,　Robert Rankin m. Susan Hogg.　3s.
　,,　,,　James Mercer m. Rachel Aitchison in Galashiels.　7s.
June　28. William Oliver in Jedburgh m. Eleanor Davidson.　6s.
　,,　28. Archibald Stewart m. Christian Paton in St. Boswels.　6s. 9d.
Aug.　11. William Orr in Lauder m. Helen Robertson.　6s.
Sept.　12. James Conquir in Dalmeny m. Mary Ann Shiels.　6s. 9d.
Oct.　6. Alexander Stenhouse m. Esther Riddell in St. Boswells.
　,,　31. Robert Young in Dunse m. Mary Stenhouse.
Nov.　21. Thomas Murray m. Anne Mercer, both of Galashiels.
　　1813.
Jan.　9. Thomas Hope m. Agnes Knox in Fala.
Feb.　6. Alexander Young m. Margaret Gillies.
　,,　,,　David Wilson in Stitchel m. Elizabeth Mien.
　,,　,,　James Learmont m. Mary Young in St. Boswells.
Mar.　20. George Stewart m. Janet Sanderson, Buckholmside and Kerrsfield.
　,,　,,　James Gray m. Mary Robison in Newtown.
　,,　27. William Ovans m. Christian Tait in Innerleithen.
　,,　,,　James Wood in Channelkirk m. Grisel Kerr.
April　3. Joseph Shillinglaw m. Margaret Bennet.
May　23. Robert Ballantyne in Selkirk m. Iellan Girvan.
June　20. Alexander Turnbull m. Agnes Blaikie.
　,,　,,　Alexander Keltie m. Ann Fair.
July　5. Thomas Richardson in Morebattle m. Jean Laidlaw.
Aug.　14. John Gray m. Isabel Wetherston.
　,,　,,　John Watson in Earlston m. Janet Fairbairn.
　,,　21. William Smith m. Helen Scott.
　,,　,,　William Willans in Ridgerton m. Jane Elder.
Oct.　23. Thomas Ballantyne m. Jean Douglas.
　,,　30. Francis Brown m. Helen Craig.
Nov.　14. Robert Scott m. Jessy Millar.
　,,　,,　Michael Broad m. Helen Walker.
　,,　,,　David Young in Ancrum m. Anne Davidson.
Dec.　24. Alexander Blaikie m. Isabel Henderson.
　　1814.
Jan.　— Robert C. Lockhart in Lesmahagow m. Eliza Kyle.
　,,　— John Lun in this parish m. Mary Clapperton in Galashiels.
　,,　— William Johnstone m. Alice Cairns.
　,,　— Thomas Fairbairn m. ——.
Feb.　— Robert Richardson m. Helen Darling.
　,,　— James Cherry m. Betty Lun.
　,,　— Duncan M. Church m. Betty Robertson in Kelso.
Mar.　7. John Hall m. Mary Ronaldson.
April　11. John Laidlaw m. Beatrix Laidlaw.
　,,　,,　Andrew Millar m. Janet Easton.
　,,　,,　George Graham m. Betty Allen.
　,,　18. Walter Thomson m. Wilhelmina Tait.
　,,　,,　James Robison m. Jean Lockie.
　,,　,,　John Scott m. Christian Coulter.
　,,　,,　William Armstrong in Earlston m. Agnes Laidlaw.
May　16. John Smith m. Mary Hume in Bowden.
　,,　,,　James Hupper in Earlston m. Grizle Waldie.
June　6. James Chisholm m. Helen Wood.
　,,　20. Thomas Taylor m. Isabel Bunzie.

1814.
June 20. William Niel m. Douglass Ainslie.
Aug. 8. Peter Maxwell m. Agnes Lees.
  „   „ Walter Ormiston m. Nancy Brown.
  „ 29. Adam Stewart m. Margaret Coldcleugh.
Sept. 6. David Brown m. Betty Mercer.
Oct. 11. John Robison m. Margaret Macclauchlan in Fala.
  „ 16. Thomas Scott m. Alison Blythe.
  „ 29. Robert Usher m. Betty Scott in Wilton.
Nov. 6. James Craig m. Isabella Cockburn in Berwick.
  „ 12. Andrew Robertson m. Elisabeth Thomson in Merton.
Dec. 2. Thomas Newton m. Agnes Robson in Kelso.
  „ 11. James Nevan m. Margaret Cochrane.
  „ 31. Nichol Brack m. Christian Linsay in Kelso.
1815.
Jan. 7. John Lambert m. Frances Fergrieve.
  „ 14. James Hall m. Helen Thorburn in Galashiels.
  „ 28. Andrew Knox m. Janet Lermont.
  „ 29. Charles Stewart Henry m. Isable Mylne. An irregular marriage, but confirmed by the session.
Feb. 18. Charles Simpson m. Margaret Romanes in Lauder.
Mar. 4. William Baxter in Melrose m. Margaret Wood in Earlston.
  „ 25. Andrew Smith m. Agnes Ketchen.
May 7. Francis Henderson m. Mary Hislop.
  „ 13. John Welsh m. Alison Lunn in Galashiels.
  „   „ William Thomson m. Janet Slight in Lauder.
  „ 28. John Dunning m. Janet Pringle.
June 4. George Wise, grocer in the parish of St. George's, Edinburgh, m. Helen Dove.
  „ 23. Oliver Young m. Isabel Slater.
July 8. Robert Gill m. Margaret Smith.
Aug. 27. George Fortune m. Elizabeth Lockie.
Sept. 23. David Spence m. Helen Brodie in Whitekirk, Haddingtonshire.
Oct. 6. John Matheson m. Jean Lisle.
  „ 28. Andrew Marr m. Elizabeth Ronaldson.
Nov. 25. Thomas Bryden m. Alison Mylne.
Dec. 9. John Bower m. Margaret Scott.——
       (A marriage forgot here.)
  „ 31. Thomas Lunn m. Margaret Ritchie.
1816.
Jan. 5. William Lee m. Margaret Inglis, both residing at Buckholmside.
  „ 21. James Sanderson in Buckholmside m. Elisabeth Walker in Galashiels.
  „   „ Thomas Ferguson in Cavers m. Ivine Walker in Newton in this parish.
  „ 27. John Grieve m. Helen Chisholm in Blainslie.
  „   „ William Drydon m. Elisabeth Dobson.
June 2. Alexander Skirvin m. Margaret Mercer in Stow.
  „   „ James Curle, writer in Melrose, m. Isabella Romanes in Lauder.
  „   „ John Drummond m. Marion Lumsdan in Borthwick.
  „ 16. Robert Crease m. Isabella Luke.
  „   „ Thomas Sanderson m. Alison Brown.
  „   „ Alexander Paterson m. Jean Sibbald.
  „ 23. George Crawford m. Elisabeth Hogg.
  „ 29. John Sinclair m. Janet Wight.
July 7. Walter Tait m. Nancy Oliver.
Aug. 4. George Davidson m. Margaret Bleakie in Selkirk.
  „ 18. Andrew Mercer, Lochbreast, m. Mary Yellowlees in West Kirk, Edinburgh.
1816.
Feb. 28. James Blackie m. Beney Hogg in Selkirk.
Sept. 9. Gordon Waynes m. Elspeth Young in Morbattle.
  „ 15. Adam Ormiston m. Margaret Wilson.

1816.

Sept. 15. George Scott in Galashiels m. Janet Fisher.
,, 29. Captain James Steedman of His Majesty's 26th Regiment of foot, son to James Steedman, Esq. of Whinfield, Kinross-shire, m. Miss Sophia Mercer of Broomhill, only child of the deceased James Mercer, Esq. of Broomhill, in the parish of Melrose and county of Roxburgh.
Oct. 6. Thomas Dickson m. Lilies Gibson.
,, 20. William Thomson m. Jean Turnbull in Bowden.
Dec. 3. Simon Bathgate m. Euphan Aitchison in Minto.

1817.

Jan. 1. Francis Tait m. Janet Goodfellow in Galashiels.
,, 20. James Leithhead in Galashiels m. Jean Chisholm in Melrose.
Feb. 17. David Knox m. May Ewans in Selkirk.
Mar. 2. Richard Laidlaw m. Janet Tait.
April 6. James Hislop in Merton m. Elizabeth Purves.
,, ,, Hugh Hall m. Margaret Coldcleugh.
,, 13. William Cowan m. Helen Anderson.
,, ,, James Turnbull m. Euphan Robson.
May 4. John Forrest m. Elisabeth Frier.
June 2. Thomas Smith m. Jean Turnbull in Minto.
,, 15. John Laing m. Agnes Anderson in Maxton.
,, 22. Thomas Davidson m. Janet Sime.
Nov. 2. George Summers m. Isabel Scott in Galashiels.
,, 9. George Long in Earlston m. Mary Pennycook.
,, ,, Alexander Matheson m. Elisabeth Notman.
,, 30. William Murray in Kelso m. Janet Bell.
Dec. — Richard Wardrobe m. Ann Brackenrige.
,, — George Frazer m. Margaret Wood.

1818.

Jan. 12. William Walker at Darlingshaugh m. Helen Inglis in Selkirk.
Mar. 15. George Fisher in Galashiels m. Mary Jamieson.
April 19. George Laudreth in Roxburgh m. Margaret Bunzie.
,, 26. Andrew Stenhouse in Appletreeleaves m. Agnes Easton in Little Catpair in Stow.
,, ,, Andrew Robertson in Blainslie m. Elisabeth Gibson.
May 10. James Brown at Haugh-head in Earlston m. Elisabeth Clerk.
,, 25. John Rae at Eildon Mains m. Agnes Ainslie at Rutherford in Maxton.
,, 31. John Smith, builder in Darnick, m. Alison Purves in Housebyres.
June 8. James Walker, stockingmaker, m. Janet Chisholm, both in Darlingshaugh.
,, ,, Andrew Ferguson in Selkirk m. Janet Boston.
Aug. 3. John Lisle in Denholm m. Jean Turnbull.
,, 10. Andrew Bruce m. Janet Darling.
,, 17. James Rickets in Sprouston m. Janet Henderson.
Sept. 27. Walter Cook m. Elisabeth Wight.
,, ,, Thomas Milton m. Helen Lunn.
Oct. 12. Robert Milne in Langlands m. Catharine Hunter in Newtown.
,, 26. James Dickson, surgeon in Darlingshaugh, m. Janet Jeffrey at New-keltoun in Loch Carron, Ross-shire.
,, ,, James Burnet m. Janet Thomson, Gattonside. An irregular marriage confirmed by the session in August 1818.
Nov. 23. Charles Hope m. Agnes Dickinson, both in Gattonside.
Dec. 21. William Fairgrieve m. Jean Bunzie.
,, 28 Thomas Dods, Drygrange mill, m. Jean Pringle in the parish of St. Cuthberts in the West Church of Edinburgh.

1819.

Jan. 18. Alexander Jaffray m. Euphemia Scott, both at Langshaw.
Feb. 2. Thomas Murray m. Margaret Sime.
,, ,, William Brown m. Margaret Waynes.
,, 28. James Scott, flesher in Melrose, m. Mary Wight. An irregular marriage confirmed.

2F

1819.

Mar. 15. William Merton m. Sara Adams, both in Gattonside.
  ,, 29. James Elliot in Newstead m. Margaret Graham in Sprouston.
April 11. John Ker in Crailing m. Elisabeth Dods.
  ,, 19. John Kemp, brewer, m. Margaret Browne.
May 18. Walter Elliot, shepherd at Hawkburn, m. Isabella Pringle at Yare in Selkirk.
  ,, ,, James Frier in Colmslie m. Janet Brown in West Kirk, Edinburgh.
  ,, ,, James Sime m. Mary Paterson, both in Darlingshaugh.
  ,, 29. William Mack in Dalkeith m. Helen Young.
  ,, ,, James Henderson m. Elisabeth Thomson.
July 12. James Lambert in Ashkirk m. Jean Melrose.
  ,, 19. Alexander Lumsden m. Elisabeth Scott in Hawick.
Aug. 2. William Douglas in the parish of St. George, Edinburgh, m. Margaret Usher.
  ,, 16. James Cochrane m. Isabell Lumsdel in Crichton.
  ,, ,, James Storie in Galashiels m. Janet Watson.
  ,, 23. George Craigie Laurence, watchmaker, m. Helen Turnbull.
  ,, ,, Gideon Brockie m. Catharine Tinline.
Nov. 8. George Redpath in Channelkirk m. Alison Welsh.
  ,, 15. Robert Turner in Earlston m. Helen Shillinglaw.
  ,, 29. James Mein in Stow m. Janet Leithhead.
  ,, ,, Thomas Suddan in Stow m. Christian Shillinglaw.
Dec. 6. James Thomson m. Ann Cochrane.
  ,, ,, William Watson in Morbattle m. Mary Tait.
  ,, 20. John Paterson in Dalkeith m. Mary Lees in Buckhamside.
  ,, ,, John Shiel in Earlston m. Janet Caverhill.

1820.

Jan. 10. Andrew Laidlaw m. Isabell Boyd.
  ,, 17. James Clerk m. Isabella Ramsey.
  ,, ,, William Johnson in Earlston m. Janet Matheson.
Feb. 14. George Mercer m. Margaret Nichol.
  ,, 28. Robert Speden in Bowden m. Elisabeth Fairgrieve.

IV.—Mortuary Roll.

The following Entries and "Mort Roll" are extracted from the volumes of the Session Minutes in the hands of the Kirk Session of Melrose, and through the kindness of the Rev. R. J. Thompson, M.A., Minister of the Parish, the Editor has been permitted to print them. The second Mort Roll from 1781 is in the Register House, Edinburgh.

A MORT ROLL OR REGISTER OF THE DEAD.

Date.	Names.	Places.	Ages.
1760			
Dec. 25	George Lawrie	Danieltown	84
1763			
June 3	James Hardie, a child	Blainslie	7
,, 5	Alexander Dalgleish	Darnick	36
July 4	Ann Wight	Darnick	—
,, 21	Francis Hoy	Melrose	18
Aug. 15	William Stonhouse	Earlstown	50
,, 28	Helen Mercer	Darnick	49
Sept. 5	John Stonhouse	Lessuden	75
,, 17	John Young, a child	Westhouses	3 mths.
,, 19	William Hood	Melrose	14
,, 30	John Milne	Newtoun	70
Oct. 23	Alexander Redfoord	Eildon	4
Nov. 5	Elspath Lumsdale	Gattonside	68
,, 11	Margaret Brown	Newstead	76
,, 25	Margaret Pringle	Bridgend	68
,, 28	Joseph Shillinglaw	Gattonside	81
Dec. 13	William Mercer	Gattonside	78
1764			
Jan. 21	Margaret Grahamslie	Danieltoun	2
,, 29	Margaret Illes	Gattonside	61
Mar. 16	Isabel Notman	Melrose	42
,, 19	Mary Mein	Newstead	82
,, 25	John Turnbull	Gattonside	75
,, 29	Margaret Riddell	Gattonside	100
April 11	Margaret Mein	Newstead	72
,, 12	Helen Pringle	Newstead	1
,, 14	Helen Smith	Darnick	38
,, 24	Isabel Hunter	Lessuden	60
May 1	Nicol Milne, a child	Newtoun	3 mths.
,, 7	Betty Brown	Melrose	12
,, 8	John Fyfe	Newstead	40
,, 10	James Young	Gattonside	30
,, 11	Christopher Walker	Newtoun	72
,, 24	James Bunzie	Newstead	81
June 10	Jean Hislop	Newstead	12
,, 16	Nelly Elliot	Melrose	36
July 2	William Wallace	Melrose	75

Date.		Names.	Places.	Ages.
1764				
Aug.	15	Andrew Main, a child	Newstead	5 mths.
„	16	John Taylor, a child	Melrose	1
Sept.	2	Margaret Paterson	Overchatto	50
„	18	Martha Inglis	Gattonside	17
„	„	John Brown	Blainslie	—
„	26	William Hopkirk	Melrose	51
Nov.	11	William Neil	—	57
„	21	Hugh Morton	Gattonside	19
Dec.	26	—— Scott, a child	Gattonside	4 mths.
„	28	Andrew Mein	Newstead	52
1765				
Jan.	28	James Wallace	Blainslie	71
Feb.	14	George Stewart	Gattonside	75
„	„	Robert Sibbald	Gattonside	44
Mar.	10	Robert Ormston	Gattonside	81
„	12	Margaret Mercer	Darnick	80
„	27	Cathrine Mercer	Cartlihole	80
April	4	John Haitlie	Hislop	18
„	7	James Wilson	Eildon	80
„	15	Jean Thomson	Brummihill	—
„	27	Janet Glendinning	Darnick	50
May	7	Isabel Fisher	Darnick	63
„	29	George Knox	Faldonside	1
June	2	George Hatton	Melrose	4½
„	4	Allison Mein	Newstead	59
„	11	Thomas Vair	Newstead	22
„	19	Betty Graham	Darnick	9
July	13	James Drummond	Old Melrose	56
Aug.	14	Mary Darling	Darnick	74
„	„	Alison Little	Newstead	74
„	18	Thomas Bunzie	Eildon	71
„	26	Robert Forsan	Melrose	75
Sept.	3	Elspath Walker	Melrose	—
„	19	Isabel Dickson	Eastfield of Newtoun	27
„	21	Andrew Bowar	Newtown	49
Nov.	14	Robert Johnston	Melrose	63
„	„	Adam Grahamslie	Danieltown	½ year
Dec.	22	Margaret Lumsdale	Newstead	27
1766				
Jan.	19	William Drummond	Bridgend	11 mths.
„	20	Mary Rutherford, a child	Bridgend	6 weeks
„	29	Jean Kerr	Bleachfield	67
Feb.	8	John Baxter	Bleachfield	7
„	18	Elizabeth Waugh	Melrose	13
„	20	Andrew Drummond	Bridgend	4 mths.
„	22	Peggy Young, a child	Gattonsidehaugh	1½
Mar.	2	Janet Grieve	Melrose	76
„	20	Elspeth Anderson	Gattonside	58
„	26	Thomas Milne	Newtown	71
April	13	James Rutherford	Melrose	7
„	14	Walter Murray	Melrose	75
„	26	Janet Turner	Calthill	74
„	28	John Vair	Newstead	21
May	6	Jean Pringle	Newstead	57
„	11	David Wood	Old Melrose	38
„	14	James Mercer, a child	Gattonside	4 mths.

Date.	NAMES.	PLACES.	Ages.
1766			
May 29	Babie Mein	Newstead	62
Aug. 13	Anne Moffat	Maxton	36
„ 25	James Fisher	Darnick	5½
Sept. 1	George Mercer lost his life in Tweed, a little below Galafoot and his body was found at Cragover Sept. 13.		
Oct. 22	Robert Ballantyne, a child	Melrose	6 mths.
„ 29	Miss Anne Elliot	Melrose	82
Nov. 1	John Burton, a child	Danieltoun	11 mths.
„ 10	Margaret Chisholm	Bridgend	68
Dec. 9	Walter Ballantyne, a child	Melrose	2 mths.
„ 13	James Howden	Darnick	21
„ 23	Susanna Rutherford	Melrose	56
„ 25	Mr. William Hunter	Gattonside	93
1767			
Jan. 6	Janet Fisher, a child	Darnick	4 mths.
„ 7	John Fiddes	Gattonside	101
„ 19	Helen Dodds	Danieltoun	16
„ 23	Janet Wilson	Danieltoun	55
„ 27	Jean Brock	Melrose	89
„ 31	Janet Mercer	Bridgend	62
Mar. 22	Agnes Mein	Newstead	55
April 19	Helen Marr	Newstead	47
„ 21	Isabel Symson	Newstead	62
„ 24	Thomas Hilson, a child	Melrose	3
May 15	Agnes Dawson	Melrose	10
„ 18	Andrew Mein, a child	Newstead	12
June 6	Anne Orr	Melrose	10½
„ 16	Margaret Darling	Melrose	54
July 7	Robert Grierson	Darnick	74
„ 14	Jean Gillies	Melrose	65
„ 27	John Skirving, a child	Bleachfield	1½
„ „	William Matheson	Gattonside	83
Aug. 25	James Smith	Darnick	55
Oct. 17	Margaret Moffat	Melrose	58
„ 31	Janet Watson	Bowden Muir	55
Nov. 5	Janet Mercer	Newstead	59
Dec. 1	Marion Myles	Darnick	
„ 3	Adam Dods	Danieltoun	24
„ 23	Isabel Ballantyne	Melrose	60
„ 27	George Paxton	Melrose	66
„ 29	Mary Brown	Bleachfield	68
1768			
Jan. 7	Alison Hunter	Gattonside	56
„ 8	Isabel Taylor	Danieltoun	59
„ 9	Agnes Smith	Gattonside	86
„ 10	Thomas Young, a child	Gattonside	3 mths.
„ 13	David Grieve	Newtown	62
„ 18	Andrew Stewart	Gattonside	52
„ 20	George Walker	Melrose	84
„ „	Robert Inglis	Gattonside	22
„ 30	John Marr	Gattonside	72
„ 31	Janet Dalgleish	Gattonside	22
Feb. 3	Thomas Marr, a child	Melrose	10 days
„ 9	Thomas Rea	Gattonside	69
„ 16	Andrew Morray, a child	Melrose	2 mths.
„ „	Katherine Sprots	Darnick	19
Mar. 6	Marion Ormiston	Melrose	80

Date.		NAMES.	PLACES.	Ages.
1768				
Mar.	29	Janet Halliwal	Gattonside	—
April	21	Elspath Grierson	Darnick	74
,,	23	George Hart	Newstead	36
May	7	Elspath Turner	Gattonside	22
June	6	James Dickson	Friarshall	61
,,	21	Thomas Vair	Newstead	66
July	6	Thomas Vair, a child	Bleachfield	2 weeks
,,	20	James Ronaldson, a child	Melrose	11 mths.
Aug.	18	Peter Notman	Darnick	47
Nov.	7	Alexander Macfaden	Melrose	84
,,	,,	Marion Lauder	Melrose	56
,,	17	James Vair, a child	Melrose	1
,,	27	John Bowie	Melrose	63
Dec.	13	Janet Frier, a child	Westerhousebyres	9 mths.
,,	26	Margaret Scott	Gattonside	76
1769				
Jan.	14	Nicol Mar, a child	Newtown	$1\frac{3}{4}$
Feb.	3	Helen Lauder	Blainslie	40
Mar.	2	Jean Scott	Westhouses	33
,,	6	Samuel Mein, a child	Newstead	4 mths.
,,	22	Janet Simpson	Gattonside	80
April	10	Isabella Smith	Darnick	31
,,	17	Isabella Ballantine	Melrose	53
,,	21	Peggy Forrest	Westhouses	22
,,	24	Miss May Gordon	Melrose	52
,,	25	Janet Rea	Melrose	45
,,	26	Andrew Hope	Melrose	30
May	26	Robert Whitelaw	Melrose	15
,,	,,	Alexander Scott	Blainslie	62
,,	27	Anne Bowie	Melrose	67
,,	29	William Hog	Newstead	24
,,	30	William Haitlie	Hilslop	63
June	22	John Bruce	Melrose	71
,,	25	Thomas Nicol, a child	Drygrange	5 mths.
July	7	Richard Nicol, a child	Drygrange	6 ,,
,,	26	Peggy Lindsay	Gattonside	9
,,	30	John Leyden, a child	Melrose	$1\frac{1}{4}$
Aug.	4	Thomas Williamson, a child	Gattonside	$1\frac{1}{4}$
,,	13	Margaret Marr, a child	Gattonside	3
,,	17	Janet Ronaldson, a child	Melrose	$3\frac{1}{2}$
,,	20	James Boston, a child	Gattonside	3
,,	21	Isabel Taket, a child	Melrose	$1\frac{1}{4}$
,,	22	William Gillies, a child	Melrose	$4\frac{1}{2}$
,,	24	Barbara Trotter	Melrose	34
,,	26	Christian Mean, a child	Newstead	$1\frac{1}{4}$
Sept.	2	Margaret Orr, a child	Melrose	$3\frac{1}{2}$
,,	7	Thomas Turnbull, a child	Gattonside	$8\frac{1}{2}$
,,	,,	Margaret Fairbairn, a child	Melrose	$1\frac{3}{4}$
,,	9	Joseph Gillies, a child	Melrose	$1\frac{3}{4}$
,,	12	Christian Forsan	Melrose	60
,,	13	Janet Heart, a child	Newstead	$2\frac{1}{2}$
,,	18	George Heart, a child	Newstead	5
,,	25	James Bunzie	Eildon	32
,,	,,	Elizabeth Marr, a child	Melrose	$4\frac{1}{4}$
,,	26	Agnes Muir, a child	Melrose	$2\frac{1}{4}$
,,	28	Jean Marr, a child	Melrose	$2\frac{1}{4}$
Oct.	1	Peggy Barclay, a child	Newtown	2

Date.		NAMES.	PLACES.	Ages.
1769				
Oct.	2	Wm. Barclay, a child	Newtown	¾
,,	3	Janet Riddell	Gattonside	—
,,	6	John Young, a child	Gattonsidehaugh	3 mths.
,,	9	Peggy Dods, a child	Melrose	,, ,,
,,	12	George Drummond	Darnick	7½
,,	14	James Lumsdale, a child	Newstead	1½
,,	15	Robert Milne, a child	Newtown	1
,,	16	Isabel Milne, a child	Newtown	4½
,,	22	Isabel Mein, a child	Newstead	⅔
,,	23	Margaret Steel	Melrose	58
,,	28	James Mein	Newstead	8
Nov.	8	Agnes Davidson	Drygrange	50
,,	11	Peggy Vair, a child	Newtown	1 7/12
,,	16	Katherine Stonehouse, a child	Newstead	6 5/12
Dec.	8	Thomas Brown	Westhouses	31
,,	11	Agnes Dods	Darnick	14
,,	12	John Dalgleish	Bridgend	74
,,	15	Peggy Mein	Newstead	40
,,	16	Robert Huntley	Gattonside	—
,,	,,	Isabel Young	Nenthorn	71
,,	18	Agnes Stonehouse	Whitelees	1½
1770				
Jan.	8	Alison Frier	Gateside	53
,,	12	Ann Macfaden	Melrose	44
Feb.	1	John Grierson	Darnick	44
,,	14	Janet Scott	Melrose	57
,,	15	John Mein	Newstead	20
,,	17	Andrew Ballantyne	Melrose	26
Mar.	5	Walter Scott	Danielton	70
,,	7	Helen Brydon	Eildon	70
,,	13	Robert Vair, a child	Melrose	7 mths.
,,	26	Jean Moodie	—	—
April	14	George Mercer, a child	Drygrange	4 mths.
,,	19	John Lun	Darnick	—
,,	,,	Meny Wright	Broadwoodshiel	—
,,	20	Christian Harvey, a child	Bleachfield	1 4/12
,,	,,	Peggy Thynn	Kedsly	21
,,	31	Agnes Brown	Darnick	55
May	3	Robert Mercer	Newstead	—
,,	10	Agnes Steel	Melrose	70
June	8	Agnes Huntley, a child	Gattonside	7/12
,,	10	John Young	Gattonside	66
,,	29	George Brown	Drygrange	—
July	11	Margaret Drummond	Newtown	60
Aug.	15	George Mercer	Darnick	—
Oct.	12	Charles Frier, a child	Maxton	¾
,,	20	Margaret Young	Melrose	80
Nov.	8	Milne Martine	Melrose	23
,,	26	Elizabeth Mein	Darnick	64
Dec.	1	William Wight	Darnick	60
,,	3	Peggie Hilson	Melrose	57
,,	10	Lilly Black	Melrose	8
1771				
Jan.	2	Janet Pringle, a child	Newstead	7 1/12
,,	10	Elizabeth Cook	Darnick	80
,,	30	Robert Myles	Gattonside	83
Feb.	17	Margaret Martin	Melrose	70

Date.		Names.	Places.	Ages.
1771				
Feb.	21	Thomas Inglis	Gattonside	27
,,	26	George Beatie	Bridgend	79
May	7	Agnes Dickson	Melrose	34
,,	19	Miss Margaret Wilkieson	Melrose	33
,,	25	William Muir, a child	Melrose	$9\frac{1}{2}$ mths.
—		Thomas Ovens	Newstead	63
June	14	John Ramsay	Melrose	62
,,	22	Robert Grieve	Maxton	26
July	4	Anne Orr, a child	Melrose	$1\frac{1}{2}$
,,	12	Anne Herdman	Melrose	62
,,	22	Thomas Skirven, a child	Bleachfield	$\frac{1}{4}$
Aug.	3	Mary Purves	Gattonside	56
,,	6	William Forrest	Westhouses	21
,,	17	Andrew Hog, a child	Melrose	$1\frac{1}{2}$
Sept.	4	James Pringle, a child	Melrose	1
,,	7	Dorothea Wilson	Melrose	50
,,	28	James Vair, a child	Melrose	$1\frac{5}{12}$
Oct.	19	John Hope, a child	Melrose	$2\frac{3}{4}$
,,	26	Anne Pringle, a child	Newstead	4
Nov.	23	Anne Lyel	Melrose	66
,,	26	Marion Henderson	Melrose	77
Dec.	2	Archibald Stewart	Gattonside	39
,,	12	Marion Ronaldson, a child	Melrose	$1\frac{1}{2}$
,,	,,	Isobel Wight	Clackmae	70
,,	13	Henry Hood	Dryburgh	19
,,	16	John Hatton	Melrose	15
1772				
Jan.	8	Helen Skirven	Darnick	60
,,	11	Hugh Pringle, a child	Newstead	$1\frac{8}{12}$
,,	16	Marion Bunnie	Melrose	68
,,	18	Colonel Peter Edmonston	Melrose	—
Feb.	2	Mary Hope	Newstead	—
,,	8	Agnes Nefley	Newstead	57
,,	12	Agnes Skirven	Melrose	54
,,	23	John Fairbairn	Newtown	66
—		Margaret Bunnie	Newstead	70
Mar.	6	John Barklay ⎫ Children all		
,,	12	Henry Barkley ⎬ born at one	Newtoun	—
,,	14	Robert Barkley ⎭ birth		
April	21	Thomas Wilson	—	72
May	9	James Wilson	Melrose	17
,,	27	James Rutherford	Melrose	87
,,	31	James Inglis	Gattonside	22
June	14	Robert Scott, a child	Danieltoun	1
,,	21	Mary Helliwall	Gattonside	—
July	5	James Mercer, a child	Newstead	10
Aug.	17	Jane Kerr	Darnick	42
Sept.	30	Nelly Darling	Darnick	55
Oct.	22	Janet Brown	Melrose	47
Nov.	3	Andrew Mein	Newtown	67
,,	28	Annie Aitchison	Newtown	38
Dec.	4	James Pringle	Newstead	13
,,	11	Nelly Fraser, a child	Eildon	2
,,	29	Isabel Broomfield, a child	Melrose	1
1773				
Jan.	1	Jean Lukup	Melrose	49
,,	8	Jean Carmichael	Newstead	78

Date.		NAMES.	PLACES.	Ages.
1773				
Jan.	—	Peggy Penman	Melrose	14
,,	12	Agner Mercer	Darnick	33
,,	14	Agnes Reul	Gattonside	—
,,	25	Elizabeth Scott	Danieltoun	26
,,	29	Alison Ferbairn	Newtoun	—
Feb.	3	Thomas Hoy	Gattonside	75
,,	22	Helen Ormiston	Melrose	19
,,	25	Alexander Cook	Melrose	84
,,	26	Isabel Young	Gattonside	63
		James Caldcleugh	Gattonside	10
Mar.	14	Isabel Wilson	Westhouses	59
,,	16	Thomas Holliwell	Westhouses	75
,,	20	Isabel Hunter	Melrose	28
,,	24	Isabel Thomson	Bridgend	42
April	5	Anne Oliver	Newtown	31
,,	,,	John Tacket	Melrose	12
,,	7	Andrew Barklay, a child	Newstead	5 mths.
,,	10	Mary Mercer	Newstead	59
,,	15	Isabel Hope, a child	Darnick	6 days
,,	—	Margaret Young, a child	Melrose	2½
,,	20	Marion Marr	Melrose	15
,,	23	John Stonehouse, a child	Mainhill	2½
,,	24	Mr. George Byers	Melrose	74
,,	26	Jean Lukup	Melrose	19
May	4	Nelly Barton	Brekenbeg (?)	55
,,	16	George Mein, a child	Newstead	2
,,	—	Betty Cook	Melrose	29
,,	17	Marion Usher	Darnick	57
,,	18	Agnes Forsan	Melrose	47
July	20	William Mein, a child	Newstead	2¼
,,	28	Nelly Drummond	Bridgend	19½
,,	31	Janet Mabon	Newstead	—
Aug.	3	James Vair	Newstead	40
,,	21	Margaret Mercer	Darnick	26
Sept.	4	William Vair	Newstead	40
,,	13	Janet Marr, a child	Melrose	3⁵⁄₁₂
,,	17	John Bell	Melrose	55¹¹⁄₁₂
,,	19	Nicol Mercer	Melrose	32
,,	20	James Smail	Darnick	56
Oct.	30	Charles Hardie	Melrose	44
Nov.	5	Margaret Coldcleugh	Gattonside	57
Dec.	3	Marion Bowie	Melrose	60
,,	8	Janet Usher, a child	Blainslie	½
,,	11	Helen Haitlie	Newstead	—
1774				
Jan.	20	Janet Sandilands	Newstead	44
,,	23	James Frier	Gattonside	53
Feb.	7	Christian Grahamslie	Melrose	70
,,	14	Thomas Bunnie	Newstead	79
,,	15	Margaret Coldcleugh	Danieltown	79
,,	20	William Williamson	Newstead	24
Mar.	1	John Young	Gattonside	9
,,	10	Margaret Mercer	Gattonside	47
,,	21	David Mein	Newstead	24
,,	30	Janet Marshall	Melrose	63
April	1	William Turner	Gattonside	—
,,	3	Janet Cochran	Nenthorn	70

Date.	Names.	Places.	Ages.
1775			
April 18	Janet Oliver, a child	Newtoun	5
May 14	Annie Park	Melrose	22
June 13	Agnes Mercer	Bridgend	24
,, 25	Helen Young	Gattonside	76
July 2	Alexander Fisher, by a fall from his horse	Phains	46
., 13	Andrew Milne, a child	Whitehill	6 mths.
,, 29	Agnes Dods	Melrose	—
Aug. 5	Robert Richardson	Westhouses	22
,, 8	William Martin	Gattonside	59
,, 11	John Young, a child	Gattonside	—
,, 16	Robert Lawrie	Danieltoun	68
Sept. 18	Margaret Wight	Melrose	73
Oct. 11	John Hutton, a child	Darnick	$1\frac{11}{12}$
Nov. 19	David Fairbairn, a child	Melrose	$2\frac{7}{12}$
,, 23	Taylor Young, a child	Gattonside	$2\frac{4}{12}$
Dec. 1	Anne Barrowman	Melrose	32
,, 9	Thomas Heiton, a child	Darnick	3
., 14	Jean Craig	Melrose	78
., ,,	Margaret Darling	Blainslie	68
,, 20	Margaret Simpson	Gattonside	—
1775			
Jan. 3	Isabel Mein	Newstead	—
., 4	Agnes Steel	Melrose	69
Feb. 15	John Stewart, burgess of Berwick	Melrose	22
Mar. 11	Elizabeth Ballantyne	Melrose	63
,, 12	James Marr, a child	Gattonside	3
April 18	Janet Scott	Gattonside	58
., 28	Peggy Boston, a child	Gattonside	5
May 16	George Maclagan, a child	Melrose	$1\frac{10}{12}$
,, 17	Agnes Muir, a child	Melrose	16 days
June 3	Janet Brown	Gattonside	20
,, 18	Iasobel Hart	Newstead	50
., 26	Margaret Boston	Gattonside	76
,, 27	John Beinston	Gattonside	80
July 1	Cornelius Mein, a child	Newstead	$1\frac{3}{4}$
,, ,,	John Burton, a child	Danieltoun	4
., 13	James Fisher	Darnick	70
Aug. 25	John Barklay, a child	Newstead	$1\frac{7}{12}$
Sept. 8	Peggy Mitchell	Westhouses	22
., 20	Robert Fairbairn, a child	Newtoun	$\frac{8}{12}$
., 25	Jean Pringle, a child	Newtoun	$1\frac{1}{2}$
Oct. 3	Peggy Cochran, a child	Newtoun	1
., 6	Jean Cochran, a child	Newtoun	$3\frac{1}{4}$
. 9	George Milne, a child	Newtoun	3
,, 12	Janet Cochran, a child	Newtoun	$3\frac{1}{12}$
Nov. 25	John Bunnie	Eildon	70
Dec. 4	Margaret Marr	Newstead	60
,, 9	Robert Forsan	Nisbet Mill	45
1776			
Feb. 5	Janet Mein, a child	Newtown	5 mths.
., 22	Janet Bulman	Danieltoun	23
Mar. 2	Beatrice Given	Gattonside	30
., 29	Robert Mercer	Bridgend	19
April 12	Agnes Turnbull	Gattonside	62
., 23	Christian Pringle	Bowdon	52
25	Thomas Mercer	Melrose	43

Date.	Names.	Places.	Ages.
1776			
April 26	Robert Huntlie	Gattonside	—
,, 28	Bettie Haitlie	Melrose	—
,, ,,	Alexander Loch, Merchant	Melrose	—
May 24	Janet Brown	Melrose	86
June 7	John Chisholm, a child	Darnick	½
,, 29	—— Anderson	Eildon	—
July 8	Peggy Rea, a child	Newtown	1½
,, 16	Janet Mitchell	Westerboathouse	19
,, 18	Thomas Marr	Melrose	76
Aug. 30	Jessie Will	Newstead	1
Sept. 10	Janet Heiton, a child	Darnick	1¼
,, 19	Andrew Martin	Melrose	75
,, 23	Katherine Wilson	Darnick	71
Oct. 6	Isabel Cuthil, a child	Melrose	2 5⁄12
Nov. 15	Robert Milne	Newtoun	6
,, 29	Peggy Turner	Gattonside	30
Dec. 8	Alison Turner	Langshaw	21
,, 14	John Marton, a child	Newstead	½
,, 18	Wm. Vair	Bridgend	57
,, 29	Thos. Haig, a child	Newstead	4
,, 30	James Hog	Darnick	—
1777			
Jan. 11	Grizel Learmond	Newtown	—
Feb. 4	Peggy Turner	Langshaw	13
,, 16	James Milne, a child	Newtown	1
Mar. 14	Betty Sibbald, a child	Eildon	1
,, 17	John Lauder	Gattonside	70
,, 20	Robert Milne	Whitehill	15
April 9	Marion Thynn, a child	Blainslie	1 1⁄12
,, 10	David Grieve	Deanshall	26
,, 17	John Fairbairn, a child	Newtown	6¾
May 1	Nelly Vair, a child	Highcross	10 days
,, 25	George Heart	Darnick	22
June 14	Agnes Hog	Darnick	46
July 8	Alexander Purves	Westhouses	91
,, 13	William Kerr	Gattonside	—
Aug. 12	James Wallace	Melrose	59
,, 20	John Usher	Toftfield	67
,, 24	John Paterson	Gattonside	60
Sept. 2	William Hog	Darnick	80
,, —	Isabel Hunter	Melrose	73
,, 24	William Rea, a child	Newtown	11 mths.
Oct. 29	Walter Ballantine	Melrose	72
Nov. 3	Jean Elliot, a child	Newstead	6 wks.
,, 4	Elizabeth Dickson	Melrose	85
,, 23	Agnes Vair, a child	Bridgend	5 mths.
,, 24	George Fairbairn, a child	Newtown	5½
Dec. 3	Isabel Moodie	Newstead	78
,, 19	Isabel Milne	Eildon	60
1778			
Jan. 10	Helen Paterson	Melrose	64
,, 12	Janet Darling	Gattonside	62
,, 15	Lilias Leslie	Darnick	65
,, 26	Jean Bunnie	Newstead	—
Feb. 1	Grizel Wilson	Westhouses	80
Mar. 8	Violet Pringle	Melrose	68
,, 20	Christian Cuthel, a child	Melrose	8 mths

Date.		Names.	Places.	Ages.
1778				
April	7	Margaret Dods	Blainslie	37
,,	18	Betty Bulman, a child	Darnick	2½
,,	24	Agnes Hopkirk, a child	Melrose	6 days
May	4	Agnes Smith, a child	Darnick	1 $\frac{7}{12}$
,,	5	Isabel Blackie	Gattonside	72
,,	24	Richard Mein, a child	Newstead	1 $\frac{10}{12}$
June	10	Walter Scott	Dingleton	18 $\frac{11}{12}$
,,	11	Janet Boston	Gattonside	55
,,	—	George Kemp	Melrose	78
July	15	Andrew Cook	Melrose	80
,,	19	Mary Brown	Eildon	39
,,	26	Peggy Elliot, a child	Newstead	2½
Aug.	17	Helen Skirven	Melrose	63
,,	23	Katherine Hope	Melrose	37
,,	—	John Cochran, a child	Newstead	1 $\frac{5}{12}$
,,	30	Margaret Deans	Melrose	—
Sept.	7	Mary Bulman	Darnick	—
,,	13	Andrew Mein	Newstead	43
,,	19	John Darling	Gattonside	15
Oct.	21	Alexander Vair	Danieltown	72
,,	25	Elizabeth Smail	Melrose	22
Nov.	6	Margaret Duncan	Gattonside	—
,,	28	Elizabeth Mercer	Newstead	55
Dec.	17	Peggy Dickson	Bowshank Mill	24
,,	23	James Marr	Melrose	10
,,	30	Christian Usher	Eildon	55
1779				
Jan.	15	Catherine Steel	Newstead	83
,,	28	Andrew Ormiston	Gattonside	57
Feb.	4	Katherine Wright, a child	Melrose	1 $\frac{3}{4}$
,,	24	John Mercer	Bridgend	65
,,	25	Peggie Mein	Longtown	31
Mar.	6	James Gardiner	Earlston	88
,,	11	William Maclagan, a child	Melrose	2 $\frac{10}{12}$
,,	21	Nicol Somerville	Holms (?)	1 $\frac{5}{12}$
April	4	Captain Robert Mein	Newstead	62
,,	18	Belly Goodfellow	Friarshall	10
May	4	Christian Scott	Newstead	50
,,	11	James Heiton, a child	Darnick	5 weeks
June	3	Agnes Scott	Blainslie	70
July	15	John Bell, a child	Melrose	$\frac{5}{12}$
,,	20	Thomas Mercer	Bemmerside	71
Aug.	6	William Milne	Faldonside	9
,,	13	Ann Pringle, a child	Newstead	$\frac{1}{12}$
Sept.	18	Elizabeth Williamson	Newstead	20
,,	23	Helen Barklay	Kittyfield	70
Oct.	17	Agnes Mein	Drygrange	35
,,	28	Agnes Friar	Topfield	95
Nov.	3	Robert Riddell	Darnick	79
,,	20	Charles Hardie	Melrose	28
,,	24	Janet Darling	Blainslie	61
,,	25	Helen Wilson	Bridgend	—
Dec.	9	Alison Haldon	Eildon	64
,,	15	Andrew Smith	Gattonside	90
,,	18	Michael Paterson	Abbotslee	30
,,	20	Nelly Gibson, a child	Melrose	1 $\frac{11}{12}$
,,	25	John Gill, a child	Melrose	1

Date.		NAMES.	PLACES.	Ages.
1780				
Dec.	27	Isobel Vair, a child	Melrose	2½
Jan.	15	Peggy Lawrie	Melrose	70
,,	16	John Helliwal	Gattonside	—
,,	—	Anaple Myles	Newstead	42
,,	19	George Lindsay	Gattonside	10
,,	27	James Sleeden	Bridgend	77
,,	29	Hugh Grieve	Toftfield	75
,,	31	Isabel Helliwal	Gattonside	65
Feb.	3	Walter Murray	Melrose	54
,,	—	Isabel Usher	Darnick	70
,,	8	Agnes Darling	Darnick	61
,,	11	Thomas Dickson, a child	Darnick	1½
,,	—	Anne Taylor	Dryburgh	—
,,	12	John Paterson, a child	Bridgend	4½
,,	14	Marjory Paterson	Gattonside	67
,,	20	Isabel Smail	Gattonside	59
,,	22	John Mercer, a child	Darnick	6
Mar.	5	Isabel Milne, a child	Faldonside	8
,,	11	Frederick Lunn	Darnick	11
,,	,,	John Fisher, a child	Darnick	3½
,,	12	John Dawson	Melrose	85
,,	15	Joseph Vair, a child	Darnick	1½
,,	24	Margaret Alexander	Melrose	68
April	4	Nelly Scott	Newstead	—
,,	9	Janet Paterson, a child	Darnick	1½
,,	—	Francis Waddell, a child	Darnick	1½
,,	11	John Sprott	Darnick	63
,,	13	Margaret Blaikie, age unknown	Newstead	—
,,	19	John Turner	Netherheath	80
,,	25	Margaret Mein	Newstead	27
May	2	William Usher, a child	Topfield	1½
,,	11	Joseph Forrest, a child	Westhouses	1½
,,	25	Margaret Kyle, a child	Melrose	1½
June	13	Isabel Thynn, a child	—	¾
,,	18	Mr. Archibald Somerville	Holms	42
,,	22	John Brown	Gattonside	42
,,	25	Andrew Pringle	Newstead	67
Aug.	17	Jean Liddel, a child	Darnick	1¾
,,	28	Andrew Heart	Newstead	71
,,	31	Janet Bell	Gattonside	71
,,	,,	Elizabeth Cook, a child	Melrose	—
Sept.	6	Charles Stewart	Melrose	27
Oct.	22	Nicol Laidlaw	Peasehill	21
Nov.	11	Christian Speeden	Newtown	40
,,	23	William Lumisden	Melrose	40
,,	,,	Thomas Friar	Easter Longlee	60
,,	26	Janet Rea	Newtown	28
Dec.	3	Thomas Hutton, a child	Darnick	5 mths.
,,	14	Thomas Sclater	Friarshall	28
,,	17	James Vair	Danieltown	35
,,	20	Isabel Shiel	Newtown	50
,,	27	Peggy Marr	Barnhill	27
1781				
Jan.	8	Peggy Drummond	Newtown	66
,,	22	Beatrice Hislop, a child	Gattonside	1½
,,	26	Margaret Tait	Melrose	67
,,	30	John Hay	Hughieshaugh	—

Date.		Names.	Places.	Ages.
1781				
Feb.	1	Elspeth Fife	Newstead	50
,,	6	John Mein	Newstead	37
,,	15	Robert Lookup	Melrose	66
,,	19	Margaret Mercer	Darnick	78
Mar.	6	Robert Grierson	Illaston	32
,,	19	William Farnig	Hayfield	19
,,	31	James Scott, a child	Danieltoun	2½
April	1	Janet Turner	Batts	32
May	3	Marion Wilson	Darnick	82
,,	4	James Bulman	Darnick	36
,,	10	Ann Little	Melrose	9
,,	16	Peggy Friar	Darnick	71
,,	20	John Anderson	Melrose	71
,,	21	Margaret Henderson	Westhouses	73
,,	22	John Hutton	Darnick	62
,,	26	Elizabeth Fiddes	Melrose	70
,,	27	Janet Simpson	Newstead	88
June	7	Margaret White	Melrose	71
,,	12	Henry Forrest	Westhouses	81
,,	,,	Jean Gordon	Melrose	66
,,	23	Thomas Oliver	Melrose	19
July	2	Janet Laurie, a child	Danieltoun	6 wks.
,,	23	Thomas Vair	Danieltoun	80
,,	24	Margaret Waugh	Gattonside	—
,,	25	John Weddell	Darnick	13
Aug.	19	Agnes Yound	Gattonside	49
,,	20	Helen Fyfe	Newstead	52
,,	21	Agnes Bunnie	Smailholm	22

RECORD of MORTCLOTHS extracted from Session Records.

1669.
July 11. Nicol Cochrane.
Oct. 31. Thomas Bell.
Andrew Heiton's mother.
Nov. 7. Andrew Usher.
Margaret Watson.
„ 28. George Wallace's father.
1670.
Jan. 16. John Lowrie.
Marion Shiel.
William Laidlaw.
„ 23. Elspeth Kair.
Feb. 20. Robert Laidlaw.
Mar. 6. Corsbie Bunall.
April 24. Bunzie.
Vair.
1671.
Jan. 29. John Mein's brother's son.
Wm. Wallace's son.
James Edgar and his wife.
Feb. 12. Margaret Baird.
„ 19. David Cook's mother.
April 9. Margaret Elliot.
Marie Mow.
Margaret Mein.
Janet Thomson.
June 18. Henry Milne's daughter.
July 9. George Turner's mother.
Aug. 13. Thomas Eiles.
Sept. 24. Thomas Turner.
James Mertene in Bridgend.
Oct. 8. Nicol Mercer.
Dec. 17. Isabel Mabon.
„ 31. John Barton.
1672.
Jan. 14. Robert Mein.
Robert Halliburton's daughter.
Feb. 28. George Burton and his wife.
Agnes Mein.
Mar. 3. James Moffat.
Barth Walker.
Malie Wilson.
„ 17. Thomas Law.
James Bunzie.
„ 26. Alexander Eiles.
June 16. Andrew Wallace's wife in Bowden.
July 14. Alexr. Mein's son.
Adam Turnbull's wife.
Aug. 11. George Wallace's son.
Oct. 27. George Laurie's wife.
Dec. 29. Isabel Lithgow's daughter.
1673.
Jan. 19. James Mein.
Feb. 2. Wm. Darling's wife.
Thomas Halliburton in Dryburgh.
Mar. 9. Edward Rolmainhouse.
April 6. James Paterson's wife.
May 4. —— Sclaitter's wife.

1673.
May   25. John Moss's mother.
  ,,   28. John Vair's wife.
July 20. Langshaw's son, Gilbert.
Aug.   3. David Brown's son.
  ,,   17. George Moffat's wife.
  ,,   31. Alexr. Redpath.
Sept. 14. Thomas Wallace.
  ,,   28. Walter Vaitche's wife.
Oct. 19. James Hunter.
    1674.
Feb. 15. James Mein's wife.
April 26. Andrew Bunzie's mother.
          John Lourie's wife.
May   10. James Bunzie's wife.
July 19. Robert Wright.
Aug.   9. James Laidlaw.
Sept. 27. Charles Watson's father.
    1675.
May   2. Elspeth Tutop's son.
    1676.
Jan. 23. John Taitt.
    1678.
Feb. 24. Alexr. Bisset's son.
Aug. 11. Wm. Wallace.
    1679.
Feb.   2. Thomas Mar Hunter in Lessuden.
May   18. Andro Heiton.
June   1. Robert Frier.
Oct. 26. Thomas Milne.
Dec.   7. John Halliwell.
          Andro Heiton.
    1680.
Feb. 22. Helen Fisher, in Earlston.
April 18. Allanshaws.
          John Pringle's wife, in Blainslie.
July 25. Alexr. Heiton.
Oct   3. Wm. Fisher's wife.
    1681.
Feb. 27. Robert Rouston's wife.
May   29. Park's wife.
July 10. John Wallace's wife.
    1682.
Jan.   1. John Shiell, in Earlestoune.
Dec. 24. James Usher.
    1683.
Aug.   5. James Pringle.
Nov.   4. Andrew Heiton.
    1684.
Mar.   2. Hilslope.
May   25. George Mercer.
Aug. 10. John Thurburn, in Lessuden.
    1685.
April 26. Thomas Mabon.
May   24. William Bell.
July 26. Marie Daes.
Nov. 25. Bartie Mein's burial.
    1702.
Aug.   5. The velvet mortcloth to the corps of Jannet Blaikie, daughter to
          James Blaikie, in Melrose, 1 : 26 : 00.
          Ane accompt recaved be Robert Hislop for the mortcloths.

1702.
June 22. For the corps of Wm. Fisher, in Newstead, 1 : 16 : 00.
July 6. For the corps of Wm. Millne, in Newtoun, 1 : 16 : 00.
Sept. 17. To corps of Jannet Bower, in Eildon, 1 : 16 : 00.
Oct. 20. To the corps of Mr. John Milne, in Newtoun, 1 : 16 : 00.
  ,, 29. To the corps of Margaret Wilkie, in Redpeth, 2 : 14 : 0.
  ,,   — To the cloth mortcloth to George Pringle child, 0 : 12 : 00.

The following Baptisms have been extracted from the Session
Minutes. Year uncertain, probably between 1652 or 1656.

Andrew Mein, a son named Thomas ; witnesses, Andrew Chisholme
  and Andrew Mein.
April 6. William Hoy, a son named George : witnesses, William and George
  Hoyes.
  ,, 13. James Pringle, a son named John ; witnesses, George Pringle and
  John Pringle.
June 4. William Cairncross, a daughter named Janet : witnesses, James Ker
  and William Wallace.
John Duinent, a daughter named Margaret ; witnesses, William Bell
  and George Halywell.
George Baittie, a daughter named Margaret ; witnesses, John Baitie
  and John Hettoun.
  ,, 29. Thomas Ridford, a son named John ; witnesses, William Wallace
  and Nellie Edgar.
July 9. James Cairncross, a daughter named Jean ; witnesses, John Pringle
  and Thomas Fairgrieve.
  ,, 17. The minister had a son born named Archibald, baptised at Selkirk,
  named William : witnesses, Sir Wm. Scot, younger, and Mr.
  William Elliot, minister at Yair.

And the following Marriages.

1695.
Feb. 10. Adam Darling produced his certificate of marriage with Helen
  Lauder on 14th December 1694.
1696.
Feb. 23. James Wallace produced certificate of his marriage with Ann Waugh.
1697.
July 21. Andrew Lithgow, son to Alexander Lithgow of Drygrange, marriage
  to Margaret Tod proved to have been at Kirknewton on 26th
  August 1696 by Mr. Wrig.
1702.
July 4. James Miln and Helen Glendinning, 12s. Scots.
  ,, 24. Wm. Crosser and Margaret Hardie, 12s. Scots.
Oct. 3. Walr. Lothian and Margaret Scot, 12s. Scots.
  ,, 8. Wm. Logan and Isabel Mersser, 12s. Scots.
Jo. Drummond and Janet Dickson, 12s. Scots.
  ,, 31. Wm. Gill and Margaret Turnbull, 12s. Scots.
Nov. 9. Geo. Lowrie and Margaret Gill, 12s. Scots.
Pat Riddell and ——, 12s. Scots.
Ja. Robson and Eliz. Davidson, 12s. Scots.
Dec. 21. Jas. Brown and Jean Waugh, 12s. Scots.
  ,, 26. Thos. Corsar and Janet Wight, 12s. Scots.
1703.
Jan. 5. Jo. Hounam and Elizabeth Dickson, 12s. Scots.
  ,, 21. James Blaikie and Marion Sclater, 12s. Scots.
James Mein and Jennet Coat, 12s. Scots.

MORT ROLL FROM 1781 IN THE REGISTER HOUSE, EDINBURGH.

Time of Death.	Names.	Places.	Ages.	Diseases or Distempers.
1781				
Sept. 8	James Williamson	Newstead	69	
,, 12	James Hunter	Melrose	62	Peripneumny
,, 23	Janet Scott	Danielton	20	
,, 27	Isabel Brownfield, a child	Gattonside	$1\frac{1}{2}$	
Oct. 6	Jean Corn, a child	Bowdon	$1\frac{11}{12}$	
,, 23	Robert Wallace	Melrose	13	
Nov. 19	Isabel Helliwall	Gattonside	86	
Dec. 5	Agnes Scott	Westhouses	72	
,, 27	Isabel Gill	Melrose	34	
,, 29	Thomas Murray	Melrose	25	
1782				
Jan. 24	William Rea	Newtown	65	
,, 26	Janet Jamieson	Gattonside	78	
Feb. 4	Margaret Bower	Newtown	33	
,, 8	Samuel Gilles	Melrose	49	
,, 16	Agnes Hardie	Yarrow Foord	93	
,, 20	John Forsan	Newstead	—	
,, ,,	Jean Rea, a child	Newtown	2	
,, 24	Thomas Bunnie	Eildon	15	Fever
,, ,,	Isabel Huntlie	Gattonside	24	
Mar. 3	Christian Brown	Gattonside	80	
,, 8	Mrs. Margaret Kerr	Edinburgh	88	
,, 20	Thomas Stonhouse	Whitelees	77	
,, 30	Margaret Matheson	Gattonside	77	
April 3	William Dickson	Bridgend-mains	34	Consumption
,, 22	James Ronaldson, child	Darnick	2	
,, 27	John Turner	Melrose	30	Fever
May 2	Marien Smith	Colmslie	—	
,, 20	Janet Myles	Bridgend	57	
,, 21	James Collier, a child	Darnick	$\frac{3}{4}$	
June 13	John Young	Melrose	45	
,, 22	George Simpson	Newstead	27	Fever
,, 24	William Cook, a child	Melrose	$\frac{7}{12}$	
,, 25	William Barklay	Newstead	$1\frac{3}{12}$	
July 1	Henry Cochran	Newtown	68	
,, 7	George Grahamslie	Danieltown	86	
,, 12	James Jamieson	Darnick	38	Consumption
,, 24	Margaret Mein	Newtown	—	
,, 30	Jean Martin, a child	Melrose	14 dys	
Aug. 16	Betty Kedzie	Melrose	28	Consumption
,, 25	Mrs Anne Paterson *alias* Wilkieson	Melrose	75	Fever
,, 31	Mrs Ann Cranstoun *alias* Simpson	Melrose	74	
Sept. 14	John Turnbull, a child	Highcross	$\frac{6}{12}$	
,, 19	Andrew Cook	Melrose	35	
,, 29	Mary Ronaldson	Darnick	—	
Oct. 4	Betty Lathin	Gattonside	—	
,, 6	John Grahamslie, a child	Jedburgh	2	Smallpox

Time of Death.	NAMES.	PLACES.	Ages.	Diseases or Distempers.
1782				
Oct. 19	Betty Cook	Melrose	20	Consumption
,, 20	Thomas Robertson	Newstead	30	Fever
,, 21	Ann Lyle	Melrose	—	in child-birth
Nov. 2	Janet Atchison	Newstead	67	Fever
,, 8	Nelly Pringle, a child	Newstead	4	An asthma
,, ,,	Robert Mein	Newstead	—	
,, 11	William Heart	Newstead	56	
,, 12	Thomas Heitton	Darnick	7	Fever
,, 20	Isabel Dickson, a child	Darnick	1	Asthma
,, 27	Agnes Beatie	Bridgend	24	
,, 30	Mary Marr, a child	Melrose	4	Smallpox
Dec. 10	Margaret Scott	Melrose	56	
,, 11	Betty Kyle, a child	Hawick	4	
,, 15	Isabel Helliburton	Bleachfield	86	
,, 16	Andrew Pringle, a child	Newstead	$\frac{3}{4}$	
,, 21	Philip Thynn	Coldeanknows	76	
,, 27	Isabel Stoddart	Darnick	67	
1783				
Jan. 29	Alison Liethen	Whitelaw	—	
,, 5	Margaret Young	Newtown	67	
Feb. 15	James Usher	Topfield	14	
,, ,,	John Mein	Newstead	19	
,, 23	Jean Fairfield, a child	Melrose	$\frac{3}{4}$	Chincough
Mar. 3	Isabel Mercer, a child	Melrose	$1\frac{1}{2}$	Chincough
,, ,,	Janet Sclaiter	Newstead	67	
,, 9	James Mein	Newtown	81	
,, 11	David Thomson, a child	Melrose	2	Chincough
,, 12	Barbara Trotter	Newstead	77	
,, 16	Thomas Gill, a child	Melrose	1	Chincough
,, 21	Ann Turnbull	Highcross	10	Chincough
,, 26	Margaret Stoddart, a child	Darnick	—	
,, 28	Elizabeth Pringle	Melrose	—	
April 7	Isabel Brunton	Gattonside	78	
,, 11	Peggy Martin	Melrose	39	Consumption
,, 15	Agnes Thynn	Melrose	70	
,, 16	Jean Elliot, a child	Newstead	$2\frac{1}{2}$	
,, 19	Isabel Heart, a child	Newstead	5	Chincough
,, 23	Janet Scott	Newstead	60	
,, 28	George Dalgliesh	Gattonside	82	
May 6	Agnes Mabon, a child	Newstead	1	Smallpox
,, 8	James Ronaldson, a child	Melrose	$2\frac{1}{4}$	Chincough
,, 9	Alexander Bunnie, a child	Newstead	$1\frac{1}{4}$	Smallpox
,, 15	Robert Baillie, a child	Bridgend	$1\frac{1}{12}$	Chincough and Smallpox
,, 16	Janet Cochran, a child	Newstead	$2\frac{1}{3}$	
,, 17	Ann Purves	Melrose	68	
,, 23	Isabel Paterson	Newstead	71	
,, 24	Andrew Pringle	Newstead	45	Fever
,, 28	Mary Pringle, a child	Newstead	1	
,, 29	James Forsyth, a child	Newstead	3	
,, 31	Mr James Dalgliesh	Melrose	—	
June 13	John Gill	Melrose	80	
,, 20	James Smith, a child	Newstead	3 mths	

Time of Death.		NAMES.	PLACES.	Ages.	Diseases or Distempers.
1783					
July	1	John Mabon	Newstead	66	
,,	2	Andrew Bell	Melrose	6	
,,	10	Robert Skirven	Melrose	12	
,,	25	Isabel Shillinglaw	Maxton	70	
Aug.	23	James Scott	Danieltown	22	
Sept.	11	James Sanderson	Melrose	56	
,,	24	William Barklie	Newstead	70	
Oct.	16	Nelly Pringle	Newstead	56	
Nov.	14	John Mabon	Newstead	4	
,,	24	Agnes Thorburn	Fairninton	52	
Dec.	4	William Goodfellow	Bimmerside	19	
,,	18	Betty Mercer	Bridgend	35	
,,	22	Janet Boston	Melrose	35	
1784.					
Jan.	6	David Mosgrove	Melrose	64	
,,	25	Robert Mercer	Langshaw	57	
,,	27	John Bunnie, a child	Newstead	1¼	
Feb.	9	William Darling	Gattonside	50	
,,	18	Christian Mackfadden	Melrose	—	
,,	,,	William Bell	Gattonside	72	
,,	22	Mary Moar	Bridgend	74	
,,	26	Jean Hoy	Galashiels	70	
Mar.	2	Jean Ormiston	Melrose	84	
April	5	Isabel Ronaldson	Melrose	22	
,,	8	Janet Waugh	Melrose	—	
,,	12	Andrew Fiddes	Gattonside	21	
May	12	James Marr	Melrose	58	
,,	31	Margaret Davidson	Newstead	86	
July	11	Bessie Easton	Melrose	—	
,,	19	Peggy Dods, a child	Lessudden	3 mths	
,,	22	Anne Pringle	Melrose	80	
Aug.	10	Janet Vair	Bridgend	21	
Sept.	1	Isabel Young	Gattonside	46	
,,	9	Janet Rea, a child	Newtown	1½	
Oct.	9	Janet Jack	Newstead	66	
Nov.	10	Helen Hunter	Gattonside	73	
,,	,,	Elizabeth Williamson, a child	Newtown	1¼	
,,	13	John Aitchison	Newstead	61	
,,	17	Janet Hervie	Drybrugh	19	Fever
,,	,,	Agnes Bunnie	Melrose	61	
,,	23	Ann Dickson, a child	Newstead	—	Measles
,,	25	William Mein	Newstead	22	Consumption
,,	26	Andrew Oliver	Newtown	46	
Dec.	10	Agnes Bunnie	Danielton	39	Hydropsy
,,	17	Christian Mitchel	Westboathouse	24	Consumption
,,	,,	Nelly Taitt	Easterhousbyr	19	Consumption
,,	22	Margaret Gaid	Melrose	—	
,,	28	Nicol Fairbairn	Melrose	19	
1785.					
Feb.	7	Janet Matheson, a child	Gattonside	3	Smalpox
,,	11	Isabel Wilson	Melrose	—	
,,	27	Agnes Brydon	Friershall	74	
Mar.	5	Bell Park	Drygrange	15	Consumption
,,	10	Robert Whitelaw	Melrose	61	Palsy
,,	14	Mary Rutherford	Melrose	71	

Time of Death.	NAMES.	PLACES.	Ages.	Diseases or Distempers.
1785				
Mar. 16	Nelly Scott	Gattonside	6	Smallpox
,, 22	Charles Morton, a child	Newstead	9 mths	
,, 23	John Mercer	Bridgend	70	
,, 24	Andrew Turnbull, a child	Gattonside	9 mths	Smallpox
,, 28	Hugh Cairncross	Newstead	—	
April 1	Andrew Ronaldson	Melrose	22	Consumption
,, 8	Christian Wight	Danielton	58	Appoplexy
,, 11	Nelly Dawson, a child	Melrose	5	Smallpox
,, ,,	Agnes Bell	Newstead	79	
,, 16	John Hardie	Melrose	19	Consumption
,, 23	John Murray	Melrose	21	
,, 27	Walter Scott	Melrose	44	Consumption
,, ,,	Margaret Hutcheson	Melrose	75	
,, 30	George Mein	Newstead	62	
May 13	John Butler, a child	Melrose	1½	
,, 23	Helen Laurie	Danielton	70	
,, 30	James Wight	Darnick	87	
,, 31	James Chisholm, a child	Melrose	1½	Smallpox
June 4	Jean Brownfield	Gattonside	40	
,, 5	Robert Trotter	Melrose	83	
,, 6	William Mercer	Darnick	6	
,, 15	William Hogg	Melrose	44	Consumption
,, 25	Robert Brown	Gateside	18	Lost his life in Tweed
July 28	James Martin	Staghall	39	
Sept. 28	Isable Edgar, a child	Melrose	1½	
Nov. 12	Andrew Mein	Newstead	—	
,, 17	Mr. William Hunter	Melrose	82	
Dec. 24	James Robertson	Newstead	19	
,, 25	Robert Bulman	Broomhouse	62	
1786.				
Jan. 29	Isabel Henderson	Melrose	33	
Feb. 3	Isabel Andison	Melrose	—	
,, 6	Thomas Boston's child in Gattonside, died at	Newstead	17 wks	
,, 11	Isabel Aitkine	Boldside	86	
,, 17	John Martin, junior, his daughter, a child	Melrose	18 wks	
Mar. 10	Jean Scott	Gattonside	84	
,, 17	James Bower's child	Melrose	—	
,, 19	Mary Maclagan, a child	Melrose	1½	
May 21	Alexander Parke	Drygrange	19	
,, 28	Janet Paterson	Darnick	—	
June 1	Isabel Liddis	Darnick	—	
,, 7	James Williamson	Newstead	21	Lost his life when bathing in Tweed
July 8	Mrs. Isabel Hepburn *alias* Wilkieson	Melrose	71	
Aug. 2	Andrew Fair	Gattonside	11	
Sept. 6	—— Ferholm, a child	Newtown	2	
,, ,,	Walter Taitt	Easterhousebyre	11	
,, 9	Jean Boston	Gattonside	34	
,, 15	James Hunter	Newstead	—	
,, 24	William Dickson, a child	Midlim	1½	
Dec. 7	John Mercer	Darnick	77	

Time of Death.	NAMES.	PLACES.	Ages.	Diseases or Distempers.
1787				
Dec. 17	Betty Grahamslie	Darnick	77	
,, ,,	Andrew Hoy	Melrose	51	
1787				
Jan. 3	William Scott	Danielton	17	
,, 13	Janet Grieve	Maxton	32	
Feb. 1	Mrs. Christian Turnbull *alias* Maclagan	Melrose	—	
,, 7	Janet Marshal	Melrose	72	
,, 8	George Bell	Melrose	42	Consumption
,, 11	Jean Brown	Melrose	52	Consumption
,, 14	John Jamieson	Darnick	21	Consumption
,, 15	Alexander Seade	Darnick	41	
,, 21	George Scott	Danieltown	81	
Mar. 24	Janet Main	Darnick	62	
,, ,,	Henry Cochron	Newtown	45	
,, 30	Betty Mercer	Haining	36	
April 28	Isabel Ballantine	Gattonside	70	
May 1	John Cochron	Eildon	38	
,, 2	Jean Hilson	Melrose	29	
,, 20	Helen Shiel	Eildon	60	
June 13	Alexander Brownfield	Kedslie	80	
,, 16	Isabel Smith	Gattonside	—	
,, 18	James Chisholm, a child	Melrose	13 mth	
,, 23	Thomas Bunzie	Eildon	60	
,, 27	Janet Mercer	Eildon	—	
July 5	Isabel Smith, a child	Caversmains	7 mths	
,, 8	Anne Mackfadon	Melrose	62	
Aug. 1	Anaple Forrest	Westhouses	56	
,, 5	Robert Dods, a child	Lessudon	2 mths	
,, 14	Robert Marr	Gattonside	61	
,, 29	John Milne	Faldonside	28	
Sept. 2	Margaret Watson	Newstead	78	
,, 9	Janet Sibbald	Gattonside	26	
Oct. 12	James Fisher of Clackmea	Clackmea	—	
,, 25	Janet Steuart	Gattonside	26	
,, 31	William Walker	Melrose	—	
Nov. 5	Jean Hogg	Newstead	1	
,, 20	Isabel Milne	Newtown	79	
,, 30	Elizabeth Walker	Melrose	60	
Dec. 1	Isabell Aillie	Hayfield	81	
,, 4	Agnes Jamieson	Darnick	—	
,, 9	Elizabeth Martin	Abbotslee	71	
,, 10	Thomas Davidson	Melrose	72	
1788				
Jan. 5	John Bunzie	Melrose	12	
,, 6	Thomas Goven	Gattonside	72	
,, 10	Janet Cochron	Newtown	—	
,, 21	Agnes Mein	Newstead	—	
,, 26	Mr. Andrew Fisher	Darnick	84	
,, 28	Helen Drummond	Bridgend	63	
,, 30	Isabel Scott, a child	Melrose	—	
Feb. 9	James Vair	Melrose	57	
,, 11	Peggy Jamieson	Darnick	14	
,, 20	Isabel Brown	Melrose	43	
Mar. 2	John Mercer	Darnick	16	

Time of Death.	NAMES.	PLACES.	Ages.	Diseases or Distempers.
1788				
Mar. 12	Peggy Gibson	Gattonside	60	
,, 24	Alexander Ronaldson	Darnick	23	
,, 27	James Hilson	Melrose	77	
April 3	William Mebon	Melrose	88	
,, 6	Isabel Bertine	Gattonside	66	
,, 12	Agnes Steuart	Gattonside	40	
,, 15	Janet Thomson	Gattonside	60	
,, ,,	Simon Haitlie	Melrose	76	
,, 22	Peggy Mercer	Gattonside	—	
,, 23	James Turner	Gattonside	79	
May 6	Margaret Gill, enrolled poor	Gattonside	76	
,, 11	Alison Stevenson	Melrose	—	Cancer
,, 30	Janet Bathgate	Newstead	42	
June 2	Robert Noble	Danielton	7	
July 10	Janet Douglas	Gattonside	44	
Aug. 18	Alexander Lockie	Melrose	85	
,, 27	A child in Gattonside, unbaptised, paid no duty			
,, 30	Jean Turnbull	Gattonside	31	
Sept. 1	James Ronaldson	Darnick	75	
,, 26	Mrs. Elder	Newtown	27	
Oct. 17	Marion Cuthel	Melrose	2½	Consumption
Nov. 27	Mein Hope	Melrose	20	
Dec. 1	George Edgar, a child	Newstead	½	
,, 17	Thomas Vair	Darnick	5	Smallpox
,, 23	Robert Fairbairn	Newtown	—	
,, 24	Agnes Hope	Melrose	7	Smallpox
1789				
Jan. 1	James Stirling	Blainslie	—	
,, 17	John Sanderson	Melrose	1	Smallpox
,, 29	Isabel Gill	Melrose	1	Smallpox
Feb. 4	Andrew Bunie	Melrose	18½	Smallpox
,, 10	Andrew Smith	Darnick	2	Smallpox
,, 17	Ann Dodds	Gattonside	3¾	Smallpox
Mar. 5	James Williamson	Newstead	3¼	Smallpox
,, 6	Peggy Laing	Melrose	¼	Fever
,, 12	Peggy Hobkirk	Melrose	4	Smallpox
,, 15	Agnes Dalgliesh	Gattonside	78	
,, 17	Mary Williamson	Newstead	1¾	Smallpox
,, 26	George Stoddart	Darnick	68	
,, 27	Elizabeth Pringle	Newstead	¼	Smallpox
,, 30	Elisabeth Henderson	Gattonside	40	
April 11	Andrew Dawson	Melrose	2	Smallpox
,, 16	Andrew Mathison, died end of Dec.	Gattonside	26	Palsy
,, 20	William Sclater	Newstead	78	
May 6	James Mercer	Darnick	76	
,, 14	Isabel Gilles	Danzielton	57	
,, 15	Agnes Clark	Newstead	3	Smallpox
,, 17	James Wright	Melrose	7	
June 10	William Drummond	Bridgend	75	
,, 12	John Thomson	Gattonside	56	Dropsy
,, 27	Elizabeth Cook	Melrose	1	Fever
Aug. 3	Isabel Milne	Melrose	68	

Time of Death.	NAMES.	PLACES.	Ages.	Diseases or Distempers.
1789				
Aug. 14	John Purves	Melrose	40	Consumption
July 14	William Ormiston	Melrose	65	
Aug. 19	Robert Lumsdale	Darnick	85	
Sept. 13	Christian Renwick	Old Boathouse	65	
,, 25	Jean Walker	Darnick	42	
Nov. 2	Thomas Familton	Gattonside	25	Consumption
,, 16	Robert Taket	Melrose	28	Consumption
,, 19	John Andison	Gateside	24	Dropsy
,, 26	Margaret Stewart	Darnick	50	
,, 29	John Boston	Gattonside	75	
Dec. 10	Margaret Laurie	Melrose	74	
,, 20	Thomas Turnbull	Gattonside	18	Consumption
1790				
Jan. 16	Andrew Fair	Gattonside	$\frac{1}{2}$	Palsy
Feb. 28	Thomas Milne	Eildon	89	
Mar. 5	Jean Scott	Melrose	10 mth	Chincough
,, ,,	John Martin	Melrose	15 ,,	Chincough
,, 21	William Bell	Gattonside	44	Convulsions
,, 24	Jean Govan	Gattonside	$2\frac{1}{2}$	Chincough
April 10	Christian Gibson	Housebyre	76	
,, 18	Janet Turner	Kelso	68	
May 15	John Thomson	Gattonside	24	Fever
,, 27	Janet Thomson	Parkhouse	26	
,, ,,	James Rutherford	Melrose	4	
June 7	William Mill	Darnick	18	
,, 20	Robert Mein	Spotswood	86	
,, ,,	John Cochran	Coomslie	14	Consumption
,, 30	Isabel Macdole	Melrose	66	
July 4	James Mathison	Gattonside	31	Consumption
Aug. 2	Alexander Mathison	Gattonside	23	Consumption
,, ,,	Robert Millar	Newstead	77	
,, 29	Marrion Bunie	Newstead	73	
Sept. 10	Nelly Thin	Gattonside	47	
Oct. 27	Andrew Carrudes	Mosshouses	$\frac{3}{4}$	
Nov. 16	John Bell	Melrose	2	
,, 17	William Colyard	Darnick	22	Consumption
1791				
Jan. 24	Margaret Common	Friarshall	33	Childbed
,, 30	Janet Usher	Darnick	40	
,, 31	Archibald Jamieson	Melrose	$1\frac{1}{3}$	Asthma
Feb. 26	Alison Bower	Newtown	46	Swelling
Mar. 6	John Baxter	Melrose	$24\frac{1}{2}$	Consumption
,, 16	Janet Lindsay	Gattonside	30	Consumption
,, 22	John Middlemas	Newstead	5	
,, ,,	Jannet Bower	Melrose	4	
,, 31	Thomas Stenhouse	Parkhouse	68	
,, ,,	John Easting	Gattonside Haugh	4	Fever
April 4	Isabel Brownfield	Gattonside	14	Consumption
,, 18	Janet Stewart	Darnick	50	
May 14	John Cochran	Newtown	90	
,, ,,	Mary Laurie	Langlee	5 mths	
,, ,,	Janet Ronaldson	Newtown	82	
,, 27	Andrew Heiton	Darnick	8	Consumption
,, ,,	Isabel Trotter	Gattonside	60	
June 1	Isabel Stoddart	Darnick	7	Fever

Time of Death.	NAMES.	PLACES.	Ages.	Diseases or Distempers.
1791				
June 3	Janet Heiton	Darnick	40	
,, 30	Andrew Murray	Melrose	68	Asthma
July 2	William Drummond	Darnick	24	Consumption
,, 3	Isabel Drummond	Darnick	10	Consumption
,, 12	Jean Scott	Melrose	—	
,, 13	William Hogg	Melrose	70	
,, 17	Robert Williamson	Gattonside	62	
,, 26	Agnes Colyard	Darnick	12	Consumption
Sept. —	William Stevenson	Newtown toll	—	
,, 15	Andrew Pringle	Newstead	23	
,, ,,	Margaret Common	Friarshall	4 mths	
Oct. 7	George Martin	Melrose	5 ,,	
,, 10	Andrew Hunter	Leith	2	Smallpox
,, 20	Adam Nicol	Drygrange	—	
,, 24	Nelly Vair	Danielton	9 mths	
Nov. 19	George Ormistone	Melrose	3 ,,	
,, 27	Janet Kyle	Melrose	2	Fever
,, 30	John Turnbull	Gattonside	73	
Dec. 3	Walter Ker	Newstead	1	
,, 26	Janet Mercer	Gattonside	—	
,, ,,	John Scot	Westhouses	2	
1792				
Jan. 16	John Mercer	Darnick	1	
,, ,,	Mary Pringle	Newstead	1	
,, 21	Janet Bartleman	Newtown	56	
Feb. 6	Margaret Pringle	Newstead	1½	
,, ,,	John Moodie	Darnick	—	
Mar. 1	Agnes Thin, say Isabel Thin	Blainslie	9	
,, 3	Isabel Ballantine, say Janet	Gattonside	71	
,, 5	Margaret Dalgliesh	Bridgend	61	
,, 7	Betty Smith	Newstead	4 mths	
,, 25	Margaret Lauder	Lochend	65	
,, 29	Zerubabel Turnbull	Gattonside	18	
April 4	Margaret Roger, wife of N. Milne, Esq.	Faldonside	—	
,, 9	Isabel Scot	Danieltoun	9 mths	
,, 12	William Hoy	Newstead	38	Consumption
,, 17	Margaret Haig	Mid Lothian	47	
,, 23	John Laurie	Danielton	14 mth	Fever
,, 24	Robert Bunzie	Newstead	77	
May 7	James Hume, a child	Gateside	1½	
June 9	Isabel Bartleman	Newtown	12	
July 10	Agnes Heiton	Melrose	—	
,, 23	Jean Forsyth	Newstead	2	Smallpox
,, 25	Jean Crawford	Melrose	4	Scarlet Fever
Aug. 8	Helen Mercer	Darnick	68	
,, 22	James Jamieson	Philliphaugh	7 wks	
,, 23	Robert Jamieson	Philliphaugh	20 ,,	Fever
Sept. 27	Jean Stenhouse	Gattonside	—	
,, 28	Isabel Crombie	Melrose	40	
Oct. 9	Janet Grieve	Melrose	61	
,, 15	Michael Allas	Melrose	40	A blow
,, 16	Agnes Morton	Newstead	7 mths	Smallpox
Nov. 19	Margaret Pearson	Darnick	84	

Time of Death.	NAMES.	PLACES.	Ages.	Diseases or Distempers.
1792				
Nov. 20	Margaret Scott	Newstead	—	Sore throat
,, 25	Alexander Kirkwood	Gattonside	4	
,, 27	Isabel Mercer	Darnick	78	
Dec. 16	Isabel Howden	Hawick	60	
,, 29	William Kirkwood	Gattonside		
,, 30	Walter Chisholm, a child	Westhouses	2	
,, ,,	Agnes Murray	Melrose	64	
1793				
Jan. 9	John Lyall	Melrose	85.8 mths	
,, 16	Walter Robison	Gattonside	—	
Feb. 4	James Martin	Gattonside	92	
,, 16	Mary Thorburn	Darnick	77	
,, 26	Thomas Laidlaw	Hiltonhill	—	Consumption
Mar. 26	George Caldcleugh	Gattonside	25	
,, 29	Charles Baxter	Melrose	66	Decay of nature
April 19	Elizabeth Marr	Melrose	78	Consumption
,, 28	Margaret Martin	Melrose	17	Decay
June 3	William Graham	Darnick	64	Consumption
,, 9	Margaret Hart	Newstead	27	
,, 26	Agnes Wight	Kayside	75	In travail
July 3	Isabel Martin	Gattonside	33.7	Inward trouble
,, 21	Janet Burton	Danielton	:9½	
,, 23	John Ronaldson, a child	Melrose	1.4 mth	Fever
Aug. 3	Janet Forsan	Newstead	21	Fever
,, 9	William Millar	Ouplaw	17	
,, 10	Nelly Speeding	Gattonside	—	Fever
,, 11	Agnes Mercer	Darnick	—	
,, 23	Peter Mein	Newtown	7 mths	Palsy
,, 30	Isabel Broomfield	Gattonside	59	Chincough
Sept. 4	David Kemp	Darnick	4 mths	
,, 18	Margaret Jamieson	Dingleton	63	
,, 27	Alexander Hopkirk	Melrose	5 mths	Chincough
Oct. 20	Mary Anne Aitchison	Melrose	,,	
,, 22	Jane Haig	Drygrange	10	
,, 29	Beatrix Scott	Dingleton	9 mths	Chincough
Nov. 6	Elspeth Milne	Whaums	77	Old age
,, 13	James Hunter, Netherbarns, killed	Greenlaw on Bowden Muir	35	A fall from horse
,, 15	Nelly Steinson	Darnick	18	Consumption
Dec. 14	Thomas Turnbull	Gattonside	7 dys	
,, ,,	Margaret Beinston	Gattonside	82	
,, 31	William Dickison	Gateside	2	Of a herring bone
1794				
Jan. 20	Mary Scott	Danieltown	20	Consumption
,, 24	Andrew Carter	Kadesly	76	Unknown
Feb. 9	William Williamson	Newstead	76½	
,, 26	Andrew Taket	Melrose	30	Nervous Fever
April 1	Mary Moffat	Melrose	4 mths	A slow fever
,, 9	George Black	Drygrangebridge	15 mth 14 dys	Chincough
,, 23	William Martin	Gattonside	65	Fever
May 2	Elizabeth Friar	Dryburgh	9 mths	Smallpox
,, 30	Jane Rae	Newtown	79	
July 3	Robert Penman	Melrose	65	Palsy
,, 10	Betty Cook	Melrose	3	

Time of Death.	NAMES.	PLACES.	Ages.	Diseases or Distempers.
1794 July 11	Robert Wight	Darnick	9	Drowned in Tweed
,, 13	Peggy Leithon	Newtown	55	Unknown
,, 25	James Smith	Darnick	9 mths	Purging and throwing
Aug. 20	Margaret Dalgliesh	Hilslap	9 wks	Chincough
Sept. 5	Thomas Friar	Over Langshaw	9 wks	Chincough
,, 9	Margaret Usher	Toftfield	27	Consumption
,, 16	Betty Kersewell	Newstead	—	Consumption
Nov. 1	Elizabeth Leithen, a pauper	Melrose	89	
,, 12	Christian Taket	Boldside	62	
Dec. 16	Elizabeth Stevenson	Darnick	83	
1795 Jan. 10	Alison Phaup	Melrose	68	
,, 12	Agnes Cranstone	Gattonside	79	
,, 14	Christian Lockie	Melrose	82	
,, 16	Margaret Heiton	Darnick	6 mths	
,, 26	James Moss	Caseside	77	
,, 28	Helen Huntly	Berryloch	70	
,, ,,	Thomas Lumsdane	Millmount	21	Consumption
Feb 1	John Hunter	Westhouses	—	Perished in snow
,, 27	Janet Mathison	Gattonside	95	
Mar. 8	Marrion Martine	Melrose	3 mths	
,, ,,	William Vair	Newtown	23	Fever
,, 10	Agnes Hope	Melrose	6	Consumption
,, 30	Janet Haig	Drygrange	8	Consumption
April 1	Andrew Bunzie	Newstead	75	
,, 12	Margaret Thomson	Gattonside	67	Sudden death
Aug. 1	Charles Young	Broomhill	3½	Smallpox
,, 9	Alexander Familton	Gattonside	63	
Sept. 14	John Thin	Blainslie	22	Fever
Oct. 9	Alexander Simpson	Old Melrose	32	Consumption
,, 24	Mary Easton	Eildon	50	
Nov. 16	William Brown	Melrose	5 mths	
,, 22	John Bunzie	Newstead	20	Consumption
,, 23	Robert Haig	Drygrange	20	
,, 30	William Miller	Kittyfield	41	Bruised
Dec. 22	Jean Haig	Drygrange	5 mths	
1796 Jan. 23	James Waldie	Drygrange	7	
Feb. 8	Isabel Stoddart	Darnick	81	
,, 27	Alexander Harper	Boldside	30	Consumption
Mar. 4	Ann Lockie	Newstead	59	
,, 9	Janet Smith	Eildon	60	
,, 18	Robert Stirling	Blainslie	76	
,, 26	Janet Bunzie	Drygrange	48	Consumption
May 26	Jean Dickson	Newstead	—	
,, 29	Jean Moffat	Newstead	31	Childbed
July 2	Anne Scott	Danielton	19½	Consumption
,, 28	John Hatton	Melrose	66	
Aug. 22	James Leech	Newstead	—	
Oct. 20	Janet Mabon	Melrose	—	
,, 22	Agnes Smith	Darnick	15	
,, 29	John Usher	Newtoun	—	

Time of Death.	NAMES.	PLACES.	Ages.	Diseases or Distempers.
1796				
Nov. 10	Andrew Pringle	Melrose	15	King's evil
,, 15	Anne Stoddart	Darnick	65	
Dec. 1	Margart Ballantyne	Melrose	70	
,, 18	Mary Ferrier	Melrose	95	
,, 24	Robert Ormistone	Gattonside	28	Consumption
1797				
Jan. 20	George Moffat	Newstead	5	Chincough
Mar. 7	Marrion Bunzie	Gattonside	60	
,, 17	Helen Hardie	Gattonside	81	
,, ,,	Jean Bunzie	Newstead	10 mth	Asthma
April 2	Janet Waddell	Westhouses	57	
,, 7	Margaret Thomson	Bowden	20	Consumption
,, 9	Janet Smith	Melrose	10 mth	
,, 11	Robert Paterson	Melrose	65	
May 14	Christian Taket	Melrose	25	Consumption
,, 24	Walter Tait	Darnick	63	
,, ,,	James Ballantyne	Darnick	7 mths	
,, 30	John Stenhouse	Cockleferry	1 mth	
,, 31	Andrew Brown	Darnick	57	
June 4	John Wright	Melrose	50	Fever
,, 11	James Sinclair	Melrose	6½ mth	
,, 20	James Marr	Gattonside	86	
Aug. 10	Betty Thomson	Dryburgh	77	
,, 18	Nicol Henderson	Melrose	19	Consumption
,, ,,	Alexander Sessford	Gattonside	20	Consumption
Oct. 29	James Mathison	Gattonside	77	
Dec. 3	Robert Hunter	Netherbarns	50	Consumption
,, 17	Margaret Thomson	Melrose	46	Consumption
1798				
Feb. 11	Robert Elliot	Melrose	1½	Convulsions
,, 15	Andrew Ronaldson	Darnick	60	Fever
,, 21	William Aillie	Newtown	88	
April 7	Janet Rutherfurd	Melrose	77	
,, 14	John Mein	Newstead	83	
,, 20	Margaret Anderson	Melrose	20	Cold
,, 30	William Goodfellow	Drygrange	76	
May 3	Thomas Rutherfurd	Melrose	½ year	Chincough
,, 7	James Waldie	Danielton	67	
,, 8	John Skirven	B.field	84	
June 9	Robert Nicol	Drygrange	37	Fall
,, ,,	John Moffat	Newstead	62	Fever
,, 16	Isabel Fairbairn	Eildon	54	
,, 26	John Martine, merchant	Melrose	57	Consumption
July 4	Margaret M'Dougal	Melrose	81	
,, 10	Janet Mercer	Darnick	61	
,, 12	John Thomson	Gattonside	2	
Aug. 16	Katharine Williamson	Roxburgh	66	
,, 27	Jean Gardner	Spottiswood	84	
,, 29	Jean Stoddart	Danielton	43	Consumption
Sept. 17	Mary Mein	Newstead	68	
,, 29	Janet Halliday	Gattonside	30	Consumption
Oct. 13	Janet Oliver	Pirn	27	
,, 25	Janet Smith	Darnick	48	
,, 30	Elizabeth Rutherfurd	Darnick	70	
Nov. 8	Margaret Dods	Newstead	63	
,, 14	Helen Bennet	Eildon	60	

Time of Death.	NAMES.	PLACES.	Ages.	Diseases or Distempers.
1798				
Nov. 28	William Stevenson	Bridgend	90	
Dec. 17	John Thomson	Newstead	—	
1799				
Jan. 1	John Fortune	Gattonside	$1\frac{1}{4}$	
,, ,,	Thomas Anderson	Newstead	6 wks	
,, 2	Janet Cochran	Newtown	—	
,, 5	Margaret Martine	Melrose	—	Smallpox
,, 9	Janet Martine	Melrose	—	Smallpox
,, 12	Alexander Hume	Gattonside	8	Consumption
,, 13	John Graham	Melrose	1	Smallpox
,, 26	Elizabeth Drummond	Melrose	$4\frac{1}{4}$	Smallpox
,, 29	Thomas Thomson	Newstead	$1\frac{1}{2}$	Smallpox
Feb. 11	Elizabeth Hobkirk	Melrose	$\frac{3}{4}$	Smallpox
,, ,,	James Gibson	Melrose	$2\frac{1}{3}$	Consumption
,, ,,	Margaret Hunter	Newstead	60	
,, ,,	Isabel Hume	Gattonside	63	
,, 20	Violet Wallace	Melrose	$1\frac{1}{4}$	Smallpox
,, ,,	John Gibson	Melrose	—	Consumption
,, 22	George Kyle	Melrose	2	Smallpox
,, ,,	Hunter Gill	Melrose	—	Smallpox
,, ,,	Violet Williamson	Newstead	$74\frac{1}{2}$	
,, ,,	Janet Bunzie	Newstead	—	Smallpox
,, ,,	Peggy Marr	Gattonside	—	Wat. head
Mar. 5	Andrew Moffat	Melrose	$1\frac{1}{2}$	Smallpox
,, 6	Janet Pitilla	Melrose	$1\frac{1}{3}$	Smallpox
,, 9	Andrew Millar	Newstead	$1\frac{1}{8}$	Smallpox
,, 11	Isabel Martine	Melrose	26	Consumption
,, 18	Agnes Crauford	Melrose	$3\frac{3}{4}$	Smallpox
,, 20	Agnes Crosby	Gattonside	25	Consumption
,, ,,	Nelly Stevenson	Bridgend	$1\frac{1}{2}$	Smallpox
,, 22	Betty Wilson	Danielton	3	Smallpox
April 8	Margaret Watson	Melrose	83	
,, 18	Thomas Baxter	Melrose	41	
,, 20	Helen Riddell	Newstead	—	
May 6	Andrew Mein	Eildon	82	
,, 8	Robert Grierson	Darnick	—	
,, 18	Robert Grieve	Melrose	1	
,, ,,	Andrew Lambert	Kittyfield	$1\frac{1}{2}$	Smallpox
,, 19	John Burnet	Newstead	$1\frac{1}{2}$	Smallpox
,, 27	Margaret Fletcher	Kittyfield	1	Smallpox
,, ,,	Margaret Welch	Newstead	5	Smallpox
,, 30	John Nicol	Drygrange	$1\frac{1}{2}$	Fever
June 2	James Lindsay	Gattonside	75	
,, 4	Elizabeth Burnet	Newstead	8	Smallpox
,, 13	William Govan	Darnick	25	Wh. Swell
,, 19	Nelly Easton	Drygrange	$3\frac{1}{4}$	Smallpox
,, ,,	Thomas Huntly	Gattonside	68	
,, 22	Agnes Nicol	Drygrange	$\frac{3}{4}$	Measles
Aug. 6	Gideon Grieve	Gattonside	2	
Oct. 6	John Anderson	Gateside	70	
,, 18	John Hoy	Melrose	80	
Nov. 23	Andrew Lumsden	Newstead	66	
,, 28	Agnes Kerr	Craighouse	3 mths	Smallpox
Dec. 5	Peggy Cook	Melrose	52	
1800				
Jan. 2	Janet Hastie	Newstead	—	

Time of Death.	NAMES.	PLACES.	Ages.	Diseases or Distempers.
1800				
Jan. 19	Janet Waugh	Gattonside	52	
,, 23	Charles Pentland	Habshill	—	
,, 29	James Laidlaw	Eildon	73	
,, ,,	Andrew Hislop	Darlingshaugh	2	Asthma
Feb. 26	Dorothy Anderson	Melrose	20	Consumption
,, 28	Alison Mercer	Gattonside	63	
Mar. 30	John Grahamslie	Danielton	$76\frac{1}{2}$	
,, 30	Robert Heart	Newstead	62	
April 1	Andrew Spence	Newstead	—	
,, 3	Betty Spalding	Gattonside	55	
,, 14	Jean Hopkirk	Melrose	16	Fever
,, 25	Margaret Stewart	Gattonside	28	Consumption
May 4	Janet Park	Newstead	—	
,, 6	James Rutherford	Melrose	76	
,, 24	Peter Thomson	Gattonside	70	
June 12	William Cochran	Fairniton	4 mths	
,, 13	Margaret Skirven	Darnick	83	
,, 25	Margaret Fiddes	Gattonside	83	
,, 28	Mr. David Brown	Melrose	64	
July 16	John Robson	Gattonside	84	
,, 22	Thomas Brodie	Melrose	73	
Sept. 20	Sarah Easton	Gateside	17	Consumption
Oct. 23	Isabel Stenhouse	Cockleferry	21	
,, ,,	Grizel Fairbairn	Newstead	69	
Nov. 13	James Pringle	Melrose	$71\frac{1}{2}$	
,, 14	John Bartle	Newtown	67	
,, 20	James Fiddes	Newstead	85	
,, 22	Elizabeth Armstrong	Newstead	55	Fever
,, ,,	Nelly Turner	Gattonside	1	
,, 26	William Farmer	Paddieslee	72	
Dec. 1	Andrew Elliot	Newstead	12	Fever
,, 2	Agnes Crawford	Melrose	9 mths	Smallpox
,, 10	Helen Johnstone	Melrose	74	
,, 15	John Martin	Melrose	77	
,, 23	Thomas Tod, Esq.	Drygrange	75	
1801.				
Jan. 6	Agnes Hatton	Melrose	11 mth	Smallpox
,, 11	Janet Tait	Gattonside	63	
,, 15	Robert Taket	Melrose	14 mth	Smallpox
,, 17	Robert Brown	Gattonside	13	A fall
,, 30	Margaret Mercer	Melrose	$1\frac{1}{2}$	Smallpox
Mar. 10	Betty Spence	Gattonsidehaugh	4	
,, 14	Mary Anderson	Newstead	79	
April 15	Agnes Haig	Newstead	60	
May 19	Henry Hope	Melrose	—	Jaundice
,, 20	Alexander Dickson	Gattonside	—	Consumption
,, 21	James Pringle	Melrose	14 mth	Water in the head
June 21	John Milne	Darnick	—	
,, 26	John Colier	Darnick	—	Consumption
Aug. 5	William Millar	Melrose	—	
,, 12	Gideon Colier	Darnick	—	
,, 26	John Henderson	Melrose	—	
,, 31	Andrew Martine	Melrose	—	
Sept. 27	James Cochran	Newtown	20	Consumption
Oct. 29	—— Millar	Threepwood	26	Consumption

Time of Death.	NAMES.	PLACES.	Ages.	Diseases or Distempers.
1801				
Oct. 29	Peggy Hoyle	Gattonside	17	Consumption
Nov. 15	Aillie Hownam	Darnick	80	
„ 29	Mary Mein	Newtown	$\frac{1}{4}$	Chincough
Dec. 7	Margaret Mercer	Melrose	69	
„ 23	Margaret Cochran	Newstead	65	
1802				
Jan. 7	James Penman	Melrose	77	
Feb. 9	Margaret Marjoribanks	Newstead	61	
„ „	Elizabeth Richardson	Eildon	66	
„ 14	William Aitken	Melrose	—	
„ 16	Janet Litterdale	Westhouses	67	
Mar. 14	Margaret Tod	Melrose	81	
April 1	—— Henderson	Newtown	—	Killed by a cart
„ 20	James Thomson	Gattonside	30	Consumption
„ 21	Janet Hunter	Gattonside	73	
„ 25	Isabel Sibbald	Melrose	70	
„ 29	Margaret Dalgliesh	Gattonside	24	Consumption
May 3	Margaret Paterson	Darnick	24	Dropsy
„ „	Jean Milne	Langlands	27	Consumption
„ 8	David Thomson	Melrose	85	
„ 22	Jean Robertson	Newstead	—	
„ „	William Mathison	Gattonside	$44\frac{3}{4}$	Consumption
„ „	—— Mack	Melrose		
July 24	Agnes Thorburn	Darnick	70	
„ 29	William Scott	Danielton	73	Fever
„ „	David Fairbairn	Melrose	72	
Aug. 6	George Hatton	Melrose	47	
„ 12	Margaret Rodger	Newtown	—	Consumption
„ 14	Andrew Luckup	Melrose	91	
„ 21	Marion Boston	Gattonside	69	
Sept. 8	Helen Fleming	Gattonside	81	
„ „	Isabel Musgrave	Melrose	15	Fever
„ 10	Barbara Marshal	Melrose	18	Fever
Nov. 23	George Skirven	Melrose	18	Fever
„ 28	William Broomfield	Melrose	99	
Dec. 21	Robert Hilson	Newstead	—	
1803				
Jan. 6	Margaret Blaikie	Earlstoun	81	
„ 16	Margaret Sinclair	Melrose	$\frac{1}{4}$	Fever
„ 19	Janet Fraser	Craigsford	21	Fever
„ 22	George Wight	Darnick	8 mths	
Feb. 2	Elizabeth Turnbull	Gattonside	77	
„ 4	Thomas Bell	Gattonside	36	Elia's passion
„ 7	Catharine Vogan	Melrose	70	Fever
„ „	A travelling child	Newstead	$\frac{3}{4}$	Smallpox
„ 9	William Muir	Newstead	10	Smallpox
„ 10	Andrew Morton	Newstead	4	Smallpox
„ 15	Robert Bunzie	Newstead	$\frac{2}{3}$	Smallpox
„ 25	Jean Burn	Midlim	$1\frac{1}{2}$	Measles
Mar. 1	Peter Anderson	Darnick	49	Consumption
„ 29	Andrew Heatlie	Melrose	69	
„ „	Thomas Cleghorn	Newtown	—	
April 2	Isabel Laurie	Melrose	63	
„ 7	George Hog	Melrose	72	
„ 16	James Walker	Halydean Mill	23	
„ 20	Elizabeth Martin	Melrose	—	Childbirth

Time of Death.	NAMES.	PLACES.	Ages.	Diseases or Distempers.
1803				
April 28	Helen Mein	Eildon	63	
May 10	Margaret Vair	Darnick	—	
,, 16	John Govan	Gattonside	—	
	Margaret Park, died about 2 months ago	Drygrange	—	
,, 31	John Moffat of Berwick-upon-Tweed	Eliestone	76	
June 2	Betty Cook	Melrose	10 wks	
,, 14	—— Williamson	Gattonside	—	
,, ,,	—— Stenhouse	—		
,, 20	Adam Laurie	Danielton	8	
,, ,,	Abigail Winter	Gattonside	1	
July 1	William Reid	Newstead	—	
,, 28	Ann Christie	Gattonside	90	
,, 31	Christian Taket	Melrose	3	
Aug. 6	George Martin	Chesters	22	Fever
,, 14	Mary Dick	Chesters	66	
,, 25	Agnes Fairbairn	Melrose	—	
,, 30	—— Spalding	Trows	71	
Oct. 2	David Taylor	Melrose	76	
,, 5	Agnes Ellis	Newstead	66	
,, 20	Thomas Usher	Darnick	84	
,, 21	Janet Lockie	Gattonside	76	
,, 28	Helen Cook	Melrose	4½	Fever
,, ,,	John Duncan	Darnick	—	Consumption
Dec. 28	William Mitchell	Old Melrose	—	Consumption
,, ,,	Jean Kyle	Melrose	21	Consumption
1804				
Jan. 7	John Muir	Melrose	72	Cancer
,, 12	John Hogg	Melrose	—	Consumption
,, ,,	Isabel Mathison	Gattonside	4½	Fever
Feb. 27	Margaret Mein	Gattonside	68	
Mar. 12	Janet Pringle *alias* Bell	Eildon	71	
,, 29	Andrew Carter	Gattonside	1½	Consumption
April 3	Alison Bunzie	Drygrange	77	
,, 23	Isabella Kyle	Melrose	17	Consumption
,, 24	Thomas Tait	Darnick	70	
May 1	Isabel Henderson	Melrose	7	Consumption
June 14	Helen Purves	Melrose	66	
,, 22	William Mathison	Gattonside	83½	
Aug. 9.	John Sclater	Melrose	54	Consumption
,, 23	Jean Gill	Melrose	12	Consumption
,, 24	Margaret Henderson	Melrose	80	Burnts
,, 25	Peter Laidlaw	Eildon	¼	
,, 27	Violet Collier	Melrose	80	
Sept. 11	James Pringle, painter	Melrose	29	Consumption
Oct. 26	Thomas Anderson	Langlee	53	
Nov. 4	Elizabeth Broomfield	Bluecairn	14 mth	
,, 18	Catharine Fisher	Melrose	60	
,, ,,	John Boston	Darnick	18	Consumption
Dec. 1	George Ronaldson	Melrose	—	
,, 9	Margaret Mien	Newstead	72	
,, 18	Walter Turnbull, schoolmaster	Melrose	46	
,, 20	Jemima Grant	Eildon	41	
,, 30	David Tait	Darnick	25	Consumption

Time of Death.	NAMES.	PLACES.	Ages.	Diseases or Distempers.
1805				
Jan. 25	Isabel Mercer	Melrose	76	
,, 27	James Sinclair	Melrose	5½ mth	
,, ,,	Isabel Laidlaw	Eildon	70	
Feb. 1	James Scott	Melrose	88	
Mar. 18	Agnes Gray	Newstead	82	
,, 29	Andrew Collier	Darnick	39	Palsy
April 7	John Turnbull	Gattonside	9	Fever
,, 12	Christian Penman	Melrose	12	Fever
,, 15	David Kyle	Melrose	52	Consumption
,, 19	Eupham Gibson	Gattonside	77	
,, 29	[sic] Heiton (Andrew)	Darnick	59	Consumption
May 16	Alexander Brown	Darnick	18	
,, ,,	Thomas Scott	Dingleton	69	Gravel
,, 24	George Mercer	Gattonside	72	
June 9	Robert Ormiston	Blainslie	80	
,, 10	Margaret Hamilton	Newstead	56	Palsy
July 27	Robert Stuart	Gattonside	74	
Aug. 1	Isabel Duncan	Darnick	25	Consumption
,, 10	Nelly Tait	Darnick	½	Consumption
,, 16	George Currer	Gattonside	6¼	
,, 29	Francis Fairbairn	Peasehill	6 wks	
Sept. 8	Peggy Lockie	Melrose	58	Consumption
,, 22	Agnes Fairbairn	Newstead	64	
,, 25	John Forest	Darnick	70	
,, 26	John Moffat	Newstead	23	Consumption
,, 27	Margaret Millar	Newstead	1 5/12	
Oct. 3	Andrew Drummond	Darnick	75	
,, 13	Archibald Ormiston	Melrose	55	Unknown
Nov. 9	Agnes Wallace	Melrose	10/12	Consumption
,, 10	Beatrice Edgar	Newstead	39	Consumption
Dec. 1	Betty Govan	Gattonside	74	
,, 8	Alexander Sibbald	Gattonside	83	
,, 14	Nelly Sibbald	Eildon	14½	Consumption
,, 17	Agnes Smith	Melrose	70	
,, 19	John Heart	Newstead	5½	Scarlet Fever
,, 20	Janet Bunzie	Newstead	58	Declining
1806				
Jan. 18	Andrew Moffat	Kelso	—	Fever
,, 19	Margaret Walker	Newstead	63	
,, 25	Mary Scott	Newstead	65	
,, 28	James Marr	Newstead	82	
Feb. 8	Agnes Stenhouse	Cloakmill	30	
,, 13	John Butler	Darnick	84	
,, 23	Margaret Shiel	Melrose	91½	
Mar. 18	John Paterson	Darnick	18	Fever
,, 19	Janet Watson	Darnick	83	
April 9	Adam Milne	Melrose	84	
,, 15	Christian Thomson	Gattonside	72	Jaundice
,, 20	Isabel Pringle *alias* Penman	Melrose	36	Consumption
,, 22	Margaret Cook	Melrose	66	
,, 30	William Smith	Darnick	55	
May 1	Jean Smith	Greenwells	85	
,, 12	Christian Penman	Melrose	10/12	
,, 13	Janet Trotter	Melrose	66	
June 8	Andrew Edgar	Melrose	19	Quarry

Time of Death.	NAMES.	PLACES.	Ages.	Diseases or Distempers.
1806				
June 18	Thomas Pringle	Newstead	9 dys	
,, ,,	Robert Clapperton	Gattonside	70	
,, 26	Betty Scott	Darnick	62	
,, 27	William Thomson	Gattonside	50	
July 23	George Graham	Melrose	59	Dropsy
,, 26	Agnes Bell	Melrose	40	Consumption
Aug. 7	Mary Marr	Melrose	20	Consumption
,, 11	Mary Smith	Darnick	17	Consumption
Sept. 11	Jean Wilson	Cobleheugh	42	Drowned
Oct. 5	Mary Paterson	Darnick	64	
,, 19	Janet Mercer	Newstead	80	
Dec. 2	Margaret Tait	Melrose	74	
,, 4	Mary Blake	Darnick	54	
,, ,,	Alexander Johnston	Melrose	26	Liver con.
1807				
Jan. 6	Jean Fairbairn	Peasehill	6 wks	
,, 16	James Crawford	Melrose	5 ,,	
,, 22	James Scott	Gattonside	—	Consumption
,, 30	Janet Beattie	Earlston	80	
Feb. 1	Isabel Harvie	Melrose	66	
,, 15	Robert Trotter	Morpeth	76	
Mar. 20	Archibald Law	Bowling	$\frac{8}{12}$	
April 3	Margaret Kyle	Melrose	26	Consumption
,, 15	Betty Pringle	Melrose	20	
,, 29	Margaret Millar	Newstead	61	
May 4	Nicol Milne	Faldonside	78	
,, 5	Agnes Wallace	Melrose	$2\frac{1}{4}$	
July 7	Elizabeth Cook	Gattonside	$74\frac{1}{2}$	
Aug. 8	Betty Anderson	Gattonside	29	Consumption and Cancer
,, 17	Margaret Milne	Faldonside	1 mth	
Sept. 8	William Vair	—	6 mths	
,, 19	John Drummond	Darnick	5 mths	
,, 29	James Scott	Gattonside	$1\frac{3}{4}$	Chincough
Oct. 7	Margaret Williamson	Gattonside	3	Chincough
,, 8	Mary Williamson	Gattonside	5	Chincough
,, 21	Betty Clapperton	Gattonside	$3\frac{10}{12}$	Chincough
,, 26	Helen Moss	Darnick	51	Gravel
Dec. 5	Agnes Bunzie	Melrose	48	
,, 16	Elizabeth Mein	Darnick	72	
,, ,,	Elizabeth Paterson	Melrose	35	Consumption
1808				
Jan. 2	Ann Chisholm	Newstead	75	
,, 27	Robert Riddell Easton	Melrose	5	Fever
,, ,,	Isabel Layel *alias* Pringle	Melrose	66	
Feb. 11	Isabel Lees	Hawkslees	75	
Mar. 14	George Mabon	Melrose	59	
,, 31	James Donaldson	Melrose	50	
Apr. 18	Robert Ronaldson	Darnick	$11\frac{1}{2}$	Consumption
,, 20	Margaret Hogg	Melrose	$5\frac{1}{2}$	Chincough
May 12	Robert Ormiston	Melrose	58	
,, 22	George Laurie	Danielton	$59\frac{3}{4}$	Fever
,, 27	George Adams	Newstead	3 wks	
,, 28	Janet Sibbald	Gattonside	52	Dropsy
,, ,,	Elizabeth Turnbull	Gattonside	16	Drowned in Tweed

Time of Death.	NAMES.	PLACES.	Ages.	Diseases or Distempers.
1808				
June 12	Peggy Harper	Darnick	45	Consumption
„ 23	Thomas Bartrem	Gattonside	2	Smallpox
„ „	Margaret Dove	Newstead	17	Dropsy
„ 31	Alexander Brodie	Melrose	11 mth	
July 16	William Forest	Darnick	32	Consumption
Aug. 3	Georgina Ronaldson	Darnick	22	Consumption
„ 22	Nicol Mercer	Melrose	33	Fever
„ 25	Jean Cochran	Bowden	1½	Chincough
„ 29	Helen Young	Melrose	3 wks	Bowel hive
Sept. 2	Betty Usher	Toftfield	3	Measles
„ 11	James Scott	Danielton	81	
„ 26	Betty Lumsden	Newtown	2½	
„ 29	Betty Vair	Darnick	44	
Oct. 28	Robert Martin	Melrose	2½	Measles
„ 29	Peggy Ramsay	Newstead	64	
Nov. 10	James Ronaldson	Darnick	25	Consumption
„ 15	Isabel Gray	Longnewton	11	Palpitation
„ 21	Miss Margaret Hunter	Musselburgh	73	Cholic
„ 27	James Morton	Newstead	12	Measles
Dec. 12	Robert Pringle	Newstead	1	Measles
„ 16	Agnes Anderson	Melrose	2	Measles
„ 20	William Currie	Drygrange	1	Measles
„ 21	Alison Freer	Langshaw	29	Consumption
1809				
Jan. 2	Mary Turnbull	Drygrange	55	Consumption
„ 7	Jean Crawford	Melrose	22	
„ 11	Nicol Henderson	Melrose	1	Measles
Feb. 1	James Tait	Berryloch	24	
„ „	Isabel Mercer	Gattonside	62	
„ 2	John Chisholm	Melrose	2½	Measles
„ 24	Elizabeth Lawrie	Toftfield	31	Consumption
Mar. 10	Isabel Freer	Langshaw	22	Fever
„ 23	Margaret Freer	Langshaw	11	Fever
April 7	Isabel Cochran	Newtown	68	
May 21	Katharine Marr	Gattonside	63	
„ 24	John Trotter	Melrose	76	
„ 25	Marrion Burnet	Bridgend	79	
„ 26	Christian Tully	Melrose	79	
„ 27	George Paterson	Melrose		
June 20	John Lumsden	Newtown	27	Consumption
July 16	James Millar	Threepwood	65	Inflammation in bowels
„ 23	Jean Robson	Leaderfoot	75	
„ „	George Cairncross of Edinburgh	Newstead	55	Dropsy
Aug. 10	Margaret Haig	Newstead	61	
Oct. 10	John Fisher, Esq.	Sorrowlessfield	84	
„ 14	Thomas Vair	Darnick	64	
„ 31	Peggy Coldcleugh	Gattonside	53	
Nov. 23	Robert Myles	Gattonside	70	Spitting of blood
„ 29	Nelly Thorburn	Faldonside	64	
Dec. 18	James Johnston	Sorrowlessfield	3	
„ „	Janet Drummond	Eildon	84	
„ 22	Mary Tait	Kaeside	38	Dropsy
1810				
Jan. 25	John Boston	Gattonside	63	Apoplexy

Time of Death.	NAMES.	PLACES.	Ages.	Diseases or Distempers.
1810				
Jan. 28	Margaret Lorrain	Melrose	79	
Mar. 2	William Pringle	Newstead	74	
,, 17	James Simson	Gattonside	27	Fever
,, ,,	John Park	Briaryhole	72	
April 1	William Coldcleugh	Langshaw mill	14	Smallpox
,, 2	James Melrose	Darnick	80	
,, 19	Betty Gillies	Darnick	70	
,, 14	William Paterson	Darnick	21	Convulsions
,, 27	Helen Heiton	Melrose	57	Cancer
May 8	Betty Herbertson	Danielton	29	Consumption
,, 12	William Young	Melrose	12	
,, 28	Nelly Scott	Darlingshaugh	46	Fever
June 11	John Brown	Melrose	22	Brain fever
,, 15	Peggy Heiton	Bridgend	51	Consumption
,, 22	Mrs. Brown *alias* Ann Hepburn	Melrose	62	
,, 25	Mrs. Janet Bowie	Melrose	80	
July 8	Elspeth Clark	Melrose	76	
,, 26	Betty Easton	Melrose	2½	Asthma
Aug. 3	Margaret Warwick Crawford	Melrose	7 mths	
,, 18	David Martin	Melrose	12	Bruise
Nov. 11	Henry Scott	Newstead	—	
,, 20	Margaret Smith	Darnick	75	
Dec. 5	Margaret Forsan	Gattonside	69	
,, 23	Jean Ramsay	Newstead	79	
1811				
Jan. 1	John Rutherford	Bridgend	86½	
,, 4	Robert Thomson	Melrose	27	
,, 17	Isabel Martin	Darnick	75	
Feb. 8	Isabel Brodie	Briaryhole	84	
,, 10	Alison Marr	Melrose	80	
,, 14	Francis Scott	Peasehill	64	Palsy
Mar. 11	David Kyle	Melrose	25	Consumption
,, 18	Andrew Moss	Kaeside	17	Consumption
,, 31	John Somerville	Peebles	57	Drowned, 5th March
April 11	Christian Speeden	Newtown	69	
,, 18	James Dove	Newstead	63	
,, 22	Andrew Ronaldson	Darnick	1	
,, 28	Mr. James Mercer	Melrose	65	Water in the chest
May 17	James Marr	Gattonside	89	
June 9	Helen Paterson	Darnick	23	Dropsy
July 2	Andrew Brown	Darnick	27	Consumption
,, 30	Jean Martin	Gattonside	72	
Aug. 11	James Notman	Melrose	83	
,, 25	Agnes Cochrane	Newtown	3	
Sept. 5	Elizabeth Raeburn	—	8	Fever
,, 17	Alexander Cook	Melrose	59	
Aug. 37 [*sic*]	Helen Easton	Craighouse	39	
Sept. 30	George Vair	Danieltown	78	Old age
Oct. 12	William Pringle	Newstead	8 mths	
,, 22	William Wallace	Melrose	46	Fever

Time of Death.	NAMES.	PLACES.	Ages.	Diseases or Distempers.
1811				
Oct. 23	Agnes Frier	Brotherstone	16	Water in the head
Nov. 3	Janet Mabon	Melrose	74	
,, 11	Agnes Lorrain	Melrose	55	Consumption
,, 14	Thomas Park	Woodhead	41	
,, 21	Margaret Broomfield	Gattonside	71	Cancer
Dec. 2	Helen Park	Carterhaugh	----	Consumption
,, 3	Agnes Gray	Leaderfoot	4	Asthma
,, 16	Betty Elliot	Melrose	74	Liver complaint
,, 29	Jean Redford	Sorrowlessfield	87	
,, 30	Margaret Pearson	Earlston	89	
1812				
Jan. 5	Mary Murray Bowie	Melrose	62	Palsy
,, 11	Catharine Ballantyne	Dingleton	57	Histerical
,, 20	William Mercer	Melrose	4	Fever
,, 27	Andrew Steuart	Greenwells	28	Consumption
Feb. 4	Helen Smith	Gattonside	65	Fever
,, 10	Peggy Bell	Eildon	41	Asphyxia
Mar. 20	Thomas Turnbull	Gattonside	9 days	
,, 24	Thomas Kenedy	Drygrange	14	Consumption
,, 25	Agnes Harvey	Newstead	85	Old age
April 5	John Paterson	—	28	
,, 7	Nelly Laidlaw	Melrose	80	Old age
May 1	Susan Ballantyne	Darnick	59	
,, 18	Hugh Walker	Plowieland	29	Consumption
,, 19	James Millar	Melrose	79	Old age
,, 26	Robert Claperton	Gattonside	9 mths	
,, ,,	Robert Boston	Darnick	57	Hernia
,, 29	Isabel Williamson	Gattonside	1	
,, ,,	Jean Mien	Darnick	70	Old age
June 10	Andrew Williamson	Gattonside	1	
July 19	Nicol Milne	Langlands	73	
,, 26	Robert Pringle	Newstead	$3\frac{1}{2}$	
Aug. 12	William Thomson	Holydean	80	Killed by a cart
,, ,.	Jessy Vair	Darnick	$1\frac{1}{2}$	
,, 18	Nicol Allie	Gattonside	31	Consumption
,, 20	George Drummond	Darnick	8 mths	
Sept. 8	Janet Lumsden	Brymerside	4	
,, 9	Thomas Turnbull	Gattonside	75	Old age
,, 23	Janet Anderson	Melrose	9 mths	
,, 26	Helen Skirvine	Chapel	26	Consumption
,, 29	Janet Paterson	Darnick	26	Smallpox
Oct. 2	Betty King	Gateside	84	Old age
,, 13	Hugh John Ballantyne	Darnick	7	Fever
,, ,,	Robert Collier	Darnick	$2\frac{1}{2}$	Smallpox
,, 16	Ralph Kennedy	Drygrange	$1\frac{1}{2}$	Asthma
,, 30	Margaret Oliver	Newtown	15	Consumption
Nov. 18	Marion Ronaldson	Darnick	37	Consumption
,, ,,	Janet Pringle	Melrose	29	Consumption
,, ,,	James Mien	Hawkeslees	74	By a fall
,, 29	James Anderson	Friarshall	$2\frac{10}{12}$	
Dec. 3	John Moss	Kaeside	13	Fever
,, 9	Robert Grant	Melrose	7 wks	
,, 10	Andrew Johnston	Melrose	85	Old age
,, 11	Dorothy Easton	Newstead	43	Consumption
,, 14	Alison Dove	Melrose	24	Consumption

Time of Death.	NAMES.	PLACES.	Ages.	Diseases or Distempers.
1812				
Dec. 15	Andrew Gray	Newstead	1	
,, 19	Alison Haliburton	Darnick	62	
,, 26	Barbara Burns	Melrose	$1\frac{6}{12}$	Pox
,, ,,	Alison Moffat	Newstead	15 dys	
1813				
Jan. 4	Isabel Milne	Darnick	72	Old age
,, 25	Nicol Mercer	Melrose	3	Smallpox
Feb. 6	Agnes Marr	Newstead	86	Old age
,, 8	Janet Dickinson	Gattonside	23	Consumption
,, 12	Margaret Bell	Eildon	75	Old age
,, 18	Andrew Taket	Melrose	$\frac{1}{2}$	Smallpox
,, 19	James Dalgliesh	Galashiels	80	Old age
Mar. 3	Isabel Rutherford	Bridgend	17	Consumption
,, ,,	Agnes Hogg	Melrose	$\frac{3}{4}$	Smallpox
April 9	Margaret Graham	Dingleton	95	Old age
,, 11	James Fisher	Darnick	41	Consumption
,, 14	Robert Carruthers	Dingleton	37	Consumption
,, 26	Isabel Scott	Hayfield	48	
May 9	Betty Dunlope	Kaeside	42	Consumption
,, ,,	Henry Richardson	Darnick	50	
June 6	Thomas Leithead	Toftfield	8 days	
,, ,,	George Laurie	Dingleton	7	
,, 13	Isabel Dalgliesh	Gattonside	74	Old age
July 9	Janet Penman	Melrose	78	Old age
Sept. 3	Mary Sibbald	Blainslie	62	Old age
Oct. 6	Isabel Beanston	Kaedslie	58	Apoplexy
Nov. 7	David Burton	Dingleton	84	Old age
,, 16	Margaret Burns	Darnick	77	
,, 21	Margaret Mason	Melrose	73	
1814				
Jan. 9	Helen Newlands	Melrose	39	
,, 24	Thomas Thomson	—	65	
Feb. 12	Margaret Mercer	Melrose	78	Old age
,, 20	Alexander M'Kenzie	Kattyfield	6 wks	
,, ,,	Isabel Martin	Gattonside	81	
Mar. 20	Mary Mathieson	Gattonside	58	
,, 30	Helen Dickson	Gattonside	74	Old age
April 1	Helena Erskine	Melrose	—	Hooping cough
,, ,,	Agnes Vair	Newtown	75	
,, 10	Isabel Burns	Melrose	2 mth	
May 1	John Milne	Darnick	38	
,, 10	Dorothy Turnbull	Newstead	—	
,, 31	Andrew Laurie	Melrose	27	Consumption
June 15	John Stoddart	Darnick	2 mth	
,, 26	Isabel Aitken	Melrose	40	
,, 27	Betty Hoyle	Gattonside	29	
July 8	Robert Pringle	Newstead	50	
,, 10	Robert Colliard	Darnick	5 mth	
,, 30	Alison Bertle	Clarilaw moor	18	Consumption
Aug. 13	Jannet Hopkirk	Darnick	$2\frac{1}{2}$	Killed by a horse
,, 24	Mary Bartle	Eildon	68	
Sept. 2	John Dickinson	Gattonside	21	Consumption
,, 7	Margaret Laurie	Darnick burn	89	Old age
,, 20	William Allie	Gattonside	62	
Oct. 31	John Mercer	Melrose	75	Old age
Nov. 4	Ann Davidson	Melrose	46	Declining

Time of Death.	NAMES.	PLACES.	Ages	Diseases or Distempers.
1814				
Nov. 6	Baillie Dods	Darnick	80	Old age
,, 15	Mary Tait	Crailing-hall	20	Fever
,, 25	Christian Baxter	Galashiels	50	Palsy
,, 28	Agnes Grierson	Newstead	74	Old age
Dec. 24	Isable Knox	Darnick	78	Old age
1815				
Jan. 15	Agnes Fairbairn	Newton	30	Declining
,, 26	John Burnet	Newstead	71	Old age
,, ,,	Janet Mercer	Darnick	60	Old age
Feb. 1	Thomas Stevenson	Clovenfords	1	
,, 24	Isabell Somerville	Clovenfords	25	Declining
Mar. 3	Thomas Yule	Blainslie	75	Old age
,, 10	Ann Wilkingson	Melrose	81	Old age
,, 14	George Wight	Darnick	74	Old age
,, 15	Katharine Mackall	Darnick	72	Old age
April 4	Euphin Gray	Darnick	64	Old age
May 1	Robert Anderson	Gattonside	21	Declining
,, 15	Thomas Mein	Eildon Hall	66	
June 28	David Erskine Hobkirk	Melrose	16	Declining
July 13	Isabel Oliver	—	9	
Aug. 1	William Kyle	Melrose	37	Declining
,, 2	John Mein	Newstead	65	Old age
Oct. 5	John Gill	Melrose	70	Old age
,, 11	Margaret Williamson	Melrose	70	Palsy
,, 16	John Smith	Darnick	67	Old age
,, 22	John Fair	Gattonside	77	Old age
,, ,,	Christian Scott	Buckhamside	47	Declining
Nov. 4	Jean Carshons	Drygrange	82	Old age
,, —	Isabell Fairbairn	Newstead	65	Old age
,, 24	Andrew Bell	Nortonhall	82	Old age
,, 27	Janet Mercer	Melrose	71	Old age
Dec. 1	Ann Dickson	Melrose	62	Old age
,, 29	Nancy Moss	Keyside	18	Declining
1816				
Jan. 3	Elisabeth Elliot	Gattonside	35	Declining
,, ,,	Isabel Robson	Faldonside	72	Old age
,, 5	Elisabeth Mein	Darnick	73	Old age
,, 14	Robert Burnet	Gattonside	46	Declining
,, 20	Helen Stenhouse, wife of John Mein	Newstead	75	Old age
,, ,,	John Cochrane	Newtown	14	Declining
,, 22	Thomas Williamson	Newstead	16	
,, 24	Margaret Oliver	Darnick	54	Palsy
,, ,,	Catharine Lauder	Newstead	77	Old age
Feb. 10	John Buckley	Newstead	4	
,, 14	Jean Stevenson	Newstead	8	Fever
,, 26	Jane Atchison	Old Melrose	34	Fever
Mar. 2	Margaret Scott	Melrose	83	Old age
April 20	Archibald Tod	Drygrange	57	Apology(?)
June 7	Robert Oliver	Langlee	an infant	
,, 10	Helen Dickson	Darnick	75	Old age
July 2	Beatrix Richardson	Danielton	52	Cancer
,, 5	George Waldie	Drygrange	55	Declining
,, ,,	Isabell Bunzie	Newstead	78	Old age
,, ,,	Sara Hirst	Newstead	23	Declining
,, 13	Robert Taket	Melrose	85	Old age

Time of Death.	NAMES.	PLACES.	Ages.	Diseases or Distempers.
1816				
July 13.	William Martin	Melrose	25	Declining
Aug. 1.	Alison Moss	Keyside	21	Declining
,, 26	Jean Wanless	—	59	Declining
,, ,,	James Clapperton	Gattonside	8 mths	
Sept. 4	George Mercer	Darnick	66	Old age
,, 13	Alexander Thain	Earlston	—	
,, 20	Alexander Clerk	—	2½	
Oct. 11	Isabell Elder	Newtown	20	Declining
,, 12	Robert Rutherford	Bridgend	13	Declining
,, ,,	Robert Burns	Melrose	41	
Nov. 15	James Usher	Darnick	78	Old age
Dec. 20	William Baxter	Gattonside	40	A fall
1817				
Jan. 23	James Bower	Melrose	71	Old age
,, 29	Margaret Ramsay	Melrose	82	Old age
Mar. 13	William Walker	Bleechfield	25	Declining
,, ,,	George Stoddart	Darnick	35	Fever
April 12	Margaret Grieve	Craiksford	62	Old age
,, ,,	John Broomfield	Kedslie	35	Declining
May 14	John Hatton	Melrose	72	Old age
,, 23	Isabell Paterson	Darnick	25	Declining
June —	William Clerk	Newstead	52	
,, —	William Nichol	Broomhill	25	Declining
,, 25	Isabell Reid	Gattonside	4	Measles
July —	George Alexander Pool	Melrose	3⅓	Fever
,, 6	James Reid	Gattonside	3½	Measles
Sept. 6	Adam Tait	Newtown	13½	Fever
Oct. 1.	Helen Armstrong	Newstead	3½	
,, 15	Ann Gray	Sorrowlessfield	63	Old age
,, ,,	William Armstrong	Newstead	43	Declining
,, ,,	Alexander Mackintosh	Melrose	36	
Nov. 5.	John Gill	Melrose	11	Fever
,, 23	Janet Scott	Danieltown	10	
Dec. 5	Christian Paton	Danieltown	31	Declining
,, 9	Margaret Hopkirk	Melrose	27	Fever
,, 20	George Turnbull	Gattonside	19	Declining
1818				
Jan. 1	Isabel Boston	Gattonside	70	Old age
,, ,,	Catharine Rutherford	Tweedbank	16	Declining
,, 14	George Moffat	Melrose	13	Typh. Fever
Feb. 22	Janet Spiding	Newtown	81	Old age
,, 28	John Rettie	Darnick	4 mths	Chincough
Mar. 29	Janet Laidlaw	Danieltown	72	Old age
April 22	Elisabeth Waldie	Sorrowlessfield	24	Declining
May 10	Charles Robson	Newstead	44	Declining
,, ,,	John Nichol	Melrose	28	Declining
,, 12	Catharine Legge	Eildon Hall	2 mths	Cold
,, 15	James Ronaldson	Darnick	70½	Old age
June 24	—— Church	Langlee	2	
July 27	Betty Wathstone	Gattonside	84	Old age
Aug. 15	George Mercer	Melrose	42	
,, 27	Mary Sibbald	Drygrange lodge	60	
,, 30	Nichol Stenhouse	Newtown	81	Old age
Nov. 24	John Morton	Newstead	36	Declining
,, 27	John Dickenson	Gattonside	80	Old age
Dec. 27	Barbara Phin *alias* Thin	Riddeltonhill	23	Declining

Time of Death.	NAMES.	PLACES.	Ages.	Diseases or Distempers.
1819.				
Jan. 19	Isabella Sharp	Newstead	79	
Feb. 3	James Frier	Dryburgh	54	Palsey
,, 4	Agnes Dickson	Gattonside	75	Old age
,, 7	Robert Vair	Darnick	83	Old age
,, 14	Elisabeth Murray	Melrose	63	Old age
,, 28	Robert Easton	Newstead	21	Declining
Mar. 9	Robert Anderson	Melrose	5	
,, 21	John Harper	Boughshank	48	
,, 27	Andrew Hart	Newstead	24	Fever
April 16	Isabell Thomson	Langlands	87	Old age
May 15	Helen Millar		3	
,, —	Andrew Maxwell	Darnick	5 mths	
June 1	Margaret Phin	Riddeltonhill	31	Declining
,, 21	Alison Mather	Newstead	44	Fever
,, 30	George Broomfield	Gattonside	70	Old age
July 8	Margaret Dunn	Danielton	76	Old age
,, 15	Anne Bunzie	Newstead	12	
Aug. 1	William Bunzie	Newstead	20	Fever
,, 15	—— Armstrong	Newstead	6	
Sept. 19	Andrew Mercer	Lochend	66	
,, 24	George Shillinglaw	Darnick	4	
Oct. 12	Thomas Milne	Newtown	82	Old age
Nov. 25	Mary Goodfellow	Broomylees	64	Dropsy
Dec. 4	William Elder	Newtown	62	
,,	Agnes Darling	Gattonside	78	Old age
,, 5	William Mercer	Melrose	4	Fever
,, 24	Janet Ormiston	Darnick	69	

Melrose Parish Registers.

INDEX OF PERSONS.

[*An Asterisk (*) signifies that the name occurs more than once on the page.*]

Alison, Thomas, 157
Allan (Allane, Allaine, Allen), Agnes,
84, 347; Alexander, 389*, 391,
395: Andrew, 115*; Betty, 447;
Elisabeth, 356, 368, 423; Helen,
356; Hugh, 62, 81*, 104, 107*;
Isabel, 75, 81, 95, 102, 107, 414;
James, 364, 367, 391: Janet, 89,
364; Jean, 62, 75, 81, 86, 92, 212,
320, 370, 413, 447; John, 364, 394,
405: Lorrain, 366: Magdalene,
166, 176, 258; Margaret, 353, 359,
423: Richard, 212; Robert, 356,
366, 368, 388; Thomas, 347, 356,
364, 366, 370, 377*, 388, 394:
William, 445; William Henry,
395; ——, 104, 231, 251
Allas, Michael, 473
Ambleton, Elizabeth, 369
Amos, Adam, 304; Alison, 301;
Barbara, 317, 320, 325, 329, 336,
340, 347, 352, 357; Edward, 273;
Helen, 307; James, 273, 301, 304*,
307*, 430, 431*
Andersone (Anderasone, Andirson),
Adam, 265, 330, 337, 348, 354,
367: Agnes, 316, 318, 320, 322,
324, 327, 335, 338, 369, 376, 435,
449, 483; Alexander, 5, 27, 29, 54,
114, 125, 364, 405; Alice, 353;
Alison, 261; Andrew, 354, 370;
Annapel, 398; Archibald, 324,
338, 342*, 348*, 437; Barbarie, 404;
Bessie, 397, 407, 408; Betty, 445,
482; Catharine, 257; Christian,
324, 437; Dorothy, 478; Elizabeth,
251, 328, 359, 364, 367, 441, 443;
Elspeth, 452; Eupham, 264, 421;
George, 12, 173, 424, 444; Helen,
164, 334, 359, 370, 389, 397, 449;
Isobel, 7, 22*, 349*; James, 91*,
169*, 254, 257, 260*, 330, 334, 355,
377, 393, 424, 426, 485; Janet, 21,
33, 209, 328, 333, 381, 383, 485:
Jean, 140, 370, 375; John, 7, 11,
25, 42, 108*, 111, 114, 118*, 200,
209, 211*, 219, 221*, 227, 251, 255,
257, 259*, 261, 265, 268, 288, 320,
334*, 339, 340, 381, 390, 398, 419,
421, 428, 432, 435*, 462, 477;
Margaret, 257, 326, 401, 476:
Marion, 264, 272, 274, 277, 280,
283, 287, 292, 478; Peter, 344,
479; Robert, 108, 268, 326, 328,
334, 338*, 359, 348, 353, 355, 359,
364, 369, 374, 376, 381, 386*, 390,
393, 441, 487, 489; Thomas, 31,
91, 118, 125, 140, 156, 157, 158,
159, 161, 236, 254, 348, 381, 403,
477, 480; Thomas John, 389:
Violet, 337; William, 7*, 12, 21, 22,

25, 27, 29*, 31, 33*, 288, 320, 374,
377, 389, 399, 403, 435, 446; Mr.,
336; ——, 267, 268, 459
Andison (Annison, Addison), Isabel,
469; Jane, 439; Janet, 440; John,
472; Michael, 176, 192, 420;
Peter, 432
Angus, James, 154; Margaret, 131,
139, 154, 186, 202, 216; Patrick,
139
Archart, Joseph, 435
Archibald, Grizel, 444
Armstrong (Armstrang), Andrew, 373;
Elizabeth, 478; George, 357, 363*,
367, 371; Hannah, 367; Helen,
92, 386, 488; Jenet, 406; Joan,
393; Lizie, 281; Margaret, 371;
William, 357, 373, 386, 444, 447,
488; Mr., 377*; ——, 489

BAILIE (Baillie), Andrew, 198; George,
377, 380; John, 220, 430;
Margaret, 166: Marion, 21;
Robert, 467; Thomas, 181;
William, 181, 198, 204, 209, 220;
——, 187
Bain (Baine), Isobel, 179, 231; Jennet,
69, 72, 79, 84, 96; Margaret, 224,
261, 410; William, 177, 208, 212,
216, 224, 260, 261, 263, 420, 422*
Baird (Beard), Margaret, 395, 463
Bald, Andro, 49, 410; John, 4; Thomas,
20, 406; Walter, 20
Balfour, Jean, 224; William, 343*, 441
Ballandane, James, 40, 41, 43, 44, 45*,
47; William, 44
Ballander, Elizabeth, 388
Ballantyne (Ballantin, Ballantine,
Ballentine, Ballentyne, Ballyntine,
Banantine, Bannatine, Bannatyne), Adam, 76*, 78, 79, 85, 86,
96, 105; Agnes, 373, 377, 379,
383, 384, 387, 390, 396, 431;
Alexander, 390; Andrew, 373, 455:
Catharine, 485; David, 74, 76, 78,
85*, 315, 441; Elizabeth, 85, 272,
424, 458; George, 24, 76, 226;
Helen, 365; Hugh John, 367, 485;
Isabel, 100, 158, 184, 190, 203,
208, 224, 254, 266, 268, 270, 296,
422, 443, 453, 454, 470, (say Janet),
473; Jacobina, 364; James, 3*, 11,
295, 337, 347*, 367, 373, 430, 433,
439, 440, 476: Janet, 107, 193,
199, 265, 268, 270, 274, 270, 276,
280, 423: Jean, 91; Joanna, 307,
310, 313; Joan, 272: John, 96,
264, 265*, 268, 270*, 272, 300, 362,
422, 423*, 424, 433; Katharine,
322, 328, 436; Margaret, 279, 289,
421, 426, 476; Mary, 315: Nelly,

359; Elizabeth, 324, 390; George, 114, 294, 303, 306*, 308*, 311, 315, 319, 385*, 418, 430, 432, 436, 443, 470; Helen, 78, 92, 131, 253, 256, 259, 281, 341, 420; Hugh, 3, 4, 5, 6, 9*, 13, 14*, 28, 265; Isabel, 14, 28, 30, 82, 204, 332, 385, 398, 412; James, 123, 125, 206, 306, 325, 327, 332, 338*, 341, 344*, 346, 347, 348*, 349*, 353, 355, 358; James Liddell, 337; Jane, 340; Janet, 21, 26, 103, 106, 111, 117, 125*, 131, 206, 261, 265, 274, 327, 385, 418, 422, 449, 461, 480; Jean, 106, 294, 296, 323, 327, 387; John, 3, 19*, 22*, 23, 25, 26, 27*, 28, 30*, 31, 32, 33*, 35*, 36*, 38*, 39*, 40*, 41*, 43*, 44, 46, 49, 50*, 65, 88, 89, 92, 98*, 103*, 106, 114, 116*, 125, 138, 209*, 274, 277, 281, 284, 296, 309, 315, 323*, 325, 353, 402, 411*, 417, 425, 435, 440, 457, 460, 472; Margaret, 25, 180, 297, 329, 347, 357, 363, 367, 371, 377, 385, 445, 486; Marion, 70, 72, 76, 82, 87, 91, 98, 106, 414; Mary, 117, 119, 124, 340, 344*, 349, 359, 363, 369, 379; Nelly, 337; Peggy, 303, 485; Robert, 434; Susanna, 443; Thomas, 9, 13, 14, 16, 30*, 31, 33*, 35*, 36*, 38, 40*, 41, 43*, 44, 46*, 98, 337, 350, 357, 441, 442, 463, 479; Walter, 31; William, 3, 13*, 14*, 15, 16*, 17*, 18*, 19, 20, 21, 22, 24*, 26, 27, 28*, 29, 30*, 33, 34*, 35*, 51, 54, 59, 61, 75, 78, 82, 87*, 102, 118*, 119, 204, 221, 256*, 261*, 263, 265, 266, 282, 299, 357, 367, 399, 415, 420, 422, 426, 430, 464, 465, 468, 472

Bemerside, Laird of, 406

Bennet, Helen, 476; John, 15; Elizabeth, 64, 69; Elspeth, 73; Margaret, 15, 376, 380, 445, 447

Berry, Euphan, 313; Isabell, 396

Bertram (Bartram, Bartrem, Bartrum), Alice, 359; Andrew, 359, 364, 368, 373, 389, 443; Beatrice, 364; George, 373; Mary, 320; Mary Ann, 389; Thomas, 320, 368, 385, 483; William, 385

Bett, Mary, 440

Biggar, Agnes, 332; Anne, 436; John, 337, 423; Robert, 332; Thomas, 337

Bishop, William, 386

Binning, Isobel, 324; James, 324

Bisset (Bicket, Bickett), Alexander, 29, 32, 34, 37*, 39, 41, 43, 47, 464; Christine, 29, 444; Isabel,

13, 65; Janet, 17; John, 2, 7, 8*, 13, 17, 25*; Margaret, 2, 414; Robert, 32; Roger, 8; Thomas, 34, 36, 38, 42, 44; William, 325, 434

Bitlestone, John, 411

Black (Blake, Blek), Adam, 434; Alexander, 262; Andrew, 264; Charles, 435; George, 474; Helen, 179, 264; Isabella, 392; Isabel, 440; James, 368, 387, 392*, 443; Janet, 286, 392; John, 262; Lilly, 455; Margaret, 62, 69, 387, 413; Mary, 324, 482; Ninian, 231; Robert, 368; Thomas, 76; William, 392; ——, 93

Blacketer, Margery, 345

Blackie (Blaikie, Blakie, Bleakie). Agnes, 80, 83, 97, 162, 164, 186, 295, 304, 329, 334, 360, 363, 371, 375, 379, 383, 384*, 396, 397, 431, 444, 447; Alexander, 25, 387, 447; Alison, 71, 145; Catharine, 164, 286; Charles, 47, 66, 68*, 70, 71*, 72, 85; Christian, 70, 75, 79, 85, 96, 414; David, 24; Elizabeth, 28, 146, 229, 254, 334, 446; George, 1, 5*, 9, 11, 13, 15, 16, 18, 20, 22*, 24, 26, 28*, 31, 33*, 34, 37, 38, 39, 41, 43, 44, 46, 47*, 48*, 49, 58, 59, 171, 182, 189, 194, 201, 205, 206, 216, 225*, 231, 250, 252, 254, 255*, 258*, 261*, 268, 269, 272, 276*, 277, 281, 284, 288, 289, 296, 298, 300, 334, 404, 430, 443; Helen, 65; Isabel, 15, 20, 63, 75, 127*, 131, 154, 167, 192, 213, 222, 225, 277*, 284, 287, 290, 294, 299, 305, 334, 398*, 403, 408, 412, 427, 430, 460; James, 6, 8, 11, 18, 30, 47, 49, 50*, 53, 54, 55*, 58*, 59, 60, 61*, 62, 63*, 64*, 65*, 66, 69*, 70, 71, 74*, 75*, 77*, 78*, 79*, 81, 82*, 84*, 87*, 88*, 89*, 91, 92*, 94*, 98*, 102, 106, 111, 112, 116*, 117*, 118*, 119*, 120*, 122*, 123, 124*, 125, 126*, 127, 128, 129, 130, 131*, 132*, 133*, 134*, 135*, 137, 138, 141*, 142*, 143*, 144, 145*, 146, 147*, 148*, 150, 151, 152, 154*, 155*, 156*, 157*, 159, 160*, 163, 164, 182, 206, 216, 250, 255, 260, 271, 276*, 277, 284, 286, 289, 293, 296, 297, 300, 302*, 303, 304, 308, 309, 324*, 326*, 327*, 328, 333, 334*, 335*, 337, 338, 341, 344, 347, 350, 351, 354*, 355*, 356, 357*, 358*, 360*, 361, 363, 364, 412, 414, 415, 432*, 441*, 448, 464, 465; Jane, 156; Janet, 1, 16, 31, 162, 174, 194, 205, 206, 254, 255, 258,

200, 215, 234; Walter, 30, 33, 37, 39, 42, 45, 56, 404, 412; William, 29, 308, 340; ——, 274

Dalziel, John, 347; Mr, 370

Darling, Adam, 18, 20, 23, 25*, 26, 30, 33, 34, 35, 38, 40*, 42*, 46, 47, 114, 151, 401, 465; Agnes, 94, 95, 131, 145, 183, 213, 254, 298, 309, 313, 316, 321, 428, 434*, 461, 489; Alexander, 194, 358; Andrew, 3*, 11, 12, 16, 20, 23*, 24, 25*, 27, 31*, 32*, 33, 34, 41, 51, 67, 70, 81, 100*, 106*, 112, 151, 159, 162, 177, 194, 200, 209, 216, 238, 250, 252*, 255, 258, 259, 262*, 264, 269*, 281, 299, 403, 415, 421, 429; Annabella, 255; Ann, 354, 360; Archibald, 23; Barbara, 12, 87; Bessie, 7, 398; Christine, 18; Edward, 7, 9, 12*, 13*, 15, 16*, 17, 18, 21, 23, 24, 27, 28, 30, 35, 38, 66, 69, 77, 80, 81*, 82, 83*, 84, 89, 92*, 93*, 94, 95*, 96, 97*, 98, 99*, 100*, 216, 404; Elizabeth, 150, 152, 220, 262, 418, 420; Elspeth, 89; Euphan, 113, 121, 139, 187, 223, 251; George, 13, 28, 38, 61, 65, 68*, 69, 73, 82, 93, 110, 262, 268, 269, 292, 295, 298, 303, 404, 418, 424, 429, 432; Helen, 24, 66, 69, 78, 84, 221, 259, 303, 358, 411, 447; Hugh, 43, 108, 113, 223, 434; Isabel, 33, 295, 327, 358, 403*, 404, 427, 428, 433; Jacob, 119, 150; James, 3, 18, 22, 33*, 34*, 38, 50, 61, 64, 78, 118, 129, 142, 176, 178*, 179, 188, 197, 204, 216, 262, 408, 420, 427; Janet, 76, 104, 180, 181, 221, 224, 238, 251, 255, 256, 258, 269, 273*, 277, 292, 358, 423, 449, 459, 460; Jean, 18, 25, 62, 112, 121; John, 24, 27, 31, 38*, 39, 43, 44, 57, 61, 64, 67, 76, 82, 84, 88*, 89, 90*, 92, 93*, 94, 95, 101, 104*, 106, 108, 110*, 113, 114, 115, 116, 121*, 150*, 159, 220, 225, 250, 252, 258, 259, 273, 286, 358*, 411, 415, 423, 428, 439, 460; Magdaline, 258; Margaret, 15, 23, 68, 70, 71, 75, 82, 86, 118, 129, 131, 164, 176, 183*, 197, 214, 227, 250, 251, 252, 255, 264, 280, 295, 296, 358, 397, 399, 402, 408, 414, 424, 427, 453, 458; Marion, 64, 65, 81, 93, 159, 194, 204, 436; Mary, 197, 209, 251, 286, 295, 300*, 419, 429, 431, 452; Nelly, 456; Nicol, 18, 401; Peter, 19, 20, 34*; Philip, 8; Robert, 88, 231, 234, 291, 327; Thomas, 12, 15, 16, 18, 24, 26, 31, 38*, 44, 53*, 54, 55*, 59, 64, 70, 72, 77, 87, 93,

96, 98, 99, 110*, 113, 115, 116, 118, 121, 123, 129, 130, 131*, 141, 142,* 148, 150, 153, 159, 162*, 164, 166, 168*, 170*, 171*, 172*, 175, 176, 177, 183, 188*, 194*, 204, 206, 209, 210, 213, 221, 225, 231, 234, 250, 252, 254, 258, 262, 281, 295, 299, 358, 398, 415, 416, 422, 427, 430, 435; William, 7, 8, 19, 23, 25, 26, 30, 33*, 49, 51*, 57*, 59, 61, 64, 65*, 66, 67*, 70, 71, 76*, 77, 83, 90, 93, 99, 101, 109*, 112, 136, 166, 176, 183*, 193, 227, 231, 236, 251, 252, 258, 286, 291, 296*, 303*, 315, 408*, 412, 413, 428, 463, 468; Mr 162; ——, 194

Davidson (Davidsone), Adam, 51, 55, 60, 80*, 85, 411, 420; Agnes, 455; Andrew, 8, 11*, 14, 171, 346; Anne, 103, 107, 112, 117, 127, 370, 447, 486; Betty, 373; Christian, 120, 127, 144; David, 363; Eleanor, 447; Elizabeth, 192, 444, 465; Eupham, 9, 388*, 447; George, 10, 396, 448; Helen, 271, 333; Isobel, 10; James, 8, 12*, 13, 14, 16*, 106*, 113, 118*, 398; Janet, 103, 208, 215, 223, 251, 332, 357, 438; Jean, 274, 315, 316, 324, 415; John, 8, 14, 29, 35, 38, 133*, 158*, 171, 357, 404, 420; Kathren, 29; Margaret, 11, 68, 110, 112, 116, 121, 125, 153, 176, 254, 394, 399, 401, 414, 419, 468; Marianne, 363; Mary, 375, 412; Michael, 113; Nelly, 320, 322, 436; Robert, 67, 316, 401, 416, 435, 442; Samuel, 324, 437; Thomas, 8, 12, 54, 74, 261, 263, 264*, 267, 270, 271, 274, 281, 282, 285, 324, 394, 424, 449, 470; Walter, 346, 357, 363; William, 9, 12, 14, 16, 41, 47, 363, 396; ——, 85, 260

Davie, Agnes, 98, 103, 107

Dawson (Dowson, Dason, Dauson), Agnes, 278, 453; Alison, 25, 76, 80, 86, 103, 122, 128, 129, 132, 153, 166, 176, 198, 246, 248, 252, 415; Andrew, 51*, 56*, 59, 61*, 69, 71, 94, 95, 101, 154, 156, 166, 181, 198, 200, 209, 223, 224*, 227*, 233, 247, 251, 253, 255*, 257*, 258*, 260, 263*, 266, 270, 322, 420, 471; Bessie, 398; George, 11, 258, 399; Isobel, 272, 398; James, 7*, 10, 33, 56, 59, 61*, 69, 71, 75, 86, 274, 320, 322*, 323, 326*, 412, 431; Jean, 266*, 431; John, 33, 48, 51, 103, 156, 173, 212, 227, 257, 258, 260, 263, 266*, 269, 270, 272, 274, 278, 281, 320, 421, 425, 431, 461;

285, 288, 299, 444; Jane, 378, 385,
388; Janet, 384, 400; Jean, 263,
273, 280, 356, 372, 442; John, 115,
197, 198, 214, 381, 384, 387, 394*,
419, 446; Margaret, 115, 180, 265,
286, 288, 291, 295*, 299, 307, 310,
366, 427, 430, 460, 476; Mary, 89,
95, 113, 289, 394, 415; Nichol, 387;
Peggy, 296, 302, 455, 468; Peter,
434; Robert, 251, 215*, 258, 260, 263,
267, 271*, 275, 280, 285, 286, 421,
470; Thomas, 254, 286, 290, 443,
449; William, 220, 285, 288, 289,
293, 296, 299, 302, 428; ——, 284,
Bailie, 434, 487

Dogherty, Jean, 279; Richard, 279

Donald, Sally, 442; Sarah, 362*

Donaldson (Donaldsone), Catherine,
21; Helene, 397; Isobel, 279, 281,
283, 286, 291, 296, 403, 426, 434;
James, 25*, 27, 246, 398, 412, 482;
Jean, 19; Joanna, 434; John, 15,
33, 49, 92, 94, 108, 156; Mary, 332,
337*, 341, 350, 354, 368; Mungo,
13, 16*, 17, 18*, 19*, 20*, 21*, 22,
23, 25, 31, 398; Peter, 19; Walter,
5, 8, 11, 13, 18; William, 325, 402;
——, 94

Douglas (Douglass, Dewglass), Agnes,
331, 358*, 360, 437; Alexander,
445; Andrew, 83, 84, 85*, 88, 91*,
92, 95*, 98*, 415; Anne, 88;
Charles, 95; Christian, 100; Elizabeth, 93, 95, 99, 445; Emilea, 106,
George, 115; Gilbert, 446; Helen,
84, 91; Isobel, 426, 432; James,
27, 90; Jennet, 410, 471; Jean,
387, 390, 395, 414, 447; John, 146,
147*, 148*, 372, 377, 435, 436;
Margaret, 85; Philip, 90, 94, 95,
100, 106, 115, 416; Robert, 356;
Thomas, 361; Walter, 98; William,
98, 173, 356, 450; ——, 88; Mr.
343; Dr. 368, 369, 370*, 374, 377,
378, 381

Dove, Alexander, 420; Alison, 376
380, 445, 485; Helen, 448; James,
484; Margaret, 483

Dow, Mark, 59

Draquhill (Draughill), Thomas, 114*,
439

Drood, James, 54

Drummond (Drumond), Agnes, 29, 92,
96, 101, 107, 110, 111, 414; Andrew,
13, 21, 25*, 29*, 31, 32, 33, 39, 41,
44*, 66, 69, 73, 76, 77*, 79, 86, 93,
94, 96, 98, 99*, 106, 112, 113*, 117,
121*, 125, 126, 127*, 128*, 129,
130*, 131*, 133*, 134, 135, 137,
138, 139, 141, 142*, 143, 144, 147*,
148*, 149*, 150, 151, 152, 153*,

154*, 155, 156*, 157*, 159, 160,
161*, 162*, 163*, 164*, 165*, 166*,
167, 169*, 170, 171, 172, 173, 174*,
175, 176*, 177*, 178*, 180*, 181,
182*, 183, 184*, 185*, 186, 187,
188*, 189*, 190*, 192*, 193*, 194*,
195*, 196*, 197*, 198*, 200*, 201*,
202*, 203*, 204, 205*, 206*, 207*
208*, 209*, 210*, 211*, 212*, 213*,
214, 215*, 217, 218, 219*, 220, 221*,
222*, 223, 224*, 225, 226*, 227*,
228*, 229, 231, 232, 233*, 234*,
235*, 236*, 237*, 238, 239, 240*,
241*, 242*, 243*, 244*, 245*, 246*,
247*, 248*, 249*, 250, 254, 262,
263, 266, 268*, 271, 274, 275, 277,
283*, 287, 290*, 292, 297*, 304*,
318, 322, 327, 332*, 335*, 338, 343,
345, 350, 353*, 357, 361, 362, 370,
374, 382, 386, 395, 398, 402*, 414,
417, 427, 435, 452, 481; Edward,
17; Elizabeth, 69, 338, 477;
George, 31, 73, 76, 107, 110, 111,
116, 268, 287, 304, 353, 362, 382,
386, 423, 424, 455, 485; Helen, 17,
121, 267, 268, 271, 273*, 274, 275,
278, 283, 287, 401, 405, 417, 423,
424, 470; Isobel, 5, 13, 18, 21, 63,
76, 113, 116, 164, 171, 177, 197
238, 258, 315, 343, 350, 354, 473,
James, 357, 452; Janet, 13, 74, 80,
91, 98*, 111, 121, 141, 271, 280,
283, 287, 292, 313, 317, 322, 328,
332, 341, 393, 398, 414, 426, 433,
483; John, 2*, 5, 7, 9, 11, 13*, 17,
21, 25*, 29*, 31*, 32, 48, 55, 56*,
65, 66*, 69*, 71, 73, 76, 80, 327,
350, 354, 362, 370, 374, 391, 395,
414, 448, 465, 482; Margaret, 2,
75, 80, 92, 213, 225, 254, 256, 266,
285, 391, 414, 455; Marion, 9, 32,
318; Mary, 361; Nelly, 432, 457;
Peggy, 461; Robert, 350; Thomas,
2, 7*, 13, 17, 18, 20, 21, 25, 34*,
35*, 36, 37, 39, 42*, 43, 44*, 45*,
47*, 48, 54, 63, 74, 80, 89, 91, 94*,
96, 98*, 99, 100, 101, 104, 414;
Walter, 76; William, 17, 44, 46,
48, 53, 56, 63, 69, 96, 271, 273,
274*, 275, 277, 278, 283, 285, 289*,
292, 315, 322, 424, 425, 427, 433,
452, 471, 473; ——, 106, 189, 259

Dryden (Drydon), James, 391; John,
431; William, 197, 391, 448

Drygrainge, 117*, 118*, 119*, 120*,
121, 122*, 123*, 124*, 125*, 126*,
127*, 128*, 129*, 130, 131, 132*,
133*, 134*, 135*, 136*, 137*, 138,
139*, 140*, 141*, 142*, 143*, 144*,
145*, 146*, 147*, 148*, 150*, 151*,
152*, 153*, 154*, 155*, 156*, 157*,

Gilchrist, Mr, 146
Gill (Guill), Alice, 364 ; Alison, 100,
104, 107, 112, 116, 141, 165, 185,
236, 366, 377, 378, 418, 431 ;
Andrew, 267, 334 ; Bessie, 3, 12,
246 ; Bettie, 220, 251, 254, 265,
268, 273 ; Elizabeth, 91*, 96, 100,
106, 212, 261, 417 ; George, 12,
79, 85 ; Helen, 100, 107, 256, 262,
356 ; Henry, 333 ; Hunter, 327,
477 ; Isobel, 158, 253, 254, 255,
260 ; Isabella, 323, 420, 466, 471 ;
James, 32, 251, 277, 313, 392 ;
Janet, 32, 63, 75, 80, 102 ; Jean,
104, 334, 411, 480 ; John, 28, 32,
33, 34, 36, 38, 45, 57, 73, 75, 80,
88, 94*, 107, 110, 111, 115*, 116,
119, 142, 172, 185, 196, 212, 221,
224*, 227*, 236, 238*, 243, 251,
253, 254, 255, 256, 259*, 260, 262,
267, 269, 270, 271, 273, 277, 289,
291, 293*, 294, 299, 304*, 307, 308,
310, 311*, 312*, 313*, 314, 315*,
316, 317*, 318*, 320, 321*, 323,
327, 334, 344, 404, 420, 431, 433*,
442, 460, 467, 487, 488 ; Margaret,
32, 72, 77, 81, 85, 86, 93, 98, 115,
165, 179, 187, 198, 221, 251, 263,
273, 414, 465, 471 ; Nelly, 304,
307, 310, 312, 315, 432 ; Peggy,
317 ; Robert, 75, 318, 329, 342,
392, 448 ; Thomas, 3*, 4, 11, 28*,
33, 63, 73, 77, 79, 80*, 81, 85, 93,
94, 100, 102, 103, 104, 107*, 111,
112, 115, 116, 141, 149, 165*, 185,
214, 221*, 236, 238, 251, 253, 255,
256, 259, 260, 262, 270, 316, 404,
418, 445, 467 ; William, 33, 34, 36,
49, 57, 60, 65, 66, 72, 73, 75, 78*,
81*, 85, 86, 92, 93*, 97, 98, 109,
141, 192, 411, 414, 465
Gillies (Giles, Gillas, Gilles, Gillis),
Agnes, 17 ; Alexander, 12 ; Betty,
304, 308, 316, 378, 440, 484 ;
Elizabeth, 296, 300, 344, 430 ;
Isabel, 282, 287, 290, 293, 296,
300, 303, 308, 426, 471 ; James,
17 ; Jean, 127, 180, 196, 453 ;
John, 303 ; Joseph, 293, 454 ;
Margaret, 188, 198, 215, 447 ;
Samuel, 289, 293, 298, 303*, 466 ;
William, 289, 454 ; Williebetty,
298 ; ——, 236, 279
Gillon (Gillan), Joseph, 323, 332 ;
Margaret, 332, 336, 339, 343, 352,
356, 366 ; Peggy, 438 ; Robert,
339 ; Thomas, 329, 332*, 336,
438 ; William, 313* ; Captain,
329, 335
Gilroy (Gilray, Gilry), Elizabeth, 431 ;
Jean, 101, 161*, 170

Girvan, Iellan, 447
Given. *See* Govan.
Gladstones (Gladstains), Cecill, 104 ;
Jean 265, 266, 270, 274, 278 ;
Robert, 442 ; ——, 272
Glass (Gleiss), Isabel, 7 ; James, 7,
Willison, 444 ; Glen, John, 290 ;
William, 290
Glendinning (Glendining), Helen, 73,
78, 92, 97, 102, 414, 465 ; Janet,
130, 172, 201, 229, 238, 253, 256,
259, 264, 266, 272, 284, 420, 445,
452 ; Jenny, 378 ; John, 63, 68,
85, 255, 413, 416 ; Margaret, 63,
145 ; Mungo, 190, 200, 217, 250,
255, 421 ; Robert, 85
Goldie, Jean, 319
Goodfellow, Belly, 460 ; Elizabeth,
366 ; Isabel, 370 ; James, 359*,
366, 370, 376, 429, 441, 442 ;
Janet, 376, 449 ; Margaret, 388,
441 ; Mary, 361*, 489 ; William,
429, 445, 468, 476
Goodsman, John, 354*, 360 ; Mary,
360
Gordon, James, 203, 430 ; Janet, 190 ;
Jean, 253, 258, 269, 462 ; John,
97, 117*, 146, 162, 183, 190, 192,
203, 218, 254, 417, 418, 420, 445 ;
Margaret, 146 ; Marion, 186 ;
May, 454 ; Thomas, 162, 186,
218, 223 ; ——, 97
Gottard, Cornet, 163
Goudie, John, 131 ; Mr, 120
Gourlay (Gurlaw, Gowrla), Isobel, 7 ;
James, 27*, 29*, 404
Govan (Givan, Goven, Govin), Agnes,
251 ; Beatrix, 255, 431, 458 ;
Betty, 481 ; Elizabeth, 80, 83, 89 ;
Isabel, 311, 336, 338, 340, 346, 349,
357, 363, 439, 442 ; James, 268,
308 ; Janet, 380, 383, 386, 394,
446 ; Jean, 472 ; John, 171, 184,
251, 255, 259*, 268, 308*, 311*,
431, 433, 437, 480 ; Thomas, 470 ;
William, 257*, 366, 373*, 430,
444, 477
Govenlock (Gavenlock, Gavinlock,
Gouvenlock, Gowanlock, Gowenlock), Agnes, 357 ; Elizabeth, 157,
158, 159, 160, 187 ; Janet, 439 ;
John, 434 ; Katharine, 430 ; Margaret, 114, 391, 395
Graham (Grahme, Grhame), Agnes,
302 ; Anne, 270 ; Betty, 452 ;
Christian, 278, 349 ; Elizabeth,
332 ; George, 49, 287, 326, 332*,
346*, 411, 437, 447, 482 ; Isobel,
285 ; James, 283, 285, 287, 292,
296*, 302, 308, 335, 355, 359, 427,
436, 445, 446 ; Jennet, 415 ; Jean,

283, 287, 290, 291*, 293, 294, 296, 299, 300, 301, 302, 303, 305*, 308, 311, 420, 421, 422, 424, 426, 427, 428, 430, 432, 461; Isabel, 372, 423, 437, 439; James, 16, 37, 39, 62*, 71*, 75, 76, 81, 86, 92, 93, 101*, 102*, 103, 104*, 107*, 110, 112, 116, 220, 252, 328, 343, 347, 370, 401, 413, 419, 440; Janet, 95, 101, 211, 279, 281, 283, 285, 288, 291, 356, 424, 426, 452, 470, 473; Jean, 92, 187, 209, 221, 232, 233, 252, 254, 256, 259, 261, 264, 267, 271, 441; John, 26, 115, 118, 147, 184, 187, 204, 231, 309, 326, 328, 338*, 339, 342*, 345*, 348, 356*, 359, 364, 372, 379, 437, 448; Margaret, 104, 130, 218, 250, 256, 291, 303, 326, 382, 409, 429, 446, 488; Mary, 309, 371, 378; Peggy, 294, 296, 300, 305, 308, 311, 316, 319, 321; Peter, 139*, 147; Rachel, 432; Robert, 347, 429, 434, 456, 477; Thomas, 204, 309*, 346, 348, 356, 440; Walter, 343; William, 184; Laird, 127; ——, 75, 199

Grinlay, Elizabeth, 444

Gullan, Robert, 426

Gunter, Sarah, 107

Guthrie, Alexander, 124; James, 400

HADDEN (Haddon, Haddone), Jannet, 139; Jean, 111, 119; John, 333, 404; Marrione, 398; Robert, 44; William, 48, 399, 410

Haig (Hague), Agnes, 327, 478; Andrew, 295; Archibald, 349; Elizabeth, 385; Elspeth, 397; George, 382, 385, 390; Hannah, 202*; Helen, 292, 295, 302, 335; Jane, 340, 474; Janet, 323, 355, 475; Jean, 189, 318, 475; John, 189, 207, 333, 390; Margaret, 207, 217, 310, 314, 363, 446, 473, 483; Nelly, 309, 313; Robert, 306, 363*, 382, 475; Thomas, 295, 302*, 306*, 310*, 314, 318, 323, 327, 335, 340, 347, 349, 355, 441, 459; William, 313*, 328*, 333, 439; Mr, 202; Mrs, 203*. *See* Bemerside.

Hair, Helen, 404; Isobel, 9; John, 9, 29

Haitly (Haitlay, Haitley, Haitlie, Heitly), Agnes, 176, 189, 207, 259, 281, 427; Alexander, 19, 252, 402; Alison, 263, 420, 422; Andrew, 166, 176, 198, 204, 252*, 258, 295, 420, 427, 431, 479; Anne, 95; Betty, 459; Elizabeth, 71; Helen, 19, 75, 78, 82, 87, 92, 415, 417, 457; Isobel, 198; James, 25, 443; Janet,

299, 305, 431, 433; Jean, 88; John, 19, 38, 67, 71, 77, 86, 88, 95, 104, 403, 452; Margaret, 258; Mary, 413; Patrick, 409; Peggie, 294, 297, 301, 312; Robert, 25, 254; Simon, 202*, 203*, 204*, 251, 254, 258, 471; Thomas, 251, 317; Walter, 27, 228; William, 77, 317, 335, 420, 435, 454; ——, 104

Haldane (Haldean, Haldon), Adam, 355; Alison, 460; David, 327; George, 430; John, 325*, 326*, 327*, 328*, 329, 339, 342, 430, 436, 437, 438, 440*; Mary, 322, 323, 355, 436; Peggy, 436; Robert, 347; William, 342*, 345*, 347*, 350, 355*, 440

Haliburton (Haliburtone, Haliburtoun, Halliburton, Halliburtune, Halyburton, Helliburton), Agnes, 259; Alexander, 21, 22, 24; Alison, 261, 264, 301, 304, 308, 317, 328, 342, 431, 486; Andrew, 257; Elizabeth, 63, 67, 70, 147, 188; Helen, 233; Isabel, 69, 131, 164*, 165*, 168, 173*, 174*, 175, 176*, 179, 204, 213, 221, 232, 251, 261, 263, 467; James, 32*, Janet, 117, 154, 193, 205, 419; John, 50*, 63, 67*, 68, 70, 233, 257, 259, 261, 264, 399; Margaret, 285, 287, 294, 297, 301, 303, 427; Mark, 7; Mary, 418; Peggy, 290; Robert, 463; Thomas, 58, 68, 69, 413, 463; Violet, 411; Walter, 58, 65, 68*, 69, 93, 414; ——, 232

Haliday (Haillyday, Halliday, Helliday, Hollyday), Agnes, 212; Andrew, 69, 72, 79, 84, 96, 131, 316, 429; Betty, 431; Catharine, 151, 190; Christian. 272; James, 273; Janet, 258, 264, 335, 421, 437, 476; Margaret, 429; Mary, 69; Robert, 154; Thomas, 79, 218, 273, 277; William, 72, 151, 167, 190, 209, 212, 218, 277; ——, 84, 96

Haliwell (Haliwall, Halliwall, Halliwell, Helliwal, Helliwall, Helliwill), Alexander, 23; Andro, 23, 30, 34, 36, 37, 44, 49, 53, 54, 58, 63, 410; Elizabeth, 197; George, 3, 5*, 6, 8*, 15, 16, 29, 465; Helen, 21, 25, 28, 403, 409; Isabel, 17, 19, 26, 63, 134, 143, 156, 203, 215, 402, 461, 466; James, 156; Janet, 5*, 21, 25, 28, 63, 67, 68, 76, 116, 130, 181, 261, 267, 287, 328, 398, 401, 402, 410, 428, 454; Jeanie, 20, 63; John, 3, 4*, 5, 6, 7, 8, 9*, 10*, 11*, 13, 14*, 15*, 16, 17*, 18*, 19*, 20*,

82, 83, 84, 412 ; Thomas, 82, 87,
90*, 92, 194, 284, 286, 288, 292,
295*, 299*, 427, 430; William, 82 ;
——, 282
Harwell, John, 20 ; Thomas, 20
Hastie (Haistie), Alexander, 4, 160 ;
Bessie, 398 ; Catharin, 63 ; George,
33 ; Isobel, 268, 423 ; Janet, 289,
295, 300, 304, 307, 312, 317, 404,
408, 429, 477 ; Margaret, 404 ;
Marion, 400 ; Patrick, 63 ; Robert,
33 ; Thomas, 33 ; William, 22,
157, 158, 159*, 160
Haswell (Hoswel), Adam, 271, 424 ;
Elliot, 271
Hatton, Agnes, 352, 363, 478 ; Anne,
300 ; Elizabeth, 296, 339, 364,
365*, 381*; George, 283, 291, 328,
336, 339, 346, 352, 357, 374, 452,
479; Isabel, 350; John, 163, 274*,
276*, 280, 283, 291, 296, 298, 300*,
307, 328*, 350, 352, 357*, 363, 364,
365, 369, 374, 425, 428, 442, 456,
475, 488 ; Margaret, 280, 336,
369; Mary, 346; Violet, 332, 339,
345, 352, 358
Haw, Nelly, 335, 337
Hay, Agnes, 326, 329, 421, 441 ;
Alexander, 365 ; Alice, 357; Alison,
355, 366, 378, 382; Betty, 365 ;
George, 36, 431; James, 277*,
350, 351*, 355*, 357, 365, 442 ;
Jessie, 377; John, 277, 366, 461 ;
Martha, 365 ; Peggy, 365 ; Thomas,
355*, 365*, 377, 378, 442 ; Mr, 367
Heggie, Margaret, 347 ; Thomas, 347
Heiton (Haton, Heaton, Heatoun,
Heiddon, Heitton, Hetton, Hiton,
Hitoun, Hitton, Hittone, Hyton),
Agnes, 32, 77, 85, 88, 95, 98, 255, 267,
306, 309, 314, 319, 322, 324, 415,
416, 431, 473; Alexander, 4*, 5,
12, 14, 16, 19, 21, 22, 42, 44, 400,
464; Alison, 8, 21; Andrew, 3, 4*,
8*, 9, 11, 12, 13*, 14*, 15, 16, 17,
19, 21, 22, 25*, 26, 27*, 29, 30,
32*, 33*, 34*, 35*, 36*, 37, 39*,
40*, 41*, 42, 43*, 45*, 47, 63, 66,
85*, 88, 91, 95, 98, 105, 111, 113,
116, 263, 297, 298, 300, 301, 302*,
303*, 304*, 305, 306*, 307, 308*,
309*, 310*, 311*, 312*, 313*, 314*,
315*, 316*, 317*, 318, 319*, 320*,
322, 323*, 327*, 328, 329*, 330,
321*, 332, 336*, 338, 340*, 343*, 346,
347, 348*, 349*, 350, 353*, 356,
357*, 359, 360*, 363*, 400, 405,
417, 419, 431*, 435, 437, 439, 440,
441, 463, 464*, 472, 481; Bessie,
109; Bettie, 275, 324, 432 ;
Christian, 402, 406; Elizabeth, 66,

69, 75, 79, 90, 94, 99*, 103, 109,
113*, 120, 138, 215, 329, 351, 413,
417, 419; George, 3, 10, 116, 285,
321, 324, 437 ; Helen, 14, 27, 273,
412, 484; Isabel, 10, 90, 166, 291,
323, 340, 401, 416, 437 ; James, 2,
6*, 7*, 8*, 13, 32, 37, 75, 112, 121,
148, 177, 213, 266, 299, 300*, 312,
357, 460; Janet, 10, 215, 238, 261,
269, 300, 305, 306, 310, 316, 321,
323, 329, 398, 421, 431, 443, 459,
473; John, 7, 10*, 14, 16*, 22*, 25,
26, 27*, 30, 31, 33*, 34*, 35, 36*,
38, 39*, 41*, 42, 43*, 47*, 69, 73,
85*, 89*, 91, 92, 93, 97, 100*, 105*,
111, 148, 211, 254, 261, 263, 266,
267*, 269*, 273, 275*, 282, 283*,
284, 285*, 287*, 288*, 289*, 290*,
291*, 292*, 293*, 294*, 295*, 296*,
297, 298*, 299*, 300*, 301*, 302,
303*, 304*, 305*, 306*, 307*, 308,
309*, 310*, 311*, 312*, 313*, 314*,
315, 321, 323, 327, 329*, 337*, 338,
349, 416, 421*, 422, 423*, 427, 437,
438, 465; Katharin, 401; Leonard,
10; Margaret, 16, 22, 92, 101, 282,
287, 327, 332, 338, 346, 362, 398,
403, 404, 413, 417, 475; Marion,
25, 288, 322, 329, 335, 338, 341,
353, 359, 366, 368, 435; Mary, 347 ;
Peggy, 318, 322, 435, 484; Robert,
3*, 294, 323, 321, 365, 366, 438,
441; Stephen, 32, 40, 413, 414 ;
Thomas, 3, 8*, 10, 12, 13*, 14, 15,
16, 17, 21, 25, 45, 47, 49, 55, 61,
121, 300, 306, 314, 363, 398, 400,
458, 461, 467; William, 19, 349;
——, 75
Helin, James, 129*
Helme, Christian, 411
Henderson (Hendersone), Agnes, 285,
296, 297, 350, 362 ; Alexander, 267,
271, 379; Alice, 359; Andrew, 109,
110, 114, 205, 250, 283, 296*, 300,
333, 367, 385, 428; Betty, 367, 438 ;
Charles, 296 ; Christian, 66 ;
David, 51, 55, 60, 66, 70, 77, 85*,
104, 411; Elizabeth, 82, 87, 313,
321, 332, 367, 373, 395, 434, 471 ;
Euphan, 299 ; Francis, 448 ;
George, 221, 257, 269, 281*, 283,
287, 288, 339, 351*, 374, 380, 421,
423, 424, 427, 441, 445; Grace,
441; Isabel, 86, 91, 112, 119, 271,
287, 319, 322, 344, 367, 374*, 380,
387, 391, 392, 416, 417, 430, 435,
440, 445, 447, 469, 480; James, 134,
143, 163, 203*, 215, 252, 294, 339,
344, 350*, 354*, 359, 362, 367, 370,
373*, 377, 379, 380, 385*, 393, 431,
433, 440*, 450; Jane, 367; Jennet,

286, 300, 319, 431*, 432, 459;
Jane, 335; Jannet, 177; Jean, 32,
182, 289, 325*, 328, 339, 345, 353,
357, 366, 376, 470; John, 29, 32,
34, 35, 140, 149, 208, 215, 222,
239, 272, 300, 327, 341, 347, 354,
360, 405, 408, 417, 480; Margaret, 24, 209, 223, 252, 258, 367,
431, 482; Mary, 275, 368; Nelly,
354, 360; Robert, 76, 163, 177,
188, 197, 198, 212, 215, 229, 236,
239, 258; Sophia, 319; Susan,
447; Thomas, 215; William, 24,
83, 119, 147, 162, 178, 182, 204,
272, 276, 286, 321, 375, 378, 383,
385, 392, 409, 424, 445, 454, 459,
469, 473

Hogarth (Hoggart), Andrew, 361;
Isobel, 141, 153, 193, 369; Jean,
369; Mary, 370; Thomas, 369*,
370; William, 361

Home (Holme, Hoome, Hume), Alexander, 12, 217, 350, 354, 477;
Alison, 174, 439; Andrew, 3, 17;
Beatrix, 351; Bell, 387; Catharine,
446; George, 311, 407; Helen,
94, 98; Henry, 143*; Isobel, 169,
370, 375, 380, 393, 443, 477;
James, 383, 386, 389, 441, 473;
Janet, 446; John, 3, 351; Margaret, 354, 399, 404; Marion, 383,
Mary, 447; Nelly, 445; Peggy,
442; Robert, 389, 432; William,
350, 351*, 354, 386, 439 442*;
Mr, 144

Hood (Houd, Hoyd, Hudd). Henry,
456; James, 287*, 431; Margaret, 434; Thomas, 443; William,
451

Hope (Hop, Hopp), Agnes, 316, 325*,
388, 471, 475; Andrew, 232, 293,
295, 297, 454; Anne, 275; Catharine, 251, 285, 287, 290, 293, 298,
301, 306, 308, 310, 460; Charles,
449; Christian, 80, 83; Elizabeth,
79, 84, 90, 95, 104; Henry, 297,
300*, 303, 306, 316, 319*, 322, 325,
435, 436, 440, 478; Isabel, 303, 457;
James, 293, 388; Jean, 422; Joan,
371*, 379, 382, 387, 390, 395;
John, 63, 115, 221, 232, 251, 295,
319, 438, 456; Magdalene, 209;
Margaret, 112, 300, 419; Mary,
456; Meina, 322; Mein, 471;
Robert, 422; Thomas, 388*, 434,
447; William, 115

Hopkirk (Hobkirk, Hopkirke), Agnes,
310, 460; Alexander, 281, 317,
320, 325, 329, 336*, 340, 344*, 347,
348, 352, 357. 359, 474; Anne,
312; Anne Mercer, 340; Betty,

317; Christian, 329, 385; David,
322, 382, 387, 393, 446; David
Erskine, 352, 487; Elizabeth (or
Bessie), 98, 103, 106, 111, 115, 122,
147, 153, 179, 186, 195, 212, 347;
364, 417, 418, 477; George, 3;
Helen, 114, 137, 161, 172, 186*,
188; Issobel, 3, 253, 270; James,
239*, 240, 246, 250*, 277, 310, 312,
315, 322, 326, 329*, 336, 338, 340,
344, 347, 359, 367*, 370, 371, 377,
426, 443; Janet, 382, 486; Jean,
320, 357, 478; John, 326, 375;
Margaret, 86, 90, 266, 329, 336,
386, 416, 488; Marion, 77, 81, 87,
91, 94, 99, 102, 107, 116, 129, 145,
377, 415; Peggy, 471; Robert,
344, 393; Thomas, 359, 393, 398;
Walter, 338; William, 44, 47,*
48, 52, 55, 58, 61*, 71, 77, 81*, 87,
90, 95*, 98, 99, 103*, 106, 107,
111*, 112, 114, 115, 116, 122, 129,
137, 145, 153*, 160, 166, 172, 179,
180, 186, 194, 203, 212, 235, 239*,
253*, 260*, 262*, 266, 267, 270,
277, 281, 325, 364, 370, 371, 375,
380*, 387, 393, 417, 420, 424, 425,
428, 443, 452

Horne (Horn), Isabella, 364; Jean,
68

Horsburgh (Horsebrugh, Horseburgh),
Alexander, 58, 70, 83, 85*, 412;
Janet, 325, 329, 333, 365, 404;
John, 64, 224, 432; Margaret, 85;
Marion, 262; Susan, 444; Walter,
224, 261; William, 261

Houlistone, William, 357

Housebyres, 202, 203*, 206

Howatson (Hewitson, Houtson,
Howetson, Howieson, Howison,
Howistown, Howyson), Agnes,
400; George, 425; Helen, 425;
Isabel, 172, 192, 400; James, 12,
14, 15, 17*, 425, 430; Janet, 17;
John, 12, 15, 17, 400, 401; Patrick,
400; Thomas, 425

Howburne, Janet, 405

Howden (Houden), George, 96, 220;
Isabel, 284, 286, 292, 297, 400, 428,
474; James, 96, 101*, 112, 416,
453

Howe (Howie), George, 11, 19; Janet,
19; Margaret, 20; Robert, 11;
Thomas, 20; William, 19, 20, 27

Hownam (Hounam, Hounim, Howname), Agnes, 114, 404*, 421;
Aillie, 479; Alexander, 22; Alison,
259, 265, 269, 272, 276, 398, 421;
Andrew, 2*, 29*, 31*, 33, 34, 35*,
37*, 39, 41*, 42, 45*, 74, 85*, 88*,
95*, 109, 110, 114, 154, 259, 265,

311*, 312, 313, 315*, 318, 364, 396,
424, 437*, 475; Margaret, 213,
477, 483; Marion, 64, 79, 84, 89,
413; Mary, 231; Nicol, 10, 267;
Nelly, 293, 296, 299, 302, 309, 319,
430; Robert, 79, 83, 93, 94, 102,
106, 112, 130, 154, 155*, 156*, 166,
203, 213, 234, 243*, 252, 259, 264*,
267, 270, 272, 274, 277, 299, 313*,
315, 323, 324, 327, 334, 418, 429,
430, 432, 433*, 476; Thomas, 24*,
31, 45, 79, 193, 210*, 262, 404;
Thomas Mar, 464; William, 10,
62, 72*, 91, 97*, 104, 106*, 123,
130, 154*, 140, 166, 167, 188*,
193, 195, 203, 213, 214*, 234,
239, 252, 253, 256, 257*, 260, 262,
272, 279, 309, 396, 416, 421*, 422*,
425, 430, 453, 469; Dr, 160; Mr,
160, 280; ——, 252
Huntlie (Huntley, Huntly), Agnes, 298,
455; George, 288, 436, 441; Helen,
475; Isobel, 234, 466; James, 181,
284, 288, 292, 298, 428; Margaret,
284, 333, 337, 345, 351, 438; Robert,
99, 104*, 107*, 118, 119, 171, 181,
187, 188, 234, 292, 418, 424, 455,
459; Thomas, 477
Huntliewood (Huntliwood), 153, 155,
199
Hupper, James, 447
Hutchison (Hutcheson), Alexander,
99; Andrew, 106; Betty, 382;
Charles, 446; George, 319, 382,
407; Isabel, 319; James, 372, 418;
Margaret, 469; William, 99, 106;
Hutton, Alexander, 404; Andro, 10,
13*, 30; Isobel, 146, 320, 333, 341,
362; James, 11; John, 458, 462

IDINTON (Idington), Isabel, 312;
Joanna, 308; John, 8, 308, 312
Inglis (Ingales, Ingles, Inglish),
Agnes, 338, 342, 348, 352;
Andrew, 337; Betty, 384*;
Charles, 359; Christian, 353;
Elizabeth, 328; Grissel, 324*, 328,
436; Harrie, 29, 30; Helen, 16,
449; Isabel, 261; James, 30, 261,
263, 328, 337, 424, 429, 434, 456;
Jean, 263; John, 139, 152, 413,
445; Margaret, 30, 307, 321, 425,
431, 448; Martha, 452; Mary, 68,
152, 296*, 300, 331*, 370, 375,
379, 383, 424, 444; Peggy, 304,
311, 314, 317; Robert, 16, 29, 30,
353, 441, 453; Thomas, 68, 254,
353, 359, 379, 456; William, 16;
Mrs, 169; ——, 68
Irvine (Irwin), Margaret, 67, 71
Ivly, Janet, 342, 350, 355, 363, 440

JACK (Jacque, Jak), Isabell, 62, 70, 126;
James, 16; Janet, 265, 266, 269,
422, 468; John, 436; Richard,
434; Thomas, 10, 13, 16, 399
Jackson, Christine, 25, 26; Gedeon,
24, 25, 26, 27, 29; Helen, 24;
Janet, 92; Jean, 27; John, 386*;
Margaret, 29, 87; Thomas, 124;
William, 434
Jamieson (Jameson, Jamison), Agnes,
470; Andrew, 352; Archibald, 345,
472; Betty, 435; Christian, 329;
David, 159; Elizabeth, 330, 398;
Grizel, say Katharine, 327;
Hannah, 250; Helen, 339; Isabel,
330, 344, 440; James, 80, 83, 84,
298*, 303, 310, 313, 330, 335, 339,
344, 345, 352*, 353, 359, 362,
409, 435, 466, 473; Janet, 171,
251, 268, 335, 466; Jean, 310,
362; John, 80, 83, 282, 284, 287,
288*, 294, 295, 326, 329, 428,
436, 470; Katharine, 323, 335,
339, 344, 353, 366; Kitty, 436;
Margaret, 87, 276, 278, 287, 288,
293, 303, 359, 374, 426, 474; Mary,
313, 386*, 444, 449; Peggy, 290,
317, 470; Robert, 330, 473;
Thomas, 352; William, 159, 326,
427; ——, 282, 284
Jeffrey (Jaffrey), Alexander, 449; Jane,
372; Janet, 449; Robert, 372,
445
Jerdan (Jerdain), Ann, 444; Annabella,
121; Magaret, 158, 166, 186, 215;
Richard, 121; Captain, 163
Johnstone (Johnson, Johnston, Johnstown, Jonson), Adam, 421; Alexander, 93, 365*, 482; Andrew, 180,
276, 280, 286, 332, 422, 429, 485;
Christian, 322, 332; David, 276,
279*, 280; Ebenezer, 327; George,
19, 60, 327, 333; Helen, 127, 272,
276, 286, 289, 344, 424, 428, 478;
Isabel, 355; James, 93, 319*, 323*,
327, 332, 338, 344, 349, 355, 361,
363, 364, 379*, 383, 385, 401, 442,
446, 483; Janet, 18, 23, 349, 425;
Jean, 87, 196, 276, 327, 446; John,
16*, 17, 18, 20, 23, 30, 38, 87, 203,
298, 323, 401, 436, 444; Laurance,
320; Margaret, 338, 424; Mary,
333, 383; Robert, 127, 151, 173,
180, 188, 195, 196, 198, 205, 215,
217, 234, 236, 272, 276*, 280, 286,
452; Samuel, 364; Thomas, 17*,
203, 391, 401; William, 17, 298,
319, 345*, 352, 385, 388*, 391, 401,
405*, 406*, 407, 408*, 421, 422,
438, 446, 447, 450; ——, 19
Jones, Agnes, 436; Margaret, 228

Mary, 275; Richard, 414; Walr.,
465; William, 70

Louden (Loudain, Loudon, Lowden,
Lowdon), Alison, 300, 305, 310,
312, 316, 327, 431; Betty, 305;
Elizabeth, 307; Isabel, 312, 430,
434; Janet, 328; John, 305*, 328,
340, 437, 438; Robert, 403;
Thomas, 340

Louis (Lowis), Margaret, 405; Thomas,
405, 406*, 407*, 408*, 409*

Lounie, Helen, 21; James, 25; John,
25, 47

Lugtown, George, 438

Luke, Isabella, 448

Lumsdale (Lumbsdaill, Lumesdean,
Lumesden, Lumsdain, Lumsden),
Alexander, 450; Andrew, 290, 291,
294, 297, 299, 300, 301*, 304*, 308*,
314*, 315, 316, 317, 318, 427, 429,
477; Barbara, 385, 446; Betty,
483; Elizabeth, 110, 138, 189;
Elspath, 451; Isabel, 73, 166, 392*,
439, 450; James, 116, 133*, 294,
301, 455; Janet, 485; Jean, 290;
John, 223, 428, 436, 483; Margaret,
299, 452; Marion, 448; Mary,
391, 395; Robert, 30*, 202, 430,
472; Thomas, 304, 475; William,
461

Lunn (Lun, Lund), Alison, 448; Betty,
321, 329, 436, 447; Frederick, 295,
461; Helen, 340, 449; Isabel, 337,
439; James, 435; John, 290, 295,
435, 447, 455; Nelly, 307, 310,
313, 433; Rachel, 332, 438; Robert,
20; Thomas, 290, 333, 340, 347,
350, 436, 438, 448

Lyall (Layal, Layel, Layen, Lile, Lisle,
Lyal, Lyell, Lyle), Agnes, 9;
Alexander, 61, 66, 69, 75, 76, 80*,
84, 89, 254, 412; Alison, 115, 419;
Anna, 158; Anne, 75, 428, 435,
456, 467; Bessie, 403; Isabel, 255,
299, 301, 304, 306, 308, 312, 315,
319, 322, 398, 430, 482; Jane, 337,
396, 448; John, 10, 80, 173, 234,
237, 254, 255, 260, 269, 270, 273,
275, 284, 289, 290, 291, 293, 295,
298, 299*, 301*, 302*, 303, 304*,
305*, 306*, 307*, 308*, 309*, 310,
311*, 312*, 313*, 314*, 315*, 316*,
317*, 318*, 319*, 320*, 321*, 322*,
323*, 335*, 337, 340, 420, 421,
428, 435, 449, 474; Margaret, 89,
404, 410; Mary, 84, 361; Thomas,
9, 14, 16*, 66, 69, 260, 398; William,
340

Lyon, Thomas, 21

Ma——, Thomas, 43

Maban (Mabane, Maben, Mabon,
Mabone, Meben, Mebon), Adam,
81, 208, 298, 306, 307*, 308*, 309,
310*, 312, 313, 316, 317, 434;
Agnes, 133, 316, 406, 467; Alison,
390; Andrew, 327; Anne, 190,
332, Katharin, 106, 266, 274, 280,
284, 288, 421; Christian, 404;
George, 166, 268, 314, 346*, 362,
482; Helen, 401; Isabel, 25, 63,
74, 78, 84, 86, 96, 149, 208, 229,
283, 285, 288, 291, 294, 297, 300,
346, 413, 427, 463; James, 12, 26,
229, 265*, 269, 324; Janet, 11, 62,
66*, 68, 71, 75, 81, 86, 94, 96, 98,
100, 103, 106, 114, 125, 172, 187,
224, 245, 253, 254, 412, 413, 417,
420, 457, 475, 485; John, 3*, 8,
14, 19*, 25, 31, 37, 39, 41, 42,
44*, 49, 54, 55*, 56, 59, 62*, 63,
66*, 68*, 69, 70, 71, 72*, 74, 75*,
76, 77*, 78*, 79*, 80, 81*, 82, 83*,
84*, 86, 90, 92, 93, 95, 96, 98, 100,
103, 104, 106, 107, 110, 113, 114,
117, 118*, 119*, 120, 121, 122*,
123*, 124*, 125*, 126, 127, 128,
129*, 130*, 131, 132*, 133*, 134*,
135*, 136*, 137, 138*, 139, 140,
141*, 142*, 143, 144*, 145*, 146*,
147*, 148*, 149*, 150*, 152*, 153*,
155*, 156*, 157*, 158*, 159*, 160*,
161*, 162*, 163*, 164*, 165*, 166,
167, 168*, 170, 171*, 172*, 173*, 174*,
175*, 176*, 177*, 178*, 179, 180*,
181*, 182*, 183*, 184*, 185*, 186*,
187*, 188*, 189*, 190*, 192*, 193*,
194*, 195*, 196*, 197*, 198*, 199,
200*, 201*, 202*, 203*, 204*, 205*,
206*, 207*, 210*, 211*, 212*, 213*,
214*, 215*, 216*, 217*, 218*, 219*,
220*, 221, 222*, 223*, 224*, 225*,
226, 227*, 228*, 229, 231*, 232*,
233*, 234, 235*, 236, 237, 238*, 240*,
241*, 242*, 243*, 244*, 245, 246*,
237*, 248, 249*, 251, 252, 253, 254,
256, 265, 266, 268*, 269, 283, 311*,
319, 362, 401, 413, 422, 468*;
Margaret, 3, 68, 75, 94, 129, 171,
178, 189, 206, 221, 237, 252, 256,
260, 263, 266, 399, 407; Nelly,
443; Robert, 12, 17, 20*, 22, 25,
34, 37, 42, 45, 399; Thomas, 2, 3,
5, 6, 31*, 36, 41, 42, 46, 71, 96, 114,
190, 207*, 208*, 253, 261, 263, 266,
332, 404, 420, 464; Walter, 3*, 17,
91, 94, 96, 100, 106, 110, 123, 202,
417; William, 11*, 19*, 44, 66, 91,
94, 95, 96*, 98, 100*, 110*, 116*,
122, 129, 149, 171, 178, 179, 184,
187, 189, 190, 202, 206, 208, 216,
218, 221, 222, 224*, 237, 252, 253,

305*, 306, 307, 401, 423*, 426, 428*, 453, 459; William, 131, 144, 222, 252, 295; ——, 161, 284

Marrer. *See* Morar.

Marshall (Marchell, Marshell, Mersel), Agnes, 417, 443; Barbara, 479; Helen, 91, 97, 103; Isobel, 434; James, 435; Janet, 457, 470; John, 27*, 68, 99; Thomas, 93*, 99, 433; William, 95, 111, 119

Martin (Mairton, Marten, Martine, Merten, Mertene, Mertin. Merton. Mertoun, Mertown), Agnes, 3, 74, 82, 211, 251, 289, 292, 293, 327, 402, 413, 427, 429*; Alexander, 183; Andrew, 19, 23*, 24, 25, 26, 27, 28*, 30, 32*, 31*, 35, 36, 39, 40, 42, 43, 47, 55, 57*, 59, 63, 68*, 71, 73*, 75*, 79*, 80, 83*, 84, 85, 86, 87, 92, 94, 95*, 100, 102*, 105*, 106*, 107, 108, 112, 115*, 116, 117, 118*, 131, 137, 140, 143, 154, 160, 161, 184, 189, 192, 193, 194, 198, 201, 205, 206, 208*, 213, 219, 224, 225, 232, 234, 244, 251*, 252, 253, 254, 256*, 257, 258*, 259, 260*, 261*, 262, 263, 264*, 268, 270, 271, 273*, 274*, 275, 278, 280*, 281, 283, 284*, 285, 290, 299, 322, 323, 327, 332, 339, 345*, 347*, 352, 354*, 358, 360, 369*, 382, 432*, 437, 439*, 459, 478; Barbara, 423; Betty, 313; Catharine, 234, 270, 358; Christian, 27, 103; David, 20, 83, 171, 253, 254, 256, 259, 362, 420, 484; Elizabeth, 5, 30, 57, 80, 90, 92, 98, 158, 188, 208, 209, 213, 215, 227, 236, 251, 322, 379, 383, 415, 442, 446, 470, 479; Esther, 262; Gavin, 2, 4, 5, 7, 12, 261; George, 4, 11, 20, 22*, 23, 24, 25, 27, 28, 29, 30*, 31, 32*, 33, 34*, 35, 39, 40, 42, 43, 44, 46*, 47, 84, 85, 87, 88*, 89*, 90, 91*, 92*, 93*, 94*, 95*, 96*, 97, 98*, 99, 100*, 101*, 102*, 103*, 104*, 105*, 107, 108, 109*, 110*, 111, 112, 113, 115*, 116, 117, 118, 119*, 121*, 127, 130, 131*, 133*, 136, 137, 138, 140, 141*, 143, 147, 149, 151, 154, 156, 157, 159, 162, 163*, 165*, 168, 170, 175, 177, 180, 183*, 184, 188, 189*, 192, 193*, 194*, 197, 200, 201*, 204*, 205, 207, 208*, 210, 211, 212*, 215*, 219, 220, 221, 222*, 224, 225*, 227, 228*, 229, 230, 232, 233, 234*, 240*, 241*, 243, 247, 251*, 252*, 253*, 254*, 255*, 256*, 257, 258*, 259*, 261*, 262*, 264*, 265*, 266*, 267, 270*, 271, 272*, 273*, 274*, 276, 277, 278*,

280*, 281, 329, 335, 362, 419, 473, 480; Grizell, 93; G., 204; Helen, 79, 259, 344, 346, 347, 350, 354, 358, 421*, 440, 445; Hugh, 259; Isabel, 18, 25, 62, 76, 79, 82, 96, 97, 102, 120, 131, 138, 175, 183, 188, 221, 225, 232, 271, 273, 283, 287, 290, 292, 297, 303, 304, 315, 317, 319, 321, 322, 327, 329, 343, 345, 346, 359, 399, 401, 406, 412, 415, 424, 427, 440, 474, 477, 484, 486; James, 4, 12, 15, 17, 19, 20, 22, 23*, 25*, 26*, 27*, 29*, 30*, 31, 32, 34*, 35*, 37, 40*, 41, 42, 43, 44, 46*, 56, 57, 80, 98*, 104, 109, 115, 125, 137, 138, 140, 155, 161, 172*, 188, 207, 208, 253, 254, 261, 327*, 332*, 354, 362*, 404, 418, 438, 443, 463, 469, 474; Janet, 5, 24, 29, 62, 72, 113, 161, 171, 267, 310, 314, 332, 351, 357, 372, 377, 383, 386, 400, 402, 429, 441, 477; Jasper, 25; Jean, 88, 93, 94, 101, 105, 114, 116, 232, 257, 280, 301, 306, 308, 312, 317, 319, 416*, 426, 431, 434, 466, 484; John, 6, 11, 12*, 15, 17, 18*, 19*, 20*, 21, 22, 23, 25*, 26*, 27*, 28, 29*, 30*, 31*, 33, 36, 37, 38, 40, 56, 59, 63, 68, 71, 75, 78*, 79*, 80*, 81*, 82*, 83*, 84*, 85*, 86*, 87*, 88*, 89*, 90*, 91*, 92, 117, 213, 225, 229, 254, 258, 272*, 276, 279, 281, 282, 283*, 284*, 285*, 288, 289*, 290, 291*, 292, 293, 294, 295*, 298, 301, 303, 306, 309, 310*, 313*, 314, 315*, 317, 318*, 319*, 320, 322*, 323, 324*, 325*, 326*, 327*, 328*, 329*, 332, 333, 334, 335*, 336*, 337*, 338, 340*, 341*, 343, 344, 346, 347*, 348, 351, 353, 354*, 355, 357, 359*, 360, 362*, 363, 368, 401, 410, 411, 421, 424*, 429, 430, 431*, 432*, 435*, 436*, 437, 439*, 440, 441, 459, 469, 472, 476, 478; J., 337; Margaret, 4, 12, 19, 22, 26, 30, 63, 65, 67, 89, 104, 114, 117, 132, 148, 149, 164, 170, 192, 194, 220, 224, 251, 252*, 253, 258*, 259, 264, 306, 339, 353, 401, 402, 403, 413, 434, 455, 474, 477; Marion, 83, 338, 432, 475; Mark, 7; Mary, 193, 210, 252, 341; Milne, 264, 455; Patrick, 30; Peggy, 306, 308, 315, 432, 467; Robert, 7*, 14*, 18, 20, 24, 26, 29, 37, 40, 42*, 44*, 46*, 47, 48, 50, 52*, 54, 60, 64, 73, 74*, 78, 79, 83*, 93*, 97, 108*, 117, 118, 119, 127, 138*, 142, 159, 161, 271, 276, 362, 368, 369, 417, 483; Stephen,

141*, 147, 164, 167, 182, 183, 188,
193, 195, 214, 218, 221, 222, 223,
239, 253*, 254, 256 257*, 259*,
260, 261*, 262, 263*, 266, 269*,
271, 273, 275, 278, 279, 287, 297*,
299*, 300*, 304, 305, 310, 316*,
321, 323*, 329*, 331, 346, 357*,
366, 378, 397, 401, 405, 413, 416,
418, 427, 428, 431, 436, 437, 439,
450, 453, 455*, 464, 481, 488*;
Gustavus, 270; Helen, 26, 62,
70, 91, 102, 108, 117, 120, 134,
214, 221, 259, 272, 292, 321, 373,
378, 400, 444, 451, 473; Hen., 418;
Isabel, 4, 17, 18, 21, 27, 32, 33,
51, 66, 70, 71, 75, 77, 78, 81, 85,
86, 89*, 92, 93, 98, 99*, 108, 109,
156, 167, 211, 224, 254, 257, 258,
261, 274, 281, 283, 287, 291, 294,
295, 298, 299, 315, 331, 358, 364,
391, 393, 404*, 414, 415*, 418,
421, 422*, 432, 465, 467, 474, 481,
483; James, 11, 18, 19, 20, 21,
23*, 25, 26*, 29, 33*, 36, 40*, 42*,
43, 44*, 45*, 46, 58, 64, 67*, 76*,
79, 80*, 84, 85, 86*, 88*, 93, 96,
97*, 99, 101, 103*, 109, 115, 119,
121*, 232, 233, 262, 263*, 266,
267, 269, 270, 271, 272, 275, 277*,
278, 282, 291, 308, 310, 352* 353,
355*, 357, 359, 366, 378, 382*,
401, 407, 415*, 422, 424, 430, 437*,
447, 449, 452, 456, 471, 484;
Janet, 3, 4, 7, 11, 13, 16, 66, 68,
75, 85, 86, 88, 89*, 92, 96, 98, 100,
101*, 104, 105, 119, 131, 145, 154,
157, 160, 193, 212, 221, 232, 238,
254, 257, 258, 260*, 261, 263,
266*, 268, 271, 272, 273, 274, 277,
285, 286, 288, 289, 292, 294, 297,
301, 305, 308, 314, 364, 366, 368,
374, 383, 398, 399, 416*, 417, 421*,
422, 423, 424, 427, 428, 429, 433,
440, 453*, 470, 473, 476, 482, 487*;
Jean, 97, 297, 379; John, 2, 3, 4,
7, 8, 9*, 11, 14, 16*, 17, 19*, 20, 21,
22, 23, 24, 25*, 26*, 27*, 30, 31,
32*, 33*, 36, 38, 40, 42, 43, 45*,
46, 47*, 48, 49, 50*, 51, 52, 53, 54*,
55, 57, 59*, 62, 63, 64, 66, 68, 69*,
71*, 72*, 73*, 74*, 75, 76, 77*,
79*, 80*, 81, 82, 83*, 85*, 86*, 87*,
88, 89*, 91*, 93*, 94*, 96*, 97*,
98*, 99*, 100*, 101*, 103*, 104,
105*, 106, 108*, 109*, 110*, 111*,
112*, 113*, 114, 115*, 116*, 117,
119, 121*, 122, 123, 124, 125, 128*,
129*, 130*, 131*, 132*, 133*, 134*,
135*, 136, 137*, 138*, 139*, 140*,
141, 142*, 143*, 144*, 145*, 146*,
147*, 148, 149*, 150, 151, 152*,

153, 154, 155, 156*, 157, 158, 159,
160*, 161, 162, 163*, 164*, 165*,
166*, 167*, 168*, 169, 170*, 171*,
172*, 173*, 174*, 175, 176*, 177*,
178*, 179*, 180*, 181*, 182*, 183*,
184, 185*, 186, 187*, 188*, 189*,
191, 193*, 194*, 195*, 198*,
199, 200*, 201*, 205, 206*, 207*,
208*, 209*, 210*, 213, 214*, 216*,
217, 218*, 219, 221, 222*, 223,
226*, 227*, 228*, 229, 231*, 232*,
233*, 234*, 235*, 237*, 238*, 239*,
240*, 241, 242*, 243*, 244*, 245,
246, 247*, 248*, 249, 250*, 253*,
254, 257*, 259*, 260*, 261*, 262,
263*, 265, 266*, 267, 268*, 269,
271, 272*, 274, 277, 278*, 281,
283, 284, 286*, 288*, 289, 291,
292, 295, 297*, 300, 304*, 305,
309, 311*, 315, 316, 319, 329, 339,
340*, 353, 356, 358, 359, 361, 362,
371, 379*, 398, 400, 401, 403*,
404, 411*, 414, 416, 417, 420, 421,
422, 423, 424*, 425, 427, 428, 431*,
432*, 433, 440*, 442, 446, 460,
461, 469*, 470, 473, 486; Lizie,
264, 279, 282; Ma., 286; Malie,
4; Margaret, 8, 22, 24*, 32, 65,
70, 71, 75, 76, 83, 86, 99, 100, 104,
113, 138, 180, 194, 195, 215, 220,
235*, 251, 253, 257, 258, 259, 260,
263, 283, 285, 287, 288, 289, 290,
294*, 296, 297, 298, 299, 303, 350,
354, 378, 379, 386, 392, 412, 418,
419, 420, 427, 428, 430, 445, 448,
452, 457*, 462, 478, 479, 486;
Maria, 379; Marion, 289, 292,
296, 302, 310; Mary, 74, 95, 115,
120, 121, 222, 252, 293, 296, 299*,
302, 305, 312, 360, 371, 421, 428,
431, 457; Michael, 367, 376, 382,
391, 442; Nelly, 436; Nicol, 3,
4*, 5, 9*, 11, 13, 14, 17*, 18*, 19*,
20*, 21, 22*, 23*, 24, 26, 27*, 29,
30*, 32, 34, 36, 38*, 40*, 41, 42,
46, 48, 50, 55, 63, 65, 68, 75*, 78,
79, 82*, 86, 92, 93, 94*, 99*, 107,
113, 117, 122, 128, 136, 145, 147,
154, 180, 182, 188, 194, 200, 209,
211, 215, 225, 232, 235, 238, 251,
252, 254, 255*, 258, 260, 263, 266,
267, 274, 290, 305, 350, 354, 360,
378, 382, 386*, 400, 402, 414, 415, 417,
422, 424, 442, 444, 457, 463, 483,
486; Peggy, 289, 291, 292, 298,
300, 301, 303, 305, 311, 471;
Peter, 10; Robert, 4*, 9, 40, 41,
42, 43*, 45*, 46, 49, 50, 52*, 56, 61,
64*, 66*, 67, 67, 99, 101, 103, 111,
115*, 121, 139, 142, 156, 165, 173,
174, 189, 200, 207*, 208*, 214, 222,

Oliver, Agnes, 23, 318; Andrew, 23,
25, 29, 31, 34, 36, 39, 41*, 46, 52,
53, 57, 392, 403, 405, 407*, 411,
429, 468; Anne, 457; Christian,
433; David, 398; Elizabeth, 304,
310; Helen, 346, 368, 375, 382,
389*, 390*; Isobel, 29, 114, 401,
487; James, 23, 25, 29, 42, 52, 53,
57, 69, 87, 92, 392*, 411, 439;
Janet, 418, 439, 458, 476; John,
43, 392; Margaret, 329, 337, 343,
346, 377, 380, 381, 383, 387, 393, 397,
436, 445, 485, 487; Nancy, 443;
Richard, 11*; Robert, 18*, 23,
25, 487; Thomas, 462; William,
17*, 113, 114, 121*, 329, 447
Ormiston (Ormeston, Ormistone,
Ormistoun, Ormistown), Adam,
284, 317*, 348, 363, 366, 435, 442,
448; Agnes, 286, 305; Andrew, 2, 3,
13, 16, 22, 49, 188, 197, 396, 428, 430,
431, 460; Anne, 75, 125*, 173*,
174, 246, 247; Archibald, 385*,
394, 481; Bessie, 18; Bettie, 278;
Charles, 232, 238, 305; Elizabeth,
161, 238; George, 25, 26, 30, 36,
120, 125*, 137, 142, 330, 399, 473;
Helen, 65, 273, 457; Isabel, 12,
15, 40, 89, 93, 96, 103, 105, 126,
287, 416, 447; James, 3, 12, 126,
317; Janet, 2, 102, 114, 154, 263,
268, 292, 323, 332*, 336, 348, 378,
394, 424, 489; Jean, 13, 156, 157*,
158*, 182*, 183*, 184, 300, 468;
John, 25, 50, 54, 57*, 59, 63, 65;
Margaret, 5, 16, 238, 276, 330,
335, 339, 345, 352, 359; Marion,
188, 197, 290, 453; Mary, 313,
317, 321, 354, 434; Peggy, 435;
Richard, 22; Robert, 5, 13, 15,
27*, 30, 37, 38, 39*, 40*, 43, 44,
45, 53, 54, 57, 65, 96, 97, 102, 105,
107, 112*, 114, 115, 126*, 128*,
131*, 137, 155, 156, 161, 172*,
188, 195, 206, 228, 232, 271, 282,
286, 290, 292, 300, 317, 330*, 344,
354, 418, 422, 428, 431, 434, 452,
476, 481, 482; Thomas, 2, 6, 9, 11,
12*, 13, 15, 16, 49, 50, 54, 57*, 59,
63*, 65, 75, 195, 197*, 411, 426;
Walter, 394*, 396, 433, 448;
William, 2*, 3, 4, 6*, 9, 12, 13, 14,
15, 16, 35, 37, 268, 271, 273, 276,
278*, 281, 282, 284, 287, 399, 423,
426*, 427, 472
Orr (Ore), Andrew, 315; Anne, 277,
290, 453, 456; James, 277, 280*,
283, 286, 291, 295, 299, 313, 315,
429*; Janet, 313; John, 283;
Margaret, 286, 291, 454; William,
295, 447

Ovens (Owens, Oynes), Anaple, 142,
156, 173, 200, 222; Annabella,
250, 255, 258; Andrew, 76; David,
436; Isabel, 266; Janet, 72, 76,
81, 89, 414; John, 4, 56, 60; Margaret, 390; Mary, 385, 395*;
Thomas, 266, 386, 421, 456;
William, 386, 390, 447

Paisley, Francis, 217
Parke (Park), Alexander, 469; Andrew,
307; Anne, 267; Annie, 458;
Archibald, 265; Bell, 468; Betty,
310, 314, 317; Elizabeth, 438;
George, 267; Helen, 92, 175*, 262,
421, 485; Isabel, 89, 117, 181,
220, 260; James, 94*, 254, 258,
394, 417; Janet, 343, 350, 478;
John, 89, 99*, 113, 238*, 239, 251,
254, 256, 257, 271, 305, 322, 343,
350, 415, 420, 423, 424*, 430, 438,
484; Joseph, 286; Margaret, 175*,
215, 274, 422, 480; Marion, 215,
269; Mary, 100; Mungo, 92, 99,
104, 108*, 113, 117, 156, 164, 174,
175*, 203, 225, 238*, 239, 251, 254,
257, 258*, 259, 260*, 261, 262*,
263, 265, 266, 267*, 269*, 270,
271*, 274*, 418, 420, 421*, 424;
Nelly, 294; Richard, 136, 166,
195, 208, 212, 215, 238*, 254, 256,
264, 268, 305, 307, 422*, 431;
Robert, 271; Thomas, 104, 195*,
286, 446, 485; William, 254, 394
Parre, James, 20, 61
Parsone, Michael, 61
Paterson (Patersone), Adam, 11, 331,
379*; Agnes, 7, 10, 63, 87, 281,
295, 366, 368; Alexander, 43, 44,
45*, 46, 107, 139, 223, 225, 227,
229*, 230*, 231*, 233*, 234, 237,
239, 243, 246, 251, 285, 309, 393,
405, 448; Alison, 74; Andrew, 1,
3, 4, 5*, 8*, 9*, 10, 11, 13, 14, 16*,
20*, 21, 22, 33, 34, 65, 66, 68, 69,
70, 73*, 74*, 75*, 77*, 78*, 80*,
81, 82, 84*, 85*, 86, 89*, 91, 92,
93*, 94, 97, 98*, 100, 101, 102*,
103, 104, 108*, 110, 112, 113, 114*,
116*, 117*, 118*, 119, 120*, 121,
122, 123, 124*, 125*, 126*, 128,
129*, 130, 131*, 132*, 133*, 134*,
135*, 136*, 137*, 138, 140, 141*,
142*, 144*, 145, 146, 147*, 148*,
149*, 341, 402, 416, 417; Anna,
186, 210, 227, 239, 253, 257, 263,
341, 466; Bessie, 399, 402; Betty,
348; Catherine, 121, 215; Christine, 9, 13, 20; Christian, 315, 319,
323; Elizabeth, 70, 74*, 78, 84, 98,
102, 225, 251, 253, 256, 369, 414,

346, 349, 358, 364, 370, 374, 414,
440; Margaret Edgar, 336; Mary,
133, 291, 349, 452, 468; Peggy, 384;
Robert, 108, 109, 113, 120, 138*,
212, 268, 288, 320, 361, 419, 423,
488; Samuel, 388, 445; Susanna,
161, 179, 221, 256, 261, 267, 453;
Thomas, 68*, 109, 165, 166, 259,
345, 346, 382, 421, 476; Walter,
29; William, 14, 107, 224, 276*,
292, 297*, 320, 321, 401, 432; Dr,
216, 239, 257, 267, 268, 272

Ruthet, Isobel, 28; John, 28

Ruthven (Riven), Elizabeth, 261;
Robert, 272; William, 261, 272

Ruttlage, Andro, 11, 399; Johne, 11

SADLER (Saidler), Adam, 414;
Christian, 122; Elizabeth, 138;
——, Jenet, 399

Salmon, Robert, 349

Salton, Isabel, 374; John, 374, 445

Sanderson (Saunderson), Adam, 370,
376, 381, 390; Agnes, 328, 342,
346, 355, 390, 395; Alexander,
109, 326, 330, 336, 340, 436, 437;
Alison, 391, 436; Andrew, 326*,
328, 332, 342*, 347, 350*, 354,
358*, 362, 436; Anne, 355,
357, 360, 407, 438; Betty,
369, 435; Christian, 331; David,
354; Elizabeth, 331, 391, 440;
Hugh, 329, 342, 438*; Isabel,
342, 344, 395, 434; James, 304,
314, 316, 322*, 323, 330, 332, 344,
360, 370, 391, 395*, 425, 431, 432,
434, 436*, 448, 468; Jane, 336;
Janet, 326, 365, 379*, 385, 388,
392, 436, 440, 447; Jean, 358, 384,
445; John, 323, 326, 350*, 354,
357, 360, 362*, 364, 369, 376, 379,
436*, 437, 440, 471; Margaret,
275, 330, 336, 381, 438, 443*;
Mary, 314, 350, 390; Peggy, 356;
Peter, 332*, 438; Robert, 326;
Thomas, 326, 341, 346*, 350*,
352*, 354*, 355*, 356, 357*, 358*,
360, 380*, 384, 390, 391, 422, 440,
441, 442, 446, 448; William, 331*,
350, 354, 360, 369, 384, 413;
Widow, 446

Sandilands (Sandlans), Agnes, 84, 88,
94; Alexander, 152, 189, 190, 211,
252, 288; Alison, 89; Andrew,
172; Beatrice, 88; Esther, 357;
Eupham, 211; Isobel, 112; James,
72, 88, 98, 102, 105*, 190, 209*,
252; Janet, 102, 171, 183, 206,
295, 398, 428, 457; Jean, 105;
John, 53, 83, 126, 357; Margaret,
114, 443; Robert, 424; Thomas,

102; Walter, 72; William, 10, 46,
81, 88, 89*, 94*, 98, 102*, 172,
180, 188, 213, 244, 287, 416; ——
83, 116

Sawers (Sawrs), Grissel, 323, 325, 336

Sclater (Sclaiter, Sclaitter, Sclatter,
Slaiter, Slater, Slatter), Agnes, 7,
65, 69, 75, 80, 86, 91, 96, 101, 105,
106, 141, 168, 401, 403, 413, 417;
Alison, 21, 62, 77; Andrew, 1, 2*,
3*, 4, 5*, 6*, 8*, 10*, 11*, 12, 13,
14, 15*, 17, 20, 21, 32, 36, 40, 47,
325; Elisabeth, 31, 71, 74, 78, 82,
87, 93, 157; Eupham, 438; Isabel,
10, 12, 69, 197, 293, 295, 390, 392,
396, 430, 448; James, 135, 137,
261, 317, 318, 320*, 323*, 325,
326, 328, 332, 335*, 351*, 430,
435*, 436; Janet, 10, 20, 99, 344,
423, 435, 439*, 467; John, 21, 26*,
29, 30*, 31, 32, 33*, 34, 36, 37*,
38*, 39*, 41*, 42*, 43, 44, 45, 46*,
47*, 49, 50, 52, 53, 56, 58*, 62, 66*,
69*, 80, 81, 85, 119, 129, 135, 138,
141, 152, 269, 307, 325, 351, 403,
413, 438, 439, 480; Malie, 400;
Margaret, 12, 16, 67, 69, 77, 81,
84, 89*, 93, 99, 112, 116, 125, 129,
146, 414*, 419; Marion, 81, 94,
96, 100, 407, 414, 417, 465; Mary,
10, 87, 293, 297, 300, 304, 307, 311,
317, 321, 328, 429; Nelly, 351;
Nicol, 26; Peggy, 309, 433;
Richard, 1, 3, 4*, 5*, 6, 7*, 8, 9*,
10*, 12*, 13, 14, 15, 16*, 17*, 18,
19, 20*, 21*, 22*, 24, 25*, 26, 28,
29*, 48, 67, 76, 80, 83, 86*, 89, 96*,
98, 99*, 100, 134, 256, 398, 415,
416*, 430*; Robert, 1*, 5*, 7, 9,
10, 30, 42, 44, 45, 47, 48, 53, 58*,
101*, 112, 116, 119, 137, 320, 419;
Thomas, 5, 6, 10, 13, 17, 86, 89,
93, 101, 119, 135, 137, 159*, 238,
256, 265, 270, 307, 397, 418, 420,
422, 461; William, 9, 31, 32, 36,
37, 41, 42*, 69, 86*, 89, 91*, 96,
99, 100, 102, 105, 107, 110, 116,
127, 149, 199, 202, 258, 261, 265,
269, 318, 404, 416, 421, 422, 471;
——, 33, 76, 169, 187, 211, 463

Scoon, Agnes, 321, 324, 327, 329, 339*,
347, 367; Anne, 436; Thomas,
329

Scot (Scott), Adam, 16, 73, 432, 433*;
Agnes, 74, 83, 109, 116, 130, 152,
159, 176, 194, 219*, 228, 244, 253*,
255, 259, 284, 316, 323, 338, 341,
404, 419, 420, 443*, 460, 466;
Alexander, 80, 91, 187, 190, 198,
234, 238*, 239, 241*, 250, 251,
253, 262, 267, 269, 271, 277, 279,

290, 293, 296, 299, 302, 304, 307, 311, 314; Euphan, 127, 136, 149, 174, 208, 323, 424, 445; Francis, 440; George, 144*, 145, 291, 294, 299, 304, 318*, 380, 429; Gilbert, 224; Helen, 116, 134, 263, 366, 369, 374, 428, 451, 485; Isabel, 227, 265, 293, 329, 387, 429, 432, 439, 445, 454, 470*; James, 20, 26, 32, 34, 38, 47, 92, 190, 229, 312, 318, 337, 340, 375, 383, 421, 428, 453, 467, 475; Janet, 85, 95, 101, 112, 180, 190, 205, 222, 251, 254, 257, 262, 269, 318*, 320, 360, 417, 435, 475, 476*; Jean, 87, 358, 392, 414, 415, 421, 481; Jeremiah, 422; John, 74, 85, 92*, 95, 97*, 101, 102*, 103*, 105*, 108*, 110*, 112*, 113, 117*, 119, 124, 131, 134*, 176*, 181, 187, 190, 194, 200, 206*, 215, 218, 219, 227*, 251, 272, 299, 303, 306, 309, 310, 312*, 315, 318*, 320, 321*, 322*, 325, 327, 329, 336, 337, 340*, 341, 342*, 343, 344, 345, 346*, 347*, 348*, 349*, 351, 353*, 354, 355*, 357*, 359, 360*, 362, 363*, 393, 410, 416, 418, 422, 431, 432*, 436*, 437*, 447, 449, 487; Margaret, 21, 26, 148, 199, 259, 286, 291, 329, 332, 343, 347, 390, 392, 395, 398, 428*, 437, 445, 448, 484; Marion, 382, 383, 389, 400, 466; Mary, 325, 482; Nelly, 300, 303, 306, 310, 313, 316, 320, 326, 431; Peggy, 289; Robert, 41, 294, 437; Thomas, 212, 321, 395, 429, 433, 449; Violet, 336; William, 2, 7, 11, 16, 43, 45*, 47*, 52, 102, 117, 300, 311, 318, 319*, 320*, 323*, 327, 332, 335, 340, 347, 358, 375, 385*, 389, 424, 425*, 426, 435, 439, 447, 481; Mr, 377*; ——, 383, 388

Snedden, Joanna, 299; John, 299

Somers (Summers), George, 449; Isabel, 377

Somerville (Somervail, Somervel, Somervell, Somervile, Sommervaill, Sommervel, Sommerville, Summervaill, Summervell, Summervil, Symervail), Archibald, 429, 461; Elizabeth, 346, 351, 355, 361, 366, 375, 440; George, 62, 290, 351*; Isabel, 444, 487; James, 355, 375; Janet, 129, 307; Jean, 402, 406; John, 32, 51, 58, 59, 62*, 69, 72, 82, 87, 89, 97, 122, 129, 346, 389, 409, 411, 412*, 414, 429, 484; Margaret, 67, 69, 73, 78, 87, 90, 195, 238, 252, 255, 259, 268, 272; Marion, 262, 264, 274, 283,

287, 290, 422; Nicol, 460; William, 389; ——, 103, 211, 233, 252

Sore (?), James, 10; John, 10

Souden (Soudon, Sudden), Alison, 22; Janet, 282; Robert, 22, 45; Thomas, 45, 46, 450

Sounness (Sonnais, Sunneyis, Sunase, Sunness), George, 7, 11*; Helen, 7; James, 49, 53, 411; Janet, 400; John, 3, 5, 8, 23, 407*

Spalding, Betty, 478; ——, 480

Speede, Mary, 299; Thomas, 299

Speeden (Speden, Speedin, Speeding, Speiden, Speidon, Spiden), Alexander, 398; Anne, 437; Betty, 429, 441; Christian, 257, 430, 461, 484; David, 75, 80, 83*, 86, 89, 99, 104, 116, 182, 187, 212; George, 252; Helen, 251, 437; Isabel, 122, 147, 187, 201, 284, 286, 288, 292, 295, 299, 427; James, 145, 192, 194, 212, 214, 221, 225, 238, 254*, 255, 257, 260, 311, 428, 430; Janet, 99, 106, 221, 286, 289, 300, 306, 428, 488; Jean, 93, 238; John, 419; Margaret, 98, 194, 201, 232, 417, 419, 422, 429; Mary, 157; Nelly, 474; Robert, 80, 114, 159, 197, 229, 251, 343, 423, 450; Thomas, 136, 144, 147, 157, 187, 201, 221, 232, 251*, 252; William, 89, 437; ——, 238

Spiers (Spear, Spears, Speirs), Adam, 351, 356; Agnes, 190, 356; Betty, 349*; Christian, 105; George, 351, Janet, 203; Jean, 118; John, 176, 183, 187, 190, 203, 205, 220, 255*, Margaret, 220

Spence, Agnes, 395; Andrew, 343, 478; Betty, 478; David, 376, 388, 395, 448; Elizabeth, 343, 376; Janet, 363, 402; Joseph, 388; Margaret, 350; Marion, 302; Thomas, 425; William, 343, 350, 358, 363, 442; Miss, 376; Mrs, 376*

Spittle, Margaret, 432; Peggy, 305

Spottiswoode (Spotswood), Alexander, 51; Alison, 403; Andro, 29; Helen, 106; Isabel, 266, 269, 272, 277, 281, 285; John, 51, 106; Margaret, 29, 81; Robert, 29, 32, 35, 37, 39, 87, 88; William, 7, 20, 25*, 28*, 29*, 31*, 32, 397

Sprate, Agnes, 264

Sprots (Sprot, Sprott, Sprotts), Alison, 281; Andrew, 270, 430; Catharine, 265, 453; Christian, 284; George, 272, 421; Henry, 274; Isobel, 280; John, 92, 101*, 150*, 151*, 182*, 258, 264*, 265, 270, 277, 281, 417, 421, 427, 461; Margaret, 258,

E

9 789354 037030